University Casebook Series

April, 1977

ACCOUNTING AND THE LAW, Third Edition (1964), with Problem Pamphlet
> The late James L. Dohr, Director, Institute of Accounting, Columbia University.
> Ellis L. Phillips, Jr., Professor of Law, Columbia University.
> George C. Thompson, Professor, Columbia University Graduate School of Business, and
> William C. Warren, Professor of Law, Columbia University.

ACCOUNTING, MATERIALS ON, (1959), with 1968 Supplement
> Robert Amory, Jr., Esq.,
> W. Covington Hardee, Esq., Third Edition by
> David R. Herwitz, Professor of Law, Harvard University, and
> Donald T. Trautman, Professor of Law, Harvard University.

ADMINISTRATIVE LAW, Sixth Edition (1974), with 1974 Problems Supplement
> Walter Gellhorn, University Professor, Columbia University, and
> Clark Byse, Professor of Law, Harvard University.

ADMIRALTY (1969) with 1972 Supplement
> Jo Desha Lucas, Professor of Law, University of Chicago.

ADVOCACY, INTRODUCTION TO, Second Edition (1976) with 1970 Supplementary Cases Pamphlet
> Board of Student Advisers, Harvard Law School.

AGENCY–ASSOCIATIONS–EMPLOYMENT–PARTNERSHIPS, Second Edition (1977)
> Reprinted from Conard, Knauss & Siegel's Enterprise Organization

AGENCY, see also Enterprise Organization

ANTITRUST AND REGULATORY ALTERNATIVES (1977)
> Louis B. Schwartz, Professor of Law, University of Pennsylvania.
> John J. Flynn, Professor of Law, University of Utah.

ANTITRUST SUPPLEMENT—SELECTED STATUTES AND RELATED MATERIALS (1977)
> John J. Flynn, Professor of Law, University of Utah.

ARBITRATION (1968)
> The late Shelden D. Elliott, Professor of Law, New York University.

BANKRUPTCY ACT (Annotated) 1967 Edition
> The late James Angell MacLachlan, Professor of Law Emeritus, Harvard University.

BIOGRAPHY OF A LEGAL DISPUTE, THE: An Introduction to American Civil Procedure (1968)
> Marc A. Franklin, Professor of Law, Stanford University.

BUSINESS ORGANIZATION, see also Enterprise Organization

CREDITORS' RIGHTS, see also Debtor-Creditor Law

CRIMINAL LAW (1973)

Fred E. Inbau, Professor of Law, Northwestern University.
James R. Thompson, U. S. Attorney for the Northern District of Illinois.
Andre A. Moenssens, Professor of Law, University of Richmond.

CONSTITUTIONAL CRIMINAL PROCEDURE (1977)

James E. Scarboro, Professor of Law, University of Colorado.
James B. White, Professor of Law, University of Chicago.

CRIMINAL PROCEDURE (1974) with 1976 Supplement

Fred E. Inbau, Professor of Law, Northwestern University.
James R. Thompson, U. S. Attorney for the Northern District of Illinois.
James B. Haddad, First Assistant State's Attorney, Cook County, Illinois.
James B. Zagel, Chief, Criminal Justice Division, Office of Attorney
General of Illinois.
Gary L. Starkman, Assistant U. S. Attorney, Northern District of Illinois.

CRIMINAL JUSTICE, THE ADMINISTRATION OF, CASES AND MATERIALS ON, Second Edition (1969)

Francis C. Sullivan, Professor of Law, Louisiana State University.
Paul Hardin III, Professor of Law, Duke University.
John Huston, Professor of Law, University of Washington.
Frank R. Lacy, Professor of Law, University of Oregon.
Daniel E. Murray, Professor of Law, University of Miami.
George W. Pugh, Professor of Law, Louisiana State University.

CRIMINAL JUSTICE ADMINISTRATION AND RELATED PROCESSES, Successor Edition (1976)

Frank W. Miller, Professor of Law, Washington University.
Robert O. Dawson, Professor of Law, University of Texas.
George E. Dix, Professor of Law, University of Texas.
Raymond I. Parnas, Professor of Law, University of California, Davis.

CRIMINAL LAW, Second Edition (1975)

Lloyd L. Weinreb, Professor of Law, Harvard University.

CRIMINAL LAW AND ITS ADMINISTRATION (1940), with 1956 Supplement

The late Jerome Michael, Professor of Law, Columbia University, and
Herbert Wechsler, Professor of Law, Columbia University.

CRIMINAL LAW AND PROCEDURE, Fifth Edition (1977)

Rollin M. Perkins, Professor of Law, University of California, Hastings
College of the Law.
Ronald N. Boyce, Professor of Law, University of Utah.

CRIMINAL PROCESS, Second Edition (1974), with 1977 Supplement

Lloyd L. Weinreb, Professor of Law, Harvard University.

DAMAGES, Second Edition (1952)

The late Charles T. McCormick, Professor of Law, University of Texas, and
The late William F. Fritz, Professor of Law, University of Texas.

DEBTOR–CREDITOR LAW (1974) with 1975 Case-Statutory Supplement

William D. Warren, Dean of the School of Law, University of California,
Los Angeles.
William E. Hogan, Professor of Law, Cornell University.

DECEDENTS' ESTATES (1971)

Max Rheinstein, Professor of Law Emeritus, University of Chicago.
Mary Ann Glendon, Professor of Law, Boston College Law School.

DECEDENTS' ESTATES AND TRUSTS, Fifth Edition (1977)

John Ritchie III, Professor of Law, University of Virginia,
Neill H. Alford, Jr., Professor of Law, University of Virginia.
Richard W. Effland, Professor of Law, Arizona State University.

DECEDENTS' ESTATES AND TRUSTS (1968)

Howard R. Williams, Professor of Law, Stanford University.

DOMESTIC RELATIONS, Second Edition (1974)

Monrad G. Paulsen, Dean of the Law School, Yeshiva University.
Walter Wadlington, Professor of Law, University of Virginia.
Julius Goebel, Jr., Professor of Law Emeritus, Columbia University.

DOMESTIC RELATIONS—Civil and Canon Law (1963)

Philip A. Ryan, Professor of Law, Georgetown University, and
Dom David Granfield, Associate Professor, Catholic University of America.

DYNAMICS OF AMERICAN LAW, THE: Courts, the Legal Process and Freedom of Expression (1968)

Marc A. Franklin, Professor of Law, Stanford University.

ELECTRONIC MASS MEDIA (1976) (paper back)

William K. Jones, Professor of Law, Columbia University.

ENTERPRISE ORGANIZATION, Second Edition (1977)

Alfred F. Conard, Professor of Law, University of Michigan.
Robert L. Knauss, Dean of the School of Law, Vanderbilt University.
Stanley Siegel, Professor of Law, University of California, Los Angeles.

ENVIRONMENTAL PROTECTION, SELECTED LEGAL AND ECONOMIC ASPECTS OF (1971)

Charles J. Meyers, Professor of Law, Stanford University.
A. Dan Tarlock, Professor of Law, Indiana University.

EQUITY AND EQUITABLE REMEDIES (1975)

Edward D. Re, Adjunct Professor of Law, St. John's University.

EQUITY, RESTITUTION AND DAMAGES, Second Edition (1974)

Robert Childres, Professor of Law, Northwestern University.
William F. Johnson, Jr., Adjunct Professor of Law, New York University.

ESTATE PLANNING PROBLEMS (1973) with 1977 Supplement

David Westfall, Professor of Law, Harvard University.

ETHICS, see Legal Profession

EVIDENCE, Third Edition (1976)

David W. Louisell, Professor of Law, University of California, Berkeley.
John Kaplan, Professor of Law, Stanford University.
Jon R. Waltz, Professor of Law, Northwestern University.

EVIDENCE, Sixth Edition (1973) with 1976 Supplement

John M. Maguire, Professor of Law Emeritus, Harvard University.
Jack B. Weinstein, Professor of Law, Columbia University.
James H. Chadbourn, Professor of Law, Harvard University.
John H. Mansfield, Professor of Law, Harvard University.

EVIDENCE (1968)

Francis C. Sullivan, Professor of Law, Louisiana State University.
Paul Hardin, III, Professor of Law, Duke University.

FAMILY LAW: STATUTORY MATERIALS, Second Edition

Monrad G. Paulsen, Dean of the Law School, Yeshiva University.
Walter Wadlington, Professor of Law, University of Virginia.

INTRODUCTION TO THE STUDY OF LAW (1970)
E. Wayne Thode, Professor of Law, University of Utah.
J. Leon Lebowitz, Professor of Law, University of Texas.
Lester J. Mazor, Professor of Law, University of Utah.

INTRODUCTION TO LAW, see also Legal Method, also On Law in Courts, also Dynamics of American Law

JUDICIAL CODE: Rules of Procedure in the Federal Courts with Excerpts from the Criminal Code, 1976 Edition
The late Henry M. Hart, Jr., Professor of Law, Harvard University, and Herbert Wechsler, Professor of Law, Columbia University.

JURISPRUDENCE (Temporary Edition Hard Bound) (1949)
Lon L. Fuller, Professor of Law, Harvard University.

JUVENILE COURTS (1967)
Hon. Orman W. Ketcham, Juvenile Court of the District of Columbia.
Monrad G. Paulsen, Dean of the Law School, Yeshiva University.

JUVENILE JUSTICE PROCESS, Second Edition (1976)
Frank W. Miller, Professor of Law, Washington University.
Robert O. Dawson, Professor of Law, University of Texas.
George E. Dix, Professor of Law, University of Texas.
Raymond I. Parnas, Professor of Law, University of California, Davis.

LABOR LAW, Eighth Edition (1977) with Statutory Supplement
Archibald Cox, Professor of Law, Harvard University, and
Derek C. Bok, President, Harvard University.
Robert A. Gorman, Professor of Law, University of Pennsylvania.

LABOR LAW (1968) with Statutory Supplement
Clyde W. Summers, Professor of Law, University of Pennsylvania.
Harry H. Wellington, Dean of the Law School, Yale University.

LAND FINANCING, Second Edition (1977)
Norman Penney, Professor of Law, Cornell University.
Richard F. Broude, of the California Bar.

LAW, LANGUAGE AND ETHICS (1972)
William R. Bishin, Professor of Law, University of Southern California.
Christopher D. Stone, Professor of Law, University of Southern California.

LEGAL METHOD, Second Edition (1952)
Noel T. Dowling, late Professor of Law, Columbia University,
The late Edwin W. Patterson, Professor of Law, Columbia University, and
Richard R. B. Powell, Professor of Law, University of California, Hastings College of the Law.
Second Edition by Harry W. Jones, Professor of Law, Columbia University.

LEGAL METHODS (1969)
Robert N. Covington, Professor of Law, Vanderbilt University.
E. Blythe Stason, Professor of Law, Vanderbilt University.
John W. Wade, Professor of Law, Vanderbilt University.
The late Elliott E. Cheatham, Professor of Law, Vanderbilt University.
Theodore A. Smedley, Professor of Law, Vanderbilt University.

LEGAL PROFESSION (1970)
Samuel D. Thurman, Dean of the College of Law, University of Utah.
Ellis L. Phillips, Jr., Professor of Law, Columbia University.
The late Elliott E. Cheatham, Professor of Law, Vanderbilt University.

PROCEDURE—CIVIL PROCEDURE, Second Edition (1974)

James H. Chadbourn, Professor of Law, Harvard University, and
A. Leo Levin, Professor of Law, University of Pennsylvania.
Philip Shuchman, Professor of Law, University of Connecticut.

PROCEDURE—CIVIL PROCEDURE, Third Edition (1973)

Richard H. Field, Professor of Law, Harvard University, and
Benjamin Kaplan, Professor of Law, Harvard University.

PROCEDURE—CIVIL PROCEDURE, Third Edition (1976)

Maurice Rosenberg, Professor of Law, Columbia University.
Jack B. Weinstein, Professor, of Law, Columbia University.
Hans Smit, Professor of Law, Columbia University.
Harold L. Korn, Professor of Law, Columbia University.

PROCEDURE—FEDERAL RULES OF CIVIL PROCEDURE, 1975 Edition

PROCEDURE PORTFOLIO (1962)

James H. Chadbourn, Professor of Law, Harvard University, and
A. Leo Levin, Professor of Law, University of Pennsylvania.

PRODUCTS AND THE CONSUMER: DECEPTIVE PRACTICES (1972)

W. Page Keeton, Dean of the School of Law, University of Texas.
Marshall S. Shapo, Professor of Law, University of Virginia.

PRODUCTS AND THE CONSUMER: DEFECTIVE AND DANGEROUS PRODUCTS (1970)

W. Page Keeton, Dean of the School of Law, University of Texas.
Marshall S. Shapo, Professor of Law, University of Virginia.

PROFESSIONAL RESPONSIBILITY (1976) with Special California Supplement

Thomas D. Morgan, Professor of Law, University of Illinois.
Ronald D. Rotunda, Professor of Law, University of Illinois.

PROPERTY, Third Edition (1972)

John E. Cribbet, Dean of the Law School, University of Illinois,
The late William F. Fritz, Professor of Law, University of Texas, and
Corwin W. Johnson, Professor of Law, University of Texas.

PROPERTY—PERSONAL (1953)

The late S. Kenneth Skolfield, Professor of Law Emeritus, Boston University.

PROPERTY—PERSONAL, Third Edition (1954)

The late Everett Fraser, Dean of the Law School Emeritus, University of Minnesota—Third Edition by
Charles W. Taintor II, late Professor of Law, University of Pittsburgh.

PROPERTY—REAL—INTRODUCTION, Third Edition (1954)

The late Everett Fraser, Dean of the Law School Emeritus, University of Minnesota.

PROPERTY—REAL PROPERTY AND CONVEYANCING (1954)

Edward E. Bade, late Professor of Law, University of Minnesota.

PROPERTY, MODERN REAL, FUNDAMENTALS OF (1974)

Edward H. Rabin, Professor of Law, University of California, Davis.

PROPERTY, REAL, PROBLEMS IN (Pamphlet) (1969)

Edward H. Rabin, Professor of Law, University of California, Davis.

PROSECUTION AND ADJUDICATION (1976) (Pamphlet)

Chapters 12–16 of Miller, Dawson, Dix & Parnas' Criminal Justice Administration, Second Edition.

TAXES AND FINANCE—STATE AND LOCAL (1974)

Oliver Oldman, Professor of Law, Harvard University.

Ferdinand P. Schoettle, Professor of Law, University of Minnesota.

TORT LAW AND ALTERNATIVES: INJURIES AND REMEDIES (1971), with 1976 Supplement

Marc A. Franklin, Professor of Law, Stanford University.

TORTS, Third Edition (1976)

The late Harry Shulman, Dean of the Law School, Yale University.

Fleming James, Jr., Professor of Law Emeritus, Yale University.

Oscar S. Gray, Professor of Law, University of Maryland.

TORTS, Sixth Edition (1976)

The late William L. Prosser, Professor of Law, University of California, Hastings College of the Law.

John W. Wade, Professor of Law, Vanderbilt University.

Victor E. Schwartz, Professor of Law, University of Cincinnati.

TRADE REGULATION (1975) with 1977 Supplement

Milton Handler, Professor of Law Emeritus, Columbia University.

Harlan M. Blake, Professor of Law, Columbia University.

Robert Pitofsky, Professor of Law, Georgetown University.

Harvey J. Goldschmid, Professor of Law, Columbia University.

TRADE REGULATION, see Free Enterprise

TRANSNATIONAL LEGAL PROBLEMS, Second Edition (1976) with Documentary Supplement

Henry J. Steiner, Professor of Law, Harvard University.

Detlev F. Vagts, Professor of Law, Harvard University.

TRIAL ADVOCACY (1968)

A. Leo Levin, Professor of Law, University of Pennsylvania.

Harold Cramer, Esq., Member of the Philadelphia Bar, (Maurice Rosenberg, Professor of Law, Columbia University, as consultant).

TRUSTS, Fourth Edition (1967)

George G. Bogert, James Parker Hall Professor of Law Emeritus, University of Chicago.

Dallin H. Oaks, President, Brigham Young University.

TRUSTS AND SUCCESSION, Second Edition (1968)

George E. Palmer, Professor of Law, University of Michigan.

UNFAIR COMPETITION, see Competitive Process and Business Torts

UNITED NATIONS IN ACTION (1968)

Louis B. Sohn, Professor of Law, Harvard University.

UNITED NATIONS LAW, Second Edition (1967) with Documentary Supplement (1968)

Louis B. Sohn, Professor of Law, Harvard University.

WATER RESOURCE MANAGEMENT (1971) with 1973 Supplement

Charles J. Meyers, Professor of Law, Stanford University.

A. Dan Tarlock, Professor of Law, Indiana University.

WILLS AND ADMINISTRATION, 5th Edition (1961)

The late Philip Mechem, Professor of Law, University of Pennsylvania, and

The late Thomas E. Atkinson, Professor of Law, New York University.

WORLD LAW, see United Nations Law

University Casebook Series

EDITORIAL BOARD

CASES AND MATERIALS

ON

CONTRACTS

SECOND EDITION

By

E. ALLAN FARNSWORTH
Alfred McCormack Professor of Law, Columbia University

WILLIAM F. YOUNG, Jr.
Professor of Law, Columbia University

HARRY W. JONES
Cardozo Professor of Jurisprudence
Columbia University

Mineola, N. Y.
THE FOUNDATION PRESS, INC.
1972

Farnsworth–Young & Jones Cs. Contracts UCB

7th Reprint—1978

PREFACE

The course in Contracts serves a twofold purpose in the first year curriculum. It is the law school's first course in commercial transactions and so must provide the necessary foundation for advanced courses and seminars in this area and ultimately for professional practice. In American legal education, however, the first year Contracts course has always had an additional and more ambitious function. Law teachers have long believed—rightly we think—that contract law offers a body of precepts and problems exceptionally well suited to development of the student's "legal mind": respect for sources, skepticism toward easy generalizations, and disciplined creativity in the use of legal materials for the accomplishment of practical professional tasks. In the selection and arrangement of the materials in this casebook, we have tried to take account of both the specific and the more general objectives served by Contracts courses.

We have tried, where possible, to ease the task of learning. Text is used for introductory exposition and for background on business practices. Notes and problems spotlight topics of current interest (such as those affecting consumers), and suggest how timely counselling and drafting may avoid later litigation. They also call attention to relevant statutes such as the Uniform Commercial Code, and to the formulations of the common law contained in the Restatement of Contracts. But this, like its predecessors, is still essentially a casebook-with-notes rather than a professor's notebook-with-cases. A law school casebook is not an encyclopedia or treatise and is designed for very different purposes. Although we have tried to indicate recurring questions of policy, no effort has been made to provide approved answers. We have tried to caution against the false assumption, to which beginning law students may be inclined, that questions of policy are somehow extrinsic and "nonlegal." In contracts, as elsewhere in the legal order, law and policy are inextricable.

We continue in the debt of our distinguished predecessors, Edwin Patterson and George W. Goble, to whose casebook this volume is the successor. Our indebtedness to many other distinguished scholars is evident throughout. Less evident, but no less real, is our obligation to the imaginative and energetic law students whom we have been privileged to meet in the classroom. We are particularly grateful for the help of the student assistants who have worked with us: Woodrow Wilson Campbell, Jr., John B. Kirkwood, and John D. Taurman.

E. ALLAN FARNSWORTH
WILLIAM F. YOUNG, JR.
HARRY W. JONES

New York
June, 1972

INTRODUCTION

This is a book about legally enforceable promises, or what lawyers call "contracts." What function do contracts serve in our society? What needs are met by private agreements among its members?

As a beginning, imagine taking an inventory of all the contracts made on a typical business day in a city with which you are familiar. How many businesses were sold? How many buildings? Cars? Television sets? How many people got jobs? Rented apartments? Opened bank accounts? Went to movies or ball games? Rode busses? What other transactions should be counted? As these questions suggest, the institution of contract is a vehicle through which the daily needs of ordinary people for goods and services are met. It is also, of course, a vehicle for mammoth enterprises in which governments and their agencies and great corporate bodies engage. Indeed, a large share of the wealth of any developed nation is embodied in contract rights.

The name "contract" is shared by documents purchased at vending machines, as air trip insurance often is, and by agreements negotiated at arm's length by parties taking advice of counsel at every step. Countless contracts are formed daily by telephone, hand signal, or other informal means. The subjects of contracts, and the objects they advance, are even more diverse, if possible, than the means of their creation. Sometimes they are used to settle disputes. Sometimes they are used to establish long-term arrangements under which thousands of individual transactions are to be conducted. Sometimes they are used to vary the effects that certain rules of law would otherwise have on the parties and their dealings. And it is largely through contracts that interests in property are created and altered.

What does this diversity signify about the character of the law of contracts? A first inference might be that the law is largely instrumental. Much of it consists of specifying means for unstated and undetermined ends. To what purposes the power to contract will be put is left very largely to the choice of those who exercise it. Within the domain of contract, as it has been said, "the liberties recognized by law block out a sphere of social life which is left to be controlled, in the absence of further group action, by the process of *autonomous legal ordering*."[a] When organized commercial activity takes place within this sphere, it is commonly described as a "market." The law of contracts has a vital supporting function in relation to markets, as has been described by a distinguished American legal historian, Professor Willard Hurst, in the context of a study of the lumber in-

---

a. Hart and Sacks, The Legal Process
147–48 (Tent. ed. 1958).

dustry in nineteenth-century Wisconsin: "Because marketing cannot go on save in a context of reasonably assured expectations, the legal order as a whole was, of course, indispensable to the existence of a market. But it was the law of contract which supplied the assurances and the procedures and tools necessary for the immediate operation and steadily expanding energy of the institution. . . . Law did not bring the market into being. But law provided essential conditions for its existence. . . . For the timber industry as for other business, contract law provided a framework of reasonably assured expectations within which men might plan and venture. The availability of the forms and procedures of contract thus helped the expansion of the market. . . . [The law] provided a framework of delegated power within which private decisions might operate. . . . The nature of contract was to disperse decision making widely. . . ." [b]

As the character and institutions of a society change, the functions of contract making and enforcement change with it. The dispersion of decision-making power in private hands may lose its attractiveness as an ideal, in competition either with anarchy or with more official forms of decision making.[c] Even if it does not, conditions may change so that contracts become instruments of concentrating power in large business units. The backing of legal force given to private agreements by contract law shows to best advantage in a community, market, or society, in which bargaining power is rather widely and evenly distributed. Professor Kessler expressed the point this way: "The individualism of our rules of contract law, of which freedom of contract is the most powerful symbol, is closely tied up with the ethics of free enterprise capitalism and the ideals of justice of a mobile society of small enterprisers, individual merchants and independent craftsmen." [d]

b. Hurst, Law and Economic Growth: The Legal History of the Lumber Industry in Wisconsin 1936–1915, 285, 294, 297, 333 (1964).

c. Would it not be possible to dispense with contracts entirely by dispensing with the need for private ordering? An attempt was made in the Soviet Union in the early revolutionary years to administer the economy without the institution of contract, to base centralized distribution of wealth on administrative norms. The experiment ended in failure, and Lenin wrote in 1921 that "we must now admit . . . if we do not want to hide our heads under our wings . . . [that] the private market proved to be stronger than we and . . . we ended up with ordinary purchase and sale, trade." Contracts were reintroduced and contract law was codified, largely along traditional lines. Loeber, Plan and Contract Performance in Soviet Law in LaFave (ed.), Law in the Soviet Society 128–29 (1965). You may take it from this that contract is at least a durable institution and it is a safe generalization that few societies have been able to develop far without recognizing at least some promises as enforceable. See Farnsworth, The Past of Promise: A Historical Introduction to Contract, 69 Colum.L.Rev. 576, 578–82 (1969).

d. Kessler, Contracts of Adhesion— Some Thoughts About Freedom of Contract, 43 Colum.L.Rev. 629, 640 (1943).

Well before the present century it was perceived that "enterprisers" of this type were sometimes overmatched in bargaining power by firms in monopoly positions. Then, and increasingly in this century, the law has responded with restraints on the process of private ordering. Lately such restraints have been addressed especially to the position of consumers, as they have become increasingly involved in consensual transactions. Their participation in contract making commonly takes the form of routine assent, or "adhesion," to a standard form contract, whether in dealings with great corporations or in dealings with neighborhood merchants. Many contract forms are like statutes, having uniform application to large classes of persons. Through such forms, the draftsman may exercise positions of authority, in the name of contract, without the necessity of debate and democratic validation that limits legislation. So exercised, it often appears oppressive. Under what circumstances should the law refuse to allow the dominant party to invoke official sanctions for the breach of such agreements? Through statutes and judicial decisions, the law of contracts is moving to answer this question by placing new controls on the manner of contracting and the allowable terms of agreement. It is coming to place a higher value on what Professor Patterson called the freedom *from* contract.[e]

No one imagines that, when promises are kept, it is ordinarily because the promisor is conscious of the rules of contract law. Far from it: both social and business engagements are generally kept for other reasons, including the sense of honor and the concern for community standing. The standards of mutual assistance that apply in conscience and in the market place are sometimes higher, sometimes lower, than those that contract law attaches to a bargain. On the other hand, painstaking attention is regularly paid to contract rules in setting out the terms of a business transaction. There is a skill in drafting agreements that ranks high in legal accomplishments, and you should attempt in this course to grasp it.

It has already been suggested that contract law is useful for supporting market transactions. But its value runs beyond this, in a way hard to measure. Contract is the principal mechanism for allocating and distributing financial risks. This is the object of guarantee and insurance contracts, in particular. If agreements could not be defined with some degree of precision, as a skilled draftsman can do, the costs of uncertainty would stifle many an enterprise, and the affliction of insecurity would be uncontrolled. In addition, if there were no means of enforcing promises, those who keep them for reasons of conscience might be at such a disadvantage, as compared with the unscrupulous, that few of us would be willing and able to pay the price of honoring our undertakings.

e. Patterson, An Apology for Consideration, 58 Colum.L.Rev. 929, 949 (1958).

Organization. The first four chapters of this book are concerned with the law relating to the enforceability of promises. Chapter 1 examines possible bases for determining enforceability and concludes (not surprisingly in the light of the excerpt from Hurst) that bargained-for exchange is the principal basis in our law. Chapter 2 explores the bargaining process through the traditional analysis of offer and acceptance, and concludes by presenting in depth four particularly troublesome problems. Chapter 3 concerns the restraints that are placed on the terms of bargains and on the bargaining process to prevent social evils such as overreaching and sharp practice. Chapter 4 asks when a writing is necessary to the enforceability of a promise.

Chapter 5 turns to a different theme. It is concerned with the remedies available to the aggrieved party when, assuming that there is a contract, the other party does not perform it.

The next four chapters are concerned with the nature and extent of the parties' obligations under the contract. As draftsmen of documents, lawyers have played a major part in this aspect of private ordering. In the words of Professor Llewellyn: "It was . . . the lawyer who devised the mortgage, who made possible the giving of security in goods or land, while leaving the beneficial use of the borrower during the period for which the security was needed; made possible, therefore, the secured production loan whereby a debtor had the chance of financing a new venture out of whose own profits he might hope to meet the debt. . . . It was the lawyer who devised the long-term lease for real estate improvement, and the collateral trust for real estate financing, or for financing new equipment for a mortgaged railroad. And, greatest perhaps of any single line of growth within our law, it was the lawyer who from the outset has shaped the thousand uses of the law of trusts. . . ."[f] Some of the materials in this book are designed to help you develop the skills in drafting that are essential to this facet of professional activity. Chapter 6 inquires into the processes, notably that of interpretation, that define the parties' obligations and repair deficiencies in their expressions, when courts are required to give them effect. Chapter 7 takes up the effects of one party's failure of performance, or prospective failure, on the other party's obligations. Chapter 8 asks when impossibility of performance or frustration of purpose relieves a party of an obligation. And Chapter 9 considers when a party's obligation extends to a third person, as distinguished from the other party to the contract.

The final chapter, Chapter 10, looks at contract rights as a kind of property, and treats of their transfer.

f. Llewellyn, The Bramble Bush 146–47 (1960).

SUMMARY OF CONTENTS

*

TABLE OF CONTENTS

TABLE OF CONTENTS

TABLE OF CASES

The principal cases are in italic type. The cited cases are in roman type. The references are to Pages.

NOTE ON EDITING

Principal cases have been edited with restraint. Cases where editing has been more extensive are presented in abbreviated form. The editors' restatements of facts and insertions within opinions (except for corrections of obvious typographical errors) are enclosed in brackets. Footnotes in opinions and quoted texts have sometimes been omitted and the remaining ones renumbered in sequence. Footnotes inserted by the editors are lettered rather than numbered.

When a problem is accompanied by a reference to a case, the facts presented are sometimes abbreviated from those before the court, but may be markedly different. In any event, the reference is only intended to support a line of thought, or an analogy, and not to supply "the answer" to the problem.

In citation, the Restatement of Contracts (1932) and the Restatement Second of Contracts (still in the process of preparation) are referred to simply as "Restatement" and "Restatement Second." The Uniform Commercial Code is cited as "UCC." Corbin on Contracts (1950–1964) is cited as "Corbin," Williston on Contracts (3d ed. by Jaeger 1957–   ) as "Williston," and Selected Readings on Contracts (Association of American Law Schools 1931) as "Selected Readings."

†

CASES ON CONTRACTS

Chapter 1

A BASIS FOR ENFORCEMENT: BARGAINED-FOR EXCHANGE AND ITS ALTERNATIVES

SECTION 1. BARGAINED–FOR EXCHANGE

What promises will the law enforce? The answer to this question under early English law was closely tied to the common law actions of covenant, debt and assumpsit, and even today no adequate answer can ignore this aspect of legal history.

The first of these actions, covenant, was used to enforce contracts made under seal. Once a written promise was sealed and delivered, the action of covenant was available to enforce it, and it made no difference whether the promisor had bargained for or received anything in exchange for his promise, or whether the promisee had in any way changed his position in reliance on it. In medieval England, the seal was a piece of wax affixed to the document and bearing an impression identifying the person who had executed it. At first its use was confined to the nobility, but later it spread to the commonalty. With the growth of literacy and the use of the personal signature as a means of authentication, the requirement of formality was so eroded that a seal could consist of any written or printed symbol intended to serve as a seal. The word "Seal" and the letters "L.S." (*locus sigilli*) were commonly used for this purpose.

Two functions performed by such legal formalities as the seal have been described by Professor Fuller as "evidentiary," that is, providing trustworthy evidence of the existence and terms of the contract in the event of controversy, and "cautionary," that is, bringing home to the parties the significance of their acts—inducing "the circumspective frame of mind appropriate in one pledging his future." Fuller, Anatomy of the Law 36–37 (1968) ; Fuller, Consideration and Form, 41 Colum.L.Rev. 799, 800 (1941). With the erosion of the solemnity of the seal, it became doubtful that it performed either of these functions well. Consequently, the distinctive effect of the seal on the enforceability of promises has been abolished in roughly half of the states of the United States and seriously curtailed in the rest. The most recent of these assaults on the seal came in UCC 2–203, which, in the words of its draftsmen, "makes it clear that every effect of the seal which relates to 'sealed instruments' as such is wiped out insofar as contracts for sale are concerned." (Comment 1 to UCC 2–203). Where the seal still retains some effect, it is often limited to raising a rebuttable presumption of consideration or making applicable a longer period of limitations. A survey of the laws on the seal in the various states is contained in the Statutory Note at the beginning of Chapter 4, Topic 3, of the Restatement Second.

The second of the three actions, that of debt, could be used to enforce some types of unsealed promises to pay a definite sum of money, including a promise to repay money that had been loaned and a promise to pay for goods that had been delivered or for work that had been done. Since these were situations in which the contemplated exchange was completed on one side, they appealed to the primitive notion that the promisor (or debtor) had something belonging to the promisee (or creditor) which he ought to surrender. The proprietary element present in this notion is reflected in the popular expression that the depositor who is owed money by a bank "*has* money in the bank." What the promisee had given the promisor was sometimes called the "*quid pro quo*," and, as the underlying principles of contract law developed, the promisor's obligation in debt was considered to rest upon his receipt of a *benefit* from the promisee.

The third and ultimately the most important action, assumpsit, grew out of cases in which the promisee sought to recover damages for physical injury to person or property on the basis of a consensual undertaking. In one such case a ferryman who undertook to carry the plaintiff's horse across a river was held liable when he overloaded the boat and the horse drowned. In another a carpenter who undertook to build the plaintiff a house was held liable when he did so unskillfully. The underlying theme of these decisions was that of misfeasance—the promisor, having undertaken (*assumpsit*) to do something, had done it in a manner inconsistent with his undertaking to the detriment of the promisee. The decisions did not go so far as to impose liability for nonfeasance—where the promisor had done *nothing* in pursuance of his undertaking—for example, where the carpenter in the case just put had failed to build the house at all. It was not until the latter half of the fifteenth century that the common law courts began to make this extension. When they did, they imposed a requirement, analogous to that in the misfeasance cases, that the promisee must have incurred a *detriment* in reliance on the promise—as where the owner had changed his position by selling his old house in reliance on the carpenter's promise to build him a new one.

Finally, by the end of the sixteenth century, the courts made a second major extension of the action of assumpsit and held that a party who had given only a promise in exchange for the other's promise had incurred a detriment by having his freedom of action fettered, since he was bound in turn by his own promise. By this circular argument, the common law courts began to enforce exchanges of promises. Here is the opinion in what is said to be the earliest case recognizing that a promise, not even partly performed, could be consideration for a return promise:

> Note, That a promise against a promise will maintain an action upon the case, as in consideration that you do give me £10 on such a day, I promise to give you £10 such a day after.

Strangborough v. Warner, 4 Leo. 3 (Q.B. 1588). See Holdsworth, Debt, Assumpsit and Consideration, 11 Mich.L.Rev. 347, 351 (1913). (How could it happen that England had reached the end of the sixteenth century without giving legal recognition to such transactions?)

Eventually, for reasons that need not be gone into here, the action of assumpsit was allowed to supplant that of debt for the enforcement of promises that would previously have been enforced in the latter action. Thus, by the beginning of the seventeenth century, the common law courts had succeeded in developing the action of assumpsit as a general basis for the enforcement of promises. By the same time, the term "consideration" had come to be used as a word of art to express the sum of the conditions necessary for such an action to lie. It was therefore a tautology that a promise, if not under seal, was enforceable only where there was "consideration," for this was to say no more than that it was enforceable only where the action of assumpsit would lie. Bound up in the concept of consideration were several elements. Most important, from the *quid pro quo* of debt came the idea that there must have been an exchange arrived at by way of bargain. To the extent that debt inspired the concept of consideration, there was the notion that there must be a *benefit* to the promisor. To the extent that assumpsit inspired it, there was the notion that there must be a *detriment* to the promisee. The interplay of these elements can be judged from the cases that follow, and from Restatement Second, § 75. They lend at least some support to the claim of the English legal historian, F. W. Maitland, that "The forms of action we have buried, but they still rule us from their graves." Maitland, The Forms of Action at Common Law 2 (1936 ed.). See, generally, Farnsworth, The Past of Promise: An Historical Introduction to Contract, 69 Colum.L.Rev. 576 (1969).

In considering what promises the law will enforce, it is useful to have some insight into how the law enforces promises, a matter that will be explored in depth in Chapter 5. Ordinarily, when a court concludes that an enforceable promise has been broken, it attempts to protect the plaintiff's expectation by putting him in the position in which he would have been had the promise been performed, i. e., had there been no breach. It may do this by decreeing specific performance of the promise, but usually does it by awarding damages calculated on this basis. The interest that it protects in this way has been called the *expectation interest* and it is said to give the promisee the "benefit of the bargain." The rest of Section 1 is devoted to a consideration of situations in which a promisee seeks the "benefit of the bargain," claiming a promise supported by consideration.

The possibility of alternative claims for relief should not, however, be overlooked. Even in the absence of a claim based on a promise supported by consideration, there may be a claim for restitution of a benefit actually conferred by the plaintiff upon the defendant. The law might protect this interest by putting the defendant back in the position in which he would have been had the promise not been made. The interest so protected has been called the *restitution interest*. And even in the absence of claims based on a promise supported by consideration or for restitution of a benefit conferred, there may be a claim arising out of the fact that the promisee has changed his position to his detriment in reliance on the promise. (He may, for example, have incurred expenses in preparing to perform or have lost opportunities to make other contracts.) The law might protect this interest by putting the plaintiff back in the position in which he would have been had the promise not been made. The interest so protected has been called the *reliance interest*. These alternative interests are explored in Sections 2 and 3. For more on the three interests, see Fuller and Perdue, The Reliance Interest in Contract Damages, 46 Yale L.J. 52, 52–54 (1936).

Which, if any, of these interests does the law protect?

HAMER v. SIDWAY

Court of Appeals of New York, 1891.
124 N.Y. 538, 27 N.E. 256.

[A judgment in favor of plaintiff entered at the trial at Special Term was reversed at General Term of the Supreme Court. Appeal to this court.]

The action was brought by plaintiff, as assignee, against defendant, as executor, upon a contract alleged to have been made between plaintiff's remote assignor and defendant's testator.

PARKER, J. The question which provoked the most discussion by counsel on this appeal, and which lies at the foundation of plaintiff's asserted right of recovery, is whether by virtue of a contract defendant's testator William E. Story became indebted to his nephew William E. Story, 2d, on his twenty-first birthday in the sum of five thousand dollars. The trial court found as a fact that "on the 20th day of March, 1869, . . . William E. Story agreed to and with William E. Story, 2d, that if he would refrain from drinking liquor, using tobacco, swearing, and playing cards or billiards for money until he should become 21 years of age, then he, the said William E. Story, would at that time pay him, the said William E. Story, 2d, the sum of $5000 for such refraining, to which the said William E. Story, 2d, agreed," and that he "in all things fully performed his part of said agreement." [The uncle's promise was made orally in the presence of many witnesses at the golden wedding anniversary of the uncle's parents. On January 31, 1875, when the nephew had turned 21, he wrote the uncle and the uncle wrote back that the nephew had earned the $5000 and that he would keep it at interest for him. The nephew consented. Twelve years later the uncle died, and this action was brought to recover the $5000 with interest.]

The defendant contends that the contract was without consideration to support it, and, therefore, invalid. He asserts that the promisee by refraining from the use of liquor and tobacco was not harmed but benefited; that that which he did was best for him to do independently of his uncle's promise, and insists that it follows that unless the promisor was benefited, the contract was without consideration, a contention which, if well founded, would seem to leave open for controversy in many cases whether that which the promisee did or omitted to do was, in fact, of such benefit to him as to leave no consideration to support the enforcement of the promisor's agreement. Such a rule could not be tolerated, and is without foundation in the law. The Exchequer Chamber, in 1875, defined consideration as follows: "A valuable consideration in the sense of the law may consist either in some right, interest, profit, or benefit accruing to the one party, or some forbearance, detriment, loss, or responsibility given, suffered, or undertaken by the other." Courts "will not ask whether the thing which forms the consideration does in fact benefit the promisee or a third party, or is of any substantial value to any one. It is enough that something is promised, done, forborne, or suffered by the party to whom the promise is made as consideration for the promise made to him." Anson's Prin. of Con. 63.

"In general, a waiver of any legal right at the request of another party is a sufficient consideration for a promise." Parsons on Contracts, 444.

"Any damage, or suspension or forbearance of a right, will be sufficient to sustain a promise." Kent, Vol. 2, 465, 12th Ed.[a]

a. James Kent (1763–1847) began practice after three years as an apprentice and was active in Federalist politics. Hamilton introduced him to the writings of European authors on the civil law, which were to influence his later work. In 1793, largely through his Federalist connections, he was made Professor of Law in Columbia College. He attracted few students, and soon resigned to become a judge on the New York Supreme Court, then the highest court in the state. In 1814 he became Chancellor. Upon his retirement in 1823, he lectured again at Columbia for three years. Out of these lectures grew the "Commentaries on American Law," in four volumes, which became the most important American law book of the century. (It is the source of the quotation above.) Kent lived to prepare six editions; subsequent ones were revised by others. For his work on the Court of Chancery, he has been called practically the creator of equity in the United States.

Pollock, in his work on contracts, page 166, after citing the definition given by the Exchequer Chamber already quoted, says: "The second branch of this judicial description is really the most important one. Consideration means not so much that one party is profiting as that the other abandons some legal right in the present or limits his legal freedom of action in the future as an inducement for the promise of the first."

Now, applying this rule to the facts before us, the promisee used tobacco, occasionally drank liquor, and he had a legal right to do so. That right he abandoned for a period of years upon the strength of the promise of the testator that for such forbearance he would give him $5000. We need not speculate on the effort which may have been required to give up the use of those stimulants. It is sufficient that he restricted his lawful freedom of action within certain prescribed limits upon the faith of his uncle's agreement, and now having fully performed the conditions imposed, it is of no moment whether such performance actually proved a benefit to the promisor, and the court will not inquire into it, but were it a proper subject of inquiry, we see nothing in this record that would permit a determination that the uncle was not benefited in a legal sense. Few cases have been found which may be said to be precisely in point, but such as have been support the position we have taken.

In Shadwell v. Shadwell, 9 C.B.N.S. 159, an uncle wrote to his nephew as follows:

"MY DEAR LANCEY—I am so glad to hear of your intended marriage with Ellen Nicholl, and as I promised to assist you at starting, I am happy to tell you that I will pay you 150 pounds yearly during my life and until your annual income derived from your profession of a chancery barrister shall amount to 600 guineas, of which your own admission will be the only evidence that I shall require.

> "Your affectionate uncle,
> "CHARLES SHADWELL."

It was held that the promise was binding and made upon good consideration.

In Lakota v. Newton, an unreported case in the Superior Court of Worcester, Mass., the complaint averred defendant's promise that "if you (meaning plaintiff) will leave off drinking for a year I will give you $100," plaintiff's assent thereto, performance of the condition by him, and demanded judgment therefor. Defendant demurred on the ground, among others, that the plaintiff's declaration did not allege a valid and sufficient consideration for the agreement of the defendant. The demurrer was overruled.

In Talbott v. Stemmons, 89 Ky. 222, the step-grandmother of the plaintiff made with him the following agreement: "I do promise and bind myself to give my grandson, Albert R. Talbott, $500 at my death, if he will never take another chew of tobacco or smoke another cigar during my life from this date up to my death, and if he breaks this pledge he is to refund double the amount to his mother." The executor of Mrs. Stemmons demurred to the complaint on the ground that the agreement was not based on a sufficient consideration. The demurrer was sustained and an appeal taken therefrom to the Court of Appeals, where the decision of the court below was reversed. In the opinion of the court it is said that "the right to use and enjoy the use of tobacco was a right that belonged to the plaintiff and not forbidden by law. The abandonment of its use may have saved him money or contributed to his health; nevertheless, the surrender of that right caused the promise, and having the right to contract with reference to the subject-matter, the abandonment of the use was a sufficient consideration to uphold the promise." Abstinence from the use of intoxicating liquors was held to furnish a good consideration for a promissory note in Lindell v. Rokes, 60 Mo. 249. The cases cited by the defendant on this question are not in point. . . .

[In an omitted part of the opinion the court held that the action was not barred by the statute of limitations because under the uncle's letter he held the money in trust and not merely as a debtor.] Order reversed and judgment of special term affirmed.

NOTE

Benefit and Detriment. On what ground did the court enforce the uncle's promise? What was the consideration for that promise? How would the measure of recovery in Hamer v. Sidway differ according to whether it was the nephew's restitution, reliance or expectation interest that was being protected? What measure is allowed? Does this mean that the benefit that is the basis of restitution and the detriment that comes from reliance play no role in the court's thinking? What role do they play under the Restatement Second, § 75? Did the circumstances under which the promise was made and the fact that it was reaffirmed play any role in the court's thinking? See generally Braucher, Freedom of Contract and the Second Restatement, 78 Yale L.J. 598, 598–607 (1969).

GRATUITOUS TRANSFERS AND GRATUITOUS PROMISES

Suppose that the uncle had given the nephew $5,000 in cash at the golden wedding anniversary and had told him that it was a gift which he could keep on condition that he refrained from drinking, smoking, swearing and gambling until he was twenty-one. Surely the nephew, having met the condition, could have kept the money if the uncle's executor had attempted to get it back. Why, if the law recognizes gratuitous transfers, should it not recognize gratuitous promises? Why did the court have to find that there was consideration? Is it arguable that gratuitous promises serve no useful economic function? That they raise dangers as to proof? What sorts of rules would you suggest if it were thought desirable to enable promisors, in appropriate cases, to make enforceable gratuitous promises? To what extent should those rules take account of such factors as the promisor's motives, the social utility of the promise, the formality with which it was made, and the availability of alternative means of making gifts?

The civil law countries (those whose legal systems are derived from Roman law) commonly have procedures involving the appearance of the promisor before a notary (a lawyer who holds an appointment from the state and who has no counterpart in common law countries), by which irrevocable gratuitous promise may be made. See von Mehren, Civil Law Analogues to Consideration: An Exercise in Comparative Analysis, 72 Harv.L.Rev. 1009, 1057–62 (1959). A few states have general statutes that facilitate the making of binding gratuitous promises by recognizing some form of writing as a substitute for a seal. One such statute, the Model Written Obligations Act, proposed by the National Conference of Commissioners on Uniform State Laws, provides:

> A written release or promise hereafter made and signed by the person releasing or promising shall not be invalid or unenforceable for lack of consideration, if the writing also contains an additional express statement, in any form of language, that the signer intends to be legally bound.

Only Pennsylvania has adopted this act, and a 1937 recommendation of the English Law Revision Commission that a similar statute be adopted in that country has not been followed.[a] A New Mexico statute provides:

> Every contract in writing hereafter made shall import a consideration in the same manner and as fully as sealed instruments have heretofore done. (N.M.Stat.Ann. § 20–2–8 (1953).)

---

a. See the 1937 Report of the [English] Law Revision Committee on the Statute of Frauds and the Doctrine of Consideration (Sixth Interim Report, Cmd. No. 5449 (1937).) This fourteen-member Committee concurred in a Report on Consideration, which took the bargain concept as the meaning of "consideration," and then gave an historical summary of the doctrine which reflected the highly critical attitude of Holdsworth. Thus it was stated that the origin of consideration was "more or less" fortuitous and that the reasons which gave rise to the requirement have "ceased to be of importance at the present day." The Committee's conclusion in principle was as follows:

"If the view is accepted that all that is necessary in order to render an agreement enforceable is that there should be evidence that the parties intend to create a relationship binding in law, then it seems to follow that this requirement can be satisfied equally well either by consideration regarded as evidence of that intention or by some other evidence of that intention. On this basis, it becomes possible to frame proposals which will carry into effect this purpose, and will, while doing as little violence as possible to any long-established theories, remove hardships arising from the technical applications of the doctrine which have crept into the law of contracts."

A more common variety of general legislation is typified by a California statute that makes a writing "presumptive evidence of consideration" (Cal.Civ.Code § 1614 (West 1954)). The specific provisions of the Uniform Commercial Code and of New York statutes, none of which applies to the simple promise of a gift, will be dealt with later at appropriate points.

NOTE

Lord Mansfield on Consideration. As long ago as 1765, Lord Mansfield [b] declared that, "In commercial cases amongst merchants, the want of consideration is not an objection." Pillans and Rose v. Van Mierop and Hopkins, 3 Burr. 1663, 97 Eng.Rep. 1035 (K.B.1765). His rule was short lived, for three years later it was rejected by the House of Lords, which concluded that, "All contracts are, by the laws of England, distinguished into agreements by specialty [i. e., agreements under seal], and agreements by parol; nor is there any such third class as some of the counsel have endeavored to maintain, as contracts in writing. If they be merely written and not specialties, they are parol, and a consideration must be proved." Rann v. Hughes, 7 T.R. 350n, 101 Eng.Rep. 1014n (1778).

PROMISE FOR PROMISE

We have already seen how, in the historical development of the action of assumpsit as a general basis for the enforcement of promises, courts came to recognize that the consideration for a promise could be found in a return promise, even if not even partly performed (see p. 3 supra). But what rationale lies behind the enforcement of a promise when the promisee cannot show that he has conferred a benefit upon the promisor nor even that he has done anything in reliance on the promise? If one of the parties to an exchange of promises has second thoughts about the transaction the instant after the exchange has occurred, why should he not be allowed to retract his promise without liability?

Consider this simple example. W. O. Lucy met with A. H. Zehmer and his wife Ida and arranged for the sale to Lucy of a farm owned by the Zehmers. The Zehmers promised to convey the land, and Lucy promised to pay $50,000. When the Zehmers refused to convey, Lucy sued for specific performance. The Zehmers claimed that, before they had left Lucy after making the agreement, they had

b. William Murray, first Earl of Mansfield (1705–1793), was a rival of the elder Pitt in school, in Parliament, and in politics. He favored strict measures with the American rebels. His friends included Dr. Johnson (although Mansfield was a Scotsman), and Alexander Pope, who helped him practice advocacy and later praised his eloquence in verse. He achieved greatness as a judge, being Lord Chief Justice from 1756 to 1788. In one important decision he discountenanced slave-holding in England (Somersett's Case). One of his chief services was in rationalizing mercantile law. He familiarized himself with commercial usages, selected a group of merchants who sat as a special jury to advise him on controversies between merchants, and thus translated custom into judicial precedent.

told him that they would not perform. Lucy claimed that the Zehmers had not told him this until three days after the agreement, and
that in the meantime he had arranged to raise half of the money
from his brother and had employed an attorney to examine the title.
The Supreme Court of Appeals of Virginia held that Lucy was entitled to specific performance. Since there had been a bargained-for
exchange of promises, the Zehmers' refusal came too late even on
their version of the facts. (The opinion, which gives other salient
facts, appears at p. 57 infra.)

Why should Lucy be allowed to enforce a promise when the Zehmers had in no way benefitted and Lucy had, on the Zehmers' version
of the facts, in no way relied to his detriment? Would it not be better
to require Lucy to prove that his version of the facts was correct and
that he had relied upon the Zehmers' promise? How much reliance
would you require? Would it be enough if Lucy had testified, without
contradiction, that he would have made an offer on another farm had
the Zehmers not agreed to sell him theirs, and that the other farm
had been sold before they told him that they would not perform?
Would promisees such as Lucy be as safe in relying on promises if
those promises were enforceable only on proof of reliance? For some
answers to these questions, see Fuller and Perdue, The Reliance Interest in Contract Damages, 46 Yale L.J. 52, 61–62 (1936).

ELEANOR THOMAS v. BENJAMIN THOMAS

In the Queen's Bench, 1842. 2 Q.B.Rep. 851, 114 Eng.Rep. 330.

[Assumpsit upon an agreement, a part of which follows:] "And
whereas the said testator, shortly before his death, declared, in the
presence of several witnesses, that he was desirous his said wife should
have and enjoy during her life, or so long as she should continue his
widow, all and singular the dwelling-house," &c., "or 100*l.* out of his
personal estate," in addition to the respective legacies and bequests
given her in and by his said will; "but such declaration and desire
was not reduced to writing in the life-time of the said John Thomas
and read over to him; but the said Samuel Thomas and Benjamin
Thomas are fully convinced and satisfied that such was the desire of
the said testator, and are willing and desirous that such intention
should be carried into full effect: Now these presents witness, and it
is hereby agreed and declared by and between the parties, that, in
consideration of such desire and of the premises," the executors would
convey the dwelling-house, &c., to the plaintiff and her assigns during
her life, or for so long a time as she should continue a widow and unmarried: "provided nevertheless, and it is hereby further agreed and
declared, that the said Eleanor Thomas or her assigns shall and will,
at all times during which she shall have possession of the said dwelling-house, &c., pay to the said Samuel Thomas and Benjamin Thom-

as, their executors, &c., the sum of 1*l.* yearly towards the ground-rent payable in respect of the said dwelling-house and other premises thereto adjoining, and shall and will keep the said dwelling-house and premises in good and tenable repair:" with other provisions not affecting the questions in this case.

The plaintiff was left in possession of the dwelling-house and premises for some time; but the defendant, after the death of his co-executor, refused to execute a conveyance tendered to him for execution pursuant to the agreement, and shortly before the trial brought an ejectment, under which he turned the plaintiff out of possession. . . . Ultimately a verdict was found for the plaintiff on all the issues; and in Easter Term last a rule nisi was obtained pursuant to leave reserved to enter a nonsuit.

LORD DENMAN, C. J.   There is nothing in this case but a great deal of ingenuity, and a little wilful blindness to the actual terms of the instrument itself.   There is nothing whatever to show that the ground-rent was payable to a superior landlord; and the stipulation for the payment of it is not a mere proviso, but an express agreement.   (His Lordship here read the proviso.)   This is in terms an express agreement, and shows a sufficient legal consideration quite independent of the moral feeling which disposed the executors to enter into such a contract.   Mr. Williams' definition of consideration is too large: the word *causa* in the passage referred to means one which confers what the law considers a benefit on the party.   Then the obligation to repair is one which might impose charges heavier than the value of the life estate.

PATTESON, J.   It would be giving to *causa* too large a construction if we were to adopt the view urged for the defendant: it would be confounding consideration with motive.   Motive is not the same thing with consideration.   Consideration means something which is of some value in the eye of the law, moving from the plaintiff: it may be some detriment to the plaintiff, or some benefit to the defendant; but at all events it must be moving from the plaintiff.   Now that which is suggested as the consideration here—a pious respect for the wishes of the testator—does not in any way move from the plaintiff: it moves from the testator; therefore, legally speaking, it forms no part of the consideration.   Then it is said that, if that be so, there is no consideration at all, it is a mere voluntary gift: but when we look at the agreement we find that this is not a mere proviso that the donee shall take the gift with the burthens: but it is an express agreement to pay what seems to be a fresh apportionment of a ground-rent, and which is made payable not to a superior landlord but to the executors.   So that this rent is clearly not something incident to the assignment of the house; for in that case, instead of being payable to the executors, it would have been payable to the landlord.   Then as to the repairs: these houses may very possibly be held under a lease containing covenants to repair; but we know nothing about it: for any thing that appears, the liability to repair is first created by this instrument. The proviso certainly struck me at first as Mr. Williams put it, that the rent and repairs were merely attached to the gift by the donors; and, had the instrument been executed by the donors only, there might have been some ground for that construction; but the fact is not so. Then it is suggested that this would be held to be a mere voluntary conveyance as against a subsequent purchaser for value: possibly that might be so: but suppose it would: the plaintiff contracts to take it, and does take it, whatever it is, for better or worse: perhaps a bonâ fide purchase for a valuable consideration might override it; but that cannot be helped.

COLERIDGE, J. The concessions made in the course of the arguments have in fact disposed of the case. It is conceded that mere motive need not be stated; and we are not obliged to look for the legal consideration in any particular part of the instrument, merely because the consideration is usually stated in some particular part: ut res magis valeat, we may look to any part. In this instrument, in the part where it is usual to state the consideration, nothing certainly is expressed but a wish to fulfil the intentions of the testator; but in another part we find an express agreement to pay an annual sum for a particular purpose, and also a distinct agreement to repair. If these had occurred in the first part of the instrument, it could hardly have been argued that the declaration was not well drawn, and supported by the evidence. As to the suggestion of this being a voluntary conveyance, my impression is that this payment of 1*l*. annually is more than a good consideration: it is a valuable consideration: it is clearly a thing newly created, and not part of the old ground-rent.

Rule discharged.

NOTES

(1) *Motive and Consideration.* Is motive irrelevant? Does it play no part in finding a bargain? Would the result have been the same if the court had concluded that the executors' sole motive in making their promise had been "a pious respect for the wishes of the testator"? Are Restatement Second, § 75(2) and § 84(1) consistent? See also § 81. Holmes [a] discussed consideration in terms of the "reciprocal conventional inducement": "It is said that consideration must not be confounded with motive. It is true that it must not be confounded with what may be the prevailing or chief motive in actual fact. A man may promise to paint a picture for five hundred dollars, while his chief motive may be a desire for fame. A

a. Oliver Wendell Holmes (1841–1935) practiced law in Boston, served briefly as professor of law at Harvard, and then for twenty years as justice and later chief justice of the Supreme Judicial Court of Massachusets. In 1902 he was appointed an associate justice of the United States Supreme Court, where the quality of his dissenting opinions won him the title of the "Great Dissenter." He resigned because of his great age in 1932. His most famous work is The Common Law (1881), based on a series of lectures.

consideration may be given and accepted, in fact, solely for the purpose of making a promise binding. But, nevertheless, it is the essence of a consideration, that, by the terms of the agreement, it is given and accepted as the motive or inducement of the promise. Conversely, the promise must be made and accepted as the conventional motive or inducement for furnishing the consideration. The root of the whole matter is the relation of reciprocal conventional inducement, each for the other, between consideration and promise." Holmes, The Common Law 293–94 (1881). "[T]he promise and the consideration must purport to be the motive each for the other, in whole or at least in part. It is not enough that the promise induces the detriment or that the detriment induces the promise if the other half is wanting." Holmes, J., in Wisconsin & Michigan Railway Co. v. Powers, 191 U.S. 379 (1903).

(2) *Consideration as Form.* Does Thomas v. Thomas mean that a promise of a gift can be raised to the status of a bargain by a mere token payment, inserted by the parties for the specific purpose of satisfying the legal requirement of consideration? Holmes concluded that since courts would not in general "inquire into the amount of such consideration . . . , consideration is as much a form as a seal." Krell v. Codman, 154 Mass. 454, 28 N.E. 578 (1891). (The term "peppercorn" is often used to deride consideration that is of trifling value.) Should such a device be permitted?

The extent to which courts will police the exchange to assure fairness, or at least the absence of unfairness, is the subject of Chapter 3, Policing the Bargain.

FEINBERG v. PFEIFFER CO.

Saint Louis Court of Appeals, Missouri, 1959.
322 S.W.2d 163.

Action on alleged contract by defendant to pay plaintiff a specified monthly amount upon her retirement from defendant's employ. The Circuit Court, City of St. Louis, rendered judgment for plaintiff, and defendant appealed.

DOERNER, COMMISSIONER. This is a suit brought in the Circuit Court of the City of St. Louis by plaintiff, a former employee of the defendant corporation, on an alleged contract whereby defendant agreed to pay plaintiff the sum of $200 per month for life upon her retirement. A jury being waived, the case was tried by the court alone. Judgment below was for plaintiff for $5,100, the amount of the pension claimed to be due as of the date of the trial together with interest thereon, and defendant duly appealed.

The parties are in substantial agreement on the essential facts. Plaintiff began working for the defendant, a manufacturer of pharmaceuticals, in 1910, when she was but 17 years of age. By 1947 she had attained the position of bookkeeper, office manager, and assistant treasurer of the defendant, and owned 70 shares of its stock out of a total of 6,503 shares issued and outstanding. Twenty shares had been given to her by the defendant or its then president, she had purchased 20, and the remaining 30 she had acquired by a stock split or stock dividend. Over the years she received substantial dividends on the stock she owned, as did all of the other stockholders. Also, in addition to her salary, plaintiff from 1937 to 1949, inclusive, received each year a bonus varying in amount from $300 in the beginning to $2,000 in the later years.

On December 27, 1947, the annual meeting of the defendant's Board of Directors was held at the Company's offices in St. Louis, presided over by Max Lippman, its then president and largest individual stockholder. The other directors present were George L. Marcus, Sidney Harris, Sol Flammer, and Walter Weinstock, who, with Max Lippman, owned 5,007 of the 6,503 shares then issued and outstanding. At that meeting the Board of Directors adopted the following resolution, which, because it is the crux of the case, we quote in full:

"The Chairman thereupon pointed out that the Assistant Treasurer, Mrs. Anna Sacks Feinberg, has given the corporation many years of long and faithful service. Not only has she served the corporation devotedly, but with exceptional ability and skill. The President pointed out that although all of the officers and directors sincerely hoped and desired that Mrs. Feinberg would continue in her present position for as long as she felt able, nevertheless, in view of the length of service which she has contributed provision should be made to afford her retirement privileges and benefits which should become a firm obligation of the corporation to be available to her whenever she should see fit to retire from active duty, however many years in the future such retirement may become effective. It was, accordingly, proposed that Mrs. Feinberg's salary which is presently $350.00 per month, be increased to $400.00 per month, and that Mrs. Feinberg would be given the privilege of retiring from active duty at any time she may elect to see fit so to do upon a retirement pay of $200.00 per month for life, with the distinct understanding that the retirement plan is merely being adopted at the present time in order to afford Mrs. Feinberg security for the future and in the hope that her active services will continue with the corporation for many years to come. After due discussion and consideration, and upon motion duly made and seconded, it was—

"Resolved, that the salary of Anna Sacks Feinberg be increased from $350.00 to $400.00 per month and that she be afforded the privilege of retiring from active duty in the corporation at any time she may elect to see fit so to do upon retirement pay of $200.00 per month, for the remainder of her life."

At the request of Mr. Lippman his sons-in-law, Messrs. Harris and Flammer, called upon the plaintiff at her apartment on the same day to advise her of the passage of the resolution. Plaintiff testified on cross-examination that she had no prior information that such a pension plan was contemplated, that it came as a surprise to her, and that she would have continued in her employment whether or not such a resolution had been adopted. It is clear from the evidence that there was no contract, oral or written, as to plaintiff's length of employment, and that she was free to quit, and the defendant to discharge her, at any time.

Plaintiff did continue to work for the defendant through June 30, 1949, on which date she retired. In accordance with the foregoing resolution, the defendant began paying her the sum of $200 on the first of each month. Mr. Lippman died on November 18, 1949, and was succeeded as president of the company by his widow. Because of an illness, she retired from that office and was succeeded in October, 1953, by her son-in-law, Sidney M. Harris. Mr. Harris testified that while Mrs. Lippman had been president she signed the monthly pension check paid plaintiff, but fussed about doing so, and considered the payments as gifts. After his election, he stated, a new accounting firm employed by the defendant questioned the validity of the payments to plaintiff on several occasions, and in the Spring of 1956, upon its recommendation, he consulted the Company's then attorney, Mr. Ralph Kalish. Harris testified that both Ernst and Ernst, the accounting firm, and Kalish told him there was no need of giving plaintiff the money. He also stated that he had concurred in the view that the payments to plaintiff were mere gratuities rather than amounts due under a contractual obligation, and that following his discussion with the Company's attorney plaintiff was sent a check for $100 on April 1, 1956. Plaintiff declined to accept the reduced amount, and this action followed. Additional facts will be referred to later in this opinion.   .   .   .

Appellant's next complaint is that there was insufficient evidence to support the court's findings that plaintiff would not have quit defendant's employ had she not known and relied upon the promise of defendant to pay her $200 a month for life, and the finding that, from her voluntary retirement until April 1, 1956, plaintiff relied upon the continued receipt of the pension installments. The trial court so found, and, in our opinion, justifiably so. Plaintiff testified, and was corroborated by Harris, defendant's witness, that knowledge of the passage of the resolution was communicated to her on December 27, 1947, the very day it was adopted. She was told at that time by Harris and Flammer, she stated, that she could take the pension as of that day, if she wished. She testified further that she continued to work for another year and a half, through June 30, 1949; that at that time her health was good and she could have continued to work, but that after working for almost forty years she thought she would take a rest. Her testimony continued:

"Q. Now, what was the reason—I'm sorry. Did you then quit the employment of the company after you—after this year and a half? A. Yes.

"Q. What was the reason that you left? A. Well, I thought almost forty years, it was a long time and I thought I would take a little rest.

"Q. Yes. A. And with the pension and what earnings my husband had, we figured we could get along.

"Q. Did you rely upon this pension? A. We certainly did.

"Q. Being paid? A. Very much so. We relied upon it because I was positive that I was going to get it as long as I lived.

"Q. Would you have left the employment of the company at that time had it not been for this pension? A. No.

"Mr. Allen: Just a minute, I object to that as calling for a conclusion and conjecture on the part of this witness.

"The Court: It will be overruled.

"Q. (Mr. Agatstein continuing): Go ahead, now. The question is whether you would have quit the employment of the company at that time had you not relied upon this pension plan? A. No, I wouldn't.

"Q. You would not have. Did you ever seek employment while this pension was being paid to you— A. (interrupting): No.

"Q. Wait a minute, at any time prior—at any other place? A. No, sir.

"Q. Were you able to hold any other employment during that time? A. Yes, I think so.

"Q. Was your health good? A. My health was good."

It is obvious from the foregoing that there was ample evidence to support the findings of fact made by the court below.

We come, then, to the basic issue in the case. While otherwise defined in defendant's third and fourth assignments of error, it is thus succinctly stated in the argument in its brief: ". . . whether plaintiff has proved that she has a right to recover from defendant based upon a legally binding contractual obligation to pay her $200 per month for life."

It is defendant's contention, in essence, that the resolution adopted by its Board of Directors was a mere promise to make a gift, and that no contract resulted either thereby, or when plaintiff retired, because there was no consideration given or paid by the plaintiff. It urges that a promise to make a gift is not binding unless supported by a legal consideration; that the only apparent consideration for the adoption of the foregoing resolution was the "many years of long and faithful service" expressed therein; and that past services are not a valid consideration for a promise. Defendant argues further that there is nothing in the resolution which made its effectiveness conditional upon plaintiff's continued employment, that she was not under contract to work for any length of time but was free to quit whenever she wished, and that she had no contractual right to her position and could have been discharged at any time.

Plaintiff concedes that a promise based upon past services would be without consideration, but contends that there were two other elements which supplied the required element: First, the continuation by plaintiff in the employ of the defendant for the period from December 27, 1947, the date when the resolution was adopted, until the date of her retirement on June 30, 1949. And, second, her change of position, i. e., her retirement, and the abandonment by her of her opportunity to continue in gainful employment, made in reliance on defendant's promise to pay her $200 per month for life.

We must agree with the defendant that the evidence does not support the first of these contentions. There is no language in the resolution predicating plaintiff's right to a pension upon her continued employment. She was not required to work for the defendant for any period of time as a condition to gaining such retirement benefits. She was told that she could quit the day upon which the resolution was adopted, as she herself testified, and it is clear from her own testimony that she made no promise or agreement to continue in the employ of the defendant in return for its promise to pay her a pension. Hence there was lacking that mutuality of obligation which is essential to the validity of a contract. [The court quoted Restatement, § 75.]

[The rest of the opinion in this case, dealing with Mrs. Feinberg's second contention, is at p. 53 infra.]

NOTES

(1) *The Missing Ingredient.* Why was not Mrs. Feinberg's 37 years of service, prior to the resolution of December 27, 1947, consideration for Pfeiffer's promise? Why was not her 18 months of service, subsequent to the resolution, consideration? Why was not her retiring consideration?

(2) *Counselling.* Suppose that Mr. Lippman had called in his lawyer in December, 1947, and said, "I want you to draw up a resolution that will make it sure that Mrs. Feinberg will get a pension of $200 a month as long as she lives." Could the promise have been made enforceable under the doctrine of consideration? How? Would it have helped to have reworded the resolution to include the words, *"in consideration of her many years of long and faithful service"*? See Perreault v. Hall, 94 N.H. 191, 49 A.2d 812 (1946).

ADAM SMITH ON CONSIDERATION

Every human society relies to some extent upon cooperation among its members to achieve social purposes. To what extent does the notion of consideration comport with the view that this cooperation can best be achieved by a system of "free enterprise"? Consider in this regard, and in connection with the following cases, these words of Adam Smith, written in 1776: "[M]an has almost constant occasion for the help of his brethren, and it is vain for him to expect it from their benevolence only. He will be more likely to prevail if he can interest their self-love in his favour, and shew them that it is for their own advantage to do for him what he requires of them. Whoever offers to another a bargain of any kind, proposes to do this: Give me that which I want, and you shall have this which you want, is the meaning of every such offer; and it is in this manner that we obtain from one another the far greater part of those good offices which we stand in need of. . . . We address ourselves, not to their humanity but to their self-love, and never talk to them of our own necessities but of their advantages. Nobody but a beggar chooses to depend chiefly upon the benevolence of his fellow-citizens." A. Smith, An Inquiry into the Nature and Causes of the Wealth of Nations 11 (1811 ed., bk. 1, ch. II).

NOTE

The Economics of Consideration. For the most part, our economic system allocates resources according to a competitive or free enterprise model, in which the role of bargain is apparent. Nevertheless, in the two centuries since Adam Smith wrote the words quoted above, economists have come to realize that the preferences of a society as a whole may not be adequately expressed by strict adherence to such a model. The result has been a substantial and growing amount of governmental regulation. When we have finished examining The Bargaining Process in Chapter 2, we shall see how some of this regulation is used in Policing the Bargain in Chapter 3.

MILLS v. WYMAN

Supreme Judicial Court of Massachusetts, 1825.
3 Pick. 207.

This was an action of assumpsit brought to recover a compensation for the board, nursing, etc. of Levi Wyman, son of the defendant, from the 5th to the 20th of February, 1821. The plaintiff then lived at Hartford, in Connecticut; the defendant at Shrewsbury, in this state. Levi Wyman, at the time when the services were rendered, was about 25 years of age, and had long ceased to be a member of his father's family. He was on his return from a voyage at sea, and being suddenly taken sick at Hartford, and being poor and in distress, was relieved by the plaintiff in the manner and to the extent above stated. On the 24th of February, after all the expenses had been incurred, the defendant wrote a letter to the plaintiff, promising to pay him such expenses. There was no consideration for this promise, except what grew out of the relation which subsisted between Levi Wyman and the defendant, and Howe, J., before whom the case was tried in the Court of Common Pleas, thinking this not sufficient to support the action, directed a nonsuit. To this direction the plaintiff filed exceptions.

PARKER, C. J. General rules of law established for the protection and security of honest and fair-minded men, who may inconsiderately make promises without any equivalent, will sometimes screen men of a different character from engagements which they are bound *in foro conscientiae* to perform. This is a defect inherent in all human systems of legislation. The rule that a mere verbal promise, without any consideration, cannot be enforced by action, is universal in its application, and cannot be departed from to suit particular cases in which a refusal to perform such a promise may be disgraceful.

The promise declared on in this case appears to have been made without any legal consideration. The kindness and services towards the sick son of the defendant were not bestowed at his request. The son was in no respect under the care of the defendant. He was twenty-five years old, and had long left his father's family. On his return from a foreign country, he fell sick among strangers, and the plaintiff acted the part of the good Samaritan, giving him shelter and comfort until he died. The defendant, his father, on being informed of this event, influenced by a transient feeling of gratitude, promised in writing to pay the plaintiff for the expenses he had incurred. But he has determined to break this promise, and is willing to have his case appear on record as a strong example of particular injustice sometimes necessarily resulting from the operation of general rules.

It is said a moral obligation is a sufficient consideration to support an express promise; and some authorities lay down the rule thus broadly; but upon examination of the cases we are satisfied that the universality of the rule cannot be supported, and that there must have been some pre-existing obligation, which has become inoperative by positive law, to form a basis for an effective promise. The cases of debts barred by the Statute of Limitations, of debts incurred by infants, of debts of bankrupts, are generally put for illustration of the rule. Express promises founded on such pre-existing equitable obligations may be enforced; there is a good consideration for them; they merely remove an impediment created by law to the recovery of debts honestly due, but which public policy protects the debtors from being compelled to pay. In all these cases there was originally a *quid pro quo*, and according to the principles of natural justice the party receiving ought to pay; but the legislature has said he shall not be coerced; then comes the promise to pay the debt that is barred, the promise of the man to pay the debt of the infant, of the discharged bankrupt to restore to his creditor what by the law he had lost. In all these cases there is a moral obligation founded upon an antecedent valuable consideration. These promises, therefore, have a sound legal basis. They are not promises to pay something for nothing; not naked pacts, but the voluntary revival or creation of obligations which before existed in natural law, but which had been dispensed with, not for the benefit of the party obliged solely, but principally for the public convenience. If moral obligation, in its fullest sense, is a good substratum for an express promise, it is not easy to perceive why it is not equally good to support an implied promise. What a man ought to do, generally he ought to be made to do whether he promise or refuse. But the law of society has left most of such obligations to the interior forum, as the tribunal of conscience has been aptly called . . . . .

Without doubt there are great interests of society which justify withholding the coercive arm of the law from these duties of imperfect obligation, as they are called; imperfect, not because they are less binding upon the conscience than those which are called perfect, but because the wisdom of the social law does not impose sanctions upon them.

A deliberate promise in writing, made freely and without any mistake, one which may lead the party to whom it is made into contracts and expenses, cannot be broken without a violation of moral duty. But if there was nothing paid or promised for it, the law, perhaps wisely, leaves the execution of it to the conscience of him who makes it. It is only when the party making the promise gains something, or he to whom it is made loses something, that the law gives the promise validity. And in the case of the promise of the adult to pay the debt of the infant, of the debtor discharged by the statute of limitations or bankruptcy, the principle is preserved by looking back to the origin of that transaction, where an equivalent is to be found . . . . .

For the foregoing reasons we are all of opinion that the nonsuit directed by the Court of Common Pleas was right, and that judgment be entered thereon for costs for the defendant.

NOTES

(1) *The Case Against "Moral Obligation."* Mills v. Wyman accurately reflects the traditional common law view that a promise made in recognition of a "moral obligation" arising out of a benefit previously received is not enforceable. A benefit conferred before a promise is made can hardly be said to have been given in "exchange" for the promise. Williston[a] says: "However much one may wish to extend the number of promises which are enforceable by law, it is essential that the classes of promises which are so enforceable shall be clearly defined. The test of moral con-

a. Samuel Williston (1861–1963) joined the faculty of the Harvard Law School in 1890, after practicing law for a short period in Boston, and taught there until his retirement in 1938. His principal fields were contracts and sales. His multi-volume work, A Treatise on the Law of Contracts, was first published in 1920 and became one of the most widely used legal treatises in the United States. He was the Reporter for the Restatement of Contracts and the draftsman of several uniform laws, including the Uniform Sales Act.

sideration must vary with the opinion of every individual. Indeed, as has been said, since there is a moral obligation to perform every promise, it would seem that if morality was to be the guide, every promise would be enforced and if the existence of a past moral obligation is to be the test, every promise which repeats or restates a prior gratuitous promise would be binding." Williston, § 148.

(2) *Recognized Exceptions.* In some exceptional situations the common law did enforce a promise on the ground that it was made in recognition of what could be viewed as a "moral obligation." Leading examples include those mentioned by the court in Mills v. Wyman: a promise to pay a debt that is no longer legally enforceable because of the running of the period of limitations or because of the discharge of the debtor in bankruptcy proceedings, and a promise by an adult to perform a duty imposed by a promise that he made as an infant and that he could have avoided on that ground. See Restatement Second, §§ 86, 87, 89. Does the court in Mills v. Wyman adequately distinguish these examples?[b]

Promises to pay debts barred by bankruptcy proceedings are sometimes made by consumers to finance companies after discharge in bankruptcy proceedings available to wage earners. The promise to pay the barred debt commonly occurs after the finance company has threatened to sue the consumer under an exception, generally applicable to all bankruptcy proceedings, that a debt is not dischargeable if credit was extended in reliance on a materially false financial statement. See Shuchman, The Fraud Exception in Consumer Bankruptcy, 23 Stan.L.Rev. 735, 755 (1971). (The possibility that the relinquishment by the finance company of even a doubtful claim might itself be consideration for the consumer's new promise should be considered in connection with Chapter 3, Policing the Bargain. The validity of promises induced by such threats is also dealt with in that chapter.)

WEBB v. McGOWIN

Court of Appeals of Alabama, 1935.
27 Ala.App. 82, 168 So. 196.
Certiorari denied 232 Ala. 374, 168 So. 199 (1936).

Action by Joe Webb against N. Floyd McGowin and Joseph F. McGowin, as executors of the estate of J. Greeley McGowin, deceased. From a judgment of nonsuit, plaintiff appeals.

BRICKEN, PRESIDING JUDGE. This action is in assumpsit. The complaint as originally filed was amended. The demurrers to the complaint as amended were sustained, and because of this adverse ruling by the court the plaintiff took a nonsuit, and the assignment of

---

b. In 1782 Lord Mansfield, whose earlier bout with the doctrine of consideration is discussed in Note, p. 9, supra, derived from such exceptions the dictum, "Where a man is under a moral obligation, which no Court of Law or Equity can inforce, and promises, the honesty and rectitude of the thing is a consideration." Hawkes v. Saunders, 1 Cowp. 289, 98 Eng.Rep. 1091 (1782). The dictum never became the law.

errors on this appeal are predicated upon said action or ruling of the court.

A fair statement of the case presenting the questions for decision is set out in appellant's brief, which we adopt.

"On the 3d day of August, 1925, appellant while in the employ of the W. T. Smith Lumber Company, a corporation, and acting within the scope of his employment, was engaged in clearing the upper floor of Mill No. 2 of the company. While so engaged he was in the act of dropping a pine block from the upper floor of the mill to the ground below; this being the usual and ordinary way of clearing the floor, and it being the duty of the plaintiff in the course of his employment to so drop it. The block weighed about 75 pounds.

"As appellant was in the act of dropping the block to the ground below, he was on the edge of the upper floor of the mill. As he started to turn the block loose so that it would drop to the ground, he saw J. Greeley McGowin, testator of the defendants, on the ground below and directly under where the block would have fallen had appellant turned it loose. Had he turned it loose it would have struck McGowin with such force as to have caused him serious bodily harm or death. Appellant could have remained safely on the upper floor of the mill by turning the block loose and allowing it to drop, but had he done this the block would have fallen on McGowin and caused him serious injuries or death. The only safe and reasonable way to prevent this was for appellant to hold to the block and divert its direction in falling from the place where McGowin was standing and the only safe way to divert it so as to prevent its coming into contact with McGowin was for appellant to fall with it to the ground below. Appellant did this, and by holding to the block and falling with it to the ground below, he diverted the course of its fall in such way that McGowin was not injured. In thus preventing the injuries to McGowin appellant himself received serious bodily injuries, resulting in his right leg being broken, the heel of his right foot torn off and his right arm broken. He was badly crippled for life and rendered unable to do physical or mental labor.

"On September 1, 1925, in consideration of appellant having prevented him from sustaining death or serious bodily harm and in consideration of the injuries appellant had received, McGowin agreed with him to care for and maintain him for the remainder of appellant's life at the rate of $15 every two weeks from the time he sustained his injuries to and during the remainder of appellant's life; it being agreed that McGowin would pay this sum to appellant for his maintenance. Under the agreement McGowin paid or caused to be paid to appellant the sum so agreed on up until McGowin's death on January 1, 1934. After his death the payments were continued to and including January 27, 1934, at which they they were discontinued. Thereupon plaintiff brought suit to recover the unpaid installments accruing up to the time of the bringing of the suit.

"The material averments of the different counts of the original complaint and the amended complaint are predicated upon the foregoing statement of facts." . . .

The action was for the unpaid installments accruing after January 27, 1934, to the time of the suit. . . .

1. The averments of the complaint show that appellant saved McGowin from death or grievous bodily harm. This was a material benefit to him of infinitely more value than any financial aid he could have received. Receiving this benefit, McGowin became morally bound to compensate appellant for the services rendered. Recognizing his moral obligation, he expressly agreed to pay appellant as alleged in the complaint and complied with this agreement up to the time of his death; a period of more than 8 years.

Had McGowin been accidentally poisoned and a physician, without his knowledge or request, had administered an antidote, thus saving his life, a subsequent promise by McGowin to pay the physician would have been valid. Likewise, McGowin's agreement as disclosed by the complaint to compensate appellant for saving him from death or grievous bodily injury is valid and enforceable.

Where the promisee cares for, improves, and preserves the property of the promisor, though done without his request, it is sufficient consideration for the promisor's subsequent agreement to pay for the service, because of the material benefit received. . . .

In Boothe v. Fitzpatrick, 36 Vt. 681, the court held that a promise by defendant to pay for the past keeping of a bull which had escaped from defendant's premises and been cared for by plaintiff was valid, although there was no previous request, because the subsequent promise obviated that objection; it being equivalent to a previous request. On the same principle, had the promisee saved the promisor's life or his body from grievous harm, his subsequent promise to pay for the services rendered would have been valid. Such service would have been far more material than caring for his bull. Any holding that saving a man from death or grievous bodily harm is not a material benefit sufficient to uphold a subsequent promise to pay for the service, necessarily rests on the assumption that saving life and preservation of the body from harm have only a sentimental value. The converse of this is true. Life and preservation of the body have material, pecuniary values, measurable in dollars and cents. Because of this, physicians practice their profession charging for services rendered in saving life and curing the body of its ills, and surgeons perform operations. The same is true as to the law of negligence, authorizing the assessment of damages in personal injury cases based upon the extent of the injuries, earnings, and life expectancies of those injured.

In the business of life insurance, the value of a man's life is measured in dollars and cents according to his expectancy, the soundness of his body, and his ability to pay premiums. The same is true as to health and accident insurance.

It follows that if, as alleged in the complaint, appellant saved J. Greeley McGowin from death or grievous bodily harm, and McGowin subsequently agreed to pay him for the service rendered, it became a valid and enforceable contract.

2. It is well settled that a moral obligation is a sufficient consideration to support a subsequent promise to pay where the promisor has received a material benefit, although there was no original duty or liability resting on the promisor. [Cases cited.]

The case at bar is clearly distinguishable from that class of cases where the consideration is a mere moral obligation or conscientious duty unconnected with receipt by promisor of benefits of a material or pecuniary nature. . . . Here the promisor received a material benefit constituting a valid consideration for his promise.

3. Some authorities hold that, for a moral obligation to support a subsequent promise to pay, there must have existed a prior legal or equitable obligation, which for some reason had become unenforceable, but for which the promisor was still morally bound. This rule, however, is subject to qualification in those cases where the promisor having received a material benefit from the promisee, is morally bound to compensate him for the services rendered and in consideration of this obligation promises to pay. In such cases the subsequent promise to pay is an affirmance or ratification of the services rendered carrying with it the presumption that a previous request for the service was made. . . .

4. The averments of the complaint show that in saving McGowin from death or grievous bodily harm, appellant was crippled for life. This was part of the consideration of the contract declared on. McGowin was benefited. Appellant was injured. Benefit to the promisor or injury to the promisee is a sufficient legal consideration for the promisor's agreement to pay. . . .

5. Under the averments of the complaint the services rendered by appellant were not gratuitous. The agreement of McGowin to pay and the acceptance of payment by appellant conclusively shows the contrary. . . .

From what has been said, we are of the opinion that the court below erred in the ruling complained of; that is to say in sustaining the demurrer, and for this error the case is reversed and remanded.

Reversed and remanded.

SAMFORD, JUDGE (concurring). The questions involved in this case are not free from doubt, and perhaps the strict letter of the rule, as stated by judges, though not always in accord, would bar a recovery by plaintiff, but following the principle announced by Chief Justice Marshall in Hoffman v. Porter, Fed.Cas.No.6,577, 2 Brock. 156, 159, where he says, "I do not think that law ought to be separated from justice, where it is at most doubtful," I concur in the conclusions reached by the court.

NOTES

(1) *Restitution.* Did Webb have a claim against McGowin in restitution? If so, the release of that claim in exchange for McGowin's promise could serve as consideration for that promise. The possibility of a claim in restitution can best be considered in connection with the cases in Section 2, Restitution as an Alternative. Does this appear to have been the basis for the decision in the case? See, in this connection, Restatement Second, § 89A.

(2) *The Case for "Moral Obligation."* "Courts have frequently enforced promises on the simple ground that the promisor was only promising to do what he ought to have done anyway. These cases have either been condemned as wanton departures fom legal principle, or reluctantly accepted as involving the kind of compromise logic must inevitably make at times with sentiment. I believe that these decisions are capable of rational defense. When we say the defendant was morally obligated to do the thing he promised, we in effect assert the existence of a substantive ground for enforcing the promise. . . . The court's conviction that the promisor ought to do the thing, plus the promisor's own admission of his obligation, may tilt the scales in favor of enforcement where neither standing alone would be sufficient. If it be argued that moral consideration threatens certainty, the solution would seem to lie, not in rejecting the doctrine, but in taming it by continuing the process of judicial exclusion and inclusion already begun in the cases involving infants' contracts, barred debts, and discharged bankrupts." Fuller, Consideration and Form, 41 Colum.L.Rev. 799, 821, 822 (1941). See also Henderson, Promises Grounded in the Past: The Idea of Unjust Enrichment and the Law of Contracts, 57 Va.L.Rev. 1115 (1971).

(3) *The Case of the Spared Spouse.* Lee Taylor assaulted his wife in Lena Harrington's house, where she had taken refuge from a previous assault. The wife knocked him down with an axe, and was about to cut his head open when Lena Harrington deflected the axe, mutilating her hand badly but saving Lee Taylor's life. Later, he orally promised her to pay her damages, but paid only a small sum. She sued him on his promise. *Held*: for defendant. "[H]owever much the defendant should be impelled by common gratitude to alleviate the plaintiff's misfortune, a humanitarian act of this kind, voluntarily performed, is not such consideration as would entitle her to recover at law." Harrington v. Taylor, 225 N.C. 690, 36 S.E.2d 227 (1945).

(4) *Statutes.* New York does not recognize "moral obligation" as an equivalent of consideration, but a New York statute enacted in 1941 and now found in General Obligations Law, § 5–1105, provides: "A promise in writing and signed by the promisor or by his agent shall not be denied effect as a valid contractual obligation on the ground that consideration for the promise is past or executed, if the consideration is expressed in the writing and is proved to have been given or performed and would be a valid consideration but for the time when it was given or performed."

California Civil Code, § 1606, enacted in 1872, provides: "An existing legal obligation resting upon the promisor, or a moral obligation originating in some benefit conferred upon the promisor, or prejudice suffered by the promisee, is also a good consideration for a promise, to an extent corresponding with the extent of the obligation, but no further or otherwise."

How would these statutes have affected the results in the preceding cases? Would the common recital "for value received" satisfy the New York statute? Would you favor the adoption of either statute by other states?[a]

THE "ZEALOUS" ADVOCATE AND "TECHNICAL" DEFENSES

Is any ethical question raised when a lawyer is asked to represent a client who has a "technical" defense to the legal enforcement of a "moral" obligation?

An extreme position on the zeal of the advocate is reflected in the famous statement of Lord Brougham, in his defense of Queen Caroline before the House of Lords, in the case of her divorce from George IV:

> I once before took occasion to remind your lordships . . . that an advocate, by the sacred duty which he owes his client, knows in the discharge of that office but one person in the world, that client and none other. To save that client by all expedient means, to protect that client at all hazards and costs, to all others, and among others to himself, is the highest and most unquestioned of his duties; and he must not regard the alarm, the suffering, the torment, the destruction which he may bring upon any other. Nay, separating even the duties of a patriot from those of an advocate, and casting them, if need be, to the wind, he must go on reckless of the consequences, if his fate it should unhappily be to involve his country in confusion for his client's protection.

For discussion of this view of the advocate's zeal, see Thurman, Phillips and Cheatham, Cases and Materials on the Legal Profession 280–81 (1970).

Canon 7 of the American Bar Association's Code of Professional Responsibility says, with more moderation, "A lawyer should represent a client zealously within the bounds of the law," and Disciplinary Rule 7–101(A) adds that he shall not intentionally "[f]ail to seek the

---

a. The Reporter who drafted Restatement Second, § 89A has expressed the belief that "this statement of principle is more useful than the statutory formula drafted by the New York Law Revision Commission. . . . [The latter] is too broad in scope and too restrictive in formal requirements; it does not seem to have had any significant effect." Braucher, Freedom of Contract and the Second Restatement, 78 Yale L.J. 598, 605 (1969).

lawful objectives of his client through reasonably available means permitted by law and the Disciplinary Rules, except as provided by DR 7–101(B)." Disciplinary Rule 7–101(B) says that a lawyer may, "[w]here permissible, exercise his professional judgment to waive or fail to assert a right or position of his client." Although Ethical Consideration 7–7 says that, except for "certain areas of legal representation not affecting the merits of the cause or substantially prejudicing the rights of a client . . . the authority to make decisions is exclusively that of the client," Ethical Consideration 7–8 says that in "assisting his client to make a proper decision, it is often desirable for a lawyer to point out those factors which may lead to a decision that is morally just as well as legally permissible." What position should he take as to his client's defense of lack of consideration for his promise to perform his "moral" obligation?

In practice, the ethical problems implicit in the use of a "technical" defense may be presented in quite another way. "Is it proper to use surprise tactics to defeat on a technical ground a claim or defense which you consider unjust upon grounds which you may not be able to establish? Does it make a difference whether such grounds (those which you may not be able to establish) are factual or legal? It is in this 'intermediate' form that the ethical question usually arises. Most cases are settled; in the smaller percentage going to trial, each lawyer generally feels that the other party is at least seeking more than that to which he is justly entitled, if not making a wholly unjustified claim or defense. Probably the answer implicit in prevailing practice is that it is permissible to use any legally supportable ground of claim or defense, though it be a surprise move, to uphold a position which the lawyer believes just, whatever the basis of his belief may be." Keeton, Trial Tactics and Methods 3–4 (1954).

NOTE

Canon Buttle's Case. Canon Buttle's case may shed some light on the problem. Trustees under a trust of land for sale orally agreed to sell it to Mrs. Simpson for £6,000 and the matter had proceeded so far that one copy of the contract had been signed by Mrs. Simpson and the other by one, but only one, trustee. Canon Buttle, one of the beneficiaries of the trust, then offered £6,500 on behalf of a charity. The trustees indicated that they felt "in honour bound" to complete the sale to Mrs. Simpson. Canon Buttle and other beneficiaries sought an order restraining the trustees, and the trustees asked for the direction of the court. Wynn-Parry, J., of the Chancery Division said:

> It is true that persons who are not in the position of trustees are entitled, if they so desire, to accept a lesser price than that which they might obtain on the sale of property. . . . It redounds to the credit of a man who acts like that in such circumstances. Trustees, however, are not vested with such complete freedom. They have an overriding duty to obtain the best price which they can for their beneficiaries. . . . The only

consideration which was present to their minds was that they had gone so far in the negotiations with Mrs. Simpson that they could not properly, from the point of view of commercial morality, resile from these negotiations. That being so, they did not, to any extent, probe Canon Buttle's offer as, in my view, they should have done. . . . There being a serious purchaser, I shall give the trustees liberty to sell to Mrs. Simpson for £6,600, that being the highest price offered.

Buttle v. Saunders, [1950] 2 All.E.R. 193 (Ch.). Does a lawyer have "complete freedom" to act according to his sense of "commercial morality," or does he have an "overriding duty" to his client?

KIRKSEY v. KIRKSEY

Supreme Court of Alabama, 1845.
8 Ala. 131.

The plaintiff was the wife of defendant's brother, but had for some time been a widow, and had several children. In 1840, the plaintiff resided on public land, under a contract of lease, she had held over, and was comfortably settled, and would have attempted to secure the land she lived on. The defendant resided in Talladega County, some sixty or seventy miles off. On the 10th October, 1840, he wrote to her the following letter:

"Dear Sister Antillico,—Much to my mortification, I heard that brother Henry was dead, and one of his children. I know that your situation is one of grief and difficulty. You had a bad chance before, but a great deal worse now. I should like to come and see you, but cannot with convenience at present. . . . I do not know whether you have a preference on the place you live on or not. If you had, I would advise you to obtain your preference, and sell the land and quit the country, as I understand it is very unhealthy, and I know society is very bad. If you will come down and see me, I will let you have a place to raise your family, and I have more open land than I can tend; and on account of your situation, and that of your family, I feel like I want you and the children to do well."

Within a month or two after the receipt of this letter, the plaintiff abandoned her possession, without disposing of it, and removed with her family, to the residence of the defendant, who put her in comfortable houses, and gave her land to cultivate for two years, at the end of which time he notified her to remove, and put her in a house, not comfortable, in the woods, which he afterwards required her to leave.

A verdict being found for the plaintiff, for $200, the above facts were agreed, and if they will sustain the action, the judgment is to be affirmed, otherwise it is to be reversed.

ORMOND, J. The inclination of my mind is that the loss and inconvenience which the plaintiff sustained in breaking up and moving

to the defendant's, a distance of sixty miles, is a sufficient consideration to support the promise to furnish her with a house, and land to
cultivate, until she could raise her family.   My brothers, however,
think that the promise on the part of the defendant was a mere gratuity, and that an action will not lie for its breach.   The judgment of
the court below must therefore be reversed, pursuant to the agreement of the parties.

NOTES

(1) *Characterization of "If" Clauses.*   How did the court read the
words, "If you will come down and see me, I will let you have a place to
raise your family"?   As words of bargain for an exchange or of condition
to a gratuitous promise of a gift?   Was not the benefit to the brother-in-
law comparable to the benefit to the uncle in Hamer v. Sidway, p. 4 supra?

(2) *Reliance as a Basis.*   Should "Sister Antillico" be allowed to
recover on the ground that she relied on the promise, even though her reliance was not bargained for?   This question will be taken up in Section
3, Reliance as an Alternative.

(3) *Problem.*   A father and a daughter became estranged after the
mother had divorced the father, and the daughter refused to see the father.
The father then wrote to his daughter: "If you will meet me at Tiffany's
next Monday at noon, I will buy you the emerald ring advertised in this
week's New Yorker."   The daughter came to Tiffany's at the time specified, and met her father there, but he failed to buy her the promised
ring.   Bargained-for exchange or conditional gratuitous promise?

BROADNAX v. LEDBETTER

Supreme Court of Texas, 1907.
100 Tex. 375, 99 S.W. 1111.

[Action by Broadnax to recover a reward of $500 offered by
Ledbetter for the recapture and return to the Dallas County jail of a
prisoner, Vann, who had escaped therefrom.   The defendant interposed demurrers on the ground that the petition stated no cause of
action because it was not alleged that the plaintiff had knowledge or
notice of the reward when the escaped prisoner was captured and returned to jail by the plaintiff.

These demurrers were sustained and judgment was entered dismissing plaintiff's case.   Plaintiff appeals.   The following question
was certified: Was notice or knowledge to plaintiff of the existence of
the reward when the capture was made essential to his right to recover?]

WILLIAMS, J. . . .   Upon the question stated there is a conflict among the authorities in other states.   All that have been cited
or found by us have received due consideration, and our conclusion is
that those holding the affirmative are correct.   The liability for a re-

ward of this kind must be created, if at all, by contract. There is no rule of law which imposes it except that which enforces contracts voluntarily entered into. A mere offer or promise to pay does not give rise to a contract. That requires the assent or meeting of two minds, and therefore is not complete until the offer is accepted. Such an offer as that alleged may be accepted by anyone who performs the service called for when the acceptor knows that it has been made and acts in performance of it, but not otherwise. He may do such things as are specified in the offer, but, in so doing, does not act in performance of it, and therefore does not accept it, when he is ignorant of its having been made. There is no such mutual agreement of minds as is essential to a contract. The offer is made to anyone who will accept it by performing the specified acts, and it only becomes binding when another mind has embraced and accepted it. The mere doing of the specified things without reference to the offer is not the consideration for which it calls. .   .   .

Some of the authorities taking the opposite view seem to think that the principles of contracts do not control the question, and in one of them, at least, it is said that "the sum offered is but a boon, gratuity, or bounty, generally offered in a spirit of liberality, and not as a mere price, or a just equivalent simply for the favor or service requested, to be agreed or assented to by the person performing it, but, when performed by him, as justly and legally entitling him to a fulfillment of the promise, without any regard whatever to the motive or inducement which prompted him to perform it." Eagle v. Smith, 4 Houst., Del., 293. But the law does not force persons to bestow boons, gratuities, or bounties merely because they have promised to do so. They must be legally bound before that can be done. It may be true that the motive of the performer in rendering service is not of controlling effect as is said in some of the authorities above cited in pointing out the misapprehension of the case of Williams v. Carwardine, 6 English Ruling Cases 133, into which some of the courts have fallen. But this does not reach the question whether or not a contractual obligation is essential.

Other authorities say that it is immaterial to the offerer that the person doing that which the offer calls for did not know of its existence; that the services are as valuable to him when rendered without as when rendered with knowledge. Dawkins v. Sappington, 26 Ind. 199; Auditor v. Ballard, 9 Bush., Ky., 572, 15 Am.Rep. 728. But the value to the offerer of the acts done by the other party is not the test. They may in supposable cases be of no value to him, or may be no more valuable to him than to the person doing them. He is responsible, if at all, because, by his promise, he has induced another to do the specified things. Unless so induced, the other is in no worse position than if no reward had been offered. The acting upon this inducement is what supplies, at once, the mutual assent and the contemplated consideration. Without the legal obligation thus arising from contract there is nothing which the law enforces.

Reasons have also been put forward of a supposed public policy, assuming that persons will be stimulated by the enforcement of offers of rewards in such cases to aid in the detection of crime and the arrest and punishment of criminals. But, aside from the fact that the principles of law to be laid down cannot on any sound system of reasoning be restricted to offers made for such purposes, it is difficult to see how the activities of people can be excited by offers of rewards of which they know nothing. If this reason had foundation in fact, it would hardly justify the courts in requiring private citizens to minister to the supposed public policy by paying rewards merely because they have made offers to pay upon which no one has acted. Courts can only enforce liabilities which have in some way been fixed by the law. While we have seen no such distinction suggested, it may well be supposed that a person might become legally entitled to a reward for arresting a criminal, although he knew nothing of its having been offered where it is or was offered in accordance with law by the government. A legal right might in such a case be given by law without the aid of contract. But the liability of the individual citizen must arise from a contract binding him to pay.

The question is answered in the affirmative. [Judgment affirmed.]

NOTES

(1) *Knowledge of Offer.* Were Broadnax's acts "bargained for"? Could he have recovered if he had captured Vann while ignorant of the reward but had learned of it before returning him to jail? Is his solution to release the criminal and capture him again? Compare Restatement, § 53 with Restatement Second, § 53. See also Restatement Second, § 23. Could Broadnax have recovered if he had known of the reward but had captured Vann and turned him in because he was a close friend and wished to save him from mob violence? See Taft v. Hyatt, 105 Kan. 35, 180 P. 213 (1919); Restatement Second, § 84(2). Could he have recovered if he had said, when he turned Vann in, that he did not want the reward? See Corbin, § 58.

The court's dictum that if the reward were "offered in accordance with law by the government . . ., [a] right might in such a case be given by law without the aid of contract," was followed in Choice v. City of Dallas, 210 S.W. 753 (Tex.Civ.App.1919), involving the offer of a reward by an ordinance of the city of Dallas, which the court characterized as "in the nature of a bounty." In some legal systems, including the German, a promise of reward is treated, "not as an offer which would require acceptance in order to ripen into a contract, but as a unilateral jural act which as such is effective and binding without acceptance." 1 Schlesinger (ed.), Formation of Contracts: A Study of the Common Core of Legal Systems 101–02 (1968). Would such a concept be a desirable one in our law? (Can a helpful analogy be found in a conditional promise under seal?)

(2) *Problem.* Diamond Jim III, a rock fish, was tagged and placed in the Chesapeake Bay on June 19 by the American Brewery in connection with its Third Annual American Beer Fishing Derby. Under the Derby's well-publicized rules, the person who caught Diamond Jim III would receive a cash prize of $25,000. On August 6, William Simmons set out to go fishing in the Bay. He had heard of the contest, but did not have it in mind on that day. He caught Diamond Jim III, and although he at first took little notice of the tag, he realized upon reexamining it a half hour later that he had caught the prize fish. Is Simmons legally entitled to the prize? See Simmons v. United States, 308 F.2d 160 (4th Cir. 1962).

(3) *Who Can Accept?* Generally, an offer can be accepted only by one whom it invites to furnish the consideration. The classic case is Boulton v. Jones, 2 H. & N. 564 (1857). Jones, a regular customer of Brocklehurst, a pipe hose manufacturer with whom he had a running account, sent an order for leather hose addressed to Brocklehurst. Earlier the same day Boulton, Brocklehurst's foreman and manager, had bought the entire business including stock in trade. Boulton furnished the hose without notifying Jones of the change in ownership. When Jones refused to pay, Boulton sued for the price. *Held*: For Jones. Bramwell, B., noted that, "When a contract is made, in which the personality of the contracting party is or may be of importance, as a contract with a man to write a book, or the like, or where there might be a set-off, no other person can interpose and adopt the contract." If Jones had used or disposed of the goods, Boulton's remedy would be in quasi contract for their reasonable value, not the price. (See Section 2, Restitution as an Alternative.) Suppose, however, that Jones still had the goods and was able to return them, but did not offer to do so. Would there be a contract? This case is criticized in Williams, Mistake as to Party in the Law of Contract II, 23 Can.B.Rev. 380, 383 (1945).

SECTION 2.   RESTITUTION AS AN ALTERNATIVE

Courts have, with reason, regarded with suspicion claims to recover for benefits voluntarily conferred. The Restatement of Restitution, § 112, Comment a, gives this rather obvious illustration:

> During A's absence and in the belief that A will be willing to pay for the work, B improves A's land, which is worth and is offered for sale at $5000, to such an extent that upon A's return he sells the land for $8000. B is not entitled to restitution from A.

The following cases pose more difficult problems in drawing the line between the "officious intermeddler" and the deserving claimant.

CALLANO v. OAKWOOD PARK HOMES CORP.

Superior Court of New Jersey, 1966.
91 N.J.Super. 105, 219 A.2d 332.

COLLESTER, J. A. D.   Defendant Oakwood Park Homes Corp., (Oakwood) appeals from a judgment of $475 entered in favor of plaintiffs Julia Callano and Frank Callano in the Monmouth County District Court.

The case was tried below on an agreed stipulation of facts. Oakwood, engaged in the construction of a housing development, in December 1961 contracted to sell a lot with a house to be erected thereon to Bruce Pendergast, who resided in Waltham, Massachusetts. In May 1962, prior to completion of the house, the Callanos, who operated a plant nursery, delivered and planted shrubbery pursuant to a contract with Pendergast. A representative of Oakwood had knowledge of the planting.

Pendergast never paid the Callanos the invoice price of $497.95. A short time after the shrubbery was planted Pendergast died. Thereafter, on July 10, 1962 Oakwood and Pendergast's estate cancelled the contract of sale. Oakwood had no knowledge of Pendergast's failure to pay the Callanos. On July 16, 1962 Oakwood sold the Pendergast property, including the shrubbery located thereon, to Richard and Joan Grantges for an undisclosed amount.

The single issue is whether Oakwood is obligated to pay plaintiffs for the reasonable value of the shrubbery on the theory of *quasi*-contractual liability. Plaintiffs contend that defendant was unjustly enriched when the Pendergast contract to purchase the property was cancelled and that an agreement to pay for the shrubbery is implied in law. Defendant argues that the facts of the case do not support a recovery by plaintiffs on the theory of *quasi*-contract.

Contracts implied by law, more properly described as *quasi* or constructive contracts, are a class of obligations which are imposed or created by law without regard to the assent of the party bound, on the ground that they are dictated by reason and justice. They rest solely on a legal fiction and are not contract obligations at all in the true sense, for there is no agreement; but they are clothed with the semblance of contract for the purpose of the remedy, and the obligation arises not from consent, as in the case of true contracts, but from the law or natural equity. Courts employ the fiction of *quasi* or constructive contract with caution.[a]   17 C.J.S. Contracts § 6, pp. 566–570 (1963).

---

a. "Quasi contract" is a useful term for describing a ground for recovering money in an action at common law, when the claim is not based either on principles of tort law or on a true contract. Together with such equi- table remedies as those discussed at p. 41, *infra*, it serves to redress unjust enrichment. "Restitution" is a broader term, propagated by American scholars in this century, to embrace all of the remedies having that func-

In cases based on *quasi*-contract liability, the intention of the parties is entirely disregarded, while in cases of express contracts and contracts implied in fact the intention is of the essence of the transaction. In the case of actual contracts the agreement defines the duty, while in the case of *quasi*-contracts the duty defines the contract. Where a case shows that it is the duty of the defendant to pay, the law imparts to him a promise to fulfill that obligation. The duty which thus forms the foundation of a *quasi*-contractual obligation is frequently based on the doctrine of unjust enrichment. It rests on the equitable principle that a person shall not be allowed to enrich himself unjustly at the expense of another, and on the principle of whatsoever it is certain a man ought to do, that the law supposes him to have promised to do. St. Paul Fire, etc., Co. v. Indemnity Ins. Co. of No. America, 32 N.J. 17, 22, 158 A.2d 825 (1960).

The key words are *enrich* and *unjustly*. To recover on the theory of *quasi*-contract the plaintiffs must prove that defendant was enriched, *viz.*, received a benefit, and that retention of the benefit without payment therefor would be unjust.

It is conceded by the parties that the value of the property, following the termination of the Pendergast contract, was enhanced by the reasonable value of the shrubbery at the stipulated sum of $475. However, we are not persuaded that the retention of such benefit by defendant before it sold the property to the Grantges was inequitable or unjust.

Quasi-contractual liability has found application in a myriad of situations. See Woodruff, Cases on Quasi-Contracts (3d ed. 1933). However, a common thread runs throughout its application where liability has been successfully asserted, namely, that the plaintiff expected remuneration from the defendant, or if the true facts were known to plaintiff, he would have expected remuneration from defendant, at the time the benefit was conferred. See Rabinowitz v. Mass. Bonding & Insurance Co., 119 N.J.L. 552, 197 A. 44 (E. & A. 1937); Power-Matics, Inc. v. Ligotti, 79 N.J.Super. 294, 191 A.2d 483 (App. Div.1963); Shapiro v. Solomon, 42 N.J.Super. 377, 126 A.2d 654 (App.Div.1956). It is further noted that *quasi*-contract cases involve either some direct relationship between the parties or a mistake on the part of the person conferring the benefit.

In the instant case the plaintiffs entered into an express contract with Pendergast and looked to him for payment. They had no dealings with defendant, and did not expect remuneration from it when

tion. It refers also to the theory on which they are based. "Quantum meruit" (as much as he deserved) is an older term, narrower, and less useful in current discourse about contract law. It describes a form of action, or short-form pleading, used for centuries in enforcing duties of payment for services. A related action for the worth of goods was "quantum valebat" (as much as it was worth).

Inexact uses of these terms are common. In particular, the term "quantum meruit" is often used interchangeably with "quasi-contract."

they provided the shrubbery.   No issue of mistake on the part of plaintiffs is involved.   Under the existing circumstances we believe it would be inequitable to hold defendant liable.   Plaintiffs' remedy is against Pendergast's estate, since they contracted with and expected payment to be made by Pendergast when the benefit was conferred. . . . A plaintiff is not entitled to employ the legal fiction of *quasi*-contract to "substitute one promisor or debtor for another." Cascaden v. Magryta, 247 Mich. 267, 225 N.W. 511, 512 (Sup.Ct. 1929).

Plaintiffs place reliance on De Gasperi v. Valicenti, 198 Pa.Super. 455, 181 A.2d 862 (Super.Ct.1962), where recovery was allowed on the theory of unjust enrichment.   We find the case inapposite.   It is clear that recovery on *quasi*-contract was permitted there because of a fraud perpetrated by defendants.   There is no contention of fraud on the part of Oakwood in the instant case.

Recovery on the theory of *quasi*-contract was developed under the law to provide a remedy where none existed.   Here, a remedy exists. Plaintiffs may bring their action against Pendergast's estate.   We hold that under the facts of this case defendant was not unjustly enriched and is not liable for the value of the shrubbery.

Reversed.

NOTES

(1) *The Case of Contractor's Claim.*   Paschall's built a bathroom onto the Doziers' house at the request and on the credit of their daughter, Mrs. Best, who lived with them, and with the knowledge and consent of the Doziers.   Paschall's was unsuccessful in collecting from Mrs. Best, who was subsequently adjudicated a bankrupt, and sued the Doziers on a theory of restitution.   The trial court sustained the Doziers' demurrer and dismissed the complaint, and Paschall's appealed.   *Held*: Reversed.   The court granted that it may be "the general rule" that "an implied undertaking cannot arise against one benefitted by the work performed, where the work is done under a special contract with another. . . . However, the situation is dissimilar where a person furnishes materials and labor under a contract for the benefit of a third party, and that contract becomes unenforceable or invalid. . . . [W]e think that before recovery can be had against the landowner on an unjust enrichment theory, the furnisher of the materials and labor must have exhausted his remedies against the person with whom he had contracted, and still has not received the reasonable value of his services."   Paschall's, Inc. v. Dozier, 219 Tenn. 45, 407 S.W.2d 150 (1966).

Can this case be distinguished from the Callano case?   On restitution in such cases, see Wade, Restitution for Benefits Conferred Without Request, 19 Vand.L.Rev. 1183, 1212 (1966); Dawson, Unjust Enrichment (1951).

(2) *Subcontactors and Mechanics' Liens.*   An application of the problem considered in the preceding case that is of great practical importance concerns the rights of subcontractors on construction jobs.   Typically

two separate contracts are involved, one between the owner and the general contractor, and another between the general contractor and the subcontractor. It is clear that if, after the subcontractor has performed, he is not paid by the general contractor, the subcontractor has no contractual rights against the owner. It is also clear, under reasoning like that in the Callano case, that even though the subcontractor has benefitted the owner by improving his property, he cannot recover in restitution. E. g., Johnson & Petersen v. Toohey, 285 Minn. 181, 172 N.W.2d 326 (1969).

In all states, however, subcontractors are protected by statutes providing for what are historically known as "mechanics' liens." These statutes began to be enacted in the late eighteenth century to spur construction in a young and growing country. They protect laborers, materialmen, subcontractors, contractors and the like, who make improvements on real property by giving them a lien, i. e., a security interest, in that property to secure payment for those improvements. Public property is generally exempt. The subcontractor's lien is limited to the reasonable value of what he has done, and in some states it may not exceed the amount then due from the owner to the general contractor. Typically the lien must be perfected by serving notice on the owner and filing a statement in a public office within prescribed times. Although the lien does not create any personal obligation from the owner to the subcontractor, it is enforceable through sale of the owner's property in foreclōsure proceedings, with the debt owed by the general contractor to the subcontractor payable out of the proceeds.[a]

COTNAM v. WISDOM

Supreme Court of Arkansas, 1907.
83 Ark. 601, 104 S.W. 164.

Appeal from Circuit Court, Pulaski County; R. J. Lea, Judge.

Action by F. L. Wisdom and another against T. T. Cotnam, administrator of A. M. Harrison, deceased, for services rendered by plaintiffs as surgeons to defendant's intestate. Judgment for plaintiffs. Defendant appeals. Reversed and remanded.

Instructions 1 and 2, given at the instance of plaintiffs, are as follows: "(1) If you find from the evidence that plaintiffs rendered professional services as physicians and surgeons to the deceased, A. M. Harrison, in a sudden emergency following the deceased's injury in a street car wreck, in an endeavor to save his life, then you are instructed that plaintiffs are entitled to recover from the estate of the said A. M. Harrison such sum as you may find from the evidence is a reasonable compensation for the services rendered. (2) The charac-

---

a. Why did not the Callanos and Paschall's have liens? The New Jersey statute provides for a lien on property "for all debts contracted by the owner thereof" for improvements, specifically including "planting thereon any shrubs." N.J.Stat.Ann. § 2A:44–66. But the facts indicate that Oakwood, not Pendergast, was the "owner" of the property. Similarly, the Tennessee statute provides for a lien where improvements have been made on a house by "contract with the owner or his agent." Tenn.Code Ann. §§ 64–1102.

ter and importance of the operation, the responsibility resting upon the surgeon performing the operation, his experience and professional training, and the ability to pay of the person operated upon, are elements to be considered by you in determining what is a reasonable charge for the services performed by plaintiffs in the particular case."

HILL, C. J. (after stating the facts). . . . The first question is as to the correctness of [the first] instruction. As indicated therein the facts are that Mr. Harrison, appellant's intestate, was thrown from a street car, receiving serious injuries which rendered him unconscious, and while in that condition the appellees were notified of the accident and summoned to his assistance by some spectator, and performed a difficult operation in an effort to save his life, but they were unsuccessful, and he died without regaining consciousness. The appellant says: "Harrison was never conscious after his head struck the pavement. He did not and could not, expressly or impliedly, assent to the action of the appellees. He was without knowledge or will power. However merciful or benevolent may have been the intention of the appellees, a new rule of law, of contract by implication of law, will have to be established by this court in order to sustain the recovery." Appellant is right in saying that the recovery must be sustained by a contract by implication of law, but is not right in saying that it is a new rule of law, for such contracts are almost as old as the English system of jurisprudence. They are usually called "implied contracts." More properly they should be called "quasi contracts" or "constructive contracts." See 1 Page on Contracts, sec. 14; also 2 Page on Contracts, sec. 771.

The following excerpts from Sceva v. True, 52 N.H. 627, are peculiarly applicable here: "We regard it as well settled by the cases referred to in the briefs of counsel, many of which have been commented on at length by Mr. Shirley for the defendant, that an insane person, an idiot, or a person utterly bereft of all sense and reason by the sudden stroke of an accident or disease may be held liable, in assumpsit, for necessaries furnished to him in good faith while in that unfortunate and helpless condition. And the reasons upon which this rests are too broad, as well as too sensible and humane, to be overborne by any deductions which a refined logic may make from the circumstances that in such cases there can be no contract or promise, in fact, no meeting of the minds of the parties. The cases put it on the ground of an implied contract; and by this is not meant, as the defendant's counsel seems to suppose, an actual contract—that is, an actual meeting of the minds of the parties, an actual, mutual understanding, to be inferred from language, acts, and circumstances by the jury—but a contract and promise, said to be implied by the law, where, in point of fact, there was no contract, no mutual understanding, and so no promise. The defendant's counsel says it is usurpation for the court to hold, as a matter of law, that there is a contract and a promise, when all the evidence in the case shows that there was not a contract, nor the semblance of one. It is doubtless a legal fiction, invented and used for the sake of the remedy. If it was originally usurpation, certainly it has now become very inveterate, and firmly fixed in the body of the law. Illustrations might be multiplied, but enough has been said to show that when a contract or promise implied by law is spoken of, a very different thing is meant from a contract in fact, whether express or tacit. The evidence of an actual contract is generally to be found either in some writing made by the parties, or in verbal communications which passed between them, or in their acts and conduct considered in the light of the circumstances of each particular case. A contract implied by law, on the contrary, rests upon no evidence. It has no actual existence. It is simply a mythical creation of the law. The law says it shall be taken that there was a promise, when in point of fact, there was none. Of course this is not good logic, for the obvious and sufficient reason that it is not true. It is a legal fiction, resting wholly for its support on a plain legal obligation, and a plain legal right. If it were true, it would not be a fiction. There is a class of legal rights, with their correlative legal duties, analogous to the obligations quasi ex contractu of the civil law which seem to lie in the region between contracts on the one hand, and torts on the other, and to call for the application of a remedy not strictly furnished either by actions ex contractu or actions ex delicto. . . ."

In its practical application it sustains recovery for physicians and nurses who render services for infants, insane persons, and drunkards. . . . And services rendered by physicians to persons unconscious or helpless by reason of injury or sickness are in the same situation as those rendered to persons incapable of contracting, such as the classes above described. . . . The court was therefore right in giving the instruction in question. . . .

There was evidence in this case proving that it was customary for physicians to graduate their charges by the ability of the patient to pay, and hence, in regard to that element, this case differs from the Alabama case [Morrissett v. Wood, 123 Ala. 384, 26 So. 307]. . . . This could not apply to a physician called in an emergency by some bystander to attend a stricken man whom he never saw or heard of before; and certainly the unconscious patient could not, in fact or in law, be held to have contemplated what charges the physician might properly bring against him. In order to admit such testimony, it must be assumed that the surgeon and patient each had in contemplation that the means of the patient would be one factor in determining the amount of the charge for the services rendered. While the law may admit such evidence as throwing light upon the contract and indicating what was really in contemplation when it was made, yet a different question is presented when there is no contract to be ascertained or construed, but a mere fiction of law creating a contract where none existed in order that there might be a remedy for a right. This fiction merely requires a reasonable compensation for the services rendered. The services are the same be the patient prince or pauper, and for them the surgeon is entitled to fair compensation for his time, service, and skill. It was therefore error to admit this evidence, and to instruct the jury in the second instruction that in determining what was a reasonable charge they could consider the "ability to pay of the person operated upon." [a]

It was improper to let it go to the jury that Mr. Harrison was a bachelor and that his estate was left to nieces and nephews. This was relevant to no issue in the case, and its effect might well have been prejudicial. While this verdict is no higher than some of the evidence would justify, yet it is much higher than some of the other evidence would justify, and hence it is impossible to say that this was a harmless error.

Judgment is reversed, and cause remanded.

BATTLE and WOOD, JJ., concur in sustaining the recovery, and in holding that it was error to permit the jury to consider the fact that his estate would go to collateral heirs; but they do not concur in holding that it was error to admit evidence of the value of the estate, and instructing that it might be considered in fixing the charge.

NOTES

(1) *Question.* Would the result have been different if Dr. Wisdom had treated Harrison in response to a call from Harrison's daughter, who had said, "Give him the best care you can and I will pay you for it"? See p. 424 infra.

(2) *Gratuitousness.* Where one's life or property is imperiled by storm, fire, accident or other casualty, and another renders assistance, the law presumes, in accordance with the mores of our society, that the services were intended to be gratuitous. Thus where a passing motorist finds an injured pedestrian on the highway, administers first aid and takes him to a hospital, there is a presumption of gratuity which will ordinarily bar recovery. However, the presumption may be rebutted if the services are excessively expensive or burdensome to the person rendering them, as where he goes out of his way a hundred miles to take the injured person to a hospital, or where his services continue for days or weeks. The presumption that services rendered in an emergency are gratuitous may also be overturned if the person rendering them does so in a business or professional capacity, as where a passing ambulance removes the injured person to the hospital or, where as in Cotnam v. Wisdom, a passing physician treats the injured person. The law of salvage in admiralty affords some interesting comparisons with land rules concerning services rendered in an emergency. See Wade, Restitution for Benefits Conferred Without Request, 19 Vand.L. Rev. 1183, 1208–11 (1966).

---

a. For a case rejecting Cotnam v. Wisdom on this point, see In re Agnew's   Estate, 132 Misc. 811, 231 N.Y.S. 4 (1928).

(3) *Amount of Recovery.* What is the proper measure of recovery in quasi contract? In Hill v. Waxberg Construction Co., 237 F.2d 936 (9th Cir. 1956), the court gave the following answer: "An 'implied in fact' contract is essentially based on the intentions of the parties. It arises where the court finds from the surrounding facts and circumstances that the parties intended to make a contract but failed to articulate their promises and the court merely implies what it feels the parties really intended. It would follow then that the general contract theory of compensatory damages should be applied. Thus, if the court can in fact imply a contract for services, the compensation therefor is measured by the going contract rate. An 'implied in law' contract, on the other hand, is a fiction of the law which is based on the maxim that one who is unjustly enriched at the expense of another is required to make restitution to the other. The intentions of the parties have little or no influence on the determination of the proper measure of damages. In the absence of fraud or other tortious conduct on the part of the person enriched, restitution is properly limited to the value of the benefit which was acquired. The distinction is based on sound reason, too, for where a contract is all but articulated, the expectations of the parties are very nearly mutually understood, and the Court has merely to protect those expectations as men in the ordinary course of business affairs would expect them to be protected, whereas in a situation where one has acquired benefits, without fraud and in a non-tortious manner, with expectations so totally lacking in such mutuality that no contract in fact can be implied, the party benefited should not be required to reimburse the other party on the basis of such party's losses and expenditures, but rather on a basis limited to the benefits, which the benefited party has actually acquired." [a]

Thus in Michigan Central R. Co. v. State, 85 Ind.App. 557, 155 N.E. 50 (1927), the railroad company delivered to the State of Indiana a carload of coal under the mistaken belief that it was the consignee. On discovering its error, the railroad company paid the proper consignee for the coal at the market price of $6.85 a ton and then sued the State for reimbursement based on that price. The evidence showed that the State was buying the same kind of coal at $3.40 a ton. The trial court gave judgment for the railroad company based on $3.40 per ton and this was affirmed. The railroad company may recover in quasi contract only the expense saved the State ($3.40 a ton) and not the outlay of the railroad ($6.85 a ton).

---

a. One important consequence of the distinction between "implied in fact" and "implied in law" arises under the Tucker Act, in which the federal government has consented to be sued in the Court of Claims on claims "founded . . . upon any express or implied contract with the United States" (28 U.S.C.A. § 1491). In Schillinger v. United States, 155 U.S. 163 (1894), the Supreme Court held that this did not confer jurisdiction upon the Court of Claims over a claim by a patentee whose patent had been used by the government without his consent since "there is no statement tending to show a coming together of minds in respect to anything." The case has given rise to the proposition that the Court of Claims has no jurisdiction over a claim based on a contract implied in law. Merritt v. United States, 267 U.S. 338 (1925).

CONSTRUCTIVE TRUST AND SUBROGATION

The common law action for damages to prevent unjust enrichment is supplemented by several types of equitable relief. The most important of these are the constructive trust and subrogation. See, generally, Dawson, Restitution or Damages?, 20 Ohio St.L.J. 175, 181–85 (1959).

The "constructive trust" is a method of giving the plaintiff restitution where the defendant has acquired title to property from him or through disposition of his property. The court impresses the property with a constructive trust and will compel its transfer to the plaintiff, subject to the rights of intervening good faith purchasers. See Restatement, Restitution, § 160.

An example is Nebraska National Bank v. Johnson, 51 Neb. 546, 71 N.W. 294 (1897). Johnson, a janitor in a bank, stole $5,000 in gold coin from his employer, and used the money to purchase and improve land in Omaha for his residence. He became insolvent and had no other property.[a] The bank sued to impress the property with a constructive trust in its favor and to have its title to the land confirmed, and the trial court granted this relief on condition that the bank pay Johnson $185 which he had contributed from his own funds to the improvement of the property. Johnson appealed and the Supreme Court of Nebraska affirmed. It rejected the argument that there could be no constructive trust because there was no fiduciary relationship–no "relation of trust and confidence"–between Johnson and the bank. "The doctrine of constructive trusts, as developed by courts of equity, was intended primarily as a remedy for fraud in cases where the established rules had proved wholly inadequate; and larceny, under the circumstances here disclosed, is none the less a fraud upon the owner of the property stolen because committed by a servant instead of one who is, in the technical sense of the term, a trustee."

"Subrogation" is a method of giving the plaintiff restitution where his property has been used in fully discharging another's obligation or a security interest upon another's property. The court allows the plaintiff to be subrogated to the position which the creditor or securityholder had occupied prior to the discharge. See Restatement, Restitution, § 162.

Ford v. United States, 115 Ct.Cl. 793, 88 F.Supp. 263 (1950), is illustrative. Ford, an American soldier in England, stole £350 from Segelman, an Englishman. When Ford was arrested, £353 was taken from him, but this was not the stolen money. After Ford had been convicted and sentenced, the United States paid Segelman pursuant

---

a. Under homestead laws in many states, including Nebraska, property occupied as a home is protected, at least in part, from ordinary claims, such as the bank would have had against Johnson in conversion, by being exempted from execution for such claims.

to a federal statute enacted "[f]or the purpose of promoting and maintaining friendly relations by the prompt settlement of meritorious claims." Ford sued the United States to recover the amount taken from him on his arrest, and the United States pleaded a set-off in the amount that it had paid Segelman. The Court of Claims held that the United States was entitled to the set-off. "Segelman of course could have maintained an action against plaintiff to recover the money which plaintiff had stolen from him. Instead, Segelman filed a claim against the United States, and the United States [under the statute] paid Segelman the debt which plaintiff owed him. This of course discharged plaintiff's liability to Segelman and, hence, it would seem that defendant is subrogated to Segelman's claim against plaintiff. In paying plaintiff's debt to Segelman, we do not think it can be said the defendant was acting as a volunteer. For the sake of promoting friendly relations with friendly countries whose soil we were occupying during the war, we assumed liability for certain acts of the members of our armed forces."

NOTE

Duty of Another. Particularly troublesome problems of "officiousness" and "gratuitousness" are posed where a claimant seeks restitution from one whose duty he has, in some measure, performed—the position of the United States in Ford v. United States, supra. Some of the most common instances arise in connection with duties owed to other members of one's family. If a husband fails to furnish his wife with necessaries, a third party who, without the husband's request, does so may generally recover their reasonable value from the husband. Similarly, if a father fails to furnish a minor child with necessaries, a third party who does so, without the father's request, may generally recover their reasonable value from the father. Such problems are more fully considered in courses in family law. For an interesting case on the liability of parents for medical services rendered to their child after they had refused to provide them, see Greenspan v. Slate, 12 N.J. 426, 97 A.2d 390 (1953).

LIABILITY FOR APPROPRIATION OF IDEAS

Claims of liability for appropriation of ideas have provided fertile ground for the development of the law relating to unjust enrichment. Schott v. Westinghouse Electric Corp., 436 Pa. 279, 259 A.2d 443 (1969), is illustrative. Schott, an employee of Westinghouse, twice submitted a suggestion concerning the construction of circuit breaker panels pursuant to a program under which Westinghouse invited its employees to submit suggestions for cash awards from $5.00 up to $15,000. On the suggestion form, above the line for the employee's signature, appeared the stipulation, "I agree that the decision of the local Suggestion Committee on all matters pertaining to this suggestion . . . will be final." The Committee twice rejected Schott's suggestion, stating that it would require heavy preliminary expenditures but would be reconsidered if circuit breaker redesign was undertaken for other reasons. Schott sued Westinghouse alleging that it had appropriated his idea by making the suggested change within the next year but had refused to pay him, giving the excuse that it had been made as "the result of independent action taken without knowledge of your suggestion."

He pleaded causes of action in both contract and unjust enrichment, but the trial court dismissed the complaint. The Supreme Court of Pennsylvania reversed as to the cause of action in unjust enrichment. The stipulation on the form precluded a claim in contract, but the allegations that the use of his "basic idea" resulted in savings to Westinghouse stated a cause of action in unjust enrichment since it did not appear that he "expected no payment or intended to confer a gratuity, nor in the context of the suggestion program . . . that the benefit was conferred officiously." Schott's case was distinguished from those in which recovery had been denied on the ground that "the 'idea' . . . was neither concrete in form nor novel in nature." Two judges concurred on the ground that Schott had stated a cause of action in contract but had relinquished any claim in unjust enrichment when he signed the form, and one judge dissented.

Courts have dealt with claims for the use of ideas in terms of breach of a contract implied in fact, restitution to prevent unjust enrichment, and breach of a fiduciary duty arising out of disclosure. Although recovery may be had regardless of whether the idea was solicited or not, courts have generally insisted that the idea "appropriated" be "concrete" and "novel" and that its disclosure be "in confidence." On the difficulty of proving "novelty," as well as "appropriation," see C. P. Flemming v. Ronson Corp., 107 N.J.Super. 311, 258 A.2d 153 (1969). For more on the use of ideas, including practices adopted by corporations to protect themselves, see Havighurst, The Right to Compensation for an Idea, 49 Nw.U.L.Rev. 924 (1954); Note, 65 Harv.L.Rev. 673 (1952).

SECTION 3.　RELIANCE AS AN ALTERNATIVE

RICKETTS v. SCOTHORN

Supreme Court of Nebraska, 1898.
57 Neb. 51, 77 N.W. 365.

SULLIVAN, J. In the District Court of Lancaster county, the plaintiff, Katie Scothorn, recovered judgment against the defendant, Andrew D. Ricketts, as executor, of the last will and testament of John C. Ricketts, deceased. The action was based upon a promissory note, of which the following is a copy: "May the first, 1891. I promise to pay to Katie Scothorn on demand, $2,000 to be at 6 per cent. per annum. J. C. Ricketts." In the petition the plaintiff alleges that the consideration for the execution of the note was that she should surrender her employment as bookkeeper for Mayer Bros., and cease to work for a living. She also alleges that the note was given to induce her to abandon her occupation, and that, relying on it, and on the annual interest, as a means of support, she gave up the employment in which she was then engaged. These allegations of the petition are denied by the administrator.

The material facts are undisputed. They are as follows: John C. Ricketts, the maker of the note, was the grandfather of the plaintiff. Early in May—presumably on the day the note bears date—he called on her at the store where she was working. What transpired between them is thus described by Mr. Flodene, one of the plaintiff's witnesses: "A. Well, the old gentleman came in there one morning about nine o'clock, probably a little before or a little after, but early in the morning, and he unbuttoned his vest, and took out a piece of paper in the shape of a note; that is the way it looked to me; and he says to Miss Scothorn, 'I have fixed out something that you have not got to work any more.' He says, 'none of my grandchildren work, and you don't have to.' Q. Where was she? A. She took the piece of paper and kissed him, and kissed the old gentleman, and commenced to cry." It seems Miss Scothorn immediately notified her employer of her intention to quit work, and that she did soon after abandon her occupation. The mother of the plaintiff was a witness, and testified that she had a conversation with her father, Mr. Ricketts, shortly after the note was executed, in which he informed her that he had given the note to the plaintiff to enable her to quit work; that none of his grandchildren worked, and he did not think she ought to. For something more than a year the plaintiff was without an occupation, but in September, 1892, with the consent of her grandfather, and by his assistance, she secured a position as bookkeeper with Messrs. Funke & Ogden. On June 8, 1894, Mr. Ricketts died. He had paid one year's interest on the note, and a short time before his death expressed regret that he had not been able to pay the balance. In the summer or fall of 1892 he stated to his daughter, Mrs. Scothorn, that if he could sell his farm in Ohio he would pay the note out of the proceeds. He at no time repudiated the obligation.

We quite agree with counsel for the defendant that upon this evidence there was nothing to submit to the jury, and that a verdict should have been directed peremptorily for one of the parties. The testimony of Flodene and Mrs. Scothorn, taken together, conclusively establishes the fact that the note was not given in consideration of the plaintiff pursuing, or agreeing to pursue, any particular line of conduct. There was no promise on the part of the plaintiff to do, or refrain from doing, anything. Her right to the money promised in the note was not made to depend upon an abandonment of her employment with Mayer Bros., and future abstention from like service.   Mr. Ricketts made no condition, requirement, or request.   He exacted no quid pro quo.   He gave the note as a gratuity, and looked for nothing in return.   So far as the evidence discloses, it was his purpose to place the plaintiff in a position of independence, where she could work or remain idle, as she might choose.   The abandonment by Miss Scothorn of her position as bookkeeper was altogether voluntary.   It was not an act done in fulfillment of any contract obligation assumed when she accepted the note.

The instrument in suit, being given without any valuable consideration, was nothing more than a promise to make a gift in the future of the sum of money therein named.   Ordinarily, such promises are not enforceable, even when put in the form of a promissory note. .   .   . But it has often been held that an action on a note given to a church, college, or other like institution, upon the faith of which money has been expended or obligations incurred, could not be successfully defended on the ground of a want of consideration.   .   .   . In this class of cases the note in suit is nearly always spoken of as a gift or donation, but the decision is generally put on the ground that the expenditure of money or assumption of liability by the donee on the faith of the promise constitutes a valuable and sufficient consideration.   It seems to us that the true reason is the preclusion of the defendant, under the doctrine of estoppel, to deny the consideration. .   .   .

Under the circumstances of this case, is there an equitable estoppel which ought to preclude the defendant from alleging that the note in controversy is lacking in one of the essential elements of a valid contract?   We think there is.   An estoppel in pais is defined to be "a right arising from acts, admissions, or conduct which have induced a change of position in accordance with the real or apparent intention of the party against whom they are alleged." .   .   . According to the undisputed proof, as shown by the record before us, the plaintiff was a working girl, holding a position in which she earned a salary of $10 per week.   Her grandfather, desiring to put her in a position of independence, gave her the note, accompanying it with the remark that his other grandchildren did not work, and that she would not be obliged to work any longer.   In effect, he suggested that she might abandon her employment, and rely in the future upon the bounty which he promised.   He doubtless desired that she should give up her occupation, but, whether he did or not, it is entirely certain that he contemplated such action on her part as a reasonable and probable consequence of his gift.   Having intentionally influenced the plaintiff to alter her position for the worse on the faith of the note being paid when due, it would be grossly inequitable to permit the maker, or his executor, to resist payment on the ground that the promise was given without consideration.   The petition charges the elements of an equitable estoppel, and the evidence conclusively establishes them.   If errors intervened at the trial, they could not have been prejudicial. A verdict for the defendant would be unwarranted. The judgment is right, and is

> Affirmed.

NOTES

(1) *Kirksey Revisited.* Would the reasoning of the court in the principal case support a recovery by the plaintiff promisee in Kirksey v. Kirksey, p. 28 supra?

(2) *Estoppel: New Wine in an Old Bottle.* Decisions like the one in the principal case involve far more than routine application of established estoppel theory. The conventional estoppel case concerns a representation of fact made by one party and relied on by the other; the estopped party is prohibited from alleging or proving facts that would contradict the truth of his own earlier representation if the other party has taken action in reliance on that representation. Cases like Ricketts v. Scothorn concern not a factual representation but a promise, and the estoppel idea is used affirmatively as the legal basis of a claim.

(3) *Bargained-For Exchange as an Alternative.* Might another court have found a bargained-for exchange in the principal case, and so have enforced the note to Katie Scothorn as a promise supported by consideration? Compare, particularly, Hamer v. Sidway, p. 4 supra.

"PROMISSORY ESTOPPEL"

Holmes said, "It would cut up the doctrine of consideration by the roots, if a promisee could make a gratuitous promise binding by subsequently acting in reliance on it." Commonwealth v. Scituate Savings Bank, 137 Mass. 301, 302 (1884). Nevertheless, Ricketts v. Scothorn is one of a number of cases that, even prior to the promulgation of the Restatement of Contracts in 1932, recognized reliance as a basis for the enforcement of promises. For the most part, these cases fall into four categories.

1. *Family Promises.* One category consisted of cases, like Ricketts v. Scothorn itself, in which the promise was made by one member of a family to another. Is there a possible connection between the growth of this category and the fact that the pattern of bargained-for exchange, so common in a commercial setting, ordinarily seems out of place in a family setting? Contrast Ricketts v. Scothorn with Hamer v. Sidway, p. 4 supra.

2. *Promises to Convey Land.* Another category consisted of cases involving promises to convey land, on which the promisee had relied by moving onto the land and making improvements. An early example is Freeman v. Freeman, 43 N.Y. 34 (1870). Would the facts in Kirksey v. Kirksey, p. 28 supra, have brought that case within this category?

3. *Promises Coupled With Gratuitous Bailments.* A third category was made up of cases in which a bailor sought to enforce a promise made by the bailee in connection with a gratuitous bailment. The leading case is Siegel v. Spear & Co., 234 N.Y. 479, 138 N.E. 414 (1923). Siegel bought furniture on credit from Spear, giving Spear a mortgage on it and agreeing not to remove it from his apartment in New York City without Spear's consent until it was paid for. When he decided to leave the city for the summer, he saw Spear's credit man, McGrath, who agreed to store it free of charge. McGrath then said, "You had better transfer your insurance policy over to our warehouse," to which Siegel answered that he had no insurance but would get some through his agent. McGrath replied, "That won't be necessary to get that from him; I will do it for you; it will be a good deal cheaper; I handle lots of insurance; when you get the next bill—you can send a check for that with the next installment." In May, Siegel sent the furniture to Spear's storehouse. About a month later it was destroyed by fire. It had not been insured. Siegel sued Spear, had judgment, and Spear appealed. The Court of Appeals affirmed. Although the gratuitous bailment itself imposed no duty on Spear to insure the furniture, such a duty arose from McGrath's promise followed by the delivery of the furniture by Siegel. The court distinguished an old New York case, Thorne v. Deas, 4 Johns. 84 (N.Y. Sup.Ct.1809), in which the court had refused to hold one of two joint owners of a ship to his promise made to the other owner to insure the ship, when he had failed to do so and the ship had been lost. There, in contrast to Siegel, the promisee "parted with nothing . . . gave up possession of none of his property" to the promisor. This category will be considered further in connection with the next case.

4. *Charitable Subscriptions.* The fourth category of cases involves charitable subscriptions. As one court put it, "This promise was made to a charitable corporation, and for that reason we are not confined to the same orthodox concepts which once were applicable to every situation arising within a common law jurisdiction. There can be no denying that the strong desire on the part of the American courts to favor charitable institutions has established a doctrine which once would have been looked upon as legal heresy." Danby v. Osteopathic Hospital Ass'n of Delaware, 34 Del.Ch. 427, 104 A.2d 903 (1954). It is sometimes possible to enforce such a promise by finding an exchange among subscribers of promises for the benefit of (and enforceable by) the charitable organization, particularly where one subscriber appears as the "bellwether" of the flock and promises a large sum on condition that other subscribers raise a specified amount. See Petition of Upper Peninsula Development Bureau, 364 Mich. 179, 110 N.W.2d 709 (1961). (How could you draft a pledge form to help your favorite charity take advantage of this possibility?)

It is perhaps curious that the most widely known and influential decision on charitable subscriptions contains only dictum concerning the effect of reliance. It is Allegheny College v. National Chautauqua County Bank of Jamestown, 246 N.Y. 369, 159 N.E. 173 (1927). Mary Yates Johnston, promised to pay $5,000 to Allegheny College, by a writing that stipulated that the gift "be known as the Mary Yates Johnston memorial fund, the proceeds from which shall be used to educate students preparing for the ministry." The sum was not payable until 30 days after her death, but $1,000 was paid while she was alive and set aside by the college for the specified purpose. She later repudiated her promise, and on the expiration of 30 days following her death the college brought an action against her executor for the unpaid balance. Cardozo, C. J.,[a] writing for the New York Court of Appeals, found consideration for her promise in the return promise of the college to set up the memorial fund which arose "by implication" from its acceptance of the $1,000. "The college could not accept the money and hold itself free thereafter from personal responsibility to give effect to the condition." But in the course of his opinion, Cardozo went out of his way to speak to the effect of reliance. "[T]here has grown up of recent days a doctrine that a substitute for consideration or an exception to its ordinary requirements can be found in what is styled 'a promissory estoppel'. . . . Whether the exception has made its way in this state to such an extent as to permit us to say that the general law of consideration has been modified accordingly, we do not now attempt to say. Cases such as Siegel v. Spear & Co. . . . may be signposts on the road. Certain, at least, it is that we have adopted the doctrine of promissory estoppel as the equivalent of consideration in connection with our law of charitable subscriptions."

Restatement. Although the doctrine of "promissory estoppel" expounded in the Allegheny College case has been accorded little honor in New York itself (see Note, p. 53 infra), Cardozo's dictum was influential in the formulation of Restatement, § 90, which was promulgated five years later. Although that section avoids the use of the words "promissory estoppel," it states in general terms the principle that had been applied in the four categories of cases just described.

---

a. Benjamin Nathan Cardozo (1870–1938) practiced in New York City after law school. He served as judge and later chief judge of the Court of Appeals of New York, and was appointed an associate justice of the Supreme Court of the United States in 1932 to fill the vacancy left by Holmes. Of his contribution to the law of contracts, Professor Corbin has written: "It cannot be said that he made any extensive changes in the existing law of contract. To state the facts of the cases, the decision, and the reasoning of his opinion will not show the overthrow of old doctrine or the establishment of new. Instead, it will show the application of existing doctrines with wisdom and discretion; an application that does not leave those doctrines wholly unaffected, but one that carries on their evolution as is reasonably required by the new facts before the court. When Cardozo is through, the law is not exactly as it was before; but there has been no sudden shift or revolutionary change." Cardozo's best known jurisprudential work is a series of lectures entitled The Nature of the Judicial Process (1921).

See generally, Boyer, Promissory Estoppel: Principle from Precedents, 50 Mich.L.Rev. 639, 873 (1952).

EAST PROVIDENCE CREDIT UNION v. GEREMIA

Supreme Court of Rhode Island, 1968.
103 R.I. 597, 239 A.2d 725.

KELLEHER, JUSTICE. This is a civil action to collect from the defendants the balance due on a promissory note. The defendants filed a counterclaim. The case was heard by a justice of the superior court. He dismissed the plaintiff's complaint and found for the defendants on their counterclaim. The case is before us on the plaintiff's appeal.

On December 5, 1963, defendants, who are husband and wife, borrowed $2,350.28 from plaintiff for which they gave their promissory note. The payment of the note was secured by a chattel mortgage on defendants' 1962 ranch wagon. The mortgage contained a clause which obligated defendants to maintain insurance on the motor vehicle in such amounts as plaintiff required against loss by fire, collision, upset or overturn of the automobile and similar hazards. This provision also stipulated that if defendants failed to maintain such insurance, plaintiff could pay the premium and " .   .   . any sum so paid shall be secured hereby and shall be immediately payable." The defendants had procured the required insurance and had designated plaintiff as a loss payee on its policy. The premium therefor was payable in periodic installments.

On October 11, 1965, defendants received a notice from the insurance carrier informing them that the premium then payable was overdue and that, unless it was paid within the ensuing twelve days, the policy would be cancelled. A copy of this notice was also sent by the insurer to plaintiff who thereupon sent a letter to defendants. The pertinent portion thereof reads as follows:

"We are in receipt of a cancellation notice on your Policy.

"If we are not notified of a renewal Policy within 10 days, we shall be forced to renew the policy for you and apply this amount to your loan."

Upon receiving this communication, defendant wife testified that she telephoned plaintiff's office and talked to the treasurer's assistant; that she told this employee to go ahead and pay the premium; that she explained to the employee that her husband was sick and they could not pay the insurance premium and the payment due on the loan; and that the employee told her her call would be referred to plaintiff's treasurer. The employee testified that she told defendant to contact this officer. We deem this difference in testimony insignificant. It is clear from the record that defendants communicated their approval of and acquiescence in plaintiff's promise to pay the insurance due on the car and that this employee notified the treasurer of such fact.

On December 17, 1965, defendants' motor vehicle was demolished in a mishap the nature of which cannot be learned from the record. It is obvious, however, that the loss was within the coverage of the policy. The automobile was a total loss. The evidence shows that at the time of the loss, the outstanding balance of the loan was $987.89 and the value of the ranch wagon prior to the loss exceeded the balance due on the loan.

Sometime after this unfortunate incident, all the parties became aware that the insurer would not indemnify them for the loss because the overdue premium had not been paid and defendants' policy had been canceled prior to the accident.

The defendants had on deposit with plaintiff over $200 in savings shares. The plaintiff, in accordance with the terms of the note, had deducted therefrom certain amounts and applied them to defendants' indebtedness so that at the time this litigation was instituted defendants allegedly owed plaintiff $779.53.

In finding for defendants on their counterclaim, the trial justice awarded them all the moneys which plaintiff had applied after the date of defendants' accident to the then outstanding balance of the loan.[1] The justice, at the conclusion of the evidence, made certain findings which were in accordance with the testimony as set forth above. He found from the evidence that plaintiff, in pursuance of its right under the mortgage contract and its letter to defendants, had agreed to renew the policy and charge any premiums paid by it on behalf of defendants to the outstanding balance on their loan.

In reaching this conclusion, the trial justice made the following observation: ". . . it seems to me quite clear that the defendants, having been given notice that the plaintiff would do this [pay the overdue premium], and calling the plaintiff's attention to the fact that they weren't going to renew and that the plaintiff had better do this to protect everybody, seems to me at that point there was agreement on the part of the plaintiff that it would procure this insurance. Or, put it another way, that they are estopped from denying that they were exercising the right that they had under the original mortgage." The superior court further found that defendants were justified in believing in plaintiff's assurance that it would pay the overdue premium.

The sole issue raised by this appeal is whether or not plaintiff is precluded from recovering on its loan contract by reason of its failure to fulfill a promise to defendants to pay the overdue insurance

---

1. Included in this amount are the moneys deducted from the savings shares, $80 received from a junkyard as the salvage value of the wrecked automobile and a $10 payment made by defendants on December 28, 1965.

premium. In urging that the trial justice erred in finding for defendants, plaintiff directs our attention to Hazlett v. First Fed. Sav. & Loan Assn., 14 Wash.2d 124, 127 P.2d 273, in which the court refused to apply the doctrine of promissory estoppel to enforce a gratuitous promise made by a mortgagee to procure fire insurance for mortgaged property even though the mortgagor suffered serious detriment in reliance on the mortgagee's promise.[a]

Until recently it was a general rule that the doctrine of estoppel was applied only to representations made as to facts past or present. Anderson v. Polleys, 54 R.I. 296, 173 A. 114; Croce v. Whiting Milk Co., R.I., 228 A.2d 574. This doctrine is commonly known as "equitable" estoppel. Over the years, however, courts have carved out a recognized exception to this rule and applied it to those circumstances wherein one promises to do or not to do something in the future. This latter doctrine is known as "promissory" estoppel. See Southeastern Sales & Service Co. v. T. T. Watson, Inc., Fla.App., 172 So.2d 239. See also Berarducci v. Diano, 60 R.I. 305, 198 A. 351.

Promissory estoppel is defined in the 1 Restatement, Contracts, § 90, p. 110, as follows:

"A promise which the promisor should reasonably expect to induce action or forbearance of a definite and substantial character on the part of the promisee and which does induce such action or forbearance is binding if injustice can be avoided only by enforcement of its promise."

Although this court has not yet applied the doctrine of promissory estoppel as it is expressed in the Restatement, we have in Mann v. McDermott, 77 R.I. 142, 73 A.2d 815, implied that in appropriate circumstances we would.

Traditionally, the doctrine of promissory estoppel has been invoked as a substitute for a consideration, rendering a gratuitous promise enforceable as a contract. 28 Am.Jur.2d, Estoppel and Waiver, § 48 at 657–658; note 20 S.W. Law Journal 656, "Extension of the Doctrine of Promissory Estoppel into Bargained-for Transactions." Viewed in another way, the acts of reliance by the promisee to his detriment provided a substitute for consideration. Hoffman v. Red Owl Stores, Inc., 26 Wis.2d 683, 133 N.W.2d 267.

While the doctrine was originally recognized and most often utilized in charitable subscription cases, it presently enjoys a much wider and more expanded application. See 1 Williston, Contracts (3d. Jaeger), § 140; 1A Corbin, Contracts, §§ 193–209; 48 A.L.R.2d 1069–1088. Relative to the problem presented in this case, we have discovered several cases in which the theory of promissory estoppel

a. The Hazlett case, in which the court held that the reliance had to take the form of affirmative conduct rather than mere forbearance, has been "overruled *sub silentio*" by a later case in the Supreme Court of Washington, according to Hellbaum v. Burwell and Morford, 1 Wash.App. 694, 463 P.2d 225 (1969), which cited with approval the Geremia case.

has been invoked. In these cases, courts have held that a gratuitous promise made by one to procure insurance on the promisee's property is made enforceable by the promisee's reliance thereon and his forbearance to procure such insurance himself. Graddon v. Knight, 138 Cal.App.2d 577, 292 P.2d 632; see also 1A Corbin, Contracts, § 208 at 265, and cases cited therein. Our research indicates, therefore, that the contrary view expressed in Hazlett v. First Fed. Sav. & Loan Assn., supra, and relied upon by plaintiff, is a minority viewpoint on the issue before us and we are disinclined to follow it.

In the instant case, however, after a careful review of the facts, we are of the opinion that plaintiff made more than a mere gratuitous or unrecompensed promise. Instead, we believe that the promise by plaintiff to pay the insurance premium on defendants' car was one made in exchange for valid consideration. The mortgage contract provided that in the event plaintiff paid a premium for defendants, it would add such expended sums to the outstanding balance of defendants' loan. We are satisfied from a close examination of plaintiff's reply to defendants' interrogatories and of the chattel mortgage agreement that plaintiff intended to compute interest on any money it expended in keeping the insurance on defendants' car active. Hence, in our opinion, the interest due on any sums paid out by plaintiff on behalf of defendants for insurance represents valid consideration and converts their promise into a binding contract. The plaintiff's failure to successfully carry out its promise must be deemed a breach of that contract entitling defendants to assert a right of action which would at the very least offset any amount of money found owing to plaintiff on their loan.

We would point out that, even if it could be shown by plaintiff that it never intended to compute any interest on amounts paid by it for insurance premiums on defendants' car and that its promise was truly a pure gratuitous undertaking, we believe such a showing would be of no avail to it since we would not hesitate in finding from this record evidence sufficient to establish a case for the application of promissory estoppel. The conditions precedent for the invocation of this doctrine are well set forth by Dean Boyer in his oft-cited article, "Promissory Estoppel: Requirements And Limitations Of The Doctrine," 98 U.Pa.L.Rev. 459. He enumerates the conditions as follows:

"(1) Was there a promise which the promisor should reasonably expect to induce action or forbearance of a definite and substantial character on the part of the promisee?

"(2) Did the promise induce such action or forbearance?

"(3) Can injustice be avoided only by enforcement of the promise?"

After a study of the facts in this case, our reply to each of the above inquiries is a definite "yes." Promissory estoppel as a legal theory is gaining in prominence as a device used by an increasing number of courts to provide a much needed remedy to alleviate the plight of those who suffer a serious injustice as a result of their good-faith reliance on the unfulfilled promises of others. As the Arkansas supreme court has so appropriately commented in Peoples Nat'l Bank of Little Rock v. Linebarger Constr. Co., 219 Ark. 11, at 17, 240 S.W.2d 12, at 16, the law of promissory estoppel exhibits ". . . an attempt by the courts to keep remedies abreast of increased moral consciousness of honesty and fair representations in all business dealings . . .." We subscribe to those sentiments.

The plaintiff's appeal is denied and dismissed and the judgment appealed from is affirmed.

NOTE

Case Comparison. What was the consideration for the Credit Union's promise? Does the discussion of promissory estoppel in the principal case go beyond Siegel v. Spear, p. 47 supra? On somewhat similar facts, a lower New York court denied recovery, explaining that Siegel v. Spear applied only to "misfeasance" as distinguished from "nonfeasance," and that the Allegheny College case "extended the doctrine of promissory estoppel only to the law relating to charitable subscriptions." A lower court, therefore, "should go no further." Comfort v. McCorkle, 149 Misc. 826, 268 N.Y. S. 192 (1933). (No assessment of the New York law in this area can ignore Spiegel v. Metropolitan Life Insurance Co., 6 N.Y.2d 91, 160 N.E.2d 40 (1959), although, because of the court's failure to deal with the precedents, that case raises more questions than it answers.)

FEINBERG v. PFEIFFER CO.

Saint Louis Court of Appeals, Missouri, 1959.
322 S.W.2d 163.

[The facts and the first part of the opinion in this case are at p. 13 supra. The court there rejected Mrs. Feinberg's contention that her continuation in the employ of Pfeiffer Co. from December 27, 1947, the date of the resolution, until the date of her retirement, June 30, 1949, was consideration for Pfeiffer's promise to pay her $200 per month for life upon her retirement. In the portion of the opinion below, the court considers Mrs. Feinberg's second contention, that the promise was enforceable because of her reliance on it, "i.e., her retirement, and the abandonment by her of her opportunity to continue in gainful employment."]

DOERNER, COMMISSIONER. . . . But as to the second of these contentions we must agree with plaintiff. By the terms of the resolution defendant promised to pay plaintiff the sum of $200 a month upon her retirement. [The court quoted Restatement, § 90.]

Was there such an act on the part of plaintiff, in reliance upon the promise contained in the resolution, as will estop the defendant, and therefore create an enforceable contract under the doctrine of promissory estoppel? We think there was. One of the illustrations cited under Section 90 of the Restatement is: "2. A promises B to pay him an annuity during B's life. B thereupon resigns a profitable employment, as A expected that he might. B receives the annuity for some years, in the meantime becoming disqualified from again obtaining good employment. A's promise is binding." This illustration is objected to by defendant as not being applicable to the case at hand. The reason advanced by it is that in the illustration B became "disqualified" from obtaining other employment *before* A discontinued the payments, whereas in this case the plaintiff did not discover that she had cancer and thereby became unemployable until *after* the defendant had discontinued the payments of $200 per month. We think the distinction is immaterial. The only reason for the reference in the illustration to the disqualification of A is in connection with that part of Section 90 regarding the prevention of injustice. The injustice would occur regardless of when the disability occurred. Would defendant contend that the contract would be enforceable if the plaintiff's illness had been discovered on March 31, 1956, the day before it discontinued the payment of the $200 a month, but not if it occurred on April 2nd, the day after? Furthermore, there are more ways to become disqualified for work, or unemployable, than as the result of illness. At the time she retired plaintiff was 57 years of age. At the time the payments were discontinued she was over 63 years of age. It is a matter of common knowledge that it is virtually impossible for a woman of that age to find satisfactory employment, much less a position comparable to that which plaintiff enjoyed at the time of her retirement.

The fact of the matter is that plaintiff's subsequent illness was not the "action or forbearance" which was induced by the promise contained in the resolution. As the trial court correctly decided, such action on plaintiff's part was her retirement from a lucrative position in reliance upon defendant's promise to pay her an annuity or pension.

The Commissioner therefore recommends, for the reasons stated, that the judgment be affirmed.

PER CURIAM. The foregoing opinion by DOERNER, C., is adopted as the opinion of the court. The judgment is, accordingly, affirmed.

NOTES

(1) *Case Comparison.* How would the court that decided the principal case have decided the case of Kirksey v. Kirksey, p. 28 supra?

(2) *Measure of Recovery.* Do the preceding cases suggest that there is any difference in the measure of recovery allowed when the enforceability of the promise is based on reliance instead of on bargained-for exchange? (Does not the etymology of "promissory estoppel" favor a negative answer?) Should there be any difference?

During the discussion of Restatement, § 90 on the floor of the American Law Institute, Professor Williston, as Reporter, made the following statement: "Either the promise is binding or it is not. If the promise is binding it has to be enforced as it is made. As I said to Mr. Coudert, I could leave this whole thing to the subject of quasi contracts so that the promisee under those circumstances shall never recover on the promise but he shall recover such an amount as will fairly compensate him for any injury incurred; but it seems to me you have to take one leg or the other. You have either to say the promise is binding or you have to go on the theory of restoring the status quo." 4 American Law Institute Proceedings, Appendix, 103–04 (1926).

Note the second sentence added in Restatement Second, § 90: "The remedy granted for breach may be limited as justice requires." Might justice have required such a limitation in any of the preceding cases in which that section would have called for enforcement of the promise?

Chapter 2

THE BARGAINING PROCESS

SECTION 1. THE OFFER

The process by which the parties arrive at a bargain will vary widely according to the circumstances. It is common to assume that it involves two distinct steps: first, an offer by one party and, second, an acceptance by the other. A discussion of whether this is inevitably the case can be deferred until later. It is helpful to begin, at least, with this assumption.

What is an offer? Corbin [a] gives this answer: "An offer is . . . an act whereby one person confers upon another the power to create contractual relations between them. . . . [T]he act of the offeror operates to create in the offeree a power . . . ; thereafter the voluntary act of the offeree alone will operate to create the new relations called a contract. . . . What kind of act creates a power of acceptance and is therefore an offer? It must be an expression of will or intention. It must be an act that leads the offeree reasonably to believe that a power to create a contract is conferred upon him. . . . It is on this ground that we must exclude invitations to deal or acts of mere preliminary negotiation, and acts *evidently* done in jest or without intent to create legal relations. All these are acts that do not lead others reasonably to believe that they are empowered 'to close the contract.'" Corbin, Offer and Acceptance, and Some of The Resulting Legal Relations, 26 Yale L.J. 169, 181–82 (1917), Selected Readings 170, 179–80. See also Restatement Second, § 24.

---

a. Arthur Linton Corbin (1874–1967) practiced law in Colorado for four years after his graduation from law school in 1899. He taught at the Yale Law School from 1903 until his retirement in 1943, and became a leading authority on the law of contracts. His eight-volume treatise, Corbin on Contracts, which began to appear in 1950, ranks as one of the great legal treatises in any field of law in this country. He also served as Special Advisor and as Reporter for the Chapter on Remedies for the Restatement of Contracts.

LUCY v. ZEHMER

Supreme Court of Appeals of Virginia, 1954.
196 Va. 493, 84 S.E.2d 516.

BUCHANAN, JUSTICE. This suit was instituted by W. O. Lucy and J. C. Lucy, complainants, against A. H. Zehmer and Ida S. Zehmer, his wife, defendants, to have specific performance of a contract by which it was alleged the Zehmers had sold to W. O. Lucy a tract of land owned by A. H. Zehmer in Dinwiddie county containing 471.6 acres, more or less, known as the Ferguson farm, for $50,000. J. C. Lucy, the other complainant, is a brother of W. O. Lucy, to whom W. O. Lucy transferred a half interest in his alleged purchase.

The instrument sought to be enforced was written by A. H. Zehmer on [Saturday,] December 20, 1952, in these words: "We hereby agree to sell to W. O. Lucy the Ferguson Farm complete for $50,000.00, title satisfactory to buyer," and signed by the defendants, A. H. Zehmer and Ida S. Zehmer.

The answer of A. H. Zehmer admitted that at the time mentioned W. O. Lucy offered him $50,000 cash for the farm, but that he, Zehmer, considered that the offer was made in jest; that so thinking, and both he and Lucy having had several drinks, he wrote out "the memorandum" quoted above and induced his wife to sign it; that he did not deliver the memorandum to Lucy, but that Lucy picked it up, read it, put it in his pocket, attempted to offer Zehmer $5 to bind the bargain, which Zehmer refused to accept, and realizing for the first time that Lucy was serious, Zehmer assured him that he had no intention of selling the farm and that the whole matter was a joke. Lucy left the premises insisting that he had purchased the farm.

Depositions were taken and the decree appealed from was entered holding that the complainants had failed to establish their right to specific performance, and dismissing their bill. The assignment of error is to this action of the court. . . .

The defendants insist that the evidence was ample to support their contention that the writing sought to be enforced was prepared as a bluff or dare to force Lucy to admit that he did not have $50,000; that the whole matter was a joke; that the writing was not delivered to Lucy and no binding contract was ever made between the parties.

It is an unusual, if not bizarre, defense. When made to the writing admittedly prepared by one of the defendants and signed by both, clear evidence is required to sustain it.

In his testimony Zehmer claimed that he "was high as a Georgia pine," and that the transaction "was just a bunch of two doggoned drunks bluffing to see who could talk the biggest and say the most." That claim is inconsistent with his attempt to testify in great detail as to what was said and what was done. It is contradicted by other evidence as to the condition of both parties, and rendered of no weight by the testimony of his wife that when Lucy left the restaurant she suggested that Zehmer drive him home. The record is convincing that Zehmer was not intoxicated to the extent of being unable to comprehend the nature and consequences of the instrument he executed, and hence that instrument is not to be invalidated on that ground. 17 C.J.S. Contracts, § 133, b., p. 483; Taliaferro v. Emery, 124 Va. 674, 98 S.E. 627. It was in fact conceded by defendants' counsel in oral argument that under the evidence Zehmer was not too drunk to make a valid contract.

The evidence is convincing also that Zehmer wrote two agreements, the first one beginning "I hereby agree to sell." Zehmer first said he could not remember about that, then that "I don't think I wrote but one out." Mrs. Zehmer said that what he wrote was "I hereby agree," but that the "I" was changed to "We" after that night. The agreement that was written and signed is in the record and indicates no such change. Neither are the mistakes in spelling that Zehmer sought to point out readily apparent.

The appearance of the contract, the fact that it was under discussion for forty minutes or more before it was signed; Lucy's objection to the first draft because it was written in the singular, and he wanted Mrs. Zehmer to sign it also; the rewriting to meet that objection and the signing by Mrs. Zehmer; the discussion of what was to be included in the sale, the provision for the examination of the title, the completeness of the instrument that was executed, the taking possession of it by Lucy with no request or suggestion by either of the defendants that he give it back, are facts which furnish persuasive evidence that the execution of the contract was a serious business transaction rather than a casual, jesting matter as defendants now contend.

.   .   .

If it be assumed, contrary to what we think the evidence shows, that Zehmer was jesting about selling his farm to Lucy and that the transaction was intended by him to be a joke, nevertheless the evidence shows that Lucy did not so understand it but considered it to be a serious business transaction and the contract to be binding on the Zehmers as well as on himself. The very next day he arranged with his brother to put up half the money and take a half interest in the land. The day after that he employed an attorney to examine the title. The next night, Tuesday, he was back at Zehmer's place and there Zehmer told him for the first time, Lucy said, that he wasn't going to sell and he told Zehmer, "You know you sold that place fair and square." After receiving the report from his attorney that the title was good he wrote to Zehmer that he was ready to close the deal.

Not only did Lucy actually believe, but the evidence shows he was warranted in believing, that the contract represented a serious business transaction and a good faith sale and purchase of the farm.

In the field of contracts, as generally elsewhere, "We must look to the outward expression of a person as manifesting his intention rather than to his secret and unexpressed intention. 'The law imputes to a person an intention corresponding to the reasonable meaning of his words and acts.'" First Nat. Exchange Bank of Roanoke v. Roanoke Oil Co., 169 Va. 99, 114, 192 S.E. 764, 770.

At no time prior to the execution of the contract had Zehmer indicated to Lucy by word or act that he was not in earnest about selling the farm. They had argued about it and discussed its terms, as Zehmer admitted, for a long time. Lucy testified that if there was any jesting it was about paying $50,000 that night. The contract and the evidence show that he was not expected to pay the money that night. Zehmer said that after the writing was signed he laid it down on the counter in front of Lucy. Lucy said Zehmer handed it to him. In any event there had been what appeared to be a good faith offer and a good faith acceptance, followed by the execution and apparent delivery of a written contract. Both said that Lucy put the writing in his pocket and then offered Zehmer $5 to seal the bargain. Not until then, even under the defendants' evidence, was anything said or done to indicate that the matter was a joke. Both of the Zehmers testified that when Zehmer asked his wife to sign he whispered that it was a joke so Lucy wouldn't hear and that it was not intended that he should hear.

The mental assent of the parties is not requisite for the formation of a contract. If the words or other acts of one of the parties have but one reasonable meaning, his undisclosed intention is immaterial except when an unreasonable meaning which he attaches to his manifestations is known to the other party. Restatement of the Law of Contracts, Vol. I, § 71, p. 74. . . .

An agreement or mutual assent is of course essential to a valid contract but the law imputes to a person an intention corresponding to the reasonable meaning of his words and acts. If his words and acts, judged by a reasonable standard, manifest an intention to agree, it is immaterial what may be the real but unexpressed state of his mind. 17 C.J.S., Contracts, § 32, p. 361; 12 Am.Jur., Contracts, § 19, p. 515.

So a person cannot set up that he was merely jesting when his conduct and words would warrant a reasonable person in believing that he intended a real agreement. . . .

Whether the writing signed by the defendants and now sought to be enforced by the complainants was the result of a serious offer by Lucy and a serious acceptance by the defendants, or was a serious offer by Lucy and an acceptance in secret jest by the defendants, in either event it constituted a binding contract of sale between the parties. . . .

The complainants are entitled to have specific performance of the contract sued on. The decree appealed from is therefore reversed and the cause is remanded for the entry of a proper decree requiring the defendants to perform the contract in accordance with the prayer of the bill.

Reversed and remanded.

NOTE

Jesting and Bluffing. What result if the price had been $50 rather than $50,000? See Thomas v. Thomas, p. 10 supra. In Keller v. Holderman, 11 Mich. 248 (1863), Holderman, as a "frolic and banter," gave Keller a $300 check for a watch worth about $15. Holderman had no money in the bank and intended to insert a condition in the check rendering him not liable. This he neglected to do. Keller sued Holderman on the check and had judgment. Holderman appealed. *Held*: Reversed. "When the Court below found as a fact that 'the whole transaction between the parties was a frolic and a banter, the plaintiff not expecting to sell, nor the defendant intending to buy the watch at the sum for which the check was drawn,' the conclusion should have been that no contract was ever made by the parties. . . ."

Note that the Zehmers, in addition to contending that "the whole matter was a joke," contended that the writing "was prepared as a bluff or dare to force Lucy to admit that he did not have $50,000." What result if the offer had been so intended by the Zehmers and if Lucy, knowing this, had "called their bluff" by raising the money from his brother through transferring a half interest to him? Should a distinction be made between jesting and bluffing in this situation?

GENTLEMEN'S AGREEMENTS

Can the parties to an agreement, by express provision, prevent the machinery of government from enforcing their promises? Consider this question in connection with two significant situations where such "gentlemen's agreements" have been used.

One arises in "firm-commitment underwriting" of corporate stock, a transaction in which the corporate issuer sells an entire issue of stock outright to a group of underwriters, who in turn sell to a larger group of dealers, who then sell to the public. Under the Securities Act of 1933, a registration statement containing specified information about the stock, the issuer, and the underwriters must be filed with the Securities and Exchange Commission before the stock is offered to either the dealers or the public. Before going to the substantial trouble and expense of preparing and printing a registration statement, the issuer wants some assurance of the availability of the underwriters. The underwriters, however, are not willing to make an enforceable promise to purchase the stock, since that would subject them to the risk of an adverse change in the market during the time before the registration statement takes effect. The solution has been found in having the underwriters write to the issuer a "letter of intent," which is then signed by the issuer, and which sets out, often in considerable detail, the terms of the proposed underwriting, but contains language, such as the following, negating legal liability.

Since this instrument consists only of an expression of our mutual intent, it is expressly understood that no liability or obligation of any nature whatsoever is intended to be created as between any of the parties hereto. This letter is not intended to constitute a binding agreement to consummate the financing outlined herein, nor an agreement to enter into an Underwriting Agreement. The parties propose to proceed promptly and in good faith to conclude the arrangements with respect to the proposed public offering and any legal obligations between the parties shall be only those set forth in the executed Underwriting Agreement. In the event that the Underwriting Agreement is not executed and/or the purchase of the securities is not consummated, we shall not be obligated for any expenses of the Company or for any charges or claims whatsoever arising out of this letter of intent or the proposed financing or otherwise and, similarly, the Company shall not be, in any way, obligated to us.

In Dunhill Securities Corp. v. Microthermal Applications, 308 F. Supp. 195 (S.D.N.Y.1969), the court held that, in view of this language, the issuer had no liability in contract to an underwriter when it refused to go through with the underwriting on the ground that it had discovered that the Securities and Exchange Commission had brought proceedings against the underwriters. The underwriter was also denied recovery "in quantum meruit, for services actually performed and expenses sustained pursuant to the letter of intent." For a fuller description of the transaction, see 1 Loss, Securities Regulation 163–71 (2d ed. 1961) and Supp.

Bonus and death benefit plans afford the second situation in which gentlemen's agreements are used. The employer may want to disclose the plan in order to take advantage of the resulting incentive, but may want to keep its administration within his uncontrolled discretion. Here is some typical language, taken from a certificate addressed to an employee promising that a specified death benefit would be paid to her designated beneficiary if she was still employed at the time of her death:

The issue and delivery of this certificate is understood to be purely voluntary and gratuitous on the part of this Company and is accepted with the express understanding that it carries no legal obligation whatsoever or assurance or promise of future employment, and may be withdrawn or discontinued at any time by this Company.

In Mabley & Carew Co. v. Borden, 129 Ohio St. 375, 195 N.E. 697 (1935), the court held that, in spite of this language, the employer was liable to the beneficiary. Why should this language be treated differently from that of the "letter of intent"? In Spooner v. Reserve Life Insurance Co., 47 Wash.2d 454, 287 P.2d 735 (1955), the court gave effect to similar language in an insurance company's announcement of a bonus plan for its agents, distinguishing the death benefit cases on the ground that there a denial of recovery would produce a "harsh result" for the beneficiary. Is this a sound distinction?

Assuming the law in this area to be uncertain in your jurisdiction, what advice would you give an employer concerning the desirability of including some such language as the following in its statement of a bonus or death benefit plan?

Benefits, if any, under the plan shall be at the sole discretion of the Benefits Committee, consisting of the Controller, the Secretary, and the Treasurer of the Company. The decision of the Benefits Committee shall be final and binding.

See Montgomery Ward & Co. v. Reich, 131 Colo. 407, 282 P.2d 1091 (1955).

NOTE

Family and Social Agreements. There are many promises made in a family setting for which the machinery of the government's judicial process is not ordinarily available. In Balfour v. Balfour, [1919] 2 K.B. 571, denying a wife recovery on her husband's promise to pay her an allowance of £30 a month, Lord Atkin expressed the prevailing judicial attitude toward such promises: "[T]hey are not contracts because the parties did not intend that they should be attended by legal consequences. To my mind it would be of the worst possible example to hold that agreements such as this resulted in legal obligations which could be enforced in the Courts. . . . Agreements such as these are outside the realm of contracts altogether. . . . In respect of these promises each house is a domain into which the King's writ does not seek to run, and to which his officers do not seek to be admitted." What assumptions might justify this attitude? Could the same have been said of the promises in Hamer v. Sidway, p. 4 supra, Kirksey v. Kirksey, p. 28 supra, and Ricketts v. Scothorn, p. 43 supra? Would it make a difference if the husband and wife put their agreement in writing? Stated that they intended it to be legally enforceable? See Note, 79 Harv.L.Rev. 1650 (1966); McDowell, Contracts in the Family, 45 B.U.L.Rev. 43 (1965). Difficult problems arise in connection with claims of implied contracts for services in the family, where courts have been prone to find that the services were gratuitous. See Havighurst, Services in the Home—A Study of Contract Concepts in Domestic Relations, 41 Yale L.J. 386 (1932).

Would you expect a court to enforce a promise made in a social setting, such as a promise to be a guest at a dinner party? Would it make a difference if the host had gone to considerable expense to make elaborate preparations?

OBJECTIVE AND SUBJECTIVE THEORIES OF CONTRACT

Two contrasting theories of contract, commonly described as "objective" and "subjective" are illustrated by these excerpts from Judge Learned Hand [a] and his colleague Judge Jerome Frank,[b] concurring in a case in which Hand wrote the opinion of the court.

According to Hand: "A contract has, strictly speaking, nothing to do with the personal or individual, intent of the parties. A contract is an obligation attached by the mere force of law to certain acts of the parties, usually words, which ordinarily accompany and represent a known intent. If, however, it were proved by twenty bishops that either party when he used the words intended something else than the usual meaning which the law imposes upon them, he would still be held, unless there were some mutual mistake or something else of the sort." Hotchkiss v. National City Bank of New York, 200 F. 287, 293 (S.D.N.Y.1911).

According to Frank: "In the early days of this century a struggle went on between the respective proponents of two theories of contracts, (a) the "actual intent" theory—or "meeting of the minds" [c] or "will" theory—and (b) the so-called 'objective' theory.[1] Without

a. Learned Hand (1872–1961) was admitted to the practice of law in New York in 1897, appointed to the United States District Court for the Southern District of New York in 1909 and to the United States Court of Appeals for the Second Circuit in 1924. He retired in 1951, after having sat on the bench longer than any other federal judge. Justice Cardozo called him "the greatest living American jurist," and he was so regarded by many of his contemporaries. His extrajudicial utterances may be sampled in The Spirit of Liberty (1952) and The Bill of Rights (1958).

b. Jerome New Frank (1889–1957) practiced in Chicago and New York for more than twenty years before going to Washington in 1933, where he served first as a government lawyer and then as a member and later chairman of the Securities and Exchange Commission. In 1941 he was appointed to the United States Court of Appeals for the Second Circuit. He also lectured at the Yale Law School and was associated with the philosophy of law known as "legal realism." One of his best known books is Law and the Modern Mind (1930).

c. For the curious origin of the term "meeting of the minds," see Farnsworth, "Meaning" in the Law of Contracts, 76 Yale L.J. 939, 943–44 (1967). It has remained a popular metaphor, e. g., "Any greater 'meeting of the minds' would require them to bump their heads together." Turner v. Worth Insurance Co., 106 Ariz. 132, 472 P.2d 1 (1970).

1. "The 'actual intent' theory, said the objectivists, being 'subjective' and putting too much stress on unique individual motivations, would destroy that legal certainty and stability which a modern commercial society demands. They depicted the 'objective' standard as a necessary adjunct of a 'free enterprise' economic system. In passing, it should be noted that they arrived at a sort of paradox. For a 'free enterprise' system is, theoretically, founded on 'individualism'; but, in the name of economic individualism, the objectivists refused to consider those reactions of actual specific individuals which sponsors of the 'meeting-of-the-minds' test purported to cherish. 'Economic individualism' thus shows up as hostile to real individualism. This is nothing new: The 'economic man' is of course an abstraction, a 'fiction.' "

doubt, the first theory had been carried too far: Once a contract has been validly made, the courts attach legal consequences to the relation created by the contract, consequences of which the parties usually never dreamed—as, for instance, where situations arise which the parties had not contemplated. As to such matters, the 'actual intent' theory induced much fictional discourse which imputed to the parties intentions they plainly did not have.

"But the objectivists also went too far. They tried (1) to treat virtually all the varieties of contractual arrangements in the same way, and (2), as to all contracts in all their phases, to exclude, as legally irrelevant, consideration of the actual intention of the parties or either of them, as distinguished from the outward manifestation of that intention. The objectivists transferred from the field of torts that stubborn anti-subjectivist, the 'reasonable man'; so that, in part at least, advocacy of the 'objective' standard in contracts appears to have represented a desire for legal symmetry, legal uniformity, a desire seemingly prompted by aesthetic impulses. Whether (thanks to the 'subjectivity' of the jurymen's reactions and other factors) the objectivists' formula, in its practical workings, could yield much actual objectivity, certainty, and uniformity may well be doubted. At any rate, the sponsors of complete 'objectivity' in contracts largely won out in the wider generalizations of the Restatement of Contracts and in some judicial pronouncements." Ricketts v. Pennsylvania R. Co., 153 F.2d 757 (2d Cir. 1946).

Does either theory adequately explain the decision in Lucy v. Zehmer?

NOTE

Problem. Father consulted Doctor about an operation to remove scar tissue from Son's hand which had resulted from a severe burn nine years before. Father asked Doctor, "How long will the boy be in the hospital," and Doctor replied, "Three or four days, not over four; then the boy can go home and it will be just a few days when he will go back to work with a good hand." Son's hand was not healed for a month after the operation. Is Doctor liable to Father for breach of contract? See Hawkins v. McGee, 84 N.H. 114, 146 A. 641 (1929).

OWEN v. TUNISON

Supreme Judicial Court of Maine, 1932.
131 Me. 42, 158 A. 926.

Action by W. H. Owen against R. G. Tunison for breach of contract.

BARNES, J. This case is reported to the law court, and such judgment is to be rendered as the law and the admissible evidence require.

Plaintiff charges that defendant agreed in writing to sell him the Bradley block and lot, situated in Bucksport, for a stated price in cash, that he later refused to perfect the sale, and that plaintiff, always willing and ready to pay the price, has suffered loss on account of defendant's unjust refusal to sell, and claims damages.

From the record it appears that defendant, a resident of Newark N. J., was, in the fall of 1929, the owner of the Bradley block and lot.

With the purpose of purchasing, on October 23, 1929, plaintiff wrote the following letter:

"Dear Mr. Tunison:

"Will you sell me your store property which is located on Main St. in Bucksport, Me. running from Montgomery's Drug Store on one corner to a Grocery Store on the other, for the sum of $6,000.00?"

Nothing more of this letter need be quoted.

On December 5, following, plaintiff received defendant's reply, apparently written in Cannes, France, on November 12, and it reads:

"In reply to your letter of Oct. 23rd which has been forwarded to me in which you inquire about the Bradley Block, Bucksport, Me.

"Because of improvements which have been added and an expenditure of several thousand dollars it would not be possible for me to sell it unless I was to receive $16,000.00 cash.

"The upper floors have been converted into apartments with baths and the b'l'dg put into first class condition.

"Very truly yours,

"[Signed] R. G. Tunison."

Whereupon, and at once, plaintiff sent to defendant, and the latter received, in France, the following message:

"Accept your offer for Bradley block Bucksport Terms sixteen thousand cash send deed to Eastern Trust and Banking Co Bangor Maine Please acknowledge."

Four days later he was notified that defendant did not wish to sell the property, and on the 14th day of January following brought suit for his damages.

Granted that damages may be due a willing buyer if the owner refuses to tender a deed of real estate, after the latter has made an offer in writing to sell to the former, and such offer has been so accepted, it remains for us to point out that defendant here is not shown to have written to plaintiff an offer to sell.

There can have been no contract for the sale of the property desired, no meeting of the minds of the owner and prospective purchaser, unless there was an offer or proposal of sale. It cannot be successfully argued that defendant made any offer or proposal of sale.

In a recent case the words, "Would not consider less than half" is held "not to be taken as an outright offer to sell for one-half." Sellers v. Warren, 116 Me. 350, 102 A. 40, 41.

Where an owner of millet seed wrote, "I want $2.25 per cwt. for this seed f. o. b. Lowell," in an action for damages for alleged breach of contract to sell at the figure quoted above, the court held: "He [defendant] does not say, 'I offer to sell to you.' The language used is general, and such as may be used in an advertisement, or circular addressed generally to those engaged in the seed business, and is not an offer by which he may be bound, if accepted, by any or all of the persons addressed." Nebraska Seed Co. v. Harsh, 98 Neb. 89, 152 N. W. 310, 311, and cases cited in note L.R.A.1915F, 824.

Defendant's letter of December 5 in response to an offer of $6,000 for his property may have been written with the intent to open negotiations that might lead to a sale. It was not a proposal to sell.

Judgment for defendant.

NOTE

Analysis of Communications. Did Tunison by his letter of November 12 indicate an intention to empower Owen "to close the contract"? Or did he indicate that he expected the offer to come from Owen? A useful technique in analyzing the language used by the parties is to redraft it twice, staying as faithful to the original as possible, so that it would clearly require a decision, first for one party, then for the other. Take, for example, the language "it would not be possible for me to sell it unless I was to receive $16,000 cash." What result if Tunison had said instead, "I will sell for $16,000"? What result if he had said, "I will not entertain an offer for less than $16,000"? Which comes closer to the meaning of the language that he used? Is the fact that there is a considerable disparity between $6,000 and $16,000 relevant? The interpretation of contract language is the subject of Section 2 of Chapter 6. On how this differs from the interpretation of communications to determine whether a contract exists in the first place, see Note 2, p. 572 infra.

HARVEY v. FACEY, [1893] A.C. 552 (P.C.) (Jamaica). [Harvey and another, solicitors in Kingston, were interested in a piece of property known as Bumper Hall Pen. Facey, the owner, had been engaged in negotiations for its sale to the town of Kingston for £900. Harvey telegraphed Facey, who was on a journey, "Will you sell us Bumper Hall Pen? Telegraph lowest cash price—answer paid." Facey replied by telegram, "Lowest price for Bumper Hall Pen £900." Harvey answered, "We agree to buy Bumper Hall Pen for the sum of nine hundred pounds asked by you." Harvey sued for specific performance of this agreement and for an injunction to restrain the town of Kingston from taking a conveyance of the property. The trial court dismissed the action on the ground that the agreement did not disclose a concluded contract; the Supreme Court of Jamaica reversed; the defendants appealed to the Judicial Committee of the Privy Council.]

LORD MORRIS. . . . [T]heir Lordships concur in the judgment of Mr. Justice Curran that there was no concluded contract between the appellants and L. M. Facey to be collected from the aforesaid telegrams. The first telegram asks two questions. The first question is as to the willingness of L. M. Facey to sell to the appellants [i. e. Harvey]; the second question asks the lowest price, and the word "telegraph" is in its collocation addressed to that second question only. L. M. Facey replied to the second question only, and gives his lowest price. The third telegram from the appellants treats the answer of L. M. Facey stating his lowest price as an unconditional offer to sell to them at the price named. Their Lordships cannot treat the telegram from L. M. Facey as binding him in any respect, except to the extent it does by its term, viz., the lowest price. Everything else is left open, and the reply telegram from the appellants cannot be treated as an acceptance of an offer to sell to them; it is an offer that required to be accepted by L. M. Facey. The contract could only be completed if L. M. Facey had accepted the appellants' last telegram. It has been contended for the appellants that L. M. Facey's telegram should be read as saying "yes" to the first question put in the appellants' telegram, but there is nothing to support that contention. L. M. Facey's telegram gives a precise answer to a precise question, viz., the price. The contract must appear by the telegrams, whereas the appellants are obliged to contend that an acceptance of the first question is to be implied. Their Lorships are of opinion that the mere statement of the lowest price at which the vendor would sell contains no implied contract to sell at that price to the persons making the inquiry. . . . [Reversed and the judgment of the trial court restored.]

NOTE

More Analysis of Communications. Redraft Facey's telegram so that it clearly would have required a decision for Harvey. Redraft it so that it clearly would have required a decision for Facey. Which seems closer to the meaning of the language that he used? Is it significant that Harvey presumably knew that he was not the only potential buyer for Bumper Hall Pen? Could Harvey's first telegram have been more skillfully drafted? What result if it had read, "What is the lowest price at which you will sell me Bumper Hall Pen?" See, in criticism of Harvey v. Facey, Russell, 1 Can.Bar Rev. 392, 398–403 (1923); in approval, MacLeod, 1 Can.Bar Rev. 694 (1923); and in rejoinder, Russell, 1 Can.Bar Rev. 713 (1923).

Appellant ——— *Appellee*

FAIRMOUNT GLASS WORKS v. CRUNDEN–MARTIN WOODENWARE CO.

Court of Appeals of Kentucky, 1899.
106 Ky. 659, 51 S.W. 196, 21 Ky.Law Rep. 264.

Action by the Crunden-Martin Woodenware Company against the Fairmount Glass Works to recover damages for breach of contract. Judgment for plaintiff, and defendant appeals. Affirmed.

HOBSON, J.   On April 20, 1895, appellee wrote appellant the following letter:

"St. Louis, Mo., April 20, 1895.   Gentlemen: Please advise us the lowest price you can make us on our order for ten car loads of Mason green jars, complete, with caps, packed one dozen in a case, either delivered here, or f. o. b. cars your place, as you prefer.   State terms and cash discount.   Very truly, Crunden-Martin W. W. Co."

To this letter appellant answered as follows:

"Fairmount, Ind.   April 23, 1895.   Crunden-Martin Wooden Ware Co., St. Louis, Mo.—Gentlemen: Replying to your favor of April 20, we quote you Mason fruit jars, complete, in one-dozen boxes, delivered in East St. Louis, Ill.: Pints, $4.50, quarts, $5.00, half gallons, $6.50 per gross, for immediate acceptance, and shipment not later than May 15, 1895; sixty days' acceptance, or 2 off, cash in ten days.   Yours truly, Fairmount Glass Works.

"Please note that we make all quotations and contracts subject to the contingencies of agencies or transportation delays or accidents beyond our control."

For reply thereto, appellee sent the following telegram on April 24, 1895:

"Fairmount Glass Works, Fairmount, Ind.: Your letter twenty-third received.   Enter order ten car loads as per your quotation. Specifications mailed.   Crunden-Martin W. W. Co."

In response to this telegram, appellant sent the following:

"Fairmount, Ind., April 24, 1895.   Crunden-Martin W. W. Co., St. Louis, Mo.: Impossible to book your order.   Output all sold.   See letter.   Fairmount Glass Works."

Appellee insists that, by its telegram sent in answer to the letter of April 23d, the contract was closed for the purchase of 10 car loads of Mason fruit jars.   Appellant insists that the contract was not closed by this telegram, and that it had the right to decline to fill the order at the time it sent its telegram of April 24.   This is the chief question in the case.   The court below gave judgment in favor of appellee, and appellant has appealed, earnestly insisting that the judgment is erroneous.

We are referred to a number of authorities holding that a quotation of prices is not an offer to sell, in the sense that a completed contract will arise out of the giving of an order for merchandise in accordance with the proposed terms.   There are a number of cases holding that the transaction is not completed until the order so made is accepted.   7 Am. & Eng.Enc.Law (2d Ed.) p. 138; Smith v. Gowdy, 8 Allen, Mass., 566; Beaupre v. Telegraph Co., 21 Minn. 155.   But each case must turn largely upon the language there used.   In this case we think there was more than a quotation of prices, although appellant's letter uses the word "quote" in stating the prices given.   The true meaning of the correspondence must be determined by reading it as a whole. Appellee's letter of April 20th, which began the transaction, did not ask for a quotation of prices. It reads: "Please advise us the lowest price you can make us on our order for ten carloads of Mason green jars. . . . State terms and cash discount." From this appellant could not fail to understand that appellee wanted to know at what price it would sell ten car loads of these jars; so when, in answer, it wrote: "We quote you Mason fruit jars . . . pints $4.50, quarts $5.00, half gallons $6.50, per gross, for immediate acceptance; . . . 2 off, cash in ten days,"—it must be deemed as intending to give appellee the information it asked for. We can hardly understand what is meant by the words "for immediate acceptance," unless the latter was intended as a proposition to sell at these prices if accepted immediately. In construing every contract, the aim of the court is to arrive at the intention of the parties. In none of the cases to which we have been referred on behalf of appellant was there on the face of the correspondence any such expression of intention to make an offer to sell on the terms indicated. . . . The expression in appellant's letter, "for immediate acceptance," taken in connection with appellee's letter, in effect, at what price it would sell it the goods, is, it seems to us, much stronger evidence of a present offer, which, when accepted immediately, closed the contract. Appellee's letter was plainly an inquiry for the price and terms on which appellant would sell it the goods, and appellant's answer to it was not a quotation of prices, but a definite offer to sell on the terms indicated, and could not be withdrawn after the terms had been accepted.

It will be observed that the telegram of acceptance refers to the specifications mailed. These specifications were contained in the following letter: "St Louis, Mo., April 24, 1895. Fairmount Glass-Works Co., Fairmount, Ind.—Gentlemen: We received your letter of 23rd this morning, and telegraphed you in reply as follows: 'Your letter 23rd received. Enter order ten car loads as per your quotation. Specifications mailed,'—which we now confirm. We have accordingly entered this contract on our books for the ten cars Mason green jars, complete, with caps and rubbers, one dozen in case, delivered to us in East St. Louis at $4.50 per gross for pint, $5.00 for quart, $6.50 for one-half gallon. Terms, 60 days' acceptance, or 2 per cent. for cash in ten days, to be shipped not later than May 15, 1895. The jars and caps to be strictly first-quality goods. You may ship the first car to us here assorted: Five gross pint, fifty-five gross quart, forty gross one-half gallon. Specifications for the remaining 9 cars we will send later. Crunden-Martin W. W. Co." It is insisted for appellant that this was not an acceptance of the offer as made; that the stipulation, "The jars and caps to be strictly first-quality goods," was not in their offer; and that, it not having been accepted as made, appellant is not bound. But it will be observed that appellant declined to furnish the goods before it got this letter, and in the correspondence with appellee it nowhere complained of these words as an addition to the contract. Quite a number of other letters passed, in which the refusal to deliver the goods was placed on other grounds, none of which have been sustained by the evidence. Appellee offers proof tending to show that these words, in the trade in which parties were engaged, conveyed the same meaning as the words used in appellant's letter, and were only a different form of expressing the same idea. Appellant's conduct would seem to confirm this evidence.

Appellant also insists that the contract was indefinite, because the quantity of each size of the jars was not fixed, that ten car loads is too indefinite a specification of the quantity sold, and that appellee had no right to accept the goods to be delivered on different days. The proof shows that "ten car loads" is an expression used in the trade as equivalent to 1,000 gross, 100 gross being regarded as a car load. The offer to sell the different sizes at different prices gave the purchaser the right to name the quantity of each size, and, the offer being to ship not later than May 15th, the buyer had the right to fix the time of delivery at any time before that. . . . The petition, if defective, was cured by the judgment, which is fully sustained by the evidence.

Judgment affirmed.

NOTES

(1) *The "Battle of the Forms" (Opening Skirmish).* The pattern of communications illustrated in the Fairmount Glass Works case remains an important one, even today. Commercial contracts for the sale of goods are often the result of an exchange of several documents by the buyer and seller rather than a single document signed by both. In routine transactions most of these documents are standardized printed forms with blanks filled in to fit the particular transaction. Typically the buyer will begin by sending his "request for quotation" form, comparable to Crunden-Martin's letter of April 20. The seller will answer by sending his "quotation" form, comparable to Fairmount's letter of April 23. The buyer will reply by sending his "purchase order" form, comparable to Crunden-Martin's telegram of April 24. Finally the seller will send his "sales acknowledgement" form, and then the goods will be shipped by the seller and received by the buyer. These final steps did not, of course, take place in the Fairmount Glass Works case. This pattern of bargaining by communication on standard forms has come to be known as the "battle of the forms." Each party strives to make a contract on the terms of *his* form. Other problems that this raises will be taken up later in this chapter. See Subsection 4(d), infra. For the present, the problem is the characterization of Fairmount's "quotation" of April 23.

(2) *Offer or Not?* Suppose Fairmount's letter of April 23 had not been in response to a preliminary letter from Crunden-Martin. Would the result have been the same? What significance should be attached to the use of the expression "we quote you" in Fairmount's letter of April 23? What facts make "quote" mean "offer"? Is the second paragraph of Fairmount's letter significant in this connection? In answering these questions, consider the following case.

Amount not definite (handwritten)

Kershaw wrote Moulton, "In consequence of a rupture in the salt trade we are authorized to offer Michigan fine salt in full car load lots of 80 to 95 barrels, delivered at your city at 85 cents per barrel to be shipped per C. & N. W. R. R. Co. only. At this price it is a bargain as the price in general remains unchanged. Shall be pleased to receive your order." Moulton immediately wired Kershaw, "Your letter of yesterday received and noted. You may ship me two thousand barrels Michigan fine salt as offered in your letter." Kershaw failed to ship the salt, and Moulton sued for breach of contract. The trial court overruled Kershaw's demurrer and Kershaw appealed. *Held:* Reversed. "The language is not such as a business man would use in making an offer to sell . . . a definite amount of property." Moulton v. Kershaw, 59 Wis. 316, 18 N.W. 172 (1884). Suppose Kershaw's communication to Moulton had read, "we are authorized to offer two thousand barrels Michigan fine salt," etc. Would the result have been different? What would be the objection to construing Kershaw's communication as an offer to sell any reasonable quantity of salt—say one to twenty-five car load lots—leaving it to the offeree to name the precise quantity? Has not Kershaw committed himself in advance to supply any reasonable quantity? What result if Kershaw's communication had read, "we are authorized to offer you all the Michigan fine salt you will order," etc.?

CRAFT v. ELDER & JOHNSTON CO.

Court of Appeals of Ohio, Montgomery County, 1941.
38 N.E.2d 416.

[Action by Craft against Elder & Johnston Co. for alleged breach of contract. From a judgment of dismissal plaintiff appeals.]

BARNES, JUDGE. . . . On or about January 31, 1940, the defendant, the Elder & Johnston Company, carried an advertisement in the Dayton Shopping News, an offer for sale of a certain all electric sewing machine for the sum of $26 as a "Thursday Only Special". Plaintiff in her petition, after certain formal allegations, sets out the substance of the above advertisement carried by defendant in the Dayton Shopping News. She further alleges that the above publication is an advertising paper distributed in Montgomery County and throughout the city of Dayton; that on Thursday, February 1, 1940, she tendered to the defendant company $26 in payment for one of the machines offered in the advertisement, but that defendant refused to fulfill the offer and has continued to so refuse. The petition further alleges that the value of the machine offered was $175 and she asks damages in the sum of $149 plus interest from February 1, 1940.

. . . .

The trial court dismissed plaintiff's petition as evidenced by a journal entry, the pertinent portion of which reads as follows: "Upon consideration the court finds that said advertisement was not an offer which could be accepted by plaintiff to form a contract, and this case is therefore dismissed with prejudice to a new action, at costs of plaintiff."

Within statutory time plaintiff filed notice of appeal on questions of law and thus lodged the case in our court. . . .

It seems to us that this case may easily be determined on well-recognized elementary principles. The first question to be determined is the proper characterization to be given to defendant's advertisement in the Shopping News. . . .

"It is clear that in the absence of special circumstances an ordinary newspaper advertisement is not an offer, but is an offer to negotiate—an offer to receive offers—or, as it is sometimes called, an offer to chaffer." Restatement of the Law of Contracts, Par. 25, Page 31.

Under the above paragraph the following illustration is given, " 'A', a clothing merchant, advertises overcoats of a certain kind for sale at $50. This is not an offer but an invitation to the public to come and purchase."

"Thus, if goods are advertised for sale at a certain price, it is not an offer and no contract is formed by the statement of an intending purchaser that he will take a specified quantity of the goods at that price. The construction is rather favored that such an advertisement is a mere invitation to enter into a bargain rather than an offer. So a published price list is not an offer to sell the goods listed at the published price." Williston on Contracts, Revised Edition, Vol. 1, Par. 27, Page 54.

"The commonest example of offers meant to open negotiations and to call forth offers in the technical sense are advertisements, circulars and trade letters sent out by business houses. While it is possible that the offers made by such means may be in such form as to become contracts, they are often merely expressions of a willingness to negotiate." Page on the Law of Contracts, 2d Ed., Vol. 1, Page 112, Par. 84.

"Business advertisements published in newspapers and circulars sent out by mail or distributed by hand stating that the advertiser has a certain quantity or quality of goods which he wants to dispose of at certain prices, are not offers which become contracts as soon as any person to whose notice they may come signifies his acceptance by notifying the other that he will take a certain quantity of them. They are merely invitations to all persons who may read them that the advertiser is ready to receive offers for the goods at the price stated." 13 Corpus Juris 289, Par. 97. . . .

We are constrained to the view that the trial court committed no prejudicial error in dismissing plaintiff's petition.

The judgment of the trial court will be affirmed and costs adjudged against the plaintiff-appellant.

NOTE

Advertisements as Offers. If advertisements such as that in the Craft case were held to be offers, what would be the position of the store if the demand were to exceed its supply? Would it arise if "first come, first served" were read into every advertisement? This last approach appears to be that of French law, under which "the great majority of authorities consider such a proposal to be an offer, even if it can be accepted only by one of those to whom it is addressed. But such an offer is subject to the condition, as to each offeree, that it has not already been accepted by a quicker-acting offeree." 1 Schlesinger (ed.), Formation of Contracts: A Study of the Common Core of Legal Systems 359 (1968). Can you see any difficulties that might arise under this approach? What if the personal qualities (e. g., integrity) of the other party will play an important role under the contract?

"BAIT–AND–SWITCH"

The term "bait-and-switch" is used to describe advertising that seeks to attract customers by advertising at a spectacularly low price a product, used as "bait," that the seller does not intend to sell, so that the seller can then try to "switch" the customer to another product on which his profit is greater. Would a rule similar to that of French law, under which advertisements were offers unless they provided otherwise, afford substantial protection to persons who are now victimized by this practice?

Nearly all states have legislation patterned after the Printer's Ink model statute, named for the advertising trade journal that sponsored it in 1911, making "untrue, deceptive, or misleading" advertising a misdemeanor. A smaller number of states also have statutes making it a misdemeanor to "offer" goods or services for sale with an "intent not to sell." Ohio has provisions of both types, which are set out below. The first paragraph, a Printer's Ink statute, dates from 1913, the second dates from 1957.

> No person, firm, or corporation shall directly or indirectly make, publish, disseminate, circulate, or place before the public, in this state, in a newspaper, magazine, or other publication, or in the form of a book, notice, handbill, poster, circular, pamphlet, letter, sign, placard, card, label, or over any radio station, or in any other way, an advertisement or announcement of any sort regarding merchandise, securities, service, employment, real estate, or anything of value offered by him for use, purchase, or sale, and which advertisement or announcement contains any assertion, representation, or statement which is untrue, or fraudulent.

> No person, firm, or corporation shall, in any manner, or by any means of advertisement, or other means of communication, offer for sale any merchandise, commodity, or serv-

ice, as part of a plan or scheme with the intent, design, or purpose not to sell the merchandise, commodity, or service so advertised at the price stated therein, or with the intent, design, or purpose not to sell the merchandise, commodity, or service so advertised. Nothing in this section shall apply to any visual or sound radio broadcasting station, to a telephone company offering announcement service according to tariffs filed with the public utilities commission of Ohio, or to any publisher or printer of a newspaper, magazine, or other form of printed advertising, who broadcasts, publishes, or prints such advertisement in good faith without knowledge of its false, deceptive, or misleading character.

Whoever violates this section shall be fined not less than two hundred nor more than one thousand dollars or imprisoned not more than twenty days, or both. (Ohio Rev.Code Ann. § 2911.41.)

A related provision empowers a state prosecuting attorney to enjoin the acts and practices proscribed above. Ohio Rev.Code Ann. § 2911.42.

Under what circumstances might the advertisement in the Craft case have been in violation of this Ohio Statute? What do the statutory words "offer for sale" mean? Suppose that the store had had a dozen of the sewing machines advertised, which it had sold to those customers who insisted on buying them after they had been encouraged to buy a more expensive machine, but that Mrs. Craft had arrived at the store after the dozen were gone. Would there have been a violation of the statute? There have been remarkably few prosecutions under statutes of this sort. See People v. Ludwig Baumann & Co., 56 Misc.2d 153, 288 N.Y.S.2d 404 (1968) (injunction obtained by attorney general); Note, 69 Yale L.J. 830 (1960).

Furthermore, in 1969 Ohio adopted the Uniform Deceptive Trade Practices Act, promulgated by the National Conference of Commissioners on Uniform State Laws in 1964. Among the things that it makes a "deceptive trade practice" is the advertising of goods or services "with intent not to sell them as advertised" or "with intent not to supply reasonably expectable public demand unless the advertisement discloses a limitation of quantity." The principal remedy under the act is an injunction by any person "likely to be damaged." Proof of "monetary damage or loss of profits" is not required.[a] Ohio Rev.Stat.Ann. §§ 4165.02(I)(K), 4165.03. How much does the uniform act expand the protection against "bait-and-switch" schemes in Ohio?

a. The comparable language of the uniform act, § 3(a), reads "monetary damage, loss of profits, or intent to deceive." On the uniform act and the Ohio amendments, see Dole, Merchant and Consumer Protection: The Uniform Deceptive Trade Practices Act, 76 Yale L.J. 485 (1967); Carpenter, Consumer Protection in Ohio Against False Advertising and Deceptive Practices, 32 Ohio St.L.J. 1 (1971).

In addition to state legislation of the type described in the preceding note, Section 5 of the Federal Trade Commission Act has since 1938 declared "unfair or deceptive acts or practices in commerce" to be unlawful. The act provides for enforcement by the Federal Trade Commission, which consists of five members. If a violation of the act is found, the Commission may issue a cease-and-desist-order, which may be reviewed by a federal court of appeals. Once such an order has become final, the violator is subject to civil penalties of up to $5,000 a day, with each day of continuing disobedience constituting a separate violation. An order restraining a respondent from false and deceptive advertising does not, of course, provide the kind of individual relief sought by Mrs. Craft.

The Commission also publishes industry guides giving its advice on the legality of specific conduct in selected areas, renders advisory opinions in response to individual inquiries concerning the legality of a proposed course of action, promulgates rules on which it may rely in future proceedings,[b] and accepts assurances that objectionable practices will be discontinued. In recent years a growing number of state and local governments have established special agencies for consumer protection.

––––––

LEFKOWITZ v. GREAT MINNEAPOLIS SURPLUS STORE, 251 Minn. 188, 86 N.W.2d 689 (1957). [The Great Minneapolis Surplus Store published the following advertisement in a Minneapolis newspaper:

"SATURDAY 9 A. M.
2 BRAND NEW PASTEL
MINK 3-SKIN SCARFS
Selling for $89.50
Out they go

Saturday.   Each $1.00
1 BLACK LAPIN STOLE
Beautiful,
worth $139.50 . . . .$1.00
FIRST COME
FIRST SERVED"

b. In 1971, for example, the Commission promulgated a rule making it, "an unfair or deceptive act or practice" for a retail foodstore, without appropriate disclosure, to offer "food and grocery products or other merchandise . . . at a stated price, by means of any advertisement disseminated in an area served by any of its stores which are covered by the advertisement which do not have such products in stock, and readily available to customers during the effective period of the advertisement," or to fail "to make the advertised items conspicuously and readily available for sale at or below the advertised prices." A retailer who does not have the products in stock is given a defense if he "maintains records sufficient to show that [they] were ordered in adequate time for delivery and delivered to the stores in quantities sufficient to meet reasonably anticipated demands." 16 C.F.R. § 424.1.

Lefkowitz was the first to present himself on Saturday and demanded the Lapin stole for one dollar. The store refused to sell to him because of a "house rule" that the offer was intended for women only. Lefkowitz sued the store and was awarded $138.50 as damages. The store appealed.]

MURPHY, JUSTICE. . . . The defendant relies principally on Craft v. Elder & Johnston Co. . . . On the facts before us we are concerned with whether the advertisement constituted an offer, and, if so, whether the plaintiff's conduct constituted an acceptance. There are numerous authorities which hold that a particular advertisement in a newspaper or circular letter relating to a sale of articles may be construed by the court as constituting an offer, acceptance of which would complete a contract. . . . The test of whether a binding obligation may originate in advertisements addressed to the general public is "whether the facts show that some performance was promised in positive terms in return for something requested." 1 Williston, Contracts (rev. ed.) § 27. The authorities above cited emphasize that, where the offer is clear, definite and explicit, and leaves nothing open for negotiation, it constitutes an offer, acceptance of which will complete the contract. . . . Whether in any individual instance a newspaper advertisement is an offer rather than an invitation to make an offer depends on the legal intention of the parties and the surrounding circumstances. . . . We are of the view on the facts before us that the offer by the defendant of the sale of the Lapin fur was clear, definite, and explicit, and left nothing open for negotiation. . . . The defendant contends that the offer was modified by a "house rule" to the effect that only women were qualified to receive the bargains advertised. The advertisement contained no such restriction. This objection may be disposed of briefly by stating that, while an advertiser has the right at any time before acceptance to modify his offer, he does not have the right, after acceptance, to impose new or arbitrary conditions not contained in the published offer. . . .

Affirmed.[a]

NOTES

(1) *Rationale.* Can the Craft and Lefkowitz cases be distinguished? In what respect was the advertisement in the latter more "clear, definite and explicit" than that in the former? Were the words "First Come First Served" significant?

a. In an omitted part of the opinion, the court discusses the fact that Lefkowitz had answered a similar advertisement of Great Minneapolis Surplus Store only a week before the publication of the advertisement in question. At that time the store had also refused to sell to him, explaining that by a "house rule" the offer was intended for women only and sales would not be made to men. Considering this additional fact, do you agree with the court's decision that he could recover under the later advertisement? See Note 3, p. 32 supra.

(2) *Auctions.* When an auctioneer puts property up for sale at an auction, is this an offer to sell to the highest bidder, which is then accepted when the highest bid is made? Or is it merely an invitation for offers by bids, which can then be accepted or rejected by the auctioneer? The law has taken the latter view, that it is the bidder that makes the offer. Nevertheless, the auctioneer may make an offer if he chooses to do so, and the usual way of doing this is by advertising the sale to be "without reserve." See Restatement Second, § 27; UCC 2–328. Note that under the Restatement and the Code, if the sale is "without reserve," the auctioneer is bound not to withdraw after a bid is made, but the bidder is not similarly bound. Local statutes may also govern auction sales.

The rather elaborate provisions of UCC 2–328 are, of course, expressly applicable only to the sale of goods. UCC 2–102. Might they be extended by analogy to the sale of land? Comment 1 to UCC 1–102 recognized the possibility of reasoning from the Code by analogy: "[Courts] have recognized the policies embodied in an act as applicable in reason to subject-matter which was not expressly included in the language of the act. . . . They have done the same where reason and policy so required, even where the subject-matter had been intentionally excluded from the act in general. . . . Nothing in this Act stands in the way of the continuance of such action by the courts." Cf. Freeman v. Poole, 37 R.I. 489, 93 A. 786 (1915), a land auction case in which the court reasoned by analogy to the auction provisions of the Uniform Sales Act, the Code's predecessor.

WILHELM LUBRICATION CO. v. BRATTRUD

Supreme Court of Minnesota, 1936.
197 Minn. 626, 268 N.W. 634, 106 A.L.R. 1279.

Action by the Wilhelm Lubrication Company against Wallace C. Brattrud, doing business under the name of the Economy Supply Company. From a judgment for plaintiff, defendant appeals.

Reversed and remanded.

DEVANEY, CHIEF JUSTICE. Action for damages for breach of contract for failure to accept delivery of 11,500 gallons of lubricating oil and 4,000 pounds of transmission grease.

On January 24, 1934, plaintiff and defendant entered into an agreement which reads as follows:

"The above seller hereby sells and agrees to hold in its storage for the Purchaser, and the above Purchaser hereby buys, the merchandise described below, which shall be shipped to Purchaser at Waseca, Minn., on Aug. 1st, 1934 unless ordered out sooner.

Quantity	Description	Per Gal.	Total.
5000 gals.	Worthmore Motor Oil SAE 10–70 Base	.21–31	
3000 gals.	Beterlube Motor Oil SAE 10–70	.26–36	
2000 gals.	Costal Motor Oil SAE 10–70	18½–28½	
1500 gals.	Penzalube Motor Oil SAE 10–70	34–44	
4000 lbs.	Black Devil Trans. Lub.	5¢	
As per Price List 34 attached			"

[Parts of the agreement not necessary to the discussion here are omitted.]

Approximately three weeks after the making of the above agreement, defendant repudiated the same. Plaintiff treated the contract as breached, and brought this action for damages.

The jury returned a verdict for plaintiff in the sum of $210. Defendant moved in the alternative for judgment notwithstanding or for a new trial. The motion was denied and judgment entered. This appeal is taken from the judgment.

Three questions are presented: (1) Is the agreement between the parties in whole or in part so indefinite in its terms as to be unenforceable? (2) If indefinite in part only, is the contract severable? (3) Did the court err in instructing the jury as to the measure of damages for breach of the contract?

1. In considering the first question it is necessary to explore the meaning of the terms used in the contract. Defendant, Brattrud, agreed to take a total of 11,500 gallons of oil of the different brands listed and 4,000 pounds of "Black Devil" lubricating grease. The technical term SAE 10–70 opposite each item in the contract signifies seven weights of oil officially designated by the Society of Automotive Engineers according to their thickness or viscosity. The lightest of these groups is designated SAE 10; the heaviest SAE 70; the intervening ones are, 20, 30, 40, 50, and 60. The price varies with the weight. Thus, for example, under this contract, defendant agreed to take 5,000 gallons of "Worthmore Motor Oil" of any weight he should choose from 10–70. The price for SAE 10 was 21 cents per gallon and the price for SAE 70 was 31 cents per gallon. The other weights varied in price between 21 cents and 31 cents per gallon. The same applies to the other brands of oil that defendant agreed to take.

The total quantity of each brand of oil purchased was definite. Defendant, however, had the right under the contract to specify any weight oil he wished within the weights listed. The weight controlled the price, the price of each weight being definite. But until the defendant chose a particular weight the price he was obligated to pay under the contract was not ascertained. Nor was there any agreement as to how many gallons of each weight defendant was to take. As to these matters there had been no meeting of the minds or expression of mutual assent of the parties to the contract. There was and could be no agreement as to these elements until the defendant indicated his wants within the specified limits of the alleged contract. This indefiniteness and uncertainty in the contract, is in our opinion, fatal to plaintiff's cause of action. The subject-matter of a contract of sale must be definite as to quantity and price. The reason for this requirement is obvious when we consider the question of damages. As the contract now stands with respect to the oil defendant agreed to take, the application of any measure of damages, which in case of breach of such contract must be based partly on the contract price, is impossible. Here the quantity of each brand to be taken and the contract price thereof cannot be determined until the defendant places an order. This was never done. The agreement was repudiated before any order was placed. The court or jury cannot be allowed to speculate as to the measure of damages, and there is no sound authority for taking an average or an arbitrary price as the contract price in a case of this kind. This, in effect, would be inserting a new term in the contract, thereby remaking the agreement for the parties, which is beyond the power of a court or jury.

In the case of Wheeling Steel & Iron Co. v. Evans, 97 Md. 305, 55 A. 373, a contract of sale involving the same problem as the one in this case was before the court. The buyer had agreed to take 100 tons of tack plate. There were four grades, two at one price and two at another. It was held that no enforceable contract was created as there was no agreement as to how much of each grade the purchaser was to take, and the purchase price could not be ascertained until the purchaser designated which he wanted. The court said: "If the purchaser had the option to specify for any or all of the four gauges, it is clear that, until such specifications had been made, there could be no definite agreement, because it was the purchaser's privilege and right to designate 100 tons of No. 12, or of No. 14, or of No. 15, or of No. 16, or 25 tons of each gauge, or any other of a vast multitude of different proportions of the whole four gauges, or of any two or three of them. The price of each gauge was definite; the total quantity of tons was definite, and the times of delivery were definite; but the proportion of each gauge, as well as which of the four would be required, is wholly indefinite and uncertain. As to that element of the alleged contract there was obviously no consensus ad idem. . . . The test . . . lies in considering what would have been the measure of damages in a suit instituted by the vendor against the vendee for a breach of the alleged contract. Would the vendor have been entitled to recover the difference between the contract price and the market price of the whole 100 tons, reckoned on the basis of $2.80 per 100 pounds or on the basis of $2.72 per 100 pounds, or on some other basis founded on an arbitrary apportionment of the whole number of tons amongst the four different gauges? . . . What quantity of each gauge could a court or jury declare that the vendee ought to have specified? If either court or jury had undertaken such a task, it would have supplied a term of the contract which the parties themselves failed to incorporate, and manifestly such a proceeding would have been unwarranted." [Cases cited.]

The compelling logic of the foregoing line of decisions, coupled with the obvious fact that the adoption of any other rule would result in innumerable difficulties and cause much confusion in actual operation, leads us to the conclusion that in an agreement of this kind, the subject-matter of the contract is too indefinite to be capable of identification, and no action will lie for breach thereof. . . .

As to the portion of the agreement which provides for defendant's purchase of 4,000 pounds of lubricating grease, the contract is clearly not indefinite. The brand, "Black Devil" is definite. The quantity, 4,000 pounds, and the price, 5 cents per pound, are likewise certain and definite. There is no discretion allowed the buyer, defendant, in either amount or price. Plaintiff is entitled to recover damages for breach of this part of the agreement if the agreement is legally severable. . . . [The court's discussion of question (2) is omitted.]

We conclude that the contract is severable and that plaintiff is entitled to recover damages for breach of this portion of the agreement. . . . [The court's discussion of question (3) is omitted.]

Because part of the contract in this case is unenforceable, and the question of damages was submitted to the jury with reference to the whole thereof, the decision of the court below must be reversed, and the case remanded for a new trial on the question of damages only in accordance with the views herein set forth.

So ordered.

NOTES

(1) *Indefiniteness.* It is often said that a court will not "make a contract for the parties." But was it not clear that Wilhelm Lubrication and Brattrud reached agreement on the terms set out in their writing of January 24? Why, then, was that agreement not enforced? Was it not possible to calculate what Wilhelm Lubrication's damages would have been had Brattrud made his selection of oil so as to minimize those damages? See Restatement Second, §§ 32, 33. Would the result be different under the Code? See UCC 2–204, 2–305, 2–311. Would it make any difference if Brattrud had, after making the agreement, given specifications for "Worthmore" but none of the other brands of oil? Note that in Fairmount Glass Works v. Crunden-Martin, p. 67 supra, the court held that there was a contract although the quantity of pint, quart and half-gallon jars agreed to be sold, was optional with the buyer. Can that case be reconciled with the Brattrud case? See Comment, 23 U.Chi.L.Rev. 499 (1956).

(2) *Counselling.* Can you draft an agreement between Wilhelm Lubrication and Brattrud that would leave Brattrud with the range of choice that he wanted and yet would leave no doubt as to its enforceability by Wilhelm Lubrication in the event of Brattrud's repudiation?

(3) *Indefiniteness in Equity.* If the reason for the requirement of definiteness is, as the court said here, "obvious when we consider the question of damages," it would seem that the requirement might be different when the remedy sought is not damages but specific performance. Would you suppose that it would be more or less stringent? The traditional answer is given in Rego v. Decker, 482 P.2d 834 (Alaska 1971): "A greater standard of certainty is required for specific performance than for damages,

because of the difficulty of framing a decree specifying the performance required, as compared with the relative facility with which a breach may be perceived for the purpose of awarding damages." See Parev Products v. Rokeach, p. 609 infra.

––––––––

SOUTHWEST ENGINEERING CO. v. MARTIN TRACTOR CO., 205 Kan. 684, 473 P.2d 18 (1970). [Southwest Engineering was interested in submitting a bid to the United States Corps of Engineers for runway lighting facilities at McConnell Air Force Base in Wichita, Kansas. On April 11, 1966, Cloepfil, its construction superintendent, called Hurt, the manager of Martin Tractor's engine department, asking for a price on a generator. Hurt telephoned back a price of $18,500. Southwest used Hurt's figure in making up its bid and was awarded the contract. On April 28, Cloepfil met with Hurt at the Springfield, Missouri airport and was "amazed" to learn that the price had been "upped" to $21,500, but they reached an agreement at this figure, of which Hurt made a handwritten memorandum. On May 2, Cloepfil wrote Hurt to proceed, and on May 24, Hurt wrote Cloepfil that Martin could not fill the order. Further negotiations ended when the president of Southwest was told over the telephone by one of Martin's officers, "Who in the hell do you think you are? We don't have to sell you a damn thing." Southwest procured the generator elsewhere for $27,541 and sued for the difference of $6,041. From a judgment for the plaintiff for this amount, the defendant appealed.]

FONTRON, JUSTICE. . . . It is quite true, as the trial court found, that terms of payment were not agreed upon at the Springfield meeting. Hurt testified that as the memorandum was being made out, he said they wanted 10 per cent with the order, 50 per cent on delivery and the balance on acceptance, but he did not recall Cloepfil's response. Cloepfil's version was somewhat different. He stated that after the two had shaken hands in the lobby preparing to leave, Hurt said their terms usually were 20 per cent down and the balance on delivery; while he (Cloepfil) said the way they generally paid was 90 per cent on the tenth of the month following delivery and the balance on final acceptance. It is obvious the parties reached no agreement on this point.

However, a failure on the part of Messrs. Hurt and Cloepfil to agree on terms of payment would not, of itself, defeat an otherwise valid agreement reached by them. K.S.A. 84–2–204(3) reads:

"Even though one or more terms are left open a contract for sale does not fail for indefiniteness if the parties have intended to make a contract and there is a reasonably certain basis for giving an appropriate remedy."

The official U.C.C. Comment is enlightening:

"Subsection (3) states the principle as to 'open terms' underlying later sections of the Article. If the parties intend to enter into a binding agreement, this subsection recognizes that agreement as valid in law, despite missing terms, if there is any reasonably certain basis for granting a remedy. The test is not certainty as to what the parties were to do nor as to the exact amount of damages due the plaintiff. Nor is the fact that one or more terms are left to be agreed upon enough of itself to defeat an otherwise adequate agreement. Rather, commercial standards on the point of 'indefiniteness' are intended to be applied, this Act making provision elsewhere for missing terms needed for performance, open price, remedies and the like.

"The more terms the parties leave open the less likely it is that they have intended to conclude a binding agreement, but their actions may be frequently conclusive on the matter despite the omissions."

The above Code provision and accompanying Comment were quoted in Pennsylvania Co. v. Wilmington Trust Co., 39 Del.Ch. 453, 166 A.2d 726, where the court made this observation:

"There appears to be no pertinent court authority interpreting this rather recent but controlling statute. In an article entitled 'The Law of Sales In the Proposed Uniform Commercial Code,' 63 Harv. Law Rev. 561, 576, Mr. Williston wanted to limit omissions to 'minor' terms. He wanted 'business honor' to be the only compulsion where 'important terms' are left open. Nevertheless, his recommendation was rejected (see note on p. 561). This shows that those drafting the statute intended that the omission of even an important term does not prevent the finding under the statute that the parties intended to make a contract." (pp. 731, 732.)

So far as the present case is concerned, K.S.A. 84–2–310 supplies the omitted term. This statute provides in pertinent part:

"Unless otherwise agreed

"(a) payment is due at the time and place at which the buyer is to receive the goods even though the place of shipment is the place of delivery;"

In our view, the language of the two Code provisions is clear and positive. Considered together, we take the two sections to mean that where parties have reached an enforceable agreement for the sale of goods, but omit therefrom the terms of payment, the law will imply, as part of the agreement, that payment is to be made at time of delivery. . . . We do not mean to infer that terms of payment are not of importance under many circumstances, or that parties may not condition an agreement on their being included. However, the facts before us hardly indicate that Hurt and Cloepfil considered the terms of payment to be significant, or of more than passing interest. Hurt testified that while he stated his terms he did not recall Cloepfil's response, while Cloepfil stated that as the two were on the point of leaving, each stated their usual terms and that was as far as it went. The trial court found that only a brief and casual conversation ensued as to payment, and we think that is a valid summation of what took place.

Moreover, it is worthy of note that Martin first mentioned the omission of the terms of payment, as justifying its breach, in a letter written by counsel on September 15, 1966, more than four months after the memorandum was prepared by Hurt. On prior occasions Martin attributed its cancellation of the Springfield understanding to other causes. In its May 24 letter, Martin ascribed its withdrawal of "all verbal quotations" to "restrictions placed on Caterpillar products, accessory suppliers, and other stipulations by the district governing agency." In explaining the meaning of the letter to Cloepfil, Hurt said that Martin was doing work for the Corps of Engineers in the Kansas City and Tulsa districts and did not want to take on additional work with them at this time.

The entire circumstances may well give rise to a suspicion that Martin's present insistence that future negotiations were contemplated concerning terms of payment, is primarily an afterthought, for use as an escape hatch. Doubtless the trial court so considered the excuse in arriving at its findings.

We are aware of Martin's argument that Southwest's letter of May 2, 1966, referring to the sale is evidence that no firm contract had been concluded. Granted that some of the language employed might be subject to that interpretation, the trial court found, on what we deem to be substantial, competent evidence, that an agreement of sale *was* concluded at Springfield. Under our invariable rule those findings are binding upon this court on appeal even though there may have been evidence to the contrary. . . .

The defendant points particularly to the following portion of the May 2 letter, as interjecting a new and unacceptable term in the agreement made at Springfield.

" . . . We are not prepared to make a partial payment at the time of placing of this order. However, we will be able to include 100% of the engine-generator price in our first payment estimate after it is delivered, and only 10% will have to be withheld pending acceptance. Ordinarily this means that suppliers can expect payment of 90% within about thirty days after delivery."

It must be conceded that the terms of payment proposed in Southwest's letter had not been agreed to by Martin. However, we view the proposal as irrelevant. Although terms of payment had not been mutually agreed upon, K.S.A. 84–2–310 supplied the missing terms, i. e., payment on delivery, which thus became part of the agreement already concluded. In legal effect the proposal was no more than one to change the terms of payment implied by law. Since

Martin did not accept the change, the proposal had no effect, either as altering or terminating the agreement reached at Springfield.
. . .

[Affirmed.]

NOTE

"Reasonable" Compensation. Suppose that a party (e.g., a dentist, a plumber, a doctor, a lawyer) is to perform services that are by their nature difficult to value in advance. Is a promise to pay "reasonable" compensation in such a case too indefinite to be enforced?

Consider Corthell v. Summit Thread Co., 132 Me. 94, 167 A. 79 (1933). Corthell, a salesman for Summit, entered into an agreement under which Summit obtained the rights to three patents that Corthell held as well as "all future inventions for developments" and, "being desirous at all times to be fair and reasonable," paid him $3,500, agreed to continue to employ him for five more years at a fixed annual salary, and promised him "reasonable recognition" for future inventions, "the basis and amount of recognition to rest entirely with the Summit Thread Company at all times. All of the above is to be interpreted in good faith on the basis of what is reasonable and intended and not technically." When Summit refused to pay for future inventions that Corthell had turned over to it, he sued. The Supreme Court of Maine held that he was entitled to $5,000. "Reasonable recognition" meant reasonable compensation. Although "a reservation to either party of an *unlimited* right to determine the nature and extent of his performance renders his obligation too indefinite for legal enforcement, . . . if parties manifest, through express words or by reasonable implication, an intent on the one hand to pay and on the other to accept a fair price, a promise to pay a 'fair price' is not, as a matter of law, too vague for enforcement, and such damages as can be proved may be recovered. . . . The company was not free to do exactly as it chose. . . . It was bound in good faith to determine and pay the plaintiff the reasonable value of what it accepted from him."

What difference does it make whether such a promise is enforceable? If the promise is unenforceable, would there not be a claim for restitution? Cf. Schott v. Westinghouse Electric Corp., p. 42 supra. This question will be considered again in Subsection 4(b) of this chapter, which deals with "pre-contractual" liability.

WILLMOTT v. GIARRAPUTO, 5 N.Y.2d 250, 184 N.Y.S.2d 97, 157 N.E.2d 282 (1959). [Giarraputo gave the Willmotts a six month option to buy property. The option agreement described the property, the price, and the amount of the purchase-money mortgage, but provided with respect to that mortgage that "the payment of interest and amortization of principal shall be mutually agreed upon at the time of entering into a more formal contract." When the Willmotts elected to exercise the option, Giarraputo's lawyer submitted a contract to them, which they declined to sign because it did not contain a pre-payment term. Their lawyer then modified the contract by inserting a pre-payment term, and they signed and returned it to Giarraputo, who refused to sign the modified contract. The Willmotts then instituted an action for specific performance. They appeal from a dismissal of their complaint.]

FULD, J.[a] . . . Few principles are better settled in the law of contract than the proposition that, "If a material element of a contemplated contract is left for future negotiations, there is no contract. . . ." Here . . . the option agreement expressly recites that the "payment of interest and amortization of principal" provided for in the mortgage were to be "mutually agreed upon at the time of entering into a more formal contract." And, as one of the plaintiffs actually testified, the parties never agreed upon that matter. Not only were the plaintiffs dissatisfied with the contract drafted by the defendant's lawyer, but their own attorney made a still further amendment to the contract, with respect to prepayment, which the parties had, so far as appears, never even discussed.

[Affirmed.]

NOTE

Alternative Grounds for Recovery. In a case like Willmott v. Giarraputo, the effect of a decision that no contract was made is to deny the aggrieved party any recovery. Are there some situations in which, even if the parties did not reach the point where a contract was made, the aggrieved party might recover on some alternative ground—in restitution or for reliance, for example? This possibility is the subject of Subsection 4(b) of this chapter, which deals with "pre-contractual" liability.

"AGREEMENT TO AGREE" AND "FORMAL CONTRACT CONTEMPLATED"

Should a distinction be made between a situation in which the parties have agreed that a term, such as the compensation or the time for performance, shall be "reasonable," and one in which they have agreed that they shall continue to negotiate in a "reasonable" manner to fix that term? Does UCC 2–204(3) recognize such a distinction? Does UCC 2–305(1)? In what sense do these provisions invite a court to "make a contract for the parties"? According to the official comment to UCC 2–204, "the fact that one or more terms are left to be agreed upon [is not] enough of itself to defeat an otherwise adequate agreement." Does the comment go beyond the text of the Code? To what extent may such rules have desirable or undesirable effects on the parties during the bargaining process?

a. Stanley H. Fuld (1903–) practiced law in New York City from 1926 to 1935 when he became assistant district attorney. In 1946 he was appointed associate judge on the New York Court of Appeals. In 1967 he became chief judge.

Willmott v. Giarraputo shows the traditional judicial attitude toward the "agreement to agree" (the "contract to make a contract"). Does the Southwest Engineering case reject this attitude? Does it support the comment to UCC 2–204?

To what extent did the decision in Willmott v. Giarraputo turn on the phrase "shall be mutually agreed upon" and to what extent did it turn on the phrase "a more formal contract"? Are the problems inherent in those two phrases the same? Would Giarraputo's position with regard to the latter phrase have been strengthened by the omission of the words "more formal"?

Not infrequently the parties, particularly following complex negotiations, agree on what they consider the essential terms and leave details to be worked out, often by their lawyers, in connection with the preparation of a formal document which they both expect to sign. The process is more fully described at p. 99 infra. (See also the "letter of intent" set out at p. 61 supra.) If one of the parties refuses to sign the formal document, can the other enforce the agreement? Consider the following case.

Dohrman, who was in Florida, reached an agreement, through an exchange of letters, with the Sullivans for the sale to them of Dohrman's home in Kentucky. In the course of this exchange, he had written to them: "If the answers are to our satisfaction, we will immediately forward the sales contract which we have prepared which contains the terms of the agreement. This of course would act as a confirmation of the sale. If a sale is confirmed, I shall forward the deed." A week later he wrote his real estate agent a letter enclosing three copies of a formal sales contract for the "prospective purchasers" to sign. The contract stated that he had "bargained and sold" the property to the Sullivans. The letter said that when the Sullivans had signed the acceptance on the contract, "we will sign them, retain one for ourselves and return to you a copy for them and a copy for your company's record." The Sullivans signed, but Dohrman did not. The Sullivans sued Dohrman for specific performance. A judgment for the Sullivans was affirmed. Dohrman's letter enclosing the contract was an offer which the Sullivans accepted. "Where all the substantial terms of a contract have been agreed on and there is nothing left for future settlement, the fact alone that the parties contemplated execution of a formal instrument as a convenient memorial or definitive record of the agreement does not leave the transaction incomplete and without binding force in the absence of a positive agreement that it should not be binding until so executed." Dohrman v. Sullivan, 310 Ky. 463, 220 S.W.2d 973 (1949).

NOTE

A Case for Contrast. Massee, who lived in Minnesota, reached an agreement through an exchange of letters with Gibbs, who lived in Illinois, on the terms under which he would sell Gibbs a farm in Minnesota. Massee then wrote: "If you wish I can draw contract covering terms as planned and send it to you. . . . If contract and terms are agreeable you do not need to come up." Gibbs wrote back his approval, and Massee then sent an initial draft of the contract, which Gibbs returned unsigned with "the changes that seemed right to complete our deal for the land," adding, "Have another copy made, and if satisfactory to you forward the two copies with your signature. . . . I see no reason why we can't close it right up." Massee had the contract redrawn as requested, signed it in duplicate, and sent both copies to Gibbs, who refused to sign. Massee sued Gibbs for damages. *Held:* For Gibbs. "The correspondence makes it clear that all through defendant did not intend to be bound, and never expressed his assent to become bound, without the formal execution of the contract. . . . This is not a case where there has been a 'mere reference to a future contract in writing' wanted by one or more of the parties as a memorial of something already finally agreed upon, but is rather one where the 'reduction of the agreement to writing and its signature' has been made a condition precedent to its completion." Massee v. Gibbs, 169 Minn. 100, 210 N.W. 872 (1926).

Can these two cases be distinguished?

FLEXIBLE PRICING

Suppose that over a long term a seller wants to be assured of an outlet for a fixed quantity of his product and that a buyer wants to be assured of a source of supply for the same quantity. But neither wants to take the risk of a shift in the market: the seller does not want the risk of a rise in prices before delivery, and the buyer does not want the risk of a fall. How can they make an agreement that will be legally enforceable and yet will allow the price of the goods to fluctuate?

One possibility is to leave the price term "open," so that under UCC 2–305 the price will then be "a reasonable price at the time for *delivery*." The opportunities for dispute over what is "reasonable" may make this solution unattractive. (Would it be useful to designate a third party to fix the price if the parties disagreed? See UCC 2–305.) Another possibility is to use an "escalator clause" under which the price will be fixed according to a formula tied in some way to the market. Would it be easier to draft such an agreement if there were an ascertainable market price for the raw materials required by the seller to produce his product? An ascertainable market price for the product itself? (On ascertainable market price, see UCC 2–723, 2–724.) Would prices charged by competing sellers or to competing buyers be useful?[a] Helpful analogies can be found in clauses in leases tied to gross profits, in clauses in collective bargaining agreements tied to the cost of living, and in clauses in construction contracts tied to costs ("cost-plus" contracts).[b] On flexible pricing, see Note, 36 Va.L.Rev. 627 (1950).

Suppose that you succeeded in devising a *perfect* formula for tying the price to the buyer's market. Would it make any difference if the agreement were legally enforceable or not? (For what loss could the buyer recover damages if he could purchase the goods for the same price on the market?)

Some of the difficulties that parties have encountered at the hands of the courts are illustrated by Sun Printing & Publishing Ass'n v. Remington Paper & Power Co., 235 N.Y. 338, 139 N.E. 470 (1923). Sun Printing agreed to buy and Remington Paper to sell 1,000 tons of paper per month over a 16-month period. The agreement fixed the price for the first four months and provided: "For the balance of the period of this agreement the price of the paper and the length of terms for which such price shall apply shall be agreed upon by and between the parties hereto fifteen days prior to the expiration of each period for which the price and length of term thereof have been previously agreed upon, said price in no event to be higher than the contract price for newsprint charged by the Canadian Export Paper Company to the large consumers, the seller to receive the benefit of any differentials in freight rates." Prices rose and after the first four months Sun Printing offered to pay the Canadian Export price, but Remington Paper refused and Sun Printing sued for damages. The New York Court of Appeals held (5–2), in an opinion by Cardozo, that the complaint did not state a cause of action since there were "two subjects to be settled in the middle of December and at unstated intervals thereafter. One was the price to be paid. The other was the length of time during which such price was to govern. . . . Seller and buyer understood that the price to be fixed in December for a term to be agreed upon would not be more than the price then charged by the Canadian Export Paper Company to the large consumers. They did not understand that, if during the term so established the price charged by the Canadian Export Paper Com-

---

a. The impact of the antitrust laws on this question must be left for a later course.

An interesting variant is patterned after the "most favored nation" clause found in treaties. See, for example, Reynolds Metals Co. v. United States, 438 F.2d 983 (Ct.Cl.1971), in which the United States promised Reynolds to amend their contract "if later agreements with the Aluminum Company of America and/or the Kaiser Aluminum and Chemical Company are, in your opinion, more favorable than the agreement which has been executed with you."

b. Such clauses may, particularly in an inflationary period, have an adverse effect on the economy. (Is this necessarily so, if the clause is a substitute for a higher initial price?) Should this be of concern to the lawyer drafting an agreement for his client?

pany was changed, the price payable to the seller would fluctuate accordingly. . . . While the term was unknown, the contract was inchoate." What result under the Code? See UCC 2–305.

Not long after the decision, Cardozo gave a series of lectures in which he said of this case: "The court subordinated the equity of a particular situation to the overmastering need of certainty in the transactions of commercial life. . . . The loss to business would in the long run be greater than the gain if judges were clothed with power to revise as well as to interpret. Perhaps, with a higher conception of business and its needs, the time will come when even revision will be permitted if it is revision in consonance with established standards of fair dealing, but the time is not yet." Cardozo, Growth of the Law 110–11 (1924).

What are the "needs" of business? "The standard contract used by manufacturers of paper to sell to magazine publishers has a pricing clause which is probably sufficiently vague to make the contract legally unenforceable. The house counsel of one of the largest paper producers said that everyone in the industry is aware of this because of a leading New York case concerning the contract, but that no one cares." Macaulay, Non-Contractual Relations in Business: A Preliminary Study, 28 Am.Sociological Rev. 55, 60 (1963).

One avenue of escape from legal rules that do not accord with business practices is through arbitration. Commercial arbitration tribunals, usually with a single arbitrator or a three-member panel, are ordinarily established temporarily for each specific case. Organizations such as the American Arbitration Association and the International Chamber of Commerce, as well as many trade associations, maintain lists of available arbitrators and have promulgated rules under which panels may be appointed and their proceedings conducted. Arbitrators need not be lawyers. According to Section 30 of the rules of the American Arbitration Association, "The Arbitrator shall be the judge of the relevancy and materiality of the evidence offered and conformity to legal rules of evidence shall not be necessary." The arbitral award is generally not subject to judicial review for errors of substantive law, and, at least in this country, the arbitrators usually do not even give the reasons for their decision.[c]

c. But cf. Granite Worsted Mills v. Aaronson Cowen, 25 N.Y.2d 451, 255 N. E.2d 168 (1969), in which the New York Court of Appeals held (4–3) that where the contract contained a clause expressly excluding the right of a buyer of goods, with a price of $984, to recover consequential damages for defects, the arbitrator exceeded his authority in awarding $3,780 without giving reasons for disregarding the clause.

Consider the following clause, found in a reinsurance agreement between two insurance companies: "In the event of Arbitration, the Arbiters are relieved from all judicial formalities and may abstain from following the strict rule of law, interpreting the present Agreement as an honorable engagement and not a mere legal obligation."

As might be supposed, judges showed initial hostility to this rival system of adjudication, which would "oust" the courts of jurisdiction, and refused to enforce arbitration clauses in contracts by which the parties agreed to send future disputes to arbitration.   Federal statute and the statutes of many states, however, now make such clauses enforceable, and a party may apply to an appropriate court for an order directing arbitration under the clause.   See, generally, Domke, The Law and Practice of Commercial Arbitration (1968); Mentschikoff, Commercial Arbitration, 61 Colum.L.Rev. 846 (1961).

NOTE

American Arbitration Association Clause.   The standard arbitration clause recommended by the American Arbitration Association reads:

> Any controversy or claim arising out of or relating to this contract, or the breach thereof, shall be settled by arbitration in accordance with the Rules of the American Arbitration Association, and judgment upon the award rendered by the Arbitrator(s) may be entered in any Court having jurisdiction thereof.

Under such a broadly worded clause, the very enforceability of the "contract," in the face of a claim of indefiniteness, is for the arbitrators to determine.

SECTION 2.   THE ACCEPTANCE

What is an acceptance?   Corbin gives this answer: "An acceptance is a voluntary act of the offeree whereby he exercises the power conferred upon him by the offer, and thereby creates the set of legal relations called a contract.   What acts are sufficient to serve this purpose?   We must look first to the terms in which the offer was expressed, either by words or by other conduct.   .   .   .   The offeror has, in the beginning, full power to determine the acts that are to constitute acceptance.   After he has once created the power, he may lose his control over it, and may become disabled to change or to revoke it; but the fact that, in the beginning, the offeror has full control of the immediately succeeding relation called a power, is the characteristic that distinguishes contractual relations from non-contractual ones. After the offeror has created the power, the legal consequences thereof are out of his hands, and he may be brought into numerous consequential relations of which he did not dream, and to which he might not have consented.   These later relations are nevertheless called contractual."   Corbin, Offer and Acceptance, and Some of the Resulting Legal Relations, 26 Yale L.J. 169, 199 (1917), Selected Readings 170, 193.

Assuming that there has been an offer, the offeree by exercising his power of acceptance "thereby creates," as Corbin puts it, "the set of legal relations called a contract." One of the most important consequences of this "set of legal relations" is that the offeror is no longer free to change his mind and withdraw from the relationship without incurring liability. By what means, then, may the offeree exercise this power of acceptance? If, as Corbin says, the offeror has "full power to determine the acts that are to constitute acceptance," the first step in answering this question is to look at the offer to see what sort of acceptance it invited.

We already know from Chapter 1 that the offeror may either have been bargaining for a performance or for a promise. If he was bargaining for (if his offer invited) a performance only, it would seem that nothing but that performance could amount to an acceptance. Merely promising to perform, or preparing for performance or even beginning performance, would not, of itself, be enough. (Some limits that the law has imposed on this simple conclusion are explored at p. 124 infra.) Similarly, if he was bargaining for (if his offer invited) a promise only it would seem that nothing but that promise could amount to acceptance. Merely preparing for performance, or beginning performance, or even completing performance would not, of itself, be enough. (Some limits that the law has imposed on this simple conclusion are explored in Subsection 4(b) infra.)

As will be seen more clearly from the cases that make up the bulk of this book, the economically significant transactions in our society usually involve the latter sort of bargain, in which the offeror seeks the assurance of another promise in return for his own. (Why should this be so? If bargaining for performance was good enough for William E. Storey in Hamer v. Sidway, p. 4 supra, and for A. L. Ledbetter in Broadnax v. Ledbetter, p. 29, supra, why should it not be good enough for any offeror?) In these economically significant transactions, in which the offeror invites a promise as acceptance, what will suffice as a promise? Are words essential? Or may a promise be inferred from other conduct? And, if so, what conduct? Preparation for performance? Beginning performance?[a] Other acts? Mere silence? This section considers these and related questions.

---

a. Note that it is one thing to suggest, as it was in the preceding paragraph, that if an offer invites a promise only, the mere preparation for or beginning of performance is not, *of itself*, an acceptance. It is another to suggest, as it is here, that it may be the basis for inferring that a promise was made.

WHITE v. CORLIES AND TIFT

Court of Appeals of New York, 1871.
46 N.Y. 467.

Appeal from judgment of the General Term of the first judicial district, affirming a judgment entered upon a verdict for plaintiff.

The action was for an alleged breach of contract.

The plaintiff was a builder, with his place of business in Fortieth Street, New York City.

The defendants were merchants at 32 Dey Street.

In September, 1865, the defendants furnished the plaintiff with specifications for fitting up a suite of offices at 57 Broadway, and requested him to make an estimate of the cost of doing the work.

On September 28th the plaintiff left his estimate with the defendants, and they were to consider upon it, and inform the plaintiff of their conclusions.

On the same day the defendants made a change in their specifications, and sent a copy of the same, so changed, to the plaintiff for his assent under his estimate, which he assented to by signing the same and returning it to the defendants.

On the day following the defendants' bookkeeper wrote the plaintiff the following note:

"New York, September 29.

"Upon an agreement to finish the fitting up of offices 57 Broadway in two weeks from date, you can begin at once.

"The writer will call again, probably between 5 and 6 this p. m.

"W. H. R.
For J. W. Corlies & Co.,
32 Dey St."

No reply to this note was ever made by the plaintiff; and on the next day the same was countermanded by a second note from the defendants.

Immediately on receipt of the note of September 29th, and before the countermand was forwarded, the plaintiff commenced a performance by the purchase of lumber and beginning work thereon.

And after receiving the countermand, the plaintiff brought this action for damages for a breach of contract.

The court charged the jury as follows: "From the contents of this note which the plaintiff received, was it his duty to go down to Dey Street (meaning to give notice of assent), before commencing the work?

"In my opinion it was not. He had a right to act upon this note and commence the job, and that was a binding contract between the parties."

To this defendants excepted. . . .

FOLGER, J. We do not think that the jury found, or that the testimony shows, that there was any agreement between the parties, before the written communication of the defendants of September 30th was received by the plaintiff. This note did not make an agreement. It was a proposition, and must have been accepted by the plaintiff before either party was bound, in contract, to the other. The only overt action which is claimed by the plaintiff as indicating on his part an acceptance of the offer, was the purchase of the stuff necessary for the work, and commencing work, as we understand the testimony, upon that stuff.

We understand the rule to be, that where an offer is made by one party to another when they are not together, the acceptance of it by that other must be manifested by some appropriate act. It does not need that the acceptance shall come to the knowledge of the one making the offer before he shall be bound. But though the manifestation need not be brought to his knowledge before he becomes bound, he is not bound, if that manifestation is not put in a proper way to be in the usual course of events, in some reasonable time communicated to him. Thus a letter received by mail containing a proposal may be answered by letter by mail, containing the acceptance. And in general, as soon as the answering letter is mailed, the contract is concluded. Though one party does not know of the acceptance, the manifestation thereof is put in the proper way of reaching him.

In the case in hand, the plaintiff determined to accept. But a mental determination not indicated by speech, or put in course of indication by act to the other party, is not an acceptance which will bind the other. Nor does an act, which in itself, is no indication of an acceptance, become such, because accompanied by an unevinced mental determination. Where the act uninterpreted by concurrent evidence of the mental purpose accompanying it, is as well referable to one state of facts as another, it is no indication to the other party of an acceptance, and does not operate to hold him to his offer.

Conceding that the testimony shows that the plaintiff did resolve to accept this offer, he did no act which indicated an acceptance of it to the defendants. He, a carpenter and builder, purchased stuff for the work. But it was stuff as fit for any other like work. He began work upon the stuff, but as he would have done for any other like work. There was nothing in his thought, formed but not uttered, or in his acts that indicated or set in motion an indication to the defendants of his acceptance of their offer, or which could necessarily result therein.

But the charge of the learned judge was fairly to be understood by the jury as laying down the rule to them, that the plaintiff need not indicate to the defendants his acceptance of their offer; and that the purchase of stuff and working on it after receiving the note, made a binding contract between the parties. In this we think the learned judge fell into error.

Judgment reversed, and new trial ordered.

NOTE

Means of Acceptance. What means of acceptance did Corlies' offer invite? What does the language of the offer and the nature of the transaction suggest? What answer if Corlies had written, "If you want to do the work, let me know by return mail and you can begin work at once"? See Restatement Second, §§ 29, 52, 61, 63. On the changes as to offer and acceptance made in the Restatement Second, see Braucher, Offer and Acceptance in the Second Restatement, 74 Yale L.J. 302 (1964).

EVER-TITE ROOFING CORPORATION v. GREEN, 83 So.2d 449 (La.App.1955). [The Greens wished to have Ever-Tite Roofing re-roof their residence, and signed a document that set out the work in detail and the price in monthly installments. This document was also signed by Ever-Tite's sales representative who, however, had no authority to bind Ever-Tite. The document contained a provision that, "This agreement shall become binding only upon written acceptance hereof, by the principal or authorized officer of the Contractor, or upon commencing performance of the work." As the Greens knew, since the work was to be done entirely on credit, it was necessary for Ever-Tite to get credit reports and obtain the approval of the lending institution that was to finance the contract. When this was accomplished, about nine days after execution of the agreement, Ever-Tite loaded two trucks and sent them with its workmen some distance to the Green's residence. Upon their arrival they found that others had been engaged two days before, and they were not permitted to work. Ever-Tite sued the Greens for breach of contract. From a judgment for defendant, plaintiff appealed.]

AYRES, JUDGE. . . . The basis of the judgment appealed was that defendants had timely notified plaintiff before "commencing performance of work". The trial court held that notice to plaintiff's workmen upon their arrival with the materials that defendants did not desire them to commence the actual work was sufficient and timely to signify their intention to withdraw from the contract. With this conclusion we find ourselves unable to agree. . . . Defendants evidently knew this work was to be processed through plaintiff's Shreveport office. The record discloses no unreasonable delay on plaintiff's part in receiving, processing or accepting the contract or in commencing the work contracted to be done. No time limit was specified in the contract within which it was to be accepted or within which the work was to be begun. It was nevertheless understood between the parties that some delay would ensue before the acceptancee of the contract and the commencement of the work, due to the necessity of compliance with the requirements relative to financing the job through a lending agency. The evidence as referred to hereinabove shows that plaintiff proceeded with due diligence. . . . [S]ince the contract did not specify the time within which it was to be accepted or within which the work was to have been commenced, a reasonable time must be allowed therefor in accordance with the facts and circumstances and the evident intention of the parties. A reasonable time is contemplated where no time is expressed. What is a reasonable time depends more or less upon the circumstances surrounding each particular case. The delays to process defendants' application were not unusual. The contract was accepted by plaintiff by the commencement of the performance of the work contracted to be done. This commencement began with the loading of the trucks with the necessary materials in Shreveport and transporting such materials and the workmen to defendants' residence. Actual commencement or performance of the work therefore began before any notice of dissent by defendants was given plaintiff. The proposition and its acceptance thus became a completed contract.

[Reversed.]

NOTE

Control of Representatives. Where one of the parties is a large organization with representatives, such as salesmen, who are expected to use a carefully prepared standard form for all contracts, there is a risk that the representatives will make written changes on the form itself during their negotiations with customers. Is it possible to minimize that risk? Draft a clause that will do this. Consider such language as: "No agent of either party to the contract has authority to alter or change the terms hereof." See Restatement Second of Agency § 167 (1958). Does a clause like the one used by Ever-Tite have any advantage over the one just quoted? Can you think of any risk for Ever-Tite in requiring written acceptance by an officer? Did the clause used by Ever-Tite take any account of that risk? Could the court have read that part of the clause more favorably to the Greens?

ALLIED STEEL & CONVEYORS, INC. v. FORD MOTOR CO., 277 F.2d 907 (6th Cir. 1960). [On August 19, 1955, Ford ordered machinery from Allied on Ford's printed form, Purchase Order No. 15145, which provided that if Allied was required to perform work of installation on Ford's premises, Allied would be responsible for all damages caused by the negligence of its own employees. Attached to and made a part of the Purchase Order was another printed form, Form 3618, which included a much broader indemnity provision requiring Allied to assume full responsibility not only for the negligence of its own employees, but also for the negligence of Ford's employees in connection with Allied's work. But because the installation of this machinery was to be done by Ford's own employees under Allied's supervision, this provision was marked "VOID." The Purchase Order was accepted by Allied and the contract performed.

Subsequently, on July 26, 1956, Ford submitted to Allied Amendment No. 2 to Purchase Order 15145, by which Ford proposed to purchase additional machinery. The Amendment provided:

> This purchase order agreement is not binding until accepted. Acceptance should be executed on acknowledgment copy which should be returned to buyer.

The copy of Ford's Form 3618 attached to the Amendment was identical to that attached to Purchase Order No. 15145, but the broad indemnity provision of Form 3618 was not marked "VOID" because installation of this machinery on Ford's premises was to be by Allied's employees. The acknowledgment copy of the Amendment was executed by Allied on November 10 and reached Ford on November 12, 1956. At that time Allied had already begun installation and on September 5, 1956, Hankins, an employee of Allied, had sustained personal injuries as a result of the negligence of Ford's employees in connection with Allied's work. Hankins later brought suit against Ford and Ford in turn impleaded Allied, relying on the indemnity provision of Form 3618. The trial resulted in a verdict for Hankins against Ford and for Ford against Allied. Allied's motion for judgment notwithstanding the verdict was denied and judgment was entered against it. Allied appealed.]

MILLER, DISTRICT JUDGE. . . . Allied first says that the contractual provisions evidenced by Amendment No. 2 were not in effect at the time of the Hankins injury because it had not been accepted at that time by Allied in the formal manner expressly required by the amendment itself. It argues that a binding acceptance of the amendment could be effected only by Allied's execution of the acknowledgment copy of the amendment and its return to Ford.

With this argument we cannot agree. It is true that an offeror may prescribe the manner in which acceptance of his offer shall be indicated by the offeree, and an acceptance of the offer in the manner prescribed will bind the offeror. And it has been held that if the offeror prescribes an exclusive manner of acceptance, an attempt on the part of the offeree to accept the offer in a different manner does not bind the offeror *in the absence of a meeting of the minds on the altered type of acceptance.* Venters v. Stewart, Ky.App., 261 S.W.2d 444, 446; Shortridge v. Ghio, Mo.App., 253 S.W.2d 838, 845. On the other hand, if an offeror merely suggests a permitted method of acceptance, other methods of acceptance are not precluded. Restatement, Contracts, Sec. 61; Williston on Contracts, Third Ed. Secs. 70,

76. Moreover, it is equally well settled that if the offer requests a return promise and the offeree without making the promise actually does or tenders what he was requested to promise to do, there is a contract if such performance is completed or tendered within the time allowable for accepting by making a promise. In such a case a tender operates as a promise to render complete performance. Restatement, Contracts, Sec. 63; Williston on Contracts, Third Ed. Sec. 75.[a]

Applying these principles to the case at bar, we reach the conclusion, first, that execution and return of the acknowledgment copy of Amendment No. 2 was merely a suggested method of acceptance and did not preclude acceptance by some other method; and, second, that the offer was accepted and a binding contract effected when Allied, with Ford's knowledge, consent and acquiescence, undertook performance of the work called for by the amendment. The only significant provision, as we view the amendment, was that it would not be binding until it was accepted by Allied. This provision was obviously for the protection of Ford, Albright v. Stegeman Motorcar Co., 168 Wis. 557, 170 N.W. 951, 952, 19 A.L.R. 463, and its import was that Ford would not be bound by the amendment unless Allied agreed to all of the conditions specified therein. The provision for execution and return of the acknowledgment copy, as we construe the language used, was not to set forth an exclusive method of acceptance but was merely to provide a simple and convenient method by which the assent of Allied to the contractual provisions of the amendment could be indicated. The primary object of Ford was to have the work performed by Allied upon the terms prescribed in the amendment, and the mere signing and return of an acknowledgment copy of the amendment before actually undertaking the work itself cannot be regarded as an essential condition to completion of a binding contract.

It is well settled that acceptance of an offer by part performance in accordance with the terms of the offer is sufficient to complete the contract. . . .

Other authorities are to the effect that the acceptance of a contract may be implied from acts of the parties. Malooly v. York Heating & Vent. Corp., 270 Mich. 240, 253, 258 N.W. 622; and may be shown by proving acts done on the faith of the order, including shipment of the goods ordered, Petroleum Products Distributing Co. v. Alton Tank Line, 165 Iowa 398, 403, 146 N.W. 52. Cf. Texas Co. v. Hudson, 155 La. 966, 971, 99 So. 714, 716. It would seem necessarily

---

a. It is curious that the court relies, even as an alternative ground, on the rule that full performance or a tender of full performance may operate as an acceptance of an offer that invites acceptance by a promise only. Allied had not fully performed and could not, since its performance was to extend over a substantial period of time, have tendered full performance. This rule is, perhaps fortunately, of limited practical importance and is not carried forward by the Restatement Second (see §§ 55(1), 63). Of course the offer may invite the offeree to choose between acceptance by promise and acceptance by performance, but that is not what the court suggests here.

to follow that an offeree who has unjustifiably led the offeror to believe that he had acquired a contractual right, should not be allowed to assert an actual intent at variance with the meaning of his acts.

It has been argued on behalf of Allied, by way of analogy, that Ford could have revoked the order when Allied began installing the machinery without first having executed its written acceptance. If this point should be conceded, cf. Venters v. Stewart, supra, it would avail Allied nothing. For, after Allied began performance by installing the machinery called for, and Ford acquiesced in the acts of Allied and accepted the benefits of the performance, Ford was estopped to object and could not thereafter be heard to complain that there was no contract. Sparks v. Mauk, 170 Cal. 122, 148 P. 926. . . .

[Affirmed.]

NOTE

Case Comparison. Can the Ever-Tite and Allied Steel cases be distinguished from White v. Corlies and Tift? What is the critical language of the offer in each case? [b] What reason did Ford have for putting the clause on its form? See Note 1, p. 70 supra.

TIME OF AGREEMENT

In the traditional conception, a contract is formed at a determinable moment through the process of offer and acceptance. According to UCC 2–204(2), however, "An agreement sufficient to constitute a contract for sale may be found even though the moment of its making is undetermined." Does this mean that a contract may be found even though there is no such thing as a "moment of its making" at all? Or merely that a contract may be found even though it is impossible to determine the "moment of its making"? Or merely that a contract may be found even though the "moment of its making" has not in fact been determined?

The Comment to the section explains that it is "directed primarily to the situation where the interchanged correspondence does not disclose the exact point at which the deal was closed, but the actions of the parties indicate that a binding obligation has been undertaken." Is it relevant that in the 1952 Official Edition of the Code, UCC 2–204(2) read: "Conduct by both parties which recognizes the existence of a contract is sufficient to establish a contract of sale even though

---

b. Consider, in this connection, the 1970 revision of Ford's Purchase Order, which reads:

"ACCEPTANCE-Unless otherwise provided herein, it is understood and agreed that the written acceptance by Seller of this purchase order or the commencement of any work or the performance of any services hereunder by Seller (including the commencement of any work or the performance of any services with respect to samples) shall constitute acceptance by Seller of this purchase order and of all of its terms and conditions, and that such acceptance is expressly limited to such terms and conditions."

the moment of its making cannot be determined"? Could the moment be determined in the Ever-Tite case? In the Allied Steel case? If so, when was it?

Consider also these examples given in 2 Schlesinger (ed.), Formation of Contracts: A Study of the Common Core of Legal Systems 1584–86 (1968): "Especially when large deals are concluded among corporations and individuals of substance, the usual sequence of events is not that of offer and acceptance; on the contrary, the businessmen who originally conduct the negotiations, often will consciously refrain from ever making a binding offer, realizing as they do that a large deal tends to be complex and that its terms have to be formulated by lawyers before it can be permitted to become a legally enforceable transaction. Thus the original negotiators will merely attempt to ascertain whether they see eye to eye concerning those aspects of the deal which seem to be most important from a business point of view. Once they do, or think they do, the negotiation is then turned over to the lawyers, usually with instructions to produce a document which all participants will be willing to sign. . . . When the lawyers take over, again there is no sequence of offer and acceptance, but rather a sequence of successive drafts. These drafts usually will not be regarded as offers, for the reason, among others, that the lawyers acting as draftsmen have no authority to make offers on behalf of their clients. After a number of drafts have been exchanged and discussed, the lawyers may finally come up with a draft which meets the approval of all of them, and of their clients. It is only then that the parties will proceed to the actual formation of the contract, and often this will be done by way of a formal 'closing' . . . or in any event by simultaneous execution or delivery, in the course of a more or less ceremonial meeting, of the document or documents prepared by the lawyers.

"In the usual negotiation of a large-scale transaction there is thus no room for offer and acceptance (except where options are involved). If the writers on contract law nevertheless continue to analyze the formation of contracts almost exclusively in terms of offer and acceptance, they may be right insofar as they speak of the majority of personal and business transactions of modest or medium size; but in the world of truly large-scale dealings, the traditional analysis is no longer in tune with present-day practice. . . .

"In the field of corporate finance, many important transactions are settled by signing and exchanging identical documents. The typical 'closing' in a financial transaction involves more than two parties, often as many as half a dozen—a factor which in itself tends to attenuate the concepts of offer and acceptance since there may be as many independent interests involved as there are parties. It is customary for the attorneys at a closing to verify that all documents are in order and that all conditions precedent have been met (or are waived). When they are satisfied, the documents are then signed and exchanged by and among all the parties. Even though the signing may not be completely simultaneous, the exchange often is. Similarly where the documents have in fact been signed previously but held 'in escrow' by the attorneys for the signers pending verification of all details, they are simultaneously exchanged." [a]

NOTE

"Unilateral" and "Bilateral" Contracts. A distinction between "unilateral" and "bilateral" contracts has long had currency. In a "unilateral" contract only one party makes promises; in a "bilateral" contract both parties make promises. See Restatement, § 12. The relationships between the parties in the two types of contract can be analyzed in terms of *right* and *duty.*

A is said to have a *right* that B shall do an act, when if B does not do the act, A can initiate legal proceedings which will result in coercing B, and B in such a situation is said to have a *duty* to do the act. *Right* and *duty* are therefore correlatives. In this strict sense there can never be a *right* without a *duty*, nor a *duty* without a *right*. The *right-duty* relationship is one between two parties. The *right* describes the relationship from one end and the *duty* from the other. Since, in a "unilateral" contract there is a promise on one side only, there is a *duty* on one side only, and a *right* on the other side; and since in a "bilateral" contract there is a promise on each side, there is a *right* and a *duty* on each side. The Restatement Second abandons the use of the terms "unilateral" and "bilateral," "because of doubt as to the utility of the distinction, often treated as fundamental, between the two types." Reporter's Note to Restatement Second, § 12.

For the precise use of terms such as *right* and *duty* the legal profession is indebted to the work of Professor Wesley Newcomb Hohfeld,[b] whose system of "Hohfeldian terminology" is set forth in Hohfeld, Fundamental Legal Conceptions (1923). In this terminology the offeree has, before the contract is made, a *power* to create a contract by means of acceptance. A *power* is the capacity to change a legal relationship. See Corbin, Legal Analysis and Terminology, 29 Yale L.J. 163 (1919); Goble, The Sanction of a Duty, 37 Yale L.J. 426 (1928).

a. Reprinted by permission of Rudolf B. Schlesinger.

b. Wesley Newcomb Hohfeld (1879–1918) practiced law briefly in San Francisco before joining the Stanford law faculty in 1905. In 1914 he left Stanford to teach at Yale until his death at the age of thirty-nine. He made a lasting contribution to legal literature through his development of the eight terms of "Hohfeldian terminology" in his book Fundamental Legal Conceptions. Corbin wrote, "He was a severe taskmaster, requiring his students to master his classification of 'fundamental conceptions' and to use accurately the set of terms by which they were expressed. They found this, in the light of the usage of the other professors [at Yale], almost impossible." Their resistance resulted in a petition to the President of Yale that Hohfeld's appointment not be extended. The petition was ignored and generations of law students have continued to master Hohfeld's terms.

SHIPMENT OF GOODS AS ACCEPTANCE

A recurring question of considerable practical importance is whether the seller's shipment of goods, in response to a buyer's order, is acceptance. The question usually arises when the buyer attempts to revoke his order after the seller has placed the goods on board a carrier in response to the order. UCC 2–206(1)(b) provides that such an order "for prompt or current shipment shall be construed as inviting acceptance either by a prompt promise to ship or by the prompt or current shipment of conforming or non-conforming goods." Under the Code the buyer's revocation comes too late if the seller has promptly shipped.

But the question can arise in another way. Suppose that the seller ships non-conforming goods. Has he bound himself to deliver goods that conform to the buyer's order? The answer under the Code must be that he has. This is clear from the provision that the seller can avoid this result if he "seasonably notifies the buyer that the shipment is offered only as an accommodation to the buyer." If the seller follows this course, his shipment is not an acceptance of the buyer's offer, but is a counter-offer to the buyer. What means of acceptance does that counter-offer invite? See the following case. See generally Restatement Second, §§ 31, 63, which are not limited to contracts for the sale of goods.

NOTE

Preparation for Shipment of Goods as Acceptance. What if the buyer attempts to revoke his order when the seller has incurred expense in preparing to ship the goods but has not actually shipped them? In Doll & Smith v. A & S Sanitary Dairy Co., 202 Iowa 786, 211 N.W. 230 (1926), the buyer, through the seller's agent, ordered advertising material from the seller. After the seller had paid its agent his commission and had incurred some expense, the buyer sent the seller a cancellation of the order. The court held that since the seller had not sent the buyer an acceptance of the order, the revocation was effective. Can this decision be reconciled with the Ever-Tite case, supra?

INDIANA MFG. CO. v. HAYES

Supreme Court of Pennsylvania, 1893.
155 Pa. 160, 26 A. 6.

Assumpsit for goods sold and delivered.

Plaintiff's claim on the trial, before Hemphill, J., was for the price of sixty-four refrigerators. Defendant claimed that he had never given the order for the refrigerators, and that it had been wrongfully sent in his name by a salesman of plaintiff.

Plaintiff introduced evidence tending to show that the refrigerators were accepted by defendant in the manner stated in the opinion of the Supreme Court. . . .

[The court instructed] "We say to you, gentlemen of the jury, there is no question of intention involved here to be submitted to you. There is no disputed question of fact. The goods were shipped to Mr. Hayes in his name, and when he took control of them by ordering the railroad company to turn them over to his agent, Mr. Cooper, the carter, the law implied an intention on his part to accept, and so far as the plaintiffs here are concerned he became the owner, and we instruct you to that effect, and must so qualify their points. . . .

"If the defendant gave no order to the plaintiffs for the goods sued for, and made no contract with them for furnishing him with refrigerators, it was his duty, when the said goods came to him, to decline to receive them from the railroad company. . . .

"If the sixty-four refrigerators were shipped to Robert L. Hayes by the plaintiffs, relying upon his order, and he received the same from the railroad company at West Chester, thereby discharging the said railroad company from liability to the shippers, the plaintiffs, the defendant, Robert L. Hayes, is bound to pay for the same, whether he authorized the sending of the order or not. . . ." [Verdict for the plaintiff.]

PER CURIAM, . . . Conceding that the defendant did not order the goods in question, yet when they arrived, and he was notified that they were upon the car, it was his duty to notify the plaintiffs of the alleged mistake. Instead of doing so he took the property out of the possession of the railroad company and had it hauled to his own place of business, and after having been fully informed of the shipment and consignment to him he sent a check to the plaintiff company for other merchandise purchased of it, without any reference to the goods in controversy. The case was submitted to the jury under proper instructions.

Judgment affirmed.[a]

NOTES

(1) *Acceptance of Part.* What result if Hayes had taken thirty-two of the refrigerators and left the other thirty-two with the railroad company? Are UCC 2–305(4), 2–601, 2–607(1) helpful?

(2) *Silence as Acceptance.* Suppose that the refrigerators had been delivered to Hayes' place of business and left there while he was away. Would he have been liable if he had merely retained them in silence? The general rule is that silence alone is not acceptance. See Restatement Second, § 72. The offeror who appends to his offer, "Unless I hear from you within 48 hours, you will be deemed to have accepted my offer," cannot hold the offeree if he fails to reject.

a. If the defendant took possession of refrigerators he had not ordered, is he not liable in tort for conversion? Ordinarily the offeree cannot avoid liability in contract on this ground, and under the "waiver of tort" doctrine the offeror may have his choice of suing in tort or in contract. See Restatement Second, § 72, Comment e.

In Hobbs v. Massasoit Whip Co., 158 Mass. 194, 33 N.E. 495 (1893), however, the court concluded that a silent retention amounted to an acceptance. A seller sued for $108.50, the price of 2,350 eelskins that he had sent to the buyer, a manufacturer of whips. Holmes wrote: "The plaintiff was not a stranger to the defendant, even if there was no contract between them. He had sent eelskins in the same way four or five times before, and they had been accepted and paid for. . . . [S]ending them [imposed] on the defendant a duty to act about them; and silence on its part, coupled with a retention of the skins for an unreasonable time, might be found by the jury to warrant the plaintiff in assuming that they were accepted, and thus to amount to an acceptance." What, beyond mere silence, was there in this case?

But what if the parties are reversed and it is the *buyer* who asserts that the seller has accepted by silent retention of his *order?* Ammons v. Wilson & Co., 176 Miss. 645, 170 So. 227 (1936), is such a case. On August 23, Wilson's travelling salesman, Tweedy, took an order from Ammons for 43,916 pounds of shortening, for prompt shipment. Wilson's form made it clear that Tweedy had no authority to make contracts and that the order was "taken subject to acceptance. by seller's authorized agent at point of shipment." Wilson waited until September 4 before refusing to ship. By that time the price of shortening had risen from 7½ to 9 cents a pound. The court reversed a judgment for Wilson entered on a directed verdict, and held that whether the delay of twelve days, "in view of the past history of such transactions between the parties, including the booking, constituted an implied acceptance," was a jury question. Tweedy had represented Wilson in the territory for six or eight months and during that time he had taken several orders from Ammons, "which orders in every case had been accepted and shipped not later than one week from the time they were given." What, beyond mere silence, was there in this case?

(3) *Acceptance by Insurer's Silence.* Similar problems arise in connection with solicitation by insurance agents. In American Life Insurance Co. v. Hutcheson, 109 F.2d 424 (6th Cir. 1940), Hutcheson, who had a life insurance policy with Lincoln National Life, was solicited by an agent of American Life, to purchase insurance with that company instead. Hutcheson applied to American and paid his first premium on October 10. On the same day his policy with Lincoln lapsed. On the following day he had a medical examination and because his blood pressure was too high he was asked to take a second examination on October 14. The results reached American on October 21 and showed that his blood pressure was still too high. No notice was sent of this fact and Hutcheson was killed by accident on October 26. American Life tendered back the first premium and refused to pay under the policy. Hutcheson's wife, as beneficiary, sued American. From an adverse judgment based on a jury verdict the defendant appealed. *Held:* Affirmed. "It is the general rule that mere delay in passing upon an application for insurance is not sufficient in and of itself to amount to acceptance even though the premium is retained. . . . But an acceptance may be implied from retention of the premium and failure to reject within a reasonable time. . . . Having accepted and retained the premium paid upon an application solicited by its agent, the company was bound to act with reasonable promptitude." The jury could find that it did not and that therefore there was a contract. On the alter-

native of liability in tort for unreasonable delay in acting on an application, see p. 151 infra.

UNSOLICITED MERCHANDISE

A persistent consumer complaint concerns the practice of sending unsolicited merchandise, often coupled with the suggestion that the recipient will be liable for the price if he does not return it. As you might suppose, this is not the law. The recipient who lays the merchandise on a shelf and does not use it incurs no liability to the sender. Restatement Second, § 72(2). Nevertheless, the practice is at best irritating and at worst deceptive. Is legislation desirable to combat this evil? What kind of legislation?

A number of states have enacted statutes dealing with unsolicited merchandise. Is the New York statute set out below adequate? Have you amendments to propose? Would it have applied to the Indiana Manufacturing Co.?

2. No person, firm, partnership, association or corporation, or agent or employee thereof, shall, in any manner, or by any means, offer for sale goods, wares or merchandise, where the offer includes the voluntary and unsolicited sending of goods, wares or merchandise not actually ordered or requested by the recipient, either orally or in writing. The receipt of any such unsolicited goods, wares or merchandise shall for all purposes be deemed an unconditional gift to the recipient who may use or dispose of the same in any manner he sees fit without any obligation on his part to the sender.

3. Whenever there shall be a violation of this section, an application may be made by the attorney general in the name of the people of the state of New York to a court or justice having jurisdiction to issue an injunction, and upon notice to the defendant of not less than five days, to enjoin and restrain the continuance of such violation; and if it shall appear to the satisfaction of the court or justice that the defendant is, in fact, violating this section, an injunction may be issued by such court or justice, enjoining and restraining such action or violation, without requiring proof that any person has, in fact, been misled or deceived or otherwise damaged thereby. (N.Y.Gen.Bus.L. § 396(2),(3).)

The practice of sending unsolicited merchandise has also been the target of regulation on the federal level. The Postal Reorganization Act of 1970 makes the mailing of "unordered merchandise" and "dunning communications" for such merchandise "an unfair method of competition and an unfair trade practice" in violation of Section 5 of the Federal Trade Commission Act. See p. 75 supra. Free samples "clearly and conspicuously marked as such" and "merchandise mailed by a charitable organization soliciting contributions" are excepted. The act provides that merchandise mailed in violation of it "may be treated as a gift by the recipient," and requires, somewhat curiously, that it have attached to it "a clear and conspicuous statement" to this effect. 39 U.S.C.A. § 3009.

For a discussion of these and other measures to deal with the problem, see Note, 1970 Duke L.J. 991. For an amusing account of one man's trials with unsolicited merchandise, see James Thurber, Thurber Country (Chapter 9, File and Forget) (1953).

NOTE

Unsolicited Credit Cards. A successful bank credit card system requires both a large number of cardholders and a large number of merchants who honor their cards. In order to launch the BankAmerica and Interbank systems, over 100 million unsolicited BankAmericards and Master Charge cards were mailed in the years from 1967 through 1970. The result was some 10 million active cardholders for each system. In 1970, Congress amended the Truth in Lending Act to add a new section 132:

> No credit card shall be issued except in response to a request or application therefor. This prohibition does not apply to the issuance of a credit card in renewal of, or in substitution for, an accepted credit card.

What was the reason behind the amendment? How could a recipient of an unsolicited credit card have incurred any liability if he neither used nor signed the card? Can you think of any disadvantages that might result from the amendment? Consider the following statement by Senator William Proxmire of Wisconsin:

> A number of consumer groups have urged that the sending of unsolicited credit cards be prohibited. I am in sympathy with the viewpoint and I believe it has much merit. On the other hand, I am also fearful that a prohibition of unsolicited credit cards would insulate from effective competition the companies that have already sent out unsolicited cards. For example, two bank credit card systems, BankAmerica and the Interbank System, now account for 95 percent of the bank credit card market. A prohibition of unsolicited cards would make it difficult for new systems to compete against these two giants.

Hearings on S. 721 before Subcommittee on Financial Institutions of the Senate Committee on Banking and Currency, 91st Cong., 1st Sess. 2 (1969).

LOS ANGELES RAMS FOOTBALL CLUB v. CANNON, 185 F.Supp. 717 (S.D.Cal.1960). [In the fall of 1959, the Los Angeles Rams had earned the right to first draft choice in the National Football League by virtue of their tie for last place in the League standings and the fortunate flip of a coin. They chose Billy Cannon, "a remarkable football player" and a senior at Louisiana State University, which was to oppose Mississippi in the Sugar Bowl on New Year's

Day of 1960. On November 30, 1959, Cannon and Pete Rozelle, the Ram's General Manager, signed three sets of National Football Player Contract forms covering 1960, 1961 and 1962 respectively, and Cannon took two checks, a bonus check of $10,000 for signing and a $500 check. Rozelle left a copy of the contract for 1960 with the League's acting Commissioner, who approved it on December 1. In December Cannon decided to play for the Houston Oilers in the newly-formed American Football League, and on December 30 he wrote the Rams that he no longer wished to play for them and returned the checks, uncashed and unindorsed. The Rams sued Cannon to enjoin him from playing for another team.]

LINDBERG, DISTRICT JUDGE. [The court first concluded that since the signed forms were, by their terms, not binding until approved by the Commissioner, Cannon was not bound by the unapproved forms for 1961 and 1962. The court then concluded that Cannon, by signing the forms, had made an offer to play for three years and that this had not been accepted by the Rams since they had requested and received the Commissioner's approval for only the first year. The court then considered whether Cannon's taking of the bonus check, which both parties understood to be conditioned upon his reporting to the Rams for the 1960 training camp period, could be construed as an acceptance of an "assumed counter-offer" by the Rams for the 1960 season only.[a]] This would depend, in part at least, upon the understanding between the parties as to whether Cannon accepted the check as payment. . . . At this juncture, however, it should be noted, that Cannon, granting his outstanding ability and prowess on the gridiron, is anything but an astute business man. His whole life and interest has been directed toward athletics and particularly football; and while he impressed me as being somewhat naive for a college senior I feel certain that he knew he couldn't accept as payment the $10,000 check that was tendered him and remain eligible to play for his school in the Sugar Bowl, nor do I believe he would intentionally disqualify himself. He didn't need to. With respect to Cannon this wasn't a chance in a lifetime to turn professional which he might lose forever if he didn't grab it immediately. By this time he must have appreciated the fact that his services were in great demand by professional football. I, therefore, am led to make the finding that Cannon did not accept the check in payment. Rather, he accepted it, believing it was not his and that he had no claim upon it until after the Sugar Bowl game.

While some, particularly those schooled—to use the vernacular—in the "game for dough" may view my interpretation of the transaction as a "Pollyanna" approach and entirely unrealistic it should be

---

a. The court did not discuss how Cannon might have been made aware of this "assumed counter-offer."

borne in mind that Cannon, while having been a highly publicized college ball player, was, in fact, and still is, it would appear, a provincial lad of 21 or 22, untutored and unwise, I am convinced, in the way of the business world. While he had entertained ambitions for years to get into professional football the proposition submitted to him by the Rams came by telephone apparently without prior notice while he was away from home and in New York for the purpose of receiving one of many rapidly accumulating honors that were being bestowed upon him. He was without counsel or advice and the whole transaction, including the signing of the alleged contracts, was completed in less than 48 hours. When Cannon arrived at the Warwick Hotel on Monday morning he did not know whether the Rams had acquired the right to draft him. He was immediately brought before the press and, as Rozelle testified, he Rozelle, heard Cannon make the statement to the effect that he would sign a contract with the Rams following the L.S.U. and Mississippi game in the Sugar Bowl on New Year's Day. . . .

At that time it is reasonable to assume that Cannon had no idea that Rozelle would expect him to sign a written contract. Thereafter, Rozelle took Cannon and no one else with him to Rozelle's room where Rozelle had waiting for signature the partially-completed forms which he presented to Cannon for signature. Just what language Rozelle used in persuading Cannon to sign the documents I do not know and I doubt if either Cannon or Rozelle have a completely accurate recollection of what was said. I am persuaded, however, that during the 30 to 45 minutes spent in the room Rozelle conveyed the impression to Cannon that the documents would not become effective or binding upon him until after the Sugar Bowl game on New Year's Day. The admitted fact that Rozelle sought to keep their existence confidential and secret as well as the fact that Rozelle did not become concerned as to the Acting Commissioner's approval of [the contract for 1960] until after he had learned on December 22, 1959 of the possibility that Cannon might go with the Houston Oilers lends support to the belief that Rozelle had so assured Cannon.

In view of the foregoing it is my conclusion that the accepting of possession of the check for $10,000 by Cannon was not an acceptance of payment under the alleged contract [for 1960] . . ..

[Judgment for defendant.]

NOTES

(1) *The Case of the Accidental Acceptance.* On June 24 Hotz executed a "Farm Offer and Acceptance Blank," offering to buy a tract of land owned by Equitable Life, and tendered his check for $3,000, which was to be returned if his offer was not accepted. On the check he had written: "To be cashed when contract is signed." The receipt for the check read: "This also acknowledges receipt of check for $3,000 . . . which is not to be cashed until and unless this offer is accepted." Stanfield, the mana-

ger of Equitable Life's Cedar Rapids office, gave the check to Miss Heald with instructions not to deposit it until they heard from the New York office. On July 3, she deposited it by mistake and it was paid. On July 5, Hotz learned that the check had been paid. On July 13, the New York office declined the offer. Hotz was notified of this on July 15. He refused Equitable's tender of $3,000 and sued for specific performance. From a decree for plaintiff, defendant appealed. *Held:* Affirmed. "Regardless of what was the mental intention of the one who made the deposit of this check, it must be said that the deposit was knowingly made." Hotz v. Equitable Life Assur. Soc., 224 Iowa 552, 276 N.W. 413 (1937).

(2) *Account Stated.* Where a debtor and creditor assent in good faith to a stated sum as an accurate computation of the amount due the creditor, a new duty arises to pay the stated sum. Such an agreement is known as an "account stated." See Restatement, § 422. When will the debtor's retention without objection of the creditor's bill give rise to an account stated?

Sunshine Dairy v. Jolly Joan, 234 Or. 84, 380 P.2d 637 (1963) is instructive. In 1953 Jolly Joan, a restaurant, paid $1,000 to Sunshine Dairy on a disputed bill of $3,300. From then until 1960, when the parties stopped doing business with each other, Sunshine sent Jolly Joan monthly statements showing the $2,300 balance in addition to the charges for the preceding month. Jolly Joan paid the monthly charges, reducing the balance each month to $2,300. In 1961, Sunshine sued Jolly Joan, alleging an account stated. The trial court set aside a verdict for Sunshine, and entered judgment for Jolly Joan. Sunshine appealed. *Held:* Affirmed. "The principal issue is whether the defendant impliedly or expressly acquiesced and promised to pay the amount shown by the statement. . . . If one sends a statement containing certain charges or a balancing of mutual accounts and the receiver of the statement makes no objection or reply within a reasonable time, the commercial world reasons that the amount is accepted and payment will be forthcoming. That was not, however, what happened here. . . . When one pays 12 times a year for eight years a specified portion of an account and each of such times does not pay another portion of the account contained in such statement a strong suspicion would arise in the mind of a man of business that the payor disputes his liability for the latter portion of the account. Certainly, no inference of acquiescence to such unpaid portion arises."

According to Corbin, "When an account has been stated, the statute of limitations begins to run anew from the time of mutual assent. . . . An account stated is not rendered invalid by the fact that debts already barred by statute of limitations or discharged in bankruptcy were included in the computation. A new promise to pay a barred debt is enforceable even though there is no other consideration than that involved in the barred debt itself." 6 Corbin, § 1309. See Note 2, p. 21 supra.

NOTICE OF ACCEPTANCE

As White v. Corlies and Tift, p. 92 supra, suggests, where an offeror invites acceptance by means of a promise it is ordinarily understood that the offeree must at least take steps to see that his promise is, in the words of the opinion in that case, "in some reasonable time communicated to him." But is this always the understanding when the offeror invites acceptance by means of performance? (The complications encountered in contracts by correspondence are deferred until we reach Subsection 4(c) infra.)

The court had occasion to answer this question in Bishop v. Eaton, 161 Mass. 496, 37 N.E. 665 (1894). "Ordinarily there is no occasion to notify the offeror of the acceptance of such an offer, for the doing of the act is a sufficient acceptance, and the promisor knows that he is bound when he sees that action has been taken on the faith of his offer. But if the act is of such a kind that knowledge of it will not quickly come to the promisor, the promisee is bound to give him notice of his acceptance within a reasonable time after doing that which constitutes the acceptance." In that case Frank Eaton, in Nova Scotia, had written to Bishop, in Illinois, that if he would help his brother, Harry Eaton, to get money, "I will see that it is paid." Bishop did help Harry get money by signing his note as surety when he got a loan. When Harry did not repay the loan, Bishop did, and sued Frank on his promise. The court thought that this was a case in which notice should have been given, since the loan was made in Illinois and Frank was in Nova Scotia, but concluded that it had been given.

Assuming that such a requirement is to be imposed, it can be framed so that Bishop does not accept Frank's offer until he both signs Harry's note and sends the notice to Frank. Or it can be framed so that Bishop accepts Frank's offer when he signs the note, but Frank's obligation is discharged if Bishop does not send a notice within a reasonable time. Would it make any difference? Suppose (putting the case in a modern context) that the day after Bishop signs the note, and before he has sent the notice to Frank, Frank telephones Bishop and tells him that he revokes. Would the revocation be effective? See Restatement Second, § 56; UCC 2–206(2); Dole, Notice Requirements of Guaranty Contracts, 62 Mich.L.Rev. 57 (1963).

CARLILL v. CARBOLIC SMOKE BALL CO., [1893] 1 Q.B. 256. [The Carbolic Smoke Ball Company ran the following newspaper advertisement: "£100 reward will be paid by the Carbolic Smoke Ball Company to any person who contracts the increasing epidemic influenza, colds or any disease caused by taking cold, after having used the ball three times daily for two weeks according to the printed directions supplied with each ball. £1000 is deposited with the Alliance Bank, Regent Street shewing our sincerity in the matter. . . ." On the faith of this advertisement a lady bought one of the balls and used it as directed, three times daily from November 20, 1891 to January 17, 1892, when she contracted influenza. She sued the Company and was awarded £100 damages. The Company appealed.]

[The opinion of Lindley, L. J., relying upon the mention of the £1000 deposit, concluded that the advertisement was not "a mere puff which meant nothing," but an offer to "anybody who performs the conditions named in the advertisement, and anybody who does perform the conditions accepts the offer." The preferable construction of the offer is "that the reward is offered to any person who contracts the epidemic or other disease within a reasonable time after having used the smoke ball."]

BOWEN, L. J.   I am of the same opinion. . . .   Then it was said that there was no notification of the acceptance of the contract. One cannot doubt that, as an ordinary rule of law, an acceptance of an offer made ought to be notified to the person who makes the offer, in order that the two minds may come together. Unless this is done the two minds may be apart, and there is not that consensus which is necessary according to the English law—I say nothing about the laws of other countries—to make a contract. But there is this clear gloss to be made upon that doctrine, that as notification of acceptance is required for the benefit of the person who makes the offer, the person who makes the offer may dispense with notice to himself, if he thinks it desirable to do so, and I suppose there can be no doubt that where a person in an offer made by him to another person, expressly or impliedly intimates a particular mode of acceptance as sufficient to make the bargain binding, it is only necessary for the other person to whom such offer is made to follow the indicated method of acceptance; and if the person making the offer, expressly or impliedly intimates in his offer that it will be sufficient to act on the proposal without communicating acceptance of it to himself, performance of the condition is a sufficient acceptance without notification. . . .

Now, if that is the law, how are we to find out whether the person who makes the offer does intimate that notification of acceptance will not be necessary in order to constitute a binding bargain? In many cases you look to the offer itself. In many cases you extract from the character of the transaction that notification is not required, and in the advertisement cases it seems to me to follow as an inference to be drawn from the transaction itself that a person is not to notify his acceptance of the offer before he performs the condition, but that if he performs the condition notification is dispensed with. It seems to me that from the point of view of common sense no other idea could be entertained. If I advertise to the world that my dog is lost, and that anybody who brings the dog to a particular place will be paid some money, are all the police or other persons whose business it is to find lost dogs to be expected to sit down and write a note saying that they have accepted my proposal? Why, of course, they at once look after the dog, and as soon as they find the dog they have performed the condition. The essence of the transaction is that the dog should be found, and it is not necessary under such circumstances, as it seems to me, that in order to make the contract binding there should be any notification of acceptance. It follows from the nature of the thing that the performance of the condition is sufficient acceptance without the notification of it, and a person who makes an offer in an advertisement of that kind makes an offer which must be read by the light of that common sense reflection. He does, therefore, in his offer impliedly indicate that he does not require notification of the acceptance of the offer. . . .

Appeal dismissed.

NOTE

Conditional Promises. Was the acceptance of the Carbolic Smoke Ball Company's offer: (1) the purchase of the smoke ball; (2) its use in accordance with directions; (3) the plaintiff's contracting influenza; or (4) all three? Which of these acts was bargained for? See Note 1, p. 31 supra.

A promise may be conditional, that is, its performance becomes due only if a specified event occurs. This does not mean that the promise is not binding before the event occurs. It means that the event must occur before there can be a claim for breach of the promise. A house owner pays $100 to an insurance company for the company's promise to pay the owner $10,000 if his house is destroyed by fire. If the house burns, performance of the promise becomes due. If it does not burn, performance of the promise does not become due. The burning of the house was not the acceptance of an offer. There was a contract before the house burned. The burning of the house was a condition. Is there an analogy between this and the Carbolic Smoke Ball case? Conditions will be dealt with in Section 4 of Chapter 6, infra.

INTERNATIONAL FILTER CO. v. CONROE GIN, ICE & LIGHT CO.

Commission of Appeals of Texas, 1925. 277 S.W. 631.

Action by the International Filter Company against the Conroe Gin, Ice & Light Company. Judgment for defendant was affirmed in 269 S.W. 210, and plaintiff brings error. Reversed and remanded.

NICKELS, J. Plaintiff in error, an Illinois corporation, is a manufacturer of machinery, apparatus, etc., for the purification of water in connection with the manufacture of ice, etc., having its principal office in the city of Chicago. Defendant in error is a Texas corporation engaged in the manufacture of ice, etc., having its plant, office, etc., at Conroe, Montgomery county, Tex.

On February 10, 1920, through its traveling solicitor, Waterman, plaintiff in error at Conroe, submitted to defendant in error, acting through Henry Thompson, its manager, a written instrument, addressed to defendant in error, which (with immaterial portions omitted) reads as follows:

"Gentlemen: We propose to furnish, f. o. b. Chicago, one No. two Junior (steel tank) International water softener and filter to purify water of the character shown by sample to be submitted. . . . Price: Twelve hundred thirty ($1,230.00) dollars. . . . This proposal is made in duplicate and becomes a contract when accepted by the purchaser and approved by an executive officer of the International Filter Company, at its office in Chicago. Any modification can only be made by duly approved supplementary agreement signed by both parties.

"This proposal is submitted for prompt acceptance, and unless so accepted is subject to change without notice.

"Respectfully submitted,

"International Filter Co.
"W. W. Waterman."

On the same day the "proposal" was accepted by defendant in error through notation made on the paper by Thompson reading as follows:

"Accepted Feb. 10, 1920.

"Conroe Gin, Ice & Light Co.,
"By Henry Thompson, Mgr."

The paper as thus submitted and "accepted" contained the notation, "Make shipment by Mar. 10." The paper, in that form, reached the Chicago office of plaintiff in error, and on February 13, 1920, P. N. Engel, its president and vice president, indorsed thereon: "O. K. Feb. 13, 1920, P. N. Engel." February 14, 1920, plaintiff in error wrote and mailed, and in due course defendant in error received, the following letter:

"Feb. 14, 1920.
"Attention of Mr. Henry Thompson, Manager.

"Conroe Gin, Ice & Light Co., Conroe, Texas—Gentlemen: This will acknowledge and thank you for your order given Mr. Waterman for a No. 2 Jr. steel tank International softener and filter, for 110 volt, 60 cycle, single phase current—for shipment March 10th.

"Please make shipment of the sample of water promptly so that we may make the analysis and know the character of the water before shipment of the apparatus. Shipping tag is inclosed, and please note, the instructions to pack to guard against freezing.

"Yours very truly,

"International Filter Co.
"M. B. Johnson."

By letter of February 28, 1920, defendant in error undertook to countermand the "order," which countermand was repeated and emphasized by letter of March 4, 1920. By letter of March 2, 1920 (replying to the letter of February 28th), plaintiff in error denied the right of countermand, etc., and insisted upon performance of the "contract." The parties adhered to the respective positions thus indicated, and this suit resulted.

Plaintiff in error sued for breach of the contract alleged to have been made in the manner stated above. The defense is that no contract was made because: (1) Neither Engel's indorsement of "O. K.," nor the letter of February 14, 1920, amounted to approval "by an executive officer of the International Filter Company, at its office in Chicago." (2) Notification of such approval, or acceptance, by plaintiff in error was required to be communicated to defendant in error; it being insisted that this requirement inhered in the terms of the proposal and in the nature of the transaction and, also, that Thompson, when he indorsed "acceptance" on the paper stated to Waterman, as agent of plaintiff in error, that such notification must be promptly given; it being insisted further that the letter of February 14, 1920, did not constitute such acceptance or notification of approval, and therefore defendant in error, on February 28, 1920, etc., had the right to withdraw or countermand, the unaccepted offer. Thompson testified in a manner to support the allegation of his statement to Waterman. There are other matters involved in the suit which must be ultimately determined, but the foregoing presents the issues now here for consideration.

The case was tried without a jury, and the judge found the facts in favor of defendant in error on all the issues indicated above, and upon other material issues. The judgment was affirmed by the Court of Civil Appeals, 269 S.W. 210.

We agree with the honorable Court of Civil Appeals upon the proposition that Mr. Engel's indorsement of "O. K." amounted to an approval "by an executive officer of the International Filter Company, at its office in Chicago," within the meaning of the so-called "proposal" of February 10th. The paper then became a "contract," according to its definitely expressed terms, and it became then, and thereafter it remained, an enforceable contract, in legal contemplation, unless the fact of approval by the filter company was required to be communicated to the other party and unless, in that event, the communication was not made.

We are not prepared to assent to the ruling that such communication was essential. There is no disposition to question the justice of the general rules stated in support of that holding, yet the existence of contractual capacity imports the right of the offerer to dispense with notification; and he does dispense with it "if the form of the offer," etc., "shows that this was not to be required." 9 Cyc. 270, 271; Carlill v. Carbolic Smoke Ball Co., 1 Q.B. 256 (and other references in note 6, 9 Cyc. 271). . . .

The Conroe Gin, Ice & Light Company executed the paper for the purpose of having it transmitted, as its offer, to the filter company at Chicago. It was so transmitted and acted upon. Its terms embrace the offer, and nothing else, and by its terms the question of notification must be judged, since those terms are not ambiguous.

The paper contains two provisions which relate to acceptance by the filter company. One is the declaration that the offer shall "become a contract . . . when approved by an executive officer of the International Filter Company, at its Chicago office." The other is thus stated: "This proposal is submitted for prompt acceptance, and unless so accepted is subject to change without notice." The first provision states "a particular mode of acceptance as sufficient to make the bargain binding," and the filter company (as stated above) followed "the indicated method of acceptance." When this was done, so the paper declares, the proposal "became a contract." The other provision does not in any way relate to a different method of acceptance by the filter company. Its sole reference is to the time within which the act of approval must be done; that is to say, there was to be a "prompt acceptance," else the offer might be changed "without notice." The second declaration merely required the approval thereinbefore stipulated for to be done promptly; if the act was so done, there is nothing in the second provision to militate against, or to conflict with, the prior declaration that, thereupon, the paper should become "a contract."

A holding that notification of that approval is to be deduced from the terms of the last-quoted clause is not essential in order to give it meaning or to dissolve ambiguity. On the contrary, such a construction of the two provisions would introduce a conflict, or ambiguity, where none exists in the language itself, and defeat the plainly expressed term wherein it is said that the proposal "becomes a contract . . . when approved by an executive officer." There is not anything in the language used to justify a ruling that this declaration must be wrenched from its obvious meaning and given one which would change both the locus and time prescribed for the meeting of the minds. The offerer said that the contract should be complete if approval be promptly given by the executive officer at Chicago; the court cannot properly restate the offer so as to make the offerer declare that a contract shall be made only when the approval shall have been promptly given at Chicago and that fact shall have been communicated to the offerer at Conroe. In our opinion, therefore, notice of the approval was not required.

The letter of February 14th, however, sufficiently communicated notice, if it was required. . . . Here the fact of acceptance in the particular method prescribed by the offerer is established aliunde the letter—Engel's "O. K." indorsed on the paper at Chicago did that. The form of notice, where notice is required, may be quite a different thing from the acceptance itself; the latter constitutes the meeting of

the minds, the former merely relates to that pre-existent fact.   The
rules requiring such notice, it will be marked, do not make necessary
any particular form or manner, unless the parties themselves have so
prescribed.   Whatever would convey by word or fair implication, notice of the fact would be sufficient.   And this letter, we think, would
clearly indicate to a reasonably prudent person, situated as was the
defendant in error, the fact of previous approval by the filter company.   If the Gin, Ice & Light Company had acted to change its position
upon it as a notification of that fact, it must be plain that the filter
company would have been estopped to deny its sufficiency.   .   .   .

We recommend that the judgment of the Court of Civil Appeals
be reversed, and that the cause be remanded to that court for its disposition of all questions not passed upon it by it heretofore and properly before it for determination.

CURETON, C. J.   Judgment of the Court of Civil Appeals reversed,
and cause remanded to the Court of Civil Appeals for further consideration by that court, as recommended by the Commission of Appeals.

NOTE

Requirement of Approval.   Can you distinguish the position of the
International Filter Company from that of the offeree who merely says
"I accept" to himself?   How could the Company redraft its forms to make
sure that it would not have to litigate the necessity of notice in other jurisdictions where it does business?   Would you like now to reconsider the
clause that you drafted in response to Note, p. 95 supra.   Are there still
risks for the seller inherent in such a clause?

SECTION 3.   TERMINATION OF THE POWER OF ACCEPTANCE

After one party has made an offer, conferring on the other party
a power of acceptance, that power can be terminated in several ways:
(1) revocation;   (2) death or incapacity;   (3) lapse;   and (4) rejection.   They will be considered in that order.

It is taken as a commonplace in common law countries that the
offeror is free to revoke his offer at any time before the offeree has
accepted it.   Grotius, the great seventeenth-century Dutch jurist, favored the same rule.   But this freedom to revoke is not inevitable, as
is shown by the law of Germany and some other civil law countries
where an offer is irrevocable for a reasonable time unless the offeror
expresses a different intention.   See 1 Schlesinger (ed.), Formation
of Contracts: A Study of the Common Core of Legal Systems 780–83
(1968).   Which rule seems preferable?   One disadvantage of the Ger-

man rule is that during the period of irrevocability, the offeree can take advantage of changing economic conditions to speculate at the expense of the offeror. Although Germany and the other countries that have this rule have experienced much greater economic upheavals than has the United States, they have been able to live with the rule, at least in part, because it can easily be avoided by expressly reserving the power to revoke or providing that the communication is not an offer at all. The extent to which the offeror in the United States can avoid the common law rule by expressly relinquishing the power to revoke is discussed at p. 121 infra.

HOOVER MOTOR EXPRESS CO. v. CLEMENTS PAPER CO., 193 Tenn. 6, 241 S.W.2d 851 (1951). [On November 19, 1949 Hoover Motor Express made a written offer to Clements Paper to buy real property. On January 13, Mr. Williams, representing Clements, told Mr. Hoover on the telephone that Clements was ready to go through with it and would like to discuss it with him. Mr. Hoover replied, "Well, I don't know if we are ready. We have not decided, we might not want to go through with it." Williams was surprised since this was the first suggestion that Hoover might not carry out its offer. Mr. Hoover also said that he did not think that they were going through with the proposal and that they would call Williams on January 17. He did not call Williams, and on January 20 Clements accepted in writing Hoover's offer of November 19. When Hoover refused to go through with the transaction, Clements sued. From a decree for Clements, Hoover appealed.]

TOMLINSON, J. . . . Although there is no Tennessee case deciding the point, in so far as we can find, the general rule is that express notice, in so many words, of withdrawal before acceptance of an offer of the character we have here is not required. . . . Restatement of the Law of Contracts, Section 41, page 49, has this to say: "Revocation of an offer may be made by a communication from the offeror received by the offeree, which states or implies that the offeror no longer intends to enter into the proposed contract, if the communication is received by the offeree before he has exercised his power of creating a contract by acceptance of the offer."

Applying to the undisputed testimony as furnished by Williams the rule clearly stated in all the authorities, . . . we think it must be concluded that Hoover's written offer of November 19 was withdrawn on January 13, thereafter prior to its attempted acceptance on January 20, and that the concurrent finding of the Chancellor and the Court of Appeals to the contrary is not supported by any material evidence. There can be no doubt as to it being a fact that on January 13 knowledge was brought home to Williams that Hoover no longer consented to the transaction. There was, therefore, no offer continuing up to the time of the attempted acceptance on January 20.

.   .   .

[Reversed.]

NOTE

Language of Revocation. Compare the court's treatment of the claimed revocation in the Hoover case with the court's treatment of the claimed offers in Owen v. Tunison, p. 64 supra, and in Harvey v. Facey, p. 66 supra. Are they in any way consistent?

DICKINSON v. DODDS

In the Court of Appeal, Chancery Division, 1876. 2 Ch.Div. 463.

On Wednesday, the 10th of June, 1874, the defendant John Dodds signed and delivered to the plaintiff, George Dickinson, a memorandum, of which the material part was as follows:

"I hereby agree to sell to Mr. George Dickinson the whole of the dwelling-houses, garden ground, stabling, and outbuildings thereto belonging, situate at Croft, belonging to me, for the sum of £800. As witness my hand this tenth day of June, 1874.

£800.   [Signed]   John Dodds."
"P. S.—This offer to be left over until Friday, 9 o'clock a. m. J.D. (the twelfth), 12th June, 1874.   [Signed]   J. Dodds."

The bill alleged that Dodds understood and intended that the plaintiff should have until Friday, 9 a. m., within which to determine whether he would or would not purchase, and that he should absolutely have until that time the refusal of the property at the price of £800, and that the plaintiff in fact determined to accept the offer on the morning of Thursday, the 11th of June, but did not at once signify his acceptance to Dodds, believing that he had the power to accept it until 9 a. m. on the Friday.

In the afternoon of the Thursday the plaintiff was informed by a Mr. Berry that Dodds had been offering or agreeing to sell the property to Thomas Allan, the other defendant. Thereupon the plaintiff, at about half past seven in the evening, went to the house of Mrs. Burgess, the mother-in-law of Dodds, where he was then staying, and left with her a formal acceptance in writing of the offer to sell the property. According to the evidence of Mrs. Burgess this document never in fact reached Dodds, she having forgotten to give it to him.

On the following (Friday) morning, at about seven o'clock, Berry, who was acting as agent for Dickinson, found Dodds at the Darlington Railway station, and handed to him a duplicate of the acceptance by Dickinson, and explained to Dodds its purport. He replied that it was too late, as he had sold the property. A few minutes later

Dickinson himself found Dodds entering a railway carriage, and handed him another duplicate of the notice of acceptance, but Dodds declined to receive it, saying: "You are too late. I have sold the property."

It appeared that on the day before, Thursday, the 11th of June, Dodds had signed a formal contract for the sale of the property to the defendant Allan for £800, and had received from him a deposit of £40.

The bill in this suit prayed that the defendant Dodds might be decreed specifically to perform the contract of the 10th of June, 1874; that he might be restrained from conveying the property to Allan; that Allan might be restrained from taking any such conveyance; that, if any such conveyance had been or should be made, Allan might be declared a trustee of the property for, and might be directed to convey the property to, the plaintiff; and for damages.

The cause came on for hearing before Vice Chancellor Bacon on the 25th of January, 1876 [who decreed specific performance for the plaintiff. From this decision the defendants appeal].

JAMES, L. J., after referring to the document of the 10th of June, 1874, continued:

The document, though beginning "I hereby agree to sell," was nothing but an offer, and was only intended to be an offer, for the plaintiff himself tells us that he required time to consider whether he would enter into an agreement or not. Unless both parties had then agreed, there was no concluded agreement then made; it was in effect and substance only an offer to sell. The plaintiff, being minded not to complete the bargain at that time, added this memorandum: "This offer to be left over until Friday, 9 o'clock a. m. 12th June, 1874." That shows it was only an offer. There was no consideration given for the undertaking or promise, to whatever extent it may be considered binding, to keep the property unsold until 9 o'clock on Friday morning; but apparently Dickinson was of opinion, and probably Dodds was of the same opinion, that he (Dodds) was bound by that promise, and could not in any way withdraw from it, or retract it, until 9 o'clock on Friday morning, and this probably explains a good deal of what afterwards took place. But it is clear settled law, on one of the clearest principles of law, that this promise, being a mere nudum pactum, was not binding, and that at any moment before a complete acceptance by Dickinson of the offer, Dodds was as free as Dickinson himself. Well, that being the state of things, it is said that the only mode in which Dodds could assert that freedom was by actually and distinctly saying to Dickinson, "Now I withdraw my offer." It appears to me that there is neither principle nor authority for the proposition that there must be an express and actual withdrawal of the offer, or what is called a retraction. It must, to constitute a contract, appear that the two minds were as one, at the same moment of time, that is, that there was an offer continuing up to the time of the acceptance. If there was not such a continuing offer, then the acceptance comes to nothing. Of course it may well be that the one man is bound in some way or other to let the other man know that his mind with regard to the offer has been changed; but in this case, beyond all question, the plaintiff knew that Dodds was no longer minded to sell the property to him as plainly and clearly as if Dodds had told him in so many words, "I withdraw the offer." This is evident from the plaintiff's own statements in the bill.

The plaintiff says in effect that, having heard and knowing that Dodds was no longer minded to sell to him, and that he was selling or had sold to some one else, thinking that he could not in point of law withdraw his offer, meaning to fix him to it, and endeavoring to bind him: "I went to the house where he was lodging, and saw his mother-in-law, and left with her an acceptance of the offer, knowing all the while that he had entirely changed his mind. I got an agent to watch for him at 7 o'clock the next morning, and I went to the train just before 9 o'clock, in order that I might catch him and give him my notice of acceptance just before 9 o'clock, and when that occurred he told my agent, and he told me,' You are too late,' and he then threw back the paper." It is to my mind quite clear that before there was any attempt at acceptance by the plaintiff, he was perfectly well aware that Dodds had changed his mind, and that he had in fact agreed to sell the property to Allan. It is impossible, therefore to say there was ever that existence of the same mind between the two parties which is essential in point of law to the making of an agreement. I am of opinion, therefore, that the plaintiff has failed to prove that there was any binding contract between Dodds and himself.

MELLISH, L. J. I am of the same opinion. . . . Well, then, this being only an offer, and the law says—and it is a perfectly clear rule of law—that, although it is said that the offer is to be left open until Friday morning at 9 o'clock, that did not bind Dodds. He was not in point of law bound to hold the offer over until 9 o'clock on Friday morning. He was not so bound either in law or in equity. Well, that being so, when on the next day he made an agreement with Allan to sell the property to him, I am not aware of any ground on which it can be said that that contract with Allan was not as good and binding a contract as ever was made. Assuming Allan to have known (there is some dispute about it, and Allan does not admit that he knew of it, but I will assume that he did) that Dodds had made the offer to Dickinson, and had given him till Friday morning at 9 o'clock to accept it, still in point of law that could not prevent Allan from making a more favorable offer than Dickinson, and entering at once into a binding agreement with Dodds.

Then Dickinson is informed by Berry that the property has been sold by Dodds to Allan. Berry does not tell us from whom he heard it, but he says that he did hear it, that he knew it, and that he informed Dickinson of it. Now, stopping there, the question which arises is this: If an offer has been made for the sale of property, and before that offer is accepted the person who has made the offer enters into a binding agreement to sell the property to somebody else, and the person to whom the offer was first made receives notice in some way that the property has been sold to another person, can he after that make a binding contract by the acceptance of the offer? I am of opinion that he cannot. . . . If a man makes an offer to sell a particular horse in his stable, and says, "I will give you until the day after to-morrow to accept the offer," and the next day goes and sells the horse to somebody else, and receives the purchase money from him, can the person to whom the offer was originally made then come and say, "I accept," so as to make a binding contract, and so as to be entitled to recover damages for the non-delivery of the horse? If the rule of law is that a mere offer to sell property, which can be withdrawn at any time, and which is made dependent on the acceptance of the person to whom it is made, is a mere nudum pactum, how is it possible that the person to whom the offer has been made can by acceptance make a binding contract after he knows that the person who has made the offer has sold the property to some one else? It is admitted law that, if a man who makes an offer dies, the offer cannot be accepted after he is dead; and parting with the property has very much the same effect as the death of the owner, for it makes the performance of the offer impossible. I am clearly of opinion that, just as when a man who has made an offer dies before it is accepted it is impossible that it can then be accepted, so when once the person to whom the offer was made knows that the property has been sold to someone else, it is too late for him to accept the offer, and on that ground I am clearly of opinion that there was no binding contract for the sale of this property by Dodds to Dickinson; and, even if there had been, it seems to me that the sale of the property to Allan was first in point of time. However, it is not necessary to consider, if there had been two binding contracts, which of them would be entitled to priority in equity, because there is no binding contract between Dodds and Dickinson.

BAGGALLAY, J. A. I entirely concur in the judgments which have been pronounced.

JAMES, L. J. The bill will be dismissed, with costs.

NOTES

(1) *Indirect Communication of Revocation.* What did Berry tell Dickinson? That Dodd had made an offer to sell the property or that he had made a contract to sell the property? Dickinson v. Dodds has been followed in the United States, but has also been criticized. Note the differences between Restatement, § 42 and Restatement Second, § 42. The problem of communication of revocation by mail is considered in Subsection 4(c) infra.

(2) *Revocation of General Offers.* In the case of a general offer, such as one addressed to the general public by an advertisement, it will ordinarily be impossible for the offeror actually to communicate a revocation to all of the persons who are aware of the offer. Illustrative are the offers in the Broadnax case, p. 29 supra, the Lefkowitz case, p. 75 supra, and the Carbolic Smoke Ball case, p. 109 supra. The offeror can, of course, be required to give his notice of revocation publicity equal (and usually similar) to that given the offer. But having done this, is he nevertheless bound by the acceptance of an offeree who was aware of the offer but missed the notice of revocation? The answer is that he is not bound, in spite of the general requirement that a revocation be actually communicated to the offeree. See Restatement Second, § 43; Corbin, § 41; Williston, §§ 59, 59A. How would you revoke an offer of a reward posted on a bulletin board? Would taking it down be sufficient? When would the revocation take effect? See Carr v. Mahaska County Bankers Ass'n, 222 Iowa 411, 269 N.W. 494 (1936). For an entertaining example of revocation by publication, involving a reward issued by Secretary of War Stanton for Suratt, one of Booth's accomplices in the assassination of President Lincoln, see Shuey v. United States, 92 U.S. 73 (1875).

(3) *Problem.* A offered in writing to sell B Blackacre for $1,000, offer to remain open five days. On the fourth day B received information from the county recorder of deeds that he had received for recording a deed of Blackacre from A to C. This information being reliable, B believed it, but thinking there might be some chance for error, notified A of his acceptance on the fifth day. The information given by the recorder proved to be erroneous, but A refused to perform. Contract?

OPTION CONTRACTS

Not only did the common law give the offeror the power to revoke his offer subject only to the offeree's exercise of his power of acceptance, but, as Dickinson v. Dodds indicates, a promise not to revoke, "being a mere nudum pactum, was not binding." Some means then had to be found to make that promise enforceable if the offeror's power to revoke were to be limited. A promise that effectively limits the offeror's power to revoke is called an "option contract" in the Restatement Second, in preference to the more traditional term "option." Restatement Second, § 24A. In the early common law, of course, an option contract could be made by making the promise under seal. With the abolition of the seal, the doctrine of consideration became the exclusive means to this end. What would have been the result if Dickinson had paid Dodds £1 and the postscript had been changed to read, "In consideration of £1 paid, this offer is left over until Friday, 9 o'clock a. m."?[a] This technique may be adequate for

a. It can be argued that Dickinson's remedy against Dodds on such a "collateral" promise would be only for breach of that promise and not for breach of the promise to sell the land, so that he could not have specific performance. But both Corbin and Williston reject this view. See Corbin, § 44; Williston, § 61C. The point would not arise if the letter read: "In con-

offers for the sale of land, where the parties might be expected to foresee the possibility of revocation and deal with it in this rather elaborate way. It is less satisfactory for more informal transactions such as those for the sale of goods, where the offeror is less likely to clothe his promise in the trappings of consideration.

The Uniform Commercial Code therefore contains an important provision on "firm offers," which enables an offeror to make an irrevocable offer "to buy or sell goods" by means of a signed writing. UCC 2–205. In addition, New York has the following comprehensive statute, first enacted in 1941 (along with the statute on "moral obligation" in Note 4, p. 25 supra), and later amended to take account of the Code:

> Except as otherwise provided in section 2–205 of the uniform commercial code with respect to an offer by a merchant to buy or sell goods, when an offer to enter into a contract is made in a writing signed by the offeror, or by his agent, which states that the offer is irrevocable during a period set forth or until a time fixed, the offer shall not be revocable during such period or until such time because of the absence of consideration for the assurance of irrevocability. When such a writing states that the offer is irrevocable but does not state any period or time of irrevocability, it shall be construed to state that the offer is irrevocable for a reasonable time. (New York General Obligations Law, § 5–1109.)

How could the form that Ever-Tite gave the Greens to sign, in the case at p. 94 supra, have been redrafted to take advantage of this provision if Ever-Tite were doing business in New York? Is the New York consumer under a contract for re-roofing, which is not governed by the Code, in any different position than the consumer under a contract for the sale of goods, which is? Which statute is preferable in this respect?

BARD v. KENT, 19 Cal.2d 449, 122 P.2d 8 (1942). [Kent, who administered the business affairs of Miss Roland, had been involved for some years in the unsuccessful operation of a restaurant known as The Cat and The Fiddle on land that he leased from her. The restaurant had finally proved successful in the hands of Kent's sublessee, McDonnell. McDonnell had spent about $30,000 on improvements which, at the end of Kent's lease, would revert to Miss Roland. When McDonnell's sublease had about five years to run, he told Miss Roland

---

sideration of £1 paid, I hereby agree to sell to Mr. George Dickinson the whole of the dwelling-houses . . . situate at Croft, belonging to me, for the sum of £800, on condition that he notify me of his acceptance and tender the £800 by Friday, 9 o'clock a. m."

and Kent that he would make further improvements that would cost about $10,000 if his sublease were extended for an additional four years. Miss Roland expressed to Kent a willingness to grant the extension if the proposed improvements would cost what McDonnell said they would, and suggested that Kent check the figures and have an architect draw sketches on which an estimate could be based. On August 17, she executed to Kent a written option to extend his lease for four more years, which recited that it was granted "For consideration of Ten Dollars ($10.00) and other valuable consideration." The $10 was never paid, but Kent paid an architect to draw sketches. On September 22, while the option was still unexercised, Miss Roland died. The administrator of her estate sued Kent to cancel the option. From judgment for the administrator, Kent appealed.]

TRAYNOR, JUSTICE.[a] [The $10 was not consideration because it had not been paid.] Defendant contends that his payment of the architect's fee for sketches of the proposed improvements is a consideration sufficient to make the option irrevocable. There is no doubt that such payment would be consideration for an option if the offeror agreed to accept it as such. . . . No act of an offeree, however, can constitute consideration binding upon the offeror unless the latter agrees to be bound . . . .. In the present case the trial court was justified in concluding from the evidence that Miss Roland did not promise to grant the option in return for Kent's engaging the architect. Under this interpretation of the evidence Miss Roland merely stated the conditions under which she was willing to extend the lease. Although, according to Kent's testimony, she suggested engaging an architect to check the figures on the proposed improvements, this suggestion did not constitute a promise by her to grant the option if that were done. Kent employed the architect to convince her that the necessary conditions existed, but she made no promise to extend the lease in the event they did, and remained free to withdraw her offer at any time before acceptance. Kent could have exercised the option as soon as it was executed, but he chose instead to wait rather than to undertake immediately the obligations incident to leasing the property for another four years. The engagement of the architect was to actuate Miss Roland to keep her offer open, but it did not constitute consideration binding her to do so. At best the evidence created a conflict for the trial court to resolve. . . .

Defendant contends that in engaging the architect he acted in reliance upon the option given him by Miss Roland to extend the lease, and that under the doctrine of promissory estoppel a promisor who has received no consideration is nevertheless bound by his promise

a. Roger Traynor (1900–   ) was a member of the law faculty of the University of California at Berkeley from 1930 to 1940 and specialized in tax law. He served from 1940 to 1964 as associate justice of the Supreme Court of California and from 1964 to 1970 as its chief justice. Some of his opinions on contract law are discussed in Macaulay, Mr. Justice Traynor and the Law of Contracts, 13 Stan.L.Rev. 812 (1961).

when he has induced another to suffer detriment in reliance thereon.
. . . There must, however, be a promise on which reliance may be
based. . . . Defendant did not plead the issue of promissory estoppel at the trial, and there is nothing in the record to show that
Miss Roland at any time promised to keep the option open or made
any other promise on which defendant could rely. She merely made
without consideration an offer, which was never accepted, to renew the
lease.

The judgment is affirmed.

NOTES

(1) *Caveats.* For more on promissory estoppel in California, see
Traynor's opinion in the Drennan case, p. 159 infra. That Kent's payment of the architect was not consideration, see Kirksey v. Kirksey, p. 28
supra. For a contrasting case, see City Stores v. Ammerman, 266 F.Supp.
766 (D.D.C.1967), affirmed 394 F.2d 950 (D.C.Cir.1968).

(2) *Recitals of Consideration.* Not all courts would agree that the
recital was inoperative. In Southern Bell Telephone & Telegraph Co. v.
Harris, 117 Ga. 1001, 44 S.E. 885 (1903), the court held that where a contract contains a recital of the payment of one dollar as consideration, the
contract is valid, though the sum named was not actually paid, since it
creates an obligation to pay that sum. How does this differ from the rule
stated in Restatement Second, § 89B(1) (a)?

THE BROOKLYN BRIDGE HYPOTHETICAL

Over half a century ago Professor Wormser put a notorious hypothetical: "Suppose A says to B, 'I will give you $100 if you walk
across the Brooklyn Bridge' . . .. B starts to walk across the
Brooklyn Bridge and has gone about one-half of the way across. At
that moment A overtakes B and says to him, 'I withdraw my offer.'
Has B then any rights against A? Again, let us suppose that after A
has said, 'I withdraw my offer,' B continues to walk across the Brooklyn Bridge and completes the act of crossing. Under these circumstances, has B any rights against A?" Wormser concluded that he had
none. "What A wanted from B, what A asked for, was the act of walking across the bridge. Until that was done, B had not given to A
what A had requested. The acceptance by B of A's offer could be
nothing but the act on B's part of crossing the bridge. It is elementary that an offeror may withdraw his offer until it has been accepted. It follows logically that A is perfectly within his rights in withdrawing his offer before B has accepted it by walking across the
bridge—the act contemplated by the offeror and the offeree as the
acceptance of the offer." Wormser, The True Conception of Unilateral Contracts, 26 Yale L.J. 136–137 (1916), Selected Readings 307–
308.

BRACKENBURY v. HODGKIN

Supreme Judicial Court of Maine, 1917.
116 Me. 399, 102 A. 106.

Suit by Joseph A. Brackenbury and another against Sarah D. P. Hodgkin and Walter C. Hodgkin. From a decree for plaintiffs, defendants appeal. Appeal dismissed, and decree affirmed as to Walter C. Hodgkin.

CORNISH, C. J. The defendant Mrs. Sarah D. P. Hodgkin on the 8th day of February, 1915, was the owner of certain real estate —her home farm, situated in the outskirts of Lewiston. She was a widow and was living alone. She was the mother of six adult children, five sons, one of whom, Walter, is the codefendant, and one daughter, who is the coplaintiff. The plaintiffs were then residing in Independence, Mo. Many letters had passed between mother and daughter concerning the daughter and her husband returning to the old home and taking care of the mother, and finally on February 8, 1915, the mother sent a letter to the daughter and her husband which is the foundation of this bill in equity. In this letter she made a definite proposal, the substance of which was that if the Brackenburys would move to Lewiston, and maintain and care for Mrs. Hodgkin on the home place during her life, and pay the moving expenses, they were to have the use and income of the premises, together with the use of the household goods, with certain exceptions, Mrs. Hodgkin to have what rooms she might need. The letter closed, by way of postscript, with the words, "you to have the place when I have passed away."

Relying upon this offer, which was neither withdrawn nor modified, and in acceptance thereof, the plaintiffs moved from Missouri to Maine late in April, 1915, went upon the premises described and entered upon the performance of the contract. Trouble developed after a few weeks, and the relations between the parties grew most disagreeable. The mother brought two suits against her son-in-law on trifling matters, and finally ordered the plaintiffs from the place, but they refused to leave. Then on November 7, 1916, she executed and delivered to her son, Walter C. Hodgkin, a deed of the premises, reserving a life estate in herself. Walter, however, was not a bona fide purchaser for value without notice, but took the deed with full knowledge of the agreement between the parties and for the sole purpose of evicting the plaintiffs. On the very day the deed was executed he served a notice to quit upon Mr. Brackenbury, as preliminary to an action of forcible entry and detainer which was brought on November 13, 1916. This bill in equity was brought by the plaintiffs to secure a reconveyance of the farm from Walter to his mother, to restrain and enjoin Walter from further prosecuting his action of forcible entry and detainer, and to obtain an adjudication that the mother holds the legal title impressed with a trust in favor of the plaintiffs in accordance with their contract.

The sitting justice made an elaborate and carefully considered finding of facts and signed a decree, sustaining the bill with costs against Walter C. Hodgkin, and granting the relief prayed for. The case is before the law court on the defendants' appeal from this decree.

Four main issues are raised.

1.   As to the completion and existence of a valid contract.

A legal and binding contract is clearly proven. The offer on the part of the mother was in writing, and its terms cannot successfully be disputed. There was no need that it be accepted in words, nor that a counter promise on the part of the plaintiffs be made. The offer was the basis, not of a bilateral contract, requiring a reciprocal promise, a promise for a promise, but of a unilateral contract requiring an act for a promise. "In the latter case the only acceptance of the offer that is necessary is the performance of the act. In other words, the promise becomes binding when the act is performed." 6 R.C.L. 607. This is elementary law.

The plaintiffs here accepted the offer by moving from Missouri to the mother's farm in Lewiston and entering upon the performance of the specified acts, and they have continued performance since that time so far as they have been permitted by the mother to do so. The existence of a completed and valid contract is clear. [Other points raised are omitted.]

Appeal dismissed.

NOTES

(1) *Restatement Rule.* Restatement Second, § 45 states a rule, derived from Restatement, § 45 and couched in language of "option contract" that supports the result in Brackenbury v. Hodgkin. (It is helpful in reading this section to understand that one cannot "tender" a performance that is to extend over a period of time, such as the crossing of the Brooklyn Bridge.) Indeed, thirty-four years after Wormser first wrote of the Brooklyn Bridge hypothetical, he admitted: "Since that time I have repented, so that now, clad in sackcloth, I state frankly, that my point of view has changed. I agree, at this time, with the rule set forth in the Restatement. . . ." Book Review, 3 J.Legal Ed. 145 (1950).

Are there any objections to the "option contract" notion? May it not, in a rapidly fluctuating market, give the offeree an unfair chance to speculate during the time when the offeror is bound but the offeree is not? Judging from the kinds of situations in which the problem of the Brooklyn Bridge hypothetical actually arises, how great is this danger likely to be?

Would there be any advantage in limiting recovery by B in the Brooklyn Bridge hypothetical to damages based on his reliance rather than his expectation interest? See Fuller and Perdue, The Reliance Interest in Contract Damages:2, 46 Yale L.J. 373, 410–17 (1937).

(2) *Is Promise or Performance Invited?* The whole problem can be avoided, of course, if the offer invites a promise as acceptance and either a promise is given in so many words or one can be spelled out from the offeree's conduct. (Suppose, for example, that Mrs. Hodgkin's letter had read: "If you will agree to move to Lewiston and care for me on the home place. . . .") In Davis v. Jacoby, 1 Cal.2d 370, 34 P.2d 1026 (1934), the court held that an offer somewhat similar to that in Brackenbury v. Hodgkin invited a promise as acceptance, relying in part on the offeror's language: "Will you let me hear from you as soon as possible. . . ." In case of doubt, Restatement Second, § 31 gives the offeree an opportunity to treat the offer as inviting a promise as acceptance and thus to avoid Professor Wormser's agreement simply by giving his promise. Would such an opportunity have been of any advantage to the Brackenburys? What if Mrs. Hodgkin had died after they had sold their home and liquidated their business in Missouri and begun the journey to Maine?

Are there circumstances in which an offeree might find an offer that invites a promise as acceptance *less* appealing than one which invites performance as acceptance? Suppose that the offeree's risk of failure is considerable, e. g., that A is seeking to get B to climb a flagpole rather than cross the Brooklyn Bridge. (Consider also the offer of a reward as in Broadnax v. Ledbetter, p. 29 supra.) How might an offeror frame an offer to make it appealing to the offeree under circumstances involving *both* substantial preparation for performance by the offeree *and* considerable risk of failure on his part, e. g., calling for him to deliver a piece of technologically sophisticated equipment which he might not be able to develop according to the required specifications?

(3) *Brokers and the Brooklyn Bridge.* The reader whose sense of relevance requires an example from the world of business may prefer to look at these problems through the optic of the real estate broker. Suppose that an owner of real property lists the property with a broker under an exclusive sale arrangement, promising the broker a commission if he arranges a sale and promising not to sell it himself or through another broker. Is the owner liable if, after the broker has incurred expenses in attempting to procure a buyer, he terminates their relationship, or sells the property himself or through another broker? Is it significant that it is the broker who commonly provides the form for the listing agreement? How might he avoid this risk?

(4) *The Case of the Maleficent Mortgagee.* Pattberg held a mortgage on Petterson's house on which $5,450 was due. On April 4, he wrote Petterson: "I hereby agree to accept cash for the mortgage. . . . It is understood and agreed as a consideration that I will allow you $780 providing said mortgage is paid on or before May 31. . . ." Late in May Petterson knocked at Pattberg's door with the cash. Pattberg demanded the name of his caller. Petterson replied: "It is Mr. Petterson. I have come to pay off the mortgage." Pattberg then said he had sold the mortgage. Petterson was obliged to pay the full amount to the purchaser. His widow sued Pattberg for $780. From a judgment for the plaintiff the defendant appealed. *Held:* Reversed. "[I]t clearly appears that the defendant's offer was withdrawn before its acceptance had been tendered. It is unnecessary to determine, therefore, what the legal situation might have been had tender been made before withdrawal." Speaking for him-

self, the writer of the opinion, Kellogg, J., thought the result would be the same since "the act requested to be performed was the complete act of payment, a thing incapable of performance unless assented to by the person paid." Lehman, J., dissented. "In unmistakable terms the defendant agreed to accept payment. . . . I recognize that in this case only an offer of payment, and not a formal tender of payment was made. . . Even so, under the fair construction of the words of the letter, I think the plaintiff had done the act which the defendant requested as consideration for his promise. . . . A formal tender is seldom made in business transactions, except to lay the foundation for subsequent assertion in a court of justice of right which spring from refusal of the tender." Petterson v. Pattberg, 248 N.Y. 86, 161 N.E. 428 (1928).

In 1937 New York enacted a statute providing that a written and signed offer to accept a performance in satisfaction of a claim, followed by a tender of performance before revocation, shall not be denied effect by reason of refusal of the tender. N.Y.Gen.Obl.L. § 15–503. Would this statute affect the result in Petterson v. Pattberg? In the Brooklyn Bridge hypothetical?

DEATH OF AN OFFEROR

Restatement Second, § 48 sets out the generally accepted rule in this country that an offeree's power of acceptance is terminated by the offeror's death or supervening incapacity. Professor Corbin said of this rule that there is not "any compelling necessity for its existence. It may be said that you cannot contract with a dead man; but neither can you force a dead man to pay his debts contracted before his death. Yet the law has no difficulty, in the latter case, in creating legal relations with the dead man's personal representative, and there would be no greater difficulty in declaring the power of acceptance to survive as against the offeror's representative or in favor of the offeree's representative." Corbin, Offer and Acceptance, and Some of the Resulting Legal Relations, 26 Yale L.J. 169, 198 (1917), Selected Readings 170, 192 (1931).

Jordan v. Dobbins, 122 Mass. 168 (1877), illustrates the rule. In February Jordan, Marsh & Co. had Dobbins guarantee the prompt payment of all sums owed by Moore to Jordan, Marsh as a result of sales of merchandise that Jordan, Marsh might make to Moore. In August Dobbins died. From the following January through May Jordan, Marsh sold Moore merchandise in ignorance of Dobbins' death. When Moore did not pay, Jordan, Marsh sued Dobbins' estate. The Supreme Judicial Court of Massachusetts denied recovery. "The agreement which the guarantor makes with the person receiving the guaranty is not that I now become liable to you for anything, but that if you sell goods to a third person, I will then become liable to pay for them if such third person does not. . . . Such being the nature of a guaranty, we are of opinion that the death of the guarantor operates as a revocation of it, and that the person holding it cannot recover against his executor or administrator for goods sold after the death. . . . It is no hardship to require traders, whose business it is to deal in goods, to exercise diligence so far as to ascertain whether a person upon whose credit they are selling is living."

Under the original draft of the first Restatement, as written by Professor Williston and his advisers, the unknown death of the offeror did not revoke the offer, but the Council of the American Law Institute changed the rule. Professor Williston concluded that "though the amount of actual authority is not impressive, there is a very general opinion among lawyers that death, even though unknown, does revoke an offer and does revoke an agency," and it was vital that the Restatement rule for contracts coincide with that for agency. 3 Proceedings of the American Law Institute 198 (1925). The Restatement Second preserves the rule, admitting that it "seems to be a relic of the obsolete view that a contract requires a 'meeting of the minds,' and it is out of harmony with the modern doctrine that a manifestation of assent is effective without regard to actual mental assent. . . . In the absence of legislation, [however,] the rule remains in effect." Comment a to Restatement Second, § 48. Should the application of the rule be limited to situations in which the offeree has not relied on the assumed contract in ignorance of the fact of the offeror's death?

Legislation changing the rule has been adopted in India, where Section 6(4) of the Indian Contract Act provides that a revocable offer is revoked "by the death or insanity of the proposer, if the fact of his death or insanity comes to the knowledge of the acceptor before acceptance." Would you favor enactment of such a statute in your state? Why do you suppose one has not already been enacted?

Death or incapacity of the offeree has the same effect as that of the offeror under Restatement Second, § 48. The death or incapacity of the offeror does not terminate the offeree's power of acceptance under an option contract. Restatement Second, § 35A.

NOTE

Problem. You are a Philadelphia lawyer. A client, Benjamin Earle, comes to see you with the following story. "About four years ago I had a conversation with my aunt, Mary Dewitt, who lived in Massachusetts, and she said to me something like this, as best I can remember: 'Ben there are few left to come to my funeral. I have thought a great deal of you for coming to your uncle's funeral and bringing that large box of flowers in the terrible snowstorm we had, when our friends could not reach here from Boston, and you coming from Philadelphia. I want you to attend my funeral, Ben, if you outlive me, and I think you will, and I will pay all expenses and I will give you five thousand dollars. I want you to come.' I replied that I would come if I was living and if they informed me in time to get there and if I was able. We talked about it a little more on the occasion of my mother's funeral two years later. Aunt Mary died a few months ago and I went to Massachusetts for her funeral. Soon after the funeral, I received in the mail this paper, bearing the date of our conversation and signed by Aunt Mary." The paper reads, "If Benjamin A. Earle should come to my funeral, I order my executor to pay him the sum of five thousand dollars. Mary Dewitt." The executor has refused to pay and Mr. Earle wants to know whether he has a claim against the estate for $5,000 and his expenses. Advise him. Do you need more facts? How should those facts be elicited? Would it be well to begin by explaining some elementary contract law to Mr. Earle?[a] See Earle v. Angell, 157 Mass. 294, 32 N.E. 164 (1892).

The American Bar Association's Code of Professional Responsibility says, in Disciplinary Rule 7–102 (Representing a Client Within the Bounds of the Law), that a lawyer shall not "Participate in the creation . . . of evidence when he knows or it is obvious that the evidence is false." Ethical Consideration 7–6 adds: "Often a lawyer is asked to assist his client in developing evidence relevant to the state of mind of the client at a particular time. He may properly assist his client in the development and preservation of evidence of existing motive, intent, or desire; obviously, he may not do anything furthering the creation or preservation of false evidence. In many cases a lawyer may not be certain as to the state of mind of his client, and in those situations he should resolve reasonable doubts in favor of his client." Does this give you adequate guidance?

For a discussion of "whether it is proper to give your client legal advice when you have reason to believe that the knowledge you give him will tempt him to commit perjury," see Freedman, Professional Responsibility of the Criminal Defense Lawyer: The Three Hardest Questions, 64 Mich.L.Rev. 1469, 1478–82 (1966). According to the author: "If the lawyer is not certain what the facts are when he gives the advice, the problem is substantially minimized, if not eliminated. It is not the lawyer's function to prejudge his client as a perjurer. He cannot presume that the client will make unlawful use of his advice. . . . Before he begins to remember essential facts, the client is entitled to know what his own interests are." Do you agree? Or is there "a point . . . at which it becomes brute rationalization to claim that the legal advice tendered to a client is meant to contribute to wise and informed decision-making." Noonan, The Purposes of Advocacy and the Limits of Confidentiality, 64 Mich.L.Rev. 1485, 1488 (1966). If so, has that point been reached here?

LAPSE OF AN OFFER

After some period of time, an offer lapses. If no period is specified in the offer, it lapses after a reasonable time. What is a reasonable time depends, of course, on the circumstances. Take an offer to buy or sell. If the subject matter undergoes rapid fluctuation in price, as is often the case for goods, this will shorten the time. If the subject matter does not undergo rapid fluctuations in price, as is generally the case for land, this will lengthen the time. The following two cases illustrate some other factors used in determining what is a reasonable time for this purpose.

a. For an example from fiction, see Paul Biegler's interview of his client, Lieutenant Manion, in Traver, Anatomy of a Murder 44–47 (1958).

In Akers v. J. B. Sedberry, 39 Tenn.App. 633, 286 S.W.2d 617 (1955), Akers, while in a conference with his employer, Mrs. Sedberry, orally offered to resign. Mrs. Sedberry ignored his offer and continued the conference. A few days later she wired her acceptance. He sued for breach of contract, and a decree in his favor was affirmed. "Ordinarily, an offer made by one to another in a face to face conversation is deemed to continue only to the close of their conversation, and cannot be accepted thereafter." But cf. Caldwell v. E. F. Spears & Sons, 186 Ky. 64, 216 S.W. 83 (1919).

In Loring v. City of Boston, 7 Metc. (Mass.) 409 (1844), the City of Boston had run in the daily papers an advertisement offering a $1,000 reward for the apprehension and conviction of any person setting fire to any building within the city limits. The advertisements continued for about a week in May, 1837, and did not appear again. In January, 1841, there was a fire in Boston, and Loring, with the reward in mind, pursued the incendiary to New York, arrested him, returned him to Boston, had him indicted and prosecuted, produced evidence that convicted him, and then sued the city for the reward. There was evidence that fire alarms had been frequent before the advertisements but much less so from that time until the end of 1841. Loring sued to recover the reward. The Supreme Judicial Court of Massachusetts denied recovery. Since the purposes of such an offer are to excite the vigilance of the public and, perhaps, to alarm offenders, the offer of the reward must be notorious in order to be effective. Three years and eight months was not a reasonable time under the circumstances. "In that length of time, the exigency under which it was made having passed, it must be presumed to have been forgotten by most of the officers and citizens of the community, and cannot be presumed to have been before the public as an actuating motive to vigilance and exertion on this subject; nor could it justly and reasonably have been so understood by the plaintiffs." But cf. Carr v. Mahaska County Bankers Ass'n, 222 Iowa 411, 269 N.W. 494 (1936).

What is the effect of an expression of acceptance that arrives too late to operate as an acceptance? Can the offeror, if he chooses, simply disregard the delay and treat it as an acceptance? Or is it a counter-offer that must in turn be accepted by the original offeror in order to create a contract? See Restatement Second, § 73.

MINNEAPOLIS & ST. LOUIS RAILWAY CO. v. COLUMBUS ROLLING–MILL CO.

Supreme Court of the United States, 1886.
119 U.S. 149.·

This was an action by a railroad corporation established at Minneapolis in the State of Minnesota against a manufacturing corporation established at Columbus in the State of Ohio. The petition alleged that on December 19, 1879, the parties made a contract by which the plaintiff agreed to buy of the defendant, and the defendant sold to the plaintiff, two thousand tons of iron rails of the weight of fifty pounds per yard, at the price of fifty-four dollars per ton gross, to be delivered free on board cars at the defendant's rolling mill in the month of March, 1880, and to be paid for by the plaintiff in cash when so delivered. The answer denied the making of the contract. It was admitted at the trial that the following letters and telegrams were sent at their dates, and were received in due course, by the parties, through their agents.

December 5, 1879. Letter from plaintiff to defendant: "Please quote me prices for 500 to 3,000 tons 50 lb. steel rails, and for 2,000 to 5,000 tons 50 lb. iron rails, March 1880 delivery."

December 8, 1879. Letter from defendant to plaintiff: "Your favor of the 5th inst. at hand. We do not make steel rails. For iron rails, we will sell 2,000 to 5,000 tons of 50 lb. rails for fifty-four ($54.00) dollars per gross ton for spot cash, F.O.B. cars at our mill, March delivery, subject as follows: In case of strike among our workmen, destruction of or serious damage to our works by fire or the elements, or any causes of delay beyond our control, we shall not be held accountable in damages. If our offer is accepted, shall expect to be notified of same prior to Dec. 20th, 1879."

December 16, 1879. Telegram from plaintiff to defendant: "Please enter our order for twelve hundred tons rails, March delivery, as per your favor of the eighth. Please reply."

December 16, 1879. Letter from plaintiff to defendant: Yours of the 8th came duly to hand. I telegraphed you to-day to enter our order for twelve hundred (1,200) tons 50 lb. iron rails for next March delivery, at fifty-four dollars ($54.00) F.O.B. cars at your mill. Please send contract. Also please send me templet of your 50 lb. rail. Do you make splices? If so, give me prices for splices for this lot of iron."

December 18, 1879. Telegram from defendant to plaintiff, received same day: "We cannot book your order at present at that price."

December 19, 1879. Telegram from plaintiff to defendant: "Please enter an order for two thousand tons rails, as per your letter of the sixth. Please forward written contract. Reply." (The word "sixth" was admitted to be a mistake for "eighth.")

December 22, 1879. Telegram from plaintiff to defendant: "Did you enter my order for two thousand tons rails, as per my telegram of December nineteenth? Answer."

After repeated similar inquiries by the plaintiff, the defendant, on January 19, 1880, denied the existence of any contract between the parties.

The jury returned a verdict for the defendant, under instructions which need not be particularly stated; and the plaintiff alleged exceptions, and sued out this writ of error.

MR. JUSTICE GRAY, after making the foregoing statement of the case delivered the opinion of the court.

The rules of law which govern this case are well settled. As no contract is complete without the mutual assent of the parties, an offer to sell imposes no obligation until it is accepted according to its terms. So long as the offer has been neither accepted nor rejected, the negotiation remains open, and imposes no obligation upon either party; the one may decline to accept, or the other may withdraw his offer; and either rejection or withdrawal leaves the matter as if no offer had ever been made. A proposal to accept, or an acceptance, upon terms varying from those offered, is a rejection of the offer, and puts an end to the negotiation, unless the party who made the original offer renews it, or assents to the modification suggested. The other party having once rejected the offer, cannot afterwards revive it by tendering an acceptance of it. . . . If the offer does not limit the time for its acceptance, it must be accepted within a reasonable time. If it does, it may, at any time within the limit and so long as it remains open, be accepted or rejected by the party to whom, or be withdrawn by the party by whom, it was made. . . .

The defendant, by the letter of December 8, offered to sell to the plaintiff two thousand to five thousand tons of iron rails on certain terms specified, and added that if the offer was accepted the defendant would expect to be notified prior to December 20. This offer, while it remained open, without having been rejected by the plaintiff or revoked by the defendant, would authorize the plaintiff to take at his election any number of tons not less than two thousand nor more than five thousand, on the terms specified. The offer, while unrevoked, might be accepted, or rejected by the plaintiff at any time before December 20. Instead of accepting the offer made, the plaintiff, on December 16, by telegram and letter, referring to the defendant's letter of December 8, directed the defendant to enter an order for twelve hundred tons on the same terms. The mention, in both telegram and letter, of the date and the terms of the defendant's original offer, shows that the plaintiff's order was not an independent proposal, but an answer to the defendant's offer, a qualified acceptance of that offer, varying the number of tons, and therefore in law a rejection of the offer. On December 18, the defendant by telegram declined to fulfil the plaintiff's order. The negotiation between the parties was thus closed, and the plaintiff could not afterwards fall back on the defendant's original offer. The plaintiff's attempt to do so, by the telegram of December 19, was therefore ineffectual and created no rights against the defendant.

Such being the legal effect of what passed in writing between the parties, it is unnecessary to consider whether, upon a fair interpretation of the instructions of the court, the question whether the plaintiff's telegram and letter of December 16 constituted a rejection of the defendant's offer of December 8 was ruled in favor of the defendant as a matter of law, or was submitted to the jury as a question of fact. The submission of a question of law to the jury is no ground of exception if they decide it aright. Pence v. Langdon, 99 U.S. 578, 25 L.Ed. 420. .   .   .

Judgment affirmed.

NOTES

(1) *Drafting.* Can you draft a telegram for the railroad, in answer to the rolling mill's letter of December 8, that would have been an offer to buy 1,200 tons of rails but not a rejection of the rolling mill's offer? See Restatement Second, §§ 37, 38.

(2) *Problem.* Suppose that the rolling mill's telegram of December 18 had read: "Cannot reduce quantity. We cannot book your order at present at that price." Would the result in the case have been the same? See Livingstone v. Evans, [1925] 4 D.L.R. 769 (Alberta Sup.Ct.).

SECTION 4. SOME TROUBLE SPOTS IN THE BARGAINING PROCESS

The three preceding sections have examined the basic rules that govern the agreement process. This section looks into four particularly troublesome sorts of problems, with special attention to the context in which they are apt to arise.

(a) Mistake: General Contractors

AMERICAN INSTITUTE OF ARCHITECTS, HANDBOOK OF ARCHITECTURAL PRACTICE III 7.02–7.03 (1958).[a] Under the

a. Reprinted by permission of The American Institute of Architects.   Further reproduction is not authorized.

system of competitive bidding *on private work* each contractor *invited* submits a proposal to execute the work for a definite sum. The list of bidders is subject to the control of owner and architect and can be as limited or open as they may desire. For *public work* any contractor may bid provided he has met prequalification requirements; and can furnish either a certified check in the amount specified or a bidder's bond to guarantee his acceptance of and ability to perform the contract if it is awarded him. Competitive bidding at first sight appears to have every advantage. The owner has before him proposals, the desirability of which would seem to be in inverse ratio to their amount. If the list of eligible bidders has been carefully screened he is in position to make the award because the bidders are of approximately equal responsibility and competence. If such screening has not been done, the best builder of a given locality may be pitted against the worst, and the lowest figure is apt to outweigh in the owner's mind the less obvious advantages afforded by the more competent bidder. For public work the law requires an award to the "lowest responsible bidder." [b] This is a condition scarcely capable of exact definition, but it leaves the awarding authority slight chance in court if an award is made to other than the low bidder. Thus the award is not always made to the best and most capable of the bidders.

In competitive bidding each contractor concentrates his effort to keep the price down. This reacts to the benefit of the owner and assures a reasonable and economical purchasing price. This is particularly true of those parts of the work which are performed by the contractor's own forces. For the remainder of the work a *general contractor* must depend upon *subcontractors* whose number varies directly with the complexity and diversity of the work to be bid upon. The *general contractor* invites a number of *subcontractors* to bid to him on the various branches of the work. Normally he has previously done business with most of them or knows their reputations. If he uses their bids in making up his own bid and he is the successful bidder, he is expected to award the subcontracts to those whose bids he has used. The architect may exercise some control over the selection of subcontractors by requiring evidence of their experience, reputation and financial responsibility. . . .

Unless care has been taken to include in the invitation only the *general contractors* with skill, responsibility and integrity, the lowest bid may come from a contractor who does not inquire closely into the honesty or competence of the lowest subbidders, or who discounts their bids in the hope that if awarded the contract, he can shop around

b. For example, subject to specific exceptions, contracts for military procurement under the Armed Services Procurement Act of 1947 "shall be made by formal advertising in all cases in which the use of such method is feasible and practicable under the existing conditions and circumstances." 10 U.S.C.A. § 2304(a). "Awards shall be made with reasonable promptness by giving written notice to the responsible bidder whose bid conforms to the invitation and will be the most advantageous to the United States, price and other factors considered." 10 U.S.C.A. § 2305(c).

among the subbidders and secure a lower price. Such contractors have little interest in the work and their selection increases the burden of the architect by drawing him into difficulties with incompetent *subcontractors* who are operating at a loss. Such results of competitive bidding from unselected and unscreened lists of *general contractors* are detrimental to the best interests of the owner. Fortunately this type of *general contractor* is becoming less common, and for involved and specialized building construction, contractors who are responsible trained engineers and business administrators are essential.

There are several ways by which an owner, unless compelled to advertise for bids, may avoid some of these difficulties of the competitive system:

(a) He may, with the advice of his architect, confine his list of bidders to the most reputable and competent. He should be made to see the importance of a well-chosen list, and be warned against offering a chance to bid to any indifferently qualified contractor in the hope that his bid will not be the lowest. He should be made to understand that the architect can not by supervision force a contractor to build properly, or better than he is able to. When bids are restricted to qualified contractors, the award should be to the lowest bidder.

(b) He may emphasize the clauses in instructions to bidders stating that "in the award of the contract not only the amount of the bid but the reputation and competence of the bidder will be taken into consideration," and that "the owner reserves the right to accept or reject any or all bids." Thus, without a restricted list, the obligation to award the work to the low bidder does not apply.

(c) He may reserve some of the more important branches of the work to be bid upon separately. . . .

(d) He may carry on the whole work under the separate contract system . . . thus attempting through his architect, to perform many of the expert duties of the *general contractor*.

(e) He may avoid the competitive system altogether and let his contract by the "Cost-plus-fee" system as explained below. Both architect and owner should recognize the considerable service of the bidders in estimating the construction cost of a project, and should not reject all bids and proceed to build by means of the separate contract system or by the direct employment of labor and purchase of materials.

NOTES

(1) *"Bid Shopping."* The preceding exerpt suggests the possibility that the general contractor may "shop around among the subbidders and secure a lower price." The construction industry regards such "bid shopping" with opprobrium, whether it occurs before or after the award.[c] Sub-

---

c. The Code of Ethical Conduct of the Association General Contractors of America provides that with respect to subcontractors: "The figures of one

contractors regard it with particular distaste when it occurs after the successful general contractor's bargaining position has been strengthened by the award.

It is objected, on the one hand, that bid shopping results in an undesirable decrease in competition, because subcontractors will pad their bids so that they can lower them later when bid shopping occurs, inflating the general contractor's bid to the ultimate disadvantage of the owner. Is this objection convincing if, as the exerpt suggests, there is a countervailing tendency among general contractors to discount their estimates on subcontractor's bids in anticipation of bid shopping?

It is objected, on the other hand, that bid shopping results in an undesirable increase in competition—that subcontractors will be driven to bid so low that they will be "operating at a loss" and tempted to use substandard work and materials, again to the ultimate disadvantage of the owner. Is this risk greater in the construction industry than in other areas of the economy?

The owner may combat post-award bid shopping by requiring that general contractors list their prospective subcontractors in their bids. This requirement is more common, however, in government than in private contracts. Why do not more private owners require listing if bid shopping is to their ultimate disadvantage? Subcontractors, whose self-interest is clearer, have attempted to combat bid shopping by organizing themselves into "bid depositories," although such concerted efforts raise serious problems under the anti-trust law. See, e. g., Mechanical Contractors Bid Depository v. Christiansen, 352 F.2d 817 (10th Cir. 1965), cert. denied, 384 U.S. 918 (1966). They have also tried to combat pre-award bid shopping by waiting until the last possible moment to submit their bids. The resulting haste with which the general contractor must then prepare his own bid may, of course, cause him to make the kinds of errors that gave rise to the next two cases. For more background, see Schultz, The Firm Offer Puzzle: A Study of Business Practice in the Construction Industry, 19 U.Chi.L.Rev. 237 (1952), an illuminating study of bidding practices in the construction industry in Indiana, based on questionaires returned by eighty general contractors and ninety-three subcontractors. For a similar survey in Virginia, see Note, 53 Va.L.Rev. 1720 (1967). See also Schueller, Bid Depositories, 58 Mich.L.Rev. 497 (1960); Notes, 18 U.C.L.A.L.Rev. 389 (1970); 39 N.Y. U.L.Rev. 816 (1964).

(2) *Offer or Not?* Is the owner's invitation for bids or the contractor's bid the offer? By analogy to the rule as to auctions, the contractor's bid is the offer. See Note 2, p. 77 supra. But it is possible to word the invitation so as to make it an offer. In Jenkins Towel Service v. Fidelity-Philadelphia Trust Co., 400 Pa. 98, 161 A.2d 334 (1960), the Su-

competitor shall not be made known to another before the award of the subcontract, nor should they be used by the contractor to secure a lower proposal from another bidder."
The counterpart of "bid shopping," sometimes known as "bid peddling," occurs when subcontractors approach the successful general contractor, after the award, and make lower offers. On the confused use of these terms, see Christiansen v. Mechanical Contractors Bid Depository, 230 F.Supp. 186, 190 n. 10 (D.C.Utah 1964), affirmed in the opinion cited in the text below.

preme Court of Pennsylvania concluded that the following letter from a trustee of real estate was an offer:

> We wish to acknowledge your letter   . . .   submitting an offer for the purchase of the group of properties . . . . As you already know, several offers have been submitted for the purchase of these properties which offers are approximately of the same amount and on the same terms and conditions. . . . In order to give each and every prospect an equal chance and in order to secure the highest and best price . . . it has been decided to ask for sealed bids from all interested parties. It is suggested, therefore, that you forward to this office on or before Wednesday, June 24, 1959, your highest offer for the properties. At that time the bids will be opened and an Agreement of Sale tendered to the highest acceptable bidder provided the offer is in excess of $92,000. cash. [The letter also contained details as to the bid deposit and a provision on broker's commissions to be included in the Agreement of Sale.] The Trustees of course, reserve the right to approve of any and all offers, or to withdraw the properties from the market.

What language from the letter would you rely on in arguing that it was not an offer? What authorities from this chapter would you cite in support of your argument?

CRENSHAW COUNTY HOSPITAL BOARD v. ST. PAUL FIRE & MARINE INSURANCE CO.

United States Court of Appeals, Fifth Circuit, 1969.
411 F.2d 213.

AINSWORTH, CIRCUIT JUDGE. This appeal is from a judgment in the amount of $10,000 (the maximum amount recoverable under a bid bond) in favor of Crenshaw County Hospital Board, a participant in federal Hill-Burton funds, for damages sustained by it as the result of appellant's alleged breach of the bond conditions. The bond, furnished by appellant St. Paul Fire and Marine Insurance Company as surety for Waller Construction Company, provided for payment to the Hospital Board in the event of a contract award to, and subsequent failure to perform by, its principal.[a]

The Hospital Board advertised for public bids in connection with certain construction work. The bid invitation announced that the lowest bid made by a responsible bidder would be accepted, and restricted withdrawal of bids for a period of thirty days after their having been opened. Waller Construction Company submitted its bid in the sum of $285,837.50. The bid opening was attended by W. A. Waller, one of

---

a. The standard form of bid bond promulgated by the American Institute of Architects obligates the surety to pay "the difference not to exceed the penalty hereof [i. e., the amount of the bond] between the amount specified in said bid and such larger amount for which the Obligee may in good faith contract with another party to perform the Work covered by said bid."

the partners of the construction company. Waller's bid, which was $24,793.50 below the next bid, was announced by the Board to be the low bid. Two Board resolutions were passed accepting the bid of Waller and awarding to it the construction contract. On the following day these resolutions were signed by the Board Chairman and mailed to Waller. In the interim, Mr. Waller discovered that a $35,000 error had been made in the amount of the bid offer as the result of an inadvertent clerical mistake. He informed the Chairman of the Hospital Board of the error that same evening by telephone, requesting that his offer be rejected, and confirmed this by letter the following day. The Hospital Board considered Waller's request but later declined it upon advice of the Director in charge of allocating Hill-Burton funds in Alabama that the Federal Government could furnish a pro rata of the construction cost on the basis of the lowest bid only. Consequently, the Board declined to release Waller from its offer. Waller failed to perform, and the contract was awarded to the next low bidder. The Board then initiated this action against Waller's surety for breach of contract, claiming the difference between the amount shown in the Waller bid and the higher amount it was obliged to pay as a result of Waller's failure to perform, subject to the limitation contained in the bond of $10,000.

Although the District Court specifically found that the bid was entered into in good faith, that the error was inadvertent, committed without gross negligence, and promptly communicated to the Board, it nevertheless held that there was a breach of contract. We affirm.

At the trial the insurance company argued that Waller's request to be excused from the contract was not tantamount to rejecting the contract and that the company stood ready to perform once the formal contract was tendered. The District Court rejected this contention, however, and found that Mr. Waller's conduct and remarks to the Board Chairman that the company "was not able to do, and could not do, the construction for the price of the bid which it had submitted" constituted a breach of the conditions of the bond sued on, which breach was subsequent to acceptance by the Hospital Board of the Waller bid.

The resolution adopted by the Board on the day of the bid opening states in pertinent part:

"BE IT FURTHER RESOLVED THAT, Mr. S. T. Windham is hereby authorized to execute said contract after final approval of the project by the State Board of Health and the U. S. Public Health Service and upon official notification thereof from the Bureau of Health Facilities Construction, Alabama State Department of Public Health."

Appellant contends that there was no binding contract inasmuch as acceptance by the Hospital Board of Waller's bid was conditional only, acceptance thereof being predicated upon final approval of the public health agencies, which approval was not forthcoming until approximately three weeks subsequent to Waller's alleged refusal to perform. Appellant urges, as it did at the trial, that under these circumstances the case is controlled by our holding in Peerless Casualty Company v. Housing Authority, 5 Cir., 1955, 228 F.2d 376. the District Court found the *Peerless* case to be inapposite. We agree with the District Court's analysis in distinguishing the two sets of fact.

In *Peerless*, starting with the common law premise that "an offer may be withdrawn at any time before it is accepted," thus aborting the creation of a binding contract, we held that a condition of approval of the Public Housing Administration which was annexed by an offeree to its attempted acceptance had the effect of delaying that acceptance, and that the withdrawal of the offer prevented a subsequent attempted acceptance from creating a contract. Id. at 378, 379. In *Peerless*, a bid bond for construction work had been entered into between Ivey, a building contractor, and its surety Peerless Casualty Company. The Housing Authority of Hazelhurst, Georgia, advertised for bids and stipulated therein that no bid was to be withdrawn without its consent for a period of thirty days subsequent to the opening of bids. Ivey's bid was low, and a motion was adopted by the local Authority to accept the bid. On the same night a clerical mistake was discovered by Ivey which had resulted in the submission of a bid lower than intended. On the following day he sent a telegram to the local Authority advising of the error. There, however, the factual similarity between the two cases ends. In reversing a verdict directed in favor of the Housing Authority, we found that there was no enforceable contract because *acceptance of the bid* was subject to approval of another agency. The resolution was to award the contract to Ivey "subject to the approval of the Public Housing Administration," which agency subsequently approved the acceptance.

In the instant case, the bid was unconditionally accepted by the Board. Subsequent approval by the other agencies of the *"project"* was a formality insofar as the contract between the parties was concerned.

We are not persuaded by appellant's "equitable" defense based on the District Court's findings of good faith and a promptly communicated, inadvertent error committed without gross negligence. While it is true that Alabama recognizes an equitable exception to the general rule that a unilateral error does not avoid a contract, where excessive hardships flow to the party responsible for an error, nevertheless, rescission based on such a mistake may be had only where no prejudice results to the other party. Ex Parte Perusini Const. Co., 1942, 242 Ala. 632, 7 So.2d 576, 578. A review of the evidence substantiates the District Court's finding that Waller's failure to perform in accordance with its bid resulted in damage to the Hospital Board in at least the amount sued for. Equity will also step in where a party through mistake names a consideration entirely disproportionate to the value of the subject involved and the other party is cognizant of the mistake. Townsend v. McCall, 1955, 262 Ala. 554, 80 So.2d 262, 266; Board of Water & Sewer Com'rs of City of Mobile v. Spriggs, 1962, 274 Ala. 155, 146 So.2d 872, 876. The consideration named by Waller was not out of all proportion to the value of the subject. It was $27,000 in excess of the projected cost of the job. An expert who had supervised more than three hundred hospital projects testified that there was not an unusual disparity between the Waller bid and the next lowest bid.[1] Also it appears that Waller had figured $25,000 profit in the job and that some of the subcontractors had offered to cut their prices to help him out of his difficulty. Thus to enforce the contract as made was not unconscionable. Townsend v. McCall, supra; Board of Water & Sewer Com'rs of City of Mobile v. Spriggs, supra; Ex Parte Perusini Const. Co., supra.

Affirmed.

NOTES

(1) *Knowledge of Mistake.* If the offeree knows or has reason to know of the offeror's material mistake when he accepts, the offeror is not bound. "One cannot snap up an offer or bid knowing that it was made in mistake." Tyra v. Cheney, 129 Minn. 428, 152 N.W. 835 (1915). Difficulty arises when the offeror claims that the magnitude of the mistake was such that it should have been apparent from the face of the offer.

Heifetz Metal Crafts, Inc. v. Peter Kiewit Sons' Co., 264 F.2d 435 (8th Cir. 1959), is a good example. There Kiewit was preparing a bid for the construction of a hospital and Heifetz offered to do the kitchen work for $99,500, $52,000 less than Kiewit's next lowest quotation. Kiewit lowered his bid by $52,000, which made it $17,942,200, the lowest by $9,000. After Kiewit was awarded the contract and had accepted the Heifetz offer, Heifetz discovered that in preparing its quotation it had overlooked some subsidiary kitchen installations required by the plans. It sought rescission and argued that since its quotation was one-third less than the next lowest, Kiewit should have realized that there had been a mistake. The court rejected this contention and held that the contract was enforceable. It relied upon testimony by Kiewit's employees that they were ignorant of the mistake, upon Kiewit's lack of familiarity with the kitchen equipment field, and upon "testimony indicating that at times some contractor would have a special reason for desiring to obtain a particular job and would submit a figure controlled by that consideration." It noted that "the figures submitted by subcontractors on the electrical work for the project has varied from $1,400,000 to $1,850,000 and on the lathing and plastering work from $672,000 to $1,028,000; and the 'mechanical spread' had been between $3,647,000 and $6,000,000."

For a case holding that a bid of $7,751.51 for a government surplus lathe was not so out of line as to create a "suspicion of error," where the

1. Compare Townsend v. McCall, 1955, 262 Ala. 554, 80 So.2d 262, in which the estimated cost of the project was $350,000, the bid of the contractor claiming justifiable mistake was $183,000 and the next lowest bid was $356,000.

other bids were $3,441, $2,429.99, $1,511 and $288, see Wender Presses v. United States, 343 F.2d 961 (Ct.Cl.1965).

Is it of any significance that a general contractor will sometimes pass over a low bid to accept one from a subcontractor with which he has a personal or business connection, and that subcontractors sometimes deliberately make losing bids to break up such combinations? Is it of any significance that subcontractors sometimes bid low in the expectation that changes will later be made to provide for profitable extra work?

In the rare case were the offeree not only knows or has reason to know that the offeror has made a mistake, but knows or has reason to know exactly what the mistake is (as where a decimal point has been misplaced), can the offeror hold the offeree, who has "snapped up" his offer, to a contract on the terms that the offer *would* have contained had the mistake not been made? Would the offeror be in a better position to make this argument in the unlikely event that the mistake was not discovered until performance had proceeded so far that rescission was no longer possible? For such a rare case in which the court gave an affirmative answer, see Chernick v. United States, 372 F.2d 492 (Ct.Cl.1967).

(2) *Problem.* Lee Calan Imports instructed the Chicago Sun-Times to advertise a used Volvo for sale at $1,795. The Sun-Times, by mistake, advertised it for $1,095. O'Brien went to look at the car and said that he wanted to buy it for $1,095. The salesman refused to sell it at the erroneous price. Is Lee Calan liable to O'Brien? Is the Sun-Times liable to Lee Calan? See O'Keefe v. Lee Calan Imports, 128 Ill.App.2d 410, 262 N.E.2d 758 (1970).

M. F. KEMPER CONSTRUCTION CO. v. CITY OF LOS ANGELES

Supreme Court of California, 1951.
37 Cal.2d 696, 235 P.2d 7.

GIBSON, CHIEF JUSTICE. M. F. Kemper Construction Company brought this action against the City of Los Angeles to cancel a bid it had submitted on public construction work and to obtain discharge of its bid bond. The city cross-complained for forfeiture of the bond and for damages. The trial court cancelled the bid, discharged the bond, and allowed appellant city nothing on its cross-complaint. The sole issue is whether the company is entitled to relief on the ground of unilateral mistake.

On July 28, 1948, the city Board of Public Works published a notice inviting bids for the construction of the general piping system for the Hyperion sewer project. Pursuant to the city charter, the notice provided that each bid must be accompanied by a certified check or surety bond for an amount not less than 10% of the sum of the bid "as a guarantee that the bidder will enter into the proposed contract if it is awarded to him," and that the bond or check and the proceeds thereof "will become the property of the city of Los Angeles, if the bidder fails or refuses to execute the required contract . . . ." [1] The charter provides: "After bids have been opened and declared, except with the consent of the officer, board or City Council having jurisdiction over the bidding, no bid shall be withdrawn, but the same shall be subject to acceptance by the city for a period of three months . . . ." Sec. 386(d). The notice inviting bids reserved to the board the right to reject any and all bids, and both it and the official bid form stated that bidders "will not be released on account of errors."

Respondent company learned of the invitation for bids on August 17 and immediately began to prepare its proposal. Over a thousand different items were involved in the estimates. The actual computations were performed by three men, each of whom calculated the costs of different parts of the work, and in order to complete their estimates, they all worked until 2:00 o'clock on the morning of the day the bids were to be opened. Their final effort required the addition and transportation of the figures arrived at by each man for his portion of the work from his "work sheet" to a "final accumulation sheet" from which the total amount of the bid was taken. One item estimated on a work sheet in the amount of $301,769 was inadvertently omitted from the final accumulation sheet and was overlooked in computing the total amount of the bid. The error was caused by the fact that the men were exhausted after working long hours under pressure. When the bids were opened on August 25, it was found that respondent company's bid was $780,305 and the bids of the other three contractors were $1,049,592, $1,183,000 and $1,278,895.

The company discovered its error several hours after the bids were opened and immediately notified a member of the board of its mistake in omitting one item while preparing the final accumulation of figures for its bid. On August 27 the company explained its mistake to the board and withdrew its bid. A few days later, at the board's invitation, it submitted evidence which showed the unintentional omission of the $301,769 item. The board, however, passed a resolution accepting the erroneous bid of $780,305, and the company refused to enter into a written contract at that figure. On October 15, 1948, without readvertising, the board awarded the contract to the next lowest bidder. The city then demanded forfeiture of the Kemper Company's bond, and the company commenced the present action to cancel its bid and obtain discharge of the bond.

1. Section 386(d) of the Charter of the City of Los Angeles provides in part that every bid shall be accompanied by a certified check or surety bond for an amount not less than ten per cent of the aggregate sum of the bid "guaranteeing that the bidder will enter into the proposed contract if the same be awarded to him." Section 386(i) provides, "If the successful bidder fails to enter into the contract awarded him . . . within ten days after the award, then the sum posted in cash or by certified check or guaranteed by the bid bond is forfeited to the city. Such forfeiture shall not preclude recovery of any sum over and above the amount posted or guaranteed to which the city sustains damage by reason of such default or failure to contract . . . ."

The trial court found that the bid had been submitted as the result of an excusable and honest mistake of a material and fundamental character, that the company had not been negligent in preparing the proposal, that it had acted promptly to notify the board of the mistake and to rescind the bid, and that the board had accepted the bid with knowledge of the error. The court further found and concluded that it would be unconscionable to require the company to perform for the amount of the bid, that no intervening rights had accrued, and that the city had suffered no damage or prejudice.

Once opened and declared, the company's bid was in the nature of an irrevocable option, a contract right of which the city could not be deprived without its consent unless the requirements for rescission were satisfied. . . . The company seeks to enforce rescission of its bid on the ground of mistake. See Civ.Code, § 1689.[a] The city contends that a party is entitled to relief on that ground only where the mistake is mutual, and it points to the fact that the mistake in the bid submitted was wholly unilateral. See Rest., Contracts § 503; Rest., Restitution, § 12; 5 Williston on Contracts [1937] § 1579. However, the city had actual notice of the error in the estimates before it attempted to accept the bid, and knowledge by one party that the other is acting under mistake is treated as equivalent to mutual mistake for purposes of rescission. . . . Relief from mistaken bids is consistently allowed where one party knows or has reason to know of the other's error and the requirements for rescission are fulfilled. . . .

Rescission may be had for mistake of fact if the mistake is material to the contract and was not the result of neglect of a legal duty, if enforcement of the contract as made would be unconscionable, and if the other party can be placed in statu quo. See Civ.Code, §§ 1577, 3406, 3407, 1689, 1691; . . . In addition, the party seeking relief must give prompt notice of his election to rescind and must restore or offer to restore to the other party everything of value which he has received under the contract. Civ.Code, § 1691; . . .

Omission of the $301,769 item from the company's bid was, of course, a material mistake. The city claims that the company is barred from relief because it was negligent in preparing the estimates, but even if we assume that the error was due to some carelessness, it does not follow that the company is without remedy. Civil Code section 1577, which defines mistake of fact for which relief may be allowed, describes it as one not caused by "the neglect of a legal duty"

a. Although the opinion makes frequent reference to the provisions of the California Civil Code on mistake, the analysis is not dissimilar to that in cases from other jurisdictions, as the citations in the paragraph after the next, and others which have been omitted suggest. Your editors have included the opinion in this case because it figures in the opinion of the same court in the Drennan case, p. 159 infra, and because it has been particularly influential in other jurisdictions. See, e. g., Boise Junior College District v. Mattefs Construction Co., 92 Idaho 757, 450 P.2d 604 (1969); Smith & Lowe Construction Co. v. Herrera, 79 N.M. 239, 442 P.2d 197 (1968).

on the part of the person making the mistake. It has been recognized numerous times that not all carelessness constitutes a "neglect of a legal duty" within the meaning of the section. . . . On facts very similar to those in the present case, courts of other jurisdictions have stated that there was no culpable negligence and have granted relief from erroneous bids. See Conduit & Foundation Corporation v. Atlantic City, 2 N.J.Super. 433, 64 A.2d 382; School District of Scottsbluff v. Olson Const. Co., 153 Neb. 451, 45 N.W.2d 164; Board of Regents v. Cole, 209 Ky. 761, 273 S.W. 508; Geremia v. Boyarsky, 107 Conn. 387, 140 A. 749; Barlow v. Jones, N.J., 87 A. 649; W. F. Martens & Co. v. City of Syracuse, 183 App.Div. 622, 171 N.Y.S. 87; R. O. Bromagin & Co. v. City of Bloomington, 234 Ill. 114, 84 N.E. 700; Board of School Com'rs v. Bender, 36 Ind.App. 164, 72 N.E. 154; Moffett, Hodgkins & Clarke Co. v. City of Rochester, 178 U.S. 373, 20 S.Ct. 957, 44 L.Ed. 1108; see 59 A.L.R. at 818–824; cf. Steinmeyer v. Schroeppel, 226 Ill. 9, 80 N.E. 564, 10 L.R.A.,N.S., 114. The type of error here involved is one which will sometimes occur in the conduct of reasonable and cautious businessmen, and, under all the circumstances, we cannot say as a matter of law that it constituted a neglect of legal duty such as would bar the right to equitable relief.

The evidence clearly supports the conclusion that it would be unconscionable to hold the company to its bid at the mistaken figure. The city had knowledge before the bid was accepted that the company had made a clerical error which resulted in the omission of an item amounting to nearly one-third of the amount intended to be bid, and, under all the circumstances, it appears that it would be unjust and unfair to permit the city to take advantage of the company's mistake. There is no reason for denying relief on the ground that the city cannot be restored to status quo. It had ample time in which to award the contract without readvertising, the contract was actually awarded to the next lowest bidder, and the city will not be heard to complain that it cannot be placed in statu quo because it will not have the benefit of an inequitable bargain. . . . Finally, the company gave notice promptly upon discovering the facts entitling it to rescind, and no offer of restoration was necessary because it had received nothing of value which it could restore. . . . We are satisfied that all the requirements for rescission have been met.

The city nevertheless contends that the company is precluded from relief because of the statement in the invitation and in the official bid form that bidders "will not be released on account of errors," and that this language required all contractors to warrant the accuracy of their bids and to waive all rights to seek relief for clerical mistake. There is a difference between mere mechanical or clerical errors made in tabulating or transcribing figures and errors of judgment, as, for example, underestimating the cost of labor or materials. The distinction between the two types of error is recognized in the cases allowing rescission and in the procedures provided by the state and federal governments for relieving contractors from mistakes in bids on public work. . . . Generally, relief is refused for error in judgment and allowed only for clerical or mathematical mistakes. . . . Where a person is denied relief because of an error in judgment, the agreement which is enforced is the one he intended to make, whereas if he is denied relief from a clerical error, he is forced to perform an agreement he had no intention of making. The statement in the bid form in the present case can be given effect by interpreting it as relating to errors of judgment as distinguished from clerical mistakes. If we were to give the language the sweeping construction contended for by the city, it would mean holding that the contractor intended to assume the risk of a clerical error no matter in what circumstances it might occur or how serious it might be. Such interpretation is contrary to common sense and ordinary business understanding and would result in the loss of heretofore well-established equitable rights to relief from certain types of mistake.

The city also argues that public interest precludes any right to rescind for mistake, and in this connection it asserts that a literal interpretation should be given to the provision in section 386(d) of the charter that "After bids have been opened and declared, except with the consent of the officer, board or City Council having jurisdiction over the bidding, no bid shall be withdrawn . . . ." As we have seen, such a bid is in the nature of an irrevocable offer or option, but the offer is subject to rescission upon proper equitable grounds, and the cases recognize no distinction between public and private contracts with regard to the right of equitable relief. . . .

There is no merit in the city's contention that, even assuming the company is entitled to cancellation of the bid and is not liable for breach of contract, the bid bond should nevertheless be enforced because the company failed to enter into a written contract. It is argued that forfeiture of the bond is provided for by charter and that equity cannot relieve from a statutory forfeiture. We do not agree however that the city charter should be construed as requiring forfeiture of bid bonds in situations where the bidder has a legal excuse for refusing to enter into a formal written contract. Under such circumstances the contingency which would give rise to a forfeiture has not occurred. . . .

The judgment is affirmed.

SHENK, EDMONDS, TRAYNOR and SCHAUER, JJ., concur.

CARTER, JUSTICE. I dissent.

The majority opinion is based upon two grounds: (1) That a bidder on a public construction job may rescind his bid for unilateral mistake after it is opened and thus escape the forfeiture provided by statute; (2) That the clause in the invitation for bids and the bid, that bidders "will not be released on account of errors" does not apply to clerical errors, and, therefore, is not applicable in the instant case. I do not agree with either premise.

The first violates one of the obvious and fundamental principles of the law of rescission for unilateral mistake, that is, that the one against whom rescission is sought *must have had knowledge of the mistake before a binding contract is made.* . . . The contract to be rescinded is a contract to make a contract to perform the work, that is, the irrevocable bid, the performance of which is guaranteed by the bid bond. At the time the bids were opened the city had no knowledge and had no means of knowing that the bidder had made a mistake. There is nothing left therefore but a naked unilateral mistake which is not ground for rescission. . . . The proof of whether or not he has made such a mistake is so completely within his control and power that the public body is helpless to refute it. Charter provisions, invitation for bids, and the forfeiture provisions, such as those here involved, are made wholly meaningless, for in practically every case the reason the bidder wants to withdraw is because he has made a mistake. The important considerations of public policy behind those provisions will be completely destroyed. . . .

In addition to the foregoing, the bidder here was advised by words printed in capital letters in the invitation for bids and also in the bid itself that *he would not be released for errors.* Nothing could be more explicit. There is no room left for claiming mistake. Yet the majority say that the "errors" to which reference is made in the above mentioned documents, are of judgment, not in computation. The term "error" has a broad meaning and is not confined to those of judgment. It means the same as mistake. . . .

To limit the errors of the bidder for which he is responsible to those of judgment, is to strike at the very purpose of the clause in question and the bid bond. The clause and bond are there to assure certainty of contract and to preserve the integrity of the bidding system in letting public contracts. In the majority of cases that purpose will be defeated by the limitation. From the standpoint of the bidder, his mistake is far more inexcusable when it is in computation rather than judgment. There is no reason why he cannot have his arithmetic correct. School boys have been disciplined for stupidity in that field. . . .

I would, therefore, reverse the judgment.

NOTES

(1) *Revocability.* Can the two preceding cases be distinguished on the ground that the general contractor attempted to withdraw his bid after it had been accepted in the first case but before it had been accepted in the second? Ordinarily a general contractor's bid on a construction contract is an offer subject to a power in the offeror to revoke before acceptance. Where, however, as in the Kemper case, the owner is a state or local government, statutes or ordinances usually provide that the general contractor may not withdraw his bid after the bids have been opened. Where the owner is the federal government, the same result has been reached on the basis of federal regulation. See Keys, Consideration Reconsidered—The Problem

of the Withdrawn Bid, 10 Stan.L.Rev. 441, 448–53 (1958). Is there any reason to treat a bid made subject to such a rule any differently from a bid that has been accepted? For a rare case in which a general contractor was allowed to recover his deposit where he had notified the owner of his mistake the day *after* his bid had been accepted, see St. Nicholas Church v. Kropp, 135 Minn. 115, 160 N.W. 500 (1916); cf. Cataldo Construction Co. v. County of Essex, 110 N.J.Super. 414, 265 A.2d 842 (1970).

(2) *Bid Bonds and Deposits.* If the general contractor retains the power to revoke his offer, that power cannot be simply circumvented by the use of a bid bond. For, if the general contractor is free to withdraw his bid, the surety on his bid bond incurs no liability. A deposit may stand on a different footing. Comment a to Restatement Second, § 47A states that subject to the rules governing liquidated damages and penalties (discussed in Chapter 5, Section 4 infra): "The agreement may be valid as a provision for liquidated damages, or as a provision of security for the payment of actual damages. In either case, the offer is treated as irrevocable for the purpose of determining rights in the deposit, but the offeror's power of revocation is not otherwise impaired. In cases of bids on government contracts, statutes often authorize forfeiture without regard to the distinction between liquidated damages and penalty." Having a deposit also gives the owner an obvious practical advantage.

MISTAKE IN TRANSMISSION

Suppose that the offeror sends his offer by telegram, and that the telegraph company makes an error in transmitting it. For example, in Ayer v. Western Union Telegraph Co., 79 Me. 493, 10 A. 495 (1887), the offeror delivered to Western Union the message: "Will sell 800 M. laths, delivered at your wharf, two ten net cash." The company omitted the word "ten" in transmission. The offeree replied by wire: "Accept your telegraphic offer on laths." Was there a contract in spite of the error? And, if so, at two or at two ten? The court held that there was a contract at two, and that therefore the offeror had suffered a loss and could recover damages from the telegraph company. There is also authority to the contrary. See Western Union Telegraph Co. v. Cowin & Co., 20 F.2d 103 (8th Cir. 1927), holding that there was no contract between the sender and the receiver in such a case.

As between the offeror and the offeree, who should bear the risk? Should it make a difference who chose to communicate by telegram? (Should the allocation of risk depend on whether the offer by telegram was in response to an inquiry by mail or by telegram?) Does it matter that the sender has a contractual relationship with the telegraph company?

By federal statute a telegraph company may classify messages and vary its rates according to class, subject to the approval of the Federal Communications Commission. The following provisions on limitations of liability have been approved and are printed on telegraph blanks:

> The Telegraph Company shall not be liable for mistakes or delays in the transmission or delivery, or for non-delivery, of any message received for transmission at the unrepeated-message rates beyond the sum of five-hundred dollars; nor for mistakes or delays in the transmission or delivery, or for non-delivery, of any message received for transmission at the repeated-message rate beyond the sum of five thousand dollars, unless specially valued; nor in any case for delays arising from unavoidable interruption in the working of its lines.

A repeated message is repeated back at each stage of transmission from point of origin to destination. How useful is this technique in preventing delays in delivery as opposed to errors in transmission? How useful is the valued message? If the sender should choose to use a valued message, how can he estimate the amount of the loss that might result from a possible default by the telegraph company?

NOTES

(1) *Question.* Would the result in the Ayer case have been different if, instead of omitting the word "ten," the telegraph company had transmitted the word "one" in place of the word "two"? See Germain Fruit Co. v. Western Union Telegraph Co., 137 Cal. 598, 70 P. 658 (1902); Note 1, p. 141 supra.

(2) *Other Kinds of Mistake.* The cases involving mistaken bids have traditionally been classified as cases of "unilateral" mistake, as distinguished from cases of "mutual" mistake, in which both parties share a mistake as to a basic assumption. Compare Restatement, Restitution § 12 (on "unilateral" mistake) with § 9(3) (on "mutual" mistake). An example of "mutual" mistake arises under a building construction contract when both builder and owner are mistaken as to subsoil conditions, which are such as to make construction much more difficult. Questions of this sort are dealt with in Chapter 7, infra. Questions of mistake in the use of language are taken up in connection with interpretation in Chapter 6, infra. On mistake as to the identity of the other party, see Note 3, p. 32 supra.

(b) "Pre-Contractual" Liability: Subcontractors and Franchisors

---

The following materials deal with claims of liability growing out of what may loosely be called "*pre*-contractual" relationships. As we have seen, conventional learning is that no contractual liability may arise until there is "a bargain in which there is a manifestation of mutual assent to the exchange," and that up to that point either party may withdraw without incurring liability. Restatement Second, § 19. If an offeror invites a promise as acceptance, nothing short of a promise will do. See p. 91 supra. The rigors of this rule are, to be sure, occasionally mitigated by stretching the facts to find early assent as a basis for contractual liability.

Take, for example, Hill's Inc. v. William B. Kessler Inc., 41 Wash. 2d 42, 246 P.2d 1099 (1952). On May 16 a Seattle retailer ordered men's fall suits through the manufacturer's salesman on a printed form, supplied by the salesman, providing that the manufacturer was not bound until acceptance by one of its officers in New Jersey. On May 23 the manufacturer, by form letter, advised the retailer that, "You may be assured of our very best attention to this order." On July 18, however, after the time for placing orders for fall suits had passed, and at the instigation of one of the retailer's large competitors in Seattle, the manufacturer wrote to "cancel" the order. The retailer sued the manufacturer and had judgment in the trial court, which found that the manufacturer's form letter had been an acceptance. The Supreme Court of Washington affirmed. For a contrary result, see Courtney Shoe Co. v. E. W. Curd & Son, 142 Ky. 219, 134 S.W. 146 (1911). In that case the manufacturer wrote, "Your order   .   .   . is at hand and will receive our prompt and careful attention," but sent a second letter only eight days later rejecting the order on the ground that the salesman had made the sale without authority. Which of these decisions accords better with the preceding materials in this chapter? Do those materials suggest any basis for distinguishing them? Can *you* suggest any basis?

At most such cases give a court only a limited degree of flexibility in applying the traditional rules that allow the parties to withdraw without liability at any time before acceptance. There are, however, instances where liability is imposed as a result of conduct during the negotiation process even though there is no contract in the traditional sense on which liability may be based. They can be gathered under four rubrics: (1) refusal to deal; (2) refusal to bargain in "good faith"; (3) restitution; and (4) reliance.

Refusal to Deal. In a few narrow fields of economic activity a doctrine of "compulsory contract" is recognized. Businesses described generally as "public utilities," such as telephone companies, gas and electric companies, and railroads, are considered to be under "a duty to serve without discrimination and on proper terms all who request [their] service." Restatement of Torts, § 763. Their duty arises without regard to whether any negotiations have taken place or not. "The duty to serve without discrimination is the result partly of historical development, partly of the nature of the services which they render and partly of their less competitive and more monopolistic character." Id., Comment a. The term "compulsory contract" is somewhat misleading because the liability for refusal to deal is not in contract, but in tort. The circumstance that the terms of the contract that should have been made are standard terms is, however, a significant factor in facilitating the assessment of damages.

Although insurance companies have not been brought within the ambit of "compulsory contract," a related sort of liability has been imposed on life insurers. When an aspiring policyholder applies for a policy insuring his life, and the insurer takes an unreasonable length of time to act on his application, the insurer has been held liable if the applicant dies during the period of delay. See, e. g., Rosin v. Peninsular Life Ins. Co., 116 So.2d 798 (Fla.App.1960). The preferred theory is that of liability in tort for negligence, with damages predicated on the assumption that had the insurer promptly rejected the application the applicant would have obtained an identical policy elsewhere. See Keeton, Basic Text on Insurance Law 45–50 (1971), where it is also suggested that on this assumption the cause of action belongs to the intended beneficiary and not to the applicant's estate.

In addition to these rare examples involving public utilities and insurers (where there is a general liability for refusal to deal), there are other important instances in which a refusal to deal may have legal consequences if it is improperly motivated. Where, for example, its purpose is to restrain trade or gain a monopoly, a refusal to deal may be wrongful under either the common law relating to business torts or statutes in the fields of antitrust and trade regulation. See, e. g., 1 Harper and James, The Law of Torts § 6.13 (1956); Turner, The Definition of Agreement Under the Sherman Act: Conscious Parallelism and Refusals to Deal, 75 Harv.L.Rev. 655, 689 (1962). And where it is motivated by racial or religious discrimination, it may be wrongful under one of the anti-discrimination laws. See, e. g., Gray v. Serruto Builders, 110 N.J.Super. 297, 265 A.2d 404 (1970), in which the court, on a showing of violation of a fair housing law, ordered the defendant to offer an apartment when available and awarded damages for mental suffering. See also Notes, 84 Harv.L.Rev. 1109 (1971); 80 Yale L.J. 516 (1971). Although these topics must be left to special courses in their respective fields, it is worth noting that to the extent that civil liability is imposed for refusal to deal, here too it generally is on a theory of tort rather than of contract. (See also pp. 73–75 supra.)

Refusal to Bargain in "Good Faith". Instead of attaching legal consequences to refusal to deal, the law may require a party to bargain according to acceptable standards, in the hope that the usual, although not the necessary, result of such bargaining will be a contract. The standard adopted, where such a requirement has been imposed, has been that of "good faith." Thus the National Labor Relations Act, § 8 imposes a duty on both employer and labor union to bargain collectively—"to meet at reasonable times and confer in good faith . . ., but such obligation does not compel either party to agree to a proposal or require the making of a concession." See Wellington, Labor and the Legal Process 52–59 (1968); Cox, The Duty to Bargain in Good Faith, 71 Harv.L.Rev. 1401 (1958). The National Labor Relations Board is empowered to promulgated orders, enforceable in the courts, to implement this provision, but although it may order a party to cease and desist from refusing to bargain, it may not order a party to include a particular term in the agreement. See H. K. Porter Co. v. NLRB, 397 U.S. 99 (D.C.Cir.1970). The collective bargaining agreement is admittedly a special sort of agreement, in good part because of what has been called the "compulsory character of the bargaining relationship," in which the employer is required to bargain with the union that represents a majority of employees, to the exclusion of all other unions. See C. Summers, Collective Agreements and the Law of Contracts, 78 Yale L.J. 525, 530–33 (1969). Its study is best left for another course. It is interesting to observe in this connection, however, that an analogous problem arises in communist countries where, as a result of state planning, the bargaining relationship between a producing enterprise and a consuming enterprise also takes on a "compulsory" character. As a consequence, in the Soviet Union, for example, a system of economic courts (*Arbitrazh*) resolves pre-contractual disputes by determining the terms of agreements.[a] See, Berman, Justice in the U.S.S.R. 131–34 (1963). It is indicative of the problems that might be encountered, in a broader application of the notion of a duty to bargain, that both of the systems just discussed have specialized agencies to implement that duty.

Nevertheless, there have been suggestions that the notion might be more generally applied. An example is Heyer Products Co. v. United States, 140 F.Supp. 409 (Ct.Cl.1956), in which Heyer, a disappointed bidder on a contract with the Army Ordnance Corps, sued the government alleging that, although its bid had been the lowest, the government had awarded the contract to another bidder in order to retaliate against Heyer for having testified against the Ordnance Corps at a Senate hearing. The court held that while the government "could accept or reject an offer as it pleased, and no contract resulted until an offer was accepted," it was "an implied condition of the request for offers that each of them would be honestly considered," and the government was under an "obligation to honestly consider [the bid] and not to wantonly disregard it."[b] It would therefore be liable

---

a. See also Winston-Salem Printing Pressman & Assistants' Union v. Piedmont Publishing Co., 393 F.2d 221 (4th Cir. 1968), in which the court held enforceable the following clause in a collective bargaining agreement between a publisher and a union which ran from April 13, 1964 to October 31, 1965. "Should either party desire to negotiate for changes in any or all of the provisions of this contract as of November 1, 1965, written notice to the effect must be given to the other party on or before September 1, 1965, together with a written statement in detail of the changes desired. Otherwise, this agreement shall continue from November 1 through October 31 from year to year and can be changed only by mutual consent or through negotiations started by written notice of one of the parties to the other, on or before September 1st of any succeeding year. Should either party propose such amendments or a new contract, and an agreement proves impossible, the difference or differences shall be arbitrated as herein provided."

b. Was this obligation implied in fact or implied in law? See footnote a, p. 40 supra.

to Heyer for its expense in preparing its bid if "bids were not invited in good faith." Accord: Continental Business Enterprises v. United States, 452 F.2d 1016 (Ct.Cl.1971). Heyer was, however, unable to prove its allegations. Heyer Products Co. v. United States, 177 F. Supp. 251 (Ct.Cl.1959). Subsequent claimants who have sought to bring themselves within the announced rule have met the same fate. E. g., Robert F. Simmons & Associates v. United States, 360 F.2d 962 (Ct.Cl.1966).[c] And the rule itself must be regarded with caution, since it was framed in the particular circumstances of an invitation to bid on a government contract where, it will be remembered, the bidder's power to revoke his bid is restricted. See Note 1, p. 147 supra. Nevertheless, one writer has hailed the decision as a unique one "in which a court has recognized, in the absence of a statutory or contractual duty to negotiate, that a cause of action exists against a party who negotiates without serious intent to contract." R. Summers, "Good Faith" in General Contract Law and the Sales Provisions of the Uniform Commercial Code, 54 Va.L.Rev. 195, 221 (1968).

The suggestion that there might be a "contractual duty to negotiate" raises a question that we first saw in Willmott v. Giarraputo, p. 84 supra, in which the court gave the orthodox answer: "If a material element is left for future negotiations, there is no contract." Could the parties, nevertheless, impose upon themselves a duty to negotiate in "good faith"?

Consider Itek Corp. v. Chicago Aerial Industries, 248 A.2d 625 (Del.1968). On January 15, after negotiations looking to the purchase by Itek of all CAI's assets, the parties executed a "letter of intent" confirming the terms of the sale and providing that, "Itek and CAI shall make every reasonable effort to agree upon and have prepared as quickly as possible a contract providing for the foregoing purchase by Itek and sale by CAI, . . . embodying the above terms and such other terms and conditions as the parties shall agree upon. If the parties fail to agree upon and execute such a contract they shall be under no further obligation to one another." On February 23, CAI insisted on three new conditions, to which Itek agreed. On March 2, CAI, evidently having received a more favorable offer from Bourns, telegraphed Itek that it was not going ahead with the transaction as a result of unforeseen circumstances and the failure of the parties to reach agreement. Itek sued CAI for breach of contract, but the trial court granted summary judgment for CAI, relying on the second sentence quoted above. The Supreme Court of Delaware reversed, reasoning that "it is apparent that the parties obligated themselves to 'make every reasonable effort' to agree upon a for-

c. On the question of the disappointed bidder's standing to sue, see Keco Industries v. United States, 428 F.2d 1233 (Ct.Cl.1970); Scanwell Laboratories v. Shaffer, 424 F.2d 859 (D.C. Cir. 1970). These cases are discussed in Grossbaum, Procedural Fairness in Public Contracts: The Procurement Regulations, 57 Va.L.Rev. 171, 227–54 (1971).

mal contract, and only if such effort failed were they absolved from 'further obligation' for having 'failed' to agree upon and execute a formal contract. We think these provisions of the January 15 letter obligated each side to attempt in good faith to reach final and formal agreement." Since there was evidence that in order to accept a more favorable offer from Bourns, "CAI willfully failed to negotiate in good faith and to make 'every reasonable effort' to agree upon a formal contract, as it was required to do," it was error to grant summary judgment. What sorts of facts might CAI show at the trial to establish its "good faith"? If Itek proves its case at trial, how should damages be measured? In support of the somewhat unconventional result in the Itek case, see Knapp, Enforcing the Contract to Bargain, 44 N.Y.U.L.Rev. 673 (1969).

Restitution. Better established as a ground for recovery growing out of "pre-contractual" relationships is restitution to prevent unjust enrichment. To take a simple example, the prospective buyer of land who makes a down payment during negotiations that fail to result in a contract is entitled to the return of his down payment. But unjust enrichment is often harder to show. So in Cronin v. National Shawmut Bank, 306 Mass. 202, 27 N.E.2d 717 (1940), National Shawmut Bank invited brokers to submit proposals for fire and theft insurance on specified property, involving premiums of about $850,000 and broker's commissions of between $30,000 and $40,000. Cronin submitted a proposal and, at the request of McCarthy, one of the bank's officers, he revised it several times until it was "the precise proposal that McCarthy wanted." The bank then gave the contract to another firm, who submitted a proposal identical to Cronin's except for the names of the broker and the insurer, because a partner in that firm was a friend of one of McCarthy's superiors. Cronin sued the bank, including a claim in restitution. The Supreme Judicial Court of Massachusetts affirmed judgment for the bank. The bank "never actually availed itself of any proposal made by the plaintiff." The contract made was with a different insurer and serviced by a different broker. "To be sure the defendant got the benefit of the rates proposed by the plaintiff, and this may have been important; but what the rates would have been if they had not been the plaintiff's rates remains speculative. It has been held in a number of cases that deriving benefit from the broker's work does not lead to liability where there has been no employment." See also Gould v. American Water Works Service Co., 52 N.J. 226, 245 A.2d 14 (1968), cert. denied 394 U.S. 943 (1969).

A contrasting case on restitution is Hill v. Waxberg, 237 F.2d 936 (9th Cir. 1956). Hill asked Waxberg, a contractor, to help him make preparations for the construction of a building on Hill's lot in Fairbanks, Alaska. It was understood that if the financing could be arranged through the Federal Housing Authority as contemplated, Waxberg would be awarded the building contract. Waxberg then made several trips to Seattle at Hill's request to confer with the architects, hired a third party to secure a drill log on the property, surveyed the property, and was instrumental in getting the data for the F.H.A. He expected to be compensated for this out of the profits from the contemplated contract. When the F.H.A. issued the commitment, Hill and Waxberg began negotiations for the building contract, but were unable to agree. Hill then made a contract with another contractor, and Waxberg sued to recover the reasonable value of his services and the expenditures made by him. The evidence showed that Waxberg's plans, ideas and efforts were of some value to Hill, and the trial court entered judgment for him on a jury verdict for $11,167.46. On Hill's appeal the Court of Appeals explained that it is a general principle of Anglo-American jurisprudence that "something in the nature of an implied contract results where one renders services at the request of another with the expectation of pay therefor, and in the process confers a benefit on the other. . . . It makes no difference whether the pay expected is in the form of an immediate cash payment, or in the form of profits to be derived from a contract, the consummation of which would or should be anticipated by reasonable men, and it follows *a fortiori* that such a rule obtains where the contract is in fact contemplated by *both* parties." The contract may be "implied in fact," in which case the general contract theory of compensatory damages applies, compensation for services being measured at "the going contract rate." Or it may be "implied in law," in which case a restitution measure of damages applies and recovery is limited to "the value of the benefit which was acquired." (This portion of the opinion is quoted in full in Note 3, p. 40 supra.) Because the trial judge did not adequately instruct the jury on this distinction, its judgment was reversed, unless the parties should agree to a reduction in its amount to $5,896.88, the asserted reasonable value of Waxberg's services plus his claimed expenses. Would not this court's reasoning have required a decision for Cronin on his claim against the bank? If so, for how much? Are the two cases distinguishable? Are the cases on liability for appropriation of ideas, discussed at p. 42 supra, relevant?

Reliance. A final ground for recovery growing out of "pre-contractual" relationships is reliance by one party during the negotiation process. To what extent, if at all, will such reliance serve as a basis for recovery by a party should the negotiations fail to produce an agreement? Some answers are suggested by the following cases.

JAMES BAIRD CO. v. GIMBEL BROS.

United States Circuit Court of Appeals, Second Circuit, 1933.
64 F.2d 344.

Action by the James Baird Company against Gimbel Brothers, Incorporated. From a judgment dismissing the complaint, plaintiff appeals.

L. HAND, CIRCUIT JUDGE. The plaintiff sued the defendant for breach of a contract to deliver linoleum under a contract of sale; the defendant denied the making of the contract; the parties tried the case to the judge under a written stipulation and he directed judgment for the defendant. The facts as found, bearing on the making of the contract, the only issue necessary to discuss, were as follows: The defendant, a New York merchant, knew that the Department of Highways in Pennsylvania had asked for bids for the construction of a public building. It sent an employee to the office of a contractor in Philadelphia, who had possession of the specifications, and the employee there computed the amount of the linoleum which would be required on the job, underestimating the total yardage by about one-half the proper amount. In ignorance of this mistake, on December twenty-fourth the defendant sent to some twenty or thirty contractors, likely to bid on the job, an offer to supply all the linoleum required by the specifications at two different lump sums, depending upon the quality used. These offers concluded as follows: "If successful in being awarded this contract, it will be absolutely guaranteed, . . . and . . . we are offering these prices for reasonable" (sic), "prompt acceptance after the general contract has been awarded." The plaintiff, a contractor in Washington, got one of these on the twenty-eighth, and on the same day the defendant learned its mistake and telegraphed all the contractors to whom it had sent the offer, that it withdrew it and would substitute a new one at about double the amount of the old. This withdrawal reached the plaintiff at Washington on the afternoon of the same day, but not until after it had put in a bid at Harrisburg at a lump sum, based as to linoleum upon the prices quoted by the defendant. The public authorities accepted the plaintiff's bid on December thirtieth, the defendant having meanwhile written a letter of confirmation of its withdrawal, received on the thirty-first. The plaintiff formally accepted the offer on January second, and, as the defendant persisted in declining to recognize the existence of a contract, sued it for damages on a breach.

Unless there are circumstances to take it out of the ordinary doctrine, since the offer was withdrawn before it was accepted, the acceptance was too late. Restatement of Contracts, sec. 35. To meet this the plaintiff argues as follows: It was a reasonable implication from the defendant's offer that it should be irrevocable in case the plaintiff acted upon it, that is to say, used the prices quoted in making its bid, thus putting itself in a position from which it could not withdraw without great loss. While it might have withdrawn its bid after receiving the revocation, the time had passed to submit another, and as the item of linoleum was a very trifling part of the cost of the whole building, it would have been an unreasonable hardship to expect it to lose the contract on that account, and probably forfeit its deposit. While it is true that the plaintiff might in advance have secured a contract conditional upon the success of its bid, this was not what the defendant suggested. It understood that the contractors would use its offer in their bids, and would thus in fact commit themselves to supplying the linoleum at the proposed prices. The inevitable implication from all this was that when the contractors acted upon it, they accepted the offer and promised to pay for the linoleum, in case their bids were accepted.

It was of course possible for the parties to make such a contract, and the question is merely as to what they meant; that is, what is to be imputed to the words they used. Whatever plausibility there is in the argument is in the fact that the defendant must have known the predicament in which the contractors would be put if it withdrew its offer after the bids went in. However, it seems entirely clear that the contractors did not suppose that they accepted the offer merely by putting in their bids. If, for example, the successful one had repudiated the contract with the public authorities after it had been awarded to him, certainly the defendant could not have sued him for a breach. If he had become bankrupt, the defendant could not prove against his estate. It seems plain therefore that there was no contract between them. And if there be any doubt as to this, the language of the offer sets it at rest. The phrase, "if successful in being awarded this contract," is scarcely met by the mere use of the prices in the bids. Surely such a use was not an "award" of the contract to the defendant. Again, the phrase, "we are offering these prices for . . . prompt acceptance after the general contract has been awarded," looks to the usual communication of an acceptance, and precludes the idea that the use of the offer in the bidding shall be the equivalent. It may indeed be argued that this last language contemplated no more than an early notice that the offer had been accepted, the actual acceptance being the bid, but that would wrench its natural meaning too far, especially in the light of the preceding phrase. The contractors had a ready escape from their difficulty by insisting upon a contract before they used the figures; and in commercial transactions it does not in the end promote justice to seek strained interpretations in aid of those who do not protect themselves.

But the plaintiff says that even though no bilateral contract was made, the defendant should be held under the doctrine of "promissory estoppel." This is to be chiefly found in those cases where persons subscribe to a venture, usually charitable, and are held to their promises after it has been completed. It has been applied much more broadly, however, and has now been generalized in section 90, of the

Restatement of Contracts. We may arguendo accept it as it there reads, for it does not apply to the case at bar. Offers are ordinarily made in exchange for a consideration, either a counter-promise or some other act which the promisor wishes to secure. In such cases they propose bargains; they presuppose that each promise or performance is an inducement to the other. . . . But a man may make a promise without expecting an equivalent; a donative promise, conditional or absolute. The common law provided for such by sealed instruments, and it is unfortunate that these are no longer generally available. The doctrine of "promissory estoppel" is to avoid the harsh results of allowing the promisor in such a case to repudiate, when the promisee has acted in reliance upon the promise. . . . But an offer for an exchange is not meant to become a promise until a consideration has been received, either a counter-promise or whatever else is stipulated. To extend it would be to hold the offeror regardless of the stipulated condition of his offer. In the case at bar the defendant offered to deliver the linoleum in exchange for the plaintiff's acceptance, not for its bid, which was a matter of indifference to it. That offer could become a promise to deliver only when the equivalent was received; that is, when the plaintiff promised to take and pay for it. There is no room in such a situation for the doctrine of "promissory estoppel."

Nor can the offer be regarded as of an option, giving the plaintiff the right seasonably to accept the linoleum at the quoted prices if its bid was accepted, but not binding it to take and pay, if it could get a better bargain elsewhere. There is not the least reason to suppose that the defendant meant to subject itself to such a one-sided obligation. True, if so construed, the doctrine of "promissory estoppel" might apply, the plaintiff having acted in reliance upon it, though, so far as we have found, the decisions are otherwise. Ganss v. Guffey Petroleum Co., 125 App.Div. 760, 110 N.Y.S. 176; Comstock v. North, 88 Miss. 754, 41 So. 374. As to that, however, we need not declare ourselves.

Judgment affirmed.

NOTE

Problem. Suppose that Gimbel's bid had included the following language instead of that quoted by the court: "If successful in being awarded this contract, it will be absolutely guaranteed. If our bid is used, wire us collect no later than the twenty-eighth or else our bid is withdrawn." And suppose that before Gimbel wired Baird of its mistake, it had already received a telegram from Baird reading, "We used your bid on the Pennsylvania job." Same result? See Williams v. Favret, 161 F.2d 822 (5th Cir. 1947).

Suppose that Gimbel had not made a mistake, but had withdrawn its bid because it had changed its mind. Same result? See Tatsch v. Hamilton-Erickson Mfg. Co., 76 N.M. 729, 418 P.2d 187 (1966).

DRENNAN v. STAR PAVING CO.

Supreme Court of California, In Bank, 1958.
51 Cal.2d 409, 333 P.2d 757.

General contractor brought action against paving subcontractor to recover damages because of refusal of subcontractor to perform paving according to bid which subcontractor submitted to general contractor. The Superior Court, Kern County, William L. Bradshaw, J., entered judgment adverse to the subcontractor, and the subcontractor appealed.

TRAYNOR, JUSTICE. Defendant appeals from a judgment for plaintiff in an action to recover damages caused by defendant's refusal to perform certain paving work according to a bid it submitted to plaintiff.

On July 28, 1955, plaintiff, a licensed general contractor, was preparing a bid on the "Monte Vista School Job" in the Lancaster school district. Bids had to be submitted before 8:00 p. m. Plaintiff testified that it was customary in that area for general contractors to receive the bids of subcontractors by telephone on the day set for bidding and to rely on them in computing their own bids. Thus on that day plaintiff's secretary, Mrs. Johnson, received by telephone between fifty and seventy-five subcontractors' bids for various parts of the school job. As each bid came in, she wrote it on a special form, which she brought into plaintiff's office. He then posted it on a master cost sheet setting forth the names and bids of all subcontractors. His own bid had to include the names of subcontractors who were to perform one-half of one per cent or more of the construction work, and he had also to provide a bidder's bond of ten per cent of his total bid of $317,385 as a guarantee that he would enter the contract if awarded the work.

Late in the afternoon, Mrs. Johnson had a telephone conversation with Kenneth R. Hoon, an estimator for defendant. He gave his name and telephone number and stated that he was bidding for defendant for the paving work at the Monte Vista School according to plans and specifications and that his bid was $7,131.60. At Mrs. Johnson's request he repeated his bid. Plaintiff listened to the bid over an extension telephone in his office and posted it on the master sheet after receiving the bid form from Mrs. Johnson. Defendant's was the lowest bid for the paving. Plaintiff computed his own bid accordingly and submitted it with the name of defendant as the subcontractor for the paving. When the bids were opened on July 28th, plaintiff's proved to be the lowest, and he was awarded the contract.

On his way to Los Angeles the next morning plaintiff stopped at defendant's office. The first person he met was defendant's construction engineer, Mr. Oppenheimer. Plaintiff testified: "I introduced myself and he immediately told me that they had made a mistake in their bid to me the night before, they couldn't do it for the price they had bid, and I told him I would expect him to carry through with their original bid because I had used it in compiling my bid and the job was being awarded them. And I would have to go and do the job according to my bid and I would expect them to do the same."

Defendant refused to do the paving work for less than $15,000. Plaintiff testified that he "got figures from other people" and after trying for several months to get as low a bid as possible engaged L & H Paving Company, a firm in Lancaster, to do the work for $10,948.60.

The trial court found on substantial evidence that defendant made a definite offer to do the paving on the Monte Vista job according to the plans and specifications for $7,131.60, and that plaintiff relied on defendant's bid in computing his own bid for the school job and naming defendant therein as the subcontractor for the paving work. Accordingly, it entered judgment for plaintiff in the amount of $3,817.00 (the difference between defendant's bid and the cost of the paving to plaintiff) plus costs.

Defendant contends that there was no enforceable contract between the parties on the ground that it made a revocable offer and revoked it before plaintiff communicated his acceptance to defendant.

There is no evidence that defendant offered to make its bid irrevocable in exchange for plaintiff's use of its figures in computing his bid. Nor is there evidence that would warrant interpreting plaintiff's use of defendant's bid as the acceptance thereof, binding plaintiff, on condition he received the main contract, to award the subcontract to defendant. In sum, there was neither an option supported by consideration nor a bilateral contract binding on both parties.

Plaintiff contends, however, that he relied to his detriment on defendant's offer and that defendant must therefore answer in damages for its refusal to perform. Thus the question is squarely presented: Did plaintiff's reliance make defendant's offer irrevocable?

Section 90 of the Restatement of Contracts states: "A promise which the promisor should reasonably expect to induce action or forbearance of a definite and substantial character on the part of the promisee and which does induce such action or forbearance is binding if injustice can be avoided only by enforcement of the promise." This rule applies in this state. . . .

Defendant's offer constituted a promise to perform on such conditions as were stated expressly or by implication therein or annexed thereto by operation of law. (See 1 Williston, Contracts [3rd ed.], § 24A, p. 56, § 61, p. 196.) Defendant had reason to expect that if its bid proved the lowest it would be used by plaintiff. It induced "action . . . of a definite and substantial character on the part of the promisee."

Had defendant's bid expressly stated or clearly implied that it was revocable at any time before acceptance we would treat it accordingly. It was silent on revocation, however, and we must therefore determine whether there are conditions to the right of revocation imposed by law or reasonably inferable in fact. In the analogous problem of an offer for a unilateral contract, the theory is now obsolete that the offer is revocable at any time before complete performance. Thus section 45 of the Restatement of Contracts provides: "If an offer for a unilateral contract is made, and part of the consideration requested in the offer is given or tendered by the offeree in response thereto, the offeror is bound by a contract, the duty of immediate performance of which is conditional on the full consideration being given or tendered within the time stated in the offer, or, if no time is stated therein, within a reasonable time." In explanation, comment *b* states that the "main offer includes as a subsidiary promise, necessarily implied, that if part of the requested performance is given, the offeror will not revoke his offer, and that if tender is made it will be accepted. Part performance or tender may thus furnish consideration for the subsidiary promise. Moreover, merely acting in justifiable reliance on an offer may in some cases serve as sufficient reason for making a promise binding (see § 90)."

Whether implied in fact or law, the subsidiary promise serves to preclude the injustice that would result if the offer could be revoked after the offeree had acted in detrimental reliance thereon. Reasonable reliance resulting in a foreseeable prejudicial change in position affords a compelling basis also for implying a subsidiary promise not to revoke an offer for a bilateral contract.

The absence of consideration is not fatal to the enforcement of such a promise. It is true that in the case of unilateral contracts the Restatement finds consideration for the implied subsidiary promise in the part performance of the bargained-for exchange, but its reference to section 90 makes clear that consideration for such a promise is not always necessary. The very purpose of section 90 is to make a promise binding even though there was no consideration "in the sense of something that is bargained for and given in exchange." (See 1 Corbin, Contracts 634 et seq.) Reasonable reliance serves to hold the offeror in lieu of the consideration ordinarily required to make the offer binding. In a case involving similar facts the Supreme Court of South Dakota stated that "we believe that reason and justice demand that the doctrine [of section 90] be applied to the present facts. We cannot believe that by accepting this doctrine as controlling in the state of facts before us we will abolish the requirement of a consideration in contract cases, in any different sense than an ordinary estoppel abolishes some legal requirement in its application. We are of the opinion, therefore, that the defendants in executing the agreement [which was not supported by consideration] made a promise which they should have reasonably expected would induce the plaintiff to submit a bid based thereon to the Government, that such promise did induce this action, and that injustice can be avoided only by enforcement of the promise." Northwestern Engineering Co. v. Ellerman, 69 S.D. 397, 408, 10 N.W.2d 879, 884; see also, Robert Gordon, Inc., v. Ingersoll-Rand Co., 7 Cir., 117 F.2d 654, 661; cf. James Baird Co. v. Gimbel Bros., 2 Cir., 64 F.2d 344.

When plaintiff used defendant's offer in computing his own bid, he bound himself to perform in reliance on defendant's terms. Though defendant did not bargain for this use of its bid neither did defendant make it idly, indifferent to whether it would be used or not. On the contrary it is reasonable to suppose that defendant submitted its bid to obtain the subcontract. It was bound to realize the substantial possibility that its bid would be the lowest, and that it would be included by plaintiff in his bid. It was to its own interest that the contractor be awarded the general contract; the lower the subcontract bid, the lower the general contractor's bid was likely to be and the greater its chance of acceptance and hence the greater defendant's chance of getting the paving subcontract. Defendant had reason not only to expect plaintiff to rely on its bid but to want him to. Clearly defendant had a stake in plaintiff's reliance on its bid. Given this interest and the fact that plaintiff is bound by his own bid, it is only fair that plaintiff should have at least an opportunity to accept defendant's bid after the general contract has been awarded to him.

It bears noting that a general contractor is not free to delay acceptance after he has been awarded the general contract in the hope of getting a better price. Nor can he reopen bargaining with the subcontractor and at the same time claim a continuing right to accept the original offer. See, R. J. Daum Const. Co. v. Child, Utah, 247 P. 2d 817, 823. In the present case plaintiff promptly informed defendant that plaintiff was being awarded the job and that the subcontract was being awarded to defendant.

Defendant contends, however, that its bid was the result of mistake and that it was therefore entitled to revoke it. It relies on the rescission cases of M. F. Kemper Const. Co. v. City of Los Angeles, 37 Cal.2d 696, 235 P.2d 7, and Brunzell Const. Co. v. G. J. Weisbrod, Inc., 134 Cal.App.2d 278, 285 P.2d 989. See also, Lemoge Electric v. San Mateo County, 46 Cal.2d 659, 662, 297 P.2d 638. In those cases, however, the bidder's mistake was known or should have been known to the offeree, and the offeree could be placed in status quo. Of course, if plaintiff had reason to believe that defendant's bid was in error, he could not justifiably rely on it, and section 90 would afford no basis for enforcing it. Robert Gordon, Inc., v. Ingersoll-Rand, Inc., 7 Cir., 117 F.2d 654, 660. Plaintiff, however, had no reason to know that defendant had made a mistake in submitting its bid, since there was usually a variance of 160 per cent between the highest and lowest bids for paving in the desert around Lancaster. He committed himself to performing the main contract in reliance on defendant's figures.

Under these circumstances defendant's mistake, far from relieving it of its obligation, constitutes an additional reason for enforcing it, for it misled plaintiff as to the cost of doing the paving. Even had it been clearly understood that defendant's offer was revocable until accepted, it would not necessarily follow that defendant had no duty to exercise reasonable care in preparing its bid. It presented its bid with knowledge of the substantial possibility that it would be used by plaintiff; it could foresee the harm that would ensue from an erroneous underestimate of the cost. Moreover, it was motivated by its own business interest. Whether or not these considerations alone would justify recovery for negligence had the case been tried on that theory (see Biakanja v. Irving, 49 Cal.2d 647, 650, 320 P.2d 16), they are persuasive that defendant's mistake should not defeat recovery under the rule of section 90 of the Restatement of Contracts. As between the subcontractor who made the bid and the general contractor who reasonably relied on it, the loss resulting from the mistake should fall on the party who caused it.

Leo F. Piazza Paving Co. v. Bebek & Brkich, 141 Cal.App.2d 226, 296 P.2d 368, 371, and Bard v. Kent, 19 Cal.2d 449, 122 P.2d 8, 139 A.L.R. 1032, are not to the contrary. In the Piazza case the court sustained a finding that defendants intended, not to make a firm bid, but only to give the plaintiff "some kind of an idea to use" in making its bid; there was evidence that the defendants had told plaintiff they were unsure of the significance of the specifications. There was thus no offer, promise, or representation on which the defendants should reasonably have expected the plaintiff to rely. The Bard case held that an option not supported by consideration was revoked by the death of the optionor. The issue of recovery under the rule of section 90 was not pleaded at the trial, and it does not appear that the offeree's reliance was "of a definite and substantial character" so that injustice could be avoided "only by the enforcement of the promise." [a]

There is no merit in defendant's contention that plaintiff failed to state a cause of action, on the ground that the complaint failed to allege that plaintiff attempted to mitigate the damages or that they could not have been mitigated. Plaintiff alleged that after defendant's default, "plaintiff had to procure the services of the L & H Co. to perform said asphaltic paving for the sum of $10,948.60." Plaintiff's uncontradicted evidence showed that he spent several months trying to get bids from other subcontractors and that he took the lowest bid. Clearly he acted reasonably to mitigate damages. In any event any uncertainty in plaintiff's allegation as to damages could have been raised by special demurrer. Code Civ.Proc. § 430, subd. 9. It was not so raised and was therefore waived. Code Civ.Proc. § 434.

The judgment is affirmed.

a.   See note 1, p. 124 supra.

NOTES

(1) *Preparing to Cross the Brooklyn Bridge.* The rationale of the Drennan case is reflected in Restatement Second, § 89B(2). Would this rule protect B in the Brooklyn Bridge hypothetical, p. 124 supra, if he had spent time and money in preparing to cross the bridge but had not begun to cross it when A revoked? Would you advise B, in such a situation, to cross the bridge in spite of the revocation? Would this rule protect the broker in Note 3, p. 127 supra, if he had done no more than advertise the property? Would it affect the result in the case in Note 4, p. 127 supra?

(2) *Problem.* Suppose that after receiving Star Paving's bid on July 28, Drennan had telephoned Star Paving and asked if it "could shave it a little," Star Paving had said it would "have to think it over," and that Star Paving's bid had then been used without further inquiry. Same result? Compare Jaybe Construction Co. v. Beco, 3 Conn.Cir. 406, 216 A.2d 208 (1965) with State ex rel. Sorenson v. Wisner State Bank, 125 Neb. 345, 250 N.W. 89 (1933). Suppose that this telephone conversation had taken place after the award to Drennan but before Star Paving had discovered its mistake, and that before any further discussion could be had it had discovered its mistake and told Drennan of its unwillingness to perform. Same result? See N. Litterio & Co. v. Glassman Construction Co., 319 F. 2d 736 (D.C.Cir.1963). See also Restatement Second, § 35A.

SOUTHERN CALIFORNIA ACOUSTICS CO. v. C. V. HOLDER, 71 Cal.2d 719, 456 P.2d 975 (1969). [Acoustics, a subcontractor, telephoned to Holder, a general contractor, an $83,400 bid on the acoustical tile work for a construction job for the Los Angeles Unified School District. Later that day, Holder submitted its bid to the school district, listing subcontractors, including Acoustics. California Government Code, § 4104, a part of the 1963 Subletting and Subcontracting Fair Practices Act, required listing of subcontractors whose work made up more than one-half of one per cent of the bid. Holder was awarded the prime contract and a local trade paper reported the award, along with the names of the subcontractors listed in its bid. When Acoustics read this, it refrained from bidding on other construction jobs in order to remain within its bonding limits. Holder then obtained the consent of the school district to substitute another subcontractor for Acoustics on the ground that the latter had been inadvertently listed in place of the former. Acoustics sought a writ of mandamus to compel the school district to rescind its consent and, when that proceeding was dismissed, sued Holder and the school district for damages. From dismissal of its complaint against both defendants, plaintiff appealed.]

TRAYNOR, CHIEF JUSTICE. . . . . There was no contract between plaintiff and Holder, for Holder did not accept plaintiff's offer. . . . The listing by the general contractor of the subcontractors he intends to retain is in response to a statutory command (Gov.Code, § 4104) and cannot reasonably be construed as an expression of acceptance. . . . Plaintiff contends, however, that its reliance on Holder's use of its bid and Holder's failure to reject its offer promptly after Holder's bid was accepted constitute acceptance of plaintiff's bid by operation of law under the doctrine of promissory estoppel. . . . Plaintiff urges us to find an analogous subsidiary promise [to that found in Drennan] not to reject its bid in this case, but it fails to allege facts showing the existence of any promise by Holder to it upon which it detrimentally relied. Plaintiff did not rely on any promise by Holder, but only on the listing of subcontractors required by section 4104 of the Government Code and on the statutory restrictions on Holder's right to change its listed subcontractors without the consent of the school district. (Gov.Code, § 4107.) [a] . . .

Plaintiff contends, however, that the [1963] Subletting and Subcontracting Fair Practices Act confers rights on listed subcontractors that arise when the prime contract is awarded and that these rights may be enforced by an action for damages. [The court then reviewed the 1963 statute, and concluded that, in contrast to the earlier statute in effect at the time of the Drennan case, its purpose was not only to allow the awarding authority to investigate and approve subcontractors, but] also to protect the public and subcontractors from the evils attendant upon the practices of bid shopping and bid peddling subsequent to the award of the prime contract for a public facility. Thus section 4107 now clearly limits the right of the prime contractor to make substitutions and the discretion of the awarding authority to consent to substitutions to . . . situations . . . keyed to the unwillingness or inability of the listed subcontractor properly to perform. . . .

[W]e hold that it confers the right on the listed subcontractor to perform the subcontract unless statutory grounds for a valid substitution exist. Moreover, that right may be enforced by an action for damages against the prime contractor to recover the benefit of the bargain the listed subcontractor would have realized had he not wrongfully been deprived of the subcontract. [The court concluded that the statute did not, however, confer on the subcontractor a right of action against the school district.]

[Affirmed as to the school district. Reversed and remanded as to Holder.]

NOTES

(1) *The Case of the Detonation Detection Team.* AT wrote to a number of companies, including GE, which were planning to bid on an Air Force contract to establish nuclear detonation detection stations, indicating

---

a. This section forbids a prime contractor whose bid has been accepted to substitute another subcontractor for a listed subcontractor without the consent of the awarding authority, and then only in situations involving the unwillingness or inability of the listed subcontractor.

its interest in being a subcontractor to provide the electromagnetic sensors. Representatives of AT and GE then met several times to discuss terms and how "AT would be a team member, subject to. Air Force approval." As the result of the success of these meetings, GE submitted a proposal contemplating a cost-plus-fixed-fee contract and listed itself, AT, and three other companies on the cover of its proposal to the Air Force. Two AT scientists participated in an oral presentation of GE's proposal to the Air Force. GE was selected as prime contractor, subject to negotiation of a suitable contract, but when that contract was concluded on a cost-plus-incentive-fee basis, giving GE a strong interest in cutting costs below its target, GE refused to deal exclusively with AT and sought other bids on the sensors. AT brought suit in equity to restrain GE from using information supplied to it by AT, for a declaration that GE had breached a fiduciary relation to AT, and for damages. AT was denied injunctive relief, but awarded $128,734. Both parties appealed. *Held:* Reversed and remanded for redetermination of damages. The master who heard the case below had concluded that since AT had furnished similar information to GE's competitors, it was not a trade secret and GE owed no duty to AT based on its appropriation alone. But the court held that the situation was distinguishable from that in the Cronin case, p. 154 supra, because GE had agreed that AT would be a "team member," which suggested "some form of joint undertaking." Although it was not technically a "joint venture," GE "may be held to its contractual responsibility to AT as a team member," which was that if GE was awarded the contract, AT would receive, subject to Air Force approval, a subcontract for the sensors that would give AT a "reasonable opportunity to recover its costs plus a fair profit." The uncertainties about the subcontract, such as those created by the prospect of bargaining with GE and the requirement of Air Force approval, do not preclude recovery by AT for its lost opportunity, but were not properly taken into account by the master in calculating damages. In no event may the damages be less than the higher of "(a) the value reasonably expended by AT in the performance of the joint arrangement, and (b) the fair value of AT's contribution to that arrangement." Air Technology Corp. v. General Elec. Co., 347 Mass. 613, 199 N.E.2d 538 (1964). What rationale lies behind this limitation on damages?

(2) *The Case of the Contractor Caught in the Act.* Page & Wirtz, a general contractor, was preparing a bid for construction on the Western Plaza Shopping Center, and already had a subcontractor's bid of about $214,000 on the masonry from Southwestern Bricklaying. At 11:00 a. m., a few hours before the 2:00 p. m. deadline for general contractors' bids, Van Doran, another subcontractor, left his bid of $204,395 with Walter Wirtz after discussing it. Van Doran was still in the building talking to Wirtz' son Jack, when Wirtz came out of his office and told Page to get Southwestern on the telephone immediately. When Wirtz turned around and saw that Van Doran had overheard him, there was "an atmosphere of embarrassment," particularly because Van Doran had accused other general contractors of bid shopping in the past. At 1:00 p. m. Southwestern submitted a second bid, $1,595 under the Van Doran bid. Page & Wirtz submitted its own bid based on Van Doran's figures by 2:00 p. m. At 4:00 p. m. Van Doran telephoned Walter Wirtz, who said "this morning I made the biggest bust I ever made in my life" and "under existing con-

ditions, I can do nothing but give you the job." Van Doran replied, "Well, Walter, now, as I understand it, if you get this job, I've got a job," and Wirtz said "Yes". Page & Wirtz was awarded the contract, and awarded the masonry contract to Southwestern. Van Doran sued Page & Wirtz for breach of contract, claiming loss of prospective profits. From a judgment for $25,000, defendant appealed. *Held:* Reversed. "Van Doran admitted throughout his testimony to numerous conditions of the contract between it and Wirtz which would have to be later negotiated." These related to lien rights, a two-year guarantee, an escalator clause, and arrangements that would have to be made if the owners refused to use the standard contract conditions of the American Institute of Architects. "It is clear in the record that before Van Doran's bid was submitted the [owners] were insisting on the conditions just related and Van Doran and Wirtz had discussed the fact that efforts would be made by Wirtz to secure modifications thereof to conform to Van Doran's bid. . . . In view of the several essential conditions Van Doran testified would have to be negotiated between his company and Wirtz we do not believe [that Air Technology Corp. v. General Electric Co., discussed in Note 1, supra] is decisive to make a binding contract between them. . . . There is not even a contention of any species of joint venture in our case." Page & Wirtz Const. Co. v. Van Doran Bri-Tico Co., 432 S.W.2d 731 (Tex.Civ.App.1968). See also Plumbing Shop Inc. v. Pitts, 67 Wash.2d 514, 408 P.2d 382 (1965).

POSSIBLE SOLUTIONS

Which of the following three solutions, suggested in the Baird and Drennan opinions, do you favor?

First, treat the subcontractor's bid as an offer revocable at any time until the general contractor has accepted it by his return promise following the award. This leaves the general contractor with only the practical sanction of refusing to do further business with a subcontractor who withdraws a bid on which the general contractor has relied.

Second, treat the subcontractor's bid as an offer irrevocable until the general contractor has had a reasonable time to accept it by his return promise following the award. This binds the subcontractor but not the general contractor, and the subcontractor who is already vulnerable to bid shopping during this period can be expected to regard it as aggravating as existing imbalance. (Market changes during this period may also cause the subcontractor concern, but these he can avoid by using an "escalator" clause.)

Third, treat the subcontractor's bid as an offer revocable until the general contractor has accepted it by his return promise before the award, the resulting contract being subject to the condition that the general contractor receive the award. This, of course, would bind both parties and prevent bid shopping. How practical is this solution? Consider the delay of subcontractors in submitting their bids and the haste in which the general contractor's bid is often submitted.

Consider also the fact that subcontractors' bids are often stated in different ways (e. g., lumping various items together) so that comparison is difficult on the basis of the bids alone. Should a return promise by the general contractor be implied from his use of the subcontractor's bid? How practical is this solution if there is no requirement of listing? What if the general contractor has discounted the bid in anticipation of bid shopping? What if he has "doctored" subcontractors' bids by combining figures from several of them?

To what extent should the solution depend on whether the subcontractor stated that his bid was irrevocable? On whether the bid was in writing? Does UCC 2–205 provide a useful analogy? [a]

NOTE

Industry Attitudes and Practices. Would your answer be affected by any of the following industry attitudes and practices, suggested by Professor Schultz' study in Indiana, cited at p. 137 supra? A substantial majority of subcontractors' bids are, by their terms, firm offers, and in most cases this is required by the general contractor. Where the subcontractor has made a firm offer, the great majority of general contractors feel bound to give him the job if they have used his bid and been awarded the contract, and the great majority of subcontractors feel bound by their bid, even if there is an unexpected rise in the price of materials. But the overwhelming majority of subcontractors who feel bound base their feeling on moral or ethical rather than legal grounds, and only a tiny minority of general contractors would even threaten a lawsuit if a subcontractor withdrew. Only a distinct minority of general contractors ever consider legal devices such as an option contract, a contract conditional on award, or a bid bond to bind the subcontractor before the award, and in most of the cases consideration is given to a bid bond. An even smaller minority of subcontractors consider legal devices, since most feel that their bargaining position does not make them practical. See also Note, 53 Va.L. Rev. 1720 (1967).

Professor Schultz' own conclusion was that the second of the three solutions in the preceding note would add further to the existing imbalance in favor of the general contractor, and that it would be better to accept the first solution and leave the matter to be worked out by the parties without the aid of legal sanctions. Do you agree?

FRANCHISES

The next cases deal with franchised dealers, who have been described by Professor Kessler as occupying a position intermediate between "the independent retailer, exemplified by the general store or the corner grocery store" and the "agent who may be a branch or subsidiary of the manufacturer." An exerpt from his article follows.

a. For a decision following the Drennan case, even though the contract came within Article 2 of the Code and the subcontractor's offer was not irrevocable under UCC 2–205, see E. A. Coronis Associates v. M. Gordon Construction Co., 90 N.J.Super. 69, 216 A. 2d 246 (1966).

KESSLER, AUTOMOBILE DEALER FRANCHISES: VERTICAL INTEGRATION BY CONTRACT, 66 Yale L.J. 1135, 1136–41 (1957).[a] The unique advantage of franchising for the manufacturer lies in the considerable control over the process of distribution he may exercise without exposure to the burdens and responsibilities of an agency relationship. Ideally, the dealers are carefully chosen from among those of proven ability. Selected dealers, experience has shown, tend to be more aggressive in cultivating a market and servicing the product. They are generally "co-operative" in carrying out the manufacturer's suggested program of selling. And the franchises of dealers who do not prove their worth may be eliminated by cancellation or non-renewal.

In return, the franchised dealer receives from the manufacturer added capacity to build and maintain a strong retail organization. Restriction of outlets tends to protect the dealer's inventory and plant investment. Moreover, the nature of the relationship fosters mutual dependence, and the dealer can expect the manufacturer to assist him in effective merchandising. The dealer also gains increased prestige through affiliation with a large organization, frequently of national extension.

Finally, the consumer, we are told, gets better service under the franchise system and is assured that the retailer carries a complete stock of the manufacturer's products.

However great these advantages, the franchise system is not free from shortcomings and frictions. The manufacturer may suffer because the dealer, sheltered by the restriction of outlets, does not exert his "best efforts." The "un-co-operative" dealer may lose his franchise and, to the extent it is built around exclusive representation, his business. Again, due to lack of outlet competition the consumer may suffer from a high price level or be at the mercy of a dealer whose services are inadequate.

Retail distribution through franchise arrangements has grown significantly during the last forty years. It has become the principal market channel for such products as automobiles, electrical appliances, farm implements, radios, television, tires and wall paper. Because of the nature of the commodity involved, the franchise system has had its most spectacular development in the automobile industry. As the system exists today, the manufactured product is channelled through the manufacturer's own sales organization directly to selected retailers. With the industry's development of its own decentralized assembly plants, the independent distributor-wholesaler, once important in the distribution process, has largely disappeared, except in low-volume lines. Large manufacturers usually regard the distribu-

a. Reprinted by permission of The Yale Law Journal Company and Fred B. Rothman & Company.

tor as an economic luxury. And direct sales by manufacturers to the consumer, always small in number, are limited to fleet vehicles or those that require special design or finish. . . .

Although the [automobile] franchise system had many staunch supporters among dealers even before recent modifications, it has been a source of conflicts and tensions. . . . Its actual operation, the dealers complained, precluded them from attaining an independence as full as that of most merchants. In reality, the argument runs, automobile dealers have been in large measure the manufacturers' agents. Through their dominant economic position, the manufacturers have employed the franchise, a "one-sided document which is neither contract, license or agreement," to gain maximum control over the management of the dealers' business without corresponding "legal" responsibility. Under the terms of the franchise, the factories "give the orders while the dealer takes the losses."

The modern franchise indeed enables the manufacturer to wield great "vertical power" in the form of supervisory control over retail operations. The franchise is embodied in a detailed standardized contract presented by the manufacturer to the dealer. The master contract is frequently accompanied by printed addenda concerning such matters as capital requirements and succession. Modern franchise contracts show great similarity; the absence of complete uniformity may be ascribed to the competition for dealers among the . . . remaining manufacturers. This high degree of standardization is best illustrated by the "entire agreement" clauses. Patterned after provisions frequently found in insurance policies, the modern franchise states that it supersedes all prior agreements, that it constitutes the "entire agreement of the parties" and that only certain executives of the manufacturer, usually the Vice-President or Sales Manager, have authority to alter the written contract.

The terms of the franchise contract, however elaborate, do not give a complete picture of the dealership as an institution. "[They] do not show [that] 'priceless ingredient' of prime importance—namely, the manner in which the contract is administered." The policies and practices of the manufacturer may be made relevant with the help of skillfully drafted clauses in the franchise agreement. But often the dealer must comply simply because of the economic power of the manufacturer. A prospective dealer, to be sure, is free to accept or reject a dealer franchise. Once he has committed his capital and entered the business, however, the power of the manufacturer comes into operation. The dealer must, on pain of cancellation or non-renewal, accede to the demands which the manufacturer, in the interest of market penetration, deems necessary and reasonable. Thus the manufacturer has an assured market in his dealers. Of course, his power to terminate or not to renew is tempered by considerations of enlightened self-interest. The manufacturer gains nothing by destroying a valuable member of a sales organization developed over the years with his own assistance and financial contribution. On the other hand, cancellation or non-renewal are valuable means of replacing inefficient dealers with new ones, selected from the waiting list prepared by field representatives. . . .

With the gradual development of the terms of the franchise, several unique features have become apparent. Today the dealer is required to develop his territory to the satisfaction of the manufacturer, a requirement buttressed by a host of ancillary provisions. Termination clauses are designed to assure adequate performance and attempt to insulate the manufacturer from liability. But franchises do not compensate the franchised dealer by giving him "territorial security," a protected sales area. Small wonder dealers complained that the modern franchise is "one-sided," "neither contract, license or agreement." In response to dealer complaints, adverse public opinion and new federal legislation, the terms of franchises have recently been considerably changed in the dealers' favor.

GOODMAN v. DICKER

United States Court of Appeals, District of Columbia, 1948.
83 U.S.App.D.C. 353, 169 F.2d 684.

PROCTOR, ASSOCIATE JUSTICE. This appeal is from a judgment of the District Court in a suit by appellees for breach of contract.

Appellants are local distributors for Emerson Radio and Phonograph Corporation in the District of Columbia. Appellees, with the knowledge and encouragement of appellants, applied for a "dealer franchise" to sell Emerson's products. The trial court found that appellants by their representations and conduct induced appellees to incur expenses in preparing to do business under the franchise, including employment of salesmen and solicitation of orders for radios. Among other things, appellants represented that the application had been accepted; that the franchise would be granted, and that appellees would receive an initial delivery of thirty to forty radios. Yet, no radios were delivered, and notice was finally given that the franchise would not be granted.

The case was tried without a jury. The court held that a contract had not been proven but that appellants were estopped from denying the same by reason of their statements and conduct upon which appellees relied to their detriment. Judgment was entered for $1,500, covering cash outlays of $1,150 and loss of $350, anticipated profits on sale of thirty radios.

The main contention of appellants is that no liability would have arisen under the dealer franchise had it been granted because, as understood by appellees, it would have been terminable at will and would have imposed no duty upon the manufacturer to sell or appellees to buy any fixed number of radios. From this it is argued that the franchise agreement would not have been enforceable (except as to acts performed thereunder) and cancellation by the manufacturer would have created no liability for expenses incurred by the dealer in preparing to do business.   Further, it is argued that as the dealer franchise would have been unenforceable for failure of the manufacturer to supply radios appellants would not be liable to fulfill their assurance that radios would be supplied.

We think these contentions miss the real point of this case.   We are not concerned directly with the terms of the franchise.   We are dealing with a promise by appellants that a franchise would be granted and radios supplied, on the faith of which appellees with the knowledge and encouragement of appellants incurred expenses in making preparations to do business.   Under these circumstances we think that appellants cannot now advance any defense inconsistent with their assurance that the franchise would be granted.   Justice and fair dealing require that one who acts to his detriment on the faith of conduct of the kind revealed here should be protected by estopping the party who has brought about the situation from alleging anything in opposition to the natural consequences of his own course of conduct.   Dair v. United States, 1872, 16 Wall. 1, 4, 21 L.Ed. 491.   In Dickerson v. Colgrove, 100 U.S. 578, 580, 25 L.Ed. 618, the Supreme Court, in speaking of equitable estoppel, said: "The law upon the subject is well settled.   The vital principle is that he who by his language or conduct leads another to do what he would not otherwise have done, shall not subject such person to loss or injury by disappointing the expectations upon which he acted.   Such a change of position is sternly forbidden. . . .   This remedy is always so applied as to promote the ends of justice."   See also Casey v. Galli, 94 U.S. 673, 680, 24 L.Ed. 168; Arizona v. Copper Queen Mining Co., 233 U.S. 87, 95, 34 S.Ct. 546, 58 L.Ed. 863.

In our opinion the trial court was correct in holding defendants liable for moneys which appellees expended in preparing to do business under the promised dealer franchise.   These items aggregated $1,150.   We think, though, the court erred in adding the item of $350 for loss of profits on radios promised under an initial order.   The true measure of damage is the loss sustained by expenditures made in reliance upon the assurance of a dealer franchise.   As thus modified, the judgment is

Affirmed.

NOTES

(1) *Amount of Recovery.*   Why did the court in Goodman v. Dicker deny recovery for the lost profits on the thirty radios?   Would it have been possible to have calculated that profit so that it did not give double recovery for some of the expenditures included in the $1,150?   How? Cf. Chrysler Corporation v. Quimby, 51 Del. 264, 144 A.2d 123, 885 (1958). Similar problems will be encountered in connection with remedies in Chapter 5.

(2) *Culpa in Contrahendo.* The German scholar Jhering, writing in 1861, formulated a doctrine of *culpa in contrahendo* (fault in negotiating), under which "damages should be recoverable against the party whose blameworthy conduct during negotiations for a contract brought about its invalidity or prevented its perfection. . . . Of course, the party who has relied on the validity of the contract to his injury will not be able to recover the value of the promised performance, the expectation interest. But, he suggested, the law can ill afford to deny the innocent party recovery altogether; it has to provide for the restoration of the *status quo* by giving the injured party his 'negative interest' or reliance damages. The careless promisor has only himself to blame when he has created for the other party the false appearance of a binding obligation. This is the meaning of *culpa in contrahendo.*" [a] Kessler and Fine, *Culpa in Contrahendo,* Bargaining in Good Faith, and Freedom of Contract: A Comparative Study, 77 Harv.L.Rev. 401, 401–02 (1964). On developments in this country, including the cases in this subsection, see Henderson, Promissory Estoppel and Traditional Contract Doctrine, 78 Yale L.J. 343 (1969); R. Summers, "Good Faith" in General Contract Law and the Sales Provisions of the Uniform Commercial Code, 54 Va.L.Rev. 195, 220–32 (1968); Note, 37 U.Chi.L.Rev. 559 (1970).

HOFFMAN v. RED OWL STORES, 26 Wis.2d 683, 133 N.W.2d 267 (1965). [Hoffman and his wife owned and operated a bakery in Wautoma, Wisconsin. In November, 1959, he contacted Red Owl, which operated a supermarket chain, seeking to obtain a franchise for a Red Owl store in Wautoma. He mentioned that he had only $18,000 to invest and was assured that this would be sufficient. In February, 1961, on the advice of Red Owl's representative, Lukowitz, he acquired a small grocery store as a means of gaining experience. After three months, the store was operating at a profit, and Lukowitz advised him to sell it, assuring him that Red Owl would find him a larger store elsewhere. Hoffman did so in June, 1961, although he was reluctant to lose the summer tourist business. He was again assured that $18,000 would suffice to obtain a franchise. In September, on Lukowitz' advice, Hoffman put $1,000 down on a lot in Chilton selected by Red Owl. Later in September, after meeting with Hoffman to prepare a financial statement, Lukowitz told him, "[E]verything is ready to go. Get your money together and we are set." Lukowitz then told Hoffman to sell his bakery, which Hoffman did in November for $10,000, a loss of $2,000. He paid a month's rent of $125 on a house in Chilton, and they spent $140 in moving his family to Neenah where Red Owl suggested that he get experience by working at their store near there. When that job did not materialize, he went to work on the night shift at an Appleton bakery.

a. The impact of the doctrine in contemporary German law has shifted to problems that we would characterize as problems of tort rather than of contract. Might it be instructive to view the following case, Hoffman v. Red Owl, through the optic of tort?

[By this time, Lukowitz and Hoffman had considered a variety of arrangements under which Red Owl would get some third party to acquire the Chilton lot, build the building, and lease it to Hoffman, and had agreed on some of the terms of a ten-year lease, with an option in Hoffman to renew the lease or purchase the property. Late in November they met with Red Owl's credit manager and drew up a proposed financing statement showing Hoffman contributing $24,100 of which $4,600 was an actual cash contribution, and another $7,500 was to be borrowed from his father-in-law. A week or two later, Lukowitz said that according to the home office, if Hoffman could get another $2,000 for promotion, the deal could go through for $26,000. Hoffman got his father-in-law to agree to put up $13,000 if he could come in as a partner. The home office, however, insisted that the father-in-law sign an agreement that the $13,000 was either a gift or a loan subordinate to all general creditors. Early in February, 1962, the negotiations collapsed when Hoffman refused to accede to a proposed financial statement that showed his contribution as $34,000, including $13,000 from his father-in-law as an outright gift. The Hoffmans sued Red Owl and the jury gave a special verdict, assessing damages as $16,735 for the sale of the Wautoma store, $2,000 for the sale of the bakery, $1,000 for taking up the option on the Chilton lot, $140 for moving expenses to Neenah, and $125 for house rental in Chilton. The trial court confirmed the verdict, except for the figure of $16,735 for the sale of the Wautoma store, as to which it ordered a new trial.]

CURRIE, CHIEF JUSTICE. . . . The record here discloses a number of promises and assurances given to Hoffman by Lukowitz in behalf of Red Owl upon which plaintiffs relied and acted upon to their detriment. . . . There remains for consideration the question of law raised by defendants that agreement was never reached on essential factors necessary to establish a contract between Hoffman and Red Owl. Among these were the size, cost, design, and layout of the store building; and the terms of the lease with respect to rent, maintenance, renewal, and purchase options. This poses the question of whether the promise necessary to sustain a cause of action for promissory estoppel must embrace all essential details of a proposed transaction between promisor and promisee so as to be equivalent of an offer that would result in a binding contract between the parties if the promisee were to accept the same.

Originally the doctrine of promissory estoppel was invoked as a substitute for consideration rendering a gratuitous promise enforceable as a contract. . . . In other words, the acts of reliance by the promisee to his detriment provided a substitute for consideration. If promissory estoppel were to be limited to only those situations where the promise giving rise to the cause of action must be so definite with respect to all details that a contract would result were the promise supported by consideration, then the defendants' instant promises to Hoffman would not meet this test. However, sec. 90 of Restatement, 1 Contracts, does not impose the requirement that the promise giving rise to the cause of action must be so comprehensive in scope as to meet the requirements of an offer that would ripen into a contract if accepted by the promisee. . . . We deem it would be a mistake to regard an action grounded on promissory estoppel as the equivalent of a breach of contract action. . . . We conclude that injustice would result here if plaintiffs were not granted some relief because of the failure of defendants to keep their promises which induced plaintiffs to act to their detriment.

[With regard to damages, all of the items properly represented losses that he had reasonably sustained in reliance on Red Owl's promises except for the $16,735 for the sale of the Wautoma store. This should have been] limited to the difference between the sales price received and the fair market value of the assets sold, giving consideration to any goodwill attaching thereto by reason of the transfer of a going business. There was no direct evidence presented as to what this fair market was [and it was error to consider Hoffman's profits, except in relation to goodwill.] Plaintiffs contend that in a breach of contract action damages may include loss of profits. However, this is not a breach of contract action. . . . Where damages are awarded in promissory estoppel instead of specifically enforcing the promisor's promise, they should be only such as in the opinion of the court are necessary to prevent injustice. . . . At the time Hoffman bought the equipment and inventory of the small grocery store at Wautoma he did so in order to gain experience in the grocery store business. . . . Thus Hoffman made this purchase more or less as a temporary experiment. Justice does not require that the damages awarded him, because of selling these assets at the behest of defendants, should exceed any actual loss sustained measured by the difference between the sales price and the fair market value.

[Affirmed.]

NOTES

(1) *The Case of the Uncertain Loan.* Wheeler owned a tract of land in Port Arthur, Texas, on which he wanted to build a commercial structure. He made a written agreement with White, under which White was to either make or obtain a loan of $70,000, payable in monthly installments over 15 years at not more than 6%, to finance the project and to receive a $5,000 fee for obtaining the loan and a 5% commission on all rentals from tenants that he procured. Later White assured Wheeler that he would make the loan himself if the money was unobtainable elsewhere, and urged him to proceed with the demolition of the existing buildings, which had a value of $58,500 and a rental value of $400 a month. After Wheeler had razed the old buildings and begun to prepare the site, White refused to perform. When Wheeler was unable to obtain a loan himself, he sued White. From judgment dismissing Wheeler's complaint, Wheeler appealed. *Held:*

Reversed. "[T]he pleaded contract did not contain essential elements to its enforceability in that it failed to provide the amount of monthly installments, the amount of interest due upon the obligation, how much interest would be computed, [and] when such interest would be paid. . . ." The court then discussed Goodman v. Dicker. "We agree with the reasoning announced in those jurisdictions that, in cases such as we have before us, where there is actually no contract the promissory estoppel theory may be invoked, thereby supplying a remedy which will enable the injured party to be compensated for his foreseeable, definite and substantial reliance. Where the promisee has failed to bind the promisor to a legally sufficient contract, but where the promisee has acted in reliance upon a promise to his detriment, the promisee is to be allowed to recover no more than reliance damages measured by the detriment sustained." Wheeler v. White, 398 S.W.2d 93 (Tex.1965). How should those damages be calculated when the case goes back for trial? Does this case go beyond Goodman v. Dicker? Beyond Hoffman v. Red Owl?

(2) *The Case of Miller High Life.* In October, 1963, Prince, an established beer distributor, undertook the Miller High Life distributorship in East Harris County, Texas, although he knew that the area had been poorly serviced in the past and that it would be two or three years before he would realize a profit. The contract provided, "Either of us can terminate this relationship at any time without incurring liability to the other." Miller terminated in June, 1965 because it had become involved in a lawsuit with a corporation that Prince controlled. Prince had just begun to make a profit, after having sustained losses of over $20,000, not including his own time and effort and that of his wife. Miller then appointed another distributor, whose operation showed a continued and substantial increase in sales volume. Prince sued Miller for the money he had spent in preparation for and operation of the distributorship and for reasonable compensation for his services. The trial court directed a verdict for the defendant and the plaintiff appealed. *Held:* Affirmed. "It is appellant's contention that where a manufacturer and a distributor enter into an arrangement whereby the distributor is to develop a market for and sell the manufacturer's products, and it is contemplated by both parties that expenditures of time and money by the distributor are necessary to build up his distributorship, though the relationship be one terminable at will, the law will not allow the manufacturer to exercise its rights of cancellation with impunity, but will imply an obligation on its part to respond in damages sufficient to compensate the distributor for his expenditures made and losses incurred in reliance upon the agreement if the manufacturer terminates the distributorship before the distributor is afforded a reasonable time to recoup his losses. . . . This statement of the law is supported by respectable authority. . . . [However], each of these cases presented situations where the contract was oral, of indefinite duration, or void, and were considered cancellable at will as a matter of law. There was no specific written agreement authorizing cancellation without liability. . . . In Wheeler v. White [Note 1, supra], the Supreme Court recognized the case of Goodman v. Dicker. . . . In this case, however, there is a legally sufficient contract. . . . Appellant cannot disregard the contract and sue for his reliance damage. Because of the valid contract the theory of promissory estoppel is not applicable." Prince v. Miller

Brewing Co., 434 S.W.2d 232 (Tex.Civ.App.1968). But cf. Clausen & Sons v. Theo. Hamm Brewing Co., 395 F.2d 388 (8th Cir. 1968).

What result if Prince had been able to show that Miller had terminated the contract in order to let a close personal friend of one of its officers have a profitable franchise? In Goodman v. Dicker, would Dicker have had any recourse if Emerson had granted him a franchise and then terminated it immediately? Would the wording of the termination clause affect your answer? What answer if it read, "Either of us can terminate this relationship at any time"? See Gellhorn, Limitations on Contract Termination Rights—Franchise Cancellations, 1967 Duke L.J. 465 (1967).

(c) Contracts by Correspondence: The "Mailbox Rule"

This subsection deals with the problems that arise when distant parties bargain by post, telegraph or similar means of communication. Suppose, for example, that one party has sent the other an offer, and that the offeree has dispatched an acceptance which has not yet been received by the offeror. Is it too late for the offeror to change his mind and revoke the offer? Is it too late for the offeree to change his mind and reject the offer? And is there a contract if the acceptance is lost and is never received by the offeror?

As will be seen, the tendency of the common law has been to answer such questions as these on the assumption that dispatch of the acceptance is ordinarily the crucial point at which the contract is made—after which the offeror's power to revoke is terminated, the offeree's power to reject is ended, and the risks of transmission are on the offeror. Because the early cases involved acceptance by post, this came to be known as the "mailbox rule." As will also be seen, the wisdom of making so many consequences flow from the same event is at least questionable.

POWER TO REVOKE

In 1818 the Court of King's Bench decided one of the most celebrated cases in the field of contracts, Adams v. Lindsell, 1 B. & Ald. 681, 106 Eng.Rep. 250 (K.B.1818). A firm of wool dealers had mailed an offer to sell "eight hundred tods of wether fleeces" to a firm of woolen manufacturers and the manufacturers had put a letter of acceptance in the post. While this letter was in transit, the dealers attempted to revoke their offer and sold the wool to another buyer.[a]

a. One of the curious features of the case is that although the dealers had sold the wool while the letter of acceptance was in transit, they had taken no steps to notify the manufacturers of their revocation until after it had been received. It would seem, therefore, under cases like Dickinson v. Dodds, p. 117, supra, that revocation had come too late in any event. The explanation appears to lie in Cooke v. Oxley, 3 T.R. 653, 100 Eng.

When the manufacturers sued for breach of contract, the dealers argued that, "Till the plaintiffs' answer was actually received, there could be no binding contract between the parties." The court rejected this argument and upheld recovery.

> The Court said, that if that were so, no contract could ever be completed by the post. For if the defendants were not bound by their offer when accepted by the plaintiffs till the answer was received, then the plaintiffs ought not to be bound till after they had received the notification that the defendants had received their answer and assented to it. And so it might go on ad infinitum. The defendants must be considered in law as making, during every instant of the time their letter was traveling, the same identical offer to the plaintiffs; and then the contract is completed by the acceptance of it by the latter.

The overwhelming weight of authority in the United States supports the "mailbox rule" of Adams v. Lindsell. See Restatement Second, § 64. The court's reasoning, however, is less than convincing. The Restatement Second, in Comment a to § 64, gives a different rationale.

> It is often said that an offeror who makes an offer by mail makes the post office his agent to receive the acceptance, or that the mailing of a letter of acceptance puts it irrevocably out of the offeree's control. Under United States postal regulations, however, the sender of a letter has long had the power to stop delivery and reclaim the letter. A better explanation of the rule that the acceptance takes effect on dispatch is that the offeree needs a dependable basis for his decision whether to accept. In many legal systems such a basis is provided by a general rule that an offer is irrevocable unless it provides otherwise. [See p. 115 supra.] The common law provides such a basis through the rule that a revocation of an offer is ineffective if received after an acceptance has been properly dispatched.

The following case is a rare departure from the prevailing rule.

————

RHODE ISLAND TOOL CO. v. UNITED STATES, 130 Ct. Cl. 698, 128 F.Supp. 417 (1955). [The United States invited bids from suppliers for a number of items. Its invitation read: "The successful bidder will *receive* Notice of Award at the earliest possible

Rep. 785 (K.B.1790), a confusing relic of the subjective theory of contracts, which evidently stood for the proposition that a person after having offered to sell goods could by a mere change of mind, as by a sale to another, prevent acceptance by the offeree. At the hearing in Dickinson v. Dodds, Cooke v. Oxley was distinguished as going solely on the pleadings by Vice Chancellor Bacon, who found it "not so clearly and satisfactorily reported as might be desired."

date, and such Award will *thereupon* constitute a binding contract between the bidder and the Government without further action on the part of the bidder." (Italics supplied by the court.) On September 10, Tool Company submitted a bid to supply fifteen lots of bolts, but in calculating the bid its sales manager failed to notice that the specifications for three of the lots had been changed from cheaper stud bolts to more expensive machine bolts, and mistakenly based the bid on the cost of stud bolts. On October 4 the government mailed to Tool Company an acceptance of its bid as to these three lots. On the same day Tool Company, having discovered its mistake, telephoned the government's representative withdrawing its bid as to these lots. The record did not show whether the government's acceptance had been mailed at this time, but the acceptance was not received by Tool Company until after the revocation. At the government's insistence Tool Company supplied machine bolts and then sued for an additional $1,640.60 over its bid.]

JONES, CHIEF JUSTICE. . . . Under the old post office regulations when a letter was deposited in the mail the sender lost all control of it. It was irrevocably on its way. After its deposit in the mail the post office became, in effect, the agent of the addressee. Naturally the authorities held that the acceptance in any contract became final when it was deposited in the post office, since the sender had lost control of the letter at that time. That was the final act in consummating the agreement. But some years ago [a] the United States Postal authorities completely changed the regulation [to permit the sender to withdraw his letter from the mail].

When this new regulation became effective, the entire picture was changed. The sender now does not lose control of the letter the moment it is deposited in the post office, but retains the right of control up to the time of delivery. The acceptance, therefore, is not final until the letter reaches destination, since the sender has the absolute right of withdrawal from the post office, and even the right to have the postmaster at the delivery point return the letter at any time before actual delivery. We have so held. Dick v. United States, 82 F. Supp. 326, 113 Ct.Cl. 94, and authorities therein cited. . . .

Does any one believe that if the mistake had been the other way, that is, if the machine bolts had been listed first and the stud bolts as later items, and that through oversight the defendant had mailed an acceptance for too high a price and the same day had wired withdrawing and cancelling the acceptance before it left the sending post office the defendant would nevertheless have been held to an excessive

a. Postal Laws and Regulations had been changed as early as 1885 to permit the sender of a letter to have it returned even after it had left the mailing post office by application to the post master of that office. United States Official Postal Guide 697 (1885). The practical problems of attempting to retrieve a letter are suggested in Macneil, Time of Acceptance: Too Many Problems for a Single Rule, 112 U.Pa.L.Rev. 947, 959 (1964).

price? Or again, if after mailing such an acceptance the defendant, discovering its mistake, had gone to the sending post office and withdrawn the letter, the plaintiff on hearing of it, could have enforced an excessive contract on the ground that the acceptance actually had been posted and became final and enforceable, notwithstanding its withdrawal and nondelivery? We cannot conceive of such an unjust enforcement. No, under the new regulation, the Post Office Department becomes, in effect, the agency of the sender until actual delivery.

We are living in a time of change. The theories of yesterday, proved by practice today, give way to the improvements of tomorrow. To apply an outmoded formula is not only unjust, it runs counter to the whole stream of human experience. It is like insisting on an oxcart as the official means of transportation in the age of the automobile. The cart served a useful purpose in its day, but is now a museum piece. The old rule was established before Morse invented the telegraph as a means of communication. Commerce must have a breaking point upon which it may rely for the completion of a contract. At that time no faster mode of communication was known. But in the light of the faster means of communication the Post Office Department wisely changed the rule. The reason for the old rule had disappeared. This does not change any principle, it simply changes the practice to suit the changed conditions, but leaves unchanged the principle of finality, which is just as definite as ever, though transferred to a different point by the new regulation.   .   .   .

Manifestly a mistake was made. The defendant is not injured by permitting its correction. It only forbids defendant's unjust enrichment by preventing its taking technical advantage of an evident mistake. Plaintiff is allowed to recover its actual losses, if any, in furnishing the machine bolts, limited, however, to the difference between its bid and that of the next lowest bidder on these particular items, that amount being not a yardstick, but a ceiling on any losses it may be able to prove; or, in the alternative, the reasonable value of the items furnished, subject to the same limitation.   .   .   .

[LARAMORE and LITTLETON concurred. WHITAKER dissented in an opinion in which MADDEN concurred.]

NOTES

(1) *Mistake and the "Mailbox Rule."* How does this case differ from the Kemper case, p. 142 supra? Could the court have based its decision on a narrower ground than the change in postal regulations? Would Rhode Island Tool have prevailed if it had made no mistake but had simply decided that it could get a better price elsewhere? See Morrison v. Thoelke, 155 So.2d 889 (Fla.App.1963). How great is the danger that an offeror, in the position of Rhode Island Tool, will make a false claim of mistake? Is it significant in this regard that Rhode Island Tool's bid was irrevocable

(see Note 1, p. 147 supra)? See Macneil, Time of Acceptance: Too Many Problems for a Single Rule, 112 U.Pa.L.Rev. 947, 955–56 (1964).

(2) *Limits of the "Mailbox Rule."* The Restatement Second, § 64 makes the mailbox rule applicable only where the acceptance is "made in a manner and by a medium invited by [the] offer." See also UCC 2–206 (1) (a). In Henthorn v. Fraser, [1892] 2 Ch. 27, the offeror at its office in Liverpool, handed to the offeree an offer to sell land in Birkenhead, where the offeree resided. The offeree took the offer to Birkenhead and posted an acceptance from there. While it was in transit, he received a letter from the offeror saying that the offer was "cancelled." The court held that the "mailbox rule" applied and there was a contract, even though the offer had not been by post. "Where the circumstances are such that it must have been within the contemplation of the parties that, according to the ordinary usages of mankind, the post might be used as a means of communicating the acceptance of an offer, the acceptance is complete as soon as it is posted." What of an offer by mail and an acceptance by telegram? An offer by telegram and an acceptance by mail?

(3) *Revocation and the "Mailbox Rule."* As might be supposed from such cases as Dickinson v. Dodds, p. 117 supra, a revocation is effective only on receipt, not on dispatch. See Restatement Second, §§ 41, 69. The leading case in Byrne v. Van Tienhoven, 5 C.P.D. 344 (1880), in which the court rejected the argument that the rule laid down in Adams v. Lindsell for acceptance should be applied to revocation as well. "If [this] contention were to prevail no person who had received an offer by post and had accepted it would know his position until he had waited such a time as to be quite sure that a letter withdrawing the offer had not been posted before his acceptance of it." Nevertheless, California, Montana, North Dakota and South Dakota have statutes providing that a revocation as well as an acceptance is effective when dispatched.

(4) *Lapse and the "Mailbox Rule."* If the offeror provides that his offer must be accepted by a specified date or within a specified period of time, is it enough that the acceptance be dispatched within that time, or must it be received within that time? Of course the offeror can dispose of the question by express provision, but what if he does not? How would you interpret a clause in a letter offering to sell land that read, "will give you eight days in which to accept"? See Caldwell v. Cline, 109 W.Va. 553, 156 S.E. 55 (1930). Should the answer depend on whether the offer was revocable or irrevocable? See Restatement Second, § 64(b) and compare Reserve Insurance Co. v. Duckett, 249 Md. 108, 238 A.2d 536 (1968), with Chanoff v. Fiala, 440 Pa. 424, 271 A.2d 285 (1970). How would you have drafted the clause?

(5) *Counselling.* Could the offeror avoid the "mailbox rule" and preserve his power of revocation until his receipt of the acceptance? Could he make his revocation effective on dispatch? How? That many of the problems in this subsection can be disposed of by careful draftsmanship is suggested in Farnsworth, Formation of International Sales Contracts: Three Attempts at Unification, 110 U.Pa.L.Rev. 305 (1962).

POWER TO REJECT

It has generally been assumed that the "mailbox rule," laid down by Adams v. Lindsell in connection with the termination of the offeror's power to revoke, applies as well in connection with the termination of the offeree's power to reject. In other words, once the offeree has dispatched an acceptance, it is too late for him to change his mind and reject the offer. See Restatement Second, § 64. This is, of course, not a necessary assumption, since it would be possible to frame a rule which would deprive the offeror of his power to revoke his offer upon dispatch of the acceptance by the offeree, but leave the offeree free to reject the offer, at least as long as the offeror receives the rejection before he receives the acceptance. The two rules can best be contrasted by considering the case of the overtaking rejection.

Suppose that on Monday Buyer receives by mail an offer from Seller of goods. On Tuesday Buyer mails Seller a letter of acceptance which arrives on Friday. On Wednesday Buyer calls Seller and tells him that he wants to revoke his acceptance and reject the offer. If the "mailbox rule" is applied, it is too late for Buyer to change his mind and Seller can hold him to a contract. If the other rule is applied, Buyer remains free to change his mind while the letter is in transit, and Seller cannot hold him to a contract. The disadvantage of this rule is that while the letter is in transit, although the Seller is unable to revoke, the Buyer is free to watch the market and speculate, having in effect an "option contract" for that period.

But does not the "mailbox rule" also have a disadvantage? Suppose that the rejection does not mention the letter of acceptance, as where Buyer on Wednesday sends an overtaking telegram which is received on Thursday and says simply, "Reject your offer." May not application of the "mailbox rule" to find a contract in such a case prejudice Seller if he relies on the telegram of rejection and sells the goods to another buyer before receiving the letter of acceptance on Friday? Might Buyer be estopped to enforce the contract in such a case? See Comment c and Illustration 7 to Restatement Second, § 64.

NOTES

(1) *More on Mistake and the Mailbox Rule.* One of the few cases to balk at applying the "mailbox rule" to a rejection is Dick v. United States, 82 F.Supp. 326 (Ct.Cl.1949), which was relied upon in the Rhode Island Tool case, p. 178 supra. After preliminary negotiations, the Coast Guard mailed to Dick an offer to buy two sets of propellers for icebreaking vessels at Dick's proposed price of $63,775. On March 15, Dick mailed his acceptance. He then discovered that he had mistakenly assumed that the government wanted and the offer called for only one set of propellers, and on March 16 he telegraphed the Coast Guard calling attention to the mistake and saying that the price should be doubled. On March 21, his acceptance reached the Coast Guard. At the government's insistence Dick furnished the two sets of propellers and sued the United States to recover for the

second set. In overruling the government's demurrer the Court of Claims pointed out that "some years ago the Post Office Department changed its regulation and provided that anyone depositing a letter in the mail might reclaim it," and concluded that even if the government was not "charged with knowledge" of Dick's mistake, he was not precluded from withdrawing his letter of acceptance by means of his later telegram.

Note that the Dick case, like the Rhode Island Tool case, involved a mistake. Is that fact significant? Had the government relied on the mistaken figure? Could the decision have been rested on any other ground? See the discussion of the problem in the Dick case in Macneil, Time of Acceptance: Too Many Problems for a Single Rule, 112 U.Pa.L.Rev. 947, 957–62 (1964).

(2) *Power to Accept.* In the case of the overtaking rejection, it is unnecessary to decide whether it is the dispatch or the receipt of the rejection that terminates the offeree's power to accept, since both dispatch and receipt of the rejection take place after the dispatch of the acceptance and before its receipt. Restatement Second, § 39 says that, in most cases, the power to accept ends at the time of receipt of the rejection. Consider the case of the overtaking acceptance.

Suppose again that on Monday Buyer receives by mail from Seller an offer to sell goods. On Tuesday Buyer mails Seller a letter of rejection, which arrives on Friday. On Wednesday Buyer sends Seller a telegram of acceptance, which overtakes the letter and arrives on Thursday. Under the Restatement Second rule there is a contract. This protects Seller if he has, for example, relied on the telegram of acceptance and passed up an opportunity to sell the goods to another buyer.

Suppose, however, that Buyer's telegram of acceptance does not overtake his letter of rejection, but arrives later on Friday. Is there still a contract, since the telegram of acceptance was *dispatched* before the letter of rejection was *received?* To so hold would be unfair to Seller if he had relied on the earlier arriving rejection and sold the goods to another buyer before he received the later arriving acceptance. What answer does the Restatement Second give in this situation?

RISKS OF TRANSMISSION

The third problem that the "mailbox rule" has been called upon to solve concerns the risks of transmission of the acceptance.[a] Household Fire and Carriage Accident Insurance Co. v. Grant, 4 Exch.Div. 216 (C.A.1879), is a leading case. Grant had paid £ 5 as a deposit and handed to the company's agent an offer to buy 100 shares of its stock, and it had posted its acceptance, addressed to him at his residence, but it had never arrived. The company then went into liquidation and suit was brought for the balance due on the shares. The Court of Appeal held that Grant was liable. According to Thesiger, L. J., the offer was made "under circumstances from

---

a. On the risks of transmission of the offer, see Ayer v. Western Union Telegraph Co., p. 148 supra.

which we must imply that he authorized the company" to send the acceptance by post.

> To me it appears that in practice a contract completed upon the acceptance of an offer being posted, but liable to be put an end to by an accident in the post, would be more mischievous than a contract only binding upon the parties to it upon the acceptance actually reaching the offeror. . . .

BRAMWELL, L. J., dissented:

> It is said that a contrary rule would be hard on the would-be acceptor, who may have made his arrangements on the footing that the bargain was concluded. But to hold as contended would be equally hard on the offeror, who may have made his arrangements on the footing that his offer was not accepted; his nonreceipt of any communication may be attributable to the person to whom it was made being absent. What is he to do but to act on the negative, that no communication has been made to him?

And so the battle has raged. Professor Langdell [a] sided with Bramwell:

> Adopting one view, the hardship consists in making one liable on a contract which he is ignorant of having made; adopting the other view, it consists in depriving one of the benefit of a contract which he supposes he has made. Between these two evils the choice would seem to be clear: the former is positive, the latter merely negative; the former imposes a liability to which no limit can be placed, the latter leaves everything *in statu quo*. As to making provision for the contingency of the miscarriage of a letter, this is easy for the person who sends it, while it is practically impossible for the person to whom it is sent.

Langdell, Summary of the Law of Contracts 21 (2d ed. 1880). Professor Llewellyn [b] sided with Thesiger:

> As between hardship on the offeror, which is really tough, and hardship on the offeree which would be even tougher, the

a. Christopher Columbus Langdell (1826–1906) was a New York lawyer who became professor of law at Harvard Law School in 1870. His principal achievement as professor and later dean was the introduction of the case method of instruction through the publication in 1871 of his casebook on contracts. He believed that instruction should be of such a character that the students "might at least derive a greater advantage from attending it, than from devoting the time to private study."

b. Karl Nickerson Llewellyn (1893–1962) practiced law in New York for two years, and taught law at Yale for several years before becoming a member of the law faculty at Columbia in 1925, where he remained until he joined the law faculty at Chicago in 1951. He was well-known for his contributions to the field of jurisprudence, as one of the school of "legal realists," and also to the fields of commercial law and contracts. He was Chief Reporter of the Uniform Commercial Code, and the author of many books, including The Bramble Bush: On Our Law and Its Study, which was written especially for first-year law students.

vital reason for throwing the hardship of an odd delayed or lost letter upon the offeror remains this: the offeree is already relying, with the best reason in the world, on the deal being on; the offeror is only holding things open; and, in view of the efficiency of communication facilities, we can protect the offerees in *all* these deals at the price of hardship on offerors in very few of them. . . . [The] ingrained usage of business is to answer letters which look toward deals, but the usage is not so clear about acknowledging letters which close deals. The absence of an answer to a letter of offer is much more certain to lead to an inquiry than is the absence of an answer to a letter of acceptance, so that the party bitten by the mischance has under our rule a greater likelihood of being aware of uncertainty and of speedily discovering his difficulty.

Llewellyn, Our Case-Law of Contract: Offer and Acceptance, II, 48 Yale L.J. 779, 795 (1939). The Restatement Second takes the same view, but with some diffidence:

In the interest of simplicity and clarity, the rule has been extended to cases where an acceptance is lost or delayed in the course of transmission. The convenience of the rule is less clear than in cases of attempted revocation of the offer, however, and the language of the offer is often properly interpreted as making the offeror's duty of performance conditional on receipt of the acceptance.

Comment b to Restatement Second, § 64.

(d) Acceptance Varying Offer: The "Mirror Image Rule" and the "Battle of the Forms"

The pattern of communications in a typical contract for the sale of goods was described briefly in Note 1, p. 70 supra. Here is a more extensive description by Professor Macaulay, based on a study of Wisconsin businessmen. In reading the cases that follow, consider what account, if any, should be taken of such findings in formulating legal rules applicable to the transactions described.

MACAULAY, NON-CONTRACTUAL RELATIONS IN BUSINESS: A PRELIMINARY STUDY, 28 Am. Sociological Rev. 55, 57–60 (1963).[a] A firm will have a set of terms and conditions for purchases, sales, or both printed on the business documents used in

a. Reprinted by permission of the American Sociological Review.

these exchanges. Thus the things to be sold and the price may be planned particularly for each transaction, but standard provisions will further elaborate the performances and cover the other subjects of planning. Typically, these terms and conditions are lengthy and printed in small type on the back of the forms. For example, 24 paragraphs in eight point type are printed on the back of the purchase order form used by the Allis Chalmers Manufacturing Company. The provisions: (1) describe, in part, the performance required, e. g., "DO NOT WELD CASTINGS WITHOUT OUR CONSENT"; (2) plan for the effect of contingencies, e. g., ". . . in the event the Seller suffers delay in performance due to an act of God, war, act of the Government, priorities or allocations, act of the Buyer, fire, flood, strike, sabotage, or other causes beyond Seller's control, the time of completion shall be extended a period of time equal to the period of such delay if the Seller gives the Buyer notice in writing of the cause of any such delay within a reasonable time after the beginning thereof"; (3) plan for the effect of defective performances, e. g., "The buyer, without waiving any other legal rights, reserves the right to cancel without charge or to postpone deliveries of any of the articles covered by this order which are not shipped in time reasonably to meet said agreed dates"; (4) plan for a legal sanction, e. g., the clause "without waiving any other legal rights," in the example just given.

In larger firms such "boiler plate" provisions are drafted by the house counsel or the firm's outside lawyer. In smaller firms such provisions may be drafted by the industry trade association, may be copied from a competitor, or may be found on forms purchased from a printer. In any event, salesmen and purchasing agents, the operating personnel, typically are unaware of what is said in the fine print on the back of the forms they use. Yet often the normal business patterns will give effect to this standardized planning. For example, purchasing agents may have to use a purchase order form so that all transactions receive a number under the firm's accounting system. Thus, the required accounting record will carry the necessary planning of the exchange relationship printed on its reverse side. If the seller does not object to this planning and accepts the order, the buyer's "fine print" will control. If the seller does object, differences can be settled by negotiation.

This type of standardized planning is very common. Requests for copies of the business documents used in buying and selling were sent to approximately 6,000 manufacturing firms which do business in Wisconsin. Approximately 1,200 replies were received and 850 companies used some type of standardized planning. With only a few exceptions, the firms that did not reply and the 350 that indicated they did not use standardized planning were very small manufacturers such as local bakeries, soft drink bottlers and sausage makers.

While businessmen can and often do carefully and completely plan, it is clear that not all exchanges are neatly rationalized. Although most businessmen think that a clear description of both the seller's and buyer's performances is obvious common sense, they do not always live up to this ideal. The house counsel and the purchasing agent of a medium size manufacturer of automobile parts reported that several times their engineers had committed the company to buy expensive machines without adequate specifications. The engineers had drawn careful specifications as to the type of machine and how it was to be made but had neglected to require that the machine produce specified results. An attorney and an auditor both stated that most contract disputes arise because of ambiguity in the specifications.

Businessmen often prefer to rely on "a man's word" in a brief letter, a handshake, or "common honesty and decency"—even when the transaction involves exposure to serious risks. Seven lawyers from law firms with business practices were interviewed. Five thought that businessmen often entered contracts with only a minimal degree of advance planning. They complained that businessmen desire to "keep it simple and avoid red tape" even where large amounts of money and significant risks are involved. One stated that he was "sick of being told, 'We can trust old Max,' when the problem is not one of honesty but one of reaching an agreement that both sides understand." Another said that businessmen when bargaining often talk only in pleasant generalities, think they have a contract, but fail to reach agreement on any of the hard, unpleasant questions until forced to do so by a lawyer. Two outside lawyers had different views. One thought that large firms usually planned important exchanges, although he conceded that occasionally matters might be left in a fairly vague state. The other dissenter represents a large utility that commonly buys heavy equipment and buildings. The supplier's employees come on the utility's property to install the equipment or construct the buildings, and they may be injured while there. The utility has been sued by such employees so often that it carefully plans purchases with the assistance of a lawyer so that suppliers take this burden.

Moreover, standardized planning can break down. In the example of such planning previously given, it was assumed that the purchasing agent would use his company's form with its 24 paragraphs printed on the back and that the seller would accept this or object to any provisions he did not like. However, the seller may fail to read the buyer's 24 paragraphs of fine print and may accept the buyer's order on the seller's own acknowledgment-of-order form. Typically this form will have ten to 50 paragraphs favoring the seller, and these provisions are likely to be different from or inconsistent with the buyer's provisions. The seller's acknowledgment form may be received by the buyer and checked by a clerk. She will read the *face* of the acknowledgment but not the fine print on the back of it because she has neither the time nor ability to analyze the small print on the 100 to 500 forms she must review each day. The face of the acknowledgment —where the goods and the price are specified—is likely to correspond with the face of the purchase order. If it does, the two forms are filed away. At this point, both buyer and seller are likely to assume they have planned an exchange and made a contract. Yet they have done neither, as they are in disagreement about all that appears on the back of their forms. This practice is common enough to have a name. Law teachers call it "the battle of the forms."

Ten of the 12 purchasing agents interviewed said that frequently the provisions on the back of their purchase order and those on the back of a supplier's acknowledgment would differ or be inconsistent. Yet they would assume that the purchase was complete without further action unless one of the supplier's provisions was really objectionable. Moreover, only occasionally would they bother to read the fine print on the back of suppliers' forms. On the other hand, one purchasing agent insists that agreement be reached on the fine print provisions, but he represents the utility whose lawyer reported that it exercises great care in planning. The other purchasing agent who said that his company did not face a battle of the forms problem, works for a division of one of the largest manufacturing corporations in the United States. Yet the company may have such a problem without recognizing it. The purchasing agent regularly sends a supplier both a purchase order and another form which the supplier is asked to sign and return. The second form states that the supplier accepts the buyer's terms and conditions. The company has sufficient bargaining power to force suppliers to sign and return the form, and the purchasing agent must show one of his firm's auditors such a signed form for every purchase order issued. Yet suppliers frequently return this buyer's form *plus* their own acknowledgment form which has conflicting provisions. The purchasing agent throws away the supplier's form and files his own. Of course, in such a case the supplier has not acquiesced to the buyer's provisions. There is no agreement and no contract.

Sixteen sales managers were asked about the battle of the forms. Nine said that frequently no agreement was reached on which set of fine print was to govern, while seven said that there was no problem. Four of the seven worked for companies whose major customers are the large automobile companies or the large manufacturers of paper products. These customers demand that their terms and conditions govern any purchase, are careful generally to see that suppliers acquiesce, and have the bargaining power to have their way. The other three of the seven sales managers who have no battle of the forms problem, work for manufacturers of special industrial machines. Their firms are careful to reach complete agreement with their customers. Two of these men stressed that they could take no chances because such a large part of their firm's capital is tied up in making any one machine. The other sales manager had been influenced by a law suit against one of his competitors for over a half million dollars. The suit was brought by a customer when the competitor had been unable to deliver a machine and put it in operation on time. The sales manager interviewed said his firm could not guarantee that its machines would work perfectly by a specified time because they are designed to fit the customer's requirements, which may present difficult engineering problems. As a result, contracts are carefully negotiated.

A large manufacturer of packaging materials audited its records to determine how often it had failed to agree on terms and conditions with its customers or had failed to create legally binding contracts. Such failures cause a risk of loss to this firm since the packaging is printed with the customer's design and cannot be salvaged once this is done. The orders for five days in four different years were reviewed. The percentages of orders where no agreement on terms and conditions was reached or no contract was formed were as follows:

1953................75.0%
1954................69.4%
1955................71.5%
1956................59.5%

It is likely that businessmen pay more attention to describing the performances in an exchange than to planning for contingencies or defective performances or to obtaining legal enforceability of their contracts. Even when a purchase order and acknowledgment have conflicting provisions printed on the back, almost always the buyer and seller will be in agreement on what is to be sold and how much is to be paid for it. The lawyers who said businessmen often commit their firms to significant exchanges too casually, stated that the performances would be defined in the brief letter or telephone call; the lawyers objected that nothing else would be covered. Moreover, it is likely that businessmen are least concerned about planning their transactions so that they are legally enforceable contracts.

POEL v. BRUNSWICK–BALKE–COLLENDER CO.

Court of Appeals of New York, 1915.
216 N.Y. 310, 110 N.E. 619.

Appeal from a judgment of the Appellate Division of the Supreme Court in the first judicial department, entered December 8, 1913, affirming a judgment in favor of plaintiffs entered upon a decision of the court at a Trial Term without a jury.

SEABURY, J. In this action the plaintiffs sued to recover damages from this defendant for the breach of an executory contract.

The plaintiffs are the general partners of the limited partnership of Poel & Arnold. The defendant is a corporation organized under the laws of the state of New York. The theory of the action is that the defendant agreed to accept and pay for certain rubber which the plaintiffs agreed to sell to it, and that the refusal of the defendant to accept and pay for said rubber caused a breach of that contract. In the transactions between the parties the defendant was represented by one C. R. Rogers, who carried on negotiations in behalf of the defendant and signed the letters purporting to come from the defendant, and which will be referred to below. In the court below several questions were litigated, viz., whether Rogers had authority to represent the defendant, and whether there was a contract and a sufficient written memorandum of such contract to satisfy the requirements of the statute of frauds. In our discussion of this case we shall assume, without deciding, that Rogers was authorized to represent the defendant in the action which he took. . . .

There are in this case four writings, and upon three of them this controversy must be determined. They set forth with accuracy and precision the transaction between the parties. The oral evidence that was presented is in no way inconsistent with the writings, and if it were, the spoken words could not be permitted to prevail over the written. The writings referred to are as follows:

"Poel & Arnold, 277 Broadway.

New York, April 2, 1910.

"Brunswick-Balke-Collender Co., Long Island City, L. I.—Gentlemen: As per telephonic conversation with your Mr. Rogers to-day, this is to confirm having your offer of $2.42 per pound for 12 tons Upriver Fine Para Rubber, for shipment either from Brazil or Liverpool, in equal monthly parts January to June, 1911, about which we will let you know upon receipt of our cable reply on Monday morning.

Thanking you for the offer we remain,

Very truly yours,

Poel & Arnold,

Per W. J. Kelly."

"Poel & Arnold, 277 Broadway.

New York, April 4, 1910.

"Brunswick-Balke-Collender Co., Long Island City, L. I.—Gentlemen: Inclosed, we beg to hand you contract for 12 tons Upriver Fine Para Rubber, as sold you to-day, with our thanks for the order.

Very truly yours,

Poel & Arnold,

Per W. J. Kelly."

Inclosed with this letter was the following:

———

"Apr. 4/10

"Brunswick-Balke-Collender Co., Long Island City, L. I.

"Sold to You:

"For equal monthly shipments January to June, 1911, from Brazil and/or Liverpool, about twelve (12) tons Upriver Fine Para Rubber at two dollars and forty-two cents ($2.42) per pound; payable in U. S gold or its equivalent, cash twenty (20) days from date of delivery here."

———

On April 6th Rogers sent the following order to the plaintiffs. It is partly printed and partly written. The part in writing is italicized:

———

"Purchase Dep't

Order No. 25409
This number must appear on
Invoices and Cases

"The Brunswick-Balke-Collender Co. of New York
Review Ave., Fox and Marsh Sts.

Long Island City, *4/6, 1910.*

"*M Poel and Arnold, 277 Broadway, N. Y. C.* Please deliver at once the following, and send invoice with goods:

"*About 12 tons Upriver Fine Para Rubber at 2.42 per lb. Equal monthly shipments January to June, 1911.*

CONDITIONS ON WHICH ABOVE ORDER IS GIVEN

"Goods on this order must be delivered when specified. In case you cannot comply, advise us by return mail stating earliest date of delivery you can make, and await our further orders.

"The acceptance of this order which in any event you must promptly acknowledge will be considered by us as a guaranty on your part of prompt delivery within the specified time.

"Terms: F.O.B.

Respectfully yours,

The Brunswick-Balke-Collender Co. of New York,
Per C. R. Rogers."

"January 7, 1911.

"Messrs. Poel & Arnold, No. 277 Broadway, City—Gentlemen: We beg herewith to advise you that within the past few weeks there has come to our attention through a statement made to us for the first time by Mr. Rogers, information as to certain transactions had by him with you in the past, and especially as to a transaction in April last relating to 12 tons of crude rubber. Mr. Rogers had no authority to effect any such transaction on our account, nor had we any notice or knowledge of his action until he made a voluntary statement disclosing the facts within the past few weeks.

"In order that you may not be put to any unnecessary inconvenience, we feel bound to give you notice at the earliest opportunity after investigating the facts, that we shall not recognize these transactions or any others that may have been entered into with Mr. Rogers which were without our knowledge or authority.

"Yours truly,

The Brunswick-Balke-Collender Co. of New York,

Per Chas. P. Miller, Vice-Prest."

The first letter is of no legal significance, and only the other three need be considered. The fundamental question in this case is whether these writings constitute a contract between the parties. If they do not, no question as to whether these writings meet the requirements of the statute of frauds need be considered. An analysis of their provisions will show that they do not constitute a contract. It is not contended, and in face of the provisions of the plaintiffs' letter of April 4th it cannot be claimed, that that letter is in itself a contract. It is a mere offer or proposal by the plaintiffs that the defendant should accept the proposed contract inclosed which is said to embody an oral order that the defendant had that day given the plaintiffs. The object of this letter was to have the terms of the oral agreement reduced to writing so that there could be no uncertainty as to the terms of the contract. The letter of the defendant of April 6th did not accept this offer. If the intention of the defendant had been to accept the offer made in the plaintiffs' letter of April 4th, it would have been a simple matter for the defendant to have indorsed its acceptance upon the proposed contract which the plaintiffs' letter of April 4th had inclosed. Instead of adopting this simple and obvious method of indicating an intent to accept the contract proposed by the plaintiffs, the defendant submitted its own proposal and specified the terms and conditions upon which it should be accepted. The defendant's letter of April 6th was not an acceptance of this offer made by the plaintiffs in their letter of April 4th. It was a counter offer or proposition for a contract. Its provisions make it perfectly clear that the defendant: (1) Asked the plaintiffs to deliver rubber of a certain quality and quantity at the price specified in designated shipments; (2) *it specified that the order therein given was conditional upon the receipt of its order being promptly acknowledged*; and (3) upon the further condition that the plaintiffs would guarantee delivery within the time specified. It may be urged that the condition specified in the defendant's order that the plaintiffs would guarantee the delivery of the goods within the time specified added nothing of substance to the agreement, because if the offer was accepted the acceptance itself would involve this obligation on the part of the plaintiffs. The other condition specified by the defendant cannot be disposed of in the same manner. That provision of the defendant's offer provided that the offer was conditional upon the receipt of the order being promptly acknowledged. It embodied a condition that the defendant had the right to annex to its offer. The import of this proposal was that the defendant should not be bound until the plaintiffs signified their assent to the terms set forth. When this assent was given and the acknowledgment made, this contract was then to come into existence and would be completely expressed in writing. The plaintiffs did not acknowledge the receipt of this order and the proposal remained unaccepted. As the party making this offer deemed this provision material, and as the offer was made subject to compliance with it by the plaintiffs, it is not for the court to say that it is immaterial. When the plaintiffs submitted this offer in their letter of April 4th to the defendant, only one of two courses of action was open to the defendant. It could accept the offer made and thus manifest that assent which was essential to the creation of a contract, or it could reject the offer. There was no middle course. If it did not accept the offer proposed it necessarily rejected it. A proposal to accept the offer it modified or an acceptance subject to other terms and conditions was equivalent to an absolute rejection of the offer made by the plaintiffs.

. . .

In Hough v. Brown, 19 N.Y. 111, 114, it was held that a letter referring to a previous verbal proposition which stated the terms of the oral proposition according to the understanding of the writers and accepted them and added to the acceptance the words, "You will acknowledge the acceptance of the above," etc., was held not to constitute a contract, but merely a proposition for a contract. In his opinion in that case Judge Comstock, referring to the requirement that the acceptance should be acknowledged, said: "This language, in such a connection, can mean nothing else than that the defendant was expected to signify his assent to the terms thus set forth. That being done, the agreement would be complete, and it would also be in writing, so as to leave no room for future controversy. This, we are satisfied, is the true interpretation of the letter; and it follows that no contract was made consisting merely of the proposal at Buffalo, and the letter of the two firms referring to that proposal."

In Barrow Steamship Co. v. Mexican Central Railway Co., 134 N. Y. 15, 22, 31 N.E. 261, 263 (17 L.R.A. 359), the parties negotiated by letter for the transportation by the plaintiff of a party of immigrants from New York to Rome. In answer to a letter from the defendant which stated that there would probably be 250 or more in the party the plaintiff wrote, confirming the understanding between the parties that the defendant would ship not less than 250. The letter closed with the words, "Please confirm this and oblige." To this letter defendant replied that there was a probability that the party would exceed 250. The number furnished was 134, and in an action to recover for the breach of a contract to furnish 250 passengers it was held that, as there was "no evidence of any definite understanding in respect to the number of pilgrims to constitute the party for transportation prior to that letter appears in the record, the statement in the letter must be treated as a proposition on the part of the plaintiff. And to give it the effect of a contract between the parties the acceptance or adoption of it by the defendant was essential."

The respondent and the courts below, while recognizing this principle of the law of contracts, failed to give it effect upon the theory that the conditions expressed in the defendant's order of April 6th were not a part of the defendant's offer.

[The remainder of the opinion rejects this contention and also concludes that the defendant's letter of January 7th disavowing the authority of the salesman could not repair the failure on the part of the plaintiffs to accept the offer which the salesman had made.]

Having reached the conclusion that there was no contract between the parties, it is unnecessary to discuss the other questions urged upon our attention by the appellant.

The judgment appealed from should be reversed, and a new trial granted, with costs to abide the event.

WILLARD BARTLETT, C. J., and HISCOCK, COLLIN, HOGAN, and CARDOZO, JJ., concur. POUND, J., dissents.

NOTES

(1) *Mitigating the "Mirror Image" Rule.* The rigors of the rule that an acceptance must be the "mirror image" of the offer are sometimes mitigated in practice.

First, a court may decide that what at first seemed to be an additional or different term in the acceptance was an "implied term" of the offer, so that what appeared to be a conditional acceptance was an unconditional one. See, e. g., Pickett v. Miller, 76 N.M. 105, 412 P.2d 400 (1966). Could the court have done this in the Poel case?

Second, a court may conclude that the language of the acceptance relating to an additional or different term is only "precatory." What result if the letter of April 6 had said simply, "We accept subject to prompt delivery within the specified time. Please acknowledge this order promptly"? Did the actual letter differ significantly from this? How? See Valashinas v. Koniuto, 308 N.Y. 233, 124 N.E.2d 300 (1954); Home Gas Co. v. Magnolia Petroleum Co., 143 Okl. 112, 287 P. 1033 (1930).

(2) *Finding a Contract*. In spite of the legal requirement that an acceptance be unconditional, as the exerpt from Macaulay suggests, parties often act on the assumption that their promises are binding when there has been no unconditional acceptance. In practice most of these transactions are carried out without incident even though there is no contract. Occasionally, however, because of altered circumstances such as a change in market price, one of the parties later seeks a justification for not performing and seizes upon the variation as an excuse. It is interesting, as the trial court opinion in the Poel case notes, that after the purchase order of April 6 was sent, the market price of rubber rose above the contract price of $2.42 a pound, but then fell well below that price by the following December. See Poel v. Brunswick, Balke, Collender Co., 78 Misc. 311, 317, 139 N.Y.Supp. 602, 606 (1912). Would it be possible to devise a satisfactory legal test to exclude from the operation of the rule requiring unconditionality those parties whose motives in asserting the variation were "impure"? How successful is UCC 2–207 in this respect? See generally, Restatement Second, §§ 58–62.

(3) *Counselling*. Should an offeree who receives an offer by telegram confirm the terms in his acceptance? Is there any risk in going beyond "I accept your offer" and adding, for example, "of ten cents per box for 9599 boxes raisins"? Consider Ayer v. Western Union, p. 148 supra, and see United States v. Braunstein, 75 F.Supp. 137 (S.D.N.Y.1947).

(4) *Problem*. On April 5, Westside gave Humble an option contract, irrevocable for 60 days, on a tract of land. On May 2, Humble wrote Westside, "Humble Oil & Refining Company hereby exercises its option to purchase . . . . The contract of sale is hereby amended to provide that Seller shall extend all utility lines to the property before the date of closing." On May 14, Humble wrote Westside, "Humble Oil & Refining Company hereby notifies you of its intention to exercise the option granted . . . . The exercise of said option is not qualified and you may disregard the proposed amendment to the contract suggested in the letter dated May 2 . . . ." Contract? See Humble Oil & Refining Co. v. Westside Investment Corp., 428 S.W.2d 92 (Tex.1968); Restatement Second, § 35A. See also Note 2, p. 164 supra.

(5) *Problem for Review*. Greenhut Construction Company was preparing to bid on the construction of 300 housing units to be built at Elgin Air Force Base in Florida. On June 21, 1967, Craddock, a mechanical subcontractor, submitted a bid on the heating and air conditioning of $322,-500, not including the cost of a payment and performance bond. On July 17, he submitted a second bid of $328,000, including the cost of the bond. On July 20, Craddock sought and obtained a letter from Greenhut stating that "in the event that we are awarded the above subject contract, . . . we will award you a contract . . . as outlined in your letter of June, 1967, providing that we are furnished with a Performance Bond two (2) weeks thereafter." On August 8, Greenhut was awarded the general contract and, on August 12, it wrote Craddock that it would "consider the

matter closed" unless it received the bond by August 17. Craddock received the letter on August 15 and replied by a letter on the same date affirming his intention to comply with Greenhut's letter of July 20 ("It is my intention to fully comply with this request.") and stating that, with respect to Greenhut's letter of August 12, he would do his best to expedite the bonding procedure. Also on the same date, Greenhut sent Craddock a telegram stating that it had been asked by the government to furnish the name of the mechanical contractor and because of Craddock's "inability to furnish a performance and payment bond, which we have requested from you several times, we deem it necessary to consider another source for the project." On August 16, Craddock succeeded in obtaining the bond and notified Greenhut. Contract? See Craddock v. Greenhut Construction Co., 423 F.2d 111 (5th Cir. 1970). What if Craddock had not obtained the bond until August 18?

   ROTO-LITH, LTD. v. BARTLETT & CO., 297 F.2d 497 (1st Cir. 1962). [Roto-Lith, a manufacturer of cellophane bags for packaging vegetables, mailed to Bartlett, a written order for a drum of emulsion for use as a cellophane adhesive. Upon receipt of the order Bartlett sent to Roto-Lith an "acknowledgment" and an "invoice", both of which bore the legend, "All goods sold without warranties, express or implied, and subject to the terms on reverse side." Among the terms on the reverse side were, "Seller's liability hereunder shall be limited to the replacement of any goods that materially differ from the Seller's sample order on the basis of which the order for such goods was made. . . . If these terms are not acceptable, Buyer must so notify Seller at once." Roto-Lith made no objection to the terms, and paid for and used the emulsion. When bags produced with the emulsion failed to adhere, Roto-Lith sued Bartlett for damages for breach of warranty. From a directed verdict for defendant, plaintiff appeals.]

   ALDRICH, CIRCUIT JUDGE. [After stating the facts, the court set out Uniform Commercial Code, § 2–207.] Plaintiff exaggerates the freedom which this section affords an offeror to ignore a reply from an offeree that does not in terms coincide with the original offer. According to plaintiff, defendant's condition that there should be no warranties constituted a proposal which "materially altered" the agreement. As to this we concur. See Uniform Commercial Code comment to this section, Mass.Gen.Laws annotation, supra, paragraph 4. Plaintiff goes on to say that by virtue of the statute the acknowledgment effected a completed agreement without this condition, and that as a further proposal the condition never became part of the agreement because plaintiff did not express assent. We agree that section 2–207 changed the existing law, but not to this extent. Its purpose was to modify the strict principle that a response not precisely in accordance with the offer was a rejection and a counteroffer. Kehlor Flour Mills Co. v. Linden, 1918, 230 Mass. 119, 123, 119 N.E.

698; Saco-Lowell Shops v. Clinton Mills Co., 1 Cir., 1921, 277 F. 349. Now, within stated limits, a response that does not in all respects correspond with the offer constitutes an acceptance of the offer, and a counteroffer only as to the differences. If plaintiff's contention is correct that a reply to an offer stating additional conditions unilaterally burdensome upon the offeror is a binding acceptance of the original offer plus simply a proposal for the additional conditions, the statute would lead to an absurdity. Obviously no offeror will subsequently assent to such conditions.

The statute is not too happily drafted. Perhaps it would be wiser in all cases for an offeree to say in so many words, "I will not accept your offer until you assent to the following: . . ." But businessmen cannot be expected to act by rubric. It would be unrealistic to suppose that when an offeree replies setting out conditions that would be burdensome only to the offeror he intended to make an unconditional acceptance of the original offer, leaving it simply to the offeror's good nature whether he would assume the additional restrictions. To give the statute a practical construction we must hold that a response which states a condition materially altering the obligation solely to the disadvantage of the offeror is an "acceptance . . . expressly . . . conditional on assent to the additional . . . terms."

Plaintiff accepted the goods with knowledge of the conditions specified in the acknowledgment. It became bound. . . .

[Affirmed.]

NOTES

(1) *Finding the Terms of the Contract.* Contrast with the situation in the Poel case, where one party attempted to back out of the contract, the situation in the Roto-Lith case, where both parties agreed that there was a contract but disagreed on its terms. What is the logic behind the court's conclusion in Roto-Lith that "a response which states a condition materially altering the obligation solely to the disadvantage of the offeror is an 'acceptance . . . expressly . . . conditional on assent to the additional terms'" under UCC 2–207(1)? Is this a fair reading of the Code? Is the court's conclusion, that when Roto-Lith "accepted the goods with knowledge of the conditions specified in the acknowledgement" it "became bound," supported by the language of UCC 2–207(3)? Could the case have been decided on any other ground? Is UCC 2–204 relevant? What is the significance of the following, which was added as a new Comment 7 to UCC 2–207 in 1966? "In many cases, as where goods are shipped, accepted and paid for before any dispute arises, there is no question whether a contract has been made. In such cases, where the writings of the parties do not establish a contract, it is not necessary to determine which act or document constituted the offer and which the acceptance. See Section 2–204. The only question is what terms are included in the contract, and subsection (3) furnishes the governing rule." Report No. 3 of the Permanent Editorial Board for the Uniform Commercial Code 23–24

(1967).[a] See generally, Murray, Intention Over Terms: An Exploration of UCC 2–207 and New Section 60, Restatement of Contracts, 37 Ford. L.Rev. 317 (1969); Notes, 57 Nw.U.L.Rev. 477 (1962); 30 U.Chi.L.Rev. 540 (1963); 32 U.Pitt.L.Rev. 209 (1970).

(2) *An International Solution.* In 1964, a diplomatic conference at the Hague, in which the United States was a participant, concluded a convention on a Uniform Law on the Formation of Contracts for the International Sale of Goods. It may be of interest to see its counterpart of UCC 2–207.

> 1. An acceptance containing additions, limitations or other modifications shall be a rejection of the offer and shall constitute a counter-offer.
>
> 2. However, a reply to an offer which purports to be an acceptance but which contains additional or different terms which do not materially alter the terms of the offer shall constitute an acceptance unless the offeror promptly objects to the discrepancy; if he does not so object, the terms of the contract shall be the terms of the offer with the modifications contained in the acceptance.

Which solution do you prefer?

CONSTRUCTION AGGREGATES CORP. v. HEWITT-ROBINS, 404 F.2d 505 (7th Cir. 1968). [Construction Aggregates Corp. (CAC) was the successful bidder on a contract to construct dikes enclosing some 60 square miles of the Dead Sea in Israel in order to form "evaporation pans" for the extraction of minerals. CAC then began negotiations with Hewitt-Robins (H-R) on a cost-plus contract for conveyors. On June 30, 1962, CAC sent H-R a letter "to set forth the final agreement" between the two companies and asking H-R to send its confirmation. On July 3 CAC sent H-R its purchase order. On July 20, H-R sent CAC a letter enclosing the executed acceptance copy of CAC's purchase order but stating that H-R's acceptance was "predicated on the following clarifications, additions or modifications to the order," including a substitute warranty clause which disclaimed liability for engineering design or component parts manufactured by others. CAC made no objection, except to telephone H-R on July 31 and get agreement, in a letter from H-R on that date, to a change in the terms of payment. CAC had difficulties with the conveyor system, which did not operate satisfactorily, and sued H-R for breach of implied warranties of fitness as to engineering design and component

---

a. A careful reading of UCC 2–207 might suggest that a distinction is to be made between "additional" and "different" terms, and that "different" terms are not subject to (2). Does this seem sensible? Comment 3 says: "Whether or not additional or different terms will become part of the agreement depends upon the provisions of subsection (2)." Is this decisive? Of what significance is it for other states that Iowa has inserted "and different" in (2)?

parts manufactured by others.   From judgment for defendant on a jury verdict, plaintiff appealed.]

CUMMINGS, CIRCUIT JUDGE.   .   .   .   Since H-R's acceptance was "expressly made conditional on assent to the additional or different terms" contained in its July 20th letter, the exception in the last clause of Section 2–207(1) of the Uniform Commercial Code was clearly applicable.   Hence the district court was justified in permitting the jury to treat that letter as a counter-offer.

Section 2–207(3) recognizes that the subsequent conduct of the parties can establish a contract for sale.   Since CAC's July 3 purchase order and H-R's July 20 counter-offer did not in themselves create a contract, Section 2–207(3) would operate to create one because the subsequent performance by both parties constituted "conduct by both parties which recognizes the existence of a contract." Such a contract by operation of law would consist only of "those terms on which the writings of the parties agree, together with any supplementary terms incorporated under other provisions of this Act." There having been no agreement on the warranty terms, the implied warranties provided in Sections 2–314 and 2–315   .   .   .   would then ordinarily become applicable.   .   .   .   Here, however, there is no occasion to create a contract by operation of law in default of further actions by the negotiating parties, for CAC can be said to have accepted the terms of H-R's counter-offer.   CAC sought a change only in the payment terms of the counter-offer, raising no objection to H-R's other modifications of the original purchase order.   H-R granted CAC's requested change in a letter of July 31 and could reasonably have assumed that CAC's single objection was an acquiescence in the remaining terms of the counter-offer.   CAC did not object to this implication in H-R's July 31st letter reference to the terms of its counter-offer and therefore CAC could appropriately be held to the terms of the July 20th letter.   .   .   .

[Affirmed.]

NOTES

(1) *Strategy in the "Battle of the Forms."*   How should the parties draft their forms to win the "battle"?   Under the common law rule, sometimes called the "mirror image rule," the advantage was with the party who "fired the last shot" before the goods were shipped and accepted.   The Roto-Lith case itself illustrates this.   Who has the advantage under the Code?   Is it better to be the offeror or the offeree?   What clauses should be included on the buyer's "request for quotation," the seller's "quotation," the buyer's "purchase order," and the seller's "sales acknowledgement" forms?   Suppose that prompt delivery is important so that local warehouses near buyers are used, and goods arrive before the seller's order form, which must be mailed from the seller's home office.   Is there any way that the seller can deal with this problem in the case of his regular customers?   Of his new customers?   For advice on strategy, see Lipman,

On Winning the Battle of the Forms: An Analysis of Section 2–207 of the Uniform Commercial Code, 24 Bus.Law. 789 (1969); Apsey, The Battle of the Forms, 34 Notre Dame Law. 556 (1959).

Would it not make sense, at least where the buyer and seller have a continuing relationship, to negotiate an overriding agreement to govern all sales between them, rather than to engage in the "battle of the forms" each time? Would you so advise a client whose bargaining position is weak? Another possibility, of course, is for a trade association to work out standard terms to which both parties can adhere.

(2) *Business Practices and the "Battle of the Forms."* Macaulay concludes, on the basis of his study, p. 185 supra, that although businessmen sometimes make carefully planned contracts, in most situations contract is not needed, both because there is usually little room for honest misunderstandings or good faith differences of opinion about the seller's performances, and because there are many effective non-legal sanctions. The detailed planning required for contract may even be undesirable, as opposed to a more flexible relationship. Furthermore, resort to litigation, or the threat of litigation, has both monetary and non-monetary costs. Are such conclusions helpful in formulating legal rules applicable to the transactions described?

(3) *Problem.* Collins & Aikman sells carpets listed in its catalog to customers who order over the telephone. Sometimes these orders are accepted over the telephone and sometimes they are simply recorded. In either case, Collins & Aikman promptly sends an "Acknowledgement" which reads: "This acceptance of your order is subject to the following terms, all of which are accepted by buyer . . .." One of those terms provides for arbitration of all disputes. Advise Collins & Aikman on the effectiveness of its arbitration clause. See Dorton v. Collins & Aikman Corp., 453 F.2d 1161 (6th Cir. 1972). Cf. Matter of Doughboy Industries, 17 A.D.2d 216, 233 N.Y.S.2d 488 (1962).

Chapter 3

POLICING THE BARGAIN

Just as the notion of freedom *of* contract came to bulk large among the objectives of our legal system during the nineteenth century, the notion of freedom *from* contract has come into its own in the twentieth. We have seen in Chapter 1 that bargain is the touchstone of enforceability for most of the promises that help to distribute wealth in our society. We have seen in Chapter 2 something of the nature of the process by which bargains are made. But that process is subject to abuse in some instances. To what extent will the law police such a bargain and show its concern for the integrity of the bargaining process by giving an aggrieved party relief from his bargain? That is the subject of this chapter.

Concern for the integrity of the bargaining process might have three different orientations, singly or in some combination. First, it might be *status* oriented and focus on the characteristics of the parties involved. This has been the traditional approach in the area of capacity to contract, where the tendency has been to limit the power to contract of certain classes of persons, such as infants and insane persons, in order to protect them from the consequences of unwise bargains. (Would it be desirable to recognize a new status, that of consumer, in order to protect the members of that class?) Second, it might be *behavior* oriented and focus on how the parties in fact bargained. This has been the traditional approach in the areas of fraud and duress, the most flagrant examples of misbehavior during the bargaining process. (Would it be desirable to single out other sorts of infringements on the ideal of free bargaining, such as the use of a standard printed form on a "take it or leave it" basis, with no opportunity to bargain over its terms?) Third, it might be *substance* oriented and focus on the resultant bargain itself. This has been the traditional approach for contracts with common carriers and public utilities, where conditions of monopoly ordinarily prevail. (Would it be desirable to extend it to contracts with dealers in automobiles and stereo sets?)

Whatever the orientation of the concern, there remains a question of who is to be the architect of the relief. The courts? The legislature? An administrative agency? Some combination of these? At least until recent years, such relief as was available was fashioned largely by the courts, and was very likely to be covertly rather than overtly directed at the real problem of abuse of the bargaining process. You can therefore expect to find examples of courts' covert pol-

201

icing of bargains under such guises as applying the traditional requirement of consideration and interpreting the language of the agreement of the parties. You will, with a little patience, also find courts overtly policing bargains in a frontal attack on the real problems. But this is a development of recent years and can best be assessed by comparison with older and more established techniques. The chapter will also explore some of the considerations that restrain courts from recasting bargains to fit the presumed ideals of the day.

Finally, it may have occurred to you that concern with the integrity of the bargaining process does not exhaust society's concern with the policing of individual bargains. What happens when the interests of the parties, as reflected in their bargain, conflict with the interests of the public at large? This question is explored in the final section of this chapter, which deals with illegal bargains.

SECTION 1.   CAPACITY

What classes of persons are considered by the law to have less than full power to contract? Since the materials in this section are confined to the two important classes of infants and insane persons, some words may here be in order concerning a few other classes.

As to intoxicated persons, a common standard of capacity is stated in Lucy v. Zehmer, p. 57 supra: "Zehmer was not intoxicated to the extent of being unable to comprehend the nature or consequences of the instrument he executed." An older case puts the test this way: "To render a transaction voidable on account of the drunkenness of a party to it, the drunkenness must have been such as to have drowned reason, memory, and judgment, and to have impaired the mental facilities to such an extent as to render the party non compos mentis for the time being." Martin v. Harsh, 231 Ill. 384, 83 N.E. 164 (1907).[a]

An important class at common law consisted of married women. The common law was so far from regarding marriage as a mark of maturity in a woman, as to make it a disabling event. The technical name of the married woman's defense, when sued in contract, was *coverture*. These incapacities were largely removed, in this country, by statutes during the nineteenth century—long before women were given the vote.

---

a. As to a transaction effected by a drunkard in a sober interval, see Olsen v. Hawkins, 90 Idaho 28, 408 P.2d 462 (1965) (change of insurance beneficiary).

Another important class consists of corporations, on which limited powers are conferred by charter. The extent to which ultra vires acts of a corporation—acts beyond its powers—may be effective is best left to a course in corporations.

KESER v. CHAGNON

Supreme Court of Colorado, 1966.
159 Colo. 209, 410 P.2d 637.

McWILLIAMS, JUSTICE. This writ of error concerns the purchase of an automobile by a minor and his efforts to thereafter avoid the contract of purchase. The salient facts are as follows:

1. on June 11, 1964 Chagnon bought a 1959 Edsel from Keser for the sum of $1025, payment therefor being in cash which Chagnon obtained by borrowing a portion of the purchase price from the Cash Credit Company on a signature note, with the balance of the money being obtained from the Public Finance Corporation, the latter loan being secured by a chattel mortgage upon the automobile;

2. as of June 11, 1964 Chagnon was a minor of the age of twenty years, ten months and twenty days, although despite this fact Chagnon nonetheless falsely advised Keser that he was then over the age of twenty-one; and

3. on about September 25, 1964, when Chagnon was then of the age of twenty-one years, two months and four days, Chagnon formally advised Keser of his desire to disaffirm the contract theretofore entered into by the parties, and thereafter on October 5, 1964 Chagnon returned the Edsel to Keser.

Based on this sequence of events Chagnon brought an action against Keser wherein he sought to recover the $1025 which he had allegedly theretofore paid Keser for the Edsel. By answer Keser alleged, among other things, that he had suffered damage as the direct result of Chagnon's false representation as to his age.

A trial was had to the court, sitting without a jury, all of which culminated in a judgment in favor of Chagnon against Keser in the sum of $655.78. This particular sum was arrived at by the trial court in the following manner: the trial court found that Chagnon initially purchased the Edsel for the sum of $995 (not $1025) and that he was entitled to the return of his $995; and then by way of set-off the trial court subtracted from the $995 the sum of $339.22, this latter sum apparently representing the difference between the purchase price paid for the vehicle and the reasonable value of the Edsel on October

5, 1964, which was the date when the Edsel was returned to Keser. By writ of error Keser now seeks reversal of this judgment.

In this court Keser summarizes his argument as follows:

1. Chagnon's attempted disaffirmance was ineffective because though he returned the automobile, he nonetheless failed to also return the certificate of title thereto which was then and there in the possession of the Public Finance Corporation;

2. Chagnon in reality ratified the contract because he failed to disaffirm within a reasonable time after reaching his majority and for such length of time retained possession of the Edsel; and

3. in connection with Keser's set-off the trial court erred in its determination of Keser's damages resulting from Chagnon's false representation as to his age.

Before considering each of these several matters, it is deemed helpful to allude briefly to some of the general principles pertaining to the longstanding policy of the law to protect a minor from at least some of his childish foibles by affording him the right, under certain circumstances, to avoid his contract, not only during his minority but also within a reasonable time after reaching his majority. In Mosko v. Forsythe, 102 Colo. 115, 76 P.2d 1106 we held that when a minor elects to disaffirm and avoid his contract, the "contract" becomes invalid ab initio and that the parties thereto then revert to the same position as if the contract had never been made. In that case we went on to declare that when a minor thus sought to avoid his contract and had in his possession the specific property received by him in the transaction, he was in such circumstance required to return the same as a prerequisite to any avoidance.

In 43 C.J.S. Infants § 75 at page 171 it is said that a minor failing to disaffirm within a "reasonable time" after reaching his majority loses the right to do so and that just what constitutes a "reasonable time" is ordinarily a question of fact. As regards the necessity for restoration of consideration, in 43 C.J.S. at page 174 it is stated that the minor after disaffirming is "usually required . . . to return the consideration, if he can, or the part remaining in his possession or control."

Finally, we believe that Doenges-Long Motors, Inc. v. Gillen, 138 Colo. 31, 328 P.2d 1077 answers most of the matters sought to be raised here by Keser. In that case it was held that the right of an infant to disaffirm his contract is absolute and is not lost by reason of the fact that the infant induced the making of the contract by a deliberate misrepresentation of his age. However, in that case it was also held that even though an infant has the right to disaffirm his contract, if he falsely represents his age and as a result thereof obtains an automobile, he is at the same time answerable to the seller for his tort. In other words, though the seller is required to return to the infant that which he, the seller, received in exchange for the automobile, the seller is entitled to set-off against such sum any damage sustained by him as a result of the infant's false representation as to his age. And in this regard the measure of damage was declared to be the difference between the reasonable value of the automobile at the time of its sale and delivery and its reasonable value at the time of its return.

Proceeding, then, to a consideration of those matters which Keser now contends require a reversal of this case, it is first urged that Chagnon's attempted disaffirmance is ineffective because, although Chagnon did return the Edsel to Keser, he did not at the same time return the certificate of ownership thereto, which certificate was then in possession of the Public Finance Corporation. And needless to say, Public Finance Corporation was not about to voluntarily give up the certificate of title! This contention, however, is without merit. It is true that Mosko v. Forsythe, supra, holds that a prerequisite to the avoidance of an executed contract by a minor is that if he then has in his possession the property which he received in the transaction, he must return the same. All that is required in this regard, however, is that the disaffirming party return only those fruits of his contract which are then in his possession and if for any reason he cannot thus place the other party in status quo, he does not because of such inability lose his right to disaffirm. To hold otherwise would strike at the very root of the well-settled principle that with certain exceptions which are not applicable to the instant controversy, he who deals with a minor does so at his own peril and with the attendant risk that the minor may at his election disaffirm the transaction because of his minority. Weathers v. Owen, 78 Ga.App. 505, 51 S.E.2d 584 presents a factual situation most analogous to the instant one. See also Dawson v. Fox, 64 A.2d 162, (D.C.Mun.App.); and Freiburghaus v. Herman, 102 S.W.2d 743 (Mo.App). In the instant case Chagnon returned to Keser all of the fruits of the transaction which were then in his possession or under his control, i. e., the Edsel. The fact that the Public Finance Corporation held the certificate of title and would not deliver it over to either Chagnon or Keser does not defeat Chagnon's right to disaffirm.

Keser's next contention that Chagnon upon attaining his majority ratified the contract by his failure to disaffirm within a reasonable time after becoming twenty-one and by his retention and use of the Edsel prior to its return to the seller is equally untenable. In this connection it is pointed out that Chagnon did not notify Keser of his desire to disaffirm until 66 days after he became twenty-one and that he did not return the Edsel until 10 days after his notice to disaffirm, during all of which time Chagnon had the possession and use of the vehicle in question. As already noted, when an infant attains his majority he has a reasonable time within which he may thereafter disaffirm a contract entered into during his minority. And this rule is not as strict where, as here, we are dealing with an executed contract. There is no hard and fast rule as to just what constitutes a "reasonable" time within which the infant may disaffirm. In Fellows v. Cantrell, 143 Colo. 126, 352 P.2d 289 we held that the failure to disaffirm for a period of five years after a minor reached his majority, together with other acts recognizing the validity of the contract, constituted ratification. In Merchants' Credit Union v. Ariyama, 64 Utah 364, 230 P. 1017 disaffirmance four months after reaching majority was held to be within a reasonable time. Similarly, in Haines v. Fitzgerald, 108 Pa.Super. 290, 165 A. 52, three months was held to be a reasonable time within which to disaffirm; and in Adamroski v. Curtis-Wright, 300 Mass. 281, 15 N.E.2d 467 "nearly a year" was also held to be "reasonable." Suffice it to say, that under the circumstances disclosed by the record we are not prepared to hold that as a matter of law Chagnon ratified the contract either by his actions or by his alleged failure to disaffirm within a reasonable time after reaching his majority. In other words, there is competent evidence to support the conclusion of the trial court that Chagnon disaffirmed the contract within a reasonable time after reaching his majority and such finding of fact cannot be disturbed by us on review.

Finally, error is predicated upon the trial court's finding in connection with Keser's set-off for the damage occasioned him by Chagnon's admitted false representation of his age. In this regard the trial court apparently found that the reasonable value of the Edsel when it was returned to Keser by Chagnon was $655.78, and accordingly went on to allow Keser a set-off in the amount of $339.22, this latter sum representing the difference between the purchase price, $995, and the value of the vehicle on the date it was returned. Finding, then, that Chagnon was entitled to the return of the $995 which he had theretofore paid Keser for the Edsel, the trial court then subtracted therefrom Keser's set-off in the amount of $339.22, and accordingly entered judgment for Chagnon against Keser in the sum of $655.78. Whether it was by accident or design we know not, but $655.78 is apparently the exact amount which Chagnon "owed" the Public Finance Corporation on his note with that company.

In this regard as concerns his set-off Keser complains that the trial court did not follow the rule regarding the measure of damages as laid down in Doenges-Long v. Gillen, supra. More particularly, Keser claims that there is no evidence which supports the trial court's finding that the value of the automobile on the date it was returned to Keser was $655.78. The evidence as to the value of the Edsel on the date Chagnon returned it to Keser was as follows:

1. Chagnon said the car was worth more when he returned it than when he bought it;

2. An expert called by Keser opined that the car was worth $245 and

3. Keser testified that if he had a clear title to the vehicle it had a reasonable value of $395.

Based on this evidence the trial court found that the reasonable value of the automobile on the date of its return to Keser was $655.78, which determination from the arithmetical standpoint, at least, permitted the trial court to then enter judgment in favor of Chagnon in an amount equal to the balance then due and owing the Public Finance Corporation. Without belaboring the point, it is apparent that on its determination of the reasonable value of the Edsel on the date of its return to Keser, the trial court was influenced by factors other than the evidence before it as to such value.

The judgment is reversed and the cause remanded with direction that the trial court determine Keser's set-off in accord with the rule in Doenges-Long v. Gillen, supra, and once this set-off has been thus determined, to then enter judgment for Chagnon in an amount equal to the difference between $995 and the amount of such set-off.

NOTES

(1) *Should Appearances Count?* If Keser reasonably believed Chagnon when he lied about his age, why should Chagnon be allowed to rely upon his infancy? Does not this clash with the objective standard advanced in Lucy v. Zehmer, p. 57 supra? Why was not Chagnon estopped to deny his representation of age? Can it be argued that every agreement a minor makes, otherwise effective as a contract, ought to be taken as implying a representation that he is competent to contract? Are there differences among infancy, mental incapacity and intoxication in this regard?

(2) *Voidable Not Void.* In many statutes and cases the promise of a person without capacity is said to be "void." As the discussion of disaffirmance in the Keser case suggests, it is more accurate to regard it as "voidable." In Holt v. Ward Clarencieux, 2 Strange 937, 93 Eng.Rep. 954 (K.B.1732), the court sustained an action for a breach of promise of marriage brought on behalf of a young woman, who had been a girl of 15 at the time of the agreement. "[W]e are all of opinion that this contract is not void, but only voidable at the option of the infant. . . . And no dangerous consequences can follow from this determination, because our opinion protects the infant even more than if we rule the contract to be absolutely void." On the effect of a promise by an adult to perform a duty imposed by a promise that he made as an infant and could have avoided on that ground, see Note 2, p. 21 supra.

KIEFER v. FRED HOWE MOTORS, INC., 39 Wis.2d 20, 158 N. W.2d 288 (1968). [Steven Kiefer bought a five-year-old Willys station wagon from Fred Howe Motors when he was married, the father of a child, working, and a few months short of 21 years. The contract that he signed stated: "I represent that I am 21 years of age or over and recognize that the dealer sells the above vehicle upon this representation." He had difficulty with the car which he claimed had a cracked block, and after becoming of age, he sought to return it, and later sued to recover the price. From judgment for plaintiff, defendant appealed.]

WILKIE, J. . . . The law governing agreements made during infancy reaches back over many centuries. The general rule is that ". . . the contract of a minor, other than for necessaries, is either void or voidable at his option." The only other exceptions to the rule permitting disaffirmance are statutory [1] or involve contracts which deal with duties imposed by law such as a contract of marriage or an agreement to support an illegitimate child. The general rule is not affected by the minor's status as emancipated or unemancipated.

Appellant does not advance any argument that would put this case within one of the exceptions to the general rule, but rather urges that this court, as a matter of public policy, adopt a rule that an emancipated minor over eighteen years of age be made legally responsible for his contracts.

The underpinnings of the general rule allowing the minor to disaffirm his contracts were undoubtedly the protection of the minor. It was thought that the minor was immature in both mind and experience and that, therefore, he should be protected from his own bad judgments as well as from adults who would take advantage of him. The doctrine of the voidability of minors' contracts often seems commendable and just. If the beans that the young naive Jack purchased from the crafty old man in the fairy tale "Jack and the Bean Stalk" had been worthless rather than magical, it would have been only fair to allow Jack to disaffirm the bargain and reclaim his cow. However, in today's modern and sophisticated society the "infancy doctrine" seems to lose some of its gloss.

Paradoxically, we declare the infant mature enough to shoulder arms in the military, but not mature enough to vote; mature enough to marry and be responsible for his torts and crimes, but not mature enough to assume the burden of his own contractual indiscretions. In Wisconsin, the infant is deemed mature enough to use a dangerous instrumentality—a motor vehicle—at sixteen, but not mature enough to purchase it without protection until he is twenty-one.

No one really questions that a line as to age must be drawn somewhere below which a legally defined minor must be able to disaffirm his contracts for nonnecessities. The law over the centuries has considered this age to be twenty-one. Legislatures in other states have lowered the age. We suggest that the appellant might better seek the change it proposes in the legislative halls rather than this court. A recent law review article in the Indiana Law Journal explores the problem of contractual disabilities of minors and points to three dif-

---

1. See for example, sec. 48.985(1), Stats. (contracts for educational loans).

ferent legislative solutions leading to greater freedom to contract.[2] The first approach is one gleaned from the statutes of California[3] and New York,[4] which would allow parties to submit a proposed contract to a court which would remove the infant's right of disaffirmance upon a finding that the particular contract is fair. This suggested approach appears to be extremely impractical in light of the expense and delay that would necessarily accompany the procedure. A second approach would be to establish a rebuttable presumption of incapacity to replace the strict rule. This alternative would be an open invitation to litigation. The third suggestion is a statutory procedure that would allow a minor to petition a court for the removal of disabilities. Under this procedure a minor would only have to go to court once, rather than once for each contract as in the first suggestion.

Undoubtedly, the infancy doctrine is an obstacle when a major purchase is involved. However, we believe that the reasons for allowing that obstacle to remain viable at this point outweigh those for casting it aside. Minors require some protection from the pitfalls of the market place. Reasonable minds will always differ on the extent of the protection that should be afforded. For this court to adopt a rule that the appellant suggests and remove the contractual disabilities from a minor simply because he becomes emancipated, which in most cases would be the result of marriage, would be to suggest that the married minor is somehow vested with more wisdom and maturity than his single counterpart. However, logic would not seem to dictate this result especially when today a youthful marriage is oftentimes indicative of a lack of wisdom and maturity.

[The court went on to rule that the dealer had not established deceit. The recital in the contract should have been supplemented by evidence of intent to defraud on the part of Kiefer, and of justifiable reliance on the part of the dealer.]

[Affirmed.]

HALLOWS, CHIEF JUSTICE (dissenting) . . . The magical age limit of 21 years as an indication of contractual maturity no longer has a basis in fact or in public policy. [Furthermore,] an automobile to this respondent was a necessity and therefore the contract could not be disaffirmed. . . . Automobiles for parents under 21 years of age to go to and from work in our current society may well be a necessity, and I think in this case the record shows it is. . . .

NOTES

(1) *Benefit or Burden.* Some of those whose capacity was limited under the common law, such as infants and married women, were describ-

---

2. 41 Ind.L.J. 140 (1965–1966).

3. Cal.Civ.Code Annot., sec. 36.

4. N.Y. General Obligations Law, Consol. Laws, c. 24–A, p. 10, sec. 3–105 (McKinney 1964).

ed as "favorites" of the law. Is lack of capacity a benefit or a burden to the "favorite"? Would married women applaud revival of the old rules that made them "favorites"? Would they refuse to take advantage of analogous rules if they were made generally applicable to all "consumers"?

Lack of capacity can obviously be a serious burden to the person who is underage and who seeks to buy a substantial item, such as an automobile, on credit. For some items the burden is avoided by the exception that makes an infant liable for "necessaries." What sort of assurances might satisfy a prospective creditor where "necessaries" are not involved?

But lack of capacity was obviously a significant benefit to Kiefer when he became dissatisfied with the performance of his Willys station wagon. What would his situation have been if he had not had his infancy as an ace up his sleeve? The student note cited by the court (fn. 2) suggested that the refuge of nonage may no longer be needed, as laws are progressively developed to protect *all* the public from unscrupulous dealings, but that such laws were at that time (1965) themselves in their infancy.

(2) *Change in the Age.* In a number of states the age of capacity for married persons has been reduced to 18 years, and other statutory changes in the common law rules on infancy are widespread. Should the change in the voting age affect the common law rule on capacity? The student note cited in the Kiefer case also invites the speculation that the age of capacity should be increased, because of the academic seclusion of modern young people and the growing complexity of commercial affairs. (It is thought that early English law may have responded to technological advances by increasing the age of maturity from 15 to 21 when the introduction of chain mail armor made military service unduly burdensome for older boys.)

ORTELERE v. TEACHERS' RETIREMENT BOARD, 25 N. Y.2d 196, 250 N.E.2d 460 (1969). [Grace Ortelere was a 60-year-old New York City schoolteacher, who had suffered a nervous breakdown diagnosed as involving "involutional psychosis, melancholia type," and was on leave for mental illness. Her psychiatrist also suspected that she suffered from cerebral arteriosclerosis. Her husband of 38 years had quit his job as an electrician to stay home and care for her. She had a reserve of $70,925 in the public retirement system in which she had participated for over 40 years. In 1965, without telling her husband she borrowed from the system the maximum possible, $8,760, and made an irrevocable election to take maximum retirement benefits of $450 a month during her lifetime. This revoked an earlier election under which she would have received only $375 a month but her husband would have taken the unexhausted reserve on her death, and it left him and their two grown children with no benefits in the event of her death. Two months later she died of cerebral arteriosclerosis.[a] Her husband sued to set aside her 1965 election on the ground of mental incompetence. Her psychiatrist testified that she was inca-

---

a. The immediate cause of death was described as "cerebral thrombosis due to H[ypertensive] H[eart] D[isease]." (Record) pable of making a decision of any kind and that victims of involutional melancholia "can't think rationally. . . . They will even tell you . . . 'I don't know whether I should get up or whether I should stay in bed.' . . . Everything is impossible to decide." From a judgment for the plaintiff, the defendant appealed to the Appellate Division, which reversed and dismissed the complaint. The plaintiff appealed.]

BREITEL, JUDGE. . . . Traditionally, in this State and elsewhere, contractual mental capacity has been measured by what is largely a cognitive test . . . . Under this standard the "inquiry" is whether the mind was "so affected as to render him wholly and absolutely incompetent to comprehend and understand the nature of the transaction" . . . . A requirement that the party also be able to make a rational judgment concerning the particular transaction qualified the cognitive test . . . . Conversely, it is also well recognized that contractual ability would be affected by insane delusions intimately related to the particular transaction . . . .

These traditional standards governing competency to contract were formulated when psychiatric knowledge was quite primitive. They fail to account for one who by reason of mental illness is unable to control his conduct even though his cognitive ability seems unimpaired. When these standards were evolving it was thought that all the mental faculties were simultaneously affected by mental illness. . . . This is no longer the prevailing view . . . .

Of course the greatest movement in revamping legal notions of mental responsibility has occurred in the criminal law. The nineteenth century cognitive test embraced in the *M'Naghten* rules has long been criticized and changed by statute and decision in many jurisdictions (see *M'Naghten's Case*, 10 Clark & Fin. 200; 8 Eng.Rep. 718 [House of Lords, 1843]; Weihofen, Mental Disorder as a Criminal Defense [1954], pp. 65–68; British Royal Comm. on Capital Punishment [1953], ch. 4; A.L.I. Model Penal Code, § 4.01, supra; cf. Penal Law, § 30.05).

It is quite significant that Restatement, 2d, Contracts, states the modern rule on competency to contract. . . . Thus, the new Restatement section reads: "(1) A person incurs only voidable contractual duties by entering into a transaction if by reason of mental illness or defect . . . (b) he is unable to act in a reasonable manner in relation to the transaction and the other party has reason to know of his condition." (Restatement, 2d, Contracts [T.D. No. 1, April 13, 1964], § 18C.) . . .

The system was, or should have been, fully aware of Mrs. Ortelere's condition. They, or the Board of Education, knew of her leave of absence for medical reasons and the resort to staff psychiatrists by the Board of Education. Hence, the other of the conditions for avoidance is satisfied.

Lastly, there are no significant changes of position by the system other than those that flow from the barest actuarial consequences of benefit selection.

Nor should one ignore that in the relationship between retirement system and member, and especially in a public system, there is not involved a commercial, let alone an ordinary commercial, transaction. It is not a sound scheme which would permit 40 years of contribution and participation in the system to be nullified by a one-instant act committed by one known to be mentally ill. This is especially true if there would be no substantial harm to the system if the act were avoided. Of course, nothing less serious than medically classified psychosis should suffice or else few contracts would be invulnerable to some kind of psychological attack. As noted earlier, the trial court's finding and perhaps some of the testimony attempted to fit into the rubrics of the traditional rules. For that reason rather than reinstatement of the judgment at Trial Term there should be a new trial under the proper standards frankly considered and applied.

[Reversed (5–2).]

JASEN, JUDGE (dissenting). [The dissent set out the full text of a letter from Grace to the Retirement System prior to her election, in which she put eight questions typified by the following (No. 6): "If I take a loan of $5,000 before retiring and select option four-a on both the pension and annuity, what would my allowance be?"] It seems clear that this detailed, explicit and extremely pertinent list of queries reveals a mind fully in command of the salient features of the Teachers' Retirement System. Certainly, it cannot be said the decedent could possess sufficient capacity to compose a letter indicating such a comprehensive understanding of the retirement system, and yet lack the capacity to understand the answers.

As I read the record, the evidence establishes that the decedent's election to receive maximum payments was predicated on the need for a higher income to support two retired persons—her husband and herself. Since the only source of income available to decedent and her husband was decedent's retirement pay, the additional payment of $75 per month which she would receive by electing the maximal payment was a necessity. . . . Under these circumstances, an election of maximal income during decedent's lifetime was not only a rational, but a necessary decision. . . . Moreover, there is nothing in the record to indicate that the decedent had any warning, premonition, knowledge or indication at the time of retirement that her life expectancy was, in any way, reduced by her condition.

The generally accepted test of mental competency to contract which has thus evolved . . . represents a balance struck between policies to protect the security of transactions between individuals and freedom of contract on the one hand, and protection of those mentally handicapped on the other hand. In my opinion, this rule has proven workable in practice and fair in result. . . . As in every situation where the law must draw a line between liability and nonliability, between responsibility and nonresponsibility, there will be borderline cases, and injustices may occur by deciding erroneously that an individual belongs on one side of the line or the other. To minimize the chances of such injustices occurring, the line should be drawn as clearly as possible. . . .[b]

NOTES

(1) *Elections Under Pension Plans.* Can you envisage any adverse consequences for a pension plan offering a choice among various modes of benefit, if the choice made by a large number of participants proved to be revocable after death? Does the Ortelere decision open up that prospect? Might the effect of the decision be limited to cases in which the employee has had psychiatric or similar consultation before the election? Would this lead to arbitrary distinctions? And how should the rule apply where the employer funds his pension plan through a professional insurer, who is not likely to know of the employee's psychosis? Should the employer's knowledge be attributable to the insurer? Why should it make any difference whether *either* was aware of the employee's condition? Should appearances count?

(2) *Contractual and Testamentary Capacity.* Should the standard for mental qualification to make a contract be the same as that to make a will? If not, which standard should be higher? In one court's opinion, "A higher degree of mental competence is required for the transaction of ordinary business and the making of contracts than is necessary for testamentary dispositions of property." In re Estate of Faris, 159 N.W.2d 417 (Iowa 1968). Do you agree? Why?

What of a contract concerning the disposition of property by will? For an opinion relying on a statement of the testamentary standard (1 Page on Wills § 12.37) in a case involving such a contract, see Simmons First National Bank v. Luzader, 246 Ark. 302, 438 S.W.2d 25 (1969) (promise of $12,000 in bank account in return for lifetime care). In such a case, is it improper to consider who the beneficiaries of the estate are? On that subject the court made the following observation: "Let it be remembered that this is not a case where a man is depriving his wife or children of needed monies—this is not a case where loved ones are cast aside for strangers. To the contrary, all heirs are collateral heirs, none of whom, from the record, had anything to do with helping Yarbrough accumulate his savings."

CUNDICK v. BROADBENT, 383 F.2d 157 (10th Cir. 1967). [Darwin Cundick was a 59-year-old sheep rancher who had sometimes sold his lamb crop to J. R. Broadbent. At a meeting between the two

---

b. Compare Moses v. Manufacturers Life Ins. Co., 298 F.Supp. 321 (D.S.C. 1968), aff'd mem. 407 F.2d 1142 (4th Cir.1969).

men in September, 1963, they signed a one-page contract in longhand by which Cundick agreed to sell all of his ranching properties to Broadbent. Mr. and Mrs. Cundick then took the contract to their lawyer, who refined and amplified it into an eleven-page document, which the parties signed in his office. In October, 1963, the agreement was amended, again with a lawyer's aid, so as to increase the price to Cundick and in another respect favorable to him. Under the amended agreement, more than 2,000 acres of range land went for about $40,000. (An expert later valued it at $89,000.) Also included was Cundick's interest in a development company of which Broadbent was a director, at a price of $46,750. (A witness for Cundick later valued this at $184,000, and one for Broadbent at $73,743.) As late as February, 1964, he was executing documents to carry out the sale. In March, 1964, when the price had been paid and the sale was almost completed, Cundick sought to rescind. His wife, who had been appointed his guardian ad litem, for the purpose of suing, brought an action against Broadbent to set aside the agreement. She asserted that her husband had been mentally incompetent to contract, and that in any event he was mentally infirm and that Broadbent had knowingly overreached him. The evidence showed that Cundick had psychiatric treatment in 1961. Thereafter his family doctor saw him many times about various ailments, but nothing was said or done about a mental condition until suit was commenced. The court ordered examinations in 1964, which disclosed premature arteriosclerosis. Two neurosurgeons and a psychologist testified that he had been incapable, the previous September, of transacting important business affairs, that he was a "confused and befuddled man with very poor judgment." There was no medical evidence to the contrary. The trial court nevertheless found: "The acts and conduct of Cundick between September 2, 1963, and the middle of February, 1964, were the acts, conduct and behavior of a person competent to manage his affairs and cognizant of the effect of his actions." It also found that the contract was not unconscionable, unfair or inequitable. From a dismissal of the action, the plaintiff appealed.]

MURRAH, CHIEF JUDGE. . . . At one time, in this country and in England, it was the law that since a lunatic or non compos mentis had no mind with which to make an agreement, his contract was wholly void and incapable of ratification. But, if his mind was merely confused or weak so that he knew what he was doing yet was incapable of fully understanding the terms and effect of his agreement, he could indeed contract, but such contract would be voidable at his option. . . . But in recent times courts have tended away from the concept of absolutely void contracts toward the notion that even though a contract be said to be void for lack of capacity to make it, it is nevertheless ratifiable at the instance of the incompetent party. The modern rule, and the weight of authority, seems to be [that] ". . . the contractual act by one claiming to be mentally deficient, but not under guardianship, absent fraud, or knowledge of such asserted incapacity by the other contracting party, is not a void act but at most only voidable at the instance of the deficient party; and then only in accordance with certain equitable principles." Rubenstein v. Dr. Pepper Co., 8 Cir., 228 F.2d 528. . . .

In recognition of different degrees of mental competency the weight of authority seems to hold that mental capacity to contract depends upon whether the allegedly disabled person possessed sufficient reason to enable him to understand the nature and effect of the act in issue. Even average intelligence is not essential to a valid bargain. . . . "Mere weakness of body or mind, or of both, do not constitute what the law regards as mental incompetency sufficient to render a contract voidable. . . . A condition which may be described by a physician as senile dementia may not be insanity in a legal sense." Kaleb v. Modern Woodmen of America, 51 Wyo. 116, 64 P.2d 605, 607. Weakmindedness is, however, highly relevant in determining whether the deficient party was overreached and defrauded. . . .

There was, to be sure, evidence of a change in his personality and attitude toward his business affairs during [the period between his mental examinations in 1961 and 1964]. But the record is conspicuously silent concerning any discussion of his mental condition among his family and friends in the community where he lived and operated his ranch. Certainly, the record is barren of any discussion or comment in Broadbent's presence. It seems incredible that Cundick could have been utterly incapable of transacting his business affairs, yet such condition be unknown on this record to his family and friends, especially his wife who lived and worked with him and participated in the months-long transaction which she now contends was fraudulently conceived and perpetrated. . . .

The narrated facts of this case amply support the trial court's finding to the effect that Broadbent did not deceive or overreach Cundick. . . . [Although] there is positive evidence that the property was worth very much more than what Broadbent paid for it, . . . there was evidence to the effect that after the original contract was signed and some complaint made about the purchase price, the parties agreed to raise the price and the contract was so modified.

[Affirmed.]

HILL, CIRCUIT JUDGE (dissenting): . . . . The evidence relied upon by the majority is actually trivial and inconsequential as compared with the undisputed medical testimony. . . . It is inconceivable to me that any mentally competent person, with a lifetime of experience as a successful rancher and stockman, would dispose of his ranch interests at a price equal to less than one-half of the actual value. . . .

NOTES

(1) *Orientation.* Are the Ortelere and Cundick cases distinguishable? At p. 201 supra mention was made of status, behavior and substance orientation. To what extent do the differences among the majority and dissenting opinions in those cases reflect different orientations? For a discussion of mental illness and contracts, see Note, 57 Mich.L.Rev. 1020 (1959).

(2) *The Case of Commercial Insanity.* Davis was acquitted of larceny by reason of insanity, and committed to the State Hospital for the Insane. He escaped and borrowed $10,000 from a bank to start a trucking business. He made installment payments for over a year on such items as a tractor, a refrigeration unit and tires, and paid insurance premiums, all amounting to many thousands of dollars. But the business did not prosper and Davis brought an action (through his wife as "next friend") to recover the amounts he had paid. One of the defendants, Montgomery Ward, made a counterclaim for the balance due on the tires. At the close of the plaintiff's evidence, his action was dismissed and the counterclaim granted. He appealed. *Held:* Affirmed. "The undisputed facts are that Davis used the equipment; that he obtained considerable monies through their use, during which time the equipment was worn and depreciated, and subsequently wrecked. . . . He returned nothing to any of the parties." The contracts were not void, and Davis's failure to do equity defeated his right to rescission. The court rejected an argument by Davis based on the following statute: "All contracts, agreements, and credits with or to any insane person, shall be absolutely void as against such person, his heirs, or personal representatives; but persons making such contracts or agreements with any insane person shall be bound thereby at the election of his conservators." The court drew the conclusion, from statutory sources, that "what is contemplated is a civil proceeding in which there is an appointment of a conservator to manage affairs of the incompetent. . . . The article also indicates a legislative intent to place in county courts *exclusive* and continuing jurisdiction over the affairs of the mental incompetent." Davis v. Colorado Kenworth Corporation, 156 Colo. 98, 396 P.2d 958 (1964).

SECTION 2.　UNFAIRNESS: CONVENTIONAL CONTROLS

In this section we turn attention to inequality of exchange, as manifested in the terms of a bargain. Is it the proper business of a court to calculate the advantages of a contract for each party, and see to it that neither of them suffers a disproportionate loss, or enjoys a disproportionate gain? Put in that form the question has an obvious answer, supported by a powerful tradition. "Parties of sufficient mental capacity for the management of their own business," it is said, "have the right to make their own bargains." [a] We have seen that the

a. Hardesty v. Smith, 3 Ind. 39 (1851).

core idea of consideration is the fact of a bargain, and the law on that subject contains an implicit judgment that a promise should be enforced whether or not something of equal value was given for it. "If the requirement of a consideration is met, there is no additional requirement of . . . equivalence in the values exchanged." [b] As the materials to follow will show, that judgment is supported by substantial reasons of policy.

Nevertheless, a number of limiting principles serve to prevent the routine enforcement of unequal bargains. Some of them have long been fixed in the law. They are the subject of this section. The less traditional means that courts have developed in recent years to police against unfairness in the substance of an exchange are explored in Section 4, infra.

The function of policing has always been something of a specialty of equity courts. Relying on the element of discretion, or grace, associated with granting specific performance, they have refused that remedy in cases where the exchange appeared highly disproportionate. In cases "at law," by contrast, the means of policing have had to be either more direct, or more devious, depending on the circumstances. A direct measure is to pronounce a public policy by which a particularly overbearing provision of a contract may be disregarded. That course is exceptional. More commonly, the courts have manipulated the doctrine of consideration to serve the ideal of fairness. It will be seen in this section that that ideal plays a part in determining whether or not any "bargain" at all has been effected.

NOTE

Good Faith. According to the Restatement Second, "Every contract imposes upon each party a duty of good faith and fair dealing in its performance and its enforcement." Section 231. This "rule" has no predecessor in the original Restatement; but see UCC 1–203. According to a comment, neither § 231 nor the Code provision deals with good faith in the formation of a contract.

Is it useful to draw a sharp distinction between the formation and performance stages of contracting? Why is there no recognition of a generalized duty of good faith in negotiation in the Code or the Restatement? In going through the chapter, you should consider how many of the problems could helpfully be approached in terms of such a duty. See p. 151 supra.

b. Restatement Second, § 81(b).

McKINNON v. BENEDICT

Supreme Court of Wisconsin, 1968.
38 Wis.2d 607, 157 N.W.2d 665.

[In 1960 Roderick McKinnon, the owner of a home on Mamie Lake, Wisconsin, amid more than a thousand acres, gave help to Mr. and Mrs. Roy Benedict in buying a resort known as Bent's Camp. It consisted of a lodge and some cabins on about 80 acres that were enclosed by the lake and McKinnon's property. McKinnon promised some help in getting business and in other minor respects, but his principal contribution was in making a loan of $5,000. The Benedicts used the advance as part of a down payment on a land purchase contract with the previous owners of the camp. The Benedicts promised McKinnon to cut no trees between the camp and his property, and to make no improvements "closer to [his] property than the present buildings." The term of these restrictions was 25 years. They did not affect all the resort tract, but did affect all the most desireable portion.

[The resort business did not prosper, after the Benedicts bought it, although they repaid the loan in about seven months. In 1964 they decided to add a trailer park and tent camp. In the fall and following spring they invested some $9,000 in bulldozing and installing utilities. The summer of 1965 brought McKinnon from Arizona, where he spent the winters, and brought also a suit against the Benedicts. The trial court enjoined them from continuing with their projected improvements, and they appealed.]

HEFFERNAN, JUSTICE. . . . No action at law has been commenced for damages by virtue of the breach of the restrictions; and, in fact, the plaintiffs in their complaint claim that they have no adequate remedy at law. [The court expounded some "ancient principles of equity," and quoted the Restatement of Contracts, § 367.]

Coupled with the general equitable principle that contracts that are oppressive will not be enforced in equity is the principle of public policy that restrictions on the use of land "are not favored in the law" (Mueller v. Schier (1926), 189 Wis. 70, 82, 205 N.W. 912, 916), and that restrictions and prohibitions as to the use of real estate should be resolved, if a doubt exists, in favor of the free use of the property. Stein v. Endres Home Builders, Inc. (1938) 228 Wis. 620, 629, 280 N. W. 316. . . .

The great hardship sought to be imposed upon the Benedicts is apparent. What was the consideration in exchange for this deprivation of use? The only monetary consideration was the granting of a $5,000 loan, interest free, for a period of seven months. The value of this money for that period of time, if taken at the same interest rate as the 5 percent used on the balance of the land contract, is approximately $145; and it should be noted that this was not an unsecured loan, since McKinnon took a mortgage on the cottage property of the Benedicts in Michigan. In addition, McKinnon stated that he would "help you try" to reach a solution of the problem posed by Mrs. Vair's occupancy of one of the cottages on a fifty-year lease at $5 per year. His one attempt, as stated above, was a failure; and McKinnon's promise to generate business resulted in an occupancy by only one group for less than a week. For this pittance and these feeble attempts to help with the operational problems of the camp, the Benedicts have sacrificed their right to make lawful and reasonable use of their property.

In oral argument it was pointed out that the value of the $5,000 loan could not be measured in terms of the interest value of the money, since, without this advance, Benedict would have been unable to purchase the camp at all. To our mind, this is evidence of the fact that Benedict was not able to deal at arm's length with McKinnon, for his need for these funds was obviously so great that he was willing to enter into a contract that results in gross inequities. Lord Chancellor Northington said "necessitous men are not, truly speaking, free men." Vernon v. Bethell (1762), 2 Eden 110, 113.

We find that the inadequacy of consideration is so gross as to be unconscionable and a bar to the plaintiffs' invocation of the extraordinary equitable powers of the court.

While there is no doubt that there are benefits from this agreement to McKinnon, they are more than outweighed by the oppressive terms that would be imposed upon the Benedicts. McKinnon testified that he and his wife spend only the summer months on their property. Undoubtedly, these are the months when it is most important that there be no disruption of the natural beauty or the quiet and pleasant enjoyment of the property, nevertheless, there was testimony that the trailer camp could not be seen from the McKinnon home, nor could the campsite be seen during the summer months of the year, when the leaves were on the trees. Thus, the detriment of which the McKinnons complain, that would be cognizable in an equity action, is minimal,[1] while the damage done to the Benedicts is severe.

Considering all the factors—the inadequacy of the consideration, the small benefit that would be accorded the McKinnons, and the oppressive conditions imposed upon the Benedicts—we conclude that this contract failed to meet the test of reasonableness that is the *sine qua non* of the enforcement of rights in an action in equity.

5A Corbin, Contracts, sec. 1164, p. 219, points out that, although a contract is harsh, oppressive, and unconscionable, it may nevertheless be enforceable at law; but, in the discretion of the court, equita-

---

1. McKinnon testified that the value of his property had depreciated in the amount of $50,000. That testimony was properly admissible, but its probative value was slight, especially since plaintiffs' expert real estate witness stated that he was unable to testify to the amount of the depreciated value.

ble remedies will not be enforced against one who suffers from such harshness and oppression.

A fair reading of the transcript indicates no sharp practice, dishonesty, or overreaching on the part of McKinnon. However, there was a wide disparity between the business experience of the parties. McKinnon was a man of stature in the legal field, an investment counsellor, a former officer of a major corporation, and had held posts of responsibility with the United States government, while, insofar as the record shows, Benedict was a retail jeweler and a man of limited financial ability. He no doubt overvalued the promises of McKinnon to assist in getting the operation "well organized" and to solve the lease problem and to "generate business." These factors, in view of Benedict's financial inability to enter into an arms-length transaction, may be explanatory of the reason for the agreement, but the agreement viewed even as of the time of its execution was unfair and based upon inadequate consideration. We, therefore, have no hesitancy in denying the plaintiffs the equitable remedy of injunction. . . .

[Reversed.[a]]

NOTES

(1) *Questions.* Has it been decided that the Benedicts may bulldoze on their property and make improvements wherever they please? If the Benedicts had begun their new business immediately after making the agreement of 1960, would the court have given McKinnon the relief then that he is now denied?

(2) *Specific Performance and Damages.* In a sense it is extraordinary for a contract claimant to be entitled to specific performance, in English and American law. The "normal" remedy is conceived to be a judgment for damages resulting from the breach, or for other relief at law. Exceptionally, when such a remedy is inadequate, specific performance may be had in a "court of equity." The power to grant this remedy was historically exercised by the English Court of Chancery, centuries ago, and is today administered in courts succeeding to the powers and traditions of that court. Owing to modern procedural reforms both legal and equitable remedies are now generally provided in the same court, but some distinctions remain.

By tradition, a decree of specific performance is not a matter of right in the same sense as damages are, but may be withheld in the court's discretion. Some of the grounds on which the remedy may be denied are that the terms of the contract reflect mistake or sharp practice, or impose disproportionate hardship. See Restatement, § 367. It is also said that an action for specific performance does not lie on a promise for which the consideration is grossly inadequate, although that has been a controversial proposition.[b]

a. Except insofar as the trial court had given relief on a separate cause of action for trespass.

b. As to inadequacy of price, Lord Eldon said that unless it is "such as shocks the conscience, and amounts in

In principle, when specific performance is denied on such a ground it may be possible for the claimant to obtain damages in a suit at law. The thought that courts of law are less sensitive than courts of equity to issues of fairness is repulsive to some. It has been described as a "moral curtain that, heavy with the mold of centuries, still hangs across our law." Newman, The Rennaissance of Good Faith in Contracting in Anglo-American Law, 54 Corn.L.Rev. 553, 554 (1969). This writer observes that the dual standard may have ceased to exist in practice, though it continues to be repeated. Only two cases have been found, it seems, in which specific performance was denied and damages awarded (and in one of these the judgment was set aside for an error in calculating it).[c]

One way to eliminate the "dual standard" would be for equity courts to rescind or cancel contracts for unfairness, using the same standards as they apply in specific performance cases. In McKinnon v. Benedict, if the Benedicts had sought to have the restrictions on their use of the property cancelled, does it appear that they would have been successful? The power to cancel has not been freely exercised. This fact may mean that damage claims are more readily available to parties who fail to get specific performance than the reported cases happen to show. "One suspects that the Chancellors thought there was a real remedy at law, and that the litigants did too; else the actions for cancellation and the judges' agonizing over them make little sense."[d]

In denying specific performance to a claimant, the courts sometimes take comfort in the thought, as many opinions show, that the decision does not deprive him of all remedy, but only remits him to the more perfunctory one of damages. But that may be an empty justification in a case like McKinnon v. Benedict. Perhaps there was no effective remedy available to the McKinnons other than specific performance: notice their allegation that they had no adequate remedy at law. This might be so because of the rule that no damages will be awarded unless the amount of loss can be calculated with some degree of certainty. Or it might be so because damages are a poor substitute for the performance agreed upon. Remedies for breach of contract are dealt with in more detail in Chapter 5, infra.

(3) *Certainty*. In going through the cases in this chapter, you should consider whether or not certainty in commercial affairs has been over-

itself to conclusive and decisive evidence of fraud in the transaction it is not in itself a sufficient ground for refusing a specific performance." Coles v. Trecothick, 9 Ves. 234, 32 Eng. Rep. 592 (1804). But this is a proposition on which very great men have differed, it has been said. Savage, C. J., in Seymour v. Delancey, 3 Cowen 445 (N.Y.1824). This was said, by the way, in a dissent. The majority overturned a decree of Chancellor Kent, who disputed Eldon's view.

See also Community Sports, Inc. v. Denver Ringsby Rockets, 429 Pa. 565, 240 A.2d 832 (1968), an action to enjoin breach of contract, in which the court said: "Although the rule in Pennsylvania is that lack of consideration will not preclude enforcement of a contract under seal, this rule does not apply in a court of equity where extraordinary relief such as this is sought."

c. See also Frank and Endicott, Defenses in Equity and "Legal Rights," 14 La.L.Rev. 380 (1954).

d. Leff, Unconscionability and the Code—The Emperor's New Clause, 115 U.Pa.L.Rev. 485, 541 n. 237 (1967).

valued or undervalued. "There does come a point where the additional costs of having personalized transactions may be too great; a little injustice may be a social good." [e]

TUCKWILLER v. TUCKWILLER, 413 S.W.2d 274 (Mo.1967). [John and Ruby Tuckwiller lived on the Hudson family farm in Missouri, and John farmed it as a renter. Almost half of the property —160 acres—was owned by Mrs. Metta Hudson Morrison. When she was about 70 years of age, Mrs. Morrison contracted Parkinson's disease, and at about the same time she gave up her residence in New York. She had been educated at Columbia and other schools, had been a teacher for many years, and had held other jobs. After leaving New York she travelled extensively, but early in 1963 she returned to the Hudson farm, where some rooms were reserved for her use. In April she was hospitalized for about a week, as a result of dizziness and falling. She was thought then to have had a "stroke," and showed some mental confusion. But at the first of May her doctor and a friend found her mentally clear—"clear as a bell." She knew, the doctor said, that Parkinsonism is a progressive disease, leaving the victim ultimately dependent entirely on outside care.

[Before the April incident, Mrs. Tuckwiller had been urged by Mrs. Morrison to quit a job she held and care for her for the rest of her life, and the subject was discussed again after Mrs. Morrison's release from the hospital. The two were quite congenial. On May 3, a Saturday, when she was with the Tuckwillers, Mrs. Morrison signed the following paper, written by Mrs. Tuckwiller:

> My offer to Aunt Metta is as follows
>
> I will take care of her for her lifetime; by that I mean provide her 3 meals per day—a good bed—do any possible act of nursing and provide her every pleasure possible.
>
> In exchange she will will me her (Corum) farm at her death keeping all money made from it during her life. She will maintain expense of her medicine.

On May 6 Mrs. Tuckwiller resigned her job, and Mrs. Morrison made an appointment with a lawyer to change her will. Later that day, however, she fainted and fell. She was taken to the hospital, where, except for four days, she remained until her death on June 14. She was 73 at that time. Mrs. Tuckwiller spent much time at the hospital during Mrs. Morrison's final illness, assisting as she could, but Mrs. Morrison was attended by special nurses.

[Before leaving for the hospital on May 6, Mrs. Morrison had the date put on the paper set out above, and obtained the signatures

---

e.   Leff, Injury, Ignorance and Spite— The Dynamics of Coercive Collection, 80 Yale L.J. 1, 42 (1970).

of the two ambulance attendants as witnesses. Her will, dated in 1961, was never changed. It provided for the sale of the farm, the proceeds to be used for a student loan fund at Davidson College. The farm had an "inventory value" of $34,400.

[Mrs. Tuckwiller brought a bill for specific performance of the contract, which was resisted by the College and Mrs. Morrison's executor. The trial court granted the relief, and the defendants appealed.]

WELBORN, COMMISSIONER. . . . [I]n determining whether or not a contract is so unfair or inequitable or is unconscionable so as to deny its specific performance, the transaction must be viewed prospectively, not retrospectively. The same rule applies with respect to sufficiency of consideration. . . . Viewed in this light, we find that plaintiff gave up her employment with which she was well satisfied and undertook what was at the time of the contract an obligation of unknown and uncertain duration, involving duties which, in the usual course of the disease from which Mrs. Morrison suffered, would have become increasingly onerous. . . . Viewed from the standpoint of Mrs. Morrison, the contract cannot be considered unfair. She was appreciative of the care and attention which plaintiff had given her prior to the agreement. Although, as defendants suggest, such prior services cannot provide the consideration essential to a binding contract, such prior services and the past relation of the parties may properly be considered in connection with the fairness of the contract and adequacy of the consideration. 5A Corbin on Contracts, § 1165, p. 227. Aware of her future outlook and having no immediate family to care for her, Mrs. Morrison was understandably appreciative of the personal care and attention of plaintiff and concerned with the possibility of routine impersonal care over a long period of time in a nursing home or similar institution. Having no immediate family which might be the object of her bounty, she undoubtedly felt more free to agree to dispose of the farm without insisting upon an exact quid pro quo. Her insistence that the contract be witnessed prior to her hospitalization is clear evidence of her satisfaction with the bargain as was her unsuccessful effort to change her will to carry out her agreement. . . .

Properly viewed from the standpoint of the parties at the time of the agreement, we find that the contract was fair, not unconscionable, and supported by an adequate consideration. Although not conceding that such conclusion is correct, defendants argue, in effect, that in view of the obviously brief duration of plaintiff's services and their value in comparison with the value of the farm, plaintiff should be obliged to accept the offered payment of the reasonable value of her services and denied the relief of specific performance. Defendants point out that the trial court found that valuing the services which plaintiff rendered might be "possible." That conclusion is undoubtedly correct and unquestionably the monetary value of plaintiff's services would have been a quite small proportion (perhaps one percent) of the value of the farm. Once, however, the essential fairness of the contract and the adequacy of the consideration are found, the fact that the subject of the contract is real estate answers any question of adequacy of the legal remedy of monetary damages. "Whenever a contract concerning real property is in its nature and incidents entirely unobjectionable—that is, when it possesses none of those features which . . . appeal to the discretion of the court—it is as much a matter of course for a court of equity to decree a specific performance of it, as it is for a court of law to give damages for the breach of it." Pomeroy's Specific Performance of Contracts (3d ed.), § 10, p. 23.[a]

[Affirmed.]

NOTES

(1) *Question.* Part of the plaintiff's evidence was that the life expectancy of a 73-year-old person is about 9 years. Do you see any reason to discount this evidence?

(2) *Equitable Discretion.* "Within the ambit of those factors of contract-producing behavior which would result in a denial of specific performance, a bewildering number of permutations work to inform the chancellor's discretion. In these cases one runs continually into the old, the young, the ignorant, the necessitous, the illiterate, the improvident, the drunken, the naive and the sick, all on one side of the transaction, with the sharp and hard on the other. Language of quasi-fraud and quasi-duress abounds. Certain whole classes of presumptive sillies like sailors and heirs and farmers and women continually wander on and off stage. Those not certifiably crazy, but nonetheless pretty peculiar, are often to be found. And in most of the cases, of course, several of these factors appear in combination. . . . Almost without exception, actions for specific performance were (and are) brought with respect to transactions involving real property." Leff, Unconscionability and the Code—the Emperor's New Clause, 115 U.Pa.L.Rev. 485, 531–34 (1967).

(3) *Problem.* George A. Shea contracted to sell twenty acres of land, worth $24,000, and a badly used Cadillac, to Dr. Joseph Hodge for $4,000 and a "new $6600 Coupe DeVille Cadillac." Shea was a man of means, but badly in need of cash to pay taxes. After accepting the car, he refused to convey. On these facts alone, should specific performance be granted, at the instance of the doctor? Which of the following circumstances, if any, should tip the scales against the plaintiff? (a) Shea was 75 years old at the time. (b) He was fatuously fond of new Cadillacs. (c) He was an inebriate of long standing, and afflicted with grievous chronic illnesses. (d) He had been the plaintiff's patient for many years. See Hodge v. Shea, 252 S.C. 601, 168 S.E.2d 82 (1969).

a. The court rejected the defendants' "hint that the contract was unfair because of evidence of mental confusion of Mrs. Morrison at her hospitalization in April and again on May 6." At the time of agreement, it said, it appeared from the evidence that she was "mentally alert and fully aware of what she was doing."

NEWMAN & SNELL'S STATE BANK v. HUNTER, 243 Mich. 331, 220 N.W. 665, 59 A.L.R. 311 (1928). [Lee Hunter died in January, 1926, owing $3,700 to Newman & Snell's State Bank. His note for that amount was secured by 50 shares of stock in the Hunter Company, which had been pledged to the bank. The company continued to do business as long as Hunter lived, but afterward it was liquidated, and its debts proved to be greater than its assets. Hunter's estate was also insolvent: there was not enough to pay his funeral expenses and the statutory allowance for his widow, Zennetta. On March 1 there was a transaction between Zennetta and the bank, on the basis of which it now sues her. The transaction was described as follows, in an agreed statement of facts: "the defendant gave the plaintiff the note described in the plaintiff's declaration in this cause, and the plaintiff surrendered to her therefor, and, in consideration thereof, the note of said Lee C. Hunter. The defendant also paid the plaintiff the earned interest due on the deceased's note." Apparently the bank retained the Hunter Company stock, as security for Zennetta's note. From judgment for the plaintiff, the defendant appealed.]

FELLOWS, J. [The court first considered the question whether or not the bank's surrender of Hunter's note was a "sufficient consideration" for Zennetta's note. Conceding a conflict in the precedents, the court ruled that it was not.] Here we have the widow's note given to take up the note of her insolvent husband, a worthless piece of paper. . . . [I]t seems clear to me that the transaction was without consideration. [Then the court considered and rejected the bank's contention that it had released a security interest in the pledged stock.] Stripped of all legal fiction, the cold facts are that, when the negotiations opened, plaintiff had this stock and the worthless note of defendant's husband. When they ended, the bank still had the stock and defendant's note.

[Reversed.]

NOTES

(1) *Questions.* Was this decision consistent with the rules stated in Restatement Second, §§ 75 and 81? Would the decision have been the same if Hunter's estate had been just large enough to pay the widow's allowance, all his debts, and a $1,000 bequest to Zennetta? If it had been large enough to pay a portion (say 10%) of his debts, but not all of them? Suppose that when Zennetta gave the bank her note it had handed her, in exchange, a document releasing its claim against the estate. What result under Restatement Second, § 76B(2)? (The bank had a "valid" claim against Hunter's estate, be it noted, only there was nothing to pay it with.) Is the decision as it stands an example of "widow's law"?

(2) *Sufficiency of Consideration.* The original Restatement embodies a conception of "insufficient consideration" for dealing with certain problems distinguished from that of "adequacy" of consideration. See §§ 76

et seq.; cf. § 81.[a] The Restatement Second dispenses with the standard of sufficiency, but states a set of rules qualifying § 75 in ways comparable to effects of that standard. See §§ 76A et seq.

How can the standard expressed in Restatement Second, § 89A(2)(b) —value disproportionate to benefit—be rationalized in relation to § 81?

(3) *The Case of the Tax Bonanza.* In 1898 the selectmen of the town of Hampton, New Hampshire, granted a lease for 99 years on a "barren" beach area to a beach improvement company. Over the years improvements were made on the property that had, by 1962, an assessed valuation of about $2.3 million. The town brought an action for a declaratory judgment that the lease was "null and void," or that certain of its provisions were. One term offensive to the town was that the tract (not the improvements) was to be free of taxation, which was said to violate a requirement of uniform taxation, as expressed in the state constitution. *Held:* For the company. It appeared that the area, with improvements, contributed about 10% of the town's tax income, although it constituted less than 2% of the town's area. The lease provided for an annual rent of $500. The land was said to be worth not less than $300,000—although what it would be worth apart from the lease was "pure speculation." The court said, "our Constitution does not require that all parties to public contracts must operate at a loss." Town of Hampton v. Hampton Beach Improvement Co., 107 N.H. 89, 218 A.2d 442 (1966).

BLACK INDUSTRIES, INC. v. BUSH

United States District Court, D. New Jersey, 1953.
110 F.Supp. 801.

FORMAN, CHIEF JUDGE. The plaintiff, Black Industries, Inc., a citizen of Ohio, is suing the defendant, George F. Bush, a citizen of New Jersey doing business as G. F. Bush Associates, for breach of a contract. The defendant has moved for a summary judgment in its favor.

The complaint alleges as a first cause of action that the plaintiff, a manufacturer of drills, machine parts and components thereof and a purchaser of subcontract work from other suppliers, obtained an invitation to bid upon certain contracts with The Hoover Company upon three parts known as anvils, holder primers and plunger supports. The plaintiff assumed the task of obtaining a supplier of these parts and on about March 22, 1951, the defendant reached an agreement with the plaintiff to manufacture 1,300,000 anvils at a price of $4.40 per thousand; 750,000 holder primers at $11.50 per thousand and 700,000 plunger supports at a price of $12 per thousand, all of which were to be made in accordance with government specifications and in conformity with certain drawings. The plaintiff agreed to "service the contract", be responsible for all dealings with The Hoover Compa-

a. See also Browning v. Johnson, 70   a representative case making the dis-
    Wash.2d 145, 422 P.2d 314 (1967), for   tinction.

ny and would be entitled to the difference between the defendant's quotations and the ultimate price. The Hoover Company agreed to purchase the parts from the plaintiff at a rate of $8.10 per thousand anvils, $16 per thousand holder primers and $21.20 per thousand plunger supports.

The complaint further alleges that after undertaking performance of this contract, the defendant failed to complete the order, which caused a loss of $14,625 to the plaintiff, for which sum, together with interest, the plaintiff demands judgment.

[As a second cause of action the plaintiff alleges "understandings" between these parties whereby the defendant agreed to manufacture other quantities of plunger supports and anvils, for which plaintiff made a re-sale contract with Standby Products Company; and that defendant's failure to comply with this undertaking caused plaintiff a loss of $4,460.95, for which plaintiff seeks judgment. To each cause of action defendant pleads various defenses not here relevant, and then alleges that the contract set forth in the complaint is void as against public policy. The defendant, on this last ground, now moves for summary judgment.]

[The contract alleged in the first count was evidenced by a letter of April 13, 1951, from plaintiff's Gepfert to defendant Bush, and signed as "agreed to" by the latter. In this letter Gepfert stated that he had "spent considerable time, effort and money in developing the contract" to the point where The Hoover Company issued a purchase order. The letter continued as follows: "The purchase order, when received, will run directly to George F. Bush and Associates . . . Your company is to ship the material directly to The Hoover Co. . . . Your company, however, is not to bill The Hoover Co. All shipping invoices, documents of transfer and title are to be forwarded to me, and I shall have the exclusive right to bill, upon (your) billing forms and receive payment therefor in your behalf . . . It is understood that I shall have the right to receive payment, cash checks made payable to your company under The Hoover Co. contract; and to remit to you (retaining sums) as compensation due me." The compensation stipulated by Gepfert "for my services" was to be the difference between Bush's price to Black and Black's price to Hoover. The products to be purchased both by Hoover and by Standby Products were to be used by them to fulfill United States government contracts in aid of "the defense effort," i. e., the Korean War of 1950–53. Defendant then alleges that plaintiff was to receive a "profit" of 84.09% on anvils, 39.13% on holder primers and 68.33% on plunger supports under the Hoover contract, and similar percentages under the Standby contract. Defendant further alleges that these contracts are void as against public policy because these "profits" of Black were passed on to the government and the public in the form of increased prices; and cites two Federal laws intended to prevent excessive profits on war contracts: Renegotiation Act, 50 U.S.C.A. Appendix, § 1211, and 41 U.S.C.A. § 51.]

In order to declare a contract, entered by the parties freely and without evidence of fraud, void as against public policy, the contract must be invalid on the basis of recognized legal principles. [In an omitted passage, the court quotes from Muschany v. United States, 324 U.S. 49, 66–67 (1945), as follows: "It is a matter of public importance that good faith contracts of the United States should not be lightly invalidated." Then it discusses three types of illegal contracts, as indicated in the following paragraph.]

The contract in the present case, however, does not fall in any of these categories. It is not a contract by the defendant to pay the plaintiff for inducing a public official to act in a certain manner; it is not a contract to do an illegal act; and it is not a contract which contemplates collusive bidding on a public contract. It should be noted that the first and third categories of cases, upon which the defendant relies most heavily, involve agreements which directly impinge upon government activities. In the case at hand, the contract's only effect on the government was that ultimately the government was to buy the product of which defendant's goods were to be a component. Neither the defendant nor the plaintiff had any dealings with the United States on account of this contract, and therefore the profit accruing to the plaintiff was not to have been earned as a result of either inducing government action or interfering with the system of competitive bidding. This contract cannot, therefore, be declared void as against public policy on the basis of the precedents cited by the defendant.

It is quite possible that the plaintiff was to have received a very high profit on the sale of the parts, either because The Hoover Company agreed to pay too high a price or because the defendant quoted too low a price. Further proof would be required to establish this as a fact. Even if it were proved that the plaintiff was to have received a far greater profit than the defendants for a much smaller contribution, the defendant would nevertheless be bound by his agreement by the familiar rule that relative values of the consideration in a contract between business men dealing at arm's length without fraud will not affect the validity of the contract. The Coast National Bank v. Bloom, 113 N.J.L. 597, 174 A. 576, 95 A.L.R. 528 (E. & A. 1934); Restatement of the Law of Contracts § 81 (1932).

The fact that the government is the ultimate purchaser of the product in which defendant's parts are used is cited by the defendant as a reason to hold that this contract is void as against public policy. To so hold would necessitate either ruling that all contracts are void if they provide for compensation for middlemen, such as Black Industries, between producer and purchaser of goods which ultimately are incorporated in products sold to the government, a result which is not supported by precedent and which would defy the realities of our economic life, or deciding in every case involving such a contract whether the compensation paid a middleman such as the plaintiff here who locates purchasers and assists the producer in other ways, is reasonable. This latter course would, in effect, impose price regulatory functions on the court. There are other and more effective methods of insuring that the government does not pay an unreasonable price for its supplies. The manufacturer selling directly to the United States must conform to procedures such as bidding designed to protect the government, and which should, in conjunction with the ordinary considerations of profits and loss, insure that prime contractors do not pay outlandish prices for the products they buy in order to fulfill a government contract. The contract may be subject to renegotiation. 50 U.S.C.A. Appendix, § 1211 et seq. I do not believe that it is the function of the court to interfere by determining the validity of a contract between ordinary business men on the basis of its beliefs as to the adequacy of the consideration. Consequently, I hold that, assuming the facts to be as stated by the defendant, the contract sued on in this case is not void as against public policy and the defendant's motion for a summary judgment will, therefore, be denied.

Let an order be submitted in accordance with this opinion.

NOTES

(1) *"Adequacy" of Consideration.* The arguments against courts' inquiring into the "relative value of the consideration in a contract between businessmen dealing at arm's length without fraud" have been summarized as follows: "(1) The efficient administration of the law of contracts requires that courts shall not be required to prescribe prices. (2) The test of enforceability should be certain and should not be beclouded by such vague terms as 'fair' or 'reasonable' as tests of validity. (3) There is still the somewhat old-fashioned theory that persons of maturity and sound mind should be free to contract imprudently as well as prudently." Patterson, An Apology for Consideration, 58 Colum.L.Rev. 929 (1958). See section 81 of the Restatement and of Restatement Second.

Does it appear that courts of equity, in specific performance actions, have undertaken price regulatory functions? Does the dispensing power exercised in McKinnon v. Benedict invite litigation in a large proportion of contracts about land? If so, it may tend to impair the value of such contracts as the Tuckwillers made with Mrs. Morrison, in Tuckwiller v. Tuckwiller. Should the courts be cautious, on that account, in attempting supervision over the values exchanged?

(2) *Middlemen.* The court acknowleges the possibility that Black might have stood to receive a "far greater profit" than Bush "for a much smaller contribution." What is the nature of the "contribution" of a middleman such as Black?

He may perform an "informational" function, by bringing together buyers and sellers who would otherwise be ignorant of each other's needs.

(See Note 3, infra.) He may also perform a "risk-shifting" function, by taking on himself risks of market fluctuations that would otherwise have to be borne by buyers or sellers. Both of these functions are highly developed in well organized markets, such as commodities exchanges, where brokers clearly perform both an "informational" function by facilitating transactions between buyers and sellers and a "risk-shifting" function through stabilizing foreseeable market fluctuations. See Samuelson, Economics, Appendix to Chap. 21 (8th ed. 1970).

Does it appear that Black's "contribution" involved either an "informational" or a "risk-shifting" function? If it involved the former, did Black supply Hoover with enough information about available suppliers to merit the compensation he received? Why did not Hoover contact Bush directly? Why did not Bush contact Hoover directly? Would Bush have been able to charge Black more if he had known how much Hoover was paying Black?

We have already spent some time on an important type of middleman, the general contractor in the construction industry. At one extreme, he may be little more than a broker between owner and subcontractors, maintaining only a small office with supervisory personnel and contracting out substantially all the work. It has been suggested that the evils of bid shopping can be avoided if the owner bypasses the general contractor and makes separate contracts directly with the subcontractors, leaving their supervision to his architect. Can you see any disadvantages to this? See Note, 39 N.Y.U.L.Rev. 816, 828–29 (1964); American Institute of Architects, Handbook of Architectural Practice III 7.04 (1958).

(3) *An Economist's View.* George Stigler, an economist, has written of the phenomenon of "search," by which, in a market economy, buyers (or sellers) canvass various sellers (or buyers). If the dispersion of prices quoted "is at all large (relative to the cost of search), it will pay, on average, to canvass several sellers." Thus the optimal amount of search varies directly with the dispersion of prices in a market and inversely with the cost of search. In markets with search the low-price sellers will attract more buyers than the high-price sellers, which will tend to force the latter out of business and decrease the dispersion. Once the dispersion is known to be low, the system becomes stable. Stigler, The Economics of Information, 69 J. Political Economy 213 (1961). See also Stigler, Information in the Labor Market, 70 J. Political Economy (Supp.) 94 (1962).

What does this have to say about the merits of the decision in Black v. Bush?

(4) *Excessive Profits in Contracts with the Government.* Should the courts, as a matter of public policy, deny enforcement to a military procurement contract or other contract with the United States, when it is demonstrable that the contractor's profits have been or will be exorbitant? The leading case is U. S. v. Bethlehem Steel Corporation, 315 U.S. 289 (1952), in which counsel for the government contended that a contract for building war vessels during World War I had yielded such great profits that it should be treated as having been induced by "duress" on the United States. But the Court, over strenuous dissenting opinions, held that the contract had not been induced by duress. In World War II, a number of

legislative and administrative devices were used to limit profits on war contracts.   These devices included: (1) compulsory renegotiation of procurement contracts so as to reduce the contractor's profits to reasonable margins; (2) administrative price regulation and priority control of scarce materials; (3) a sharply graduated "excess profits" tax; and (4) elimination of the cost-plus-percentage-of-cost contract in government procurement.

One of Bush's arguments was that Black's profits were passed on to the government and the public in the form of excessive prices, contrary to "public policy."   If Bush had been granted the relief that he sought, what would have been the probable impact on prices paid by the government in similar transactions?

STRONG v. SHEFFIELD

Court of Appeals of New York, 1895.
144 N.Y. 392, 39 N.E. 330.

[Action on a promissory note.   A judgment for plaintiff against defendant, Louisa A. Sheffield, was reversed by the General Term of the Supreme Court.   The facts are stated in the opinion.]

ANDREWS, C. J.   The contract between a maker or endorser of a promissory note and the payee forms no exception to the general rule that a promise, not supported by a consideration, is nudum pactum. The law governing commercial paper which precludes an inquiry into the consideration as against bona fide holders for value before maturity, has no application where the suit is between the original parties to the instrument.   It is undisputed that the demand note upon which the action was brought was made by the husband of the defendant and endorsed by her at his request and delivered to the plaintiff, the payee, as security for an antecedent debt owing by the husband to the plaintiff.   The debt of the husband was past due at the time, and the only consideration for the wife's endorsement, which is or can be claimed, is that as part of the transaction there was an agreement by the plaintiff when the note was given to forbear the collection of the debt, or a request for forbearance, which was followed by forbearance for a period of about two years subsequent to the giving of the note. There is no doubt that an agreement by the creditor to forbear the collection of a debt presently due is a good consideration for an absolute or conditional promise of a third person to pay the debt or for any obligation he may assume in respect thereto.   Nor is it essential that the creditor should bind himself at the time to forbear collection or to give time.   If he is requested by his debtor to extend the time, and a third person undertakes in consideration of forbearance being given to become liable as surety or otherwise, and the creditor does in fact forbear in reliance upon the undertaking, although he enters into no enforceable agreement to do so, his acquiescence in the request, and an actual forbearance in consequence thereof for a reasonable time, furnishes a good consideration for the collateral undertaking.

In other words, a request followed by performance is sufficient, and mutual promises at the time are not essential unless it was the understanding that the promisor was not to be bound, except on condition that the other party entered into an immediate and reciprocal obligation to do the thing requested. . . . The note in question did not in law extend the payment of the debt. It was payable on demand, and although being payable with interest it was in form consistent with an intention that payment should not be immediately demanded, yet there was nothing on its face to prevent an immediate suit on the note against the maker or to recover the original debt. . . .

In the present case the agreement made is not left to inference, nor was it a case of request to forbear, followed by forbearance, in pursuance of the request, without any promise on the part of the creditor at the time. The plaintiff testified that there was an express agreement on his part to the effect that he would not pay the note away, nor put it in any bank for collection, but (using the words of the plaintiff) "I will hold it until such time as I want my money, I will make a demand on you for it." And again: "No, I will keep it until such time as I want it." Upon this alleged agreement the defendant endorsed the note. It would have been no violation of the plaintiff's promise if, immediately on receiving the note, he had commenced suit upon it. Such a suit would have been an assertion that he wanted the money and would have fulfilled the condition of forbearance. The debtor and the defendant, when they became parties to the note, may have had the hope or expectation that forbearance would follow, and there was forbearance in fact. But there was no agreement to forbear for a fixed time or for a reasonable time, but an agreement to forbear for such time as the plaintiff should elect. The consideration is to be tested by the agreement, and not by what was done under it. It was a case of mutual promises, and so intended. We think the evidence failed to disclose any consideration for the defendant's endorsement, and that the trial court erred in refusing so to rule.

The order of the General Term reversing the judgment should be affirmed, and judgment absolute directed for the defendant on the stipulation with costs in all courts.

Ordered accordingly.

NOTES

(1) *Questions.* The Restatement Second, § 79, mentions the "illusory" or "apparent" promise as a type that is not consideration. Did the plaintiff, Strong, make any promise of substance to the Sheffields, or either of them? Was his promise alternative in any sense? See the Restatement section cited.

Suppose Mrs. Sheffield had written to Strong: "I will be responsible for my husband's debt if you will not bother him about it for two years." Would she have been accountable to Strong if he had done nothing about the note for that period? What difference is there between this situation and the case as it stands?

(2) *Statutory Change.* The precise rule of this case is reversed by UCC 3–408, and may have been reversed by the enactment of the Negotiable Instruments Law, soon after the decision. See First National City Bank v. Valentine, 61 Misc.2d 554, 306 N.Y.S.2d 227 (Sup.Ct.1969), rearg. denied, 62 Misc.2d 719, 309 N.Y.S.2d 563 (1970). However, inasmuch as these statutes purport to apply only to negotiable instruments, the principle of the case is presumably still viable in the absence of such an instrument.

(3) *Problems.* Consult Restatement Second, § 89C. (*a*) Under the rule of clause (c), what additional fact would have reversed the decision in Strong v. Sheffield? (*b*) Would the following signed writing have satisfied clause (a) of the section?—"I, Louisa Sheffield, promise to pay my husband's note to you, Strong, if he does not. I make this promise in consideration of your forbearance to enforce the note until you have a mind to."

(4) *The Bonus Case.* For a case in which the conception of illusory promise was used in favor of a consumer, see Sentinel Acceptance Corporation v. Colgate, 162 Colo. 64, 424 P.2d 380 (1967). The defendant, a buyer on credit of home fire- and burglar-alarm systems, had been promised a bonus for a list of names of twenty prospects, provided the seller's agent succeeded in making a full presentation to each of them. The seller was made the sole judge of compliance with the condition. In an action for the unpaid purchase price, the doctrine of mutuality was applied to excuse the buyer.

(5) *Extensions of Time.* Many contracts involve a more or less continuous exchange of values between the parties. Contracts of employment and lease contracts are examples. If there is an agreement for the term of such a contract to be extended, without other change, it can be understood that each party makes a further commitment, and there is scarcely a problem of consideration.

The same analysis can be applied to the extension of an interest-bearing debt.[a] But suppose the creditor promises the debtor an extra year to pay, and authorizes the debtor to stop the running of interest by making payment anytime during the year when he is ready. Is the creditor bound to the extension? After some part of the year has elapsed, the debtor may contend that the accumulated interest for that period serves as consideration for the creditor's promise of forbearance. But is that plausible? Does Strong v. Sheffield tend to refute such a contention?[b]

Consult Restatement Second, § 76B(2). If a debtor renews, in writing, his promise to pay, and in exchange the creditor agrees to extend the time for payment, is the creditor bound under this rule?

a. See Adamson v. Bosick, 82 Colo. 309, 259 P. 513 (1927); Rogers v. First National Bank, 282 Ala. 379, 211 So.2d 796 (1968).

b. "The law is well settled that the extension of a note must be for a definite period in order to be enforceable as an extension agreement." Shepherd v. Erickson, 416 S.W.2d 450 (Tex. Civ.App.1967).

WOOD v. LUCY, LADY DUFF–GORDON

Court of Appeals of New York, 1917.
222 N.Y. 88, 118 N.E. 214.

Appeal from Supreme Court, Appellate Division, First Department.

Action by Otis F. Wood against Lucy, Lady Duff-Gordon. From a judgment of the Appellate Division (177 App.Div. 624, 164 N.Y. Supp. 576), which reversed an order denying defendant's motion for judgment on the pleading, and which dismissed the complaint, plaintiff appeals. Reversed.

CARDOZO, J. The defendant styles herself "a creator of fashions." Her favor helps a sale. Manufacturers of dresses, millinery, and like articles are glad to pay for a certificate of her approval. The things which she designs, fabrics, parasols, and what not, have a new value in the public mind when issued in her name. She employed the plaintiff to help her to turn this vogue into money. He was to have the exclusive right, subject always to her approval, to place her indorsements on the designs of others. He was also to have the exclusive right to place her own designs on sale, or to license others to market them. In return she was to have one-half of "all profits and revenues" derived from any contracts he might make. The exclusive right was to last at least one year from April 1, 1915, and thereafter from year to year unless terminated by notice of 90 days. The plaintiff says that he kept the contract on his part, and that the defendant broke it. She placed her indorsement on fabrics, dresses, and millinery without his knowledge, and withheld the profits. He sues her for the damages, and the case comes here on demurrer.

The agreement of employment is signed by both parties. It has a wealth of recitals. The defendant insists, however, that it lacks the elements of a contract. She says that the plaintiff does not bind himself to anything. It is true that he does not promise in so many words that he will use reasonable efforts to place the defendant's indorsements and market her designs. We think, however, that such a promise is fairly to be implied. The law has outgrown its primitive stage of formalism when the precise word was the sovereign talisman, and every slip was fatal. It takes a broader view today. A promise may be lacking, and yet the whole writing may be "instinct with an obligation," imperfectly expressed (Scott, J., in McCall Co. v. Wright, 133 App.Div. 62, 117 N.Y.S. 775; Moran v. Standard Oil Co., 211 N.Y. 187, 198, 105 N.E. 217). If that is so, there is a contract.

The implication of a promise here finds support in many circumstances. The defendant gave an exclusive privilege. She was to have no right for at least a year to place her own indorsements or market her own designs except through the agency of the plaintiff. The acceptance of the exclusive agency was an assumption of its duties.

Phoenix Hermetic Co. v. Filtrine Mfg. Co., 164 App.Div. 424, 150 N. Y.S. 193; W. G. Taylor Co. v. Bannerman, 120 Wis. 189, 97 N.W. 918; Mueller v. Mineral Spring Co., 88 Mich. 390, 50 N.W. 319. We are not to suppose that one party was to be placed at the mercy of the other. Hearn v. Stevens & Bro., 111 App.Div. 101, 106, 97 N.Y.S. 566; Russell v. Allerton, 108 N.Y. 288, 15 N.E. 391. Many other terms of the agreement point the same way. We are told at the outset by way of recital that:

"The said Otis F. Wood possesses a business organization adapted to the placing of such indorsements as the said Lucy, Lady Duff-Gordon, has approved."

The implication is that the plaintiff's business organization will be used for the purpose for which it is adapted. But the terms of the defendant's compensation are even more significant. Her sole compensation for the grant of an exclusive agency is to be one-half of all the profits resulting from the plaintiff's efforts. Unless he gave his efforts, she could never get anything. Without an implied promise, the transaction cannot have such business "efficacy, as both parties must have intended that at all events it should have." Bowen, L. J., in the Moorcock, 14 P.D. 64, 68. But the contract does not stop there. The plaintiff goes on to promise that he will account monthly for all moneys received by him, and that he will take out all such patents and copyrights and trademarks as may in his judgment be necessary to protect the rights and articles affected by the agreement. It is true, of course, as the Appellate Division has said, that if he was under no duty to try to market designs or to place certificates of indorsement, his promise to account for profits or take out copyrights would be valueless. But in determining the intention of the parties the promise has a value. It helps to enforce the conclusion that the plaintiff had some duties. His promise to pay the defendant one-half of the profits and revenues resulting from the exclusive agency and to render accounts monthly was a promise to use reasonable efforts to bring profits and revenues into existence. For this conclusion the authorities are ample. [Ten citations omitted.]

The judgment of the Appellate Division should be reversed, and the order of the Special Term affirmed, with costs in the Appellate Division and in this court.

CUDDEBACK, McLAUGHLIN, and ANDREWS, JJ., concur. HISCOCK, C. J., and CHASE and CRANE, JJ., dissent.

NOTES

(1) *Factual Basis?* Was it the only justification for implying a return promise in the principal case that injustice could not otherwise be avoided? Or was there a factual basis for the implication?

The principle of Wood v. Lucy appears in legislative form in UCC 2–306(2).

(2) *Problem.* About Christmastime one year, Tim's employment was terminated by the Scrooge Company, a small firm that he had served as a bookkeeper since its inception several years before. About a year before his discharge, the directors of Scrooge had "Voted, That Scrooge Company does contract to pay monthly to Tim not less than $200 beginning January 1, for such services as he, in his sole discretion may render. The term of this contract to be not less than five years." How would you argue that Scrooge committed a breach of contract in firing Tim? See Griswold v. Heat Incorporated, 108 N.H. 119, 229 A.2d 183 (1967); cf. Pacific Pines Construction Corporation v. Young, 477 P.2d 894 (Ore.1970).

McMICHAEL v. PRICE

Supreme Court of Oklahoma, 1936.
177 Okl. 186, 58 P.2d 549.

Action by Harley T. Price, doing business as the Sooner Sand Company, against W. M. McMichael, wherein defendant filed a counterclaim. From a judgment for plaintiff, defendant appeals.

Affirmed.

OSBORN, VICE CHIEF JUSTICE. This action was instituted in the district court of Tulsa county by Harley T. Price, doing business as Sooner Sand Company, hereinafter referred to as plaintiff, against W. M. McMichael, hereinafter referred to as defendant, as an action to recover damages for the breach of a contract. The cause was tried to a jury and a verdict returned in favor of plaintiff for $7,512.51. The trial court ordered a remittitur of $2,500, which was duly filed. Thereafter the trial court rendered judgment upon the verdict for $5,012.51, from which judgment defendant has appealed.

The pertinent provisions of the contract, which is the basis of this action, are as follows: . . .

"Now, therefore, in consideration of the mutual promises herein contained, the said second party [defendant, McMichael] agrees to furnish all the sand of various grades and qualities which the first party can sell for shipment to various and sundry points outside of the City of Tulsa, Oklahoma, and to load all of said sand in suitable railway cars . . . for delivery to said Frisco Railway Company as said initial carrier. Said second party agrees to furnish the quantity and quality of sand at all and various times as the first party [Price] may designate by written or oral order, and agrees to furnish and load same within a reasonable time after said verbal or written order is received.

"In consideration of the mutual promises herein contained, first party agrees to purchase and accept from second party all of the sand of various grades and quality which the said first party can sell, for shipment to various and sundry points outside of the City of Tulsa, Oklahoma, provided that the sand so agreed to be furnished and loaded by the said second party shall at least be equal to in quality and comparable with the sand of various grades sold by other sand companies in the City of Tulsa, Oklahoma, or vicinity. First party agrees to pay and the second party agrees to accept as payment and compensation for said sand so furnished and loaded, a sum per ton which represents sixty per cent (60%) of the current market price per ton of concrete sand at the place of destination of said shipment. . . .

"This contract and agreement shall cover a period of ten years from the date hereof, . . ."

Defendant contends that the contract between the parties was a mere revocable offer and is not a valid and binding contract of purchase and sale for want of mutuality. The general rule is that in construing a contract where the consideration on the one side is an offer or an agreement to sell, and on the other side an offer or agreement to buy, the obligation of the parties to sell and buy must be mutual, to render the contract binding on either party, or, as it is sometimes stated, if one of the parties, not having suffered any previous detriment, can escape future liability under the contract, that party may be said to have a "free way out" and the contract lacks mutuality. Consolidated Pipe Line Co. v. British American Oil Co., 163 Okl. 171, 21 P.2d 762. Attention is directed to the specific language used in the contract binding the defendant to "furnish all of the sand of various grades and qualities which the first party can sell" and whereby plaintiff is bound "to purchase and accept from second party all of the sand of various grades and qualities which the said first party (plaintiff) can sell." It is urged that plaintiff had no established business and was not bound to sell any sand whatever and might escape all liability under the terms of the contract by a mere failure or refusal to sell sand. In this connection it is to be noted that the contract recites that plaintiff is "engaged in the business of selling and shipping sand from Tulsa, Oklahoma, to various points." The parties based their contract on this agreed predicate. . . .

At the time the contract involved herein was executed, plaintiff was not the owner of an established sand business. The evidence shows, however, that he was an experienced salesman of sand, which fact was well known to defendant, and that it was anticipated by both parties that on account of the experience, acquaintances, and connections of plaintiff, he would be able to sell a substantial amount of sand to the mutual profit of the contracting parties. The record discloses that for the nine months immediately following the execution of the contract plaintiff's average net profit per month was $516.88.

By the terms of the contract the price to be paid for sand was definitely fixed. Plaintiff was bound by a solemn covenant of the contract to purchase all the sand he was able to sell from defendant and for a breach of such covenant could have been made to respond in damages. The argument of defendant that the plaintiff could escape liability under the contract by going out of the sand business is without force in view of our determination, in line with the authorities hereinabove cited, that it was the intent of the parties to enter into a contract which would be mutually binding. . . .

The judgment is affirmed.

NOTES

(1) *Sand v. Glue.* Peter Cooper's Glue Factory wrote to a jobber in glue, agreeing to supply "your requirements of 'Special BB' glue for the year 1916, price to be 9¢ per lb." The jobber was misleadingly named Schlegel Manufacturing Company; in fact it had no manufacturing business in which glue was used. During 1916 the jobber ordered about five times as much glue as it had ordered in any of the preceding five years. The Glue Factory supplied less than half of the amount ordered, and Schlegel sued it. From a judgment for the plaintiff, the defendant appealed. *Held:* Reversed. The court remarked: "The price of glue having risen during the year 1916 from nine to twenty-four cents per pound, it is quite obvious why orders for glue increased correspondingly." In ruling that consideration was lacking for the defendant's promise, the court made these observations about the agreement: "there is no standard mentioned by which the quantity of glue to be furnished can be determined with any approximate degree of accuracy. . . . [T]here was no obligation on the part of the plaintiff to sell any of the defendant's glue, to make any effort towards bringing about such sale, or not to sell other glues in competition with it." Schlegel Manufacturing Co. v. Cooper's Glue Factory, 231 N.Y. 459, 132 N.E. 148 (1921).

In what respects was the glue agreement like the sand agreement in the main case? In what respects different? What was the decisive difference?

(2) *Requirements Contracts.* The contract in McMichael v. Price is known as a "requirements" contract, in that the quantity of sand to be supplied was to be determined by the needs of Price in supplying his customers.[a] A contract which calls on the buyer to take all of the goods, or all of a certain sort, that may be produced by a seller is known as an "output" contract. Contracts of these types are commonly bracketed together in discussion, as presenting common problems. In this note output contracts will not be further noticed, but what is said about requirements contracts may usually be understood as bearing on output contracts as well. For a Note examining the difficulties to be faced in drafting such contracts, and some solutions, see 78 Harv.L.Rev. 1212 (1965).

An initial problem as to requirements contracts is the one addressed in the main case: does the buyer have a "free way out"? Though there are some older precedents to the contrary,[b] the consensus now is that the requirement of mutuality is satisfied without a commitment by the buyer to take a fixed quantity of goods. On the distinction between a mere "pric-

---

a. For another example, see HML Corp. v. General Foods Corp., p. 606 infra.

b. See Miami Butterine Co. v. Frankel, 190 Ga. 88, 8 S.E.2d 398 (1940); Miami Coca-Cola Bottling Co. v. Orange Crush Co., 296 Fed. 593 (5th Cir. 1924).

ing arrangement" and a requirements contract, see Brightwater Paper Co. v. Monadnock Paper Mills, 161 F.2d 869 (1st Cir. 1947).

A more elusive problem is how to define the obligation of a buyer under a requirements contract. See UCC 2–306. Comment 2 after this section states: "The essential test is whether [he] is acting in good faith;" and another comment observes that this section "removes . . . most of the 'personal discretion' element by substituting the reasonably objective standard of good faith operation of the plant or business to be supplied." [c] How may this standard be applied to Price's contract for sand, considering that he had no established sand business at the time of contracting? Did the contract entail a possible gain for him, with no possibility of loss? If the contract had specified a fixed price per ton, would it have been entirely one-sided? The problem is most acute in relation to a jobber, such as Price, as opposed to a buyer who makes use of the goods in question. Is the Code provision addressed only to the latter situation? See Note, 102 U.Pa.L.Rev. 654 (1954), commenting on the section.

(3) *Problem.* A distributor of wines contracts for the supply of all the domestic wines he may order from a producer, and engages not to sell wines under certain brand names (Sunlight, Ramona) unless they are supplied by the producer. In the absence of any other commitment by the distributor, is the agreement enforceable against the producer? See G. Loewus & Co. v. Vischia, 2 N.J. 54, 65 A.2d 604 (1949). Compare Mag Construction Company v. McLean County, 181 N.W.2d 718 (N.D.1970).

DI BENNEDETTO v. DI ROCCO

Supreme Court of Pennsylvania, 1953.
372 Pa. 302, 93 A.2d 474.

HORACE STERN, CHIEF JUSTICE. In this action for specific performance of a contract for the sale of real estate the court below—in our opinion erroneously—held that the agreement was lacking in mutuality of obligation; accordingly it sustained preliminary objections and dismissed plaintiff's bill in equity.

In the written agreement between the parties, dated March 11, 1949, defendants, the owners of premises 6441 Haverford Avenue, Philadelphia, agreed to sell that property to plaintiff for the sum of $8,500, of which $100 was to be paid, and was paid, at the time of the signing of the agreement, and the balance of $8,400 in cash at the settlement; by written addition to the agreement made June 21, 1949, plaintiff was to pay a further sum of $602. There were two provisions in the agreement which have given rise to the present controversy. The one was that "In the event that the buyer *cannot* make the settlement, he may cancel this agreement, without any further liability on his part, and deposit money returned." The other was that "It is hereby further agreed that the purchaser will give to the seller six

---

c. UCC 2–210, Comment 4. See also Restatement Second, § 231, Illustration 1; Humble Oil & Refining Company v. Cox, 207 Va. 197, 148 S.E.2d 756 (1966) (implied promise by gasoline station operator not to quit business).

(6) months notice prior to July 1, 1951, of his intention to exercise the herein agreement to purchase, ..." Settlement was to be made on or before July 1, 1951, said time to be the essence of the agreement. The agreement was signed by plaintiff and by one P. DiBenedetto as agent for defendants, but defendants themselves added: "we hereby approve the above contract," and signed the agreement with seals opposite to their names.

On December 7, 1950, plaintiff's attorneys, acting on his behalf, wrote to defendants advising them that, in accordance with the clause as to the giving of six months' notice prior to July 1, 1951 of plaintiff's "intention to exercise the agreement to purchase," they thereby gave notice of his intention to make settlement on that date or the nearest legal date thereto. On June 20, 1951, the same attorneys wrote to defendants, enclosing settlement certificate and informing them that arrangements had been made for settlement at the Broad Street Trust Company on Friday, June 29, 1951, at 3 p. m. On that day and at that time plaintiff appeared at the Trust Company, ready, willing and able to carry out the terms of the agreement on his part to be performed, but defendants failed to appear and have ever since refused to convey title.

The first question in the case is whether plaintiff, by reason of the first of the two clauses above quoted, had an absolute, arbitrary right to cancel the agreement without any further liability on his part. We think that he had no such right. The determinative, crucial word in that regard is *"cannot"*. "Cannot" connotes, not unwillingness, but inability. Cf. Hannock v. Tope & Tope, 77 Pa.Super. 101, 104; Wilker v. Jenkins, 88 Pa.Super. 177. If defendants had brought action against plaintiff to compel performance of his agreement to purchase the property he could have successfully defended only by proving that he was *unable* to complete the transaction, not merely that he did not *desire* to do so. Plaintiff, however, by notifying defendants more than six months prior to the time fixed for settlement that it was his intention to make settlement at the time specified, admitted thereby that he was *not unable* to make settlement and therefore that he had no *right* to cancel the agreement. The agreement constituted, therefore, a contract binding on both parties alike, and did not lack mutuality of obligation.

Even were we to assume, however, that the agreement did not obligate plaintiff from the very beginning but should be interpreted as the mere grant of an *option* to him to purchase the property, he certainly became bound when the notice of December 7, 1950, was given. The agreement being under seal, and accompanied by the payment of $100 at the time of its execution, there was consideration sufficient to entitle him to the right to exercise the option, and even had there been no consideration the exercise of the option before any revocation of it by defendants converted it into a contract with mutuality of obli-

gation. Driebe v. Fort Penn Realty Co., 331 Pa. 314, 200 A. 62, 117
A.L.R. 1091.   . . .

Defendants question the legal sufficiency of the notice of December 7, 1950, on the ground that it was not shown that the agents who wrote the letter were authorized so to do by plaintiff in writing. This overlooks the well established principle that the Statute of Frauds does not require an agreement for the sale of real estate to be signed by the purchaser but only by the "parties making or creating" the interest in the land. Stevenson v. Titus, Administrators, 332 Pa. 100, 2 A.2d 853.

Decree reversed and the record remanded with a procedendo; costs to abide the event.

NOTES

(1) *The Concealed Offer.* Seller promises to fill all the orders for sand, at a stated price, that Buyer cares to send him, and Buyer promises to pay for any sand he orders. There is no contract on the face of this "exchange." However, if Buyer orders five carloads of sand before Seller retracts his promise or it lapses, there is a contract for that number. What the parties may have *thought* was a contract did at least amount to an offer by Seller.

Similarly, if there were no contract of sale in the main case, there was at least an offer to sell, and an acceptance occurred before revocation. As the court says, "even had there been no consideration the exercise of the option before any revocation of it by defendants converted it into a contract. . . ." Compare the analysis of a check-credit agreement in First Wis. National Bank v. Oby, 52 Wis. 1, 188 N.W.2d 454 (1971).

(2) *Questions.* The court mentions the deposit of $100 as binding an option. Is that view tenable, in view of the provision, "deposit money to be returned" if the buyer cannot make settlement? Is it possible that the owner bargained for the use of $100 for some months, as the consideration for an option? Cf. Kowal v. Day, 20 Cal.App.3d 720, 98 Cal.Rptr. 118 (1971).

Consult Restatement Second, § 89B. As a test of the rule stated in subsection (1) (a), consider the following changes in the main case: no deposit money is paid, the agreement permits the buyer to cancel if he desires to do so, and the seller repudiates shortly after signing. Does the rule apply to bind the seller?

(3) *Problem.* North, the owner of a going business, wishes to live in a warmer climate. He finds a similar business in a southern state, owned by South, who wishes to sell. South's business is in rented quarters. North and South come to terms, which they put in writing. The "sale contract" provides for closing in six months, "but only if North is able to sell his present business for $50,000 cash within that time." It also provides: "The agreement is conditioned upon North getting a five-year extension of South's current lease." If South repudiates the agreement soon after signing it, does North have a contract claim against him? If South does not repudiate, and North does nothing about selling his business, does South

have a contract claim against him? Compare Paul v. Rosen, 3 Ill.App.2d
423, 122 N.E.2d 603 (1954), with Carlton v. Smith, 285 Ill.App. 380, 2 N.E.
2d 116 (1936).

SYLVAN CREST SAND & GRAVEL CO. v. UNITED STATES

United States Circuit Court of Appeals, Second Circuit, 1945.
150 F.2d 642.

Appeal from the District Court of the United States for the District of Connecticut.

Action by the Sylvan Crest Sand & Gravel Company, a legal corporation of the Town of Trumbull, County of Fairfield, and State of Connecticut, against the United States for breach of four alleged contracts to purchase trap rock from plaintiff. From a summary judgment for the government, plaintiff appeals.

SWAN, CIRCUIT JUDGE. This is an action for damages for breach of four alleged contracts under each of which the plaintiff was to deliver trap rock to an airport project "as required" and in accordance with delivery instructions to be given by the defendant. The breach alleged was the defendant's refusal to request or accept delivery within a reasonable time after the date of the contracts, thereby depriving the plaintiff of profits it would have made in the amount of $10,000. The action was commenced in the District Court, federal jurisdiction resting on 28 U.S.C.A. § 41(20). Upon the pleadings, consisting of complaint, answer and reply, the defendant moved to dismiss the action for failure of the complaint to state a claim or, in the alternative, to grant summary judgment for the defendant on the ground that no genuine issue exists as to any material fact. The contracts in suit were introduced as exhibits at the hearing on the motion. Summary judgment for the defendant was granted on the theory that the defendant's reservation of an unrestricted power of cancellation caused the alleged contracts to be wholly illusory as binding obligations. The plaintiff has appealed.

The plaintiff owned and operated a trap rock quarry in Trumbull, Conn. Through the Treasury Department, acting by its State Procurement Office in Connecticut, the United States invited bids on trap rock needed for the Mollison Airport, Bridgeport, Conn. The plaintiff submitted four bids for different sized screenings of trap rock and each bid was accepted by the Assistant State Procurement officer on June 29, 1937. The four documents are substantially alike and it will suffice to describe one of them. It is a printed government form, with the blank spaces filled in in typewriting, consisting of a single sheet bearing the heading:

"Invitation, Bid, and Acceptance
"(Short Form Contract)"

Below the heading, under the subheadings, follow in order the "Invitation," the "Bid," and the "Acceptance by the Government."

The Invitation, signed by a State Procurement Officer, states that "Sealed bids in triplicate, subject to the conditions on the reverse hereof, will be received at this office . . . for furnishing supplies . . . for delivery at WP 2752—Mollison Airport, Bridgeport, Ct." Then come typed provisions which, so far as material, are as follows:

"Item No. 1. ½″ Trap Rock to pass the following screening test . . . approx. 4000 tons, unit price $2.00 amount $8000. To be delivered to project as required. Delivery to start immediately. Communicate with W. J. Scott, Supt. W.P.A. Branch Office, 147 Canon Street, Bridgeport, Ct., for definite delivery instructions. Cancellation by the Procurement Division may be effected at any time."

The Bid, signed by the plaintiff, provides that

"In compliance with the above invitation for bids, and subject to all of the conditions thereof, the undersigned offers, and agrees, if this bid be accepted . . . to furnish any or all of the items upon which prices are quoted, at the prices set opposite each item, delivered at the point(s) as specified, . . ."

The Acceptance, besides its date and the signature of an Assistant State Procurement Officer, contains only the words "Accepted as to items numbered 1." The printing on the reverse side of the sheet under the heading "Conditions" and "Instructions to Contracting Officers" clearly indicates that the parties supposed they were entering into an enforcible contract. For example, Condition 3 states that "in case of default of the contractor" the government may procure the articles from other sources and hold the contractor liable for any excess in cost; and Condition 4 provides that "if the contractor refuses or fails to make deliveries . . . within the time specified . . . the Government may by written notice terminate the right of the contractor to proceed with deliveries . . ." The Instructions to Contracting Officers also presupposes the making of a valid contract; No. 2 reads:

"Although this form meets the requirements of a formal contract (R.S. 3744), if the execution of a formal contract with bond is contemplated, U. S. Standard Forms 31 and 32 should be used."

No one can read the document as a whole without concluding that the parties intended a contract to result from the Bid and the Government's Acceptance. If the United States did not so intend, it certainly set a skillful trap for unwary bidders. No such purpose should be attributed to the government. See United States v. Purcell Envelope Co., 249 U.S. 313, 318, 39 S.Ct. 300, 63 L.Ed. 620. In construing the document the presumption should be indulged that both parties were acting in good faith.

Although the Acceptance contains no promissory words, it is conceded that a promise by the defendant to pay the stated price for rock delivered is to be implied.[1] Since no precise time for delivery was specified, the implication is that delivery within a reasonable time was contemplated. Allegheny Valley Brick Co. v. C. W. Raymond Co., 2 Cir., 219 F. 477, 480; Frankfurt-Barnett v. William Prym Co., 2 Cir., 237 F. 21, 25. This is corroborated by the express provision that the rock was "to be delivered to the project as required. Delivery to start immediately." There is also to be implied a promise to give delivery instructions; nothing in the language of the contracts indicates that performance by the plaintiff was to be conditional upon the exercise of the defendant's discretion in giving such instructions. A more reasonable interpretation is that the defendant was placed under an obligation to give instructions for delivery from time to time when trap rock was required at the project. Such were the duties of the defendant, unless the cancellation clause precludes such a construction of the document.

Beyond question the plaintiff made a promise to deliver rock at a stated price; and if the United States were suing for its breach the question would be whether the "acceptance" by the United States operated as a sufficient consideration to make the plaintiff's promise binding. Since the United States is the defendant the question is whether it made any promise that has been broken. Its "acceptance" should be interpreted as a reasonable business man would have understood it. Surely it would not have been understood thus: "We accept your offer and bind you to your promise to deliver, but we do not promise either to take the rock or pay the price." The reservation of a power to effect cancellation at any time meant something different from this. We believe that the reasonable interpretation of the document is as follows: "We accept your offer to deliver within a reasonable time, and we promise to take the rock and pay the price unless we give you notice of cancellation within a reasonable time." Only on such an interpretation is the United States justified in expecting the plaintiff to prepare for performance and to remain ready and willing to deliver. Even so, the bidder is taking a great risk and the United States has an advantage. It is not "good faith" for the United States to insist upon more than this. It is certain that the United States intended to bind the bidder to a "contract," and that the bidder thought that the "acceptance" of his bid made a "contract." A reasonable interpretation of the language used gives effect to their mutual intention. Consequently we cannot accept the contention that the defendant's power of cancellation was unrestricted and could be exercised merely by failure to give delivery orders. The words "cancellation may be effected at any time" imply affirmative action, namely, the giving of notice of intent to cancel. The defendant itself so construed the clause by giving notice of cancellation on July 11, 1939, as alleged in its answer. While the phrase "at any time" should be liber-

---

1. The answer alleges that certain deliveries were made, all of which were duly paid for by the United States, and the reply admitted this.

ally construed, it means much less than "forever."   If taken literally, it would mean that after the defendant had given instructions for delivery and the plaintiff had tendered delivery in accordance therewith, or even after delivery had actually been made, the defendant could refuse to accept and when sued for the price give notice of cancellation of the contract.   Such an interpretation would be not only unjust and unreasonable, but would make nugatory the entire contract, contrary to the intention of the parties, if it be assumed that the United States was acting in good faith in accepting the plaintiff's bid.   The words should be so construed as to support the contract and not render illusory the promises of both parties.   This can be accomplished by interpolating the word "reasonable", as is often done with respect to indefinite time clauses.   See Starkweather v. Gleason, 221 Mass. 552, 109 N.E. 635.   Hence the agreement obligated the defendant to give delivery instructions or notice of cancellation within a reasonable time after the date of its "acceptance."   This constituted consideration for the plaintiff's promise to deliver in accordance with delivery instructions, and made the agreement a valid contract.

It must be conceded that the cases dealing with agreements in which one party has reserved to himself an option to cancel are not entirely harmonious.   Where the option is completely unrestricted some courts say that the party having the option has promised nothing and the contract is void for lack of mutuality.   Miami Coca-Cola Bottling Co. v. Orange Crush Co., 5 Cir., 296 F. 693; Oakland Motor Car Co. v. Indiana Automobile Co., 7 Cir., 201 F. 499.   These cases have been criticized by competent text writers and the latter case cited by this court "with distinct lack of warmth", as Judge Clark noted in Bushwick-Decatur Motors v. Ford Motor Co., 2 Cir., 116 F.2d 675, 678.   But where, as in the case at bar, the option to cancel "does not wholly defeat consideration", the agreement is not nudum pactum. Corbin, The Effect of Options on Consideration, 34 Yale L.J. 571, 585; see Hunt v. Stimson, 6 Cir., 23 F.2d 447; Gurfein v. Werbelovsky, 97 Conn. 703, 118 A. 32.   A promise is not made illusory by the fact that the promisor has an option between two alternatives, if each alternative would be sufficient consideration if it alone were bargained for.   A.L.I. Contracts, § 79.   As we have construed the agreement the United States promised by implication to take and pay for the trap rock or give notice of cancellation within a reasonable time. The alternative of giving notice was not difficult of performance, but it was a sufficient consideration to support the contract.

The judgment is reversed and the cause remanded for trial.

NOTES

(1) *Termination Clauses and Mutuality of Obligation.*   If the contractor (plaintiff in the principal case) had refused to deliver gravel under the contract, would he have been liable for damages for breach of contract?   What was the government's side of the exchange, that is, the con-

sideration for the contractor's promise to deliver gravel as called for? On the general subject, see Patterson, "Illusory" Promises and Promisors' Options, 6 Iowa L.Bull. 129, 209 (1921), Selected Readings 425–27, 431.

(2) *Interpretation of Termination Clauses.* With the approach of the court in the Sylvan Crest case, compare UCC 2–309(3). What if a termination clause explicitly negates any duty of notification? As to this, Comment 8 to UCC 2–309 includes the following statement: "An agreement dispensing with notification or limiting the time for the seeking of a substitute arrangement is, of course, valid under this subsection unless the results of putting it into operation would be the creation of an unconscionable state of affairs."

(3) *Good Faith.* An illustration based on the facts of this case appears in the Restatement Second, under the following rule: "Every contract imposes upon each party a duty of good faith and fair dealing in its performance and its enforcement." (Section 231, Illustration 5) According to the illustration, good faith requires the buyer to order and accept the rock within a reasonable time unless he has given the seller notice of intent to cancel. Is this proposition essential to the decision in the actual case? Is the rule of the case logically prior to the Restatement proposition? Or are the two logically unrelated?

(4) *The Underwriters' Out.* The distribution of new securities (chiefly stocks and bonds) to the public in this country requires the services of investment bankers ("underwriters") who must, for technical reasons, contract to accept new securities in bulk a day or two before they are free to negotiate resales. The contract may contain a "market out" clause, excusing the underwriters in certain described circumstances, such as the closing of a stock exchange, or a declaration of war, in the interim. More broadly, the clause may excuse them if there is a change in political or market conditions which, in their judgment, makes it inadvisable to market the securities at the price agreed on for public sales. The practice is described in Loss, 1 Securities Regulation 166 (2d ed. 1961), and Supplement 2295 (1969), where it is said that "in practice it is not considered 'cricket' to take advantage" of the clause. If it is expressed in terms of the underwriters' "absolute judgment," does it make the agreement unenforceable by the underwriters, for want of mutuality? See Blish v. Thompson Automatic Arms Corp., 30 Del.Ch. 538, 64 A.2d 581 (1948).

(5) *The Case of the Student's Insurance.* The Travelers Indemnity Company issued a policy of automobile liability insurance to Norman McVean, a student at S.M.U., insuring him and "any other person using [the described] automobile with the permission of the named insured, provided his actual operation . . . thereof is within the scope of such permission." Some months later, through its local agent, Travelers obtained McVean's signature on the following "Student Restrictive Endorsement" form:

> In consideration of the premium at which this policy is written, it is agreed that no insurance is afforded under this policy to any student other than [McVean].

Still later, McVean was killed in a collision. He was riding as a passenger in his own car, and it was driven by a fellow-student named Edwards. Despite the endorsement, Edwards claimed to be an unnamed insured in the policy. It was a one-year contract, and the premium had been paid in ad-

vance. However, it was cancellable by Travelers on ten days' notice. In
a suit brought by Edwards, Travelers contended that its forbearance to cancel was ample consideration for the change by endorsement. From judgment for the plaintiff, the defendant appealed. *Held:* Affirmed. "The
evidence only shows that Travelers made repeated attempts for four months
to obtain the signed forms, but there is no evidence to show that they had
determined to cancel Norman McVean's policy if he did not sign. On the
basis of this record we are unable to hold that Travelers refrained from
exercising its cancellation right in consideration for the insured's signing
the restriction." Travelers Indemnity Company v. Edwards, 462 S.W.2d
533 (Tex.1970). Is this decision consistent with the principles stated in
Strong v. Sheffield, p. 231 supra? Would you expect a comparable decision on facts involving a business firm as an insured? The Court of Civil
Appeals, an intermediate court, wrote as follows on the case: "The insurance company, with its superior bargaining power, should inform the
insured of its intention and permit the insured an intelligent choice."
Travelers Indemnity Company v. Edwards, 451 S.W.2d 313 (Tex.Civ.App.
1970), aff'd, supra.

YORK CHRYSLER–PLYMOUTH, INC. v. CHRYSLER CREDIT CORP.

United States Court of Appeals, Fifth Circuit, 1971.
447 F.2d 786.

RONEY, CIRCUIT JUDGE. . . . This case had its genesis in 1963,
when C. C. York and his son, Jerry A. York, purchased 100% of the
stock of Barnes Motors, Inc., a Chrysler-Plymouth dealership located
in the downtown section of Mobile, Alabama. The purchase price
was $75,000.00, of which $70,000 was borrowed from Commercial
Credit Corporation and the remaining $5,000 was provided by Jerry
A. York. C. C. York, who served as president of the dealership corporation, took title to two-thirds of the capital stock. Jerry A. York,
who served as vice-president, owned the other third.

In 1964, a representative of Chrysler Motors Corporation approached the Yorks with the proposition that they move their business from its downtown location to the new "automobile row" being developed on the outskirts of Mobile. The Yorks agreed to this suggestion, and on October 21, 1964, they entered into a Dealer Relocation
Agreement with Chrysler Motors. This agreement contemplated that
Chrysler Motors would buy land and construct a new facility which
would then be leased to the dealership corporation.

There were two other significant occurrences in 1964. First, the
Yorks became short of working capital and had to obtain from Commercial Credit Corporation a three month moratorium on the $70,000
loan which had been taken out in connection with purchase of the dealership. Second, Chrysler Motors Corporation performed a "Dealership Survey," which pointed out that the cash flow position of the
dealership was precarious. The survey recommended, among other

things, that the capital loan with Commercial Credit be renegotiated. The Yorks declined, however, to take this step.

Chrysler Motors then suggested that the Yorks might obtain needed working capital by reorganizing the dealership under the "Dealer Enterprise Plan." In general terms, the Dealer Enterprise Plan works this way. Chrysler Motors Corporation provides as much as 75% of the dealership's required capital, taking preferred stock in the dealership corporation in exchange. The dealer contributes a minimum of 25% of the capital, taking common stock in exchange. The preferred stock is retired gradually, out of the profits of the business, so that the individual dealer eventually becomes sole owner of the business. Until the preferred stock is retired, however, Chrysler Motors controls the dealership's board of directors.

The Yorks initially expressed an interest in the Dealer Enterprise Plan (D. E.) and, in fact, submitted a D. E. application in December of 1964. By the time the application had been approved, however, they had become concerned over the fact that under the D. E. Plan they would have to give up control of the dealership, so they advised Chrysler that they were no longer interested in a Dealer Enterprise operation.

In the fall of 1965, the Yorks accomplished the relocation of their dealership. In conjunction with the move, a number of changes were made. The dealership's name was changed from Barnes Motors to York Chrysler-Plymouth, Inc. The Yorks also changed their financing, severing their relationship with Commercial Credit Corporation and placing their retail and wholesale financing with Chrysler Credit Corporation. In addition, Chrysler Credit made the dealership a $40,000 capital loan, which was used to pay off the balance of the outstanding loan with Commercial Credit and an outstanding bank loan.

Since the name and location of the dealership had changed, it was necessary for the Yorks to enter into a new franchise agreement with Chrysler Motors. Chrysler Motors was dissatisfied with the financial condition of the dealership, however, and refused to give the Yorks the same "Direct Dealer Agreement" under which they had previously operated. Instead the parties entered into a "Term Sales Agreement," which differed from the Direct Dealer Agreement in two respects.[1] First, it ran for only a one year term. Second, it obligated the Yorks to increase their working capital. At the time the agreement was signed, however, Chrysler Motors informed the Yorks orally that it would not hold them to the strict requirements of the agreement, but would be satisfied with a good faith effort at increasing the working capital.

---

1. This agreement was not signed until April, 1966. Until that time the York dealership simply operated without any formal franchise.

In January, 1967, Chrysler Credit performed an audit of the dealership's books in connection with renewal of the $40,000 capital loan. According to this audit, (the accuracy of which is not admitted by plaintiffs) the dealership's net worth was a deficit of $2,000 and its working capital was a deficit of some $34,000. Chrysler Credit then performed a physical inventory of the automobiles in possession of the dealership and discovered that 22 new and used cars had been "sold out of trust." [2] The value of the cars sold out of trust amounted to slightly over $50,000.

On Monday, January 23, 1967, following the audit and discovery of the out of trust condition, representatives of Chrysler Motors Corporation met at the offices of York Chrysler-Plymouth with the regional manager of Chrysler Credit to discuss the future of the York dealership. The Yorks did not participate in this meeting, but were told that Chrysler Motors Corporation was trying to "work something out." The following day Chrysler Credit asked the Yorks to surrender the assets of the dealership corporation, in accordance with the security agreements held by Chrysler Credit. That evening, after the necessary papers had been reviewed by the Yorks' attorney, Chrysler Credit took over the assets of the dealership corporation. At the same time Chrysler Motors Corporation asked the Yorks to sign a mutual termination of the franchise. On advice of their attorney, they refused. Wednesday Chrysler Motors again asked the Yorks to resign from the dealership and the Yorks again refused.

This action was instituted on February 16, 1967. The Term Sales Agreement was allowed to expire by its own terms two months later.

[The action was brought under what is known as the Automobile Dealers Day in Court Act, a federal statute of 1956. The two Yorks and their company were the plaintiffs. Among the defendants were the Chrysler Corporation and its sales subsidiary, Chrysler Motors. All three plaintiffs obtained a judgment against these two defendants, for $107,000. Other parties and claims in the action are disregarded here.

[On appeal, the court concluded that the individual plaintiffs were so "inextricably woven into" the franchise agreement that they were entitled to the benefits of the Act, but that the judgment should have run only against Chrysler Motors. It would be liable, under the Act, for failure "to act in good faith in performing or complying with any of the terms or provisions of the franchise." 15 U.S.C.A. § 1222.[a]

---

2. "Sold out of trust" or "SOT" are terms used in automobile floor-plan financing to refer to the condition which exists when an automobile dealer has sold automobiles and failed to pay its liability with respect thereto to the financing institution, in this case, Chrysler Credit.

a. "Authorization of suits against manufacturers; amount of recovery; defenses—An automobile dealer may

[The court affirmed the judgment against Chrysler Motors, disposing of two objections by Chrysler Motors as follows.]

C. Legal Right to Terminate.

The fact that Chrysler Motors may have had grounds for lawful termination of the automobile dealership does not permit this court to set aside a jury verdict after a trial which provided ample opportunity for this defense to be asserted. Frank Chevrolet Co. v. General Motors Corp., 419 F.2d 1054 (6th Cir. 1969) does not hold otherwise. There the court affirmed a summary judgment which merely held that the sales performances of the dealer in that case consistently fell below acceptable standards in violation of the agreement between the parties and that the refusal to renew the contract did not constitute an act of bad faith under the statute.

The Dealers Day in Court Act contemplates a cause of action even upon the assertion of legal rights if there is a failure of good faith in the exercise thereof. Assuming issues of fact which would support a finding of lack of "good faith in performing or complying with any of the terms or provisions of the franchise, or in terminating, canceling, or not renewing the franchise," it is up to the jury to determine the redemption value of the facts indicating that the action could have been taken in good faith. The Act specifically permits the assertion of the dealer's failure to act in good faith as a defense. 15 U.S.C.A. § 1222. The Act is not as concerned with what the parties did as it is concerned with why they did it.

We hold that to the extent that this issue was presented, the jury must have resolved it against Chrysler, and to any extent that it was not presented below, we cannot consider it on appeal. Hanley v. Chrysler Motors, 433 F.2d 708 (10th Cir. 1970) ; Pan-American Life Ins. Co. v. Alvarez, 374 F.2d 92 (5th Cir. 1967), cert. den., 389 U.S. 829, 88 S.Ct. 89, 19 L.Ed.2d 85.

D. Sufficiency of the Evidence.

Chrysler Motors finally urges that there was insufficient evidence to support the jury's verdict of a violation of the Dealers Act. Although not necessarily compelling, the evidence provides a sufficient basis for the jury's decision, as viewed most favorably to the plaintiffs. Boeing Co. v. Shipman, 411 F.2d 365 (5th Cir. 1969).

bring suit against any automobile manufacturer engaged in commerce, in any district court of the United States in the district in which said manufacturer resides, or is found, or has an agent, without respect to the amount in controversy, and shall recover the damages by him sustained and the cost of suit by reason of the failure of said automobile manufacturer from and after August 8, 1956 to act in good faith in performing or complying with any of the terms or provisions of the franchise, or in terminating, canceling, or not renewing the franchise with said dealer: *Provided*, That in any such suit the manufacturer shall not be barred from asserting in defense of any such action the failure of the dealer to act in good faith."

The pivotal question that the jury had to determine concerned the alleged failure of the defendant to exercise "good faith" in its dealings with the plaintiffs and the coercive or intimidating effect of such dealings upon them. By its very nature, this determination must be made on inferences drawn from the evidence. It is derived from a subjective analysis of the facts. Reasonable men might differ. Thus, the jury verdict must stand.

Section 1221(e) of the Act defines the "good faith" against which defendants' acts were to be considered.

> "(e) The term 'good faith' shall mean the duty of each party to any franchise, and all officers, employees, or agents thereof to act in a fair and equitable manner toward each other so as to guarantee the one party freedom from coercion, intimidation, or threats of coercion or intimidation from the other party: Provided, That recommendation, endorsement, exposition, persuasion, urging or argument shall not be deemed to constitute a lack of good faith."

The broad theory which the Yorks presented at trial was that Chrysler Motors wanted a high volume Chrysler-Plymouth dealership in the Mobile area without regard to the advantage or disadvantage to the dealer.[3] The most expeditious method of obtaining such a goal was to establish a Dealer Enterprise operation in which Chrysler moved into a position of control. When the Yorks refused to go along with this plan, Chrysler Motors and Chrysler Credit Corporation[4] strung together a series of acts which were designed to coerce and intimidate the Yorks into bending to Chrysler's desires or suffering a termination of their franchise. They contended that this is the kind

---

3. The case of Madsen v. Chrysler Corporation, 261 F.Supp. 488 (N.D.Ill. 1966) vacated for mootness, 375 F.2d 773 (7th Cir. 1967) with similar facts set forth the following analysis of Chrysler's D. E. Program.

"By giving the dealer the use of Chrysler's funds (in whole or in part) and by restricting his obligation to purchase any of the manufacturer's interest to only those situations where the dealership has shown a profit for the year, the DE system effects a substantial reduction in the risks which the dealer takes. As a result, the dealer's primary concern becomes synonymous with that of the manufacturer: selling more cars. He is under less pressure to sell each car at a satisfactory profit. The record shows that DE dealerships have often operated at an overall loss for substantial periods of time and, when profitable, their profit per new car sold is substantially lower than that of private dealers.

The DE outlet is also equipped to handle a large volume of service, thus adding an additional factor enabling the dealer to forego profit in the sale of new cars. In short, the DE dealerships are designed to obtain volume and to increase the manufacturer's share of the market beyond that which even an aggressive private dealer can obtain." 261 F.Supp. at 499.

Also see: Swartz v. Chrysler Motors Corporation, 297 F.Supp. 834 (C.D.N.J. 1969); Mt. Lebanon Motors, Inc. v. Chrysler Corp., 283 F.Supp. 453 (W.D. Pa.1968); aff'd, 417 F.2d 622 (3rd Cir. 1969).

4. Although not a party defendant, Chrysler Credit Corporation was a related company to Chrysler Motors and we think that its actions could be properly considered by the jury in determining the good faith of Chrysler Motors.

of evil in the manufacturer-dealer power struggle that the Act was designed to cover.[5]

That certain specific conduct has been held not to constitute a violation of the Act in certain cases does not lead to the conclusion that such conduct would not violate the Act in the setting of another case.[6] The actions of the manufacturer must be considered under the circumstances arising in each particular case. The entire course of dealing between manufacturer and dealer may be considered and it may then be concluded by the jury that the total conduct was violative of the Act.[7] American Motors Sales Corp. v. Semke, 384 F.2d 192 (10th Cir. 1967).

. . . .

5. The legislative history of the Dealer Act states that "The existence of coercion or intimidation depends upon the circumstances arising in each particular case and may be inferred from a course of conduct." United States Code, Congressional and Administrative News, (1956) 84th Congress, Second Session, Vol. 3, p. 4603. In further explanation of the remedial intent of the Act to correct "the manifest disparity in the ability of franchised dealers . . . to bargain with their manufacturers" (p. 4597) the Committee of the House explained as follows:

"Manufacturer coercion or intimidation or threats thereof is actionable by the dealer where it relates to performing or complying with any of the terms or provisions of the franchise, or where it relates to the termination, cancellation, or nonrenewal of the dealer's franchise. Thus, where a dealer's resistance to manufacturer pressure is related to cancellation or nonrenewal of his franchise a cause of action would arise." At p. 4603.

6. In other cases, it has been held that there was no violation of the Act in (1) requiring the dealer to submit monthly financial statements, Garvin v. American Motors Corp., 318 F.2d 518 (3rd Cir. 1963); (2) requiring the dealer to maintain satisfactory and competitive business facilities, Woodard v. General Motors Corp., 298 F.2d 121 (5th Cir. 1962), cert. den., 369 U.S. 887, 82 S.Ct. 1161, 8 L.Ed.2d 288 (1962); (3) requiring the dealer to meet reasonable minimum sales responsibilities, Victory Motors of Savannah, Inc. v. Chrysler Motors Corp., 357 F.2d 429 (5th Cir. 1966); (4) requiring the

dealer to provide working capital in accordance with reasonable standards set by the manufacturer, Globe Motors Inc. v. Studebaker-Packard Corp., 328 F.2d 645 (3rd Cir. 1964); (5) insisting that a dealer sell more cars, advertise in a certain way and hire more salesmen, Victory Motors of Savannah, Inc. v. Chrysler Motors Corp., supra; (6) urging a dealer to adopt better business practices and insisting that he devote full time to his business, Kotula v. Ford Motor Co., 338 F.2d 732 (8th Cir. 1964), cert. den., 380 U.S. 979, 85 S.Ct. 1333, 14 L.Ed.2d 273 (1965); (7) threatening to assert contract rights, Fabert Motors v. Ford Motor Company, 355 F.2d 888 (7th Cir. 1966); (8) establishing competitive dealerships, Southern Rambler Sales v. American Motors Corp., supra; (9) soliciting the dealer's agreement to a mutual termination of the franchise, *Victory-Motors*, supra; *Kotula*, supra; (10) demanding relocation to better facilities, Unionvale Sales, Ltd. v. World-Wide Volkswagen Corp., 299 F. Supp. 1365 (S.D.N.Y.1969); (11) engaging in arbitrary conduct, Berry Bros. Buick v. General Motors Corp., 257 F. Supp. 542, aff'd, 377 F.2d 552 (3rd Cir. 1967); (12) cancelling a franchise because of an unauthorized transfer of ownership, General Motors Corp. v. Mac Co., 247 F.Supp. 723 (D.Colo. 1965).

7. The Yorks argued that the following activity was sufficient basis for the jury to find lack of good faith and coercion: (1) Chrysler told the Yorks that if they didn't move out to automobile row, Chrysler would put another dealer there. (2) Chrysler had already decided to put a D. E. dealer in the new facility. (3) In order to

NOTES

(1) *Performance Standards.* For some two-hundred pages of discussion of the Dealers' Day in Court Act, and related topics, see Macaulay, Changing a Continuing Relationship Between a Large Corporation and Those Who Deal With It: Automobile Manufacturers, Their Dealers, and the Legal System, 1965 Wis.L.Rev., 483, 740 (cited hereafter as "Macaulay".[b]) On Chrysler's need for new dealers, and for relocating old ones, in the early '60's, see pp. 822 n. 778, 827.

One of the pressures of which dealers complain is demands for a high volume of sales, of the type, "you must beat the Thunderwagen sales in your area." Dealers' contracts subject them to volume standards in two general ways. They may (as some Chrysler contracts do) provide incentives through complex formulas incorporating such objective elements as the dealer's sales in prior years, and the total of car registrations in his locality. On the other hand, they may set standards in vague terms, such as "adequate" or "sufficient" performance. Which type of provision is more likely to open a manufacturer to a charge of bad faith, under the Act, when it threatens to terminate a dealership for poor sales performance?

make the Yorks move, Chrysler promised (a) no change in working capital would be required, (b) a new dealer agreement would be issued, as a mere formality, (c) the Yorks would have an exclusive dealership in Mobile, (d) the Yorks would receive financial assistance in making the move. (4) In the summer of 1964 Chrysler was aware of the Yorks' short working capital position. (5) In the spring of 1965 Chrysler "exerted pressure" on the Yorks to increase working capital and sales volume. (6) Even after the Yorks withdrew their D. E. application, Chrysler kept "offering" them that "opportunity." (7) After September, 1965, when the relocation took place, there "was no turning back" for the Yorks, because if they didn't get a new franchise agreement within 30 days, the termination of their old franchise remained effective. (8) At trial Mr. Smith, of Chrysler Motors, stated he didn't know that Chrysler Credit was financing the Yorks. The Yorks argued that this was untrue. (9) In January, 1966, the Yorks were told that they would have to go D. E., borrow additional capital, or take a Term Sales Agreement. (10) The Yorks did not receive the relocation money which Chrysler had promised them until they agreed to sign the Term Sales Agreement. (11) In the summer of 1966 the Yorks' Minimum Sales Requirement (MSR) was raised 17%. In order to get the cars they

wanted, the Yorks had to take the cars which the regional sales manager forced upon them. (12) Chrysler had actual knowledge that the Yorks had not increased their working capital, despite what was on the monthly financial reports. (13) Chrysler Motors and Credit contributed to the Yorks' shortage of cash by offsetting parts account with rebate moneys which were given to Credit. (14) In September, 1966, Credit froze 50% of the dealer reserve account, which contributed to shortage of capital. (15) Chrysler owed the dealership $23,000 in holdback and warranty moneys. The Yorks claimed that if they had had this money, they wouldn't have run out of working capital. (16) Neither Chrysler nor Credit met with the Yorks to explore ways out of the SOT condition. (17) Until presented with the turn-over agreement, the Yorks had been led to believe that Chrysler would work something out. (18) Chrysler falsely promised that the Yorks' employees could keep their jobs after the turn-over agreement was signed. (19) It was contemplated that the dealership would be taken over by John Gimma, the very person with whom C. C. York had been trying to negotiate a sale.

b. These articles appeared also as a book, in slightly different form: Macaulay, Law and the Balance of Power (1966).

(2) *Dealer's Good Faith.* In the section of the Act authorizing suit by a dealer it is said that "the manufacturer shall not be barred from asserting in defense of any such action the failure of the dealer to act in good faith." Section 1222. In this connection the sales of cars made by York "out of trust" should be considered. The floor-planning, or "wholesale" financing by Chrysler Credit implies that it advanced funds to Chrysler Motors, on York's behalf, to enable York to maintain an inventory of cars, which were subject to a security interest in favor of the lender. Upon making retail sales, York was doubtless required to account promptly for the proceeds to Chrysler Credit. (Proceeds might take the form of payment rights under conditional sale contracts with York's customers—"retail" financing agreements—cash, and other items.) York's failure to account promptly may have placed Chrysler Credit under a heavy handicap in competition with other creditors, in the event of York's bankruptcy or other liquidation. Selling out of trust commonly signifies extreme financial pressure on the dealer.

On what reasoning could it be found that York acted in good faith?

SETTING OF THE STATUTE

Shortly before and after the Act was passed, the manufacturers revised their dealer franchises, imposing on many of them a term of one year, or a few years. Consider how the main case might have stood if the Yorks had never had more than successive, one-year "term sales agreements" with Chrysler, and Chrysler had simply let the 1966–67 agreement expire. Could the court have approved a verdict resting on bad faith in that situation? See Macaulay, 563 ff. In a few states there are statutes prohibiting the non-renewal of an automobile dealer's franchise without "just cause." [c]

The enactment of the federal statute was preceded by intensive lobbying efforts by the National Automobile Dealers Association and

c. In 1964 the legislature of Puerto Rico enacted a "Dealer's Contract Law," including this provision: "Notwithstanding the existence in a dealer's contract of a clause reserving to the parties the unilateral right to terminate the existing relationship, no principal or grantor may terminate said relationship or refuse to renew said contract on its normal expiration, except for just cause." The act contains a definition of just cause: "non-performance of any of the essential obligations of the dealer's contract, on the part of the dealer, or any action or omission on his part that adversely and substantially affects the interests of the principal or grantor in promoting the marketing or distribution of the merchandise or service."

"In spite of this legislation a number of manufacturers acted to terminate or otherwise change their dealers' agreements, and much litigation has ensued." Fornaris v. Ridge Tool Co., 423 F.2d 563 (1st Cir. 1970). In this case the court held the statute violative of the due process clause of the federal Constitution. (It did not decide whether Puerto Rico is a "state" within the prohibition against impairing the obligation of contracts: Art. I, § 10.) The Supreme Court reversed, saying, "It is conceivable that 'just cause' might be judicially confined to a more narrow ambit which would avoid all constitutional questions." It directed the federal court to "hold its hand" until construction of the statute could be had in the Supreme Court of Puerto Rico. Fornaris v. Ridge Tool Co., 400 U.S. 41 (1970).

the manufacturers, as recited by Macaulay in considerable detail. The terms of the Act were a compromise.[d] Of 89 suits under the Act that Macaulay unearthed, only one went to final judgment against the manufacturer. Modest settlements were made in a fair proportion of the others. What might explain the rarity of a dealer's recovery under the Act? [e]

One of the debated issues of construction concerns the phrase beginning "so as to guarantee". Does it make coercion (intimidation, or threat) an indispensable element of a dealer's claim? Or is a failure to act generally "in a fair and equitable manner" also a failure of good faith? Was this issue involved in the main case?

NOTES

(1) *Common-Law Good Faith?* Why has legislation been called for, in relation to the termination of dealerships and franchise contracts? Was it not possible for the courts to develop suitable controls, using the materials at hand in the common law? In Bushwick-Decatur Motors, Inc. v. Ford Motor Co., 116 F.2d 675 (2d Cir. 1940), a former dealer sued Ford for unjustifiable termination of the dealership. Their agreement provided, in standard form: "This agreement may be terminated at any time at the will of either party . . .." A summary judgment was given for Ford, and affirmed on appeal. The court said:

"With a power of termination at will here so unmistakably expressed, we certainly cannot assert that a limitation of good faith was anything the parties had in mind. Such a limitation can be read into the agreement only as an overriding requirement of public policy. This seems an extreme step for judges to take. The onerous nature of the contract for the successful dealer and the hardship which cancellation may bring him have caused some writers to advocate it, however; and an occasional case has seized upon elements of overreaching to come to such a result on particular facts. . . . But, generally speaking, the situation arises from the strong bargaining position which economic factors give the great automobile manufacturing companies: the dealers are not misled or imposed upon, but accept as nonetheless advantageous an agreement in form bilateral, in fact one-sided. To attempt to redress this balance by judicial action without legislative authority appears to us a doubtful policy. We have not proper facilities to weigh economic factors, nor have we before us a showing of the supposed needs which may lead the manufacturers to require these seemingly harsh bargains. [Here the court mentioned a

---

d. Ford's legal department is said to have drafted the proviso in § 1221 (e).

One of the interesting interchanges in hearings on the bill occurred between Mr. William T. Gossett, General Counsel for Ford, and Congressman Celler, when Mr. Gossett referred to the probable weight that local dealers would carry with juries. Mr. Celler asked, "Have you no faith in the jury system?" Gossett: "Sir, I have the same faith in the jury system that you, as a distinguished and experienced lawyer, have. [Laughter.]" Macaulay, 550n.

e. One partial explanation may be that the manufacturers have established elaborate internal procedures for making decisions to terminate a dealership, and for reviewing such a decision if contested. See Macaulay, 557–60.

Wisconsin statute limiting the power of automobile manufacturers to terminate dealers' contracts. It was not applicable to this case.[f]] But it suggests the proper source of remedy, if one is needed."

More recently, it has been suggested that the courts may properly apply an "objective" test of unconscionability to the problem of this case. See Gellhorn, Limitations on Contract Termination Rights—Franchise Cancellations, 1967 Duke L.J. 465, 479–82, and especially pp. 502–05. But see Sinkoff Beverage Co. v. Jos. Schlitz Brewing Co., 51 Misc.2d 446, 273 N.Y. S.2d 364 (Sup.Ct.1966). This case is commented on in Ellinghaus, In Defense of Unconscionability, 78 Yale L.J. 757, 808–12 (1969), where it is also suggested that the rule of Bushwick-Decatur Motors may have been altered by the adoption of the Code. Compare Restatement Second, §§ 231, 234.

(2) *Questions.* Refer again to the Note on Franchises, p. 169 supra. How much truth remains in the statement there that, for a manufacturer (of automobiles), cancellation and non-renewal "are valuable means of replacing inefficient dealers with new ones"? Refer again to the Case of Miller High Life, p. 176 supra. Would you favor the enactment of a Beer Dealers Day in Court Act, parallel to the auto dealers act? What is unusual, if anything, about the position of an automobile dealer, requiring special safeguards against arbitrary action by his supplier? See Fornaris v. Ridge Tool Co., 423 F.2d 563, 568 (1st Cir.), rev'd, 400 U.S. 41 (1970).

(3) *Problem.* The operator of a service station has a location owned by Octane Oil Company, his supplier of gasoline and other products. For six years he has been operating under two agreements with the company, expressed on standard forms common to the industry. One is a lease binding him to pay monthly rent varying with the volume of his business. The other is a dealer's contract, in which he agreed to buy, and the company agreed to sell, his requirements of certain products, with yearly limits as to quantity. Each contract provides for a three-year term, automatically renewed, except that either party might prevent renewal by a 90-day notice. The company has notified the operator that it will not renew. It has other plans for the leased premises, and does not complain of the dealer's performance under the agreements. He now seeks an order to compel the company to renew. For some of the legal issues that may emerge, see Division of Triple T Service, Inc. v. Mobil Oil Corp., 60 Misc.2d 720, 304 N.Y.S.2d 191, aff'd mem., 34 A.D.2d 618, 311 N.Y.S.2d 961 (2d Dept. 1970). Does the Code reach franchise agreements? If relief is proper under UCC 2–302 as to the sale of gasoline, but the lease is not renewed, is it like giving the plaintiff a "paddle in a dry creek"? Does that Code section authorize an injunction?

What other issues does the claim raise?

f. For a description of this statute and its operation, see Macaulay, op. cit. supra.

SECTION 3.   OVERREACHING: CONVENTIONAL CONTROLS

Under the leadership, again, of equity, the courts have traditionally been insistent that no advantage should be gained through gross unfairness in the process of bargaining. The means reprobated in classical equity are fraud, mistake, and duress. The ordinary remedy, when a contract is found to be subject to one of these infirmities, is to rescind or avoid it, at the instance of the victim. Not only fraud, in the more shameful sense, but an innocent misrepresentation made in the bargaining process may be a ground for avoiding a contract. Indeed, it is sometimes required that a party possessed of information material to the exchange either disclose it or refrain from imposing on the ignorance of the other. What privilege of exploiting superior knowledge for a bargaining advantage should be recognized? How should the risks of inaccuracy in statements and of errors of fact be allocated between the parties? What pressures may conscientiously be exerted by one party on another to gain his assent to a bargain or the settlement of a dispute? These are questions examined here.

Some further aspects of the doctrine of consideration are also presented. The doctrine has sometimes been extended to prevent overreaching in bargaining. Is it too blunt an instrument for that purpose? If so, how should it be reshaped?

The subject of this section has a complex relation to the problems of capacity and of unfairness in the substance of bargains, presented above. If the parties are fully competent to contract, and the bargaining process is cleansed of overreaching, is there any need for the courts to concern themselves with possible imbalances in the resulting exchange? Should all of these elements be considered together, from case to case? Or is it important, for purposes of predictability, that when a court declines to enforce a contract it specify a single deficiency of the bargain, or in the capacity of a party? Do you find instances of each method?

NOTE

Law and Equity. As the successors to equity powers, virtually all courts in which contract litigation is conducted are now competent to avoid a contract without requiring an independent proceeding for rescission. (The procedure of the court may reflect the origin in equity of these defenses, however; notably, it may not be necessary to submit them to juries. Courses in civil procedure examine this difference.) Quite apart from equity "jurisdiction," there are instances of fraud, mistake and duress that serve as invalidating causes in contract law: the contract affected is said to be "void."

(a) Pressure in Bargaining

When a person has used compulsion on another to obtain a benefit, he may sometimes be required to give it up. Money paid and property transferred under duress may be recovered; if assent to a contract is obtained by duress it may not be enforced against the victim. At p. 289 infra an example is given of duress in a contemporary form. In early English cases from which the current doctrine stems, relief was confined to situations in which imprisonment and threats of confinement or bodily harm were the instruments of coercion. Threats of purely economic injury became a ground for relief when "duress of goods" was recognized. In comparatively recent times, duress has been recognized in a greatly enlarged range of situations, and the general conception of "economic coercion" has won a place as a sort of junior partner of duress in redressing oppression.[a]

These developments have not yet made duress a commonplace defense in contract actions. Freehanded applications of the doctrine are still prevented by a number of policy considerations, as well as some surviving technical obstacles. A mention of these will be useful as a prelude to the materials that follow.

In some courts a reasonable degree of temerity in the face of a threat is insisted on. This requirement serves to restrict relief for duress by denying it to persons who yield to pressure too readily. As one court puts it, duress consists of "restraint or danger, either actually inflicted or impending, which is sufficient in severity or apprehension to overcome the mind of a person of ordinary firmness." [b] Some expressions of the courts imply an even stricter test: it is duress, as they describe it, to deprive a person of free choice,[c] or to destroy his volition,[d] or to obtain his consent only in form.[e] Such expressions, often somewhat metaphorical, appear largely in cases where relief was *granted*, and it has often been granted where no such total mastery existed. A classical passage rejecting the "no will" conception of duress is this from Holmes:

> It always is for the interest of a party under duress to choose the lesser of two evils. But the fact that a choice was

---

a. See McCubbin v. Buss, 180 Neb. 624, 144 N.W.2d 175 (1966).

b. Carrier v. William Penn Broadcasting Company, 426 Pa. 427, 233 A.2d 519 (1967).

c. Joannin v. Ogilvie, 49 Minn. 564, 52 N.W. 217 (1892).

d. See Konsuvo v. Nitzke, 91 N.J.Super. 353, 220 A.2d 424 (1966); cf. Kaplan v. Kaplan, 25 Ill.2d 181, 182 N.E.2d 706 (1962).

e. See United States v. Huckabee, 16 Wall. (83 U.S.) 414 (1873) (alleged duress by a rebel government).

made according to interest does not exclude duress. It is the characteristic of duress properly so called.[f]

On the other hand, it is regularly acknowledged that a perfectly honorable agreement may be made with a person who must either accede to it or face some repugnant alternative.[g] "The question is one of degree." [h]

Duress is sometimes associated with unlawful conduct. One who yields to a threat of criminal or tortious injury may be given relief on this ground. On cognate reasoning, it has been held that a threat of lawful action cannot be wrongful. "It is not duress to threaten to do what there is a legal right to do." [i]

Such reasoning has particular application to cases in which a dispute is compromised under a threat of suit.[j] As it is not unlawful to institute legal proceedings, a person threatened with suit may not buy his way out and thereafter complain of the bargain: such is a usual argument in support of settlements. Yet it is not now accepted as a general proposition that one may rightfully threaten what he may rightfully do. "An unjust and inequitable threat is wrongful, although the threatened act would not be a violation of duty in the sense of an independent actionable wrong in the law of crimes, torts, or contracts." [k] This view is illustrated in cases of benefit that an employer exacts from an employee, under threat to discharge him, where the employment contract is terminable at will.[1]

Professor Dawson has pointed out that preventing unjust enrichment is a principal function of the doctrines of duress, and that the limitations on relief mentioned above tend to obscure that function.[m] These limitations have been considerably relaxed, at least in some situations.[n] Instances are given at a later point in this chapter, following materials on related topics.

f. Union Pacific R. Co. v. Public Service Commission, 248 U.S. 67 (1918) (duress by a state agency).

g. See Sheraton Hawaii Corporation v. Poston, 51 Haw. 142, 172, 454 P.2d 369 (1969).

h. Hellenic Lines, Ltd. v. Louis Dreyfus Corporation, 372 F.2d 753 (2d Cir. 1967) (valuable discussion).

i. This proposition, in one form or another, is relied on in a mass of American cases. For a collection, see 17A Am.Jur., Duress and Undue Influence, § 18.

j. See Dunbar v. Dunbar, 102 Ariz. 357, 429 P.2d 949 (1967): "It is not duress to declare an intention to resort to the courts for the purpose of insisting on what one believes are one's legal rights."

k. McCubbin v. Buss, footnote a, supra. See also Silsbee v. Webber, 171 Mass. 378, 50 N.E. 555 (1898): "When it comes to the question of obtaining contracts by threats, it does not follow that, because you cannot be made to answer for the act, you may use the threat."

l. See Laemmar v. J. Walter Thompson Company, 435 F.2d 680 (7th Cir. 1970).

m. Dawson, Economic Duress—An Essay in Perspective, 45 Mich.L.Rev. 253, 282 ff. (1947). See also Patterson, Compulsory Contracts in the Crystal Ball, 43 Colum.L.Rev. 731, 741 (1943).

n. See Hellenic Lines, Ltd. v. Louis Dreyfus Corporation, footnote h, supra.

NOTES

(1) *Duress by Threat of Suit.* When a person seeks relief from a contract on the ground of coercion, it is not uncommon to find that he is himself adept at coercive practices. An example is Undersea Eng. & Const. Co. v. International Tel. & Tel. Corp., 429 F.2d 548 (9th Cir. 1970).[o] In that case the plaintiff, Undersea, had been a subcontractor on a job for which the defendant, ITT, was the general contractor. Disputes between them led to extended negotiations, and to a settlement which the plaintiff later sought to void. The defendant was depicted as a billion-dollar corporation having elephantine power over the plaintiff. The court observed, however, that before the settlement "Undersea was using every threat of economic and moral pressure to coerce and force ITT to settle rather than face a law suit with threatened world-wide publicity."

If a settlement of a disputed claim does not put a period to the dispute, the claimant may usually begin second-round negotiations with the valuable advantage that he has already been paid a portion of his claim. If it were the rule that a settlement *never* puts an end to a dispute, the rule might put an end to settlements. The courts are quite alive to the demerit of prolonging controversy indefinitely. They do not, for instance, regard a threat of civil suit as coercive, in ordinary circumstances. Nevertheless, it is generally recognized that a threat to bring a civil action is sometimes an instrument of duress.[p]

(2) *Restitution.* Duress is a ground not only for avoiding an agreement or settlement, but also for recovering a payment exacted by lawless compulsion. The fountainhead case on the law of restitution, Moses v. Macferlan,[q] speaks to the point. In that case Lord Mansfield said that an action for money had and received lies "for money got through imposition (express or implied); or extortion; or oppression; or an undue advantage taken of the plaintiff's situation, contrary to laws made for the protection of persons under those circumstances."

(3) *The Overpaid Mortgage.* Hensel contracted to convey a piece of property he owned free and clear of mortgages. He had already given

o. See also Grad v. Roberts, 14 N.Y.2d 70, 198 N.E.2d 26 (1964); Hellenic Lines, Ltd. v. Louis Dreyfus Corporation, footnote h, supra.

p. E. g., Link v. Link, 278 N.C. 181, 179 S.E.2d 697 (1971): "corrupt intent to coerce a transaction grossly unfair to the victim and not related to the subject of such proceedings." On the topic of this note, see especially Dawson, Duress Through Civil Litigation, 45 Mich.L.Rev. 571(I) and 679(II) (1947).

As to a threat of criminal prosecution, see Buhrman v. International Harvester Company, 181 Neb. 633, 150 N.W.2d 220 (1967).

q. 2 Burr. 1005, 97 Eng.Rep. 676 (K.B. 1760).

For a case of pressure exerted by Charles Kemble, the actor, see Dana v. Kemble, 34 Mass.(17 Pick.) 545 (1836). Kemble and his daughter were booked into the Tremont Theater, in Boston, for 25 evenings. A dispute arose about the amount of pay he was entitled to. The theater manager, Francis W. Dana, seems to have made some threat to withhold part of the pay Kemble claimed. It is not clear that any pay was owing, however, at the critical time, just before the final performance. Kemble became "much excited," and said, "I shall not play tomorrow night unless I am paid." This threat worked, but Dana later sued. The result reported above was inconclusive.

a mortgage on the property to Cahill, payable "within 15 years in monthly installments." Hensel was willing to pay the principal of the mortgage plus interest at 5% to date. But Cahill refused to record satisfaction of the mortgage unless he received $233 in addition. (This would have been the interest earned at 2½% if the mortgage were not prepaid.) He explained that, as trustee of the real owner of the mortgage, an estate, he would "be obliged to reinvest the proceeds most likely in Government Bonds." Hensel paid the whole sum demanded, completed the sale transaction, and then sued to recover the $233 as money paid under duress. Prior to this one there was no controlling judicial determination of the right to pre-pay a mortgage containing similar terms. From judgment for the defendant, the plaintiff appealed. *Held:* Affirmed. "Duress was not proven. . . . [I]t is not unreasonable to assume that if plaintiffs were not satisfied with their agreement they would have paid the balance of principal with 5% interest into court under [a Pennsylvania statute], where after satisfaction of the mortgage the question of their liability for interest could have been determined." Hensel v. Cahill, 179 Pa.Super. 114, 116 A.2d 99 (1955).

THE PRE–EXISTING DUTY RULE

"Performance of a legal duty owed to a promisor which is neither doubtful nor the subject of honest dispute is not consideration . . . ." Restatement Second, § 76A. This is a recent version of an old rule that has given rise to some dissatisfaction. Professor Edwin W. Patterson [r] observed that it is, "on the whole, that adjunct of the doctrine of consideration which has done most to give it a bad name." Patterson, An Apology for Consideration, 58 Colum.L.Rev. 929, 936 (1958). On the other hand, some decisions that can be referred to the rule are generally applauded. In such cases there is commonly an element of coercion, as illustrated in the following well-known case.

A group of workmen had individually signed a contract to work on Alaska Packers' ship during the salmon canning season, from San Francisco to Pyramid Harbor, Alaska, and return, for a specified compensation. Upon arrival at the canning factory in Alaska, they presented a demand to Alaska Packers' superintendent for a very substantial increase in compensation, and they refused to work any further unless this demand was agreed to. Since it was impossible to get other men to replace them, the superintendent signed an agreement to pay the larger amount. Upon the return of the men to San Francisco at the end of the season, Alaska Packers paid them in accordance with the first agreement, and the employees sued in admiralty to recover the additional compensation. From judgment for the libelants, the defendant appealed. *Held*: Reversed. The agreement to pay the increased compensation was without consideration and was in-

---

r. Edwin W. Patterson (1889–1965) practiced for four years in Kansas City and then taught at Texas, Colorado, Iowa and Columbia. Among his writings are books on contracts, in-surance and jurisprudence, including four editions of the predecessor of this casebook. He was one of the Advisers for the Restatement of Restitution.

duced by the coercion of libelants' unjustified refusal to perform their contracts. Alaska Packers Ass'n v. Domenico, 117 Fed. 99 (9th Cir. 1902).

How would the foregoing case have been decided under the following provision of New York law?

Written agreement for modification or discharge

> An agreement, promise or undertaking to change or modify, or to discharge in whole or in part, any contract, obligation, or lease, or any mortgage or other security interest in personal or real property, shall not be invalid because of the absence of consideration, provided that the agreement, promise or undertaking changing, modifying, or discharging such contract, obligation, lease, mortgage or security interest, shall be in writing and signed by the party against whom it is sought to enforce the change, modification or discharge, or by his agent.[s]

For another statutory modification of the pre-existing duty rule, see UCC 2–209(1). How would the case in Note 1 have been decided under the Code?

NOTES

(1) *The Case of the Complaisant Customer.* In Rexite Casting Co. v. Midwest Mower Co., 267 S.W.2d 327 (Mo.App.1954), Rexite, a manufacturing company, had contracted in November, 1947, to make for and sell to Midwest, a manufacturer of lawn mowers, 100,000 cast aluminum side frames at 52 cents each; Midwest reserved the right to cancel the purchase on 30 days' written notice. After 17,000 to 20,000 frames had been shipped to Midwest, Rexite notified it that it was necessary, owing to increased costs of metal, to increase the price, and that Midwest could "take it or leave it." After some objection Midwest "acquiesced" in an "adjusted price" of 78¾ cents each for all castings made thereafter. Midwest at that time had substantial orders for deliveries at prices based on the original price of castings, and could not obtain another supplier (of molds and castings) in time to keep its plant in operation. Midwest paid the increased price for several lots of castings in the fall of 1948. Midwest then found another supplier (at 57 cents each), refused to buy any more castings from Rexite, and demanded repayment of the excess over contract price. Rexite then sued to recover $783.22 for castings delivered at 78¾ cents; Midwest admitted liability of $578.25 (at the original price) and sought to recover the amount paid because of the "price hike", $2,301.75. From judgment for the defendant, the plaintiff appealed. *Held*: Affirmed. The alleged modification was invalid because of want of consideration, since Rexite promised nothing new, and threatened a breach of its contractual duty.

(2) *Duress?* Might a modifying agreement that is within UCC 2–209 (1) or the New York statute quoted above still be voidable for duress where it was induced by one party's threat to break his contract? Comment 2 to

---

s. New York General Obligations Law,
  § 5–1103.

UCC 2–209 states, in part, that "modifications made thereunder must meet the test of good faith imposed by this Act . . . and the extortion of a 'modification' without legitimate commercial reason is ineffective as a violation of the duty of good faith." See Farnsworth, Good Faith Purchase and Commercial Reasonableness Under the Uniform Commercial Code, 30 U. Chi.L.Rev. 666, 675–76 (1963).

SCHWARTZREICH v. BAUMAN–BASCH, INC.

Court of Appeals of New York, 1921.
231 N.Y. 196, 131 N.E. 887.

[On August 31, 1917, the plaintiff contracted in writing to work for the defendant as a designer of coats and wraps at $90 per week, the employment to continue for one year from November 22, 1917. The plaintiff was later offered similar employment by another at $115 per week. Upon plaintiff's informing the defendant of the offer, the defendant suggested that he would pay the plaintiff $100 per week if he would stay. The plaintiff agreed. Whereupon, on October 17, 1917, a new agreement, exactly like the first except as to the amount of pay, was drawn up and signed by the parties. Simultaneously with the signing of the new contract, the signatures were torn off the old one by the plaintiff and his copy surrendered to the defendant. The plaintiff was discharged in the following December and brought this action on the contract of October 17th, in the City Court of the city of New York. A verdict was rendered for the plaintiff for the amount due on the contract of October 17th, the court instructing that if the old contract was canceled "prior to or at the time of the execution" of the new there was consideration for the new. The trial court set aside the verdict and dismissed the complaint. The Appellate Term reversed and reinstated the verdict. The defendant appealed unsuccessfully to the Appellate Division First Department, and appealed again.]

CRANE, J. . . . The question remains, therefore, whether the charge of the court as above given, was a correct statement of the law, or whether on all the evidence in the plaintiff's favor a cause of action was made out.

Can a contract of employment be set aside or terminated by the parties to it and a new one made or substituted in its place? If so, is it competent to end the one and make the other at the same time?

It has been repeatedly held that a promise made to induce a party to do that which he is already bound by contract to perform is without consideration. But the cases in this state, while enforcing this rule, also recognize that a contract may be canceled by mutual consent and a new one made. Thus Vanderbilt v. Schreyer, 91 N.Y. 392, 402, held that it was no consideration for a guaranty that a party promise to do only that which he was before legally bound to perform. This court stated, however:

"It would doubtless be competent for parties to cancel an existing contract and make a new one to complete the same work at a different rate of compensation, but it seems that it would be essential to its validity that there should be a valid cancellation of the original contract.   Such was the case of Lattimore v. Harsen, 14 Johns. 330."

In Cosgray v. New England Piano Co., 10 App.Div. 351, 353, 41 N.Y.S. 886, it was decided that where the plaintiff had bound himself to work for a year at $30 a week, there was no consideration for a promise thereafter made by the defendant that he should notwithstanding receive $1,800 a year.   Here it will be noticed that there was no termination of the first agreement which gave occasion for Bartlett, J., to say in the opinion:

"The case might be different if the parties had, by word of mouth, agreed wholly to abrogate and do away with a pre-existing written contract in regard to service and compensation, and had substituted for it another agreement."

Any change in an existing contract, such as a modification of the rate of compensation, or a supplemental agreement, must have a new consideration to support it.   In such a case the contract is continued, not ended.   Where, however, an existing contract is terminated by consent of both parties and a new one executed in its place and stead, we have a different situation and the mutual promises are again a consideration.   Very little difference may appear in a mere change of compensation in an existing and continuing contract and a termination of one contract and the making of a new one for the same time and work, but at an increased compensation.   There is, however, a marked difference in principle.   Where the new contract gives any new privilege or advantage to the promisee, a consideration has been recognized, though in the main it is the same contract.   Triangle Waist Co., Inc. v. Todd, 223 N.Y. 27, 119 N.E. 85.

If this which we are now holding were not the rule, parties having once made a contract would be prevented from changing it no matter how willing and desirous they might be to do so, unless the terms conferred an additional benefit to the promisee.

All concede that an agreement may be rescinded by mutual consent and a new agreement made thereafter on any terms to which the parties may assent.   Prof. Williston in his work on Contracts says (Vol. 1, sec. 130a): "A rescission followed shortly afterwards by a new agreement in regard to the same subject-matter would create the legal obligations provided in the subsequent agreement."

The same effect follows in our judgment from a new contract entered into at the same time the old one is destroyed and rescinded by mutual consent.   The determining factor is the rescission by consent. Provided this is the expressed and acted upon intention, the time of the rescission, whether a moment before or at the same time as the making of the new contract, is unimportant.

The decisions are numerous and divergent where one of the parties to a contract refuses to perform unless paid an additional amount. Some states hold the new promise to pay the demand binding though there be no rescission. It is said that the new promise is given to secure performance in place of an action for damages for not performing (Parrot v. Mexican Central Railway Co., 207 Mass. 184, 93 N.E. 90, 34 L.R.A.,N.S., 261), or that the new contract is evidence of the rescission of the old one and it is the same as if no previous contract had been made (Coyner v. Lynde, 10 Ind. 282; Connelly v. Devoe, 37 Conn. 570; Goebel v. Linn, 47 Mich. 489, 11 N.W. 284, 41 Am.Rep. 723), or that unforeseen difficulties and hardships modify the rule (King v. Duluth, M. & N. Ry. Co., 61 Minn. 482, 63 N.W. 1105), or that the new contract is an attempt to mitigate the damages which may flow from the breach of the first.   Endriss v. Belle Isle Ice Co., 49 Mich. 279, 13 N.W. 590.   .   .   .

The contrary has been held   .   .   .   .   In none of these cases, however, was there a full and complete rescission of the old contract and it is this with which we are dealing in this case.   Rescission is not presumed; it is expressed; the old contract is not continued with modifications; it is ended and a new one made.

The efforts of the courts to give a legal reason for holding good a promise to pay an additional compensation for the fulfillment of a pre-existing contract is commented upon in note upon Abbott v. Doane, 163 Mass. 433, 40 N.E. 197, in 34 L.R.A. 33, 39, 47 Am.St. Rep. 465, and the result reached is stated as follows: "The almost universal rule is that without any express rescission of the old contract, the promise is made simply for additional compensation, making the new promise a mere nudum pactum." As before stated, in this case we have an express rescission and a new contract.

There is no reason that we can see why the parties to a contract may not come together and agree to cancel and rescind an existing contract, making a new one in its place. We are also of the opinion that reason and authority support the conclusion that both transactions can take place at the same time.

For the reasons here stated, the charge of the trial court was correct, and the judgments of the Appellate Division and the Appellate Term should be affirmed, with costs.

CHASE, J., dissents.

NOTES

(1) *Case Analysis*. Does the court in the principal case find that the parties made two contracts or three? What was the legal significance, if any, of the ceremony in which the signatures were torn off the original employment contract? Would the decision have been different if the sig-

natures had not been torn off the old contract until after the parties had signed the new one?

In a study of agreements modifying contracts, the New York Law Revision Commission was critical of the Schwartzreich case: "Whether the evidence shows an intention by both parties to rescind the old contract will in most cases be a question for the jury. Thus, until the jury decides, the contractual rights of the parties can only be described by a prediction of what a jury will do, always an uncertain process." Second Annual L.R.C. Report 255 (Leg.Doc.No.65, 1936).

The Commission proposed the statute that has become N.Y.Gen.Obl. L. § 5–1103, p. 262 supra.

(2) *Question.* Consult Restatement Second, § 89D(a). Should the job offer at $115 a week be regarded as a circumstance not anticipated when the contract was made, such that a $10 raise was "fair and equitable"?

ARZANI v. PEOPLE, 149 N.Y.S.2d 38 (Sup.Ct., Onondaga County, 1956). [The State of New York let a contract for the reconstruction of a highway to Kranz and Martin, as general contractors. They entered into a written subcontract with Victor Arzani, by which he agreed to do part of the work, including contract paving. After doing it, and being paid $106,000, Arzani brought suit against Kranz and Martin (including the State as a defendant) for an unpaid balance. After adjusting for various charges and credits, the court gave judgment for Arzani, in the amount of $19,520.62. It rejected Arzani's claim for an additional amount of some $1,500, based on an oral promise made to him by Kranz.]

GORMAN, JUSTICE. . . . The proposal issued by the State listed the minimum wage for laborers as $1.95 per hour, which amount was in effect when the plaintiff commenced work on his subcontract. A few days later, the union representative demanded an increase of twenty cents per hour or he would call a strike and shut down the job. The plaintiff says that he then told the defendant Kranz that he, himself, would pull off the job if Kranz did not agree to pay one-half of the additional labor cost, and that Kranz agreed. This testimony is uncontradicted. The plaintiff further stated on cross-examination that it constituted the entire conversation with Kranz and was not reduced to writing. The proof showed that the plaintiff thereafter paid his laborers the sum of $3,003.40 over the amount he would have paid at the lesser rate, and that the work proceeded to a satisfactory conclusion.

It is the contention of the defendant contractors that there is no enforceable contract between the interested parties as to this item because of failure of consideration. It is competent for the parties to a contract to abandon it or to substitute another in its place. Merger of the rescission and promise into one transaction does not destroy them as elements composing the transaction. See Schwartzreich v.

Bauman-Basch, Inc., 231 N.Y. 196, 131 N.E. 887.   But there must be a new consideration, and there is general acceptance in this state that where A is under a contract with B, a promise made by one to the other to induce performance is void.   Consideration is not necessary to an act of rescission, waiver, release or discharge, but rather to the enforceability of executory promises.   But it is necessary that there be a valid abrogation of the existing contract, and this by mutual agreement.   This fact has not been established, whether the test be factual or legal.

It is true that this is not a situation where coercion or expediency has been utilized by the plaintiff in a mere attempt to exact more money.   The conceded circumstances might spell out factually a mutual acceptance of immediate danger to the completion of one of interrelated contracts.   But termination is not shown.   The most that the plaintiff shows beyond the promise is his reliance upon his capacity to breach the contract, and his statement that he would do so if the excess labor cost was not shared.   See McGowan & Connolly Co., Inc., v. Kenny-Moran Co., Inc., 207 App.Div. 617, 202 N.Y.S. 513.   Judged from the standpoint of ordinary business morality, the situation of the promisor contractor may well be less defensible than that of the plaintiff.   But termination is not presumed.   It must be proved and upon this record the plaintiff has failed to sustain his burden.   .   .   .

NOTES

(1) *Question.*   Would this decision have been different under the rule of Restatement Second, § 89D?

(2) *The Sheep and the Goats.*   It has been urged that the courts should endeavor "to separate the sheep from the goats" by enforcing the new promise in favor of the honest contractor and refusing to enforce it in favor of the dishonest or extortionate contractor.   Corbin, Does a Preexisting Duty Defeat Consideration?, 27 Yale L.J. 362, 373 (1918), Selected Readings 504, 514.   What facts, provable in court, can provide the basis for separating "the sheep from the goats"?   How would the plaintiff in the present case be characterized, as "sheep" or "goat"?   Is it clear that he used no coercion to secure the agreement about labor costs?   (Part of the court's opinion in Arzani—"Judged from the standpoint of ordinary business morality   .   .   . "—is an unacknowledged excerpt from Corbin's writing.)

(3) *The Forgiving Creditor.*   Mrs. Beer had a judgment against Dr. Foakes for £2,000.   In order to induce him to pay it, she agreed to accept part payment at once, and stated installments in the future, foregoing her right to interest.   After Foakes paid the principal in full, Mrs. Beer sued for the interest.   The House of Lords found a controlling precedent in Pinnel's Case, decided by Lord Coke in 1602.[a]   There it was said that "pay-

a.   Cited as 5 Coke's Rep. 117a (in Vol. 3, Part V), 77 Eng.Rep. 237 (Common Pleas).

ment of a lesser sum on the day, i. e., on or after the due date of a money debt cannot be any satisfaction for the whole." In agreeing to pay the judgment, Dr. Foakes did no more than he was obliged to do in any event. Hence Mrs. Beer was not bound by the agreement.[b]

(4) *Dropping the Rule?* Among many who have doubted or denounced the rule of Foakes v. Beer, one was Justice Stone, of Minnesota. He wrote: "The doctrine thus invoked is one of the relics of antique law which should have been discarded long ago. It is evidence of the former capacity of lawyers and judges to make the requirement of consideration an overworked shibboleth rather than a logical and just standard of actionability." Rye v. Phillips, 203 Minn. 567, 282 N.W. 459 (1938). (However, on the facts of the case he said that the creditor's concession was supported by "plenty of consideration.")[c]

Taking broader ground, some courts and scholars have challenged the general rule about pre-existing duty, as it affects the modification of contracts. One thoughtful appraisal is that of Patterson, in An Apology for Consideration, 58 Colum.L.Rev. 929, 936–38 (1958), concluding: "The nineteenth century, striving to bring unity out of diversity, included too many different ideas under the general heading of consideration."

(5) *The Case of the Change of Course.* Black Diamond Lines, Inc. agreed to charter two vessels to the United States Navigation Company for stated periods, and prepared the charters which it submitted to Navigation to sign. Navigation did so, but returned them with a cover letter saying that the charters "do not correctly state the periods . . . which we agreed upon. We return them . . . under protest, and reserve our rights." The charters limited the use of the vessels to a single round-trip voyage, whereas the prior oral agreement had given Navigation optional time for a second voyage for each vessel. After a first voyage for each of the vessels, Black Diamond refused to permit Navigation to make further use of them, and Navigation sued for damages. From a decree dismissing the suit, the libelant appealed. *Held:* Reversed. The written charters did not supersede the oral agreements, but were agreements for partial performance, and signing them was a proper way to mitigate damages. Black Diamond had refused to permit Navigation to make any use of the vessels unless it signed the charters.

Learned Hand, dissenting, would have applied the New York statute set out at p. 262 supra. He said, however: "it is a rather curious irony that a statute, designed generally to avoid injustice, should in this instance operate so harshly." Of Navigation's attempt to reserve its rights, Judge Hand wrote as follows: "The situation is the not uncommon one in which a party to a contract actually, but unwillingly, consents; the charterer knew it could not get even one voyage without consenting and consent it

---

b. Foakes v. Beer, 1884 L.R. 9 A.C. 605 (H.L.). (Some of the law lords doubted that the operative document purported to foreclose Mrs. Beer's interest claim. Others did not acquiesce in the authority of Pinnel's Case. But there was a majority ruling as stated in the text.)

c. See also Kramas v. Beattie, 107 N.H. 321, 221 A.2d 236 (1966).

For another assault on the rule of Foakes v. Beer, see Comment, 11 Ariz.L.Rev. 344 (1969). The writer describes the historical "quagmire" out of which the rule developed, and a set of real or apparent exceptions to it.

did. Reserving its rights under the oral contract did not withdraw that consent; it merely expressed the belief that the law would not sanction the supposed wrong. Its position was like that of a man who signs a contract with the reservation of a right to repudiate it because he had been forced to do so through his poverty; his defense can rest only upon the validity of the excuse and is not aided by the reservation." United States Navigation Co. v. Black Diamond Lines, 124 F.2d 508 (2d Cir. 1942), cert. denied, 315 U.S. 816 (1942).

LEASES AND ECONOMIC ADVERSITY

The Great Depression of the 30's gave rise to a number of cases in which a landlord agreed to a reduction in rent for the unexpired term of the lease, and afterward sought to charge the tenant with the difference between what he had paid and the amount originally stipulated. In some cases these claims prevailed; in others not. In a New Jersey case, Levine v. Blumenthal,[d] the court referred to Pinnel's Case, and said: "General economic adversity, however disastrous it may be in its individual consequences, is never a warrant for judicial abrogation of this primary principle of the law of contracts." The landlord prevailed. Was the decision consistent with Restatement Second, § 89D?

In Green v. Millman Brothers, Inc., 7 Mich.App. 450, 151 N.W.2d 860 (1967), a landlord accepted monthly rent checks for three years, each being $150 less than the amount called for in the lease.[e] Then he sued the tenant for unpaid rent of $3,600. He conceded that he had agreed orally to a reduction of rent for one year.[f] The tenant contended that the concession was for the whole unexpired term of the lease—about 15 years. In affirming a judgment for the landlord, the court said: "It is necessary to distinguish the instant case from those where the lessee experiences unforeseeable conditions of hardship. . . . The failure of the location under lease here to be productive of a volume of business such as would produce a profit was not such an extraordinary or unforeseen condition as would fall within the ambit of the aforementioned exception." What was to prevent the landlord from recovering $5,400?

In Haun v. Corkland, 399 S.W.2d 519 (Tenn.App.1965), cert. denied, a merchant's rent was reduced when a large department store across the street moved to a new location, with grave effects on his sales volume. At the same time, he began paying rent weekly, rather

---

d. 117 N.J.L. 23, 186 A. 457 (1936), aff'd on opinion of Supreme Court, 117 N.J.L. 426, 189 A. 54 (Ct. of Err. & App. 1937).

e. That is, the minimum stipulated rent. There was also a provision for the payment of a percentage of the

tenant's gross sales, but the court disregarded this feature. Consider how it might affect the merits of the controversy.

f. In Michigan there is a statute like the New York provision set out at p. 262 supra.

than monthly as called for in the lease. The landlord sought to retract his rent concession. How does this case compare with the foregoing ones?

NOTES

(1) *Avoiding the Rule.* In Levine v. Blumenthal, discussed in the preceding note, the court also said: "any consideration for the new undertaking,
however insignificant, satisfies this rule. For instance, an undertaking to
pay part of the debt before maturity, or at a place other than that where
the obligor was legally bound to pay, or to pay in property, regardless of
its value, or to effect a composition with creditors by the payment of less
than the sum due, has been held to constitute a consideration sufficient in
law." The same thought was expressed by Lord Coke, in Pinnel's Case: "by
no possibility, a lesser sum can be satisfaction to the plaintiff for a greater
sum: but the gift of a horse, hawk or robe, etc. in satisfaction is good."

What modern equivalent of a "horse, hawk or robe" might suitably be
used to make a creditor's concession to his debtor irreversible? In Restatement Second, § 76A it is said that a performance "similar" to that
owing "is consideration if it differs from what was required . . . in a
way which reflects more than a pretense of a bargain." Does the concluding phrase encourage lawyers to make a pioneering search for trivial new
objects of bargaining?

A landlord's agreement to accept a reduced rent has sometimes been
enforced on the ground that the tenant gave consideration by agreeing not
to vacate the premises. Is this to say that the tenant may supply consideration for the landlord's concession by threatening him with a breach?
In the Michigan case described in the foregoing note, the tenant relied
on the fact that he had not vacated, but the court answered by pointing
to a covenant in the lease binding him to "operate 100% of the leased
premises during the entire term."

(2) *Assignment.* In Foakes v. Beer (Note 3, p. 267 supra), if Dr.
Foakes had anticipated Mrs. Beer's change of heart, and the result of her
suit, it might have occurred to him to set up the agreement differently.
Consider this arrangement: Foakes agrees to pay the principal amount of
the judgment, in installments, and Beer assigns to him her right to interest
on the judgment. An assignment of a contract (or judgment) claim, having the character of a present transfer, is generally effective without regard to consideration. Given certain formalities, at least, a gift assignment
is irrevocable. However, it is arguable that an assignment of a claim by
its holder *to the obligor* is a distinct species, less favored than an assignment to a third party. Given the rule of Foakes v. Beer, is it a logical
corollary that a gift assignment of this species is impossible?

In the following case the court justified its decision, in part, by reference to the law of gifts. (That part of the opinion is omitted.) However,
the facts did not lend themselves to an assignment analysis, for the agreement in question was oral. The rule as to an *oral* gift assignment, acknowledged by the court, is that it may be revoked. The court refused, therefore, to peg its decision on the law of assignments: "when a creditor releases his debtor, without full payment of the debt, no assignment is involved." (Chapter 10 presents assignment law in some detail.)

WATKINS & SON v. CARRIG

Supreme Court of New Hampshire, 1941.
91 N.H. 459, 21 A.2d 591, 138 A.L.R. 131.

Assumpsit, for work done. By a written contract between the parties the plaintiff agreed to excavate a cellar for the defendant for a stated price. Soon after the work was commenced solid rock was encountered. The plaintiff's manager notified the defendant, a meeting between them was held, and it was orally agreed that the plaintiff should remove the rock at a stipulated unit price about nine times greater than the unit price for excavating upon which the gross amount to be paid according to the written contract was calculated. The rock proved to constitute about two-thirds of the space to be excavated.

A referee found that the oral agreement "superseded" the written contract, and reported a verdict for the plaintiff based on the finding. To the acceptance of the report and an order of judgment thereon the defendant excepted. Further facts appear in the opinion. Transferred by Burque, C. J.

ALLEN, CHIEF JUSTICE. When the written contract was entered into, no understanding existed between the parties that no rock would be found in the excavating. The plaintiff's manager made no inquiry or investigation to find out the character of the ground below the surface, no claim is made that the defendant misled him, and the contract contains no reservations for unexpected conditions. It provides that "all material" shall be removed from the site, and its term that the plaintiff is "to excavate" is unqualified. In this situation a defence of mutual mistake is not available. A space of ground to be excavated, whatever its character, was the subject matter of the contract, and the offer of price on that basis was accepted. Leavitt v. Dover, 67 N.H. 94, 32 A. 156, 68 Am.St.Rep. 640. If the plaintiff was unwise in taking chances, it is not relieved, on the ground of mistake, from the burden incurred in being faced with them. The case differs from that of King Co. v. Aldrich, 81 N.H. 42, 121 A. 434, in which the parties did not contract for the property delivered in purported performance of the contract actually made.

The referee's finding that the written contract was "superseded" by an oral contract when the rock was discovered is construed to mean that the parties agreed to rescind the written contract as though it had not been made and entered into an oral one as though it were the sole and original one. The defendant either thought that the contract did not require the excavation of rock on the basis of the contract price or was willing to forego his rights under the contract in respect to rock. It was important to him that the work should not be delayed, and other reasons may have contributed to induce him to the concession he made. In any event, he consented to a special price for excavating rock, whatever his rights under the contract. The plaintiff on the strength of the promise proceeded with the work.

But the defendant contends that the facts do not support a claim of two independent and separate transactions, one in rescission of the written contract as though it were nugatory, and one in full substitution of it. All that is shown, as he urges, is one transaction by which he was to pay more for the excavating than the written contract provided, with that contract otherwise to remain in force. And upon the basis of this position he relies upon the principle of contract law that his promise to pay more was without consideration, as being a promise to pay the plaintiff for performance of its obligation already in force and outstanding. Whether the contract was rescinded with a new one to take its place or whether it remained in force with a modification of its terms, is not important. In the view of a modification, the claim of a promise unsupported by consideration is as tenable as under the view of a rescission. A modification involves a partial rescission.

In the situation presented the plaintiff entered into a contractual obligation. Facts subsequently learned showed the obligation to be burdensome and the contract improvident. On insistent request by the plaintiff, the defendant granted relief from the burden by a promise to pay a special price which overcame the burden. The promise was not an assumption of the burden; the special price was fair and the defendant received reasonable value for it.

The issue whether the grant of relief constituted a valid contract is one of difficulty. The basic rule that a promise without consideration for it is invalid leads to its logical application that a promise to pay for what the promisor already has a right to receive from the promisee is invalid. The promisee's performance of an existing duty is no detriment to him, and hence nothing is given by him beyond what is already due the promisor. But the claim is here made that the original contract was rescinded, either in full or in respect to some of its terms, by mutual consent, and since any rescission mutually agreed upon is in itself a contract, the claim of a promise to pay for performance of a subsisting duty is unfounded. The terms of the contract of rescission are of course valid if the rescission is valid. The defendant's answer to this claim is well stated in this quotation from Williston, Contr., 2d Ed., § 130a: "But calling an agreement an agreement for rescission does not do away with the necessity of consideration, and when the agreement for rescission is coupled with a further agreement that the work provided for in the earlier agreement shall be completed and that the other party shall give more than he originally promised, the total effect of the second agreement is that one party promises to do exactly what he had previously bound himself to do, and the other party promises to give an additional compensation therefor."

With due respect for this eminent authority, the argument appears to clothe consideration with insistence of control beyond its proper demands. With full recognition of the legal worthlessness of a bare promise and of performance of a subsisting duty as a void consideration, a result accomplished by proper means is not necessarily bad because it would be bad if the means were improper or were not employed.

It is not perceived that the requirement of consideration is necessarily disregarded in spite of the net result of a promise to pay more for less, without additional obligation of the promisee. If the process in reaching such a result is inoffensive to the doctrine of consideration, the result does not become a naked promise. If in analysis of the transaction compliance with the elements of a valid contract may be found, it is hardly a perversion of principle to give the steps taken recognition. The result being reasonable, the means taken to reach it may be examined to determine their propriety.

In common understanding there is, importantly, a wide divergence between a bare promise and a promise in adjustment of a contractual promise already outstanding. A promise with no supporting consideration would upset well and long-established human interrelations if the law did not treat it as a vain thing. But parties to a valid contract generally understand that it is subject to any mutual action they may take in its performance. Changes to meet changes in circumstances and conditions should be valid if the law is to carry out its function and service by rules conformable with reasonable practices and understandings in matters of business and commerce.

Rescission in full or in modification being intended, it should be effective although the result benefits only one party and places a burden only on the other. It is the fact of rescission rather than the effect of it that determines its legal quality. The difference between a rescission unrelated to a new contract and one interdependent with a new contract, with the result the same in each case, signifies no failure of consideration in the latter case. The result, whatever it may be, is indecisive of the contractual character of the transaction. The steps taken being pointed out by the law, the result should not be held an idle one. Merger of the rescission and promise into one transaction does not destroy them as elements composing the transaction.

. . .

Whether the gift to a debtor of an intangible right be termed a waiver, a surrender, an abandonment, or a release, seems broadly immaterial. Its nature, in yielding the right, or in forgiving the obligation, is determinative, rather than its appellation. There may be distinctions and discriminations in the required manner of their metaphysical delivery, but here . . . no symbolism or particular form of evidence is an essential of proof. The case is one of a simple relinquishment of a right pertaining to intangible personalty. The defendant intentionally and voluntarily yielded to a demand for a special price for excavating rock. In doing this he yielded his contract right to the price it provided. Whether or not he thought he had the right, he intended, and executed his intent, to make no claim of the right. The promise of a special price for excavating rock necessarily imported a release or waiver of any right by the contract to hold the plaintiff to the lower price the contract stipulated. In mutual understanding the parties agreed that the contract price was not to control. The contract right being freely surrendered, the issue of contract law whether the new promise is valid is not doubtful. If the totality of the transaction was a promise to pay more for less, there was in its inherent makeup a valid discharge of an obligation. Although the transaction was single, the element of discharge was distinct in precedence of the new promise.

The foregoing views are considered to meet the reasonable needs of standard and ethical practices of men in their business dealings with each other. Conceding that the plaintiff threatened to break its contract because it found the contract to be improvident, yet the defendant yielded to the threat without protest, excusing the plaintiff, and making a new arrangement. Not insisting on his rights but relinquishing them, fairly he should be held to the new arrangement. The law is a means to the end. It is not the law because it is the law, but because it is adapted and adaptable to establish and maintain reasonable order. If the phrase justice according to law were transposed into law according to justice, it would perhaps be more accurately expressive. In a case like this, of conflicting rules and authority, a result which is considered better to establish "fundamental justice and reasonableness" (Cavanaugh v. Boston & M. Railroad, 76 N.H. 68, 72, 79 A. 694, 696), should be attained. It is not practical that the law should adopt all precepts of moral conduct, but it is desirable that its rules and principles should not run counter to them in the important conduct and transactions of life.

Exceptions overruled.

NOTES

(1) *The Hawaiian Housing Case.* Richards contracted to build housing in Hawaii for the Marine Air Corps, using a subcontractor's bid for the metal work, by the Air Conditioning Company (AC). By error, AC had calculated its bid on the assumption that galvanized sheet metal would be used, rather than zinc alloy. When AC informed Richards that it would not do the work for the bid price, Richards "blew up." Over the next two months, hard bargaining ensued, during which Richards insisted that AC was bound by its bid price. At length, Richards and AC executed a contract for the metal work at $62,000. (The AC bid had been less than $49,-000). After paying some $50,000 as the work progressed, Richards refused to pay more. In fact, Richards never intended to pay the agreed price. When sued for the remainder, Richards relied on the pre-existing duty rule, and cited Alaska Packers Ass'n v. Domenico. (See brief of the case at p. 261 supra.) From judgment for the plaintiff, the defendant appealed. *Held:* Affirmed. Richards Construction Company v. Air Conditioning Co. of Hawaii, 318 F.2d 410 (9th Cir. 1963).

Was the Alaska Packers case easily distinguishable? Was Richards in a good position to assert the rule, having retreated from the position that AC was bound by its bid?

An additional fact in the case was that AC did not inform Richards of its error for about a month after it had learned of the award of the main contract, and after it had discovered the error. What conclusion does this suggest? Another fact was that the second lowest bid was $83,000.[a] What conclusion does this suggest?

(2) *Problem.* A lawyer is appointed by the court to represent an indigent person accused of murder, under a statute requiring the county to pay a fee to be fixed by the court. After he makes an unsuccessful defense, relatives of the accused promise to pay him $1,000 for taking an appeal[l], if it is successful. He obtains a reversal of the conviction, but the relatives refuse to pay. May the lawyer enforce their promise? See Commonwealth v. Wormsley, 294 Pa. 495, 144 A. 428 (1928); Hale v. Brewster, 81 N.M. 342, 467 P.2d 8 (1970). Regarding the problem as one of consideration, is it different from all the other situations so far given in which the pre-existing duty rule was invoked? If so, how?

A JUDICIAL TOUR DE FORCE

De Cicco v. Schweizer [b] is a well-known New York case in which Cardozo wrote for the court on the subject of consideration. Its chief interest is not the decision itself, but the dazzling ingenuity he displayed in reaching it.

On the merits, the plaintiff's claim had a strong intrinsic appeal, but the pre-existing duty rule presented an obstacle. Blanche Schweizer and Count Oberto Gulinelli were engaged to be married. Four days before the wedding occurred the Count and the bride's parents executed "articles of agreement" in which the father, Joseph Schweizer, promised to make an annual payment to Blanche of $2,500 as long as he (Joseph) and Blanche should both live.[c] The sentence containing this promise began as follows: [d] "Whereas, Miss Blanche Josephine Schweizer . . . is now affianced to and is to be married to the above said Count Oberto Giacomo Giovannia Francesco Maria Gulinelli: Now in consideration of all that is herein set forth the said Mr. Joseph Schweizer promises," etc. The first payment was made on the wedding day. After the tenth payment, no more were made. The couple assigned their rights in the contract to Attilio De Cicco, and he sued Schweizer.[e]

a. Richards' architect had estimated the cost of the metal work at $16,000. One of the bids it received was for more than $173,000.

b. 221 N.Y. 431, 117 N.E. 807 (1917).

c. Mrs. Schweizer covenanted to continue the payments after her husband's death, and there were testamentary provisions as well.

d. Translated; the agreement was in Italian.

e. The court assumed, properly, that Attilio's right to enforce the contract was as good as that of either Blanche

Cardozo first stated the defendant's contention: "that Count Gulinelli was already affianced to Miss Schweizer, and that the marriage was merely the fulfillment of an existing legal duty." Turning to the law, he accepted the premise of the defendant's argument: "The courts of this state are committed to the view that a promise by A. to B. to induce him not to break his contract with C. is void." He then developed at length a distinction, showing that Schweizer's promise was not of that character. Instead, he reasoned, it was a promise to induce the Count not to join with Blanche in a voluntary rescission of their engagement. Although neither could rightfully withdraw without the other's consent, *together* they were free to terminate the engagement or postpone the marriage. The consideration, then, for Schweizer's promise was that they did not do so.[f]

In some beautifully articulated paragraphs the opinion seeks to make this reading plausible: "It does not seem a far-fetched assumption [in relation to contracts to marry] that one will release where the other has repented . . . one does not commonly apply pressure to coerce the will and action of those who are anxious to proceed. The attempt to sway their conduct by new inducements is an implied admission that both may waver . . . . The springs of conduct are subtle and varied. One who meddles with them must not insist upon too nice a measure of proof that the spring which he released was effective to the exclusion of all others." And in a final paragraph, Cardozo takes higher ground, appealing to "those considerations of public policy which cluster about contracts that touch the marriage relation."[g]

NOTES

(1) *Questions.* Is the principle of this case usable in any situation that does not involve a marriage? In Arzani v. People, p. 266 supra, would it have been plausible for the plaintiff to cite De Cicco v. Schweizer? If not, what change in the facts would make the two cases comparable?

In a later opinion, Cardozo cited De Cicco v. Schweizer as a "signpost on the road" toward general acceptance of the doctrine of promissory estoppel. See Allegheny College v. National Chautauqua County Bank, referred to at p. 48 supra. Do you see a connection between the case and that doctrine? See also Restatement Second, § 90(2), Illustration 17.

(2) *The Case of the Disbursing Bank.* Cisco Aircraft, Inc. obtained a contract with the Government for some aerial spraying of timber land. Cisco let a contract for some necessary supplies and aircraft to the Morrison Flying Service. Cisco also assigned to the Deming Bank its right to earnings under the contract, as security for a loan. Morrison's president,

---

or the Count. It did not indicate which of them might have enforced it, or when the assignment was given, or for what consideration, if any.

f. Along the way, Cardozo rejected the contention that Schweizer had only

made a promise of a gift: "One does not commonly pledge one's self to generosity in the language of a covenant."

g. One judge concurred in a separate opinion.

concerned about Cisco's ability to pay, wrote to the bank: "we are wondering if your bank could send us a letter assuring us of payment for our services." To which the bank's president responded: "I can assure you that once the money is received from the Forest Service, we will pay all the bills submitted, without delay." (Morrison's president later testified that if she had not received this letter she would have approached the Forest Service about paying her directly, as another subcontractor on the job successfully did.) Although the bank received proceeds from the spraying job, Morrison was not paid. In an action by Morrison against the bank, a question of consideration was raised. From an adverse judgment, Morrison appealed. *Held*: Reversed. "We recognize that there is a conflict among the authorities as to whether there is a sufficient consideration for a promise by a third person made to induce a party to an existing contract to perform. Professor Corbin recognizes this conflict and his comment about it has the approval of this court. . . . 'The reasons that may be advanced to support the rule that is applied in the two-party cases, weak enough as they often are in the cases, are scarcely applicable at all in three-party cases.' Corbin, Contracts, § 176." Morrison Flying Service v. Deming National Bank, 404 F.2d 856 (10th Cir. 1968), cert. denied, 393 U.S. 1020 (1969).[h]

Could Morrison have exerted coercion on the bank to make the promise, if the bank had been less compliant? See Restatement Second, § 76A, Comment d, where it is said that the rule of the section may apply to three-party situations, but that unfair pressure is less likely in such situations than in two-party ones.

(3) *The Jockey's Case.* Mike McDevitt was a jockey who had accepted employment from Shaw to drive a mare named Grace in the Kentucky Futurity. Stokes owned "relatives" of the mare, and stood to gain if she should win. Stokes promised McDevitt a bonus of $1,000 for riding in and winning the race. McDevitt won, but Stokes refused to pay, and McDevitt sued him. From judgment for the defendant on a demurrer to the plaintiff's complaint, the plaintiff appealed. *Held:* Affirmed. "To hold that [plaintiff] would not have won the race with Grace but for the agreement of [defendant] to pay him the $1,000 . . . would be to say that he would have been recreant to the obligation arising out of his employment by Shaw . . ." McDevitt v. Stokes, 174 Ky. 515, 192 S.W. 681 (1917). Does this case illustrate (to use Cardozo's words) "a promise by A. to B. to induce him not to break his contract with C."?

CLAIM SETTLEMENTS

Settlements of disputed claims have beneficial effects, such as alleviating discord and eliminating sources of uncertainty. These effects are achieved, of course, largely by judicial action foreclosing claims that have resulted in settlement and compromise. It is a commonplace observation in opinions that the law favors settlements. The law does not, however, give effect to every attempt at settlement,

h. For a comparable case, relying on the first Restatement (§ 84), see Philips Electronics & Pharmaceutical Ind. Corp. v. Leavens, 421 F.2d 39 (3d Cir. 1970).

for various reasons. Sometimes a settlement is avoided because the parties entered into it under a mistake. (As to this topic, see subsection (b), infra.) An attempted settlement may also fail by reason of duress, as observed above.

May it also fail for want of consideration? Virtually every settlement of a disputed claim embodies an agreement not to seek enforcement of the claim, at least for a time, whether the agreement be expressed or not. When suit is brought on a settlement agreement, consideration is regularly found in the plaintiff's promise to forbear suit on the disputed claim. But what if the claim had no substance? Can it be said in that case that the "settlement" removed any uncertainties? Should it be possible to claim a reward for abandoning a worthless claim? These are the questions to be addressed next.

NOTE

The Accord. Sometimes a settlement is ineffective because of the form it takes. At common law an agreement in the form of an "executory accord" was unenforceable. That is an agreement by which a supposed liability is to be terminated upon a performance in the future by the obligor. The accord as such is wholly ineffective, either to foreclose assertion of the old liability, or to create a new one upon the promise. Only after full performance of the promise is the attempted settlement effective; it is then known as an "accord and satisfaction." The common-law rule has been modified by statute in some states,[a] and limited by a number of refined distinctions.[b] It retains a certain force, however, possibly because promissory settlements do not ameliorate discord and uncertainty very well.

FIEGE v. BOEHM

Court of Appeals of Maryland, 1956.
210 Md. 352, 123 A.2d 316.

DELAPLAINE, JUDGE. This suit was brought in the Superior Court of Baltimore City by Hilda Louise Boehm against Louis Gail Fiege to recover for breach of a contract to pay the expenses incident to the birth of his bastard child and to provide for its support upon condition that she would refrain from prosecuting him for bastardy.

Plaintiff alleged in her declaration substantially as follows: (1) that early in 1951 defendant had sexual intercourse with her although she was unmarried, and as a result thereof she became pregnant, and defendant acknowledged that he was responsible for her pregnancy; (2) that on September 29, 1951, she gave birth to a female child; that defendant is the father of the child; and that he acknowledged on many occasions that he is its father; (3) that before the child was born, defendant agreed to pay all her medical and miscellaneous ex-

---

a. E. g., N.Y.Gen.Obl.L. § 15–501.

b. See Goldbard v. Empire State Mutual Life Ins. Co., 5 A.D.2d 230, 171 N.Y.S.2d 194 (1st Dept. 1958).

penses and to compensate her for the loss of her salary caused by the child's birth, and also to pay her ten dollars per week for its support until it reached the age of 21, upon condition that she would not institute bastardy proceedings against him as long as he made the payments in accordance with the agreement; (4) that she placed the child for adoption on July 13, 1954, and she claimed the following sums: Union Memorial Hospital, $110; Florence Crittenton Home, $100; Dr. George Merrill, her physician, $50; medicines $70.35; miscellaneous expenses, $20.45; loss of earnings for 26 weeks, $1,105; support of the child, $1,440; total, $2,895.80; and (5) that defendant paid her only $480, and she demanded that he pay her the further sum of $2,415.80, the balance due under the agreement, but he failed and refused to pay the same.

Defendant demurred to the declaration on the ground that it failed to allege that in September, 1953, plaintiff instituted bastardy proceedings against him in the Criminal Court of Baltimore, but since it had been found from blood tests that he could not have been the father of the child, he was acquitted of bastardy. The Court sustained the demurrer with leave to amend.

Plaintiff then filed an amended declaration, which contained the additional allegation that, after the breach of the agreement by defendant, she filed a charge with the State's Attorney that defendant was the father of her bastard child; and that on October 8, 1953, the Criminal Court found defendant not guilty solely on a physician's testimony that "on the basis of certain blood tests made, the defendant can be excluded as the father of the said child, which testimony is not conclusive upon a jury in a trial court."

Defendant also demurred to the amended declaration, but the Court overruled that demurrer.

Plaintiff, a typist, now over 35 years old, who has been employed by the Government in Washington and Baltimore for over thirteen years, testified in the Court below that she had never been married, but that at about midnight on January 21, 1951, defendant, after taking her to a moving picture theater on York Road and then to a restaurant, had sexual intercourse with her in his automobile. She further testified that he agreed to pay all her medical and hospital expenses, to compensate her for loss of salary caused by the pregnancy and birth, and to pay her ten dollars per week for the support of the child upon condition that she would refrain from instituting bastardy proceedings against him. She further testified that between September 17, 1951, and May, 1953, defendant paid her a total of $480.

Defendant admitted that he had taken plaintiff to restaurants, had danced with her several times, had taken her to Washington, and had brought her home in the country; but he asserted that he had never had sexual intercourse with her. He also claimed that he did not enter into any agreement with her. He admitted, however, that he had paid her a total of $480. His father also testified that he stated "that he did not want his mother to know, and if it were just kept quiet, kept principally away from his mother and the public and the courts, that he would take care of it."

Defendant further testified that in May 1953, he went to see plaintiff's physician to make inquiry about blood tests to show the paternity of the child; and that those tests were made and they indicated that it was not possible that he could have been the child's father. He then stopped making payments. Plaintiff thereupon filed a charge of bastardy with the State's Attorney.

The testimony which was given in the Criminal Court by Dr. Milton Sachs, hematologist at the University Hospital, was read to the jury in the Superior Court. In recent years the blood-grouping test has been employed in criminology, in the selection of donors for blood transfusions, and as evidence in paternity cases. The Landsteiner blood-grouping test is based on the medical theory that the red corpuscles in human blood contain two affirmative agglutinating substances, and that every individual's blood falls into one of the four classes and remains the same throughout life. According to Mendel's law of inheritance, this blood individuality is an hereditary characteristic which passes from parent to child, and no agglutinating substance can appear in the blood of a child which is not present in the blood of one of its parents. The four Landsteiner blood groups, designated as AB, A, B, and O, into which human blood is divided on the basis of the compatibility of the corpuscles and serum with the corpuscles and serum of other persons, are characterized by different combinations of two agglutinogens in the red blood cells and two agglutinins in the serum. Dr. Sachs reported that Fiege's blood group was Type O, Miss Boehm's was Type B, and the infant's was Type A. He further testified that on the basis of these tests, Fiege could not have been the father of the child, as it is impossible for a mating of Type O and Type B to result in a child of Type A.

Although defendant was acquitted by the Criminal Court, the Superior Court overruled his motion for a directed verdict. In the charge to the jury the Court instructed them that defendant's acquittal in the Criminal Court was not binding upon them. The jury found a verdict in favor of plaintiff for $2,415.80, the full amount of her claim.

Defendant filed a motion for judgment n. o. v. or a new trial. The Court overruled that motion also, and entered judgment on the verdict of the jury. Defendant appealed from that judgment.

Defendant contends that, even if he entered into the contract as alleged, it was not enforceable, because plaintiff's forbearance to prosecute was not based on a valid claim, and hence the contract was without consideration. . . .

It was originally held at common law that a child born out of wedlock is *filius nullius*, and a putative father is not under any legal liability to contribute to the support of his illegitimate child, and his promise to do so is unenforceable because it is based on purely a moral obligation. . . .

However, where statutes are in force to compel the father of a bastard to contribute to its support, the courts have invariably held that a contract by the putative father with the mother of his bastard child to provide for the support of the child upon the agreement of the mother to refrain from invoking the bastardy statute against the father, or to abandon proceedings already commenced, is supported by sufficient consideration. Jangraw v. Perkins, 77 Vt. 375, 60 A. 385; Beach v. Voegtlen, 68 N.J.L. 472, 53 A. 695; Thayer v. Thayer, 189 N.C. 502, 127 S.E. 553, 39 A.L.R. 428.

In Maryland it is now provided by statute that whenever a person is found guilty of bastardy, the court shall issue an order directing such person (1) to pay for the maintenance and support of the child until it reaches the age of eighteen years, such sum as may be agreed upon, if consent proceedings be had, or in the absence of agreement, such sum as the court may fix, with due regard to the circumstances of the accused person; and (2) to give bond to the State of Maryland in such penalty as the court may fix, with good and sufficient securities, conditioned on making the payments required by the court's order, or any amendments thereof. Failure to give such bond shall be punished by commitment in the jail or the House of Correction until bond is given but not exceeding two years. Code Supp.1955, art. 12, § 8.

Prosecutions for bastardy are treated in Maryland as criminal proceedings, but they are actually civil in purpose. . . . Accordingly a contract by the putative father of an illegitimate child to provide for its support upon condition that bastardy proceedings will not be instituted is a compromise of civil injuries resulting from a criminal act, and not a contract to compound a criminal prosecution, and if it is fair and reasonable, it is in accord with the Bastardy Act and the public policy of the State.

Of course, a contract of a putative father to provide for the support of his illegitimate child must be based, like any other contract, upon sufficient consideration. . . .

In 1867 the Maryland Court of Appeals, in the opinion delivered by Judge Bartol in Hartle v. Stahl, 27 Md. 157, 172, held: (1) that forbearance to assert a claim before institution of suit, if not in fact a legal claim, is not of itself sufficient consideration to support a promise; but (2) that a compromise of a doubtful claim or a relinquishment of a pending suit is good consideration for a promise; and (3) that in order to support a compromise, it is sufficient that the parties entering into it thought at the time that there was a *bona fide* question between them, although it may eventually be found that there was in fact no such question.

We have thus adopted the rule that the surrender of, or forbearance to assert an invalid claim by one who has not an honest and reasonable belief in its possible validity is not sufficient consideration for a contract. 1 Restatement, Contracts, sec. 76(b). We combine the subjective requisite that the claim be *bona fide* with the objective requisite that it must have a reasonable basis of support. Accordingly a promise not to prosecute a claim which is not founded in good faith does not of itself give a right of action on an agreement to pay for refraining from so acting, because a release from mere annoyance and unfounded litigation does not furnish valuable consideration.

Professor Williston was not entirely certain whether the test of reasonableness is based upon the intelligence of the claimant himself, who may be an ignorant person with no knowledge of law and little sense as to facts; but he seemed inclined to favor the view that "the claim forborne must be neither absurd in fact from the standpoint of a reasonable man in the position of the claimant, nor, obviously unfounded in law to one who has an elementary knowledge of legal principles." 1 Williston on Contracts, Rev.Ed., sec. 135. We agree that while stress is placed upon the honesty and good faith of the claimant, forbearance to prosecute a claim is insufficient consideration if the claim forborne is so lacking in foundation as to make its assertion incompatible with honesty and a reasonable degree of intelligence. Thus, if the mother of a bastard knows that there is no foundation, either in law or fact, for a charge against a certain man that he is the father of the child, but that man promises to pay her in order to prevent bastardy proceedings against him, the forbearance to institute proceedings is not sufficient consideration.

On the other hand, forbearance to sue for a lawful claim or demand is sufficient consideration for a promise to pay for the forbearance if the party forbearing had an honest intention to prosecute litigation which is not frivolous, vexatious, or unlawful, and which he believed to be well founded. Snyder v. Cearfoss, 187 Md. 635, 643, 51 A.2d 264; Pullman Co. v. Ray, 201 Md. 268, 94 A.2d 266. Thus the promise of a woman who is expecting an illegitimate child that she will not institute bastardy proceedings against a certain man is sufficient consideration for his promise to pay for the child's support, even though it may not be certain whether the man is the father or whether the prosecution would be successful, if she makes the charge in good faith. . . .

Another analogous case is Thompson v. Nelson, 28 Ind. 431. There the plaintiff sought to recover back money which he had paid to compromise a prosecution for bastardy. He claimed that the prosecuting witness was not pregnant and therefore the prosecution was fraudulent. It was held by the Supreme Court of Indiana, however, that the settlement of the prosecution was a good consideration for the payment of the money and it could not be recovered back, inasmuch as it appeared from the evidence that the prosecution was instituted in good faith, and at that time there was reason to believe that the prosecuting witness was pregnant, although it was found out afterwards that she was not pregnant. [The court's summary of a similar decision on similar facts in Illinois is here omitted. Heaps v. Dunham, 95 Ill. 583, 590.]

In the case at bar there was no proof of fraud or unfairness. Assuming that the hematologists were accurate in their laboratory tests and findings, nevertheless plaintiff gave testimony which indicated that she made the charge of bastardy against defendant in good faith. For these reasons the Court acted properly in overruling the demurrer to the amended declaration and the motion for a directed verdict.

[The court's discussion of alleged errors in the trial court's charge to the jury is here omitted.]

As we have found no reversible error in the rulings and instructions of the trial court, we will affirm the judgment entered on the verdict of the jury.

Judgment affirmed, with costs.

NOTES

(1) *The Objective Requisite.* Examine Restatement Second, § 76B (1). What has happened to the requirement of the first Restatement, that the forbearing party have a *reasonable* belief in his position? On a close reading of the main case, does it appear that the new Restatement rule is substantially identical to the rule of the case?

(2) *Questions.* If Miss Boehm had made two or more agreements of the kind she made with Fiege, obtaining identical commitments from more than one man, at the same time, is it clear that none of them could be enforced? Only one of them?

(3) *The Case of the Church's Immunity.* Ralston suffered injuries, as she alleged, in a fall on a church stairway, which resulted from its negligence. An adjuster for the church's insurance company called on her and promised that it would pay all her expenses if she would refrain from suing the church or the insurer. Not being paid, she sued the insurer on its promise. The trial court sustained its demurrer to the plaintiff's petition alleging these facts, and she appealed. *Held:* Reversed. The insurer based its argument on holdings of the court that churches and charitable organizations are immune from liability for their torts. Referring to other holdings, however, the court concluded that a claim by the plaintiff, based on negligence, would not have been "obviously invalid or frivolous." If it promised to pay the plaintiff, the court said, the insurer was hardly in a position to make that contention. Ralston v. Mathew, 173 Kan. 550, 250 P.2d 841 (1952).

Was the decision in this case parallel to that in Fiege v. Boehm? Of course there was this difference: the challenge to Boehm's claim was based on its factual weakness, whereas Ralston's claim was questioned on a legal ground. Should this make a difference in the standard applied? Should the viewpoint of a layman or that of a lawyer be used to answer the question whether or not a claim was "obviously invalid" in law?[a] Do you see any harmful result for the law of *torts* that may result from a decision like Ralston v. Mathew?

(4) *Rescinding the Unenforceable.* Robert Browning, an osteopath in Tacoma, agreed to sell his practice and equipment to Arthur Johnson, a fellow-practitioner. Before the date of transfer Browning asked to be released from the sale. Another agreement was reached, by which Browning promised to pay Johnson $40,000, and the sale contract was canceled. Still later, Browning sought a declaratory judgment that the promise of payment was not binding on him. The trial court found that the original agreement could not have been enforced, for want of mutuality, and for indefiniteness in its terms. Nevertheless, it denied the relief sought by Browning and he appealed. *Held:* Affirmed. "The legal detriment suffered by Johnson through Browning's inducement will support Browning's promise to pay." Browning v. Johnson, 70 Wash.2d 145, 422 P.2d 314 (1967). What was the detriment suffered by Johnson?

KIBLER v. FRANK L. GARRETT & SONS, INC.

Supreme Court of Washington, 1968.
73 Wash.2d 523, 439 P.2d 416.

[William Kibler harvested the wheat on 37 acres owned by Frank L. Garrett & Sons, Inc., under an agreement that he would be paid 18¢ a bushel, "and perhaps more, depending on the circumstances." He sent Garrett a bill for $826.20, calculated at 20¢ a bushel. He justified the price by reference to obstructions encountered in the fields. Garrett responded with a check for $444 ($12 an acre), and a covering letter explaining the basis for this figure ("50% more than we paid last year," etc.). The letter concluded: "Billing on this acreage for approximately $30 an acre is ridiculous." Kibler called his lawyer to ask if he could safely deposit the check. The lawyer asked him to read the notations on it. He read the typing on the check, including the notation, "Harvesting Wheat Washington Ranch." He did not read or notice a line of fine print as follows: "By endorsement this check when paid is accepted in full payment of the following account." On the lawyer's advice, Kibler deposited the check. Then he brought an action against Garrett for the difference between his bill and the amount of the check. The trial court dismissed the action, and the plaintiff appealed.]

ROSELLINI, JUDGE. [The court first concluded that the letter did not contain an unequivocal statement that the check was to be

---

a. See Renney v. Kimberly, 211 Ga. 396, 86 S.E.2d 217 (1955), in which a deed of a non-existent interest in land was held not to be a consideration for promises made by the gran- tees to the grantor. The court analyzed its prior decisions to determine that the deed conveyed no interest.

payment in full.]   Since there were no conditions attached to the acceptance of the check in this case, the letter was not an offer of an accord.

Was the condition sufficiently expressed on the check itself?   It is unquestioned that the plaintiff did not see the fine print, and his attorney did not see it.   The defendant's attorney did not notice it, apparently, until it was called to his attention at the trial.   This was a form check, presumably used in the payment of all of the defendant's accounts, whether the payments made were payments in full or partial payments.   There was nothing on the check to indicate that the language was particularly applicable to the plaintiff's claim.   The trial court felt that the tone of the letter cast upon the plaintiff the duty to examine the check minutely or cash it at his peril.   We do not agree.   The burden is upon the party alleging an accord and satisfaction to show that there was indeed a meeting of the minds.   See Brear v. Klinker Sand & Gravel Co., 60 Wash.2d 443, 374 P.2d 370 (1962).   If the language contained in the fine print on the check was of significance in forming an accord, it must appear that the fact of its significance was brought to the plaintiff's attention.   The evidence is to the contrary.

In the case of Washington Fish & Oyster Co. v. G. P. Halferty & Co., 44 Wash.2d 646, 269 P.2d 806 (1954), the respondent sued to recover the balance due on a contract.   A partial payment had been made by a check with a voucher attached bearing a similar notation, accompanied by a detailed statement showing the "balance" as that amount which was contained in the check.   This court held that the language on the check was of no significance, inasmuch as it was a form voucher apparently attached to all checks of the company.   It is true that in that case the respondent had received checks previously from the company, presumably with the same form of voucher attached, and that in this case there was no evidence that the parties had had previous dealings, but we do not think that fact is determinative.   It is the fact that the notation is obviously formal and applies to all payments made by check, whether or not they are intended as full payment, that renders the language ineffective, and also the fact that it is in print so small that no recipient can be presumed to have read it.

We hold that the proof in this case did not show an accord and satisfaction, since while the claim was disputed, there was no showing that the defendant manifested to the plaintiff his intention to pay no more than the amount which he remitted.   To sustain the trial court would necessitate a holding that payment of an amount less than that claimed by the creditor operates as an accord and satisfaction if the amount paid is all that the debtor admits that he owes.   This . . . would place a creditor at a disadvantage in accepting partial payments from a reluctant debtor, since by doing so he would be jeopardizing his right to receive the balance, even though in law that balance was in fact due him.   It is true that the courts look with favor on compromise, but this means genuine compromise, arrived at through mutual agreement, and not compromise fallen into inadvertently.

The plaintiff's witnesses testified that the reasonable value of his services was close to the amount which he claimed was due him.   The defendant did not present evidence on this question, since the court dismissed the action at the close of the plaintiff's case.   As the record now stands, there is no evidence of overreaching on the part of the plaintiff.

The judgment is reversed and the cause remanded for a new trial.

[Three judges dissented, relying on the terms and circumstances of the letter alone.]

NOTES

(1) *The Embarrassing Choice.*   "A debtor paying his own money may couple the payment with such conditions as he pleases. . . .   From this the rule has grown up in connection with the satisfaction of unliquidated demands that one who sends a check to another upon a condition explicitly declared, that the demand shall be extinguished or the check sent back unused, may hold the creditor to the condition, however embarrassing the choice."   Hudson v. Yonkers Fruit Co., p. 287 infra.   In Toledo Edison Co. v. Roberts, 50 Ohio App. 74, 197 N.E. 500 (1934), the payee of a check tried to evade the choice by erasing a statement on the instrument; he failed. In Hoeppner Construction Co. v. United States, 273 F.2d 835 (10th Cir. 1960), a debtor contended that an accord resulted from the way his check had been dealt with, but the contention was rejected.   The payee had been advised by counsel not to cash the check and had made unavailing efforts to return it.

Can the payee escape his dilemma by notifying the debtor that he is cashing the check in part payment?   See Olson v. Wilson & Co., 244 Iowa 895, 58 N.W.2d 381 (1953); Nassoiy v. Tomlinson, 148 N.Y. 326, 42 N.E. 715 (1896); Restatement, § 420.   On reservation of rights, see UCC 1–207.

(2) *A Close Question.*   Palladi contracted to build a house and convey it to Ohlinger and his wife, but he retained the "option to cancel" if prices for material should increase prior to the date of settlement.   Ohlinger paid Palladi $1,500 at the time of contracting.   A year later, when prices had advanced, Palladi sent Ohlinger a notice of cancellation and a check for $1,500.   The Ohlingers believed that the notice at that juncture was ineffective, and they brought an action against Palladi for specific performance. They prayed the court to be allowed to pay $1,500 to be held "to the credit of the cause."   When the court so ordered, Ohlinger endorsed Palladi's check and the clerk deposited it.   The court decreed specific performance, and Palladi appealed.   *Held:* Affirmed.   The attempted cancellation was not timely.   On another point the court said: "Three members of the Court hold that the use made of the check constituted an acceptance of the conditions upon which it was tendered even though this was contrary to the intention of the appellees.   The other three are equally firm in their view that the deposit of the check in court in the case in which the appellees were

attempting to enforce the contract was not a tortious exercise of dominion over the appellant's money. In view of this situation, the ruling of the chancellor on this point will be affirmed without discussion." Palladi Realty Co. v. Ohlinger, 190 Md. 303, 58 A.2d 125 (1948).

(3) *Problem.* A landlord cashed his tenant's monthly rent check, bearing the notation "Final and termination payment under the lease." The tenant had asserted the right to terminate the lease for inadequacy in the heat supply. Was the lease terminated by the landlord's conduct? See Kramas v. Beattie, 107 N.H. 321, 221 A.2d 236 (1966). Cf. Gottlieb v. Charles Scribner's Sons, 232 Ala. 33, 166 So. 685 (1936).

HUDSON v. YONKERS FRUIT CO., Inc., 258 N.Y. 168, 179 N. E. 373, 80 A.L.R. 1052 (1932). CARDOZO, C. J. Plaintiff [George C. Hudson], then the owner and in possession of a quantity of apples, requested the defendant to procure a purchaser. This the defendant did, and collected the price. The plaintiff says that the service was to be rendered without charge; a friendly accommodation. The defendant says that there was an express agreement for the payment of a commission at the rate of ten per cent.

The defendant, after collecting the proceeds of the sales, sent a statement of the account to the plaintiff, in which items amounting in their total to $1,017.60, ten per cent. of the price, were deducted for commissions. With this statement there was sent a check for $3,184.50, the balance then due if the deduction was correct. The plaintiff kept the check, but made protest at once that the deduction was erroneous. In an action to recover the amount withheld, the jury returned a verdict in favor of the plaintiff, thereby finding that the defendant's service was to be gratuitous. The Appellate Division reversed and dismissed the complaint, holding that the acceptance by the plaintiff of the balance conceded to be his was an accord and satisfaction.

We discover nothing in the record to give support to that conclusion. . . . [A tender of payment by a debtor may, the court conceded, be coupled with a condition, such that the payee is bound by an accord and satisfaction—his assent being "imputed"—if he makes use of the money.]

In the case at hand, the condition was not lawfully imposed, if we assume provisionally that it was imposed at all. The defendant was not merely a debtor, paying its own money, which it would have been free to retain or to disburse according to its pleasure. It was an agent, a fiduciary, accounting for money belonging to its principal. No matter whether the deduction of a commission was proper or improper, the balance represented by the check was due in any event. The law will not suffer an agent to withhold moneys collected for a principal's account by the pressure of a threat that no part of the moneys will be remitted to the owner without the approval of deductions beneficial to the agent. Such conduct is a flagrant abuse of the opportunities and powers of a fiduciary position. Britton v. Ferrin, 171 N.Y. 235, 63 N.E. 954; Morris v. Windsor Trust Co., 213 N.Y. 27, 106 N.E. 753, Ann.Cas.1916C, 972. We do not need to determine whether a condition would be lawful if the tender by the agent were to involve some abatement of deductions that might otherwise be his. Sufficient for the decision of this case is the ruling that the condition is unlawful when what is paid is no more than must certainly be due. A payment so made is not within Nassoiy v. Tomlinson, and other cases of that type. There, as the court was careful to point out (page 331 of 148 N.Y., 42 N.E. 715, 716), "the money tendered belonged to them [i. e., to the makers of the tender], and they had the right to say on what condition it should be received." The payment in this case is within the doctrine of such cases as Mance v. Hossington, 205 N.Y. 33, 36, 98 N.E. 203, and Eames Vacuum Brake Co. v. Prosser, 157 N.Y. 289, 51 N.E. 986. What was paid had no connection with what was disputed and reserved. "The payment of an admitted liability is not a payment of or consideration for, an alleged accord and satisfaction of another and independent alleged liability." Mance v. Hossington, supra; cf. Hettrick Mfg. Co. v. Barish, supra, at page 684 of 120 Misc.Rep., 199 N.Y.S. 755, 766, and cases there cited. The doctrine of accord and satisfaction by force of an assent that is merely constructive or imputed assumes as its foundation stone the existence of a condition lawfully imposed. The rationale of the doctrine fails if submission to the alternative would be submission to a crime. A principal does not put himself in the wrong by repudiating a condition where the agent by withholding payment would be guilty of embezzlement.

[The court ruled, as an alternate ground of decision, that the statement of account sent by the defendant with its check was insufficient to inform the plaintiff that he was being offered the check in full settlement of a disputed account.

[Judgment of the Appellate Division reversed, and that of the trial court affirmed.]

NOTES

(1) *What is a "Fiduciary"?* The law of express trusts provides the model of a fiduciary relation. It is an ancient body of law, created in equity, and it imposes high standards of conduct on the trustee. Loosely speaking, a trustee is one appointed to hold and manage property that belongs ("in equity") to another. The manner of creating the relation, trustee and beneficiary, and the extent of fiduciary duties, must be studied in another course. Here it may be noted that fiduciary duties attach to other relations as well, such as an agent's relation to his principal. Indeed, they are sometimes ascribed to relations far removed from trust law. Sometimes the term "fiduciary" seems to be applied to express a pre-determined

conclusion.[a] Among the persons most regularly charged with fiduciary duties, in a strict sense, are corporate directors, in transactions between them and the firms they serve, and lawyers, in their business dealings with clients.

(2) *Questions.* Is there a policy basis for the distinction here drawn between a fiduciary and a debtor, as concerns the attachment of conditions when a check is offered in settlement of a disputed account? Was the defendant in Kibler v. Frank L. Garrett & Sons a "debtor" or a "fiduciary"?

(3) *Insurance Settlements.* An insurance company seeking to make a final settlement with an insured or a benficiary under its insurance contract has frequently been held to owe a duty to act in good faith and to give the other party full information as to the effects of cashing the check. Kellogg v. Iowa State Traveling Men's Ass'n, 239 Iowa 196, 29 N.W.2d 559 (1947) ("the relationship between the parties is closely akin to a fiduciary one"). Compare Connell v. Provident Life & Acc. Ins. Co., 148 Tex. 311, 224 S.W.2d 194, 196 (1949) (insurer took exceptional care to inform the insured that the final draft, written on paper of a different color from the prevous ones, was in final settlement, and check-cashing was deemed a final discharge) with Metropolitan Life Ins. Co. v. Richter, 173 Okl. 489, 49 P.2d 94 (1935) (routine "payment-in-full" endorsement on check was insufficient notice of finality).

AUSTIN INSTRUMENT, INC. v. LORAL CORPORATION

Court of Appeals of New York, 1971.
29 N.Y.2d 124, 272 N.E.2d 533.

FULD, CHIEF JUDGE. The defendant, Loral Corporation, seeks to recover payment for goods delivered under a contract which it had with the plaintiff Austin Instrument, Inc., on the ground that the evidence establishes, as a matter of law, that it was forced to agree to an increase in price on the items in question under circumstances amounting to economic duress.

In July of 1965, Loral was awarded a $6,000,000 contract by the Navy for the production of radar sets. The contract contained a schedule of deliveries, a liquidated damages clause applying to late deliveries and a cancellation clause in case of default by Loral. The latter thereupon solicited bids for some 40 precision gear components needed to produce the radar sets, and awarded Austin a subcontract to supply 23 such parts. That party commenced delivery in early 1966.

In May, 1966, Loral was awarded a second Navy contract for the production of more radar sets and again went about soliciting bids.

a. It has beeen suggested, for example, that a lender is in a fiduciary position as to a borrower, at least in one aspect of the loan transaction. See Background Study of the Regulation of Credit Life and Disability Insurance (N. A. I. C. staff, 1970), at pp. 132 et seq. The suggestion extends also to a credit seller, vis-a-vis a buyer. The situation underlying the suggestion is a specialized one: the sale of life or health insurance in connection with "consumer debt" transactions.

Austin bid on all 40 gear components but, on July 15, a representative from Loral informed Austin's president, Mr. Krauss, that his company would be awarded the subcontract only for those items on which it was low bidder. The Austin officer refused to accept an order for less than all 40 of the gear parts and on the next day he told Loral that Austin would cease deliveries of the parts due under the existing subcontract unless Loral consented to substantial increases in the prices provided for by that agreement—both retroactively for parts already delivered and prospectively on those not yet shipped—and placed with Austin the order for all 40 parts needed under Loral's second Navy contract. Shortly thereafter, Austin did, indeed, stop delivery. After contacting 10 manufacturers of precision gears and finding none who could produce the parts in time to meet its commitments to the Navy,[1] Loral acceded to Austin's demands; in a letter dated July 22, Loral wrote to Austin that "We have feverishly surveyed other sources of supply and find that because of the prevailing military exigencies, were they to start from scratch as would have to be the case, they could not even remotely begin to deliver on time to meet the delivery requirements established by the Government. . . . Accordingly, we are left with no choice or alternative but to meet your conditions."

Loral thereupon consented to the price increases insisted upon by Austin under the first subcontract and the latter was awarded a second subcontract making it the supplier of all 40 gear parts for Loral's second contract with the Navy.[2] Although Austin was granted until September to resume deliveries, Loral did, in fact, receive parts in August and was able to produce the radar sets in time to meet its commitments to the Navy on both contracts. After Austin's last delivery under the second subcontract in July, 1967, Loral notified it of its intention to seek recovery of the price increases.

On September 15, 1967, Austin instituted this action against Loral to recover an amount in excess of $17,750 which was still due on the second subcontract. On the same day, Loral commenced an action against Austin claiming damages of some $22,250—the aggregate of the price increases under the first subcontract—on the ground of economic duress. The two actions were consolidated and, following a trial, Austin was awarded the sum it requested and Loral's complaint against Austin was dismissed on the ground that it was not shown that "it could not have obtained the items in question from other sources in time to meet its commitment to the Navy under the first contract." A closely divided Appellate Division affirmed (35 A.D.2d 387, 316 N. Y.S.2d 528, 532). There was no material disagreement concerning the facts; as Justice Steuer stated in the course of his dissent below,

---

1. The best reply Loral received was from a vendor who stated he cou'd commence deliveries sometime in October.

2. Loral makes no claim in this action on the second subcontract.

"[t]he facts are virtually undisputed, nor is there any serious question of law. The difficulty lies in the application of the law to these facts." (35 A.D.2d 392, 316 N.Y.S.2d 534.)

The applicable law is clear and, indeed, is not disputed by the parties. A contract is voidable on the ground of duress when it is established that the party making the claim was forced to agree to it by means of a wrongful threat precluding the exercise of his free will. . . . The existence of economic duress or business compulsion is demonstrated by proof that "immediate possession of needful goods is threatened" . . . or, more particularly, in cases such as the one before us, by proof that one party to a contract has threatened to breach the agreement by withholding goods unless the other party agrees to some further demand. . . . However, a mere threat by one party to breach the contract by not delivering the required items, though wrongful, does not in itself constitute economic duress. It must also appear that the threatened party could not obtain the goods from another source of supply [3] and that the ordinary remedy of an action for breach of contract would not be adequate.[4]

We find without any support in the record the conclusion reached by the courts below that Loral failed to establish that it was the victim of economic duress. On the contrary, the evidence makes out a classic case, as a matter of law, of such duress.[5]

It is manifest that Austin's threat—to stop deliveries unless the prices were increased—deprived Loral of its free will. As bearing on this, Loral's relationship with the Government is most significant. As mentioned above, its contract called for staggered monthly deliveries of the radar sets, with clauses calling for liquidated damages and possible cancellation on default. Because of its production schedule, Loral was, in July, 1966, concerned with meeting its delivery requirements in September, October and November, and it was for the sets to be delivered in those months that the withheld gears were needed. Loral had to plan ahead and the substantial liquidated damages for which it would be liable, plus the threat of default, were genuine possibilities. Moreover, Loral did a substantial portion of its busi-

---

3. See, e. g., Du Pont de Nemours & Co. v. J. I. Hass Co., 303 N.Y. 785, 103 N.E.2d 896, supra; Gallagher Switchboard Corp. v. Heckler Elec. Co., 36 Misc.2d 225, 226, 232 N.Y.S.2d 590, 591, supra; 30 East End v. World Steel Prods. Corp., Sup., 110 N.Y.S. 2d 754, 757.

4. See, e. g., Kohn v. Kenton Assoc., 27 A.D.2d 709, 280 N.Y.S.2d 520; Colonie Constr. Corp. v. De Lollo, 25 A.D.2d 464, 465, 266 N.Y.S.2d 283, 285; Halperin v. Wolosoff, 282 App.Div. 876, 124 N.Y.S.2d 572; J. R. Constr. Corp. v. Berkeley Apts., 259 App.Div. 830,

19 N.Y.S.2d 500; Boss v. Hutchinson, 182 App.Div. 88, 92, 169 N.Y.S. 513, 516.

5. The suggestion advanced that we are precluded from reaching this determination because the trial court's findings of fact have been affirmed by the Appellate Division ignores the question to be decided. That question, undoubtedly one of law (see Cohen and Karger, Powers of the New York Court of Appeals [1952], § 115, p. 492), is, accepting the facts found, did the courts below properly apply the law to them.

ness with the Government, and it feared that a failure to deliver as agreed upon would jeopardize its chances for future contracts. These genuine concerns do not merit the label " 'self-imposed, undisclosed and subjective' " which the Appellate Division majority placed upon them. It was perfectly reasonable for Loral, or any other party similarly placed, to consider itself in an emergency, duress situation.

. . . [T]he parts needed for the October schedule were delivered in late August and early September. Even so, Loral had to "work . . . around the clock" to meet its commitments. Considering that the best offer Loral received from the other vendors it contacted was commencement of delivery sometime in October, which, as the record shows, would have made it late in its deliveries to the Navy in both September and October, Loral's claim that it had no choice but to accede to Austin's demands is conclusively demonstrated.

We find unconvincing Austin's contention that Loral, in order to meet its burden, should have contacted the Government and asked for an extension of its delivery dates so as to enable it to purchase the parts from another vendor. Aside from the consideration that Loral was anxious to perform well in the Government's eyes, it could not be sure when it would obtain enough parts from a substitute vendor to meet its commitments. The only promise which it received from the companies it contacted was for *commencement* of deliveries, not full supply, and, with vendor delay common in this field, it would have been nearly impossible to know the length of the extension it should request. It must be remembered that Loral was producing a needed item of military hardware. Moreover, there is authority for Loral's position that nonperformance by a subcontractor is not an excuse for default in the main contract. (See, e. g., McBride & Wachtel, Government Contracts, § 35.10, [11].) In light of all this, Loral's claim should not be held insufficiently supported because it did not request an extension from the Government.

Loral, as indicated above, also had the burden of demonstrating that it could not obtain the parts elsewhere within a reasonable time, and there can be no doubt that it met this burden. The 10 manufacturers whom Loral contacted comprised its entire list of "approved vendors" for precision gears and none was able to commence delivery soon enough.[6] As Loral was producing a highly sophisticated item of military machinery requiring parts made to the strictest engineering standards, it would be unreasonable to hold that Loral should have gone to other vendors, with whom it was either unfamiliar or dissatisfied, to procure the needed parts. As Justice Steuer noted in his dissent, Loral "contacted all the manufacturers whom it believed capa-

---

6. Loral, as do many manufacturers, maintains a list of "approved vendors," that is, vendors whose products, facilities, techniques and performance have been inspected and found satisfactory.

ble of making these parts" (35 A.D.2d at p. 393, 316 N.Y.S.2d at p. 534), and this was all the law requires.

It is hardly necessary to add that Loral's normal legal remedy of accepting Austin's breach of the contract and then suing for damages would have been inadequate under the circumstances, as Loral would still have had to obtain the gears elsewhere with all the concomitant consequences mentioned above. In other words, Loral actually had no choice, when the prices were raised by Austin, except to take the gears at the "coerced" prices and then sue to get the excess back.

Austin's final argument is that Loral, even if it did enter into the contract under duress, lost any rights it had to a refund of money by waiting, until July, 1967, long after the termination date of the contract, to disaffirm it. It is true that one who would recover moneys allegedly paid under duress must act promptly to make his claim known. . . . In this case, Loral delayed making its demand for a refund until three days after Austin's last delivery on the second subcontract. Loral's reason—for waiting until that time—is that it feared another stoppage of deliveries which would again put it in an untenable situation. Considering Austin's conduct in the past, this was perfectly reasonable, as the possibility of an application by Austin of further business compulsion still existed until all of the parts were delivered.

In sum, the record before us demonstrates that Loral agreed to the price increases in consequence of the economic duress employed by Austin. Accordingly, the matter should be remanded to the trial court for a computation of its damages.

The order appealed from should be modified, with costs, by reversing so much thereof as affirms the dismissal of defendant Loral Corporation's claim and, except as so modified, affirmed.

BERGAN, JUDGE (dissenting).

Whether acts charged as constituting economic duress produce or do not produce the damaging effect attributed to them is normally a routine type of factual issue.

Here the fact question was resolved against Loral both by the Special Term and by the affirmance at the Appellate Division. It should not be open for different resolution here. . . .

When the testimony of the witnesses who actually took part in the negotiations for the two disputing parties is examined, sharp conflicts of fact emerge. Under Austin's version the request for a renegotiation of the existing contract was based on Austin's contention that Loral had failed to carry out an understanding as to the items to be furnished under that contract and this was the source of dissatisfaction which led both to a revision of the existing agreement and to entering into a new one.

This is not necessarily and as a matter of law to be held economic duress. On this appeal it is needful to look at the facts resolved in favor of Austin most favorably to that party. Austin's version of events was that a threat was not made but rather a request to accommodate the closing of its plant for a customary vacation period in accordance with the general understanding of the parties.

Moreover, critical to the issue of economic duress was the availability of alternative suppliers to the purchaser Loral. . . .

Austin asserted and Loral admitted on cross-examination that there were many suppliers listed in a trade registry but that Loral chose to rely only on those who had in the past come to them for orders and with whom they were familiar. It was, therefore, at least a fair issue of fact whether under the circumstances such conduct was reasonable and made what might otherwise have been a commercially understandable renegotiation an exercise of duress.

The order should be affirmed.

BURKE, SCILEPPI and GIBSON, JJ., concur with FULD, C. J.

BERGAN, J., dissents and votes to affirm in a separate opinion in which BREITEL and JASEN, JJ., concur.

NOTES

(1) *Objective Standard?* Does the court apply the test for duress that the danger must have been sufficient to "overcome the mind of a person of ordinary firmness"? See Note, p. 258 supra. Holmes once remarked that to apply a requirement of ordinary courage in duress cases is "an attempt to apply an external standard of conduct in the wrong place." Silsbee v. Webber, 171 Mass. 378, 50 N.E. 555 (1898).[a] And Holmes was usually insistent on objective criteria in the law.

(2) *Questions.* What cases do you find earlier in this chapter that might have been decided as they were on grounds of coercion but were reasoned in other terms?

Suppose that Loral had renounced its agreement with Austin a year before it did, shortly after acceding to Austin's demands. Laying aside the problem of duress, would it have been justified in renouncing the price increases? Would it have been justified in renouncing the purchase order under the second Navy contract? What is the answer to these questions under the New York Gen.Obl.L., § 5–1103, p. 262 supra? What is the answer apart from such a statute?

(3) *Problem.* Mitchell, a truckdriver for the Herrin Transportation Company, was injured in a collision with a garbage truck driven by Crane. The accident was arguably Crane's fault. Crane's employer, the Sanitation Company, offered to pay all loss and expense suffered to date by Mitchell and Herrin if both would execute a release discharging Sanitation and Crane of any further liability. Mitchell was reluctant to sign, fearing fur-

a. See also Rubenstein v. Rubenstein,
20 N.J. 359, 120 A.2d 11 (1956).

ther medical expense from his injury, but Herrin was eager for reimbursement for the damage to its truck. Herrin threatened to fire Mitchell unless he signed the release, and he did so. His injury has since caused further expense. May he avoid the release for duress? If Sanitation's offer was designed to induce Herrin to exercise its influence over Mitchell, would that make a difference? See Mitchell v. C. C. Sanitation Company, 430 S.W.2d 933 (Tex.Civ.App.1968), writ ref. n. r. e.

Judge Jerome Frank maintained that when a corporate employer takes a release from an ordinary employee who has been injured on the job it should be scrutinized with special care. Such an employee, he said, is entitled to protection from the courts after the fashion of that given to seamen as "wards of admiralty." Ricketts v. Pennsylvania R. Co., 153 F.2d 757, 760, 767–68, 164 A.L.R. 387 (1946) (concurring opinion). If that view were accepted, how would it apply to Mitchell's case?

VICTIM'S OPTIONS

Some threats are so empty ("last opportunity to buy at this low price") that they cannot well amount to duress in a legal sense. In most cases where an issue of duress is fairly arguable, it has to be asked whether the victim of the threat was opportunistic in yielding to it, or might have resisted it and found a reasonably satisfactory remedy for any resulting injury. In the leading case on duress of goods, the defendant, a pawnbroker, argued that the plaintiff borrower might have gone to law to regain the property being wrongfully withheld from him. (Instead, he overpaid his debt to get it.) But the court said, "plaintiff might have had such an immediate want of his goods that an action of trover would not do his business." [a] Since then, allowance has regularly been made for the delay attendant on legal proceedings. [b]

If the threat is one to sue for a money judgment, the obvious mode of resistance is to make a defense. Some legal proceedings, however, such as mortgage foreclosure and body seizure, commonly put the debtor in a situation of greater urgency. Even so, he may have recourse to injunctive relief, or to damages for abuse of legal process. To forego such a remedy, in favor of a settlement, is naturally prejudicial to the debtor when he later complains of duress. Should the law insist on its preference that wrongful threats be met

---

a. Astley v. Reynolds, 2 Str. 915, 93 Eng.Rep. 939 (K.B. 1732). See Goff and Jones, The Law of Restitution 148 ff. (1966).

b. E. g., Pecos Const. Co. v. Mortgage Invest. Co. of El Paso, 80 N.M. 680, 459 P.2d 842 (1960); Ross Systems v. Linden Dari-Delite, 35 N.J. 329, 173 A.2d 258 (1961) ("no immediate and adequate remedy in the courts"). See also Silsbee v. Webber, 171 Mass. 378, 50 N.E. 555 (1898), as to the shortfall in the law of its own aspirations.

In a somewhat related connection, it has been said that "the notion of the arms' length transaction still requires that the 'arm' hold a boxing glove, rather than a mace." Roberts, J., dissenting in Fratto v. New Amsterdam Casualty Co., 434 Pa. 136, 252 A. 2d 606, 609, 610 (1969).

by resort to the courts? Professor Dawson observes that if the "freedom to litigate" is prized, to control abuses of it by injunction or tort recoveries impairs that freedom more directly than to do so through relief for duress. "The most that is sought," in the latter form, "is judicial review of a settlement, after surrender to the pressure. The object is neither to transfer nor to prevent losses but to cancel out the gain."c

NOTES

(1) *Problem.* In wartime, when the national interest requires a program of rapid production of ships for the Government, a large shipbuilding firm drives a hard bargain for its services, yielding immense profits. The Government seeks later to reclaim part of its cost, charging the firm with duress. Is there a common-law remedy? Apart from making a one-sided bargain, what responses to the pressure might the Government have made? Should the courts pass judgment on its choice of responses? When it seeks a judicial remedy for duress, is there any way for the courts to avoid passing such a judgment? See United States v. Bethlehem Steel Corporation, 315 U.S. 289 (1952).d

(2) *Problem.* The Smith Company gave an estimate to the King Company for the price of supplying an overhead crane—about $17,000—to be part of an Atomic Energy Commission plant. The next day King, having bid for the job of building the plant, was awarded a contract which contained "penalties" for noncompliance. On the following day Smith agreed orally to supply the crane specified for the plant at the stated price. Smith repudiated the agreement soon afterward. King looked for another supplier, but found that Smith was the only one who could supply a crane that the Commission would approve. Therefore he contracted in writing to buy the same crane from Smith for more than $30,000. King received the crane, installed it, and paid about $26,000. Then he refused to pay more. Smith sued for the balance, and King asserted a counterclaim for overpayment. The trial court found that King had agreed to abandon and rescind the oral contract by reason of fear of economic loss, but it allowed Smith to recover some $4,000, the unpaid part of the price under the written contract. What argument would you make for reversal of the judgment? See King Construction Co. v. W. M. Smith Electric Co., 350 S.W. 2d 940 (Tex.Civ.App.1961), writ ref. n. r. e.

(b) Concealment, Misrepresentation and Mistake

According to Chancellor Kent: *"Cicero de Officiis,* lib. 3. sec. 12–17, states the case of a corn merchant of Alexandria arriving at Rhodes in a time of great scarcity, with a cargo of grain, and with

c. Dawson, Duress Through Civil Litigation: I, 45 Mich.L.Rev. 571, 577 (1947).

d. For a review of cases in which an official of the Government has exerted sharp pressure on one of its contractors, see Urban Plumbing & Heating Co. v. United States, 408 F.2d 382 (Ct.Cl.1969).

knowledge that a number of other vessels, with similar cargoes, had already sailed from Alexandria for Rhodes, and whom he had passed on the voyage. He then puts the question, whether the Alexandrine merchant was bound in conscience to inform the buyers of that fact, or to keep silence, and sell his wheat for an extravagant price; and he answers it by saying, that, in his opinion, good faith would require of a just and candid man, a frank disclosure of the fact." a

What is the requirement that the law makes, as opposed to the demand of conscience, for disclosing facts in a bargaining context? Many courts have said that they will not insist on the degree of disclosure that a person of exceptional scruple might make. On the other hand, in allowing bargaining advantages to be secured by persons of little scruple, the law may attach a competitive disadvantage to conscientious conduct.

NOTE

Expert Knowledge. Should there be special rules about information derived from training and experience? It is generally understood that dealers in certain types of merchandise, such as antiques and rare coins, for example, trade on their expertness, and they are not expected to disclose to their customers all the elements that enter into their evaluations. Similarly, in purchasing mineral interests, firms engaged in prospecting for oil and gas preserve high secrecy over the information they have acquired through drilling and seismological tests. The expense of acquiring such expertness would not be justified if it did not yield bargaining advantages. To some extent the same consideration affects the degree of disclosure required in most commercial exchanges. Compare the market expertness of middlemen, mentioned in Note 2, p. 229 supra.

The case that follows is a suit in tort, for deceit, rather than in contract. It demonstrates, however, the wide extent of the privilege commonly allowed to keep silent about material facts in the bargaining process.

SWINTON v. WHITINSVILLE SAV. BANK

Supreme Judicial Court of Massachusetts, 1942.
311 Mass. 677, 42 N.E.2d 808, 141 A.L.R. 965.

QUA, JUSTICE. The declaration alleges that on or about September 12, 1938, the defendant sold the plaintiff a house in Newton to be occupied by the plaintiff and his family as a dwelling; that at the time of the sale the house "was infested with termites, an insect that is most dangerous and destructive to buildings"; that the defendant

---

a. 2 Kent's Commentaries 491 * n. c (3d ed. 1836). Kent cited Grotius, Puffendorf, and Pothier for the contrary opinion, but he added, "It is a little singular, however, that some of the best ethical writers under the Christian dispensation, should complain of the moral lessons of Cicero, as being too austere in their texture, and too sublime in speculation, for actual use."

knew the house was so infested; that the plaintiff could not readily observe this condition upon inspection; that "knowing the internal destruction that these insects were creating in said house", the defendant falsely and fraudulently concealed from the plaintiff its true condition; that the plaintiff at the time of his purchase had no knowledge of the termites, exercised due care thereafter, and learned of them about August 30, 1940; and that, because of the destruction that was being done and the dangerous condition that was being created by the termites the plaintiff was put to great expense for repairs and for the installation of termite control in order to prevent the loss and destruction of said house.

There is no allegation of any false statement or representation, or of the uttering of a half truth which may be tantamount to a falsehood.   There is no intimation that the defendant by any means prevented the plaintiff from acquiring information as to the condition of the house.   There is nothing to show any fiduciary relation between the parties, or that the plaintiff stood in a position of confidence toward or dependence upon the defendant.   So far as appears the parties made a business deal at arm's length.   The charge is concealment and nothing more; and it is concealment in the simple sense of mere failure to reveal, with nothing to show any peculiar duty to speak. The characterization of the concealment as false and fraudulent of course adds nothing in the absence of further allegations of fact. Province Securities Corp. v. Maryland Casualty Co., 269 Mass. 75, 92, 168 S.E. 252.

If this defendant is liable on this declaration every seller is liable who fails to disclose any nonapparent defect known to him in the subject of the sale which materially reduces its value and which the buyer fails to discover.   Similarly it would seem that every buyer would be liable who fails to disclose any nonapparent virtue known to him in the subject of the purchase which materially enhances its value and of which the seller is ignorant.   See Goodwin v. Agassiz, 283 Mass. 358, 186 N.E. 659.   The law has not yet, we believe, reached the point of imposing upon the frailties of human nature a standard so idealistic as this.   That the particular case here stated by the plaintiff possesses a certain appeal to the moral sense is scarcely to be denied.   Probably the reason is to be found in the facts that the infestation of buildings by termites has not been common in Massachusetts and constitutes a concealed risk against which buyers are off their guard. But the law cannot provide special rules for termites and can hardly attempt to determine liability according to the varying probabilities of the existence and discovery of different possible defects in the subjects of trade.   The rule of nonliability for bare nondisclosure has been stated and followed by this court in [seven cases cited].   It is adopted in the American Law Institute's Restatement of Torts, § 551. See Williston on Contracts, Rev.Ed., §§ 1497, 1498, 1499.

The order sustaining the demurrer is affirmed, and judgment is to be entered for the defendant. Keljikian v. Star Brewing Co., 303 Mass. 53, 55–63, 20 N.E.2d 465.

So ordered.

NOTES

(1) *Questions.* Does it follow from this holding that the plaintiff could not have rescinded the sale, on establishing the facts he alleged? If the decision had been to the contrary, overruling the demurrer, would it follow that the plaintiff *could* have rescinded the sale? (An answer to this question is suggested by the next main case.) If the sale had not been executed, and the seller had brought an action against the buyer for specific performance, would it have succeeded?

(2) *Authorities.* Although the Swinton holding has been approved in several courts, there are some contrary decisions. For a twenty-page Annotation on the duty of a vendor to give information to a purchaser as to termite infestation, see 27 A.L.R.3d 972 (1968).

(3) *Concealment and Stocks.* With respect to transactions in securities, Congress has committed a major role in protecting investors from deceptive "devices" to the Securities and Exchange Commission. In turn, the S. E. C. has formulated rules for identifying fraud, including omissions to disclose material facts. The effects of these rules must be studied in another course, but it may be observed here that corporate officials are expected to strike a nice balance between optimism and pessimism in preparing press releases. For a thoughtful set of opinions on this problem, see S. E. C. v. Great American Industries, Inc., 407 F.2d 453 (2d Cir. 1968), cert. denied, 395 U.S. 920 (1969). One of the judges, referring to the main case, remarked: "The Securities and Exchange Commission, seeking to enjoin manipulation of such 'intricate merchandise' as securities . . ., should not be fettered by such a wholehearted embrace of the doctrine of caveat emptor." (Irving R. Kaufman, J., concurring, at 462, 463)

KANNAVOS v. ANNINO

Supreme Judicial Court of Massachusetts, 1969.
356 Mass. 42, 247 N.E.2d 708.

[In 1961 or 1962, Mrs. Carrie Annino bought a one-family dwelling in Springfield: No. 11, Ingersoll Grove.[a] She converted it into a multi-family building with eight apartments, without obtaining a building permit, and in knowing violation of the city zoning ordinance. The house was in a "Residence A" district, where multi-family uses were prohibited. In 1965 a real-estate broker was employed to try to sell the property. He placed newspaper ads, of which the following is an example: "Income gross $9,600 yr in lg. single house,

---

a. Throughout the transactions described, Mrs. Annino acted as the authorized agent for the Annino Realty Trust. Her co-defendants, not mentioned hereafter, were Samuel Annino and Joseph Santospirito.

converted to 8 lovely, completely furn. (includ. TV and china) apts. 8 baths, ideal for couple to live free with excellent income. By apt. only. Foote Realty."

[Apostolos Kannavos read one of the ads, and got in touch with the broker, Foote. Foote showed him the house, and gave him income and expense figures supplied by Mrs. Annino. Without the aid of a lawyer, Kannavos contracted to buy the property, and did so, borrowing money from a bank for the purpose, and giving it a mortgage. At the closing, attorneys for the seller and for the mortgagee were present, and the latter prepared the papers. Mrs. Annino and Foote knew that Kannavos' reason for buying was to rent the apartments. He was unaware of any zoning or building permit violation, and would not have purchased the property if he had known of any such violation. It was worth substantially less if operated only as a single-family dwelling than it was as an apartment building.

[Soon after the sale, the city started legal proceedings to abate the non-conforming use of the building.[b] Kannavos brought a bill in equity against Mrs. Annino to rescind the purchase. The trial court overruled a demurrer, and granted rescission on the basis of findings by a master. Mrs. Annino appealed.

[It appeared that Kannavos had immigrated from Greece in 1957, when he was about thirty years old. In this country he had learned English, and become a self-employed hairdresser. It was found that he made no inquiry of anyone about zoning or building permits before or during the closing, and that no statements were made to him on these subjects. Everything that was said to him by or on behalf of the seller was substantially true.]

CUTTER, JUSTICE. . . . We assume that, if the vendors had been wholly silent and had made no references whatsoever to the use of the Ingersoll Grove houses, they could not have been found to have made any misrepresentation. See Swinton v. Whitinsville Sav. Bank, 311 Mass. 677, 678–679, 42 N.E.2d 808, 141 A.L.R. 965,[1] where this court affirmed an order sustaining a demurrer to a declaration in an action of tort brought by a purchaser of a house. . . . The court (p. 679) indicated that it was applying a long standing "rule of nonliability for *bare nondisclosure*" (emphasis supplied).

---

b. As to other, similar properties that Kannavos (and an associate) also bought from Mrs. Annino, the city also asserted violations of the building code, but the opinion does not make it clear whether or not No. 11 was in question on this score.

1. The *Swinton* case may not represent the law elsewhere. See Restatement 2d: Torts, § 551 (Tent. Draft No. 11, April 15, 1965), p. 43; Prosser, Torts (3d ed.), § 101, p. 711. Cf. discussions of situations in landlord and tenant cases like Cutter v. Hamlen, 147 Mass. 471, 474, 18 N.E. 397, 1 L.R.A. 429; Stumpf v. Leland, 242 Mass. 168, 172–174, 136 N.E. 399; Cooper v. Boston Housing Auth., 342 Mass. 38, 40, 172 N.E.2d 117. For general consideration of silence as misrepresentation, see Restatement: Restitution, § 8; Williston, Contracts (2d ed.) § 1497.

As in the *Swinton* case, the parties here were dealing at arm's length, the vendees were in no way prevented from acquiring information, and the vendors stood in no fiduciary relationship to the vendees. In two aspects, however, the present cases differ from the *Swinton* case: viz. (a) The vendees themselves could have found out about the zoning violations by inquiry through public records, whereas in the *Swinton* case the purchaser would have probably discovered the presence of termites only by retaining expert investigators; and (b) there was something more here than the "bare nondisclosure" of the seller in the *Swinton* case.

(a) We deal first with the affirmative actions by the vendors, their conduct, advertising, and statements. Was enough said and done by the vendors so that they were bound to disclose more to avoid deception of the vendees and reliance by them upon a half truth? In other words, did the statements made by the vendors in their advertising and otherwise take the cases out of the "rule of nonliability for bare nondisclosure" applied in the *Swinton* case?

Although there may be "no duty imposed upon one party to a transaction to speak for the information of the other . . . if he does speak with reference to a given point of information, voluntarily or at the other's request, he is bound to speak honestly and to divulge all the material facts bearing upon the point that lie within his knowledge. Fragmentary information may be as misleading . . . as active misrepresentation, and half-truths may be as actionable as whole lies . . .." See Harper & James, Torts, § 7.14. See also Restatement: Torts, § 529; Williston, Contracts (2d ed.) §§ 1497–1499. The existence of substantially this principle was assumed in the *Swinton* case, 311 Mass. 677, 678, 42 N.E.2d 808, 141 A.L.R. 965, in the first sentence of the passage from that case quoted above. Massachusetts decisions have applied this principle. See Kidney v. Stoddard, 7 Metc. 252, 254–255 (a father represented that his son was entitled to credit but failed to disclose that the son was a minor; statement treated as a fraudulent representation); Burns v. Dockray, 156 Mass. 135, 137, 30 N.E. 551 (assertion that title was good [see Lyman v. Romboli, 293 Mass. 373, 374, 199 N.E. 916] but omitting to refer to the possible insanity of one whose incompetence might cloud title); Van Houten v. Morse, 162 Mass. 414, 417–419, 38 N.E. 705, 26 L.R.A. 430 (partial disclosure by a woman to her fiancé about a prior divorce). See also . . . Boston Five Cents Sav. Bank v. Brooks, 309 Mass. 52, 55–56, 34 N.E.2d 435, 437 ("Deception need not be direct . . .. Declarations and conduct calculated to mislead . . . which . . . do mislead one . . . acting reasonably are enough to constitute fraud"). Cf. Wade v. Ford Motor Co., 341 Mass. 596, 597–598, 171 N.E.2d 282.

The master's report provides ample basis for treating the present cases as within the decisions just cited. The original advertisements in effect offered the houses as investment properties and referred to them as single houses converted to apartments. The investment aspect of the houses was emphasized by Foote's action in furnishing income and expense figures. There was an express assertion that 11 Ingersoll Grove was "being rented to the public for multi-family purposes" and that Kannavos and Bellas "could continue to operate . . . [the other properties] as multi-dwelling property." The master's conclusions indicate that this statement applied to all the properties.[2] The buildings were divided into apartments. The sales included refrigerators, stoves, and other furnishings appropriate for apartment use, as well as real estate. The vendors knew that the vendees were planning to continue to use the buildings for apartments, and yet the vendors still failed to disclose the zoning and building violations. We conclude that enough was done affirmatively to make the disclosure inadequate and partial, and, in the circumstances, intentionally deceptive and fraudulent.

(b) The second difference between these cases and the *Swinton* case is the character of the defect not disclosed.

In the *Swinton* case, the presence of predatory insects threatened the structure sold. In the absence of any seller's representations whatsoever, there was no duty to disclose this circumstance, even though doubtless it would have been difficult to discover. In the present cases, the defect in the premises related to a matter of public regulation, the zoning and building ordinances. Its applicability to these premises could have been discovered by these vendees or by the vendees' counsel if, acting with prudence, they had retained counsel, which they did not. The bank mortgagee's counsel presumably was looking only to the protection of the bank's security position. Nevertheless, where there is reliance on fraudulent representations or upon statements and action treated as fraudulent, our cases have not barred plaintiffs from recovery merely because they "did not use due diligence . . . [when they] could readily have ascertained from . . . records" what the true facts were. See Yorke v. Taylor, 332 Mass. 368, 373, 124 N.E.2d 912. There this court allowed rescission because of the negligent misrepresentation, innocent but false, of the current assessed value of the property being sold. Here the representations made by the advertising and the vendors' conduct and statements in effect were that the property was multi-family housing suitable for investment and that the housing could continue to be used for that purpose. Because the vendors did as much as they did do, they were bound to do more. Failing to do so, they were responsible for misrepresentation. We think the situation is comparable to that in Yorke v. Taylor, 332 Mass. 368, 374, 124 N.E.2d 912, even though

---

2. In any event some discussions with respect to all these properties in the same neighborhood were going on about the same time and the later transaction appears to have been commenced either before or about the time the earlier one was completed.

there the misrepresentation was "not consciously false" and here it was by half truth.

We hold that the vendors' conduct entitled the vendees to rescind. See Yorke v. Taylor, 332 Mass. 368, 371–372, 374, 124 N.E.2d 912; Restatement: Contracts, §§ 472, 489; Restatement: Restitution, § 28; Williston, Contracts (2d ed.) §§ 1497–1500. There was, in our opinion, much more than "bare nondisclosure" as in the *Swinton* case. Cf. Spencer v. Gabriel, 328 Mass. 1, 2, 101 N.E.2d 369; Donahue v. Stephens, 342 Mass. 89, 92, 172 N.E.2d 101.

[The court affirmed the decree below overruling the demurrer. However, it reversed the final decree so that there might be further consideration of the relief, in view of a fire that had occurred at No. 11 after that decree.]

NOTES

(1) *Question.* Does it follow from this decision that Kannavos could have maintained an action in deceit against Mrs. Annino? The requisites of that action, and the remedy it affords, are dealt with in detail in courses on torts. It should be noted, however, that contract remedies are not the only guarantees of minimum decencies in the bargaining process.

(2) *Another Termite Case.* After the death of their mother, Ray and Ralph Lind sold her house and two smaller buildings on the premises to Mr. and Mrs. Fred Maser. Mr. Maser discovered termites about a month after taking possession. He called an expert, who found serious damage in the principal structures, caused by general termite infestation. The Masers sued the Linds for damages, alleging fraud.

Maser was a man in his 40's, employed in a manufacturing firm, and had lived about three blocks away from the property. He testified that he had never heard of a termite. The sale was effected without advertising, and without the services of a broker or attorney. On two occasions Maser made an ordinary examination of the living quarters, but the damage was not exposed to view. According to him, Ray Lind said to him, "Well, these are good, sound buildings and they will make you a good investment." The Linds testified that they did not know there were termites in the houses, but there was some impeaching evidence. The purchase price was $16,250. After a jury trial, the Masers obtained a judgment for some $3,-000, and the Linds appealed.

Held: Affirmed. "A misrepresentation of the condition of buildings is not always remedial, and may constitute a mere expression of opinion upon which a purchaser may not rely, depending on the circumstances of the particular case. Such a misrepresentation may be actionable if made and relied upon as a positive statement of an existing fact where the purchaser by the exercise of ordinary prudence is unable to discover the true damaged condition. . . . We have consistently held that proof of scienter is unnecessary, a misrepresentation being actionable even though made innocently and with honest belief of its truth." Maser v. Lind, 181 Neb. 365, 148 N.W.2d 831, 22 A.L.R.3d 965 (1967).

How would this case have been decided by the Massachusetts court?

MISREPRESENTATION

Misrepresentation is a ground for rescinding a contract, closely related to concealment. As a predicate for a tort action, it may be necessary for the plaintiff to establish that the defendant made the misrepresentation knowing it to be false, or at least with reckless disregard for its truth. This element in deceit actions is known as *scienter*. The requirement was insisted on in 19th century English cases, and remains influential in many courts.[a] In contract law it generally has never had the same force, owing partly to the equitable character of rescission. See Halpert v. Rosenthal, —— R.I. ——, 267 A.2d 730 (1970), a "termite case" making the distinction. As a rule, a party to a contract may avoid it if the other party obtained his assent by an innocent misrepresentation, i. e., one that the party making it believed to be true. What difference between the functions of tort and contract law might explain this difference in sensitivity to the nature of a falsehood?

In both tort and contract law relief for misrepresentation is restricted in some ways that merit at least a mention. (To the extent that they are distinctive, the principles of tort law will not be pursued here.)

It has sometimes been held that a misrepresentation of law is innocuous. The same thought underlies the view that *mistake* of law is not a ground for relief: everyone should know the law. Apart from the general discredit that has fallen on such reasoning, its influence on misrepresentation cases has been limited in practice. One reason is that the author of a misrepresentation of law is frequently one better placed to know the law than the victim of it is: a lawyer speaking to his client, an insurance agent to a customer, and so on. In such cases the inequality of competence is perceived as a reason for giving relief.

A misrepresentation of opinion, as opposed to one of fact, is not a ground for relief, by tradition.[b] Doubtless the distinction retains considerable force as it affects ordinary "puffing" of the style, "This property is worth every cent I am asking for it." Yet the distinction has lost much of its clarity, as witness the foregoing note case in which the seller's statement was: "these are good, sound buildings and they will make you a good investment." Again, the relative positions of the parties may influence the decision more than the form of words that was used.

---

a. See Jo Ann Homes at Bellmore, Inc. v. Dworetz, 25 N.Y.2d 112, 250 N.E.2d 214 (1969).

b. See Fifty Associates v. Prudential Insurance Co. of America, 450 F.2d 1007 (9th Cir. 1971) (appraisal of property value).

The misrepresentation must be a material one.[c] This requirement is prominent in insurance litigation, where a misrepresentation by a policy buyer relating to his health is a commonplace ground for rejecting a claim. A policy of medical expense insurance, for example, was voidable because the application for it omitted reference to various prior occasions of hospital treatment, including one for angina pectoris. As to the applicant's prior treatment for an infected toenail, however, the judges thought that the misrepresentation was immaterial.[d] Various standards of materiality have been expressed, and none of them is applied uniformly. They serve the common function, however, of justifying a certain control by judges over the more volatile behavior of juries.

When a contract is enforced in favor of a party who made a misrepresentation, a reason sometimes given is that the other party was negligent in relying on it. Naturally, the degree of diligence required of a party in detecting a falsehood is a function partly of his capacities, partly of the nature of the transaction, and partly of the plausibility of the representation. The question of diligence should be distinguished from the question whether any credence was placed in the representation at all. If it was not relied upon in that sense, no legal consequences follow from a misrepresentation. There can be no complaint about a statement by one who heard it and proceeded to satisfy himself about its accuracy: "reliance and verification are incompatible." [e] There is a necessary dimension in a complaint about misrepresentation, however, that goes beyond the fact of reliance. In the currently preferred formulation, the complainant must show *justifiable* reliance.

Other limitations on relief for misrepresentation mentioned above, notably those having to do with statements of law and statements of opinion, have been considerably relaxed, if not subsumed entirely under the issue last mentioned. There is a plain tendency to consider the character of the statement in question as only one aspect of the broader issue whether or not the complainant justifiably relied upon it.

NOTES

(1) *Problem.* An automobile dealer advertised a four-year-old car as a "CHRYSLER Imperial 2 door hardtop . . .; full power including FACTORY AIR CONDITIONING: there aren't many around like this.
 . . ." Herbert Williams and his brother visited the dealer's lot, examined the car, and took it for an hour's test run. A salesman told him it was air conditioned, "and that Chrysler was a nice car, and all that jazz."

c. For a fascinating problem in materiality and business morality, see Earl v. Saks & Co., 36 Cal.2d 602, 226 P.2d 340 (1951), and a comment on the case in Cahn, The Moral Decision 123 ff. (1959 paperback edition).

d. Delaney v. Prudential Ins. Co., 29 Wis.2d 345, 139 N.W.2d 48 (1966).

e. Hayat Carpet Cleaning Co., Inc. v. Northern Assur. Co., 69 F.2d 805 (2d Cir. 1934) (L. Hand).

Williams bought the car. Several days later he discovered that the knobs marked "air" were for ventilation and that the car was not air conditioned. May he rescind the purchase? Does it matter what time of year the purchase was made? See Williams v. Rank & Son Buick, Inc., 44 Wis.2d 239, 170 N.W.2d 807 (1969) (fraud action; 4–3 decision).

(2) *Confidential Relations.* In attempting to avoid contracts on the ground of overreaching, the key to success often lies in establishing that a relation of trust and confidence existed between the parties, so that the bargain was not an arm's length transaction. In the absence of such a relation, it is said, fraud must be affirmatively shown, and will not be presumed. Furthermore, it is the tradition derived from equity practice that the evidence required to establish fraud must be "clear and convincing"— meeting a more exacting standard than that applied to most issues in civil litigation.

By contrast, when a confidential relation existed, and the party asserting rights under the contract is the one in whom confidence was reposed, he is required to show that the bargain was "fair, conscientious, and beyond the reach of suspicion." Young v. Kaye, 443 Pa. 335, 279 A.2d 759 (1971). In this case, representative of many like it, an elderly man was imposed upon by an ex-convict who provided him services and won his confidence as a "tax consultant." As examples of confidential relations, the court mentioned attorney and client, guardian and ward, principal and agent, and trustee and cestui que trust. (See Note 1, p. 288 supra, on fiduciaries.) But a comprehensive definition of the relation cannot be given, the court said: "It is not restricted to any specific association . . . but is deemed to exist whenever the relative position of the parties is such that one has power and means to take advantage of or exert undue influence over the other." f

(3) *Insurance Law.* The doctrines of concealment and misrepresentation have somewhat specialized application to insurance cases. When an applicant for life insurance is asked whether or not he uses alcohol to excess, the response is likely to be treated as a "matter of opinion," so that all the insurer is entitled to is an honest expression of the applicant's view. In this fashion, and in others more or less direct, it is often made a requirement that the insurer show scienter in order to avoid the contract. See, for instance, Metropolitan Life Ins. Co. v. Fugate, 313 F.2d 788 (5th Cir. 1963): "In his own mind, the decedent may have thought that he was not suffering from alcoholism." But in this case the policy, a contract of life insurance, was avoided because the applicant had actively concealed medical treatments for his affliction. The court said: "There is no room for opinion about the hospital visits."

Innocent misrepresentation is sometimes called "equitable fraud," when used as a basis for rescinding a contract. The implied moral judgment is that one who obtains a contract by making such a misrepresentation should not insist on rights under it, after he learns the truth. Do you see why this judgment might be less forceful in relation to insurance contracts than in relation to other sorts of contracts? See Johnson v. Metropolitan Life Ins. Co., 53 N.J. 423, 251 A.2d 257 (1969).

---

f. See also Ruggieri v. West Forum Corporation, 444 Pa. 175, 282 A.2d 304 (1971), as to trust reposed in a son by his parents.

As to concealment it has been said, in an influential case: "[I]f a man, about to fight a duel, should obtain life insurance without disclosing his intention, it would seem that no argument or additional evidence would be needed to show the fraudulent character of the non-disclosure. On the other hand, where men may reasonably differ as to the materiality of a fact concerning which the insurer might have elicited full information, and did not do so, the insurer occupies no such position of disadvantage in judging of the risk as to make it unjust to require that before the policy is avoided it shall appear, not only that the undisclosed fact was material, but also that it was withheld in bad faith." [g]

MISTAKE

Like concealment and misrepresentation, mistake is sometimes a ground for rescinding a contract. Mistakes in the computation and communication of prices have been explored in Chapter 2. A kind of mistake that may be described as misunderstanding is to be examined in Chapter 6. At this point, by contrast, we consider mistakes having to do with the relative advantages of the bargain as between the parties. The configuration of the law on this subject somewhat resembles that of the law relating to concealment and misrepresentation, the most notable difference being that the element of fault is less prominent in mistake cases.

One limitation commonly placed on relief for mistake, when the relief sought is avoidance of a contract, is that the mistake must be "mutual", i. e., common to the parties. Examples may be found of relief for unilateral mistake, but they are somewhat exceptional. In a concealment case, there is invariably a unilateral mistake. However, in the usual case of that type the party charged with concealment is aware, or should be, that the other party is less well informed than he is. By contrast, the assumption in a "pure" mistake case is that each party supposed the other to be equally informed about the material facts.

A second limitation on relief has to do with the character of the mistake, in relation to the transaction. The operative word, in some formulations of the rule, is "basic".[a] Or it is said that the parties must have been mistaken in an essential point, or that the mistake must go to the root of the contract. Something more than materiality is implied. If it is concluded that the parties to a contract entered into it under a mistake about a fact so basic as to justify rescission,

g. Taft, Cir. J., in Penn Mutual Life Ins. Co. v. Mechanics Savings Bank & Trust Co., 72 F. 413 (6th Cir. 1896); on reh., 73 F. 653 (1896).

a. See Restatement, § 502: "parties . . . both under a mistake regarding a fact assumed by them as the basis on which they entered into the transaction." See Raddue v. Le Sage, 138 Cal.App.2d 852, 292 P.2d 522 (1956).

it would therefore follow that if one party had misrepresented that fact to the other the victim would have had no difficulty, on the score of materiality, in obtaining relief. The converse is not entailed: the subject of a mistake may not be regarded as fundamental to the bargain resulting from it, although it would be characterized as deceit for either party to *induce* a mistake on the point in the mind of the other party.

Identifying basic mistake is sometimes a nice problem of judgment: "In the vital areas the answer will depend upon the magnitude of the mistake, the degree of certainty in the minds of the parties, and the attitude towards the type of transaction involved." [b] An example concerning uncertainty in the minds of the parties is Wood v. Boynton, 64 Wis. 265, 25 N.W. 42 (1885). A girl found a pretty stone, about the size of a canary bird's egg. She did not know what it was. She showed it to a jeweler, who bought it from her for a dollar, although he too did not know what it was. The stone turned out to be an uncut diamond worth an estimated $700. The girl tendered the price back and sued the jeweler for rescission. Judgment for the defendant was affirmed on appeal. "There is no pretense of any mistake as to the identity of the thing sold. . . . When this sale was made the value of the thing sold was open to the investigation of both parties, neither knew its intrinsic value, and, so far as the evidence in this case shows, both supposed that the price paid was adequate." Similarly, it is supposed that if a second-hand book dealer places a valuable first edition on a shelf of $5 books, a sale at that price would not be rescinded, at least if the customer was bargain hunting, and had no reason to suppose the book was misplaced. Professor Warren A. Seavey, co-reporter for the Restatement of Restitution, put this case as one where the book dealer "matches his judgment against that of a purchaser." [c] But he added: "I would suppose that if a valuable first edition, by mistake of the bookseller's clerk, got mixed with a current cheap edition, the $5 purchaser would have to return it." [d]

A celebrated case of avoidance is Sherwood v. Walker, 66 Mich. 568, 33 N.W. 919 (1887), in which the parties were a cattle breeder, Walker, and a banker, Sherwood. Walker sold Sherwood a cow of distinguished ancestry named Rose 2d of Aberlone. Rose went for $80 because both parties believed that she was sterile. When Walker discovered that Rose was pregnant and therefore worth between $750 and $1000, he refused to deliver her and Sherwood sued in replevin. Judgment for plaintiff was reversed on appeal. "If there is a difference or misapprehension as to the substance of the thing bargained for . . . and intended to be sold, then there is no contract; but if it be only a difference in some quality or accident, even though the mistake may have been the actuating motive to the purchaser or sell-

b. Seavey, Problems in Restitution, 7   c. Id., 268.
   Okla.L.Rev. 257, 267 (1954).

        d. Ibid.

er, or both of them, yet the contract remains binding. . . . A barren cow is substantially a different creature than a breeding one. . . . She was not in fact the animal, or the kind of animal, the defendants had intended to sell or the plaintiff to buy." [e]

Referring to Sherwood v. Walker and cases like it, Professor Seavey observed: "Through these cases, where the older common-law rules of contracts would demand the pound of flesh, the rules of restitution help to create a limit beyond which the customs of the horse trader will not be permitted to control the rules of normal bargaining." [f]

NOTES

(1) *Case Comparison.* Can Sherwood v. Walker be distinguished from Wood v. Boynton on the ground that when the suits were brought the diamond had been delivered, but the cow had not? Note that in the former case the court assumed that if an enforceable contract had been made Sherwood could have had a remedy (replevin) based on his ownership of the cow. Can the cases be distinguished at all? Is it helpful to view them as involving the allocation of risks?

(2) *Unilateral Mistake.* Is either the diamond case or the cow case difficult to square with the rule in M. F. Kemper Const. Co. v. City of Los Angeles, p. 142 supra? If the jeweler had known that the stone was a diamond, and Sherwood had known that Rose was pregnant, the cases would have presented problems of unilateral mistake. Compare Restatement Restitution § 9(3) (on "mutual" mistake) with § 12 (on "unilateral" mistake). With that change in the facts, would there have been a different result in either case? Assuming a unilateral mistake in each case, how might it be argued that the results should have been different in *both*?

For discussion of mistake in general, and criticism of the distinction between "unilateral" and "mutual" mistake in particular, see 3 Corbin, §§ 597–600, 605–612; Palmer, Mistake and Unjust Enrichment (1962); Rabin, A Proposed Black-Letter Rule Concerning Mistaken Assumptions in Bargain Transactions, 45 Tex.L.Rev. 1273 (1967).

(3) *Conscious Ignorance.* The firm of Wright and Pierce contracted to prepare a "tax map" of the Town of Wilmington, Massachusetts, upon

---

e. There was a vigorous dissent.

Literati will want to consult Professor Brainerd Currie's ballad about Rose of Aberlone in Student Law., April 1956, 1965, p. 4, Harv.L.S.Record, March 4, 1954, p. 3. The final lines of this epic read:

> She rules the cases, she stalks the page
> Even in this atomic age.
> In radioactive tracts of land,
> In hardly collectible notes of hand,
> In fiddles of dubious pedigree,
> In releases of liability,
> In zoning rules unknown to lessors,
> In weird conceits of law professors,
> In printers' bids and ailing kings,
> In all mutations and sorts of things,
> In many a hypothetical
> With characters alphabetical,
> In many a subtle and sly disguise
> There lurks the ghost of her sad brown eyes.
> That she will turn up in some set of facts is
> Almost as certain as death and taxes:
> For students of law must still atone
> For the shame of Rose of Aberlone.

f. Seavey, op. cit. supra footnote b, at 268.

a bid of $11,350. The town assessors had previously informed the firm that the number of individual properties in the town was about 4,500. They offered to let the firm inspect the town records, but said that an examination would not disclose the true number because of confusion in the records. No examination was made. The number proved to be 5,820. When it appeared that there were many more parcels than expected, the firm complained of losing money, and a town official requested that the work be completed pending negotiations. When the work was done, the town refused to pay more than the contract price, and the firm sued it. From judgment for the town, the plaintiff appealed. *Held:* Affirmed. The case was not a proper one for rescission and recovery in quantum meruit. "Plaintiff realized fully that the actual number was unascertained . . . Plaintiff not only had reason to suspect that the estimate was not accurate, but also failed to request the protection against inaccuracy which it utilized in such instances 'whenever possible' [according to the evidence]. We do not subscribe to the district court's pronouncement that further payment was 'morally due.' " Wright and Pierce v. Town of Wilmington, 290 F.2d 30 (1st Cir. 1961).

(4) *Questions.* When mistake is asserted as a reason for avoiding the compromise of a dispute, is the problem different in kind from that of rescinding a sale of goods? If a difference of approach is required at all, how would you express it? Refer to Fiege v. Boehm, p. 278 supra, and the cases cited in the notes after it. Was any of these a case where the court could properly have ruled that the agreement was voidable for mistake? The second agreement in Browning v. Johnson (Note 4, p. 284 supra) for instance? Do you see distinctions among the cases in this respect?

WARRANTY COMPARED

Many problems arising in sales of goods that might otherwise be solved in terms of concealment, mistake, or the like, are dealt with instead by reference to warranties given by a seller, and particularly "implied" warranties. The following section of this chapter touches on some of the means used to qualify a seller's warranty, or to limit a buyer's remedy for breach of warranty, but the content and scope of warranties must be examined in a course on commercial transactions. A series of Code provisions on the subject begins with UCC 2–312, which states a warranty by the seller that "the title conveyed shall be good, and its transfer rightful." In this manner the risk of mistake about ownership of the article sold is placed largely on the seller, unless the warranty is excluded or modified as permitted by the section.

When a warranty on a given subject is disclaimed, obviously the buyer may have difficulty establishing a right to relief for mistake on that subject. If he can establish a misrepresentation by the seller he is more likely to find a remedy, owing to the grounding that fraud claims have in tort law. Sometimes a recovery for "fraud" is permitted when it seems to be only a surrogate for the seller's liability on a warranty, which is foreclosed by a provision of the sale contract.

This is the case especially when the seller's expression characterized as fraudulent is in the form of a promise, and he is held accountable without a showing that he intended any deception. For a notable case of this character, see Clements Auto Co. v. Service Bureau Corp., 444 F.2d 169 (8th Cir. 1971).

Implied warranties are traditionally associated with sales of goods, but transactions of other types have been subjected to warranty analysis with increasing frequency in recent years. See Note, Implied Warranties, p. 615 infra. Buyers of newly-built houses have recently found an expanded remedy on this basis in some courts.[a] Developments along this line tend to narrow the range in which principles of mistake and misrepresentation operate. In large part, however, the extension of implied warranties to non-sale transactions has occurred in relation to personal injury claims. Problems such as termite infestation in old houses are not, as yet, within the purview of the law of implied warranties.

NOTE

Promissory Fraud. For a promise made in bargaining with the intent not to keep it, it is clear in most courts that the promisee is entitled at least to rescission.[b] It may be said that the fact misrepresented is the promisor's intention—a state of mind. A claim for damages is more questionable, especially in the face of disclaimer clauses such as appeared in the Clements Auto case. As against oral assurances in the bargaining process, the provisions of a written contract are commonly reinforced by the parol evidence rule. Cases concerning this doctrine are presented in Chapter 6.

SEARS, ROEBUCK AND CO. v. JARDEL CO.

United States Court of Appeals, Third Circuit, 1970.
421 F.2d 1048.

VAN DUSEN, CIRCUIT JUDGE. This is an appeal from a District Court order entering summary judgment for the third-party defendant, Hirsch, Arkin, Pinehurst, Inc.

John A. Robbins Co., Inc. (Robbins, Inc.) is a Pennsylvania general construction corporation, wholly owned by John A. Robbins (Robbins) and his wife. In 1958 Robbins, Inc. formed Jardel Co., Inc.

a. E. g., House v. Thornton, 76 Wash. 2d 586, 457 P.2d 199 (1969); Theis v. Heuer, 270 N.E.2d 764 (Ind.App.1971). Contra: Allen v. Wilkinson, 250 Md. 395, 243 A.2d 515 (1968). See Roberts, The Case of the Unwary Home Buyer, 52 Corn.L.Q. 835 (1967).

b. Sabo v. Delman, 3 N.Y.2d 155, 143 N.E.2d 906 (1957); Perma Research and Development Co. v. Singer Co., 410 F.2d 572 (2d Cir. 1969). See also Rose v. Rose, 385 Pa. 427, 123 A.2d 693 (1956) (promise of peace in the family); Entron, Inc. v. General Cablevision of Palatka, 435 F.2d 995 (5th Cir. 1970). Contra: Sachs v. Blewett, 206 Ind. 151, 185 N.E. 856 (1933); cf. Classic Bowl, Inc. v. AMF Pinspotters, Inc., 403 F.2d 463 (7th Cir. 1968). As for a damage claim, see Paiva v. Vanech Heights Construction Company, 159 Conn. 12, 271 A.2d 69 (1970).

(Jardel), the appellant in this action, as a wholly owned Delaware subsidiary with principal offices in Pennsylvania. Robbins has at all times been the president and controlling figure in both corporations.

In 1962 Jardel began the development of Price's Corner Shopping Center on land it owned in Delaware. Jardel hired Robbins, Inc. as general contractor under a contract that prevented Robbins, Inc., and apparently its subcontractors, from securing a lien against Jardel's property, thus protecting the mortgagee's interest. Robbins, Inc. in turn subcontracted the plumbing, heating and air-conditioning work to Hirsch, Arkin, Pinehurst, Inc. (Hirsch), a Pennsylvania corporation and appellee in this action. Hirsch agreed to payment on a time and material basis, plus fixed fee.

When Hirsch completed its portion of the construction in the fall of 1963, it was still owed approximately $70,000. by Robbins, Inc. Robbins, Inc. refused to pay, demanding that Hirsch rectify certain errors in the construction. Hirsch made several attempts to correct the problems, but, feeling that it could not satisfy Robbins, finally instituted negotiations for a settlement. As a result of these negotiations, on January 7, 1964, Hirsch agreed to accept $36,000. in full payment of Robbins, Inc.'s obligation to it, in return for which Robbins, Inc. released Hirsch of all liability arising or to arise out of its Price's Corner contract. Jardel was not a party to the release, nor did it participate as a corporation in the negotiations.

On July 9, 1965, a substantial portion of one of the buildings in Price's Corner Shopping Center collapsed. The tenant, Sears, Roebuck and Co., demanded that Jardel rebuild the destroyed portion of the building, which Jardel did as required by the lease. In addition, Sears sued Jardel for $150,000., alleging that its loss of supplies, payroll and other expenses, equipment and profits was due to Jardel's breach of the construction provisions of the contract under which Sears had agreed to rent the building, as well as to Jardel's breach of its duty of maintenance and to negligence.[1] Jardel then sued Hirsch in a third-party action, alleging that "Hirsch breached its agreement with the contractor and was negligent" in failing to meet the Sears' specifications which had been incorporated into Hirsch's contract with Robbins, Inc. Judgment was asked against Hirsch to cover any judgment that Sears might recover against Jardel.[2]

---

1. Sears alleged that the collapse was caused by the breaking of a water pipe leading from the building to an outside service island. Specifically, Sears claimed that Jardel, in constructing the building, failed to use thick pipe, soft rather than hard pipe, and "sleeving" where the pipe passed through the building's foundation, all of which were required by contract. Another allegation of breach is not relevant here.

2. Jardel later moved to amend its complaint to include a prayer for $73,000., the cost to Jardel of repairing the building. After ruling that judgment would be entered for Hirsch, the District Court said, " . . . the Court need not consider Jardel's motion . . .."

Hirsch filed an answer generally denying the allegations of the third-party complaint.   After interrogatories were answered, it amended its answer to plead the release between it and Robbins, Inc. as an affirmative defense against Jardel's claim "because of the relationship between [Jardel] and [Robbins, Inc.]".[3]   After depositions were taken, Hirsch moved for summary judgment.

The District Court granted the motion, holding [4] that (a) the general release was valid to bar Jardel's claim if the release bound Jardel as well as Robbins, Inc., and (b) the release bound Jardel because "justice" required the disregard of the corporate distinction between Jardel and its parent, Robbins, Inc.   The appellant, Jardel, challenges both these findings.

It is undisputed that the parties negotiating the release did not specifically mention or consider the leaking pipe causing the collapse of the Sears' building, nor can it be disputed, for the purposes of a motion for summary judgment, that the pipe was not installed in accordance with the contract or that this breach was the cause of the building's collapse.[5]   Because of these facts, Jardel argues that the release would not be binding even against Robbins, Inc.; it argues that there can never be an enforceable accord and satisfaction to claims that neither party discussed or knew existed at the time of settlement.

We do not believe that the law of Pennsylvania [6] goes this far.   A general release, by its terms discharging a party of "all manner of actions and causes of action, suits, debts, dues, accounts, bonds, covenants, contracts, agreements, judgments, claims and demands whatsoever in law or equity arising or to arise from a contract between the parties," [7] will ordinarily be enforced absent a showing that the parties did not intend what they wrote:

> "It is well settled that where the terms of a release and the facts and circumstances existing at the time of its execution indicate

3. In support of its motion to amend, Hirsch declared that it had learned that Jardel was a wholly-owned subsidiary of Robbins, Inc. only after Jardel's answers to the interrogatories.

4. The District Court opinion is not reported.

5. Hirsch, in its answer, denied that the pipe was not in conformity with the contract specifications and that any fault on its part caused the collapse.

6. Under Klaxon Co. v. Stentor Mfg. Co., 313 U.S. 487, 61 S.Ct. 1020, 85 L. Ed. 1477 (1941), the conflict of laws principles of the forum state, Delaware, must be applied to this action.

Delaware follows a strict jurisdiction selection test, looking to the law of the place of contracting to determine the validity and construction of a contract. [Citations omitted]; Restatement of Conflict of Laws, § 332(f) (1934).   In the instant case, the Jardel-Robbins, Inc. contract, the Robbins, Inc.-Hirsch contract, and the release were all executed in Pennsylvania.   The Robbins, Inc.-Hirsch contract specifically provided that Pennsylvania law would govern its interpretation.   The release made no provision as to applicable law.

7. The release, in pertinent part, provided:

"JOHN A. ROBBINS CO., INC. . . . does hereby remise, release and forever discharge HIRSCH, ARthe parties had in mind a general settlement of accounts, the release will be given effect according to its terms. . . .''

Brill's Estate, 337 Pa. 525, 528, 12 A.2d 50, 52 (1940) ; *see* Cockcroft v. Metropolitan Life Ins. Co., 125 Pa.Super. 293, 299, 189 A. 687, 689 (1937) (dictum).

The facts leading to the release were related in depositions by two of the three principals of Hirsch, and their statements have not been refuted by Jardel. After completing the plumbing, heating and air-conditioning work at the Price's Corner project, Hirsch demanded payment from Robbins, Inc. It was met with a series of alleged defects that Hirsch corrected, while denying that the defects were its responsibility. Hirsch again demanded payment, and again it was met with a different list of defects that, once again, it corrected. Finally, upon once again demanding payment and once again being met with a different list of defects, Hirsch asked to negotiate a settlement. Hirsch's purpose in these negotiations was clear—it wished to terminate its relationship with the Robbins organization completely.[8] The negotiations took place at the office of Robbins, Inc.'s (and Jardel's) attorney in Philadelphia; both parties were represented by counsel. Although it does not appear that the principals of Hirsch were directly involved, both Robbins and Mr. Anglin [9] were present for Robbins, Inc. The principals of Hirsch deposed that it was told to their attorney that if Hirsch signed the release, "at no future time would we

---

KIN, PINEHURST, INC., its successors and assigns of and from all, and all manner of, actions and causes of action, suits, debts, dues, accounts, bonds, covenants, contracts, agreements, judgments, claims and demands whatsoever in law or equity arising or to arise from a contract between the parties . . . for the performance of plumbing, heating, air-conditioning and ventilation work, in connection with a project known as Price's Corner . . . or arising out of any addendum or oral or written modification or extension of these contracts, which against the said HIRSCH . . ., JOHN A. ROBBINS CO., INC. ever had, now has, or which its successors or assigns, or any of them, hereafter can, shall or may have, for, or by reason of any cause, matter or thing whatsoever, from the beginning of the world to the date of these presents.''

8. Abraham Hirsch's testimony was as follows:
"Q. What was the purpose which your organization had in mind in obtaining a release from the Robbins organization?

"A. Just to get our money and get away from this nut.
"Q. Did you intend that after the release was executed that there would be any further negotiations or further claims?
"A. It was definitely told to our lawyers that if we signed any release it was on the basis that at no future time were we to even hear the name John A. Robbins, if I can say it that way. We wanted nothing further to do with that man."

David Hershman's testimony was to the same effect:
"[W]e wanted to make sure that we weren't going to be pinned against the wall for something we had no responsibility for or anything on the job if he was going to negotiate us out of something like $35,000, which he ended up doing."

9. Mr. Anglin was executive vice president of Robbins, Inc. at the time of the negotiations. Although he was an employee also of Jardel, it is not clear whether he was an officer.

even hear the name John A. Robbins." And it was on this basis that they accepted:

"We wanted to make sure we would not be responsible for anything else when we signed this and accepted the final payment; that we would not be responsible for anything else.

. . . .

"[O]ur attorney came out and said, 'Will you accept this? This is what they offer.'

"We said, 'We will accept it on the condition that we are released of all possible claims that come out of it [the Price's Corner project],' and he went back in and apparently, obviously they agreed on it and this is what came out of it."

The release, as signed by Robbins and attested to by the secretary of Robbins, Inc., stated that Robbins, Inc. released all its claims against Hirsch in exchange for $34,000.[10]

Jardel now seeks to challenge the release by the allegation that Hirsch "failed to disclose" the defects of the piping.[11] Even if it were true that Hirsch knew of the alleged defects,[12] this fact would not defeat the validity of the general release. Under Pennsylvania law, the only question open to challenge is whether the parties intended the release to be honored according to its terms.[13] There is ample evidence

---

10. Robbins, Inc. owed $70,000. on the contract. It paid Hirsch, under the terms of the release, $36,000.

11. In its brief before this court, Jardel also argued that it was the intention of the parties to release Hirsch only of those claims specifically enumerated in the list presented by Robbins to Hirsch immediately before the negotiations. We find nothing in the record to support this contention. In fact, the only mention of the list came from Hirsch's principals, who asserted that at no time did they consider the list a relevant factor:

"Q. Was it your intention that this release would release you only from those claims [contained in the list] or from all claims in contact with the job?

"A. [by Hershman] At the moment I couldn't tell you what the claims were. They were very unimportant as far as we were concerned. As I say, we considered them a smoke screen to stop us from what was directly due us. The release was to get us out of the job completely one hundred per cent. It had nothing to do with the claim as far as we were concerned because

the claims were unjust to start off with."

12. Hirsch argues that the mere "averment" by Robbins in his affidavit of these facts does not create a "genuine" issue of fact as contemplated by Rule 56(e) of the Federal Rules of Civil Procedure. Because of our disposition of the underlying dispute, we need not reach this issue.

13. Jardel has cited many cases to support the general proposition that a mistake by one of the parties to a release, such as "to amount to a complete difference between what he supposed he was receiving or giving up and what was in fact received or given up." 1 C.J.S. Accord and Satisfaction § 3(c), at p. 471 (1936), makes the release unenforceable. In this case, however, the only evidence is that the parties bargained for and received a general release, covering all claims having arisen or "to arise," which Robbins, Inc. "ever had, now has, or which . . . [it] hereafter can, shall or may have." By its own terms, therefore, the release covered claims unknown to the parties at the time of execution.

in the record supporting the conclusion that the parties intended so to honor the release, and there is no evidence to the contrary. Since it was Jardel's burden to refute the explicit language of the instrument and the corroborating testimony of the Hirsch principals, and since it made no attempt to do so, summary judgment on this issue, against Jardel, was proper.

[The court proceeded to consider whether or not the release given by Robbins to Hirsch was binding on Jardel. This portion of the opinion appears at p. 920 infra.]

[Affirmed.]

NOTES

(1) *Questions.* Note the testimony for Hirsch (footnote 11) that the defects listed by Robbins were "very unimportant as far as we were concerned." If Hirsch had known that the plumbing was improperly installed, should it be deemed to have known that Robbins was dealing under a material mistake of fact? What would justify its failure to correct that mistake, under the rule in Kannavos v. Annino, p. 299 supra? Suppose that a principal of Hirsch had said to Robbins during the negotiations, "We believe there are no significant defects in our work." Different result? Note that Hirsch apparently conducted the negotiations through its attorney as a go-between. Do you see an advantage for Hirsch in this procedure?

(2) *Personal Injury Claims.* Two cars collided at an intersection, injuring one of the drivers, Simon Mitzel. He consulted a doctor, and the other driver, Kasper Schatz, reported the accident to his insurance company. Three days after the accident an insurance adjuster called on Mitzel and made an "amiable" settlement with him for $100. As far as they knew, Mitzel had only some bruises and "a big black eye." Some time later his injury was diagnosed as a subdural hematoma (blood clot on the brain). He required surgery, incurred medical expenses of more than $1,-600, and suffered continuing disability.

By the terms of the settlement, Mitzel released Schatz from "any and all known and unknown actions, causes of action, claims, demands, damages, costs, loss of services, expenses, compensation, rights of contribution and all consequent damages on account or in any way growing out of any and all known and unknown personal injuries and property damage and death resulting or to result from an accident that occurred on or about the 15th day of November, 1965, near Zeeland, North Dakota." Mitzel sued Schatz. From an order rescinding the release, Schatz appealed. *Held:* Affirmed. Mitzel v. Schatz, 175 N.W.2d 659 (N.D.1970).

This case typifies a large class of settlement cases, in which the results are discordant. What grounds are there for differentiating between settlements of this character and a settlement like that in the main case? See Frank, J., concurring, in Ricketts v. Pennsylvania R. Co., 153 F.2d 757, 760, 767, 164 A.L.R. 387 (1946). What merits would you see in a rule avoiding any release of a personal injury claim given within a month after the injury? (Mitzel's injury was not properly diagnosed for a month and a half after the accident.) What demerits would you see in such a rule?

(3) *Statute.* Would the following statute, effective in North Dakota at the time of the Mitzel-Schatz settlement, have been a better ground for the decision? "A general release does not extend to claims which the creditor does not know or suspect to exist in his favor at the time of executing the release, which if known by him, must have materially affected his settlement with the debtor." N.D.Cent.Code, § 9–13–02. For an application of a like statute to facts somewhat comparable, see Casey v. Proctor, 59 Cal.2d 97, 378 P.2d 579 (1963).

Would this statute have altered the result in Sears, Roebuck and Co. v. Jardel Co.?

SECTION 4.   UNCONSCIONABILITY AND PROBLEMS OF ADHESION CONTRACTS

In the preceding sections of this chapter a number of familiar principles aimed at preserving the decencies of bargaining have been seen at work, both limiting and supplementing the process. In this section some newly established or newly expanded ones are presented. The notion of unconscionability in contracts is by no means new, but it has taken on new life since it was embodied as a test of enforceability in the Uniform Commercial Code; a substantially new body of case law has formed about it, and there has been an explosion of literature on the subject. Also, the "contract of adhesion" has emerged in this century as a type of agreement requiring distinctive treatment. The principles mentioned thus far have been developed largely through judicial decisions. In this section it will be seen that legislative and administrative measures have an important and developing role in policing bargains. The question arises whether or not these are better means for dealing with overreaching by contract than any remedies the courts can devise.

In the policing rules to be illustrated, elements of status, behavior, and substance are often combined. That being so, it is perhaps inevitable that the rules are largely undefined. The notions of unconscionability and adhesion have not yet become fixed quantities in the law. Is it desirable that they should be? Would they cease to be useful as agents for the law's renewal if they were rigorously defined? Or do they cause needless uncertainty and confusion?

NOTE

Strict Construction. It is often objected that courts introduce uncertainty and confusion by interpreting and construing agreements in accordance with their predispositions. The opinion that follows speaks of "strict construction" of provisions in leases whereby landlords attempt to immunize themselves from liability for negligence to their tenants. In reading the case, it will be well to have in mind the fact that a court's idea of fairness between the parties can sometimes be imposed on them by a purposive reading of their agreement. Many examples might be given, but one must suffice here: Galligan v. Arovitch, 421 Pa. 301, 219 A.2d 463 (1966).[a] The plaintiff was a tenant in an apartment building who suffered injury in a fall on the lawn. She sued the owner, charging that he was accountable for negligence in maintenance. Judgment was given for the defendant on the pleadings. The plaintiff's lease excluded liability of the owner for injury arising from her use of the hallways and six other common areas, including sidewalks. On appeal, the judgment was reversed. One judge declared the provision violative of public policy, and another expressed serious doubt on that score. The opinion of the court, however, was based on the location of the injury—the lawn was not mentioned in the lease. "A lawn and a sidewalk are clearly different locations." Two judges dissented. Might the decision have been based on a better ground? Consider the view of Professor Llewellyn:

"A court can 'construe' language into patently not meaning what the language is patently trying to say. It can find inconsistencies between clauses and throw out the troublesome one. It can even reject a clause as counter to the whole purpose of the transaction. . . . Indeed, the law of agreeing can be subjected to divers modes of employment, to make the whole bargain or a clause stick or not stick according to the status of the party claiming under it. . . . The difficulty with these techniques of ours is threefold. First, since they all rest on the admission that the clauses in question are permissible in purpose and content, they invite the draftsman to recur to the attack. Give him time, and he will make the grade. Second, since they do not face the issue, they fail to accumulate either experience or authority in the needed direction: that of marking out for any given type of transaction what the *minimum decencies* are which a court will insist upon as essential to an enforceable bargain of a given type, or as being inherent in a bargain of that type. Third, since they purport to construe, and do not really construe, nor are intended to, but are instead tools of intentional and creative misconstruction, they seriously embarrass later efforts at true construction, later efforts to get at the true meaning of those wholly legitimate contracts and clauses which call for their meaning to be got at instead of avoided. The net effect is unnecessary confusion and unpredictability, together with inadequate remedy, and evil persisting that calls for remedy. Covert tools are never reliable tools." Llewellyn, Book Review, 52 Harv.L.Rev. 700, 702 (1939). See also Kessler, Contracts of Adhesion—Some Thoughts About Freedom of Contract, 43 Colum.L.Rev. 629, 631 (1943).

a. Problems of interpreting agreements are dealt with in detail in Chapter 6, infra.

O'CALLAGHAN v. WALLER & BECKWITH REALTY CO.

Supreme Court of Illinois, 1958.
15 Ill.2d 436, 155 N.E.2d 545.

SCHAEFER, JUSTICE.[a] This is an action to recover for injuries allegedly caused by the defendant's negligence in maintaining and operating a large apartment building. Mrs. Ella O'Callaghan, a tenant in the building, was injured when she fell while crossing the paved courtyard on her way from the garage to her apartment. She instituted this action to recover for her injuries, alleging that they were caused by defective pavement in the courtyard. Before the case was tried, Mrs. O'Callaghan died and her administrator was substituted as plaintiff. The jury returned a verdict for the plaintiff in the sum of $14,000, and judgment was entered on the verdict. Defendant appealed. The Appellate Court held that the action was barred by an exculpatory clause in the lease that Mrs. O'Callaghan had signed, and that a verdict should have been directed for the defendant. 15 Ill.App.2d 349, 146 N.E.2d 198. It therefore reversed the judgment and remanded the cause with directions to enter judgment for the defendant. We granted leave to appeal.

In reaching its conclusion the Appellate Court relied upon our recent decision in Jackson v. First National Bank, 415 Ill. 453, 114 N. E.2d 721. There we considered the validity of such an exculpatory clause in a lease of property for business purposes. We pointed out that contracts by which one seeks to relieve himself from the consequences of his own negligence are generally enforced "unless (1) it would be against the settled public policy of the State to do so, or (2) there is something in the social relationship of the parties militating against upholding the agreement." 415 Ill. at page 460, 114 N.E.2d at page 725. And we held that there was nothing in the public policy of the State or in the social relationship of the parties to forbid enforcement of the exculpatory clause there involved.

The exculpatory clause in the lease now before us clearly purports to relieve the lessor and its agents from any liability to the lessee for personal injuries or property damage caused by any act or neglect of the lessor or its agents. It does not appear to be amenable to the strict construction to which such clauses are frequently subjected. See 175 A.L.R. 8, 89. The plaintiff does not question its applicability, and she concedes that if it is valid it bars her recovery. She argues vigorously, however, that such a clause is contrary to public policy, and so invalid, in a lease of residential property.

a. Walter V. Schaefer (1904–) practiced law and served in a variety of governmental posts in Chicago between 1928 and 1940, when he became a professor of law at Northwestern University. Since 1951 he has been a member of the Illinois Supreme Court. He is one of the Advisers for the Restatement Second of Contracts.

Freedom of contract is basic to our law. But when that freedom expresses itself in a provision designed to absolve one of the parties from the consequences of his own negligence, there is danger that the standards of conduct which the law has developed for the protection of others may be diluted. These competing considerations have produced results that are not completely consistent. This court has refused to enforce contracts exculpating or limiting liability for negligence between common carriers and shippers of freight or paying passengers (Chicago and Northwestern Railway Co. v. Chapman, 133 Ill. 96, 24 N.E. 417, 8 L.R.A. 508), between telegraph companies and those sending messages (Tyler, Ullman & Co. v. Western Union Telegraph Co., 60 Ill. 421), and between masters and servants (Campbell v. Chicago, Rock Island and Pacific Railway Co., 243 Ill. 620, 90 N.E. 1106). The obvious public interest in these relationships, coupled with the dominant position of those seeking exculpation, were compelling considerations in these decisions, which are in accord with similar results in other jurisdictions. See 175 A.L.R. 8.

On the other hand, as pointed out in the Jackson case, the relation of lessor and lessee has been considered a matter of private concern. Clauses that exculpate the landlord from the consequences of his negligence have been sustained in residential as well as commercial leases. [Citations omitted.] There are intimations in other jurisdictions that run counter to the current authority. See Kuzmiak v. Brookchester, Inc., 1955, 33 N.J.Super. 575, 111 A.2d 425; Kay v. Cain, 1946, 81 U.S.App.D.C. 24, 154 F.2d 305. The New Hampshire court applies to exculpatory clauses in all leases its uniform rule that any attempt to contract against liability for negligence is contrary to public policy. Papakalos v. Shaka, 1941, 91 N.H. 265, 18 A.2d 377. But apart from the Papakalos case we know of no court of last resort that has held such clauses invalid in the absence of a statute so requiring.

A contract shifting the risk of liability for negligence may benefit a tenant as well as a landlord. See Cerny-Pickas & Co. v. C. R. Jahn Co., 7 Ill.2d 393, 131 N.E.2d 100. Such an agreement transfers the risk of a possible financial burden and so lessens the impact of the sanctions that induce adherence to the required standard of care. But this consideration is applicable as well to contracts for insurance that indemnify against liability for one's own negligence. Such contracts are accepted, and even encouraged. See Ill.Rev.Stat.1957, chap. 95½, pars. 7—202(1) and 7—315.

The plaintiff contends that due to a shortage of housing there is a disparity of bargaining power between lessors of residential property and their lessees that gives landlords an unconscionable advantage over tenants. And upon this ground it is said that exculpatory clauses in residential leases must be held to be contrary to public policy. No attempt was made upon the trial to show that Mrs. O'Callaghan was at all concerned about the exculpatory clause, that she tried to negotiate with the defendant about its modification or elimination, or that she made any effort to rent an apartment elsewhere. To establish the existence of a widespread housing shortage the plaintiff points to numerous statutes designed to alleviate the shortage (see Ill.Rev.Stat.1957, chap. 67½, *passim*) and to the existence of rent control during the period of the lease. 65 Stat. 145 (1947), 50 U.S.C.A. Appendix, § 1894.

Unquestionably there has been a housing shortage. That shortage has produced an active and varied legislative response. Since legislative attention has been so sharply focused upon housing problems in recent years, it might be assumed that the legislature has taken all of the remedial action that it thought necessary or desirable. One of the major legislative responses was the adoption of rent controls which placed ceilings upon the amount of rent that landlords could charge. But the very existence of that control made it impossible for a lessor to negotiate for an increased rental in exchange for the elimination of an exculpatory clause. We are asked to assume, however, that the legislative response to the housing shortage has been inadequate and incomplete, and to augment it judicially.

The relationship of landlord and tenant does not have the monopolistic characteristics that have characterized some other relations with respect to which exculpatory clauses have been held invalid. There are literally thousands of landlords who are in competition with one another. The rental market affords a variety of competing types of housing accommodations, from simple farm house to luxurious apartment. The use of a form contract does not of itself establish disparity of bargaining power. That there is a shortage of housing at one particular time or place does not indicate that such shortages have always and everywhere existed, or that there will be shortages in the future. Judicial determinations of public policy cannot readily take account of sporadic and transitory circumstances. They should rather, we think, rest upon a durable moral basis. Other jurisdictions have dealt with this problem by legislation. McKinney's Consol.Laws of N.Y.Ann., Real Property Laws, sec. 234, Vol. 49, Part I; Ann.Laws of Mass., Vol. 6, c. 186, sec. 15. In our opinion the subject is one that is appropriate for legislative rather than judicial action.

The judgment of the Appellate Court is affirmed.

BRISTOW, JUSTICE, and DAILY, CHIEF JUSTICE (dissenting). We cannot accept the conclusions and analysis of the majority opinion, which in our judgment not only arbitrarily eliminates the concept of negligence in the landlord and tenant relationship, but creates anomalies in the law, and will produce grievous social consequences for hundreds of thousands of persons in this State.

According to the undisputed facts in the instant case, this form lease with its exculpatory clause, was executed in a metropolitan area in 1947, when housing shortages were so acute that "waiting lists" were the order of the day, and gratuities to landlords to procure shelter were common. (U.S.Sen.Rep.1780, Committee on Banking & Currency, vol. II, 81st Cong., 2nd Sess. (1950), p. 2565 et seq.; Cremer v. Peoria Housing Authority, 399 Ill. 579, 589, 78 N.E.2d 276.) While plaintiff admittedly did not negotiate about the exculpatory clause, as the majority opinion notes, the record shows unequivocally that the apartment would not have been rented to her if she had quibbled about any clause in the form lease. According to the uncontroverted testimony, "If a person refused to sign a [form] lease in the form it was in, the apartment would not be rented to him."

Apparently, the majority opinion has chosen to ignore those facts and prevailing circumstances, and finds instead that there were thousands of landlords competing with each other with a variety of rental units. Not only was the element of competition purely theoretical—and judges need not be more naive than other men—but there wasn't even theoretical competition, as far as the exculpatory clauses were concerned, since these clauses were included in all form leases used by practically all landlords in urban areas. Simmons v. Columbus Venetian Stevens Building, Inc., Ill.App., 155 N.E.2d 372; 1952 Ill.L.Forum, 321, 328. This meant that even if a prospective tenant were to "take his business elsewhere," he would still be confronted by the same exculpatory clause in a form lease offered by another landlord.

Thus, we are *not* construing merely an isolated provision of a contract specifically bargained for by one landlord and one tenant, "a matter of private concern," as the majority opinion myoptically [sic] views the issue in order to sustain its conclusion. We are construing, instead, a provision affecting thousands of tenants now bound by such provisions, which were foisted upon them at a time when it would be pure fiction to state that they had anything but a Hobson's choice in the matter. Can landlords, by that technique, immunize themselves from liability for negligence, and have the blessings of this court as they destroy the concept of negligence and standards of law painstakingly evolved in the case law? That is the issue in this case, and the majority opinion at no time realistically faces it.

In resolving this issue, it is evident that despite the assertion in the majority opinion, there is no such thing as absolute "freedom of contract" in the law. West Coast Hotel Co. v. Parrish, 300 U.S. 379, 392, 57 S.Ct. 578, 582, 81 L.Ed. 703. As Mr. Justice Holmes stated, "pretty much all law consists in forbidding men to do some things that they want to do, and contract is no more exempt from law than other acts." Dissent, Adkins v. Children's Hospital of District of Columbia, 261 U.S. 525, 568, 43 S.Ct. 394, 405, 67 L.Ed. 785. Thus, there is no freedom to contract to commit a crime; or to contract to give a reward for the commission of a crime; or to contract to violate essential morality; or to contract to accomplish an unlawful purpose, or to contract in violation of public policy. 12 I.L.P. Contracts §§ 151, 154.

In the instant case we must determine whether the exculpatory clause in the lease offends the public policy of this State. We realize that there is no precise definition of "public policy" or rule to test whether a contract is contrary to public policy, so that each case must be judged according to its own peculiar circumstances. First Trust & Savings Bank of Kankakee v. Powers, 393 Ill. 97, 102, 65 N.E.2d 377. None would dispute, however, that there is a recognized policy of discouraging negligence and protecting those in need of goods or services from being overreached by those with power to drive unconscionable bargains.

Even the majority opinion recognizes this policy as a possible limitation on the concept of "freedom of contract" in its statement, "when that freedom expresses itself in a provision designed to absolve one of the parties from the consequences of his own negligence, there is danger that the standards of conduct which the law has developed for the protection of others may be diluted." Diluted? As applied in the instant case, the word is "destroyed." When landlords are no longer liable for failure to observe standards of care, or for conduct amounting to negligence by virtue of an exculpatory clause in a lease, then such standards cease to exist. They are not merely "diluted." Negligence cannot exist in abstraction. The exculpatory clause destroys the concept of negligence in the landlord-tenant relationship, and the majority opinion, in sustaining the validity of that clause, has given the concept of negligence in this relationship a "judicial burial."

This court, however, has refused to countenance such a destruction of standards of conduct and of the concept of negligence in other relationships. We have invalidated such exculpatory clauses as contrary to our public policy in contracts between common carriers and shippers or paying passengers [citations omitted]; between telegraph companies and those sending messages [citation omitted], and between employers and employees [citations omitted].

By what logic and reasoning can you hold that such clauses are void and contrary to public policy in an employer-employee contract, but valid in contracts between landlords and tenants, as the majority opinion does? If the criterion for invalidating exculpatory clauses is the presence of "monopolistic characteristics" in the relationship, as the majority opinion suggests, then do employers have a greater monopoly on the labor market than landlords have on the tenant market? Is there less competition among employers for employees than among landlords for tenants? The facts defy any such reasoning. Nor are there any other cogent grounds for distinguishing between these categories. . . .

The basis of voiding exculpatory clauses is that they are contrary to the public policy of discouraging negligence and protecting those in need of goods or services from being overreached by those with power to drive unconscionable bargains. Bisso v. Inland Waterways Corp., 349 U.S. 85, 91, 75 S.Ct. 629, 99 L.Ed. 911. In determining whether such clauses should be deemed void, the courts have weighed such factors as the importance which the subject has for the physical and economic well-being of the group agreeing to the release; their bargaining power; the amount of free choice actually exercised in agreeing to the exemption; and the existence of competition among the group to be exempted. (Williston, Contracts, vol. 6, p. 4968; "The Significance of Bargaining Power in the Law of Exculpation," 37 Col.L.Rev. 248; 175 A.L.R. 8, 48; 15 Univ.Pitt.L.Rev. 493.) Adjudged by such criteria, it is evident that the subject matter of the exculpatory clause herein—shelter—is indispensable for the physical well being of tenants; that they have nothing even approaching equality of bargaining power with landlords and no free choice whatever in agreeing to the exemption, since they will be confronted with the same clause in other form leases if they seek shelter elsewhere. Although the majority opinion claims that such clauses may also benefit tenants, it is hard for us to envisage a tenant on a waiting list for an apartment, insisting that the lease include a provision relieving him from liability for his negligence in the maintenance of the premises. Consequently, in our judgment, every material ground for voiding the exculpatory clause exists in the lease involved in the instant case. . . .

NOTES

(1) *Public Policy Revisited.* In 1959 the Illinois legislature enacted a statute similar to those of Massachusetts and New York, cited in Judge Schaefer's opinion. It condemned agreements in connection with real property leases, exempting a lessor from liability for his negligence in operating or maintaining the property, as "void as against public policy." Certain business leases were excepted, however, including leases granted by "regulated" corporations.

In 1969 the Illinois Supreme Court had to consider a lease in the excepted class, when a freight train was derailed and damaged an adjacent bulk oil station. The oil company brought a negligence action against the railroad. The oil station was on ground leased by the railroad, and a provision in the lease was held to preclude recovery. The oil company asserted a disparity of bargaining power, saying that by common knowledge a firm in its position is required either to accept the railroad's terms or to forego essential rail services. But the court found no support in the evidence for this contention. Sweney Gasoline & Oil Company v. Toledo, P. & W. R. Co., 42 Ill.2d 265, 247 N.E.2d 603 (1969). The rule of O'Callaghan, the court said, "accords to the individual the dignity of being considered capable of making and standing by his own agreements." The court also ruled that the statute violated the state constitution, in that it made a "discriminatory classification without any reasonable basis" and unlawfully granted a special privilege and immunity to "regulated" corporations.

Justice Schaefer dissented from the result, although he agreed that the statute was invalid. Remembering that he wrote the opinion of the court in O'Callaghan, what do you suppose his reasoning was?

(2) *An Apartment-Building Rule.* In McCutcheon v. United Homes Corporation, 79 Wash.2d 443, 486 P.2d 1093 (1971), the court denied ef-

fect to a landlord's exculpation clause in circumstances like those in O'Callaghan, emphasizing the "not" clause in Restatement, § 574: "A bargain for exemption from liability for the consequences of negligence not falling greatly below the standard established by law for the protection of others against unreasonable risk of harm, is legal. . ." The court relied also on census figures showing the growth of apartment use in the state. It declined to pass judgment on such clauses as they might appear in various agreements not presented for decision, such as those for the occasional rental of rooms in private homes, a specific bargain for exculpation on the basis of reduced rental payment, a business lease exculpating the landlord from liability for property damage. If the courts develop a rule distinguishing between residential and business leases, is it subject to constitutional challenge on the ground of unreasonable classification? If a judge-made rule is immune to constitutional questioning, though a statute in the same terms would not be, what might explain the difference?

STANDARD FORM CONTRACTS

Standard form contracts have become a commonplace aspect of daily life. Their use in business affairs is so prevalent that they provide a vehicle for every step in the dealings of consumers with merchants and others.[a] Take, for example, a man who buys a car "on time." The contract of sale will be on a standard form prepared by a finance company. The car will be insured under a standard form prepared by an insurance company. The check with which he makes his down payment will be drawn on an account governed by a standard form prepared by a bank. When he parks the car in a parking lot he will receive a ticket on a standard form prepared by a parking lot operator. And so it goes. Sometimes such items as quantity, quality and price will be open to actual bargain; sometimes they will not.

Mass production of contracts, like mass production of goods, may serve the interests of all parties. Among the advantages claimed for the use of standard form contracts are these: it takes advantage of the lessons of experience and enables a judicial interpretation of one contract to serve as an interpretation of all contracts; it reduces uncertainty and saves time and trouble; it simplifies planning and administration and makes the skill of the draftsman available to all personnel; it makes risks calculable and "increases that real security

a. A study of 500 contracts cases reported in 1951 revealed that written contracts were involved in 341, and that of these 187 seemed to have been the product of bargaining and negotiation, 123 to have been printed form contracts, with the remainder uncertain. Shepherd, Contracts in a Prosperity Year, 6 Stan.L.Rev. 208, 212 (1954). In another study, "Requests for copies of business documents used in buying and selling were sent to approximately 6,000 manufacturing firms which do business in Wisconsin. Approximately 1,200 replies were received and 850 companies used some type of standardized planning. With only a few exceptions, the firms that did not reply and the 350 that indicated they did not use standardized planning were very small manufacturers such as local bakeries, soft drink bottlers and sausage makers." Macaulay, Non-Contractual Relations in Business: A Preliminary Study, 28 Am. Sociological Rev. 55, 58 (1963).

which is the necessary basis of initiative and the assumption of fore-seeable risks." Cohen, The Basis of Contract, 46 Harv.L.Rev. 553, 558 (1933). See also Llewellyn, Book Review, 52 Harv.L.Rev. 700, 701 (1939). Professor Kessler has discussed some of these advantages more fully.

"The development of large scale enterprise with its mass production and mass distribution made a new type of contract inevitable—the standardized mass contract. A standardized contract, once its contents have been formulated by a business firm, is used in every bargain dealing with the same product or service. The individuality of the parties which so frequently gave color to the old type of contract has disappeared. The stereotyped contract of today reflects the impersonality of the market. It has reached its greatest perfection in the different types of contracts used on the various exchanges. Once the usefulness of these contracts was discovered and perfected in the transportation, insurance, and banking business, their use spread into all other fields of large scale enterprise, into international as well as national trade, and into labor relations. It is to be noted that uniformity of terms of contracts typically recurring in a business enterprise is an important factor in the exact calculation of risks. Risks which are difficult to calculate can be excluded altogether. Unforeseeable contingencies affecting performance, such as strikes, fire, and transportation difficulties can be taken care of. The standard clauses in insurance policies are the most striking illustrations of successful attempts on the part of business enterprises to select and control risks assumed under a contract. The insurance business probably deserves credit also for having first realized the full importance of the so-called 'juridical risk', the danger that a court or jury may be swayed by 'irrational factors' to decide against a powerful defendant. Ingenious clauses have been the result. Once their practical utility was proven, they were made use of in other lines of business. It is highly probable that the desire to avoid juridical risks has been a motivating factor in the widespread use of warranty clauses in the machine industry limiting the common law remedies of the buyer to breach of an implied warranty of quality and particularly excluding his right to claim damages. The same is true for arbitration clauses in international trade. Standardized contracts have thus become an important means of excluding or controlling the 'irrational factor' in litigation. In this respect they are a true reflection of the spirit of our time with its hostility to irrational factors in the judicial process, and they belong in the same category as codifications and restatements." Kessler, Contracts of Adhesion—Some Thoughts About Freedom of Contract, 43 Colum.L.Rev. 629, 631–32 (1943).

But there are dangers inherent in standardized contract as well, for it may be the means by which one party imposes his will upon another unwilling or even unwitting party. Such contracts have come to be known generally as "contracts of adhesion" [b] but courts and writers have not always been careful to articulate precisely the means of the imposition. There are at least three distinct possibilities, which often appear in combination. First, bargaining over terms may not be between equals. The standardized contract may be used by an enterprise with such disproportionately strong economic power that it can dictate its terms to the weaker party. Second, there may be no opportunity to bargain over terms at all. The standardized contract may be a take-it-or-leave-it proposition in which the only alternatives are adherence or outright rejection. Third, one party may be completely, or at least relatively, unfamiliar with the terms. The standardized contract may be used by a party who has had the advantage of time and expert advice in preparing it while the other party may have no real opportunity to scrutinize it. This may be compounded by the use of fine print and convoluted clauses.[c]

NOTE

Status to Contract, and Back. One of the great generalizations about social history is the thesis of Sir Henry Maine that the history of progressive societies may be described as a movement from status to contract. His influential book, Ancient Law, developing this thesis, was published in 1864. More recently, some writers have detected a reverse tendency in the law. Curiously, a high regard for freedom of contract may be seen as providing a climate for the reverse movement. The prevalence of standard form contracts is conducive to a regime of status, as the argument goes, and they are implemented in the name of freedom to contract. The following excerpts represent these views:

(a) Maine, Ancient Law 163–65: "The movement of the progressive societies has been uniform in one respect. Through all its course it has been distinguished by the gradual dissolution of family dependency and the growth of individual obligation in its place. The individual is steadily substituted for the Family, as the unit of which civil laws take account. . . . Nor is it difficult to see what is the tie between man and man which replaces by degrees those forms of reciprocity in rights and duties which have their origin in the Family. It is Contract. Starting, as from one terminus of history, from a condition of society in which all the rela-

---

b. The term "contract of adhesion" was first used in the United States by Patterson, The Delivery of a Life-Insurance Policy, 33 Harv.L.Rev. 198, 222 (1919). It was coined by Raymond Saleilles as "contrat d'adhésion" to describe contracts "in which one predominant unilateral will dictates its law to an undetermined multitude rather than to an individual . . . as in all employment contracts of big industry, transportation contracts of big railroad companies and all those contracts which, as the Romans said, resemble a law much more than a meeting of the minds." Saleilles, De

la Declaration de Volonté 229 (1901). It has been popularized in the United States by scholars who were educated on the continent of Europe and who later taught in this country. See Kessler, Contracts of Adhesion—Some Thoughts About Freedom of Contract, 43 Colum.L.Rev. 629 (1943); Ehrenzweig, Adhesion Contracts in the Conflict of Laws, 53 Colum.L.Rev. 1072 (1953). Both articles were cited by the court in the Henningsen case, infra.

c. See Note, 63 Harv.L.Rev. 494 (1950).

tions of Persons are summed up in the relations of Family, we seem to have steadily moved towards a phase of social order in which all these relations arise from the free agreement of individuals. . . . All the forms of Status taken notice of in the Law of Persons were derived from, and to some extent are still coloured by, the powers and privileges anciently residing in the Family. If then we employ Status, agreeably with the usage of the best writers, to signify these personal conditions only, and avoid applying the term to such conditions as are the immediate or remote result of agreement, we may say that the movement of the progressive societies has hitherto been a movement *from Status to Contract.*"

(b) Kessler, op. cit. supra, 640: "With the decline of the free enterprise system due to the innate trend of competitive capitalism towards monopoly, the meaning of contract has changed radically. Society, when granting freedom of contract, does not guarantee that all members of the community will be able to make use of it to the same extent. On the contrary, the law, by protecting the unequal distribution of property, does nothing to prevent freedom of contract from becoming a one-sided privilege. Society, by proclaiming freedom of contract, guarantees that it will not interfere with the exercise of power by contract. Freedom of contract enables enterprisers to legislate by contract and, what is even more important, to legislate in a substantially authoritarian manner without using the appearance of authoritarian forms. Standard contracts in particular could thus become effective instruments in the hands of powerful industrial and commercial overlords enabling them to impose a new feudal order of their own making upon a vast host of vassals. . . . Thus the return back from contract to status which we experience today was greatly facilitated by the fact that the belief in freedom of contract has remained one of the firmest axioms in the whole fabric of the social philosophy of our culture."

TICKETS, PASSES AND STUBS

Printed slips and tickets are issued to their customers by firms offering services of many kinds: laundries, parking lot operators, and firms storing and carrying baggage, for examples. It is common to find a provision on such a ticket that purports to limit the liability of the issuer for injury or loss. To what extent are these provisions effective?

Consider this case: visitors are admitted by ticket to an ocean liner when it is about to set sail. A person wishing to attend a *bon voyage* party for a friend, held on board, is required to pay 50 cents for the privilege of boarding. He is issued a ticket at the foot of the gangway, to be turned in at the top. A sign over the counter where the money is paid indicates that it is a "contribution" to the seamen's welfare fund. The ticket contains the legend: "The steamship line is not responsible for any injury suffered by a visitor while on board." The print is not distinguished in size or color from other material on the ticket. The visitor's attention is not called to the printing on the ticket, and he does not read it. On these facts it can be said with assurance that the legend has no effect on any claim that he may thereafter make against the line. The reasoning might be that the visitor has not manifested assent to any contract with the steamship line. In contrast, the traveller who has purchased a steamship ticket is likely to be held bound by a limitation of liability appearing in it whether or not it is conspicuous, and whether or not he reads it.[a] What is the difference? Imagine an apartment lease having signatures on the front of a sheet and printed terms continued on the back. Could it be held, on the authority of a ruling about a boarding pass, that the terms on the back do not affect the tenant's rights?

In one well-known case the ticket reproduced was issued by a firm offering a checking service to the public.

H. & M. PARCEL ROOM, INC.

BROADWAY & 33rd ST. HUDSON TUNNELS
OPEN 7:00 A.M. – CLOSE 1:00 A.M.
(E. S. Time Except When Another Time is in Effect)

■ CONTRACT ■

This CONTRACT is made on the following conditions and in consideration of the low rate at which the service is performed, and its acceptance by the depositor. Expressly binds both parties to the CONTRACT.

Charge—10 cents for every 24 hours or fraction thereof. For each piece covered by this contract.

Loss or damage—no claim shall be made in excess of $25.00 for loss or damage to any piece.

Unclaimed articles remaining after 90 days may be sold at public or private sale to satisfy accrued charges.

PHONE PEnnsylvania 6–2467: H. & M. PARCEL ROOM, INC.

34--971

[A5309]

One Ellis, acting for a patron, left a package for storage at the parcel room and received the ticket but did not read it. Two days later, when the patron went to reclaim the package, he was told that it had been delivered to someone else by mistake. He sued the storage firm for the alleged value of the contents: $1,000. The trial court gave judgment for nearly that amount. On successive appeals, the judges were in disagreement, some believing that the recovery should be limited to $25. One judge holding that view wrote as follows: "The parcel check . . . had conspicuously printed the word "Contract" on the face thereof near the top in bold face type, clearly legible in red ink. . . . The whole form was exceptionally brief. . . . Plaintiffs . . . had ample opportunity to read the notice on the check stub . . . The package, alleged to contain valuable furs, was tied up with a piece

a. See Secoulsky v. Oceanic Steam Nav. Co., 223 Mass. 465, 112 N.E. 151 (1916) (loss of baggage; plaintiff not literate in language of ticket). Compare Polonsky v. Union Federal Savings & Loan Ass'n, 334 Mass. 697, 138 N.E.2d 115, 60 A.L.R.2d 702 (1956) (provision on the inside of the cover of a savings bank book that the bank was not responsible for money paid to any person unlawfully presenting the book).

of cord in a brown paper parcel. The charge for checking was the trivial sum of ten cents." [b]

The court affirmed the trial court's judgment, however. An excerpt from the opinion is as follows: " 'The coupon was presumptively intended as between the parties to serve the special purpose of affording a means of identifying the parcel left by the bailor. In the mind of the bailor the little piece of cardboard . . . did not arise to the dignity of a contract by which he agreed that in the event of the loss of the parcel, even through the negligence of the bailee itself, he would accept therefor a sum which, perhaps, would be but a small fraction of its actual value.' . . . While the defendant bailee should be protected in its legal right to limit its responsibility, the public should also be safeguarded against imposition. If the bailee wishes to limit its liability for negligence, it must at least show that it has given adequate notice of the special contract and that it has received the assent thereto of those with whom it transacts business." Klar v. H. & M. Parcel Room, Inc., 270 App.Div. 538, 61 N.Y.S.2d 285, aff'd mem. 296 N.Y. 1044, 73 N.E.2d 912 (1947).

Compare the case of the steamship boarding pass. Even if the parcel room's liability had been limited to $25, what distinguishing reasons could be given for disregarding the legend on the boarding pass?

Would the parcel-room case have been decided differently if the defendant had posted a placard, plainly visible to customers, stating the limitation on its liability? [c] Would it have been decided differently if the customer had read the ticket when he deposited the package? [d] If he had not read the ticket, but had previously read this note?

The Restatement Second deals with the problem in § 237. What distinction does it make between persons who read the tickets handed to them and those who do not? Does it satisfactorily explain why a limitation of liability on a travel ticket is given effect, whereas one on a checking stub is not? (The comments after the section are more helpful in making the distinction, and are generally valuable on the subject of standard form contracts.)

---

b. The relation between Ellis and the plaintiff is not known.

A conceivable one is suggested by the following report: "Public lockers in Penn Station. Locked trunks in parked cars. This is where the contraband is hidden, deposited there surreptitiously by one party and picked up quietly by another. Is it narcotics, jewels, gold bullion? No, it is furs, or, more accurately, parts of fur garments, awaiting sewing so that the complete garment can be made available for sale. The lined skins are placed in lockers or car-trunks by fur-garment producers willing to use non-union contractors, usually a one-man sewing shop or a shop with a few workers. After picking up the garments at their convenience, the contractors sew them for 50 per cent less than a unionized shop would. They then return the garments via the same conduits to their unionized clients. Although outlawed in labor-management contracts, the increasing use of such contractors has produced consternation in an already-troubled industry."—The New York Times, March 26, 1972, Business Section, p. 1.

c., d. See notes c and d on p. 331.

NOTES

(1) *Bargaining Process.* In Klar v. Parcel Room and similar cases, it may be said that the courts have policed against overreaching in contracts by manipulating the principles of contract formation. What are the limits of this method? Specialized conceptions of offer and acceptance doubtless have something to contribute to substantive fairness in enforcing contracts, as these cases show. See also the note on knowledge of mistake, p. 141 supra. Are the ticket cases based on the principle stated there?

(2) *Tariffs and Filings.* The common-law rules of liabilities of carriers and storers for the loss of, or damage to goods have generally been codified, and in some respects reshaped by statute. A shipper of goods, for example, has rights against an interstate common carrier as stated by the Interstate Commerce Act, which may not be disclaimed by agreement. However, carriers are permitted under the Act to file tariffs, or rate schedules "dependent upon the value declared in writing by the shipper or agreed upon in writing as the released value of the property," and with the approval of the Interstate Commerce Commission a limitation is effective as a "released value." According to the Act, a carrier "may establish rates varying with the value so declared and agreed upon." [e]

In Shirazi v. Greyhound Corporation, 145 Mont. 421, 401 P.2d 559 (1965), a limitation of $25 was stated on a baggage receipt given by the defendant bus company to the plaintiff when he checked his suitcase. When it was lost, his recovery was limited to that amount, although he was an immigrant who had only 400 words of English. The defendant's tariff filing afforded it protection. It has been said, however, that "the law as it relates to standardized form contracts" is particularly pertinent in determining whether or not a shipper's assent to the released value has been obtained. "Congress no doubt used these words [agreed upon in writing] to indicate that a shipper should agree in the same sense that one agrees or assents to enter into a contractual obligation." Chandler v. Aero Mayflower Transit Co., 374 F.2d 129 (4th Cir. 1967).[f] Is this statement consistent with the Greyhound case, supra? Whether or not it will

---

c. The wording of a sign meant to call attention to a limitation of liability must evidently be chosen with some care. See McAshan v. Cavitt, 149 Tex. 147, 226 S.W.2d 1016 (1950), concerning a sign posted at a parking lot: "We close at 6 P.M. Cars left later at owner's risk." Do you see an ambiguity, with respect to a car brought to the lot at 5 o'clock and stolen at 7? In U Drive & Tour v. System Auto Parks, 28 Cal.App.2d Supp. 782, 71 P.2d 354 (1937), it was said that a similar sign, of modest size, was "psychologically" concealed by the advertising signs of the lot operator.

d. For an analysis of the "duty to read," in relation to a structured set of legal policies, see Macaulay, Private Legislation and the Duty to Read, 19 Vand.L.Rev. 1051 (1966). This com-ment makes special reference to the liability of a credit card holder for its unauthorized use—a liability now considerably curtailed by legislation. See 15 U.S.C.A. § 1643, part of the Truth-in-Lending Act of 1968. For an amusing discussion of methods employed to prevent the written word from conveying any message, see Mellinkoff, How to Make Contracts Illegible, 5 Stan.L. Rev. 418 (1953). On buying at auction a painting bearing a master's name without reading the seller's disclaimer of genuineness in the catalog, see Weisz v. Parke-Bernet Galleries, Inc., 67 Misc.2d 1077, 325 N.Y.S.2d 576 (Civ. Ct.1971).

e. 49 U.S.C.A. § 20(11).

f. Compare Insurance Co. of North Amer. v. Krieck Furriers, Inc., 36

be borne out in further litigation over the statute, in light of changing attitudes toward standard form contracts, remains to be seen.

(3) *The Case of the Golfer's Mishap.* The document set out below was executed by Robert Baker when he played golf at the Jackson Municipal Course. As he was returning the golf cart rented to him by Westweld Metal Works the brakes failed and it overturned, causing him personal injury; so he alleged in suing Westweld. The defendant moved for summary judgment. What arguments for and against the motion occur to you? See Baker v. City of Seattle, 79 Wash.2d 198, 484 P.2d 405 (1971), citing Farnsworth, Implied Warranties of Quality in Non-Sales Cases, 57 Colum. L.Rev. 653 (1957).

GOLF CART RENTAL AGREEMENT

LESSOR - Westweld Metal Works

GOLF COURSE___ JA _____ DATE 7/7 19 67

LESSEE - CUSTOMER ___ Robert R. Baker ___

ADDRESS___ 20723 54th Ave W. ___

CITY - STATE ___ Lynnwood, Wash ___

CART NO.___ O ___ NO. OF HOLES 18 ___ AMOUNT 3 66

The above numbered MODEL TEE Golf Cart is hereby leased to the lessee for the number of holes of play on the date and on the golf course indicated above. If Lessee retains said cart after expiration thereof, such retention shall be construed as a new rental at the same rate of rental, and under the same terms and conditions as contained in this agreement. Said cart is not to be removed from the above named golf course and is to be returned promptly to the Lessor after use. Lessee represents that he is familiar with the use and operation of said cart. Lessee agrees to keep said cart in the Lessee's custody and not to sub-lease or re-rent same. Lessee agrees to keep and return said cart in the same condition as when received. Lessee agrees that in using said cart, he does so at his own risk. It is expressly understood and agreed that the Lessor shall not be liable for any damages whatsoever arising from injuries to the person and/or property damage or loss, of the Lessee arising from the use of, operation of, or in any way connected with said cart or any part thereof, from whatever cause arising. All provisions contained herein constitute the entire and exclusive agreement between the parties. Any promises, representations, understanding and/or agreement pertaining directly or indirectly to the agreement which are not contained herein, are hereby waived. The receipt of the above described cart, in good order and repair, is hereby acknowledged by Lessee.

THIS CART SHALL BE USED SOLELY FOR THE PURPOSES DESIGNED AND NO MORE THAN ONE PERSON AND TWO GOLF BAGS SHALL BE ON SAID CART AT ANY ONE TIME.

3448 _____ Robert R. Baker _____
(CUSTOMER) - LESSEE

[A3994]

Flatpakit © Moore Business Forms, Inc.

(4) *Problem.* The Rev. Elmer Russell took his wife, Bertha, to the Kansas City airport, from which she flew to attend a brother's funeral in Texas. They stopped at a booth for air-trip insurance. The attendant ask-

Wis.2d 563, 153 N.W.2d 532 (1967); Holmes v. National Van Lines, Inc., 55 Wash.2d 861, 350 P.2d 864 (1960); Sorenson-Christian Indus., Inc. v. Railway Express Ag., Inc., 434 F.2d 867 (4th Cir. 1970).

ed about the duration of the trip, and Russell said that four days should be allowed. The policy was written for that period, at a premium of $2.25. Mrs. Russell died in a crash on the return flight, about twelve hours after the policy expired. (The brother's funeral had been delayed.) Russell brought an action against the insurer for reformation of the policy, extending it to the return flight. The trial court found that the Russells intended to buy insurance for the round trip, which they thought would occur within four days. He found also that the attendant did not warn them of the expiration time, or explain the policy, or mention any other available policies. For a lesser premium, they could have purchased straight flight insurance in the same amount for the round trip (limited to 12 months), either at the booth or at a nearby vending machine. (It would not have afforded coverage, however, for risks unrelated to air travel, as the policy in question did.)

The trial court reformed the policy, and gave judgment for its face amount: $20,000. Both parties appealed, Russell contending that the judgment should have been for the amount of the straight flight insurance his premium would have bought: $90,000. The appellate opinion begins as follows: "Does the speed of the modern jet age and the restless, irrepressible, increased tempo of all who are in its vortex impose on a flight insurer the obligation toward prospective policy buyers of explaining the distinctive differences of the several available coverages? Does the insurer's attractive sales booth, neon signs heralding the need for and availability of 'flight insurance', and the other catchy advertising come-ons carry the inevitable message to scurrying people on the move the notion that the coverage is for the traveler's intended round trip rather than for a definitive period of time? And to avoid this misreading by people in a hurry of printed contracts plain enough that even those who run may read, must the insurer affirmatively take steps by extra-contract informational statements to overcome such misapprehension?"

What is your answer to these questions? See Mutual of Omaha Ins. Co. v. Russell, 402 F.2d 339, 29 A.L.R.3d 753, cert. denied, 394 U.S. 973 (1969).[g]

INCORPORATION BY REFERENCE

The following paragraph represents a technique of contract drafting closely connected with standard form contracts. It appeared in two contracts, each on one page, largely printed, each covering the sale of a quantity of cotton fabric to an export firm.

This Salesnote is subject to the provisions of Standard Cotton Textile Salesnote [a] which, by this reference, is incorpo-

---

g. Limitations in policies of air trip insurance, sold through vending machines, have sometimes been disregarded in suits by beneficiaries on the ground, apparently, that the buyer had insufficient opportunity to appreciate their effect. For notable discussions of this problem, see Lachs v. Fidelity & Casualty Co., 306 N.Y. 357, 118 N.E. 2d 555 (1954); Steven v. Fidelity & Casualty Co., 58 Cal.2d 862, 377 P.2d 284 (1962); Corbin, The Interpretation of Words and the Parol Evidence Rule, 50 Corn.L.Q. 161, 177, 184 (1965).

a. The Standard Cotton Textile Salesnote is the joint product of about a dozen trade associations representing

rated as a part of this agreement and together herewith constitutes the entire contract between buyer and seller.

Incorporation of standard terms by reference is common practice in many trades in which such terms have been prepared by trade associations. On private lawmaking by trade associations, see Note, 62 Harv.L.Rev. 1346 (1949).

As will be seen in Chapter 6, an agreement may be supplemented or qualified by a "usage of trade." This effect is usually confined, however, to cases in which each party is acquainted with the usage in question, or is situated so that he can fairly be expected to know of it. See Restatement Second, § 248. The technique of incorporating trade terms by reference may have the effect to imposing them on "outsiders". With reference to the paragraph quoted above it was said: "The effect of the foregoing contract provisions was to adopt, and to integrate into each purchase agreement, the terms of the standard cotton textile salesnote." Level Export Corp. v. Wolz, Aiken & Co., 305 N.Y. 82, 111 N.E.2d 218 (1953).

In the case quoted, the fabric seller sought arbitration of a dispute between the parties, provided for in the standard salesnote. The buyer, Level Export, moved to stay the arbitration proceedings, and one of its officers gave this affidavit in support of the motion : "Neither the petitioner [Level Export] nor any of its officers or directors is a member of any association or any textile group; none of us has ever seen the Worth Street Rules; we have never been provided with a copy thereof . . . . At the time that the petitioner signed the contracts . . . neither the petitioner nor any of its officers or directors was aware of any provision requiring arbitration under the contracts." The court ruled, however, in view of the character of the buyer—"an exporter of wide experience"—that its ignorance of the arbitration clause did not warrant the relief it sought.[b]

In international trade there are particular advantages in pre-defined terms, and organizations concerned with such trade have prepared two sets that are in current use by American firms engaged in foreign trade. Among the terms defined are "F.O.B." and "C.I.F.", both of which are given extensive definition in the Uniform Commercial Code. Do you see why the Code definitions do not meet the needs of such traders? And why incorporation by reference is important to them? See Farnsworth, Formation of International Sales Contracts: Three Attempts at Unification, 110 U.Pa.L.Rev. 305 (1962).[c]

the principal interests in the cotton textile markets—mills, selling houses, and buyers. It was published in 1935 as part of the Worth Street Rules, which also contain the rules of the General Arbitration Council of the Textile Industry. It was revised in 1941.

b. Compare Riverdale Fabrics Corp. v. Tillinghast-Stiles Co., 306 N.Y. 288, 118 N.E.2d 104, 41 A.L.R.2d 867 (1954), where the Level Export case was narrowly distinguished.

c. See also Schmitthoff, The Unification or Harmonization of Law by

NOTE

Problem. Seller takes a telephone order for goods, making no mention of arbitration. He then sends Buyer, in another state, an invoice reciting the terms agreed upon, and adding: "All controversies arising from the sale are to be settled by arbitration in Seller's state." If Buyer retains the invoice without objection, is he foreclosed from suing Seller for a defect in the goods? Would it matter where he sues? Would it matter if the invoice did not state the place for arbitration? Would it matter that the arbitration provision appeared in a distinctive type and color? Compare *Tanenbaum Textile Co. v. Schlanger*, 287 N.Y. 400, 40 N.E.2d 225 (1942), with *Southeastern Enameling Corp. v. General Bronze Corp.*, 434 F.2d 330 (5th Cir. 1970).[d]

Compare the variations mentioned above with the issues raised in the problem in Note 3, p. 200 supra. Which do you regard as the more appropriate as factors in deciding problems such as these?

HENNINGSEN v. BLOOMFIELD MOTORS, INC.

Supreme Court of New Jersey, 1960.
32 N.J. 358, 161 A.2d 69, 75 A.L.R.2d 1.

[Claus Henningsen purchased a new Plymouth automobile from Bloomfield Motors. His wife Helen was injured when the steering mechanism failed while she was driving it ten days after it had been delivered. They both sued Bloomfield Motors and the manufacturer, Chrysler Corporation, for breach of an implied warranty of merchantability imposed by the Uniform Sales Act. The defendants claimed that the warranty had been disclaimed, as permitted by the Act, and relied upon a provision contained on the back of the purchase contract, among eight and a half inches of fine print, which purported to limit liability for breach of warranty to replacement of defective parts for the period of 90 days after delivery or 4,000 miles of driving, whichever was shorter. The provisions on the back of the purchase contract were referred to on the front, above the signature elements, in language printed in six point type, as follows, although most of the language on the front was in twelve point type:[a]

Means of Standard Contracts and General Conditions, 17 Int. & Comp.L.Q. 551 (1968), distinguishing between model contracts, sets of standard conditions, and contracts of adhesion. On problems of incorporation by reference generally, see Whitman, Incorporation by Reference in Commercial Contracts, 21 Md.L.Rev. 1 (1961).

d. In the former case the seller testified: "I never speak to a customer about arbitration. It would be bad policy." As to the "cross-country" aspect of the arbitration provision, com-

pare the second case cited with *Player v. Geo. M. Brewster & Son, Inc.*, 18 Cal.App.3d 526, 96 Cal.Rptr. 149 (1971).

a. The cases in this book are set in 10 point type, the notes in 9 point type, and the footnotes in 8 point type. To a considerable extent, however, the readability of type depends not only on its size but also upon the width of the column, a point that is humorously made in "A Contract with Cunard," The New Yorker magazine, February 4, 1961, p. 36.

"The front and back of this Order comprise the entire agreement affecting this purchase and no other agreement or understanding of any nature concerning same has been made or entered into, or will be recognized. I hereby certify that no credit has been extended to me for the purchase of this motor vehicle except as appears in writing on the face of this agreement.

"I have read the matter printed on the back hereof and agree to it as a part of this order the same as if it were printed above my signature. I certify that I am 21 years of age, or older, and hereby acknowledge receipt of a copy of this order."

From judgment for the plaintiffs the defendant appealed.]

FRANCIS, J.[b] . . . In assessing [the disclaimer's] significance we must keep in mind the general principle that, in the absence of fraud, one who does not choose to read a contract before signing it, cannot later relieve himself of his burdens. . . . And in applying that principle, the basic tenet of freedom of competent parties to contract is a factor of importance. But in the framework of modern commercial life and business practices, such rules cannot be applied on a strict, doctrinal basis. . . . The traditional contract is the result of free bargaining of parties who are brought together by the play of the market, and who meet each other on a footing of approximate economic equality. In such a society there is no danger that freedom of contract will be a threat to the social order as a whole. But in present-day commercial life the standardized mass contract has appeared. It is used primarily by enterprises with strong bargaining power and position. "The weaker party, in need of the goods or services, is frequently not in a position to shop around for better terms, either because the author of the standard contract has a monopoly (natural or artificial) or because all competitors use the same clauses. His contractual intention is but a subjection more or less voluntary to terms dictated by the stronger party, terms whose consequences are often understood in a vague way, if at all." Kessler, "Contracts of Adhesion—Some Thoughts About Freedom of Contract," 43 Colum.L.Rev. 639, 632 (1943); Ehrenzweig, "Adhesion Contracts in the Conflict of Laws," 53 Colum.L.Rev. 1072, 1075, 1089 (1953). Such standardized contracts have been described as those in which one predominant party will dictate its law to an undetermined multiple rather than to an individual. They are said to resemble a law rather than a meeting of the minds. Siegelman v. Cunard White Star, 221 F.2d 189, 206 (2 Cir. 1955). . . .

b. The official report of this case fills sixty pages. It has been severely edited here to save space.

The warranty before us is a standardized form designed for mass use. It is imposed upon the automobile consumer. He takes it or leaves it, and he must take it to buy an automobile. No bargaining is engaged in with respect to it. In fact, the dealer through whom it comes to the buyer is without authority to alter it; his function is ministerial—simply to deliver it. The form warranty is not only standard with Chrysler but, as mentioned above, it is the uniform warranty of the Automobile Manufacturers Association. Members of the Association are: General Motors, Inc., Ford, Chrysler, Studebaker-Packard, American Motors (Rambler), Willys Motors, Checker Motors Corp., and International Harvester Company. Automobile Facts and Figures (1958 Ed., Automobile Manufacturers Association) 69. Of these companies, the "Big Three" (General Motors, Ford, and Chrysler) represented 93.5% of the passenger-car production for 1958 and the independents 6.5%. Standard & Poor (Industrial Surveys, Autos, Basic Analysis, June 25, 1959) 4109. And for the same year the "Big Three" had 86.72% of the total passenger vehicle registrations. Automotive News, 1959 Almanac (Slocum Publishing Co., Inc.) p. 25.

The gross inequality of bargaining position occupied by the consumer in the automobile industry is thus apparent. There is no competition among the car makers in the area of the express warranty. Where can the buyer go to negotiate for better protection? Such control and limitation of his remedies are inimical to the public welfare and, at the very least, call for great care by the courts to avoid injustice through application of strict common-law principles of freedom of contract. Because there is no competition among the motor vehicle manufacturers with respect to the scope of protection guaranteed to the buyer, there is no incentive on their part to stimulate good will in that field of public relations. Thus, there is lacking a factor existing in more competitive fields, one which tends to guarantee the safe construction of the article sold. Since all competitors operate in the same way, the urge to be careful is not so pressing. See "Warranties of Kind and Quality," 57 Yale L.J. 1389, 1400 (1948).

Although the courts, with few exceptions, have been most sensitive to problems presented by contracts resulting from gross disparity in buyer-seller bargaining positions, they have not articulated a general principle condemning, as opposed to public policy, the imposition on the buyer of a skeleton warranty as a means of limiting the responsibility of the manufacturer. They have endeavored thus far to avoid a drastic departure from age-old tenets of freedom of contract by adopting doctrines of strict construction, and notice and knowledgeable assent by the buyer to the attempted exculpation of the seller. 1 Corbin, supra, 337; 2 Harper & James [Law of Torts], 1590; Prosser, "Warranty of Merchantable Quality," 27 Minn.L.Rev. 117, 159 (1932). Accordingly to be found in the cases are statements that disclaimers and the consequent limitation of liability will not be given effect if "unfairly procured," . . . International Harvester Co. of America v. Bean, 159 Ky. 842, 169 S.W. 549 (Ct.App.1914) ; if not brought to the buyer's attention and he was not made understandingly aware of it . . . or if not clear and explicit. . . .

The rigid scrutiny which the courts give to attempted limitations of warranties and of the liability that would normally flow from a transaction is not limited to the field of sales of goods. Clauses on baggage checks restricting the liability of common carriers for loss or damage in transit are not enforceable unless the limitation is fairly and honestly negotiated and understandingly entered into. If not called specifically to the patron's attention, it is not binding. It is not enough merely to show the form of a contract; it must appear also that the agreement was understandingly made. . . . The same holds true in cases of such limitations on parcel check room tickets . . . and on storage warehouse receipts . . . ; on automobile parking lot or garage tickets or claim checks . . . ; as to exculpatory clauses in leases releasing a landlord of apartments in a multiple dwelling house from all liability for negligence where inequality of bargaining exists, see Annotation, 175 A.L.R. 8 (1948). And the validity of release clauses in orders signed by a depositor directing a bank to stop payment of his check, exonerating the bank from liability for negligent payment, has been seriously questioned on public policy grounds in this State. . . . Elsewhere they have been declared void as opposed to public policy. . . .

It is true that the rule governing the limitation of liability cases last referred to is generally applied in situations said to involve services of a public or semi-public nature. Typical, of course, are the public carrier or storage or parking lot cases. Kuzmiak v. Brookchester, 33 N.J.Super. 575, 111 A.2d 425 (App.Div.1954); Annotation, supra, 175 A.L.R. at pp. 14–17. But in recent times the books have not been barren of instances of its application in private contract controversies. . . .

Basically, the reason a contracting party offering services of a public or *quasi*-public nature has been held to the requirements of fair dealing, and, when it attempts to limit its liability, of securing the understanding consent of the patron or consumer, is because members of the public generally have no other means of fulfilling the specific need represented by the contract. Having in mind the situation in the automobile industry as detailed above, and particularly the fact that the limited warranty extended by the manufacturers is a uniform one, there would appear to be no just reason why the principles of all of the cases set forth should not chart the course to be taken here.

It is undisputed that the president of the dealer with whom Henningsen dealt did not specifically call attention to the warranty on the back of the purchase order. The form and the arrangement of its face, as described above, certainly would cause the minds of reasonable men to differ as to whether notice of a yielding of basic rights stemming from the relationship with the manufacturer was adequately given. The words "warranty" or "limited warranty" did not even appear in the fine print above the place for signature, and a jury might well find that the type of print itself was such as to promote lack of attention rather than sharp scrutiny. The inference from the facts is that Chrysler placed the method of communicating its warranty to the purchaser in the hands of the dealer. If either one or both of them wished to make certain that Henningsen became aware of that agreement and its purported implications, neither the form of the document nor the method of expressing the precise nature of the obligation intended to be assumed would have presented any difficulty.

But there is more than this. Assuming that a jury might find that the fine print referred to reasonably served the objective of directing a buyer's attention to the warranty on the reverse side, and, therefore, that he should be charged with awareness of its language, can it be said that an ordinary layman would realize what he was relinquishing in return for what he was being granted? Under the law, breach of warranty against defective parts or workmanship which caused personal injuries would entitle a buyer to damages even if due care were used in the manufacturing process. Because of the great potential for harm if the vehicle was defective, that right is the most important and fundamental one arising from the relationship. Difficulties so frequently encountered in establishing negligence in manufacture in the ordinary case make this manifest. 2 Harper & James, supra, §§ 28.14, 28.15; Prosser, supra, 506. Any ordinary layman of reasonable intelligence, looking at the phraseology, might well conclude that Chrysler was agreeing to replace defective parts and perhaps replace anything that went wrong because of defective workmanship during the first 90 days or 4,000 miles of operation, but that he would not be entitled to a new car. It is not unreasonable to believe that the entire scheme being conveyed was a proposed remedy for physical deficiencies in the car. *In the context* of this warranty, only the abandonment of all sense of justice would permit us to hold that, as a matter of law, the phrase "its obligation under this warranty being limited to making good at its factory any part or parts thereof" signifies to an ordinary reasonable person that he is relinquishing any personal injury claim that might flow from the use of a defective automobile. Such claims are nowhere mentioned. The draftsmanship is reflective of the care and skill of the Automobile Manufacturers Association in undertaking to avoid warranty obligations without drawing too much attention to its effort in that regard. No one can doubt that if the will to do so were present, the ability to inform the buying public of the intention to disclaim liability for injury claims arising from breach of warranty would present no problem. . . .

The task of the judiciary is to administer the spirit as well as the letter of the law. On issues such as the present one, part of that burden is to protect the ordinary man against the loss of important rights through what, in effect, is the unilateral act of the manufacturer. The status of the automobile industry is unique. Manufacturers are few in number and strong in bargaining position. In the matter of warranties on the sale of their products, the Automobile Manufacturers Association has enabled them to present a united front. From the standpoint of the purchaser, there can be no arms length negotiating on the subject. Because his capacity for bargaining is so grossly unequal, the inexorable conclusion which follows is that he is not permitted to bargain at all. He must take or leave the automobile on the warranty terms dictated by the maker. He cannot turn to a competitor for better security.

Public policy is a term not easily defined. Its significance varies as the habits and needs of a people may vary. It is not static and the field of application is an ever increasing one. A contract, or a particular provision therein, valid in one era may be wholly opposed to the public policy of another. . . . Courts keep in mind the principle that the best interests of society demand that persons should not be unnecessarily restricted in their freedom to contract. But they do not hesitate to declare void as against public policy contractual provisions which clearly tend to the injury of the public in some way.

. . . .

[Affirmed.]

NOTES

(1) *Warranty Disclaimers.* Was there any suggestion that Henningsen was concerned about the disclaimer clause or sought to negotiate for its modification? Does the result in Henningsen depend on the fact that other members of the industry followed the language proposed by the Association? Was there an agreement to do so? If the accident had occurred four months after the car had been delivered, would the disclaimer have been ineffective to bar recovery? The Henningsen case, which has become a landmark in the field of warranty disclaimers, will be discussed further in a course on sales or commercial law. Compare UCC 2–316(2) with 2–719 (1)(a), (3).

In 1963 the Chrysler Corporation began to give a warranty on parts of its cars for an extended term—as long as five years. For several years thereafter the automobile makers jockeyed for competitive advantage by extending and advertising their warranties. "The experience proved beyond doubt that consumers do care enough about warranties to make their selections felt competitively *if they are sufficiently informed to do so.*" Slawson, Standard Form Contracts, 84 Harv.L.Rev. 529, 548 (1971).

(2) *Contracts Compared.* Is the Henningsen case distinguishable from the O'Callaghan case, p. 319 supra? The opinion in Henningsen refers to a decision of a New Jersey intermediate court (Kuzmiak v. Brookchester, Inc.) on facts similar to those in O'Callaghan. In that case the court re-

versed a summary judgment for the defendant landlord, emphasizing the presumed inequality of bargaining power between the parties.

Is an apartment lease any less a contract of adhesion than a new-car purchase contract? Compare these with an automobile dealership contract. Was the one in York Chrysler-Plymouth v. Chrysler Credit Corp., p. 247 supra, an adhesion contract? Which is most like a gasoline service-station lease? See Weaver v. American Oil Co., — Ind. —, 276 N.E.2d 144 (1971).

Do the following remarks relate to each of these kinds of contract?

"The management of the large and successful corporation as a rule represents the ultimate in dependability. There is little doubt that, with the possible exception of political bosses, no persons as a class are more scrupulous in keeping promises. . . . But in nearly all these situations the corporation is subject to minimal competitive pressures, the services of the small man are not unique, and if relations with him are severed, many other small men are available to take his place. . . . It is far simpler to require adhesion to a contract that commits the business legally to a performance far less than it expects to render, to hedge promises about with conditions that it does not expect to insist upon, unless the other party proves to be evil or unstable. If carefully prepared, the contract, supplemented by verbal assurances, has the advantage of raising the expectations necessary to induce the desired performance and at the same time insulate against liability . . . [But] the contract of adhesion, though conceived in a worthy cause, has the effect of depriving every adherent of a day in court." Havighurst, The Nature of Private Contract 78, 115–17 (1961).

(3) *Overservice by the Profession.* "The lawyer who serves his client without regard to the public welfare, though he succeed in getting the decision in a particular case, in the long run does his client no real service, and, if you want an illustration, let me briefly refer to the extraordinary service which insurance lawyers rendered the insurance business in years gone by, in exaggerating warranties to the point where they were almost one hundred per cent protection against claims, only to develop a public atmosphere resulting in judicial decision and legislation which puts the insurer under his contract in a worse position today than is any other contracting party. That is overservice by the profession." Parkinson, Are the Law Schools Adequately Training for the Public Service?, 8 Am.Law School Rev. 291, 294 (1935).

(4) *Problem.* For $6,000 Robert Reid bought a new Lincoln Continental car from a Ford dealer, under an express warranty: "each part . . . to be free . . . from defects in material and workmanship," for twelve months or 24,000 miles. "All the warranties shall be fulfilled by the Selling Dealer . . . replacing with a genuine [Ford] part, or repairing . . . free of charge . . . any such defective part." Implied warranties were excluded. While the car was parked in Reid's garage, attached to his house, a fire was observed in the electrical harness under the front seat, and in a few minutes the fire spread, consuming car, garage, and house. Suing the Ford Motor Company, Reid obtained a verdict and

judgment for $89,000, and Ford appealed. On these facts alone, what result? See Ford Motor Co. v. Reid, 465 S.W.2d 80 (Ark.1971).[c]

JUDICIAL CONTROL OF STANDARD FORM CONTRACTS

For the courts to be concerned about standard form contracts is no new thing. In 1873 Chief Justice Doe of New Hampshire described with passion and irony the difficulty an insurance buyer would face in appreciating the terms of an elaborate insurance policy. "The compound, if read by him, would, unless he were an extraordinary man, be an inexplicable riddle, a mere flood of darkness and confusion. . . . [I]t was printed in such small type, and in lines so long and so crowded, that the perusal of it was made physically difficult, painful, and injurious. Seldom has the art of typography been so successfully diverted from the diffusion of knowledge to the suppression of it. There was ground for the premium payer to argue that the print alone was evidence, competent to be submitted to a jury, of a fraudulent plot." Delancey v. Insurance Co., 52 N.H. 581.

As a main counterpoise to such "plots," the courts have developed the principle that ambiguities in an insurance contract are to be resolved against the draftsman. In some cases the principle has been pressed beyond the limits of common sense. "The conclusion is inescapable that courts have sometimes invented ambiguity where none existed, then resolving the invented ambiguity contrary to the plainly expressed terms of the contract document." Keeton, Insurance Law (Basic Text) 356 (1971). To some degree the same technique is evident in cases concerning standard form contracts of many other types as well. In particular, some courts have shown a perverse inability to understand the terms of contracts that purport to exculpate a party from the consequences of his own negligence.

Decisions of this character have been regarded by some judges, and others, as discreditable. In one case of strained interpretation of an insurance form, for example, Judge Charles E. Clark[a] concurred on the ground that the insurer's conduct was "unpardonable." He wrote: "I do not think we can properly or should rest upon an ambiguity of the company's forms. . . . [A] result placed not squarely upon inequity, but upon interpretation, seems sure to pro-

---

c. See Ellinghaus, In Defense of Unconscionability, 78 Yale L.J. 757, 766–67 (1969): "Just because the contract I signed was proffered to me by Almighty Monopoly Incorporated does not mean that I may subsequently argue exemption from any or all obligation: at the very least, some element of deception or substantive unfairness must presumably be shown."

a. Charles Edward Clark (1889–1963) practiced in New York City for six years, joined the faculty of the Yale Law School in 1919, and became its dean in 1929. In 1939 he was appointed to the United States Court of Appeals for the Second Circuit, and he served as its chief judge from 1954–1959. As a scholar, he was particularly active in the field of civil procedure.

duce continuing uncertainty in the law of insurance contracts." [b]   In similar vein, Judge Frank dissented from a decision which denied a steamship passenger recovery for personal injuries because of clauses printed on her ticket.   (The case was Siegelman v. Cunard White Star, cited in Henningsen v. Bloomfield Motors, p. 335 supra.)   Judge Frank appealed for a forthright approach:

"I call attention to another factor which, while unnecessary to my conclusion, I think supports it: The ticket is what has been called a 'contract of adhesion' or a 'take-it-or-leave-it' contract.   In such a standardized or mass-production agreement, with one-sided control of its terms, when the one party has no real bargaining power, the usual contract rules, based on the idea of 'freedom of contract,' cannot be applied rationally.   For such a contract is 'sold not bought.'   The one party dictates its provisions; the other has no more choice in fixing those terms than he has about the weather.   The insurance policy cases are outstanding examples, but there are many others.   Our courts, in particular contexts, have, in effect, nullified many provisions of such agreements, if unfair to the weaker party who must take-or-leave.   Often our courts have done so by rather strained constructions of seemingly unambiguous language or by other indirect or 'back-door' methods.   Referring to such decisions, several brilliant commentators [including Kessler, Llewellyn and Patterson] have suggested that the courts forthrightly adopt a general doctrine which calls for refusal to enforce directly—i. e., without recourse to such indirect devices—highly unfair provisions of all so-called 'contracts of adhesion' where there was no possibility of real bargaining.   These writers urge that some decisions, in cases where this point of view was not presented to, or considered by, the courts should not now be deemed controlling.   Their position is that of Holmes and Corbin, i. e., that the courts will do justice better by forthrightly, not obliquely, articulating important doctrines of public policy.   The commentators on 'adhesion' contracts do not at all suggest that all standardized contracts be stricken down, for they recognize that such contracts often serve a highly useful purpose when the parties are not markedly unequal in bargaining power (as in many 'commercial' contracts)."   Siegelman v. Cunard White Star, 221 F.2d 189, 204–05 (2d Cir. 1955).

NOTES

(1) *Adhesion and Democracy.* The courts have been urged to develop a "set of legal principles" for treating standard form contracts, by analogy to those for reviewing administrative regulations, so as to "reconcile the interests of issuers in setting such terms as they wish on an agreement and of the consumer in having his reasonable expectations fulfilled." Slawson, Standard Form Contracts and Democratic Control of Lawmaking Pow-

b. Gaunt v. John Hancock Mut. Life
   Ins. Co., 160 F.2d 599, cert. denied
   331 U.S. 849 (1947).

er, 84 Harv.L.Rev. 529, 532 (1971). Some premises of the argument are these:

(a) That standard forms are undemocratic, in the sense that they amount to private lawmaking without the legitimacy conferred by the "consent of the governed," [c] that they necessarily tend toward unfairness, and that indeed they are hardly ever contracts at all, "as customarily used in consumer transactions;" but

(b) That standardized undertakings are essential to many business undertakings, and that it would be "unrealistic to confer on courts broad powers to rewrite standard forms."

"There being no private consent to support a contract of adhesion, its legitimacy rests entirely on its compliance with standards in the public interest." Id., 566. The principle of unconscionability, according to Professor Slawson, should be reserved for terms that are not "adhered to" in the usual way of standard forms.[d]

Would it be a better technique for a court, dealing with an adhesion contract, to construct a hypothetical bargaining process between the parties, and to implement only those terms that would survive, with the judge acting as "impartial arbiter"? See Oldfather, Toward a Usable Method of Judicial Review of the Adhesion Contractor's Lawmaking, 16 U.Kan.L.Rev. 303 (1968).

(2) *Brokers' Commissions.* Determining when a real estate broker's commission is earned has been a continuing problem in the law. The answer depends in part, of course, on the character of the arrangement between the broker and the person promising to pay him: the conditions agreed upon, and the court's construction of them. To this extent, the matter is dealt with in Chapter 6, infra. In a notable New Jersey case, however, considerations of public policy were brought to bear on the problem in a novel way.

Ordinarily a broker looks to the seller for his fee. Sometimes the seller agrees to pay only if a sale is consummated through the broker's efforts, and the fee is not earned at the point when the seller and a buyer enter into a contract for sale. In that manner the seller is protected from having to pay a broker's fee in the event a contract for sale is made, but the buyer refuses to perform it. In the New Jersey case the court indicated that such protection is a reasonable expectation of owners, and consistent with the expectations of conscientious brokers.

But the question then arises whether or not, by an explicit agreement in the broker's contract, he may earn a commission by producing a responsible buyer and effecting a contract, whatever happens thereafter. To this the court answered with an (almost) categorical No. It discussed uncon-

c. Automobile manufacturers, Professor Slawson observes, "make more warranty law in a day than most legislatures or courts make in a year." Op. cit. supra, 530.

d. But compare Ellinghaus, In Defense of Unconscionability, 78 Yale L.J. 757, 773 (1969), on UCC 2–302: "Comment 1 goes to some lengths to establish a climate in which courts will feel emboldened to strike directly at contracts or contractual terms which appear too heavily weighted in favor of one of the parties; that is to act, in some measure at least, as a tribunal of constitutional review applying 'bill-of-rights' prescriptions to the parties' private legislation."

scionability at length, citing the Henningsen case and UCC 2–302. In support of its position, the court adverted to the standardization of brokers' contracts and the statutory licensing of brokers. It described brokers as fiduciaries. Apparently it concluded that in all his usual employment the broker enjoys such bargaining power that the agreement described is contrary to public policy, calling it contrary to the common understanding of men, and contrary to common fairness. The opinion leaves open only the faintest possibility that a clearly expressed agreement of this nature might be given effect between bargaining equals. Ellsworth Dobbs, Inc. v. Johnson, 50 N.J. 528, 236 A.2d 843 (1967).

For further comment on the case, see p. 638 infra; Note, 23 Rutgers L.Rev. 83 (1968).

LEGISLATIVE CONTROL OF STANDARD FORM CONTRACTS

As the foregoing materials show, the problems associated with standard form contracts have been given legislative as well as judicial attention. Other examples are to follow.

Under legislative auspices, some progress has also been made in redressing imbalances of bargaining power which underlie the problems. For example, in labor relations law, federal statutes have not only facilitated the organization of individual employees into unions, whose bargaining power may equal or exceed that of an employer, but they also direct that both unions and employers bargain "in good faith." The anti-trust laws may also have an incidental effect by helping to preserve a party's opportunity to choose among those with whom he may deal, but they have no immediate concern with ensuring that his choice is among parties whose bargaining power approximates his own.

Most legislation directly germane to standard form contracts has one or both of the following objects: to compel *disclosure* of contract terms, and to *control* the terms employed. The contracts affected by such statutes are commonly those offered to the general public by some well-organized segment of business or industry. Insurance policies and consumer sale contracts are examples.

Disclosure. The decade of the 60's featured legislative battles over required disclosures in a wide range of consumer credit transactions, both sales and loans. It culminated in the federal Truth-in-Lending Act of 1968,[a] and Regulation Z issued thereunder by the Federal Reserve Board, requiring certain disclosures as to credit terms. The same legislative technique is manifested in many state and local enactments affecting merchants: they are required to give their customers ready access to certain information thought essential to the making of intelligent choices among products.

---

a. Part of the Consumer Credit Protection Act, 15 U.S.C.A. §§ 1601 et seq.

It is a common adjunct of such legislation to require that the required information be disclosed in a particular form: that the nature of the agreement be clearly set forth in the title, or that printed terms be in type of at least a certain size or (less frequently) in red ink. The Uniform Commercial Code occasionally demands in more general terms that a provision be "conspicuous", and other legislation has followed suit. (The Code definition of the word is at UCC 1–201(10).[b])

For some purposes it is required in the Code that the recipient of a writing have "reason to know of its contents." See, e. g., UCC 2–201(2). The Code also requires in a few instances that terms be "separately signed" as a protection against inadvertent signing. See, e. g., UCC 2–209(2); UCC 1–201(39) (definition of "signed" includes initials). On a simpler level, there is the requirement in a New York statute on retail installment sales contracts that they include this admonition to buyers: "Do not sign this agreement until you read it." [c]

Do any of the foregoing statutory provisions go to the point made in the Henningsen case that the "ordinary layman would [not] realize what he was relinquishing in return for what he was being granted," even if he were aware of the language of the agreement? Until recently at least, attempts to deal with this aspect of the problem by statute have been uncommon. Do you see why? Some attempts made in the Code, in relation to warranties, are presented in the following materials.

The utility of disclosure requirements is intrinsically limited, and especially so as to groups who suffer most from an imbalance of bargaining power. The following comment makes the point in relation to the low-income consumer: "In sum, the new wave of informational legislation will be of little help to the poor because it presupposes values, motivation and knowledge which do not generally exist among them. The actual problem is not just a shortage of a narrowly defined sort of information—such as the price per pound of prepackaged food—but a total breakdown in the function the consumer is supposed to play in the market. 'Bad buys' are the rule and price and quality competition the exception. As one merchant in New York put it: 'People do not *shop* in this area . . . . It is just up to who catches him.' " Note, Consumer Legislation and the Poor, 76 Yale L.J. 745, 754 (1967).

b. For a case refusing to give effect to a disclaimer of an implied warranty on the ground that it did not meet the Code standard of conspicuousness, see Entron, Inc. v. General Cablevision of Palatka, 435 F.2d 995 (5th Cir. 1970). Note that the court applied the Code to a *construction* contract. But it ruled also that the purported disclaimer was ineffective under applicable state law (other than the Code), even if the contract were to be regarded as one for services.

c. Pers.Prop.L. § 402.

Control of Terms. The classic example of statutes controlling the terms of agreements is usury legislation. Statutes that restrict charges for credit (not only usury laws, but also many specialized provisions for consumer credit) are characterized by precise limits. A very different example of statutory intervention in agreements is UCC 2–302, directing courts to refuse enforcement of a contract or term found to be "unconscionable". (Materials on this topic appear below.) Considered as approaches to the problems of standard form contracts, rules about usury and about unconscionability show that legislative and judicial methods do not confront one another along a simple line.

Statutes about exculpation clauses in leases, mentioned in the O'Callaghan case and the notes after it, illustrate legislative *prohibitions* on the use of particular terms. A Code illustration is UCC 2–318, forbidding a provision by which a buyer's family or guests might be deprived of the benefit of the seller's warranties. More generally, the Code prohibits disclaimer of "the obligations of good faith, diligence, reasonableness and care prescribed by this Act." UCC 1–102(3). Many other state statutes, again concentrated in fields such as insurance and consumer sales, also deny effect to proscribed terms.

Another legislative technique for controlling the terms of an agreement is to *require the inclusion* of a term. In some instances a complete contract is prescribed. A standard form of fire insurance policies is generally set out in state statutes or departmental regulations, and the terms of ocean bills of lading are set out in the federal Carriage of Goods by Sea Act. A more usual form of statute is one that prescribes one or more standard provisions for a given type of contract, leaving the remainder to be created by the parties. This is a common method of control in the fields of life, accident and health, and liability insurance. Whether the entire contract or only some of its provisions are prescribed, the statute may provide that the dominant party may use language different from that set out in the statute as long as this does not result in a "lessening" of his liability, or as long as it is "not less favorable" to the other party. But the risks involved in tampering with the statutory formulations are obvious.

The sanctions provided for violation of legislative controls over the contract vary widely. Among the most common are invalidation of the offending provision or of so much of it as is offensive, revocation of a license to engage in the business involved, and the criminal penalties of fine and imprisonment. Legislation dealing with contract clauses in fine print is discussed in Note, 63 Harv.L.Rev. 494 (1950). See Kimball and Pfennigstorf, Legislative and Judicial Control of the Terms of Insurance Contracts: A Comparative Study of American and European Practice, 39 Ind.L.J. 675 (1964).

A novelty in legislative control over agreements is the now-usual provision of state law about an element of automobile insurance known as "uninsured motorists coverage." An insured driver is compensated under this coverage by his own insurer when he is injured by the fault of another, lacking insurance against liability, as if the other driver had been so insured. The terms of the coverage are more or less prescribed, but it is commonly not required to be included in the basic contract. Rather, the statutes require that it be *tendered* in connection with a sale of automobile insurance, with the thought that few buyers will actively decline the offer. A statute in Michigan requires that the policy "contain a notice, displayed prominently on the front page of the policy, in at least 8-point type that such protection coverage was explained to [the named insured] and that he can reject such coverage by notice in writing." [d] Apart from such a provision, it has been held that the insurer has no duty to explain the coverage to a customer unless he asks about it.[e]

NOTES

(1) *Knowledge and Behavior.* The Truth-in-Lending Act, and some comparable state statutes, require that merchants and lending institutions provide their customers with certain information about their credit terms, when making installment sales and loans in the consumer market, as defined. Among other figures to be disclosed, it is required that the finance charge be stated as a percentage of the amount financed, on an annual basis. "The purpose in requiring a creditor or seller to state the charges on the loan in terms of simple annual interest is to allow a consumer to make intelligent comparisons between different creditors and alternate forms of financing that were not directly comparable prior to the acts unless one had a sophisticated knowledge of principles of accounting." White and Munger, Consumer Sensitivity to Interest Rates, 69 Mich.L.Rev. 1209 n. 7 (1971). This article reports a study of a group of car buyers, and several lenders making credit available in their community, to test the hypothesis that the disclosures required have little effect on buyers' choices among available sources of credit. It tended to confirm that hypothesis.

(2) *Judicial or Legislative Solution?* Owing to the nature of the judicial process, the role of the courts in dealing with standardized contracts is restricted to case-by-case consideration of specific contracts ordinarily based on information presented by the parties, and characteristically limited to a decision either to enforce or not to enforce the contract or a term in the contract. It is therefore natural to ask whether these problems, or at least some of them, could be dealt with more effectively by legislation than by case law. The three excerpts that follow suggest some of the arguments on both sides.

"Attempts to revise the more basic unequal distribution of coercive power among individuals which is registered in normal market prices themselves, would require remedies which courts alone would be incapable of furnishing, and inquiries for which they are not fitted. . . . But because courts can do nothing to revise the underlying pattern of market relationships, it does not follow that other organs of government should make

---

d. Mich.Stat.Ann.1969 Cum.Supp. § 24.-10310.

e. Lopez v. Midwest Mutual Ins. Co., 223 So.2d 550 (Fla.App.1969).

no attempt to accord greater freedom to the economically weak from the restrictions which stronger individuals place upon them by means of the coercive bargaining power which the law now permits or enables them to assert." Hale, Bargaining, Duress, and Economic Liberty, 43 Colum.L.Rev. 603, 625 (1943).

"It is hard to prove the factual justification of laissez faire capitalism; it is also hard to disprove it. In practical politics, in disputes about the wisdom of particular legislation, the issue is framed differently. The immediate effects of restrictive legislation, in mitigating or removing certain evils, can often be measured with as much precision as the value of the conclusions requires. On the contrary, the effects of such a restriction in diminishing the beneficent effects of freedom of enterprise often cannot be measured at all. The economic evaluation of compulsory contract vs. freedom of enterprise is thus a weighing of ponderables against imponderables." Patterson, Compulsory Contracts in the Crystal Ball, 43 Colum.L.Rev. 731, 746 (1943).

"[Legislation] has a serious disadvantage. It does away with the flexibility without which only very few trades can do. It enlarges the business man's risk and does not allow him to take measures against its increase, measures which only he can devise and which must be applied rapidly. Legislative compulsion works best where a trade has grown into a quasi-governmental function, as, e. g., insurance or traffic; it is almost impossible in all other branches." Prausnitz, The Standardization of Commercial Contracts in English and Continental Law 145 (1937).

(3) *The Red-Letter Auto Policy.* An insurer doing business in Maine proposed to issue an automobile liability policy containing this warning, in red letters, on its cover: "This is not a Standard Automobile Policy . . [and] in general does not cover operation of the insureds' automobiles by others." The Insurance Commissioner disapproved the form, one of his findings being (in summary) as follows: "it is so limited as to be beyond the reasonable comprehension of the average policyholder, who through the years, has been educated to a broadening of coverages under liability policies insuring his automobile."

The insurer appealed against the Commissioner's action, and observed that the charge for the policy would be less than that for more conventional coverages. The action was based on a statute prohibiting the use of forms found to be illegal, misleading, or "capable of a construction which is unfair to the assured or the public."

The appeal was allowed in part. Most of the Commissioner's specific objections were unwarranted, except in the opinion of one justice. The court observed that affording the coverage might induce more motorists to insure themselves, particularly those in the "less endowed financial group." American Fidelity Co. v. Mahoney, 157 Me. 507, 174 A.2d 446 (1961).

ADMINISTRATIVE CONTROL OF STANDARD FORM CONTRACTS

Some of the disadvantages associated with legislation, such as inflexibility, can be avoided if control over contract terms is given by the legislature to an administrative agency. Agencies on the federal, state and local levels play a significant role in controlling contract terms in many areas. In some instances they act in a quasi-judicial way, as when the Federal Trade Commission charges a merchant with deceptive practices. Some agencies have a policing function with respect to statutory controls over contract terms. This is notably true of insurance departments. For example, in New York a life insurer may employ a suicide clause as stated by statute, or one which is in the opinion of the superintendent of insurance "substantially the same or more favorable to policyholders." [a] As to certain policies, he has the larger function of disapproving a form "if it contains provisions which encourage misrepresentation or are unjust, unfair, unequitable, misleading, deceptive, contrary to law or to the public policy of this state." [b]

The charge given to many administrative agencies has to do more with controlling the charges made within a given business or industry than with the language of agreements employed in it. That is so with respect to the regulation of common carriers and public utilities. Yet agencies engaged in such regulation have on occasion used their powers so as to exert control over contract language as well as rates.[c]

NOTES

(1) *Agencies v. Courts.* The fact that oversight of a business has been committed to an administrative agency is sometimes a handicap to one of its customers when he objects in litigation to the application of a burdensome provision in a standard form used by the business. If the business is a regulated carrier, for example, whose rates are approved by a public agency in conjunction with its contract forms, a court may be reluctant to declare that the contract favors the carrier unduly. For reasoning tending to sustain a regulated firm's contract exculpating it from liability for negligence, see Southwestern Sugar & Molasses Co. v. River Terminals Corp., 360 U.S. 411 (1959), in which the Court said: "For all

a. Ins.L. § 155.

b. Ins.L. § 141.

In 1971 the New York department was directed to regulate accident and health insurance policies so as to achieve, among other objectives, "reasonable standardization and simplification of coverages to facilitate understanding and comparisons," and the elimination of provisions which "may be contrary to the health care needs of the public," and of "coverages which are so limited in scope as to be of no substantial economic value to the holders thereof." N.Y.Ins.L. § 174–2(2).

c. The Natural Gas Act requires that every natural gas company file with the Federal Power Commission not only information relating to its rates, but also all contracts relating to its rates. Under its rate-making power, the Commission has issued an administrative regulation declaring that any contract term providing for a change in price shall be of no effect unless it comes within one of three types specified in the regulation. See 15 U.S.C.A. §§ 717c, 717d; 18 C.F.R. § 154.93. Similarly, the Federal Communications Commission under its statutory power to license radio and television stations has issued regulations providing that no station will be licensed if it has a contract with a network that contains certain provisions specified in the regulations. See, e. g., 47 U.S.C. § 308; 47 C.F.R. § 73.658, concerning television stations.

we know, it may be that the rate specified in the relevant tariff is computed on the understanding that the exculpatory clause shall apply . . ., and is a reasonable rate so computed. . . . The rule of [liability], however applicable where the towboat owner has 'the power to drive hard bargains,' may well call for modification when that power is effectively controlled by a pervasive regulatory scheme." [d] An instance of the same tendency appears in some litigation over insurance contracts, which are usually construed in favor of the policyholder. If the form of the contract has been approved by an insurance department, should the courts strive for a "neutral" interpretation? For the view that terms prescribed by statute are to be literally interpreted, see Goldman v. Piedmont Fire Ins. Co., 198 F.2d 712 (3d Cir. 1952). But see Kimball and Pfennigstorf, Legislative and Judicial Control of the Terms of Insurance Contracts, 39 Ind.L.J. 674, 703–4, 729 (1964), referring to "the significant role of industry representatives in drafting standard policies."

(2) *Israeli Law.* By the Israeli Standard Contracts Law of 1958 an administrative board was empowered to act on applications to approve "restrictive" terms that suppliers propose to use in standard contracts. Clauses within a broad range are made ineffective in the absence of prior approval; those approved are not to be judicially questioned for a period specified by the board. The issue is framed for the board in terms of unfair advantage to suppliers, and prejudice to customers. Evidence from various sources is contemplated, and the board's decisions are reviewable in the Supreme Court. The board's first application came from the American firm, Dun & Bradstreet. How readily could this arrangement be adapted to conditions in this country? See Comment, Administrative Regulation of Adhesion Contracts in Israel, 66 Colum.L.Rev. 1340 (1966).

CONFESSION OF JUDGMENT

By statutes and rules in Pennsylvania, dating back to the forepart of the 19th century, it has been possible for a creditor to obtain a judgment against his debtor without service of process on, or other notification to him. For this purpose it is necessary to prepare a contract by which the debtor authorizes, or "warrants," an attorney or court officer of the creditor's choosing to appear for the debtor and confess judgment, and a provision to this effect is known as a "confession of judgment" clause. It is also known as a *cognovit*, and it has a lengthy common-law history. Many standard form contracts, such as retail installment sale contracts, contain such a clause.[a]

---

d. On remand, the case was ultimately decided on other grounds. River Terminals Corp. v. Southwestern Sugar and Molasses Co., 274 F.2d 36 (5th Cir. 1960). See, also, as to the problems of towing contracts, Fluor Western, Inc. v. G & H Offshore Towing Co., 447 F.2d 35 (5th Cir. 1971).

a. The following example is taken from Swarb v. Lennox, cited below: "Each buyer and co-buyer, jointly and severally, hereby authorize and empower the Prothonotary, Clerk or any attorney, or any court of record within the United States or elsewhere, at any time, to appear for each buyer and a co-buyer and to confess judgment as often as necessary against each buyer and of co-buyer and in favor of the holder, as of any term, with or without declaration filed for

Commonly the debtor, who signs such a contract, first learns that proceedings have been taken against him when he learns that a judgment has been entered against him and that a sheriff's sale has been scheduled to dispose of his property to satisfy the judgment. He may then apply to open the judgment on various grounds, but there are certain burdens and expenses attendant on obtaining this relief.

In some other states, Ohio being one, confession of judgment provisions are given comparable effect. In D. H. Overmyer Co. v. Frick Co., 405 U.S. 174, 92 S.Ct. 775 (1972), the contention was made by a judgment debtor (Overmyer) that the Ohio courts had deprived it of due process in giving effect to its cognovit note. The Court disagreed, observing that Overmyer "voluntarily, intelligently and knowingly waived the rights it otherwise possessed to pre-judgment notice and hearing, and that it did so with full awareness of the legal consequences." [b]

On the same day the Court affirmed the decision in Swarb v. Lennox, a Pennsylvania case.[c] That was a class action brought by 47 persons against whom confessed judgments had been entered, seeking to enjoin court officials in Philadelphia County from acting on such judgments. The federal district court concluded that the procedure transgressed the Fourteenth Amendment, to the extent that the clauses did not represent an understanding waiver of notice. The order it entered included a prohibition on entering judgments against a defined class of persons "on the basis of confession of judgment clauses . . . unless it has been shown that the signers of such clauses have intentionally, understandingly, and voluntarily waived" the rights impaired by the clauses, when executing a document containing such a clause. The court left it for state authorities to determine what would constitute an understanding waiver, but it made

such sum or sums as may be payable hereunder with the cost of suit with 20 per cent added as attorney's fees. With respect to any judgment and exemption under any law now or hereafter in force, and each hereby agrees that real estate may be sold under a writ or execution and voluntarily condemns the same and authorize the Prothonotary or Clerk to enter said condemnation on such writ; and each buyer and co-buyer agrees that a true copy hereof, verified by affidavit made by the holder or someone acting on its behalf, may be filed in such proceeding in lieu of filing the original as warrant of attorney, any rule of court, custom to practice to the contrary notwithstanding. Any judgment entered hereon or of any prior note for which the note is in whole or in part mediately or immediately renewal shall be secured, security for the payment hereof and of any future note which is in whole or in part mediately or immediately renewal hereof."

b. Overmyer was a corporate enterprise with widespread activities. The note was given in the process of readjusting an obligation for a refrigeration system costing about a quarter of a million dollars. Overmyer's counsel advised it in this transaction, and it received ample consideration.

The Court said: "Our holding, of course, is not controlling precedent for other facts of other cases. For example, where the contract is one of adhesion, where there is great disparity in bargaining power, and where the debtor receives nothing for the cognovit provision, other legal consequences may ensue."

c. 314 F.Supp. 1091 (E.D.Pa.1970).

these remarks: "Where the debtor is an attorney, all that may be necessary to prove that he understood the meaning and consequences of such a clause in a consumer financing note is an affidavit of such a debtor's profession. On the other hand, more proof may be required of non-high school graduates . . .." The court defined the class of persons entitled to the protection of its decree as follows: "individual natural persons, resident in Pennsylvania and having incomes . . .[d] of less than $10,000. per year at the time of the execution of . . . leases and consumer financing documents," excepting certain mortgage documents.[e] The court also defined "consumer transaction" as one in which the money, property, or services received is "primarily for personal, family, or household purposes."

The decision was appealed to the Supreme Court by the *complainants*. They were represented by a legal services organization. The Attorney General of Pennsylvania did not seek to sustain the validity of the state statutes. In affirming, the Supreme Court observed that "the impact and effect of Overmyer [the decision in the Ohio case cited above] upon the Pennsylvania system are not to be delineated in the one-sided appeal in this case and we make no attempt to do so." [f]

In Cutler Corp. v. Latshaw, 374 Pa. 1, 97 A.2d 234 (1953), the court ordered that a confessed judgment be stricken on the ground, largely, that the authorization for it appeared in the contract on the back of a page, in a mass of fine-type verbiage. The court did not rely on the due process clause.

Do any other problems encountered in this chapter appear to have a constitutional dimension?

d. "or conjugal incomes where both spouses have signed the documents."

e. One of the judges on the three-judge court dissented from the dollar limitation.

The evidence on which the court relied included a study by Dr. David Caplovitz, in which questions were addressed to a sample of defaulting debtors in Philadelphia. His report was that only 4% of those surveyed had incomes of over $10,000, and that of 236 debtors who were aware of signing a contract only 14% knew that it contained a confession of judgment clause. Numerous firms and organizations appeared in the case either as parties or as amici curiae, including finance companies, trade associations, consumer-protection groups, and the like.

f. Swarb v. Lennox, 405 U.S. 191, 92 S.Ct. 767 (1972). The Court noted the "pervasive and drastic character of the Pennsylvania system," and cited these cases for further description of it: Cutler Corp. v. Latshaw, infra; Kine v. Forman, 404 Pa. 301, 172 A. 2d 164 (1961); Atlas Credit Corp. v. Ezrine, 25 N.Y.2d 219, 303 N.Y.S.2d 382, 250 N.E.2d 474 (1969).

Justice Douglas dissented, believing that the Court should have discussed the merits and reached all the issues tendered.

NOTE

Questions. Was the district court's decree in Swarb v. Lennox unwarranted because it usurped a legislative or rule-making function? Does it portend a displacement of contract law by principles of constitutional law? See Skilton and Helstad, Protection of the Installment Buyer of Goods Under the UCC, 65 Mich.L.Rev. 1465, 1475 (1967): "We should not sell the future short. Notions of what constitute fundamental justice, due process, and equal protection are dynamic, not static." Was the court's reliance on the Caplovitz survey appropriate? For a parody of the opinion suggesting that it was not, see P. S., In re: Social Science in the Eastern District of Pennsylvania, 32 U.Pitt.L.Rev. 463 (1971). How would the decision apply to a young doctor, beginning practice, who buys a car on credit for mixed personal and professional use?

UNCONSCIONABLE CONTRACTS UNDER THE UNIFORM COMMERCIAL CODE

One of the most controversial sections of the Uniform Commercial Code is UCC 2–302, which authorizes a court to refuse enforcement or to limit the application of a contract or clause that it determines to have been "unconscionable." The comment to that section reads in part:

"This section is intended to make it possible for the courts to police explicitly against the contracts or clauses which they find to be unconscionable. In the past such policing has been accomplished by adverse construction of language, by manipulation of the rules of offer and acceptance or by determinations that the clause is contrary to public policy or to the dominant purpose of the contract. . . . The principle is one of the prevention of oppression and unfair surprise (Cf. Campbell Soup Co. v. Wentz, 172 F.2d 80, 3d Cir. 1948) and not of disturbance of allocation of risks because of superior bargaining power." [a]

Professor Llewellyn, the Chief Reporter of the Code, defended the section at the hearings of the New York Law Revision Commission in 1954 in these words:

"Business lawyers tend to draft to the edge of the possible. Any engineer makes his construction within a margin of safety, and a wide margin of safety, so that he knows for sure that he is getting what he is gunning for. The practice of business lawyers has been, however —it has grown to be so in the course of time—to draft, as I said before, to the edge of the possible.

"Let me rapidly state that I do not find that this is desired by the business lawyers' clients. In all the time that I have been working

---

a. The comment is reprinted in full in the Supplement. The section itself appears there and in Jones v. Star Credit Co., p. 379 infra.

on this Code, and before, one of the more striking phenomena has been to me that the lawyers insist on having all kinds of things that their clients don't want at all.   If I get together with a gang of business lawyers in regard to a portion of the Code, I have a perfectly terrible time trying to make them see any sense at all.   If, on the other hand, I can get some of their clients into the same room, when the lawyer insists, 'Under no circumstances!' the client says, 'why not?' He is apparently satisfied in the main with reasonable business judgment, and that kind of drafting is going to be very easy under the unconscionable clause, because that kind of drafting in which you get for your client or ask for your client things only within the margin of safety and don't try to take more than 80 per cent of the pie, is never going to be regarded as unconscionable.   The only doubt that comes up in regard to unconscionability is, if you start drafting to the absolute limit of what the law can conceivably bear.   At that point you run into what they run into now, and what you run into now is, the court kicks it over.

"We have all of us seen this kind of series of cases, haven't we? Case No. 1 comes up.   The clause is perfectly clear and the court said, 'Had it been desired to provide such an unbelievable thing, surely language could have been made clearer.'   Then counsel redrafts, and they not only say it twice as well, but they wind up saying, 'And we mean it,' and the court looks at it a second time and says, 'Had this been the kind of thing really intended to go into an agreement, surely language could have been found,' and so on down the line.

"This kind of thing does not make for good business, it does not make for good counseling, and it does not make for certainty.   It means that you never know where you are, and it does a very bad thing to the law indeed.   The bad thing that it does to the law is to lead to precedent after precedent in which language is held not to mean what it says and indeed what its plain purpose was, and that upsets everything for everybody in all future litigation.

"We believe that if you take this and bring it out into the open, if you say, 'When it gets too stiff to make sense, then the court may knock it out,' you are going to get a body of principles of construction instead of principles of misconstruction, and the precedents are going to build up so that the language will be relied upon and will be construed to mean what it says."   Report of the New York State Law Revision Commission for 1954, N.Y.Leg.Doc. (1954) No. 65, pp. 177–78.

The Campbell Soup case, cited in the comment to the Code, involved a standard grower-canner contract for the sale to the canner of the growers' entire harvest of Chantenay carrots during the coming season for up to $30 per ton.   Because of a scarcity of Chantenay carrots, they were virtually unobtainable at the time for delivery and their price had risen to at least $90 per ton.   The growers began to sell some of the carrots to others in violation of the contract, and the canners brought suit against the growers to enjoin further sales and to compel specific performance. The court of appeals refused to grant equitable relief, saying that the "form has quite obviously been drawn by skilful draftsmen with the buyer's interests in mind," and "it is too hard a bargain to entitle the plaintiff to relief in a court of conscience." Of the several clauses that the court found objectionable, the "hardest of all" was a provision that excused the canner from performance if production was curtailed due to circumstances beyond its control, but prohibited the grower, even though he could no longer require the canner to take the carrots, from selling them elsewhere without the canner's written consent. But the court added, "we are not suggesting that the contract is illegal. Nor are we suggesting any excuse for the grower in this case who has deliberately broken an agreement. . . ." Presumably the canner could have recovered damages from the grower, but these would have been limited by a liquidated damage clause in the contract. Does this case support the rule of UCC 2–302? [b]

NOTES

(1) *Code Drafting.* For an illuminating and amusing account of the development, in successive Code drafts, of what became UCC 2–302, see Leff, Unconscionability and the Code—The Emperor's New Clause, 115 U. Pa.L.Rev. 485 (1967). Early drafts focussed on improprieties in bargaining, or the absence of it. Then the focus shifted: at one stage there was a comment condemning a "lopsided bargain," though deliberately entered into, with full knowledge and awareness. By Professor's Leff's account, the element of "naughty bargaining conduct" proved impossible to formulate, and a prohibition on lopsided terms proved unacceptable to important backers of the Code. "Thus faced with a dilemma, the difficulty of the first alternative and the unpopularity of the second, the draftsmen opted for a third solution. They fudged." Id., 501.

(2) *Restatement Second.* Section 234 of the Restatement Second states a rule in virtually the same terms as UCC 2–302(1). It is without parallel in the original Restatement. The comments and Reporter's Note cite some twenty cases, running back to 1750. More than half of them, however, were decided in the 1960's. Illustration 1 is based on the Campbell Soup case. Is the subject ripe for restatement? What weight might the Restatement section carry in the states where the legislatures omitted UCC 2–302 in enacting the Code?

(3) *Equal Treatment.* Professor Robert Keeton has proposed the following generalization as a mode of striking down or modifying overly restrictive provisions in insurance policies:

> If the enforcement of a policy provision would defeat the reasonable expectations of the great majority of policyholders to whose claims it is relevant, it will not be enforced even against those who know of its restrictive terms.[c]

Many of the precedents he relies on purport to be interpretations of policy terms, rather than "policing of the bargain." As to these he says: "A bet-

---

b. The case is discussed in 58 Yale L.J. 1161 (1949).

c. Keeton, Insurance Law (Basic Text) 358 (1971).

ter explanation of these precedents is that the language of the policy provision unambiguously provides so little coverage that it would be unconscionable to permit the insurer to enforce it . . . " [d] Professor Keeton maintains that it would be unconscionable to enforce a harsh term, appearing in many similar policies, only against the few policyholders who are aware of its existence and purport. Is "unconscionability" the same in Professor Keeton's lexicon as it is in the Code?

POST-CODE LEGISLATION

There is a general agreement that UCC 2–302 commits a sizable set of critical problems to judicial solution, on relatively uncontrolled terms. Objections have been voiced to this mode of solution, on several grounds. One is that no concrete and objective guides are provided to assist the courts in applying the section. Another is that the judicial system does not provide adequate relief for the victim of an unconscionable contract, since he must bear the expense of contesting the contract, and can expect at most to avoid loss on the transaction. A seller may enjoy the fruits of unconscionable dealing with all his customers who do not protest, and write off contested claims at no great cost. From another side it is objected that the principle of the section should not be limited to sale transactions, and should at least be extended to *loan* transactions with consumers, the other great mechanism for providing them with credit. For an unsuccessful attempt to apply the principle of unconscionability to a consumer loan, secured by the borrower's household furniture, see Hernandez v. S. I. C. Finance Co., 79 N.M. 673, 448 P.2d 474 (1968).

Legislation has been proposed, and enacted in a few states, to meet some of these objections.[a] There is the Uniform Consumer Credit Code, prepared by the Commissioners on Uniform State Laws, and adopted in several states, and there is the National Consumer Act, advanced by a conference of "consumer experts." The differences are instructive. The Code features injunctive relief against unconscionable conduct, whereas the Act encourages private actions (including class actions) by permitting the recovery of attorneys' fees and penalties.[b] An excerpt from the Code appears at p. 385 infra.

---

d. Id., 360.

a. The proposals mentioned here are meant to serve many other purposes as well, of course.

Consumer-protection laws exist also at the purely local level. Pawnbrokers have long been regulated by municipal law in some states, for example. For a much more recent and elaborate example, see the New York City Administrative Code, ch. 64, and regulations pursuant to it. Note particu-

larly the definition of "unconsionable trade or practice," in § 2203d–2.0(b), which refers indirectly to "rulings and decisions of legislative or judicial bodies in this state or elsewhere."

b. Is UCC 2–302 itself a sufficient basis for recovering punitive damages, when the claimant shows that he was subjected to an unconscionable contract or clause? See Pearson v. National Budgeting Sys., Inc., 31 A.D.2d 792, 297 N.Y.S.2d 59 (1969).

What chance of enactment would you expect these proposals to have in the two states where the legislature rejected UCC 2–302, in enacting the Code? How would you expect the courts to handle the notion of unconscionability in those states? (In California, which is one of them, the courts are notably benign toward class actions.)

NOTE

What is a "Consumer"? In formulating rules for the protection of consumers, it is a constant legislative problem to decide what class of transactions to single out for special treatment. As obvious examples, it may be asked whether a rule favoring consumer buyers should extend to the buyers in such "business" transactions as the purchase of a car by a doctor, or a light bulb by a factory.[c] The Uniform Consumer Credit Code contains elaborate definitions and scope provisions to express the range of its numerous consumer-protection rules. Similarly, in requiring that lenders and merchants disclose rates and other information when extending credit to consumers, the Congress experienced difficulty in singling out the transactions to be affected: see the Truth-in-Lending Act, 15 U.S.C.A. §§ 1601 et. seq.

Because we are all consumers, it has been observed, it is somewhat crass to classify any of us as such. Skilton and Helstad, Protection of the Installment Buyer of Goods Under the Uniform Commercial Code, 65 Mich. L.Rev. 1465 (1967). The Code does not give special treatment to "consumers," and so has no definition of that class. It does, however, embody special rules about "consumer goods," and transactions in them as defined in section 9–109(1).[d] As compared with some later legislative efforts, this distinction appears rather primitive.

WILSON TRADING CORPORATION v. DAVID FERGUSON, LTD.

Court of Appeals of New York, 1968.
23 N.Y.2d 398, 244 N.E.2d 685.

JASEN, JUDGE. The plaintiff, Wilson Trading Corporation, entered into a contract with the defendant, David Ferguson, Ltd., for the sale of a specified quantity of yarn. After the yarn was delivered, cut and knitted into sweaters, the finished product was washed. It was during this washing that it was discovered that the color of the yarn had "shaded"—that is, "there was a variation in color from piece to piece and within the pieces." This defect, the defendant claims, rendered the sweaters "unmarketable".

c. These examples were considered by the (English) Law Commission and the Scottish Law Commission, in connection with a recommendation that a disclaimer of implied warranties be ineffective in consumer sales. The commissions produced a complex set of definitions for "consumer sale" but concluded that "no legal definition, however sophisticated, could adequately cater for all borderline cases . . .." Exemption Clauses in Contracts, First Report of The Law Commission, etc., 30–32 (1969).

d. For examples see UCC 9–204(4) (b), 9–206(1), and 9–505.

This action for the contract price of the yarn was commenced after the defendant refused payment.   As a defense to the action and as a counterclaim for damages, the defendant alleges that "[p]laintiff has failed to perform all of the conditions of the contract on its part required to be performed, and has delivered . . . defective and unworkmanlike goods".

The sales contract provides in pertinent part:

"2.   No claims relating to excessive moisture content, short weight, count variations, twist, quality or shade shall be allowed *if made after weaving, knitting, or processing,* or more than 10 days after receipt of shipment. . . .   The buyer shall within 10 days of the receipt of the merchandise by himself or agent examine the merchandise for any and all defects." (Emphasis supplied.)

"4.   This instrument constitutes the entire agreement between the parties, superseding all previous communications, oral or written, and no changes, amendments or additions hereto will be recognized unless in writing signed by both seller and buyer or buyer's agent.   It is expressly agreed that no representations or warranties, express or implied, have been or are made by the seller except as stated herein, and the seller makes no warranty, express or implied, as to the fitness for buyer's purposes of yarn purchased hereunder, seller's obligations, except as expressly stated herein, being limited to the *delivery of good merchantable yarn of the description stated herein*". (Emphasis supplied.)

Special Term granted plaintiff summary judgment for the contract price of the yarn sold on the ground that "notice of the alleged breach of warranty for defect in shading was not given within the time expressly limited and is not now available by way of defense or counterclaim."   The Appellate Division affirmed, without opinion.

The defendant on this appeal urges that the time limitation provision on claims in the contract was unreasonable since the defect in the color of the yarn was latent and could not be discovered until after the yarn was processed and the finished product washed.

Defendant's affidavits allege that its sweaters were rendered unsaleable because of latent defects in the yarn which caused "variation in color from piece to piece and within the pieces."   This allegation is sufficient to create a question of fact concerning the merchantability of the yarn (Uniform Commercial Code, § 2–314, subd. [2]).   Indeed, the plaintiff does not seriously dispute the fact that its yarn was unmerchantable, but instead, like Special Term, relies upon the failure of defendant to give notice of the breach of warranty within the time limits prescribed by paragraph 2 of the contract.

Subdivision (3) (par. [a]) of section 2–607 of the Uniform Commercial Code expressly provides that a buyer who accepts goods has a reasonable time after he discovers or should have discovered a breach to notify the seller of such breach. (Cf. 5 Williston, Contracts [3d ed.], § 713.) Defendant's affidavits allege that a claim was made immediately upon discovery of the breach of warranty after the yarn was knitted and washed, and that this was the earliest possible moment at which the defects could reasonably be discovered in the normal manufacturing process. Defendant's affidavits are, therefore, sufficient to create a question of fact concerning whether notice of the latent defects alleged was given within a reasonable time. (Cf. Ann., 17 A.L.R.3d 1010, 1112–1115 [1968].)

However, the Uniform Commercial Code allows the parties, within limits established by the code, to modify or exclude warranties and to limit remedies for breach of warranty. The courts below have found that the sales contract bars all claims not made before knitting and processing. Concededly, defendant discovered and gave notice of the alleged breach of warranty after knitting and washing.

We are, therefore, confronted with the effect to be given the time limitation provision in paragraph 2 of the contract. Analytically, paragraph 2 presents separate and distinct issues concerning its effect as a valid limitation on remedies for breach of warranty (Uniform Commercial Code, § 2–316, subd. [4]; § 2–719) and its effect as a modification of the express warranty of merchantability (Uniform Commercial Code, § 2–316, subd. [1]) established by paragraph 4 of the contract.

Parties to a contract are given broad latitude within which to fashion their own remedies for breach of contract (Uniform Commercial Code, § 2–316, subd. [4]; §§ 2–718–2–719). Nevertheless, it is clear from the official comments to section 2–719 of the Uniform Commercial Code that it is the very essence of a sales contract that at least minimum adequate remedies be available for its breach. "If the parties intend to conclude a contract for sale within this Article they must accept the legal consequence that there be at least a fair quantum of remedy for breach of the obligations or duties outlined in the contract. Thus any clause purporting to modify or limit the remedial provisions of this Article in an *unconscionable manner* is subject to deletion and in that event the remedies made available by this Article are applicable as if the stricken clause had never existed." (Uniform Commercial Code, § 2–719, official comment 1; emphasis supplied.)

It follows that contractual limitations upon remedies are generally to be enforced unless unconscionable. This analysis is buttressed by the fact that the official comments to section 2–302 of the Uniform Commercial Code, the code provision pertaining to unconscionable contracts or clauses, cites Kansas City Wholesale Grocery Co. v. Weber Packing Corp. (93 Utah 414, 73 P.2d 1272 [1937]), a case invalidating a time limitation provision as applied to latent defects, as illustrating the underlying basis for section 2–302.[1]

Whether a contract or any clause of the contract is unconscionable is a matter for the court to decide against the background of the contract's commercial setting, purpose, and effect, and the existence of this issue would not therefore bar summary judgment.[2]

However, it is unnecessary to decide the issue of whether the time limitation is unconscionable on this appeal for section 2–719 (subd. [2]) of the Uniform Commercial Code provides that the general remedy provisions of the code apply when "circumstances cause an exclusive or limited remedy to fail of its essential purpose". As explained by the official comments to this section: "where an apparently fair and reasonable clause because of circumstances fails in its purpose or operates to deprive either party of the substantial value of the bargain, it must give way to the general remedy provisions of this Article." (Uniform Commercial Code, § 2–719, official comment 1.) Here, paragraph 2 of the contract bars all claims for shade and other specified defects made after knitting and processing. Its effect is to eliminate any remedy for shade defects not reasonably discoverable within the time limitation period. It is true that parties may set by agreement any time not manifestly unreasonable whenever the code "requires any action to be taken within a reasonable time" (Uniform Commercial Code, § 1–204, subd. [1]), but here the time provision eliminates all remedy for defects not discoverable before knitting and processing and section 2–719 (subd. [2]) of the Uniform Commercial Code therefore applies.

Defendant's affidavits allege that sweaters manufactured from the yarn were rendered unmarketable because of latent shading de-

---

1. We recognize that the Superior Court of Pennsylvania in Vandenberg & Sons, N. V. v. Siter (204 Pa.Sup. 392, 204 A.2d 494 [1964]) held that the manifest unreasonableness of a time limitation clause presented a question of fact for trial (citing Uniform Commercial Code, § 1–204 and two pre-Uniform Commercial Code cases). However, the Pennsylvania Superior Court did not consider the sections of the code pertaining to limitation of remedies for breach of warranty. (Uniform Commercial Code, § 2–316, subd. [4]; §§ 2–718, 2–719.) When these interrelated sections are considered in light of the official comments to section 2–719 of the Uniform Commercial Code it is clear that the issue of the reasonability of limitations upon contractual remedies presents a question of unconscionability for the court. For this reason we decline to follow Vandenberg & Sons, N. V. v. Siter (supra).

2. In construing section 2–302 (subd. [2]) as a matter of first impression, Sinkoff Beverage Co. v. Schlitz Brewing Co. (51 Misc.2d 446, 273 N.Y.S.2d 364) acknowledges that the issue of unconscionability is a matter of law for the court, but holds that a hearing to determine the commercial setting, purpose, and effect of a contract is mandatory rather than discretionary when the court accepts the possibility of unconscionability. Neither party argues that Special Term should have held an evidentiary hearing on the issue of unconscionability, and accordingly we express no opinion on this issue. (Cf. Cohen and Karger, Powers of the New York Court of Appeals [Rev. ed., 1952], §§ 161, 162.)

fects not reasonably discoverable before knitting and processing of the yarn into sweaters. If these factual allegations are established at trial, the limited remedy established by paragraph 2 has failed its "essential purpose" and the buyer is, in effect, without remedy. The time limitation clause of the contract, therefore, insofar as it applies to defects not reasonably discoverable within the time limits established by the contract, must give way to the general code rule that a buyer has a reasonable time to notify the seller of breach of contract after he discovers or should have discovered the defect. (Uniform Commercial Code, § 2–607, subd. [3], par. [a].) As indicated above, defendant's affidavits are sufficient to create a question of fact concerning whether notice was given within a reasonable time after the shading defect should have been discovered.

It can be argued that paragraph 2 of the contract, insofar as it bars all claims for enumerated defects not reasonably discoverable within the time period established, purports to exclude these defects from the coverage of the express warranty of merchantability. By this analysis, the contract not only limits remedies for its breach, but also purports to modify the warranty of merchantability. An attempt to both warrant and refuse to warrant goods creates an ambiguity which can only be resolved by making one term yield to the other (cf. Hawkland, Limitation of Warranty under the Uniform Commercial Code, 11 How.L.J. 28 [1965]). Section 2–316 (subd. [1]) of the Uniform Commercial Code provides that warranty language prevails over the disclaimer if the two cannot be reasonably reconciled.

Here, the contract expressly creates an unlimited express warranty of merchantability while in a separate clause purports to indirectly modify the warranty without expressly mentioning the word merchantability. Under these circumstances, the language creating the unlimited express warranty must prevail over the time limitation insofar as the latter modifies the warranty. It follows that the express warranty of merchantability includes latent shading defects and defendant may claim for such defects not reasonably discoverable within the time limits established by the contract if plaintiff was notified of these defects within a reasonable time after they were or should have been discovered.

The result reached under the Uniform Commercial Code is, therefore, similar to the pre-code case law holding unreasonable contractual provisions expressly limiting the time for inspection, trial or testing of goods inapplicable or invalid with respect to latent defects. (Randy Knitwear Inc. v. American Cyanamid Co., 7 N.Y.2d 791, 194 N.Y.S.2d 530, 163 N.E.2d 349 . . .) In fact, in Randy Knitwear (supra) this court held a contractual provision remarkably similar to the time limitation clause in the instant case to present a factual question for trial concerning the reasonableness of the time limitation.

In sum, there are factual issues for trial concerning whether the shading defects alleged were discoverable before knitting and processing, and, if not, whether notice of the defects was given within a reasonable time after the defects were or should have been discovered. If the shading defects were not reasonably discoverable before knitting and processing and notice was given within a reasonable time after the defects were or should have been discovered, a further factual issue of whether the sweaters were rendered unsaleable because of the defect is presented for trial.

The order of the Appellate Division should be reversed, with costs, and plaintiff's motion for summary judgment should be denied.

FULD, CHIEF JUDGE (concurring). I agree that there should be a reversal—but on the sole ground that a substantial question of fact has been raised as to whether the clause limiting the time in which to make a claim is "manifestly unreasonable" (Uniform Commercial Code, § 1–204) as applied to the type of defect here complained of. In this view, it is not necessary to consider the relevancy, if any, of other provisions of the Uniform Commercial Code (e. g., §§ 2–302, 2–316, 2–719), dealing with "unconscionable" contracts or clauses, exclusion of implied warranties or limitations on damages.[a]

NOTES

(1) *Disclaimer and Unconscionability.* Can you envisage an exclusion or modification of warranty that is effective under UCC 2–316, but may be found to be unconscionable under UCC 2–302? Professor Leff considers it incredible that a term passing muster under the former section should fail under the latter. Notice that unconscionability is employed as a limitation in section 2–719, which is in turn referred to in section 2–316(4). Does this fact support or impair Professor Leff's argument?

Comment 1 after UCC 2–302 illustrates the "underlying basis" of the section with a series of ten cases. It has often been observed that about half of these concern unsuccessful attempts to disclaim warranties, and that all of them are in the range of topics dealt with in UCC 2–316, 2–718, 2–719. It seems curious that the comment writer could not find instances of unconscionability that are not curable by the Code's more explicit proscriptions.

The careful comment-reader may be further mystified by Comment 3 after section 2–719, which seems to revive Professor Leff's argument after

---

a. For a comparable case see Neville Chemical Corp. v. Union Carbide Corp., 422 F.2d 1205 (3d Cir. 1970), in which the trial court said: "Like tulip bulbs shipped in the fall which did not bloom in the spring, a time limitation of a few days after receipt of shipment renders any warranties ineffective as to defects not discoverable on ordinary inspection," and cited Vandenberg & Sons N. V. v. Siter, footnote 1 supra (a bulb case). The appellate court construed the seller's disclaimers of warranties as inapplicable to the buyer's claim of negligence.

See also Cree Coaches, Inc. v. Panel Suppliers, Inc., 384 Mich. 646, 186 N.W.2d 335 (1971), and Burton-Dixie Corp. v. Timothy McCarthy Const. Co., 436 F.2d 405 (5th Cir. 1971), as to construction work.

other comments have done it in. One sentence in the comment is: "The seller in all cases is free to disclaim warranties in the manner provided in Section 2–316." See Leff, Unconscionability and the Code—The Emperor's New Clause, 115 U.Pa.L.Rev. 485, 520–32 (1967). But see Ellinghaus, In Defense of Unconscionability, 78 Yale L.J. 757, 793–97, 800–802 (1969).[b]

Alter the facts in Wilson Trading so that they provide a test of the proposition, "seller in all cases is free to disclaim warranties." How would your hypothetical case be decided by the New York court? By Chief Judge Fuld?

(2) *Misperformance.* When Glen Riley bought a new Lincoln Mark III for nearly $8,500, the Ford Motor Company extended him a warranty that it would repair or replace defective parts, but not assume responsibility for the loss of use of the car, or other consequential expense. Many malfunctions appeared. In an action brought by Riley against the company, it was found by the jury (implicitly) that the remedy had failed of its essential purpose: see UCC 2–719(2). On appeal, this finding was approved: "at some point after the purchase of a new automobile, the same should be put in good running condition." However, Riley's judgment was reversed, as excessive. He had established some $400 as the cost of substitute transportation, and declared that the car had not been worth anything to him. The court said that the judgment should not have been for more than some $8,900. The jury had awarded $30,000. Riley v. Ford Motor Company, 442 F.2d 670 (5th Cir. 1971). See also Adams v. J. I. Case Company, 125 Ill.App.2d 388, 261 N.E.2d 1 (1970), on the effect of delay in performing a warranty of repair.

In Jones & McKnight Corp. v. Birdsboro Corporation, 320 F.Supp. 39 (N.D.Ill.1970), it was held that a buyer may recover consequential damages for a defect in goods, notwithstanding a disclaimer that would otherwise be binding on him, if the seller has been "willfully or unreasonably dilatory" in performing an express warranty of repair. The court seemed to rely on UCC 2–719(2); but was this necessary?

(3) *Problem.* A contract for the sale of an executive-type aircraft provides that the seller "shall not be liable for failure or delay in making delivery for any cause whatsoever. If delivery is not made within 30 days of the specified delivery date, purchaser may cancel this order and have the full deposit refunded." Is this a clause liquidating damages for breach, within UCC 2–718? If not, does it provide an "optional" remedy for the buyer within UCC 2–719? If it purports to be an exclusive remedy, what circumstances would justify the buyer in claiming damages under UCC 2–719(2)?

In Dow Corning Corporation v. Capitol Aviation, Inc., 411 F.2d 622 (7th Cir. 1969), a plane manufacturer, relying on such a provision, "pointed out that it is common to the industry . . . to obtain a release from liability in the event of failure to deliver," and that the plaintiff buyer encountered the same term when it bought a substitute plane from a competitor of the defendant. Does this circumstance indicate that the limitation of remedy is acceptable? Or that it is unconscionable? Would it affect

---

b. For an indication of the international al character of the problem of disclaimers and exculpation clauses, and a comparative study, see Hippel, The Control of Exemption Clauses, 16 Int. & Comp.L.Q. 591 (1967).

your evaluation that the plane was of a type never before placed in production?

(4) *Problem.* A fisherman signed an order for a new diesel engine on a salesman's multicopy form, interleaved with carbons. The reverse side contained, in bold-face capitals, an exclusion of the implied warranty of merchantability, under the heading "Terms and Conditions." The face of the form contained certain provisions, both printed and written, and the following legend in bold-face capitals: BOTH THIS ORDER AND ITS ACCEPTANCE ARE SUBJECT TO 'TERMS AND CONDITIONS' STATED IN THIS ORDER. Was the warranty effectively excluded? Compare Hunt v. Perkins Machinery Co., 352 Mass. 535, 226 N.E.2d 228 (1967), with Childers & Venters, Inc. v. Sowards, 460 S.W.2d 343 (Ky. 1970). Does it make any difference whether or not the fisherman read the back of the form?

WARRANTY LEGISLATION FOR CONSUMERS

A beginning has been made, in sporadic legislation, to differentiate the law of warranties as it relates to consumers from warranty law generally, and to undergird the protection of consumers. An example is an addition to the Uniform Commercial Code in Massachusetts, which excepts sales of consumer goods and services from UCC 2–316, and provides: "Any language, oral or written, used by a seller or manufacturer of consumer goods and services, which attempts to exclude or modify any implied warranties of merchantability and fitness for a particular purpose or to exclude or modify the consumer's remedies for breach of those warranties, shall be unenforceable." [a] In California, a much more elaborate statute permits a disclaimer of such warranties, but only by specified means for warning the buyer.[b] Each statute also contains incentives for a manufacturer to maintain facilities for service and repair in the state. These provisions would seem to operate in favor of distribution systems like those of automobile manufacturers, and against those relying on independent merchants, discount houses, and the like. The Congress has also been urged to intervene against disclaimer of warranties and to grant the Federal Trade Commission increased authority to deal with the problem.

NOTE

Proposed Statutes. According to federal bills of 1971, the FTC would be granted rule-making and other powers with respect to warranties in consumer transactions. It would be made a deceptive practice for a supplier to attempt disclaimer of implied warranties while using the word "guaranty" or "warranty" in advertising, and it would be necessary to formulate express warranties "in simple and readily understood terms." It would of course be possible in addition to require that sales of certain

a. Mass.Gen.L., Ch. 106, § 2–316A.   b. Cal.Civ.Code, §§ 1790 et seq. Both of these statutes were enacted in 1970.

products be accompanied by specified warranties, but the bills cited clearly disavow that purpose.[c]

How do you evaluate the following provision of the National Consumer Act?

"Notwithstanding any other provisions of law, with respect to goods which are the subject of or are intended to become the subject of a consumer transaction, no merchant shall:

(1) Exclude, modify or otherwise attempt to limit any warranty, express or implied, including the warranties of merchantability and fitness for a particular purpose; or

(2) Exclude, modify or attempt to limit any remedy provided by law, including the measure of damages available, for a breach of warranty, express or implied." [d]

LLEWELLYN ON BOILER-PLATE

Professor Llewellyn adverted many times to the problems posed by standard form contracts. He was not sanguine about an approach to them through legislation, "which seems to me dubious, uncertain, and likely to be both awkward in manner and deficient or spotty in scope." Instead, he wrote, the true answer to the whole problem seems, amusingly, to be one which could occur to any court or any lawyer, at any time, as readily as to a scholar who had spent a lifetime on the subject—though I doubt if it could occur to anyone without the inquiry and analysis in depth which we owe to the scholarly work.

"The answer, I suggest, is this: Instead of thinking about 'assent' to boiler-plate clauses, we can recognize that so far as concerns the specific, there is no assent at all. What has in fact been assented to, specifically, are the few dickered terms, and the broad type of the transaction, and but one thing more. That one thing more is a blanket assent (not a specific assent) to any not unreasonable or indecent terms the seller may have on his form, which do not alter or eviscerate the reasonable meaning of the dickered terms. The fine print which has not been read has no business to cut under the reasonable meaning of those dickered terms which constitute the dominant and only real expression of agreement, but much of it commonly belongs in. . . .

" . . . There has been an arm's-length deal, with dickered terms. There has been accompanying that basic deal another which, if not on any fiduciary basis, at least involves a plain expression of confidence, asked and accepted, with a corresponding limit on the powers granted: the boiler-plate is assented to en bloc, 'unsight, unseen,' on the implicit assumption and to the full extent that (1) it does not alter or impair the fair meaning of the dickered terms when read

---

c. The bills are S. 1221 and H.R. 6314, 92d Cong., 1st Sess.

d. Section 3.302 (Official Text, First Final Draft, 1970).

alone, and (2) that its terms are neither in the particular nor in the net manifestly unreasonable and unfair. Such is the reality, and I see nothing in the way of a court's operating on that basis, to truly effectuate the only intention which can in reason be worked out as common to the two parties, granted good faith. And if the boiler-plate party is not playing in good faith, there is law enough to bar that fact from benefiting it. . . . [A]ny contract with boiler-plate results in *two* several contracts: the *dickered* deal, and the collateral one of *supplementary* boiler-plate. Rooted in sense, history, and simplicity, it is an answer which could occur to anyone." Llewellyn, The Common Law Tradition: Deciding Appeals 370–71 (1960).

NOTES

(1) *Fundamental Breach.* A series of English cases has given currency to the expression "fundamental breach." The doctrine it describes is at best rather ill-defined, but it bears some resemblance to Professor Llewellyn's view. One writer's attempt to summarize the cases is as follows: "Every contract contains a 'core' or fundamental obligation which must be performed. If one party fails to perform this fundamental obligation, he will be guilty of a breach of the contract whether or not any exempting clause has been inserted which purports to protect him. Closely allied with this principle is yet another: that a party will only be protected by an exemption clause in a contract while he is performing that contract and not when he has deviated from it in a substantial manner." Guest, Fundamental Breach of Contract, 77 L.Q.Rev. 98, 99 (1961).[a]

In Suisse Atlantique Société, etc. v. N. V. Rotterdam, etc., [1966] 2 All.E.R. 61, the House of Lords severely limited the doctrine of fundamental breach, so far as it was ever established. One of the law lords said there that a rule nullifying a limitation of liability, for fundamental breach, "would involve a restriction on the freedom to contract and in the older cases I can find no trace of it."[b]

(2) *Question.* How might either of these approaches have been used in the cases included in this section?

(3) *An Ethical Issue.* Something might be gained by inserting a provision in a form contract, such as the limitation of remedy in the Wilson Trading case, p. 358 supra, even if it is known to be unenforceable. It may serve to discourage some of the parties assenting to the term, and not fully advised of the law, from asserting their rights.[c] What attitude should

---

a. See also Meyer, Contracts of Adhesion and the Doctrine of Fundamental Breach, 50 Va.L.Rev. 1178 (1964).

b. The doctrine continues under discussion, however. See, for example, Silverberg, The Doctrine of Fundamental Breach Revisited, 1971 J.Bus.L. 197, 280. It should be noted that the case cited concerned a liquidated damages clause in a ship charter, providing a payment to the owner of $1,000 a day for certain idle periods. The owner sought damages in a larger amount. Only one of the lord justices (Reid) considered the problem in relation to standardized contracts common to consumer transactions, and he said: "This is a complex problem which intimately affects millions of people, and it appears to me that its solution should be left to Parliament."

c. As to this and other advantages, see Comment, Administrative Regulation of Adhesion Contracts in Israel, 66 Colum.L.Rev. 1340, 1342–43 (1966).

a lawyer take to drafting a contract in this fashion? An ethics committee has given this opinion:

"You inquire if it is ethical for a lawyer to insert in a contract a waiver of a right, which waiver is void 'as against public policy.'

"You state that the right in question is a tenant's right to a sixty-day period to reconsider and cancel an agreed upon increase of rent under the Emergency Rent Laws. You further state that many times a layman does not know his rights and could be deceived into compliance by such an illegal clause.

"In the opinion of our Committee it is not within the proper standards of ethics for a lawyer to insert such a waiver in a contract if the lawyer knows that such a waiver is against public policy and void as a matter of law.

"A lawyer must himself observe and advise his client to observe the statute law (Canon 32). If a waiver in a contract has been held by a court of last resort to be void as against public policy as a matter of law, he should so advise his client. If the client should nevertheless insist on its incorporation in the contract, the lawyer should refuse to do so, for if he should comply with his client's request he would thereby become a party to possible deception of the other party to the contract.

"In the language of Canon 29 as to the lawyer's duty to uphold the honor of the profession, 'He should strive at all times to uphold the honor and to maintain the dignity of the profession and to improve not only the law but the administration of justice.' " [d]

BETTER FOOD MARKETS v. AMERICAN DISTRICT TELEGRAPH CO.

Supreme Court of California, 1953.
40 Cal.2d 179, 253 P.2d 10.

[In June of 1947 the parties made a written agreement whereby the defendant was to install and maintain a burglar alarm system in the plaintiff's food market. On receipt of a signal, the defendant was to dispatch its own guards to the premises and to notify the police. The contract contained the following clause: "It is agreed by and between the parties that the Contractor is not an insurer, that the payments hereinbefore named are based solely on the value of the service in the maintenance of the system described, that it is impracticable and extremely difficult to fix the actual damages, if any, which may proximately result from a failure to perform such services and in case of failure to perform such services and a resulting loss its liability hereunder shall be limited to and fixed at the sum of fifty dollars as liquidated damages, and not as a penalty, and this liability shall be exclusive." At 7:30 p. m. on November 16, 1947, the assistant manager of the market set the system and locked the building. As he en-

---

d. Committee on Professional Ethics of the Association of the Bar of the City of New York, Opinions on Professional Ethics 435 (1956).

tered his car in the parking lot, an armed robber forced him at gunpoint to return to the store and open the safe. The robber emptied the safe of $35,930, taped the assistant manager, and fled. Signals were received at the defendant's central station for about fourteen minutes after the store door was reopened and for nine minutes after the safe was opened, but the defendant's operators did not call a guard or inform the police until the end of that time, at 7:51. At about 7:50 the assistant manager succeeded in knocking a telephone off the hook and calling for help. The police arrived at the market at 7:52, within one minute after receiving a call. The defendant's guards arrived shortly thereafter. The plaintiff sued the defendant in tort and contract for failure to transmit the signals to their own guards and to the police. The plaintiff appeals from judgment for the defendant entered on its motion for a directed verdict.]

SHENK, JUSTICE. [After concluding that there was substantial evidence from which a jury could have found that the plaintiff's loss was the proximate result of the defendant's breach of its contract, so that it was error to direct a verdict for the defendant, the court came to the question of the validity of the liquidated damage clause.] It is generally recognized that a valid agreement may be made for the payment of liquidated damages, whereas an agreement for the payment of a penalty is invalid. Under the law generally the parties are allowed to contract for liquidated damages if it is necessary to do so in order that they may know with reasonable certainty the extent of liability for a breach of the agreement. Where the parties exercise their business judgment in providing that it is impracticable and extremely difficult to fix the damages which may result from the defendant's failure to render its service such a provision is not controlling as to the actual difficulty in fixing damages, although it is entitled to some weight.   .   .   .

The statutory law and its interpretation in this state are in accord with the general law. Civil Code section 1670 states that a provision in a contract which provides for the amount of damages to be paid in the event of a breach of the contract is void, except as expressly provided in section 1671 as follows: "The parties to a contract may agree therein upon an amount which shall be presumed to be the amount of damage sustained by a breach thereof, when, from the nature of the case, it would be impracticable or extremely difficult to fix the actual damage."   .   .   .

The plaintiff argues that there is no difficulty in the present case in fixing the actual damage and that the amount of money stolen should be the actual damage. Its contention is that the time for the determination of the question of the impracticability and difficulty in fixing the damages is after the loss has occurred. This is not the rule. In determining this question the court should place itself in the position of the parties at the time the contract was made and should consider the nature of the breaches that might occur and any consequences that were reasonably foreseeable. . . .

The possibilities of the consequences of a failure of the defendant to perform its obligation under the contract are innumerable. A failure to receive the signals, or to respond to them, or to report them to the plaintiff would be a violation of the agreement. Entrances to the building after working hours might be made by persons having authority as well as by burglars or by persons bent upon mischief. They might or might not cause damage. There might be the theft of a ham, or of a truckload of goods, or the contents of a safe. There might be a breaking in for the purpose of theft and no theft. If money was taken it might be a few dollars or many thousands. Books might be tampered with, or papers abstracted. Damage might be caused in many ways that were not foreseeable. In short, it was extremely difficult to predict the nature and extent of the loss. Furthermore, there was no way of ascertaining what portion of any loss sustained could be attributed to the defendant's failure to perform. The contract specifically provided that the defendant was not an insurer. Therefore, if it should have fully performed on the contract and a loss resulted nevertheless it could in no way be liable. The parties recognized, then, that losses might have resulted which were not causally connected with the defendant's failure of performance. Where there had been a failure of performance and a loss, what part of that loss could be attributed to the failure of performance; or how much of that loss would have resulted had there not been a failure of performance? Under the complexity of the circumstances in this case the parties could not answer this question. There being no reasonable basis upon which to predict the nature and extent of any loss, or how much of that loss the defendant's failure of performance might account for, it is certain that it would have been "impracticable or extremely difficult to fix the actual damage" § 1671, Civ.Code.

The validity of a clause for liquidated damages requires that the parties to the contract "agree therein upon an amount which shall be presumed to be the amount of damage sustained by a breach thereof . . . .." Civ.Code § 1671. This amount must represent the result of a reasonable endeavor by the parties to estimate a fair average compensation for any loss that may be sustained. . . . It had been suggested that the greater the difficulty encountered by the parties in estimating the damages which might arise from a breach, the greater should be the range of estimates which the courts should uphold as reasonable. (5 Corbin on Contracts, § 1059, p. 291). The plaintiff's contention that the agreed amount did not represent an endeavor by the parties to estimate the probable damage is based on evidence that the liquidation clause was part of the printed material in a form contract generally used by the defendant in dealing with subscribers such as the plaintiff, and that the defendant did not investigate the plaintiff's manner of conducting its business or the character and value of its stock. Nevertheless the parties agreed to the liquidation provisions, and there is no evidence that they were not fully aware of circumstances making it desirable that liquidated damages be provided for.

In the present case the impracticability or extreme difficulty in fixing actual damages appeared as a matter of law. In the exercise of their business judgment the parties reasonably agreed that in all cases of breach by the defendant the damages would be fixed at $50 whether in fact the defendant's loss for a given breach was greater or less than that amount. As previously stated the stipulation that the amount was to be paid "as liquidated damages and not as a penalty" while entitled to some weight is not conclusive. Nevertheless, it is clear that the actual loss resulting from a breach could in many cases be less than the amount provided for. It is equally clear that in many other cases the actual loss would exceed that amount. To construe this as a penalty it would have to be said that the amount provided to be paid bore no reasonable relation to the losses the parties thought might be sustained. This may not rightly be stated. . . .

The order directing a verdict for the defendants involved questions of fact which could have been found in the plaintiff's favor. However, the error warrants only a qualified reversal of the judgment, as the plaintiff's recovery is limited to $50 if he should prevail on a retrial.

The judgment of the trial court is modified to provide as follows: "It is ordered, adjudged and decreed that plaintiff recover from the defendant, American District Telegraph Company, the sum of $50.00 without costs." As so modified the judgment is affirmed. Each party shall bear its own costs on appeal.

GIBSON, C. J., and EDMONDS, TRAYNOR, SCHAUER and SPENCE, JJ., concur.

CARTER, JUSTICE. I dissent. . . . In order to uphold the so-called $50 liquidated damage provision, it was necessary for the majority to find that damages were "impracticable and extremely difficult" to fix at the time the contract was entered into, and further that the $50 provision bore a reasonable relation to any loss which the parties contemplated might be sustained as a result of a breach of the contract. . . . Placing myself in the position of the parties at the time the contract was entered into, I would say that one way of ascertaining the loss which might occur, was to take an average of the amount of cash left in the safe in the store overnight; an inventory of the average merchandise kept in the store. . . .

[T]his court goes to great lengths to uphold the validity of a provision such as this. Note the "possibilities" which it considers might have happened from a failure of the burglar detection system.

. . . If persons having authority to enter did so, plaintiff would, in all probability, not have sued the defendant, or, if it had done so, that would have been a matter of defense at the trial. If a ham had been stolen, the provision for $50 in all probability, would have been held a penalty as disproportionate to the loss involved. These same arguments apply to the balance of the "reasoning" of the majority.

It is also necessary that the amount agreed upon by the parties "represent the result of a reasonable endeavor by the parties to estimate a fair average compensation for any loss that may be sustained. . . . In other words, the amount agreed upon must bear some reasonable relation to the losses which might occur as a result of a breach. In my opinion, the $50 provision bears no reasonable relation to any amount which might have been lost by a failure of the system to operate.

NOTES

(1) *References.* For a companion to the main case, see Atkinson v. Pacific Fire Extinguisher Co., 40 Cal.2d 192, 253 P.2d 18 (1953). The main case was followed in Zurich Insurance Company v. Kings Industries, Inc., 255 Cal.App.2d 919, 63 Cal.Rptr. 585 (1968). Compare Shaer Shoe Corp. v. Granite State Alarm, Inc. 110 N.H. 132, 262 A.2d 285 (1970). For an application of the "unconscionable" argument, see Bonhard v. Gindin, 104 N.J.L. 599, 142 A. 52 (1928). See generally, Fritz, "Underliquidated" Damages as Limitation of Liability, 33 Tex.L.Rev. 196 (1954); McCormick, Damages, § 149.

(2) *Questions.* Would a liquidated damages clause be acceptable as a way of limiting the liability of the seller in cases such as Henningsen v. Bloomfield Motors, p. 335 supra, and Wilson Trading Corp. v. David Ferguson, Ltd., p. 358 supra? See UCC 2–718 and 2–719. Is the latter section germane to this question? In Comment 1 after the former section it is said: "A term fixing unreasonably large liquidated damages is expressly made void as a penalty.[a] An unreasonably small amount would be subject to similar criticism and might be stricken under the section on unconscionable contracts or clauses."

What would the decision have been in the main case if the agreement had provided that the Contractor would be liable for any actual damages *not to exceed* $50? If such a provision had to be tested under the Code, which of the sections cited above would be controlling?

(3) *Policing by the Justice Department.* The American District Telegraph Company was one of four interlocked companies sued by the United States in U. S. v. Grinnell Corp., 384 U.S. 563 (1966). The evidence showed that ADT did 73% of the business done throughout the country, in providing "accredited" central-station alarm services.[b] It had the only such

a. Problems associated with *large* liquidated damages clauses are examined in Chapter 5.

b. These services require sensors at a subscriber's premises, electrically connected to a station staffed at all times to send guards or raise an alarm, the whole being approved by insurance associations for rate credits.

system in 92 of the 115 cities in which it operated. If such evidence had been advanced by Better Food Markets, would it have had any effect on the decision in the main case?

The Government's suit charged ADT with monopolistic practices under the Sherman Act, and the court ordered divestiture of some of its holdings.[c] The figures given above relate to fire- and sprinkler-alarm, as well as burglar-alarm business, and the Court ruled that in the circumstances it was proper to consider the defendants' share of the whole. If that is correct in testing for "monopoly" under the statute, is it equally so in testing for equality of bargaining power? How would you argue that ADT's share of the fire-alarm business was irrelevant to the contract in the main case?

WILLIAMS v. WALKER–THOMAS FURNITURE CO.

United States Court of Appeals, District of Columbia Circuit, 1965.
350 F.2d 445, 18 A.L.R.3d 1297.

J. SKELLY WRIGHT, CIRCUIT JUDGE. Appellee, Walker-Thomas Furniture Company, operates a retail furniture store in the District of Columbia. During the period from 1957 to 1962 each appellant in these cases purchased a number of household items from Walker-Thomas, for which payment was to be made in installments. The terms of each purchase were contained in a printed form contract which set forth the value of the purchased item and purported to lease the item to appellant for a stipulated monthly rent payment. The contract then provided, in substance, that title would remain in Walker-Thomas until the total of all the monthly payments made equaled the stated value of the item, at which time appellants could take title. In the event of a default in the payment of any monthly installment, Walker-Thomas could repossess the item.

The contract further provided that "the amount of each periodical installment payment to be made by (purchaser) to the Company under this present lease shall be inclusive of and not in addition to the amount of each installment payment to be made by (purchaser) under such prior leases, bills or accounts; *and all payments now and hereafter made by (purchaser) shall be credited pro rata on all outstanding leases, bills and accounts* due the Company by (purchaser) at the time each such payment is made." (Emphasis added.) The effect of this rather obscure provision was to keep a balance due on every item purchased until the balance due on all items, whenever purchased, was liquidated. As a result, the debt incurred at the time of purchase of each item was secured by the right to repossess all the

c. The Court recited the following findings: "ADT over the years reduced its minimum basic rates to meet competition and renewed contracts at substantially increased rates in cities where it had a monopoly of accredited central station service. ADT threatened retaliation against firms that contemplated inaugurating central station service."

items previously purchased by the same purchaser, and each new item purchased automatically became subject to a security interest arising out of the previous dealings.

On May 12, 1962, appellant Thorne purchased an item described as a Daveno, three tables, and two lamps, having total stated value of $391.10. Shortly thereafter, he defaulted on his monthly payments and appellee sought to replevy all the items purchased since the first transaction in 1958. Similarly, on April 17, 1962, appellant Williams bought a stereo set of stated value of $514.95.[1] She too defaulted shortly thereafter, and appellee sought to replevy all the items purchased since December, 1957. The Court of General Sessions granted judgment for appellee. The District of Columbia Court of Appeals affirmed, and we granted appellants' motion for leave to appeal to this court.

Appellants' principal contention, rejected by both the trial and the appellate courts below, is that these contracts, or at least some of them, are unconscionable and, hence, not enforceable. In its opinion in Williams v. Walker-Thomas Furniture Company, 198 A.2d 914, 916 (1964), the District of Columbia Court of Appeals explained its rejection of this contention as follows:

> "Appellant's second argument presents a more serious question. The record reveals that prior to the last purchase appellant had reduced the balance in her account to $164. The last purchase, a stereo set, raised the balance due to $678. Significantly, at the time of this and the preceding purchases, appellee was aware of appellant's financial position. The reverse side of the stereo contract listed the name of appellant's social worker and her $218 monthly stipend from the government. Nevertheless, with full knowledge that appellant had to feed, clothe and support both herself and seven children on this amount, appellee sold her a $514 stereo set.

> "We cannot condemn too strongly appellee's conduct. It raises serious questions of sharp practice and irresponsible business dealings. A review of the legislation in the District of Columbia affecting retail sales and the pertinent decisions of the highest court in this jurisdiction disclose, however, no ground upon which this court can declare the contracts in question contrary to public policy. We note that were the Maryland Retail Installment Sales Act, Art. 83 Sections 128–153, or its equivalent, in force in the District of Columbia, we could grant appellant appropriate relief. We

---

1. At the time of this purchase her account showed a balance of $164 still owing from her prior purchases. The total of all the purchases made over the years in question came to $1,800. The total payments amounted to $1,-400.

think Congress should consider corrective legislation to protect the public from such exploitive contracts as were utilized in the case at bar."

We do not agree that the court lacked the power to refuse enforcement to contracts found to be unconscionable. In other jurisdictions, it has been held as a matter of common law that unconscionable contracts are not enforceable.[2] While no decision of this court so holding has been found, the notion that an unconscionable bargain should not be given full enforcement is by no means novel. In Scott v. United States, 79 U.S. (12 Wall.) 443, 445, 20 L.Ed. 438 (1870), the Supreme Court stated:

> " . . . If a contract be unreasonable and unconscionable, but not void for fraud, a court of law will give to the party who sues for its breach damages, not according to its letter, but only such as he is equitably entitled to. . . . "

Since we have never adopted or rejected such a rule, the question here presented is actually one of first impression.

Congress has recently enacted the Uniform Commercial Code, which specifically provides that the court may refuse to enforce a contract which it finds to be unconscionable at the time it was made. (Section 2–302) The enactment of this section, which occurred subsequent to the contracts here in suit, does not mean that the common law of the District of Columbia was otherwise at the time of enactment, nor does it preclude the court from adopting a similar rule in the exercise of its powers to develop the common law for the District of Columbia. In fact, in view of the absence of prior authority on the point, we consider the congressional adopting of Section 2–302 persuasive authority for following the rationale of the cases, from which the section is explicitly derived.[3] Accordingly, we hold that where the element of unconscionability is present at the time a contract is made, the contract should not be enforced.

Unconscionability has generally been recognized to include an absence of meaningful choice on the part of one of the parties together with contract terms which are unreasonably favorable to the other party. Whether a meaningful choice is present in a particular case can only be determined by consideration of all the circumstances sur-

---

2. Campbell Soup Co. v. Wentz, 3 Cir., 172 F.2d 80 (1948); Indianapolis Morris Plan Corp. v. Sparks, 132 Ind.App. 145, 172 N.E.2d 899 (1961); Henningsen v. Bloomfield Motors, Inc., 32 N.J. 358, 161 A.2d 69, 84–96, 75 A.L.R.2d 1 (1960). Cf. 1 Corbin, Contracts Section 128 (1963).

3. See Comment, Sec. 2–302, Uniform Commercial Code (1962). Compare Note, 45 Va.L.Rev. 583, 590 (1959), where it is predicted that the rule of Sec. 2–302 will be followed by analogy in cases which involve contracts not specifically covered by the section. Cf. 1 State of New York Law Revision Commission, Report and Record of Hearings on the Uniform Commercial Code 108–110 (1954) (remarks of Professor Llewellyn).

rounding the transaction. In many cases the meaningfulness of the choice is negated by a gross inequality of bargaining power.[4] The manner in which the contract was entered is also relevant to this consideration. Did each party to the contract, considering his obvious education or lack of it, have a reasonable opportunity to understand the terms of the contract, or were the important terms hidden in a maze of fine print and minimized by deceptive sales practices? Ordinarily, one who signs an agreement without full knowledge of its terms might be held to assume the risk that he has entered a one-sided bargain.[5] But when a party of little bargaining power, and hence little real choice, signs a commercially unreasonable contract with little or no knowledge of its terms, it is hardly likely that his consent, or even an objective manifestation of his consent, was ever given to all the terms. In such a case the usual rule that the terms of the agreement are not to be questioned [6] should be abandoned and the court should consider whether the terms of the contract are so unfair that enforcement should be withheld.[7]

In determining reasonableness or fairness, the primary concern must be with the terms of the contract considered in light of the circumstances existing when the contract was made. The test is not simple, nor can it be mechanically applied. The terms are to be considered "in the light of the general commercial background and the commercial needs of the particular trade or case." [8] Corbin suggests the

---

4. See Henningsen v. Bloomfield Motors, Inc., supra Note 2, 161 A.2d 69 at 86, and authorities there cited. Inquiry into the relative bargaining power of the two parties is not an inquiry wholly divorced from the general question of unconscionability, since a one-sided bargain is itself evidence of the inequality of the bargaining parties. This fact was vaguely recognized in the common law doctrine of intrinsic fraud, that is, fraud which can be presumed from the grossly unfair nature of the terms of the contract. See the oft-quoted statement of Lord Hardwicke in Earl of Chesterfield v. Janssen, 28 Eng.Rep. 82, 100 (1751):
". . . (Fraud) may be apparent from the intrinsic nature and subject of the bargain itself; such as no man in his senses and not under delusion would make . . ."

5. See Restatement, Contracts Sec. 70 (1932); Note, 63 Harv.L.Rev. 494 (1950). See also Daley v. People's Building, Loan & Savings Ass'n, 178 Mass. 13, 59 N.E. 452, 453 (1901), in which Mr. Justice Holmes, while sitting on the Supreme Judicial Court of

Massachusetts, made this observation: ". . . Courts are less and less disposed to interfere with parties making such contracts as they choose, so long as they interfere with no one's welfare but their own. . . . It will be understood that we are speaking of parties standing in an equal position where neither has any oppressive advantage or power. . . ."

6. This rule has never been without exception. In cases involving merely the transfer of unequal amounts of the same commodity, the courts have held the bargain unenforceable for the reason that "in such a case, it is clear, that the law cannot indulge in the presumption of equivalence between the consideration and the promise." 1 Williston, Contracts Sec. 115 (3d ed. 1957).

7. See the general discussion of "Boiler-Plate Agreements" in Llewellyn, The Common Law Tradition 362–371 (1960).

8. Comment, Uniform Commercial Code Sec. 2–307.

test as being whether the terms are "so extreme as to appear unconscionable according to the mores and business practices of the time and place." 1 Corbin, op. cit. supra Note 2.[9] We think this formulation correctly states the test to be applied in those cases where no meaningful choice was exercised upon entering the contract.

Because the trial court and the appellate court did not feel that enforcement could be refused, no findings were made on the possible unconscionability of the contracts in these cases. Since the record is not sufficient for our deciding the issue as a matter of law, the cases must be remanded to the trial court for further proceedings.

So ordered.

DANAHER, CIRCUIT JUDGE (dissenting) :

The District of Columbia Court of Appeals obviously was as unhappy about the situation here presented as any of us can possibly be. Its opinion in the *Williams* case, quoted in the majority text, concludes: "We think Congress should consider corrective legislation to protect the public from such exploitive contracts as were utilized in the case at bar."

My view is thus summed up by an able court which made no finding that there had actually been sharp practice. Rather the appellant seems to have known precisely where she stood.

There are many aspects of public policy here involved. What is a luxury to some may seem an outright necessity to others. Is public oversight to be required of the expenditures of relief funds? A washing machine, e. g., in the hands of a relief client might become a fruitful source of income. Many relief clients may well need credit, and certain business establishments will take long chances on the sale of items, expecting their pricing policies will afford a degree of protection commensurate with the risk. Perhaps a remedy when necessary will be found within the provisions of the "Loan Shark" law, D. C.Code Sections 26–601 et seq. (1961).

I mention such matters only to emphasize the desirability of a cautious approach to any such problem, particularly since the law for so long has allowed parties such great latitude in making their own contracts. I dare say there must annually be thousands upon thousands of installment credit transactions in this jurisdiction, and one can only speculate as to the effect the decision in these cases will have.[10]

9. See Henningsen v. Bloomfield Motors, Inc., supra Note 2; Mandel v. Liebman, 303 N.Y. 88, 100 N.E.2d 149 (1951). The traditional test as stated in Greer v. Tweed . . ., 13 Abb. Pr.,N.S. (N.Y.1872), at 429, is "such as no man in his senses and not under delusion would make on the one hand, and as no honest or fair man would accept, on the other."

10. However the provision ultimately may be applied or in what circumstances, D.C.Code Sec. 28–2–302 (Supp. IV, 1965) did not become effective until January 1, 1965.

I join the District of Columbia Court of Appeals in its disposition of the issues.[a]

NOTES

(1) *Effect of Repossession.* The contract provision authorizing the seller to repossess one item for the buyer's failure to pay for another is known as a cross-collateral, or "dragnet" provision. Is it clear that the furniture company would be overpaid by the enforcement of this provision? If the repossessed items are resold for less than the buyer's indebtedness, the seller is entitled to a deficiency judgment for the difference, plus certain expenses. (The right to such a judgment is curtailed, however, in some consumer credit legislation, such as section 5.103 of the Uniform Consumer Credit Code.) If they are resold for more than is due, the seller must account to the buyer for the surplus. What is the likelihood of a surplus, on a resale of second-hand consumer goods? On the subject of enforcing security interests, Article 9, Part 5, of the Uniform Commercial Code may be consulted, but the subject must be pursued in a course concerning security interests in personal property.

(2) *Questions.* If the furniture company's contracts had not contained a cross-collateral provision, would there have been anything offensive about them? Should Mrs. Williams have been permitted to keep the stereo set without paying for it? To keep it on paying part of the price? To return it and keep the other furniture she had bought? Do your answers depend in part on what you know of her financial position? Note the remarks of the lower court on the subject. Do they contain a patronizing implication that storekeepers may decide who can and who cannot afford their merchandise?

(3) *Pro-Rata Payments.* Mrs. Williams was represented by the legal assistance office of the bar association.[b] "The Legal Assistance Office was willing to concede that the store could repossess the stereo record player for nonpayment, but what stirred them to action was that the seller sought to scoop up all that it had ever sold to Ora. . . . The store's records showed that of a combined total claim of $444 as of December 26, 1962, Ora still owed 25¢ on item 1, purchased December 23, 1957 (price $45.65); 3¢ on item 2, purchased December 31, 1957 (price $13.21); . . . and similarly for subsequent purchases . . . ." Skilton and Helstad, Protection of the Installment Buyer of Goods under the UCC, 65 Mich. L.Rev. 1465 (1967).[c] Mrs. Williams had made payments of more than $1,000. Apparently the store applied each payment in the proportion that the outstanding balances on the several items bore to one another at the time of the payment.

Another way to apportion a payment is in relation to the *original* debt for each item. If the store had applied Mrs. Williams' payments that way,

a. The case is the basis for Illustration 5 after Restatement Second, § 234, referring especially to the clause, "all payments . . . shall be credited pro rata on all outstanding . . . accounts." The Illustration concludes: "It may be determined that either the quoted clause or the contract as a whole was unconscionable when made."

b. In addition, the court of appeals appointed amicus curiae.

c. Of many comments on the Williams case, this is an outstanding one.

she would evidently have paid in full for about a dozen of the 16 items she bought from the store. Could the store have been compelled to reallocate her payments in that manner, as a plausible reading of the contract?

The manner of apportioning payments is widely prescribed by legislation on retail installment sales. For a case like that of Mrs. Williams the Uniform Consumer Credit Code states this rule: "payments received by the seller . . . are deemed, for the purpose of determining the amount of the debt secured by the various security interests, to have been first applied to the payment of the debts arising from the sales first made. To the extent debts are paid according to this section, security interests in items of property terminate as the debts [sic] originally incurred with respect to each item is paid." UCCC 2.409(1).[d]

The specific legislation germane to the Williams case, and many concrete prohibitions on particular practices, suggest some questions: Is a court less likely to declare a contract unconscionable by reason of the fact that the legislature has placed contracts of its type in a straitjacket of exact proscriptions designed to protect one of the parties? That is, does statutory control of contract terms, as it grows, limit the range of unconscionability doctrine? If so, is this a good thing?

(4) *The Lawyer's Role.* As a legal precedent, the court's ruling on unconscionability is more significant for consumers generally than any victory Mrs. Williams could have won on the basis of interpretation of her contract. Sometimes a client's interest is better served by seeking relief on a narrow basis than by treating his problem as a test case on a broader principle, such as unconscionability. In this situation, what is the duty of the lawyer? If he is dedicated to the interests of consumers at large, should he seek to advance them by risking the interest of an individual client? Legal-aid lawyers report that they can commonly settle complaints of consumer debtors on favorable terms, with little effort. Should they urge such a client to forego settlement in the hope of obtaining a landmark ruling? What are the ethical considerations? For a legal-aid lawyer, who is not compensated by individual clients, is it necessary to enlist himself in general causes more than for a lawyer charging fees? Permissible?

JONES v. STAR CREDIT CORP.

Supreme Court of New York, Nassau County, 1969.
59 Misc.2d 189, 298 N.Y.S.2d 264.

WACHTLER, J. On August 31, 1965 the plaintiffs, who are welfare recipients, agreed to purchase a home freezer unit for $900 as the result of a visit from a salesman representing Your Shop At Home Service, Inc. With the addition of the time credit charges, credit life insurance, credit property insurance, and sales tax, the

---

d. The section excepts sales pursuant to a revolving charge account. On this subject, however, see In re Jackson, 8 UCC Rep. 1152 (Bankruptcy Referee's opinion, W.D.Mo.1971).

The Uniform Commercial Code affords a modest measure of protection for buyers of successive consumer items in UCC 9–204(4)(b).

purchase price totalled $1,234.80. Thus far the plaintiffs have paid $619.88 toward their purchase. The defendant claims that with various added credit charges paid for an extension of time there is a balance of $819.81 still due from the plaintiffs. The uncontroverted proof at the trial established that the freezer unit, when purchased, had a maximum retail value of approximately $300. The question is whether this transaction and the resulting contract could be considered unconscionable within the meaning of Section 2–302 of the Uniform Commercial Code which provides in part:

(1) If the court as a matter of law finds the contract or any clause of the contract to have been unconscionable at the time it was made the court may refuse to enforce the contract, or it may enforce the remainder of the contract without the unconscionable clause, or it may so limit the application of any unconscionable clause as to avoid any unconscionable result.

(2) When it is claimed or appears to the court that the contract or any clause thereof may be unconscionable the parties shall be afforded a reasonable opportunity to present evidence as to its commercial setting, purpose and effect to aid the court in making the determination. L.1962, c. 553, eff. Sept. 27, 1964.

There was a time when the shield of "caveat emptor" would protect the most unscrupulous in the marketplace—a time when the law, in granting parties unbridled latitude to make their own contracts, allowed exploitive and callous practices which shocked the conscience of both legislative bodies and the courts.

The effort to eliminate these practices has continued to pose a difficult problem. On the one hand it is necessary to recognize the importance of preserving the integrity of agreements and the fundamental right of parties to deal, trade, bargain, and contract. On the other hand there is the concern for the uneducated and often illiterate individual who is the victim of gross inequality of bargaining power, usually the poorest members of the community.

Concern for the protection of these consumers against overreaching by the small but hardy breed of merchants who would prey on them is not novel. The dangers of inequality of bargaining power were vaguely recognized in the early English common law when Lord Hardwicke wrote of a fraud, "which may be apparent from the intrinsic nature and subject of the bargain itself; such as no man in his senses and not under delusion would make." The English authorities on this subject were discussed in Hume v. United States, 132 U.S. 406, 10 S.Ct. 134, 33 L.Ed. 393 (1889) where the United States Supreme Court characterized these as "cases in which one party took advantage of the other's ignorance of arithmetic to impose upon him, and the fraud was apparent from the face of the contracts."

The law is beginning to fight back against those who once took advantage of the poor and illiterate without risk of either exposure or interference. From the common law doctrine of intrinsic fraud we have over the years, developed common and statutory law which tells not only the buyer but also the seller to beware. This body of laws recognizes the importance of a free enterprise system but at the same time will provide the legal armor to protect and safeguard the prospective victim from the harshness of an unconscionable contract.

Section 2–302 of the Uniform Commercial Code enacts the moral sense of the community into the law of commercial transactions. It authorizes the court to find, as a matter of law, that a contract or a clause of a contract was "unconscionable at the time it was made", and upon so finding the court may refuse to enforce the contract, excise the objectionable clause or limit the application of the clause to avoid an unconscionable result. "The principle", states the Official Comment to this section, "is one of the prevention of oppression and unfair surprise". It permits a court to accomplish directly what heretofore was often accomplished by construction of language, manipulations of fluid rules of contract law and determinations based upon a presumed public policy.

There is no reason to doubt, moreover, that this section is intended to encompass the price term of an agreement. In addition to the fact that it has already been so applied (State by Lefkowitz v. ITM, Inc., 52 Misc.2d 39, 275 N.Y.S.2d 303; Frostifresh Corp. v. Reynoso, 52 Misc.2d 26, 274 N.Y.S.2d 757, affd. 54 Misc.2d 119, 281 N.Y.S.2d 964; American Home Improvement, Inc. v. MacIver, 105 N.H. 435, 201 A.2d 886, 14 A.L.R.3d 324), the statutory language itself makes it clear that not only a clause of the contract, but the contract in toto, may be found unconscionable as a matter of law. Indeed, no other provision of an agreement more intimately touches upon the question of unconscionability than does the term regarding price.

Fraud, in the instant case, is not present; nor is it necessary under the statute. The question which presents itself is whether or not, under the circumstances of this case, the sale of a freezer unit having a retail value of $300 for $900 ($1,439.69 including credit charges and $18 sales tax) is unconscionable as a matter of law. The court believes it is.

Concededly, deciding the issue is substantially easier than explaining it. No doubt, the mathematical disparity between $300, which presumably includes a reasonable profit margin, and $900, which is exhorbitant on its face, carries the greatest weight. Credit charges alone exceed by more than $100 the retail value of the freezer. These alone, may be sufficient to sustain the decision. Yet, a caveat is warranted lest we reduce the import of Section 2–302 solely to a mathematical ratio formula. It may, at times, be that; yet it may also be much more. The very limited financial resources of the pur-

382 POLICING THE BARGAIN Ch. 3

chaser, known to the sellers at the time of the sale, is entitled to weight in the balance. Indeed, the value disparity itself leads inevitably to the felt conclusion that knowing advantage was taken of the plaintiffs. In addition, the meaningfulness of choice essential to the making of a contract, can be negated by a gross inequality of bargaining power. (Williams v. Walker-Thomas Furniture Co., 121 U.S. App.D.C. 315, 350 F.2d 445.)

There is no question about the necessity and even the desirability of instalment sales and the extension of credit. Indeed, there are many, including welfare recipients, who would be deprived of even the most basic conveniences without the use of these devices. Similarly, the retail merchant selling on instalment or extending credit is expected to establish a pricing factor which will afford a degree of protection commensurate with the risk of selling to those who might be default prone. However, neither of these accepted premises can clothe the sale of this freezer with respectability.

Support for the court's conclusion will be found in a number of other cases already decided. In American Home Improvement, Inc. v. MacIver, supra, the Supreme Court of New Hampshire held that a contract to install windows, a door and paint, for the price of $2,568.60, of which $809.60 constituted interest and carrying charges and $800. was a salesman's commission was unconscionable as a matter of law. In State by Lefkowitz v. ITM, Inc., supra, a deceptive and fraudulent scheme was involved, but standing alone, the court held that the sale of a vacuum cleaner, among other things, costing the defendant $140 and sold by it for $749 cash or $920.52 on time purchase was unconscionable as a matter of law. Finally, in Frostifresh Corp. v. Reynoso, supra, the sale of a refrigerator costing the seller $348 for $900 plus credit charges of $245.88 was unconscionable as a matter of law. . . .

Having already paid more than $600 toward the purchase of this $300 freezer unit, it is apparent that the defendant has already been amply compensated. In accordance with the statute, the application of the payment provision should be limited to amounts already paid by the plaintiffs and the contract be reformed and amended by changing the payments called for therein to equal the amount of payment actually so paid by the plaintiffs.

NOTES

(1) *The Question of Remedies.* If Mr. and Mrs. Jones had paid $1,000 before complaining of the contract, would the court have permitted them to recover a part of it? If they had paid only $300, would the court have required them to pay more? What is the rationale of stopping the payments at $619.88?

One of the cases cited by the court, Frostifresh Corp. v. Reynoso, is a well-known action by the seller of a freezer for the unpaid balance of the price. The Reynosos had made only one payment, of $32. The plaintiff had paid $348 for the appliance. The trial court made a simple deduction, and gave judgment for $316. On appeal, the judgment was reversed, and the trial court was directed to give judgment for the "net cost for the refrigerator-freezer, plus a reasonable profit, in addition to trucking and service charges necessarily incurred and reasonable finance charges." Two comments on the case are as follows:

"This case means that sellers can charge the most exorbitant rates, secure in the knowledge that at the worst they will be able to recover a reasonable profit plus all their expenses." Narral, interview, in The Law and the Low Income Consumer 330 ff. (Katz, ed., 1968).

"It must be recognized that even in the poverty situations, putting aside the cases of fraud and high pressure in home sales, the buyers do want the goods. Even in the famous *Frostifresh* case, the question of remedies was complicated by the fact that the Spanish-speaking people deceived into buying a home freezer at a high price *chose to keep the freezer*. Thus we cannot adopt restrictions on remedies so punitive as to put the credit sellers in the poverty areas, and their financers, out of business. Despite the present high social cost, they serve a social purpose." Kripke, Consumer Credit Regulation: A Creditor-Oriented Viewpoint, 68 Colum.L.Rev. 455, 478 ff. (1968).

(2) *Tactics.* Who passes on unconscionability under UCC 2–302, judge or jury? At a hearing on an issue of unconscionability, the evidence might tend to prejudice or confuse the jury about other issues in the case, so it has been suggested. If so, the party supporting the agreement may well try to get a ruling that it is not unconscionable before the court proceeds to other issues. For a particular strategy for dealing with this problem, see County Asphalt, Inc. v. Lewis Welding & Eng. Corp., 444 F.2d 372 (2d Cir. 1971), cert. denied, 404 U.S. 939 (1971). The court there ruled, in favor of the defendant, that a provision excluding consequential damages was not unconscionable. Without holding a separate hearing, it was held, the court had complied with UCC–302(2).[a]

A bare allegation of unconscionability in the price of an item, it has been held, does not require the seller to respond to disclosure proceedings aimed at ascertaining his costs. Patterson v. Walker-Thomas Furniture Company, 277 A.2d 111 (D.C.App.1971). See also Morris v. Capitol Furniture & Appliance Co., 9 UCC Rep. 577 (D.C.App.1971). If the seller insists that evidence of "retail value" as established by purchases from other merchants are beside the point, because they do not reflect *his* costs, what reply can be made?

On the difficulties of procedure, and delaying tactics, in maintaining an action for affirmative relief on behalf of an impoverished consumer, on grounds of fraud and unconscionability, see Schrag, Bleak House 1968: A Report on Consumer Test Litigation, 44 N.Y.U.L.Rev. 115 (1969).

a. The plaintiff argued that it had a right, under the Seventh Amendment, to jury consideration of the issue of unconscionability. The court responded as follows: "Plaintiff's argument . . . hardly merits consideration. In 1791, when the amendment was adopted, the discretionary power to grant equitable relief according to the 'conscience' of the chancellor was so unmistakably a matter for the equity side rather than the law side of the court no further discussion of the constitutional ground is warranted. *Cf.* Rose v. Bernhard, 396 U.S. 531 (1970)."

(3) *Unconscionability: Two Varieties.* The unconscionability provision of the Code is criticized in Leff, Unconscionability and the Code—The Emperor's New Clause, 115 U.Pa.L.Rev. 485 (1967), and defended in Ellinghaus, In Defense of Unconscionability, 78 Yale L.J. 757 (1969). That debate draws a helpful distinction between unfairness in the content of the agreement (which is termed "substantive unconscionability") and unfairness in the bargaining process by which agreement is reached (which is termed "procedural unconscionability"). Among the questions that the authors raise are the following:

To what extent are substantive and procedural unconscionability either necessary or sufficient? For example, when, if ever, will a showing of procedural unconscionability be enough, without regard to whether or not there is substantive unconscionability? Or, when, if ever, will a showing of *fairness* in the bargaining process "insulate" an otherwise objectionable agreement from a claim of substantive unconscionability? And what is the significance of potential as opposed to actual, unfairness in the form of inequality of bargaining power? What account is to be taken of the peculiar social and economic status of the weaker party in such a situation? To what extent are unfairness in the entire contract (which has been termed "overall imbalance") and unfairness in a particular part of the contract either necessary or sufficient? To the extent that unfairness in a particular part is sufficient, what is the impact of an excessive price, a disclaimer of warranties, a limitation of remedies, and so on? And which sorts of cases justify a refusal to enforce the entire contract and which sorts call for a more limited response?

Is it helpful to regard the problem of unconscionability as one of allocating risks? See Murray, Unconscionability: Unconscionability, 31 U. Pitt.L.Rev. 1 (1969), and comments beginning at id., 333 (1970).

(4) *Two Aspects.* In concluding that a charge for goods or services is "too high," either or both of two somewhat distinct judgments may be implied: it is too much for the buyer to pay, and it is too much for the seller to charge. On which of these aspects should attention be focussed, in applying the test of price unconscionability? As the following note shows, the Uniform Consumer Credit Code emphasizes the buyer's viewpoint and measures prices by what others in his class must pay for similar goods or services. In contrast, the seller's viewpoint is advocated in Note, 67 Mich.L.Rev. 1248, 1259 (1969): "It is submitted that a price should be held sufficiently excessive to render a contract unconscionable if it gives the seller a greater profit than similarly situated sellers ordinarily receive." On this view, what significance attaches to the fact that a merchant's costs of doing business are exceptionally high? See Note, Unconscionable Sales Prices, 20 Me.L.Rev. 159 (1968).

UNCONSCIONABILITY IN THE UCCC

The Uniform Consumer Credit Code contains a section on unconscionability derived from UCC 2–302, incorporating much of the same language: UCCC 5.108. It is designed to be given effect in private litigation with respect to consumer sales, consumer leases, and consumer loans. The Code also contains a section on the subject, reproduced below, which is not designed to apply in suits between the parties to a consumer transaction, but which authorizes actions by an administrator. (The "administrator" is not identified in the Code, but it is contemplated that each enacting state will designate an official, or agency, or more than one, to oversee consumer credit practices.) A notable feature of the section is that it emphasizes a *course* of unconscionable conduct, rather than isolated instances of unconscionability.

_____

Section 6.111   [Injunctions Against Unconscionable Agreements and Fraudulent or Unconscionable Conduct]

(1) The Administrator may bring a civil action to restrain a creditor or a person acting in his behalf from engaging in a course of

(a) making or enforcing unconscionable terms or provisions of consumer credit sales, consumer leases, or consumer loans;

(b) fraudulent or unconscionable conduct in inducing debtors to enter into consumer credit sales, consumer leases, or consumer loans; or

(c) fraudulent or unconscionable conduct in the collection of debts arising from consumer credit sales, consumer leases, or consumer loans.

(2) In an action brought pursuant to this section the court may grant relief only if it finds

(a) that the respondent has made unconscionable agreements or has engaged or is likely to engage in a course of fraudulent or unconscionable conduct;

(b) that the agreements or conduct of the respondent has caused or is likely to cause injury to consumers; and

(c) that the respondent has been able to cause or will be able to cause the injury primarily because the transactions involved are credit transactions.

(3) In applying this section, consideration shall be given to each of the following factors, among others:

(a) belief by the creditor at the time consumer credit sales, consumer leases, or consumer loans are made that there was no reasonable probability of payment in full of the obligation by the debtor;

(b) in the case of consumer credit sales or consumer leases, knowledge by the seller or lessor at the time of the sale or lease of the inability of the buyer or lessee to receive substantial benefits from the property or services sold or leased;

(c) in the case of consumer credit sales or consumer leases, gross disparity between the price of the property or services sold or leased and the value of the property or services measured by the price at which similar property or services are readily obtainable in credit transactions by like buyers or lessees;

(d) the fact that the creditor contracted for or received separate charges for insurance with respect to consumer credit sales or consumer loans with the effect of making the sales or loans, considered as a whole, unconscionable; and

(e) the fact that the respondent has knowingly taken advantage of the inability of the debtor reasonably to protect his interests by reason of physical or mental infirmities, ignorance, illiteracy or inability to understand the language of the agreement, or similar factors.

(4) In an action brought pursuant to this section, a charge or practice expressly permitted by this Act is not in itself unconscionable.

NOTES

(1) *National Consumer Act.* The NCA authorizes the administrator, as the Code does not, to issue an order to a creditor to "cease and desist" from engaging in unconscionable conduct, and to promulgate rules declaring specific practices unconscionable.[a] It authorizes him, "or any consumer," to bring an action to restrain a merchant from engaging in unconscionable conduct.[b] It contains a list of considerations bearing on the issue of unconscionability, which are comparable to those in the Code section set out above, but more comprehensive.[c] Unlike the Code, however, the NCA incorporates such a list in the section concerning private enforcement of consumer transactions.

Comment 1 to that section refers to UCC 2-302 as follows: "Nearly fifteen years of experience with [it] has shown that 'unconscionability' is so broad and undefined as to enable courts to run roughshod over the legitimate interests of merchants. In fact, the experience has been quite to the contrary; the few cases reported on Section 2-302 have been markedly conservative in their interpretation."

(2) *Questions.* Do you find reference in UCCC 6.111 to both "substantive" and "procedural" unconscionability? What is the justification for centralizing in an "administrator," as the Code does, the function of policing the unconscionable conduct of creditors? What is the justification for requiring the administrator to proceed in court against unconscionability, as the Code does, rather than permitting him to issue cease-and-desist orders, as the NCA does? What is the justification for permitting a consumer to take action against unconscionable conduct whether or not he is affected by it, as the NCA does?

The Code section on unconscionability in private enforcement proceedings (UCCC 5.108) includes a sentence that is notably missing from the corresponding NCA section: "For the purpose of this section, a charge or

a. Section 6.108(1), section 6.109.   c. Section 5.107.

b. Section 6.110.

practice expressly permitted by this Act is not in itself unconscionable." In what way could this sentence serve to protect a creditor? Why did the draftsmen of the NCA not say the same in their act?

(3) *F.T.C. Action.* The Federal Trade Commission has taken action, particularly in the District of Columbia, against deceptive credit practices by some merchants. A seminal instance is the case, Leon A. Tashoff, No. 8714 (F.T.C.1968), CCH Trade Reg.Rep. ¶ 18,606. The case resulted in a cease-and-desist order against a seller of eyeglasses and jewelry. The following quotations will suggest the tenor of the lengthy, thoughtful opinion:

"We conclude, therefore, that respondent has deceived his customers and dealt unfairly with them, through its use of 'easy credit' advertising and its markup and other promotion practices. When the entire format of respondent's business is considered, it is clear that it is attracting customers who cannot obtain credit elsewhere by the two pronged, doubly deceptive gimmick of 'discount' prices and 'easy' credit. As utilized by this respondent, both practices are deceptive and are in violation of Section 5 of the Federal Trade Commission Act. . . . [I]t is manifestly unfair to adopt a marketing policy which has the effect of luring unsophisticated customers into entering contractual obligations which in all likelihood they have little understanding of, convincing them that the credit is 'easy' and prices are low and at the same time following a rigid collection policy resulting in default judgments and garnishments being levied against their meager wages."

On the suggestion that a merchant of a certain character be required to disclose to his customers that merchandise like his is available elsewhere at a lower price, see Kripke, Consumer Credit 228–29 (1970).

OF HIGH PRICES AND LOW INCOMES

How may a court determine that the price charged for goods is so high that the contract is unconscionable, if there is no other element of overreaching? Must the court be prepared to say what the "intrinsic" value of the goods is? Must it be prepared to say what a "reasonable" profit to the seller is? See UCCC 6.111(3), supra. Under this section, if the buyer is an unusually weak credit risk, does that fact tend to justify what would otherwise appear to be a gross disparity? See subsection (c). If the individual buyer's risk characteristics are unknown, but he lives in a low-income neighborhood, is a disparity explainable by that fact?[a] How do you evaluate that factor in the UCCC by comparison with the corresponding one in the National Consumer Act, as follows?—"Gross disparity between the price of goods

---

a. With reference to the section cited, Professor Kripke has put these questions: "Does it declare it to be unconscionable for a chain store to charge more for an item in the ghetto than for the same item in its suburban store? . . . for a merchant in the ghetto to charge more for a television than the same set sells for in a downtown store? . . . for the door-to-door salesman to charge more for an item than the price charged for the same item in stores of that neighborhood?" And should these margins be made unconscionable? Kripke, Consumer Credit 228 (1970).

or services and their value as measured by the price at which similar goods or services are readily obtainable by other consumers, or by other tests of true value." [b]

In Toker v. Westerman, 8 UCC Rep. 789 (N.J.Dist.Ct.1970), there was an installment sale of a refrigerator-freezer priced at $900 (less 2¢). Resisting payment, the buyers produced an appliance dealer as a witness, who estimated the reasonable retail price of the item as between $350 and $400. The court expressed its shock at the price, "particularly so where, as here, the sale was made by a door-to-door salesman for a dealer who therefore would have less overhead expense than a dealer maintaining a store or showroom. In addition it appeared that the defendants during the course of the payments they made to the plaintiff were obliged to seek welfare assistance."

If the seller had shown that he paid high commissions to his salesmen, would that have helped to justify his price? Does the court's reasoning tend to justify the higher prices charged by storekeepers in urban slum areas than those charged for similar merchandise in more affluent areas? That such disparity in pricing exists is one of the conclusions of a survey conducted by the Federal Trade Commission in the District of Columbia. [c] Retailers there were classified into two groups: those appealing primarily to low-income customers and those appealing to a more general market. "The survey disclosed that without exception low-income market retailers had high average markups and prices. On the average, goods purchased for $100 at wholesale sold for $255 in the low-income market store, compared with $159 in general market stores." But it was found that the latter enjoyed higher average returns on net worth (13% for department stores, 20.3% for appliance, radio, and TV retailers). The average return after taxes for low-income market retailers was 10.1%. The returns on net sales for the two groups were 4.6% and 4.7%. "Despite their substantially higher prices, net profit on sales for low-income market retailers was only slightly higher and net profit return on net worth was considerably lower when compared to general market retailers. It appears that salaries and commissions, bad-debt losses, and other expenses are substantially higher for low-income market retailers."

Another finding of the survey cited above was that low-income market retailers, unlike others, take legal action to enforce their claims "as a normal order of business." These retailers resorted to repossession and garnishment with great frequency. If this finding is reliable, what does it indicate about unconscionability in their pricing policies? The finance charges imposed by low-income market retailers were higher, on the average, than those imposed by others, but

b. Section 6.109(3).

c. F.T.C., Economic Report on Installment Credit and Retail Sales Practices of District of Columbia Retailers (1968).

not markedly so: on one class of contracts the comparable annual rates for credit were 19% and 23%. What does this indicate about the way slum-area merchants cover their exceptional expenses?

According to one judge in the District of Columbia, "It is a fact of common knowledge that mark-up on furniture frequently exceeds 100%." [d] This was said as an indication that a large mark-up of furniture prices by a retail merchant is not of itself unconscionable. According to the F.T.C. study, representative mark-ups on furniture in the District range from 47.5 to 56.2% for different groups of retailers. How might the judge have made use of this finding?

NOTE

Ghetto Market Improvement. The "Riot Commission" report of 1968 —Report of the National Advisory Commission on Civil Disorders—contained a section on Exploitation of Disadvantaged Consumers By Retail Merchants, including these remarks: "Forced to use credit, [ghetto residents] have little understanding of the pitfalls of credit buying. But because they have unstable incomes and frequently fail to make payments, the cost to the merchants of serving them is significantly above that of serving middle-income consumers. Consequently, a special kind of merchant appears to sell them goods on terms designed to cover the high cost of doing business in ghetto neighborhoods. . . . While higher prices are not necessarily exploitative in themselves, many merchants in ghetto neighborhoods take advantage of their superior knowledge of credit buying by engaging in various exploitative tactics—high-pressure salesmanship, bait advertising, misrepresentation of prices, substitution of used goods for promised new ones, failure to notify consumers of legal actions against them, refusal to repair or replace substandard goods, exorbitant prices or credit charges, and use of shoddy merchandise. Such tactics affect a great many low-income consumers." [e]

Various remedial measures for improving the quality of the marketing process described here have been attempted or proposed, including buyers' strikes and consumer education programs. One of the most elaborate is designed to make property insurance available to slum-area merchants. Cooperative efforts to this end by Congress, state legislatures, administrators, and the insurance industry have resulted in FAIR plans in many states—Fair Access to Insurance Requirements.[f]

---

d. Capitol Furniture & Appliance Co., Inc. v. Morris, 8 UCC Rep. 321 (D.C. Gen.Sess.1970).

It has been suggested that a price is prima facie unconscionable if it exceeds the "average" by 100%. Speidel, Unconscionability, Assent and Consumer Protection, 31 U.Pitt.L.Rev. 359, 372–73 (1970) (by analogy to the civil-law doctrine of *laesio enormis*).

e. Report, 274–76 (Bantam ed. 1968).

f. The workings of such a plan are described in Pohorily v. Kennedy, 269 A. 2d 240 (Del.Super.1970). For an appraisal by the Federal Insurance Administrator, see Bernstein, Critical Evaluation of FAIR Plans, 38 J. Risk & Ins. 269 (1971).

HOME SOLICITATION SALES AND "COOLING OFF" PERIODS

Since 1963, following the lead of Parliament, a number of American legislatures have enacted statutes directed at door-to-door selling, and providing what is known as a cooling-off period. A representative one, embodied in the Uniform Consumer Credit Code, is quoted below. There is a federal provision of this character, in the Consumer Credit Protection Act of 1968. It applies only when a security interest is granted "in any real property which is used or is expected to be used as a residence of the person to whom credit is extended." Naturally, there are many home-improvement contracts that this provision does not affect. There are significant variances in the state statutes, both as to scope and as to the mechanics of cancellation.

The basic rule of the UCCC is stated in section 2.502:

(1) Except as provided in subsection (5),[a] in addition to any right otherwise to revoke an offer, the buyer has the right to cancel a home solicitation sale until midnight of the third business day after the day on which the buyer signs an agreement or offer to purchase which complies with this Part.

The definition of "home solicitation sale" embraces most consumer credit sales "in which the seller or a person acting for him engages in a personal solicitation of the sale at a residence of the buyer and the buyer's agreement or offer to purchase is there given to the seller or a person acting for him." [b]

The power to cancel cannot be terminated until the end of the statutory period *following* the time when the buyer signs a document containing this statement:

BUYER'S RIGHT TO CANCEL [c]

If this agreement was solicited at your residence and you do not want the goods or services, you may cancel this agreement by mailing a notice to the seller. The notice must say that you do not want the goods or services and must be mailed before midnight of the third business day after you sign this agreement. The notice must be mailed to: (insert name and mailing address of seller). If you

---

a. According to subsection (5), the buyer may not cancel in certain circumstances, if he "requests the seller to provide goods or services without delay because of an emergency."

b. Section 2.501.

c. This caption must be conspicuous. The Code definition of "conspicuous" follows that of the Truth in Lending Act: "A term or clause is conspicuous when it is so written that a reasonable person against whom it is to operate ought to have noticed it. Whether a term or clause is conspicuous or not is for decision by the court." Section 1.301(6). It is derived in part from UCC 1–201(10).

cancel, the seller may keep all or part of your cash down payment.[d]

The seller's cancellation fee may not exceed the cash down payment, or 5% of the cash price. Special provisions are made for the home sale of services, for goods traded in, and for the safe return of goods after cancellation.

NOTES

(1) *Questions.* Would it be well to extend the principle of this legislation to in-store sales? What arguments might be made for and against such an extension? It is a well-known practice in some stores to let customers take merchandise out of stock "on approval," or virtually so. If it could be shown that this practice is least prevalent among merchants catering to poor persons, would the distinction seem invidious?

House-to-house selling affords full- or part-time employment to many persons of modest income, including college students. This fact is sometimes brought forward in argument against "cooling off" legislation, as applied to home sales. How do you appraise the argument?

(2) *Unconscionability and Incapacity.* Should the principle of unconscionability be regarded as defining a new class of persons lacking the capacity to contract? An analogy between unconscionability cases and those on capacity has been drawn by Professor Leff. As he sees it, the notion of Williams v. Walker-Thomas Furniture Company, p. 373 supra, is that the poor should be discouraged from frill-buying, and is comparable to the premise in infancy cases ("all persons under twenty-one lack sufficient probity"). Both of them illustrate a tendency toward stereotyping of parties. He writes: "One can see it enshrined in the old English equity courts' jolly treatment of English seamen as members of a happy, fun-loving race (with, one supposes, a fine sense of rhythm), but certainly not to be trusted to take care of themselves. What effect, if any, this had upon the sailors is hidden behind the judicial chuckles as they protected their loyal sailor boys, but one cannot help wondering how many sailors managed to get credit at any reasonable price. In other words, the benevolent have a tendency to colonize, whether geographically or legally." [e]

Is this fair criticism of the Williams case? Should new conceptions of capacity to contract be framed as a solution to consumer credit problems, or should the focus remain on the characteristics of the credit *transactions*?

---

d. Section 2.503(2).

e. Leff, Unconscionability and the Code —The Emperor's New Clause, 115 U. Pa.L.Rev. 485, 556–58 (1967). Professor Leff regards the Williams case as an example of certain decisions which have relied on UCC 2–302 as a way of escape from difficult policy judgments. (He regards the opinion in Henningsen with favor: "it is most significant that the court did *not* have § 2–302 to work with.").

With these views compare Ellinghaus, In Defense of Unconscionability, 78 Yale L.J. 757, 766–67, 773 (1969) ("nothing could be more misconceived").

UNCONSCIONABILITY AS "CONSUMER FRAUD"

The New Jersey Consumer Fraud Act authorizes the courts to enter orders as necessary, including injunctions, to prevent certain prohibited practices, or to restore "to any person in interest" money acquired by such practices, all at the instance of the attorney general.[a] In Kugler v. Romain, 58 N.J. 522, 279 A.2d 640 (1971), the attorney general brought an action under the act against Romain, trading as Educational Services Company. The action sought relief against contracts entered into between Romain and 24 named customers, and sought relief also for "those consumers similarly situated." The one aspect said to be common to each of these transactions was the price, "Which the testimony showed was about two and a half times a reasonable price in the relevant market." (The item sold was an "educational package" of books and related materials.) "[T]he Attorney General pointed out that in addition to being excessive in relation to defendant's cost, the books had very little and in some cases no value for the purpose for which the consumers were persuaded to buy them. Consequently he urged that under the circumstances the price was unconscionable under § 2–302 of the Uniform Commercial Code and, as such, was within the proscription of § 2 of the Consumer Fraud Act."

An apparent difficulty with the attorney general's position was that the New Jersey act makes no mention of unconscionability. But the court said that "the concept of fraud and unconscionability are interchangeable"—at least in the context of sales by professionals to the uneducated, the inexperienced and people of low incomes. Unconscionability as intended in UCC 2–302, the court said, is "an amorphous concept obviously designed to establish a broad business ethic. . . . The intent of the clause is not to erase the doctrine of freedom of contract, but to make realistic the assumption of the law that the agreement has resulted from real bargaining between parties who had freedom of choice and understanding and ability to negotiate in a meaningful fashion."

The court ruled that "the price for the book package was unconscionable in relation to defendant's cost and the value to the consumers and was therefore a fraud within the contemplation of" the Consumer Fraud Act.

NOTES

(1) *Class Action.* The New Jersey act makes fraud, deception and the like unlawful "whether or not any person has in fact been misled, deceived or damaged thereby." According to Comment 1 to UCC 2–302, the principle of the section is "one of the prevention of oppression and unfair surprise." Is it possible under the section to find unconscionability in a contract because one of the parties *might* have been oppressed or surprised, although in fact he was not?

a. N.J.Stat.Ann. §§ 56:8–1 et seq.

This question might be critical in deciding whether or not a consumers' class action may be mounted under the section. Such an action, the New Jersey court said, is "not maintainable if the right of each individual claimant to relief depended upon a separate set of facts applicable only to him." It left the question open whether or not the attorney general can maintain a class action based solely on UCC 2–302. Certainly the court did not hold that an individual buyer may base an action on that section, on behalf of himself and all others similarly situated. The conditions in which such an action lies must be left for courses in procedure and consumer protection. It is one of the liveliest and most vexing aspects of those subjects.[b]

(2) *Extension by Analogy.* One of the controversies over UCC 2–302 is whether or not it is a novelty in the law. Compare Williams v. Walker-Thomas Furniture Company, p. 373 supra, with United States Leasing Corp. v. Franklin Plaza Apartments, Inc., 8 UCC Rep. 1026 (N.Y.Civ.Ct.1971). Assuming that it is, should the principle of the section be applied, by analogy, to leases of goods, sales of services, and other contracts not within Article 2? See the case last cited (a very dubious one on the point decided, however).

SECTION 5.　ILLEGALITY

In the preceding sections our concern was with protecting one party to an agreement against imposition by the other party. In this section our concern is with protecting the public at large against imposition by both parties. When will a court refuse to enforce an agreement, fairly and freely entered into by both parties, on the ground that to enforce it would contravene "public policy"?

To begin with, where do courts get their notions of public policy? In some cases they formulate them for themselves, or rely on prior formulations by other courts. Examples, from the following pages, include the common law policies against improper restraint of competition and against improper influence in public affairs. In other cases they derive them from legislation. Rarely, however, do statutes proscribing conduct speak to the enforceability of contracts involving such conduct. (The main exceptions are the usury and gambling statutes which characteristically state that contracts in violation of them are "void.") But courts often look to statutes as sources of public policy, even when they are silent on enforceability itself. This phenomenon is not, of course, peculiar to the law of contracts, but is merely one aspect of the broader problem of adjusting the body of ex-

---

b. Even if a class action is not available, an individual buyer complaining of unconscionability may be permitted to use as evidence a successful charge against the seller by a public official, based on unlawful selling practices; so it was held in Milford Finance Corp. v. Lucas, 8 UCC Rep. 801 (Mass. App.1970).

isting law to take account of statutory directions. A comparable phenomenon can be seen in the law of torts when conduct in violation of a criminal statute is held to constitute negligence per se.

It may at first seem strange that the impact of public policy upon the enforceability of agreements is relegated to a single section at the end of this chapter. The explanation lies in the fact that most of the conduct that society finds objectionable (e. g., pollution, discrimination, crime in the streets) involves private agreement only peripherally or not at all. In discouraging such conduct, the threat of the conventional criminal sanctions of fine and imprisonment is far more likely to be effective than is the threat of the unenforceability of private agreement. Even where the conduct (e. g., usury, gambling, restraint of competition) is more intimately connected with private agreement, the relative efficacy of the threat of unenforceability may be questionable. In short, policing the bargain in the interests of society is not likely to be a very effective way of furthering those interests.

KARPINSKI v. INGRASCI

Court of Appeals of New York, 1971.
28 N.Y.2d 45, 268 N.E.2d 751.

FULD, CHIEF JUDGE. This appeal requires us to determine whether a covenant by a professional man not to compete with his employer is enforceable and, if it is, to what extent.

The plaintiff, Dr. Karpinski, an oral surgeon, had been carrying on his practice alone in Auburn—in Cayuga County—for many years. In 1953, he decided to expand and, since nearly all of an oral surgeon's business stems from referrals, he embarked upon a plan to "cultivate connections" among dentists in the four nearby Counties of Tompkins, Seneca, Cortland and Ontario. The plan was successful, and by 1962 twenty per cent of his practice consisted of treating patients referred to him by dentists located in those counties. In that year, after a number of those dentists had told him that some of their patients found it difficult to travel from their homes to Auburn, the plaintiff decided to open a second office in centrally-located Ithaca. He began looking for an assistant and, in the course of his search, met the defendant, Dr. Ingrasci, who was just completing his training in oral surgery at the Buffalo General Hospital and was desirous of entering private practice. Dr. Ingrasci manifested an interest in becoming associated with Dr. Karpinski and, after a number of discussions, they reached an understanding; the defendant was to live in Ithaca, a locale with which he had no prior familiarity, and there work as an employee of the plaintiff.

A contract, reflecting the agreement, was signed by the defendant in June, 1962. It was for three years and, shortly after its execution, the defendant started working in the office which the plaintiff rented and fully equipped at his own expense. The provision of the contract with which we are concerned is a covenant by the defendant not to compete with the plaintiff. More particularly, it recited that the defendant

"promises and covenants that while this agreement is in effect and forever thereafter, he will never practice dentistry and/or Oral Surgery in Cayuga, Cortland, Seneca, Tompkins or Ontario counties except: (a) In association with the [plaintiff] or (b) If the [plaintiff] terminates the agreement and employs another oral surgeon".

In addition, the defendant agreed, "in consideration of the . . . terms of employment, and of the experience gained while working with" the plaintiff, to execute a $40,000 promissory note to the plaintiff, to become payable if the defendant left the plaintiff and practiced "dentistry and/or Oral Surgery" in the five enumerated counties.[1]

When the contract expired, the two men engaged in extended discussions as to the nature of their continued association—as employer and employee or as partners. Unable to reach an accord, the defendant, in February, 1968, left the plaintiff's employ and opened his own office for the practice of oral surgery in Ithaca a week later. The dentists in the area thereupon began referring their patients to the defendant rather than to the plaintiff, and in two months the latter's practice from the Ithaca area dwindled to almost nothing and he closed the office in that city. In point of fact, the record discloses that about 90% of the defendant's present practice comes from referrals from dentists in the counties specified in the restrictive covenant, the very same dentists who had been referring patients to the plaintiff's Ithaca office when the defendant was working there.[2]

The plaintiff, alleging a breach of the restrictive covenant, seeks not only an injunction to enforce it but also a judgment of $40,000 on the note. The Supreme Court, after a nonjury trial, decided in favor of the plaintiff and granted him both an injunction and damages as requested. On appeal, however, the Appellate Division reversed the resulting judgment and dismissed the complaint; it was that court's view that the covenant was void and unenforceable on the ground that its restriction against the practice of both dentistry and oral surgery was impermissibly broad.

There can be no doubt that the defendant violated the terms of the covenant when he opened his own office in Ithaca. But the mere fact of breach does not, in and of itself, resolve the case. Since there

1. Either party was privileged to terminate the agreement on 60 days' notice within the three-year period and, if the plaintiff were to do so, the contract recited, the defendant was released from the restrictive covenant and the note.

2. There are two other oral surgeons, in addition to the plaintiff and the defendant, serving the Ithaca area.

are "powerful considerations of public policy which militate against sanctioning the loss of a man's livelihood," the courts will subject a covenant by an employee not to compete with his former employer to an "overriding limitation of 'reasonableness' ".   (Purchasing Assoc. v. Weitz, 13 N.Y.2d 267, 272, 246 N.Y.S.2d 600, 603, 196 N.E.2d 245, see Millet v. Slocum, 5 N.Y.2d 734, 177 N.Y.S.2d 716, 152 N.E.2d 672, affg. 4 A.D.2d 528, 167 N.Y.S.2d 136; Lynch v. Bailey, 300 N.Y. 615, 90 N.E.2d 484, affg. 275 App.Div. 527, 90 N.Y.S.2d 359; Interstate Tea Co. v. Alt, 271 N.Y. 76, 80, 2 N.E.2d 51, 53; see, also, Note, An Employer's Competitive Restraints on Former Employees, 17 Drake L.Rev. 69; Blake, Employee Agreements Not to Compete, 73 Harv.L. Rev. 625; Wetzel Employment Contracts and Noncompetition Agreements, 1969 U.Ill.L.F. 61.)   Such covenants by physicians are, if reasonable in scope, generally given effect.   (See Millet v. Slocum, 5 N. Y.2d 734, 177 N.Y.S.2d 716, 152 N.E.2d 672, affg. 4 A.D.2d 528, 167 N.Y.S.2d 136, supra; Foster v. White, 273 N.Y. 596, 7 N.E.2d 710, affg. 248 App.Div. 451, 290 N.Y.S. 394; see, also, Ann., Restriction on Practice of Physician, 58 A.L.R. 156; 6A Corbin, Contracts [1962], § 1393.)   "It is a firmly established doctrine", it has been noted, "that a member of one of the learned professions, upon becoming assistant to another member thereof, may, upon a sufficient consideration, bind himself not to engage in the practice of his profession upon the termination of his contract of employment, within a reasonable territorial extent, as such an agreement is not in restraint of trade or against public policy" (Ann., Restriction on Practice of Physician, 58 A.L.R. 156, 162).

Each case must, of course, depend, to a great extent, upon its own facts.   It may well be that, in some instances, a restriction not to conduct a profession or a business in two counties or even in one, may exceed permissible limits.   But, in the case before us, having in mind the character and size of the counties involved, the area restriction imposed is manifestly reasonable.   The five small rural counties which it encompasses comprise the very area from which the plaintiff obtained his patients and in which the defendant would be in direct competition with him.   Thus, the covenant's coverage coincides precisely with "the territory over which the practice extends", and this is proper and permissible.   (6A Corbin, Contracts [1962], § 1393, p. 87; see Interstate Tea Co. v. Alt, 271 N.Y. 76, 80, 2 N.E.2d 51, 53, supra; see, also, Ann., Employees—Restrictive Covenant—Area, 43 A.L.R.2d 94, 162.)   In brief, the plaintiff made no attempt to extend his influence beyond the area from which he drew his patients, the defendant being perfectly free to practice as he chooses outside the five specified counties.

Nor may the covenant be declared invalid because it is unlimited as to time, forever restricting the defendant from competing with the plaintiff.   It is settled that such a covenant will not be stricken merely because it "contains no time limit or is expressly made unlimited as to time". (37 N.Y.Jur., Master and Servant, § 179, p. 60; see Diamond Match Co. v. Roeber, 106 N.Y. 473, 484, 13 N.E. 419, 422; Goos v. Pennisi, 10 A.D.2d 643, 644, 197 N.Y.S.2d 253, 254; Foster v. White, 248 App.Div. 451, 456, 290 N.Y.S. 394, 399, affd. 273 N.Y. 596, 7 N.E.2d 710, supra; see, also, Ann.—Employee—Restrictive Covenant—Time, 41 A.L.R.2d 15, 35.) "According to the weight of authority as applied to contracts by physicians, surgeons and others of kindred profession," the court wrote in *Foster* (248 App.Div., at p. 456, 290 N.Y.S. at p. 399), "relief for violation of these contracts will not be denied merely because the agreement is unlimited as to time, where as to area the restraint is limited and reasonable." In the present case, the defendant opened an office in Ithaca, in competition with the plaintiff, just one week after his employment had come to an end. Under the circumstances presented, we thoroughly agree with the trial judge that it is clear that nearly all of the defendant's practice was, and would be, directly attributable to his association with his former employer.

This brings us to the most troublesome part of the restriction imposed upon the defendant. By the terms of the contract, he agreed not to practice "dentistry and/or Oral Surgery" in competition with the plaintiff. Since the plaintiff practices only "oral surgery," and it was for the practice of that limited type of "dentistry" that he had employed the defendant, the Appellate Division concluded that the plaintiff went beyond permissible limits when he obtained from the defendant the covenant that he would not engage in any "dentistry" whatsoever.[3] The restriction, *as formulated*, is, as the Appellate Division concluded, too broad; it is not reasonable for a man to be excluded from a profession for which he has been trained when he does not compete with his former employer by practicing it.

The plaintiff seeks to justify the breadth of the covenant by urging that, if it had restricted only the defendant's practice of oral surgery and permitted him to practice "dentistry"—that is, to hold himself out as a dentist generally—the defendant would have been permitted, under the Education Law (§ 6601, subd. 3), to do all the work which an oral surgeon could. We have no sympathy with this argument; the plaintiff was not privileged to prevent the defendant from working in an area of dentistry in which he would not be in competition with him. The plaintiff would have all the protection he needs if the restriction were to be limited to the practice of oral surgery, and this poses the question as to the court's power to "sever" the impermissible from the valid and uphold the covenant to the extent that it is reasonable.

---

3. Some of the things a dentist may do, which a practitioner who limits himself to oral surgery is ethically prevented from doing include the filling of teeth, placing crowns on teeth, doing reconstruction work of the mouth, dentures, prophylaxis or straightening of the teeth.

Although we have found no decision in New York directly in point, cases in this court support the existence of such a power. (See, e. g., Purchasing Assoc. v. Weitz, 13 N.Y.2d 267, 272, 246 N.Y.S.2d 600, 603, supra; Carpenter & Hughes v. De Joseph, 10 N.Y.2d 925, 224 N.Y.S.2d 9, 179 N.E.2d 854, affg. 13 A.D.2d 611, 213 N.Y.S.2d 860; Interstate Tea Co. v. Alt, 271 N.Y. 76, 80, 2 N.E.2d 51, 53, supra.) Moreover, a number of out-of-state decisions, and they are supported by authoritative texts and commentators, explicitly recognize the court's power of severance and divisibility in order to sustain the covenant insofar as it is reasonable.[4] As Professor Blake put it (73 Harv.L.Rev., at pp. 674–675), "If in balancing the equities the court decides that his [the employee's] activity would fit within the scope of a reasonable prohibition, it is apt to make use of the tool of severance, paring an unreasonable restraint down to appropriate size and enforcing it." In short, to cull from the Washington Supreme Court's opinion in Wood v. May, 73 Wash.2d 307, 314, 438 P.2d 587, 591, "we find it just and equitable to protect appellant [employer] by injunction to the extent necessary to accomplish the basic purpose of the contract insofar as such contract is reasonable." Accordingly, since his practice is solely as an oral surgeon, the plaintiff gains all the injunctive protection to which he is entitled if effect be given only to that part of the covenant which prohibits the defendant from practicing oral surgery.

The question arises, however, whether injunctive relief is precluded by the fact that the defendant's promissory note for $40,000 was to become payable if he breached the agreement not to compete. We believe not. The mere inclusion in a covenant of a liquidated damages provision does not automatically bar the grant of an injunction. (See Rubinstein v. Rubinstein, 23 N.Y.2d 293, 298, 296 N.Y.S.2d 354, 358, 244 N.E.2d 49, 51; Wirth & Hamid Fair Booking v. Wirth, 265 N.Y. 214, 224, 192 N.E. 297, 301; Diamond Match Co. v. Roeber, 106 N.Y. 473, 486, 13 N.E. 419, 423, supra; Foster v. White, 248 App.Div. 451, 457, 290 N.Y.S. 394, 400, affd. 273 N.Y. 596, 7 N.E.2d 710, supra; see, also, 5 Corbin, Contracts [1964], § 1071; Ann.—Restriction on Practice of Physician, 58 A.L.R. 156, 172–174.) As this court wrote in the *Diamond Match Co.* case (106 N.Y. at p. 486, 13 N.E., at p. 424.), "It is a question of intention, to be deduced from the whole instrument and the circumstances; and if it appear that the performance of the covenant was intended, and not merely the payment of damages in case of a breach, the covenant will be enforced." The covenant under consideration in this case may not reasonably be read to render "the liquidated damages provision . . . the sole remedy." (Rubinstein v. Rubinstein, 23 N.Y.2d 293, 298, 296 N.Y.S.2d 354,

---

4. [Citations omitted.] Some of these authorities would only sever by applying the so-called "blue pencil" rule —that is, dividing the contract only when it is grammatically severable. Even this limited approach, however, would be sufficient in the case before us.

358, 244 N.E.2d 49, 51, supra.)   On the other hand, it would be grossly unfair to grant the plaintiff, in addition to an injunction, the full amount of damages ($40,000) which the parties apparently contemplated for a total breach of the covenant, since the injunction will halt any further violation.   The proper approach is that taken in *Wirth* (265 N.Y. 214, 192 N.E. 297, supra).   The court, there faced with a similar situation, granted the injunction sought and, instead of awarding the amount of liquidated damages specified, remitted the matter for determination of the *actual* damages suffered during the period of the breach.

The hardship necessarily imposed on the defendant must be borne by him in view of the plaintiff's rightful interest in protecting the valuable practice of oral surgery which he built up over the course of many years.   The defendant is, of course, privileged to practice "dentistry" generally in Ithaca or continue to practice "oral surgery" anywhere in the United States outside of the five small rural counties enumerated.   The covenant, part of a contract carefully negotiated with no indication of fraud or overbearing on either side, must be enforced, insofar as it reasonably and validly may, according to its terms.   In sum, then, the plaintiff is entitled to an injunction barring the defendant from practicing oral surgery in the five specified counties and to damages actually suffered by him in the period during which the defendant conducted such a practice in Ithaca after leaving the plaintiff's employ.

The order appealed from should be reversed, with costs, and the case remitted to Supreme Court, Cayuga County, for further proceedings in accordance with this opinion.

NOTES

(1) *Agreements Not to Compete.*   How does the court's concern in this case differ from that in the cases in the preceding section?   From what source did the court derive the "powerful considerations of public policy which militate against sanctioning the loss of a man's livelihood"?   Does it cite statutory authority on this point?   On the general subject, see Blake, Employee Agreements Not to Compete, 73 Harv.L.Rev. 625 (1960).   Contracts in restraint of trade are dealt with in more detail in courses on trade regulation and antitrust law.

(2) *Severability.*   The concept of severability is an important one in illegality cases.   (On clauses providing for penalties, see Chapter 5, Section 4, infra.)   What result would the court have reached if Dr. Ingrasci had promised not to practice anywhere in the state of New York instead of the five counties listed?   See Restatement, § 518, to the effect that a promise involving an unreasonable restraint, and not "in terms" divisible, is "not enforceable even for so much of the performance as would be a reasonable restraint."   But see Ceresia v. Mitchell, 242 S.W.2d 359 (Ky. 1951).

(3) *Inducing Official Action.*   Influence peddling is a common subject of judicial denunciation, but lawyers above all should be aware that services

in procuring favorable official action are worthy of a price.[a]   Contracts to pay lobbyists are by no means condemned as such.   The proper line has been stated as follows: "The authorities very generally hold that a contract to pay for services to be performed in the endeavor to obtain or defeat legislation by other means than the use of argument addressed to the reason of the legislators, such as, for example, for the exertion of personal or political influence apart from the appeal to reason as applied to the consideration of the merits or demerits of the legislation in question, is an illegal contract."   Campbell County v. Howard & Lee, 133 Va. 19, 112 S.E. 876 (1922).   The consequence of stepping over the line is illustrated in Ewing v. National Airport Corporation, 115 F.2d 859 (4th Cir. 1940), cert. denied, 312 U.S. 705 (1941).

In the latter case the court said: "Contingent fees for services in securing the passage of legislation are especially regarded with disfavor by the courts."   Why should this be?   Tort litigation in this country is customarily conducted by lawyers for claimants under contracts for contingent fees.   It has been said that in such cases, "Because of the very fact that [the contingent fee] does insure the most humble citizen equal justice under law, while at the same time preserving the lawyer's independence of judgment and action, it serves the highest public interest."   Cohen, Book Review, 24 Vand.L.Rev. 433, 441 (1971).   Is it significant that in some courts there are disclosure requirements and regulations designed to control immoderate contingent fees for lawyers, and there are schedules and ceilings for the compensation of lawyers pressing certain types of claims? In addition, bar associations issue "recommended fee schedules."

(4) *Problem for Review.*   The Atomic Energy Commission (AEC) invited several general contractors, including Miller-Davis, to bid on a Meson Building Addition at the Argonne National Laboratories.   Bids were to be divided into a base bid plus five alternates, among which the AEC might choose in order to stay within its budget.   Bids were to be opened at 2:00 p. m. on March 3.   At 12:30 on March 3, Stanley Wielgos, the manager of Premier Electrical Construction Company, called Miller-Davis' chief estimator, Paul Hunsberger, and gave Hunsberger a base bid of $247,000 and the following alternatives: Alt. 1 $1,500; Alt. 2 $4,500; Alt. 3 $14,000; Alt. 4 $21,000; Alt. 5 $90,000.   Hunsberger said that the bid was the lowest so far and "very interesting."   Wielgos asked, "Do we have a job if you have one?"   Hunsberger said he would like some "sizeable protection."   (This was understood by both men to mean that Premier would submit higher bids to Miller-Davis' competitors so that Miller-Davis would have the lowest electrical costs.)   Wielgos said he would give Hunsberger "what he asked" and added "we are banking on you getting the job and we are willing to gamble on you and you only."   Hunsberger said that in that case Premier would have the contract if its figures remained the lowest and if Miller-Davis used them and got the bid.   Huns-

a. Agreements that have been questioned range from an agreement supposedly made by a justice of the peace to collect a doctor's bills "under color of his office" (In re Robertson, 7 N.C. App. 186, 171 S.E.2d 801 (1970)) to an agreement made by a lawyer with good political connections to present to President Kennedy, on behalf of a railroad, the case for the intervention of the Department of Justice in a proceeding involving the I.C.C. (Troutman v. Southern Railway Co., 441 F.2d 586 (5th Cir. 1971) (the presentation was successful)).

berger told Wielgos, "I am not going to tell anybody else what your number [bid] is." An hour later he reassured Wielgos that his bid was still the lowest, when the latter called to ask about the situation because, if their bid was not the lowest, they wanted to publish their price to the other contractors bidding on the job.

In spite of these assurances, however, Hunsberger telephoned St. Arnaud, a competitor of Premier with whom Miller-Davis had dealt many times, and asked if they could beat Premier's bid. In the meantime, Miller-Davis had sent Richard Larsen to Argonne Laboratories with the official bid form so that he could insert the figures at the last moment. (Miller-Davis was not required to, and did not, list its subcontractors on the bid form.) At 1:30 Larsen called the office and Hunsberger gave him Miller-Davis' figures for the five alternates, each based on Premier's figures, to be entered by Larsen on the bid form, leaving the base bid blank. At 1:40 Hunsberger received a $255,000 base bid figure from St. Arnaud. At 1:50 Larsen called the Miller-Davis office again and was given a base bid figure of $1,019,000, based on St. Arnaud's figure. He entered it on the form which he submitted to the AEC a few minutes later. The AEC awarded the contract to Miller-Davis and chose Alternative 3. Miller-Davis then made a contract with St. Arnaud for the electrical work. Does Premier have a claim against Miller-Davis? See Premier Electrical Construction Co. v. Miller-Davis Co., 291 F.Supp. 295 (N.D.Ill.1968), aff'd, 422 F.2d 1132 (7th Cir. 1970), cert. denied, 400 U.S. 828 (1970).

SIRKIN v. FOURTEENTH ST. STORE, 124 App.Div. 384, 108 N.Y.S. 830 (1908). [Sirkin sued the Fourteenth Street Store for $1,555, the purchase price of hosiery and wrappers that he had sold and delivered to the store. The store alleged as a defense that Sirkin had bribed McGuiness, its purchasing agent, by promising him 5% on all orders he placed with it, and that he had paid the purchasing agent $75 for the transaction sued on. The New York Penal Code made it a misdemeanor, punishable by a fine of up to $500 and imprisonment of up to one year, for a seller to offer an agent "authorized to procure materials, supplies or other articles either by purchase or contract for his principal . . . a commission, discount or bonus," or for an agent to receive it. The trial court directed a verdict for the plaintiff, without allowing the defendant to prove the defense alleged, reasoning that since the goods had been delivered, the defendant could not retain them and decline to pay. The defendant appealed.]

LAUGHLIN, J. . . . There can be no doubt that the act of the plaintiff in bribing the purchasing agent of the defendant was a violation of . . . the Penal Code. . . . The Legislature has not expressly declared either that the contract to pay the bribe or the contract induced by the bribe is void or unenforceable. A contract, however, made in violation of a penal statute, although not expressly prohibited or declared to be void, is prohibited, void, and unenforceable, whether executory or executed . . .. A contract to do an illegal act or to aid another in violating the law is likewise void and unenforceable, whether executory or executed. . . . Upon the same principle one who is required by law to procure a license to conduct any trade, calling, or profession may not recover for services rendered or property sold, without first obtaining such license, regardless of whether or not it was known by the person for whom the services were rendered or to whom the property was sold that the license had not been obtained. . . . It is therefore quite clear that the purchasing agent could not enforce the contract to recover the consideration agreed to be paid to him; and it may be here observed that this would have been so under the common law, if the statute had not been enacted, for the contract contravened public policy. The question appears to be presented now for the first time as to whether this is the limitation of the disability for violating the penal statute, or whether the court may refuse its aid to the party obtaining the contract for the purchase or sale of property, or for work, in violation of the statute, upon the same ground that it leaves a party to a contract which is void as against public policy, or offends against good morals, where it finds him. It is manifest that the Legislature in enacting this penal statute intended to emphasize and extend the public policy of the common law, which rendered such contracts by agents for their own benefit void. It being the province of the Legislature to declare the public policy of the state, it is the duty of the court to be guided thereby in administering the law. The acts of the plaintiff not only offended against good morals and public policy at common law, but constituted a crime under the statutory law of this state; and he is here seeking the aid of the court to enforce a contract which he procured by violating our penal statute. Nothing could be more corrupting, nor have a greater tendency to lead to disloyalty and dishonesty on the part of servants, agents, and employés, and to a betrayal of the confidence and trust reposed in them, than these practices which the Legislature has endeavored to stamp out; and I think nothing will be more effective in stopping the growth and spread of this corrupting and now criminal custom than a decision that the courts will refuse their aid to a guilty vendor or vendee, or to any one who has obtained a contract by secretly bribing the servant, agent, or employé of another to purchase or sell property, or to place the contract with him. . . .

The servant would be accountable to his master or employer for any moneys thus received, but that affords no adequate remedy, for the reason that such contracts are made secretly, and it would be difficult to discover or prove the facts. The vice lies in making the agreement without the knowledge of the master. Of course, it is perfectly competent for a master to employ a servant as a purchasing or selling agent, and to give him a commission upon the purchase price or allow a commission to be paid by the vendee upon the selling price, and it may well be, as was recently held in Ballin v. Fourteenth Street Store, 54 Misc. 359, 105 N.Y.S. 1028, affirmed (Sup.) 108 N.Y.S. 26, that, where the bribe is received with the knowledge of the master, the statute does not apply, and the contract of sale will be enforced. It is perfectly plain that, if the contract had not been performed by the plaintiff, the defendant, upon discovering the fact that its agent had been bribed to place the contract, would have had the right to rescind. . . . It is contended that its only remedies upon discovering the facts were to rescind the contract, or, if that were impracticable, to counterclaim for any damages it has sustained by reason of the plaintiff's fraud in inducing the contract, and that by a failure to rescind or thus counterclaim it is deemed to have ratified and affirmed the contract. I am of opinion that this is not a case in which the rule of ratification, applicable to ordinary contracts induced by fraud, should be applied. The public policy of our state forbids the ratification, as well as the making, of such a contract. Usually private contracts concern only the parties thereto, and it is optional with a person who has discovered that he has been defrauded whether to ratify the contract or to rescind it. There is ordinarily, at least, no general public policy involved in such cases. . . .

    [Reversed (3–2).]

    SCOTT, J. (dissenting) . . . Undoubtedly the secret agreement to pay a commission to plaintiff was a fraud on defendant, and rendered the contract voidable at its option. It might, if it had discovered the fraud in time, have refused to receive the goods, or, having received them, might have tendered them back, or might even now counterclaim for the damages it suffered from the fraud, if, in fact and law, it could show that it had suffered damage. The statute which has made that a crime, which heretofore was merely immoral, has affixed to that crime an appropriate penalty. It is no part of our duty to assume legislative power and prescribe an additional punishment, nor are we to assume, in the absence of allegations to that effect, that the defendant did, in fact, suffer damage as a result of plaintiff's unlawful agreement with McGuiness. . . .

NOTES

    (1) *Recovery of the Bribe.* Could the Fourteenth Street Store have kept the goods, refused to pay for them, and recovered the bribe from McGuiness? In Reading v. Attorney General, [1951] A.C. 507 (P.C.), a British Army sergeant, stationed in Cairo, gave color to an illicit traffic in liquor by riding the criminals' truck in uniform to avoid police inspection. The British government seized the money that he earned in this way and successfully resisted his claim to it. Consider also McDevitt v. Stokes, p. 277 supra, as to which the Restatement Second proposes as a solution that the jockey's driving in the race is consideration for the promise of a bonus, but the employer may be entitled to it. Restatement Second, § 76A, Illustration 12.

(2) *Unjust Enrichment.* Does not the decision in the Sirkin case result in the unjust enrichment of the Fourteenth Street Store? Recovery in restitution is not generally allowed a party for benefits conferred under a contract unenforceable because of illegality. (See p. 413 infra.) Is it possible to avoid such enrichment in some other way?

Rush v. Curtiss-Wright Export Corp., 175 Misc. 873, 25 N.Y.S.2d 597 (1941), suggests a possible approach. An ex-naval officer was employed by the Republic of Colombia as its full-time military aircraft procurement advisor for $21,000 a year. He took this job at the urging of Export Co., an aircraft manufacturer, which promised to supplement his Colombia salary by paying him commissions and bonuses on its sales of aircraft to Colombia. In an action by his assignee against Export Co. to recover $41,000 in commissions and bonuses, the trial court refused to dismiss the complaint and directed entry of judgment for the plaintiff "as trustee for the Republic of Colombia." On appeal, however, the judgment was reversed, the Appellate Division concluding that the agreement was "corrupt and illegal," but ordering that the complaint be dismissed for that reason. Rush v. Curtiss-Wright Export Co., 263 App.Div. 69, 31 N.Y.S.2d 550 (1942), aff'd, 289 N.Y. 562, 43 N.E.2d 712 (1943). Do you agree? In the case in the preceding note, would it have been better to have required the sergeant to account to the government of Egypt, whose laws he had flouted? See Seavey, Problems in Restitution, 7 Okla.L.Rev. 257, 259 (1954).

Under Soviet law, "in the event a contract is invalid [because of illegality], neither of the parties shall have the right to demand from the other the return of whatever has been performed under the contract; instead it may be treated as unjust enrichment to be forfeit to the state." Berman, Justice in the U.S.S.R. 141 (1963).

(3) *Two Views.* In 1692 Lord Holt expressed the following influential view: "Every contract made for or about any matter or thing which is prohibited and made unlawful by any statute is a void contract though the statute itself doth not mention that it shall be so, but only inflicts a penalty on the offender, because a penalty implies a prohibition, though there are no prohibitory words in the statute." Bartlett v. Vinor, Carth. 251, 252, 90 Eng.Rep. 750. In 1936 Professor Gellhorn wrote: "The judges are not bound to regard as void every contract which seems in some way to fall within the general aura of the criminal law, but only those whose enforcement, they are persuaded, after respectfully studying the 'public policy' involved, will disserve the general interest as it has been indicated by the legislature." Contracts and Public Policy, 35 Colum.L.Rev. 679, 686 (1936).

Consider in this connection Coules v. Pharris, 212 Wis. 558, 250 N.W. 404 (1933). Charles Coules was an alien who had entered and remained in the United States in violation of the Immigration Laws and who was employed by Alex Pharris to work in his Palace of Sweets. When Coules sued Pharris for unpaid wages, the Supreme Court of Wisconsin ordered the complaint dismissed. The statute "creates a public policy" to exclude persons such as Coules, resulting in "the deprivation of the right to sue for wages in the courts of the land he has secretly invaded against the express command of the government thereof. . . . Denied the means of collecting for his labor, he will not be likely to succeed in maintaining himself and accomplishing his cheat upon the government."

Which view does this case support? Which view do you favor?

LICENSING

The court in the Sirkin case goes too far when it says that "one who is required by law to procure a license to conduct any trade, calling, or profession may not recover for services rendered or property sold, without first obtaining such license." In Cope v. Rowlands, 2 M. & W. 149, 150 Eng.Rep. 707 (Exch.1836), a London stockbroker sued for a commission and was met by a plea that he was not licensed by the Mayor and Aldermen as required by statute. According to the court, the question is, "whether the enactment of the statute is meant merely to secure a revenue to the city . . . or whether one of its objects be the protection of the public, and the prevention of improper persons acting as brokers." The court concluded that since the statute provided for licensing of brokers "under such restrictions and limitations for their honest and good behavior as the [Mayor and Aldermen] should think fit and reasonable," it was of the latter sort and denied recovery. In Howard v. Lebby, 197 Ky. 324, 246 S.W. 828, 30 A.L.R. 830 (1923), the same analysis led to upholding a claim by a painter who had worked without a license required by city ordinance. The question, said the court, is "was the ordinance primarily designed as a revenue measure, or as a police regulation?" Finding that the licensing requirement was only an incident to an occupation tax, the court held that it did not afford a defense to the claim. "His occupation . . . is one that has been followed in all communities from time immemorial. From no rational point of view can it be regarded as deleterious to the health, morals or welfare of the public."

What is the justification for the distinction between "regulation" and "revenue" measures? How can they be distinguished?

NOTES

(1) *Brokerage.* Licenses are universally required of persons acting professionally as real estate brokers in this country. An unlicensed person so acting may not enforce a promise of payment for his services. Does the rule extend to a person who acts as broker in the sale of a *business*, if an interest in real property passes under the sale? The question has been answered variously by the courts. See Quick Shops of Mississippi v. Bruce, 232 So.2d 351 (Miss.1970). By one view, if the non-real-estate values are the dominant element in the sale, the broker may have his commission. By another, he may recover that part of the commission attributable to such values. On a third view, he is denied compensation altogether. Which is preferable?

(2) *Liquor Distinguished from Milk.* In John E. Rosasco Creameries, Inc. v. Cohen, 276 N.Y. 274, 11 N.E.2d 908, 118 A.L.R. 641 (1937), an

agreement for a dealer-to-dealer sale of milk was enforced although the seller who sued for the price of approximately $11,000 was unlicensed. The statutory provision read: "No milk dealer shall buy milk . . . or deal in . . . milk unless such dealer be duly licensed. . . . It shall be unlawful for a milk dealer to buy milk from . . . a milk dealer who is unlicensed, or in any way deal in or handle milk which he has reason to believe has previously been dealt in or handled in violation of the provisions of this chapter." Violations were made punishable, as misdemeanors, by fine of up to $200 and imprisonment for up to six months. The purpose of the statute was economic regulation, as shown by the fact that exemptions were authorized for dealers in a small way, and in small communities. The court said: "If the contract is declared unenforceable, the effect will be to punish the plaintiff to the extent of a loss of approximately $11,000 and permit the defendants to evade the payment of a legitimate debt." Was this decision consistent with the reasoning in the cases of the stockbroker and the painter?

Four years later, however, the same court refused to allow an unlicensed liquor dealer to recover $6,400, the price of liquor sold and delivered by him. The Alcoholic Beverage Control Law of New York makes it a criminal offense to sell liquor without a permit from the proper state authority but does not expressly provide that contracts made by unlicensed dealers are unenforceable. In Carmine v. Murphy, 261 App.Div. 17, 23 N.Y.S.2d 723 (1940), the court held that an unlicensed liquor dealer could recover: "The reasoning in that [Rosasco] case should apply with equal force to the controversy here under consideration." But the Court of Appeals reversed in a cryptic opinion which said merely: "The present case is not excepted from the general rule of law that no right of action can spring out of an illegal contract." 285 N.Y. 413, 35 N.E.2d 19 (1941).

Are the cases distinguishable?

McCONNELL v. COMMONWEALTH PICTURES CORPORATION

Court of Appeals of New York, 1960.
7 N.Y.2d 465, 166 N.E.2d 494.

DESMOND, CHIEF JUDGE. The appeal is by defendant from so much of an Appellate Division, First Department, order as affirmed that part of a Special Term order which struck out two defenses in the answer.

Plaintiff sues for an accounting. Defendant had agreed in writing that, if plaintiff should succeed in negotiating a contract with a motion-picture producer whereby defendant would get the distribution rights for certain motion pictures, defendant would pay plaintiff $10,000 on execution of the contract between defendant and the producer, and would thereafter pay plaintiff a stated percentage of defendant's gross receipts from distribution of the pictures. Plaintiff negotiated the distribution rights for defendant and defendant paid plaintiff the promised $10,000 but later refused to pay him the commissions or to give him an accounting of profits.

Defendant's answer contains, besides certain denials and counterclaims not now before us, two affirmative defenses the sufficiency of which we must decide. In these defenses it is asserted that plaintiff, without the knowledge of defendant or of the producer, procured the distribution rights by bribing a representative of the producer and that plaintiff agreed to pay and did pay to that representative as a bribe the $10,000 which defendant paid plaintiff. The courts below (despite a strong dissent in the Appellate Division) held that the defenses were insufficient to defeat plaintiff's suit. Special Term's opinion said that, since the agreement sued upon—between plaintiff and defendant—was not in itself illegal, plaintiff's right to be paid for performing it could not be defeated by a showing that he had misconducted himself in carrying it out. The court found a substantial difference between this and the performance of an illegal contract. We take a different view. Proper and consistent application of a prime and long-settled public policy closes the doors of our courts to those who sue to collect the rewards of corruption.

New York's policy has been frequently and emphatically announced in the decisions. " 'It is the settled law of this State (and probably of every other State) that a party to an illegal contract cannot ask a court of law to help him carry out his illegal object, nor can such a person plead or prove in any court a case in which he, as a basis for his claim, must show forth his illegal purpose', Stone v. Freeman, 298 N.Y. 268, 271, 82 N.E.2d 571, 572, 8 A.L.R.2d 304, citing the leading cases. The money plaintiff sues for was the fruit of an admitted crime and 'no court should be required to serve as paymaster of the wages of crime'. Stone v. Freeman, supra, 298 N.Y. at page 271, 82 N.E.2d at page 572. And it makes no difference that defendant has no title to the money since the court's concern 'is not with the position of the defendant' but with the question of whether 'a recovery by the plaintiff should be denied for the sake of public interests', a question which is one 'of public policy in the administration of the law'. Flegenheimer v. Brogan, 284 N.Y. 268, 272, 30 N.E.2d 591, 592, 132 A.L.R. 613. That public policy is the one described in Riggs v. Palmer, 115 N.Y. 506, 511–512, 22 N.E. 188, 190, 5 L.R.A. 340: 'No one shall be permitted to profit by his own fraud, or to take advantage of his own wrong, or to found any claim upon his own iniquity, or to acquire property by his own crime. These maxims are dictated by public policy, have their foundation in universal law administered in all civilized countries, and have nowhere been superseded by statutes' " (Carr v. Hoy, 2 N.Y.2d 185, 187, 158 N.Y.S.2d 572, 574–575, 139 N.E.2d 531, 533).

We must either repudiate those statements of public policy or uphold these challenged defenses. It is true that some of the leading decisions (Oscanyan v. Arms Co., 103 U.S. 261, 26 L.Ed. 539; Stone v. Freeman, 298 N.Y. 268, 82 N.E.2d 571, 8 A.L.R.2d 304) were in suits on intrinsically illegal contracts but the rule fails of its purpose unless it covers a case like the one at bar. Here, as in Stone v. Freeman and Carr v. Hoy (supra), the money sued for was (assuming the truth of the defenses) "the fruit of an admitted crime." To allow this plaintiff to collect his commissions would be to let him "profit by his own fraud, or to take advantage of his own wrong, or to found [a] claim upon his own iniquity, or to acquire property by his own crime" (Riggs v. Palmer, 115 N.Y. 506, 511, 22 N.E. 188, 190, 5 L.R.A. 340). The issue is not whether the acts alleged in the defenses would constitute the crime of commercial bribery under section 439 of the Penal Law, Consol.Laws, c. 40, although it appears that they would. "A seller cannot recover the price of goods sold where he has paid a commission to an agent of the purchaser (Sirkin v. Fourteenth Street Store, 124 App.Div. 384, 108 N.Y.S. 830); neither could the agent recover the commission, even at common law and before the enactment of section 384–r of the Penal Law (now section 439)" (Judge Crane in Reiner v. North American Newspaper Alliance, 259 N.Y. 250, 261, 181 N.E. 561, 565, 83 A.L.R. 23). The Sirkin opinion (124 App.Div. 384, 108 N.Y.S. 830) has been cited with approval by this court in Merchants' Line v. Baltimore & Ohio R. Co.; 222 N.Y. 344, 347, 118 N.E. 788, and Morgan Munitions Supply Co. v. Studebaker Corp., 226 N.Y. 94, 99, 123 N.E. 146. In unmistakable terms it forbids the courts to honor claims founded on commercial bribery.

We are not working here with narrow questions of technical law. We are applying fundamental concepts of morality and fair dealing not to be weakened by exceptions. So far as precedent is necessary, we can rely on Sirkin v. Fourteenth Street Store, 124 App.Div. 384, 108 N.Y.S. 830, supra, and Reiner v. North American Newspaper Alliance, 259 N.Y. 250, 181 N.E. 564, 83 A.L.R. 23, supra. Sirkin is the case closest to ours and shows that, whatever be the law in other jurisdictions, we in New York deny awards for the corrupt performance of contracts even though in essence the contracts are not illegal. Sirkin had sued for the price of goods sold and delivered to defendant. Held to be good was a defense which charged that plaintiff seller had paid a secret commission to an agent of defendant purchaser. There cannot be any difference in principle between that situation and the present one where plaintiff (it is alleged) contracted to buy motion-picture rights for defendant but performed his covenant only by bribing the seller's agent. In the Reiner case (supra), likewise, the plaintiff had fully performed the services required by his agreement with the defendant but was denied a recovery because his performance had involved and included "fraud and deception" practiced not on defendant but on a third party. It is beside the point that the present plaintiff on the trial might be able to prove a prima facie case without the bribery being exposed. On the whole case (again assuming that the defenses speak the truth) the disclosed situation would be within the rule of our precedents forbidding court assistance to bribers.

It is argued that a reversal here means that the doing of any small illegality in the performance of an otherwise lawful contract will deprive the doer of all rights, with the result that the other party will get a windfall and there will be great injustice. Our ruling does not go as far as that. It is not every minor wrongdoing in the course of contract performance that will insulate the other party from liability for work done or goods furnished. There must at least be a direct connection between the illegal transaction and the obligation sued upon. Connection is a matter of degree. Some illegalities are merely incidental to the contract sued on (see Messersmith v. American Fidelity Co., 187 App.Div. 35, 175 N.Y.S. 169, affirmed 232 N.Y. 161, 133 N.E. 432, 19 A.L.R. 876; De Persia v. Merchants Mut. Cas. Co., 268 App.Div. 176, 49 N.Y.S.2d 324, affirmed 294 N.Y. 708, 61 N.E.2d 449; Ferkin v. Board of Education, 278 N.Y. 263, 268, 15 N.E.2d 799, 800). We cannot now, any more than in our past decisions, announce what will be the results of all the kinds of corruption, minor and major, essential and peripheral. All we are doing here is labeling the conduct described in these defenses as gross corruption depriving plaintiff of all right of access to the courts of New York State. Consistent with public morality and settled public policy, we hold that a party will be denied recovery even on a contract valid on its face, if it appears that he has resorted to gravely immoral and illegal conduct in accomplishing its performance.

Perhaps this application of the principle represents a distinct step beyond Sirkin and Reiner (supra) in the sense that we are here barring recovery under a contract which in itself is entirely legal. But if this be an extension, public policy supports it. We point out that our holding is limited to cases in which the illegal performance of a contract originally valid takes the form of commercial bribery or similar conduct and in which the illegality is central to or a dominant part of the plaintiff's whole course of conduct in performance of the contract.

There is no pertinence here of the rule which makes such defenses unavailable to one who is a mere depository or escrowee—that is, one who is holding money or goods for one of the parties without himself being a party to the transaction sued upon (see Southwestern Shipping Corp. v. National City Bank of New York, 6 N.Y.2d 454, 190 N. Y.S.2d 352, 160 N.E.2d 836) [p. 417 infra]. That exception is used when, in execution or satisfaction of an illegal transaction, one of the parties thereto turns over money or property to a third person (not a party to the illegal deal) for the use of one who is a party. In our case there were two parties only—plaintiff and defendant. There is no third person holding money or property.

The sufficiency of defendant's counterclaim (for the return of its $10,000) was litigated below but it is not before us on this appeal.

The order appealed from should be reversed, with costs, the certified question answered in the negative, and plaintiff's motion, insofar as it attacks the sufficiency of the two separate defenses, should be denied.

FROESSEL, JUDGE (dissenting). . . .

This is not a case where the contract *sued upon* is intrinsically illegal (cf. Stone v. Freeman, 298 N.Y. 268, 82 N.E.2d 571, 8 A.L.R.2d 304; Reiner v. North American Newspaper Alliance, 259 N.Y. 250, 181 N.E. 561, 83 A.L.R. 23); or was *procured* by the commission of a crime (Sirkin v. Fourteenth Street Store, 124 App.Div. 384, 108 N. Y.S. 830); or where a beneficiary under a will murdered his ancestor in order to obtain the speedy enjoyment of his property (Riggs v. Palmer, 115 N.Y. 506, 22 N.E. 188, 5 L.R.A. 340). In the Sirkin case, so heavily relied upon by the majority, the plaintiff obtained the very contract he was seeking to enforce by paying secret commissions to defendant's own purchasing agent. In Merchants' Line v. Baltimore & Ohio R. Co., 222 N.Y. 344, 347, 118 N.E. 788, we pointed out that in Sirkin "the plaintiff reached and bribed the man who made *the contract under which he was seeking to recover*" (emphasis supplied). In Morgan Munitions Supply Co. v. Studebaker Corp., 226 N.Y. 94, 99, 123 N.E. 146, 147, we likewise cited the Sirkin case for the proposition that "a contract *procured by* the commission of a crime is unenforceable even if executed" (emphasis supplied).

In the instant case, the contract which plaintiff is seeking to enforce is perfectly valid, and it was not intended or even contemplated that plaintiff would perform the contract by illegal or corrupt means. Having received and retained the full benefits of plaintiff's performance, defendant now seeks to "inject into" its contract with plaintiff, "which was fair and legal in itself, the illegal feature of the other independent transaction" Messersmith v. American Fidelity Co., 187 App.Div. 35, 37, 175 N.Y.S. 169, 170, affirmed 232 N.Y. 161, 133 N. E. 432, 19 A.L.R. 876. This court is now adopting a rule that a party may retain the benefits of, but escape his obligations under, a wholly lawful contract if the other party commits some illegal act not contemplated nor necessary under the contract. By way of a single illustration an owner may thus avoid paying his contractor for the cost of erecting a building because the contractor gave an inspector a sum of money to expedite an inspection.

The majority opinion seeks to distinguish between "major" and "minor" illegality and "direct" and "peripheral" corruption. It decides this case on the ground that the manner in which plaintiff performed his admittedly valid contract with defendant was "gravely immoral and illegal". Such distinctions are neither workable nor sanctioned by authority. If a contract was lawfully made, and did not contemplate wrongdoing, it is enforcible; if, on the other hand, it was *procured* by the commission of a crime, or was in fact for the performance of illegal services, it is not enforcible. These are the criteria distinguishing enforcible from unenforcible contracts—not "nice" distinctions between degrees of illegality and immorality in the performance of lawful contracts, or whether the illegal act of performance was "directly" or "peripherally" related to the main contract.

Moreover, a reversal here would be contrary to the spirit, if not the letter, of our holding in Southwestern Shipping Corp. v. National City Bank, 6 N.Y.2d 454, 190 N.Y.S.2d 352, 160 N.E.2d 836. The broad proposition for which that case stands is that a party unconnected with an illegal agreement should not be permitted to reap a windfall by pleading the illegality of that agreement, to which he was a stranger. There, the contract between the plaintiff and the bank was entirely lawful, and the bank attempted to avoid the consequences of its breach of contract and negligence by asserting the illegality of a different contract between plaintiff and a third party. Here, the contract between plaintiff and defendant was perfectly legal, and defendant is seeking to avoid its obligations under the contract—of which it has reaped the benefits for some 12 years—by asserting the illegality of a *different* and subsequent agreement between plaintiff and a third party. This it should not be permitted to do.

The order appealed from should be affirmed, with costs, and the question certified answered in the affirmative.

Van Voorhis, Judge (dissenting). Public morals and fair dealing are likely to be advanced by limiting rather than by enlarging the rule that is being extended to the facts of this case. This rule is grounded on considerations of public policy. Courts will not intervene between thieves to compel them to divide the spoils. But in a situation like the present, it seems to me that the effect of this decision will not be to restrain the corrupt influencing of agents, employees or servants but to encourage misappropriation of funds and breaches of faith between persons who do not stand in corrupt relationships with one another. The public interest is not served best by decisions which put a premium on taking unconscionable advantage of such situations, or which drive the enforcement of obligations of this kind underground. I concur in the dissenting opinion by Judge Froessel.

Dye, Fuld, Burke and Foster, JJ., concur with Desmond, C. J. Froessel, J., dissents in an opinion in which Van Voorhis, J., concurs in a separate memorandum.

Order reversed, with costs in all courts, and matter remitted to the Appellate Division for further proceedings in accordance with the opinion herein. Question certified answered in the negative.

NOTE

Question. The dissent gives the illustration of "an owner [who] may thus avoid paying his contractor for the cost of erecting a building because the contractor gave an inspector a sum of money to expedite an inspection." How would the majority have decided that case? See Tocci v.

Lembo, 325 Mass. 707, 92 N.E.2d 254 (1950), in which the contractor used materials then, in 1946, in short supply and under federal priorities control, without securing or applying for the required authorization from the Civilian Production Administration.

DEGREE OF INVOLVEMENT

The court in the McConnell case says, "There must at least be a direct connection between the illegal transaction and the obligation sued upon." For a contrasting conclusion as to "connection," consider Graves v. Johnson, 179 Mass. 58, 60 N.E. 383 (1901). A buyer defaulted on an agreement to buy liquor in Massachusetts, where such a sale was lawful. When sued by the seller for the price, his defense was that he had intended to resell the liquor in Maine, in violation of a statute of that state, and that the seller was aware of his purpose. Rejecting the defense, Holmes wrote: "All that is necessary for us to say now is that in our opinion a sale otherwise lawful is not connected with subsequent unlawful conduct by the mere fact that the seller correctly divines the buyer's unlawful intent, closely enough to make the sale unlawful. It will be observed that the finding puts the plaintiffs' knowledge of the defendant's intent no higher than an uncommunicated inference as to what the defendant was likely to do. Of course the defendant was free to change his mind, and there was no communicated desire of the plaintiffs to co-operate with the defendant's present intent . . . but on the contrary an understood indifference to everything beyond an ordinary sale in Massachusetts. It may be that, as in the case of attempts, . . . the line of proximity will vary somewhat according to the gravity of the evil apprehended, . . . and in different courts with regard to the same or similar matters. . . . But the decisions tend more and more to agree that the connection with the unlawful act in cases like the present is too remote."

Hull v. Ruggles, 56 N.Y. 424 (1874), shows that the seller may not fare as well if he exhibits more than an "understood indifference" to the buyer's unlawful purpose. The goods sold were 300 packages of candy and 60 pieces of silverware. Packed inside 60 of the candy boxes were tickets, each identifying a piece of silverware. The buyer intended to induce his customers to buy the candy at an inflated price in the hope of getting a piece of silverware "free," in violation of the statute against lotteries. In denying the seller recovery of the price, the court relied on "the not unfamiliar English cases, in which it is held, that if goods be bought with the purpose of smuggling them into England, though the vendor have knowledge of the purpose, he may recover the price of the goods, if he do nothing to aid in carrying out the design . . . ; but if he has so packed the goods as to facilitate the smuggling, he is regarded as particeps criminis and cannot recover."

Do you agree with the distinction drawn in these cases?

NOTES

(1) *A Prize-Fight Case.* Florida imposes heavy criminal penalties on persons who engage in "any pugilistic exhibition" for which admission is charged. However an exception permits prize fighting "under the auspices of" various groups, including the Y.M.C.A., the Junior Chamber of Commerce, and the Veterans of Foreign Wars. In 1964, Cassius Clay, as he then was, became world heavyweight champion by knocking out Charles "Sonny" Liston. An agent for the fighters, which had procured their services, sued the promoter who had made all the local arrangements, for $400,-000, alleging an agreement to pay that amount. A witness for the defendant testified that the promoter had "used the name" of the VFW (Miami Post 3559) "and paid them a contribution for that." A VFW member testified that $500 was "given to our organization for attending the fight." The chairman of its boxing committee was told "Be here with the men," and about twenty were in attendance. An officer of the Miami Beach Boxing Commission testified that their presence was necessary to make it a legal venture. The tickets indicated VFW sponsorship. A public relations man for the plaintiff testified: "I think there was some kind of a handout that these guys had been having for years in this town." From judgment for the plaintiff, the defendant appealed. *Held:* Reversed. "The conclusion is inescapable that the Liston-Clay fight was not held under the auspices of the VFW. The use of the organization's name was a mere fiction. . . ." Inter-Continental Promotions v. Miami Beach First Nat. Bank, 441 F.2d 1356 (5th Cir. 1971), cert. denied, 404 U.S. 850 (1971).

What reasoning might have been used to sustain the opposite result?

(2) *Problem.* Fineman sold an Edison phonograph to Mamie Faulkner, on credit, for use in her home. Fineman "knew by general reputation that she was a prostitute carrying on her trade at her home." Can Fineman recover the price of the phonograph? See Fineman v. Faulkner, 174 N.C. 13, 93 S.E. 384, L.R.A.1918A, 337 (1917). Compare Pearce v. Brooks, L.R. 1 Exch. 213 (1866).

RESTITUTION

Courts, in cases of illegal bargains, are fond of citing the maxim: *In pari delicto potior est conditio defendentis* (In a case of equal fault, the condition of the party defending is the stronger). It is applied not only to deny enforcement of the bargain, but to bar restitution as well. There are, however, two mitigating doctrines that may be invoked to allow restitution.

First, the party seeking restitution may not be considered to be *in pari delicto* with the other. He may be allowed restitution if, for example, he has been the victim of fraud or duress, or of overreaching based on a superior bargaining position. (It has, however, been urged that the doctrine not be extended to cases in which the only fraud consists of representations as to the profitability, as opposed to the legality, of the transaction. Williston, § 1791.) Second, even though the party seeking restitution is *in pari delicto* with the other, he may have decided to withdraw from the bargain before the attainment of the illegal purpose. He is ordinarily given a *locus poenitentiae* and allowed restitution if his withdrawal comes in time to prevent its attainment. On the limits of the theory of restitution in actions to recover for benefits conferred on another pursuant to an illegal bargain, see Wade, Benefits Obtained Under Illegal Transactions, 25 Texas L.Rev. 31 (1946); and Wade, Restitution of Benefits Acquired Through Illegal Transactions, 95 U.Pa.L.Rev. 261 (1947).

Much of the discussion of these two mitigating doctrines has come in the context of gambling agreements. Although the decisions of courts in contract cases are unlikely to have substantial impact on the incidence of this sort of activity,[a] a few of them are discussed in the notes that follow as illustrations of the two doctrines.

NOTES

(1) *The Case of the Penitent Pledgor.* Gehres lost $225 to Ater in a social crap game, giving rise to an unenforceable gambling debt. Lacking the cash to pay, Gehres pledged a municipal bond to Ater as security for the claim. Some months later Gehres tendered $225 to Ater and asked for his bond back. Ater could not comply because he had sold it. Gehres sued for $540, the market value of the bond. From judgment for the defendant on his demurrer to the plaintiff's petition, the plaintiff appealed. *Held:* Reversed. The court saw two competing principles. One is the broad principle that courts will leave parties who are in pari delicto where they find them. The other is that repentance should be encouraged. "At common law one who makes a wager with another may always withdraw from the wager and retain or recover his property or money before it goes into the hands of the winner, even after the result of the wager is known. So long as the title to the property or money has not passed to the winner, the loser may repudiate the wager and retain his money or property or recover it in a common-law action. . . . One who places money or property in the hands of a stakeholder may, while such money or property remains in the stakeholder's hands, withdraw his wager or repudiate the illegal contract, under which the money or property was deposited, and demand the return of such money or property, and if the stakeholder refuses to return the money or property the loser may bring an action against him for its recovery." The bond was not given in payment, but merely as security. "Title to the bond did not pass to the defendant but remained in the plaintiff." Gehres v. Ater, 148 Ohio St. 89, 73 N.E.2d 513 (1947).

(2) *The Case of the Bested Bookie.* Watts, an amateur gambler, placed bets on horse races with Malatesta, a professional bookmaker. At the

a. "Law enforcement officials agree almost unanimously that gambling is the greatest source of revenue for organized crime. It ranges from lotteries, such as 'numbers' or 'bolita,' to off-track horse betting, bets on sporting events, large dice games and illegal casinos. . . . There is no accurate way of ascertaining organized crime's gross revenue from gambling in the United States. Estimates of the annual intake have varied from $7 to $50 billion." President's Commission on Law Enforcement and Administration of Justice (Task Force Report: Organized Crime) 2-3 (1967).

end of two years he sued to recover $37,535 that he had lost during that time, under a New York statute that provides: "Any person who shall pay . . . any money . . ., upon the event of any wager or bet prohibited, may sue for and recover the same of the winner . . . whether any such wager be lost or not." (N.Y.Gen.Obl.L., § 5–419) Malatesta counterclaimed for $95,938, alleging that Watts' winnings had exceeded his losses by that amount. From judgment for the plaintiff in the full amount of his claim, the defendant appealed. *Held:* Affirmed (4–2). "The evil which the law chiefly condemns and makes criminal . . . is betting and gambling organized and carried on as a systematic business . . . . Curb the professional with his constant offer of temptation coupled with ready opportunity, and you have to a large extent controlled the evil. It is clear that in the eyes of the law the professional gambler and his customer do not stand in the same place. They are not in pari delicto." Watts v. Malatesta, 262 N.Y. 80, 186 N.E. 210 (1933).

LIEBMAN v. ROSENTHAL, 185 Misc. 837, 57 N.Y.S.2d 875 (N.Y.Sup.Ct.1945). [Liebman sued Rosenthal for the value of jewelry delivered to Rosenthal, alleging the following facts. In May of 1941 when they both resided in Paris and were sojourning in Bayonne, France, Liebman was desirous of getting his family and himself to Portugal in order to escape the oncoming German army. Rosenthal represented that he was an intimate friend of the Portuguese consul in Bayonne, and that he could get visas for Liebman and his family if he gave the consul $30,000. Liebman gave Rosenthal $28,000 worth of diamond jewelry, but Rosenthal absconded with the jewelry and did not obtain the visas. Liebman later met Rosenthal in New York City and demanded the jewelry. Rosenthal moved for summary judgment on the ground that the agreement was illegal.]

HOOLEY, JUSTICE. . . . In Morgan v. Groff, 4 Barb. 524, 526, the court said: 'There is a distinction between executory and executed illegal contracts. Where money has been paid on an illegal contract which has been executed, and both the parties are in pari delicto, neither of them can recover from the other the money so paid; but if the contract is executory, and the party paying the money is desirous of rescinding the contract, he may do so, and recover back his money by action of assumpsit for money had and received.' " . . .

From the complaint in the case at bar it appears that this contract was wholly unexecuted and that the action is not brought to enforce the contract but rather to obtain moneys paid to one who is alleged to have defrauded the plaintiff by false representations.

Moreover, it sufficiently appears from the complaint that the plaintiff's actions were motivated by the desire of saving the lives of himself and his family from the Hitlerian army. If it be true that in such a situation this plaintiff delivered property in a large amount to the defendant, it may not be successfully contended that, acting under such pressure, the plaintiff was in pari delicto with the defendant upon whose representations and promises of action the plaintiff alleges he relied. There is no question of public policy involved in a case like this where a man is attempting to save himself from an enemy who has violated all the laws of civilization. Protection of one's self and one's family is among the first laws of nature and this court can appreciate that under similar conditions the most law-abiding man would enter into such an agreement as this plaintiff is alleged to have made. In the light of what we now know as to what happened in the internment camps of Germany and the cruelties and barbarities therein and the uncertainty of the fate of those in the path of the Nazi horde who might become lodged therein, who shall say that such a contract was against public policy? Rather it may be said that public policy should not permit the defendant to profit by what plaintiff maintains happened here. . . .

[Motion denied.]

[On appeal by Rosenthal, the Appellate Division affirmed, stating only that, "The determination of illegality should await all the proof to be adduced upon the trial." Adel, J., dissented: "The agreement in suit, being malum in se, is contrary to public policy, and though it be unexecuted, the law will neither enforce its terms nor direct restitution of moneys paid thereunder. . . . There is no authority for the holding that urgency of motive provides an excuse for entering into an illegal engagement." Liebman v. Rosenthal, 269 App.Div. 1062, 59 N.Y.S.2d 148 (1945).]

NOTES

(1) *The Case of the Lost Lire.* In 1947 Bousted, a British subject, was advised by his doctor to send his thirteen-year-old daughter abroad to avoid a recurrence of pleurisy, from which she had suffered for three winters. In order to obtain more than the £115 which the Treasury would allow his daughter and her mother together, he made a contract with Mrs. Bigos, in contravention of the Exchange Control Act of 1947, whereby Mrs. Bigos was to make £150 worth of Italian money available to Bousted in Italy and Bousted was to repay Mrs. Bigos with English money in England. As security, Bousted deposited a valuable stock certificate with Mrs. Bigos. Mrs. Bigos failed to make the Italian money available, and Bousted demanded a return of his stock certificate. Mrs. Bigos, instead, sued to recover £150 from Bousted, and Bousted counterclaimed for return of his certificate. Mrs. Bigos abandoned her claim, but Bousted continued his counterclaim, asserting that, since the illegal contract was still executory, he had a locus poenitentiae. *Held:* Against Bousted on his counterclaim for return of the stock certificate. The doctrine of locus poenitentiae is unavailable to Bousted, since the fact that the illegal transaction was not carried out was due to no intervening repentance of Bousted but to Mrs. Bigos' nonperformance of her part of the illegal bargain. Bigos v. Bousted [1951] 1 All E.R. 92 (K.B.).

(2) *"Clean Hands."* Courts of equity have traditionally demanded greater moral rectitude of suitors than have courts of law. One of the colorful maxims of equity runs: "He who comes into equity must come with clean hands." See New York Football Giants v. Los Angeles Chargers Football Club, 291 F.2d 471, 473 (5th Cir. 1961), in which the Giants were denied an injunction to prevent Charles Flowers from playing with the Chargers, in violation of his contract with the Giants, since the Giants lacked "clean hands" by virtue of having kept the contract secret so that Flowers could play in the Sugar Bowl. But cf. Houston Oilers v. Neely, 361 F.2d 36 (10th Cir. 1966), cert. denied, 385 U.S. 840 (1966).

The interplay of notions related to illegality with the application of the "clean hands" doctrine is well illustrated by West Los Angeles Institute for Cancer Research v. Mayer, 366 F.2d 220 (9th Cir. 1966), cert. denied, 385 U.S. 1010 (1967). The Mayers sold their business to the Institute for Cancer Research in a complex transaction designed to produce a three-fold tax advantage. The Mayers wanted a provision that if the Internal Revenue Service disapproved any of the three tax features, the parties would be restored, as nearly as possible, to their original positions. But the chairman of the Institute's board assured him that the provision was unnecessary since the board members, honorable men, would do this anyway, and that "an examining Revenue Agent might be led to believe that no one would be hurt by IRS disapproval and would for that reason disapprove it." After the transfer the IRS denied two of the expected tax advantages and cast doubt on the third. The Mayers brought an action to recover the property. From a decision granting the relief sought, the Institute appealed. In affirming, the court concluded that the IRS ruling rejected the tax premises on which the transaction was based and frustrated the transaction (see Chapter 8 infra).

"The Institute argues that equitable relief is barred by the doctrine of 'unclean hands' since the parties deliberately omitted from the contract an express provision . . . in order to conceal this understanding from the Internal Revenue Service. . . . We think the circumstances of this case justified the district court's determination that the clean-hands maxim should not be applied. No injury resulted to the public generally, since the anticipated tax benefits were denied despite the concealment. . . . The Mayers' offense, though serious, was mitigated by the circumstance that their motive . . . was not to gain an unjustified tax advantage by concealing a relevant fact, but rather to assure an evaluation of the transaction on its merits by excluding an extraneous fact which might improperly influence the examining agent. The parties were not in pari delicto. The agents of the Institute, purportedly possessing an expertise which the Mayers lacked, stood in a superior position. They were the active parties. . . . And the forfeiture . . . if relief were denied would be extreme."

SOUTHWESTERN SHIPPING CORP. v. NATIONAL CITY BANK, 6 N.Y.2d 454, 160 N.E.2d 836 (1959). [Garmoja, an Italian concern, ordered 300 tons of fatty acid at $37,222 from Southwestern Shipping, its purchasing agent in New York. Garmoja did not have a permit license to pay dollars as required by Italian foreign exchange regulations. It therefore made an agreement with Corti, another Italian concern, which had a permit license to pay dollars to an American named Anlyan for rags to be imported from the United States. Under the agreement, Garmoja paid lire to Corti in Italy, Corti used its permit license to transmit a credit for $37,222 to National City Bank of New York "in favor of" Anlyan; Anlyan in advance of the transfer had executed an assignment of the dollars to Southwestern Shipping, which had an account with National City Bank. The Garmoja-Corti agreement and the Anlyan assignment violated both Italian law and the Bretton Woods International Monetary Agreement. By mistake, National City Bank improperly paid $37,222 to Anlyan, who absconded. Upon National City Bank's refusal to pay Southwestern Shipping, the latter sued. From a judgment setting aside a jury verdict in favor of plaintiff and granting defendant's motion for a directed verdict, plaintiff appealed.]

FROESSEL, J. . . . It is well settled in this State "that a party to an illegal contract cannot ask a court of law to help him carry out his illegal object, nor can such a person plead or prove in any court a case in which he, as a basis for his claim, must show forth his illegal purpose". . . . To this well-established principle of law, however, there is an equally well-established exception. If a party to an illegal transaction turns over money or property to a third person for the use of the other party to the transaction, the latter can enforce the express or implied promise or trust of the third party to turn over the money or property, notwithstanding the fact that he could not have enforced payment or delivery by the party who voluntarily made the payment or deposit. A mere agent or depository of the proceeds of an illegal transaction will not be permitted to assert the defense of illegality in an action to recover the proceeds by a party to the illegal transaction. . . . In the instant case, defendant was merely a conduit through which dollars were to pass from one principal, Corti, to plaintiff, as alter ego of the other principal, Garmoja. It had no beneficial interest in or claim to the $37,222, and its position was that of a depository into whose hands moneys were delivered for payment to another. . . .

Defendant seeks to distinguish the controlling New York cases on three grounds: (1) the agent in those cases refused to pay the proceeds of the illegal transaction to its *own* principal; (2) the illegal transaction was completed, and (3) to have sustained the defense would have left the agent with a windfall. None of these alleged distinctions will withstand analysis. In all the relevant cases, the third party, who received the proceeds from one principal to the illegal transaction, was obligated to the other principal by virtue of a contract or trust, express or implied, to pay over the proceeds. The triers of the facts here found that defendant, after verifying the authenticity of the assignment, promised to transfer the proceeds to the account of its own depositor, plaintiff. This clearly bound defendant to transmit the funds to plaintiff and created a legally enforcible obligation on its part to make such payment. . . .

As to the second claimed basis of distinction, the illegal transaction in the relevant cases was completed only in the sense that both principals had performed their part of the illegal bargain—as Garmoja did here by paying the lire and as Corti did by transmitting the dollar equivalent—and the fruits were in the hands of an agent or depository. In all the cases, as here, one of the principals was seeking to recover the proceeds from the agent or depository; however, this was regarded not as a suit to consummate the illegal bargain, but to enforce an independent promise or trust to pay over the proceeds. . . .

Finally, by being permitted to successfully maintain the affirmative defense of illegality, defendant was enabled to avoid liability for the stated sum, which the jury verdict had fastened on it. Having been found liable for breach of contract and for negligence in the sum of $37,222, defendant, solely by virtue of the illegality of the antecedent agreement, to which it was not a party, has been allowed to escape the consequences of its own wrongdoing. This constitutes a windfall as surely as if defendant had kept the proceeds and refused to turn them over. . . .

[Reversed, 5–2.]

DESMOND, J. (dissenting). . . . [J]udgment for the plaintiff here would in effect compel the taking of the final step in the transaction itself—a step without which the transaction would be meaningless—that is, the assignment to plaintiff. . . . [I]t would seem that this defendant, had it learned the purpose for which this assignment was made, could have refused to recognize that document and could have stood on its right not to aid in carrying out an essentially illegal transaction. That being so, its position is not made worse by the fact that by error or negligence it paid out the money to the assignor instead of holding it for the assignee and thus rounding out the whole forbidden transaction.

NOTES

(1) *Problem.* Suppose that two friends, in a state where gambling is illegal, make a $1,000 bet on the outcome of a prize fight. Each deposits $1,000 with a third friend, who agrees to act as stakeholder pending the event. After the fight, the successful better demands the money from the stakeholder. The stakeholder, who has become financially embarrassed, refuses to turn the money over and the successful better sues to recover the $2,000 from the stakeholder. Decision? Is the case distinguishable from *Southwestern Shipping Corp. v. National City Bank,* and, if so, on what ground?

(2) *Rambling and Gambling.* The Southwestern Shipping case calls into question the extent to which a court will recognize the "public policy" of another jurisdiction. Although this is a problem that can best be left for a course in conflict of laws, one illustration may be enlightening here.

Jack Golden, a resident of New York, visited Puerto Rico, gambled at a casino operated by International Hotels under government license, and left behind a check for $3,000 and I.O.U.s for $9,000—so International Hotels alleged in suing Golden in New York. The trial court gave judgment for the plaintiff, the Appellate Division reversed, and the plaintiff appealed. *Held:* Reversed (5–2). The court referred to cases holding Nevada gambling debts unenforceable there and elsewhere. In contrast, the law of Puerto Rico permits enforcement of such debts, except to the extent that they represent losses that "exceed the customs of a good father of a family." On the problem of migratory suits, the court referred to Paulsen and Sovern, "Public Policy" in the Conflict of Laws, 56 Colum.L. Rev. 969 (1956). It said: "Informed public sentiment in New York is only against unlicensed gambling. . . ." Intercontinental Hotels Corp. (P.R.) v. Golden, 15 N.Y.2d 9, 203 N.E.2d 210 (1964). Consider also Liebman v. Rosenthal, p. 415 supra, in this connection.

(3) *Problem.* Some "Onassis' companies," ship operators, were persuaded to switch their purchases of paint to the Red Hand Compositions Company by the efforts of Costa Colyvas, who then sued Red Hand for a 5% commission that it had promised him on the sales. He gave evidence that his main contact in the Onassis companies was a department head named Paizis, with whom he had agreed to divide the commission evenly. The agreement was not disclosed to Paizis' employer for, according to Colyvas, "if anything of this would leak out, it would not be very nice for this person mentioning the five percent." Red Hand moved for summary judgment, citing the McConnell case, p. 406 supra. Colyvas countered with the Intercontinental Hotels case, Note 2 supra (apparently the transactions in question had occurred in Monte Carlo). On these facts alone, what decision? See Colyvas v. Red Hand Compositions Co., 318 F.Supp. 1376 (S.D. N.Y.1970).

Chapter 4

THE REQUIREMENT OF A WRITING (THE STATUTE OF FRAUDS)

SECTION 1. CONTRACTS WITHIN THE STATUTE

(a) The Text of the Statute

Most legal systems require a writing for the enforcement of some sorts of promises. In this country the most important requirement of this kind is derived from the British Statute of Frauds enacted by Parliament in 1677 (The Statute of Frauds, An Act for Prevention of Frauds and Perjuries, Stat. 29, Car. II, c. 3). This chapter deals with four major categories of contracts which are subjected to this requirement in nearly every state: (1) contracts to answer for the duty of another; (2) contracts not to be performed within one year; (3) contracts for the sale of an interest in land; and (4) contracts for the sale of goods. State law should be consulted for other categories.[a] The California statute below affords a good example of a contemporary American statute of frauds.

The following contracts are invalid, unless the same, or some note or memorandum thereof, is in writing and subscribed by the party to be charged or by his agent:

1. An agreement that by its terms is not to be performed within a year from the making thereof;

2. A special promise to answer for the debt, default, or miscarriage of another . . . ;

---

a. Two of these categories (contracts obligating executors and administrators to pay out of their own estates; contracts in consideration of marriage) are derived from the original British statute. Others (e. g., brokerage contracts) have been added to suit American conditions.

Some writing requirements are not ordinarily regarded as related to the statute of frauds. One example is the requirement of a writing for an agreement to arbitrate disputes. California Code of Civil Procedure § 1281, for example, provides: "A written agreement to submit to arbitration an existing controversy or a controversy thereafter arising is valid, enforceable and irrevocable, save on such grounds as exist for the revocation of any contract." Note that, in contrast to the statute of frauds, this statute does not state that the writing must be signed.

3. An agreement made upon consideration of marriage other than a mutual promise to marry;

4. An agreement for the leasing for a longer period than one year, or the sale of real property, or of an interest therein; and such agreement, if made by an agent of the party sought to be charged, is invalid, unless the authority of the agent is in writing, subscribed by the party sought to be charged;

5. An agreement authorizing or employing an agent or broker to purchase or sell real estate for compensation or a commission;

6. An agreement which by its terms is not to be performed during the lifetime of the promisor, or an agreement to devise or bequeath any property, or to make any provision for any person by will;

7. An agreement by a purchaser of real property to pay an indebtedness secured by a mortgage or deed of trust upon the property purchased, unless assumption of said indebtedness by the purchaser is specifically provided for in the conveyance of such property. [West's Ann.Calif.Civil Code § 1624.]

[The requirement of a writing for contracts for the sale of goods was the subject of a special section in the British Statute of Frauds, passed into the Uniform Sales Act, and is now contained in Section 2–201 of the Uniform Commercial Code, which has been enacted in California. See pp. 432, 441 infra.]

The requirement of a writing is not an alternative to the requirement of consideration but an addition to it. What is its justification? Consider Professor Fuller's discussion of the "evidentiary" and "cautionary" functions of legal formalities at p. 1 supra. It is significant that in 1954, after 277 years, the British Parliament repealed all of the Statute of Frauds except those provisions requiring a writing for promises to answer for the debt of another and contracts for the sale of land (Act, 1954, 2 & 3 Eliz. 2, c. 34). Why do you suppose these exceptions were made? Here are some of the reasons given by the English Law Revision Committee for repeal:

"(1) First and foremost, it is urged that the Act is a product of conditions which have long passed away. At the time when it was passed, essential kinds of evidence were excluded (e. g., the parties themselves could not give evidence), and objectionable types of evidence were admitted (e. g., juries were still in theory entitled to act on their own knowledge of the facts in dispute). It was an improvement on this state of affairs to admit the evidence of the parties, even though only to the extent that such evidence was in signed writing.

To-day, when the parties can freely testify, the provisions . . . are an anachronism. A condition of things which was advanced in relation to 1677 is backward in relation to 1937.

"(2) 'The Act', in the words of Lord Campbell already cited 'promotes more frauds than it prevents'. True, it shuts out perjury; but it also and more frequently shuts out the truth. It strikes impartially at the perjurer and at the honest man who has omitted a precaution, sealing the lips of both. Mr. Justice Fitz James Stephen . . . went so far as to assert that 'in the vast majority of cases its operation is simply to enable a man to break a promise with impunity, because he did not write it down with sufficient formality'. (Law Quarterly Review, 1885, Vol. 1 p. 1.)

"(3) The classes of contracts to which [it] applies seem to be arbitrarily selected and to exhibit no relevant common quality. There is no apparent reason why the requirement of signed writing should apply to these contracts, and to all of them, and to no others.

"(4) The Section is out of accord with the way in which business is normally done. Where actual practice and legal requirement diverge, there is always an opening for knaves to exploit the divergence.

"(5) The operation of the Section is often lopsided and partial. A and B contract: A has signed a sufficient note or memorandum, but B has not. In these circumstances B can enforce the contract against A, but A cannot enforce it against B." Law Revision Committee, Sixth Interim Report, Cmd. No. 5449, pp. 6–7 (1937).

The situation in England may, however, be distinguishable from that in this country in several respects. Chief among these are: first, the fact that in England trial by jury in contract actions is within the discretion of the judge, makes it possible to keep from the jury a case formerly within the statute; and second, the fact that in England counsel's fees are included in the costs assessed against the losing party, makes it more likely that the technicalities and uncertainties of the statute will discourage litigants from suing on otherwise meritorious claims. See 68 Harv.L.Rev. 383 (1954). The materials that follow are intended to suggest some of the problems that the statute has raised in the United States.

(b) Contracts to Answer for the Duty of Another

One of the most important of the provisions of the statute of frauds is that which requires a writing for a "special promise to answer for the debt, default, or miscarriage of another." The provision is directed generally at suretyship contracts. Suretyship is defined in Section 82 of the Restatement of Security as "the relation which exists where one person has undertaken an obligation and another person is also under an obligation or other duty to the obligee, who is entitled to but one performance, and as between the two who are bound, one rather than the other should perform."

As a simple example, suppose that A wishes to obtain services on credit from C. In order to induce C to extend credit, A not only promises to pay the price but has B add his own promise to pay C the price. Both A and B are under obligation to pay the full amount to C; C is entitled to but one performance; and as between A and B, A rather than B should perform. The relation thus fits the Restatement definition of suretyship: A is the *principal*, B is the *surety*, and C is the *creditor*. B's promise is one to answer for the duty of A and so comes within the statute of frauds.

"Why should such promises, more than others, be subject to that requirement? Doubtless because the promisor has received no benefit from the transaction. This circumstance may make perjury more likely, because while in the case of one who has received something the circumstances themselves which are capable of proof show probable liability, in the case of a guaranty nothing but the promise is of evidentiary value. Moreover, as the lack of any benefit received by the guarantor increases the hardship of his being called upon to pay, it also increases the importance of being very sure that he is justly charged." 3 Williston, § 452. Consider also the "evidentiary" and "cautionary" functions of formalities discussed at p. 1 supra. Which of them applies here?

Suppose, however, that instead of the tripartite agreement described above, B and C agree that C will perform services to A in return for which B will repay C the price at a later time. This is not a suretyship relation. B's promise is not one to answer for the debt of A, because A is under no obligation to C, and so B's promise to C is not within the statute.[a] But do not all of the reasons just given for requiring a writing apply with equal force to this situation?

Much litigation has been devoted to characterizing specific transactions to determine whether the promise in suit is one to answer for the duty *of another*. Suppose, for example, that in Cotnam v. Wisdom, p. 36 supra, Dr. Wisdom had treated Harrison in response to a call from Harrison's daughter, who had said, "Give him the best care you can and I will pay you for it." Does the statute apply to the daughter's promise? The Supreme Court of Vermont said in Lawrence v. Anderson, 108 Vt. 176, 184 A. 689 (1936): "Such a promise is not collateral or secondary, but primary and original. . . . To such a contract the Statute of Frauds does not apply, for the simple reason that it is not a promise to pay the debt of another, but is a promise to pay the debt of the promisor—one that he makes his own

---

a. As will be seen in Chapter 9, A may, as a third party beneficiary, be entitled to enforce the promise that C made to B.

by force of his engagement." The court, however, went on to hold that the doctor by first charging the patient, billing his estate, and engaging a lawyer to proceed against the estate, "elected to accept the [daughter's] engagement as collateral" to the father's, so that when he sued the daughter a year and a half after the accident "he could not hold the defendant, though she had tendered an engagement direct, in form." Would it have been better to say that the daughter was not bound because the doctor did not accept her offer? Was there any way out of the doctor's dilemma? If he had first pressed a claim against the daughter, without success, could he then have recovered from the estate? See Note 1, p. 39 supra.

NOTES

(1) *"Main Purpose"* or *"Leading Object" Rule.* Even where the promise is plainly one to answer for the duty of another, some courts have made an exception where the promisor's "main purpose" or "leading object" is to further his own economic advantage. See Restatement Second, § 184. What is the reason for this exception? Yarbro v. Neil B. McGinnis Equipment Co., 101 Ariz. 378, 420 P.2d 163 (1966), is instructive.

Russell bought a tractor from McGinnis under a conditional sales contract calling for twenty-three monthly payments of $574 each. When he failed to make the first payment, at Russell's suggestion a representative of McGinnis met with Yarbro to ask if he would help with the payments. Yarbro agreed and paid one installment. Russell then failed to pay any subsequent installments and Yarbro gave repeated oral assurances that he would cover the delinquent payments, but did not do so. Finally, McGinnis repossessed the tractor, resold it for $5,000 at auction, and sued Yarbro for the balance. The trial court rejected Yarbro's defense of the statute of frauds and gave judgment for McGinnis. Yarbro appealed, and the Supreme Court of Arizona affirmed on the basis of the "leading object" rule.

The rule, said the court, "is based upon the underlying fact that the Statute does not apply to promises related to debts created at the instance, and for the benefit, of the promisor (i. e. 'original' promises), but only to those by which the debt of one party is sought to be charged upon and collected from another (i. e. 'collateral' promises). . . . The leading object may be inferred from that which he expected to get as the exchange for his promise. Thus, it is neither 'consideration' alone (for there must be consideration to make any promise enforceable, including one of guaranty) nor 'benefit' alone (for in most every guaranty situation at least some benefit will flow to the promisor-guarantor) that makes an oral promise to pay the debt of another enforceable. Rather, there must be consideration and benefit *and* that benefit must be the primary object of making the promise as distinguished from a benefit which is merely incidental, indirect, or remote. . . . The facts in the present case show that before the McGinnis Co. ever began its dealings with Russell, Yarbro had sought to purchase the tractor in question for himself, but that no sale had resulted because the financing institution with which the McGinnis Equipment Co. financed such deals would not accept Yarbro's credit. It was at this point that Yarbro said that he thought he could get Russell to buy the tractor. Further evidence of Yarbro's interest in the tractor comes from the fact that after its purchase he had borrowed it on a series of occasions. When repairs were needed shortly after Yarbro had made the first installment payment, the McGinnis Co. repairman found the machine on Yarbro's land. He admits that a number of times he used the tractor for jobs around his ranch, and witnesses stated at the trial that Yarbro had asked on several occasions that the McGinnis Co. not repossess the tractor because he needed it. These requests were usually in conjunction with a promise to pay what was owing on the tractor. . . . We find that there was substantial evidence to support the trial court's conclusion that the main and leading object of Yarbro in making his promises to McGinnis Co. was not to become Russell's guarantor but rather was to serve interests of his own." However, since Yarbro's promise had only been to pay the then delinquent installments, he was not liable for later installments.

(2) *Novation.* If A is already under an obligation to C, and C agrees to release A from liability in exchange for B's promise to pay, the transaction is known as a *novation.* The statute of frauds is construed so as not to apply to B's promise in such a case. Why? Is it not a promise to answer for the debt of A? See Restatement Second, § 183.

(3) *Promise Made to Debtor.* A promise made to the debtor is not within the statute. For a promise to come within the statute it "must be one to pay the debt of another, and while 'another' might have been construed to mean merely another than the promisor, it has been construed to mean another than either the promisee or the promisor, and, therefore, the statute applies only to promises made to the person or persons to whom another is answerable. . . . That is seemingly due to the notion that the mischief sought to be remedied by the statute was perjured claims by creditors that promises had been made to them." Costigan, Cases on Contracts 832–33 (1932). If, therefore, B promises A that he will pay A's debt to C, the statute does not apply. This is so even though, as will be seen in Chapter 9, Third Party Beneficiaries, C may recover from B as a creditor beneficiary of B's promise. See Restatement Second, § 180.

(c) Contracts Not to be Performed Within One Year

Of all the classes of contracts brought within the original statute of frauds, the most difficult of rationalization is that consisting of contracts "not to be performed within the space of one year from the making thereof." If the one-year limitation is based upon the tendency of memory to fail and evidence to grow stale with the passage of time, it is ill-contrived: for the one-year period is not between fact and proof of that fact, but between the making of the contract and completion of performance. Suppose, for example, that an oral contract that cannot be performed within a year is broken the day after its making. No action can be maintained upon it, although its terms are still fresh in the minds of the parties. But suppose that an oral contract that can be performed within a year is broken, and suit is not brought until nearly six years (the usual statute of limitations for contract) after the breach. The action can be maintained upon it although its terms are no longer fresh in the minds of the parties.

If the one-year limitation is an attempt to separate significant contracts of long duration for which writings should be required from insignificant contracts of short duration for which writings are unnecessary, it is equally ill-contrived: for the one-year period is not between the commencement of performance and the completion of performance, but between the making of the contract and the completion of performance. Suppose, for example, that an oral contract to work for one day, thirteen months from now, is broken. No action can be maintained upon it, although its duration is only one day. But suppose that an oral contract to work for a year beginning today [a] is broken. An action can be maintained upon it although its duration is a full year.

Perhaps because of the difficulty in justifying the one-year provision, it has been subjected to a number of judicial limitations. The most important of these is that in most states in order to fall within the statute, the contract must be one which *cannot* be performed within a year. The mere possibility that performance may take less than a year is ordinarily sufficient to take the contract out of the statute. For example, if A agrees to work for B for A's life, the contract is not within the statute because it *could* be completely performed within a year in the event that A should die within that time. See Restatement, § 198, Illustration 2.[b] The materials that follow explore the limits of this limitation.

GILLIAM v. KOUCHOUCOS, 161 Tex. 299, 340 S.W.2d 27 (1960). [Kouchoucos had a written contract with Gilliam to serve as manager of the Ridgewood Motor Hotel, Inc. He entered into an oral contract with Gilliam to serve as manager of the Beaumont Petroleum

---

a.   Where the contract is to be performed over the term of a year beginning on the day of the making of the contract, the statute is clearly inapplicable. Where the contract is to be performed over the term of a year beginning on the day following the day of the making of the contract, there is disagreement as to the applicability of the statute. Some courts have been willing to disregard fractions of a day and have held the statute inapplicable; others have calculated the period exactly and have held the statute applicable. See 3 Williston, § 502.

b.   A simple illustration is Co-Op Dairy v. Dean, 102 Ariz. 573, 435 P.2d 470

(1967), which involved a contract of employment as sales manager "for a minimum period of one year" in which the employee could have reported for work in Phoenix, Arizona, the day after the contract was made, but instead went home to Oklahoma, moved his family to Phoenix, and reported for work two weeks later. The court held that the contract was not within the statute. It agreed that the statute, as applied to an employment contract, "is an anachronism in modern life" and that for it to be applied "there must not be the *slightest possibility* that it can be fully performed within one year."

Club for the same term. That term was set forth in the written contract as follows:

> The term of this contract and agreement shall be for a term of ten years from the date of completion of the premises.
> . . . This contract and agreement shall, however, terminate on the death of the Operator, and any further operation by his heirs, assigns or successors shall be under a renegotiated contract.

Kouchoucos sued Gilliam for breach of their oral agreement. The trial court held that Kouchoucos' claim was barred by the statute of frauds. The Court of Civil Appeals reversed, and Gilliam appealed.]

SMITH, JUSTICE. . . . The question here is whether the agreement is within the prohibition of the statute, notwithstanding the possibility of termination within less than a year by reason of respondent's death. An analogous question was before this court in the case of Chevalier v. Lane's, Inc., 1948, 147 Texas 106, 213 S.W.2d 530, 6 A.L.R.2d 1045. In that case, the question was answered in the affirmative. . . . The respondent contends that in the case of Chevalier v. Lane's, Inc., the court was considering an oral agreement which contained no reference to the possible death of plaintiff or other contingency that might prematurely terminate the arrangement. Respondent reasons further that since the present agreement contains the language that "This contract and agreement shall, however, terminate on the death of the operator . . ." the contract of employment for ten years is not within the prohibition of the statute, and such provision brings the case squarely within the rule that the statute does not apply where the agreement may, *by its own terms*, be fully performed within the year. . . . With this construction we cannot agree. . . . The statute relates to a contract "not to be *performed* within the space of one year from the making thereof." It thus has application only to contracts which are terminated *by performance*, and does not apply to contracts which may be terminated within a year by some means other than performance. All personal service contracts are terminated by death. Therefore, the addition of the words "but the agreement shall terminate on the death of the operator", added nothing. . . .

[Judgment of Court of Civil Appeals reversed and that of trial court affirmed.]

GRIFFIN, JUSTICE (dissenting). . . . [T]he error of the majority opinion [is that it] applies the rule whereby the contract of the parties is terminated *by operation of law* to a case where the parties themselves have agreed that the death of the plaintiff is performance. . . .

NOTES

(1) *Applicability of One-Year Provision.* To which of the following oral agreements does the one-year clause of the statute of frauds apply?

(a) A agrees to work for B for 5 years.

(b) A agrees to work for B for A's life.

(c) A agrees to work for B for A's life, but not exceeding 5 years.

(d) A agrees to work for B for 5 years, if A lives that long.

(e) A agrees to work for B for 5 years, but if A dies the contract is to be terminated.

Is there a rational basis for requiring a writing in some of these cases and not in others? See 3 Williston, § 499.

(2) *Lifetime Provision.* The New York act requires a writing for an agreement that "is not to be performed within one year from the making thereof or the performance of which is not to be completed before the end of a lifetime." New York General Obligations Law § 5–701. See also Calif.Civil Code § 1624(6), p. 422 supra. How would the questions in the preceding note be answered under these provisions? Is this a desirable modification of the statute?

(3) *Promises Not to Compete.* Dixon sold his grocery business to Doyle and orally promised Doyle that he would not go into the grocery business in Chicopee for five years. Doyle sued for breach of that promise and Dixon set up the defense of the statute of frauds. From a judgment for the plaintiff, the defendant appealed. *Held:* Affirmed. "[I]f the death of the promisor within the year would merely prevent full performance of the agreement, it is within the statute; but if his death would leave the agreement completely performed and its purpose fully carried out, it is not. It has accordingly been repeatedly held by this court that an agreement not hereafter to carry on a certain business at a particular place was not within the statute, because, being only a personal engagement to forbear doing certain acts, not stipulating for anything beyond the promisor's life, and imposing no duties upon his legal representatives, it would be fully performed if he died within the year." Doyle v. Dixon, 97 Mass. 208 (1867).

Professor Williston has criticized this decision: "It is obvious, however, that the contract would not be fully performed under the circumstances; it would merely have become certain that the contract would be performed since the promisor being dead could not longer break a negative promise; but no one can refrain from competition for [five] years within a year." 3 Williston, § 497.

Suppose that Dixon, in his contract to sell his business, had promised not to engage in the grocery business in Chicopee for five years, in return for which Doyle had promised to pay him $5,000 at the end of that time. If Dixon had died in six months, could his executor have maintained an action against Doyle for $5,000, either then or at the end of the five years, on the ground that there had been complete performance?

(4) *Problem.* Carl Coan, a first-year law student, entered into an oral agreement with Victor Orsinger, under which Coan was to be resident

manager of an apartment development owned by Orsinger "until [Coan] completed his law studies as a student duly matriculated in Georgetown University Law Center, Washington, D. C. or was obliged to discontinue these studies." Five weeks after Coan undertook his duties, he was fired. Does the statute of frauds bar recovery by Coan? See Coan v. Orsinger, 265 F.2d 575 (D.C.Cir. 1959).

HOPPER v. LENNEN & MITCHELL, 146 F.2d 364 (9th Cir. 1944). [Hedda Hopper, a columnist and radio personality, orally contracted with Lennen & Mitchell, an advertising agent, to do weekly radio broadcasts over a term of five years, which was broken down into ten twenty-six week periods. Lennen & Mitchell had the right to cancel by written notice four weeks before the end of any period. When Lennen & Mitchell refused to perform, she sued for damages. The trial court held that her claim was barred by the California statute of frauds, and she appealed.]

STEPHENS, CIRCUIT JUDGE. . . . Appellant claims . . . that since the contract by its terms can be terminated in less than a year, it is not within the statute which declares void any contract which is not to be performed within a year. . . . At the outset of our consideration of the point at issue, we direct attention to the fact that the identical point has been the subject of judicial expression in England and in many, and probably all, of the states. A rather sharp cleavage in decision has resulted in a "majority" and a "minority" rule, and we shall now proceed to discover upon which side of the cleavage the California law falls. . . .

It is a well established rule in California that if, by its terms, performance of a contract is possible within one year, the contract does not fall within the statute even though it is probable that it will extend beyond one year. . . . Obviously the contract in question was to run for five years, but only in the event appellees did not exercise their option to terminate the same within any one of ten twenty-six week periods within the period of five years. It is clear that appellees were to be bound for a longer period than twenty-six weeks only at their discretion. Thus, the reason for the statutory rule is preserved, for at no time is appellee bound for a period greater than the prescribed limitation for oral contracts. . . .

[Reversed.]

NOTES

(1) *Hopper and Gilliam.* Is the Hedda Hopper case distinguishable from Gilliam v. Kouchoucos? Did not both involve unilateral termination? Would the result in the Hedda Hopper case have been the same if the power of cancellation had been Miss Hopper's and not Lennen & Mitchell's?

(2) *The Commission Cases.* Zupan, a freelance advertising solicitor, was promised orally by Blumberg that he would receive a 25% commission

on any account that he brought in so long as the account remained active. When Blumberg stopped paying commissions, Zupan sued and Blumberg set up the statute of frauds. From judgment for the plaintiff, the defendant appealed. *Held:* Reversed. "It was within the contemplation of the parties to the contract that the customer might give orders for years, as actually occurred." And "a salesman's right to commissions cannot be defeated by the arbitrary refusal of his employer to accept orders from the procured customer." Zupan v. Blumberg, 2 N.Y.2d 547, 141 N.E.2d 819 (1957). Does this mean that a seller's oral promise to pay a salesman a 5% commission on all sales that he may make is also unenforceable? Compare Nat Nal Service Stations v. Wolf, 304 N.Y. 332, 107 N.E.2d 473 (1952), with Burkle v. Superflow Manufacturing Co., 137 Conn. 488, 78 A.2d 698 (1951). What of a brewer's promise to make a distributor "the exclusive wholesale distributor in Queens County of Schmidt beer . . . for as long as Schmidt sold beer in the New York metropolitan area"? See North Shore Bottling Co. v. C. Schmidt & Sons, 22 N.Y.2d 171, 239 N.E.2d 189 (1968).

(3) *Effect of Performance on One Side.* A wholly executory oral contract that is performable within a year on one side but not on the other is within the statute and is unenforceable on both sides. It is generally held, however, that if the one party who could do so had actually completely performed within a year, the contract is no longer within the statute and is enforceable. The Restatement and some courts have extended this exception to cases in which the plaintiff has performed without regard to whether his performance took place within a year. See Restatement Second, § 198. Professor Corbin has argued that it is the "fact that full performance has been rendered that affords a reason for enforcement." 2 Corbin, § 457. Indeed, in Professor Corbin's view, where the restitutionary remedy is inadequate, a *part* performance by one party should be sufficient to remove the bar of the statute in contracts not to be performed within a year. 2 Corbin, § 459; see Note, p. 450 supra. Are these incursions into the one-year provision best explained on logical grounds or on the basis of hostility to the provision?

(d) Contracts for the Sale of an Interest in Land

The original statute of frauds provides that "no action shall be brought . . . upon any contract or sale of lands, tenements or hereditaments, or any interest in or concerning them" unless the contract is in writing. An interest in land includes, among other interests, a lease, a mortgage, an easement, and sometimes it includes trees, buildings, or other things attached to the soil. Under what circumstances these and other interests are "land" within the meaning of the statute may be considered in courses in the field of real property.

Suppose that S orally agrees with B to convey to him land, for which B orally promises to pay $10,000. The failure of either S or B to perform this agreement does not give the other a cause of action, either at law for damages or in equity for specific performance. Even if B pays $500 down to "bind the bargain" the agreement will not be enforceable. But, although the statute makes no express exception, if S makes the agreed transfer he is allowed to recover the purchase price on the rather tenuous ground that the part of the transaction that brought it within the statute has been performed. And in some cases involving the sale of land the contract may be "taken out" of the statute by what is called "part performance."

The doctrine of part performance originated in suits in equity for specific performance. Its basis has been stated as follows: "The ground upon which a court, notwithstanding the statute of frauds, may compel the complete performance of an oral contract for the sale of real estate which has been partly performed is that such a decree may be necessary in order to avoid injustice toward one who in reliance upon the agreement has so altered his position that he cannot otherwise be afforded adequate relief. His mere entry into possession with the consent of the owner does not in and of itself meet this condition. . . . True, whenever he has made permanent improvements upon the property the courts are ready to order a conveyance, even though it might be possible to provide compensation in damages. A sufficient reason for this is that alterations in the artificial features of real estate are so largely a matter of individual taste that the loss to their designer in being deprived of their benefit might not be adequately measured either by the increased value of the property, or by his expenditures in making them. And whenever possession is taken under such circumstances that its relinquishment involves a disadvantage apart from the mere loss of the benefits of the bargain, a case may be presented for equitable relief, dependent upon the special circumstances. Nothing having been shown here beyond the bare fact of possession, we think the court erred in [allowing specific performance]." Baldridge v. Centgraf, 82 Kan. 240, 108 P. 83 (1910).

There is considerable difference of opinion as to what constitutes a sufficient part performance to take the contract out of the statute. See, e. g., Wilson v. La Van, 22 N.Y.2d 131, 238 N.E.2d 738 (1968).

(e) Contracts for the Sale of Goods

The original requirement of a writing for contracts "for the sale of any goods, wares and merchandizes, for the price of ten pounds sterling or upwards" was contained in a separate section, section seventeen, rather than in section four, which listed the other classes of contracts that came within the statute.

Although the seventeenth section of the British Statute of Frauds was repealed by Parliament in 1954, the draftsmen of the Uniform Commercial Code concluded that the requirement of a writing for contracts for the sale of goods should be retained in the United States. "[T]he spread of literacy, the rise of metropolitan living, the drive toward internal records, and the Code's removal of those unwise misinterpretations which so largely influenced the English decision, leave reasonable room for some Statute of Frauds in the sales area." Supplement No. 1 to the 1952 Official Draft of Text and Comments of the Uniform Commercial Code, p. 98 (1955). The Code's version of the statute for the sale of goods is found in UCC 2–201. See also UCC 1–206. For an empirical study of the statute as it applies to the sale of goods, see Note, 66 Yale L.J. 1038 (1957).

One of the problems in defining the scope of this branch of the statute has been in distinguishing contracts for the sale of goods from contracts for work and labor. The distinction is significant because the statute of frauds does not apply to contracts for work and labor unless, of course, they happen to fall within the one-year provision. The difficulty is most acute where the contract involves both the supplying of goods and the furnishing of work and labor. Consider, for example, a contract for a set of false teeth to be made by a dentist, for a portrait to be painted by an artist, for a suit to be made to measure by a tailor, for a machine to be designed and produced by an engineering firm. The Uniform Sales Act resolved a conflict which had arisen in the prior case law under section seventeen with respect to such contracts as these by adopting the prevailing view that the statute of frauds applies even though the goods have not been made at the time of the contract, but with an exception for the case of goods to be specially manufactured which are not suitable for sale to others in the ordinary course of the seller's business. Is this exception to the rule justifiable? On what grounds? The rule with its exception is carried on, in substantially the same form, in the Uniform Commercial Code.

A similar problem has arisen in distinguishing between the sale of goods and the sale of land. Here the distinction is significant because, although the statute of frauds applies to both, its requirements as to the sale of goods are considerably less exacting than as to the sale of land. The problem may arise in a contract for the sale of timber as it stands, of minerals to be extracted, or of a building to be removed. For the Code solution to such problems, see UCC 2–107.

SECTION 2.   SATISFACTION OF THE STATUTE

The last section was concerned with determining which contracts are within the statute of frauds; this section is concerned with determining how the statute may be satisfied, assuming that the contract comes within it.   Here it is important to keep in mind that the sale of goods was the subject of a special section, section seventeen, in the original British version, while all of the other classes of contracts within the statute were dealt with in section four.   The latter and its statutory progeny provide for satisfaction of the statute only by a writing.   The former and its statutory progeny (notably UCC 2–201) provide for satisfaction not only by a writing, but in the alternative by acceptance and receipt of goods and by part payment.   Furthermore, as will be seen, there are important differences in the kind of writing required under the present-day versions of these two original sections of the statute.

In the case of the statutes derived from section four, the writing must state "with reasonable certainty the essential terms and conditions."   Restatement Second, § 207.   The attitude of courts toward this requirement is suggested by the opinion of Cardozo in Marks v. Cowdin, 226 N.Y. 138, 123 N.E. 139 (1919), in which he said: "The statute must not be pressed to the extreme of a literal and rigid logic. .   .   .   The memorandum which it requires, like any other memorandum, must be read in the light of reason."

Marks went to work as sales manager for Cowdin's ribbon business, under a contract that ran from 1911 to 1913.   Cowdin sent out notices to salesmen describing him as "sales-manager."   In 1913 the contract was orally renewed for three years, at a larger compensation. Later that year, after a disagreement with Cowdin, Marks asked for and received a memorandum signed by Cowdin and reciting that the arrangement made earlier that year for Marks' employment at a salary of $15,000 per year plus a stated share of gross profits "continues in force until Jan. 1st, 1916," but omitting any mention of his title or duties.   When, in 1914, Cowdin told Marks that he was to work under a new sales manager, McLaren, Marks refused and was fired. Marks sued Cowdin, who raised the one-year provision of the statute as a defense.   The Court of Appeals rejected this defense.   The contract had been made in January; the memorandum had been signed the following December.   "It assumes the existence of a position that the plaintiff is then filling.   It says that the employment shall be continued for a term and at a salary prescribed .   .   .. We are not left to gather the relation between the parties from executory promises.   We are informed that the relation existing is the one to be maintained   .   .   .. In this case the plaintiff does not need the aid of one spoken word of promise to identify his place.   His first contract was for two years, from January 1, 1911, to January 1, 1913. During that period, writings subscribed by the defendants attest the nature of his position. The memorandum exacted by the statute does not have to be in one document. It may be pieced together out of separate writings, connected with one another either expressly or by the internal evidence of subject matter and occasion."

CRABTREE v. ELIZABETH ARDEN SALES CORP.

Court of Appeals of New York, 1953.
305 N.Y. 48, 110 N.E.2d 551.

Action for damages for breach of employment contract employing plaintiff as sales manager of defendant corporation.

FULD, JUDGE. In September of 1947, Nate Crabtree entered into preliminary negotiations with Elizabeth Arden Sales Corporation, manufacturers and sellers of cosmetics, looking toward his employment as sales manager. Interviewed on September 26th, by Robert P. Johns, executive vice-president and general manager of the corporation, who had apprised him of the possible opening, Crabtree requested a three-year contract at $25,000 a year. Explaining that he would be giving up a secure well-paying job to take a position in an entirely new field of endeavor—which he believed would take him some years to master—he insisted upon an agreement for a definite term. And he repeated his desire for a contract for three years to Miss Elizabeth Arden, the corporation's president. When Miss Arden finally indicated that she was prepared to offer a two-year contract, based on an annual salary of $20,000 for the first six months, $25,000 for the second six months and $30,000 for the second year, plus expenses of $5,000 a year for each of those years, Crabtree replied that that offer was "interesting". Miss Arden thereupon had her personal secretary make this memorandum on a telephone order blank that happened to be at hand:

"EMPLOYMENT AGREEMENT WITH
NATE CRABTREE   Date Sept. 26–1947
At 681—5th Ave.   6: P.M.
*   *   *

Begin	20000.
6 months	25000.
6 "	30000.

5000.—per year, Expense money
[2 years to make good]

"Arrangement with Mr. Crabtree, By Miss Arden, Present Miss Arden, Mr. John, Mr. Crabtree, Miss OLeary"

A few days later, Crabtree 'phoned Mr. Johns and telegraphed Miss Arden; he accepted the "invitation to join the Arden organization", and Miss Arden wired back her "welcome". When he reported for work, a "pay-roll change" card was made up and initialed by Mr. Johns, and then forwarded to the payroll department. Reciting that it was prepared on September 30, 1947, and was to be effective as of October 22d, it specified the names of the parties, Crabtree's "Job Classification" and, in addition, contained the notation that "This employee is to be paid as follows:

> "First six months of employment $20,000. Per annum
> Next six months of employment   25,000.   "   "
> After one year of employment   30,000.   "   "

> Approved by RPJ [initialed]"

After six months of employment, Crabtree received the scheduled increase from $20,000 to $25,000, but the further specified increase at the end of the year was not paid. Both Mr. Johns and the comptroller of the corporation, Mr. Carstens, told Crabtree that they would attempt to straighten out the matter with Miss Arden, and, with that in mind, the comptroller prepared another "pay-roll change" card, to which his signature is appended, noting that there was to be a "Salary increase" from $25,000 to $30,000 a year, "per contractual arrangements with Miss Arden". The latter, however, refused to approve the increase and, after further fruitless discussion, plaintiff left defendant's employ and commenced this action for breach of contract.

At the ensuing trial, defendant denied the existence of any agreement to employ plaintiff for two years, and further contended that, even if one had been made, the statute of frauds barred its enforcement. The trial court found against defendant on both issues and awarded plaintiff damages of about $14,000, and the Appellate Division, two justices dissenting, affirmed. Since the contract relied upon was not to be performed within a year, the primary question for decision is whether there was a memorandum of its terms, subscribed by defendant, to satisfy the statute of frauds, Personal Property Law, § 31.

Each of the two payroll cards—the one initialed by defendant's general manager, the other signed by its comptroller—unquestionably constitutes a memorandum under the statute. That they were not prepared or signed with the intention of evidencing the contract, or that they came into existence subsequent to its execution, is of no consequence, see Marks v. Cowdin, 226 N.Y. 138, 145, 123 N.E. 139, 141; Spiegel v. Lowenstein, 162 App.Div. 443, 448–449, 147 N.Y.S. 655, 658; see, also, Restatement, Contracts, §§ 209, 210, 214; it is enough, to meet the statute's demands, that they were signed with intent to authenticate the information contained therein and that such information does evidence the terms of the contract. See . . . 2 Corbin on Contracts [1951], pp. 732–733, 763–764; 2 Williston on Contracts [Rev. ed., 1936], pp. 1682–1683. Those two writings contain all of the essential terms of the contract—the parties to it, the position that plaintiff was to assume, the salary that he was to receive —except that relating to the duration of plaintiff's employment. Accordingly, we must consider whether that item, the length of the contract, may be supplied by reference to the earlier unsigned office memorandum, and, if so, whether its notation, "2 years to make good", sufficiently designates a period of employment.

The statute of frauds does not require the "memorandum . . . to be in one document. It may be pieced together out of separate writings, connected with one another either expressly or by the internal evidence of subject-matter and occasion." . . . Where each of the separate writings has been subscribed by the party to be charged, little if any difficulty is encountered. . . . Where, however, some writings have been signed, and others have not —as in the case before us—there is basic disagreement as to what constitutes a sufficient connection permitting the unsigned papers to be considered as part of the statutory memorandum. The courts of some jurisdictions insist that there be a reference, of varying degrees of specificity, in the signed writing to that unsigned, and, if there is no such reference, they refuse to permit consideration of the latter in determining whether the memorandum satisfies the statute. . . . That conclusion is based upon a construction of the statute which requires that the connection between the writings and defendant's acknowledgment of the one not subscribed, appear from examination of the papers alone, without the aid of parol evidence. The other position—which has gained increasing support over the years—is that a sufficient connection between the papers is established simply by a reference in them to the same subject matter or transaction. . . . The statute is not pressed "to the extreme of a literal and rigid logic", Marks v. Cowdin, supra, 226 N.Y. 138, 144, 123 N.E. 139, 141, and oral testimony is admitted to show the connection between the documents and to establish the acquiescence, of the party to be charged, to the contents of the one unsigned. . . .

The view last expressed impresses us as the more sound, and, indeed—although several of our cases appear to have gone the other way, . . . —this court has on a number of occasions approved the rule, and we now definitively adopt it, permitting the signed and unsigned writings to be read together, provided that they clearly refer to the same subject matter or transaction. . . .

The language of the statute—"Every agreement . . . is void, unless . . . some note or memorandum thereof be in writing, and subscribed by the party to be charged", Personal Property Law, § 31—does not impose the requirement that the signed acknowledgment of the contract must appear from the writings alone, unaided by oral testimony. The danger of fraud and perjury, generally attendant upon the admission of parol evidence, is at a minimum in a case such as this. None of the terms of the contract are supplied by parol. All of them must be set out in the various writings presented to the court, and at least one writing, the one establishing a contractual relationship between the parties, must bear the signature of the party to be charged, while the unsigned document must on its face refer to the same transaction as that set forth in the one that was signed. Parol evidence—to portray the circumstances surrounding the making of the memorandum—serves only to connect the separate documents and to show that there was assent, by the party to be charged, to the contents of the one unsigned. If that testimony does not convincingly connect the papers, or does not show assent to the unsigned paper, it is within the province of the judge to conclude, as a matter of law, that the statute has not been satisfied. True, the possibility still remains that, by fraud or perjury, an agreement never in fact made may occasionally be enforced under the subject matter or transaction test. It is better to run that risk, though, than to deny enforcement to all agreements, merely because the signed document made no specific mention of the unsigned writing. . . .

Turning to the writings in the case before us—the unsigned office memo, the payroll change form initialed by the general manager Johns, and the paper signed by the comptroller Carstens—it is apparent, and most patently, that all three refer on their face to the same transaction. The parties, the position to be filled by plaintiff, the salary to be paid him, are all identically set forth; it is hardly possible that such detailed information could refer to another or a different agreement. Even more, the card signed by Carstens notes that it was prepared for the purpose of a "Salary increase per contractual arrangements with Miss Arden". That certainly constitutes a reference of sorts to a more comprehensive "arrangement," and parol is permissible to furnish the explanation.

The corroborative evidence of defendant's assent to the contents of the unsigned office memorandum is also convincing. Prepared by defendant's agent, Miss Arden's personal secretary, there is little likelihood that that paper was fraudulently manufactured or that defendant had not assented to its contents. Furthermore, the evidence as to the conduct of the parties at the time it was prepared persuasively demonstrates defendant's assent to its terms. Under such circumstances, the courts below were fully justified in finding that the three papers constituted the "memorandum" of their agreement within the meaning of the statute.

. . . Only one term, the length of the employment, is in dispute. The September 26th office memorandum contains the notation, "2 years to make good". What purpose, other than to denote the length of the contract term, such a notation could have, is hard to imagine. Without it, the employment would be at will, see Martin v. New York Life Ins. Co., 148 N.Y. 117, 121, 42 N.E. 416, 417, and its inclusion may not be treated as meaningless or purposeless. Quite obviously, as the courts below decided, the phrase signifies that the parties agreed to a term, a certain and definite term, of two years, after which, if plaintiff did not "make good", he would be subject to discharge. And examination of other parts of the memorandum supports that construction. Throughout the writings, a scale of wages, increasing plaintiff's salary periodically, is set out; that type of arrangement is hardly consistent with the hypothesis that the employment was meant to be at will. The most that may be argued from defendant's standpoint is that "2 years to make good", is a cryptic and ambiguous statement. But, in such a case, parol evidence is admissible to explain its meaning. . . . Having in mind the relations of the parties, the course of the negotiations and plaintiff's insistence upon security of employment, the purpose of the phrase—or so the trier of the facts was warranted in finding—was to grant plaintiff the tenure he desired.

The judgment should be affirmed, with costs.

NOTES

(1) *Reason and the Statute of Frauds.* How many of the following propositions involving the statute of frauds make sense to you?

(a) When a writing satisfying the statute is signed by only one party, it makes the contract enforceable *against* that party even though it is not enforceable *by* that party. See 2 Corbin, § 282.

(b) The printed firm name of the defendant appearing in the letterhead at the top of a writing is a sufficient signature if it is adopted by the defendant with the intention of authenticating the writing. See 2 Corbin, § 522; UCC 1–201(39) and Comment 39.

(d) If a writing satisfying the statute of frauds has been lost, the statute may be satisfied by parol evidence of its making and contents. See 2 Corbin, § 529.

(e) Parol evidence may be used to show that a memorandum, complete on its face, is not a correct representation of all the terms of the agreement and is, for this reason, insufficient. See 2 Corbin, §§ 288, 498. On reformation, see Palmer, Reformation and the Statute of Frauds, 65 Mich.L.Rev. 421 (1967).

(2) *The Case of the Careless Cancellation.* On October 16, a salesman for Varnish Company took an oral order from Lorick & Lowrance for paint and varnish, noted it in his memorandum book and sent a copy to Varnish Company. On October 17, Lorick & Lowrance wrote Varnish Company, "Gents: Don't ship paint ordered through your salesman. We have concluded not to handle it." Varnish Company shipped the goods before this letter was received. Lorick & Lowrance refused to take them and Varnish Company sued. From a nonsuit based on the statute of frauds, the plaintiff appealed. *Held:* Reversed. The letter clearly referred to the order, which, although unsigned, was in writing and otherwise satisfied the statute of frauds. "We have, then, an admission in writing that an order for the goods in question through the salesman had been given, and we have the order referred to, likewise in writing, and the two together fully satis-

fy the requirements of the statute." Louisville Asphalt Varnish Co. v. Lorick & Lowrance, 29 S.C. 533, 8 S.E. 8 (1888).

Consider the position of Lennen & Mitchell under the agreement in the Hedda Hopper case, p. 430 supra. Assume that they are uncertain as to the applicability of the statute of frauds to their contract. Do they run any risk if they send a notice of cancellation? Do they run any risk if they send no notice of cancellation? Advise them.

(3) *The Case of the Chary Chanteuse.* George Scheck had for many years been the manager of Connie Francis, a popular singer. About a year after an earlier employment agreement had expired, they began negotiations for a new agreement. After the final negotiation session, her lawyer mailed Scheck four copies of a new five-year contract with a covering letter, signed by the lawyer on her behalf, asking Scheck to "sign all copies" and "have Connie sign them." Scheck signed them, but Miss Francis did not. He continued to work for Miss Francis until about a year later, when a dispute arose and he sued Miss Francis for damages. From dismissal of his complaint on the ground that it was barred by the statute of frauds, he appealed, arguing that the statute was satisfied by the contract (unsigned by Miss Francis) when read together with the letter (signed on her behalf). *Held:* Affirmed. "The plaintiff's reliance upon the Crabtree case . . . is misplaced . . . . In the present case, unlike Crabtree, the letter signed by the defendants' attorney . . . does not serve to establish a contractual relationship between the parties . . . . Quite obviously, it was written for the sole purpose of forwarding the documents to the parties for signature . . . . The signatures which would authenticate the existence of the contracts within the meaning of the statute were to be made later after the parties read and approved the terms set forth in the proposed documents." Scheck v. Francis, 26 N.Y.2d 466, 260 N.E.2d 493 (1970).

ETHICS AND THE STATUTE OF FRAUDS

In a thoughtful article, Dean Stevens pointed out that, "It is probably a prevailing practice automatically to plead the Statute of Limitations to a stale claim and the Statute of Frauds when there is known to be no writing signed by the defendant, or his agent, evidencing the contract sued upon. The statutes are there, they supply the defenses, and the attorney would not be giving full and competent service to his client if he did not advise him of them and advance them for him." As to the Statute of Frauds, Dean Stevens saw a problem of ethics in which "the lawyer's conscience may be in conflict, not merely with a custom of the profession habitually to plead the defense, as in the case of the Statute of Limitations, but with judge-made law, that is all but unanimously adopted, to the effect that the defendant can admit an honest obligation and yet defeat its enforcement by pleading that the agreement was only oral and that there is no written evidence of the obligation as required by the Statute of Frauds. In the conflict between conscience and judicially approved practice, what is the lawyer to do? Conscience tells him that the practice is wrong, but the literature from insurance companies reminds him of liability for malpractice." Stevens, Ethics and the Statute of Frauds, 37 Cornell L.Q. 355 (1952).

NOTE

Statutory Solutions. Consider the solution to this dilemma found in the following Iowa statutes:

> The above regulations [the Iowa counterpart of section four of the original statute of frauds], relating merely to the proof of contracts, shall not prevent the enforcement of those not denied in the pleadings, except in cases when the contract is sought to be enforced, or damages recovered for the breach thereof, against some person other than him who made it. (Iowa Code Ann. § 622.34.) The oral evidence of the maker against whom the unwritten contract is sought to be enforced shall be competent to establish the same. (Iowa Code Ann. § 622.35.)

What effect will UCC 2–201(3) (b) have upon this problem? Does it include an involuntary admission resulting from a failure to deny the allegations of the complaint? See Alaska Code § 09.25.020(4).

UCC 2–201

As we saw earlier, contracts for the sale of goods were the subject of a special section in the original statute of frauds. This passed into Uniform Sales Act § 4, and then into UCC 2–201. Although the draftsmen of the Code did not abolish the requirement of a writing, they relaxed it very considerably. The original statute spoke of "some note or memorandum in writing of the said bargain," and the Uniform Sales Act of "some note or memorandum in writing of the contract or sale." But UCC 2–201(1) requires only "some writing sufficient to indicate that a contract for sale has been made between the parties," but couples this with an insistence on the quantity term. Comment 1 to UCC 2–201 explains:

> The required writing need not contain all the material terms of the contract and such material terms as are stated need not be precisely stated. All that is required is that the writing afford a basis for believing that the offered oral evidence rests on a real transaction. It may be written in lead pencil on a scratch pad. It need not indicate which party is the buyer and which the seller. The only term which must appear is the quantity term which need not be accurately stated but recovery is limited to the amount stated. The price, time and place of payment or delivery, the general quality of the goods, or any particular warranties may all be omitted. . . . Only three definite and invariable requirements as to the memorandum are made by this subsection. First, it must evidence a contract for the sale of

goods; second, it must be "signed", a word which includes any authentication which identifies the parties to be charged; and third, it must specify a quantity.

To what extent do these requirements differ from those applicable to other contracts that come within the statute? Why must the writing specify the *quantity* but not the *price*? The same Comment gives this answer:

> In many valid contracts for sale the parties do not mention the price in express terms, the buyer being bound to pay and the seller to accept a reasonable price which the trier of fact may well be trusted to determine. Again, frequently the price is not mentioned since the parties have based their agreement on a price list or catalogue known to both of them and this list serves as an efficient safeguard against perjury. Finally, "market" prices and valuations that are current in the vicinity constitute a similar check. Thus if the price is not stated in the memorandum it can normally be supplied without danger of fraud.

How convincing is the argument that the market is a check on perjury as to price, in view of the fact that the relief sought by the injured party usually consists of damages based on the difference between the contract price and a real or hypothetical transaction on the market? (Will not relatively small increments in price bulk large in the calculation of damages?) [a]

This insistence of the draftsmen on some evidence of the quantity term is carried over to the provisions on part payment and acceptance of the goods. The original statute could be satisfied not only by a writing, but also if "the buyer shall accept part of the goods . . . sold, and actually receive the same, or give something in earnest to bind the contract, or in part payment." A comparable provision was inserted in the Uniform Sales Act. Its application is illustrated by Helen Whiting v. Trojan Textile Corp., 307 N.Y. 360, 121 N.E.2d 367 (1954), in which the seller orally agreed to sell the buyer 83,000 yards of three different kinds of cloth goods. The seller then sent the buyer five yards of each kind of cloth with a separate writing covering each kind. The buyer kept the cloth, but signed only one of the writings and repudiated the other two. It was held that there was a sufficient acceptance and receipt to satisfy the statute as to all three kinds of cloth. "[T]he three five-yard pieces were not samples sent for approval but were 'part of the goods' accepted and received by the buy-

---

a. Professor Williston, who drafted the Uniform Sales Act, attacked the provisions of UCC 2–201, as, with one exception, "the most iconoclastic in the Code." With regard to the relaxation in the requirements of the writing he wrote: "No such inaccuracy is permitted under existing law, and the value of a memorandum open to such contradiction is questionable." Williston, The Law of Sales in the Proposed Uniform Commercial Code, 63 Harv.L. Rev. 561, 573, 574 (1950). Do you agree?

er. . . . Of course they were very small deliveries, but they were billed as deliveries under the contracts." The draftsmen of the Code dealt with this problem in UCC 2–201(3)(c). Note the language, "with respect to goods for which payment has been made and accepted, or which have been received and accepted." Comment 2 to that section explains that, "If the court can make a just apportionment, therefore, the agreed price of any goods actually delivered can be recovered without a writing or, if the price has been paid, the seller can be forced to deliver an apportionable part of the goods." [b] And what if it cannot make a just apportionment as, for example, in the case of acceptance and receipt of some but not all the parts of a dismantled machine, or part payments against an indivisible unit of goods? Compare Williamson v. Martz, 11 Pa.D. & C.2d 33 (1956) (statute not satisfied by such part payment), with Starr v. Freeport Dodge, 54 Misc.2d 271, 282 N.Y.S.2d 58 (1967) (statute satisfied by such part payment).

The most interesting innovation in UCC 2–201 is in subsection (2). It is the subject of the following opinion.

NOTE

The Southwest Engineering Case (Reprise). You will recall that in the Southwest Engineering case, p. 81 supra, an agreement for the sale of generators was held enforceable against the seller, Martin Tractor. The court concluded that the handwritten memorandum made by Hurt at the airport on April 28 satisfied UCC 2–201. On it Hurt listed the generator's component parts and its accessories, noting their prices including a discount. In the top left-hand corner he printed "Ken Hurt, Martin Tractor, Topeka, Caterpillar." He gave it to Cloepfil as a record of what they had done. Was the writing "sufficient to indicate that a contract for sale has been made between the parties"? Was it "signed by the party against whom enforcement is sought or by his authorized agent"? See UCC 1–201(39).

Hurt's letter of May 24 read, "Due to restrictions placed on Caterpillar products, accessory suppliers, and other stipulations by the district governing agency, we cannot accept your letter to proceed dated May 2, 1966, and hereby withdraw all verbal quotations." Assuming that Cloepfil's letter of May 2 contained details of the transaction, did Hurt's letter of May 24 satisfy the statute?[c] See Note 2, p. 439 supra. But in that case

---

b. Professor Corbin has written: "The present writer would have preferred to leave unchanged the old provisions as to part payment and acceptance and receipt. This is for two reasons . . . : first, he believes that the statutory provisions should be wholly abandoned because they increase litigation, greatly promote dishonest repudiation, and do not greatly aid our judicial system to frustrate fraud and perjury; and secondly, because a true apportionment of the goods or the

price can not be made without first proving the terms of the contract, and having proved them the contract should be enforced in full." Corbin, The Uniform Commercial Code— Sales; Should It be Enacted?, 59 Yale L.J. 821, 831 n. 7 (1950).

c. Although the opinion does not quote Cloepfil's May 2 letter, the record on appeal, p. 6, shows that it read in part: "We hereby authorize you to proceed with the preparation of shop

was not UCC 2–201(2) applicable without regard to Hurt's letter? What does the following case have to say on this point?

HARRY RUBIN & SONS v. CONSOLIDATED PIPE CO.

Supreme Court of Pennsylvania, 1959.
396 Pa. 506, 153 A.2d 472.

BENJAMIN R. JONES, JUSTICE. This is an appeal from the action of the Court of Common Pleas No. 1 of Philadelphia County, which sustained, in part, the appellees' preliminary objections to the appellants' complaint in assumpsit.

Rubin-Arandell, in their complaint, alleged that on three different dates—August 22nd, 25th and 28th, 1958—they entered into three separate oral agreements, all for the sale of goods in excess of $500, with one Carl Pearl, an officer and agent of Consolidated-Lustro, for the purchase of plastic hoops and materials, for use in assembling plastic hoops, and that Consolidated-Lustro failed to deliver a substantial portion of the hoops and material as required by the terms of the oral agreements. The court below, passing upon Consolidated-Lustro's preliminary objections, held that two of the alleged oral agreements violated the statute of frauds provision of the Uniform Commercial Code and were unenforceable. Rubin-Arandell contend that certain memoranda [1] (attached as exhibits to the complaint)

---

drawings and submittal documents for the engine generator set for McDonnell AFB lighting job. . . . If we furnish [the] cabinet, how will it affect the $705.00 price you showed on your sheet to me? . . . 'You are required to follow the provisions of DMS Reg. 1 and all other applicable regulations and orders of BDSA in obtaining controlled materials and other products and materials need [sic] to bill this order.' "

---

1.   "Purchase Order . . .
"Lustro Plastic Tile Company   No. 2859
          General Office & Warehouse
          1066 Home Avenue
          AKRON 10, OHIO
          POrtage 2–8801

"Ordered From
          Consolidated Tile Co.

		Date		
		Ship to		
Ship when		Route Via	FOB	
Quantity	Number		Description	Price
30,000			Hoops Te-Vee	36½¢

Red, Green, Blue
as per sample
From Lengths 8'–10"
to 9'–3"   So they can
nest
          "Lustro Plastic Tile Co.
          By /s/ Harry Rubin & Sons Inc.
               Leonard R. Rubin, V. Pres."

[*Footnote 1 continued on following page.*]

were sufficient to take both oral agreements out of the statute of frauds. . . .

The statute of frauds provision of the Uniform Commercial Code, supra, states: "§ 2–201. Formal Requirements: Statute of Frauds (1) Except as otherwise provided in this section a contract for the sale of goods for the price of $500 or more is not enforceable by way of action or defense unless there is some writing sufficient to indicate that a contract for sale has been made between the parties and signed by the party against whom enforcement is sought or by his authorized agent or broker. A writing is not insufficient because it omits or incorrectly states a term agreed upon but the contract is not enforceable under this paragraph beyond the quantity of goods shown in such writing. (2) Between merchants if within a reasonable time a writing in confirmation of the contract and sufficient against the sender is received and the party receiving it has reason to know its contents, it satisfies the requirements of subsection (1) against such party unless written notice of objection to its contents is given within ten days after it is received."

As between merchants, the present statute of frauds provision (i. e. under Section 2–201(2), supra) significantly changes the former law by obviating the necessity of having a memorandum signed by the party sought to be charged. The present statutory requirements are: (1) that, within a reasonable time, there be a writing in confirmation of the oral contract; (2) that the writing be sufficient to bind the sender; (3) that such writing be received; (4) that no reply thereto has been made although the recipient had reason to know of its contents. Section 2–201(2) penalizes a party who fails to "answer a written confirmation of a contract within ten days" of the receipt of the writing by depriving such party of the defense of the statute of frauds.[2]

"Consolidated Pipe Co.   "August 25, 1958
1066 Homes Ave.
Akron, Ohio
Att.: Mr. Carl Pearl
"Dear Carl,

       "As per our phone conversation of today kindly enter our order for the following:

> 60,000 Tee-Vee Hoops made of rigid polyethylene tubing from lengths of 8′ 10″ to 9′ 2″; material to weigh 15 feet per lb., colors red, green and yellow packed 2 Dozen per carton
> 39¢ each

       "It is our understanding that these will be produced upon completion of the present order for 30,000 hoops.

                      "Very truly yours,
                      Harry Rubin & Sons, Inc.
                      /s/ Leonard R. Rubin, Vice-pres."

2.   Comment to Section 2–201, 12A P.S.
     p. 87.

The memoranda upon which Rubin-Arandell rely consist of the purchase order on the Lustro form signed by Rubin stating the quantity ordered as 30,000 hoops with a description, the size and the price of the hoops listed and the letter of August 25th from Rubin to Consolidated requesting the entry of a similar order for an additional 60,000 hoops at a fixed price: "As per our phone conversation of today." This letter closes with the significant sentence that: "It is our understanding that these [the second order for 60,000 hoops] will be produced upon completion of the present order for 30,000 hoops."

Consolidated-Lustro's objection to the memoranda in question is that by employment of the word "order" rather than "contract" or "agreement", the validity of such memoranda depended upon acceptance thereof by Consolidated-Lustro and could not be "in confirmation of the contract[s]" as required by Section 2–201(2). We believe, however, that the letter of August 25th sufficiently complies with Section 2–201(2) to remove both oral contracts from the statute of frauds. The word "order" as employed in this letter obviously contemplated a binding agreement, at least, on the part of the sender, and, in all reason, should have been interpreted in that manner by the recipient. The sender in stating that "It is our understanding that these will be produced upon completion of the present order for 30,000 hoops," was referring to the initial order as an accomplished fact, not as an offer depending upon acceptance for its validity. Any doubt that may exist as to the sender's use of the word "order" is clearly dispelled by its use in the communication confirming a third contract.[3] This letter of August 28th, 1958, states: "Pursuant to our phone conversation of yesterday, *you may enter our order* for the following [number, description and price]. . . . *This order is to be entered* based upon our phone conversation, in which you *agreed* to ship us your entire production of this Hoop material at the above price . . .." (Emphasis supplied.) The letter of August 25th was a sufficient confirmation in writing of the two alleged oral contracts, and, in the absence of a denial or rejection on the part of the recipient within ten days, satisfied the requirements of Section 2–201(2) of the Uniform Commercial Code.

Under the statute of frauds as revised in the Code "All that is required is that the writing afford a basis for believing that the offered oral evidence rests on a real transaction."[4] Its object is the elimination of certain formalistic requirements adherence to which often resulted in injustice, rather than the prevention of fraud. The present memoranda fulfill the requirement of affording a belief that the oral contracts rested on a real transaction and the court below erred in holding otherwise. Nor are Consolidated-Lustro harmed by

---

3. As to this alleged oral contract, the court below held Consolidated-Lustro's defense of the statute of frauds provision was without merit.

4. See "Uniform Commercial Code Comment" under "Purpose of Changes 1", 12A P.S. § 2–201.

such a determination since Rubin-Arandell must still sustain the burden of persuading the trier of fact that the contracts were in fact made orally prior to the written confirmation.[5] . . .

The order of the court below, as modified, is affirmed and the record remanded for proceedings consistent with this opinion.

NOTES

(1) *Question.* What result if the letter had read: "As per our telephone conversation of today we are pleased to offer . . . "? See Alice v. Robett Manufacturing Co., 328 F.Supp. 1377 (N.D.Ga.1970), aff'd per curiam, 445 F.2d 316 (5th Cir. 1971).

(2) *UCC 2–201(2) and UCC 2–207(2).* Compare the rule as to merchants in UCC 2–201(2) with that in UCC 2–207(2). Comment 3 to UCC 2–201 explains that the only effect of the former "is to take away from the party who fails to answer the defense of the Statute of Frauds; the burden of persuading the trier of fact that a contract was in fact made orally prior to the written confirmation is unaffected. Compare the effect of failure to reply under Section 2–207." [a] Reconsider the advice that you gave in response to Note 3, p. 200 supra.

(3) *Multiple Application of the Statute.* Where more than one provision of the statute of frauds applies to a contract, all the applicable provisions must be satisfied if the contract is to be enforceable. So, for example, if the contract is one for the sale of goods which cannot be performed within one year, both the sale of goods and the one year provisions must be satisfied. As a result, acceptance and receipt of part of the goods or part payment will not make the contract enforceable because these do not satisfy the one year provision.

(4) *Oral Rescission and Modification.* Generally, a written contract that comes within the statute of frauds may be completely rescinded or abrogated orally. E. g., ABC Outdoor Advertising v. Dolhun's Marine, 38 Wis.2d 457, 157 N.W.2d 680 (1968). But in the case of a modification or variation, the statute of frauds must be satisfied if the contract as modified comes within its provisions. Where the contract as modified is not within the statute, however, even though the original contract was, an oral modification has been held effective. See Restatement Second, §§ 222, 223. The Code rule is set out in UCC 2–209(3).

---

5. Appellees also argue that parties not named in the communications cannot be bound. Oral testimony to establish that the addressee of the letter was an agent of the unnamed appellees is admissible and does not violate the Statute of Frauds. See Penn Discount Corp. v. Sharp, 125 Pa.Super. 171, 189 A. 749.

a. Of UCC 2–201(2) Professor Williston wrote, "This provision, though entirely novel, would be desirable if it were not for the permission of extreme inaccuracy in the memorandum. . . . Furthermore, the provision, if accept-

able between merchants, should be applied also where only one party or neither party is a merchant." Williston, The Law of Sales in the Proposed Uniform Commercial Code, 63 Harv.L.Rev. 561, 575 (1950). Do you agree? Consider, in this connection, the following quotation: "The advice of Wm. Randolph Hearst, 'Throw [it] in the wastebasket. Every letter answers itself in a couple of weeks.' Koenigsberg, King News, 273 (1941), is not a safe legal principle." Gateway Co. v. Charlotte Theatres, 297 F. 2d 483, 486 (5th Cir. 1961).

SECTION 3. ALTERNATIVES TO EXPECTATION

What alternatives are open to the injured party who has already done something in performance of, or at least in preparation for, an agreement that later turns out to be unenforceable because of the statute of frauds? Can he have a recovery based on his restitution interest, or perhaps even his reliance interest, although he is barred from a recovery based on his expectation interest? Many cases recognize the right of such a plaintiff to recover the reasonable value of his performance, to the extent that it has benefitted the defendant, and evidence of the unenforceable oral agreement is admissible on the question of the value of the plaintiff's performance.[a] See Restatement, § 355; Restatement, Restitution, § 108(d). Cf. Campbell v. Tennessee Valley Authority, 421 F.2d 293 (5th Cir. 1969).[b]

Where, however, there has been only reliance, without benefit, courts have generally denied relief. As the court put it in the leading case of Boone v. Coe, 153 Ky. 233, 154 S.W. 900 (1913), "Having received no benefit, no obligation to pay is implied." The following cases explore this proposition.

MONARCO v. LO GRECO, 35 Cal.2d 621, 220 P.2d 737 (1950). [In 1926 Natale and Carmela Castiglia promised Christie Lo Greco, Carmela's son by a former marriage, that if he would abandon his plans to leave home and would stay on the farm which they had acquired a few years before for $4,000, he would have the farm when they died. Christie worked for 20 years for room and board and spending money, and the value of the farm rose to $100,000. But Natale, shortly before his death, secretly changed his will to leave his interest to his grandson, Carmen Monarco. Monarco sought a partition of the property and an accounting, claiming that the 1926 agree-

a. The California statute (p. 422 supra) is typical of those of many states in including a special provision on brokerage contracts. How would the reasonable value of the broker's services to his principal, if he were allowed to recover in restitution, differ from the amount provided in the unenforceable contract? On the assumption that it would differ little if at all, it is usually held that the broker cannot recover in restitution, because to allow him to do so would circumvent the statute. E. g., Baugh v. Darley, 112 Utah 1, 184 P.2d 335 (1947).

b. Is the plaintiff who is in default under an agreement unenforceable because of the statute of frauds entitled to restitution for his part performance from a defendant who is willing and able to perform? Certainly the plaintiff in default under an unenforceable agreement should be put in no *worse* position than the plaintiff in default under an enforceable agreement. (The latter's rights will be explored in Chapter 7.) The question is whether he should be put in a *better* position. The prevailing view is that he should not, and that the contract may be set up as a defense. See 2 Corbin, § 332.

ment was unenforceable under the California statute of frauds as one "not to be performed during the lifetime of the promisor" (see p. 422 supra). From an adverse judgment, Monarco appealed.]

TRAYNOR, JUSTICE. . . . The doctrine of estoppel to assert the statute of frauds has been consistently applied by the courts of this state to prevent fraud that would result from refusal to enforce oral contracts in certain circumstances. Such fraud may inhere in the unconscionable injury that would result from denying enforcement of the contract after one party has been induced by the other seriously to change his position in reliance on the contract. . . . or in the unjust enrichment that would result if a party who has received the benefits of the other's performance were allowed to rely upon the statute. . . . In this case both elements are present. In reliance on Natale's repeated assurances that he would receive the property when Natale and Carmela died, Christie gave up any opportunity to accumulate property of his own and devoted his life to making the family venture a success. . . . Christie forebore from demanding any present interest in the venture in exchange for his labors on the assurance that Natale's and Carmela's interest would pass to him on their death. . . . On the other hand, Natale reaped the benefits of the contract. He and his devisees would be unjustly enriched if the statute of frauds could be invoked to relieve him from performance of his own obligations thereunder.

It is contended, however, that an estoppel to plead the statute of frauds can only arise when there have been representations with respect to the requirements of the statute indicating that a writing is not necessary or will be executed or that the statute will not be relied upon as a defense. . . . Those cases, however, that have refused to find an estoppel have been cases where the court found either that no unconscionable injury would result from refusing to enforce the oral contract, . . . or that the remedy of quantum meruit for services rendered was adequate. . . . In those cases, however, where either an unconscionable injury or unjust enrichment would result from refusal to enforce the contract, the doctrine of estoppel has been applied whether or not plaintiff relied upon representations going to the requirements of the statute itself. . . . In reality it is not the representation that the contract will be put in writing or that the statute will not be invoked, but the promise that the contract will be performed that a party relies upon when he changes his position because of it. It is settled that neither the remedy of an action at law for damages for breach of contract nor the quasi-contractual remedy for the value of services rendered is adequate for the breach of a contract to leave property by will in exchange for services of a peculiar nature involving the assumption or continuation of a close family relationship. . . .

[Affirmed.]

NOTE

Estoppel by Performance. Does estoppel "swallow up" the doctrine of part performance as applied to contracts for the sale of land (p. 432 supra) and of full performance on one side as applied to contracts not to be performed within one year (Note 3, p. 431 supra)? See McIntosh v. Murphy, 52 Haw. 29, 469 P.2d 177 (1970), in which the court relied on Monarco v. Lo Greco to permit an automobile sales manager to enforce an oral one-year employment contract after he had moved 2,200 miles from Los Angeles to Honolulu and worked for two and a half months. Monarco v. Lo Greco is discussed, approvingly, in Traynor, Unjustifiable Reliance, 42 Minn.L.Rev. 11, 18 (1957). See Notes, 66 Mich.L.Rev. 170 (1967); 53 Calif.L.Rev. 590 (1965).

OZIER v. HAINES, 411 Ill. 160, 103 N.E.2d 485 (1952). [Ozier, who ran a grain elevator, sued Haines, alleging that Haines had orally sold Ozier 5,000 bushels of corn at $1.24 a bushel, and that relying on this Ozier had immediately resold the corn over the telephone to a broker while Haines was still in Ozier's office. Ozier also alleged that it was the custom of the grain trade to buy and sell on oral contracts. He claimed $4,450, the difference between the price which he had to pay for the corn on the open market and the contract price. The complaint was dismissed on the ground that the contract was unenforceable under the statute of frauds, and the plaintiff appealed.]

DAILEY, CHIEF JUSTICE. . . . [One of the elements of equitable estoppel is:] "Words or conduct by the party against whom the estoppel is alleged amounting to a misrepresentation or concealment of material facts. . . ." [Ozier's] position is that the promisee's reliance upon an unenforcible promise will validate the promise. To adopt such a view would render the Statute of Frauds useless and unmeaning. It is true that harsh results, or moral fraud as plaintiffs choose to term it, may occur where one has changed his position in reliance on the oral promise of another, but it is a result which is invited and risked when the agreement is not reduced to writing in the manner prescribed by law. The present case is a patent example, for although the parties were in each other's presence and in a business office, no attempt was made to reduce their agreement to the simplest writing . . . . [Furthermore,] the customs pleaded could not render nugatory the provision of the Statute of Frauds. . . .

[Affirmed.]

NOTE

The Case of the Free Legal Advice. Ann sued Paul, alleging that when they were divorced in 1957, after twenty years of marriage and three children, the property settlement incorporated into the decree provided that Paul would pay Ann $900 a month until 1967, payments to cease in the event of her remarriage. In 1958 Ann had an offer of remarriage, but told Paul that she would not accept it unless he would continue to pay her at least part of the monthly sums. Paul then orally agreed to a compromise under which he would continue to make monthly payments in a reduced amount after her remarriage until 1967. When Ann asked if she would need a lawyer and if the agreement should be put on paper, Paul, himself a lawyer, told her that she did not need the advice of an independent counsel, and promised her that he would confirm their agreement in writing. Ann then remarried. After a few payments under the oral agreement, which was never confirmed in writing, Paul defaulted and Ann sued, also alleging that Paul's promise to confirm by letter was made with no intention of carrying it out, but only to induce Ann to act on his promise to her detriment. The trial court granted Paul's motion to dismiss the complaint under the one-year provision of the statute of frauds and Ann appealed. *Held:* Reversed. The Supreme Court of Illinois, citing Ozier v. Haines, agreed with Paul that, "The moral wrong alone of refusing to be bound by an agreement because it fails to comply with the statute does not suffice to estop a defendant from asserting the statute as a defense." But it concluded that, "According to the facts charged in the present complaint and the reasonable inferences therefrom, the plaintiff's failure to have the agreement put in writing was induced by defendant's intentionally misleading advice and promises. . . .   If, contrary, to his representations, he can now interpose the Statute of Frauds and thereby render the agreement void and unenforcible, the effect will be the accomplishment of a virtual fraud." Loeb v. Gendel, 23 Ill.2d 502, 179 N.E.2d 7 (1961).

How would the Supreme Court of Illinois have decided Monarco v. Lo Greco?

Chapter 5

REMEDIES FOR BREACH

SECTION 1. FUNDAMENTAL ASSUMPTIONS

(a) Compulsion or Relief?

What objectives underlie our law of remedies for breach of contract? Llewellyn concluded "that the real major effect of law will be found not so much in the cases in which law officials actually intervene, nor yet in those in which such intervention is consciously contemplated as a possibility, but rather in contributing to, strengthening, stiffening attitudes toward performance as what is to be expected and what 'is done'. If the contract-dodger *cannot* be bothered, if all he needs is a rhinoceros hide to thumb his nose at his creditor with impunity, more and more men will become contract-dodgers. Only saps will work, in an economy of indirect, non-face-to-face contacts. And as between individual enterprises, the competition of the contract-dodger will drive the contract-keeper into lowering his own standards of performance, on pain of destruction. This work of the law machine at the margin, in helping keep the level of social practice and expectation up to where it is, as against slow canker, is probably the most vital single aspect of contract law. For in this aspect each hospital case is a case with significance for the hundreds of thousands of normal cases." Llewellyn, What Price Contract?—An Essay in Perspective, 40 Yale L.J. 704, 725 n. 47 (1931).

Nevertheless, our law of remedies, like that of most of the rest of the world, is not directed at *compulsion* of *promisors* to *prevent* breach, but at *relief* to *promisees* to *redress* breach. Breach of contract is nowhere a crime and is not, with rare exceptions, a basis for the award of punitive damages.

Not all legal systems are as tolerant of breach of contract. In the communist countries, where the contracts of state enterprises are designed to carry out an economic plan and the aggrieved party ordinarily does not have alternative sources of supply or demand, penalties for breach of contract are common. Professor Berman says this of the Soviet system:

"Although under the Soviet legal system the money payable by the defaulting party goes to the other party, and not to the state (ex-

452

cept where both parties have violated the law), the power to use money received for breach of contract is limited; while it forms part of the enterprise's circulating capital, it does not necessarily serve to enable the enterprise to perform the same kinds of operations that were contemplated in the contract. Indeed, the main reason contract penalties are paid to the other party rather than to the state seems to be to give the other party an incentive to sue and thus to expose defects in planning, violations of contract discipline, and the like. In recent years, however, there has been an increasing emphasis upon the compensatory functions of contract remedies in planned economies. Under Soviet law—at least since 1959—the defaulting party in a contract of delivery may be required to compensate for losses (including lost profits) incurred as a result of the breach. It would appear, however, that it is extremely difficult in the Soviet planned economy to measure losses (and especially lost profits) resulting from breach of contracts of delivery." Berman, Protection of Rights Arising Out of Economic Contracts Under Socialist Legal Systems: A Comparative Approach, 14 Osteuropa-Recht 213, 217 (1968).

The limitations on the use of the money recovered tend to diminish the incentive to invoke these sanctions and lead to informal settlements. However, higher planning agencies may have an interest in preventing such informal settlements since suits for breach of contract have the advantage, from the planner's point of view, of exposing defects in the implementation of the plan. See also Loeber, Plan and Contract Performance in Soviet Society in La Fave (ed.), Law in the Soviet Society 128, 169–72 (1965).

In sharp contrast, our courts not only shun penalties but purport to be blind to fault. Innocent and aggravated breaches are traditionally treated alike, for as Holmes said, "If a contract is broken the measure of damages generally is the same, whatever the cause of the breach." Globe Refining Co. v. Landa Cotton Oil Co., 190 U.S. 540, 544 (1903). We shall have the occasion, in the pages that follow, to see whether even men of judicial temperament are immune from the temptation to depart from a rule so oblivious to blame. In its essential design, however, our law of remedies for breach of contract is directed at relief rather than compulsion.

NOTES

(1) *The Case of the Sexagenarian Swinger.* Mrs. Syester, a widow in her sixties who worked in Des Moines as a "coffee girl," went to an Arthur Murray Dance Studio because of a gift from a friend. As the result of an "astoundingly successful selling campaign" in which the manager promised her that she "would be a professional dancer," she was sold over 4,000 hours of instruction (including three lifetime memberships), of which she used about 3,100 at a cost of nearly $30,000. She became dissatisfied when her 25 year-old instructor was dismissed, quit and, after protracted negotiations, sued the studio for fraud and misrepresentation. From a judgment on a jury verdict of $14,300 actual damages and $40,000 punitive dam-

ages, the defendant appealed. *Held:* Affirmed. There was sufficient "malice" to support an award of punitive damages. "The jury award of $40,000 was large. However, the evidence of greed and avariciousness on the part of defendants is shocking to our sense of justice as it obviously was to the jury. The allowance of exemplary damages is wholly within the discretion of the jury where there is a legal basis for the allowance of such damages." Syester v. Banta, 257 Iowa 613, 133 N.W.2d 666 (1965).[a] How did Mrs. Syester's claim differ from one for "malicious" breach of contract? Is the "malicious" making of promises more culpable than the "malicious" breaking of promises?

Would the defendant's conduct have been criminal under an Iowa statute, enacted in 1965, which makes it a misdemeanor, punishable by a fine of up to $100 and imprisonment for up to 30 days, for anyone conducting a course of instruction for profit to "Falsely advertise or represent to any person any matter material to such course of instruction" or "to sell more than one lifetime contract to any one person." Iowa Code Ann. §§ 713A.1, 713A.4.

(2) *California Statute.* Under a statute enacted in California in 1965: "Any person who receives money for the purpose of obtaining or paying for services, labor, materials or equipment and willfully fails to apply such money for such purpose by either willfully failing to complete the improvements for which funds were provided or willfully failing to pay for services, labor, materials or equipment provided incident to such construction, and wrongfully diverts the funds to a use other than that for which the funds were received, shall be guilty of a public offense [punishable by imprisonment for up to five years and a fine of up to $5,000]." Cal.Penal Code § 484b. Does this statute make breach of contract a crime? It has been held not to violate the state constitutional prohibition against imprisonment for debt except in cases of fraud. People v. William Howard, 70 Cal.2d 618, 451 P.2d 401 (1969).

(b) Restitution, Reliance or Expectation?

As "bargain" is commonly the talisman of enforceability in our law on contract, "benefit of the bargain" is ordinarily the measure of enforcement. In general the disappointed promisee is entitled to relief based on his *expectation* interest, as measured by the net gain that he would have enjoyed had the promise been performed, rather than on his *reliance* or *restitution* interest. See pp. 3–4 supra. Where, as we have seen, a claim is not founded on bargain, recovery may be more limited. For examples of recovery limited to the reliance interest, see Goodman v. Dicker, p. 171 supra, and Hoffman v. Red Owl Stores, p. 173 supra. For examples of recovery limited to

---

a. The report of this case should be consulted for its full flavor, including, for example, a reference to the revised edition of the studio's "Eight Good Rules For Interviewing" with a part on "How to prevent a prospect from consulting his banker, lawyer, wife or friend."

the restitution interest, see Callano v. Oakwood Park Homes Corp., p. 33 supra and Cotnam v. Wisdom, p. 36 supra. But where a claim is founded on bargain, recovery measured by the more generous expectation interest is generally allowed. But cf. Heyer Products Co. v. United States, p. 153 supra.

The choice of expectation interest was not inevitable. In Flureau v. Thornhill, 2 Bl.W. 1078, 96 Eng.Rep. 635 (K.B.1776), the court chose to protect the promisee's reliance interest instead. That case announced the rule that recovery against a vendor who promised to convey land, but is unable without any bad faith to give a good title, is limited to the expense incurred by the purchaser in reliance on the promise, including any down payment. As DeGrey, C. J., stated, "I do not think that the purchaser can be entitled to any damages for the fancied goodness of the bargain, which he supposes he has lost." But the subsequent development of the law of damages did not follow this course. Although the rule has persisted in England as to contracts for the sale of land and has found its way into the law of a number of states, the tendency even in these jurisdictions has been to restrict its application. See 5 Corbin, § 1098. The dominant theme, then, is one of relief based on expectation.

NOTE

The Case of the Missing Masterpiece. In 1932 the Menzels bought a painting by Marc Chagall in Brussels for about $150. When the Germans invaded Belgium in 1940, the Menzels fled, leaving the Chagall in their apartment. When they returned six years later, the Chagall was gone, and a receipt by the German authorities had been left in its place. In 1955, the Perls, who ran an art gallery in New York bought the Chagall from a Paris art gallery for $2,800, unaware of its history and relying on the reputation of the Paris gallery as to title. Later that year, the Perls sold it to List for $4,000. In 1962, Mrs. Menzel noticed a reproduction of the missing Chagall in an art book, together with List's name, and demanded its return. When List refused, she sued him for replevin, and he impleaded the Perls, claiming liability for breach of an implied warranty of title. Mrs. Menzel had judgment against List, who returned the Chagall to her. List had judgment against the Perls for $22,500, the value of the Chagall at the time of the trial. The Perls appealed and the Appellate Division reduced the judgment to $4,000, the amount List had paid. List appealed to the Court of Appeals. *Held*: Order of the Appellate Division reversed and judgment of the trial court reinstated. "The Perls support their position by reference to the damages recoverable for the breach of the warranty of quiet possession as to real property. However this rule has been severely criticized by [Williston who characterizes it as] '. . . a violation of general principles of contracts to deny him in an action on the contract such damages *as will put him in as good a position as he would have occupied had the contract been kept.*' . . . Clearly, List can only be put in the same position he would have occupied if the contract had been kept by the Perls if he recovers the value of the painting at the time when . . . he was required to surrender the painting . . . ." Menzel v. List, 24 N.Y.2d 91, 246 N.E.2d 742 (1969).

(c) Specific or Substitutional Relief?

FARNSWORTH, LEGAL REMEDIES FOR BREACH OF CON-
TRACT, 70 Colum.L.Rev. 1145, 1149–56 (1970).[a] The relief available to the promisee is of two main kinds. It is said to be "specific"
when it is intended to secure for the promisee the very benefit
that he was promised, as where the court confers the promised
benefit on the injured party or orders the defaulting promisor to
do so. It is said to be "substitutional" when it is intended to provide him with something in substitution for that benefit, as where
the court awards the injured party money damages.[1]

Although damages will, in some cases, permit the injured party
to arrange an adequate substitute for the expected benefit, specific
relief is clearly the form better suited to the objective of putting the
promisee in the position in which he would have been had the promise
been performed. Of course the passage of time may reduce the effectiveness even of specific relief. The benefit will at best usually be delayed since contract remedies are ordinarily not available until after
breach has occurred.[2] And there are some situations in which specific relief is simply not possible at all. For example, the promise may
have been one to deliver particular goods which turn out to be defective, or to have been destroyed, or to have been sold to a third person.
But there remain many instances in which specific relief will be both
timely and feasible. They can be put into two broad categories.

In one category of cases, specific relief does not require the cooperation of the defaulting promisor. If the promise is to deliver

a. Reprinted by permission of the Columbia Law Review.

1. Substitutional redress need not be
limited to money, but may be in kind.
Isaac Schapera tells of a case among
the Tswana in which a man who broke
his promise to deliver a cow to another was obliged to deliver four
cows, one in substitution for the cow
he should have given and three in
substitution for its offspring. Schapera, Contract in Tswana Case Law,
9 J. African L. 142, 148 (1965). Charles
Wright notes the incidence of this in
everyday dealing—"If I lose the ski
poles I have borrowed from a friend,
I buy a new pair and return them to
him"—and suggests that legal sanctions of this sort might be considered.
Wright, The Law of Remedies as a
Social Institution, 18 U.Det.L.J. 376,
378 (1955). In a society with a market
economy, however, the tendency is to
assume that the injured party can
procure a substitute himself and need
only be compensated for the expense
involved. In French law, for example,
if the promisor fails to perform his
duty to do work, as where a landlord
fails to repair the leased premises, the
court may authorize the promisee to
have it done at the promisor's expense. P. Herzog, Civil Procedure in
France 557 (1967). Cf. the buyer's
remedy of "cover" under UCC 2–712
. . . .

2. In the exceptional case where a
party repudiates his obligation in advance of the time for performance,
specific relief might be given without
delay. And where a declaratory judgment is granted before the time for
performance, it at least reinforces the
extra-legal compulsions to perform,
although it adds no legal compulsion.

goods, an officer of the court may seize and deliver them; if it is to convey land, he may execute a binding conveyance; if it is to pay money, he may seize and sell enough of the promisor's assets to yield the required sum. In this category the practical impediments to specific relief are at a minimum. In the other category of cases, however, specific relief does require the cooperation of the promisor. Consider, for example, a promise to act in a play, to paint a house, or to build a building. To assure specific relief in each of these cases some form of coercion may be needed, so that the practical impediments are substantial.

The civil law systems, i. e., those descended from Roman law, have by and large proceeded on the premise that specific redress should be ordered whenever possible, not only for cases in the first category, but even for those in the second category as well, unless the disadvantages of the remedy outweigh its advantages. As Dawson has said of the German law,

> The main reservations are for cases where specific relief is impossible, would involve disproportionate cost, would introduce compulsion into close personal relationships or compel the expression of special forms of artistic or intellectual creativity. Presumably German courts, like French courts and our own, would not affirmatively order painters to paint pictures or singers to sing.[3]

The logic of the civil law is reenforced by practical considerations in communist countries that lack markets on which aggrieved parties can arrange substitute transactions. The task of manufacture imposed on a state enterprise by a government plan, for example, can only be accomplished if the enterprise receives the specific raw materials that it has been promised for production; money damages are not an adequate substitute.

The common law countries escape both the civil law's doctrinal logic and communism's practical need for compulsion. The early common law courts did know specific relief, for many of the first suits after the Norman Conquest were proprietary in nature, designed to regain something of which the plaintiff had been deprived. Even the action of debt was of this character, since it was based on the notion of an unjust detention of something belonging to the plaintiff. But it became the practice in these actions to allow money damages for the detention in addition to specific relief, and with the development of new forms of action, such as assumpsit, that were in no way proprietary, substitutional relief became the usual form.

The typical judgment at common law declared that the plaintiff recover from the defendant a sum of money, which in effect imposed

3. Dawson, Specific Performance in France and Germany, 57 Mich.L.Rev. 495, 530 (1959).

on him a new obligation as redress for the breach of the old. The new obligation required no cooperation on his part for its enforcement since, if the sum was not paid, a writ of execution would issue empowering the sheriff to seize and sell so much of the defendant's property as was required to pay the plaintiff. The proprietary actions remained, so that there were a few instances where relief at common law was specific; for example, in an action by a buyer for replevin of goods sold to him but not delivered, the sheriff might first seize them from the seller and turn them over to the buyer, and the judgment would then declare that the buyer was entitled to them. And, of course, where the claim was to a sum of money that the defendant had promised to pay, the effect, as in the original action for debt, was to give the promisee specific relief; for example, in an action by the seller for the price of goods delivered but not paid for, judgment would be given against the buyer for the full amount of the price. But these instances were the exception rather than the rule, and even where the common law courts granted specific redress, they were unwilling to exert pressure directly on the defendant to compel him to perform. The judgment itself was seen as a mere declaration of rights as between the parties, and the process for its execution was directed not at the defendant but at the sheriff, ordering him to put the plaintiff in possession of real or personal property or to seize the defendant's property and sell such of it as was necessary to satisfy a money judgment.

The enforcement of promises in equity developed along very different lines. Prior to the development of assumpsit by the common law courts in the sixteenth century, most of the cases brought before the chancellor were based on promises that would not have been enforceable at common law, and the question was whether they would nevertheless be enforced in equity. After the development of assumpsit, equity accepted the test for enforcement that had been developed by the rival common law courts, and refused to enforce simple promises made without "consideration." To this extent its jurisdiction in contract became concurrent with that of the common law courts, and its concern shifted from the enforceability of the promise to the nature of its enforcement.

Under the influence of the canon law (for the early chancellors were usually clerics), decrees in equity came to take the form of a personal command to the defendant to do or not to do something. His cooperation was assumed, and if he disobeyed he could be punished not only for criminal contempt, at the instance of the court, but also for civil contempt, at the instance of the plaintiff. This put into the plaintiff's hands the extreme sanction of imprisonment, which might be supplemented by fines payable to the plaintiff and sequestration of the defendant's goods.[4] So it was said that equity acted *in*

---

4. The development of these supplementary sanctions is traced in C. A.   Huston, The Enforcement of Decrees in Equity 76–83 (1915) . . . .

personam, against the person of the defendant, while the law acted *in rem,* against his property. But it did not follow that the chancellor stood ready to order every defaulting promisor to perform his promise. Equitable relief was confined to special cases in light of both practical and historical limitations.

The practical limitations grew out of the problems inherent in coercion. Our courts, like those of civil law countries, will not undertake to coerce a performance that is personal in nature—to compel an artist to paint a picture or a singer to sing a song. (They have, to be sure, been ingenious in framing orders enjoining contracted parties from acting inconsistently with their promises as a substitute for orders directing them to perform them—the court that will not order the singer to sing may enjoin him from singing elsewhere.)[5] Our courts have also been reluctant to order specific performance where difficulties of supervision or enforcement are foreseen, e. g., to order a building contractor specifically to perform his contract to repair a house. It has been suggested that "in their origins these ideas carried a load of snobbery, expressed in distaste for menial tasks—'how can a Master judge of repairs in husbandry?' "[6] Today they are more often justified as a means of avoiding conflict and unfairness where no clear standards can be framed in advance. The practical exigencies of drafting decrees to guide future conduct under threat of contempt have also moved courts to require that contract terms be expressed with somewhat greater certainty if specific performance is to be granted than if damages are to be awarded. But these practical limitations are on the whole far less significant than the historical ones.

The most important of the historical limitations derives from the circumstance that, since the chancellor had first granted equitable relief in order to supply the deficiencies of the common law, equitable remedies were readily characterized as "extraordinary." When, during the long jurisdictional struggle between the two systems of courts, some means of accommodation were needed, an "adequacy" test was

---

Huston notes the measures required "to coerce obedience from the stubborn seventeenth-century Englishman. Thus in 1598, after one Walter had been already subjected in vain to close imprisonment for some time, the court ordered him to perform within a fortnight 'which if he shall not do . . . then his Lordship mindeth without further delay not only to shut the defendant close prisoner but also to lay as many irons on him as he may bear.' " Id. at 79, citing Clerk v. Walter, Monro 718.

5. Lumley v. Wagner, 1 De G.M. & G. 618, 42 Eng.Rep. 687 (Ch.App.1852). A more extreme example is that of a suit for specific performance of a contract to run street cars to connect with the plaintiff's trains, in which the court enjoined the defendant from operating any cars unless it performed its contract. Prospect Park & Coney Island R. R. v. Coney Island & Brooklyn R. R., 144 N.Y. 152, 39 N.E. 17 (1894).

6. Dawson, supra note 3, at 537, quoting from Rayner v. Stone, 2 Eden 128, 130, 28 Eng.Rep. 845, 846 (1762). . . .

developed to prevent encroachment by the chancellor on the powers of the common law judges. Equity would stay its hand if the remedy at law was "adequate." To this test was added the gloss that the money damages awarded by the common law courts were ordinarily "adequate"—a gloss encouraged by the philosophy of free enterprise, since in a market economy money ought to enable an aggrieved promisee to arrange a substitute transaction. As one writer put it:

> The law, concerning itself more and more with merchandise bought or sold for money, with things having a definite and calculable exchange value, came to conceive that the money compensation, which was an entirely adequate remedy in the common case, and in many cases the only possible one when once the wrong complained of had been committed, was [generally] the only remedy available for their use . . . .[7]

So it came to be that, in sharp contrast to the civil law approach, money damages were regarded as the norm and specific relief as the deviation, even where the law could easily have provided specific relief without any cooperation from the defaulting promisor.

Land, which the common law viewed with particular esteem, was singled out for special treatment. Each parcel, however ordinary, was considered to be "unique," and from this it followed that if a vendor defaulted on his promise to convey land, not even money would enable an injured purchaser to find a substitute. The remedy at law being in this sense "inadequate," a decree of specific performance would ordinarily issue.[8] Although the case for allowing the vendor to have specific performance when the purchaser defaulted was less compelling, equity also granted him relief. But no such reason applied to the contract for the sale of goods, for in a market economy it was supposed that, with rare exceptions for such "unique" items as heirlooms and objects of art, substantially similar goods were available elsewhere. Some attempts have been made to liberalize this restriction. The draftsmen of the Uniform Commercial Code state in its Comments that it introduces "a new concept of what are 'unique' goods," and they assert that "where the unavailability of a market price is caused by a scarcity of goods of the type involved, a good case is normally made for specific performance under this Article." But specific performance is still the exception, not the rule, and in contrast to the view held in socialist countries, it is to be justified on the basis of the peculiar needs of the aggrieved party and not the general welfare of society as a whole. Although a court, in determin-

---

7. C. A. Huston, supra note 4, at 74. Holmes, with some overstatement, wrote that "The duty to keep a contract at common law means a prediction that you must pay damages if you do not keep it—and nothing else." Holmes, The Path of the Law, 10 Harv.L.Rev. 457, 462 (1897).

8. E. g., Kitchen v. Herring, 42 N.C. 190 (1851) (principle in regard to land adopted, not because it was fertile or rich in minerals, or valuable for timber, but simply because it was land— a favorite and favored subject in England, and in every country of Anglo-Saxon origin).

ing the adequacy of an award of damages, may take account of such factors as the difficulty of their ascertainment (e. g., under a long-term "output" or "requirements" contract) and the improbability of their collection (e. g., against an insolvent defendant), the typical buyer of goods must still content himself with money as a substitute for the goods in the event of breach.

A second historical limitation, or group of limitations, is premised on the notion that equitable relief is "discretionary." Since the chancellor was to act according to "conscience" (a circumstance that prompted the famous charge that his conscience might vary with the length of his foot [9]), he might withhold relief where considerations of "fairness" or "morality" dictated. Some of the most renowned of these equitable restrictions are embodied in equity's colorful maxims: "he who seeks equity must do equity"; "he who comes into equity must come with clean hands"; and "equity aids the vigilant." One of the most troublesome is the now largely discredited "mutuality of remedy" rule, under which specific performance would not be granted to the aggrieved party unless it would have been available to the other party had the aggrieved party been the one in breach. It is one of the curious inconsistencies to arise out of the dual jurisdiction of law and equity that these restrictions operated to bar only equitable relief and did not prevent the award of damages at law.

The historical development of the parallel systems of law and equity may afford an adequate explanation of the reluctance of our courts to grant specific relief; it is scant justification for it. A more rational basis might be the severity of the sanctions available under the contempt power for their enforcement. In any event, the current trend is clearly in favor of the extension of specific relief. The fusion of law and equity into a single court system at least facilitates a major change in this direction, and commentators have urged such a change.

> Why not, as in both French and German law, give specific performance as to any physical object that can be found and is reachable by direct execution? It is true that whenever speed is a factor and markets reasonably organized, promisees will not often ask for it . . . . But why not leave this to the promisee's choice?[10]

Still, for the present, the promisee must ordinarily be content with money damages.

---

9. " 'Tis all one, as if they should make his foot the standard for the measure we call a Chancellor's foot; what an uncertain measure this would be! One Chancellor has a long foot, another a short foot, a third an indifferent foot; 'tis the same thing in the Chancellor's conscience." Selden, Table Talk, quoted in Gee v. Pritchard, 2 Swanst. 402, 414, 36 Eng.Rep. 670, 679, (Ch.1818).

10. Dawson, supra note 3, at 532. . . .

McCALLISTER v. PATTON

Supreme Court of Arkansas, 1948.
214 Ark. 293, 215 S.W.2d 701.

MILLWEE, JUSTICE.   A. J. McCallister was plaintiff in the chancery court in a suit for specific performance of an alleged contract for the sale and purchase of a new Ford automobile from the defendant, R. H. Patton.   The complaint alleges:

"That on or about the 15th day of September, 1945, the Plaintiff entered into a contract with the Defendant, whereby the Plaintiff contracted to purchase and the Defendant to sell, one Ford super deluxe tudor sedan and radio.

"That the Defendant is an automobile dealer and sells Ford automobiles and trucks within the city of Jonesboro, Craighead County, Arkansas and that at the time this Plaintiff entered into this contract the Defendant had no new Ford automobiles in stock of any kind and was engaged in taking orders by contract, numbering the contracts in the order that they were executed and delivered to him.   As the cars were received the Defendant would fill the orders as he had previously received the contracts.   The Plaintiff's number was number 37.

"As consideration and as part of the purchase price the Plaintiff paid to this Defendant the sum of $25.00 and at all times stood ready, able and willing to pay the balance upon the purchase price in accordance with the terms of the contract.   That a copy of this contract is hereto attached marked Exhibit 'A' and made a part of this Complaint, the original being held subject to the orders of this Court and the inspection of the interested parties.

"The Plaintiff is informed and verily believes and the Defendant has admitted to this Plaintiff that he has received more than 37 cars since the execution of this contract.   The Defendant refuses to sell an automobile of the above make and description to this Plaintiff.

"Since the execution of this contract and to the present date, new Ford automobiles have been hard to obtain and this Plaintiff is unable to purchase an automobile at any other place or upon the open market of the description named in this contract and there is not an adequate remedy at law and the Court should direct specific performance of this contract."

The prayer of the complaint was that the defendant be ordered to sell the automobile to plaintiff in compliance with the contract, and for all other proper relief.   Under the terms of the "New Car Order" attached to the complaint as Exhibit "A," delivery of the car was to be made "as soon as possible out of current or future production" at defendant's regularly established price.   Plaintiff was not required to trade in a used car but might do so, if the price of such car could be agreed upon and, if not, plaintiff was entitled to cancel the order and to the return of his deposit. The deposit of $25 was to be held in trust for the plaintiff and returned to him at his option on surrender of his rights under the agreement. There was no provision for forfeiture of the deposit in the event plaintiff refused to accept delivery of the car.

Defendant demurred to the complaint on the grounds that it did not state facts sufficient to entitle plaintiff to the relief of specific performance, and that the alleged contract was lacking in mutuality of obligation and certainty of subject matter. There were further allegations in the demurrer constituting an answer to the effect that plaintiff was engaged in the sale of used cars and had contracted to resell whatever vehicle he obtained from the defendant; and that upon being so informed, defendant tendered and plaintiff refused to accept return of the $25 deposit. Plaintiff filed a motion to strike this part of the pleading.

The chancellor sustained the demurrer to the complaint and overruled the motion to strike. The plaintiff refused to plead further and his complaint was dismissed. This appeal follows.

In testing the correctness of the trial court's ruling in sustaining the demurrer we first determine whether the allegations of the complaint are sufficient to bring plaintiff within the rule that equity will not grant specific performance of a contract for the sale of personal property if damages in an action at law afford a complete and adequate remedy. Our cases on the question are in harmony with the rule recognized generally that, while equity will not ordinarily decree specific performance of a contract for the sale of chattels, it will do so where special and peculiar reasons exist such as render it impossible for the injured party to obtain adequate relief by way of damages in an action at law. In Cooper v. Roland, 95 Ark. 569, 130 S.W. 559, 560, the general rule and various exceptions thereto are discussed. It was there held that the trial court properly sustained a demurrer to a complaint in a suit for specific performance of a contract for the sale of county scrip notwithstanding an allegation that the scrip had no stable market value. Chief Justice McCulloch said in the opinion:

"The general rule, subject to some exceptions, undoubtedly is that courts of equity will not enforce specific performance of executory contracts for the sale of chattels, and this court has announced its adherence to that general rule. Collins v. Karatopsky, 36 Ark. 316. The rule established by the authorities is well stated in a note in volume 5 of American & English Annotated Cases, page 269: 'Courts of equity decree the specific performance of contracts, not upon any distinction between realty and personalty, but because damages at law may not, in the particular case, afford a plain, adequate and complete remedy. Therefore a court of equity will not, generally, decree performance of a contract in respect of personalty, not because of its personal nature, but because damages at law are as complete a remedy as the delivery of the property itself, inasmuch as with the damages like property may be purchased.' "

In Block v. Shaw, 78 Ark. 511, 95 S.W. 806, specific performance of an executory contract for the sale of cotton was denied on the ground that the purchaser had an adequate remedy at law in an action for damages for breach of the contract.

Among the various exceptions to the general rule are those cases involving contracts relating to personal property which has a peculiar, unique or sentimental value to the buyer not measurable in money damages. In Chamber of Commerce v. Barton, 195 Ark. 274, 112 S. W.2d 619, 625, this court held that the purchaser, Barton, was entitled to specific performance of a contract for the sale of Radio Station KTHS as an organized business. Justice Baker, speaking for the court, said:

"A judgment for a bit of lumber from which a picture frame might be made and also for a small lot of tube paint and a yard of canvas would not compensate one who had purchased a great painting.

"By the same token Barton would not be adequately compensated by a judgment for a bit of wire, a steel tower or two, more or less, as the mere instrumentalities of KTHS when he has purchased an organized business including these instrumentalities, worth perhaps not more than one-third of the purchase price. Moreover, he has also contracted for the good will of KTHS, which is so intangible as to be incapable of delivery or estimation of value. So the property is unique in character and, so far as the contract is capable of enforcement, the vendee is entitled to relief."

Exhaustive annotations involving many cases of specific performance of contracts for the sale of various types of personal property are found in L.R.A.1918E, 597 and 152 A.L.R. 4. Comparatively few cases involving suits for specific performance of contracts for the sale of new automobiles have reached the appellate courts. Plaintiff relies on the case of De Moss v. Conart Motor Sales, Inc., 72 N.E.2d 158, where an Ohio Common Pleas Court directed specific performance of a contract similar to the one under consideration on the ground that the purchaser was without an adequate remedy at law due to the fact that new automobiles were difficult to obtain.

A different result was reached in Kirsch v. Zubalsky, 139 N.J.Eq. 22, 49 A.2d 773, 775, where the court sustained defendant's motion to strike the bill of complaint for specific performance in which plaintiff alleged that he was unable to purchase an identical automobile elsewhere at regular O.P.A. price limitations because of the extreme scarcity of such cars and would be forced to pay an illegal bonus above O.P.A. regulations for any similar automobile available on the market. The court said: "The complainant mentions no characteristic which adds a special value to the automobile so as to put it in the category of an unique chattel; and he presents no facts which can be considered by this court as elements of value adding to the intrinsic worth of the automobile itself, so as to permit it to be classed as special or unique. While automobiles may be difficult to procure under the economic or industrial conditions of the present day, they are not in the category of unique chattels."

In Welch v. Chippewa Sales Co., 252 Wis. 166, 31 N.W.2d 170, 171, the plaintiff contended that the vehicle contracted for was invested with the quality of uniqueness due to a current shortage of automobiles and that a judgment for damages did not furnish an adequate remedy. In holding that the complaint did not state a cause of action for specific performance, the court cited Kirsch v. Zubalsky, supra, and said: "In spite of the failure of production fully to meet the demands of customers, automobiles, and indeed, the very make and type of automobile ordered by plaintiff in this case, are being produced by the thousands. There is no sentimental consideration worth while protecting that has to do with the particular make, color or style of automobile. Hence, the mere contention that plaintiff needs cars in his business is not impressive. . . ."

In the still more recent case of Poltorak v. Jackson Chevrolet Co., 322 Mass. 699, 79 N.E.2d 285, the plaintiff contracted for the purchase of a new passenger automobile and delivered to the dealer his automobile for which he was to be allowed a credit on the purchase price of a new car. It was held that plaintiff was not entitled to specific performance of the contract upon showing a scarcity of automobiles and in the absence of a showing of substantial harm of a character which could not be adequately compensated in an action at law for damages.

Efforts to obtain specific performance of similar contracts under Sec. 68 of the Uniform Sales Act, Act 428 of 1941, have been denied by the New York courts. This section provides that a court of equity may, "if it thinks fit," direct specific performance of a contract to deliver "specific or ascertained goods." In Kaliski v. Grole Motors, Inc., Sup., 69 N.Y.S.2d 645, the court held that a contract for the sale of a "New 1947 Studebaker two or four-door Champion automobile" was for the sale of an "unascertained" automobile and hence not specifically enforceable by the buyer. See also, Goodman v. Henry Caplan, Inc., 188 Misc. 242, 65 N.Y.S.2d 576; Cohen v. Rosenstock Motors, Inc., 188 Misc. 426, 65 N.Y.S.2d 481; Gellis v. Falcon Buick Co., Inc., 191 Misc. 566, 76 N.Y.S.2d 94.

Section 68 of the Uniform Sales Act, supra, follows Sec. 52 of the Sale of Goods Act of England. Some English courts, and a few courts of our own states which have adopted the uniform act, have construed this section as broadening the power of equity to grant relief by specific performance, while other courts in both countries have held that it merely recodified the law theretofore existing and did not give the remedy where it had not previously existed. Ann. 152 A.L.R.

45 et seq.; Williston on Sales, Rev.Ed., Vol. 3, Sec. 601. However, under all the decisions, a court of equity will not grant specific performance if a law action for damages affords an adequate remedy to the buyer.

Plaintiff says we will take judicial knowledge of the scarcity of new automobiles as a result of the recent world war. If so, we would also take judicial notice of the fact that large numbers of cars of the type mentioned in the alleged contract have been produced since 1945, and sold through both new and used car dealers in the open market. Although the complaint alleges inadequacy of the remedy at law, it does not set forth facts sufficient to demonstrate such conclusion. It is neither alleged nor contended that the car ordered has any special or peculiar qualities not commonly possessed by others of the same make so as to make it practically impossible to replace it in the market. While it is alleged that new Ford automobiles have been hard to obtain, no harm or inconvenience of a kind which could not be fully compensated by an award of damages in a law action is set forth in the complaint.

We conclude that the allegations of the complaint are insufficient to entitle plaintiff to equitable relief and that his remedy at law is adequate. The demurrer was, therefore, properly sustained. In view of this conclusion we do not find it necessary to examine the contention that lack of consideration and mutuality renders the contract specifically unenforceable.

The decree is affirmed.

NOTES

(1) *The Automobile Cases.* As the opinion indicates, McCallister v. Patton is typical of a number of cases that arose after the Second World War. In most of these the courts reached the same result as did the Arkansas court. But for a case allowing specific performance, see Heidner v. Hewitt Chevrolet Co., 166 Kan. 11, 199 P.2d 481 (1948). There the dealer had attempted to impose the additional requirement of a trade-in upon the buyer, and the trial court had found that "it was possible, but highly improbable, that plaintiff [buyer] could have bought in the open market, for cash alone, the type of automobile he [buyer] was willing to accept." Might the Arkansas court have allowed specific performance if additional facts had been alleged? What facts? Would UCC 2–716 have changed the result in the McCallister case?

(2) *The Case of the Cowboy's Lament.* Archie Sparrow, a cowboy, agreed to work on Chip Morris' cattle ranch for 16 weeks, in return for which Morris agreed to pay him $400 and give him a horse called Keno. When Sparrow went to work, Keno was practically unbroken, but during his spare time he trained him so that, with a little additional training, he would have been a first class roping horse. At the end of the 16 week term, Morris paid Sparrow the $400, but refused to give him the horse. Sparrow sued for specific performance. *Held:* For plaintiff. "Although it has been held that equity will not ordinarily enforce, by specific performance, a contract

for the sale of chattels, it will do so where special and peculiar reasons exist which render it impossible for the injured party to obtain relief by way of damages in an action at law. McCallister v. Patton, 214 Ark. 293, 215 S.W.2d 701. . . . Certainly when one has made a roping horse out of a green, unbroken pony, such a horse would have a peculiar and unique value; if Sparrow is entitled to prevail, he has a right to the horse instead of its market value in dollars and cents." Morris v. Sparrow, 225 Ark. 1019, 287 S.W.2d 583 (1956).

EASTERN ROLLING MILL CO. v. MICHLOVITZ

Supreme Court of Maryland, 1929.
157 Md. 51, 145 A. 378.

[Eastern Rolling Mill, a manufacturer of sheet steel agreed to sell to Michlovitz, a dealer in scrap, its entire accumulation of steel scrap, which was a by-product of its manufacture of sheet, for a period of five years. Michlovitz was to take delivery at Eastern's plant in Baltimore. The contract price was $3 per ton less than the prices quoted as the Philadelphia market in "Iron Age," a trade publication, at the beginning of every quarter. The deduction was to cover a freight rate which was a minimum of $2.27 a ton to Michlovitz' yards and to every market within the Philadelphia market area except for the Bethlehem Steel plant, together with overhead, transportation costs, and a net profit to Michlovitz. There was a chance that Bethlehem Steel might take the scrap from Michlovitz, which would have increased its profit because the freight rate to Bethlehem's plant was only 90 cents per ton. There was also the chance that if Bethlehem did not take the scrap Michlovitz' costs might have been so high that it would have sustained a loss. After less than a year of performance under the contract, during which time Bethlehem Steel did take the scrap and Michlovitz made a handsome profit, Eastern repudiated and Michlovitz sued for specific performance. From a decree in favor of Michlovitz, Eastern appealed.]

PARKE, J. . . . In the present case section 246 of article 16 of the Code [a] has no application, since the defendant's proof satisfactorily showed that the defendant has property from which the plaintiffs may recover any damages and costs which might be adjudged for a breach of the contracts, therefore, apart from statute, Code, art. 83, § 89 [Uniform Sales Act, § 68], the court, as a general rule, will

---

a. This section, which is now Md.Ann. Code art. 16, § 169 (1957), provides: "No court shall refuse to specifically enforce a contract on the mere ground that the party seeking its enforcement has an adequate remedy in damages, unless the party resisting its specific enforcement shall show to the court's satisfaction that he has property from which such damages may be made, or shall give bond, with approved security, in a penalty to be fixed by the court, to perform the contract or pay all such costs and damages as may, in any court of competent jurisdiction, be adjudged against him for breach or nonperformance of such contract."

refuse to decree specific performance in respect of chattels because damages are a sufficient remedy. This principle does not apply in all cases of chattels, so there are many exceptions to this rule, because, principally, of the inadequacy of the remedy at law in the particular case or of the special nature and value of the subject-matter of the contract. Passing by other illustrations of the exceptions to one more clearly in point, Pomeroy on Specific Performance (3d Ed.) § 15, puts it thus: "Again contracts for the delivery of goods will be specifically enforced, when by their terms the deliveries are to be made and the purchase price paid in installments running through a considerable number of years. Such contracts 'differ from those that are immediately to be executed.' Their profits depending upon future events cannot be estimated in present damages, which must, of necessity, be almost wholly conjectural. To compel a party to accept damages under such circumstances is to compel him to sell his possible profits at a price depending upon a mere guess." This statement of the law is supported by the Maryland decisions. . . .

Under the cases, the right to specific performance turns upon whether the plaintiffs can be properly compensated at law. The plaintiffs are entitled to compensatory damages, and, if an action at law cannot afford them adequate redress, equity will specifically enforce the contracts, which would not impose upon the court any difficulties in enforcement, as the subject-matter of the contracts is the accumulated scrap at the plant of the defendant. The defendant relied upon the case of Fothergill v. Rowland, L.R. 17 Eq. 132, but there the contract was one whose performance involved the working of a coal mine, which required personal skill, and this with its different facts distinguishes that case from the one at bar. The goods which the parties here had bargained for were not procurable in the neighborhood, and, moreover, they possessed a quality and concentrated weight which could not be secured anywhere within the extensive region covered by the "Philadelphia Market." In addition, the delivery of the scrap at Baltimore was one of the valuable incidents of the purchase. It follows that the right to these specific goods is a consideration of great importance, and this and the difficulty of securing scrap of the same commercial utility are factors making for the inadequacy of damages.

The scrap is not to be delivered according to specified tonnage, but as it accumulates, which in the past has been at the rate of one and two, and occasionally three, carloads of scrap a day, so the quantities vary from quarter to quarter. If the plant should cease to operate or suffer an interruption, there would be no scrap accumulating for delivery under the contracts, and its deliveries would end or be lessened. Neither are the prices for the scrap constant during the period of the contracts, but change from quarter to quarter according to the quotations of two specified materials on the Philadelphia market whose quarterly prices are accepted as the standards upon which the contract prices are quarterly computed. The contracts run to September 30, 1932. By what method would a jury determine the future quarterly tonnage, the quarterly contract price, and quarterly market price during these coming years? How could it possibly arrive at any fair ascertainment of damages? Any estimate would be speculative and conjectural, and not, therefore, compensatory. It follows that the defendant's breach of its contracts is not susceptible of fair and proper compensation by damages; and that to refuse to compel the defendant to do merely what it bound itself to do, and to remit the plaintiffs to their action at law, is to permit the defendant to relieve itself of the contracts and to force the plaintiffs to sell their profits at a conjectural price. To substitute damages by guess for due performance of contract could only be because "there's no equity stirring."

The equitable remedy of specific performance is indicated by the facts and circumstances; and would seem to be authorized by section 89 of article 83 of the Code [Uniform Sales Act, § 68], providing as follows:

"89. Where the seller has broken a contract to deliver *specific or ascertained goods*, a court having the powers of a court of equity may, if it thinks fit, on the application of the buyer, by its judgment or decree, direct that the contract shall be performed specifically without giving the seller the option of retaining the goods on payment of damages. The judgment or decree may be unconditional, or upon such terms and conditions as to damages, payment of the price and otherwise, as to the court may seem just."

[In the remainder of its opinion the court concluded that the scrap was "specific or ascertained goods."]

For the reasons given, the decree will be affirmed.

Decree affirmed, with costs.

NOTES

(1) *The Code.* What effect would UCC 2–716 have on the Michlovitz case? One obvious effect would be to relieve the court of the embarrassment caused by the words "specific or ascertained goods." Comments 1 and 2 to UCC 2–716 explain: "[W]ithout intending to impair in any way the exercise of the court's sound discretion in the matter, this Article seeks to further a more liberal attitude than some courts have shown in connection with the specific performance of contracts of sale. . . . In view of this Article's emphasis on the commercial feasibility of replacement, a new concept of what are 'unique' goods is introduced under this section. Specific performance is no longer limited to goods which are already specific or ascertained at the time of contracting. The test of uniqueness under this section must be made in terms of the total situation which characterizes the contract. Output and requirements contracts involving a particular or peculiarly available source or market present today the typical commercial specific performance situation, as contrasted with

contracts for the sale of heirlooms or priceless works of art which were usually involved in the older cases. However, uniqueness is not the sole basis of the remedy under this section for the relief may also be granted 'in other proper circumstances' and inability to cover is strong evidence of 'other proper circumstances.' "

(2) *The Case of the Slowdown in Steel.* Bliss, a general contractor, contracted to expand and modernize Phoenix Steel's plant, which was spread over a 60-acre site, for $27,500,000. Work did not progress as rapidly as contemplated in the contract, and Phoenix sought a court order of specific performance to compel Bliss to comply with the contract by putting on the job the 300 more workmen required to make up a full second shift during the period that one of the mills had to be shut down because of the work. *Held:* Specific performance denied. "It is not that a court of equity is without jurisdiction in a proper case to order the completion of an express- ly designed and largely completed construction contract, particularly where the undertaking is tied in with a contract for the sale of land and the construction in question is largely finished. . . . The point is that a court of equity should not order specific performance of any building con- tract in a situation in which it would be impractical to carry out such an order, . . . unless there are special circumstances or the public in- terest is directly involved. . . . I conclude that to grant specific per- formance . . . would be inappropriate in view of the imprecision of the contract provision relied upon and the impracticability if not impossibility of effective enforcement by the Court of a mandatory order designed to keep a specific number of men on the job at the site of a steel mill which is undergoing extensive modernization and expansion. If plaintiffs have sustained loss as a result of actionable building delays . . ., they may, at an appropriate time, resort to law for a fixing of their claimed dam- ages." On a motion for reargument, Phoenix argued that it sought only an order "directing the performance of a ministerial act, namely, the hiring by defendant of more workers." The court denied the motion, relying on "the well established principle that performance of a contract for personal services, even of a unique nature, will not be affirmatively and directly enforced." Northern Delaware Industrial Development Corp. v. E. W. Bliss Co., —— Del.Ch. ——, 245 A.2d 431 (1968). See also Parev Products v. I. Rokeach & Sons., p. 609 infra. Consider the remark of Chancellor Walworth, in denying a decree of specific performance against an opera singer: "I am not aware that any officer of this court has that perfect knowledge of the Italian language, or possesses that exquisite sensibility in the auricular nerve which is necessary to understand, and to enjoy with a proper zest, the peculiar beauties of the Italian opera, so fascinating to the fashionable world." DeRivafinoli v. Corsetti, 4 Paige 263, 270 (N.Y. 1833). Are general contractors distinguishable from opera singers?

Suppose that Bliss and Phoenix had included in their contract a bind- ing provision for arbitration of all disputes under the rules of the Ameri- can Arbitration Association, which empower the arbitrators in their award to grant any just or equitable remedy "including . . . specific per- formance." Would the court have enforced an arbitral award granting the relief that it refused in the actual case? See Grayson-Robinson Stores v. Iris Construction Co., 8 N.Y.2d 133, 168 N.E.2d 377 (1960) (a 4–3 deci- sion).

(3) *The Game for Dough.* In recent years the world of professional athletics, with its warring leagues, has been more productive of notable decisions in this field than has the world of opera. Sports fans will want to consult New York Football Giants v. Los Angeles Chargers Football Club, 291 F.2d 471 (5th Cir. 1961) (Were the Giants, who sought an injunction to prevent Charles Flowers from playing with the Chargers in violation of his contract with the Giants, barred by "unclean hands" as a result of having kept that contract a secret so that Flowers could play in the Sugar Bowl?); Washington Capitols Basketball Club v. Barry, 419 F.2d 472 (9th Cir. 1969) (Were the Caps, who sought, as assignees of the Oakland Oaks, to enjoin "Rick" Barry from playing with the San Francisco Warriors, barred by "unclean hands" as a result of dealings of the Oaks' organizers with Barry while he was under contract with the Warriors?). And cf. Los Angeles Rams Football Club v. Cannon, p. 105 supra.

(d) Cost to Complete or Diminution in Value?

How is the injured party's expectation to be measured in terms of money? One basis would be the cost to complete, that is, the additional financial sacrifice that the injured party would have had to incur in order to obtain a substitute performance considered adequate to put him in the position in which he would have been had there been no breach. Another would be the diminution in value, that is, the loss of advantage that resulted in not being in that position.

The first basis, cost to complete, may have initial appeal, as seeming to come closer to assuring the injured party's expectation. The general preference in our legal system, however, is for the diminution in value. Are there good reasons for this? Is diminution in value a better measure of expectation in cases in which the cost to complete greatly exceeds it, so that the injured party would not even consider completion if awarded the larger sum needed to complete? And are there not situations in which completion is impossible at any cost, as where the party in breach is uniquely capable of performing (e. g., disclosing a secret process), or in which the delay occasioned by his breach has made performance impossible (e. g., performing an emergency operation)? And, in any event, is not the injured party entitled to compensation for any delay occasioned by the breach, for which cost to complete is not a suitable basis since no amount of money can turn the clock back? Are there other reasons?

In principle the diminution in value sought is that to the injured party himself, quite without regard to the diminution in value to anyone else, and depends on his own particular circumstances or those of his enterprise. Where the injured party's expected advantage consists largely or exclusively of the realization of profit, as is the case for most commercially significant exchanges, it can be expressed in money with some assurance. Its calculation depends on two ingredients.

The first is his *loss on the bargain,* which he suffers by the frustration of the exchange for which he bargained. It may have two components. One is the *loss in value* to the injured party of the other party's performance, and represents the difference in the value to the injured party of what the other party was to have done and of what he did. This component is always present, whether the breach is partial or total. Where the breach is total, and the injured party has been relieved of the balance of his own performance, a second component enters into the calculation. This is the cost that he avoided as a result of being excused. His *loss on the bargain* is then the difference between *loss in value* and *cost avoided.*

The second ingredient is *other loss,* such as physical harm to the injured party's person or property and expenses incurred by him in an attempt to salvage the transaction after breach. The general measure, then, is the sum of these two ingredients, which gives Formula A.

(A) *Damages* = *loss in value* − *cost avoided* + *other loss.*

Since, in most agreements, one of the parties (here called the "recipient") is required to pay money, the estimation of *loss in value* and *cost avoided* usually poses problems only in connection with the performance of the other party (here called the "supplier"), who may be required, for example, to furnish goods, land, or services in return. Where the supplier is the injured party, and the breach consists of the recipient's promise to pay, the difficulty lies in the determination of the supplier's *cost avoided,* since his *loss in value* is simply the amount of money that the recipient has failed to pay. Where the recipient is the injured party, and the supplier is in breach, the difficulty lies in the determination of the recipient's *loss in value,* since his *cost avoided* is simply the amount of money that he has not yet paid.

The building contract cases afford a simple illustration. Suppose that Builder contracts with Owner to construct a factory on Owner's land for $1,000,000 payable on completion. If the recipient (Owner) is the party in breach and the supplier (Builder) has used the breach to excuse his further performance, the controversy will center on the *cost avoided* by Builder in his not having to complete construction of the factory. The *loss in value* to Builder will be simply the amount remaining unpaid. If, for example, Builder can show that it would have cost him $400,000 more to complete the job, his recovery under Formula A (ignoring *other loss*) would be $1,000,000 less $400,000 or $600,000. Builder will often calculate his *cost avoided* by determining the cost already incurred in reliance on the contract. Assuming that this sum is $500,000, the *cost of complete per-*

formance would be the total of the *cost of reliance* and the *cost avoided*, that is $500,000 plus $400,000, or $900,000. In other words:

Cost avoided = *cost of complete performance* − *cost of reliance*.

Substituting the right hand side of this equation for *cost avoided* in Formula A, and remembering that the difference between *loss in value* and *cost of complete performance* is Builder's expected *profit*, we get Formula B as the equivalent of Formula A.[a]

(B) *Damages* = *cost of reliance* + *profit* + *other loss*.

In the illustration given, Builder's recovery under Formula B (ignoring *other loss*) would be $500,000 plus $100,000 or $600,000, just as under Formula A. How should items of overhead be treated under either Formula A or Formula B?

VITEX MANUFACTURING CORP. v. CARIBTEX CORP.

United States Court of Appeals, Third Circuit, 1967.
377 F.2d 795.

STALEY, CHIEF JUDGE. This is an appeal by Caribtex Corporation from a judgment of the District Court of the Virgin Islands finding Caribtex in breach of a contract entered into with Vitex Manufacturing Company, Ltd., and awarding $21,114 plus interest to Vitex for loss of profits. The only substantial question raised by Caribtex is whether it was error for the district court, sitting without a jury, not to consider overhead as part of Vitex's costs in determining the amount of profits lost. We conclude that under the facts presented, the district court was not compelled to consider Vitex's overhead costs, and we will affirm the judgment.

Before discussing the details of the controversy between the parties, it will be helpful to briefly describe the peculiar legal setting in which this suit arose. At the time of the events in question, there were high tariff barriers to the importation of foreign wool products. However, under § 301 of the Tariff Act of 1930, 19 U.S.C.A. § 1301a, repealed but the provision continued under Revised Tariff Schedules, 19 U.S.C.A. § 1202, note 3(a) (i) (ii) (1965), if such goods were imported into the Virgin Islands and were processed in some manner so that their finished value exceeded their importation value by at least 50%, then the high tariffs to importation into the continental United States would be avoided. Even after the processing, the foreign wool enjoyed a price advantage over domestic products so that the business flourished. However, to keep the volume of this business at such levels that Congress would not be stirred to change the law, the Virgin Islands Legislature imposed "quotas" on persons engaging in processing, limiting their output. 33 V.I.C. § 504 (Supp.1966).

a. For the sake of simplicity, it is assumed that Builder has not received any payment from Owner. If he has, the amount of the payment must be subtracted in applying Formula B.

Vitex was engaged in the business of chemically shower-proofing imported cloth so that it could be imported duty-free into the United States. For this purpose, Vitex maintained a plant in the Virgin Islands and was entitled to process a specific quantity of material under the Virgin Islands quota system. Caribtex was in the business of importing cloth into the islands, securing its processing, and exporting it to the United States.

In the fall of 1963, Vitex found itself with an unused portion of its quota but no customers, and Vitex closed its plant. Caribtex acquired some Italian wool and subsequently negotiations for a processing contract were conducted between the principals of the respective companies in New York City. Though the record below is clouded with differing versions of the negotiations and the alleged final terms, the trial court found upon substantial evidence in the record that the parties did enter into a contract in which Vitex agreed to process 125,000 yards of Caribtex's woolen material at a price of 26 cents per yard.

Vitex proceeded to re-open its Virgin Islands plant, ordered the necessary chemicals, recalled its work force and made all the necessary preparations to perform its end of the bargain. However, no goods were forthcoming from Caribtex, despite repeated demands by Vitex, apparently because Caribtex was unsure that the processed wool would be entitled to duty-free treatment by the customs officials. Vitex subsequently brought this suit to recover the profits lost through Caribtex's breach.

Vitex alleged, and the trial court found, that its gross profits for processing said material under the contract would have been $31,250 and that its costs would have been $10,136, leaving Vitex's damages for loss of profits at $21,114. On appeal, Caribtex asserted numerous objections to the detailed computation of lost profits. While the record below is sometimes confusing, we conclude that the trial court had substantial evidence to support its findings on damages. It must be remembered that the difficulty in exactly ascertaining Vitex's costs is due to Caribtex's wrongful conduct in repudiating the contract before performance by Vitex. Caribtex will not be permitted to benefit by the uncertainty it has caused. Thus, since there was a sufficient basis in the record to support the trial court's determination of substantial damages, we will not set aside its judgment. Stentor Elec. Mfg. Co. v. Klaxon Co., 115 F.2d 268 (C.A.3, 1940), rev'd other grounds 313 U.S. 487, 61 S.Ct. 1020, 85 L.Ed. 1477 (1941) ; 5 Williston, Contracts § 1345 (rev. ed. 1937).

Caribtex first raised the issue at the oral argument of this appeal that the trial court erred by disregarding Vitex's overhead expenses in determining lost profits. In general, overhead "* * * may be said to include broadly the continuous expenses of the business, irrespective of the outlay on a particular contract." Grand

Trunk W. R. R. Co. v. H. W. Nelson Co., 116 F.2d 823, 839 (C.A.6, 1941). Such expenses would include executive and clerical salaries, property taxes, general administration expenses, etc.[1] Although Vitex did not expressly seek recovery for overhead, if a portion of these fixed expenses should be allocated as costs to the Caribtex contract, then under the judgment of the district court Vitex tacitly recovered these expenses as part of its damages for lost profits, and the damages should be reduced accordingly. Presumably, the portion to be allocated to costs would be a pro rata share of Vitex's annual overhead according to the volume of business Vitex would have done over the year if Caribtex had not breached the contract.

Although there is authority to the contrary, we feel that the better view is that normally, in a claim for lost profits, overhead should be treated as a part of gross profits and recoverable as damages, and should not be considered as part of the seller's costs. A number of cases hold that since overhead expenses are not affected by the performance of the particular contract, there should be no need to deduct them in computing lost profits. E. g., Oakland California Towel Co. v. Sivils, 52 Cal.App.2d 517, 520, 126 P.2d 651, 652 (1942); Jessup & Moore Paper Co. v. Bryant Paper Co., 297 Pa. 483, 147 A. 519, 524 (1929); Annot., 3 A.L.R.3d 689 (1965) (collecting cases on both sides of the controversy). The theory of these cases is that the seller is entitled to recover losses incurred and gains prevented in excess of savings made possible, Restatement, Contracts § 329 (made part of the law of the Virgin Islands, 1 V.I.C. § 4); since overhead is fixed and nonperformance of the contract produced no overhead cost savings, no deduction from profits should result.

The soundness of the rule is exemplified by this case. Before negotiations began between Vitex and Caribtex, Vitex had reached a lull in business activity and had closed its plant. If Vitex had entered into no other contracts for the rest of the year, the profitability of its operations would have been determined by deducting its production costs and overhead from gross receipts yielded in previous transactions. When this opportunity arose to process Caribtex's wool, the only additional expenses Vitex would incur would be those of re-opening its plant and the direct costs of processing, such as labor, chemicals and fuel oil. Overhead would have remained the same whether or not Vitex and Caribtex entered their contract and whether or not Vitex actually processed Caribtex's goods. Since this overhead remained constant, in no way attributable-to or affected-by the Caribtex contract, it would be improper to consider it as a cost of Vitex's performance to be deducted from the gross proceeds of the Caribtex contract.

1. Caribtex could not be referring to overhead expenses as including labor costs and the like, because the trial judge did charge as costs all the expenses directly associated with the reactivation of Vitex's plant, and the actual processing of Caribtex's goods according to the terms of the contract.

However, Caribtex may argue that this view ignores modern accounting principles, and that overhead is as much a cost of production as other expenses. It is true that successful businessmen must set their prices at sufficient levels to recoup all their expenses, including overhead, and to gain profits. Thus, the price the businessman should charge on each transaction could be thought of as that price necessary to yield a pro rata portion of the company's fixed overhead, the direct costs associated with production, and a "clear" profit. Doubtless this type of calculation is used by businessmen and their accountants. Pacific Portland Cement Co. v. Food Mach. & Chem. Corp., 178 F.2d 541 (C.A.9, 1949). However, because it is useful for planning purposes to allocate a portion of overhead to each transaction, it does not follow that this allocate share of fixed overhead should be considered a cost factor in the computation of lost profits on individual transactions.

First, it must be recognized that the pro rata allocation of overhead costs is only an analytical construct. In a similar manner one could allocate a pro rata share of the company's advertising cost, taxes and/or charitable gifts. The point is that while these items all are paid from the proceeds of the business, they do not normally bear such a direct relationship to any individual transaction to be considered a cost in ascertaining lost profits.

Secondly, even were we to recognize the allocation of overhead as proper in this case, we should uphold the tacit award of overhead expense to Vitex as a "loss incurred." Conditioned Air Corp. v. Rock Island Motor Transit Co., 253 Iowa 961, 114 N.W.2d 304, 3 A.L.R.3d 679, cert. denied, 371 U.S. 825, 83 S.Ct. 46, 9 L.Ed.2d 64 (1962). By the very nature of this allocation process, as the number of transactions over which overhead can be spread becomes smaller, each transaction must bear a greater portion or allocate share of the fixed overhead cost. Suppose a company has fixed overhead of $10,000 and engages in five similar transactions; then the receipts of each transaction would bear $2000 of overhead expense. If the company is now forced to spread this $10,000 over only four transactions, then the overhead expense per transaction will rise to $2500, significantly reducing the profitability of the four remaining transactions. Thus, where the contract is between businessmen familiar with commercial practices, as here, the breaching party should reasonably foresee that his breach will not only cause a loss of "clear" profit, but also a loss in that the profitability of other transactions will be reduced. Resolute Ins. Co. v. Percy Jones, Inc., 198 F.2d 309 (C.A.10, 1952); Cf. In re Kellett Aircraft Corp., 191 F.2d 231 (C.A.3, 1951). Therefore, this loss is within the contemplation of "losses caused and gains prevented," and overhead should be considered to be a compensable item of damage.

Significantly, the Uniform Commercial Code, adopted in the Virgin Islands, 11A V.I.C. §§ 1–101 et seq., and in virtually every state today, provides for the recovery of overhead in circumstances similar to those presented here. Under 11A V.I.C. § 2–708, the seller's measure of damage for non-acceptance or repudiation is the difference between the contract price and the market price, but if this relief is inadequate to put the seller in as good position as if the contract had been fully performed, " . . . then the measure of damages is the *profit (including reasonable overhead)* which the seller would have made from full performance by the buyer . . .." 11A V.I.C. § 2–708(2). (Emphasis added.) While this contract is not controlled by the Code, the Code is persuasive here because it embodies the foremost modern legal thought concerning commercial transactions. Indeed, it may overrule some of the cases denying recovery for overhead. E. g., Wilhelm Lubrication Co. v. Brattrud, 197 Minn. 626, 632, 268 N.W. 634, 636, 106 A.L.R. 1279 (1936).

Caribtex also argued that the contract should not be enforced because it was unconscionable. While Vitex was to make a large profit on the processing and Caribtex did bear the risk of failure to meet customs standards, the contract was freely entered-into, after much negotiation, between parties of apparently equal bargaining strength. This was not a contract of adhesion—Vitex was not the only processor in the Virgin Islands and Caribtex's bargaining strength was evidenced by the successive and substantial price reductions it wrested from Vitex during the negotiations. Compare, Campbell Soup Co. v. Wentz, 172 F.2d 80 (C.A.3, 1948); Henningsen v. Bloomfield Motors, Inc., 32 N.J. 358, 161 A.2d 69, 75 A.L.R.2d 1 (1960).

The judgment of the district court will be affirmed.

NOTE

Overhead. Vitex's *loss on the bargain* was the difference between *loss in value* and *cost avoided* (see Formula A, supra). Did the trial court include overhead costs in *cost avoided*? Should it have? Or, from a different perspective, Vitex's *loss on the bargain* was the sum of *cost of reliance* and *profit* (see Formula B, supra). Did the trial court include overhead costs in *cost of reliance* and in *profit*? Should it have? On the computation of *cost avoided*, see Harris, A General Theory for Measuring Seller's Damages for Total Breach of Contract, 60 Mich.L.Rev. 577 (1962).

JACOB & YOUNGS v. KENT

Court of Appeals of New York, 1921.
230 N.Y. 239, 129 N.E. 889, 23 A.L.R. 1429.

CARDOZO, J. The plaintiff built a country residence for the defendant at a cost of upwards of $77,000, and now sues to recover a balance of $3,483.46, remaining unpaid. The work of construction ceased in June, 1914, and the defendant then began to occupy the dwelling. There was no complaint of defective performance until March, 1915. One of the specifications for the plumbing work provides that "all wrought iron pipe must be well galvanized, lap welded pipe of the grade known as 'standard pipe' of Reading manufacture." The defendant learned in March, 1915, that some of the pipe, instead of being made in Reading, was the product of other factories. The plaintiff was accordingly directed by the architect to do the work anew. The plumbing was then encased within the walls except in a few places where it had to be exposed. Obedience to the order meant more than the substitution of other pipe. It meant the demolition at great expense of substantial parts of the completed structure. The plaintiff left the work untouched, and asked for a certificate that the final payment was due. Refusal of the certificate was followed by this suit.[a]

The evidence sustains a finding that the omission of the prescribed brand of pipe was neither fraudulent nor willful. It was the result of the oversight and inattention of the plaintiff's sub-contractor. Reading pipe is distinguished from Cohoes pipe and other brands only by the name of the manufacturer stamped upon it at intervals of between six and seven feet. Even the defendant's architect, though he inspected the pipe upon arrival, failed to notice the discrepancy. The plaintiff tried to show that the brands installed, though made by other manufacturers, were the same in quality, in appearance, in market value and in cost as the brand stated in the contract—that they were, indeed, the same thing, though manufactured in another place. The evidence was excluded, and a verdict directed for the defendant. The Appellate Division reversed, and granted a new trial.

We think the evidence, if admitted, would have supplied some basis for the inference that the defect was insignificant in its relation to the project. The courts never say that one who makes a contract fills the measure of his duty by less than full performance. They do say, however, that an omission, both trivial and innocent, will sometimes be atoned for by allowance of the resulting damage, and will not always be the breach of a condition to be followed by a forfeiture (Spence v. Ham, 163 N.Y. 220, 57 N.E. 412; Woodward v. Fuller, 80 N.Y. 312; Glacius v. Black, 67 N.Y. 563, 566; Bowen v. Kimbell, 203 Mass. 364,

---

a. The record on appeal indicates that, under the contract, payments were to be made monthly as the work progressed, on the certificate of the architect in an amount which "in his judgment" represented the amount due less 15% to be withheld. The specifications attached to the contract made the architect's decision "as to the character of any material or labor furnished by the Contractor . . . final and conclusive." Furthermore, "Any work furnished by the Contractor, the material or workmanship of which is defective or which is not fully in accordance with the drawings and specifications, in every respect, will be rejected and is to be immediately torn down, removed and remade or replaced in accordance with the drawings and specifications, whenever discovered. . . . The Owner will have the option at all times to allow the defective or improper work to stand and to receive from the Contractor a sum of money equivalent to the difference in value of the work as performed and as herein specified." Record pp. 98–108.

370, 89 N.E. 542.)   The distinction is akin to that between dependent
and independent promises, or between promises and conditions (Anson on Contracts, Corbin's Ed., sec. 367: 2 Williston on Contracts, sec.
842).   Some promises are so plainly independent that they can never
by fair construction be conditions of one another.   (Rosenthal Paper
Co. v. Nat. Folding Box & Paper Co., 226 N.Y. 313, 123 N.E. 766;
Bogardus v. N. Y. Life Ins. Co., 101 N.Y. 328, 4 N.E. 522.)   Others
are so plainly dependent that they must always be conditions.   Others,
though dependent and thus conditions when there' is departure in
point of substance, will be viewed as independent and collateral when
the departure is insignificant (2 Williston on Contracts, secs. 841,
842; Eastern Forge Co. v. Corbin, 182 Mass. 590, 592, 66 N.E. 419;
Robinson v. Mollett, L.R., 7 Eng. & Ir.App. 802, 814; Miller v. Benjamin, 142 N.Y. 613, 37 N.E. 631).   Considerations partly of justice
and partly of presumable intention are to tell us whether this or that
promise shall be placed in one class or another.   The simple and the
uniform will call for different remedies from the multifarious and the
intricate.   The margin of departure within the range of normal expectation upon a sale of common chattels will vary from the margin
to be expected upon a contract for the construction of a mansion or a
"skyscraper."   There will be harshness sometimes and oppression in
the implication of a condition when the thing upon which labor has
been expended is incapable of surrender because united to the land,
and equity and reason in the implication of a like condition when the
subject-matter, if defective, is in shape to be returned.   From the
conclusions that promises may not be treated as dependent to the extent of their uttermost minutiae without a sacrifice of justice, the
progress is a short one to the conclusion that they may not be so
treated without a perversion of intention.   Intention not otherwise revealed may be presumed to hold in contemplation the reasonable and
probable.   If something else is in view, it must not be left to implication.   There will be no assumption of a purpose to visit venial faults
with oppressive retribution.

Those who think more of symmetry and logic in the development
of legal rules than of practical adaptation to the attainment of a
just result will be troubled by a classification where the lines of division are so wavering and blurred.   Something, doubtless, may be said
on the score of consistency and certainty in favor of a stricter standard.   The courts have balanced such considerations against those of
equity and fairness, and found the latter to be the weightier.   The decisions in this state commit us to the liberal view, which is making its
way, nowadays, in jurisdictions slow to welcome it (Dakin & Co. v. Lee,
1916, 1 K.B. 566, 579).   Where the line is to be drawn between the
important and the trivial cannot be settled by a formula.   "In the nature of the case precise boundaries are impossible" (2 Williston on
Contracts, sec. 841).   The same omission may take on one aspect or
another according to its setting.   Substitution of equivalents may not

have the same significance in fields of art on the one side and in those of mere utility on the other. Nowhere will change be tolerated, however, if it is so dominant or pervasive as in any real or substantial measure to frustrate the purpose of the contract (Crouch v. Gutmann, 134 N.Y. 45, 51, 31 N.E. 271). There is no general license to install whatever, in the builder's judgment, may be regarded as "just as good" (Easthampton L. & C. Co., Ltd. v. Worthington, 186 N.Y. 407, 412, 79 N.E. 323). The question is one of degree, to be answered, if there is doubt, by the triers of the facts (Crouch v. Gutmann; Woodward v. Fuller, supra), and, if the inferences are certain, by the judges of the law (Easthampton L. & C. Co., Ltd. v. Worthington, supra). We must weigh the purpose to be served, the desire to be gratified, the excuse for deviation from the letter, the cruelty of enforced adherence. Then only can we tell whether literal fulfillment is to be implied by law as a condition. This is not to say that the parties are not free by apt and certain words to effectuate a purpose that performance of every term shall be a condition of recovery. That question is not here. This is merely to say that the law will be slow to impute the purpose, in the silence of the parties, where the significance of the default is grievously out of proportion to the oppression of the forfeiture. The willful transgressor must accept the penalty of his transgression (Schultze v. Goodstein, 180 N.Y. 248, 251, 73 N.E. 21; Desmond-Dunne Co. v. Friedman-Doscher Co., 162 N.Y. 486, 490, 56 N.E. 995). For him there is no occasion to mitigate the rigor of implied conditions. The transgressor whose default is unintentional and trivial may hope for mercy if he will offer atonement for his wrong (Spence v. Ham, supra).

In the circumstances of this case, we think the measure of the allowance is not the cost of replacement, which would be great, but the difference in value, which would be either nominal or nothing. Some of the exposed sections might perhaps have been replaced at moderate expense. The defendant did not limit his demand to them, but treated the plumbing as a unit to be corrected from cellar to roof. In point of fact, the plaintiff never reached the stage at which evidence of the extent of the allowance became necessary. The trial court had excluded evidence that the defect was unsubstantial, and in view of that ruling there was no occasion for the plaintiff to go farther with an offer of proof. We think, however, that the offer, if it had been made, would not of necessity have been defective because directed to difference in value. It is true that in most cases the cost of replacement is the measure (Spence v. Ham, supra). The owner is entitled to the money which will permit him to complete, unless the cost of completion is grossly and unfairly out of proportion to the good to be attained. When that is true, the measure is the difference in value. Specifications call, let us say, for a foundation built of granite quarried in Vermont. On the completion of the building, the owner learns that through the blunder of a subcontractor part of the foundation has been built of granite of the same quality quarried in New Hampshire. The measure of allowance is not the cost of reconstruction. "There may be omissions of that which could not afterwards be supplied exactly as called for by the contract without taking down the building to its foundations and at the same time the omission may not affect the value of the building for use or otherwise, except so slightly as to be hardly appreciable" (Handy v. Bliss, 204 Mass. 513, 519, 90 N.E. 864. Cf. Foeller v. Heintz, 137 Wis. 169, 178, 118 N.W. 543; Oberlies v. Bullinger, 132 N.Y. 598, 601, 30 N.E. 999; 2 Williston on Contracts, sec. 805, p. 1541). The rule that gives a remedy in cases of substantial performance with compensation for defects of trivial or inappreciable importance, has been developed by the courts as an instrument of justice. The measure of the allowance must be shaped to the same end.

The order should be affirmed, and judgment absolute directed in favor of the plaintiff upon the stipulation, with costs in all courts.

McLAUGHLIN, J. (dissenting). I dissent. The plaintiff did not perform its contract. Its failure to do so was either intentional or due to gross neglect which, under the uncontradicted facts, amounted to the same thing, nor did it make any proof of the cost of compliance, where compliance was possible. . . .

I am of the opinion the trial court was right in directing a verdict for the defendant. The plaintiff agreed that all the pipe used should be of the Reading Manufacturing Company. Only about two-fifths of it, so far as appears, was of that kind. If more were used, then the burden of proving that fact was upon the plaintiff, which it could easily have done, since it knew where the pipe was obtained. The question of substantial performance of a contract of the character of the one under consideration depends in no small degree upon the good faith of the contractor. If the plaintiff had intended to, and had complied with the terms of the contract except as to minor omissions, due to inadvertence, then he might be allowed to recover the contract price, less the amount necessary to fully compensate the defendant for damages caused by such omissions. Woodward v. Fuller, 80 N.Y. 312; Nolan v. Whitney, 88 N.Y. 648. But that is not this case. It installed between 2,000 and 2,500 feet of pipe, of which only 1,000 feet at most complied with the contract. No explanation was given why pipe called for by the contract was not used, nor was any effort made to show what it would cost to remove the pipe of other manufacturers and install that of the Reading Manufacturing Company. The defendant had a right to contract for what he wanted. He had a right before making payment to get what the contract called for. It is no answer to this suggestion to say that the pipe put in was just as good as that made by the Reading Manufacturing Company, or that the difference in value between such pipe and the pipe made by the Reading Manufacturing Company would be either "nominal or nothing." Defendant contracted for pipe made by the Reading Manufacturing Company. What his reason was for requiring this kind of pipe is of no importance. He wanted that and was entitled to it. . . . The rule, therefore, of substantial performance, with damages for unsubstantial omissions, has no application. (Crouch v. Gutmann, 134 N.Y. 45, 31 N.E. 271; Spence v. Ham, 163 N.Y. 220, 57 N.E. 412.) . . .

HISCOCK, CH. J., HOGAN and CRANE, JJ., concur with CARDOZO, J.; POUND and ANDREWS, JJ., concur with McLAUGHLIN, J.

Order affirmed, etc.

NOTES

(1) *Substantial Performance.* Kent promised to pay Jacob & Youngs if it built him a house as specified. Building the house as specified was therefore a condition of Jacob & Youngs' right to recover from Kent on that promise. In the first part of the opinion, Cardozo explains why Jacob & Youngs can recover from Kent on that promise in spite of the fact that it did not strictly fulfill that condition. As to this, three judges dissent. This notion of substantial, as opposed to strict, performance and the law of conditions in general are taken up in Chapter 7, Performance and Breach. For present purposes, we are concerned only with the second part of Cardozo's opinion, in which he considers how much, if anything, should be deducted from that recovery as Kent's damages. (To remove the problem of substantial performance from the picture, assume that Kent had paid Jacob & Youngs in full and was suing them for damages.)

(2) *Determining Diminution in Value.* Do you agree that the "difference in value" *to Kent* "would be either nominal or nothing"? It may be that the difference between the *market price* of a house with Reading pipe and one with Cohoes pipe is zero, because buyers of houses consider the two kinds of pipe to be of equal value *to them.* But why should *Kent's* recovery be limited by this? Should it not be the law that, as one court put it, if a man "chooses to erect a monument to his caprice or folly on his premises, and employs and pays another to do it, it does not lie with a defendant who has been so employed and paid for building it, to say that his own performance would not be beneficial to the plaintiff." Chamberlain v. Parker, 45 N.Y. 569 (1871).

Diminution in market price is, however, useful in fixing a lower limit for recovery, since the value of property to its owner is usually no less than the net price at which he could sell it. Similarly, cost to complete is useful in fixing an upper limit for recovery since, even if that cost is less than the diminution in value to him, the lesser sum will enable him to complete and avoid any diminution in value.

The problem of determining diminution in value is most acute when, as in the principal case, there is great disparity between the minimum of diminution in market price and the maximum of cost to complete. Which better approximates diminution in value? Although the opinion gives us no insight into why Kent might have specified Reading rather than some other brand of pipe, it does suggest one reason for the disparity between the maximum and minimum. Does that reason suggest which better approximates diminution in value? (If a very large fraction of the disparity represents the cost of undoing and redoing the work, how large a fraction represents the difference in value to Kent?)

GROVES v. JOHN WUNDER CO.

Supreme Court of Minnesota, 1939.
205 Minn. 163, 286 N.W. 235.

STONE, J. Action for breach of contract. Plaintiff got judgment for a little over $15,000. Sorely disappointed by that sum, he appeals.

In August, 1927 S. J. Groves & Sons Company, a corporation (hereinafter mentioned simply as Groves), owned a tract of 24 acres of Minneapolis suburban real estate. It was served or easily could be reached by railroad trackage. It is zoned as heavy industrial property. But for lack of development of the neighborhood its principal value thus far may have been in the deposit of sand and gravel which it carried. The Groves company had a plant on the premises for excavating and screening the gravel. Nearby defendant owned and was operating a similar plant.

In August, 1927, Groves and defendant made the involved contract. For the most part it was a lease from Groves, as lessor, to defendant, as lessee; its term seven years. Defendant agreed to remove the sand and gravel and to leave the property "at a uniform grade, substantially the same as the grade now existing at the roadway . . . on said premises, and that in stripping the overburden . . . it will use said overburden for the purpose of maintaining and establishing said grade."

Under the contract defendant got the Groves screening plant. The transfer thereof and the right to remove the sand and gravel made the consideration moving from Groves to defendant, except that defendant incidentally got rid of Groves as a competitor. On defendant's part it paid Groves $105,000. So that from the outset, on Groves' part the contract was executed except for defendant's right to continue using the property for the stated term. (Defendant had a right to renewal which it did not exercise.)

Defendant breached the contract deliberately. It removed from the premises only "the richest and best of the gravel" and wholly failed, according to the findings, "to perform and comply with the terms, conditions, and provisions of said lease . . . with respect to the condition in which the surface of the demised premises was required to be left." Defendant surrendered the premises, not substantially at the grade required by the contract "nor at any uniform grade." Instead, the ground was "broken, rugged and uneven." Plaintiff sues as assignee and successor in right of Groves.

As the contract was construed below, the finding is that to complete its performance 288,495 cubic yards of overburden would need to be excavated, taken from the premises, and deposited elsewhere. The reasonable cost of doing that was found to be upwards of $60,000. But, if defendant had left the premises at the uniform grade required by the lease, the reasonable value of the property on the determinative date would have been only $12,160. The judgment was for that sum,[a] including interest, thereby nullifying plaintiff's claim that cost of completing the contract rather than difference in value of the land was the measure of damages. The gauge of damage adopted by the decision was the difference between the market value of plaintiff's land in the condition it was [in] when the contract was made and what it would have been if defendant had performed. The one question for us arises upon plaintiff's assertion that he was entitled, not to that difference in value, but to the reasonable cost to him of doing the work called for by the contract which defendant left undone.

1. Defendant's breach of contract was wilful. There was nothing of good faith about it. Hence, that the decision below handsomely rewards bad faith and deliberate breach of contract is obvious. That is not allowable. Here the rule is well settled, and has been since Elliott v. Caldwell, 43 Minn. 357, 45 N.W. 845, 9 L.R.A. 52, that, where the contractor wilfully and fraudulently varies from the terms of a construction contract, he cannot sue thereon and have the benefit of the equitable doctrine of substantial performance. That is the rule generally. See Annotation, "Wilful or intentional variation by contractor from terms of contract in regard to material or work as affecting measure of damages," 6 A.L.R. 137.

Jacob & Youngs, Inc. v. Kent, 230 N.Y. 239, 243, 244, 129 N.E. 889, 891, 23 A.L.R. 1429, [p. 938 infra] is typical. It was a case of substantial performance of a building contract. (This case is distinctly the opposite.) Mr. Justice Cardozo, in the course of his opinion, stressed the distinguishing features. "Nowhere," he said, "will change be tolerated, however, if it is so dominant or pervasive as in any real or substantial measure to frustrate the purpose of the contract." Again, "the willful transgressor must accept the penalty of his transgression."

2. In reckoning damages for breach of a building or construction contract, the law aims to give the disappointed promisee, so far as money will do it, what he was promised. 9 Am.Jur. Building and Construction Contracts, sec. 152. It is so ruled by a long line of decisions in this state beginning with Carli v. Seymour, Sabin & Co., 26 Minn. 276, 3 N.W. 348, where the contract was for building a road. There was a breach. Plaintiff was held entitled to recover what it would cost to complete the grading as contemplated by the contract. For our other similar cases, see 2 Dunnell, Minn.Dig., 2 Ed. & Supp., secs. 2561, 2565.

a. This was on the assumption that the land as it was left could not have been sold on the market.

Never before, so far as our decisions show, has it even been suggested that lack of value in the land furnished to the contractor who had bound himself to improve it [gave] any escape from the ordinary consequences of a breach of the contract.   .   .   .

Even in case of substantial performance in good faith, the resulting defects being remediable, it is error to instruct that the measure of damage is "the difference in value between the house as it was and as it would have been if constructed according to contract." The "correct doctrine" is that the cost of remedying the defect is the "proper" measure of damages. Snider v. Peters Home Building Co., 139 Minn. 413, 414, 416, 167 N.W. 108.

Value of the land (as distinguished from the value of the intended product of the contract, which ordinarily will be equivalent to its reasonable cost) is no proper part of any measure of damages for wilful breach of a building contract. The reason is plain.

The summit from which to reckon damages from trespass to real estate is its actual value at the moment. The owner's only right is to be compensated for the deterioration in value caused by the tort. That is all he has lost.[1] But not so if a contract to improve the same land has been breached by the contractor who refuses to do the work, especially where, as here, he has been paid in advance. The summit from which to reckon damages for that wrong is the hypothetical peak of accomplishment (not value) which would have been reached had the work been done as demanded by the contract.

The owner's right to improve his property is not trammeled by its small value. It is his right to erect thereon structures which will reduce its value. If that be the result, it can be of no aid to any contractor who declines performance. As said long ago in Chamberlain v. Parker, 45 N.Y. 569, 572: "A man may do what he will with his own,   .   .   .   and if he chooses to erect a monument to his caprice or folly on his premises, and employs and pays another to do it, it does not lie with a defendant who has been so employed and paid for building it, to say that his own performance would not be beneficial to the plaintiff." To the same effect is Restatement, Contracts, sec. 346, p. 576, Illustrations of Subsection (1), par. 4.

Suppose a contractor were suing the owner for breach of a grading contract such as this. Would any element of value, or lack of it, in the land have any relevance in reckoning damages? Of course not. The contractor would be compensated for what he had lost, i. e., his profit. Conversely, in such a case as this, the owner is entitled to compensation for what he has lost, that is, the work or structure which he has been promised, for which he has paid, and of which he has been deprived by the contractor's breach.

---

1.   So also in condemnation cases, where the owner loses nothing of promised contractual performance.

To diminish damages recoverable against him in proportion as there is presently small value in the land would favor the faithless contractor. It would also ignore and so defeat plaintiff's right to contract and build for the future. To justify such a course would require more of the prophetic vision than judges possess. This factor is important when the subject matter is trackage property in the margin of such an area of population and industry as that of the Twin Cities. . . .

The genealogy of the error pervading the argument contra is easy to trace. It begins with Seely v. Alden, 61 Pa. 302, 100 Am.Dec. 642, a tort case for pollution of a stream. Resulting depreciation in value of plaintiff's premises, of course, was the measure of damages. About 40 years later, in Bigham v. Wabash-Pittsburg T. Ry., 223 Pa. 106, 72 A. 318, the measure of damages of the earlier tort case was used in one for breach of contract, without comment or explanation to show why. . . .

It is at least interesting to note Morgan v. Gamble, 230 Pa. 165, 79 A. 410, decided two years after the Bigham case. The doctrine of substantial performance is there correctly stated, but plaintiff was denied its benefit because he had deliberately breached his building contract. It was held that: "Where a building contractor agrees to lay an extra strong lead water pipe, and he substitutes therefor an iron pipe, he will be required to allow to the owners in a suit upon the contract, not the difference [in value] between the iron and lead pipes, but the cost of laying a lead pipe as provided in the agreement."

To show how remote any factors of value were considered, it was also held that: "Where a contractor of a building agrees to construct two gas lines, one for natural gas, and one for artificial gas, he will not be relieved from constructing both lines, because artificial gas was not in use in the town in which the building was being constructed."

The objective of this contract of present importance was the improvement of real estate. That makes irrelevant the rules peculiar to damages to chattels, arising from tort or breach of contract. . . . In tort, the thing lost is money value, nothing more. But under a construction contract, the thing lost by a breach such as we have here is a physical structure or accomplishment, a promised and paid for alteration in land. That is the "injury" for which the law gives him compensation. Its only appropriate measure is the cost of performance.

It is suggested that because of little or no value in his land the owner may be unconscionably enriched by such a reckoning. The answer is that there can be no unconscionable enrichment, no advantage upon which the law will frown, when the result is but to give one party to a contract only what the other has promised; particularly where, as here, the delinquent has had full payment for the promised performance.

3. It is said by the Restatement, Contracts, sec. 346, comment b: "Sometimes defects in a completed structure cannot be physically remedied without tearing down and rebuilding, at a cost that would be imprudent and unreasonable. The law does not require damages to be measured by a method requiring such economic waste. If no such waste is involved, the cost of remedying the defect is the amount awarded as compensation for failure to render the promised performance."

The "economic waste" declaimed against by the decisions applying that rule has nothing to do with the value in money of the real estate, or even with the product of the contract. The waste avoided is only that which would come from wrecking a physical structure, completed, or nearly so, under the contract. The cases applying that rule go no further. Illustrative are Buchholz v. Rosenberg, 163 Wis. 312, 156 N.W. 946; Burmeister v. Wolfgram, 175 Wis. 506, 185 N.W. 517. Absent such waste, as it is in this case, the rule of the Restatement, Contracts, sec. 346, is that "the cost of remedying the defect is the amount awarded as compensation for failure to render the promised performance." That means that defendants here are liable to plaintiff for the reasonable cost of doing what defendants promised to do and have wilfully declined to do.

It follows that there must be a new trial. The initial question will be as to the proper construction of the contract. Thus far the case has been considered from the standpoint of the construction adopted by plaintiff and acquiesced in, very likely for strategic reasons, by defendants. The question has not been argued here, so we intimate no opinion concerning it, but we put the question whether the contract required removal from the premises of any overburden. The requirement in that respect was that the overburden should be used for the purpose of "establishing and maintaining" the grade. A uniform slope and grade were doubtless required. But whether, if it could not be accomplished without removal and deposit elsewhere of large amounts of overburden, the contract required as a condition that the grade everywhere should be as low as the one recited as "now existing at the roadway" is a question for initial consideration below.

The judgment must be reversed with a new trial to follow.

So ordered.

[JULIUS J. OLSON, J., dissenting in an opinion in which HOLT, J. concurred, urged that the diminished value rule be applied in the absence of evidence to show that the completed product was to satisfy the personal taste of the promisee, and denied that the wilfulness of the breach should affect the measure of damages. HILTON and LORING JJ., took no part.]

NOTE

Purpose of Owner. One commentator on the Groves case has suggested that courts tend to use diminution in market price where "it appears from all the facts that the promisee was interested in the construction solely for its immediate effect upon the sale value of his adjacent property," and to use cost to complete "if he was interested in the construction either for its use value or as one step in a comprehensive scheme." He concludes that in Groves diminution in market price is indicated since "it appears that a level grade was not uppermost in the mind of the promisee at the time the contract was made; it dealt mainly with the removal of gravel, and it was covenanted that the overburden which had to be removed to get at the gravel, instead of being disposed of in the ordinary manner, would be deposited in such a way as to leave the land graded." Note, 40 Colum.L.Rev. 323, 325–27 (1940).

After the decision in Groves, the lessee paid the owner $55,000 to settle the claim. The land was left until 1951, when some grading was done on a portion at a cost of $6,000, and in 1953 this portion was sold for $45,000 to a buyer who planned to use it for a factory. Dawson and Harvey, Cases on Contracts and Contract Remedies 12 (2d ed. 1969). Does this suggest anything about the proper measure of recovery?

PEEVYHOUSE v. GARLAND COAL & MINING CO., 382 P.2d 109 (Okla.1962), cert. denied, 375 U.S. 906 (1963). [In 1954 Willie and Lucille Peevyhouse leased their farm for five years to Garland Coal & Mining Co. to strip mine coal. In addition to the usual covenants, Garland agreed to perform specified restorative and remedial work at the end of the lease. It failed to do this work, which would have involved the moving of many thousands of cubic yards of dirt at a cost of about $29,000. Had the work been done, the market price of the farm would have been increased by only $300. The Peevyhouses sued for $25,000 in damages. The trial court gave judgment on a verdict for $5,000. Both parties appealed.]

JACKSON, JUSTICE. . . . On appeal, the issue is sharply drawn. Plaintiffs contend that the true measure of damages in this case is what it will cost plaintiffs to obtain performance of the work that was not done because of defendant's default. Defendant argues that the measure of damages is the cost of performance "limited, however, to the total difference in the market value before and after the work was performed". It appears that this precise question has not heretofore been presented to this court. . . .

Plaintiffs rely on Groves v. John Wunder Co., 205 Minn. 163, 286 N.W. 235, 123 A.L.R. 502. In that case, the Minnesota court, in a substantially similar situation, adopted the "cost of performance" rule as opposed to the "value" rule. The result was to authorize a jury to give plaintiff damages in the amount of $60,000, where the real estate concerned would have been worth only $12,160, even if the work contracted for had been done.

It may be observed that Groves v. John Wunder Co., supra, is the only case which has come to our attention in which the cost of performance rule has been followed under circumstances where the cost of performance greatly exceeded the diminution in value resulting from the breach of contract. Incidentally, it appears that this case was decided by a plurality rather than a majority of the members of the court. . . .

We do not think [that] either [the] analogy [of a "building and construction" or a "grading and excavation" contract] is strictly applicable to the case now before us. The primary purpose of the lease contract between plaintiffs and defendant was neither "building and construction" nor "grading and excavation". It was merely to accomplish the economical recovery and marketing of coal from the premises, to the profit of all parties. The special provisions of the lease contract pertaining to remedial work were incidental to the main object involved.

Even in the case of contracts that are unquestionably building and construction contracts, the authorities are not in agreement as to the factors to be considered in determining whether the cost of performance rule or the value rule should be applied. The American Law Institute's Restatement of the Law, Contracts, Volume 1, Sections 346(1) (a) (i) and (ii) submits the proposition that the cost of performance is the proper measure of damages "if this is possible and does not involve *unreasonable economic waste*"; and that the diminution in value caused by the breach is the proper measure "if construction and completion in accordance with the contract would involve *unreasonable economic waste*". (Emphasis supplied.) In an explanatory comment immediately following the text, the Restatement makes it clear that the "economic waste" referred to consists of the destruction of a substantially completed building or other structure. Of course no such destruction is involved in the case now before us.

On the other hand, in McCormick, Damages, Section 168, it is said with regard to building and construction contracts that " . . . in cases where the defect is one that can be repaired or cured without *undue expense*" the cost of performance is the proper measure of damages, but where " . . . the defect in material or construction is one that cannot be remedied without *an expenditure for reconstruction disproportionate to the end to be attained*" (emphasis supplied) the value rule should be followed. The same idea was expressed in Jacob & Youngs, Inc. v. Kent, 230 N.Y. 239, 129 N.E. 889, 23 A.L.R. 1429, as follows: "The owner is entitled to the money which will permit him to complete, unless the cost of completion is grossly and unfairly out of proportion to the good to be attained. When that is true, the measure is the difference in value."

It thus appears that the prime consideration in the Restatement was "economic waste"; and that the prime consideration in McCormick, Damages, and in Jacob & Youngs, Inc. v. Kent, supra, was the relationship between the expense involved and the "end to be attained"—in other words, the "relative economic benefit". . . .

We . . . hold that where, in a coal mining lease, lessee agrees to perform certain remedial work on the premises concerned at the end of the lease period, and thereafter the contract is fully performed by both parties except that the remedial work is not done, the measure of damages in an action by lessor against lessee for damages for breach of contract is ordinarily the reasonable cost of performance of the work; however, where the contract provision breached was merely incidental to the main purpose in view, and where the economic benefit which would result to lessor by full performance of the work is grossly disproportionate to the cost of performance, the damages which lessor may recover are limited to the diminution in value resulting to the premises because of the non-performance. . . .

[Judgment reduced to $300 and affirmed (4–3).]

IRWIN, JUSTICE (dissenting). . . . Although the contract speaks for itself, there were several negotiations between the plaintiffs and defendant before the contract was executed. Defendant admitted in the trial of the action, that plaintiffs insisted that the above provisions be included in the contract and that they would not agree to the coal mining lease unless the above provisions were included. . . .

[I]n my opinion, the plaintiffs were entitled to specific performance of the contract and since defendant has failed to perform, the proper measure of damages should be the cost of performance. Any other measure of damage would be holding for naught the express provisions of the contract; would be taking from the plaintiffs the benefits of the contract and placing those benefits in defendant which has failed to perform its obligations; would be granting benefits to defendant without a resulting obligation; and would be completely rescinding the solemn obligation of the contract for the benefit of the defendant to the detriment of the plaintiffs by making an entirely new contract for the parties. . . .

NOTES

(1) *Explanation.* Are Groves and Peevyhouse distinguishable? Can a distinction be based on the proposition advanced by the court in Peevyhouse that "the contract provision breached was merely incidental to the main purpose in view"?

Leaving aside the possibility of a dramatic increase in cost or a similar decrease in market price during the term of the contract, in how many ways can one explain the disparity in each case between the minimum of diminution in market price and the maximum of cost to complete? Which figure, diminution in market price or cost to complete, gives the better approximation of diminution in value under each of these assumptions? Would there be any way to show which of these (or combination of them) actually caused the discrepancy? (Would it be instructive if the parties had discussed the terms of a lease that did not include the restorative work? Was there any such evidence in either case?) In the absence of such a showing, is it clear that the $5,000 awarded to the Peevyhouses by the trial court was not the diminution in value to them? See Farnsworth, Legal Remedies for Breach of Contract, 70 Colum.L.Rev. 1145, 1167–75 (1970).

(2) *"Economic Waste."* The Restatement, we are told by the court in Peevyhouse, speaks of "economic waste" in the sense of destruction of a substantially completed structure. Assuming that Kent had been awarded damages measured by the cost to replace the pipe with Reading pipe, would he then have been required to do so? Does it seem likely that he would have done so? In what sense is there "economic waste" if he is awarded damages measured by the cost to complete?

(3) *"Wilfulness."* The court says that John Wunder's "breach of contract was wilful." [a] What does "wilful" mean in this connection? If John Wunder must pay $60,000 if the breach is "wilful" and $12,160 if it is not, how is the $47,840 difference to be characterized? As a penalty for "wilfulness"? Would such a penalty be consistent with the objectives of contract remedies in our society?

THE ECONOMICS OF BREACH

Suppose that a party, after having made a contract, discovers that it is less advantageous to him than he had supposed, and considers breaking it. To what extent, if at all, should the law attempt to discourage him from doing so? On this question the economist has something to say.

From his competitive or free enterprise model, the economist has derived a set of decisional rules to enable individual economic units to make optimal allocations of their own resources. He has also derived a set of normative rules to guide society in the allocation of its resources. The economist's goal in formulating normative rules is that of "efficiency." The allocation of resources in a society is considered to be "efficient" if no alteration in that allocation will make some economic unit better off without making some other unit worse off. (Such an allocation is often called "Pareto optimal.")

In order to determine whether a unit is "better" or "worse" off, however, account must be taken of the preferences of that unit. The determination of these preferences is not a task for the economist. But given a set of individual preferences, the normative rules formu-

---

a. In H. P. Droher & Sons v. Toushin, 250 Minn. 490, 85 N.W.2d 273 (1957), the court distinguished Groves on the ground that, "The majority opinion is based, at least in part, on the fact that the breach of the contract was wilful and in bad faith".

lated by the economist will help society to achieve an efficient alloca-tion of its resources in terms of those preferences.

Furthermore, the economist insists that, for the good of society, its resources be allocated efficiently at every point in time. It is therefore in the interest of society that each economic unit shift its resources whenever this would lead to an efficient allocation. But what if that unit is bound by a contract not to shift its resources? Should it break it and re-allocate them?

The answer for each party to a contract is, of course, affected not only by his preferences but by the legal consequences that would follow from a breach of contract. (For present purposes, we will as-sume, somewhat unrealistically, that available legal remedies are al-ways exacted, and that they are the only sanctions for breach.) The law could, for example, provide such a large measure of recovery for breach that re-allocation through breach would seldom be advanta-geous to a party. Or it could provide such a small measure of recov-ery that re-allocation through breach would usually be advantageous to him. Normative economics suggests, however, that the measure of re-covery should be the diminution in value to the injured party. Why?

Lowering the measure of recovery *below* the diminution in value caused him by the breach would not put him at the same level of satis-faction of his preferences that he expected and would fail to protect his expectations and preserve his planned allocation of resources. Raising the measure of damages *above* this level would discourage the breaking of contracts when society would want them broken and im-pair the efficient allocation of its resources. For it is in society's in-terest that each individual re-allocate his resources whenever it makes him better off without making some other unit worse off. Since re-al-location through breach will not make the injured party worse off if his expectations are protected by preserving his planned allocation of resources, and will, by hypothesis, make the party in breach better off, it is in society's interest that the contract be broken and the re-sources reallocated.

What does this suggest about the measure of damages for "wil-ful" breach? What does it suggest about the efficacy of the law of contracts in encouraging the performance of socially desirable prom-ises? See generally, Birmingham, Breach of Contract, Damage Meas-ures, and Economic Efficiency, 24 Rutgers L.Rev. 273 (1970).

SECTION 2.   ALTERNATIVES TO EXPECTATION

FARNSWORTH, LEGAL REMEDIES FOR BREACH OF CONTRACT, 70 Colum.L.Rev. 1145, 1175–78 (1970).[a]   Ordinarily the injured party will be content to base his recovery on his expectation interest, since this will be more favorable to him than recovery based on either his restitution interest or his reliance interest.   There are, however, some exceptions.

One instance in which restitution may appear an attractive alternative occurs when the party in breach has committed a total breach in spite of the fact that the bargain has turned out to favor him— that is, when the value to the party in breach of the benefit conferred upon him would exceed the value of his promised performance to the injured party.   Needless to say, this sort of situation is not common since there is usually no reason for the more favored party to refuse to perform his part of a bargain that is favorable to him.   Nevertheless, when this situation does arise, restitution is allowed if the benefit conferred on the party in breach consists simply of the payment of money.[1]

> *Illustration 1.* Builder contracts with Owner to construct a factory on Owner's land for $1,000,000 payable in advance. Owner pays the $1,000,000 and Builder breaches by failing to construct the factory. Owner sues Builder for return of the full $1,000,000, although the value of the factory to Owner would in fact have been only $700,000.

Owner will be allowed restitution of the full $1,000,000, with no deduction for the $300,000 loss he would have suffered had Builder constructed the factory.   Owner's position after the breach is consequently better than it would have been had Builder performed.

Restitution is not, however, generally allowed where the benefit conferred on the party in breach consists of something other than the payment of money.[2]

> *Illustration 2.* Builder contracts with Owner to construct a factory on Owner's land for $1,000,000 payable on completion. Builder constructs the factory and Owner breaches by failing to pay the price. Builder sues Owner for $2,000,000, the actual value of the factory to Owner, rather than for the $1,000,000 that Owner promised to pay.

a. Reprinted and slightly adapted by permission of the Columbia Law Review.

Defendant's Breach, 20 Ohio St. L.J. 264–65 (1959); Restatement § 347(1) (a).

1. Bush v. Canfield, 2 Conn. 485 (1818) discussed in Palmer, The Contract Price as a Limit on Restitution for

2. E. g., Oliver v. Campbell, 43 Cal.2d 298, 273 P.2d 15 (1954); Restatement § 350.

Here Builder's recovery will be limited to the $1,000,000 promised, which was the limit of his expectation. The results in Illustrations 1 and 2 both of which favor the party who has agreed to pay money, can be reconciled on the ground that in each case the court chooses the measure of recovery that permits it to avoid the problem of determining loss in value due to nonperformance of the promise to do something other than pay money.[3] If, however, the benefit conferred on the party in breach consists of other than the payment of money, and if the injured party has performed only in part, as where Owner breaches by repudiating when Builder is in the process of constructing the factory, the problem of valuation cannot be avoided. Here courts have generally allowed recovery based on the restitution interest, a point that will be illustrated shortly in connection with the protection of the reliance interest in this situation.[4]

Dawson points out a second instance in which recovery based on the restitution interest, broadly conceived, might exceed the expectation.[5] This occurs where one party refuses to perform so that he may take advantage of another, more attractive, opportunity.

> *Illustration 3.* Builder contracts with Owner to construct a factory on Owner's land for $1,000,000 payable on completion. Builder would have made a profit of $100,000 on this contract. Immediately after making the contract, he receives from another owner an offer of a contract under which he can make a profit of $300,000. He accepts it, although he cannot do both jobs, and repudiates his contract with Owner. Owner sues Builder for restitution of the $200,000 additional profit that Builder made as a result of his breach, although it appears that Owner would not have made a profit had the factory been built.

Dawson concludes, however, that Owner would be denied recovery of the $200,000:

> This kind of recovery could not be explained as restitution under present day tests; there would be a fatal break in the chain of causation, for the asset or conduct that was merely promised would not have come *from* the promisee [Owner].

3. For this reason Restatement § 350 allows restitution where, for example, the injured party has parted with goods in return for a promise to perform services. See Palmer, supra note 1, at 267.

4. Restatement §§ 347(1) (a), 351. See United States v. Zara, p. 496 infra. The formulas for recovery based on the expectation interest and the restitution interest, respectively, have a discontinuity at the line between part and full performance. An example is Oliver v. Campbell, 43 Cal.2d 298, 273 P.2d 15 (1954), in which a five-judge majority held that a lawyer had fully performed his services for his client and was limited to the $750 fee that they had fixed, while two dissenting judges contended that the services were not fully performed so that he was entitled to their reasonable value, $5,000.

5. Dawson, Restitution or Damages?, 20 Ohio St. L.J. 175, 186–87 (1959).

Perhaps another way to express the idea is that the prevention of profit through mere breach of contract is not yet an approved aim of our legal order, as it is with breach of "fiduciary" duties.[6]

The limits on the restitution interest as a basis of recovery, therefore, usually make it unattractive to the injured party as an alternative to the expectation interest. The reliance interest, however, is more promising.

One instance in which the injured party might prefer recovery based on his reliance interest occurs when his expectations under the contract were less than his expectations under some other bargain that he declined in reliance on the contract.

> *Illustration 4.* The facts being otherwise as stated in Illustration 3, Builder would have made a profit of $100,000 on this contract. Builder rejects the other offer because he cannot do both jobs. Owner then breaches by repudiating the contract after it is too late for Builder to accept the other offer. Builder sues Owner for $300,000 in damages, based on what he lost in reliance on his contract with Owner, rather than for $100,000 based on what he lost in disappointed expectations upon its breach.

Although $300,000 would be required to put Builder in the position in which he would have been had he not made the contract with Owner,[7] no court would allow him this larger sum. A court will not, as Fuller and Perdue stated it, "knowingly put the plaintiff in a better position than he would have occupied had the contract been fully performed."[8] Expectation here operates as an upper limit on recovery, a defensible limit since one of the justifications for the protection of the expectation interest in the first place is that it yields rules that are superior, because of their certainty and ease of application, to those derived

---

6. Dawson, supra note 5, at 187. He cites Acme Mills & Elevator Co. v. Johnson, 141 Ky. 718, 133 S.W. 784 (1911), in which a seller failed to deliver wheat which he had contracted to sell for $1.03 a bushel, sold it before the delivery date to another buyer for $1.16 a bushel, and was held liable for nominal damages only when the market dropped below the contract price by the delivery date. See also Restatement (Second) of Agency § 404 (1957), Illustration 2. But in Timko v. Useful Homes Corp., 114 N.J.Eq. 433, 168 A. 824 (1933), it was held that a vendor of lots, for which the purchaser had partly paid, held them in trust for the purchaser and was liable to him for damages based on the price at which he wrongfully sold them to a third party.

7. To eliminate the possibility that Builder might have repudiated the contract with Owner and accepted the more profitable offer, remaining liable to Owner for damages, assume that those damages would be at least $200,000, so that this course of action would have been less desirable for Builder.

8. Fuller & Perdue, The Reliance Interest in Contract Damages 1, 46 Yale L.J. 52, 79. See also their discussion of the compensability of gains prevented through reliance at 417–18.

from the reliance interest.[9] Businessmen regularly rely on contracts by foregoing other opportunities and adjusting their business to the expected performance, and basing recovery on such reliance would pose grave problems of measurement.

A second exceptional case, in which the injured party may prefer damages based on reliance to those based on expectation, arises when the breach has relieved him from finishing performance of what has turned out to be a losing contract.[10]

> *Illustration 5.* Builder contracts with Owner to construct a factory on Owner's land for $1,000,000 payable on completion. Owner breaches by repudiating the contract after Builder has begun performance. Builder has already spent $500,000 and would have to spend $600,000 more to finish performance, which would result in a $100,000 loss on the contract. Builder sues Owner for $500,000 in damages, based on his expenditures in reliance on the contract and ignoring the $100,000 loss, rather than for the $400,000 to which he would otherwise be entitled.

NOTE

Losing Contracts. What result in Illustration 5 under Formula A? Under Formula B? For a case applying Formula A, see Millen v. Gulesian, 229 Mass. 27, 118 N.E. 267 (1918).

UNITED STATES v. ZARA CONTRACTING CO., 146 F.2d 606 (2d Cir. 1944). [Zara contracted with the United States to extend the runways at the Tri-Cities Airport at Endicott, New York, and subcontracted all but a $100 item out to Susi and to D'Agostino & Curcio. Unanticipated clay in the soil caused the subcontractors extra expenses and led to a contract dispute with Zara, which took over the subcontractors' equipment and completed the performance itself. The United States paid a claim by Zara for extra work due to the clay. The subcontractors sued Zara, abandoned any claim for prof-

9. Id. at 61–62. They also suggest that in a hypothetical society in which all values were available on the market and where all markets were "perfect" in the economic sense . . . there would be no difference between the reliance interest and the expectation interest. The plaintiff's loss in foregoing to enter another contract would be identical with the expectation value of the contract he did make.

Id. at 62. They give the illustration of a "physician who by making one appointment deprives himself of the opportunity of making a precisely simi-

lar appointment with another patient . . . ." Id. at 74.

10. It may be that the injured party entered into the contract because of some special advantage, such as the enhancement of his experience or reputation or good will, with respect to which his proof fails to meet the standard of certainty, discussed in Subsection 3(c) infra. What he then regarded as an advantageous contract may thus appear as a "losing" contract.

its, and had judgment for $39,107.10 for work done at the contract rate, and $18,600 for the increased cost of excavation due to the soil conditions encountered, plus an allowance for the use of their equipment by Zara, less sums already paid them by Zara, plus interest. Zara appealed and denied liability for the $18,600 increased cost.]

CLARK, J. [Zara wrongfully prevented the plaintiffs from completing the contract. Although their increased cost was not separately compensable as "extra work," and although they could not take advantage of the terms of the main contract under which Zara had been compensated, the plaintiffs were entitled to recover that cost on another theory.] For it is an accepted principle of contract law, often applied in the case of construction contracts, that the promisee upon breach has the option to forego any suit on the contract and claim only the reasonable value of his performance. This is well settled in the New York cases. . . . It also appears to be the general view, save for an occasional case viewed as illogical by the text writers, who are solidly in support of the doctrine. . . . These authorities make it quite clear that under the better rule the contract price or the unit price per cubic yard of a construction or excavation contract does not limit recovery. . . . This doctrine is particularly applicable to unit prices in construction contracts; as Professor Patterson points out, 31 Col.L.Rev. at page 1303, a plaintiff may well have completed the hardest part of a job for which an average cost had been set. But it seems settled now in New York that with the breach fall all the other parts of the contract. . . . Hence it is clear that plaintiffs are not limited to the contract prices in the situation disclosed here.

As we have noted, the trial court granted recovery for $39,107.10 for the work done at the contract price, together with an additional sum of $18,600 for the extra cost of excavation of the clay, computed as 62,000 cubic yards at the additional expense of 30 cents per cubic yard. The amount of the clay excavation was vigorously disputed by Zara, who offered three mathematical computations each indicating a different amount. But the facts were complicated, and the District Court, having before it not only the estimates of the various witnesses, including engineers on the job, but the claims of Zara made in seeking the extra allowance from the United States, reached a reasonable figure, substantially below the plaintiffs' claims, which we are not disposed to disturb. As to the monetary amounts, these are based on the cost of the work to Zara, as well as expert testimony for the plaintiffs, and are not seriously disputed. Indeed, in fixing the additional allowance at 30 cents per cubic yard, the judge relied particularly on Zara's claim to the United States wherein it stated that its records showed an actual cost to it of the extra work, amounting to 28.7 cents per cubic yard for the excavating, and 2½ cents per cubic yard for placing the excavated material in the runways. Professor Williston points out that the measure of recovery by way of restitution, though often confused with recovery on the contract, should not be measured or limited thereby; but he does point out that the contract may be important evidence of the value of the performance to the defendant, as may also the cost of the labor and materials. 5 Williston on Contracts, Rev.Ed., §§ 1482, 1483, 1485. It is therefore appropriate here, particularly in default of any challenging evidence, to base recovery on proper expenditures in performance, . . . or for extra work, . . . and to make use of the contract as fixing the basic price. . . .

It is to be noted that, since it is the defendant who is in default, and plaintiffs' performance here is "part of the very performance" for which the defendant had bargained, "it is to be valued, not by the extent to which the defendant's total wealth has been increased thereby, but by the amount for which such services and materials as constituted the part performance could have been purchased from one in the plaintiff's position at the time they were rendered." Restatement, Contracts, § 347, comment c. . . . It is to be noted that in fact defendant Zara did receive benefits most substantial from plaintiffs' performance. Plaintiffs had actually excavated 211,390 cubic yards, for which Zara's profit, as determined by the spread between the main and the subcontract of 5½ cents per cubic yard as a minimum, with higher amounts for a part, would be around $12,000; it had already collected $17,115.79 from the United States for the additional cost of removing the "cohesive silt," of which most was done by plaintiffs, and it had pending a claim against the United States for $18,840.10 more; and what is perhaps most important, it had received a performance which it needed to make to ensure recovery of these profits and sums from the United States and avoid the danger of being in default, and which it would have had to do itself or purchase in the market. Hence the allowance made by the District Court is justified on the evidence and the law, and we find no error, therefore, in this item of recovery. . . .

[Affirmed.]

NOTES

(1) *"Benefits Most Substantial."* What result in Illustration 5, p. 496 supra, under the Zara case? The court notes that Zara "did receive benefits most substantial from plaintiffs' performance." Was recovery based on the value of those benefits to Zara?

The Zara case was cited with approval in Acme Process Equipment Co. v. United States, 347 F.2d 509 (Ct.Cl.1965). The United States, interested in obtaining a new arms supplier, awarded a contract to Acme, which had never before had a defense contract, to manufacture recoilless rifles for $385 each. The government wrongfully terminated after it had received and paid for about one-third of the rifles. Acme sued to recover its costs, which were $1,179 each at first and dropped to $690 each by the time of the termination. The trial commissioner based recovery on the amount by which Acme could have reduced its loss if it had been allowed to complete performance. On appeal, the Court of Claims remanded, quoting Comment a to Restatement, § 348, to the effect that the value of the service may be recovered "even though there never was any product created by the service that added to the wealth of the defendant." But it concluded that only reasonable costs can be recovered and sent the case back for a determination of whether Acme's costs were excessive. The case is discussed in Childres and Garamella, The Law of Restitution and the Reliance Interest in Contract, 64 Nw.U.L.Rev. 433, 444–51 (1969): Note, 79 Harv.L.Rev. 1307 (1966). See also, Palmer, The Contract Price as a Limit on Restitution for Defendant's Breach, 20 Ohio St.L.J. 264 (1959).

(2) *"A Proper Penalty."* Fuller and Perdue ask whether shifting to the defendant the loss that the plaintiff would otherwise have suffered is "a proper penalty" to impose for the defendant's breach. They suggest that to consider it as such goes but "a step farther" than the many cases that allow "the plaintiff to recover the value of benefits conferred on the defendant, even though this value exceeds that of the return performance promised by the defendant." Fuller and Perdue, The Reliance Interest in Contract Damages: 1, 46 Yale L.J. 52, 77 (1936).

In support of the argument that defendant should not be allowed to take advantage of a contract which he has broken, it may be noted that various factors may have influenced plaintiff to name a smaller price, in proportion, for a large performance than he would have named for a small performance, and that he may have suffered various inconveniences from defendant's breach, which are not compensated for by giving him only a pro rata part of the total contract price. For further discussion, see Patterson, Builder's Measure of Recovery for Breach of Contract, 31 Colum.L.Rev. 1286, 1299–1303 (1931.)

KEHOE v. RUTHERFORD, 56 N.J.L. 23, 27 A. 912 (1893). [Kehoe contracted to grade Montrose Avenue in the borough of Rutherford, New Jersey, for 65 cents per running foot. After he had done part of the work, and had been paid $1,850, the borough defaulted. He sued for breach of contract and for quantum meruit. Plaintiff was non-suited and appealed.]

Dixon, J. . . . [T]he plaintiff's evidence tended to prove that the length of the whole work required by the contract was four thousand two hundred and twenty feet, which, at the contract rate, sixty-five cents per lineal foot, made the aggregate price $2,743; that about three thousand five hundred feet in length had been substantially graded, but still needed trimming up and finishing; that in doing this work he had excavated about eight thousand cubic yards of earth, and had put in about one thousand three hundred cubic yards of filling; that, to complete the job, about fourteen thousand cubic yards of filling were still necessary, besides the trimming up and fin-

ishing of the entire length of the street.   His evidence further indicated that the fair cost of the work done was—

8,000 cubic yards of excavation, at 35 cents $2,800
900 cubic yards of filling, at 21 cents   189
400 cubic yards of filling, at 41 cents   164

Making a total of $3,153

And that the fair cost of the work remaining to be done in completely performing the contract was—

14,000 cubic yards of filling, at 12 cents $1,680
4,220 feet of finishing, at 5 cents   211

Making a total of $1,891

Thus showing the fair cost of the whole work required by the contract to be $5,044.   .   .   .

The non-suit was ordered upon the theory that a plaintiff could
recover, for the work done, only such a proportion of the contract
price as the fair cost of that work bore to the fair cost of the whole
work required, and, in respect of the work not done, only such profit
(if any) as he might have made by doing it, for the unpaid balance of
the contract price.   Under this theory, his recovery for the work done
was to be limited to such a proportion of $2,743 as three thousand one
hundred and fifty-three bears to five thousand and forty-four, viz.,
$1,715; and as to the work not done, since it would cost him $1,891 to
do it, while the unpaid balance of the price was only $893, no profit
could be earned by doing it.   Hence it was considered that he had
been overpaid to the extent of the difference between $1,850 and
$1,715.

But the contention of the plaintiff was and is that, as he was prevented from completing the contract without fault on his part, he is
entitled to the reasonable value of the work done, without reference to
the contract price; and if this be the correct rule, undoubtedly the
case should have gone to the jury.   But at the very threshold we are
confronted with this possible result of the application of the rule contended for, that the plaintiff might recover $3,153 for doing about
three-fifths of the work, while if he had done it all he could have recovered only $2,743.   The absurdity of the result condemns the appli-
cation of such a rule.   .   .   .

Some of the obscurity surrounding this subject springs, I think,
from a failure to distinguish between the right to sue upon the quantum meruit when the contract remains uncompleted through the fault
of the defendant and the measure of damages in such a state of facts.
It is well settled that, if the plaintiff has fully performed his contract,
so that nothing remains but the duty of the defendant to pay, the
plaintiff may declare upon the quantum meruit, ignoring the special
contract, and the plaintiff's readiness and offer to perform are to

this extent—but to this extent only (Shannon v. Comstock, 21 Wend., N.Y., 457)—equivalent to actual performance. In both cases, however, the amount which the plaintiff deserves to recover is regulated by the contract. The refusal of the defendant to pay after all the work is done is no less a breach of the contract than is his refusal to permit the plaintiff to do all that the bargain entitled him to do; but neither breach does or ought to put the parties in the position they would have occupied if no contract had been made. In both cases, what is done was done under the contract and should be paid for accordingly.

If, on partial performance, the plaintiff confines himself to the common counts, he excludes, by his pleading, any claim for what he has not performed, but he does not thereby enhance his desserts for what he has performed, and therefore, in order to obtain complete justice on breach of a profitable bargain, he must resort to a special count. . . .

[Affirmed.]

NOTES

(1) *Possible Solutions.* What result in Illustration 5, p. 496 supra, under Kehoe v. Rutherford?[a] What solution do you prefer? What position does the Restatement take? See Restatement, §§ 333, 346 and 347.

(2) *Burden of Proof.* Consider the following as a possible solution. "In cases where the venture would have proved profitable to the promisee, there is no reason why he should not recover his expenses. On the other hand, on those occasions in which the performance would not have covered the promisee's outlay, such a result imposes the risk of the promisee's contract upon the promisor. We cannot agree that the promisor's default in performance should under this guise make him an insurer of the promisee's venture; yet it does not follow that the breach should not throw upon him the duty of showing that the value of the performance would in fact have been less than the promisee's outlay. It is often very hard to learn what the value of the performance would have been; and it is a common expedient, and a just one, in such situations to put the peril of the answer upon that party who by his wrong has made the issue relevant to the rights of the other. On principle therefore the proper solution would seem to be that the promisee may recover his outlay in preparation for the performance, subject to the privilege of the promisor to reduce it by as much as he can show that the promisee would have lost, if the contract had been performed." Learned Hand in L. Albert & Son v. Armstrong Rubber Co., 178 F.2d 182, 189 (2d Cir. 1949).

The case just quoted from involved material delay by a seller of machines to be used by the buyer to reclaim old rubber during World War II. The buyer did not ask for loss of profits when the delay caused this speculative venture to fall through, but did claim expenses in reliance on the

a. The percentage-of-completion method is one commonly used in accounting practice. See Herwitz, Accounting for Long-Term Construction Contracts: A Lawyer's Approach, 70 Harv.L.Rev. 449, 452, n. 11 (1952).

seller's promise to deliver on time, including the cost of laying foundations for the machines. It was this claim to which Hand spoke. Note that in the preceding cases in this section the profit in question was profit to be made from the transaction between the parties, while here the profit in question was profit to be made from *other* transactions which were to be made possible by the one between the parties. Similarly, in the preceding cases the reliance in question was reliance in performing or at least in preparing to perform in the transaction between the parties, while here the reliance was in preparing to perform in *other* transactions which were to be made possible by this transaction. Should this make a difference?

(3) *The Case of the Severable Subdivision.* Day contracted to pay Shapiro Enginering $43,000 for constructing storm sewers in Oakwood Knolls Subdivision, Bethesda, Maryland. The subdivision was laid out in two sections. Lots had been sold and some homes were under construction on Section I, but not on Section II. An addendum to the contract read, "Section I . . . shall amount to $23,000, and Section II will amount to $20,000, for purposes of paying on account of this contract only." Day defaulted after Shapiro Engineering had completed Section I. Shapiro Engineering sued for $23,000. At the trial Day offered an estimate that it would have cost Shapiro Engineering $27,347 to have completed Section II. From a judgment for the plaintiff for $23,000, the defendant appealed, contending that the trial court erred in making no finding on the cost to complete Section II. *Held:* Affirmed. "The contract itself made an apportionment for purposes of payment, and upon the facts stated the two parts of the work were separate and distinct. [Moreover, in its correspondence] the defendant itself recognized that the payments on account would completely pay for the first section, without regard to the completion of Section II. A clearer acknowledgement of the severability of the contract in relation to payment can hardly be imagined." Shapiro Engineering Corp. v. Francis O. Day Co., 215 Md. 373, 137 A.2d 695 (1958).

Is this decision simply an application of the principle laid down in Kehoe v. Rutherford? Is the contract there "severable" in this sense? Is the contract in Illustration 5, p. 496 supra, "severable" in this sense?

(4) *Problem.* Security Stove in Kansas City had developed a furnace which it was anxious to exhibit at a trade association convention in Atlantic City, although it was not yet on the market. Since it was too late to ship it by freight, Security Stove made a contract for its shipment with Express Company, explaining its need, asking that it be shipped to arrive by October 8, and reminding Express Company of the urgency shortly before the date for shipment. Express Company picked up the shipment of 21 numbered packages, but the package containing the gas manifold, the most important part of the exhibit, was mislaid and did not arrive until the convention closed. Security Stove sues to recover from Express Company for express charges to Atlantic City, freight charges back to Kansas City, travel and hotel expenses and salaries for its employees who went to the convention to exhibit the furnace, and rental for the booth. What decision? See Security Stove & Mfg. Co. v. American Ry. Express Co., 227 Mo.App. 175, 51 S.W.2d 572 (1932).

SECTION 3.   LIMITATIONS ON DAMAGES

(a) Avoidability

In Virtue v. Bird, 3 Keble 766, 84 Eng.Rep. 1000, (same case) 1 Ventris 310, 86 Eng.Rep. 200 (1678), a quaint case from three centuries ago, the plaintiff contracted to carry timber to Ipswich and to deliver it to a place to be appointed by the defendant.   When the plaintiff arrived in Ipswich, however, "the defendant delayed by the space of six hours the appointment of the place; insomuch that his horses being so hot .   .   .   and standing in aperto aere, they died soon after."   The court denied him recovery of this loss on the ground that "it was the plaintiff's folly to let the horses stand," "for the plaintiff might have taken his horses out of the cart, or have laid down the [timber] anywhere in Ipswich."   Although it is sometimes said that in such cases the injured party is under a "duty" to mitigate damages, he incurs no liability to the party in breach for his failure to mitigate.   His recovery is the same regardless of whether he takes steps in mitigation or not.   He is simply precluded from recovering for loss that he could reasonably have avoided.

ROCKINGHAM COUNTY v. LUTEN BRIDGE CO.

United States Circuit Court of Appeals, Fourth Circuit, 1929.
35 F.2d 301, 66 A.L.R. 735.

[Action at law, instituted in the district court, to recover an amount alleged to be due under a contract for the construction of a bridge in North Carolina.   The contract was entered into, by the Board of County Commissioners, on January 7, 1924; but there was considerable public opposition to the building of the bridge, and on February 21, 1924, the board notified the plaintiff not to proceed any further under the contract, which it refused (unjustifiably, as the court found) to recognize as valid.   At that time plaintiff had expended about $1900 for labor done and material on the ground.   Despite this notice from the county commissioners, plaintiff continued to build the bridge in accordance with the terms of the contract.   The present action is brought to recover $18,301.07, the amount alleged to be due plaintiff for work done before November 3, 1924.   The trial court directed a verdict for plaintiff for this sum.   Defendant appealed.]

PARKER, CIRCUIT JUDGE.   .   .   .   Coming, then, to the third question—i. e., as to the measure of plaintiff's recovery—we do not think that, after the county had given notice, while the contract was still executory, that it did not desire the bridge built and would not pay for it, plaintiff could proceed to build it and recover the contract price. It is true that the county had no right to rescind the contract, and the notice given plaintiff amounted to a breach on its part; but, after plaintiff had received notice of the breach, it was its duty to do nothing to increase the damages flowing therefrom. If A enters into a binding contract to build a house for B, B, of course, has no right to rescind the contract without A's consent. But if, before the house is built, he decides that he does not want it, and notifies A to that effect, A has no right to proceed with the building and thus pile up damages. His remedy is to treat the contract as broken when he receives the notice, and sue for the recovery of such damages as he may have sustained from the breach, including any profit which he would have realized upon performance, as well as any other losses which may have resulted to him. In the case at bar, the county decided not to build the road of which the bridge was to be a part, and did not build it. The bridge, built in the midst of the forest, is of no value to the county because of this change of circumstances. When, therefore, the county gave notice to the plaintiff that it would not proceed with the project, plaintiff should have desisted from further work. It had no right thus to pile up damages by proceeding with the erection of a useless bridge.

The contrary view was expressed by Lord Cockburn in Frost v. Knight, L.R. 7 Ex. 111, but, as pointed out by Prof. Williston (Williston on Contracts, vol. 3, p. 2347), it is not in harmony with the decisions in this country. The American rule and the reasons supporting it are well stated by Prof. Williston as follows:

"There is a line of cases running back to 1845 which holds that, after an absolute repudiation or refusal to perform by one party to a contract, the other party cannot continue to perform and recover damages based on full performance. This rule is only a particular application of the general rule of damages that a plaintiff cannot hold a defendant liable for damages which need not have been incurred; or, as it is often stated, the plaintiff must, so far as he can without loss to himself, mitigate the damages caused by the defendant's wrongful act. The application of this rule to the matter in question is obvious. If a man engages to have work done, and afterwards repudiates his contract before the work has been begun or when it has been only partially done, it is inflicting damage on the defendant without benefit to the plaintiff to allow the latter to insist on proceeding with the contract. The work may be useless to the defendant, and yet he would be forced to pay the full contract price. On the other hand, the plaintiff is interested only in the profit he will make out of the contract. If he receives this it is equally advantageous for him to use his time otherwise."   .   .   .

Judgment reversed.

NOTE

The Code. Under UCC 2–704(2), a seller who is to manufacture goods may proceed to complete their manufacture upon the buyer's repudiation, instead of halting manufacture and salvaging them while in process, "in the exercise of reasonable commercial judgment for the purposes of avoiding loss and of effective realization." If he does so he may then base his recovery on the goods as completed, even if his "reasonable commercial judgment" turned out to be wrong. Is the manufacturer's situation in any way distinguishable from that of the Luten Bridge Co.?

"CONSTRUCTIVE SERVICE"

It is one thing to say that the injured party cannot recover for cost that he could have avoided by simply stopping performance. It is another to say that he cannot recover for loss that he could have avoided by taking affirmative steps to arrange a substitute transaction. In Gandell v. Pontigny, 4 Camp. 375, 171 Eng.Rep. 119 (1816), the court refused to take this second step. A merchant was sued by his clerk, whom he had wrongfully discharged in the middle of a quarter. The clerk was allowed to recover the agreed compensation for the entire quarter, including the part when he had not worked, on Lord Ellenborough's reasoning that:

> Having served a part of the quarter and being willing to serve the residue, in contemplation of law he may be considered to have served the whole.

In Howard v. Daly, 61 N.Y. 362 (1875), a leading American case, Dwight [a] rejected this doctrine of "constructive service" as

> so wholly irreconcilable to that great and beneficent rule of law, that a person discharged from service must not remain idle, but must accept employment elsewhere if offered, that we cannot accept it . . . .   The doctrine of "constructive service" is not only at war with principle but with the rules of political economy, as it encourages idleness and gives compensation to men who fold their arms and decline service, equal to those who perform with willing hands their stipulated amount of labor.

---

a. Theodore William Dwight (1822–1892) served as a professor of law at Hamilton College, and then as a professor of law and later as warden of the law school at Columbia from 1858 to 1891. His principal field was contracts. His method of teaching involved interrogation of his students on an assigned text, and it is reported that, "He could so cross-examine a dunce that the dunce would come off amazed at his own unconscious cerebration." From 1873 to 1875 he was a member of the New York Commission of Appeals, which had been created to help the Court of Appeals dispose of its backlog of undecided cases. It was said that his sixty-eight opinions were "monographs, exhausting the particular subject," and it was doubted "whether in any reports a greater amount of learning is anywhere condensed into an equal number of pages."

PARKER v. TWENTIETH CENTURY–FOX FILM CORP.

Supreme Court of California, 1970.
3 Cal.3d 176, 474 P.2d 689.

BURKE, JUSTICE.　Defendant Twentieth Century-Fox Film Corporation appeals from a summary judgment granting to plaintiff the recovery of agreed compensation under a written contract for her services as an actress in a motion picture.　As will appear, we have concluded that the trial court correctly ruled in plaintiff's favor and that the judgment should be affirmed.

Plaintiff is well known as an actress [a], and in the contract between plaintiff and defendant is sometimes referred to as the "Artist."　Under the contract, dated August 6, 1965, plaintiff was to play the female lead in defendant's contemplated production of a motion picture entitled "Bloomer Girl."　The contract provided that defendant would pay plaintiff a minimum "guaranteed compensation" of $53,571.42 per week for 14 weeks commencing May 23, 1966, for a total of $750,000.　Prior to May 1966 defendant decided not to produce the picture and by a letter dated April 4, 1966, it notified plaintiff of that decision and that it would not "comply with our obligations to you under" the written contract.

By the same letter and with the professed purpose "to avoid any damage to you," defendant instead offered to employ plaintiff as the leading actress in another film tentatively entitled "Big Country, Big Man" (hereinafter, "Big Country").　The compensation offered was identical, as were 31 of the 34 numbered provisions or articles of the original contract.[1]　Unlike "Bloomer Girl," however, which was to have been a musical production, "Big Country" was a dramatic "western type" movie.　"Bloomer Girl" was to have been filmed in California; "Big Country" was to be produced in Australia.　Also, certain terms in the proffered contract varied from those of the original.[2]

a.　Mrs. Parker may be better known to the reader under her professional name, Shirley MacLaine. The following listing from Who's Who in America (1970–1971) may be of interest in connection with the case. "Broadway plays include Me and Juliet, 1953, Pajama Game, 1954; actress movies The Trouble With Henry, 1954, Artists and Models, 1954, Around the World in 80 Days, 1955–56, Hot Spell, 1957, The Matchmaker, 1957, The Sheepman, 1957, Some Came Running, 1958 (Fgn. Press award 1959), Ask Any Girl, 1959 (Silver Bear award as best actress Internat. Berlin Film Festival 1959), Career, 1959, Can-Can, 1959, The Apartment, 1959 (best actress prize Venice Film Festival 1960); Two for the Seesaw, 1962; Irma La Douce, 1963;

What A Way To Go!, 1964; The Yellow Rolls Royce, 1964; John Goldfarb Please Come Home, 1965; Gambit [1966]; Woman Times Seven [1967]."

1.　Among the identical provisions was the following found in the last paragraph of Article 2 of the original contract: "We [defendant] shall not be obligated to utilize your [plaintiff's] services in or in connection with the Photoplay hereunder, our sole obligation, subject to the terms and conditions of this Agreement, being to pay you the guaranteed compensation herein provided for."

2.　Article 29 of the original contract specified that plaintiff approved the director already chosen for "Bloomer

Plaintiff was given one week within which to accept; she did not and the offer lapsed. Plaintiff then commenced this action seeking recovery of the agreed guaranteed compensation.

The complaint sets forth two causes of action. The first is for money due under the contract; the second, based upon the same allegations as the first, is for damages resulting from defendant's breach of contract. Defendant in its answer admits the existence and validity of the contract, that plaintiff complied with all the conditions, covenants and promises and stood ready to complete the performance, and that defendant breached and "anticipatorily repudiated" the contract. It denies, however, that any money is due to plaintiff either under the contract or as a result of its breach, and pleads as an affirmative defense to both causes of action plaintiff's allegedly deliberate failure to mitigate damages, asserting that she unreasonably refused to accept its offer of the leading role in "Big Country."

Plaintiff moved for summary judgment under Code of Civil Procedure section 437c, the motion was granted, and summary judgment for $750,000 plus interest was entered in plaintiff's favor. This appeal by defendant followed. . . .

The general rule is that the measure of recovery by a wrongfully discharged employee is the amount of salary agreed upon for the period of service, less the amount which the employer affirmatively proves the employee has earned or with reasonable effort might have earned from other employment. . . . However, before projected earnings from other employment opportunities not sought or accepted by the discharged employee can be applied in mitigation, the employ-

---

Girl" and that in case he failed to act as director plaintiff was to have approval rights of any substitute director. Article 31 provided that plaintiff was to have the right of approval of the "Bloomer Girl" dance director, and Article 32 gave her the right of approval of the screenplay.

Defendant's letter of April 4 to plaintiff, which contained both defendant's notice of breach of the "Bloomer Girl" contract and offer of the lead in "Big Country," eliminated or impaired each of those rights. It read in part as follows: "The terms and conditions of our offer of employment are identical to those set forth in the 'BLOOMER GIRL' Agreement, Articles 1 through 34 and Exhibit A to the Agreement, except as follows:

"1. Article 31 of said Agreement will not be included in any contract of employment regarding 'BIG COUNTRY, BIG MAN' as it is not a musical and it thus will not need a dance director.

"2. In the 'BLOOMER GIRL' agreement, in Articles 29 and 32, you were given certain director and screenplay approvals and you had preapproved certain matters. Since there simply is insufficient time to negotiate with you regarding your choice of director and regarding the screenplay and since you already expressed an interest in performing the role in 'BIG COUNTRY, BIG MAN,' we must exclude from our offer of employment in 'BIG COUNTRY, BIG MAN' any approval rights as are contained in said Articles 29 and 32; however, we shall consult with you respecting the director to be selected to direct the photoplay and will further consult with you with respect to the screenplay and any revisions or changes therein, provided, however, that if we fail to agree . . . the decision of . . . [defendant] with respect to the selection of a director and to revisions and changes in the said screenplay shall be binding upon the parties to said agreement."

er must show that the other employment was comparable, or substantially similar, to that of which the employee has been deprived; the employee's rejection of or failure to seek other available employment of a different or inferior kind may not be resorted to in order to mitigate damages.   .   .   .

In the present case defendant has raised no issue of *reasonableness of efforts* by plaintiff to obtain other employment; the sole issue is whether plaintiff's refusal of defendant's substitute offer of "Big Country" may be used in mitigation. Nor, if the "Big Country" offer was of employment different or inferior when compared with the original "Bloomer Girl" employment, is there an issue as to whether or not plaintiff acted reasonably in refusing the substitute offer. Despite defendant's arguments to the contrary, no case cited or which our research has discovered holds or suggests that reasonableness is an element of a wrongfully discharged employee's option to reject, or fail to seek different or inferior employment lest the possible earnings therefrom be charged against him in mitigation of damages.[3]

Applying the foregoing rules to the record in the present case, with all intendments in favor of the party opposing the summary judgment motion—here, defendant—it is clear that the trial court correctly ruled that plaintiff's failure to accept defendant's tendered substitute employment could not be applied in mitigation of damages because the offer of the "Big Country" lead was of employment both different and inferior, and that no factual dispute was presented on that issue. The mere circumstance that "Bloomer Girl" was to be a musical review calling upon plaintiff's talents as a dancer as well as an actress, and was to be produced in the City of Los Angeles, whereas "Big Country" was a straight dramatic role in a "Western Type" story taking place in an opal mine in Australia, demonstrates the difference in kind between the two employments; the female lead as a

---

3. Instead, in each case the reasonableness referred to was that of the *efforts* of the employee to obtain other employment that was not different or inferior; his right to reject the latter was declared as an unqualified rule of law. Thus, Gonzales v. Internat. Assn. of Machinists, supra, 213 Cal. App.2d 817, 823–824, 29 Cal.Rptr. 190, 194, holds that the trial court correctly instructed the jury that plaintiff union member, a machinist, was required to make "such *efforts* as the average [member of his union] desiring employment would make at that particular time and place" (italics added); but, further, that the court *properly rejected* defendant's *offer of proof of the availability of other kinds of employment* at the same or higher pay than plaintiff usually received and all outside the jurisdiction of his union, as plaintiff could not be required to accept different employment or a nonunion job.

In Harris v. Nat. Union, etc., Cooks and Stewards, supra, 116 Cal.App.2d 759, 761, 254 P.2d 673, 676, the issues were stated to be, inter alia, whether comparable employment was open to each plaintiff employee, and if so whether each plaintiff made a *reasonable effort* to secure such employment. It was held that the trial court *properly sustained an objection to an offer to prove a custom of accepting a job in a lower rank* when work in the higher rank was not available, as "The duty of mitigation of damages * * * does not require the plaintiff 'to seek or to accept other employment of a different or inferior kind.'" (p. 764 [5], 254 P.2d p. 676.)   .   .   .

dramatic actress in a western style motion picture can by no stretch of imagination be considered the equivalent of or substantially similar to the lead in a song-and-dance production.

Additionally, the substitute "Big Country" offer proposed to eliminate or impair the director and screenplay approvals accorded to plaintiff under the original "Bloomer Girl" contract (see fn. 2, *ante*), and thus constituted an offer of inferior employment. No expertise or judicial notice is required in order to hold that the deprivation or infringement of an employee's rights held under an original employment contract converts the available "other employment" relied upon by the employer to mitigate damages, into inferior employment which the employee need not seek or accept. (See Gonzales v. Internat. Assn. of Machinists, *supra*, 213 Cal.App.2d 817, 823–824, 29 Cal.Rptr. 190; and fn. 3, *ante*.) . . .

In view of the determination that defendant failed to present any facts showing the existence of a factual issue with respect to its sole defense—plaintiff's rejection of its substitute employment offer in mitigation of damages—we need not consider plaintiff's further contention that for various reasons, including the provisions of the original contract set forth in footnote 1, *ante*, plaintiff was excused from attempting to mitigate damages.

The judgment is affirmed.

SULLIVAN, Acting Chief Justice (dissenting). . . . Over the years the courts have employed various phrases to define the type of employment which the employee, upon his wrongful discharge, is under an obligation to accept. Thus in California alone it has been held that he must accept employment which is "substantially similar" (Lewis v. Protective Security Life Ins. Co. (1962) 208 Cal.App.2d 582, 584, 25 Cal.Rptr. 213; De La Falaise v. Gaumont-British P. Corp. (1940) 39 Cal.App.2d 461, 469, 103 P.2d 447); "comparable employment" (Erler v. Five Points Motors, Inc. (1967) 249 Cal.App. 2d 560, 562, 57 Cal.Rptr. 516; Harris v. Nat. Union, etc., Cooks and Stewards (1953) 116 Cal.App.2d 759, 761, 254 P.2d 673); employment "in the same general line of the first employment" (Rotter v. Stationers Corporation (1960) 186 Cal.App.2d 170, 172, 8 Cal.Rptr. 690, 691); "equivalent to his prior position" (De Angeles v. Roos Bros., Inc. (1966) 244 Cal.App.2d 434, 443, 52 Cal.Rptr. 783); "employment in a similar capacity" (Silva v. McCoy (1968) 259 Cal.App.2d 256, 260, 66 Cal.Rptr. 364); employment which is "not . . . of a different or inferior kind. . . ." (Gonzales v. Internat. Assn. of Machinists (1963) 213 Cal.App.2d 817, 822, 29 Cal.Rptr. 190, 193.)

For reasons which are unexplained, the majority cite several of these cases yet select from among the various judicial formulations which contain one particular phrase, "Not of a different or inferior kind," with which to analyze this case. I have discovered no historical or theoretical reason to adopt this phrase, which is simply a negative restatement of the affirmative standards set out in the above cases, as the exclusive standard. Indeed, its emergence is an example of the dubious phenomenon of the law responding not to rational judicial choice or changing social conditions, but to unrecognized changes in the language of opinions or legal treatises. However, the phrase is a serviceable one and my concern is not with its use as the standard but rather with what I consider its distortion.

The relevant language excuses acceptance only of employment which is of a *different kind*. . . . It has never been the law that the mere existence of *differences between two jobs in the same field* is sufficient, as a matter of law, to excuse an employee wrongfully discharged from one from accepting the other in order to mitigate damages. Such an approach would effectively eliminate any obligation of an employee to attempt to minimize damage arising from a wrongful discharge. The only alternative job offer an employee would be required to accept would be an offer of his former job by his former employer.

Although the majority appear to hold that there was a difference "in kind" between the employment offered plaintiff in "Bloomer Girl" and that offered in "Big Country", an examination of the opinion makes crystal clear that the majority merely point out differences between the two *films* (an obvious circumstance) and then apodictically assert that these constitute a difference in the *kind* of *employment*. The entire rationale of the majority boils down to this: that the *"mere circumstances"* that "Bloomer Girl" was to be a musical review while "Big Country" was a straight drama "demonstrates the difference in kind" since a female lead in a western is not "the equivalent of or substantially similar to" a lead in a musical. This is merely attempting to prove the proposition by repeating it. It shows that the vehicles for the display of the star's talents are different but it does not prove that her employment as a star in such vehicles is of necessity different *in kind* and either inferior or superior.

I believe that the approach taken by the majority (a superficial listing of differences with no attempt to assess their significance) may subvert a valuable legal doctrine.[1] The inquiry in cases such as this should not be whether differences between the two jobs exist (there will always be differences) but whether the differences which are present are substantial enough to constitute differences in the *kind* of employment or, alternatively, whether they render the substitute work employment of an *inferior kind*. . . .

---

1. The values of the doctrine of mitigation of damages in this context are that it minimizes the unnecessary personal and social (e. g., nonproductive use of labor, litigation) costs of contractual failure. If a wrongfully discharged employee can, through his own action and without suffering financial or psychological loss in the process, reduce the damages accruing from the breach of contract, the most sensible policy is to require him to do so. I fear the majority opinion will encourage precisely opposite conduct.

I remain convinced that the relevant question in such cases is whether or not a particular contract provision is so significant that its omission create employment of an inferior kind. This question is, of course, intimately bound up in what I consider the ultimate issue: whether or not the employee acted reasonably. This will generally involve a factual inquiry to ascertain the importance of the particular contract term and a process of weighing the absence of that term against the countervailing advantages of the alternate employment. In the typical case, this will mean that summary judgment must be withheld. . . .

NOTES

(1) *Substitute Employment.* The court lays no stress on the fact that the offer of substitute employment came from the employer who had broken the contract in suit. Might this fact ever be significant? Would this be affected by the circumstances of the breach? Would it make a difference if the offer of substitute employment were conditioned on the injured party's surrender of rights under the old contract? See Gilson v. F. S. Royster Guano Co., 1 F.2d 82 (3d Cir. 1924). Since the court held that Mrs. Parker can recover the full $750,000 for "Bloomer Girl," even though she rejected the "different or inferior" role in "Big Country," does it not follow that she could have recovered the full $750,000 if she had taken (and been paid for) that role? Compare Buck v. Mueller, 221 Ore. 271, 351 P.2d 61 (1960), with Standard Oil Co. v. Lloyd, 26 Ala.App. 306, 159 So. 371 (1935).

(2) *Unemployment Compensation.* Should the employer's liability be reduced by the amount of unemployment compensation or similar benefits received by the wrongfully discharged employee? The court held that it should not in Pennington v. Whiting Tubular Products, 370 Mich. 590, 122 N.W. 692 (1963). "The purpose of the employment security act as set forth by the legislature in section 2 thereof indicates the object sought to be attained was the promotion of the public good and general welfare of the people of the State. There is nothing in the act to suggest that the payment of unemployment compensation is to be construed as in lieu of wages."

However, in United Protective Workers v. Ford Motor Co., 223 F.2d 49 (7th Cir. 1955), the court held that the employer's liability for wrongful compulsory retirement of an employee was properly reduced by the amount of social security and retirement payments received by the employee. "The status of social security and annuity payments is not material to the decision here. The question for us to decide concerns only the proper damages for breach of contract. If [the employee] had not been improperly retired, he would not have received the payments in question. . . . The well established rule that a tortfeasor cannot escape any of his liability because the injured party was compensated by a third party might appear to be analogous to the situation here. . . . This rule of tort law has a flavor of punitive damages. . . . In the insurance cases there is, in addition, the feeling that since the plaintiff paid for the insurance, he, and not the defendant should get the use of it. . . . A tort always involves fault or negligence (with the exception of the few areas in which there is strict liability); otherwise the harm is not compensable. The dispute before us arose because the parties interpreted their contract differently, and the principles of law involved had not been clearly settled previously. There was no bad faith or misconduct on either side. . . . There is no justification for an award with even the flavor of punitive damages. The only appropriate measure of damages is compensation." Which view do you prefer?

(3) *Problem.* Seller agreed to deliver lumber to Buyer in installments, payment for each installment to be made 90 days after delivery. After the delivery of the first installment, Seller wrongfully refused to deliver the remainder of the lumber on credit, but offered to supply it for cash at the same price less a discount sufficient to offset the interest for 90 days. Although the market for lumber had risen substantially, Buyer insisted upon his rights under the contract and refused to buy for cash from Seller. Can Buyer recover damages for Seller's breach based upon the difference between contract and market value? See Lawrence v. Porter, 63 F. 62 (6th Cir. 1894).

THE "PRINCIPLE OF SUBSTITUTION"

The "principle of substitution," under which the injured party is denied recovery for loss that he could have avoided by arranging a substitute transaction, is the source of some of the most important of the rules used in the calculation of damages. Particularly is this true for the sale of goods since, in a free enterprise economy, it is assumed that the injured party generally has available to him a market on which he can arrange a substitute transaction. If the seller fails to deliver goods, the assumption is that the buyer can go into the market and "cover" by obtaining substitute goods, so that his damages should be based on the difference between the (presumably) greater market price that he will have to pay and the (presumably) lesser contract price. If the buyer fails to take and pay for goods, the assumption is that the seller can go into the market and resell to a substitute buyer, so that his damages should be based on the difference between the (presumably) greater contract price and the (presumably) lesser market price he will receive. Is there reason to suppose that in most cases where sellers fail to deliver, buyers will have to pay more if they cover in the market, and that in most cases where buyers fail to take and pay, sellers will have to take less if they resell in the market?

ORESTER v. DAYTON RUBBER MFG. CO.

Court of Appeals of New York, 1920.
228 N.Y. 134, 126 N.E. 510.

Action by Jacob Orester against the Dayton Rubber Manufacturing Company. Judgment for the plaintiff was affirmed by the Appellate Division (176 N.Y.Supp. 914), and defendant appeals. Reversed, and new trial granted.

ANDREWS, J.　It seems that motor tires are made by various manufacturers and sold under different trade names. The defendant makes what is known as the "Dayton pneumatic tire." Apparently it had never been introduced in Syracuse. For the purpose, therefore, of creating a demand for it and of distributing it through authorized dealers, the defendant agreed to manufacture, sell, and deliver to the plaintiff such tires as he might require at a reduction from its list prices as they might be fixed from time to time and further agreed that the plaintiff should have the sole right to distribute and sell these tires in Onondaga and some neighboring counties. In return he was to "aggressively push" the sale, to provide showrooms, to carry in stock a sufficient supply to meet the trade requirements, and to sell only in the territory allotted to him.

Under this contract some 200 tires were received and sold by the plaintiff, both at wholesale and retail. He also fulfilled all the obligations imposed upon him. Yet the contract was broken by the defendant. It refused to supply 1,000 tires which he had ordered. The question before us is as to the proper measure of damages under such circumstances.

The jury was instructed that this measure was the difference between the market value of these tires in Syracuse and the price fixed in the contract. It was told further that because of the plaintiff's sales there was such a market value. In effect, the jury was permitted to award as damages the gross profits which the plaintiff might have made had he sold the whole 1,000 tires at the prices he had fixed.

For a wrong, the law's ideal, not always realized, is compensation, neither more nor less. Theoretically the loss to an injured party because of a broken contract is its value to him. Yet this rule may not always be safely applied. He may have in mind or claim that he had in mind some special object which would make the contract of extraordinary value. It is well to avoid temptation. It is well to have some theory applicable to the majority of cases. The rule is therefore limited. As such value, for such loss, he may recover as damages only those that would naturally arise from the breach itself, or those that might reasonably be supposed to have been contemplated by the parties when the contract was made. True this is an arbitrary rule. By it full justice is not always done. But it has seemed a politic one.

Further, the methods by which the result is reached are often standardized. In the case of sales, where the articles may be purchased in the market, the value of the contract to the purchaser is the difference between the price at which in like quantities they may be bought at the time and place of delivery and the price which he would have had to pay under the contract. This rule assumes, however, the possibility of such a purchase in the market. Then the injured party may obtain the articles, but at a greater price. If this is made good, he is compensated. But it may be none can be bought. Then the rule is inapplicable. Some other method by which his loss may be fixed must be used. Saxe v. Penokee Lumber Co., 159 N.Y. 371, 54 N.E. 14.

Such is the case before us. The plaintiff could not purchase the tires from others in Syracuse. He himself was the sole source of supply. Under the circumstances the charge of the trial court was erroneous.

Nor is the error cured by the submission to the jury of other evidence than that of the plaintiff's sales as bearing upon the market price of Dayton tires. There was before it the list price issued by the defendant. This the plaintiff claimed "was the only evidence of market price, aside from the price at which the plaintiff sold." But, as the court said, it did not appear that anything was sold at the list price, nor had it any tendency to show a market in Syracuse at which such tires might be purchased.

As there must be a new trial, we should determine the proper rule of damages. If there was a market elsewhere at which tires in the quantity desired by the plaintiff could be freely purchased the damages would be the difference between the contract price and the price at that market plus the transportation charges to Syracuse. Cahen v. Platt, 69 N.Y. 348, 25 Am.Rep. 203; Wemple v. Stewart, 22 Barb. 154; Berry v. Dwinel, 44 Me. 255. Possibly there was such a market, although, if other buyers from the defendant were limited as was he to sales in specified localities, this may be doubtful. In the absence of such a foreign market, if the plaintiff might purchase a substitute tire, equally available for his reasonable purposes, then his damages would be the difference between the market price of such substitute and the contract price. Saxe v. Penokee Lumber Co., 159 N.Y. 371, 54 N.E. 14. It should be remarked, however, that this contract contemplated building up a business for the sale of the "Dayton pneumatic tire" and creating a demand for that particular tire. Whether another tire, even equally as good, but sold under another trade-name, would be a satisfactory substitute to a dealer in Dayton tires, may be at least doubtful. It is, however, a question of fact.

Finally, if none of these tests are practicable, another must be adopted. We are not dealing here with circumstances known to both parties at the time the contract was executed, which made it of peculiar value to the plaintiff. We are not concerned with collateral engagements or consequential damages. We seek some formula under which the jury may determine the natural, the usual, value of such a contract to any one, under ordinary conditions. Baldwin v. U. S. Tel. Co., 45 N.Y. 744, 6 Am.Rep. 165. No one rule can be adapted to fit every case. As the circumstances vary so must the rule. Gallagher v. Baird, 54 App.Div. 398, 66 N.Y.Supp. 759; Masterton v. Mayor, etc., of Brooklyn, 7 Hill, 61, 42 Am.Dec. 38; Den Bleyker v. Gaston,

97 Mich. 354, 56 N.W. 763. Here the tires were purchased to be resold at a profit. This profit, if reasonably certain, may be said to measure the value of the contract to the plaintiff. It was this that he lost by the default of the defendant. Not the gross profit, however, which is what the jury was permitted to allow. What the plaintiff might have made had the contract been carried out was this gross profit less the expenses of the business properly chargeable to the sale of the Dayton tire. What this would have been it is for him to show by such evidence as would afford a fair basis for the finding of a jury. A party injured by a broken contract must prove the damages he receives as well as the other elements necessary to permit a recovery.

We decide nothing as to special damages which must be alleged in the complaint. That question is not now before us. We hold only that upon the facts presented, in determining the natural and proximate damages suffered by the plaintiff for the breach of this contract, if the other tests fail, he may prove the ordinary and usual net profits resulting from business conducted in the ordinary and usual way, which he has lost by reason of such breach. Talcott v. Freedman, 149 Mich. 577, 113 N.W. 13; Todd v. Gamble, 148 N.Y. 382, 42 N.E. 982, 52 L.R.A. 225.

The judgments of the Appellate Division and the trial court should be reversed, and a new trial granted, with costs to abide the event.

NOTE

Damages Under the Code. How could Orester have shown his damages under the Code? See UCC 2–713. In the event that there was a market for "Dayton pneumatic tires" outside of Syracuse, could Orester have recovered damages based on the price in that market? See UCC 2–723, 2–724. In the absence of any suitable market, could Orester have recovered damages based on his expected profit? See UCC 2–715, 1–106. Would Orester have had a right to specific performance if he had been unable to purchase suitable tires as a replacement? See UCC 2–716 and Note 1, p. 469 supra. Comment 3 to UCC 2–713 says that, "Where the unavailability of a market price is caused by a scarcity of goods of the type involved, a good case is normally made for specific performance under this Article."

The comparable Code provisions on the seller's damages for the buyer's non-acceptance or repudiation are found in UCC 2–708(1).[a] Suppose that the seller is to tender the goods by putting them in the hands of a carrier, such as a railroad, which will receive them on the buyer's behalf and

---

a.　Here too, of course, the principle of substitution does not apply where no substitute transaction is available to the seller. In that case he may recover damages based on lost profit under UCC 2–708(2) or perhaps the price under UCC 2–709(1) (b). For an interesting example, see Centennial Development Co. v. Van Wormer & Rodriguez, 443 P.2d 596 (Alaska 1968), involving a buyer's breach of its contract to buy 50,000 gold-colored coins to be specially made to commemorate the one hundredth anniversary of the purchase of Alaska.

transport them to Buyersville, where the buyer will then receive and inspect them. If the goods conform to the contract, but the buyer wrongfully rejects them, how is market price to be determined for the purpose of calculating the seller's damages? On what hypothetical substitute transaction is this rule based? Does the rule make sense? If goods do not conform to the contract, and the buyer rightfully rejects them, how is market price to be determined for the purpose of calculating the buyer's damages? On what hypothetical substitute transaction is this rule based? Does this rule make more sense? On remedies under the Code in general and on these questions in particular, see Peters, Remedies for Breach of Contracts Relating to the Sale of Goods Under the Uniform Commercial Code: A Roadmap for Article Two, 73 Yale L.J. 199, 270–71 (1963).

ACTUAL OR HYPOTHETICAL SUBSTITUTION?

What if the injured party has arranged an actual substitute transaction on *less* favorable terms than the market price? Can he still recover damages based on the price in that actual transaction rather than on the market price in a hypothetical transaction? His right to do so before the Code was less than clear. See Rees v. Bowers Co., 280 Pa. 474, 124 A. 653 (1924). The Code gives a generally affirmative answer.

Under UCC 2–712 the aggrieved buyer may "cover" by procuring substitute goods and, if he has met the requirements of good faith and reasonableness laid down by that section, may recover from the seller damages based on the difference between the cost of cover and the contract price, even if they are greater than those based on market price. Under UCC 2–706 the aggrieved seller may resell and, under similar conditions, recover from the buyer damages based on the difference between the contract price and the resale price, even if they are greater than those based on market price. (Would this section help the seller to avoid the anomaly of the rule of UCC 2–708(1), suggested in the Note above?) Although the injured party is not obliged to arrange an actual substitute transaction, he will ordinarily prefer to do so, because the proof of the price in that actual transaction will be simpler than proof of market price. What would you advise the aggrieved party to do following breach in order to lay the foundation for a possible action for damages under one of these two sections? Note also that under UCC 2–715(2)(a) the buyer's failure to cover may bar him from consequential damages.

NOTES

(1) *Specific Relief.* The possibility of specific relief for the buyer in the form of a decree of specific performance under UCC 2–716(1) has already been discussed. See Note 1, p. 469 supra. Under some circumstances the buyer may also obtain specific relief through an action to replevy the goods under UCC 2–716(3). Can he do so if he can cover? What would

you advise an aggrieved buyer to do following breach in order to lay the foundation for a possible action for replevin under this section? Would Orester have been able to replevy the 1,000 tires? (Does it appear that they were "identified" under UCC 2–501(1)?)

Under some circumstances the seller may also obtain what amounts to specific relief through an action for- the price under UCC 2–709(1)(b). Can he do so if he can resell? What would you advise an aggrieved seller to do following breach in order to lay the foundation for a possible action for the price under this section?

(2) *Problem.* Seller contracts with Buyer to deliver goods on a specified date for $100,000. Buyer makes a contract to resell the goods to another purchaser at $125,000. Seller fails to deliver. The market price of similar goods at and immediately after the delivery date is $110,000. Since Buyer's resale contract does not require him to deliver for six months, Buyer waits and does not go into the market for six months, by which time the market price has dropped to $90,000. How much should Buyer recover? Suppose that the market price had risen to $120,000 during Buyer's delay. How much should Buyer recover? See Farnsworth, Legal Remedies for Breach of Contract, 70 Colum.L.Rev. 1145, 1190 n. 190 (1970).

ILLINOIS CENTRAL RAILROAD CO. v. CRAIL, 281 U.S. 57 (1930). [A coal dealer in Minneapolis purchased, while in transit, a carload of coal weighing at shipment 88,700 pounds. On delivery there was a shortage of 5,500 pounds, for which the carrier was liable under a federal statute to the extent of "the full actual loss, damage or injury." The coal was added to the dealer's stock for resale, but the shortage did not interfere with the maintenance of his usual stock. He lost no sales by reason of it, and purchased no coal to replace the shortage, except in carload lots. He regularly purchased similar coal in carload lots of 60,000 pounds or more for $5.50 per ton plus freight. The market price in Minneapolis for like coal sold at retail in less than carload lots was $13.00 per ton, including $3.30 freight. The coal dealer sued the carrier.[a] From a judgment awarding him damages based on the retail price, the carrier appealed.]

a. From these figures, it is evident that the difference in damages based on the two markets was less than twelve dollars. See Crail v. Illinois Central R. Co., 21 F.2d 836, 842 (D.C.Minn.1927). The railroad's petition for writ of certiorari explained: "While the amount involved is small the effect of the judgment is far reaching and the case most important, not alone to your petitioner but to all carriers and shippers. . . . The decision of this case by this court will settle the troublesome, important, and constantly arising question as to what is the proper measure of damages in a case where a part of a carload of coal is lost in transit. . . . This has been an ever present source of dispute and controversy between the carriers and shippers. . . . In fact the carriers and shippers all over the country are awaiting the decision of this case by this court. Hundreds of cases have been built up and will not be disposed of until your Honors pass on and decide this case." Petition of Illinois Central Railroad Co., pp. 2–4 (1929).

MR. JUSTICE STONE.[b] . . . [R]espondent contends, as was held below, that the established measure of damage for non-delivery of a shipment of merchandise is the sum required to replace the exact amount of the shortage at the stipulated time and place of delivery, which, in this case, would be its retail value, and that convenience and the necessity for a uniform rule require its application here. This contention ignores the basic principle underlying common law remedies that they shall afford only compensation for the injury suffered . . ., and leaves out of account the language of the amendment, which likewise gives only a right of recovery for "actual loss." The rule urged by respondents was applied below in literal accordance with its conventional statement. As so stated, when applied to cases as they usually arise, it is a convenient and accurate method of arriving at an amount of recovery which is compensatory. As so stated, it would have been applicable here if there had been a failure to deliver the entire carload of coal, since the wholesale price, at which a full carload could have been procured at point of destination, would have afforded full compensation . . ., or, in some circumstances, if respondent had been under any constraint to purchase less than a carload lot to repair his loss or carry on his business, for in that event the measure of his loss would have been the retail market cost of the necessary replacement. Haskell v. Hunter, 23 Mich. 305, 309. But in the actual circumstances the cost of replacing the exact shortage at retail price was not the measure of the loss, since it was capable of replacement and was, in fact, replaced in the course of respondent's business from purchases made in carload lots at wholesale market price without added expense. There is no greater inconvenience in the application of the one standard of value than the other and we perceive no advantage to be gained from an adherence to a rigid uniformity, which would justify sacrificing the reason of the rule, to its letter. The test of market value is at best but a convenient means of getting at the loss suffered. It may be discarded and other more accurate means resorted to if, for special reasons, it is not exact or otherwise not applicable. . . .

Reversed.

NOTE

Actual or Hypothetical Substitute (Reprise)? Who should get the benefit if the injured party is able to arrange an actual substitute transaction on *more* favorable terms than the market price? The injured party? The party in breach? Comment 5 to UCC 2–713 asserts that, "The present

b. Harlan Fiske Stone (1872–1946) both taught and practiced law after his graduation from law school. He served as dean of the Columbia School of Law from 1910 to 1923. His writing up to this time was largely in the field of equity. In 1924 he was appointed Attorney General of the United States. In 1925 he was appointed to the Supreme Court of the United States and in 1941 he succeeded Charles Evans Hughes as Chief Justice.

section provides a remedy which is completely alternative to cover . . . and applies only when and to the extent that the buyer has not covered." Where the buyer makes frequent purchases, as in the Crail case, and the price fluctuates, how is a court to determine which goods are "in substitution for those due from the seller"?

WHAT IS A "SUBSTITUTE"?

It is sometimes no simple matter to decide whether another comparable opportunity accepted by the injured party after breach should be treated as a "substitute" within the "principle of substitution." Where the injured party is the supplier of personal services, under a contract of fulltime employment for example, another comparable opportunity may be viewed as a substitute transaction since "No man can serve two masters" and the employee could not have taken advantage of the second opportunity had not the first contract been broken. Where, however, the injured party is a supplier of services that are not personal, under a contract for construction of a building, for example, another comparable opportunity is not viewed as a substitute. Rather, it is assumed that the contractor could have expanded his business to undertake additional jobs so that the breach of the original contract resulted in "lost volume" that could not be recaptured by a second similar contract. The materials that follow explore the borderlines of this distinction.

OLDS v. MAPES-REEVE CONSTRUCTION CO., 177 Mass. 41, 58 N.E. 478 (1900). [Mapes-Reeve, a general contractor, engaged Olds, a subcontractor, to do the marble work on a building for $3,000. Mapes-Reeve wrongfully ordered Olds to stop work, at a time when it would have cost $717 to complete it. Olds at once made a contract with the owner to complete it at a price of $1,053. Olds sued for $2,283 ($3,000 minus $717). The trial court allowed $1,947 ($3,000 minus $1,053). Plaintiff appealed.]

KNOWLTON, J. . . . The rule which is applicable to one who is under a contract to render personal services, and who, being discharged without cause before the end of his term, sues for damages, requires him, in estimating the damages, to allow for his services, during the unexpired term whatever he is able to obtain for them, or if damages are assessed before the end of the term, whatever he reasonably can be expected to obtain for them during the time covered by the contract. . . . But there is this difference between the case of one who is discharged while under a contract to render personal services, and a case like the present. In the former case, the person discharged, whose personal services come back to him, is bound to dispose of them in a reasonable way, so as to make the damages to the other party not unreasonably large, while, in a case like the present, one deprived of his contract is under no obligation to enter into new contracts with a view to make profits for the other party. In a contract of the kind before the court, personal services are not necessarily included. The labor or supervision may be personally performed by the contractor or may be furnished through agents or employees. In either case the value of it is all included for the benefit of the other party when the contractor is charged with the whole cost of completing the work, as an amount to be deducted from the contract price in estimating his damages. Since the damages properly are assessable in this way immediately after the breach of the contract, can it make any difference that the contractor afterwards makes a new contract with the owner which includes the unfinished work?" . . . The plaintiffs were at liberty to leave this work entirely to the care of hired servants, and to take as many other contracts as they chose elsewhere, and to give their personal time and attention to any occupation that they might choose. The question is, whether the profits from the new contract with the landowner were a direct result of the defendant's breach of contract, or whether they came from an independent intervening cause. It does not appear, and it is not to be assumed that the plaintiffs were not competent to carry on several contracts at one time, and the making of profits on a new contract does not appear to be because of relief from the obligations of the old one. There is usually plenty of work to be contracted for, and the addition of one more possible job for which contractors may bid does not make the subsequent contract to do the work a direct result of the increase of opportunities for work. The addition of a new piece of work is merely a condition of the subsequent contract to do the work, and not a direct or proximate cause of it. Moreover, the making of such a contract involves many considerations besides the existence of the work to be done. There must be calculations and estimates. In making a contract of this kind there is always a risk of loss as well as a possibility of gain. To say nothing of the fact that the plaintiffs' new contract included work which was not included in the old one, the cost of which could be fixed only as matter of estimate, this contract with the landowner was a new undertaking, in which the plaintiffs were under no obligation to engage, and which involved risks that they could assume for themselves alone. If the contract had resulted in a loss to them, they could not have charged the defendant with the loss, to the increase of their damages. As the contract resulted in a gain to them, there is no reason why the defendant should receive this gain in diminution of the damages for which it was liable. . . . If another person had taken this contract and made profits on it, as the plaintiffs did, it would hardly have been contended that the plaintiffs' damages were to be diminished on that account; or if the plaintiffs, instead of taking this contract after the breach of the former one, had gone elsewhere and taken another contract which afforded them similar profits, there would be no ground for a claim of the defendant to be allowed these profits in diminution of the damages.

[Reversed.]

NOTES

(1) *Contract for Same Performance.* The few cases that have dealt with this problem are in accord. See Kunkle v. Jaffe, 71 N.E.2d 298 (Ohio Ct.App.1946); Grinnell Co. v. Voorhees, 1 F.2d 693 (3d Cir. 1924), cert. denied, 266 U.S. 629 (1924). The latter decision was criticized in 34 Yale L.J. 553 (1925), and the following rule proposed: "[T]he repudiator should not be entitled to the benefit of any contract of the injured party except such as the injured party could not have made but for the repudiation." But suppose the other contract turned out to be a losing one?

What would have been the subcontractor's recovery if he had refused the owner's offer of a new contract? Suppose that when the contractor had repudiated his agreement with the subcontractor no offer from the owner had been forthcoming, but the contractor himself had offered the sub-contractor $2,800 instead of $3,000 for the completed job, with no surrender of any rights the subcontractor might have on the original contract. What would have been the subcontractor's recovery if he had refused the contractor's offer of a new contract? What if he had accepted it?

(2) *Contractors and "Lost Volume."* Should the general rule, that other contracts are not regarded as substitutes where personal services are not involved, be applied where the injured party obtains other contracts that exhaust his capacity? See Harrington-Wiard Co. v. Blomstrom Co., 166 Mich. 276, 131 N.W. 559 (1911).

STEWART v. HANSEN, 62 Utah 281, 218 P. 959 (1923). [Stewart, an Oldsmobile dealer in Ogden, Utah, contracted to sell an automobile to Hansen, who refused to take and pay for it. After keeping it for several months, Stewart returned it to Oldsmobile, receiving full credit for the price he had paid them for it. He sued Hansen for $200 based on the difference between the invoice price to him of $1,150 and his selling price of $1,395. He testified that he had expenses for advertising, salesmen and demonstrations, and that Hansen had had a demonstration. From a judgment for the plaintiff for $200, the defendant appealed.]

FRICK, J. . . . [The court quoted from Uniform Sales Act, § 64, then in effect in Utah:]

"2. The measure of damages is the estimated loss directly and naturally resulting, in the ordinary course of events, from the buyer's breach of contract.

"3. Where there is an available market for the goods in question, the measure of damages is, in the absence of special circumstances showing proximate damage of a greater amount, the difference between the contract price and the market or current price at the time or times when the goods ought to have been accepted, or, if no time was fixed for acceptance, then at the time of the refusal to accept." . . .

The undisputed facts of this case, in my judgment, bring it clearly within the provisions of subdivision 2 . . . and . . . subdivision 3 . . ., which permit damages beyond those stated in the general rule there stated in the event of "special circumstances, showing proximate damage of a greater amount" than the "difference between the contract price and the market or current price," etc. If we keep in mind the fact that if in cases like the one at bar the general rule of damages for breaches of contracts of sale by the purchaser is adopted, then the dealer of necessity must in every case be the loser by reason of the fact that he loses all compensation for his time and efforts in attempting to effect a sale, or in effecting it, of a car and in demonstrating it to the prospective purchaser and receives nothing for rent, advertising, and other "overhead" expenses. . . . Moreover, the rule adopted gives the seller the fruits of his bargain, which is a matter that should always be considered in applying the measure of damages in any case. The evidence in this case shows that both the dealer's price and the selling price to the public were the same at the time of the purchase that they were at the time the contract was entered into. In the nature of things such must nearly always be the case in transactions like the one in question here, for the reason that the sale and the breach, where one occurs, are seldom far apart in time. . . .

To further demonstrate that the loss of profits in this case is the natural and proximate result of its breach it is only necessary to say that in a case like the one at bar the amount of damage is ascertained in precisely the same way as they would be ascertained under the general rule, namely, by a mere process of subtraction. When the difference between the contract price and the market price is allowed, we merely subtract the lesser from the greater, and the difference, if there be any, fixes the amount of damages to be allowed. That is precisely what happens in a case like the one at bar. When that rule is applied, in case the seller refuses to consummate the contract, the purchaser obtains the full benefit of his bargain by being allowed the advanced price he was required to pay for a like article in the market, if there was any advance in price. If he has contracted for a price less than the current market price, he would again be given the benefit of his bargain by receiving the difference. If, therefore, the buyer obtains the benefit of his bargain in case the seller fails to consummate the sale, why should not the seller likewise receive the fruits of his bargain if the buyer refuses to perform the terms of his contract. This the seller cannot do in cases like the one at bar, unless he is allowed the profits that he would have received if the sale had been consummated. The general rule relied on by the defendant, therefore, has no application to this case. . . .

In my judgment there is no escape from the conclusion that while the district court did not allow the plaintiff the full amount to which he was entitled, but of which plaintiff does not complain, yet the court adopted the correct measure of damages, and therefore the judgment should be affirmed, with costs to respondent.

GIDEON, J. (dissenting). . . . The facts in this case do not authorize the contention that there were "special circumstances" surrounding this sale. . . . The testimony is without dispute that the market value of the car contracted to be purchased was the same at the date of the contract and at the date appellant refused to accept the car, and that the price remained the same to the date of trial. There is nothing in the record to indicate that the respondent purchased the car to enable him to comply with his contract with appellant. Neither is there anything to indicate that the respondent lost a sale to any other purchaser by reason of the contract of sale in question. There is some testimony tending to show that a dealer in automobiles is required to, and that this plaintiff did, employ salesmen, and also had in his employ a demonstrator; that is, a person to instruct prospective purchasers as to the method of operating automobiles. It is therefore concluded that because of these facts the sale of an automobile surrounds the transaction with "special circumstances." If that be true, a dealer in merchandise, and especially farm machinery, is surrounded by facts and circumstances constituting special circumstances. Any merchant, of necessity, employs salesmen whose duty it is to explain to prospective purchasers the quality of the article to be sold. The sale of an automobile should not be clothed with more sanctity than a sale of other property. . . .

In this case the testimony is indisputable that the plaintiff had suffered no damage. He had the property in his possession at the time of the contract of sale and he had it at the date of the breach. Its market value was the same at both dates. To allow him profits is to give him the benefits of the sale and retain the goods. It has never been recognized in this state that the mere fact of loss of sale entitles the dealer to damages. . . .

NOTES

(1) *Middlemen and "Lost Volume."* Do you agree with the result? Why? Think of the dealer, Stewart, as a middleman between the manufacturer, Oldsmobile, and the customer, Hansen. Does your answer depend on whether the customer's breach resulted in "lost volume" that the middleman could not recapture by a second similar contract? Does the determination of "lost volume" turn on the relationship between the middleman's supply from the manufacturer and the demand by his customers? Is the situation of the automobile dealer in Stewart v. Hansen distinguishable in this regard from that of the automobile dealer in McCallister v. Patton, p. 462

supra? Does the court's opinion pay adequate attention to the problem of "lost volume"? See Harris, A General Theory for Measuring Seller's Damages for Total Breach of Contract, 60 Mich.L.Rev. 577, 599–605 (1962).

(2) *The Code and "Lost Volume."* What result under UCC 2–708? According to Comment 2, "The provision of this section permitting recovery of expected profit including reasonable overhead where the standard measure of damages is inadequate, together with the new requirement that price actions may be sustained only where resale is impractical, are designed to eliminate the unfair and economically wasteful results arising under the older law when fixed price articles were involved. This section permits the recovery of lost profits in all appropriate cases, which would include all standard priced goods. The normal measure there would be list price less cost to the dealer or list price less manufacturing cost to the manufacturer. It is not necessary to a recovery of 'profit' to show a history of earnings, especially if a new venture is involved." Does the Code pay adequate attention to the problem of "lost volume"? Does that problem arise only where a middleman is dealing in "standard priced goods"? One writer concludes that "while it is easy to reach bad results under section 2–708, it is not absolutely necessary." Harris, A Radical Restatement of the Law of Seller's Damages: Sales Act and Commercial Code Results Compared, 18 Stan.L.Rev. 66, 101 (1965).

What result in Stewart v. Hansen under the Code? Could Stewart have recovered the price under UCC 2–709? Should he have resold under UCC 2–706?

(3) *Problem.* Seller contracts with Buyer to deliver goods on a specified date for $100,000. Buyer then makes a contract to resell the goods to another purchaser for $125,000. Seller fails to deliver. The market price of similar goods at and immediately after the delivery date is $130,000. How much should Buyer recover? Would your answer be different if Buyer, in making his resale contract had protected himself by reserving the power to cancel on breach by Seller? (Would the circumstances of Seller's breach be relevant in that case?) Would your answer be different if Buyer had not so protected himself but his purchaser had released him from his obligation on the resale contract? Would your answer be different if Buyer had made no resale contract? See Farnsworth, Legal Remedies for Breach of Contract, 70 Colum.L.Rev. 1145, 1190 n. 189 (1970); Iron Trade Products Co. v. Wilkoff, p. 679 infra.

(b) Foreseeability

HADLEY v. BAXENDALE

Court of Exchequer, 1854.
9 Ex. 341, 156 Eng.Rep. 145.

[Plaintiffs, who operated a mill at Gloucester, sued defendants, who were common carriers, for damages for breach of a contract of carriage. The declaration contained two counts but prior to the trial plaintiffs entered a *nolle prosequi* as to the first. In the second count plaintiffs alleged that they were forced to shut their mill down because the crank shaft of the steam engine, by which their mill was operated, became broken; that they arranged with W. Joyce & Co., of Greenwich, the manufacturers of the engine, to make a new shaft from the pattern of the old one; that they delivered the broken shaft to defendants who, in consideration of the payment of their charges, promised to use due care to deliver it to W. Joyce & Co. within a reasonable time but that defendants failed to do so; that by reason of defendants' negligence the completion of the new shaft and the reopening of plaintiffs' mill were delayed five days longer than would otherwise have been the case; and that during that period plaintiffs were compelled to pay wages and lost profits aggregating 300£ for which amount plaintiffs sought judgment. Defendants pleaded that they had paid 25£ into court in satisfaction of plaintiffs' claim; plaintiffs replied that this sum was insufficient for that purpose; and issue was joined upon this replication.]

At the trial before Crompton, J., at the last Gloucester Assizes, it appeared that the plaintiffs carried on an extensive business as millers at Gloucester; and that, on the 11th of May, their mill was stopped by a breakage of the crank shaft by which the mill was worked. The steam-engine was manufactured by Messrs. Joyce & Co., the engineers at Greenwich, and it became necessary to send the shaft as a pattern for a new one to Greenwich. The fracture was discovered on the 12th, and on the 13th the plaintiffs sent one of their servants to the office of the defendants, who are the well known carriers trading under the name of Pickford & Co., for the purpose of having the shaft carried to Greenwich. The plaintiffs' servant told the clerk that the mill was stopped, and that the shaft must be sent immediately; and in answer to the inquiry when the shaft would be taken, the answer was, that if it was sent up by twelve o'clock any day, it would be delivered at Greenwich on the following day. On the following day the shaft was taken by the defendants, before noon, for the purpose of being conveyed to Greenwich, and the sum of 2£ 4s. was paid for its carriage for the whole distance; at the same time the defendants' clerk was told that a special entry, if required, should be made to hasten its delivery. The delivery of the shaft at Greenwich was delayed by some neglect; and the consequence was, that the plaintiffs did not receive the new shaft for several days after they would otherwise have done, and the working of their mill was thereby delayed, and they thereby lost the profits they would otherwise have received.

On the part of the defendants, it was objected that these damages were too remote, and that the defendants were not liable with respect to them. The learned Judge left the case generally to the jury, who found a verdict with 25£ damages beyond the amount paid into Court.

Whateley, [for defendants], in last Michaelmas Term, obtained a rule nisi for a new trial, on the ground of misdirection.

[The arguments of counsel are omitted. After they were completed the court took the case under consideration until the next term.]

The judgment of the Court was now delivered by

ALDERSON, B. We think that there ought to be a new trial in this case; but, in so doing, we deem it to be expedient and necessary to state explicitly the rule which the Judge, at the next trial, ought, in our opinion, to direct the jury to be governed by when they estimate the damages.

It is, indeed, of the last importance that we should do this; for, if the jury are left without any definite rule to guide them, it will, in such cases as these, manifestly lead to the greatest injustice. The Courts have done this on several occasions; and, in Blake v. Midland Railway Company, 21 L.J., Q.B. 237, the Court granted a new trial on this very ground, that the rule had not been definitely laid down to the jury by the learned judge at Nisi Prius.

"There are certain established rules," this Court says, in Alder v. Keighley, 15 M. & W. 117, "according to which the jury ought to find." And the Court, in that case, adds: "and here there is a clear rule, that the amount which would have been received if the contract had been kept is the measure of damages if the contract is broken."

Now we think the proper rule in such a case as the present is this: Where two parties have made a contract which one of them has broken, the damages which the other party ought to receive in respect of such breach of contract should be such as may fairly and reasonably be considered either arising naturally, i. e., according to the usual course of things, from such breach of contract itself, or such as may reasonably be supposed to have been in the contemplation of both parties, at the time they made the contract, as the probable result of the breach of it. Now, if the special circumstances under which the contract was actually made were communicated by the plaintiffs to the defendants, and thus known to both parties, the damages resulting from the breach of such a contract, which they would reasonably contemplate, would be the amount of injury which would ordinarily follow from a breach of contract under these special circumstances so known and communicated. But, on the other hand, if these special circumstances were wholly unknown to the party breaking the contract, he, at the most, could only be supposed to have had in his contemplation the amount of injury which would arise generally, and in the great multitude of cases not affected by any special circumstances, from such a breach of contract. For, had the special circumstances been known, the parties might have specially provided for the breach of contract by special terms as to the damages in that case; and of this advantage it would be very unjust to deprive them. Now the above principles are those by which we think the jury ought to be guided in estimating the damages arising out of any breach of contract. It is said, that other cases, such as breaches of contract in the nonpayment of money, or in the not making a good title to land, are to be treated as exceptions from this, and as governed by a conventional rule. But as, in such cases, both parties must be supposed to be cognizant of that well-known rule, these cases may, we think, be more properly classed under the rule above enunciated as to cases under known special circumstances, because there both parties may reasonably be presumed to contemplate the estimation of the amount of damages according to the conventional rule. Now, in the present case if we are to apply the principles above laid down, we find that the only circumstances here communicated by the plaintiffs to the defendants at the time the contract was made, were, that the article to be carried was the broken shaft of a mill, and that the plaintiffs were the millers of that mill. But how do these circumstances show reasonably that the profits of the mill must be stopped by an unreasonable delay in the delivery of the broken shaft by the carrier to the third person? Suppose the plaintiffs had another shaft in their possession put up or putting up at the time, and that they only wished to send back the broken shaft to the engineer who made it; it is clear that this would be quite consistent with the above circumstances, and yet the unreasonable delay in the delivery would have no effect upon the intermediate profits of the mill. Or, again, suppose that, at the time of the delivery to the carrier, the machinery of the mill had been in other respects defective, then, also, the same results would follow. Here it is true that the shaft was actually sent back to serve as a model for a new one, and that the want of a new one was the only cause of the stoppage of the mill, and that the loss of profits really arose from not sending down the new shaft in proper time, and that this arose from the delay in delivering the broken one to serve as a model. But it is obvious that, in the great multitude of cases of millers sending off broken shafts to third persons by a carrier under ordinary circumstances, such consequences would not, in all probability, have occurred; and these special circumstances were here never communicated by the plaintiffs to the defendants. It follows, therefore, that the loss of profits here cannot reasonably be considered such a consequence of the breach of contract as could have been fairly and reasonably contemplated by both the parties when they made this contract. For such loss would neither have flowed naturally from the breach of this contract in the great multitude of such cases occurring under ordinary circumstances, nor were the special circumstances, which, perhaps, would have made it a reasonable and natural consequence of such breach of contract, communicated to or known by the defendants. The Judge ought, therefore, to have told the jury that, upon the facts then before him, they ought not to take the loss of profits into consideration at all in estimating the damages. There must therefore be a new trial in this case.

Rule absolute.

NOTES

(1) *Rule of Hadley v. Baxendale.* Do you think that in Hadley v. Baxendale the court applied the rule which it formulated correctly or incorrectly? Cf. Victoria Laundry (Windsor) Ltd. v. Newman Industries Ltd., 2 K.B. 528, 537 (1949): "In considering the meaning and application of these rules, it is essential to bear clearly in mind the facts on which Hadley v. Baxendale proceeded. The head-note is definitely misleading in so far as it says that the defendant's clerk, who attended at the office, was told that the mill was stopped and that the shaft must be delivered immediately. The same allegation figures in the statement of facts which are said on page 344 to have 'appeared' at the trial before Crompton J. If the Court of Exchequer had accepted these facts as established, the court must, one would suppose, have decided the case the other way round. . . . But it is reasonably plain from Alderson B.'s judgment that the court rejected this evidence, for on page 355 he says: 'We find that the only circumstances here communicated by the plaintiffs to the defendants at the time when the contract was made were that the article to be carried was the broken shaft of a mill and that the plaintiffs were the millers of that mill.' . . . ." Compare the rule laid down in Hadley v. Baxendale with the formulation of Restatement, § 330.

(2) *Meaning of "Contemplation."* In British Columbia Saw Mill Co. v. Nettleship, L.R. 3 C.P. 499 (1868), plaintiff delivered to defendant's ship at Glasgow machinery needed for construction of a mill at Vancouver, British Columbia, as defendant knew. As a result of the loss of one box of machinery somewhere in transit the mill could not be put into operation for almost a year, the time required to replace the missing machinery. The court awarded damages for the cost of replacing the machinery, including the cost of procuring new machinery from England, plus interest at 5% for the time plaintiffs were delayed, but denied recovery for the loss incurred due to stoppage of the mill. "Bovill, C. J. . . . [A defendant] is not to be made liable for damages beyond what may fairly be presumed to have been contemplated by the parties at the time of entering into the contract. It must be something which could have been foreseen and reasonably expected, and to which he has assented expressly or impliedly by entering into the contract. . . . Willes, J. . . . If that had been presented to the mind of the shipowner at the time of making the contract, as the basis upon which he was contracting, he would at once have rejected it. And, though he knew from the shippers the use they intended to make of the articles, it could not be contended that the mere fact of knowledge without more, would be a reason for imposing upon him a greater degree of liability than would otherwise have been cast upon him." In this case Willes, J. rejected the result reached in an old case "said to have been decided two centuries ago where a man going to be married to an heiress, his horse having cast a shoe on the journey, employed a blacksmith to replace it, who did the work so unskilfully that the horse was lamed, and the rider not arriving in time, the lady married another; and the blacksmith was held liable for the loss of the marriage."[a] What would have been the result under the test laid down by Restatement, § 330? What *should* have been the result?

a. But cf. Coppola v. Kraushaar, 102 App.Div. 306, 92 N.Y.S. 436 (1905), in which a disappointed suitor whose betrothed broke their engagement after

In Globe Refining Co. v. Landa Cotton Oil Co., 190 U.S. 540 (1903), Justice Holmes declared that "the extent of liability . . . should be worked out on terms which it fairly may be presumed he would have assented to if they had been presented to his mind. . . . [It] depends on what liability the defendant fairly may be supposed to have assumed consciously, or to have warranted the plaintiff reasonably to suppose that it assumed, when the contract was made. . . . [M]ere notice to a seller of some interest or probable action of the buyer is not enough." Would you favor such a test?

(3) *The Code.* What is the impact of UCC 2–715(2), which allows the buyer consequential damages for "any loss resulting from general or particular requirements and needs of which the seller at the time of contracting had reason to know"? In Harry Rubin & Sons v. Consolidated Pipe Co., p. 444 supra, the case of the failure to deliver "hula hoops," the Supreme Court of Pennsylvania rejected the buyer's claim for loss of his customers' good will. "Our research fails to reveal any judicial authority in Pennsylvania which sustains, under the [prior Uniform] Sales Act, a recovery for a loss of good will occasioned either by nondelivery or by the delivery of defective goods. . . . There is no indication that the Uniform Commercial Code was intended to enlarge the scope of a buyer's damages to include a loss of good will. In the absence of a specific declaration in this respect, we believe that damages of this nature would be entirely too speculative . . . ." For a different view on recovery for loss of good will, see Stott v. Johnston, 36 Cal.2d 864, 229 P.2d 348 (1951). On the problem of damages being "too speculative," see Subsection 3(c), Certainty, infra.

(4) *Problem.* Federal contracted to sell 75,000 tons of sugar to Czarnikow, to be delivered directly to Czarnikow's customers. In the contracts that Czarnikow then made in turn with its customers, it described the sugar as "Federal" brand, but this was not known to Federal. When the sugar delivered by Federal turned out to be defective, Czarnikow spent $340,000 in the settlement of claims and the defense of law suits brought by its customers, an amount that was inflated because Czarnikow's obligations to them could not be met by delivery of sugar from other suppliers, which it might have obtained on the market. Is Federal liable for $340,-000? Czarnikow-Rionda Co. v. Federal Sugar Refining Co., 255 N.Y. 33, 173 N.E. 913 (1930).

Assuming that Federal is liable for $340,000, could Czarnikow recover an additional $100,000 by showing that it had lost this much in profits when its volume dropped because it was deprived of $340,000 in capital? See Lewis v. Mobil Oil Corp., 438 F.2d 500 (8th Cir. 1971).

their wedding was delayed, sued to recover five hundred dollars, expended uselessly on the wedding, from the defendant, whose failure to deliver two gowns, ordered for the bride, had caused the postponement of the wedding. The court said: "Before the defendant can be held to these alleged damages . . . I think that the parties must have had in contemplation that the wedding would never occur if the defendant failed to furnish the 'two dresses' on the day before the appointed time. . . . While such a disappointment would naturally be keen to any prospective bride, it was hardly to be contemplated, in the absence of specific warning, that she would forever refuse to wed if those 'two dresses' were not forthcoming before the day set for the ceremony. The damages are too remote. (Hadley v. Baxendale, 9 Exch. 341. . . .)"

LIMITATION OF RISK

"The rule of Hadley v. Baxendale is an attempt to restrict the promisor's liability for breach of promise to those consequences, the risk of which he knew about, or must be taken to have known about, when he made the contract. The scope of damage for breach of contract is much narrower than the 'proximate consequence' rule which prevails in actions to recover for a tort. If we may assume that the defaulting promisor is usually an *entrepreneur*, a business man who has undertaken a risky enterprise, the law here manifests a policy to encourage the *entrepreneur* by reducing the extent of his risk below that amount of damage which, it might be plausibly argued, the promisee has actually been caused to suffer." Patterson, The Apportionment of Business Risks Through Legal Devices, 24 Colum.L.Rev. 335, 342 (1924).

Another limitation on contract damages that can be viewed as an attempt to restrict the promisor's liability is the traditional reluctance of courts to allow damages for mental distress. Many states do allow recovery in some situations, often involving defendants who occupy a special position toward the public—telegraph companies, innkeepers, common carriers, and the like. Because the obligations of such persons are to a large extent imposed by law, without regard to contract, it is often difficult to tell whether recovery was on a theory of contract or of tort. Should the rules as to recovery for mental distress be different in contract and in tort?

An analogy may be drawn from these restrictions on the extent of liability in terms of the amount for which a promisor may be held liable to restrictions on the extent of liability in terms of the persons to whom a promisor may be held liable. The latter will be explored in Chapter 9, Third Party Beneficiaries.

NOTE

The Case of the "Whole Damned Business." Mrs. Lamm employed the Shingletons, undertakers, to inter her first husband, Mr. Waddell, in a vault guaranteed to be watertight. About three months later, during a heavy rain, the vault rose above the ground, and the Shingletons undertook to reinter the body. In her presence, they raised the vault and found that the casket was wet. The sight "caused her considerable shock and made her extremely nervous as a result of which she became a nervous wreck." One of the Shingletons said he would not get the mud out of the vault and "to hell with the whole damned business, it's no concern of mine." This made her "so nervous she could hardly stand up." She sued for breach of contract and, from judgment that she take nothing, she appealed. *Held*: Reversed. Although "as a general rule," damages for mental anguish are not recoverable in a contract action, the law is "in a state of flux . . . ." Where the contract is personal in nature and the contractual duty or obligation is so coupled with matters of mental concern or solicitude, or with the sensibilities of the party to whom the duty is owed, that a breach of that duty will necessarily or reasonably result in mental anguish or suffering, and it should be known to the parties from the nature of the contract that such suffering will result from its breach, compensatory damages therefor may be recovered. . . . The tenderest feelings of the human heart center around the remains of the dead. . . . The contract was predominantly personal in nature and no substantial pecuniary loss would follow its breach. Her mental concern, her sensibilities, and her solicitude were the prime considerations for the contract, and the contract itself was such as to put the defendants on notice that a failure on their part to inter the body properly would probably produce mental suffering on her part." Lamm v. Shingleton, 231 N.C. 10, 55 S.E.2d 810 (1949).

(c) Certainty

EVERGREEN AMUSEMENT CORP. v. MILSTEAD

Court of Appeals of Maryland, 1955.
206 Md. 610, 112 A.2d 901.

HAMMOND, JUDGE. The Evergreen Amusement Corporation, the appellant, operator of a drive-in movie theater, was held liable by the court, sitting without a jury, to Harold D. Milstead, the appellee, a contractor, for the balance due on a written contract for the clearing and grading of the site of the theater and certain extras, less the cost of completing a part of the work and damages for delay in completion, based on rental value of the theater property during the period of delay and out-of-pocket costs for that time.

The appellant, by counterclaim, sought recovery of lost profits for the period of delay. The court held the amount claimed to have been so lost to be too uncertain and speculative, and refused evidence proffered to support appellant's theory. . . .

. . .

The real reliance of the Evergreen Amusement Corporation is on the slowness of the contractor in completing the work. It says that the resulting delay in the opening of the theater from June first to the middle of August cost it twelve thousand five hundred dollars in profits. It proffered a witness to testify that he had built and operated a majority of the drive-in theaters in the area, that he is in the theater equipment business and familiar with the profits that drive-in theaters make in the area, that a market survey was made in the area before the site of the theater was selected, and that it had shown the need for such a theater in the neighborhood. It was said he would testify as to the reasonably anticipated profits during the months in question by comparing the months in its second year of operation with those in which it could not operate the year before, and would say that the profits would have been the same. His further testimony would be, it was claimed, that weather conditions, the population, and competition were all approximately the same in the year the theater opened and the following year.

We think the court did not err in refusing the proffered evidence. Under the great weight of authority, the general rule clearly is that loss of profit is a definite element of damages in an action for breach of contract or in an action for harming an established business which has been operating for a sufficient length of time to afford a basis of estimation with some degree of certainty as to the probable loss of profits, but that, on the other hand, loss of profits from a business which has not gone into operation may not be recovered because they are merely speculative and incapable of being ascertained with the requisite degree of certainty. Restatement, Contracts, Sec. 331, states the law to be that damages are recoverable for profits prevented by breach of contract "only to the extent that the evidence affords a sufficient basis for estimating their amount in money with reasonable certainty", and that where the evidence does not afford a sufficient basis, "damages may be measured by the rental value of the property." Comment "d" says this: "If the defendant's breach has prevented the plaintiff from carrying on a *well-established business*, the amount of profits thereby prevented is often capable of proof with reasonable certainty. On the basis of its past history, a reasonable prediction can be made as to its future." (Italics supplied.) That damages for profits anticipated from a business which has not started may not be recovered, is laid down in 25 C.J.S., Damages § 42, and 15 Am.Jur., Damages, § 157; 5 Corbin, Contracts, §§ 1022, 1023; Cramer v. Grand Rapids Show Case Co., 223 N.Y. 63, 119 N.E. 227, 1 A. L.R. 156; Sinclair Ref. Co. v. Hamilton & Dotson, 164 Va. 203, 178 S.E. 777, 99 A.L.R. 938. See also The Requirement of Certainty for Proof of Lost Profits, 64 Harvard Law 317. The article discusses the difficulties of proving with sufficient certainty the profits which were lost, and then says: "These difficulties have given rise to a rule in some states that no new business can recover for its lost profits." While this Court has not laid down a flat rule (and does not hereby do so), nevertheless, no case has permitted recovery of lost profits under comparable circumstances. In Abbott v. Gatch, 13 Md. 314, the claim for loss of profits arose because of delay in completion of a flour mill. The Court held that the mill owner's loss was to be established by fair rental value for the time of the delay resulting from failure to complete it according to contract, that he could not recover estimated profits, because it was dependent, as they were, upon the quality of flour available, the fluctuation of prices of flour, continuance of the mill in running order and other variants. The Court labelled the damages claimed speculative and refused to follow a Vermont case which had allowed them to be shown. The rule laid down in this case has been followed in a number of others. . . .

. . .

Judgment affirmed, with costs.

BRUNE, C. J., dissents in part.

NOTES

(1) *Requirement of Certainty.* Ordinarily the injured party's burden of persuasion requires only that he make out his case by the "preponderance or greater weight of the evidence." See James, Civil Procedure § 7.6 (1965). Why should he have to meet a higher standard of "reasonable certainty" as to damages? Are there similarities between the requirement of certainty and that of foreseeability? In principle? In function?

Do you agree with the following criticism of the requirements? "In the century since the certainty rule was formulated, the rules of admissibility have moved closer to commercial practice. Business records and market summaries, constantly used by businesssmen to analyze their own problems, have gained increasing acceptance in the courts. . . . Further simplification can be achieved by using expert opinion based upon these records. . . . As the sciences of analyzing business costs and market behavior achieve maturity, expert witnesses, particularly court-appointed experts, promise to be of great service in facilitating problems of proof. . . . Aside from its obsolescence as a standard of admissibility, the certainty rule contains a second defect: it promotes a theory of damages which supports all-or-nothing recovery rather than compromise. The rule precludes weighing relative probabilities or awarding partial recoveries." Note, Lost Profits as Contract Damages, 65 Yale L.J. 992, 1018–20 (1965). Is it a sufficient answer that loss-splitting, as opposed to loss-shifting, is not an objective of the law of contracts?

(2) *The Value of a Chance.* In some cases the requirement is taken to mean that the *fact*, as distinguished from the *amount*, of the loss must be proved with reasonable certainty. "The law requires, and properly so, that the fact of damage be proved with reasonable certainty. . . . Uncertainty as to the fact of damage, that is, as to the nature, existence or cause of the damage, is fatal. But the same certainty as to the amount of the damage is not required. . . . The law only requires that some reasonable basis of computation be used, and will allow damages so computed even if the result reached is only an approximation." Allen v. Gardner, 126 Cal. App.2d 335, 340, 272 P.2d 99, 102 (1954).

In Collatz v. Fox Wisconsin Amusement Corp., 239 Wis. 156, 300 N.W. 162 (1941), plaintiff, one of two finalists in a quiz contest held at the defendant's theater, claimed a half interest in the automobile offered as a prize, on the ground that it had been arbitrarily awarded to the other finalist before completion of the contest. The court held for the defendant. "He (the plaintiff) suffered no damage because of the defendant's breach of the contract, for it cannot be assumed nor is it susceptible of proof that had the contest proceeded to a proper finish he would have become the winner." Is this an example of uncertainty in the sense of the preceding paragraph? But cf. Wachtel v. National Alfalfa Journal Co., 190 Iowa 1293, 176 N.W. 801 (1920).

(3) *The Right to Work.* In Shirley MacLaine Parker's case, p. 506 supra, could she have recovered more than $750,000? Was not the right to star in "Bloomer Girl" a valuable right which would have enhanced her reputation as an actress? A few courts have recognized such a right in cases such as Mrs. Parker's. See, e. g., Herbert Clayton & Jack Waller, Ltd.

v. Oliver, [1930] A.C. 209, in which the court said: "Here both parties knew that as flowing from the contract the plaintiff would be billed and advertised as appearing at the Hippodrome, and in the theatrical profession this is a valuable right." Can the value of such a right be established with sufficient certainty? What advice would you have given Mrs. Parker concerning her chances of recovery of damages based on such a right?

(4) *Nominal Damages.* The plaintiff who proves a breach of contract but fails to prove damages is traditionally awarded nominal damages (six cents or one dollar). Such an award may serve as a declaration of the plaintiff's rights. It may also serve as a "peg on which to hang costs," in the minority of states that retains the common law rule that even an award of nominal damages carries with it an award of costs against the losing party.

SECTION 4. "LIQUIDATED DAMAGES" AND "PENALTIES"

At the beginning of this chapter, it was pointed out that our law's concern is directed at relief to the promisee to redress breach rather than at compulsion of the promisor to prevent breach, and that for this reason punitive damages are not ordinarily awarded for breach of contract. The *promisee* may, however, be concerned with compulsion of the promisor. Consider the following explanation given by a bridge engineer for the California Division of Highways of the completion assessment, the per-day assessment against a contractor for each day he overruns the specified contract time. "The sole purpose of a completion assessment is to assure that the contract work will be done within the time specified, . . . to threaten the Contractor with sufficient monetary loss so that he will find it advantageous to apply sufficient men and equipment to the work to get it done on time. Whereas moderate liquidated damages such as $100 per day may well be used to insure the completion of a normal project having no special urgency, higher amounts are used to force faster work on jobs which must be finished in less than a normal construction time. High assessments may be used to emphasize the need for haste and should be of sufficient size to make it economically desirable that the contractor expedite his work by the use of multiple shifts or additional equipment." Elliott, A Study of Liquidated Damages on Highway Contracts 5 (1956). Should courts lend their aid to the enforcement of such penalties where the parties have bargained for and agreed to them?

One answer is suggested by article 1152 of the French Civil Code: "When the agreement provides that the party who fails to carry it out shall pay a certain sum as damages, no larger or smaller amount can be awarded to the other party." As the following cases show, this is not the answer in our legal system, which distinguishes between provisions for "liquidated damages," which are enforced, and provisions for "penalties," which are not. As Corbin has said, "The non-enforcement of penalties and forfeitures is a limitation on freedom of contract and is based upon the notions of public policy held by courts of equity." 5 Corbin, § 1055. What "notions of public policy" would justify such a limitation? Are terms providing for penalties more onerous than other contract terms? Are the techniques that are generally used in our legal system to police the bargaining process in order to prevent overreaching inadequate to deal with the problems that would arise if we had the rule of the French Civil Code? Does it make a difference whether it is a *"larger* or *smaller* amount" that is in issue? See pp. 368–372 supra.

The attitude of English and American courts toward "penalties" and "liquidated damages" has been strongly influenced by the development of equitable relief in cases arising under penal bonds. A penal bond, originally a sealed instrument, takes the form of a promise to pay a stated sum, coupled with a condition of defeasance. Here is an example:

> Know All Men By These Presents that A. B. is held and firmly bound to C. D. in the sum of $10,000 for the payment of which the said A. B. binds himself, his executors, administrators and assigns. The condition of the foregoing obligation is such that if A. B. shall well and truly pay unto C. D. the sum of $5,000 on . . . , the above obligation to be void; otherwise to be in full force and effect. A. B. (Seal).

The persistence of legal forms can be seen in the A.I.A.'s standard performance bond which, after setting out the amount of the bond, goes on to provide:

> Now, therefore, the condition of this obligation is such that, if Contractor shall promptly and faithfully perform said Contract, then this obligation shall be null and void; otherwise it shall remain in full force and effect.

At common law, unless the obligor had strictly performed the condition of the bond, a court would give judgment in debt against him for the penal sum, regardless of the amount of loss caused the obligee by the non-performance of the condition. By the time of the Restoration it had become settled that equity would enjoin the collection of the penal sum by the obligee and send the case to trial at law for ascertainment of the amount of damage caused by the breach of condition.[a] Upon this equity practice were based statutes under which the obligee was required at common law to state the breach of condition, and (although he was at first given a judgment for the entire penal sum) was allowed to have execution only for the amount of dam-

---

a. This development was analogous to that of the mortgagor's "equity of redemption." See p. 659 infra.

ages actually proved.   American courts, usually by virtue of similar statutes, took over the notion that the obligee under a penal bond must plead and prove the damages caused by the breach of condition. See Loyd, Penalties and Forfeitures, 29 Harv.L.Rev. 117 (1915).

The principles developed first for penal bonds were later extended to apply to penalties in contracts of all kinds.   They have also been invoked where a sum has actually been paid as a deposit, if that sum is so unreasonably large as to appear to be a penalty.   On the effect of a deposit on the revocability of an offer, see Note 2, p. 148 supra.

Once the "non-enforcement of penalties" is granted, there remains the not inconsiderable task of drawing a line between "penalties" and "liquidated damages."   It is to this task that the following cases address themselves.   It will be helpful to ask yourself, as to each case, what damages would have been awarded, under the authorities that you have just studied in this chapter, had no provision been included in the contract.   See generally, Macneil, Power of Contract and Agreed Remedies, 47 Cornell L.Q. 495 (1962).

DAVE GUSTAFSON & CO. v. STATE

Supreme Court of South Dakota, 1968.
83 S.D. 160, 156 N.W.2d 185.

HANSON, PRESIDING JUDGE.   In this action by a contractor against the State of South Dakota and its Highway Commission the single question is whether a provision in a state highway construction contract is one for liquidated damages, as the trial court found, or is a penalty.

On October 5, 1963 plaintiff, Dave Gustafson & Company, entered into a contract with the State Highway Commission for the construction of the subbase, base and bituminous surfacing of a new public highway between Wessington Springs and Woonsocket.   Plaintiff performed a total dollar amount of work in the amount of $530,724.14.   Upon completion the new highway replaced the pre-existing portion of State Trunk Highway No. 34 between the two towns. During construction the old portion of Highway 34 remained open for travel by the public in substantially the same manner as it had been for the past five years.   After the new highway was completed the old portion of the road was also left open for use as a public highway.

Plaintiff failed to complete the new highway on the date fixed. There was a delay of 67 working days for which there was no extension of time requested or granted.   Therefore the state withheld $14,070.00 as liquidated damages from the amount due plaintiff computed according to the contract scale of daily damage for delay in construction.   As this project totaled $530,742.14, the per diem daily damage was $210.   This daily damage multiplied by the 67 day delay equals the sum withheld. According to an interrogatory answered by the state any damage, loss, or expense incurred by reason of the delay was "unknown". This did not necessarily mean there were no damages.

The pertinent contract provision reads:

"8.9 FAILURE TO COMPLETE THE WORK ON TIME: —Time is an essential element of the contract and it is important that the work be pressed vigorously to completion. [1] The cost to the Department of the administration of the contract including engineering, inspection, and supervision, will be increased as the time occupied in the work is lengthened. [2] The public is subject to detriment and inconvenience when full use cannot be made of an incomplete project.

"Should the Contractor fail to complete the work within the time agreed upon in the contract or within such extra time as may have been allowed by increases in the contract or by formally approved extensions granted by the Department there shall be deducted from any monies or amount due or that may become due the Contractor, the sum set forth in the schedule shown in Section 8.10 herein, for each and every weather working day, that the work shall remain uncompleted. [3] This sum shall be considered and treated not as penalty but as fixed, agreed liquidated damage due the State from the Contractor by reason of inconvenience to the public, added cost of Engineering and supervision, and other items which have caused an expenditure of public funds resulting from his failure to complete the work within the time specified in the contract."

Section 8.10 provides the following graduated scale of per diem liquidated damages:

"Original Contract Amount		Amount of Liquidated Damages per day
From more than	To and including	
0	25,000	42
25,000	50,000	70
50,000	100,000	105
100,000	500,000	140
500,000	1,000,000	210
1,000,000	2,000,000	280
2,000,000	. . . .	420"

An unexcused delay in performing a contract after the time fixed for performance constitutes a breach of contract for which damages are recoverable. The measure of damages, except as otherwise provided by statute, is the amount which would "compensate the party aggrieved for all the detriment proximately caused thereby, or which, in the ordinary course of things, would be likely to result therefrom." SDC 1960 Supp. 37.1801. Such actual damages would have to be alleged and proved.

Stipulated sums in the nature of "Penalties imposed by contract . . . are void", and unenforceable. SDC 10.0703. However, parties to a contract may agree "upon an amount presumed to be the damage for breach in cases where it would be impracticable or extremely difficult to fix actual damage." SDC 10.0704. "The effect of a clause for stipulated damages in a contract is to substitute the amount agreed upon as liquidated damages for the actual damages resulting from breach of the contract, and thereby prevents a controversy between the parties as to the amount of damages. If a provision is construed to be one for liquidated damages, the sum stipulated forms, in general, the measure of damages in case of a breach, and the recovery must be for that amount. No larger or smaller sum can be awarded even though the actual loss may be greater or less." 22 Am.Jur.2d, Damages, § 235, page 321. In such case, evidence of the actual loss or harm suffered is immaterial and irrelevant. Willgohs v. Buerman, 262 Minn. 415, 115 N.W.2d 59.

Our statutes reflect the common law on the subject. Restatement, Contracts, § 339 comparatively reads:

> "An agreement, made in advance of breach, fixing the damages therefor, is not enforceable as a contract and does not affect the damages recoverable for the breach, unless
>
> (a) the amount so fixed is a reasonable forecast of just compensation for the harm that is caused by the breach, and
>
> (b) the harm that is caused by the breach is one that is incapable or very difficult of accurate estimation."

The difficult problem, in each case, is to determine whether or not the stipulated sum is an unenforceable penalty or an enforceable provision for liquidated damages. This is a question of law for the court to determine. Anderson v. Cactus Heights Country Club, 80 S.D. 417, 125 N.W.2d 491, and usually "the reasonableness or unreasonableness of the stipulation is decisive." 5 Williston, Contracts, 3rd Ed., § 779, page 698.

One of the primary concerns is whether or not damages imposed by contract involve a breach where it would be impracticable or extremely difficult to fix actual damages. . . . In the recent case of Anderson v. Cactus Heights Country Club, 80 S.D. 417, 125 N.W.2d 491, this court upheld a stipulated damage provision of $8,000, which was reducible according to the extent of performing a contract to design, construct, and supervise a golf course. The court said "A provision for payment of a stipulated sum as a liquidation of damages will ordinarily be sustained if it appears that at the time the contract was made the damages in the event of a breach will be incapable or very difficult of accurate estimation, that there was a reasonable endeavor by the parties as stated to fix fair compensation, and that the amount stipulated bears a reasonable relation to probable damages and not disproportionate to any damages reasonably to be anticipated."

This case reflects the modern tendency not to "look with disfavor upon 'liquidated damages' provisions in contracts. When they are fair and reasonable attempts to fix just compensation for anticipated loss caused by breach of contract, they are enforced . . . They serve a particularly useful function when damages are uncertain in nature or amount or are unmeasurable, as is the case in many government contracts." Priebe & Sons v. United States, 332 U.S. 407, 68 S.Ct. 123, 92 L.Ed. 32. See also Williston on Contracts, Vol. 5, 3rd Ed., § 788, page 760. In 43 Am.Jur., Public Works and Contracts, § 78, page 822 it is pointed out that "In many instances the governing law requires contracts for public work to contain stipulations for liquidated damages for delay, and in the absence of statute it is customary in many jurisdictions to insert such stipulations. Such a provision requiring liquidated damages for delay is not against public policy and is an appropriate means of inducing due performance, or of giving compensation, in case of failure to perform; the courts give effect to a stipulation of this kind in accordance with its terms."

Judged in this light and by the standards established in Anderson v. Cactus Heights Country Club, 80 S.E. 417, 125 N.W.2d 491, the provision in question must be considered to be one for liquidated damages rather than a penalty for the following reasons: I. Damages for delay in constructing a new highway are impossible of measurement. II. The amount stated in the contract as liquidated damages indicates an endeavor to fix fair compensation for the loss, inconvenience, added costs, and deprivation of use caused by delay. Daily damage is graduated according to total amount of work to be performed. It may be assumed that a large project involves more loss than a small one and each day of delay adds to the loss, inconvenience, cost and deprivation of use. As stated in Vol. 5, Williston on Contracts, 3rd Ed., § 785, page 733 "It is commonly provided in building and construction contracts that there shall be deducted from the contractor's compensation a fixed sum for each day's delay in performing the contract beyond the day fixed therein. Such damages are obviously graded according to the extent of the breach, increasing proportionately with each day's delay. Moreover, each day's delay, while unquestionably injurious, is injurious frequently in ways that are difficult to estimate. Accordingly, unless the sum fixed in the contract is very unreasonable the provision is treated as one for liquidated damages." . . . III. For the same reasons we must conclude the amount stipulated in the contract bears a reasonable relation to probable damages and is not, as a matter of law, disproportionate to any and all damage reasonably to be anticipated from the unexcused delay in performance.

Affirmed.

NOTES

(1) *What the Traffic Will Bear.* How much should the draftsman ask for in preparing a liquidated damage clause? As much as the traffic will bear, consistent with the cases in this section? Or are there practical limitations as well? Consider the following analysis. "High liquidated damages have a tendency to make the contractors jittery. A fear of the high cost of delay will cause an involuntary rise in bid prices. All of the bidders' thinking on prices must inevitably be colored by the specter of the high damages lurking in the background. This only emphasizes the need to use this specialized treatment and high liquidated damages only on those projects where the urgency really exists. Otherwise the State will be paying extra for expediting jobs which do not need the hurry and will not justify the higher cost. High liquidated damages make a contractor susceptible to considerable labor pressure. When a contractor is working under high liquidated damages, it gives the unions a powerful lever to force compliance with demands which may or may not be justified. The contractor is forced to give in because he cannot afford a delaying argument or strike. This pressure also may have a widespread effect. When labor unions make an advance by this sort of a squeeze play against the contractor working under high liquidated damages, other contractors in the area find that they too must give the same benefits or face considerable trouble." Elliott, A Study of Liquidated Damages on Highway Contracts 21–22 (1956).

(2) *Equitable Relief.* Should a valid liquidated damage clause bar equitable relief that would otherwise be available? See Karpinski v. Ingrasci, p. 394 supra; Bauer v. Sawyer, 8 Ill.2d 351, 134 N.E.2d 329 (1956).

(3) *Problem.* Seller contracts to deliver to Buyer a machine which is readily available on the market for $1,000 more than the contract price. If Seller fails to deliver, what are the rights of the parties under each of the following provisions?

(a) "In the event of Seller's failure to deliver, he shall pay Buyer a penalty of $10,000."

(b) "In the event of Seller's failure to deliver, he shall be liable to Buyer for $10,000 in liquidated damages."

(c) "Seller hereby agrees, at his option, to either deliver the machine to Buyer or to pay Buyer $10,000."

(d) "In the event of Seller's failure to deliver, Buyer shall be entitled to keep the $10,000 deposit that Seller has made to secure performance of this contract."

SEEMAN v. BIEMANN, 108 Wis. 365, 84 N.W. 490 (1900). [A contractor agreed with the owner of a building to do carpenter and joiner work by a specified date. The contract provided that if the work was not completed by this date, the contractor "should forfeit the sum of $10 as liquidated damages for each day's delay." The same provision was contained in six other contracts made by the owner for work on the building. The total amount of all the contracts was $5,000 and the value of the building and land was less than $6,000. The work was completed with a delay of fifty-three days, and the owner claimed liquidated damages under the clause.]

MARSHALL, J. . . . The law is too well settled to permit any reasonable controversy in regard to it at this time, that where parties stipulate in their contract for damages in the event of a breach of it, using appropriate language to indicate that the damages are agreed upon in advance, and such damages are unreasonable considered as liquidated damages, the stipulated amount will be construed to be a mere forfeiture or penalty and the recoverable damages be limited to those actually sustained. While courts adhere to the doctrine that the intention of the parties must govern in regard to whether damages mentioned in their contract are liquidated, they uniformly take such liberties in regard to the matter, based on arbitrary rules of construction, so called, as may be necessary to effect judicial notions of equity between parties, guided of course by precedents that are considered to have the force of law, sometimes calling that a penalty which the parties call stipulated damages, and that which the parties call a penalty stipulated damages, where otherwise an unconscionable advantage would be obtained by one person over another. The judicial power thus exercised cannot properly be justified under any ordinary rules of judicial construction. . . .

This court, in harmony with the weight of authority, early adopted the rule that where damages may be readily computed and the stipulated damages, so called, are largely in excess of actual damages, the court will disregard what the parties say they intended, and presume that they intended what is fair and reasonable under the circumstances, however much that may violate their language. . . .
Applying [this rule] to the case before us, the stipulation of $10 per day for delay must be held to be a penalty merely, and not necessarily recoverable to the whole amount. The rental value of the property as found by the court was $38 per month. This is the true measure of actual damages, since there were no special circumstances shown by the evidence, brought home to the knowledge of the contractor at the time of the making of the contract, from which we can say the damages which the parties then had in contemplation as the probable result of a breach of contract as to time of completing the building were other than loss of use for the period of delay. . . .

The rental value of the building is trifling in amount as compared with the stipulated damages, so called, of $10 per day. There was, in the nature of the case, at the time the contract was made, no difficulty to be apprehended in arriving at the actual damages that might arise from mere delay in completing the building. So we have the two elements recognized as controlling the language of parties respecting stipulated damages, first, the amount the parties say they agreed upon is grossly in excess of the actual damages sustained or that could have been reasonably apprehended at the time of making the contract; second, the damages actually sustained are readily ascertainable. It follows that we must hold that the parties intended the $10 per day as a mere penalty to secure the performance of the contract, and limit the recoverable damages to such as were actually sustained, to wit $38 per month for fifty-three days, or $67.12, with six per cent interest thereon from the date the breach of the contract was complete. . . .

NOTES

(1) *Bonus.* Would the court have refused to enforce a provision calling for a bonus of $10 a day if the contractor finished the work earlier than the specified date?

(2) *Intention.* What did the court in Seeman v. Biemann mean by its remarks that "courts adhere to the doctrine that the intention of the parties must govern in regard to whether damages mentioned in their contract are liquidated" and that "[t]he judicial power thus exercised cannot properly be justified under any ordinary rules of judicial construction"? Is the principal problem involved in the preceding cases one of interpretation?

(3) *"Difficult of Accurate Estimation."* The requirement that the damages be, as Restatement, § 339 puts it, "difficult of accurate estimation" is generally accepted. Why should this be so, as long as the estimate is a reasonable one? Does the Code adopt this requirement? See UCC 2–718(1).

(4) *"Blunderbuss" Clauses.* A clause in which a single sum is provided for any breach, regardless of its nature, is sometimes characterized as a "blunderbuss" clause. Such clauses have usually been held to be invalid. See, e. g., Seidlitz v. Auerbach, 230 N.Y. 167, 129 N.E. 461 (1920), in which a lease containing many covenants of varying importance provided for a deposit by the tenant of $7,500 "as security for the faithful performance by the tenant of all the covenants and agreements herein contained" and that as damages for any default by the tenant the landlord could retain the full amount of the deposit. Occasionally, however, a court may so interpret the clause as to limit its application to substantial breaches and then hold it valid. See, e. g., Hackenheimer v. Kurtzmann, 235 N.Y. 57, 138 N.E. 735 (1923), in which the same court as in the case just cited interpreted a provision for $50,000 damages "in case of breach" to apply only to important breaches and held it valid. Cf. Karpinski v. Ingrasci, p. 394 supra.

"REASONABLE FORECAST"

How is a court to determine whether the parties made what the Restatement, § 339 calls a "reasonable forecast"? Should it receive evidence of the actual damages? In Frick Co. v. Rubel Corporation, 62 F.2d 765 (2d Cir. 1933), the seller sought and the court allowed liquidated damages for the buyer's delay in accepting delivery of ice-making machines manufactured by the seller.   Judge Learned Hand wrote:

"There remains however the further question whether the judge was in error in refusing to allow the defendant to prove that the liquidated damages were wholly disproportionate to the *actual* losses suffered by the plaintiff because of the delay.   The defendant had gone only a short way on this point in its cross-examination of the plaintiff's superintendent, when it was stopped.   It then offered to prove that 'the actual loss which was made necessary,' 'the cost entailed by this alleged delay,' was 'infinitesimally small as compared with this penalty.'   The judge refused to allow such proof, and the defendant excepted.   It will be observed that the defendant did not offer to prove disparity between the amount fixed as liquidated damages and the losses which were in *contemplation* when the contract was signed. Unless proof of the *actual* losses was material to that issue, the offer was of irrelevant evidence, and no question arose whether gross disproportion between liquidated damages and losses in contemplation would be evidence that the clause was penal.   .   .   .   My brothers think, though I do not, that evidence as to the *actual* loss was not material to the issue of the losses in *contemplation,* though we all agree that it is the comparison of the liquidated damages with the last, not the first, which can raise the point at all.   On their view, the offer did not therefore raise the question, and it follows that the judge was right, and that the judgment on the second and third causes of action must also be affirmed."   What is the position of the Code on this question?   See UCC 2–718(1)

NOTES

(1) *The Case of the Double Eagle.*   Norwalk Door Closer Co. owned the right to manufacture door closers.   Eagle Lock and Screw Co. contracted to manufacture door closers exclusively for Norwalk for seven years, with an option in Norwalk to renew for another five years.   The contract provided that if Eagle went out of business, Norwalk could treat it as a breach and Eagle would be liable to pay $100,000 in liquidated damages. After four years, Eagle sold its business to another corporation, which immediately formed a subsidiary named Eagle Lock Co., moved into Eagle's premises, employed Eagle's management, and arranged to make door closers for Norwalk without loss of business or time.   Norwalk therefore suffered no damage as a result of Eagle's going out of business.   Norwalk sued Eagle for $100,000.   From judgment for Norwalk, Eagle appealed. *Held:* Reversed.   "It is not the function of the court to determine by hindsight the reasonableness of the expectation of the parties at the time the contract was made, but it is the function of the court at the time of enforcement to do justice.   .   .   .   Implicit in the transaction is the premise that the sum agreed upon will be within the fair range of those just damages which would be called for and provable had the parties resorted to proof.   Consequently, if the damage envisioned by the parties never occurs, the whole premise for their agreed estimate vanishes, and, even if the contract was to be construed as one for liquidated damages rather than one

for a penalty, neither justice nor the intent of the parties is served by enforcement." Norwalk Door Closer Co. v. Eagle Lock and Screw Co., 153 Conn. 681, 220 A.2d 263 (1966).

(2) *Other Bases of Recovery.* Granting that the parties cannot shift the basis of recovery from relief to compulsion, can they make other fundamental shifts? From expectation to restitution or reliance? From substitutional to specific relief? From diminution in value to cost to complete? Could they do away with the requirements of unavoidability, foreseeability and certainty? In the Problem in Note 4, p. 529 supra, what sort of clause would you have advised Czarnikow to include in its contract with Federal?

(3) *Injunctive Relief.* What is the effect of the following provision of the Standard Player Contract of the National Football League?

> The Player hereby represents that he has special, exceptional and unique knowledge, skill and ability as a football player, the loss of which cannot be estimated with any certainty and cannot be fairly or adequately compensated by damages and therefore agrees that the Club shall have the right, in addition to any other rights which the Club may possess, to enjoin him by appropriate injunction proceedings against playing football or any other professional sport, without the consent of the Club, or engaging in activities related to football for any person, firm, corporation, institution, or on his own behalf, and against any other breach of this contract.

(4) *Problem.* Give your opinion on the suitability of the following clause for inclusion by a lessor of juke boxes in its printed leases:

> Should the Location Owner discontinue the Phonograph in breach of this contract, his right to continue in possession shall cease and there shall become immediately due and payable, as liquidated damages and not as a penalty, an amount to be computed as follows: The total receipts from the operation of the Phonograph, less the amount paid over to the Location Owner for the weeks preceding his breach shall be totalled and divided by the number of weeks that have elapsed under the agreement and the result shall be the "net average weekly payment." This "net average weekly payment" shall be multiplied by the number of weeks remaining under the terms of the agreement.

See Knutton v. Cofield, 273 N.C. 355, 160 S.E.2d 29 (1968).

SECTION 5.   EPILOGUE

By this time it will probably have occurred to the reader that in providing for relief through damages, the law by and large assumes a frictionless system and ignores the cost to the claimant of obtaining that relief. It is, of course, true that the successful party may ordinarily recover the rather modest court costs that he has incurred as well as damages and interest, and it is also true that both parties can avail themselves of machinery of justice that is largely paid for by others. But in contrast to the situation in many countries, including Great Britain, an award of costs does not traditionally include attorney's fees, and even the winner is left to pay his own lawyer, not to mention the many other costs, some monetary and some not, of litigation.

This helps to explain why, as we have already seen, businessmen often put little stock in the legal enforceability of agreements (see pp. 185–89 supra), and why so many disputes are settled out of court. But at least, where the transaction is a substantial one between businessmen, the cost of litigation may not seem overwhelming in relation to the amount in dispute. But what of the typical consumer transaction in which the amount in dispute is likely to be much smaller, whether the aggrieved party is the merchant or the consumer?

The merchant is clearly in the better position to cope with this problem. He has enough disputes to have them handled in bulk by specialists in collection. He can provide for liquidated damages and for attorney's fees. He engages the professionals who write the contract. He may also be able to secure himself in some way, e. g., by taking a deposit where he has not yet delivered goods or by preserving the right to repossess goods where he has delivered them. Indeed, our concern in Chapter 3, Policing the Bargain, was not that he could do too little but that he could do too much.

That leaves the consumer. He may not know a lawyer. He adhered to the contract. He could not have changed its terms even if he had known what changes he had wanted. He may, depending on how trusting the merchant has been, be able to stop payment on a check or to refuse to pay for goods delivered on credit, but even here he risks the onslaught of the merchant's specialists in collection. It is not that "The customer is always right." He is often wrong and sometimes a "deadbeat." The problem is that he and the merchant stand on an unequal footing in attempting to show who is right.

A wide variety of solutions has been suggested and attempted in limited areas. One sort of solution is to "sweeten the pot" by increasing the successful consumer's recovery: by allowing him a civil penalty, multiple (e. g., treble) damages, or attorney's fees. Another sort of solution is to give him support by having others subsidize his representation: by providing free or inexpensive legal services, by allowing him to join with claimants similarly situated in a class action, or by having a public agency handle the claim and distribute any recovery to the aggrieved consumers. Another sort of solution is to reduce the cost of litigation through special tribunals: by expanding the use of small claims courts or by instituting a system of arbitration.

Since most of these solutions are essentially procedural, this is not the place to explore them in detail. For an elaborate discussion of the problem in general, see Leff, Injury, Ignorance and Spite—The Dynamics of Coercive Collection, 80 Yale L.J. 1 (1970).

Chapter 6

FINDING THE LAW OF THE CONTRACT

Much of what we think of as "contract law" consists of the legal framework within which parties may create their own rights and duties. Thus far this book has been largely concerned with this framework—with enforceability and enforcement. And yet in many contract disputes the disagreement relates not to such matters but rather to the nature and extent of the rights and duties that have been created. These disputes, over what are commonly called the "interpretation" and "construction" of contracts, are representative of a hefty and growing fraction of contract disputes. They are referred to here as disputes over the "law of the contract," to distinguish them from disputes over "contract law." [a]

The purpose of this chapter is to introduce some of the problems encountered and the techniques used by the courts in finding the law of the contract. At the same time it would be well to remember that many potential disputes of this kind do not arise at all because the language of the contract is clear, and that many actual disputes would not have arisen had the language of the contract been clearer. It would not, therefore, be amiss to ask yourself how the parties, or their lawyers, in each case might have drafted a contract which would have avoided litigation.

SECTION 1. DETERMINING THE SUBJECT MATTER TO BE INTERPRETED

A threshold problem goes to the limitations on the sources that a court may consider in finding the law of the contract. Our initial concern is with a rule, or complex of rules, that goes under the name of "the parol evidence rule." Typically it is called into play where a contract has been reduced to writing after oral or written negotiations during which the parties have given assurances, made promises, or reached understandings. In the event of litigation, one of them may

---

a. Although the term "law of the contract" may be unfamiliar to lawyers in common law countries, it would not startle lawyers in civil law countries, such as France, where article 1134 of the Civil Code provides: "Agreements legally entered into have the force of law between the parties."

546

seek to introduce evidence of the negotiations in order to establish that the terms of the contract are other than as shown in the writing. Here he will be met with the parol evidence rule which, where the parties have embodied their agreement in writing, may preclude reliance on such extrinsic evidence as negotiations.

Professor Thayer said of the parol evidence rule that, "Few things are darker than this, or fuller of subtle difficulties," and it is not purposed to explore it fully here. Certain it is that, in spite of its name, it is not limited to oral agreements; it also operates to exclude writings, such as letters or telegrams. There is also a general consensus that it is not, strictly speaking, a rule of evidence (such as the hearsay rule), which bars the use of some types of evidence to prove an ultimate matter of fact but which permits that fact to be established in a different way; rather it is a rule of substantive law, which precludes any showing of the ultimate matter of fact itself, that is, that the terms of the contract are other than as expressed in the writing.[a] So much for what the rule is not. It is more difficult to state what it is.

GIANNI v. R. RUSSEL & CO., INC.

Supreme Court of Pennsylvania, 1924.
281 Pa. 320, 126 A. 791.

Action by Frank Gianni against R. Russell & Co., Inc. From judgment for plaintiff, defendant appeals.

Reversed, and judgment entered for defendant.

SCHAFFER, J. Plaintiff had been a tenant of a room in an office building in Pittsburgh wherein he conducted a store, selling tobacco, fruit, candy and soft drinks. Defendant acquired the entire property in which the storeroom was located, and its agent negotiated with plaintiff for a further leasing of the room. A lease for three years was signed. It contained a provision that the lessee should "use the premises only for the sale of fruit, candy, soda water," etc., with the further stipulation that "it is expressly understood that the tenant is not allowed to sell tobacco in any form, under penalty of instant forfeiture of this lease." The document was prepared following a discus-

---

a. In our adversary trial system it is traditionally incumbent upon the aggrieved party to make timely objection to the admission of evidence in order to give the trial judge an opportunity to rule on its admissibility. Under an exclusionary rule of evidence, failure to object at trial is ordinarily a waiver of any ground of complaint against admission, and the evidence becomes part of the proof in the case. That an objection based on the parol evidence rule is not lost by failure to raise it at trial, see Tahoe National Bank v. Phillips, 4 Cal.3d 11, 480 P.2d 320 (1971). But for a contrary view, see Higgs v. DeMaziroff, 273 N.Y. 473, 189 N.E. 555 (1934). Compare Restatement Second, § 239 with §§ 241 and 242. Comment a to § 239 declares that the parol evidence rule there stated is "not a rule of evidence but a rule of substantive law."

sion about renting the room between the parties and after an agreement to lease had been reached. It was signed after it had been left in plaintiff's hands and admittedly had been read over to him by two persons, one of whom was his daughter.

Plaintiff sets up that in the course of his dealings with defendant's agent it was agreed that, in consideration of his promises not to sell tobacco and to pay an increased rent, and for entering into the agreement as a whole, he should have the exclusive right to sell soft drinks in the building. No such stipulation is contained in the written lease. Shortly after it was signed defendant demised the adjoining room in the building to a drug company without restricting the latter's right to sell soda water and soft drinks. Alleging that this was in violation of the contract which defendant had made with him, and that the sale of these beverages by the drug company had greatly reduced his receipts and profits, plaintiff brought this action for damages for breach of the alleged oral contract, and was permitted to recover. Defendant has appealed.

Plaintiff's evidence was to the effect that the oral agreement had been made at least two days, possibly longer, before the signing of the instrument, and that it was repeated at the time he signed; that, relying upon it, he executed the lease. Plaintiff called one witness who said he heard defendant's agent say to plaintiff at a time admittedly several days before the execution of the lease that he would have the exclusive right to sell soda water and soft drinks, to which the latter replied if that was the case he accepted the tenancy. Plaintiff produced no witness who was present when the contract was executed to corroborate his statement as to what then occurred. Defendant's agent denied that any such agreement was made, either preliminary to or at the time of the execution of the lease.

Appellee's counsel argues this is not a case in which an endeavor is being made to reform a written instrument because of something omitted as a result of fraud, accident, or mistake, but is one involving the breach of an independent oral agreement which does not belong in the writing at all and is not germane to its provisions. We are unable to reach this conclusion.

"Where parties, without any fraud or mistake, have deliberately put their engagements in writing, the law declares the writing to be not only the best, but the only evidence of their agreement." Martin v. Berens, 67 Pa. 459, 463; Irvin v. Irvin, 142 Pa. 271, 287, 21 A. 816.

"All preliminary negotiations, conversations and verbal agreements are merged in and superseded by the subsequent written contract, . . . and 'unless fraud, accident, or mistake be averred, the writing constitutes the agreement between the parties, and its terms cannot be added to nor subtracted from by parol evidence.' " Union Storage Co. v. Speck, 194 Pa. 126, 133, 45 A. 48, 49; Vito v. Birkel, 209 Pa. 206, 208, 58 A. 127.

The writing must be the entire contract between the parties if parol evidence is to be excluded, and to determine whether it is or not the writing will be looked at, and if it appears to be a contract complete within itself, "couched in such terms as import a complete legal obligation without any uncertainty as to the object or extent of the engagement, it is conclusively presumed that the whole engagement of the parties, and the extent and manner of their undertaking, were reduced to writing." Seitz v. Brewers' Refrigerating Machine Co., 141 U.S. 510, 517, 12 S.Ct. 46, 48, 35 L.Ed. 837.

When does the oral agreement come within the field embraced by the written one? This can be answered by comparing the two, and determining whether parties, situated as were the ones to the contract, would naturally and normally include the one in the other if it were made. If they relate to the same subject-matter, and are so interrelated that both would be executed at the same time and in the same contract, the scope of the subsidiary agreement must be taken to be covered by the writing. This question must be determined by the court.

In the case at bar the written contract stipulated for the very sort of thing which plaintiff claims has no place in it. It covers the use to which the storeroom was to be put by plaintiff and what he was and what he was not to sell therein. He was "to use the premises only for the sale of fruit, candy, soda water," etc., and was not "allowed to sell tobacco in any form." Plaintiff claims his agreement not to sell tobacco was part of the consideration for the exclusive right to sell soft drinks. Since his promise to refrain was included in the writing, it would be the natural thing to have included the promise of exclusive rights. Nothing can be imagined more pertinent to these provisions which were included than the one appellee avers.

In cases of this kind, where the cause of action rests entirely on an alleged oral understanding concerning a subject which is dealt with in a written contract it is assumed that the writing was intended to set forth the entire agreement as to that particular subject.

"In deciding upon this intent [as to whether a certain subject was intended to be embodied by the writing], the chief and most satisfactory index . . . is found in the circumstance whether or not the particular element of the alleged extrinsic negotiation is dealt with at all in the writing. If it is mentioned, covered, or dealt with in the writing, then presumably the writing was meant to represent all of the transaction on that element, if it is not, then probably the writing was not intended to embody that element of the negotiation." Wigmore on Evidence, 2d Ed., vol. 5, p. 309.

As the written lease is the complete contract of the parties, and since it embraces the field of the alleged oral contract, evidence of the latter is inadmissible under the parol evidence rule.

"The [parol evidence] rule also denies validity to a subsidiary agreement within [the] scope [of the written contract] if sued on as a separate contract, although except for [that rule], the agreement fulfills all the requisites of a valid contract." 2 Williston, Contracts, 1222; Penn Iron Co. v. Diller, 1 Sad., Pa., 82, 1 A. 924; Krueger v. Nicola, 205 Pa. 38, 54 A. 494; Wodock v. Robinson, 148 Pa. 503, 24 A. 73.

There are, of course, certain exceptions to the parol evidence rule, but this case does not fall within any of them. Plaintiff expressly rejects any idea of fraud, accident, or mistake, and they are the foundation upon which any basis for admitting parol evidence to set up an entirely separate agreement within the scope of a written contract must be built. The evidence must be such as would cause a chancellor to reform the instrument, and that would be done only for these reasons (Pioso v. Bitzer, 209 Pa. 503, 58 A. 891) and this holds true where this essentially equitable relief is being given, in our Pennsylvania fashion, through common-law forms.

We have stated on several occasions recently that we propose to stand for the integrity of written contracts. . . . We reiterate our position in this regard.

The judgment of the court below is reversed, and is here entered for defendant.

NOTE

Rationale. What is the reason behind the parol evidence rule? Professor McCormick, an authority on the law of evidence, pointed out that "usually the one who sets up the spoken against the written word is economically the under-dog," and that jurors would tend to favor him in spite of the unreliability of evidence of spoken words when given months or years later, even by a disinterested witness and particularly by a party himself. McCormick, Handbook of the Law of Evidence § 210 (1954).

Professor Corbin, an authority on the law of contracts, saw a different basis for the rule. "Any contract . . . can be discharged or modified by subsequent agreement of the parties. . . . If the foregoing is true of antecedent contracts that were once legally operative and enforceable, it is equally true of preliminary negotiations that were not themselves mutually agreed upon or enforceable at law. The new agreement is not a discharging contract, since there were no legal relations to be discharged; but the legal relations of the parties are now governed by the terms of the new agreement." 3 Corbin, § 574.

MASTERSON v. SINE

Supreme Court of California, 1968.
68 Cal.2d 222, 436 P.2d 561.

TRAYNOR, CHIEF JUSTICE. Dallas Masterson and his wife Rebecca owned a ranch as tenants in common. On February 25, 1958, they conveyed it to Medora and Lu Sine by a grant deed "Reserving unto the Grantors herein an option to purchase the above described property on or before February 25, 1968" for the "same consideration as being paid heretofore plus their depreciation value of any improvements Grantees may add to the property from and after two and a half years from this date." Medora is Dallas' sister and Lu's wife. Since the conveyance Dallas has been adjudged bankrupt. His trustee in bankruptcy and Rebecca brought this declaratory relief action to establish their right to enforce the option.

The case was tried without a jury. Over defendants' objection the trial court admitted extrinsic evidence that by "the same consideration as being paid heretofore" both the grantors and the grantees meant the sum of $50,000 and by "depreciation value of any improvements" they meant the depreciation value of improvements to be computed by deducting from the total amount of any capital expenditures made by defendants grantees the amount of depreciation allowable to them under United States income tax regulations as of the time of the exercise of the option.

The court also determined that the parol evidence rule precluded admission of extrinsic evidence offered by defendants to show that the parties wanted the property kept in the Masterson family and that the option was therefore personal to the grantors and could not be exercised by the trustee in bankruptcy.

The court entered judgment for plaintiffs, declaring their right to exercise the option, specifying in some detail how it could be exercised, and reserving jurisdiction to supervise the manner of its exercise and to determine the amount that plaintiffs will be required to pay defendants for their capital expenditures if plaintiffs decide to exercise the option.

Defendants appeal. They contend that the option provision is too uncertain to be enforced and that extrinsic evidence as to its meaning should not have been admitted. The trial court properly refused to frustrate the obviously declared intention of the grantors to reserve an option to repurchase by an overly meticulous insistence on completeness and clarity of written expression. . . . It properly admitted extrinsic evidence to explain the language of the deed . . . to the end that the consideration for the option would appear with sufficient certainty to permit specific enforcement . . . . The trial court erred, however, in excluding the extrinsic evidence that the option was personal to the grantors and therefore nonassignable.

When the parties to a written contract have agreed to it as an "integration"—a complete and final embodiment of the terms of an agreement—parol evidence cannot be used to add to or vary its terms. . . . When only part of the agreement is integrated, the same rule applies to that part, but parol evidence may be used to prove elements of the agreement not reduced to writing. . . .

The crucial issue in determining whether there has been an integration is whether the parties intended their writing to serve as the exclusive embodiment of their agreement. The instrument itself may help to resolve that issue. It may state, for example, that "there are no previous understandings or agreements not contained in the writing," and thus express the parties' "intention to nullify antecedent understandings or agreements." (See 3 Corbin, Contracts (1960) § 578, p. 411.) Any such collateral agreement itself must be examined, however, to determine whether the parties intended the subjects of negotiation it deals with to be included in, excluded from, or otherwise affected by the writing. Circumstances at the time of the writing may also aid in the determination of such integration. . . .

California cases have stated that whether there was an integration is to be determined solely from the face of the instrument and that the question for the court is whether it "appears to be a complete . . . agreement . . . ." (See Ferguson v. Koch (1928) 204 Cal. 342, 346, 268 P. 342, 344, 58 A.L.R. 1176; . . .) Neither of these strict formulations of the rule, however, has been consistently applied. The requirement that the writing must appear incomplete on its face has been repudiated in many cases where parol evidence was admitted "to prove the existence of a separate oral agreement as to any matter on which the document is silent and which is not inconsistent with its terms"—even though the instrument appeared to state a complete agreement. . . . Even under the rule that the writing alone is to be consulted, it was found necessary to examine the alleged collateral agreement before concluding that proof of it was precluded by the writing alone. (See 3 Corbin, Contracts (1960) § 582, pp. 444–446.) It is therefore evident that "The conception of a writing as wholly and intrinsically self-determinative of the parties' intent to make it a sole memorial of one or seven or twenty-seven subjects of negotiation is an impossible one." (9 Wigmore, Evidence (3d ed. 1940) § 2431, p. 103.) For example, a promissory note given by a debtor to his creditor may integrate all their present contractual rights and obligations, or it may be only a minor part of an underlying executory contract that would never be discovered by examining the face of the note.

In formulating the rule governing parol evidence, several policies must be accommodated. One policy is based on the assumption that written evidence is more accurate than human memory. . . . This policy, however, can be adequately served by excluding parol evidence of agreements that directly contradict the writing. Another policy is based on the fear that fraud or unintentional invention by witnesses interested in the outcome of the litigation will mislead the finder of facts. (. . . Mitchill v. Lath (1928) 247 N.Y. 377, 388, 160 N.E. 646, 68 A.L.R. 239. . . .) . . . McCormick has suggested that the party urging the spoken as against the written word is most often the economic underdog, threatened by severe hardship if the writing is enforced. In his view the parol evidence rule arose to allow the court to control the tendency of the jury to find through sympathy and without a dispassionate assessment of the probability of fraud or faulty memory that the parties made an oral agreement collateral to the written contract, or that preliminary tentative agreements were not abandoned when omitted from the writing. (See McCormick, Evidence (1954) § 210.) He recognizes, however, that if this theory were adopted in disregard of all other considerations, it would lead to the exclusion of testimony concerning oral agreements whenever there is a writing and thereby often defeat the true intent of the parties. (See McCormick, op. cit. supra, § 216, p. 441.)

Evidence of oral collateral agreements should be excluded only when the fact finder is likely to be misled. The rule must therefore be based on the credibility of the evidence. One such standard, adopted by section 240(1) (b) of the Restatement of Contracts, permits proof of a collateral agreement if it "is such an agreement as might *naturally* be made as a separate agreement by parties situated as were the parties to the written contract." (Italics added; see McCormick, Evidence (1954) § 216, p. 441; see also 3 Corbin, Contracts (1960) § 583, p. 475, § 594, pp. 568–569; 4 Williston, Contracts (3d ed. 1961) § 638, pp. 1039–1045.) The draftsmen of the Uniform Commercial Code would exclude the evidence in still fewer instances: "If the additional terms are such that, if agreed upon, they would *certainly* have been included in the document in the view of the court, then evidence of their alleged making must be kept from the trier of fact." (Com. 3, § 2–202, italics added.) [1]

The option clause in the deed in the present case does not explicitly provide that it contains the complete agreement, and the deed is silent on the question of assignability. Moreover, the difficulty of accommodating the formalized structure of a deed to the insertion of

---

1. Corbin suggests that, even in situations where the court concludes that it would not have been natural for the parties to make the alleged collateral oral agreement, parol evidence of such an agreement should nevertheless be permitted if the court is convinced that the unnatural actually happened in the case being adjudicated. (3 Corbin, Contracts, § 485, pp. 478,

480; cf. Murray, The Parol Evidence Rule: A Clarification (1966) 4 Duquesne L.Rev. 337, 341–342.) This suggestion may be based on a belief that judges are not likely to be misled by their sympathies. If the court believes that the parties intended a collateral agreement to be effective, there is no reason to keep the evidence from the jury.

collateral agreements makes it less likely that all the terms of such an agreement were included. . . . The statement of the reservation of the option might well have been placed in the recorded deed solely to preserve the grantors' rights against any possible future purchasers and this function could well be served without any mention of the parties' agreement that the option was personal. There is nothing in the record to indicate that the parties to this family transaction, through experience in land transactions or otherwise, had any warning of the disadvantages of failing to put the whole agreement in the deed. This case is one, therefore, in which it can be said that a collateral agreement such as that alleged "might naturally be made as a separate agreement." *A fortiori*, the case is not one in which the parties "would certainly" have included the collateral agreement in the deed.

It is contended, however, that an option agreement is ordinarily presumed to be assignable if it contains no provisions forbidding its transfer or indicating that its performance involves elements personal to the parties. . . . The fact that there is a written memorandum, however, does not necessarily preclude parol evidence rebutting a term that the law would otherwise presume. . . .

In the present case defendants offered evidence that the parties agreed that the option was not assignable in order to keep the property in the Masterson family. The trial court erred in excluding that evidence.

The judgment is reversed.

PETERS, TOBRINER, MOSK, and SULLIVAN, JJ., concur.

BURKE, JUSTICE (dissenting). I dissent. The majority opinion:

(1) Undermines the parol evidence rule as we have known it in this state since at least 1872 by declaring that parol evidence should have been admitted by the trial court to show that a written option, absolute and unrestricted in form, was intended to be limited and nonassignable;

(2) Renders suspect instruments of conveyance absolute on their face;

(3) Materially lessens the reliance which may be placed upon written instruments affecting the title to real estate; and

(4) Opens the door, albeit unintentionally to a new technique for the defrauding of creditors.

The opinion permits defendants to establish by parol testimony that their grant to their brother (and brother-in-law) of a written option, absolute in terms, was nevertheless agreed to be nonassignable by the grantee (now a bankrupt), and that therefore the right to exercise it did not pass, by operation of the bankruptcy laws, to the trustee for the benefit of the grantee's creditors.

And how was this to be shown? By the proffered testimony of the bankrupt optionee himself! Thereby one of his assets (the option to purchase defendants' California ranch) would be withheld from the trustee in bankruptcy and from the bankrupt's creditors. Understandably the trial court, as required by the parol evidence rule, did not allow the bankrupt by parol to so contradict the unqualified language of the written option.

The court properly admitted parol evidence to explain the intended meaning of the "same consideration" and "depreciation value" phrases of the written option to purchase defendants' land, as the intended meaning of those phrases was not clear. However, there was nothing ambiguous about the *granting* language of the option and not the slightest suggestion in the document that the option was to be nonassignable. Thus, to permit such words of limitation to be added by parol is to *contradict* the absolute nature of the grant, and to directly violate the parol evidence rule.

Just as it is unnecessary to state in a deed to "lot X" that the house located thereon goes with the land, it is likewise unnecessary to add to "I grant an option to Jones" the words *"and his assigns"* for the option to be assignable. As hereinafter emphasized in more detail, California statutes expressly declare that it *is* assignable, and only if I add language in writing showing my intent to withhold or restrict the right of assignment may the grant be so limited. Thus, to seek to restrict the grant by parol is to *contradict* the written document in violation of the parol evidence rule.

The majority opinion arrives at its holding via a series of false premises which are not supported either in the record of this case or in such California authorities as are offered. .   .   .

At the outset the majority in the present case reiterate that the rule against contradicting or varying the terms of a writing remains applicable when only part of the agreement is contained in the writing, and parol evidence is used to prove elements of the agreement not reduced to writing. But having restated this established rule, the majority opinion inexplicably proceeds to subvert it. .   .   .

Options are property, and are widely used in the sale and purchase of real and personal property. One of the basic incidents of property ownership is the right of the owner to sell or transfer it. .   .   . These rights of the owner of property to transfer it, are elementary rules of substantive law and not the mere disputable presumptions which the majority opinion in the present case would make of them. Moreover, the right of transferability applies to an option to purchase, unless there are words of limitation in the option forbidding its assignment or showing that it was given because of a peculiar trust or confidence reposed in the optionee. .   .   .

The right of an optionee to transfer his option to purchase property is accordingly one of the basic rights which accompanies the option unless limited under the language of the option itself. To allow an optionor to resort to parol evidence to support his assertion that the written option is not transferable is to authorize him to limit the option by attempting to restrict and reclaim rights with which he has already parted. A clearer violation of two substantive and basic rules of law—the parol evidence rule and the right of free transferability of property—would be difficult to conceive. . . .

[D]espite the law which until the advent of the present majority opinion has been firmly and clearly established in California and relied upon by attorneys and courts alike, that parol evidence may *not* be employed to vary or contradict the terms of a written instrument, the majority now announce that such evidence "should be excluded only when the fact finder is *likely to be misled*," and that "The rule must therefore be based on the *credibility of the evidence*." (Italics added.) But was it not, inter alia, to avoid misleading the fact finder, and to further the introduction of only the evidence which is most likely to *be* credible (the written document), that the Legislature adopted the parol evidence rule as a part of the substantive law of this state?

Next, in an effort to implement this newly promulgated "credibility" test, the majority opinion offers a choice of two "standards": one, a "certainty" standard, quoted from the Uniform Commercial Code, and the other a "natural" standard found in the Restatement of Contracts, and concludes that at least for purposes of the present case the "natural" viewpoint should prevail.

This new rule, not hitherto recognized in California, provides that proof of a claimed collateral oral agreement is admissible if it is such an agreement as might *naturally* have been made a separate agreement by the parties under the particular circumstances. I submit that this approach opens the door to uncertainty and confusion. Who can know what its limits are? Certainly I do not. For example, in its application to this case who could be expected to divine as "natural" a separate oral agreement between the parties that the assignment, absolute and unrestricted on its face, was intended by the parties to be limited to the Masterson family?

Or, assume that one gives to his relative a promissory note and that the payee of the note goes bankrupt. By operation of law the note becomes an asset of the bankruptcy. The trustee attempts to enforce it. Would the relatives be permitted to testify that by a separate oral agreement made at the time of the execution of the note it was understood that should the payee fail in his business the maker would be excused from payment of the note, or that, as here, it was intended that the benefits of the note would be *personal* to the payee? I doubt that trial judges should be burdened with the task of conjuring whether it would have been "natural" under those circumstances for such a separate agreement to have been made by the parties.

Yet, under the application of the proposed rule, this is the task the trial judge would have, and in essence the situation presented in the instant case is no different.

Under the application of the codes and the present case law, proof of the existence of such an agreement would not be permitted, "natural" or "unnatural." But conceivably, as loose as the new rule is, one judge might deem it natural and another judge unnatural. And in each instance the ultimate decision would have to be made ("naturally") on a case-by-case basis by the appellate courts.

In an effort to provide justification for applying the newly pronounced "natural" rule to the circumstances of the present case, the majority opinion next attempts to account for the silence of the writing in this case concerning assignability of the option, by asserting that "the difficulty of accommodating the formalized structure of a deed to the insertion of collateral agreements makes it less likely that all the terms of such an agreement were included." What difficulty would have been involved here, to add the words "this option is nonassignable"? The asserted "formalized structure of a deed" is no formidable barrier.   .   .   .

Comment hardly seems necessary on the convenience to a bankrupt of such a device to defeat his creditors. He need only produce parol testimony that any options (or other property, for that matter) which he holds are subject to an oral "collateral agreement" with family members (or with friends) that the property is nontransferable "in order to keep the property in the family" or in the friendly group. In the present case the value of the ranch which the bankrupt and his wife held an option to purchase has doubtless increased substantially during the years since they acquired the option. The initiation of this litigation by the trustee in bankruptcy to establish his right to enforce the option indicates his belief that there is substantial value to be gained for the creditors from this asset of the bankrupt. Yet the majority opinion permits defeat of the trustee and of the creditors through the device of an asserted collateral oral agreement that the option was "personal" to the bankrupt and nonassignable "in order to keep the property in the family"!   .   .   .

I would hold that the trial court ruled correctly on the proffered parol evidence, and would affirm the judgment.

MᶜCOMB, J., concurs.

NOTES

(1) *"Integrated" Agreements and the Restatement.* According to the Restatement Second, where a writing has been adopted by the parties as "a final expression of one or more terms of an agreement" that writing is known as an "integrated agreement," and "evidence of prior agreements or negotiations is not admissible in evidence to contradict a term of the writing." Restatement Second, §§ 235, 241. Where the writing has been

"adopted by the parties as a complete and exclusive statement of the terms of the agreement," it is known as a "completely integrated agreement," and not even evidence of "a consistent additional term is admissible to explain or supplement" it. Restatement Second, §§ 236, 242. Such evidence is, however, admissible if the writing is only a "partially integrated agreement."

Are Gianni v. Russel and Masterson v. Sine distinguishable? How would the writings in those cases be characterized in Restatement Second terms? Who characterized them? See Restatement Second, § 235(2). On the basis of what evidence were they characterized? See Restatement Second, § 240. For what purpose did Gianni and the Sines seek to introduce extrinsic evidence? What rationale for the parol evidence rule was relied on in reaching each decision?

The Code's version of the parol evidence rule is found in UCC 2–202. It does not, of course, apply to transactions like those in the preceding two cases. Are its provisions consistent with the results in those cases?

For recent criticism of the parol evidence rule, see Calamari and Perillo, A Plea for a Uniform Parol Evidence Rule and Principles of Contract Interpretation, 42 Ind.L.J. 333 (1967); Murray, The Parol Evidence Rule: A Clarification, 4 Duquesne L.Rev. 337 (1966); Sweet, Contract Making and Parol Evidence: Diagnosis and Treatment of a Sick Rule, 53 Cornell L.Rev. 1036 (1968); Note, 44 N.Y.U.L.Rev. 972 (1969).

(2) *"Collateral Agreements."* The fact that the parties have adopted a writing as an integration of one agreement has, of course, no effect on another entirely separate agreement. Note that Chief Justice Traynor speaks of a "collateral agreement" in Masterson v. Sine. What was that agreement? What was its consideration? Does the notion of a "collateral agreement," as he uses it, differ from that of "partial integration"?

He cites Mitchill v. Lath, 247 N.Y. 377, 160 N.E. 646 (1928). In that case the buyer of land under a written contract attempted to show a prior agreement by the seller to remove an unsightly ice house from a nearby tract. The court held that the parol evidence rule precluded such a showing. For evidence of a contemporaneous oral agreement to be admissible: "(1) The agreement must in form be a collateral one; (2) it must not contradict express or implied provisions of the written contract; (3) it must be one that parties would not ordinarily be expected to embody in the writing." The court thought that "an inspection of this contract shows a full and complete agreement, setting forth in detail the obligations of each party. On reading it, one would conclude that the reciprocal obligations of the parties were fully detailed." Judge Lehman dissenting says: "[T]he question we must decide is whether or not, *assuming* an agreement was made for the removal of an unsightly icehouse from one parcel of land as an inducement for the purchase of another parcel, the parties would ordinarily or naturally be expected to embody the agreement for the removal of the icehouse from one parcel in the written agreement to convey the other parcel." He thought they would not and that therefore the oral agreement was valid.

(3) *Merger Clauses.* Chief Justice Traynor observed that the "instrument may help to resolve" the issue of integration. It is a common practice to include in written contracts a clause known as a "merger clause,"

which may read somewhat as follows: "There are no promises, verbal understandings, or agreements of any kind, pertaining to this contract other than specified herein." Such clauses have usually been given effect, in situations like those in the two preceding cases, to show integration.

BOLLINGER v. CENTRAL PENNSYLVANIA QUARRY STRIPPING AND CONSTRUCTION CO.

Supreme Court of Pennsylvania, 1967.
425 Pa. 430, 229 A.2d 741.

MUSMANNO, JUSTICE.   Mahlon Bollinger and his wife, Vinetta C. Bollinger, filed an action in equity against the Central Pennsylvania Quarry Stripping Construction Company asking that a contract entered into between them be reformed so as to include therein a paragraph alleged to have been omitted by mutual mistake and that the agreement, as reformed, be enforced.

The agreement, as executed, provided that the defendant was to be permitted to deposit on the property of the plaintiffs, construction waste as it engaged in work on the Pennsylvania Turnpike in the immediate vicinity of the plaintiffs' property. The Bollingers claimed that there had been a mutual understanding between them and the defendant that, prior to depositing such waste on the plaintiffs' property, the defendant would remove the topsoil of the plaintiffs' property, pile on it the waste material and then restore the topsoil in a way to cover the deposited waste. The Bollingers averred that they had signed the written agreement without reading it because they assumed that the condition just stated had been incorporated into the writing.

When the defendant first began working in the vicinity of the plaintiffs' property, it did first remove the topsoil, deposited the waste on the bare land, and then replaced the topsoil. After a certain period of time, the defendant ceased doing this and the plaintiffs remonstrated. The defendant answered there was nothing in the written contract which required it to make a sandwich of its refuse between the bare earth and the topsoil. It was at this point that the plaintiffs discovered that that feature of the oral understanding had been omitted from the written contract. The plaintiff husband renewed his protest and the defendant's superintendent replied he could not remove the topsoil because his equipment for that operation had been taken away. When he was reminded of the original understanding, the superintendent said, in effect, he couldn't help that.

The plaintiffs then filed their action for reformation of the contract, the Court granted the requested relief, and the defendant firm appealed. We said in Bugen v. New York Life Insurance Co., 408 Pa. 472, 184 A.2d 499: "A court of equity has the power to reform the written evidence of a contract and make it correspond to the understanding of the parties. . . . However, the mistake must be mutual to the parties to the contract." The fact, however, that one of the parties denies that a mistake was made does not prevent a finding of mutual mistake. Kutsenkow v. Kutsenkow, 414 Pa. 610, 612, 202 A.2d 68.

Once a person enters into a written agreement he builds around himself a stone wall, from which he cannot escape by merely asserting he had not understood what he was signing. However, equity would completely fail in its objectives if it refused to break a hole through the wall when it finds, after proper evidence, that there was a mistake between the parties, that it was real and not feigned, actual and not hypothetical.

The Chancellor, after taking testimony, properly concluded: "We are satisfied that plaintiffs have sustained the heavy burden placed upon them. Their understanding of the agreement is corroborated by the undisputed evidence. The defendant did remove and set aside the top soil on part of the area before depositing its waste and did replace the top soil over such waste after such depositing. It follows it would not have done so had it not so agreed. Further corroboration is found in the testimony that it acted similarly in the case of plaintiffs' neighbor Beltzner."

After the Court handed down its Decree Nisi, the defendant petitioned for a rehearing on the ground of after-discovered evidence. Even assuming, without so deciding, that the so-called after-discovered evidence qualified as such, it is not clear that it was sufficiently material or relevant to bring about a change in the result reached by the Chancellor, and he so stated in his Opinion. We are satisfied that the proffered evidence would not be inconsistent with the Chancellor's findings.

Decree affirmed, costs on the appellant.

NOTES

(1) *Mistake.* How did the situation of the Bollingers differ from that of Gianni? What would he have had to show in order to bring himself within the rule of the Bollinger case? See Restatement Second, § 240(d); Palmer, Reformation and the Parol Evidence Rule, 65 Mich.L.Rev. 833 (1967).

(2) *Fraud.* It is also generally held that the parol evidence rule does not preclude the use of extrinsic evidence to show fraud. Restatement Second, § 240.[a] Is the rule the same under UCC 2–202? For an affirmative answer, see Associated Hardware Supply Co. v. Big Wheel Distributing Co., 355 F.2d 114 (3d Cir. 1965). What language of UCC 2–202 supports such a result? Is UCC 1–103 relevant?

(3) *Merger Clauses and Fraud.* Might a carefully drafted merger clause preclude the use of extrinsic evidence to show fraud? Consider the

---

a. For an interesting case involving a writing that intentionally omitted a provision for a contingent fee to be paid for procuring government contracts in order to "avoid any possible stigma which might result," see Zell v. American Seating Co., 138 F.2d 641 (2d Cir. 1943), rev'd, 322 U.S. 709 (1944).

following language, which was incorporated in a contract of sale of a lease of a building: "Purchaser hereby expressly acknowledges that no such representations have been made, and the Purchaser further acknowledges that it has inspected the premises and agrees to take the premises 'as is' . . . and that [this contract] is entered into after full investigation, neither party relying upon any statement, not embodied in this contract, made by the other." See Danann Realty Corp. v. Harris, 5 N.Y.2d 317, 157 N.E.2d 597 (1959).

HULL–DOBBS, INC. v. MALLICOAT

Court of Appeals of Tennessee, 1966.
57 Tenn.App. 100, 415 S.W.2d 344.

McAmis, Presiding Judge.   Walter H. Mallicoat, Jr., brought this action in the General Sessions Court to recover of Hull-Dobbs, Inc. "damages in an amount to be determined by the court and caused by breach of contract and fraud in the sale to plaintiff of a 1956 Ford." The Sessions Court rendered judgment for $628.58 which, on appeal to the Circuit Court, was affirmed. The present appeal to this court by Hull-Dobbs, Inc., resulted.

The assignments are (1) that the court erred in allowing oral testimony to contradict a written instrument and (2) erred in failing to dismiss the case against the plaintiff in error under the provisions of the Uniform Commercial Code. There is no assignment that the evidence preponderates against the finding of the Circuit Judge that the car was not as represented. If this question of the preponderance of the proof should be considered as raised by the supporting brief when taken in connection with the assignments we would be compelled, after a careful review of the proof, to concur in that finding.

Being unable to locate the trouble, plaintiff had the car examined by Arthur Creswell, a mechanic. Mr. Creswell testified a hole had rusted through the control arm where it fastens on the frame and "that it was just laying where it should have been tightened in there." This defect left the driver with little control over the car. He further testified the defect would not be noticed without getting under the car and was such that he might have failed to see it himself, although a mechanic.

As to the admissibility of parol evidence, it appears from the record the objection was based upon the provision of the Security Agreement that the debtor "has this day examined and accepted *in its present condition*" the described automobile. (Italics ours) There is in the record another document entitled "Retail Buyer's Order" signed by plaintiff which undertakes to exclude warranties or parol representations, but the objection to plaintiff's testimony as to representations made by the salesman, as above said, was predicated solely on the language of the Security Agreement.[1]

We think the evidence was properly admitted. [The court quoted UCC 2–202.]

The Security Agreement states that it constitutes the entire "agreement" between the parties but as to "warranties, representations and promises" the language is that they are not "to be binding on any *assignee*" of the seller. Since the "agreement" and "representations, warranties and promises" are treated as being separate and distinct and representations as to the condition of property sold are not generally considered a part of the agreement but an inducement to the execution of the sale agreement, we can not say the parties intended the Security Agreement to be a final statement of the terms of the sale. Representations as to the condition of the car are not inconsistent with any provision of the contract even if it should be held that the Security Agreement was intended as a final statement of the terms of the sale. So, if we are mistaken in holding the representations an inducement to the contract rather than a part of it, we hold the Security Agreement as written was not intended as the final expression of the agreement of the parties.

In the absence of plainer language we are not warranted in changing the previously existing rule that: "The parol evidence rule does not apply where the parol evidence in no way contradicts or alters the terms of the written contract but the representations or statements are made as an inducement to the contract and form the basis or consideration of it." Haynes v. Morton, 32 Tenn.App. 251, 222 S. W.2d 389.

Under comment 3 appearing under this Section of Tennessee Code Annotated it is said: "Under paragraph (b) consistent additional terms, not reduced to writing, may be proved unless the court finds that the writing was intended by both parties as a complete and exclusive statement of all the terms. If the additional terms are such that, if agreed upon, they would certainly have been included in the document in the view of the court, then evidence of their alleged making must be kept from the trier of fact."

As above said, representations are generally to be considered the inducement to, or the consideration for the agreement. So, we would not expect them to be included in the written agreement. In holding they are not inconsistent with the terms of the contract we have not overlooked the words "accepted in its present condition." This language refers to acceptance and is not to be taken as synonymous with "as is," "with all faults" and other like expressions which according to

---

1. Failure to interpose these provisions of the Buyer's Order may be due to the fact that it states on its face that it was not an order until accepted by an official of the company and the space opposite the word "Accepted" was never filled in, or due to the recognition that it became merged in the "Security Agreement".

common usage call the buyer's attention to the exclusion of representations and warranties and under T.C.A. 47–2–316, tend to exclude implied warranties of merchantability.

Since we hold there were express representations and warranties not in conflict with the terms of the contract, it becomes unnecessary to consider whether there was also an implied warranty of fitness.

Affirmed at the cost of Hull-Dobbs, Inc., and appeal sureties.

NOTES

(1) *Rationale.* Were the salesman's representations fraudulent? If they were not, why did the merger clause not bar Mallicoat from showing them? Is the court's definition of "agreement" consistent with that in UCC 1–201(3)? Should the court have considered UCC 2–316(1)? For support for its decision, see Broude, The Consumer and the Parol Evidence Rule: Section 2–202 of the Uniform Commercial Code, 1970 Duke L.J. 881.

(2) *Consideration and the Parol Evidence Rule.* Does the parol evidence rule prevent a promisor from showing that a recital of consideration (e. g., "in consideration of the described automobile, receipt of which is hereby acknowledged") in a completely integrated agreement is untrue? See Restatement Second, § 240(d). Does it prevent a promisee from showing that there was consideration other than that recited (e. g., "in consideration of our mutual love and affection") in a completely integrated agreement? See Thomas v. Thomas, p. 10 supra; Note 2, p. 124 supra.

INTRODUCTORY NOTE

Suppose that one of the parties seeks to prove that the provisions of a carefully drafted written contract were varied by a conversation between the parties *after* the contract was made. The parol evidence rule does not speak to this problem. Yet to the party who seeks to exclude such proof it is not dissimilar from the problems to which the rule does speak. If one wants to do business on the basis of the written word (preferably one's own), to the exclusion of oral agreements, one has as much interest in excluding subsequent as in excluding prior oral agreements. The following cases deal with this problem.

WAGNER v. GRAZIANO CONSTRUCTION CO.

Supreme Court of Pennsylvania, 1957.
390 Pa. 445, 136 A.2d 82.

MUSMANNO, JUSTICE. Edward J. Wagner entered into a contract with Graziano Construction Company to paint and supply materials in connection with the construction of the Heights Plaza Shopping Center in Natrona Heights by the Graziano Company as general contractors.   The agreement between Wagner and Graziano provided, inter alia:

> Without invalidating this contract the Contractor may add to or reduce the work to be performed hereunder.   No extra work or changes from plans and specifications under this contract will be recognized or paid for, unless agreed to in writing before the extra work is started or the changes made, in which written order shall be specified in detail the extra work or changes desired, the price to be paid or the amount to be deducted should said change decrease the amount to be paid hereunder.

Wagner claims that while fulfilling his obligations under the contract he was orally requested by the defendant's general superintendent to perform some extra work and supply additional material, the superintendent assuring him that such orders did not need to be in writing despite the provision to that effect in the contract.   Wagner states that then after acceding to the oral demands of the defendant's general superintendent, Graziano refused to pay for the supplemental work and additional materials.   He accordingly brought suit against Graziano for the amount of $5,192.22.   Graziano filed preliminary objections demurring on the ground that the complaint failed to state a cause of action because it was based on oral orders which were excluded by the contract.   The lower Court sustained the objections and dismissed the complaint.   Wagner appealed.

In his complaint Wagner averred:

> "In directing plaintiff to perform work not within the scope of work to be performed under the written contract, defendant's general superintendent refused to sign written work orders as required by said written contract: he informed plaintiff that written work orders signed by him would not be required and directed him to perform the extra work without the written work orders, informing plaintiff that appropriate adjustments would be agreed upon at a later date."

For the purposes of the demurrer, this allegation, together with those averring the superintendent's authority, must be accepted as established fact.   Thus, if we assume that the defendant's authorized agent informed Wagner that the requirement for written orders for extra work was being waived, we are then concerned only with a determination of the question as to whether parties to a written contract may alter it by an oral understanding.   There is nothing sacrosanct about a written agreement.   Granted that writing makes for specificity and clarity, reduces the chances for errors, and allows for constant reference as to what was agreed upon, it nevertheless holds no superior position over an oral compact in the realm of authoritative utterances, except where the Statute of Frauds intervenes or is invoked.

The most ironclad written contract can always be cut into by the acetylene torch of parol modification supported by adequate proof. In Achenbach v. Stoddard, 253 Pa. 338, 98 A. 604, 605, this Court held:

> "'It is always competent for the parties to a written contract to show that it was subsequently abandoned in whole or in part, modified, changed, or a new one substituted. And this may be shown by parol, by showing either an express agreement or actions necessarily involving the alterations.'"

Even where the contract specifically states that no non-written modification will be recognized, the parties may yet alter their agreement by parol negotiation. The hand that pens a writing may not gag the mouths of the assenting parties. The pen may be more precise in permanently recording what is to be done, but it may not still the tongues which bespeak an improvement in or modification of what has been written. In the case of Prudden-Winslow v. Stipp, 76 Pa.Super. 530, the contract there under consideration provided: "No verbal understanding or agreement not contained in writing on the face of the order (and these conditions) shall be considered of any force whatever." A dispute later arose between the parties as to whether this provision of the contract had been violated. Judge Maxey of the Court of Common Pleas of Lackawanna County (later Chief Justice of this Court) held that modification of a contract was always in order. The Superior Court affirmed his position, Judge Trexler saying: "Notwithstanding the written contract, the parties were still free agents. They could change it if they so desired."

In the case of Knight v. Gulf Refining Co., 311 Pa. 357, 360, 166 A. 880, 882, Justice Kephart (later Chief Justice) said:

> "Parties may, by subsequent oral agreement, modify a written contract which they previously have entered into. The new contract thus agreed upon is a substitute for the original one in so far as it alters, modifies, or changes it."

We, therefore, hold that Graziano's agent and Wagner could legally covenant to waive a specific stipulation in the contract. Minds may meet in the field of oral concord as well as between the borders of parchment or paper. . . .

Order reversed. Complaint to be reinstated and case remanded with a procedendo.

NOTE

Subsequent History. Wagner v. Graziano has had a checkered career in Pennsylvania. Eight years later Justice Musmanno again spoke for the Supreme Court of Pennsylvania in a case involving a contract for the sale of goods in which it was urged that a written contract may be modified by subsequent oral agreement even though the written contract prohibits oral modification. "This is true but there must first be a waiver of the requirement which has been spelled out in the contract. Otherwise, written documents would have no more permanence than writings penned in disappearing ink . . ., contractual obligations would become phantoms, solemn obligations would run like pressed quicksilver, and the whole edifice of business would rest on sand dunes supporting pillars of rubber and floors of turf. Chaos would envelop the commercial world." C.I.T. Corporation v. Jonnet, 419 Pa. 435, 214 A.2d 620 (1965). What facts, beyond those necessary to establish the oral modification itself, would have to be proved in order to establish the "waiver of the requirement"? Justice Musmanno did not cite UCC 2–209(2). Should he not have done so?

UNIVERSAL BUILDERS v. MOON MOTOR LODGE, 430 Pa. 550, 244 A.2d 10 (1968) [Universal Builders made a written contract with Moon Motor Lodge to build a motel and restaurant. The contract provided that all change orders had to be in writing and signed by Moon or the architect. Universal performed and sued Moon to recover $127,760, the balance due on the contract price together with extras. From a judgment for the plaintiff, the defendant appealed.]

EAGEN, JUSTICE. . . . Unless a contract is for the sale of goods, see the Uniform Commercial Code-Sales, the Act of April 6, 1953, P. L. 3, § 2–209(3), as amended, 12A P.S. § 2–209(2), it appears undisputed that the contract can be modified orally although it provides that it can be modified only in writing. E. g., Wagner v. Graziano Construction Co., 390 Pa. 445, 136 A.2d 82 (1957); 4 Williston on Contracts § 591 (3rd ed. 1961); 6 Corbin on Contracts § 1295 (1962); Restatement of Contracts § 407 (1932). Construction contracts typically provide that the builder will not be paid for extra work unless it is done pursuant to a written change order, yet courts frequently hold that owners must pay for extra work done at their oral direction. See generally Annot., 2 A.L.R.3rd 620, 648–82 (1965). This liability can be based on several theories. For example, the extra work may be said to have been done under an oral agreement separate from the written contract and not containing the requirement of a written authorization. 3A Corbin on Contracts, § 756 at p. 505 (1960). The requirement of a written authorization may also be considered a condition which has been waived. 5 Williston on Contracts § 689 (3rd ed. 1961).

On either of the above theories, the chancellor correctly held Moon liable to pay for the extras in spite of the lack of written change orders. The evidence indicates that William Berger, the agent of Moon, requested many changes, was informed that they would involve extra cost, and promised to pay for them. In addition, Berger frequently was on the construction site and saw at least some of the extra work in progress. The record demonstrates that he was a keen observer with an extraordinary knowledge of the project in general and the contract requirements in particular. Thus it is not unreasonable to infer that he was aware that extra work was being done without proper authorization, yet he stood by without protesting while the extras were incorporated into the project. Under these circumstances there also was an implied promise to pay for the extras.

C.I.T. Corp. v. Jonnet, 419 Pa. 435, 214 A.2d 620 (1965), does suggest that such non-written modifications are ineffective unless the contract provision requiring modifications to be in writing was first waived. That case, however, is misleading. Although it involved a contract for the sale of movable bar and restaurant equipment, which is a contract for the sale of "goods" controlled by the Uniform Commercial Code-Sales, supra, § 2–101 et seq., as amended, 12A P.S. § 2–101 et seq., it overlooks that legislation, in particular § 2–209. [The court quoted UCC 2–209.] From subsection (5) it can be inferred that a provision in a contract for the sale of goods that the contract can be modified only in writing is waived, just as such a provision in a construction contract is waived, under the circumstances described by Restatement of Contracts § 224 (1932), which provides: "The performance of a condition qualifying a promise in a contract within the Statute [of Frauds or in a contract containing a provision requiring modifications to be in writing (§ 407)] may be excused by an oral agreement or permission of the promisor that the condition need not be performed, if the agreement or permission is given while the performance of the condition is possible, and in reliance on the agreement or permission, while it is unrevoked, the promisee materially changes his position." Obviously a condition is considered waived when its enforcement would result in something approaching fraud. 5 Williston on Contracts § 689 at pp. 306–07 (3rd ed. 1961). Thus the effectiveness of a non-written modification in spite of a contract condition that modifications must be written depends upon whether enforcement of the condition is or is not barred by equitable considerations, not upon the technicality of whether the condition was or was not expressly and separately waived before the non-written modification.

In view of these equitable considerations underlying waiver, it should be obvious that when an owner requests a builder to do extra work, promises to pay for it and watches it performed knowing that it is not authorized in writing, he cannot refuse to pay on the ground that there was no written change order. Focht v. Rosenbaum, 176 Pa. 14, 34 A. 1001 (1876). When Moon directed Universal to "go ahead" and promised to pay for the extras, performance of the condition requiring change orders to be in writing was excused by implication. It would be manifestly unjust to allow Moon, which misled Universal into doing extra work without a written authorization, to benefit from non-performance of that condition. .   .   .

The decree of the lower court therefore was correct, except [on a point omitted here].

MUSMANNO, JUSTICE (Dissenting). I believe an injustice is being done the defendant in this case. . . . [T]he agreement specifically provides that, except in an emergency endangering life or property, no claim for an addition to the contract price was to be valid unless the work was done pursuant to the owner's written, signed order, and after written notice given by the contractor before proceeding with the work. I am disturbed that the Majority could have reached its conclusion when the record shows that *there was no such writing*.

Even the plaintiff did not contend that the requirement in writing was waived by agreement of the parties, as in Wagner v. Graziano Construction Co., 390 Pa. 445, 136 A.2d 82, relied upon by the Majority. The most that the plaintiff has shown are oral modifications of the work called for under the contract, which is exactly what is prohibited by the solemn agreement entered into between the parties. The oral modification certainly cannot be used as evidence of a waiver, for otherwise, a requirement of writing would become meaningless. This Court clearly pointed out this fundamental proposition of law in C. I. T. Corp. v. Jonnet, 419 Pa. 435, 438, 214 A.2d 620, 622. . . .

NOTES

(1) *"No Oral Modification" Clauses.* Comment a to Restatement, § 407 says: "The rule [of that section] is applicable even though the earlier contract provides that it can be rescinded or varied only by a written instrument." Does this accurately describe the common law in Pennsylvania? What is the law under the Code? (The subject of "waiver" is considered in more detail at p. 770 infra.) Why does a party like Graziano or Moon insert such a clause in a contract? To prevent the other party from making false claims of oral modifications? (If so, is not the clause analogous to a statute of frauds?)[a] To prevent his own representative (Graziano's general superintendent or Moon's agent William Berger) from making oral modifications? (If so, is not the clause analogous to the one in the International Filter case, p. 111 supra?)

Does the fact that the Code (see UCC 2–209(1)) has gone further than has the common law (see Restatement Second, § 89D) in abolishing the requirement of consideration for a modification make it more desirable for the Code to give effect to a "no oral modification" clause?[b] (See Note 2,

---

a. Comment 3 to UCC 2–209 states: "Subsections (2) and (3) are intended to protect against false allegations of oral modifications. . . . Subsection (2) permits the parties in effect to make their own Statute of Frauds as regards any future modification of the contract by giving effect to a clause in a signed agreement which expressly requires any modification to be by signed writing."

b. Consider Comment 7 to UCC 2–313: "The precise time when words of description or affirmation are made . . . is not material. The sole question is whether the language . . . [is] fairly to be regarded as part of the contract. If language is used after the closing of the deal (as when the buyer when taking delivery asks and receives an additional assurance), the warranty becomes a modification, and need not be supported by consideration if it is otherwise reasonable and in order (Section 2–209)." Would the same be true of language used to placate a buyer who complains about the goods after delivery?

p. 13 supra, on consideration as form.)   Does Pennsylvania law reflect this?

(2) *Drafting.* What circumstances might make it desirable or undesirable to limit the terms of the contract to those contained in a writing and to exclude prior, contemporaneous and subsequent oral agreements? Draft a clause to accomplish this result for a contract such as that in Wagner v. Graziano. For a contract such as that in Hull-Dobbs v. Mallicoat. Compare them with the clause that you drafted in response to Note, p. 95 supra and Note 1, p. 115 supra.

SECTION 2. INTERPRETATION OF CONTRACT LANGUAGE

" 'When *I* use a word,' Humpty Dumpty said, in rather a scornful tone, 'it means just what I choose it to mean—neither more nor less.'

" 'The question is,' said Alice, 'whether you *can* make words mean so many different things.'

" 'The question is,' said Humpty Dumpty, 'which is to be master —that's all.' "   Lewis Carroll, Through the Looking Glass, Chapter VI.

As this familiar excerpt suggests, the problem of interpretation of language is not peculiar to the law. However, language is commonly involved in social control through law, and the interpretation of this language may have consequences of great practical moment. The critical language may come from one of a variety of sources, such as a constitution, a statute, an administrative regulation, a will, a deed, or a contract. We are concerned with contracts.

Scholars less boastful than Humpty Dumpty have cautioned us on what Professor Chafee has called "the disorderly conduct of words." There is no "lawyers Paradise" where, in Professor Thayer's language, "all words have a fixed, precisely ascertained meaning, . . . and where, if the writer has been careful, a lawyer, having a document referred to him may sit in his chair, inspect the text, and answer all questions without raising his eyes." As Justice Holmes put it, "A word is not a crystal, transparent and unchanged, it is the skin of a living thought and may vary greatly in color and content according to the circumstances and the time in which it is used." Towne v. Eisner, 245 U.S. 418 (1918). One of the most perceptive of these scholars, Professor Willard van Orman Quine, has emphasized a distinction between *vagueness* and *ambiguity.* See Quine, Word and Object (1960).

According to Quine, "stimulations eliciting a verbal response, say 'red', are best depicted as forming not a neatly bounded class but a distribution about a central *norm.*" A word is vague to the extent that its applicability in marginal situations is uncertain. The parties, for example, contract for the removal of "all the dirt" on a given tract. May sand from a stratum of subsoil be taken?[a]

Ambiguity, as Quine defines it, is an entirely distinct concept from that of vagueness. A word that may or may not apply in marginal situations is vague. But a word may also have two entirely different connotations so that it may be at the same time both appropriate and inappropriate, as the word "light" may be when applied to dark feathers. Such a word is ambiguous.[b] Ambiguities may be classified into those of term and those of syntax.

Ambiguities of term are relatively rare in contract cases. A contract specifies "tons." Are they to be long or short tons?[c] Ambiguity of syntax is, in the strictest sense, an ambiguity of grammatical structure, of what is syntactically connected to what. It is more common a cause of contract disputes than is ambiguity of term. A health insurance policy excludes any "disease of organs of the body not common to both sexes." Does the policy cover a fibroid tumor (which can occur in any organ) of the uterus?[d]

Consideration of whether such distinctions as these, between vagueness and ambiguity, play a meaningful role in the interpretation of contracts can be deferred until later. It is plain that they are useful in describing disputes about language. Here are two simple techniques to the same end.

The first is to state the issue in terms of the contract language, much as an issue arising under a statute is stated in terms of the statutory language. It should be framed so that it can be answered "yes" or "no," as a court ordinarily must do. It should be framed so that it contains the controlling language of the contract, with such emphasis as is helpful. And it should be framed so that it recognizes that different meanings are attached to words in different contexts. For example:

> Is a fibroid tumor of the uterus a *"disease* of *organs* of the body *not common to both sexes"* within the insured's contract of insurance?

The second technique is to redraft the language twice, staying as faithful to the original as possible, so that it would clearly require a

---

a. See Highley v. Phillips, 176 Md. 463, 5 A.2d 824 (1939) (held: yes).

b. Since "ambiguous" is often used to comprehend vague, as well as ambiguous in the narrow sense, some writers prefer to use "equivocal" for this purpose.

c. Compare Chemung Iron & Steel Co. v. Mersereau Metal Bed Co., 179 N.Y.

S. 577 (App.Div.1920) (short tons) with Higgins v. California Petroleum & Asphalt Co., 120 Cal. 629, 52 P. 1080 (1898) (long tons).

d. Business Men's Assur. Ass'n v. Read, 48 S.W.2d 678 (Tex.Civ.App.1932) (held: yes).

decision, first for one party, then for the other. (See Note, p. 66 supra.) For example:

> (For insured) "disease of organs of the body that is not common to both sexes"

> (For insurer) "disease of organs of the body that are not common to both sexes"

Try, in each of the following problems: (1) to describe the problem in Quine's terms; (2) to state the issue in terms of the contract language; and (3) to redraft the contract language, first for one party and then for the other. (Consider, also, what additional information would be useful in answering the problems.)

(a) A contract for the sale of a photography studio provides that the seller will not compete with the buyer "for the school photography work in any school in Grant County, with the exception of Marion High School and Bennett High School." May the seller compete with the buyer for the photography of Marion College students? See Lawrence v. Cain, 144 Ind.App. 210, 245 N.E.2d 663 (1969).

(b) A contract for the sale of a grocery store provides that the seller will not engage in a similar business "within a radius of five city blocks from the above mentioned premises." May the seller establish a grocery four blocks north and two blocks east of his old store before the five years are up? See Kunin v. Weller, 296 Pa. 161, 145 A. 719 (1929).

(c) A construction contract provides that "All domestic water piping and rainwater piping installed above finished ceilings under this specification shall be insulated." Must the contractor insulate domestic water piping installed below finished ceilings? See Paul W. Abbott v. Axel Newman Heating & Plumbing, 282 Minn. 493, 166 N.W.2d 323 (1969).

The cases that follow are concerned with how to answer questions like those raised in these problems. A threshold problem is posed by the fact that unlike a will, which expresses the intention of a single testator, or even a statute, which expresses the collective intention of a single legislature, a contract involves *two* parties who may attach very different meanings to language and have very different expectations. The next cases deal with this problem.

On interpretation in general, see Farnsworth, "Meaning" in the Law of Contracts, 76 Yale L.J. 939 (1967); Farnsworth, Some Considerations in the Drafting of Agreements: Problems in Interpretation and Gap-Filling, 23 Record of N.Y.C.B. Ass'n 105 (1968); Patterson, The Interpretation and Construction of Contracts, 64 Colum. L.Rev. 833 (1964); Williams, Language and the Law, 61 L.Q.Rev. 71, 179, 293, 384 (1945), 62 L.Q.Rev. 387 (1946); Friedman, Law, Rules, and the Interpretation of Written Documents, 59 Nw.U.L.Rev. 751 (1965).

NOTES

(1) *Care in Drafting.* "It is a popular belief, especially prevalent amongst lawyers, that the efficient business man requires that obligations incurred in business should be expressed in writing in simple, intelligible and unambiguous language. It is a belief encouraged by the sayings of business men themselves. But in practice nothing appears to be further from the truth. Business men habitually adventure large sums of money on contracts which, for the purpose of defining legal obligations, are a mere jumble of words. They trust to luck or the good faith of the opposite party, with the comfortable assurance that any adverse result of litigation may be attributed to the hairsplitting of lawyers and the uncertainty of the law." Lord Atkin in Phoenix Insurance Co. of Hartford v. DeMonchy, 141 L.T. 439, 445 (H.L.1929).

One of the most common results of carelessness in drafting is a conflict between different parts of the contract. For an example, see Robinhorne Construction Corp. v. Snyder, 47 Ill.2d 349, 265 N.E.2d 670 (1970), in which Justice Schaefer wrote: "This is the kind of case that has been described as 'one where no principle of law is involved, but only the meaning of careless and slovenly documents.' . . . The parties used a standard cost-plus contract form. They modified it to specify a maximum contract price, but they failed to modify the termination provision. The conditions that they attached had been prepared for use with a lump-sum contract." For another example, see Schauerman v. Haag, 68 Wash.2d 868, 416 P.2d 88 (1966) ("Glaziers should glaze and lawyers should scriven, and neither ought do the other; for, when glaziers write and lawyers glaze, they are apt to make porous contracts and drafty windows.").

(2) *Interpretation in the Agreement Process.* We have already encountered problems of interpretation in the agreement process. See, for example, Owen v. Tunison, p. 64 supra, and Harvey v. Facey, p. 66 supra. Consider in this connection the remarks of Judge Medina in United States v. Braunstein, 73 F.Supp. 137 (S.D.N.Y.1947): "It is true that there is much room for interpretation once the parties are inside the framework of a contract, but it seems that there is less in the field of offer and acceptance. Greater precision of expression may be required, and less help from the court given, when the parties are merely at the threshold of a contract." This view was echoed in Henry Simons Lumber Co. v. Simons, 232 Minn. 187, 44 N.W.2d 726 (1950): "Because of strict rules governing offer and acceptance, which require that an acceptance be in terms of the offer, we are reluctant to follow by analogy rules laid down with respect to contracts already formed. In passing upon questions of offer and acceptance, courts may wisely require greater exactitude than when they are trying to salvage an existing contract. Where no contract has been completed and neither party has acted to his detriment, there is no compulsion on a court to guess at what the parties intended."

FRIGALIMENT IMPORTING CO. v. B. N. S. INTERNATIONAL SALES CORP.

United States District Court, S.D.N.Y., 1960.
190 F.Supp. 116.

FRIENDLY, CIRCUIT JUDGE.   The issue is, what is chicken?[a] Plaintiff says "chicken" means a young chicken, suitable for broiling and frying.   Defendant says "chicken" means any bird of that genus that meets contract specifications on weight and quality, including what it calls "stewing chicken" and plaintiff pejoratively terms "fowl".   Dictionaries give both meanings, as well as some others not relevant here.   To support its, plaintiff sends a number of volleys over the net; defendant essays to return them and adds a few serves of its own.   Assuming that both parties were acting in good faith, the case nicely illustrates Holmes' remark "that the making of a contract depends not on the agreement of two minds in one intention, but on the agreement of two sets of external signs—not on the parties' having *meant* the same thing but on their having *said* the same thing." The Path of the Law, in Collected Legal Papers, p. 178.   I have concluded that plaintiff has not sustained its burden of persuasion that the contract used "chicken" in the narrower sense.

The action is for breach of the warranty that goods sold shall correspond to the description, New York Personal Property Law, McKinney's Consol.Laws, c. 41, § 95.   Two contracts are in suit.   In the first, dated May 2, 1957, defendant, a New York sales corporation, confirmed the sale to plaintiff, a Swiss corporation, of

"US Fresh Frozen Chicken, Grade A, Government Inspected, Eviscerated
2½–3 lbs. and 1½–2 lbs. each
all chicken individually wrapped in cryovac, packed in secured fiber cartons or wooden boxes, suitable for export
75,000 lbs. 2½–3 lbs. .... @$33.00
25,000 lbs. 1½–2 lbs. .... @$36.50
per 100 lbs. FAS New York
scheduled May 10, 1957 pursuant to instructions from Penson & Co., New York."

The second contract, also dated May 2, 1957, was identical save that only 50,000 lbs. of the heavier "chicken" were called for, the price of

---

a.   In the 1940's, American chicken producers began to differentiate chickens raised for meat from those raised for eggs, and started using "assembly-line" techniques for the former, giving rise to a new consumer product, the "broiler chicken."   Production grew phenomenally, prices dropped correspondingly, and exports to Europe increased sharply.   Between 1956 and 1962, German chicken consumption went from 136 million pounds (of which 2.5 million or 1% was exported from the United States) to 716 million pounds (of which 169.6 million or 26% was exported from the United States). For more on chickens in international trade and the resulting "chicken war," see Chayes, Ehrlich and Lowenfeld, International Legal Process 249–306 (1968).

the smaller birds was $37 per 100 lbs., and shipment was scheduled for May 30. The initial shipment under the first contract was short but the balance was shipped on May 17. When the initial shipment arrived in Switzerland, plaintiff found, on May 28, that the 2½–3 lbs. birds were not young chicken suitable for broiling and frying but stewing chicken or "fowl"; indeed, many of the cartons and bags plainly so indicated. Protests ensued. Nevertheless, shipment under the second contract was made on May 29, the 2½–3 lbs. birds again being stewing chicken. Defendant stopped the transportation of these at Rotterdam.

This action followed. Plaintiff says that, notwithstanding that its acceptance was in Switzerland, New York law controls under the principle of Rubin v. Irving Trust Co., 1953, 305 N.Y. 288, 305, 113 N.E.2d 424, 431; defendant does not dispute this, and relies on New York decisions. I shall follow the apparent agreement of the parties as to the applicable law.

Since the word "chicken" standing alone is ambiguous, I turn first to see whether the contract itself offers any aid to its interpretation. Plaintiff says the 1½–2 lbs. birds necessarily had to be young chicken since the older birds do not come in that size, hence the 2½–3 lbs. birds must likewise be young. This is unpersuasive—a contract for "apples" of two different sizes could be filled with different kinds of apples even though only one species came in both sizes. Defendant notes that the contract called not simply for chicken but for "US Fresh Frozen Chicken, Grade A, Government Inspected." It says the contract thereby incorporated by reference the Department of Agriculture's regulations, which favor its interpretation; I shall return to this after reviewing plaintiff's other contentions.

The first hinges on an exchange of cablegrams which preceded execution of the formal contracts. The negotiations leading up to the contracts were conducted in New York between defendant's secretary, Ernest R. Bauer, and a Mr. Stovicek, who was in New York for the Czechoslovak government at the World Trade Fair. A few days after meeting Bauer at the fair, Stovicek telephoned and inquired whether defendant would be interested in exporting poultry to Switzerland. Bauer then met with Stovicek, who showed him a cable from plaintiff dated April 26, 1957, announcing that they "are buyer" of 25,000 lbs. of chicken 2½–3 lbs. weight, Cryovac packed, grade A Government inspected, at a price up to 33¢ per pound, for shipment on May 10, to be confirmed by the following morning, and were interested in further offerings. After testing the market for price, Bauer accepted, and Stovicek sent a confirmation that evening. Plaintiff stresses that, although these and subsequent cables between plaintiff and defendant, which laid the basis for the additional quantities under the first and for all of the second contract, were predominantly in German, they used the English word "chicken"; it claims this was done because it understood "chicken" meant young chicken whereas the

German word, "Huhn," included both "Brathuhn" (broilers) and "Suppenhuhn" (stewing chicken), and that defendant, whose officers were thoroughly conversant with German, should have realized this. Whatever force this argument might otherwise have is largely drained away by Bauer's testimony that he asked Stovicek what kind of chickens were wanted, received the answer "any kind of chickens," and then, in German, asked whether the cable meant "Huhn" and received an affirmative response. . . .

Plaintiff's next contention is that there was a definite trade usage that "chicken" meant "young chicken." Defendant showed that it was only beginning in the poultry trade in 1957, thereby bringing itself within the principle that "when one of the parties is not a member of the trade or other circle, his acceptance of the standard must be made to appear" by proving either that he had actual knowledge of the usage or that the usage is "so generally known in the community that his actual individual knowledge of it may be inferred." 9 Wigmore, Evidence (3d ed. 1940) § 2464. Here there was no proof of actual knowledge of the alleged usage; indeed, it is quite plain that defendant's belief was to the contrary. In order to meet the alternative requirement, the law of New York demands a showing that "the usage is of so long continuance, so well established, so notorious, so universal and so reasonable in itself, as that the presumption is violent that the parties contracted with reference to it, and made it a part of their agreement." Walls v. Bailey, 1872, 49 N.Y. 464, 472–473.

Plaintiff endeavored to establish such a usage by the testimony of three witnesses and certain other evidence. Strasser, resident buyer in New York for a large chain of Swiss cooperatives, testified that "on chicken I would definitely understand a broiler." However, the force of this testimony was considerably weakened by the fact that in his own transactions the witness, a careful businessman, protected himself by using "broiler" when that was what he wanted and "fowl" when he wished older birds. Indeed, there are some indications, dating back to a remark of Lord Mansfield, Edie v. East India Co., 2 Burr. 1216, 1222 (1761), that no credit should be given "witnesses to usage, who could not adduce instances in verification." 7 Wigmore, Evidence (3d ed. 1940), § 1954; see McDonald v. Acker, Merrall & Condit Co., 2d Dept.1920, 192 App.Div. 123, 126, 182 N.Y.S. 607. While Wigmore thinks this goes too far, a witness' consistent failure to rely on the alleged usage deprives his opinion testimony of much of its effect. Niesielowski, an officer of one of the companies that had furnished the stewing chicken to defendant, testified that "chicken" meant "the male species of the poultry industry. That could be a broiler, a fryer or a roaster," but not a stewing chicken; however, he also testified that upon receiving defendant's inquiry for "chickens," he asked whether the desire was for "fowl or frying chickens" and, in fact, supplied fowl, although taking the precaution of asking defendant, a day or two after plaintiff's acceptance of the contracts in suit, to change its confirmation of its order from "chickens," as defendant had originally prepared it, to "stewing chickens." Dates, an employee of Urner-Barry Company, which publishes a daily market report on the poultry trade, gave it as his view that the trade meaning of "chicken" was "broilers and fryers." In addition to this opinion testimony, plaintiff relied on the fact that the Urner-Barry service, the Journal of Commerce, and Weinberg Bros. & Co. of Chicago, a large supplier of poultry, published quotations in a manner which, in one way or another, distinguish between "chicken," comprising broilers, fryers and certain other categories, and "fowl," which, Bauer acknowledged, included stewing chickens. This material would be impressive if there were nothing to the contrary. However, there was, as will now be seen.

Defendant's witness Weininger, who operates a chicken eviscerating plant in New Jersey, testified "Chicken is everything except a goose, a duck, and a turkey. Everything is a chicken, but then you have to say, you have to specify which category you want or that you are talking about." Its witness Fox said that in the trade "chicken" would encompass all the various classifications. Sadina, who conducts a food inspection service, testified that he would consider any bird coming within the classes of "chicken" in the Department of Agriculture's regulations to be a chicken. The specifications approved by the General Services Administration include fowl as well as broilers and fryers under the classification "chickens." Statistics of the Institute of American Poultry Industries use the phrases "Young chickens" and "Mature chickens," under the general heading "Total chickens." and the Department of Agriculture's daily and weekly price reports avoid use of the word "chicken" without specification.

Defendant advances several other points which it claims affirmatively support its construction. Primary among these is the regulation of the Department of Agriculture, 7 C.F.R. §§ 70.300–70.370, entitled, "Grading and Inspection of Poultry and Edible Products Thereof." and in particular § 70.301 which recited:

"*Chickens*. The following are the various classes of chickens:

(a) Broiler or fryer . . .

(b) Roaster . . .

(c) Capon . . .

(d) Stag . . .

(e) Hen or stewing chicken or fowl . . .

(f) Cock or old rooster . . ."

Defendant argues, as previously noted, that the contract incorporated these regulations by reference. Plaintiff answers that the contract provision related simply to grade and Government inspection and did not incorporate the Government definition of "chicken," and also that the definition in the Regulations is ignored in the trade. However, the latter contention was contradicted by Weininger and Sadina; and there is force in defendant's argument that the contract made the regulations a dictionary, particularly since the reference to Government grading was already in plaintiff's initial cable to Stovicek.

Defendant makes a further argument based on the impossibility of its obtaining broilers and fryers at the 33¢ price offered by plaintiff for the 2½–3 lbs. birds. There is no substantial dispute that, in late April, 1957, the price for 2½–3 lbs. broilers was between 35 and 37¢ per pound, and that when defendant entered into the contracts, it was well aware of this and intended to fill them by supplying fowl in these weights. It claims that plaintiff must likewise have known the market since plaintiff had reserved shipping space on April 23, three days before plaintiff's cable to Stovicek, or, at least, that Stovicek was chargeable with such knowledge. It is scarcely an answer to say, as plaintiff does in its brief, that the 33¢ price offered by the 2½–3 lbs. "chickens" was closer to the prevailing 35¢ price for broilers than to the 30¢ at which defendant procured fowl. Plaintiff must have expected defendant to make some profit—certainly it could not have expected defendant deliberately to incur a loss.

Finally, defendant relies on conduct by the plaintiff after the first shipment had been received. On May 28 plaintiff sent two cables complaining that the larger birds in the first shipment constituted "fowl." Defendant answered with a cable refusing to recognize plaintiff's objection and announcing "We have today ready for shipment 50,000 lbs. chicken 2½–3 lbs. 25,000 lbs. broilers 1½–2 lbs.," these being the goods procured for shipment under the second contract, and asked immediate answer "whether we are to ship this merchandise to you and whether you will accept the merchandise." After several other cable exchanges, plaintiff replied on May 29 "Confirm again that merchandise is to be shipped since resold by us if not enough pursuant to contract chickens are shipped the missing quantity is to be shipped within ten days stop we resold to our customers pursuant to your contract chickens grade A you have to deliver us said merchandise we again state that we shall make you fully responsible for all resulting costs." Defendant argues that if plaintiff was sincere in thinking it was entitled to young chickens, plaintiff would not have allowed the shipment under the second contract to go forward, since the distinction between broilers and chickens drawn in defendant's cablegram must have made it clear that the larger birds would not be broilers. However, plaintiff answers that the cables show plaintiff was insisting on delivery of young chickens and that defendant shipped old ones at its peril. Defendant's point would be highly relevant on another disputed issue—whether if liability were established, the measure of damages should be the difference in market value of broilers and stewing chicken in New York or the larger difference in Europe, but I cannot give it weight on the issue of interpretation. Defendant points out also that plaintiff proceeded to deliver some of the larger birds in Europe, describing them as "poulets"; defendant argues that it was only when plaintiff's customers complained about this that plaintiff developed the idea that "chicken" meant "young chicken." There is little force in this in view of plaintiff's immediate and consistent protests.

When all the evidence is reviewed, it is clear that defendant believed it could comply with the contracts by delivering stewing chicken in the 2½–3 lbs. size. Defendant's subjective intent would not be significant if this did not coincide with an objective meaning of "chicken." Here it did coincide with one of the dictionary meanings, with the definition in the Department of Agriculture Regulations to which the contract made at least oblique reference, with at least some usage in the trade, with the realities of the market, and with what plaintiff's spokesman had said. Plaintiff asserts it to be equally plain that plaintiff's own subjective intent was to obtain broilers and fryers; the only evidence against this is the material as to market prices and this may not have been sufficiently brought home. In any event it is unnecessary to determine that issue. For plaintiff has the burden of showing that "chicken" was used in the narrower rather than in the broader sense, and this it has not sustained.

This opinion constitutes the Court's findings of fact and conclusions of law. Judgment shall be entered dismissing the complaint with costs.

NOTES

(1) *"What is Chicken"?* Judge Friendly says that "The issue is, what is chicken?" Is this the issue that the court had to decide? He also says that the case "nicely illustrates Holmes' remark 'that the making of a contract depends . . . not on the parties' having *meant* the same thing but on their having *said* the same thing." Does it? Would the result have been the same if *both* parties had *meant* broilers although they had *said* "chicken?" [a] Is there any reason to hold the parties to a meaning that *neither* attached to their language? The Frigaliment case is discussed in Corbin, The Interpretation of Words and the Parol Evidence Rule, 50 Cornell L.Q. 161, 164–70 (1965).[b]

a. Since both parties were corporations, the notion that either "meant" anything or had any "intention" may seem somewhat strained. It would seem even more strained if other persons, including lawyers, had participated in the negotiations along with Bauer and Stovicek. Courts have not been greatly troubled by the problems of finding a collective "intention" in such cases. (For example, Judge Friendly states that B.N.S. "was only beginning in the poultry trade." Would it have been significant if Bauer had been hired by B.N.S. be-

cause of his long experience in that trade?) For a rare instance where such a problem was raised, see Franklin Life Insurance Co. v. Mast, 435 F.2d 1038 (9th Cir. 1970), where the court said, "Whatever may have been the secret intent of Mast, it is clear that the intent of his attorney in fact, Attorney Lohse, was to enter into a bona fide agreement."

b. For an afterthought by Judge Friendly, see Dadourian Export Corp. v. United States, 291 F.2d 178, 187 n. 4 (2d Cir. 1961).

(2) *Incorporation by Reference.* Are there any special problems that arise in the interpretation of terms, such as the regulations of the Department of Agriculture, that have been incorporated in a contract by reference? Cf. Wilcox v. Wilcox, 406 S.W.2d 152 (Ky.1966), involving a divorce settlement in which the husband agreed to make maintenance payments until his daughter reached "the age of majority." The court held that the husband's obligation continued until the child reached 21, the statutory age of majority at the time of the agreement, even though the statutory age had subsequently been lowered to 18.

OBJECTIVE AND SUBJECTIVE THEORIES OF CONTRACT INTERPRETATION

Just as the objective and subjective theories have influenced the law of contract formation (see p. 63 supra), they have also influenced the law of contract interpretation. There would be little disagreement with the proposition that, where the parties have in fact attached different meanings to their language, an objective standard should determine which meaning will prevail. But the objectivists argue that, even where the parties have in fact attached the same meaning to their language, an objective standard should determine the meaning, which might be different from their shared meaning. Hand, for example, said: "It is quite true that we commonly speak of a contract as a question of intent, and for most purposes it is a convenient paraphrase, accurate enough, but, strictly speaking, untrue. It makes not the least difference whether a promisor actually intends that meaning which the law will impose upon his words. The whole House of Bishops might satisfy us that he had intended something else, and it would make not a particle of difference in his obligation. That obligation the law attaches to his act of using certain words, provided, of course, the actor be under no disability. The scope of those words will, in the absence of some convention to the contrary, be settled, it is true, by what the law supposes men would generally mean when they used them; but the promisor's conformity to type is not a factor in his obligation. Hence it follows that no declaration of the promisor as to his meaning when he used the words is of the slightest relevancy, however formally competent it may be as an admission. Indeed, if both parties severally declared that their meaning had been other than the natural meaning, and each declaration was similar, it would be irrelevant, saving some mutual agreement between them to that effect. When the court came to assign the meaning to their words, it would disregard such declarations, because they related only to their state of mind when the contract was made, and that has nothing to do with their obligations." Eustis Mining Co. v. Beer, Sondheimer & Co., 239 F. 976 (S.D.N.Y.1917). The currency of this view can be judged from the following cases. See Restatement Second, §§ 226, 227.

NOTE

The Case of the Contractor with Experience. The National Park Service, a Division of the Department of the Interior, engaged Perry and Wallis, a contractor, to construct guard houses, fences and sidewalks at the White House. Later, when a change order was issued, Perry and Wallis engaged a subcontractor to make the changes. Perry and Wallis' contract with the Park Service allowed it the "actual necessary cost" of changes plus a fixed fee of 15 percent, the cost "in no case" to include "general expense not directly attributable to the extra work." Perry and Wallis claimed that "actual necessary cost" meant cost to it, the contractor, and therefore included the subcontractor's overhead and profits. The Park Service rejected this claim on the ground that "actual necessary cost" meant cost to the subcontractor only. After an unsuccessful appeal to the Interior Board of Contract Appeals, Perry and Wallis sued the United States in the Court of Claims, and both parties moved for summary judgment. *Held:* United States' motion granted and petition dismissed. The court relied on three prior decisions of the Interior Board of Contract Appeals, which had reached the same conclusion. In one of those cases, "the Department of Interior was, as here, the agency of the government involved and our present plaintiff was the subcontractor of the complaining contractor in the case. . . . [P]laintiff, as subcontractor, was aware of the ruling and of defendant's interpretation of the clause involved. Therefore, when he signed the instant contract, he did so with knowledge of the defendant's past interpretation of this phase of the contract. A party who willingly and without protest enters into a contract with knowledge of the other party's interpretation of it is bound by such interpretation and cannot later claim that it thought something else was meant." Perry and Wallis, Inc. v. United States, 427 F.2d 722 (Ct.Cl.1970). What does this suggest as to the point in the Lefkowitz case discussed in footnote a, p. 76 supra?

RAFFLES v. WICHELHAUS

Court of Exchequer, 1864.
2 H. & C. 906, 159 Eng.Rep. 375.

Declaration. For that it was agreed between the plaintiff and the defendants, to wit, at Liverpool, that the plaintiff should sell to the defendants, and the defendants buy of the plaintiff, certain goods, to wit, 125 bales of Surat cotton, guaranteed middling fair merchant's Dhollorah, to arrive ex Peerless from Bombay; and that the cotton should be taken from the quay, and that the defendants would pay the plaintiff for the same at a certain rate, to wit, at the rate of 17¼d. per pound, within a certain time then agreed upon after the arrival of the said goods in England. Averments: that the said goods did arrive by the said ship from Bombay in England, to wit, at Liverpool, and the plaintiff was then and there ready and willing and offered to deliver the said goods to the defendants, etc. Breach: that the defendants refused to accept the said goods or pay the plaintiff for them.

Plea. That the said ship mentioned in the said agreement was meant and intended by the defendants to be the ship called the Peerless, which sailed from Bombay, to wit, in October; and that the plaintiff was not ready and willing, and did not offer, to deliver to the defendants any bales of cotton which arrived by the last-mentioned ship, but instead thereof was only ready and willing, and offered to deliver to the defendants 125 bales of Surat cotton which arrived by another and different ship, which was also called the Peerless, and which sailed from Bombay, to wit, in December.

Demurrer, and joinder therein.

MILWARD in support of the demurrer. The contract was for the sale of a number of bales of cotton of a particular description, which the plaintiff was ready to deliver. It is immaterial by what ship the cotton was to arrive, so that it was a ship called the Peerless. The words "to arrive ex Peerless," only mean that if the vessel is lost on the voyage, the contract is to be at an end. [Pollock, C.B. It would be a question for the jury whether both parties meant the same ship called the Peerless.] That would be so if the contract was for the sale of a ship called the Peerless; but it is for the sale of cotton on board a ship of that name. [Pollock, C.B. The defendant only bought that cotton which was to arrive by a particular ship. It may as well be said, that if there is a contract for the purchase of certain goods in warehouse A that is satisfied by the delivery of goods of the same description in warehouse B.] In that case there would be goods in both warehouses; here it does not appear that the plaintiff had any goods on board the other Peerless. [Martin, B. It is imposing on the defendant a contract different from that which he entered into. Pollock, C.B. It is like a contract for the purchase of wine coming from a particular estate in France or Spain, where there are two estates of that name.] The defendant has no right to contradict by parol evidence a written contract good upon the face of it. He does not impute misrepresentation or fraud, but only says that he fancied the ship was a different one. Intention is of no avail, unless stated at the time of the contract. [Pollock, C.B. One vessel sailed in October and the other in December.] The time of sailing is no part of the contract.

MELLISH (Cohen with him) in support of the plea. There is nothing on the face of the contract to show that any particular ship called the Peerless was meant; but the moment it appears that two ships called the Peerless were about to sail from Bombay there is a latent ambiguity, and parol evidence may be given for the purpose of showing that the defendant meant one Peerless and the plaintiff another. That being so, there was no consensus ad idem, and therefore no binding contract. He was then stopped by the court.

PER CURIAM. There must be judgment for the defendants.

Judgment for the defendants.

NOTES

(1) *The Meaning of "Peerless."* Can the result be explained only on the subjective theory? Holmes thought not: "By the theory of our language, while other words may mean different things, a proper name means one person or thing and no other. . . . In theory of speech your name means you and my name means me, and the two names are different. They are different words. . . . In the use of common names and words a plea of different meaning from that adopted by the court would be bad, but here the parties have said different things and never have expressed a contract." Holmes, The Theory of Legal Interpretation, 12 Harv.L.Rev. 417, 418 (1899).

According to Professor Young: "Roughly speaking, the rule is restricted to differences of understanding which have their source in the ambivalence or 'double meaning' of an expression. Neither the courts nor the logicians have succeeded, so far as I am aware, in establishing a criterion by which we can readily decide whether or not a particular expression has a 'double meaning.' Holmes's formulation would have limited the application of the Peerless rule too narrowly. The [original] Restatement test is too broad." Young, Equivocation in the Making of Agreements, 64 Colum. L.Rev. 619, 646–47 (1964).

See also Palmer, The Effect of Misunderstanding on Contract Formation and Reformation Under the Restatement of Contracts Second, 65 Mich. L.Rev. 33 (1966). For a recent version of the Peerless case, see Oswald v. Allen, 417 F.2d 43 (2d Cir. 1969).

(2) *"What is Chicken"? (Reprise).* If the court in the Frigaliment case had concluded that neither the buyer nor the seller had known nor had any reason to know of the meaning attached by the other to the word "chicken," what would have been the result? According to Holmes? According to Young? According to the Restatement? According to the Restatement Second?

PACIFIC GAS & ELECTRIC CO. v. G. W. THOMAS DRAYAGE & RIGGING CO.

Supreme Court of California, 1968.
69 Cal.2d 33, 442 P.2d 641.

TRAYNOR, CHIEF JUSTICE. Defendant appeals from a judgment for plaintiff in an action for damages for injury to property under an indemnity clause of a contract.

In 1960 defendant entered into a contract with plaintiff to furnish the labor and equipment necessary to remove and replace the upper metal cover of plaintiff's steam turbine. Defendant agreed to perform the work "at [its] own risk and expense" and to "indemnify" plaintiff "against all loss, damage, expense and liability resulting from . . . injury to property, arising out of or in any way connected with the performance of this contract." Defendant also agreed to procure not less than $50,000 insurance to cover liability for injury to property. Plaintiff was to be an additional named insured, but the policy was to contain a cross-liability clause extending the coverage to plaintiff's property.

During the work the cover fell and injured the exposed rotor of the turbine. Plaintiff brought this action to recover $25,144.51, the amount it subsequently spent on repairs. During the trial it dismissed a count based on negligence and thereafter secured judgment on the theory that the indemnity provision covered injury to all property regardless of ownership.

Defendant offered to prove by admissions of plaintiff's agents, by defendant's conduct under similar contracts entered into with plaintiff, and by other proof that in the indemnity clause the parties meant to cover injury to property of third parties only and not to plaintiff's property. Although the trial court observed that the language used was "the classic language for a third party indemnity provision" and that "one could very easily conclude that . . . its whole intendment is to indemnify third parties," it nevertheless held that the "plain language" of the agreement also required defendant to indemnify plaintiff for injuries to plaintiff's property. Having determined that the contract had a plain meaning, the court refused to admit any extrinsic evidence that would contradict its interpretation.

When a court interprets a contract on this basis, it determines the meaning of the instrument in accordance with the " . . . extrinsic evidence of the judge's own linguistic education and experience." (3 Corbin on Contracts (1960 ed.) [1964 Supp. § 579, p. 225, fn. 56].) The exclusion of testimony that might contradict the linguistic background of the judge reflects a judicial belief in the possibility of perfect verbal expression. (9 Wigmore on Evidence (3d ed. 1940) § 2461, p. 187.) This belief is a remnant of a primitive faith in the inherent potency [1] and inherent meaning of words.[2]

The test of admissibility of extrinsic evidence to explain the meaning of a written instrument is not whether it appears to the court to be plain and unambiguous on its face, but whether the offered evidence is relevant to prove a meaning to which the language of the instrument is reasonably susceptible. . . .

---

1. E. g., "The elaborate system of taboo and verbal prohibitions in primitive groups; the ancient Egyptian myth of Khern, the apotheosis of the word, and of Thoth, the Scribe of Truth, the Giver of Words and Script, the Master of Incantations; the avoidance of the name of God in Brahmanism, Judaism and Islam; totemistic and protective names in mediaeval Turkish and Finno-Ugrian languages; the misplaced verbal scruples of the 'Précieuses'; the Swedish peasant custom of curing sick cattle smitten by witchcraft, by making them swallow a page torn out of the psalter and put in dough. * * *" from Ullman, The Principles of Semantics (1963 ed.) 43. (See also Ogden and Richards, The Meaning of Meaning (rev. ed. 1956) pp. 24–47.)

2. " 'Rerum enim vocabula immutabilia sunt, homines mutabilia,' " (Words are unchangeable, men changeable) from Dig. XXXIII, 10, 7, § 2, de sup. leg. as quoted in 9 Wigmore on Evidence, op. cit. supra, § 2461, p. 187.

A rule that would limit the determination of the meaning of a written instrument to its four-corners merely because it seems to the court to be clear and unambiguous, would either deny the relevance of the intention of the parties or presuppose a degree of verbal precision and stability our language has not attained.

Some courts have expressed the opinion that contractual obligations are created by the mere use of certain words, whether or not there was any intention to incur such obligations.[3] Under this view, contractual obligations flow, not from the intention of the parties but from the fact that they used certain magic words. Evidence of the parties' intention therefore becomes irrelevant.

In this state, however, the intention of the parties as expressed in the contract is the source of contractual rights and duties. A court must ascertain and give effect to this intention by determining what the parties meant by the words they used. Accordingly, the exclusion of relevant, extrinsic evidence to explain the meaning of a written instrument could be justified only if it were feasible to determine the meaning the parties gave to the words from the instrument alone.

If words had absolute and constant referents, it might be possible to discover contractual intention in the words themselves and in the manner in which they were arranged. Words, however, do not have absolute and constant referents. "A word is a symbol of thought but has no arbitrary and fixed meaning like a symbol of algebra or chemistry, ..." (Pearson v. State Social Welfare Board (1960) 54 Cal.2d 184, 195, 5 Cal.Rptr. 553, 559, 353 P.2d 33, 39.) The meaning of particular words or groups of words varies with the ". . . verbal context and surrounding circumstances and purposes in view of the linguistic education and experience of their users and their hearers or readers (not excluding judges). . . . A word has no meaning apart from these factors; much less does it have an objective meaning, one true meaning." (Corbin, The Interpretation of Words and the Parol Evidence Rule (1965) 50 Cornell L.Q. 161, 187.) Accordingly, the meaning of a writing ". . . can only be found by interpretation in the light of all the circumstances that reveal the sense in which the writer used the words. The exclusion of parol evidence regarding such circumstances merely because the words do not appear ambiguous to the reader can easily lead to the attribution to a written instrument of a meaning that was never intended. [Citations omitted.]" (Universal Sales Corp. v. Cal. Press Mfg. Co., supra, 20 Cal.2d 751, 776, 128 P.2d 665, 679 (concurring opinion); . . ..)

Although extrinsic evidence is not admissible to add to, detract from, or vary the terms of a written contract, these terms must first

3. "A contract has, strictly speaking, nothing to do with the personal, or individual, intent of the parties. A contract is an obligation attached by the mere force of law to certain acts of the parties, usually words, which ordinarily accompany and represent a known intent." (Hotchkiss v. National City Bank of New York (S.D.N.Y. 1911) 200 F. 287, 293. . . .)

be determined before it can be decided whether or not extrinsic evidence is being offered for a prohibited purpose. The fact that the terms of an instrument appear clear to a judge does not preclude the possibility that the parties chose the language of the instrument to express different terms. That possibility is not limited to contracts whose terms have acquired a particular meaning by trade usage, but exists whenever the parties' understanding of the words used may have differed from the judge's understanding.

Accordingly, rational interpretation requires at least a preliminary consideration of all credible evidence offered to prove the intention of the parties.[4] (Civ.Code, § 1647; Code Civ.Proc. § 1860; see also 9 Wigmore on Evidence, op. cit. supra, § 2470, fn. 11, p. 227.) Such evidence includes testimony as to the "circumstances surrounding the making of the agreement . . . including the object, nature and subject matter of the writing . . . " so that the court can "place itself in the same situation in which the parties found themselves at the time of contracting." (Universal Sales Corp. v. Cal. Press Mfg. Co., supra, 20 Cal.2d 751, 761, 128 P.2d 665, 671.) If the court decides, after considering this evidence, that the language of a contract, in the light of all the circumstances, is "fairly susceptible of either one of the two interpretations contended for . . .." (Balfour v. Fresno C. & I. Co. (1895) 109 Cal. 221, 225, 44 P. 876, 877; . . .) extrinsic evidence relevant to prove either of such meanings is admissible.[5]

In the present case the court erroneously refused to consider extrinsic evidence offered to show that the indemnity clause in the contract was not intended to cover injuries to plaintiff's property. Although that evidence was not necessary to show that the indemnity clause was reasonably susceptible of the meaning contended for by defendant, it was nevertheless relevant and admissible on that issue. Moreover, since that clause was reasonably susceptible of that meaning, the offered evidence was also admissible to prove that the clause had that meaning and did not cover injuries to plaintiff's property.[6] Accordingly, the judgment must be reversed. . . .

The judgment is reversed.

4. When objection is made to any particular item of evidence offered to prove the intention of the parties, the trial court may not yet be in a position to determine whether in the light of all of the offered evidence, the item objected to will turn out to be admissible as tending to prove a meaning of which the language of the instrument is reasonably susceptible or inadmissible as tending to prove a meaning of which the language is not reasonably susceptible. In such case the court may admit the evidence conditionally by either reserving its ruling on the objection or by admitting the evidence subject to a motion to strike. (See Evid.Code, § 403.)

5. Extrinsic evidence has often been admitted in such cases on the stated ground that the contract was ambiguous (e. g., Universal Sales Corp. v. Cal. Press Mfg. Co., supra, 20 Cal.2d 751, 761, 128 P.2d 665). This statement of the rule is harmless if it is kept in mind that the ambiguity may be exposed by extrinsic evidence that reveals more than one possible meaning.

6. The court's exclusion of extrinsic evidence in this case would be error

NOTES

(1) *Extrinsic Evidence in California.* This opinion followed by four months that in Masterson v. Sine, p. 551 supra. Six months later the same court, again speaking through Chief Justice Traynor, handed down its opinion in Delta Dynamics v. Arioto, 69 Cal.2d 525, 446 P.2d 785 (1968), an action by a lock manufacturer against a distributor for damages caused by the distributor's failure to meet its yearly quota. Although the distributor had promised to sell not less than a stated number of units each year, it attempted to show by extrinsic evidence that the manufacturer's power to terminate the contract was its exclusive remedy for failure to meet this quota, and that the distributor was not, therefore, liable for damages. The court held that the trial judge had erred in excluding evidence of conversations during the negotiations leading to the contract. The termination clause was "reasonably susceptible of the meaning contended for" and there was "nothing in the rest of the contract to preclude that interpretation." Justice Mosk spoke for the three of seven judges who dissented: "Once again this court adopts a course leading toward emasculation of the parol evidence rule. During this very year Masterson v. Sine . . . and Pacific Gas & Elec. Co. v. G. W. Thomas Drayage & Rigging Co. . . . have contributed toward that result. Although I had misgivings at the time, I must confess to joining the majority in those cases. Now, however, that the majority deem negotiations leading to the execution of contracts admissible, the trend has become so unmistakably ominous that I must urge a halt. . . . Given two experienced businessmen dealing at arm's length, both represented by competent counsel, it has become virtually impossible under recently evolving rules of evidence to draft a written contract that will produce predictable results in court. The written word, heretofore deemed immutable, is now at all times subject to alteration by self-serving recitals based upon fading memories of antecedent events. This, I submit, is a serious impediment to the certainty required in commercial transactions." Would drawing a line to exclude at least some extrinsic evidence contribute to that certainty? If so, does it make sense to draw the line between negotiations and other extrinsic evidence?

To what extent are the policies for or against the use of legislative history as an aid to statutory interpretation similar to those for or against the use of negotiations ("transactional history") as an aid to contract interpretation?

(2) *Variation by Contract.* Could the parties, by a provision in their contract, prevent the court from admitting extrinsic evidence that it would

even under a rule that excluded such evidence when the instrument appeared to the court to be clear and unambiguous on its face. The controversy centers on the meaning of the word "indemnify" and the phrase "all loss, damage, expense and liability." The trial court's recognition of the language as typical of a third party indemnity clause and the double sense in which the word "indemnify" is used in statutes and defined in dictionaries demonstrate the existence of an ambiguity. (Compare Civ.Code, § 2772, "Indemnity is a contract by which one engages to save another from a legal consequence of the conduct of one of the parties, or of some other person," with Civ.Code, § 2527, "Insurance is a contract whereby one undertakes to indemnify another against loss, damage, or liability, arising from an unknown or contingent event."

otherwise admit as an aid to interpretation? In Garden State Plaza Corp. v. S. S. Kresge Corp., 78 N.J.Super. 485, 189 A.2d 448 (1963), certif. denied, 40 N.J. 226, 191 A.2d 63 (1963), the court held void as against public policy a clause providing that no "previous negotiations, arrangements, agreements and understandings . . . shall be used to interpret or construe this lease." The clause would, the court said, have it construe the contract "wearing judicial blinders. We are requested to conform to a private agreement mandating our performance of a judicial function in a manner which, under our precedents, is not the path to justice in arriving at the binding meaning of a contract." Do you agree? See also United States v. Waterman Steamship Corp., 397 F.2d 577 (5th Cir. 1968).

(3) *Private Conventions or Codes.* Even the objectivists disagreed on the admissibility of private conventions or codes. Note that Learned Hand, in the excerpt quoted in Note 2, p. 579 supra, made a distinction between the case where "both parties severally declared that their meaning had been other than the natural meaning, and each declaration was similar," and that where there was "some mutual agreement between them to that effect." Holmes, on the contrary did "not suppose that you could prove, for purposes of construction . . . for instance, that the parties to a contract orally agreed that when they wrote five hundred feet it should mean one hundred inches, or that Bunker Hill Monument should signify Old South Church." [a] Holmes, The Theory of Legal Interpretation, 12 Harv.L.Rev. 417, 420 (1899).

Ward contracted in writing to furnish crushed stone at $2.75 per cubic yard to Smith, the general contractor for the construction of a state highway. Shortly thereafter they orally agreed that each of Ward's trucks, fully loaded, contained four cubic yards of crushed stone. Ward was paid for 12,955 cubic yards, figured on this basis. He sued Smith for $24,432, claiming that the quantity actually delivered was 21,538 cubic yards, and introduced, over objection, the testimony of a civil engineer that by a more accurate method of measurement Ward had delivered the larger amount. From judgment for plaintiff, defendant appealed. *Held:* Reversed. "When a contract specifies the mode of measurement to be adopted such mode should be followed." Ward v. Smith, 140 W.Va. 791, 86 S.E.2d 539 (1955). Was the case rightly decided? Under Holmes' view? Under Hand's? Is Hand's distinction justifiable?

(4) *Reformation and Interpretation.* As the Bollinger case, p. 559 supra, indicates, if by mistake the parties have omitted an agreed term from a writing, a court, exercising its equity powers, will decree reformation to include it. It is sometimes assumed that where the parties have used words in an unclear way, reformation is also appropriate to clarify their meaning for the purpose of enforcement. Is not there an adequate remedy "at law" in such cases, through interpretation? See 3 Corbin, § 540.

General Discount Corp. v. Sadowski, 183 F.2d 542 (6th Cir. 1950), is illustrative. Sadowski and General Discount entered into a two-year contract under which he was to create and sell mortgages through General Discount on a commission basis. On mortgages where General Discount

---

a. " 'That's a great deal to make one word mean,' Alice said in a thoughtful tone. 'When I make a word do a lot of work like that,' said Humpty Dumpty, 'I always pay it extra.' " Lewis Carroll, Through the Looking-Glass, Chapter VI.

received an additional service fee over the life of the mortgage, it was to "pay such excess to second party [Sadowski] monthly." When the contract term expired after two years, Sadowski contended that he was still entitled to receive the payments on each such mortgage monthly for the life of the *mortgage*, while General Discount contended that he had been entitled to them only monthly for the life of the *contract*. The court held that Sadowski was entitled to reformation to have the writing reflect his interpretation and to a judgment for the amount due under that interpretation. Was reformation necessary?[b]

FUNCTION OF JUDGE AND JURY

A detailed consideration of the respective roles of judge and jury, where trial is had by jury, in matters of contract interpretation is best left to a course in evidence or procedure. Nevertheless, a few elementary generalizations may be in order. It is clear that the meaning of language is, strictly speaking, a question of fact. Yet the interpretation of written agreements, as to which there is no dispute over the words used by the parties, has often been withdrawn from the jury by calling it a question of "law" for the judge, rather than a question of "fact" for the jury. This has been done for a variety of reasons, including a distrust of unsophisticated, uneducated, and—at least at one time—illiterate jurors, and a desire for consistency in interpretation of some kinds of contracts, such as standard insurance policies.

The difficulty in drawing a line between the province of the judge and that of the jury is suggested by this dictum of Justice Story: [a] "It is certainly true, as a general rule, that the interpretation of written instruments properly belongs to the court, and not to the jury. But there certainly are cases in which, from the different senses of the words used, or their obscure and indeterminate reference to unexplained circumstances, the true interpretation of the language may be

---

b. Sadowski had already brought an action in a state court to recover his compensation and had lost, the Supreme Court of Michigan deciding (5–2) in favor of General Discount on the ground that the contract "is not ambiguous and the definite contract period of two years controls . . . and, in the absence of fraud or mistake, excludes prior, contemporaneous and subsequent talks as to its scope and purport." Sadowski v. General Discount Corp., 295 Mich. 340, 294 N.W. 703 (1940). He then sought reformation in the federal courts. The decision in his favor was based in part on the testimony of General Discount's lawyer, that the understanding of the parties was monthly for the life of the mortgage. (In spite of the decision of the Supreme Court of Michigan, he still considered that the language reflected that understanding.)

a. Joseph Story (1779–1845) was appointed to the United States Supreme Court in 1811. In 1829, while retaining his seat on the Court, he became a professor of law at the Harvard Law School, where he reorganized the curriculum and revitalized the school. From his lectures developed his nine commentaries, on subjects ranging from the Constitution to conflict of laws, which played an important role in promoting uniformity in the development of American law during the first half of the nineteenth century.

left to the consideration of the jury for the purpose of carrying into effect the real intention of the parties. This is especially applicable to cases of commercial correspondence, where the real objects, and intentions, and agreements of the parties are often to be arrived at only by allusions to circumstances which are but imperfectly developed." Brown & Company v. M'Gran, 39 U.S. (14 Pet.) 479 (1840).

But Judge Friendly has pointed out: "With the courts' growing appreciation of Professor Corbin's lesson that words are seldom so 'plain and clear' as to exclude proof of surrounding circumstances and other extrinsic aids to interpretation, . . . the exception bids fair largely to swallow the supposed general rule. . . . Whether determination of meaning be regarded as a question of fact, a question of law, or just itself, reliance on the jury to resolve ambiguities in the light of extrinsic evidence seems quite as it should be, save where the form or subject-matter of a particular contract outruns a jury's competence . . . ." Meyers v. Selznick Co., 373 F. 2d 218 (2d Cir. 1966).

NOTES

(1) *The Case of John's Other Wife.* In 1921, Ira Soper penned several suicide notes to Adeline, his wife of ten years, parked his car containing his hat and some clothing by a canal, and left Louisville, Kentucky, without a trace, for Minneapolis, Minnesota, where he began a new life under the name of John W. Young. There he married Gertrude Whitby, took out a $5,000 insurance policy on his own life, payable to a trust company, and made an "escrow" agreement with his partner Karstens and the trust company by which the company would pay the proceeds to "the wife" of the insured. In 1932 he actually did commit suicide, and the trustee paid the proceeds to Gertrude as his surviving wife. Several months later Adeline appeared and brought suit against Gertrude for the proceeds. From a judgment for defendant, plaintiff appealed. *Held*: Affirmed. Although Gertrude was not the legal wife of the deceased, evidence was admissible to show that she was intended as beneficiary. "Were we to award the insurance fund to plaintiff Adeline, it is obvious that we would thereby be doing violence to the contract . . . . That agreement points to no one else than Gertrude as Young's 'wife'. To hold otherwise is to give the word 'wife' 'a fixed symbol,' as 'something inherent and objective, not subjective and personal'. . . . The trust agreement has become 'susceptible of construction' because 'ambiguity appears when attempt is made to operate the contract.' " One judge dissented, arguing: "A man can have only one wife. . . . The contract in this case designates the 'wife' as the one to whom the money was to be paid. I am unable to construe this word to mean anyone else than the only wife of Soper then living." In re Soper's Estate (Cochran v. Whitby), 196 Minn. 60, 264 N.W. 427 (1935). But cf. State Farm Mutual Automobile Ins. Co. v. Thompson, 372 F.2d 256 (9th Cir. 1967).

(2) *Purpose Interpretation.* Is there an analogy in the field of contract interpretation to what is known as "purpose interpretation" in the field of statutory interpretation? According to the formulation in Heydon's

Case, 3 Coke 7a, 76 Eng.Rep. 637 (Ex. 1584), it involves these steps: examination of the law before enactment of the statute; ascertainment of the "mischief or defect" for which the law did not provide; analysis of the remedy provided by the legislature to "cure the disease"; determination of the "true reason of the remedy"; and then application of the statute so as to "suppress the mischief, and advance the remedy." Can you formulate an analogous technique for contract interpretation?

(3) *Recitals.* In the case of a statute, purpose interpretation does not depend on the availability of legislative history, and the court may even find a helpful statement of the purpose of enactment set forth in the preamble or purpose clause of the statute itself. Similarly, it is not uncommon for written contracts to begin with a series of recitals of the surrounding circumstances and of the objectives of the parties. Usually prefixed by the word "whereas," contract recitals are not ordinarily drafted as promises or conditions, and their proper rule in the interpretation of the main body of the contract has been a source of bafflement to many a judge and lawyer. Courts in this country have frequently repeated with approval Lord Esher's "three rules": "If the recitals are clear and the operative part is ambiguous, the recitals govern the construction. If the recitals are ambiguous, and the operative part is clear, the operative part must prevail. If both the recitals and the operative part are clear, but they are inconsistent with each other, the operative part is to be preferred." Ex parte Dawes, 17 Q.B.D. 275, 286 (1886). But these, like many rules of interpretation, are easier of statement than of application.

NORTH GATE CORPORATION v. NATIONAL FOOD STORES

Supreme Court of Wisconsin, 1966.
30 Wis.2d 317, 140 N.W.2d 744.

[In 1960, North Gate Corporation leased premises in its shopping center to National Food Stores, for a minimum of 13 years with two five-year extensions at National's option, and with rent dependent on gross sales with a substantial minimum. Under the lease "neither Lessor nor his heirs or legal representatives, or its beneficiaries, subsidiaries, affiliates, successors, or assigns, or any entity in which they or any of them have an interest, will demise, lease, sub-lease, use or permit the use of, for the purpose of a retail food store any portion of any property, now or hereafter owned, acquired or leased by them or any of them within 5280 feet from the premises hereby demised to the Lessee, except such property or portion thereof now owned by them and as of the date hereof occupied by a retail food store."

[The provision was part of a printed form prepared by National for its stores throughout the country and, although various blank spaces were filled in and there were interlineations and deletions at several places, there was no change in the quoted provision except the insertion of "5280" in a blank space. The shares of North Gate were owned equally by Carl Roth and his two sons and Paul Roth and his two sons. When the lease was signed, both parties knew that several of the Roths owned land within a mile of the leased premises. In 1963 Carl and his wife conveyed one of these parcels, which was adjacent to the shopping center, to his two sons and his daughter. Seven months later they conveyed it to Copps Realty Corporation under an agreement that restricted the use to a department store and parking lot, but did not exclude the sale of food at retail. When National learned that the proposed department store would include a retail food department, it notified North Gate that it would treat this as a violation of the lease. North Gate brought an action for a declaratory judgment. From a judgment declaring that the sale of the land did not constitute a breach, National appealed.]

FAIRCHILD, JUSTICE. The sole issue debated by the parties is whether, the lessor being a corporation, the words "its beneficiaries" in paragraph Fifth of the lease, mean or include "its shareholders." National takes the position that North Gate, the lessor, warranted that its shareholders would not permit the use of land owned by them individually, if within a mile, for a retail food store. . . .

Contract terms being construed are to be considered in context. Words used in a contract are generally given their plain or ordinary meaning but ". . . technical words are to be interpreted as usually understood by persons in the profession or business to which they relate, unless the context of the contract or an applicable custom or usage clearly indicates that a different meaning was intended." Neither the ordinary meaning nor any technical meaning of "beneficiary" is equivalent to "shareholder."

Black's Law Dictionary (4th ed.), defines "beneficiary" as "One for whose benefit a trust is created; a *cestui que trust*. A person having the enjoyment of property of which a trustee, executor, etc., has the legal possession. The person to whom a policy of insurance is payable. One receiving benefit or advantage, or one who is in receipt of benefits, profits, or advantage."

Where various meanings can be given a term, the term is to be strictly construed against the draftsman of the contract. Here the draftsman was National. Further, the intent of the provision in question is to restrict trade and the use of land. Such provisions are to be strictly construed. The legal term "beneficiaries" normally refers to persons designated to receive benefit from a trust, an estate or an insurance contract.

National contends that the term as used in paragraph Fifth cannot refer to a *cestui que trust* because of the grammatical context. National suggests that the form was devised for use by either an individual or by a corporation. Where the lessor is an individual, the phrase "nor his heirs or legal representatives" is applicable. But where the lessor is a corporation, National claims that the entire phrase "or its beneficiaries, subsidiaries, affiliates, successors, or assigns" becomes operative, and each of the terms must be relevant to a corporation. National rejects the possibility that a trust or estate might be named as lessor as if it were an entity, and that the term "its beneficiaries" was intended to refer to the beneficiaries of a lessor trust or estate. National makes the nice point that the trustee or the executor properly should be named lessor in such case, and that the beneficiaries of the trust or estate are not properly called beneficiaries of the trustee or executor. This particular argument does not explain, however, why we should prefer the assumption that a draftsman would not name a trust as lessor over the assumption that he would not refer to the beneficiaries of a corporation if he meant its shareholders.

Canons of construction are designed to aid courts in ascertaining the intention of the parties. Normally the words used by the contracting parties are the best indicators of their intention. Occasionally words not used are also instructive. Here National contends that it was the intention of the parties that paragraph Fifth apply to shareholders of a corporation. If that were the intention of the parties, the intention could easily have been manifested merely by using the common term "shareholders." We cannot ignore the draftsman's failure to use an obvious term, especially where it is the draftsman who is urging a tenuous interpretation of a term in order to make it applicable to a situation which would clearly have been covered if the obvious term had been chosen.

National argues that a construction of an agreement which leaves a part of the language useless or creates surplusage is to be avoided. This is the general rule but it has much less force where, as here, a standard form, designed for use in varying fact situations, is used, and it is obvious that in each transaction where the form is used, some of its terms will necessarily be surplusage.

We think the term "beneficiaries" may have meaning where this form of lease is used for property held in trust, and that it ordinarily has no meaning with respect to a corporate lessor which is not a fiduciary. We say "ordinarily" because we note, for example, that it is possible for the directors of a dissolved corporation to become trustees for the benefit of creditors and shareholders by operation of law. Whether in that instance or any other extraordinary one, not present here, the shareholders would be deemed beneficiaries under paragraph Fifth, we need not and do not decide.

National has based its case against North Gate upon a construction of the words of the lease, and has not claimed that there are any facts present here which would justify a departure from the ordinary rule that a corporation is an entity separate from its shareholders.

National contends that certain observations of the trial court with respect to available remedies for breach were erroneous. If there were error in any of such statements, it would not be prejudicial since there was no breach.

Judgment affirmed.

NOTES

(1) *Maxims.* In contrast to the Pacific Gas and Electric case, p. 582 supra, where the aids to interpretation were described as "extrinsic," the aids relied upon in the North Gate case were largely "intrinsic." The court makes special mention of maxims, or canons, of interpretation. As this may suggest, many of the same rules of thumb that are used in the interpretation of statutes are also used in the interpretation of contracts. See J. E. Faltin Motor Transportation v. Eazor Express, 273 F.2d 444 (3d Cir. 1960). Their reliability is as questionable here as it is there. A classic discussion of maxims appears in Llewellyn, The Common Law Tradition—Deciding Appeals 521–35 (1960), a later version of Llewellyn, Remarks on the Theory of Appellate Decision and the Rules or Canons About How Statutes Are To Be Construed, 3 Vand.L.Rev. 395 (1950).

(2) *Public Interest.* Observe that the court in the North Gate case says that, because the provision in question is intended "to restrict trade and the use of land," it is "to be strictly construed." In Chapter 3, Policing the Bargain, we saw that contracts involving performance that would be in violation of some strongly rooted public interest, often expressed in a statute, may be held to be unenforceable. As the North Gate case shows, public interest may also affect interpretation and construction of contracts.

In State v. Calhoun, 231 S.W. 647 (Mo.App. 1921), a physician sold his practice, agreeing not to "establish [himself] as a practicing physician and surgeon within a radius of five miles" of his former office. The court held that he was not precluded from making calls within this area or treating patients from this area who might call at his office outside the area. "The contract in question is clearly one in restraint of trade and personal liberty, and as such should not be construed to extend beyond its fair import." Why? Because of the intention of the parties?

See also Sun Oil Co. v. Vickers Refining Co., 414 F.2d 383 (8th Cir. 1969), in which the court remarked, in rejecting Sunray's interpretation under which the contract would have been void because in violation of the antitrust laws: "Sunray's attorneys, experienced in antitrust work, approved the contract without any question of antitrust consequences."

INTERPRETATION CONTRA PROFERENTEM

When the court in the North Gate case states that here "the term is to be strictly construed against the draftsman," it invokes one of the most time-honored maxims of contract interpretation, according to which a contract is to be interpreted *contra proferentem*—against the author ("profferer"). Why? To carry out the intention of the parties? To penalize sloppy draftsmen? To encourage careful draftsmen? In many of the instances where the rule has been applied, the party who chose the contract language also had superior bargaining power. Does this appear to have been true in the North Gate case? Consider in this connection the problems raised in Chapter 3, Policing the Bargain, supra.

The United States Court of Claims, in applying the rule to government contracts, has explained: "This rule is fair both to the drafters and to those who are required to accept or reject the contract as proffered, without haggling. Although the potential contractor may have some duty to inquire about a major patent discrepancy, or obvious omission, or a drastic conflict in provisions, . . . he is not normally required (absent a clear warning in the contract) to seek clarification of any and all ambiguities, doubts, or possible differences in interpretation. The Government, as the author, has to shoulder the major task of seeing that within the zone of reasonableness the words of the agreement communicate the proper notions—as well as the main risk of a failure to carry that responsibility. If the defendant chafes under the continued application of this check, it can obtain a looser rein by a more meticulous writing of its contracts and especially of the specifications. Or it can shift the burden of ambiguity (to some extent) by inserting provisions in the contract clearly calling upon possible contractors aware of a problem-in-interpretation to seek an explanation before bidding." WPC Enterprises v. United States, 323 F.2d 874, 877 (Ct.Cl.1963). ª

Should it make a difference if the party who proffered the contract invited suggestions for change from the other party? See Acme Markets v. Dawson Enterprises, 253 Md. 76, 251 A.2d 839 (1969), in which the court noted that the other party had kept the contract for sixty days before signing it, that its president was a member of the bar, and that it had, at least earlier in the negotiations, been represented by "a member of a prominent Washington law firm." The court quoted with approval its suggestion in an earlier case that "perhaps [the *contra proferentem* rule] should have but slight force in a situation where both parties are represented by counsel."

NOTES

(1) *"Woe Unto You, Lawyers."* Should it make a difference, in interpreting a contract, whether the parties were represented by lawyers? In Gulf Oil Corporation v. American Louisiana Pipe Line Co., 282 F.2d 401 (6th Cir. 1960), the court relied on a difference in language between two sections of a contract in interpreting the contract. "We cannot believe that the difference in language in the two sections of the contract was inadvertent, particularly in view of the extended negotiations of the parties who were represented by lawyers presumably skilled in this field of the law, and observed great care in drafting and redrafting various provisions of the contract."

a. But see Shedd, Resolving Ambiguities in Interpretation of Government Contracts, 36 Geo.Wash.L.Rev. 1, 21 (1967), where the author concludes, "The rule of interpreting against the drafter, if not discarded entirely, should be relegated to a rule of last resort in contract interpretation . . . ." For dispute in the Supreme Court of the United States over the application of the rule, see United States v. Seckinger, 397 U.S. 203 (1970). See also Restatement Second, § 232.

In Weiland Tool & Mfg. Co. v. Whitney, 44 Ill.2d 105, 251 N.E.2d 242 (1969), the court wrote: "In interpreting the letter . . . we have taken into consideration not only that inferences from ambiguous language must be resolved against its author . . . , but also that he is a lawyer with a number of years of trial experience and experience as a legal adviser in commercial transactions. He must have had the ability to express [his intention] in concise and clear English . . . if that were his intention. Since he did not do so, we are further persuaded that this was not his intention."

(2) *Course of Performance.* Restatement Second, § 228(4) and UCC 2–208 are concerned with the use in interpretation of a course of performance by one party, acquiesced in by the other party. Courts have often resorted to "course of performance" or, as it is also called, "practical interpretation." Why? Because the conduct indicates what the intention of the parties was at the time of original agreement? Because the parties are free to modify their contract by subsequent conduct? What would be the effect of a merger clause on this rule? Of a no-oral-modification clause? Course of performance should be considered again in connection with waiver at p. 770 infra.

HURST v. W. J. LAKE & CO.

Supreme Court of Oregon, 1932.
141 Or. 306, 16 P.2d 627.

Action by Roscoe P. Hurst against W. J. Lake & Co., Inc., in the nature of assumpsit to recover an alleged balance of $5 per ton on 140 tons of horse meat scraps purchased by defendant from plaintiff pursuant to a written contract. From a judgment for defendant allowing defendant's motion for judgment on the pleadings after the complaint, answer, and reply had been filed, plaintiff appeals.

ROSMAN, J. From the portion of the pleadings which we are required to deem true, it appears that March 20, 1930, the plaintiff and the defendant entered into an agreement in writing, a copy of which follows:

"March 20, 1930.

"Messrs. Roscoe P. Hurst, Yeon Building, Portland, Oregon.

Dear Sirs: We confirm our purchase from you today as follows:

Buyer:	W. J. Lake & Co., Inc. Seattle, Washington.
Commodity:	Horse meat scraps.
Quantity:	350 tons of 2000 lbs. each.
Price:	$50.00 per ton f. o. b. cars Portland.
Terms of Payment:	Net cash in Portland on delivery with analysis certificate.
Time of Shipment:	Prior to April 20th, 1930.
Route:	As directed by buyer.

Specifications: Minimum 50% protein, ground and sacked in 100 lb. net each.

Additional specifications on supplementary page.

Yours truly,

W. J. Lake & Company, Inc.,

By L. E. Branchflower.

Accepted by:

"Roscoe P. Hurst."

"March 20, 1930.

"Mr. Roscoe P. Hurst, Yeon Building, Portland, Oregon.

Dear Sir: In case any of the Horse Meat Scraps, covered by our purchase order No. 1352 analyzes less than 50% of protein, it is understood that W. J. Lake & Company, Inc., the buyers, are to receive a discount of $5.00 per ton.

"It is further understood that in case the buyer does not take delivery of the entire lot by April 20th, 1930, the seller agrees to carry the stock one (1) month more for 50¢ per ton additional.

"The Northwest Testing Laboratories are to instruct the warehouse in the loading and are to furnish analysis certificates, at the buyer's expense. In case of an analysis dispute findings of a refree (sic) chemist, who shall be mutually agreed upon, shall be final.

Yours very truly,

W. J. Lake & Co., Inc.,

[Signed] L. E. Branchflower.

L. E. Branchflower.

LEB:G

Accepted by:

[Signed] Roscoe P. Hurst."

Pursuant to the contract, the plaintiff delivered to the defendant 349.25 tons of horse meat scraps which contained the following per centages of protein, and for which the defendant paid the following sums of money: 180 tons contained an excess of 50 per cent. protein, and the defendant paid for it $50 per ton; 29.25 tons contained 48.66 per cent. protein, and the defendant paid therefor $45 per ton; 140 tons contained protein varying from 49.53 per cent. to 49.96 per cent., for which the defendant paid $45 per ton.

[It appears from the pleadings, which we are required to deem true,] (1) that there is a group of dealers who trade in the commodity known as horse meat scraps; (2) that both plaintiff and defendant are members of that group; (3) that the terms "minimum 50% protein" and "less than 50% protein" are trade terms to which the group has attached meanings different from their common ones; (4) that this usage, prevalent among this group, demanded that, whenever those terms appeared in a contract for the sale of horse meat scraps, it became the duty of the buyer to accept all scraps containing 49.5 per cent. protein or more, and to pay for them at the rate provided for scraps containing full 50 per cent. protein; and (5) that the defendant was aware of all of the foregoing when it attached its signature to the aforementioned contract.

The flexibility of or multiplicity in the meaning of words is the principal source of difficulty in the interpretation of language. Words are the conduits by which thoughts are communicated, yet scarcely any of them have such a fixed and single meaning that they are incapable of denoting more than one thought. In addition to the multiplicity in meaning of words set forth in the dictionaries, there are the meanings imparted to them by trade customs, local uses, dialects, telegraphic codes, etc. One meaning crowds a word full of significance, while another almost empties the utterance of any import. The various groups above indicated are constantly amplifying our language; in fact, they are developing what may be called languages of their own. Thus one is justified in saying that the language of the dictionaries is not the only language spoken in America. For instance, the word "thousand" as commonly used has a very specific meaning; it denotes ten hundreds or fifty scores, but the language of the various trades and localities has assigned to it meanings quite different from that just mentioned. Thus in the bricklaying trade a contract which fixes the bricklayer's compensation at "$5.25 a thousand" does not contemplate that he need lay actually 1,000 bricks in order to earn $5.25, but that he should build a wall of a certain size. Brunold v. Glasser, 25 Misc. 285, 52 N.Y.S. 1021; Walker v. Syms, 118 Mich. 183, 76 N.W. 320. In the lumber industry a contract requiring the delivery of 4,000 shingles will be fulfilled by the delivery of only 2,500 when it appears that by trade custom two packs of a certain size are regarded as 1,000 shingles, and that hence the delivery of eight packs fulfills the contract, even though they contain only 2,500 shingles by actual count. Soutier v. Kellerman, 18 Mo. 509. And, where the custom of a locality considers 100 dozen as constituting a thousand, one who has 19,200 rabbits upon a warren under an agreement for their sale at the price of 60 pounds for each thousand rabbits will be paid for only 16,000 rabbits. Smith v. Wilson, 3 Barn. & Adol. 728. Numerous other instances could readily be cited showing the manner in which the meaning of words has been contracted, expanded, or otherwise altered by local usage, trade custom, dialect influence, code agreement, etc. In fact, it is no novelty to find legislative enactments preceded by glossaries or brief dictionaries defining the meaning of the words employed in the act. Technical treatises dealing with aeronautics, the radio, engineering, etc., generally contain similar glossaries defining the meaning of many of the words employed by the craft. A glance at these glossaries readily shows that the different sciences and trades, in addition to coining words of their own, appropriate common words and assign to them new meanings. Thus it must be evident that one cannot understand accurately the language of such sciences and trades without knowing the peculiar meaning attached to the words which they use. It is said that a court in construing the language of the parties must put itself into the shoes of the parties. That alone would not suffice; it must also adopt their vernacular.

Wigmore on Evidence (2d) § 2460, points out that the interpretation of language may be thus approached: "The standard of the community, or popular standard, meaning the common and normal sense of words; the local standard including the special usages of a religious sect, a body of traders, an alien population or a local dialect; the mutual standard covering those meanings which are peculiar to both or all the parties to a transaction but shared in common by them; and the individual standard of one party to an act, as differing from that of the other party or parties, if any."

After Dean Wigmore has reviewed at length the overthrow of what he calls the traditional rule which insists that the meaning of all words is rigid and inflexible, and the development of what he terms the liberal rule which recognizes, to some extent at least, the four aforementioned standards of interpretation, he continues (section 2463): "The liberal rule, on the other hand, is today conceded practically everywhere, to permit resort in any case to the usage of a trade or locality, no matter how plain the apparent sense of the word to the ordinary reader; and some of the extreme instances are persuasive to demonstrate the fallacy of ignoring the purely relative meaning of words and the injustice of attempting to enforce a supposed rigid standard."

From Williston on Contracts, § 650, we quote: "Though Professor Thayer has said that 'In contracts it was always recognized that familiar words may have different meanings in different places, so that "every bargain as to such a thing shall have relation to the custom of the country where it is made," ' it may be doubted how far it was allowable under early law to show that a word in a written contract (or perhaps in an oral agreement) having a clear and fixed ordinary meaning bore a meaning contrary to its usual significance, if nothing in the context showed that a particular meaning was intended. But there are now numerous decisions (not all of them of recent date) where words with a clear, normal meaning have been shown by usage to bear a meaning which nothing in the context would suggest. This is not only true of technical terms, but of language which, at least on its face, has no peculiar or technical significance; though even today it is still occasionally said by courts that usage cannot control words having 'a definite legal meaning'; or cannot be used to interpret a contract unless there is an uncertainty on the face of the instrument."

The defendant cites numerous cases in many of which the courts held that, when a contract is expressed in language which is not ambiguous upon its face the court will receive no evidence of usage, but will place upon the words of the parties their common meaning; in other words, in those decisions the courts ran the words of the parties through a judicial sieve whose meshes were incapable of retaining anything but the common meaning of the words, and which permitted the meaning which the parties had placed upon them to run away as waste material. Surely those courts did not believe that words are always used in their orthodox sense. The rulings must have been persuaded by other considerations. The rule which rejects evidence of custom has the advantage of simplicity; it protects the writing from attack by some occasional individual who will seek to employ perjured testimony in proof of alleged custom; and, if one can believe that the parol evidence rule is violated when common meaning is rejected in favor of special meaning, then the above rule serves the purpose of the parol evidence rule. Without setting forth the manner in which we came to our conclusion, we state that none of these reasons appeals to us as sufficient to exclude evidence of custom and assign to the words their common meaning only, even though the instrument is nonambiguous upon its face. The defendant argues that this court has held that custom or usage cannot be resorted to in the interpretation of the meaning of an instrument where no ambiguity appears upon its face, and cites in support of his contention Williams v. Ledbetter, 132 Or. 145, 285 P. 214; Darling-Singer Lbr. Co. v. Oriental Navigation Co., 127 Or. 655, 259 P. 420, 272 P. 275; Interior Warehouse Co. v. Dunn, 80 Or. 528, 157 P. 806; Oregon Fisheries Co. v. Elmore Packing Co., 69 Or. 340, 138 P. 862; Barnard & Bunker v. Houser, 68 Or. 240, 137 P. 227; Savage v. Salem Mills Co., 48 Or. 1, 85 P. 69, 10 Ann.Cas. 1065; Abraham v. Oregon & California R. R. Co., 37 Or. 495, 60 P. 899, 64 L.R.A. 391, 82 Am.St.Rep. 779; and Holmes v. Whitaker, 23 Or. 319, 31 P. 705. It must be admitted that language can be found in some of these decisions which lends weight to his argument. But a reading of these cases will disclose that in all of them, with the exception of Abraham v. Oregon & California R. R. Co., the party was not resorting to custom for the purpose of interpreting the language of the instrument, but for the purpose of annexing or engrafting on to the contract an additional term; in other words, he sought to prove that the written instrument did not embody the entire agreement. Such a contention invoked a principle quite different from the one with which we are now concerned. For comment see Wigmore on Evidence (2d) § 2440. In Abraham v. Oregon & California R. R. Co., the decision does not mention custom. The appellant in that case sought to prove that he and the party with whom he dealt had placed upon one of the terms of the instrument a mutual meaning distinct from its normal one.

Without setting forth herein our review of the many authorities cited in the briefs, all of which we have read with care, we state our conclusion that members of a trade or business group who have employed in their contracts trade terms are entitled to prove that fact in their litigation, and show the meaning of those terms to assist the court in the interpretation of their language.

Finally, it is suggested that the employment of the terms "minimum 50% protein" and "less than 50% of protein" indicates that the parties rejected the mercantile custom in effecting their contract. It will be recalled that under the state of the record we are compelled to regard these two terms as trade terms possessed of a special significance. We believe that it is safe to assume, in the absence of evidence to the contrary, that, when tradesmen employ trade terms, they attach to them their trade significance. If, when they write their trade terms into their contracts, they mean to strip the terms of their special significance and demote them to their common import, it would seem reasonable to believe that they would so state in their agreement. Otherwise they would refrain from using the trade term and express themselves in other language. We quote from Nicoll v. Pittsvein Coal Co. (C.C.A.) 269 F. 968, 971: "Indeed when tradesmen say or write anything, they are perhaps without present thought on the subject, writing on top of a mass of habits or usages which they take as matter of course. So (with Prof. Williston) we think that any one contracting with knowledge of a usage will naturally say nothing about the matter unless desirous of excluding its operation; if he does wish to exclude, he will say so in express terms. Williston, Contracts, § 653." Nothing in the contract repels the meaning assigned by the trade to the two above terms unless the terms themselves reject it. But, if these terms repel the meaning which usage has attached to them, then every trade term would deny its own meaning. We reject this contention as being without merit. We have considered all other contentions presented by the respondent, but have found no merit in them.

It follows that, in our opinion, the circuit court erred when it sustained the defendant's motion for judgment on the pleadings.

Reversed.

NOTES

(1) *Proof of Usage.*[a] State the issue in Hurst v. Lake in terms of the contract language. How will usage help resolve that issue at the trial?

a. The terms "usage" and "custom" are often used interchangeably. "Custom" has the more ancient tradition, and the Uniform Commercial Code adopts "usage of trade" to reject some of the restrictions that had been traditionally placed upon the use of "custom." Comments 4 and 5 to UCC 1–205 say: "By adopting . . . the term 'usage of trade' this Act expresses its intent to reject those cases which see evidence of 'custom' as representing an effort to displace or negate 'established rules of law.' . . . The ancient English tests for 'custom' are abandoned . . . . Therefore, it is not required that a usage of trade be 'ancient or immemorial,' 'universal' or the like." Williston, however, attaches different meanings to the two terms. "Usage derives its efficacy from the assent thereto of parties to the transaction; custom derives its efficacy from its adoption into the law, and when once established is binding irrespective of

How can Hurst prove usage? Why did the buyer fail in his attempt to prove usage in the Frigaliment case, p. 573 supra? Would he have succeeded under the Code? See UCC 1–205.

(2) *Role of Usage.* Professor Lawrence Friedman has criticized what he calls "pure" contract law, which is "blind to details of subject matter and person," and "does not ask who buys and who sells, and what is bought and sold." Friedman, Contract Law in America: A Social and Economic Case Study 20 (1965). May acceptance of usage help to meet this criticism? Professor Hurst, in his study of the lumber industry in Wisconsin, found this "generality in contract concepts . . . a source of strength, so far as it meant that the legal order could efficiently and smoothly adapt itself to varied circumstances. But there was weakness, so far as contract law achieved this generality by intense devotion to a quite limited range of policies, abstracted from the living context in which they arose." He went on to suggest that "lumber-contract case law made its most distinctive adaptation to the peculiarities of the industry" by allowing proof of usage. Hurst, Law and Economic Growth: The Legal History of the Lumber Industry in Wisconsin 1836–1915 290 (1964).

On usage and custom generally, see Note, 55 Colum L.Rev. 1192 (1955); Restatement Second, §§ 245–49. Hibernians may be interested in Ermolieff v. R.K.O. Radio Pictures, Inc., 19 Cal.2d 543, 122 P.2d 3 (1942), in which a usage of the motion picture industry was admitted to establish that the term "The United Kingdom," as used in an agreement granting movie rights, included Eire, the Irish Free State.[b] Devotees of detective stories in general and of Sam Spade in particular may be interested in an entertaining case in which the court, in construing a contract, took judicial notice that, "It has long been common practice among detective-fiction writers to make use of the same central and supporting characters in subsequent works." Warner Bros. Pictures v. Columbia Broadcasting System, 102 F.Supp. 141 (S.D.Cal.1951), affirmed as to this point but reversed in part in 216 F.2d 945 (9th Cir. 1954).

KREGLINGER & FERNAU v. CHARLES J. WEBB SONS CO., 162 F.Supp. 695 (E.D.Pa.1957), aff'd 255 F.2d 680 (3d Cir. 1958). [On February 27, 1951, Kreglinger, a New Zealand seller of wool and Webb, a Philadelphia buyer, contracted in Philadelphia for the sale of 100 bales of wool, for "prompt" shipment from New Zealand. On the date of the contract all New Zealand ports were strikebound. The parties were aware of this when they contracted and the seller's representative had explained that he had been advised by his "people" in

any manifestation of assent by the parties concerned. Usage is, therefore, of importance only in consensual agreements since it is the assent of the parties which gives it its force." 5 Williston, § 649.

b. Even Holmes endorsed usage, as distinguished from private codes or conventions. After the passage quoted in Note 3, p. 587 supra, he continued: "On the other hand, when you have the security of a local or class custom or habit of speech, it may be presumed that the writer conforms to the usage of his place or class when that is what a normal person in his situation would do." Does this give some insight into Holmes' reasons for espousing the objective theory?

New Zealand that the strike would be over very shortly. Because of the strike, the wool was not loaded in New Zealand until April 20, 52 days later. On its arrival in Philadelphia the buyer refused to accept it, and the seller sued for damages.]

KIRKPATRICK, CHIEF JUDGE. . . . The whole controversy centers around the single question, What did the parties intend when they inserted the word "prompt" in the contract? Each side attempted to prove the mutual intention by calling evidence intended to establish the existence of a usage in the wool trade which gave a special meaning to the word. The plaintiff contended that it was generally accepted as meaning "by the first available ship", the defendant, as meaning "30 days". Neither party has satisfied me by the measure of proof required by the law of Pennsylvania of the existence of the trade custom or usage for which it contends and I must endeavor to find the intention of the parties from all the circumstances surrounding their agreement, without reference to custom or usage. . . .

It must be kept in mind that this was a shipment from New Zealand and that shipping facilities in New Zealand, in perfectly normal times, were and had been for a long time "notoriously irregular" and that, for that reason, what would be considered prompt in Philadelphia, or even in Australia, would not be the standard by which shipments from New Zealand are to be judged.

The plaintiff produced an analysis of a number of contracts calling for "prompt" shipment of wool from New Zealand, a study of which is illuminating upon the question of what the trade generally accepted as fulfilling that requirement. In all of them, of course, Kreglinger was the seller but the contracts were made with more than 30 different buyers or importers in the principal centers of the wool trade on the east coast, so that it would seem to fairly cover the trade. Taking the period between August 19, 1949, and ending February 19, 1951, (the last loading date before the strike began) in order to eliminate the unusual strike situation and to get a fair idea of the accepted practice under normal conditions, it appears that the word "prompt" was used in 69 out of 155 contracts and in only 27 of the 69 was the shipment made within 30 days and, what is more significant, in only one was the letter of credit for a period as short as 31 days. It thus appears that on 67 occasions some 25 buyers who had ordered wool for prompt shipment, bound themselves irrevocably to pay for it if shipped anywhere from 32 to 190 days. In 9 contracts it was 32 to 40 days. In 8 it was 41 to 52 and in 50 it was over 52 days—the number of days between the contract and the shipment of the wool in this case.

It seems to me that only one conclusion can be drawn from the evidence of this analysis, namely, that the word "prompt" in New Zealand wool contracts has no relation to any specific number of days allowed the seller to make shipment. It seems to have been a word inserted in all contracts where neither the specific date was fixed nor a

ship designated. If it has any meaning at all it would seem to be equivalent to "without undue delay" or possibly, as the Court, in the Connecticut case cited, held, something more than ordinary diligence, a standard to be determined from the circumstances which condition the seller's ability to make shipment. Leaving the strike out of consideration altogether, I am satisfied that, taking into account shipping facilities from New Zealand, the trade generally would have accepted, in normal times, 52 days as prompt shipment, and both parties with their wide experience in the wool business must have known what the trade considered prompt. I think that the plaintiff acted without undue delay and shipped within a reasonable time. It follows that the plaintiff in this case complied with the terms of the contract.
. . .

The plaintiff is, therefore, entitled to recover damages in this action. . . .

NOTES

(1) *Intentional Vagueness.* In view of the fact that the parties must have foreseen the risk of delay due to the strike, why were they not more precise in stating the time for delivery? Are there reasons why draftsmen might be intentionally vague?

(2) *Course of Dealing, Course of Performance and Usage of Trade.* On what basis did the court rely on the 155 contracts? Would they have been admissible under the Code? To show a course of dealing? To show a course of performance? To show a usage of trade? See UCC 1–205, 2–208.

(3) *Problem.* Black telegraphed Cage, a dealer in rice, asking him to "name price of carload Honduras rice." Cage answered, "Have 200 sacks left, second year, highly graded, $5.75, f. o. b. here. Wire quick. Very scarce." Black replied, "Ship one hundred and seventy sacks rice. Instructions in letter." Cage who had meant $5.75 a barrel, according to an understanding in the rice trade, wrote Black, "In accordance with telegrams exchanged between us, we confirm sale to you 170 sacks Honduras seed rice, highly graded, at $5.75 per barrel." Black had understood the offer to mean $5.75 a sack. There are 195 barrels in 170 sacks. Advise Black. Would additional facts be helpful? What facts? See Cage v. Black, 97 Ark. 613, 134 S.W. 942 (1911).

SECTION 3. DECIDING "OMITTED CASES"

Thus far we have concerned ourselves with finding the law of the contract by interpreting its language. But what is the law of the contract if the language, when interpreted, does not cover the case at hand—what if it is an "omitted case"? As we have already seen as far back as in the Southwest Engineering case, p. 81, *supra,* and again in Wood v. Lucy, p. 234, supra, a term may be implied in such a situation.

The French sociologist Emile Durkheim pointed out that "we can neither foresee the variety of possible circumstances in which our contract will involve itself, nor fix in advance with the aid of simple mental calculus what will be in each case the rights and duties of each, save in matters in which we have a very definite experience." If, at the time of contracting "it were necessary each time to begin the struggles anew, to again go through the conferences necessary to establish firmly all the conditions of agreement for the present and the future, we would be put to rout." Implied terms, the handwork of society and tradition, provide for "what we cannot foresee individually" and regulate "what we cannot regulate." Contract imposes on us duties "that we did not desire," which we can, but rarely do, change. "In principle, the rule applies; innovations are exceptional." Durkheim, On the Division of Labor in Society 213–15 (Simpson's tr. 1933). See also Restatement Second, § 230 (a section that has no counterpart in the earlier Restatement); Farnsworth, Disputes Over Omissions in Contracts, 68 Colum.L.Rev. 860 (1968). But when will a court imply a term in a contract? Justice Holmes wrote: "Behind the logical form lies a judgment as to the relative worth and importance of competing legislative grounds, often an inarticulate and unconscious judgment, it is true, and yet the very root and nerve of the whole proceeding. You can give any conclusion a logical form. You can always imply a condition in a contract. But why do you imply it? It is because of some belief as to the practice of the community or of a class, or because of some opinion as to policy, or, in short, because of some attitude of yours upon a matter not capable of exact quantitative measurement, and therefore not capable of founding exact logical conclusions. Such matters really are battle grounds where the means do not exist for determinations that shall be good for all time, and where the decision can do no more than embody the preference of a given body in a given time and place." Holmes, The Path of the Law, 10 Harv.L.Rev. 457, 466 (1897); also in Holmes, Collected Legal Papers 167, 181 (1920).

NOTES

(1) *Implied Terms.* We are speaking here of terms that are "implied in law" rather than "implied in fact." Corbin explains that difference in this way: "When a promise is said to be 'implied in fact' we are describing one that is found by interpretation of a promisor's words or conduct. When a promise is said to be 'implied in law,' we are declaring the existence of legal duty created otherwise than by assent and without any words or conduct that are interpreted as promissory." 3 Corbin, § 561. Corbin's distinction found its way into the Uniform Commercial Code, which defines "agreement" as "the bargain of the parties in fact" and "contract" as "the total legal obligation which results." Compare UCC 1–201(3) with (11).

(2) *"Interpretation" and "Construction."* Although the words "interpretation" and "construction" are often used interchangeably, attempts

have been made to give them distinct meanings. Professor Corbin proposed the following distinction: "By 'interpretation of language' we determine what ideas that language induces in other persons. By 'construction of the contract,' as that term will be used here, we determine its legal operation— its effect upon the action of courts and administrative officials. If we make this distinction, then the construction of a contract starts with the interpretation of its language but does not end with it; while the process of interpretation stops wholly short of a determination of the legal relations of the parties. . . . When a court is filling gaps in the terms of an agreement, with respect to matters that the parties did not have in contemplation and as to which they had no intention to be expressed, the judicial process should not be called interpretation."[a]   3 Corbin, § 534.

WOOD v. LUCY, LADY DUFF-GORDON

Court of Appeals of New York, 1917.
222 N.Y. 88, 118 N.E. 214.

[For the report of this case, see p. 234 supra.]

NOTES

(1) *Cardozo on Holmes.* What answer would Cardozo give to Holmes' question, "why do you imply it?" Cardozo says that "implication of a promise here finds support in many circumstances." What circumstances? What support? Comment 5 to UCC 2–306, which lays down a similar rule, has this to say: "Subsection (2), on exclusive dealing, makes explicit the commercial rule embodied in this Act under which the parties to such contracts are held to have impliedly, even when not expressly, bound themselves to use reasonable diligence as well as good faith in their performance of the contract. . . . An exclusive dealing agreement brings into play all of the good faith aspects of the output and requirement problems of subsection (1)." Why?

(2) *Problem.* In 1881 Dr. J. J. Lawrence granted J. W. Lambert the exclusive commercial use of the secret formula for an antiseptic known as Listerine for which Lambert bound himself and his successors "to pay monthly to the said Dr. J. J. Lawrence his heirs, executors or assigns, the sum of twenty dollars for each and every gross of said Listerine hereafter

---

a. Corbin succeeded in popularizing the term "constructive condition," to refer to conditions implied *in law*, in order to distinguish them from conditions implied *in fact.* 3A Corbin, §§ 632, 653; Corbin, Conditions in the Law of Contract, 28 Yale L.J. 739, 743–44 (1919), Selected Readings 871, 876. Its analogue, "constructive promise," is not used, however, and lawyers speak, somewhat inconsistently, of *"implied* promises" and *"constructive* conditions." For more on conditions, see Section 4, infra.

Lawyers from civil law systems tend not to think of specific terms "im- plied" in the particular case but of generalized rules which apply to all such cases unless the parties provide otherwise. In France these rules are called *facultative, interprétative* or *suppletive,* in contrast to those that are *impérative* and which the parties are powerless to alter. Perhaps the happiest English equivalents are "suppletive" and "mandatory." Since civil law lawyers are accustomed to finding such rules spelled out in a code in advance of controversy, they are less tempted to attribute them to the supposed "intentions" of the parties.

sold by myself, my heirs, executors or assigns." There was no termination date. Although the amount of the royalties was later reduced, royalties rose to a million and a half dollars a year. Gradually the formula unavoidably became a matter of public knowledge, so that the same antiseptic can now be produced by anyone. Lambert's successor inquires whether it is still obligated to pay royalties. What advice? See Warner-Lambert Pharmaceutical v. John J. Reynolds, Inc., 178 F.Supp. 655 (S.D.N.Y.1959), aff'd, 280 F.2d 197 (2d Cir. 1960); 74 Harv.L.Rev. 409 (1960). But cf. April Productions v. G. Schirmer, Inc., 308 N.Y. 366, 126 N.E.2d 283 (1955).

(3) *Problem.* In 1892 the town of Readsboro and the Deerfield River Railroad Company agreed that the expense of maintaining a bridge, which was then used for both a narrow gauge railroad and a highway, "shall be borne equally" by the two parties. There was no termination date. The bridge is too weak for standard gauge equipment, and its use has been discontinued by the railroad company. Must the company continue to pay for half of the repairs? Town of Readsboro v. Hoosac Tunnel & W. R. Co., 6 F.2d 733 (2d Cir. 1925).

HML CORPORATION v. GENERAL FOODS CORPORATION, 365 F.2d 77 (3d Cir. 1966). [In 1956, General Foods began to distribute a dessert topping mix called "Dream Whip" and applied for trademark protection. Its application was successfully opposed by Cream Wipt Foods, which since 1934 had marketed a salad dressing under the trademarked name "Cream Wipt." When the court's decision in favor of Cream Wipt was announced in 1960, General Foods sought to protect its four-year investment in the name "Dream Whip" by entering into two contracts with Cream Wipt and its president and principal shareholder, Harry M. Levin. Under the "Main Agreement," it agreed to pay $250,000 for the exclusive rights to the "Cream Wipt" trademark, the process and a patent. Cream Wipt was to change its name and neither it nor Levin was to compete with General Foods in the manufacture of salad dressing for ten years. Under the "Supply Agreement," Cream Wipt agreed to sell and General Foods to buy 85% of the latter's requirements of salad dressing, up to a stated maximum, in a designated area for 32 months, at a price equal to Cream Wipt's cost plus a fixed profit plus half of General Foods' profit above 28%. After four months, during which time General Foods made market tests, it notified Cream Wipt's successor, HML, that it could not profitably market the salad dressing and would require no further deliveries. HML sued General Foods for breach of contract. At the trial Levin testified that he had originally asked for a $750,000 settlement and had accepted $250,000 because General Foods' representatives had assured him that it would use its best efforts to promote the salad dressing and that a great success was likely "if it clicked." At the close of the case, the trial court held that no duty to promote the sale of salad dressing would be implied, and that Levin's testimony was inadmissible under the parol evidence rule to prove such an undertaking. It also held that it had not been proved that General Foods' decision had been made in bad faith. HML appealed.]

FREEDMAN, CIRCUIT JUDGE. . . . [The court applied New York law and discussed Wood v. Lucy, Lady Duff-Gordon.] That rule is inapplicable here. While plaintiff originally was the owner of the product, this was not the simple grant of an exclusive distributorship in return for a share of the profits. Defendant bought from the plaintiff its interest and good will in the product, as well as the name, in return for a substantial cash payment. The court below found that the primary purpose of the "Supply Agreement" was for the benefit of the defendant so that it would have a ready source of supply of the product in accordance with its requirements. We cannot say from an examination of the agreements and the record that this conclusion is erroneous. Nor need we definitively determine the precise limits of the defendant's obligation in the peculiar circumstances of this case. Cases such as percentage leases and the distinctions which have been drawn regarding an implied obligation of the lessee to use and occupy the premises where a substantial minimum rental is provided and those where there is no minimum rental may be looked to for some analogy. In these and similar circumstances the seller or lessor is not at the mercy of the buyer or lessee and the terms of the contract which provide a substantial minimum payment therefore negative an implication of a duty to promote, drawn from equitable considerations. The choice lies between implying a promise to correct an apparent injustice in the contract, as against holding the parties to the bargain which they have made. The latter alternative has especial force where the bargain is the result of elaborate negotiations in which the parties are aided by counsel, and in such circumstances it is easier to assume that a failure to make provision in the agreement resulted not from ignorance of the problem, but from an agreement not to require it. In this case the plaintiff argues that in a requirements contract the buyer impliedly promises to maintain his requirements. Here, as in percentage lease cases, the decisions are not all uniform in the strength assigned to the effort to equalize the agreement on the one hand and the reliance on the parties' bargain on the other. The better view, however, is that generally the buyer in a requirements contract is required merely to exercise good faith in determining his requirements and the seller assumes the risk of all good faith variations in the buyer's requirements even to the extent of a determination to liquidate or discontinue the business. The rule is based on a reliance on the self-interest of the buyer, who ordinarily will seek to have the largest possible requirements. Protection against abuse is afforded by penetrating through any device by which the requirement is siphoned off in some other form to the detriment of the seller. The requirement of good faith is the means by which this is enforced and self-interest in its undistorted form is maintained as the standard. . . .

The parties were well aware that the contract arose out of the defendant's desire to use the trademarked name. And in the circumstances if defendant after acquiring it and having the plaintiff's obligation to supply the product needed was to be bound by any specific obligations of performance the usual desirability of providing for it in the agreement was here even more pronounced. The absence of such a provision in the agreement therefore has greater significance in this case than in the ordinary requirements contract. . . .

There remains then the question whether defendant acted in good faith in deciding that it had no need for the product. There is not much dispute on whether this was shown. On the contrary, it is argued by plaintiff that the burden was upon the defendant to establish the good faith of its decision. Since the contract made no provision for a minimum requirement by defendant, its notice to plaintiff that it had no requirement did not of itself constitute a breach of the agreement. It follows that since plaintiff claimed a breach it was its duty to prove it, and the burden, therefore, rested upon it to show that defendant had acted in bad faith. See New York Central Iron Works Co. v. United States Radiator Co., supra, 174 N.Y. at 335–336, 66 N.E. 967. The court below found that this burden was not met and we cannot say that its finding was so clearly erroneous that it must be set aside. . . .

[Affirmed.]

NOTES

(1) *The Obligation of Good Faith.* Judge Freedman speaks of the "requirement of good faith." UCC 1–203 provides that "Every contract or duty within this Act imposes an obligation of good faith in its performance or enforcement." "Good Faith" is generally defined in the Code to mean only "honesty in fact in the conduct or transaction concerned," a purely subjective test. UCC 1–201(19). But the Sales Article, Article 2, contains a special definition of "good faith" which "in the case of a merchant means honesty in fact and the observance of reasonable commercial standards of fair dealing in the trade." UCC 2–103(1)(b).

The notion of an obligation of good faith in the performance of contract duties is a familiar one to civil law systems, most notably the German. Article 242 of the German Civil Code imposes an obligation of "performance according to the requirements of good faith [*Treu und Glauben*], common habits being duly taken into consideration." It is a novel one to the common law and the Code provisions have already occasioned considerable discussion. See Farnsworth, Good Faith Performance and Commercial Reasonableness under the Uniform Commercial Code, 30 U.Chi.L.Rev. 666 (1963); Summers, "Good Faith" in General Contract Law and the Sales Provisions of the Uniform Commercial Code, 54 Va.L.Rev. 195 (1968).

To what extent is there, by analogy or otherwise, an obligation of good faith in the performance of contract duties that do not fall within the scope of the Code? Can the rules relating to mitigation of damages be considered as merely a specific application of such a general obligation?

(2) *The Case of the Bad Faith Order.* Massachusetts Gas & Electric Light Supply, a distributor of appliances, had a distributorship agreement with V-M, a manufacturer, cancellable by V-M on 30 days' notice. In June, Massachusetts learned that V-M was about to cancel and on June 28 it ordered 892 units, its estimated need for the rest of the year, although its normal inventory was about 100 units. V-M cancelled and refused to fill the order, but offered to fill a part of it. Massachusetts took the position that it wanted the whole order or nothing, and sued. From judgment for the defendant, the plaintiff appealed. *Held:* Affirmed. "The agreement was a distributorship and not a mere sales agreement, and it was the disclosed intention that when plaintiff ceased to be a distributor it should, at least shortly, cease to carry defendant's goods. . . . [T]he maximum June 28 order which defendant should have had to respect was to maintain an appropriate inventory through July. Plaintiff's order was not a good faith attempt to accomplish this, see U.C.C. §§ 1–203, 2–103 (1)(b), 2–306, but an effort to nullify the termination clause." Massachusetts Gas & Electric Light Supply Corp. v. V-M Corp., 387 F.2d 605 (1st Cir. 1967).

PAREV PRODUCTS CO. v. I. ROKEACH & SONS

United States Circuit Court of Appeals, Second Circuit, 1941.
124 F.2d 147.

CLARK, CIRCUIT JUDGE. This appeal involves the question whether or not an injunction should issue to enforce an asserted implied negative covenant in a contract granting an exclusive license to use a secret formula for a food product. In the District Court the complaint was dismissed on the merits, D.C.E.D.N.Y., 36 F.Supp. 686, on the ground that the parties to the contract did not intend a negative covenant. Although the District Court may perhaps have emphasized "intent" more than is realistic as to matters concerning which the parties have not revealed their thinking processes, it is, of course, obvious that the terms of the contract and the status arising out of those terms are of paramount importance. We turn, therefore, at once to the facts of the case.

In 1924, plaintiff, Parev Products Co., Inc., entered into a contract with defendant, I. Rokeach & Sons, Inc. At that time, as can be reasonably inferred from some of the terms of the contract, plaintiff was not in the best of financial condition. So far as apppears, its principal product of manufacture was Parev Schmaltz, a cooking oil made from coconut oil in such a way as to be Kosher, that is, usable with meat and dairy products without violation of the Jewish dietary laws. Parev Schmaltz was then supposed to be manufactured by a secret formula made by plaintiff's president, Aaron Proser, and, as the contract warranted, known only to him, Solomon Proser, and Julius Proser, though at the time a patent had been applied for on the formula and process. Defendant, on the other hand, was a successful business house of long standing. It engaged in extensive merchandising of food and cleansing products, mostly to orthodox Jews. The purpose of the contract, so far as appears, was to enable plaintiff to get out of its difficulties and to provide defendant with a Kosher semisolid vegetable oil.

By the terms of the contract, defendant obtained the exclusive use of all the necessary secret formulae, etc., for a period of twenty-five years, with an option to renew for another twenty-five years. In return, plaintiff was to receive royalties on all sales of Parev Schmaltz. Defendant had several powers to terminate, however. It could terminate the contract at any time it found the formula not to have been secret. Up to two years after the date of the contract, it could terminate the contract without cause upon payment of $100; and after two years, upon payment of $500. If any patents were judicially declared invalid, the contract was to terminate automatically. In defending any patent actions, plaintiff was to bear the full cost if suits arose during the first two years; after that, costs were to be split.

Under the agreement, defendant was privileged to use Parev Schmaltz as it should "think fit for its use and benefit absolutely." This same privilege was restated in another part of the contract with a complete specification of what was included, such as labels, trademarks, good will, and so on. For its part, plaintiff agreed not to engage or aid in the manufacture or sale of any product "similar" to Parev Schmaltz or in any business incidental thereto during the life of the contract; moreover, it agreed to deliver the agreement of the three Prosers not to "engage or aid, either severally or collectively, directly or indirectly, in the manufacture, sale or distribution of any article that might be in competition with [defendant] in the sale, manufacture and distribution of Parev Schmaltz or of any similar product." Defendant promised after termination or expiration of the contract "not to engage in, directly or indirectly, in [sic] the manufacture, sale or distribution of the product Parev Schmaltz, or any product of a similar nature." Defendant was privileged to discard the name Parev Schmaltz, however, and any name which was substituted would always remain defendant's property.

It should be noted that the contract therefore contained at least three express negative covenants, none directly applicable to the case before the court, and that the one to be made by the Prosers as individuals is the more extensive in mode of expression at least.

Thereafter defendant immediately dropped the name Parev Schmaltz, adopted Nyafat in its stead, and commenced production. From the beginning, Nyafat was a success and during the fifteen-year period from 1924 to 1939, royalties of approximately $135,000 were paid over. In 1940, however, a disturbing factor entered the picture. Defendant began the distribution of Kea, a semisolid cooking oil made almost wholly from cottonseed oil. Although defendant does not manufacture Kea, it distributes it under its own label as a Kosher product to the same orthodox Jewish trade. Defendant, of course, has not paid any royalties to plaintiff on its sales of Kea. Plaintiff claims that, since the royalties on Nyafat are based on an absolute sum per ounce and since the price obtained by defendant has been falling, defendant has undertaken the sale of Kea to avoid its royalty obligation. Defendant, on the other hand, asserts that Crisco and Spry, widely selling cooking oils, were cutting into the Nyafat market. This was aggravated, defendant says, by a nationwide price war which occurred as soon as Spry went on the market. Consequently, it is urged, defendant had to obtain a new product "similar" to Spry and Crisco, and in the same price range.

In this action, plaintiff seeks an injunction against any further sales of Kea by defendant. The theory is that we should imply a negative covenant on the part of defendant not to compete with its own Nyafat, or in any other way to interfere with the sales of Nyafat. Defendant's argument is that no covenant should be implied beyond what it calls conduct on its part of a "tortious" nature, or, in the alternative, that any covenant would forbid only the sale of products of a "similar nature." Kea, it says, is not similar. One is made from coconut oil, one from cottonseed oil. One is yellow, one is white; one is neutral in flavor, the other has an onion flavor. Other, somewhat esoteric, differences can be spelled out.

Although the District Court placed considerable reliance on this argument, we do not think that this should be finally conclusive. If any covenant is to be implied, it must be one which reaches the core of this dispute, which is the claim that a directly competitive product is produced by defendant. Whatever reasons there are for imposing on defendant such a strict obligation are hardly vitiated by the difference in composition of the two products. They are used for exactly the same purpose—shortening; if any covenant is to be implied, it would be hollow unless it took note of this fact. Thus, it seems rather unlikely that had plaintiff undertaken the manufacture of Kea today a court would have been content to say, as against a suit by the defendant, that the products were not similar under plaintiff's express covenant not to distribute a similar shortening.

Should, therefore, a covenant be implied under all the present circumstances? When we turn to the precedents we are met at once with the confusion of statement whether a covenant can be implied only if it was clearly "intended" by the parties, or whether such a covenant can rest on principles of equity. Expressions can be found which insist on "intention," . . . which seem to combine both a requirement of "intention" and of "equity and justice," . . . and which by-pass "intention" and rely solely on equity. . . . One may perhaps conclude that in large measure this confusion arises out of the reluctance of courts to admit that they were to a considerable extent "remaking" a contract in situations where it seemed necessary and appropriate so to do. "Intention of the parties" is a good formula by which to square doctrine with result. That this is true has long been an open secret. See 3 Williston on Contracts, Rev.Ed.1936, § 825; Holmes, The Path of the Law, 10 Harv.L.Rev. 457, 466; Fuller, Legal Fictions, 25 Ill.L.Rev. 363, 369; Chafee, The Disorderly Conduct of Words, 41 Col.L.Rev. 381, 398.[1] Of course, where intent, though obscure, is nevertheless discernible, it must be followed; but a certain sophistication must be recognized—if we are to approach the matter frankly—where we are dealing with changed circumstances, fifteen years later, with respect to a contract which does not touch this exact point and which has at most only points of departure for more or less pressing analogies.

Here defendant has a strong point in stressing the various extensive grants to it of the contract, as well as the express negative covenants which do not touch the present case. Undoubtedly extensive freedom of action was intended it. And yet that could not have been wholly unlimited, as indeed, defendant properly concedes when it admits that at least tortious competition or destruction of the Nyafat market was not open to it. And we must consider that in the period of time since the making of the contract there have been various developments which present a situation not clearly, if at all, within the contemplation of the parties at the time. Here a status exists upon which each party should be entitled to rely. What we should seek is therefore that which will most nearly preserve the status created and developed by the parties.

If we thus emphasize the situation existing today, two facts stand out. Plaintiff must clearly rely on defendant for any future benefit to be derived from its original formula; and defendant, if it is to continue to remain in the vegetable oil market, must be able to prevent the inroads of outside products, such as Crisco and Spry. So far as the plaintiff is concerned, it has long since lost its hold on its own formula. Nyafat is known to the public as a Rokeach product. Even were the defendant to release the formula, plaintiff would have some difficulty. This is not the controlling factor, for if it were, defendant might very well terminate the contract. Instead, the sales of Nyafat continue. And yet if no covenant is found, defendant to some extent can let Nyafat slip in sales, while Kea is boosted. In other words, if the defendant does not terminate the contract, it can keep Nyafat under its control until Kea is successfully built up, and then it can safely forget Nyafat. The advantage is all to defendant. But a court of

---

1. Cf. Chafee, loc. cit.: "My first suggestion is, that we should firmly resolve never to speak of the intention of a testator or other writer on a given point except after we have carefully convinced ourselves that that point was actually in his mind when he wrote the words in question. For example, we will never say 'He intended this result' when we merely think that if he had foreseen the present contingency (which he didn't) then he would have intended this result. That consideration may be helpful, but it is not his intention."

equity should grant some protection to a person who parts with his formula for exploitation. Thus, a court would hardly have permitted the defendant from the inception of this contract to lock up the plaintiff's formula in a vault and freely market Kea. There is no reason to do so now.

But defendant has an equally justifiable complaint to make. Kea, it asserts, is marketed only to compete with other products; and no attempt is made to injure Nyafat's market. Certainly we cannot say that defendant must market Nyafat, come what may, down to the sale of a mere can a year, while the vegetable oil business goes to outsiders. That would as violently alter the status of the parties as would a decree of complete freedom to defendant. It is thus clear that a strict injunction against any marketing of Kea is unjustified. Yet a complete denial of relief to the plaintiff under any circumstances would not be fair either.

As we have previously suggested, defendant indirectly acknowledges the need for a middle ground when it argues that cases implying a negative covenant, . . . have as their rationale the requirement that the conduct enjoined be tortious. This, presumably, amounts to saying that so long as defendant acts in good faith in judging the extent to which Kea must be sold to meet the competition of Crisco and Spry, no cause of action lies. But this, it seems to us, is to state the rule too narrowly; a limited rule of good faith, valid so far as it goes, does not exhaust the possibilities. See Harper Bros. v. Klaw, D.C.S.D.N.Y., 232 F. 609. The really equitable solution is to permit defendant to sell Kea so long as it does not invade Nyafat's market if that point is susceptible of proof, as we think it is. Thus, assuming that defendant is correct in its assertions, Kea sells only to people who no longer buy Nyafat.[2] Hence, all the plaintiff is entitled to is the market Nyafat has created and will retain, regardless of outside competition.

An injunction to reach such a conclusion would be so vague as to be meaningless under present circumstances. Its practical effect would be to restrain defendant from any sales of Kea—which we have held to be unfair. Only by inserting "good faith" in the restraining order could defendant be protected; and this would be equivalent to the rule we have found too narrow. It follows, then, that on the present record plaintiff cannot obtain an injunction. A broad one would be unfair to defendant; a narrow one would be an empty gesture.

But plaintiff could not be denied the opportunity to show a loss of the Nyafat market as we have thus defined it. Plaintiff may be

2. It is only fair to state that plaintiff produced two housewives who said they had discontinued the use of Nyafat because Kea was cheaper. These witnesses did not say, however, that they would not have switched to Spry or Crisco.

protected if it can be determined what sales of Kea represent loss to outside products, what sales represent loss to Nyafat. Expert appraisal of market conditions would, it seems to us, answer this.[3] If loss were established, the measure of damages would be the amount of royalties on the displaced jars of Nyafat. On this record, the evidence is too fragmentary to be conclusive. Since an injunction was sought, the action was brought too soon to reflect the nature of the competition among the various cooking oils. If the plaintiff has further evidence of the inroads of Kea, it should be entitled to present it, either hereinafter in this case or in a later action.

Judgment affirmed, with costs to defendant and with leave to plaintiff either to move to reopen the action, or to bring a subsequent action, for relief not inconsistent with this opinion.

NOTES

(1) *Meaning of "Good Faith."* Judge Clark rejects the contention "that so long as defendant acts in good faith in judging the extent to which Kea must be sold to meet the competition of Crisco and Spry, no cause of action lies." What did he mean by "good faith"? Would the provisions of the Uniform Commercial Code have met his objections in this respect? Compare UCC 1–201(19) with 2–103(1)(b).

(2) *Technological Breakthroughs.* Troublesome problems are posed when an unanticipated technological breakthrough drastically changes the situation, in which the contracting parties find themselves, from that which they had expected. The development of "talkie" moving pictures in the 1920's gave rise to some particularly interesting cases, of which a leading example is Kirke La Shelle Co. v. Paul Armstrong Co., 263 N.Y. 79, 188 N.E. 163 (1933).

In 1921, when "talkies" were unknown commercially, the Paul Armstrong Co., in settlement of a lawsuit, agreed to pay to Kirke La Shelle Co. half of the receipts from revivals of Armstrong's plays "Alias Jimmy Valentine" and "Salomy Jane." The contract provided that "all contracts . . . affecting the title to the dramatic rights (exclusive of motion picture rights) to the above two plays" would be subject to the approval of the Kirk La Shelle Co. In 1928, the Paul Armstrong Co. sold the exclusive "talkie" rights to "Salomy Jane" to Metro-Goldwyn Mayer, receiving $13,500, and the Kirke La Shelle Co. claimed the right to half of that sum, and prevailed in the New York Court of Appeals. The court concluded that since talkies were unknown when the contract was made, they were not "within the contemplation of the parties either as a subject for the transfer of an interest . . . or as included in the motion picture rights specifically excepted." Nevertheless, "[b]y entering into the contract and

---

3. Assume, for example, that sales of Nyafat dropped steadily from 1933 to 1936, then from 1936 to 1939 Nyafat held its own. And assume Kea was introduced in 1939. If from 1939 on, Nyafat still held its own, Kea was not injuring Nyafat. On the other hand, if Nyafat again declined while Kea went up, Kea would be invading Nyafat's own irreducible minimum market. To be sure, this is an oversimplified example, and many extraneous factors affecting marketing would have to be eliminated. This would be the task of expert witnesses.

accepting and retaining the consideration therefor, [Kirke La Shelle] assumed a fiduciary relationship which had its origin in the contract and which imposed on them the duty of utmost good faith. . . . From the inclusion in the contract of the express agreement . . . not to enter into any contract affecting the title to the dramatic rights . . . without . . . approval, may be implied the obligation to hold the profits resulting from such breach for the benefit of the parties to the agreement in accordance with their rights under the contract." Why did Judge Clark limit Parev to damages based on the sales of Kea that "represent loss to Nyafat"? Why should not Parev have damages based on *all* the sales of Kea?

Further problems posed by technological breakthroughs will be considered in connection with impossibility and frustration in Chapter 8.

IMPLIED WARRANTIES

Perhaps the most noted of the many terms that courts have supplied for omitted cases are the warranties implied in contracts for the sale of goods. See UCC 2–314, 2–315 and p. 310 supra. They have, however, been creatures of statute for so long that it is easy to lose sight of their judicial origins. Of greater current interest is the question of the extent to which similar implied warranties will be imposed in other fields. The Supreme Court of New Jersey has provided some striking examples. In just over five years, it handed down leading decisions imposing implied warranties, by analogy to those in the sale of goods, in the lease of personal property (a truck), the sale of real property (a development house), the lease of real property (both commercial and residential), and the furnishing of goods in connection with a contract for services (a permanent wave).[a] For an interesting opinion, relying on such cases, holding that "a warranty of habitability, measured by the standards set out in the Housing Regulations for the District of Columbia, [is] implied by operation of law into leases of urban dwelling units covered by those Regulations," see Javins v. First National Realty Corp., 428 F. 2d 1071 (D.C.Cir.1970). See also Farnsworth, Implied Warranties of Quality in Non-Sales Cases, 57 Colum.L.Rev. 653 (1957).

DICKEY v. PHILADELPHIA MINIT-MAN CORP., 377 Pa. 49, 105 A.2d 580 (1954). [In 1947 Dickey leased to Minit-Man a vacant tract of land for ten years with option to the lessee of an additional ten-year term. The lease provided that the premises were to be

---

a. Cintrone v. Hertz Truck Leasing & Rental Service, 45 N.J. 434, 212 A.2d 769 (1965) (lease of truck); Schipper v. Levitt & Sons, 44 N.J. 70, 207 A.2d 314 (1965) (sale of development house); Reste Realty Corp. v. Cooper, 53 N.J. 444, 251 A.2d 268 (1969) (lease of offices); Marini v. Ireland, 56 N.J. 130, 265 A.2d 526 (1970) (lease of apartment); Newmark v. Gimbel's Inc., 54 N.J. 585, 258 A.2d 697 (1969) (furnishing of permanent wave solution).

occupied by the lessee "in the business of washing and cleaning automobiles within the scope of the business of the Philadelphia Minit-Man Corporation, . . . and for no other purpose." As rent Minit-Man agreed to pay 12½% on the amount of annual gross sales but a minimum of $1,800 per year; the term "gross sales" was to include "the sales price of all merchandise of every sort whatsoever sold, including all charges for all services performed by the Lessee in the course of the business aforesaid." Minit-Man agreed "to erect and complete all necessary buildings on the said demised premises in order to begin and carry on the business aforesaid"; all buildings and fixtures erected by Minit-Man were to become the property of Dickey as and when the lease should expire for any reason whatever. On default in the observance or performance of any of the conditions or agreements Dickey was to have the right to terminate the lease and reenter the premises. Minit-Man erected the buildings, installed the equipment, and washed and cleaned cars until August, 1952, when it discontinued that feature of its business except as incidental to simonizing and polishing. But it continued to pay at least the minimum rental. In September, 1953, Dickey filed an action in ejectment seeking recovery of possession on the ground that Minit-Man had defaulted by discontinuing the business specified in the lease. From dismissal of his action, plaintiff appeals.]

HORACE STERN, CHIEF JUSTICE. . . . The question involved is whether there was any implied obligation on the part of the lessee to continue to conduct the business on the premises of washing and cleaning cars if its failure to do so resulted in a diminution of rental payable to the lessor.

Generally speaking, a provision in a lease that the premises are to be used only for a certain prescribed purpose imports no obligation on the part of the lessee to use or continue to use the premises for that purpose; such a provision is a covenant against a noncomplying use, not a covenant to use. Plaintiff urges, however, that in a lease such as that here involved, in which the amount of rental to be paid is based upon the lessee's gross sales, there arises an implied obligation on his part to continue the business on the premises to the fullest extent reasonably possible. Defendant, on the other hand, contends that, where such an obligation is intended, it must be expressly inserted in the lease, and that the raising of an implied covenant is never justified except where obviously necessary to effectuate the intention of the parties and so clearly within their contemplation that they deemed it unnecessary to express it, and that this is especially true where a substantial minimum rental is provided the obvious purpose of which is to protect the lessor from any unfavorable circumstances that might subsequently arise whether caused by voluntary conduct of the lessee or by events beyond his control. . . .

If an implied covenant, as claimed by plaintiff, should be held to arise in such cases what would be the extent of the restriction thereby imposed upon the lessee? Would it extend to each and every act on his part that might serve to reduce the extent of his business and thereby the percentage rental based thereon? Would it forbid him, for example, if operating a retail store, from keeping it open for a fewer number of hours each day than formerly? Would it forbid him from dismissing salesmen whereby his business might be reduced in volume? Would it forbid him from discontinuing any department of his business even though he found it to be operating at a loss? It would obviously be quite unreasonable and wholly undesirable to imply an obligation that would necessarily be vague, uncertain and generally impracticable. . . . Defendant has not moved any part of its business to another location nor deliberately sought to decrease the percentage of rent payable in order to induce plaintiff to declare a termination of the lease; on the contrary, it is seeking to maintain the lease. Nor is there anything in the present case to indicate that defendant's action in discontinuing the washing and cleaning of cars except as incidental to simonizing and polishing was taken other than in good faith and in the exercise of legitimate business judgment. In our opinion it was not forbidden by any implied obligation in the lease.

. . .

[Affirmed.]

MUSMANNO, JUSTICE (dissenting). . . . In the most unambiguous language that one could desire, the lease-contract here states that the premises are: "to be used and occupied by said Lessee in the business of *washing and cleaning automobiles . . . and for no other purpose*". The majority opinion makes no attempt to explain the all-exclusive finality of the phrase *for no other purpose*. Instead, it discusses hypothetical situations. . . . There is nothing in the contract about a retail store; the agreement is empty of any reference to the dismissing of salesmen; the lease is silent on any subject referring to discontinuance of a department of business. The lease, however, is saturated with provisions and conditions to the effect that the lessee may not use the premises except for the purpose of washing and cleaning automobiles. But the majority avoids discussing the washing and cleaning of automobiles. . . .

The lower Court made the following observation in its opinion: "We are told the lease before us was drawn by plaintiff's attorney; it would have been a simple matter for him to have inserted in the lease, as he drew it, a clause requiring full use of defendant's operation and a forfeiture in the event of his failure." There is no doubt that if the drawer of the contract could have anticipated that the meaning of simple English could be so beclouded in its reading, he might have added the suggested clause and perhaps even illustrated it with pictures, but I doubt that even *that* could have made it clearer that the lessee agreed, promised, covenanted and obligated himself to use the demised premises for cleaning and washing automobiles.

The majority opinion says that there is nothing "in the present case to indicate that defendant's action in discontinuing the washing and cleaning of cars except as incidental to simonizing and polishing was taken other than in good faith and in the exercise of legitimate business judgment." The record is absolutely devoid of any factual foundation upon which to erect a superstructure of such laudation. Furthermore, the defendant corporation has no right in the law to use business judgment which will work an advantage to itself at the expense and loss of the other party to the agreement. The *plaintiff* also used what he considered was "legitimate business judgment" when he offered to lease his property to the defendant on the basis that the defendant would use the premises for the business of washing and cleaning automobiles. Even the name of the defendant corporation is one identified throughout the area with the cleaning and washing of automobiles.

The lower Court says that the phrase "cleaning and washing automobiles" is descriptive, rather than directive. The paragraph in the lease describing the premises is certainly descriptive. Is it any less effective on that account? The manner in which the rent is to be paid is descriptive. Does that mean it can be ignored?

I dissent in this case not only on legal principles but in defense of the integrity of the English language. . . . I can only conclude that cleaning and washing automobiles means the cleaning and washing of automobiles.

NOTES

(1) *Meaning of "Good Faith" (Reprise).* Chief Justice Stern pointed out that there was no indication that the lessee had acted "other than in good faith and in the exercise of legitimate business judgment." What did he mean by "good faith"? How could Dickey have shown "bad faith"? What result if Minit-Man *had* moved part of its business to another location?

(2) *Percentage Leases.* A percentage lease, like that in the principal case, is an example of flexible pricing (see p. 87 supra) that is especially favored among retailers, particularly in areas under development where success is uncertain. Although a wide variety of formulas is possible, the most common is based, for obvious reasons of accounting convenience, on gross receipts. Under such a lease, it is in the lessor's interest that the lessee maximize his gross receipts, while it is in the lessee's own interest that he maximize his net profit. When these goals become markedly inconsistent, as may happen when the profit margin dwindles, trouble is the likely result.

In deciding whether there is "any implied obligation on the part of the lessee to continue to conduct the business on the premises," many courts have, like that in the principal case, taken account of whether "a substantial minimum rental is provided." Why should this be influential? How can a court determine whether a minimum rental is "substantial" or not? Was it significant that Minit-Man was to build the necessary buildings? Might the result have been different if the lease had required Dickey to build the buildings? The opinion does not disclose the extent, if any, by which the rental during the first five years of operation exceeded the minimum. Would it be interesting to know? To what extent could the parties have avoided the dispute by careful drafting? On percentage leases generally, see Notes, 51 Minn.L.Rev. 1139 (1967); 60 Nw.U.L.Rev. 677 (1965).

(3) *The Case of the Tailored Woman's Furs.* The Tailored Woman, a retail store, had a percentage lease on the lower floors of a Fifth Avenue building. Later it acquired from the same landlord a fixed rental lease on the fifth floor, where it opened a custom-made dress department. When this venture failed, it moved its fur department from the second to the fifth floor. The landlord sued for additional rental based on a percentage of sales of furs on the fifth floor. From an adverse judgment, the landlord appealed. *Held:* Affirmed. "In deciding this case as we do, we are not moving away from the good old rule that there is in every contract an implied covenant of fair dealing. Kirke La Shelle Co. v. Paul Armstrong Co. [Note 2, p. 614 supra]. Defendant, as we see it, was merely exercising its rights." There was no "unconscionable diversion of business from percentage-lease premises to others." Two judges dissented. "[I]n every contract there is an implied covenant that neither party shall do anything which shall have the effect of injuring or destroying the right of the other party to receive the fruits of the contract." Mutual Life Ins. Co. v. Tailored Woman, 309 N.Y. 248, 128 N.E.2d 401 (1955).

---

407 E. 61ST GARAGE v. SAVOY FIFTH AVENUE CORP.

Court of Appeals of New York, 1968.
23 N.Y.2d 275, 244 N.E.2d 37.

BREITEL, JUDGE. Plaintiff 407 East 61st Garage, Inc., appeals from an order of the Appellate Division unanimously affirming, without opinion, an order of the Supreme Court, New York County. The Supreme Court, in an opinion, denied plaintiff's motion for an order striking defendant's answer, granting summary judgment, and directing an assessment of damages, and instead granted the cross motion of defendant Savoy Fifth Avenue Corporation for summary judgment.

Plaintiff garage seeks damages for defendant Savoy's alleged breach, by termination, of a contract between the parties, resulting from Savoy's discontinuance of its operation of the Savoy Hilton Hotel. Under a written agreement the garage had undertaken to furnish garage services for a period of five years to guests of the Savoy Hilton and to pay Savoy 10% of its gross transient storage charges to the hotel guests. Savoy agreed to use all reasonable efforts to provide the garage with exclusive opportunity for storage of the motor vehicles of the hotel guests.

The issue is whether the closing of the hotel prior to the expiration of the contract period, due to the asserted financial inability of

Savoy to remain in the hotel business, subjects it to continued liability under the contract. The Supreme Court, characterizing the agreement as a requirements contract, held that, absent an express contract provision requiring Savoy to remain in the hotel business, and absent allegations of bad faith, Savoy is not liable for anticipatory breach of contract.

It is concluded that, by ceasing operation of its hotel, Savoy is not excused, as a matter of law, from obligations under its agreement with the garage, and that there is, at least, an issue of fact as to implied conditions in the agreement.

Pursuant to the written agreement, dated October 1, 1963, plaintiff garage undertook to furnish adequate garage services and facilities to any guests of the Savoy Hilton Hotel who requested them. The garage was fully responsible for the billing and collection of charges for its services. Any damage to an automobile between its delivery to a representative of the garage and its return was the responsibility of the garage. The garage also agreed to have adequate supplies on hand, to obtain all necessary insurance and permits, to conform to applicable regulations of the Savoy, and to have its employees act in such a manner as to "promote the best interests" of Savoy. Savoy on its part agreed "to use all reasonable efforts to enable [the garage] to have, throughout the term of this agreement, the exclusive right and privilege of storing the motor vehicles of [the hotel's] guests, tenants and patrons". Savoy was not responsible, however, for any charges incurred by its guests for services rendered by the garage. The garage was allowed to maintain, at its own expense, a direct telephone line between the hotel and the garage. In exchange, the garage agreed to pay to Savoy 10% of the transient storage charges incurred by hotel guests. The term of the agreement was from October 1, 1963 to September 30, 1968.

In late June, 1965, due to substantial financial losses, Savoy ceased operating the hotel. The hotel building was demolished and an office building erected on its site. The garage asserts that a one-half interest in the property was sold to General Motors Corporation, and that the office building is owned jointly by General Motors and Savoy. Savoy apparently claims that it sold 50% of its capital stock to General Motors.

The agreement does not explicitly obligate Savoy to remain in the hotel business during the contract term or, put another way, to fulfill its obligations for the term even if it should wish to cease operation of a hotel. On the other hand, the only provision concerning termination allows Savoy to terminate the contract should the garage default in the performance of any condition, including the provision of adequate service, and then fail to cure the default within 30 days after receiving written notice. It was provided further that all duties of each of the parties were to be performed "during the term" of the contract.

The Supreme Court, in granting defendant Savoy's cross motion for summary judgment, relied on Du Boff v. Matam Corp., 272 App. Div. 502, 71 N.Y.S.2d 134, which held that a party to a "requirements" contract may cease doing business in good faith without incurring liability for breach of contract. However, the agreement between the garage and Savoy is not a "requirements" contract, but is akin to the grant of a license or franchise by Savoy to the garage. Thus, services were to be rendered by the garage not to Savoy but to third parties, that is, the guests of the hotel. Savoy did not undertake to compensate the garage, but was instead to be compensated by the garage for the exclusive opportunities granted. The garage benefited by gaining a preferred position in obtaining the hotel guests as customers for its services. The hotel benefited by receiving a guarantee that its guests would be able to obtain adequate garage services when and if they desired them, thus making their stay at the hotel more convenient and desirable.

Categorization of the agreement, whether as a "requirements" contract, a "license" or a "franchise", in order to determine the obligations of the parties, is only partially helpful. Under the "requirements" contract analysis used by the Supreme Court, it would seem that, absent an allegation of bad faith, there was no cause of action stated for breach of contract (see, e. g., Du Boff v. Matam Corp., supra; but see, contra, Wells v. Alexandre, 130 N.Y. 642, 645–646, 29 N.E. 142, 143, 15 L.R.A. 218). Analogically, in the context of agreements for the use of space, if the contract is considered a license or concession, the general rule is that revocation of a license granted for a stipulated term may be a breach of contract and may result in the imposition of liability for damages (Dickinson v. Hart, 142 N.Y. 183, 187, 36 N.E. 801, 802; 17 N.Y.Jur., Easements and Licenses, §§ 213, 217, 221; cf. Melodies, Inc. v. Mirabile, 7 A.D.2d 783, 179 N.Y.S.2d 991, modfg. 4 Misc.2d 1062, 163 N.Y.S.2d 131; Schusterman v. C & F Caterers, 192 Misc. 564, 567, 77 N.Y.S.2d 718, 722). Thus, if the garage had been granted a license to operate its enterprise on Savoy's premises, liability might persist after sale of the building.

Additionally, if the contract is construed as one granting an exclusive agency for the rendition of services, then again, Savoy, by ceasing operation of the business to which the services were incident, may be liable for breach of contract (Wilson Sullivan Co. v. International Paper Makers Realty Corp., 307 N.Y. 20, 25, 119 N.E.2d 573, 574; Hudak v. Hornell Ind., 304 N.Y. 207, 213–214, 106 N.E.2d 609, 611–612; but see Wolf Studebaker v. Studebaker-Packard Corp., 50 Misc.2d 226, 229–230, 270 N.Y.S.2d 158, 162–163, affd. 26 A.D.2d 992, 276 N.Y.S.2d 839 [involving an automobile sales agency for an indefinite period and the relocation of the manufacturing plant]).

In ultimate analysis, however, an attempt to categorize or "pigeonhole" the contract is a circuitous way of answering what is basically a simple question of contract interpretation or construction.

The real issue in this case is not what kind of contractual relationship is involved, but whether this agreement imports an implication that Savoy was obligated to remain in the hotel business, or, better, had undertaken indefeasible obligations for the full term.

Under familiar rules a promise that a party will continue to remain in business may be implied in fact as part of an agreement for the rendition of services to a business (Wigand v. Bachmann-Bechtel Brewing Co., 222 N.Y. 272, 277–280, 118 N.E. 618, 620; Horton v. Hall & Clark Mfg. Co., 94 App.Div. 404, 407, 88 N.Y.S. 73, 74; see Restatement, Contracts, § 314, esp. Illustrations 5 and 6; see, also, involving substantial changes of method in business operations, West, Weir & Bartel v. Mary Carter Paint Co., 25 A.D.2d 81, 86, 267 N.Y. S.2d 29, 34, app. dsmd. 19 N.Y.2d 812, 279 N.Y.S.2d 971, 226 N.E.2d 704; Carlton Illustrators v. American Locomotive Co., 168 App.Div. 289, 292, 153 N.Y.S. 1018, 1022).

Such a promise to remain in business will be implied particularly where the promisee has undertaken certain burdens or obligations in expectation of and reliance upon the promisor's continued activity (Wigand v. Bachmann-Bechtel Brewing Co., supra). Here, the garage may have undertaken certain additional continuing responsibilities, such as the obtaining of adequate insurance and perhaps even the signing of employment contracts and agreements for the purchase of supplies for the lifetime of the contract.

Savoy, based on inferences, contends that the garage was aware, prior to the signing of the agreement, that the hotel was in financial difficulty, and should be charged with acceptance of the likelihood that the hotel would close. Savoy, of course, was at least equally or better aware of this situation. The obvious solution would have been an express provision that the agreement would terminate upon specified notice to the garage or would terminate if the hotel should close. Yet, the only right of termination by Savoy expressed in the agreement was based upon default in performance by the garage. Certainly the inference by Savoy that the garage knew of the hotel's financial difficulties does not give rise, as a matter of law, to the conclusion that the contract implies a conditional termination, should the hotel cease operation. It could be just as easily concluded that such a provision was intentionally omitted and that otherwise the garage would not have entered into the agreement.

There is another inchoate issue raised by Savoy's argument. It emphasizes, as it well might, the incongruity of an enterprise, as large as a metropolitan hotel, being obligated to "continue in the hotel business" merely because of various relatively minor incidental service contracts, such as that involved here. The mere incongruity would not lessen Savoy's liability, but it does suggest that there may be a custom or usage in this industry to regard incidental service contracts for a period terminable on the hotel's going out of business. If there be such custom and usage, there is nothing in the record to show it. Upon a trial, of course, the hotel would be able to show such a custom and usage, or any other circumstances which would, subject to the parol evidence rule, establish the correct interpretation or understanding of the agreement as to its term. Certainly, the mere statement of a term in this kind of incidental service agreement is not so free from ambiguity as to preclude extrinsic evidence.

At the very least, therefore, an issue of fact is presented whether the agreement did import an implied promise by Savoy to fulfill its obligations for an entire five-year period.

Assuming such an implication, Savoy might, nevertheless, assert the hotel's financial situation as a legal excuse for its failure to continue operation of the hotel. It does point out that it was economically impossible (or rather extremely burdensome) for it to remain in the hotel business. Thus, it may be argued that the basic purpose of the contract, to insure that guests of the hotel would receive adequate garage services, was rendered impossible of performance, or, perhaps, was frustrated, when the hotel was no longer in a financial position to cater to guests. Phrased in these terms, the issue is sometimes regarded as a matter of excuse from performance, apart from the contract, rather than being treated as an implied condition for performance derived from the contractual arrangements between the parties.

Generally, however, the excuse of impossibility of performance is limited to the destruction of the means of performance by an act of God, *vis major,* or by law (International Paper Co. v. Rockefeller, 161 App.Div. 180, 184, 146 N.Y.S. 371, 374; 6 Williston, Contracts [Rev. ed.], § 1935; 10 N.Y.Jur., Contracts, § 357; Restatement, Contracts, § 457). Thus, where impossibility or difficulty of performance is occasioned only by financial difficulty or economic hardship, even to the extent of insolvency or bankruptcy, performance of a contract is not excused (Central Trust Co. of Illinois v. Chicago Auditorium, 240 U.S. 581, 36 S.Ct. 412, 60 L.Ed. 811; Cameron-Hawn Realty Co. v. City of Albany, 207 N.Y. 377, 380–381, 101 N.E. 162, 163, 164, 49 L. R.A.,N.S., 922; Updike v. Oakland Motor Car Co., 229 App.Div. 632, 635, 242 N.Y.S. 329, 331; Downey v. Shipston, 206 App.Div. 55, 58, 200 N.Y.S. 479, 480; International Paper Co. v. Rockefeller, 161 App.Div. 180, 185, 146 N.Y.S. 371, 375, supra; Stannard v. Robert H. Reid & Co., 114 App.Div. 135, 136, 99 N.Y.S. 567, 568; 6 Williston, Contracts [Rev. ed.], § 1963; see, generally, 10 N.Y.Jur., Contracts, §§ 356, 357, 359, 372; Ann.: Contract-Performance-Impossibility, 84 A.L.R.2d 12, esp. pp. 21–24, 28–29 and 52–55; Restatement, Contracts, §§ 454, 455, 457, 467). Notably, in this case, Savoy does not even assert that bankruptcy or insolvency was a likely consequence of continuing operation of the hotel. Further, in view of its admittedly contemporaneous financial difficulties, Savoy could and should have insisted that the agreement provide for the anticipated contingency of economic hardship (cf. Restatement, Contracts, § 457). In sum, performance by Savoy was at all times possible, although unprofitable, since the hotel could simply have remained in business, and the legal excuse of impossibility of performance would not be available to it.

Cases involving frustration of the purpose of the contract are inapposite. Here, the purpose of providing garage services to hotel guests was frustrated only when Savoy itself made a business decision to close the hotel, and did not result from unanticipated circumstances (see Frenchman & Sweet, Inc. v. Philco Discount Corp., 21 A. D.2d 180, 182, 249 N.Y.S.2d 611, 613; cf. Ewing Co. v. New York State Teachers' Retirement System, 14 A.D.2d 113, 115, 218 N.Y.S.2d 253, 255, affd. 11 N.Y.2d 749, 226 N.Y.S.2d 690, 181 N.E.2d 628; Marks Realty Co. v. Hotel Hermitage Co., 170 App.Div. 484, 156 N. Y.S. 179; 6 Williston, Contracts [Rev. ed.], §§ 1951, 1959; Restatement, Contracts, § 288). Moreover, rather than relying on a circumstance that was unanticipated, Savoy itself argues that its financial stringency was always known.

In short, the applicable rules do not permit a party to abrogate a contract, unilaterally, merely upon a showing that it would be financially disadvantageous to perform it; were the rules otherwise, they would place in jeopardy all commercial contracts. If, in fact, the agreement expresses or implies a promise that the hotel would remain liable for the contract term, that promise should be honored, regardless of financial hardship.

Concededly, it would not have made sense for Savoy to stay in the hotel business solely to avoid liability for breach of its contract with the garage. Such lack of business reason does not nullify the liability for damages, whatever effect it may have on a right to specific performance. However, if the patronage at the hotel had declined, proof of that situation, although perhaps not justifying termination of the garage's contract right, may have a significant bearing on the measure of damages sustained by the garage through loss of future profits (see, e. g., West, Weir & Bartel v. Mary Carter Paint Co., 25 A.D.2d 81, esp. 87–89, 267 N.Y.S.2d 29, 35–37, supra; see, also, Dickinson v. Hart, 142 N.Y. 183, 187–188, 36 N.E. 801, 802–803, supra).

Accordingly, the order should be modified, with costs, by denying defendant's cross motion for summary judgment and, as so modified, affirmed.

NOTES

(1) *Rationale.* Could Savoy have escaped liability by showing that it discontinued operation of the Savoy Hilton *in good faith?* The court suggests that different rules have evolved to deal with "requirements" contracts, contracts granting a "license" or "franchise," and contracts granting an "exclusive agency." How do the rules appear to differ? How can those differences be explained? The topics of impossibility and frustration, discussed at the end of the opinion, are explored in Chapter 8.

(2) *Expressio Unius.* The maxim *expressio unius est exclusio alterius* is a staple in dealing with contracts as well as statutes. How damaging to Savoy's position is the fact that it had expressly reserved a right to terminate on default of the garage?

In Bergum v. Weber, 136 Cal.App.2d 389, 288 P.2d 623 (1955), a seller of a business, including good will, expressly covenanted not to compete with the buyer for a year. After that time he went back into business and solicited his old customers. The court held that the express covenant did not exclude an implied obligation to act in good faith and not solicit these customers. "The implied covenant of good faith and the express restrictive covenant contained in the contract here do not deal with the same subject matter and are not inconsistent."

(3) *Contract Policies.* Look back at the quotation from Holmes at p. 604 supra. Can you formulate any of the policies that appear to have guided the courts in the preceding cases in determining whether to "imply a term in a contract"? See Macaulay, Justice Traynor and the Law of Contract, 13 Stan.L.Rev. 812, 813–17 (1961).

COLLECTIVE BARGAINING AGREEMENTS AND TREATIES

Problems similar to those just considered are encountered in the interpretation of other kinds of legal writings, such as wills. In the case of a will, however, there is only one testator, while in the case of a contract there are two parties. More interesting analogies can be found by turning to two types of agreements that are often considered to be distinct from "ordinary" contracts: collective bargaining agreements and treaties. Here are some comments on these analogies by two experts in the respective fields.

Speaking of collective bargaining agreements and contracts, Professor Archibald Cox explains that, in the case of the former, "neither the employer nor the employees collectively have the freedom to disagree which characterizes typical contracts between business firms and individuals. . . . The compulsion . . . partially explains the gaps and deliberate ambiguities in collective bargaining agreements which create distinctive problems of interpretation. The pressure to reach an agreement is so great that the parties are willing to contract although each knows that the other places a different meaning on the words and they share only the common intent to postpone the issue and take a gamble upon an arbitrator's ruling if decision is required. . . . These consequences of the practical compulsion to sign . . . mean that intepretation must assume a more creative role than in most commercial or property litigation." Professor Cox also stresses the "governmental nature of a collective bargaining agreement [which] results partly from the number of people affected and the diversity of their interests," as well as from the fact that, "since it also operates prospectively over a long period, a labor agreement must provide for countless unforeseeable contingencies. One consequence is that many provisions of the labor agreement must be expressed in general and flexible terms. . . . One simply cannot spell out every detail of life in an industrial establishment, or even of that portion which both management and labor agree is a matter of mutual concern. . . . The governmental nature of a collective bargaining agreement should have predominant influence in its interpretation. The generalities, the deliberate ambiguities, the gaps, the unforeseen contingencies, the need for a rule although the agreement is silent—all require a creativeness quite unlike the attitude of one construing a deed or a promissory note or a three-hundred page corporate trust indenture." Professor Cox goes on to urge that, as in the case of a statute, so too with a collective bargaining agreement, "the best guide to . . . meaning is its policy or purpose." Cox, The Legal Nature of Collective Bargaining Agreements, 57 Mich.L.Rev. 1, 3–26 (1958).[a] For more on collective bargaining agreements and contracts, see Summers, Collective Agreements and the Law of Contracts, 78 Yale L.J. 525 (1969); Wellington, Labor and the Legal Process, ch. 3 (1968). See also the discussion of "good faith" bargaining at p. 151 supra.

How different is the compulsion on management and labor from, say, that on landlord and tenant negotiating a renewal of a lease? Do any of the preceding cases in this chapter involve "gaps and deliberate ambiguities" that might be explained by such compulsion? Have you encountered in this course any agreements that partake of the "governmental nature" ascribed by Professor Cox to collective bargaining agreements?

Speaking of treaties and contracts, Professor Abram Chayes argues that "the analogy . . . is by no means perfect. . . . [C]ontract analogies lead treaty lawyers astray [not only] in the orientation to judicial remedies . . ., but in positing the discrete purchase and sale as the archtypal contract." The analogy afforded by the contract of sale is imperfect on two counts. First, "[t]he functional setting was the impersonal market relationships of perfect competition," a setting that is not analogous to that of agreements among nations. Second, the typical contract of sale is "a one-shot proposition," while a treaty is only one event in "an ongoing relationship." For this reason, Professor Chayes contends, "security of ex-

---

a. Professor Cox, however, also says: "The ease with which one can show that collective bargaining agreements have characteristics which preclude the application of some of the familiar principles of contracts . . . creates the danger that those who are knowledgeable about collective bargaining will demand that we discard all the precepts of contract law and create a new law of collective bargaining agreements. I have already expressed the view that courts would ignore the plea but surely it is unwise even if they would sustain it. Many legal rules have hardened into conceptual doctrines which lawyers invoke with little thought for the underlying reasons, but the doctrines themselves represent an accumulation of tested wisdom, they are bottomed upon notions of fairness and sound policy, and it would be a foolish waste to climb the ladder all over again just because the suggested principles were developed in other contexts and some of them are demonstrably inapposite." Id. at 14.

pectations becomes a decidedly secondary consideration. What matters is that the bargain reflect on a current basis the needs and bargaining power of the parties in respect of that relationship." Indeed, "the original intentions must often give way to what the situation requires at the point of breakdown or dispute over the content of the obligation. . . . [T]he international legal system, in practice, at least, if not in theory, takes account of [the relationship of the parties and the duration of their agreement] by providing for adjustment of treaty relations over time, depreciating, as a consequence, the original expectations of the parties." Professor Chayes goes on to discuss types of contracts that afford more apt analogies to treaties. Chayes, "Consent and Coercion: Reflections from International Law" (Sherril Lecture at Yale Law School, 1970).

To what extent is the contract analogy misleading "in the orientation to judicial remedies"? See the excerpt at pp. 185–89 supra, which suggests that businessmen pay little attention to those remedies. What types of contracts would you choose as more apt analogies if you were to write the rest of Professor Chayes' piece? Would Judge Clark, in deciding the Parev Products case, p. 609 supra, have found a more helpful analogy in the contract of sale or in the treaty?

NOTE

The Case of the Discharged Driver. Lucas Flour and Local 174 of the Teamsters union were parties to a collective bargaining agreement which provided: "The Employer reserves the right to discharge any man in his employ if his work is not satisfactory." There was one arbitration clause which provided that "any difference . . . between the employer and the employee . . . shall be submitted to arbitration," and that the arbitrators' decision "shall be final and binding." There was also a second arbitration clause which provided for arbitration of "any difference as to the true interpretation of this agreement." In contrast to the first arbitration clause, it contained a "no-strike" clause, which provided that "during such arbitration, there shall be no suspension of work." Welsh, an employee, was discharged for unsatisfactory work after he had run a new forklift truck off a loading platform onto some railroad tracks. In an attempt to force Lucas to rehire Welsh, the union struck Lucas for eight days, until Lucas obtained an injunction and the issue of Welsh's discharge was submitted to arbitration. The arbitrator upheld Lucas, with both parties agreeing that the dispute came within the first of the two arbitration clauses quoted above. In the meantime, Lucas had sued the union for damages caused by the strike. A judgment for Lucas was affirmed by the Supreme Court of Washington, and the Supreme Court of the United States granted certiorari. *Held:* Affirmed. Justice Stewart wrote that "a strike to settle a dispute which a collective bargaining agreement provides shall be settled exclusively and finally by compulsory arbitration constitutes a violation of the agreement. . . . To hold otherwise would obviously do violence to accepted principles of traditional contract law [and] would be completely at odds with the basic policy of national labor legislation to promote the arbitral process as a substitute for economic warfare." Local 174,

Teamsters, Chauffeurs, Warehousemen & Helpers of America v. Lucas Flour Co., 369 U.S. 95 (1962).

Justice Black dissented, calling attention to the difference in language in the two arbitration provisions. "[I]t seems to me plain that the parties to this contract, knowing how to write a provision binding a union not to strike, deliberately included a no-strike clause with regard to disputes over broad questions of contractual interpretation and deliberately excluded such a clause with regard to the essentially factual disputes arising out of the application of the contract in particular instances. . . . I had supposed . . . that the job of courts enforcing contracts was to give legal effect to what the contracting parties actually agreed to do, not to what courts think they ought to do. In any case, I have been unable to find any accepted principle of contract law—traditional or otherwise—that permits courts to change completely the nature of a contract by adding new promises that the parties themselves refused to make in order that the new court-made contract might better fit into whatever social, economic, or legal policies the courts believe to be so important that they should have been taken out of the realm of voluntary contract by the legislative body and furthered by compulsory legislation. . . . Both parties to collective bargaining discussions have much at stake as to whether there will be a no-strike clause in any resulting agreement. It is difficult to believe that the desire of employers to get such a promise and the desire of the union to avoid giving it are matters which are not constantly in the minds of those who negotiate these contracts. In such a setting, to hold—on the basis of no evidence whatever—that a union, without knowing it, impliedly surrendered the right to strike by virtue of 'traditional contract law' or anything else is to me just fiction."

In support of Justice Black, see Wellington, Freedom of Contract and the Collective Bargaining Agreement, 112 U.Pa.L.Rev. 467, 484–87 (1964). Which result would Professor Cox favor? Do "accepted principles of traditional contract law" compel a decision in favor of Lucas?

HAYDEN v. HOADLEY

Supreme Court of Vermont, 1920.
94 Vt. 345, 111 A. 343.

Action by Howard G. Hayden and another against Melvin A. Hoadley and another. Judgment for plaintiffs, and defendants except. Reversed and remanded.

POWERS, J. The parties to this action exchanged properties, and as a part of the arrangement the defendants gave the plaintiffs the following writing, which all signed:

"Memorandum of agreement made this 2d day of May, A.D.1919, by and between Melvin A. Hoadley and George A. Peck, both of Montpelier, in the county of Washington and state of Vermont, and Howard G. and Georgia V. Hayden, both of Worcester, in the county of Washington and state of Vermont, witnesseth: We, the said Hoadley and Peck, in consideration of the said Haydens having this day conveyed to us their farm in Worcester aforesaid, and whereas, we, the said Hoadley and Peck, have this day conveyed to the said Haydens certain land and premises situated on the westerly side of North street in the city of Montpelier, as and for additional consideration for such exchange of properties, bind ourselves and agree to make, without expense to said Haydens, the following repairs upon the premises conveyed to the said Haydens as aforesaid, viz.: The said Hoadley and Peck agree to straighten up and shingle the bar on said premises; to straighten up the house; repair and paint the roof, and paint the same back of said house; to repair the cellar wall; and to install a pump in said house."

It is for the noncompliance with this agreement that suit is brought.

At the trial, the defendants offered to show that at the time the writing was signed it was agreed that they should have until October 1, 1919, in which to make the repairs, that only $60 need be expended therefor, and that No. 2 shingles were to be used on the barn. These offers were excluded, and the defendants excepted. The rulings were correct. The case calls for the application of a rule so often and so recently reaffirmed by this court that we need take no time in its discussion. A written contract which contains no latent ambiguity cannot be qualified, controlled, contradicted, enlarged, or diminished by any contemporaneous or antecedent understanding or agreement; and oral testimony can no more be received to vary or contradict the legal intendment of such a contract than to vary or contradict its express terms. . . . The legal effect of the contract before us—it being silent as to the time of performance—was to require the repairs specified to be completed within a reasonable time. . . . This is a provision of the contract implied by the law, and that which is so implied is as binding as that which is expressed. In legal consequence, then, this contract is just what it would be if it was therein expressly provided that the repairs were to be made within a reasonable time. . . . To admit the testimony offered by the defendants to the effect that the parties agreed upon October 1 as the limit of the time given for the repairs would be to allow the plain legal effect of the written contract to be controlled by oral evidence. That is not permissible. . . . The contract before us is unequivocal and complete, and to say that parol evidence can be received to fix the time of performance, on the ground that the contract is incomplete, is wholly illogical and wrong, and so much of Dunnett & Slack v. Gibson, 78 Vt. 439, 63 A. 141, as is to that effect is overruled. From this it is not to be inferred that we question the proposition that an incomplete writing may be supplemented by parol, for this is a rule of unquestioned soundness.

The evidence under discussion was not offered on the ground that it was admissible on the question of what was a reasonable time under the circumstances, so we give that question no attention. For the same reason, the questions asked Hayden in cross-examination regarding the understanding about the amount of money to be paid out in the repairs, and the kind of a wall that should be made, were properly excluded. The record does not show when the conversations referred to in this connection took place, so in support of the ruling we assume that it was before the written contract was executed. . . .

Judgment reversed, and cause remanded [because of erroneous instructions as to alleged misrepresentations by plaintiff].

NOTES

(1) *Implied Terms and the Parol Evidence Rule.* Was the agreement integrated, in the court's view? Do you agree? Corbin disagrees with the decision in the case on the ground that if the parties have orally agreed to such matters as price, place of payment, and time of performance, but have omitted these items from the writing, it is probable that the parties did not intend the agreement to be integrated. Oral testimony, therefore, should be admissible to "rebut the usual presumptions and inferences." 3 Corbin, § 593.

If, before offering the evidence, the attorney for the defendant had stated that it was being offered to show what was a reasonable time for performance, would the evidence have been admissible? In support of an affirmative answer, see American Bridge Co. v. American District Steam Co., 107 Minn. 140, 119 N.W. 783 (1909). Should the admissibility of the evidence turn upon the inference it was to support?

(2) *The Code.* Under UCC 2–315, in order to show an implied warranty of fitness for a particular purpose, a buyer must show that the seller "has reason to know [the] particular purpose . . . and that the buyer is relying on the seller's skill and judgment." Could the buyer establish this by showing conversations that he had with the salesman prior to signing an integrated agreement? Note that under UCC 2–202, an integrated agreement excludes even "consistent additional terms." But is an implied warranty of fitness a "term"? See UCC 1–201(42). Compare the definition of "agreement" in UCC 1–201(3) with that of "contract" in UCC 1–201(11).

(3) *Problem.* Good Deal Super Markets leased premises in a shopping center to Renee Cleaners for ten years, under an integrated agreement which provided that "the Landlord or any person, firm or corporation, directly or indirectly controlled by Landlord will not lease to [a dry cleaning business] within 500' of the premises." Rickarjef, a wholly owned subsidiary of Good Deal, then sold an adjacent tract of land to an independent corporation, W.M.S. Co., which leased premises on it within 500' of Renee to an automatic dry cleaning business. Is Good Deal liable to Renee? See Renee Cleaners v. Good Deal Super Markets, 89 N.J.Super. 186, 214 A.2d 437 (1965).

Does this problem involve the interpretation of language or the deciding of an omitted case? Does it make any difference? What if one of the parties sought to introduce evidence of prior negotiations?

FISHER v. CONGREGATION B'NAI YITZHOK, 177 Pa.Super. 359, 110 A.2d 881 (1955). [Fisher, an orthodox Jewish rabbi-cantor, contracted in writing with an orthodox Jewish congregation to officiate as cantor at its synagogue during the High Holiday Season of 1950. At this time the congregation conducted its services in accordance with orthodox practices, including the separate seating of men and women. The contract, however, was silent as to the orthodox character of the congregation and its seating practices. Shortly thereafter, on the eve of moving into a new synagogue, the congregation determined to modify its practice of separate seating by setting aside the first four rows for men, the next four rows for women, and the remainder for mixed seating. When Fisher was informed of this, he notified the congregation that, as a rabbi of the orthodox faith, he would be unable to officiate during the coming season because to do so would be a violation of his beliefs. When the congregation refused to change its decision, he refused to officiate and sued for breach of contract. Three rabbis testified on his behalf that orthodox Judaism required the separation of the sexes in the synagogue and that an orthodox rabbi-cantor could not conscientiously officiate in a synagogue that violated this law. From judgment for the plaintiff, the defendant appealed.]

HIRT, JUDGE. . . . Although the contract is silent as to the nature of the defendant congregation, there is no ambiguity in the writing on that score and certainly nothing was omitted from its terms by fraud, accident, or mistake. The terms of the contract therefore could not be varied under the parol evidence rule. Bardwell v. Willis Co., 375 Pa. 503, 100 A.2d 102; Mathers v. Roxy Auto Co., 375 Pa. 640, 101 A.2d 680. Another principle controls the interpretation of this contract. . . . In determining the right of recovery in this case the question is to be determined under the rules of our civil law, and the ancient provision of the Hebrew law relating to separate seating is read into the contract only because implicit in the writing as to the basis—according to the evidence—upon which the parties dealt. Cf. Canovaro v. Brothers of Order of H. of St. Aug., 326 Pa. 76, 86, 191 A. 140. In our law the provision became a part of the written contract under a principle analogous to the rule applicable to the construction of contracts in the light of custom or immemorial and invariable usage. It has been said that: "When a custom or usage is once established, in absence of express provision to the contrary it is considered a part of a contract and binding on the parties though not mentioned therein, the presumption being that they knew of and contracted with reference to it". 1 Henry, Pa.Evid., 4th Ed., § 203. Cf. Restatement, Contracts, § 248(2) and § 249. In this case there was more than a presumption. From the findings of the trial judge supported by the evidence it is clear that the parties contracted on the common understanding that the defendant was an orthodox synagogue which observed the mandate of the Jewish law as to separate seating. That intention was implicit in this contract though not referred to in the writing, and therefore must be read into it. It was on this ground that the court entered judgment for plaintiff in this case.

Judgment affirmed.

NOTES

(1) *Usage and the Parol Evidence Rule.* The court concedes that the "terms of the contract . . . could not be varied under the parol evidence rule," and claims to be engaged only in "interpretation," although it produces no contract language to interpret. Contrast this reasoning with UCC 2–202, which makes it plain that usage of trade (as well as course of dealing and course of performance) may be used to show consistent additional terms to supplement even an integrated agreement.

(2) *Usage and Omitted Cases.* Look back at the Bard and Drennan cases, pp. 156, 159 supra. Could a general contractor use usage of trade to show that a subcontractor's bid, which was silent as to revocability, was irrevocable? What facts would be sufficient to establish such a usage? See Albert v. R. P. Farnsworth & Co., 176 F.2d 198 (5th Cir. 1949); cf. Industrial Electric-Seattle v. Bosko, 67 Wash.2d 783, 410 P.2d 10 (1966).

For a suggestion of the role that usages might play in consumer claims, see Carroll, Harpooning Whales . . ., 12 B.C.Ind. & Com.L.Rev. 139, 166 (1970).

(3) *The Case of the Cantor Who Couldn't.* Richard Tucker, the renouned opera singer and cantor, was engaged to conduct the 1964 Passover Seder at the Eden Roc Hotel in Miami Beach under a standard American Guild of Variety Artists form for the first Seder Service, with the typewritten provision: "If second Seder service to be held, same price as first night." He performed the first service but, although the second service had been advertised nationally and he had hired a choir and turned down other engagements, he was told by a waiter at the end of the first service and without further explanation that there would be no second service. He sued for breach of contract, and was denied recovery for the second night. He appealed. *Held:* Affirmed. The court quoted "the Passover Haggadah itself—'Wherein is this night different from all other nights?' For purposes of our legal analysis, this may be paraphrased to be: Wherein is a contract for the performance of a Passover Seder different from all other contracts? . . . We first consider whether a different result might have been reached had the controversy been resolved by construing the agreement in light of prevailing religious custom. Although Tucker testified that in the Orthodox Jewish religion two Sedarim are always held, the period of observance is, for us at least, a problematical one. Owing to the unsettled state of the Jewish calendar in olden times, Passover was celebrated for seven days in Palestine and eight days elsewhere. This meant that those outside of Palestine (now Israel) conducted two Sedarim, while those in Palestine conducted only one. The Reform Jews in America today have adopted the latter procedure and observe but one Seder. It appears that while Tucker may have been Orthodox in his observance, the Eden Rock had traditionally followed the Reform view and had only one Seder in each year prior to 1964. We cannot therefore treat the instant

agreement as different from any other agreement, and must look to the common, every day principles of law to resolve the dispute." The court decided that the trial court had not erred in concluding that there was no legally binding contract for the second Seder. Tucker v. Forty-Five Twenty-Five, 199 So.2d 522 (Fla.App.1967).

(4) *Problem.* Seller sues buyer for breach of a written contract, containing a merger clause, for the sale of a stated quantity of fertilizer over a three-year period. You are the trial judge. Rule on the admissibility of the following testimony for buyer.

"I have never heard of a contract of this type being enforced legally. It undoubtedly sounds ridiculous to people from other industries, but there are several very definite reasons why the fertilizer business is always operated under gentlemen's agreements. Weather conditions, farming practices, and government control programs change requirements from time to time. The contract is the buyer's best estimate of his anticipated requirements for a given period of time and is considered binding on him morally to the extent that he uses the tonnage. The custom, regardless of the contractual provisions, is that these contracts were not worth the cost of the paper they were printed on."

See Columbia Nitrogen Co. v. Royster Co., 451 F.2d 3 (4th Cir. 1971); see also the discussion of gentlemen's agreements at p. 60 supra.

SECTION 4. INTERPRETATION AND CONDITIONS

So far, this book has been largely concerned with *duties*. What follows deals with the process of interpretation in connection with *conditions*. It is designed as a continuation of our examination of that process and, more important, as an introduction to the concept of condition, which is essential to an understanding of the remaining chapters of the book.

We have already encountered conditions. See, e. g., Carlill v. Carbolic Smoke Ball Co., p. 109 supra, and Note following that case. The word "condition" refers to an event, assumed to be in some measure not certain to occur, by reference to which the undertaking of a contracting party is limited or qualified.[a] It is sometimes used in another sense, to refer to the term of the contract which has the effect of so limiting or qualifying an undertaking.

Our present interest is with the interpretation of language relating to conditions. Two sorts of problems arise. First, does the language make an event a condition? And second, if it does make an event a condition, what is the nature of that event? Which of these questions was involved in the following case?

---

a. If the event is fortuitous, i. e., not within the power of the parties, the promise is sometimes said to be "aleatory." See Restatement, § 291.

BEATTIE–FIRTH, INC. v. COLEBANK

Supreme Court of Appeals of West Virginia, 1958.
143 W.Va. 740, 105 S.E.2d 5, 74 A.L.R.2d 431.

DONLEY, JUDGE.   This is an action of assumpsit brought by
Beattie-Firth, Inc., against Harry G. Colebank and Ruth F. Colebank,
to recover damages for the alleged breach of a contract. The defendants refused to pay to the plaintiff a commission upon the sale of real
estate owned by the defendants, the contract for the sale of which was
procured through the plaintiff as broker. The circuit court sustained
the defendants' demurrer to the plaintiff's declaration, and, the plaintiff declining to amend it, entered an order dismissing the action.

The allegations of the declaration are to the effect that on July
7, 1956, the defendants owned certain real estate in the City of
Charleston, and engaged the plaintiff to find a purchaser for it at the
price of $29,500, and on that date the parties entered into a written
agreement, which provided as follows:

"Seller agrees to pay Broker a commission of 5 per cent of the
gross sale price of any sale or exchange of said property during the
life of this contract whether made by Broker or not, Seller further
agrees to pay the same Commission on any sale or exchange of said
property, made by seller or by any agent for seller other than another
member of the Charleston Board of Realtors, made within six
months after the termination hereof, directly or indirectly to any person with whom Broker had negotiations, or whose attention was
brought to said property by Broker. In the event Broker arrange a
sale thereof in accordance herewith *and said sale is not consummated
by reason of any default of Seller,* including Seller's failure or inability to make conveyance or convey good and marketable fee simple title, Seller agrees to pay Broker for his services a sum equal to such
commission had the sale been consummated   .   .   . " (Italics supplied.)

Pursuant to this agreement, the plaintiff procured one Carl D.
Anderson, as a purchaser, and on August 20, 1956, a contract for the
sale of the real estate was entered into between the defendants, as sellers, and Carl D. Anderson, as purchaser. Under the terms of this
contract Anderson agreed to pay $28,000 for the property, payable
$500 cash in hand, and the balance to be paid as follows: "   .   .   .
all cash at time of closing and upon delivery of proper deed. Purchaser will obtain a mortgage loan of $18,000 on subject property and
will pay $9,500 in cash at closing time."

Other provisions of the contract, which are not here material,
were followed by paragraphs (8) and (9), which provide that:

"(8) Seller and Purchaser recognize Beattie-Firth, Inc., as the
Broker who made this sale. *If this sale be consummated, or if it be
not consummated by reason of any default of Seller,* including Seller's

failure or inability to make conveyance or convey good and marketable title in accordance with the terms hereof, Seller agrees to pay a commission of five per cent (5%) of the gross sale price above set out to Broker as his commission on this sale. If Purchaser fails or refuses to perform this contract for any reason other than the failure or inability of Seller to make conveyance, or convey good and marketable title in accordance with the terms thereof, so much of any payments made by the Purchaser as equals said commission shall be retained as his own by the Broker as said commission, and the balance returned to the Purchaser; provided, however, that such retention and return of said payments by Broker shall in no way affect or impair the remedies of Seller at law or equity for any breach of this contract by Purchaser. (Italics supplied.)

"(9) Broker incurs no liability by reason of Seller's failure or refusal to sign this contract, or by reason of the failure or refusal of Seller or Purchaser to perform this contract. *Broker joins in the execution hereof to evidence his agreement to the provisions hereof affecting Broker's compensation.*" (Italics supplied.)

This contract was signed by the defendants, by the plaintiff, and by Carl D. Anderson.

Upon the execution of the contract, Anderson deposited with the plaintiff, as agent for the defendants, the sum of $500, which plaintiff deposited in its bank in a so-called "trust account", where the same still remains.

By mutual agreement of the parties the date for the closing of the purchase was extended to March 15, 1957, but upon that date Anderson informed the plaintiff and the defendants that he did not propose to purchase the property in compliance with his contract of August 20, 1956, as extended, because he had decided not to move to Charleston. The defendants acquiesced in this repudiation of the contract, and failed and refused to take any action to enforce it against Anderson.

The plaintiff now claims that it is entitled to recover the sum of $1,400, together with interest thereon, being five per cent of the contract price of $28,000.

Ordinarily, when a broker has fully performed his contract of agency to sell property, he cannot be deprived of his commission by the failure of his principal to enforce a valid contract against a solvent purchaser of the property, so as to bring about the contingency on which the broker's compensation was made to depend. Dillon v. Turkey Gap Coal & Coke Co., 89 W.Va. 395, 109 S.E. 334.

However, this general rule has no application where the express terms of the contract otherwise provide. Linton v. Johnson, 81 W.Va. 569, 94 S.E. 945; Hugill v. Weekley, 64 W.Va. 210, 61 S.E. 360, 15 L. R.A.,N.S., 1262.

There is no conflict between the provisions of the preliminary contract entered into by the plaintiff and the defendants, and those of the sale contract in which the plaintiff joined "to evidence his agreement to the provisions hereof affecting Broker's compensation," and, if there were, the latest expression of the intention of the parties controls.

It is therefore necessary to examine the terms of the contract in the present case to ascertain whether or not there is a condition precedent which must be performed before the broker is entitled to receive his compensation. Express conditions precedent have been known to the law for centuries. If one promises another to pay if a ship sailed with the next wind, the promisee must allege and prove that the ship went with the next wind. Constable v. Cloberie, (K.B. 1626) Palmer 397. If a promisor agrees to provide a cargo for a ship provided that she arrive by the twenty-fifth of June, the arrival of the ship by that date is a condition precedent. Shadforth v. Higgin (1813), 3 Camp. 385.[a] No particular form of words is necessary in order to create an express condition, and words such as "provided that", or "if", qualifying a promise, are perhaps the most commonly used expressions to indicate that the duty of the promisor is expressly conditional. 1 Restatement, Contracts, Section 258.

The provisions of paragraph (8) of the contract entered into between the three parties, hereinbefore quoted, plainly create such a condition. This is made apparent by a transposition of the words which makes their meaning quite clear. The substance of the contract is this: "Seller agrees to pay a commission of five per cent of the gross sale price above set out to broker as his commission on this sale, if this sale be consummated, or if it be not consummated by reason of any default of the seller . . ." It thus appears that the promise to pay the five per cent commission was expressly conditioned upon the occurrence of one of the two alternative events: (1) Consummation of the sale; or (2) non-consummation of the sale by reason of any default of the seller. Neither of these conditions has occurred, and the duty of the defendants to perform their promise did not, therefore, arise.

It is contended by the plaintiff that the defendants were under the duty to institute a suit against Anderson for specific performance of the contract in order to bring about the contingency upon the occurrence of which the commission was payable. We know of no authority in this jurisdiction which goes so far, and we would hesitate to enunciate a rule which would require a vendor whose promise is so

a. This was a case in which the defendant failed to provide a cargo of sugar and rum for the ship "Fanny" when she arrived in Jamaica on July 3. He had agreed to do so provided she arrived by June 25. Lord Ellenborough denied recovery: "If the freighter is liable, although the ship does not arrive till a week after the day agreed upon,—where is the line to be drawn?"

conditioned to engage in expensive and perhaps fruitless litigation in order that a broker might become entitled to a commission. A burden so onerous cannot be imposed by implication. The failure of a condition to occur, even though the condition is some performance by a party to the contract, is not a breach of contractual duty by him unless he has made an enforceable promise that the condition exists or shall occur; and whether he has done so is a question of interpretation. 1 Restatement, Contracts, Section 251. And, we think, it is clear in the present case that the defendants made no promise, express or implied, that the condition of consummation of the sale should occur. Especially is this true where, as here, the nature of the condition is such that it cannot be performed by the vendor alone. He cannot force the vendee to accept a deed in consummation of the contract of sale; nor, indeed, is he required to part with it until he receives the agreed consideration therefor. . . . In contracts such as that which we now have under examination, the words "consummation" or "sale be consummated" mean the delivery of a deed of conveyance from the vendor to the vendee. . . . Amies v. Wesnofske, 255 N.Y. 156, 174 N.E. 436, 73 A.L.R. 918; Annotation, 73 A.L.R. at page 930; 4 Williston on Contracts, Rev.Ed., 1030A, page 2878, footnote 4; "Special Conditions in Real Estate Brokerage Contracts", 32 Columbia Law Rev. 1194. In 31 Columbia Law Review 701–702, the authorities are collected and it is stated that:

"But the majority of jurisdictions impose upon the vendor no duty of compelling the purchaser to perform, and hence default by the purchaser, whether followed by mere non-action on the part of the vendor, or a release by him of the purchaser, defeats the broker's claim for commissions. . . . The intention of the parties in inserting a clause providing for payment of the balance of commissions 'on the closing of title' is probably to throw the risk of the purchaser's default on the broker. A contrary result would compel the vendor to undergo the delays and uncertainties of prolonged litigation in order to avoid the payment of commissions. This would defeat the very purpose of such allocation of risk."

Although what we have said disposes of the case, if any fortification of our views is necessary, it may be found in the further provisions of the contract between the parties in paragraph (8) of the contract, which provides, as above quoted, that if the purchaser fails or refuses to perform the contract for any reason other than the failure or inability of the seller to make conveyance or convey good and marketable title in accordance with the terms thereof, "so much of any payments made by the Purchaser as equals said commission shall be retained as his own by the Broker as said commission, and the balance returned to the Purchaser; . . . ."

There would seem to be no purpose in this provision, except to protect the broker upon the failure to consummate the sale because of the default of the purchaser; and it gives rise to a strong implication, at least, that in such event the broker's compensation is to be limited to the down payment or earnest money received by him from the purchaser. Such a position has been upheld by other Courts in construing similar, if not identical, contracts. Green v. Snodgrass, 79 Ariz. 319, 289 P.2d 191; Kline v. Johnson, 121 Cal.App.2d Supp. 851, 263 P.2d 494.

In any event, if it had been the intention of the parties that the defendants should pay the plaintiff the full commission, even though the failure to consummate the sale was solely because of the default of the purchaser, it would have been a simple matter to say so in plain language. If the broker failed to guard his interests, the court is not at liberty to rewrite the contract. As stated by Learned Hand, C. J., in Baird Co. v. Gimbel Bros., Inc., 2 Cir., 64 F.2d 344, 346 [p. 156 supra]: " . . . in commercial transactions it does not in the end promote justice to seek strained interpretations in aid of those who do not protect themselves."

The order of the Circuit Court of Kanawha County sustaining the demurrer to the declaration is affirmed.

Affirmed.

NOTES

(1) *Analysis.* Whose obligation was limited or qualified by the language in question? State the issue in terms of that language. What would have been the result if the Colebanks had sued Anderson and recovered damages from him? (Would the Colebanks' damages include Beattie-Firth's commission?)

The court quotes a law review note which analyzes the broker's situation in terms of the allocation of "the risk of the purchaser's default." Is it helpful to think in terms of the allocation of risk where conditions are involved?

(2) *Brokerage Contracts.* In Ellsworth Dobbs v. Johnson, 50 N.J. 528, 236 A.2d 843 (1967), Justice Francis addressed himself to the broker's situation where the buyer was financially unable to perform a signed contract of sale. Although that contract provided that a broker's commission was "to be paid in consideration of services rendered in consummating this sale," the court held that the trial court had erred in allowing recovery to the broker against the seller. Justice Francis admitted that earlier New Jersey cases had laid down the rule that, absent a provision to the contrary, "if the owner accepted the purchaser brought by the broker and executed a contract to sell to him, that ended the matter as far as the broker's right to commission was concerned." But the court thought that there was "no doubt that ordinarily when an owner of property lists it with a broker for sale, his expectation is that the money for the payment of commission will come out of the proceeds of the sale." Therefore, "public policy requires the courts to read into every brokerage agreement or contract of sale a requirement that barring default by the seller, commissions shall not be deemed earned against him unless the contract of sale is performed." (The court then discussed the unconscionability of a contrary agreement. See Note

2, p. 344 supra.)   But the broker had also had judgment against the buyer in the trial court, on a jury finding that the buyer had "impliedly agreed" with the broker that if the broker found property satisfactory for residential development purposes, and a contract for that property was entered into, the buyer would perform that contract and enable the broker to earn his commission.   The court sent the case back for retrial on the broker's claim against the buyer.   "[O]nce the broker finds a prospective vendee, he becomes an agent of both parties" and the buyer becomes "subject to an implied obligation to [the broker] to complete the purchase, and upon default in completion he [becomes] liable to pay the commission which [the broker] was thereby deprived of."   It was for the jury to determine whether this obligation of the buyer was subject, in this case, to a condition that the buyer be able to obtain adequate financing.   Did Beattie-Firth sue the wrong party?   Would more facts be helpful?   What facts?

LACH v. CAHILL, 138 Conn. 418, 85 A.2d 481 (1951).   [On November 10, 1949, Waldemar Lach, a lawyer with about a year in practice and a wife and three small children, made a contract with James Cahill to buy the latter's house for $18,000.   He paid Cahill a $1,000 deposit and signed an agreement which provided: "This agreement is contingent upon buyer being able to obtain mortgage in the sum of $12,000.00 on the premises   . . . ."   The conveyance was to be within 30 days.   Rabbett, who represented Cahill in the transaction, knew Lach's financial situation and that he contemplated a bank mortgage payable in installments over a reasonable period of time. By November 21, Lach had been turned down by six banks and the Federal Housing Administration, which advised him that although he was a veteran, his income did not qualify him for an F.H.A. guaranteed loan.   Rabbett then told Lach that Cahill was not interested in taking a purchase money mortgage himself.   On December 1, Lach wrote Cahill that he could not get a mortgage and requested the return of his deposit.   On Cahill's refusal, he sued to recover it.   From a judgment for Lach, Cahill appealed.]

BALDWIN, JUSTICE.   . . .   The decisive issues in the case are whether the ability of the plaintiff to secure a $12,000 mortgage was a condition precedent to his duty to perform his promise to purchase and whether he made a reasonable effort to secure the mortgage. Unless both questions are answered in the affirmative the plaintiff cannot recover.   A condition precedent is a fact or event which the parties intend must exist or take place before there is a right to performance.   . . .   A condition is distinguished from a promise in that it creates no right or duty in and of itself but is merely a limiting or modifying factor.   . . .   If the condition is not fulfilled, the right to enforce the contract does not come into existence. . . .   Whether a provision in a contract is a condition the nonfulfilment of which excuses performance depends upon the intent of the parties, to be ascertained from a fair and reasonable construction of the language used in the light of all the surrounding circumstances when they executed the contract. . . .

The plaintiff was a young man of limited means, just starting in his profession and under the necessity of finding a home for his wife and their three small children. He required a mortgage payable in reasonable instalments over a period of time if he was to complete the prospective purchase of Cahill's house. The court properly concluded that the language used, read in the light of the situation of the parties, expressed an intention that the plaintiff should not be held to an agreement to purchase unless he could secure a mortgage for $12,000 on reasonable terms as to the amount and time of instalment payments.

The condition in the contract implied a promise by the plaintiff that he would make reasonable efforts to secure a suitable mortgage. . . . The performance or nonperformance of this implied promise was a matter for the determination of the trial court. The conclusion reached upon the facts was proper. . . .

[Affirmed.]

NOTES

(1) *The Deposit.* The case preceding this involved a condition qualifying the Colebanks' duty. This case involved a condition qualifying Lach's duty. But Lach was the *plaintiff* and the Colebanks were the *defendants*. Why does the court assume that if Lach cannot be held for breach of his duty, he is entitled to the return of his deposit? In Chapter 7, Section 2, we consider the right to restitution of a party who is in default under the contract. Is Lach's situation distinguishable from that of such a party?

(2) *Drafting.* Try to draft a term in a few words that would excuse Lach from further payment, but would permit Cahill to retain the deposit, in the event that a suitable loan could not be arranged. What difficulties are involved?

(3) *Financing Conditions.* A poll of Wisconsin lawyers and brokers on terms like that in Lach v. Cahill is reported in Raushenbush, Problems and Practices with Financing Conditions in Real Estate Purchase Contracts, 1963 Wis.L.Rev. 566. According to the responses: such terms are in widespread use; general language like "subject to financing" was not favored by most of the respondents; and a majority of them felt unable to say what would be a "reasonable loan" for a buyer. Did the court in Lach v. Cahill seem prepared to say what is a reasonable mortgage for a young lawyer with three children?[a] Would an agreement "contingent upon the purchaser's obtaining the proper amount of financing" have been enforceable? See Southwest Engineering v. Martin Tractor, p. 81 supra, and Willmott v. Giarraputo, p. 84 supra; Gerruth Realty Co. v. Pire, 17 Wis. 2d 89, 115 N.W.2d 557 (1962).

a. As to whether the condition is satisfied by an offer of a purchase money mortgage by the seller himself, compare Simms Co. v. Wolverton, 232 Ore. 291, 375 P.2d 87 (1962), with Kovarick v. Vesely, 3 Wis.2d 573, 89 N.W.2d 279 (1958).

GIBSON v. CRANAGE

Supreme Court of Michigan, 1878.
39 Mich. 49.

MARSTON, J. Plaintiff in error brought assumpsit to recover the contract price for the making and execution of a portrait of the deceased daughter of defendant. It appeared from the testimony of the plaintiff that he at a certain time called upon the defendant and solicited the privilege of making an enlarged picture of his deceased daughter. He says "I was to make an enlarged picture that he would like, a large one from a small one, and one that he would like and recognize as a good picture of his little girl, and he was to pay me."

The defendant testified that the plaintiff was to take the small photograph and send it away to be finished, "and when returned if it was not perfectly satisfactory to me in every particular, I need not take it or pay for it. I still objected and he urged me to do so. There was no risk about it; if it was not perfectly satisfactory to me I need not take it or pay for it."

There was little if any dispute as to what the agreement was. After the picture was finished it was shown to defendant who was dissatisfied with it and refused to accept it. Plaintiff endeavored to ascertain what the objections were, but says he was unable to ascertain clearly, and he then sent the picture away to the artist to have it changed.

On the next day he received a letter from defendant reciting the original agreement, stating that the picture shown him the previous day was not satisfactory and that he declined to take it or any other similar picture, and countermanded the order. A further correspondence was had, but it was not very material and did not change the aspect of the case. When the picture was afterwards received by the plaintiff from the artist, he went to see defendant and to have him examine it. This defendant declined to do, or to look at it, and did not until during the trial, when he examined and found the same objections still existing.

We do not consider it necessary to examine the charge in detail, as we are satisfied it was as favorable to plaintiff as the agreement would warrant.

The contract (if it can be considered such) was an express one. The plaintiff agreed that the picture when finished should be satisfactory to the defendant, and his own evidence showed that the contract in this important particular had not been performed. It may be that the picture was an excellent one and that the defendant ought to have been satisfied with it and accepted it, but under the agreement the defendant was the only person who had the right to decide this question. Where parties thus deliberately enter into an agreement which violates no rule of public policy, and which is free from all taint of fraud or mistake, there is no hardship whatever in holding them bound by it.

Artists or third parties might consider a portrait an excellent one, and yet it prove very unsatisfactory to the person who had ordered it and who might be unable to point out with clearness or certainty the defects or objections. And if the person giving the order stipulates that the portrait when finished must be satisfactory to him or else he will not accept or pay for it, and this is agreed to, he may insist upon his right as given him by the contract. McCarren v. McNulty, 7 Gray, 141; Brown v. Foster, 113 Mass., 136; 18 Amer., 465.

The judgment must be affirmed with costs.

NOTE

Satisfaction. Would the result have been the same if Gibson's promise had been to paint Cranage's barn? In Mattei v. Hopper, 51 Cal.2d 119, 330 P.2d 625 (1958), the court noted that "satisfaction" clauses have been divided into two categories. "First, in those contracts where the condition calls for satisfaction as to commercial value or quality, operative fitness, or mechanical utility, dissatisfaction cannot be claimed arbitrarily, unreasonably, or capriciously, . . . and the standard of a reasonable person is used in determining whether satisfaction has been received. [Second, in those contracts] involving fancy, taste, or judgment. . . . the promisor's determination that he is not satisfied, when made in good faith, has been held to be a defense to an action on the contract. . . . Although these decisions do not expressly discuss the issues of mutuality of obligation or illusory promises, they necessarily imply that the promisor's duty to exercise his judgment in good faith is an adequate consideration to support the contract. None of these cases voided the contracts on the ground that they were illusory or lacking in mutuality of obligation." Would the result have been the same if Cranage had refused to look at the portrait at all?

Can you draft language that would make an objective test applicable to the painting of a portrait? That would make a subjective test applicable to the painting of a barn?

DEVOINE CO. v. INTERNATIONAL CO., 151 Md. 690, 136 A. 37 (1927). [By written contract, International sold Devoine, a manufacturer of candles, 400 50-gallon barrels of cherries in syrup, "quality satisfactory." After accepting 97 barrels, Devoine refused to take more, claiming that the quality was not satisfactory. International sued Devoine for damages. From a judgment for the plaintiff, the defendant appealed.]

BOND, C. J. . . . Taking up the . . . question . . . of the construction and effect of the provision, "quality satisfactory," we assume there can be no doubt that this means of a quality satisfactory to the buyer. . . . When parties to a valid contract refer any question of performance to the decision of the other party, or of a third person, the decision contracted for is final. . . . But it is only the decision contracted for that is final. . . . And in those cases in which there may be a question open to decision, if the person to whom it is referred decides, not on the question submitted, but on some question of interest or advantage not made the basis of rights or obligations by the contract, the decision is outside of the contract and is given no effect by it.[a] Apart from any possible difficulty in proof, and assuming it to be made clear in any case, as, for instance, by a clear admission to that effect, that the tendered performance did meet the test stipulated for, that it was satisfactory or sufficient, as the case might be, a rejection on the ground of dissatisfaction or insufficiency would be beyond the right of the party who is to approve, in bad faith, and ineffectual. . . .

It is furthermore settled by our decisions that, on the issue of good faith in rejection of performance, the evidence may take a wide range, and facts such as the appellant sought to elicit in this case against objections of the appellee should be admitted. . . . He accordingly introduced testimony that of the 97 barrels of cherries delivered on the contract before refusal of further deliveries, none were rejected, and there was no complaint. Testimony was given of careful selection and putting up of the cherries in the seller's factory, and of a quality up to the highest grade known to the trade. A letter written by the buyer during the progress of deliveries, and expressing satisfaction, was read in evidence. It had been used by the seller as an advertisement. Further testimony was given to the effect that calls from this buyer for deliveries slackened to such an extent as to cause the seller some inconvenience, and that when the president of the seller company called on the buyer, the president of the latter explained, first, that his own sales had slackened, and, later, that he had an arrangement for putting up his own supply of cherries and therefore could not use the undelivered portion of the International Company's cherries, but would try to dispose of them to other consumers. Two letters followed from the International Company to the Devoine Company on a suggestion for deliveries in small installments, and these were answered by the final letter from the Devoine Company, stating that, as the International Company's president had previously been informed, the Devoine Company found the cherries unsatisfactory and would take no more. This evidence was met by contradictory testimony on behalf of the Devoine Company, but no exception brings that up for review. Our conclusion is that the evidence of the International Company just outlined was relevant to prove a rejection for reasons other than dissatisfaction with the cherries . . ., and that it was sufficient, no matter how strong the evidence of the De-

a. "The promisor may in fact be satisfied with the performance, but not with the bargain." Learned Hand, J., in Thompson-Starrett Co. v. La Belle Iron Works, 17 F.2d 536 (2d Cir. 1927).

voine Company may have been to the contrary, to require submission to the jury of the question of good faith in making the rejection.
. . .

[Affirmed.]

NOTE

Good Faith. Compare the court's discussion of "good faith" with UCC 1–203. Cf. UCC 1–208. Is the test of good faith subjective (honesty) or objective (reasonableness)? Compare UCC 1–201(19) with 2–103(1) (b).

ARCHITECTS' CERTIFICATES

Some of the problems inherent in making a party's duty conditional on his own satisfaction can be eliminated by making his duty conditional instead on the satisfaction of an independent third party, usually an expert of some kind. Widespread use is made of such terms in construction contracts, where the owner's duty to pay the contractor is often conditional on satisfaction of the architect.[a] The next two cases arise in this setting.

SECOND NATIONAL BANK v. PAN-AMERICAN BRIDGE CO., 183 F. 391 (6th Cir. 1910). [Pan-American Bridge furnished structural steel for Second National's bank building under a contract providing for payments as the work progressed "upon a certificate of the architect," 15% to be retained from the amount of each certificate and paid within 30 days of completion of the work "and the acceptance of the same by the architects." According to the specifications, Pan-American was to furnish the architect with detail drawings for approval and to do the work "in strict accordance with such approved drawings," but the architect, in approving them, "approves them in a general manner as being in or out of conformance with the general requirements of his drawings and specifications and does not relieve the contractor of responsibility for the correctness of the work shown by them." Pan-American's drawings, approved in writing by the architect, plainly showed 8 holes for the connections of beams and columns. After the steel had reached the sixth story, however, the architect insisted that Pan-American replace the 8-rivet connections with 10-rivet connections. On its refusal, Second National made the changes at a cost of $2,370 and withheld this sum. Pan-American sued. The trial judge instructed the jury that if Pan-American's work conformed to the contract, it could recover, although the architect refused to accept or certify it, if it was withheld "unreasonably

---

a. It is also possible to make the architect's approval conclusive on the owner, that is, to make his approval the *sole* condition of the owner's duty. Such provisions are discussed in Note 2, p. 752 infra.

and unfairly." Second National insisted that relief from the refusal could be had only in equity. From judgment for the plaintiff, the defendant appealed.]

KNAPPEN, CIRCUIT JUDGE. . . . We cannot accede to the proposition that resort to equity is necessary in order to avoid the effect of failure to obtain the architect's certificate. The contention most strongly urged seems to be that the plaintiff must, as condition precedent to recovery on the contract, procure the setting aside of the contract provisions requiring such certificate, although the suggestion is also made that the architect's action needs reforming. Neither of those contentions is, in our opinion, maintainable. The plaintiff does not attack the validity of the contract provision requiring the architect's certificate as a condition precedent to recovery. Nor is there any certificate of the architect standing in the way and requiring reformation. The plaintiff's complaint in this respect is not that the contract is wrong, nor that any certificate of the architect is wrong. Its grievance is that the architect has improperly refused, as alleged, to accept the work and to certify accordingly. . . .

The right of a party to a building contract to show in an action at law thereon that the certificate required by the contract as a condition precedent to action was fraudulently withheld has been at least impliedly recognized in numerous cases, . . . and has never, so far as we have seen, been denied. But in our opinion the trial judge erred in holding that the architect's certificate could be dispensed with if the jury were satisfied that it was "unreasonably and unfairly" withheld. It is true that this instruction finds apparent support in several decisions of state courts cited in plaintiff's brief. But the rule is well settled in the federal courts that under contract provisions such as those existing here the certificate of acceptance is a condition precedent to recovery upon the contract in the absence of fraud or of mistake so gross as to imply bad faith; in other words, that the withholding of the certificate must have been in bad faith. . . .

In other words, the actual conformity of the work and materials to the plans and specifications was made the test of the bad faith which the law requires for setting aside the action of the architect. It is strongly insisted that the bad faith of the architect is clearly shown by his refusal to accept the plaintiff's work on account of defects apparent in the detail drawings approved by the architect. While the record was such as to justify submitting to the jury the question whether the architect acted in bad faith in refusing the certificate, and while it is possible that the defendant and the architect as well, in requiring the substituted connections, were influenced by a fear of criticism upon the sufficiency of the building, we cannot say, as a matter of law, that the admitted facts lead only to a conclusion of bad faith on the architect's part. . . .

[Reversed and new trial ordered.]

NOTES

(1) *A. I. A. Provisions.* The American Institute of Architects General Conditions of the Contract for Construction (AIA Document A201, 12th ed. 1970) contain elaborate provisions on the role of the architect. He "will provide general Administration of the Construction Contract, . . . will be the Owner's representative during construction and until final payment, [and] will be, in the first instance, the interpreter of the requirements of the Contract Documents and the judge of the performance thereunder by both the Owner and the Contractor" (arts. 2.2.1, 2.2.2, 2.2.6). His decisions "in matters relating to artistic effect will be final if consistent with the intent of the Contract Documents," but his decisions on other matters, except any claims that have been waived by making or accepting final payment, are subject to arbitration (arts. 2.2.9, 2.2.10). He "will determine the amounts owing to the Contractor and will issue Certificates for Payment . . . not more than seven days after the receipt of the Application . . . for such amount as he determines to be properly due, or state in writing his reasons for withholding a Certificate" (arts. 2.2.5, 9.4.1). He "may decline to approve an application for Payment and may withhold his Certificate . . . to the extent necessary reasonably to protect the Owner, if in his opinion he is unable to make representations to the owner . . . that the Work has progressed to the point indicated; that to the best of his knowledge, information and belief, the quality of the Work is in accordance with the Contract Documents . . .; and that the Contractor is entitled to payment in the amount certified" (arts. 9.5.1, 9.4.2).

What would have been the results in the preceding cases if these provisions had been applicable?

(2) *Satisfaction in New York.* New York courts have tended to read "satisfaction" to mean "reasonable satisfaction." An early example is Duplex Safety Boiler Co. v. Garden, 101 N.Y. 387, 4 N.E. 749 (1886), in which an owner of boilers agreed to pay for repairs only if "satisfied that the boilers, as changed, were a success." The Court of Appeals concluded that it "cannot be presumed" that the parties supposed that the owner was "to be sole judge in [his] own cause." This tendency carries over into cases involving architects' certificates.

In the leading case of Nolan v. Whitney, 88 N.Y. 648 (1882), a contractor, who had agreed to do masonry work to the satisfaction of the architect, sued for a $2,700 final payment on the total price of $11,700, although the architect had refused to give a certificate for that payment. The Court of Appeals affirmed a judgment for the contractor for the $2,700 less a $200 deduction for trivial defects in the plastering. "[W]hen he had substantially performed his contract, the architect was bound to give him the certificate, and his refusal to give it was unreasonable, and it is held that an unreasonable refusal on the part of an architect in such a case to give the certificate dispenses with its necessity."[a]

a. Does this help to explain why the failure of Jacob & Youngs to obtain the architect's certificate troubled neither Cardozo for the majority nor MacLaughlin for the dissenters in Jacob & Youngs v. Kent, p. 477 supra.

In Van Iderstine Co. v. Barnet Leather Co., 242 N.Y. 425, 152 N.E. 250 (1926), a seller of vealskins sued the buyer for failure to take and pay for some of the skins. The contract made the buyer's obligation subject to the approval of the skins by an expert broker. The trial judge charged the jury that the plaintiff could recover if approval was unreasonably withheld. On appeal this instruction was disapproved. The court explained the rule applied in Nolan v. Whitney on the ground that "enforcement of the contract according to its strict terms would cause forfeiture of compensation for work done and materials furnished.[b] The rule should not be extended by analogy where the reason for the rule fails." If the avoidance of forfeiture lies behind the decision in Nolan v. Whitney, why is not recovery in restitution the solution?

RIZZOLO v. POYSHER, 89 N.J.L. 618, 99 A. 390 (1916). [Rizzolo, a contractor, brought a mechanics' lien suit against Stahl, the owner, whose defenses included Rizzolo's failure to procure the architect's certificate required for payment under the contract. Rizzolo's complaint alleged "fraud on the part of the architect." A judgment of the trial court for Rizzolo was reversed on appeal, and he appeals from the reversal.]

PARKER, J. . . . It is inferable from the architect's own testimony that he was ready to issue the certificate, but that the defendants wished to cut down the final payment by several hundred dollars on account of a counterclaim which the architect refused to recognize or support except for a much smaller sum; that he advised the plaintiff to "get after them and get his money;" and that when plaintiff asked for the certificate, it was on the day before suit was begun, after plaintiff had retained counsel, and that he then refused it because he "did not want it to appear that he was issuing a certificate for a case." Such a reason was, of course, no reason at all, and led the judge very naturally to inquire of the witness whether he did not think that he had assumed responsibilities not belonging to his duties as architect. If the witness' statement was true, and there was no reason to believe the contrary, his refusal under such circumstances was fraudulent in the sense in which the court understood it in Chism v. Schipper, [51 N.J.L. 1, 16 A. 316], and Bradner v. Roffsell, [57 N.J.L. 412]. It is claimed that, to constitute such fraud, the owner must be a participant. If this were the rule, a corrupt architect would be greatly aided in extorting money from the contractor as a condition of awarding a certificate that was fully earned. . . .

[Reversed and judgment of trial court affirmed.]

b. Does this line of reasoning assume that the builder would have no right to recover from the owner on a theory of unjust enrichment if he were barred from suit on the contract by his failure to get a certificate? This question will be deferred until the next chapter.

NOTE

The Case of Constructive Fraud. A contract for the construction of low rent housing required the Wilmington Housing Authority to extend the time for completing the work "when in its judgment the findings of fact of the [Authority's] Contracting Officer justify such an extension, and his findings of fact thereon shall be final and conclusive upon the parties." The contractor gave notice of a delay resulting from a shortage of plumbers, and the officer found that a delay of 15 days was justifiable on this account. In an action against the Authority, the contractor complained that the officer had arrived at the figure of 15 days by taking 8% of the actual delay of 182 days because the plumbing cost was only that percentage of the cost of the entire contract. The Authority moved for summary judgment. *Held*: Summary judgment denied. The officer's finding may be set aside, and the issue of allowable delay presented to a jury. "It is unfortunate that a finding of constructive fraud must be made in so many words when, in fact, we are actually dealing with serious errors in calculations. However, the decisions refer to such miscalculations as constructive fraud and I find it necessary to pin that label upon the contracting officer's erroneous findings here although, actually, there is no hint of bad faith, dishonesty or deliberate wrongful conduct upon the part of the contracting officer or the Authority. I am sure that these errors were the product of inexperience and mistaken judgment." Anthony P. Miller, Inc. v. Wilmington Housing Authority, 179 F.Supp. 199 (D.Del.1959). Is a contracting officer the same sort of third party as an architect?

DUTY OR CONDITION?

At the beginning of this section (p. 633 supra), two sorts of interpretation questions were singled out. The preceding cases have been concerned with the question: If the occurrence of an event is required as a condition, what is the nature of that event? We now turn to the other question: Does the language require the occurrence of an event as a condition at all? Since contract language is ordinarily intended to serve some purpose, one can begin in a doubtful case by asking why the particular language was included if not to require a condition. The most common response is that it is language of promise, used to impose a duty. The question then becomes: Does the language impose a duty or require a condition?

The significance of this question derives from the fact that the two most common contractual devices by which an obligor may attempt to induce an obligee to do an act are, first, by having the obligee undertake a duty to do it and, second, by making the obligee's doing of the act a condition of the obligor's duty.[a] Here is an exam-

----

a. They are not the only devices used for this purpose. Another is the "unilateral" offer in which, for example, A attempts to induce B to walk across the Brooklyn Bridge by saying, "I will give you $100 if you walk across the Brooklyn Bridge." See p. 124 supra. It would, to be sure, be possible to call walking across the bridge a "condition" of A's promise, even

ple based on the venerable case of Constable v. Cloberie, Palmer 397, 81 Eng.Rep. 1141 (K.B.1626).

A cargo owner desires a ship owner to sail from England to Cadiz and back carrying his cargo. This the ship owner agrees to do in return for the cargo owner's promise to pay freight. In addition, the cargo owner wants the ship owner to sail with the next wind. To induce the ship owner to do this, he can have the ship owner undertake a duty to sail with the next wind, or can make sailing with the next wind a condition of his own duty to pay the freight, or can do both. The consequences will, however, be different in each case.

Suppose that he has the ship owner undertake a duty to sail with the next wind. If the ship owner delays in sailing, the cargo owner can recover any damages caused by the ship owner's breach of duty, but will not be excused from his own duty to pay the freight.[b]

Suppose that he makes sailing with the next wind a condition of his own duty to pay the freight. If the ship owner delays in sailing, the cargo owner can not recover damages but will be excused from his own duty to pay the freight.

Suppose that he does both.[c] If the ship owner delays in sailing, the cargo owner can recover damages caused by the ship owner's breach of duty *and* will be excused from his own duty to pay the freight. (In calculating damages, however, the court will have to take account of the fact that the cargo owner will not have to pay the freight. See p. 472 supra.)

What are the relative advantages to the cargo owner of these three solutions? Plainly the third, which gives him the advantages of both the first two, would be the best. But how much better is it, assuming that freight rates vary according to the relative disadvantage to the ship owner? As between the first two solutions, what are the relative advantages to the cargo owner?

NOTES

(1) *Drafting.* Assume that the contract begins: "In consideration of Ship Owner's promise to sail to Cadiz and return with cargo, Cargo Owner promises to pay freight at [a specified rate]." Draft clauses to follow which would make sailing with the next wind: (1) a duty of Ship

---

though it is also the acceptance of A's offer, but the term is not ordinarily used in this broad sense. According to Comment c to Restatement Second, § 250: "Events which must occur before there is a contract, such as offer and acceptance, are . . . excluded under the definition in this section. It is not customary to call such events conditions. . . . For the most part, they are required by law and may not be dispensed with

by the parties, while conditions are the result of, or at least subject to, agreement."

b. This ignores the impact of the doctrine of "constructive conditions of exchange," which is taken up in the next chapter.

c. Corbin uses the term "promissory condition" to describe this case. 3A Corbin, § 633.

Owner; (2) a condition of Cargo Owner's duty; (3) both a duty of Ship Owner and a condition of Cargo Owner's duty.[d]

(2) *Conditions and Promises of Satisfaction.* Note that in Gibson v. Cranage, p. 641 supra, the court said that Gibson "agreed that the picture when finished should be satisfactory" to Cranage. Did the court hold that Gibson was under a duty to furnish a picture satisfactory to Cranage? Could Cranage have recovered damages from Gibson for his failure to do so?

Fursmidt v. Hotel Abbey Holding Corp., 10 App.Div.2d 447, 200 N.Y.S. 2d 256 (1960), sheds some light on this last question. Fursmidt had a three-year contract with the Hotel Abbey to supply its patrons with valet and laundry services. It was "distinctly understood and agreed that the services . . . shall meet with the approval of the [Hotel], who shall be the sole judge of the sufficiency and propriety of the services." After six months, the Hotel put Fursmidt out of his space in the basement and brought in someone else to render the services. He sued and the Hotel counterclaimed for his failure to render proper services. The jury was instructed to find for Fursmidt if it believed that the Hotel's dissatisfaction was unreasonable, even if honest. From a judgment entered on a verdict in Fursmidt's favor, the Hotel appealed. *Held*: Reversed. "[A] literal construction of the 'satisfaction' provisions is made where the agreements provide for performance involving 'fancy, taste, sensibility, or judgment,'" and this contract was sufficiently of this character to make the test of "dissatisfaction honestly arrived at" appropriate under the quoted clause. The court went on to say, however, that the trial court's charge may be "correct for the purpose of determining whether the plaintiff breached the agreement so as to entitle the defendant to damages on its counterclaim as distinguished from its right to terminate the contract. Honest dissatisfaction . . . will not, in and of itself, entitle it to recover damages on its counterclaim. . . . [W]e do not pass on that phase of the case at this time."

GENERAL CREDIT CORPORATION v. IMPERIAL CASUALTY & INDEMNITY CO.

Supreme Court of Nebraska, 1959.
167 Neb. 833, 95 N.W.2d 145.

[General Credit financed the purchase of two automobiles by the Service Trucking Company, taking a security interest in the automobiles to secure the debt.[a] In order to protect that interest in the

---

d. Those with a penchant for law French may find assistance in the facts of the actual case. The cargo owner covenanted to pay freight "si le niefe [ship] va le intended voyage [to Cadiz], & retorn." The ship owner covenanted that his ship would go with "le prochien vent," and the cargo owner denied that it did so, and refused to pay the freight. The ship owner sued, and the cargo owner's plea was held bad on demurrer, "car le substance del covenant . . . est que le niefe vaera le voyage, & ceo fuit primary intention del parties." Sailing with the next wind was not a condition to the plaintiff's right to the freight. The reference to the case in Beattie-Firth v. Colebank, at p. 634 supra, as one involving a condition is therefore puzzling. The case is discussed in 3A Corbin, § 633.

a. For a description of such a transaction, see p. 966 infra.

event of loss of or damage to the automobiles, General Credit had Service Trucking agree to insure General Credit's interest, as well as Service Trucking's. Service Trucking obtained a policy of insurance against damage to these and other automobiles from Imperial Casualty & Indemnity Company. The two automobiles were damaged by collision, and it was stipulated that Imperial Casualty became liable to pay General Credit $1,839.20 as a result. General Credit's claim arose under the following "loss payable" clause:

> Loss or damage, if any, under the policy shall be payable as interest may appear to General Credit Corp., Hastings, Nebraska and this insurance as to the interest of the Bailment Lessor, Conditional Vendor or Mortgagee or Assignee of Bailment Lessor, Conditional Vendor or Mortgagee (herein called the Lienholder) shall not be invalidated by any act or neglect of the Lessee, Mortgagor or Owner of the within described automobile . . .; provided, however, that . . . in case the Lessee, Mortgagor or Owner shall neglect to pay any premium due under such policy the Lienholder shall, on demand, pay the same.

After the loss, Imperial Casualty made demand on General Credit for $1,786.86 in premiums which Service Trucking had not paid. General Credit sued Imperial Casualty for its insured loss of $1,839.20, and Imperial Casualty sought to have the unpaid premiums deducted from that claim. The trial court awarded the plaintiff judgment for $1,839.20 with interest and costs, and the defendant appealed.]

SIMMONS, CHIEF JUSTICE. . . . As stated by defendant the appeal here presents primarily the question of whether the language in the loss payable clause "provided, also, that in case the Lessee, Mortgagor or Owner shall neglect to pay any premium due under such policy the Lienholder shall, on demand, pay the same" is a condition or a covenant. . . .

In Restatement, Contracts, § 260, p. 373, it is stated: "If in an agreement words that state that an act is to be performed purport to be the words of the person who is to do the act, the words are interpreted, unless a contrary intention has been manifested, as a promise by that person to perform the act. If the words purport to be those of a party who is not to do the act they are interpreted, unless a contrary intention has been manifested, as limiting the promise of that party by making performance of the act a condition." In the comment it is said: "b. If a contract is clearly unilateral as is the case with many if not most policies of insurance, the answer to the question to whom must the language be attributed admits of no doubt. In such a contract only one party speaks, and that is the covenantor or promisor. Any clause, therefore, in a policy of insurance, requiring any act to be done by the insured, will make that act a condition of the covenant or promise of insurance." [b]

A discussion citing the above statement in Restatement is made by Williston in his work on contracts. 3 Williston on Contracts (Rev. Ed.), § 672, p. 1930. He states: "The matter has been well expressed by Professor Langdell: 'Moreover, the words of such a clause will have, in fact, a different meaning, according to the party who uses them. If they are used in a contract by the party who is to do the act, they plainly import that he binds himself to do it; while, if they are used by the party for whose benefit the act is to be done, they fairly mean that he will require it to be done, i. e., that his own obligation shall be conditional upon its being done. How then shall it be ascertained to whom the language of such a clause is to be imputed? If the contract be clearly unilateral (e. g., a policy of insurance), of course the answer to this question admits of no doubt. In such a contract only one party speaks, and that is the covenantor or promisor. Any clause, therefore, in a policy of insurance, requiring any act to be done by the insured, will be a condition of the covenant or promise of insurance, though its language may more naturally import a covenant or promise by the insured.' "

It is stated in 14 Appleman, Insurance Law and Practice, § 7842, p. 39, that: "One of the most puzzling results reached by the courts arises in connection with the type of mortgage clause which has been variously termed the 'standard', 'New York', or 'union' clause. It will be recalled from the previous discussion that this clause gives great rights to the mortgagee and protects him under circumstances where the mortgagor would receive no indemnification. However, in return for that special protection, the mortgagee is to pay upon demand, if the mortgagor defaults, such premiums as may be due. This would seem to be clear in itself, to be fair, based upon a proper consideration, and to be an agreement of the mortgagee arising through his request of the loss payable clause, acceptance of the policy, or silent acquiescence. [c] However, the vast majority of courts have reached the somewhat surprising conclusion that such agreement to pay is not a covenant on the part of the mortgagee to pay premiums which can be enforced by the insurer, but is merely a condition to his right to recover the insurance proceeds. Mortgagees are not to be blamed for striving to achieve this result, as it places them in the enviable position of being able to harvest a crop without first sowing seed."

We state his reasons with the comment that the courts do not seem to have been of like mind. [Here the court reviewed the cases

---

b. For a case relying on the first sentence of Restatement, § 260, see Charles Ilfeld Co. v. Taylor, 156 Colo. 204, 397 P.2d 748 (1964). Cf. Restatement, § 261.

c. See the agreement in Talbott v. Stemmons, as quoted in Hamer v. Sidway, p. 4 supra. If Albert Talbott assented to the agreement, what legal consequences would his chewing of tobacco entail?

on the issue, finding a division of authority. It referred to Restatement, § 236: "an interpretation (of doubtful words) is preferred which operates more strongly against the party from whom they proceed."]

Commenting on the rule the Restatement says: "This rule finds frequent application in regard to policies of insurance, which are ordinarily prepared solely by the insurance company, and therefore, the words of the policies are construed most strongly against it." Restatement, Contracts, § 236, p. 330. . . .

We conclude then that the clause here involved is a condition and that the condition requires the plaintiff to pay the premium on the insurance involved from and after the date of the demand if plaintiff desires to keep the insurance in force. Such a conclusion is in accord with the authorities above cited that construe this language to be a condition. . . .

The judgment of the trial court is affirmed.

NOTES

(1) *Issues.* What was the issue in the case? Is there a condition? What is its scope? Both? What if Imperial Casualty had made demand on General Credit for premiums *before* the loss. Would it then have preferred to have regarded the language in question as language of condition or of promise? "A complete defense is generally more beneficial to an insurer than is a mere counterclaim for breach of a promise." 3A Corbin, § 635, n. 43. (In an omitted part of the opinion, the court observed that all the unpaid premiums save $45.92 were chargeable to vehicles in which General Credit had no interest, and suggested that Imperial Casualty could not have claimed the whole premium, even if a covenant had been found in the policy.) Can it be argued that the court's construction of the loss payable clause is actually in *favor* of insurers generally?

(2) *Earlier Authorities.* Apparently all the cases prior to the main case concerned fire insurance on real property. The New York Standard Mortgagee Clause is in general use for such insurance, and it is, so far as relevant, substantially the same as that in the main case. In almost all previous cases the action was brought for the payment of premiums against the mortgagee as defendant, there having been no loss within the policy.

MASCIONI v. MILLER, INC.

Court of Appeals of New York, 1933.
261 N.Y. 1, 184 N.E. 473.

Appeal from a judgment entered July 16, 1932, upon an order of the Appellate Division of the Supreme Court in the second judicial department which reversed a judgment in favor of defendant entered upon a decision of the court at a Trial Term without a jury, and directed judgment, upon new findings, in favor of plaintiffs.

LEHMAN, J. The plaintiffs and the defendant entered into a written contract whereby the plaintiffs, described in the contract as the "Sub-Contractor," agreed to provide all the materials and all the work for the erection of concrete walls, and the defendant, described in the contract as the "Contractor," agreed to pay therefor the sum of fifty-five cents per cubic foot. The concrete walls were to be erected as "specified in a certain contract between the Contractor and Village Apartments, Inc., described therein as Owner" and the defendant's promise to pay contained the proviso: "Payments to be made as received from the Owner." In spite of the fact that the Owner has made no payments to the defendant for the work and materials, or any part thereof, performed and furnished by the plaintiffs, the plaintiffs have recovered a judgment against the defendant for the agreed price.

The problem presented on this appeal is whether the defendant assumed an absolute obligation to pay, though for convenience payment might be postponed till moneys were received from the Owner, or whether the defendant's obligation to pay arose only if and when the Owner made payment to the defendant. At the trial the plaintiffs, claiming that the contract was ambiguous, were permitted to introduce testimony to show that before the written contract was signed, much of the work had been performed under an oral contract by which the defendant assumed an absolute obligation to pay; and the defendant, though claiming that the written contract, in unambiguous terms, annexed a contingency to the defendant's obligation to pay, produced parol testimony to show that the plaintiffs expressly assumed the risk that they might never be paid. A judgment in favor of the defendant was reversed by the Appellate Division on the ground that the contract is unambiguous and that the provision with respect to payment "merely fixed the time of payment and did not create a condition precedent." (236 App.Div. 688, 257 N.Y.S. 1001.)

A provision for the payment of an obligation upon the happening of an event does not become absolute until the happening of the event. Whether the defendant's express promise to pay is construed as a promise to pay "if" payment is made by the owner or "when" such payment is made, "the result must be the same; since if the event does not befall, or a time coincident with the happening of the event does not arrive, in neither case may performance be exacted." Amies v. Wesnofske, 255 N.Y. 156, 162, 174 N.E. 436, 73 A.L.R. 918.

[The court here quotes at length from Langdell, Summary of Contracts, sec. 36, and also quotes Restatement, § 301, dealing with impossibility as a basis of relief against a forfeiture.]

Here on its face the contract provides for a promise to perform in exchange for a promise to pay as payments are "received from the Owner." Performance by the plaintiff would enure directly to the benefit of the Owner and indirectly to the benefit of the defendant, because the defendant had a contract with the Owner to perform the work for a stipulated price. The defendant would not profit by the plaintiffs' performance unless the Owner paid the stipulated price. That was the defendant's risk, but the defendant's promise to pay the plaintiffs for stipulated work on condition that payment was received by the defendant shifted that risk to the plaintiffs, if the condition was a material part of the exchange of plaintiffs' promise to perform for defendant's promise to pay.

In many cases similar conditions in contracts for compensation of brokers have been enforced in accordance with the letter of the promise to pay. In principle, brokerage contracts cannot be distinguished from other contracts to pay compensation for services rendered or materials furnished. "In each case the intention of the parties to make the debt contingent or otherwise, must be gathered from the language used, the situation of the parties, and the subject matter of the contract, as presented by the evidence." (DeWolfe v. French, 51 Me. 420; Lighton v. City of Syracuse, 188 N.Y. 499, 504, 81 N.E. 464; 2 Williston on Contracts, sec. 799.)

Here we are not called upon to decide whether the language of the contract, read in the light of the situation of the parties and the subject-matter of the contract, shows clearly and unambiguously that the condition attached to the debt or obligation to pay, and did not merely fix the time of payment. Certainly on its face it is open to the construction that the plaintiffs accepted the condition as a material part of the exchange for their own promise or performance. The trial judge, after receiving parol evidence of the actual intention of the parties, gave it this construction, and that construction was not erroneous as matter of law.

The judgment of the Appellate Division should be reversed, and that of the Special Term affirmed, with costs in this court and in the Appellate Division.

NOTES

(1) *Condition or Not?* Do you agree with the court that the brokerage contract cases cannot be distinguished "in principle"? State the issue in Mascioni v. Miller in terms of the contract language. Was this a controversy over the nature of an event required as a condition or one over whether an event was required as a condition at all? Redraft the clause for Mascioni, the subcontractor. Does your draft subject his right of recovery to a condition? See the definition of "condition" in Restatement Second, § 250. Can you explain the Restatement's exclusion of events "not certain to occur"?

(2) *Tactics.* Additional facts appear from the record on appeal. The contract was made on December 18, 1930. Samuel J. Winterbérg, secretary of Miller, Inc., testified that in a conversation about payments "previous to the drawing up of the written contract, I explained to Mr. Mascioni that his contract would be made out contingent upon our contract with the owners. . . . Mr. Mascioni at that time said he wanted to check into the

worth of the owner before he entered into such a contract with us." He testified that the disputed provision "is used in the business because during these times, which are not normal, we receive contracts from other contractors in that manner and we give contracts out in that manner." (Record, p. 47.) Did Mascioni make a tactical error in "claiming that the contract was ambiguous? Would it have helped Mascioni if he could have shown that at the beginning of negotiations he had made an informal bid to do the work at 55 cents per cubic foot? That Miller had told him that he would be short of funds until the job was completed?

———

THOS. J. DYER CO. v. BISHOP INTERNATIONAL ENGINEERING CO., 303 F.2d 655 (6th Cir. 1962). [Dyer, a subcontractor, made a contract with Engineering Company, a contractor, who was engaged in construction of the Latonia Race Track for the Kentucky Jockey Club. The contract provided for a total price, "no part of which shall be due until five (5) days after Owner shall have paid Contractor therefor." Engineering Company paid Dyer $119,133, but refused to pay an additional $108,519, for work as to which it had not been paid by the Jockey Club. Dyer sued Engineering Company for this amount. The trial court granted Dyer's motion for summary judgment and Engineering Company appealed.]

SHACKLEFORD MILLER, JR., CHIEF JUDGE. . . . [I]t is the intention of the parties which is the controlling factor in each particular case. It is, of course, basic in the construction business for the general contractor on a construction project of any magnitude to expect to be paid in full by the owner for the labor and material he puts into the project. He would not remain long in business unless such was his intention and such intention was accomplished. That is a fundamental concept of doing business with another. The solvency of the owner is a credit risk necessarily incurred by the general contractor, but various legal and contractual provisions, such as mechanics' liens and installment payments, are used to reduce this to a minimum. These evidence the intention of the parties that the contractor be paid even though the owner may ultimately become insolvent. This expectation and intention of being paid is even more pronounced in the case of a subcontractor whose contract is with the general contractor, not with the owner. In addition to his mechanic's lien, he is primarily interested in the solvency of the general contractor with whom he has contracted. He looks to him for payment. Normally and legally, the insolvency of the owner will not defeat the claim of the subcontractor against the general contractor. Accordingly, in order to transfer this normal credit risk incurred by the general contractor from the general contractor to the subcontractor, the contract between the general contractor and subcontractor should contain an express condition clearly showing that to be the intention of the parties. . . .

In the case before us we see no reason why the usual credit risk of the owner's insolvency assumed by the general contractor should be transferred from the general contractor to the subcontractor. It seems clear to us under the facts of this case that it was the intention of the parties that the subcontractor would be paid by the general contractor for the labor and materials put into the project. We believe that to be the normal construction of the relationship between the parties. If such was not the intention of the parties it could have been so expressed in unequivocal terms dealing with the possible insolvency of the owner. . . . Paragraph 3 of the subcontract does not refer to the possible insolvency of the owner. On the other hand, it deals with the amount, time and method of payment, which are essential provisions in every construction contract, without regard to possible insolvency. In our opinion, paragraph 3 of the subcontract is a reasonable provision designed to postpone payment for a reasonable period of time after the work was completed, during which the general contractor would be afforded the opportunity of procuring from the owner the funds necessary to pay the subcontractor. . . . To construe it as requiring the subcontractor to wait to be paid for an indefinite period of time until the general contractor has been paid by the owner, which may never occur, is to give to it an unreasonable construction which the parties did not intend at the time the subcontract was entered into. . . .

[Affirmed.]

NOTES

(1) *Reconciliation.* Can the preceding two cases be reconciled? On the basis of differences in contract language? On procedural grounds?

(2) *Problem.* A printed form of a contract for sale supplied by a real estate broker provided that the seller would pay the broker a stated commission "which commission is earned by agent when this agreement is signed by both parties [seller and buyer]." A typewritten sentence was added at the bottom: "Seller agrees to pay the agent at the consummation of sale the amount of the commission in cash." The agreement was signed by seller and buyer, but the sale was never consummated because the buyer refused to take title. Must the seller pay the broker the commission? See Kuhn v. Stan A. Plauche Real Estate Co., 249 La. 85, 185 So.2d 210 (1966).

FERGUSON v. PHOENIX ASSURANCE CO., 189 Kan. 459, 370 P.2d 379 (1962). [Ferguson, who ran a Rexall drug store, had a storekeeper's safe burglary policy under which Phoenix Assurance promised to pay $1,000 for loss by safe burglary, which was defined, under the heading "CONDITIONS," so as to require "felonious entry . . . provided such entry shall be made by actual force and violence, of which force and violence there are visible marks made by tools, explosives, electricity or chemicals upon the exterior of . . . all of said doors of such vault or such safe and any vault containing the safe, if entry is made through such doors." Ferguson's safe was opened by a thief who took $400 after opening the outer locked door by manipulating its combination lock, and the inner locked door by punching out the lock. When Phoenix denied liability, Ferguson sued and recovered. Phoenix appealed.]

SCHROEDER, JUSTICE. . . . The reason for such restrictions, quite obviously, is to protect the companies from what are commonly known as "inside jobs," and from frauds that would inevitably result, but for such protection. . . . The recital that there be visible marks upon the exterior of all of the doors to the safe has reference only to evidence of the force and violence used in making the felonious entry into the safe. In other words, the substantive condition of the proviso is that entry into the safe be made by actual force and violence. The further condition that there be visible marks upon the exterior of all doors to the safe, if entry is made through such doors, is merely evidentiary to show an entry into the safe by actual force and violence. . . . Had the insurance carrier desired to exclude loss by safe burglary where the combination of the outer door is worked by manipulation, such provision should have been incorporated under the "EXCLUSIONS" in the policy. . . .

[Affirmed.]

PRICE, JUSTICE (dissenting). . . . In my opinion this court has no business making another contract for the parties—its function is to enforce the contract as made. . . .

NOTES

(1) *Rationale.* What effect does the court give to the language relating to "visible marks"? Would it make good sense to reach the opposite result under a policy which contained the same language under the heading "exclusions"?

(2) *Problem.* Clark agreed to write a lawbook for West, and did produce a treatise on "Corporations." The author was to receive a royalty on sales not to exceed $6 per page. The manuscript, which was to be satisfactory to West, was paid for at the rate of $2 per page. Because of a dispute between the parties the remaining $4 was not paid, although sales were large. One provision of the contract required Clark "to totally abstain from the use of intoxicating liquors during the continuance of this contract, and the payment to him of any money in excess of $2 per page is dependent on the faithful performance of this as well as the other conditions of this contract." In suing on the contract Clark conceded that he had not abstained from liquor. See Clark v. West, 193 N.Y. 349, 86 N.E. 1 (1908). Was the condition quoted an "evidentiary" one? The court said: "It is not a contract to write books in order that the plaintiff shall keep sober, but a contract containing a stipulation that he shall keep sober so that he may write satisfactory books." Is the condition inconsistent with any public policy? (The holding in the case was that the condition was waivable, and that Clark had alleged an express waiver of it.)

CONDITIONS, FORFEITURE, AND MORTGAGES

It should be apparent by now that the law of conditions is more tolerant of the Draconian draftsman than is the law of liquidated damages. Courts have shown more tolerance for the forfeiture that results from the non-occurrence of an event that the draftsman has made a condition than for the penalty that he has provided as the consequence of breach. But there are limits even to the former, and they can be usefully considered against the background of the history of the mortgage.

A mortgage is a conveyance by a debtor, the mortgagor, to his creditor, the mortgagee, of an interest in property, whose purpose is to secure the payment of the debt. The advantages to the creditor of having this kind of security interest (which is usually called a lien) are of two sorts. First, a secured creditor has an array of remedies in case of non-payment in addition to those available to an unsecured creditor. Second, in the event of the distribution of the debtor's assets in insolvency proceedings, an effective security interest preempts the claims of unsecured creditors against the property subject to the interest. Details may be left to courses on land transactions, commercial transactions, creditors' rights, and the like. Our immediate concern is with the first of these sorts of advantages.

Although contemporary mortgage forms simply recite that the mortgagor "mortgages" the property to the mortgagee, the mortgage formerly took the form of a conveyance subject to a condition. Littleton, writing in the fifteenth century, explained it in this way. "If a feoffment be made upon such condition, that if the feoffor pay to the feoffee at a certain day, etc., 40*l.* of money, that then the feoffor may re-enter, etc., in this case the feoffee is called tenant in mortgage . . . and if he doth not pay, then the land which is put in pledge upon condition for the payment of the money, is taken from him for ever, and so dead to him upon condition, etc." Littleton's Tenures § 332.

Here is a description of the historical development that followed. "In [this] earlier era, the mortgagee obtained title to the mortgagor's property subject to divestment if the debt were paid on the due or law day. Often this arrangement meant hardship for the mortgagor, for a late tender of payment, late even by so little as one day, would not bring a return of title unless the mortgagee volunteered to give it. In time, chancery intervened in behalf of defaulting mortgagors by letting them 'redeem' the property from the mortgagee if they tendered payment within a reasonable period after the law day. This equitable right of redemption grew into an implied term of every mortgage bargain.

"Now the mortgagee faced hardship—the hardship of uncertainty—for he could not be sure, after default, when his title would indefeasibly vest. A late tendering mortgagor might yet persuade chancery that the tender was not unreasonably delayed. Taking the initiative, mortgagees began to petition the courts to cut off, or foreclose, the mortgagor's equity of redemption. In this way, the procedural remedy of foreclosure was born. The decree of foreclosure, which was issued some months after the law date and upon notice to the defaulting mortgagor, vested the mortgagee's title to the real estate security; prior to the decree redemption was possible, but after the decree, it was not.

"If, when foreclosure occurred, the real estate was worth more than the mortgage debt, still another source of hardship remained for the mortgagor. Since foreclosure vested title in the mortgagee, he stood to benefit, while the mortgagor stood to lose, from any surplus in property value. No restitution was necessary. By the early 1800s, state legislatures began to respond to the evident harshness of this situation; mortgagees who applied for a foreclosure decree were ordered to sell the property at a public sale and to pay over to the mortgagor (and to any junior lienors) the surplus moneys from the sale, i. e., the moneys not needed to satisfy the claims of the foreclosing mortgagee. (Sometimes, of course, the sales price fails to satisfy the debt, and this may give rise to further claim for a deficiency judgment.) In a substantial majority of states, *foreclosure by judicial sale* has become the exclusive or generally used process, and it is available everywhere. The process it supplanted, which for obvious reasons became known as *strict foreclosure*, survives in only a few states as a permitted remedy.

"One other form of foreclosure deserves mention, for it does not depend upon judicial decree. Where the mortgage instrument gives the mortgagee the power, and state law does not prevent its exercise, a sale arranged for by the mortgagee may be held to transfer the interest of the defaulted mortgagor. . . . In the United States the sale is invariably public and statutes carefully regulate the conduct of the sale and the method of giving notice."[a] Axelrod, Berger, and Johnstone, Land Transfer and Finance 138–40 (1971).

HOLIDAY INNS OF AMERICA, INC. v. KNIGHT

Supreme Court of California, 1969.
70 Cal.2d 327, 450 P.2d 42.

TRAYNOR, CHIEF JUSTICE. Plaintiffs appeal from a judgment for defendants in an action seeking a declaration that a contract was still effective. The judgment was entered after plaintiffs' motion for summary judgment was denied and defendants' motion for summary judgment was granted.

a. Reproduced by permission of Little,
Brown and Company.

The pleadings and affidavits of the parties establish the following undisputed facts.

Plaintiffs are the successors in interest to the optionee under a written option contract between the optionee and the owners of the option property, defendant D. Manley Knight and his mother, Mary Knight. Mary Knight is now deceased and D. Manley Knight is the sole owner of the property. Although his wife is also named a defendant herein, she has no interest in the contract or the option property. We will therefore refer to D. Manley Knight as defendant.

The contract, executed on September 30, 1963, granted an option to purchase real property in Orange County for $198,633, the price to be subject, however, to prescribed adjustments for changes in the cost of living. Unless cancelled as provided in the agreement, the option could be exercised by giving written notice thereof no later than April 1, 1968. The contract provided for an initial payment of $10,000 and for four additional payments of $10,000 to be made directly to the optionors on July 1 of each year, commencing in 1964, unless the option was exercised or cancelled before the next such payment became due. These payments were not to be applied to the purchase price. The cancellation provision provided that "it is mutually understood that failure to make payment on or before the prescribed date will automatically cancel this option without further notice." On December 9, 1963, the parties amended the contract by executing escrow instructions that provided that the annual payments were to be deposited in escrow with the Security Title Insurance Company, and that, in "the event you [Security Title] do not receive the $10,000 annual payments [by July 1] and upon receiving notice from Optionors to cancel the option, without further instructions from Optionee you are to terminate the escrow."

The initial payment of $10,000 and the annual installments for 1964 and 1965 were paid. After the execution of the contract, plaintiffs expended "great amounts of money" to develop a major residential and commercial center on the land adjacent to the option property. These expenditures have caused the option property to increase substantially in value since the contract was executed. Plaintiffs' purpose in entering into the contract was to put themselves in a position to secure the advantage of this increase in value resulting from their development efforts.

In 1966 plaintiffs mailed a check for $10,000 to defendant. It was made out to D. Manley Knight and his wife, Lavinia Knight, and dated June 30, 1966. Defendant received the check on July 2, 1966 and returned it to plaintiffs on July 8, stating that the option contract was cancelled. On July 8 plaintiffs tendered another check directly to defendant, and he again refused it. On July 15 plaintiffs deposited a $10,000 check with Security Title payable to defendant. Security Title tendered the check to defendant, but his attorney returned it to plaintiffs on July 27 and advised them that the agreement was terminated pursuant to the cancellation provision.

Plaintiffs contend that payment of the annual installment was timely on the ground that the check became the property of defendant when mailed; that even if the payment was late, the trial court should have relieved them from forfeiture and declared the option in force under section 3275 of the Civil Code; and that, in any event, the trial court erred in excluding extrinsic evidence offered to prove that the escrow instructions modified the contract to permit payment at any time before defendant notified the title company that the option was cancelled. Since the undisputed facts establish that plaintiffs are entitled to relief from forfeiture pursuant to section 3275, it is unnecessary to consider plaintiffs' other contentions.

Section 3275 provides: "Whenever, by the terms of an obligation, a party thereto incurs a forfeiture, or a loss in the nature of a forfeiture, by reason of his failure to comply with its provisions, he may be relieved therefrom, upon making full compensation to the other party, except in case of a grossly negligent, willful, or fraudulent breach of duty." The tumultuous history of this section has been recorded in a lengthy series of major decisions in the area of property and contract law.

Although most of the cases considering section 3275 have involved land sale contracts, its proscriptions against forfeiture apply in any case in which the party seeking relief from default has brought himself within the terms of the section by pleading and proving facts that justify its application. (Barkis v. Scott, supra, 34 Cal.2d at pp. 118, 120, 208 P.2d 367.) In determining whether a given case falls within section 3275, however, it is necessary to consider the nature of the contract and the specific clause in question. Although the contract in the instant case is an option contract, the question is not whether the exercise of the option was timely, but whether the right to exercise the option in the future was forfeited by a failure to pay the consideration for that right precisely on time. Defendant's reliance on Cummings v. Bullock (9th Cir. 1966) 367 F.2d 182, and Wilson v. Ward (1957) 155 Cal.App.2d 390, 317 P.2d 1018, is therefore misplaced. Both those cases dealt with the time within which an option must be exercised and correctly held that such time cannot be extended beyond that provided in the contract. To hold otherwise would give the optionee, not the option he bargained for, but a longer and therefore more extensive option. In the present case, however, plaintiffs are not seeking to extend the period during which the option can be exercised but only to secure relief from the provision making time of the essence in tendering the annual payments. (See Scarbery v. Bill Patch Land & Water Co. (1960) 184 Cal.App.2d 87, 102, 103, 7 Cal.Rptr. 408.) In a proper case, relief will be granted under section 3275 from such a provision. (Barkis v. Scott, supra, 34 Cal.2d at p. 122, 208 P.2d 367.)

The sole issue in this case is whether the plaintiffs have brought themselves within section 3275; whether there would be a loss in the nature of a forfeiture suffered by plaintiffs if the option contract were terminated. Essentially, the position of defendant is that there is no forfeiture since plaintiffs got precisely what they bargained for, namely, the exclusive right to buy the property for the three years during which they made payments. Cancellation because of the late 1966 payment amounts to nothing more than terminating a contract providing for that exclusive right during 1966. As viewed by defendant, this contract is in effect wholly executory and therefore its termination would not result in a forfeiture to either party. (Martin v. Morgan (1890) 87 Cal. 203, 25 P. 350.)

To sustain defendant's argument, the contract would have to be viewed as a series of independent contracts, each for a one-year option. Only if this were true, could it be said that plaintiffs received their bargained for equivalent of the $30,000 payments. (Sheveland v. Reed (1958) 159 Cal.App.2d 820, 822, 324 P.2d 633.) The economic realities of the transaction, however, do not support this analysis. First, the language of the agreement states that the "Optioners hereby grant to Optionee the exclusive right and option for a five year period . . .." The parties agreed to bind themselves to a period of five years with the price payable in five installments. On the basis of risk allocation, it is clear that each payment of the $10,000 installment was partially for an option to buy the land during that year and partially for a renewal of the option for another year up to a total of five years. With the passage of time, plaintiffs have paid more and more for the right to renew, and it is this right that would be forfeited by requiring payment strictly on time. At the time the forfeiture was declared, plaintiffs had paid a substantial part of the $30,000 for the right to exercise the option during the last two years. Thus, they have not received what they bargained for and they have lost more than the benefit of their bargain. In short, they will suffer a forfeiture of that part of the $30,000 attributable to the right to exercise the option during the last two years.[1]

Plaintiffs have at all times remained willing and able to continue with the performance of the contract and have acted in good faith to accomplish this end. Defendant has not suffered any injury justifying termination of the contract, and none of his reasonable expecta-

---

1. Plaintiffs also allege forfeiture of "great amounts of money" expended for the development of surrounding land. Evidently none of the investment was made in the option property. Since there is nothing to indicate that the development was not highly profitable in its own right or that inclusion of defendant's property was necessary to make the development a success, it would not seem that any part of these expenditures can be considered forfeited by a termination of the contract. (Cf. Scarbery v. Bill Patch Land & Water Co., supra, where the plaintiff offered evidence justifying the allocation of collateral development expenditures to the amounts forfeited by cancellation.)

tions have been defeated.[2]   Moreover, he will receive the benefit of his bargain, namely, the full price of the option granted plaintiffs.   As we stated in *Barkis*, "when the default has not been serious and the vendee is willing and able to continue with his performance of the contract, the vendor suffers no damage by allowing the vendee to do so." (Barkis v. Scott, supra, 34 Cal.2d at p. 122, 208 P.2d at p. 371.)

The judgment is reversed and the trial court is directed to enter a summary judgment for plaintiffs in accord with the views herein expressed.

NOTES

(1) *Rule of the Case.*   Consider again the few lines of legal history on p. 659 above, with special reference to the development of the mortgagor's equity of redemption: "In time, chancery intervened in behalf of defaulting mortgagors by letting them 'redeem' the property from the mortgagee if they tendered payment within a reasonable period after the law day."   This development was complete by the middle of the 17th century, it should be added.[a]   Do you consider the main case a ruling peculiar to "installment option" contracts, or as a twentieth century extension of an ancient principle about land financing?

(2) *Mailing or Receipt?*   On the face of it, an attractive basis for the foregoing decision is the plaintiffs' contention that their check became the property of defendant when mailed.   Cases may be cited to support it, but they chiefly concern checks sent in payment of *debts*.   Pronouncing the same rule for one sent to keep an option alive might have led the court into difficulties.   How strong is the analogy to the "mailbox rule" (see Note 4, p. 181 supra)?   At least the court would have had to think about the tangled questions of checks that bounce and are stopped, and of those that are lost or delayed in the mail.   The Uniform Commercial Code specifies when a person "receives" a notice (§ 1–201(26)), what constitutes the "receipt" of goods (§ 2–103(1)(c)), and when the "issue" of an instrument such as a check takes place (§ 3–102(1)(a)), but it carefully avoids passing on what constitutes receipt of such an instrument by the payee.   Can you think why?

(3) *Land Pricing.*   Holiday Inns was not the original optionholder, be it noted.   But it may have been his undisclosed principal.   A developer beginning a program of land acquisition will often employ a "front" or "straw" man to conceal its identity, fearing that a disclosure would drive up local land values prematurely.   The possible effect of such a program is dramatically shown in Banner v. Elm, 251 Md. 694, 248 A.2d 452 (1969).   There the buyer contracted to buy nearby parcels from A at 30 cents per square foot in October, from B at 75 cents in November, and from C at $1 in De-

---

2.   Although the initial tender was made to defendant and his wife and not to the Security Title Insurance Company as the escrow instructions specified, it gave defendant notice within one day of the due date that plaintiffs sought to keep the contract in force.

a.   See Turner, The Equity of Redemption, Chapter 2 (Cambridge Studies in English Legal History 1931).

cember.[b] Subsequently A reneged on his contract, and the question in the case was whether or not the buyer should be granted specific performance. On the facts given here, can you formulate any principle for granting specific enforcement of the Holiday Inns option, while denying similar enforcement against A?

CONDITIONS: PLEADING AND PROOF

"The elements of a cause of action or claim for breach of contract are these: (1) a contract or agreement supported by consideration (or by the presence of some other factor which under substantive law makes an agreement binding without consideration); (2) performance by plaintiff of all conditions precedent to be performed by him; and (3) breach of the contract by defendant." James, Civil Procedure § 3.12 (1965). See also Cleary, Presuming and Pleading, 12 Stan.L.Rev. 5 (1959).

With respect to the second of these, the plaintiff's burden of pleading is commonly eased by statutes and rules of court which permit him to allege generally that all conditions precedent have occurred. For example, Rule 9(c) of the Federal Rules of Civil Procedure provides: "In pleading the performance or occurrence of conditions precedent, it is sufficient to aver generally that all conditions precedent have been performed or have occurred." The defendant may prove that the allegation is not true only if he pleads facts showing the failure to perform. For example, Rule 9(c) continues: "A denial of performance or occurrence shall be made specifically and with particularity."

It is commonly said that the burden of proof, as well as of pleading, is on the plaintiff as to conditions precedent, but that the burden of proof, as well as of pleading, is on the defendant as to other conditions which are described as conditions subsequent. The question then becomes how to distinguish conditions subsequent from conditions precedent. Take a promise to pay 60 cents a gallon for a quantity of sperm oil, with an obligation to pay an additional 25 cents a gallon

> on the condition that if a greater quantity of sperm oil should arrive in whaling vessels at Nantucket and New Bedford, on or between the first day of April and the first day of October of the present year, both inclusive, than arrived at said places, in whaling vessels, on or within the same term of time the last year, then this obligation to be void.

Three tests may be applied: (1) verbal; (2) logical; and (3) functional.

---

b. A's property may, unlike that of the others, have been unimproved.

In Gray v. Gardner, 17 Mass. 188 (1821), from which the clause is taken, the court applied the verbal test and concluded that there was a condition subsequent. "The very words of the contract shew that there was a promise to pay, which was to be defeated by the happening of an event, *viz.* the arrival of a certain quantity of oil, at the specified places in a given time . . . . The defendants in this case promise to pay a certain sum of money, on condition that the promise shall be void on the happening of an event. It is plain that the burthen of proof is upon them . . . ." Under this test the result would have been different had the clause been reworded to make the sum payable on condition that *no greater* quantity of oil should arrive than during the comparable period of the preceding year. Yet the two clauses are the same in substance. A test that shifts the burden according to form and without regard to substance is of doubtful value.

The Restatement, § 250 lays down a logical test. An event whose occurrence is required, before a duty of immediate performance arises, is a condition precedent. An event whose occurrence will extinguish a claim for a breach of contract that has already occurred, is a condition subsequent. Under this test, since no duty to pay the additional sum in Gray v. Gardner would arise until after October 1, however the contract was worded, the condition was a condition precedent. Indeed, most conditions are conditions precedent under this test and a true condition subsequent is a rarity. One example is a term in an insurance policy under which the insured may not maintain an action unless he commences it within a stated period, for example, one year after the insured event.[a] The courts have not often made use of the Restatement logic in allocating burdens of pleading and proof, and Holmes remarked that the distinction based on a time-sequence of events is "of the slightest possible importance." Holmes, The Common Law 318 (1881). Restatement Second abandons it. See Restatement Second, § 250 and Comment c.

More satisfactory is a functional test, in which one goes directly to the ultimate question: Which party should bear the burden of proof in the light of the fundamental considerations for allocating that burden (either in the sense of the burden of producing evidence or of the burden of persuasion)? Which party has easier access to the facts? Which party's contention departs more from common experience? Is one party's contention less favored by the law? And so on.[b]

a. Another is a term in the A.I.A. performance bond form: "Any suit under this bond must be instituted before the expiration of two (2) years from the date on which final payment under the Contract falls due."

b. Consider, for example, a term such as that in the Fairmount Glass case, p. 67 supra: "subject to the contingencies of agencies or transportation, delays or accidents beyond our control." What is the condition of the seller's duty to deliver under such a term? Who should bear the burden of proof with respect to it? See 3A Corbin, § 642. Who should bear the burden of proof in the personal satisfaction cases?

At this point the analysis leaves the realm of substantive contract law and can best be dealt with in a course in procedure. See James, Civil Procedure § 7.8 (1965).

HICKS v. BUSH

Court of Appeals of New York, 1962.
10 N.Y.2d 488, 180 N.E.2d 425.

FULD, JUDGE. In this action for specific performance of a written agreement, we granted the plaintiff leave to appeal to consider whether the parol evidence rule was violated by the receipt of testimony tending to establish that the parties had orally agreed that the legal effectiveness of the written agreement should be subject to a stated condition precedent.

On July 10, 1956, the plaintiff Frederick Hicks, together with defendant Michael Congero and one Jack McGee, executed a written agreement with the individual defendants, members of defendant Clinton G. Bush Company, whereby the parties were to merge their various corporate interests into a single "holding" company in order to achieve more efficient operation and greater financial strength. The document recited, among other things, that the plaintiff would subscribe for some 425,000 shares of stock in the new holding corporation, known as Bush-Hicks Enterprises, Inc., and that the defendants comprising the Bush Company would subscribe for more than a million shares. The other parties to the agreement were to subscribe for a total of less than 50,000 shares. The principal consideration for the subscription was the transfer to the holding company of stock in the operating corporations which the several parties owned.

The written agreement provided expressly that the subscriptions for the stock in Bush-Hicks Enterprises were to be made "within five days after the date of this Agreement" and that, "If within twenty-five days after the date hereof Bush-Hicks shall have failed to accept any of said subscriptions delivered to it * * * then and in any such event the obligations of all of the parties hereto shall be terminated and cancelled." The subscriptions were promptly made and accepted and, although the plaintiff turned over the stock of his corporations, the defendants did not transfer the stock of their companies to Bush-Hicks Enterprises. In consequence, the plaintiff never received the Bush-Hicks stock as provided in the agreement and the merger never eventuated.

Alleging a breach of contract, the plaintiff brought this suit for specific performance and for an accounting. In their answer, the defendants urged, as an affirmative defense, that the written agreement was executed "upon a parol condition" that it "was not to operate" as a contract and that the contemplated merger was not "to become effective" until so-called "equity expansion funds", amounting to

$672,500, were first procured.   And to support that allegation, the defendants upon the trial offered evidence of such an oral understanding.   The court admitted the evidence, over the plaintiff's objection that it varied and contradicted the terms of the writing, and finding that the oral condition asserted had actually been agreed on by the parties, rendered judgment in favor of the defendants.

A reading of the record unquestionably supports the decision of the courts below, that the parties, have concluded that $672,500 was essential to successful operation of the proposed merger, agreed that the entire merger deal was to be subject to the condition precedent that that sum be raised.   Thus, one witness, the president of the defendant Bush Company, declared that everyone "understood" that the writing was not to become operative as a binding contract until the specified equity expansion funds were obtained.   Indeed, his expressive and colorful testimony leaves no doubt as to the nature of the agreement arrived at: "I used the Chinese slang phrase of 'No tickie, no shirtie.'   Let's get signed so we would be ready.   I said, 'You all know what that means, that if we do not get the funds, this document [the written agreement] does not become operative * * *.' * * *   There is only one understanding, verbal understanding that we have had.   That speaks of 'Get the money or no deal.' "

The expansion capital of $672,500, which the parties hoped would be procured by December 31, 1956, was never raised.

The applicable law is clear, the relevant principles settled.   Parol testimony is admissible to prove a condition precedent to the legal effectiveness of a written agreement (see Saltzman v. Barson, 239 N.Y. 332, 337, 146 N.E. 618, 619; Grannis v. Stevens, 216 N.Y. 583, 587, 111 N.E. 263, 265; Reynolds v. Robinson, 110 N.Y. 654, 18 N.E. 127; see, also, 4 Williston, Contracts [3d ed., 1961], § 634, p. 1021; 3 Corbin, Contracts [1960 ed.], § 589, p. 530 et seq.),[a] if the condition does not contradict the express terms of such written agreement.   (See Fadex Foreign Trading Corp. v. Crown Steel Corp., 297 N.Y. 903, 79 N.E.2d 739, affg. 272 App.Div. 273, 274–276, 70 N.Y.S.2d 892, 893–894; see, also, Restatement, Contracts, § 241.)   A certain disparity is inevitable, of course, whenever a written promise is, by oral agreement of the parties, made conditional upon an event not expressed in

a.   The classic case is Pym v. Campbell, 6 El. & Bl. 370, 119 Eng.Rep. 903 (Q.B. 1856).   Pym, an inventor, was negotiating with Campbell and his associates for the sale to them of Pym's invention.   The parties prepared a written agreement containing the terms of the proposed sale and were awaiting an opinion from Abernathie, an engineer.   In order to avoid having to meet again, they signed the agreement on the oral understanding that it would be an agreement only if Abernathie approved of the invention.   When Pym sued on the agreement, Campbell and his associates prevailed at the trial by proving that Abernathie had not approved.   The reasoning of the court in upholding this decision is suggested by Earle, J.: "The distinction in point of law is that evidence to vary the terms of an agreement in writing is not admissible, but evidence to show that there is not an agreement at all is admissible."

the writing. Quite obviously, though, the parol evidence rule does not bar proof of every orally established condition precedent, but only of those which in a real sense contradict the terms of the written agreement. (See, e. g., Illustration to Restatement, Contracts, § 241.) Upon the present appeal, our problem is to determine whether there is such a contradiction.

The Fadex case (297 N.Y. 903, 79 N.E.2d 739, supra) is illustrative. The plaintiff, seeking damages for nondelivery of certain goods, relied upon written agreements which specifically provided that the goods were "Ready now" and that the time of delivery was to be "Prompt" and "Within 4 to 6 weeks, if possible earlier". Despite these express recitals, plus the further explicit notation that no oral arrangement or modification was to be binding upon the parties, the defendant sought to show a contemporaneous oral agreement that the sales were conditioned upon its ability to obtain the goods within a month. In connection with a motion for partial summary judgment, this court decided that an oral condition precedent to the formation of a contract could be established when not contradictory of the written agreement itself, but concluded that the condition attempted to be proved by the defendant Crown Steel Corporation would, if ruled operative, actually annul the express terms of the writing.

The present case differs materially from Fadex. There is here no direct or explicit contradiction between the oral condition and the writing; in fact, the parol agreement deals with a matter on which the written agreement, as in some of the cases cited (10 N.Y.2d p. 491, 225 N.Y.S.2d 36, 180 N.E.2d 427, supra), is silent. The plaintiff, however, contends that, since the written agreement provides in terms that the obligations of the parties were to be terminated if the merged corporation failed to accept any of their stock subscriptions within 25 days, the additional oral condition—that the writing "was [not] to become operative" and that the merger was "not to become effective" until the expansion funds had been raised—is irreconcilable with the written agreement.

As already indicated, and analysis confirms it, the two conditions may stand side by side. The oral requirement that the writing was not to take effect as a contract until the equity expansion funds were obtained is simply a further condition—a condition added to that requiring the acceptance of stock subscriptions within 25 days—and not one which is contradictory. If both provisions had been contained in the written agreement, it is clear that the defendants would not have been under immediate legal duty to transfer the stock in their companies to Bush-Hicks Enterprises until both conditions had been fulfilled and satisfied. And it is equally clear that evidence of an oral condition is not to be excluded as contradictory or "inconsistent" merely because the written agreement contains other conditions precedent. . . .

In short, the parties in the case before us intended that their respective rights and duties with respect to the contemplated transfers of stock in the operating companies to the holding company be subject to two conditions, each independent of the other—the acceptance of the stock subscription within a specified period and the procuring of expansion funds of $672,500. As the courts below found, the parties did not contemplate performance of the written agreement until such funds were first received. In other words, it was their desire and understanding that the merger was to be one of proposal only and that, even though the formal preliminary steps were to be taken, the writing was not to become operative as a contract or the merger effective until $672,500 was raised. It is certainly not improbable that parties contracting in these circumstances would make the asserted oral agreement; the condition precedent at hand is the sort of condition which parties would not be inclined to incorporate into a written agreement intended for public consumption. The challenged evidence was, therefore, admissible and, since there was ample proof attesting to the making of the oral agreement, the trial court was fully warranted in holding that no operative or binding contract ever came into existence.

The judgment appealed from should be affirmed, with costs.

NOTES

(1) *Conditions and the Parol Evidence Rule.* Were the defendants attempting to show that the writing was not to have any effect until the funds were procured or that the obligations of the parties under the instrument were conditional on the procurement of the funds? If the former, was there an integrated agreement? If the latter, does the case stand for the proposition that the parol evidence rule does not apply to conditions precedent? That it does not apply to a condition like that in Lach v. Cahill? Like that in Mascioni v. Miller?

A written offer is made to supply 60,000 cases of evaporated milk, packed for export. It states: "This offer is subject to the government's acceptance for export." The recipient wires his assent to the sale prior to obtaining an export license. Suppose the buyer changes his mind, and takes the position that he had no power of acceptance under the "offer" as written. Is there another way of understanding the language quoted? Cf. National Dairymen Ass'n v. Dean Milk Co., 183 F.2d 349 (7th Cir. 1950), cert. denied, 340 U.S. 876 (1950). If it is held that the messages create a contract, but the government's action is unfavorable, is the legal position of the parties the same as if no contract existed?

(2) *The Code.* What would have been the result in Hicks v. Bush if UCC 2–202 had been applicable? See Hunt Foods & Industries v. Doliner, 26 A.D.2d 41, 270 N.Y.S.2d 937 (1st Dept. 1966).

(3) *Merger Clauses and Conditions.* In Kryl v. Mechalson, 259 Wis. 204, 47 N.W.2d 899 (1951), the court held that an oral condition to the contract could be established in spite of the following language: "It is un-

derstood that this contract is complete in itself, and that the party of the first part is not bound by any other terms or agreements other than are herein contained." Can you draft a clause which would be more likely to be effective? See Edward T. Kelly Co. v. Von Zakobiel, 168 Wis. 579, 171 N.W. 75 (1919).

Review the clause that you drafted in response to Note 2, p. 569 supra. Can you improve it in the light of Hicks v. Bush?

Chapter 7

PERFORMANCE AND BREACH

What kinds of conduct amount to a breach of contract? Are there varieties and grades of breach, such that some have more serious consequences than others? What are the permissible responses to a breach by the injured party?

The idea of exchange has had much to do with problems of breach in contract law. An important way to secure the fair expectations of a contracting party is to protect him against liability for breach on his part, prematurely asserted. Ordinarily a promisor may protect himself, as we have seen, by using appropriate express conditions, so that he is not chargeable unless the promisee has rendered some qualifying performance on his part. In this chapter we shall see that a measure of protection is given to most promisors, in an exchange relation, reflecting the law's own ideas of appropriate conditions. It came to be noticed, by Lord Mansfield and others, that implied conditions are a natural inference from an exchange of promises. More recently, Professor Corbin devised the useful term "constructive conditions" to describe the means of established rules to limit contract accountability, so as to protect the expectation of exchange.

Many justifiable expectations cannot be sufficiently protected, however, by the law of conditions, if it only supports a promisor in a defensive posture. One who has committed himself in exchange for a return performance is entitled, as stated in a Code comment, to "a continuing sense of reliance and security that the promised performance will be forthcoming when due." [a] In various ways the law affords protection for this interest, notably by the common-law doctrine of anticipatory breach, and by the statutory right to assurance of performance. These subjects are examined here.

A different sort of expectation arises when a contracting party has invested substantially in his performance, expending labor, materials, or the like. If he fails after all to meet his commitment, does he lose all under the doctrine of constructive conditions? The answer is compounded of many elements. Section 2 considers the possibility of restitutionary relief. Section 3, focussing on construction contracts, develops the doctrine of substantial performance. Ideas of divisibility, and of waiver and the like, also play a part. There is a

a. UCC 2–609, Comment 1.

connection, of course, between this problem and that of "forfeiture," broached in Chapter 3 supra.

Problems of performance and breach associated with sale contracts in particular are grouped in Section 4 (goods) and Section 5 (land).

SECTION 1.   SECURING EXPECTATIONS

GODBURN v. MESERVE

Supreme Court of Errors of Connecticut, 1944.
130 Conn. 723, 37 A.2d 235.

Action by Lulu Godburn and another against George Meserve and another, executors of the estate of Carrie J. Wells, deceased, to recover damages for breach of a contract by defendants' decedent and for value of services rendered to her, which action was tried to a jury.

BROWN, JUDGE.   In this action based on an agreement by the plaintiffs to provide and care for the defendants' decedent in her house in Stratford in consideration of her promise to leave the property to them by will, the jury rendered a verdict for the plaintiffs which, it was undisputed, was predicated upon the decedent's breach of an express agreement alleged in the first count.   There was a second count based on quantum meruit.   The defendants have appealed from the court's denial of their motion to set aside the verdict and from the judgment, assigning error in the court's charge to the jury.   In the view which we take of the case it is necessary to consider only the claimed error in the court's denial of the motion.

For more than three years prior to February 21, 1936, the plaintiffs had lived as tenants of the decedent in a house owned by her in Stratford.   As of the above date, the decedent, seventy-six years of age, was living alone in the house next door, which she also owned. On that date, the parties entered into an express written agreement which provided that for the remainder of the decedent's life they were to live together in her homestead, she occupying the front upstairs room and they furnishing her with board, heat, light and laundry, providing care for her in case of any minor ailments or sickness not requiring a nurse or hospital service, and paying ten dollars per month rent.   It further provided that the plaintiffs' family was to be limited to themselves and daughter, and that the decedent was to leave the property to them by will at her death.   The decedent made a will in accordance with the agreement and the plaintiffs occupied the house with the decedent and provided for her as stipulated until on or about August 5, 1941, when the plaintiffs moved out and did nothing

further in performance of the contract. Thereupon the decedent revoked her will. She died May 21, 1942, at the age of eighty-three.
During the first two years that the parties lived together their relations were generally harmonious and mutually agreeable, but thereafter increasing friction developed. Just before the plaintiffs moved
out Mr. Godburn proposed a modification of the agreement whereby
the decedent would have two rooms, get her own meals and do her own
laundry, and the plaintiffs would make an increased cash payment
monthly. The decedent refused to modify the agreement. These
facts are undisputed.

The jury could reasonably have further found that the plaintiffs
faithfully and fully performed their part of the contract up to the
time they left; that the decedent objected to the plaintiffs' having
their grandchildren and others stay in the home as their guests; that
she objected to being left alone in the house at night and thus prevented the plaintiffs from going out or away on vacation; that she
constantly found fault with many minor things around the house;
that she, without reason, objected to the amount of water used by the
plaintiffs which she had to pay for; that she, likewise without reason,
demanded food other than that which the plaintiffs provided; constantly objected to the manner in which Mrs. Godburn cooked food
and at times refused to eat it, developed a habit of tapping her foot
on the floor while eating, and once when Mr. Godburn was seriously ill
made a disturbance because her meal was not served on time; and
that this course of conduct so disturbed the plaintiffs' home life that
they became very nervous, and rendered it very disagreeable and difficult for them to continue to reside with her.

The contract was bilateral containing mutual and dependent covenants demanding of each of the parties readiness and willingness to
perform. It therefore required, "as a condition of judicial enforcement or redress for breach at the complaint of either such readiness
and willingness on his part or a showing of sufficient excuse for their
absence. Phillips v. Sturm, 91 Conn. 331, 335, 99 A. 689; Smith v.
Lewis, 24 Conn. 624, 625, 63 Am.Dec. 180." Stierle v. Rayner, 92
Conn. 180, 183, 102 A. 581, 582; Lunde v. Minch, 105 Conn. 657, 659,
136 A. 552. Therefore here, if the plaintiffs on their part were prevented by the decedent from completing the contract, they were entitled to bring their action for damages for her breach of it. Valente
v. Weinberg, 80 Conn. 134, 135, 67 A. 369, 13 L.R.A.,N.S., 448; Dadio
v. Dadio, 123 Conn. 88, 92, 192 A. 557; Restatement, 1 Contracts, §
295, Conn.Annot., § 295. However, "In order to amount to a prevention of performance by the adversary party, the conduct on the part
of the party who is alleged to have prevented performance must be
wrongful, and, accordingly, in excess of his legal rights." 5 Page,
Contracts, § 2919, p. 5145; Lansdowne v. Reihmann, Ky., 124 S.W.
353. Although " 'where a party stipulates that another shall do a certain thing, he thereby impliedly promises that he will himself do

nothing which will hinder or obstruct that other in doing that thing' "
(3 Williston, Contracts, Rev.Ed., § 677, p. 1956), manifestly this principle has no application where the hindrance is due to some action of
the promisor which he was permitted to take under either the express
or implied terms of the contract.   See Restatement, 1 Contracts, §
295.   The mere fact that permitted conduct of this nature by one
promisor renders unpleasant or inconvenient performance by the other of his agreement effects no discharge of that obligation.   See 5
Page, Contracts, § 2919, p. 5146; Smoot's Case, 15 Wall. 36, 46, 82 U.
S. 36, 46, 21 L.Ed. 107; Thompson & Son v. Brown, 106 Iowa 367,
372, 76 N.W. 819.

Accordingly, the question for determination is whether the
decedent's conduct complained of was wrongful in the sense of being
violative of her obligations under the contract.   In other words was it
or was it not conduct which must be said to have been fairly within the
contemplation of the parties when the agreement was entered into?
See Huminsky v. Gary Nat. Bank, 107 W.Va. 658, 150 S.E. 9.   In addition to the facts already mentioned, the undisputed testimony was
that for twenty years prior to the agreement Mr. Godburn had known
the decedent as a customer in the grocery store where he was employed, that during the last three and one-half years of this period,
while he and his family were living next door as her tenants, the
plaintiffs came to know the decedent very well, that she was regularly
and frequently in their home as a guest and ate meals there, and that
they knew she was an elderly lady apparently about seventy-six or sev-
en years of age.   It is a matter of common knowledge that a gradually
increasing impairment of powers and a not unusual tendency to more
or less eccentricity naturally are to be expected as incident to the advancing years of one of that age, and under the circumstances the
only reasonable conclusion upon the record before us is that the
decedent's conduct was fairly within the contemplation of the parties
under their contract as made.   The gist of the situation is apparently
well summarized by Mr. Godburn's testimony that "the only thing she
complained about was the eats," which everybody else thought were all
right, that her conduct was upsetting and disturbing to the plaintiffs
and that they "didn't have to take it" and they "wouldn't."   It follows
from what we have said that not only is there no evidence that the
decedent "forced the plaintiffs to leave said premises in violation of
the terms of the contract," as alleged in the complaint, but furthermore there is none that what she did was "wrongful, and, accordingly,
in excess of [her] legal rights" within the principle quoted above.
The defendants' motion to set aside the verdict should therefore have
been granted.

There is error, the judgment is set aside, and a new trial is ordered.

In this opinion, the other Judges concurred.

NOTES

(1) *The Rationale.* If it had been found that some of Carrie Wells' behavior was designed to irritate the Godburns, should the trial court's judgment have been affirmed? The plaintiff's complaint contained one count based on the express agreement and one based on quasi contract. If the evidence had been such as to warrant recovery, on which theory should it have been granted? Could the plaintiffs recover the same amount of damages *as if* they had fully performed the condition precedent to defendant's promise? "In general," Holmes wrote, "when one party, by his fault, prevents the other party to a contract from entitling himself to a benefit under it according to its terms, the former is liable for the value of that benefit less the value or cost of what the plaintiff would have had to do to get it." St. Louis Dressed Beef & Provision Co. v. Maryland Cas. Co., 201 U.S. 173 (1906). On prevention of performance generally, see Restatement, §§ 262, 295, 315.

(2) *Constructive Condition.* The failure of the plaintiffs' claim evidently resulted from their want of "readiness and willingness to perform." To state the matter technically, their performance was (unless excused) a *condition* limiting Carrie Wells' duty to perform. The court does not say that the written agreement contained an express condition to this effect. Rather, it derives the condition from the character of the contract: it was a "bilateral [one] containing mutual and dependent covenants." The case therefore illustrates the very common variety of conditions known as *constructive* conditions, and sometimes called implied conditions. The notion of constructive conditions has been an extraordinarily fruitful one in the law of contracts, and looking only to current law it seems an inevitable one. The proposition that if the Godburns wrongfully failed to care for Carrie she was not obliged to leave her property to them may appear self-evident.

At one stage of the common law, however, it was not at all self-evident. Instead, the doctrine of constructive conditions developed rather slowly and fitfully. Something of that history will be developed below. For the present, it is enough to notice that the Godburns were entitled not only to the letter of Carrie's promise, but also to a measure of cooperation from her in fulfilling the objects of the contract.

BARRON v. CAIN, 216 N.C. 282, 4 S.E.2d 618 (1939). [Barron brought an action in which he alleged that in 1932 he was induced by Cain, his grand-uncle, then 85 years of age, to go and live with Cain and care for him during his life, upon an understanding that plaintiff, at the death of the defendant, would be well paid for his services. The defendant moved to strike paragraphs 5, 6 and 7 of the complaint. Insofar as the motion was denied, defendant excepted and appealed. *Held:* Affirmed.]

BARNHILL, JUSTICE. . . . In paragraph No. 6, the plaintiff alleges that during the seven years he lived with the defendant the defendant was constantly under the influence of liquor and that notwithstanding the indignities, lonesomeness and inconvenience to which the plaintiff was subjected by reason thereof, he remained with and was at all times, ready, able and willing to serve the defendant until his death in compliance with the understanding between him and the defendant. In paragraph No. 5 the plaintiff alleges that while the defendant was under the influence of liquor he was disagreeable and subjected the plaintiff to abuse and every manner of indignity, notwithstanding which, the plaintiff, in compliance with his agreement, continued to live with and serve the defendant. These allegations constitute allegations in aggravation of damages. The plaintiff has a right to allege, and to attempt to prove, that by reason of the condition, temperament and attitude of the defendant, services rendered to him were of much greater value than similar services rendered to a sober and well-disposed person.

In paragraph No. 7 plaintiff alleges that the defendant assaulted him with a deadly weapon and ordered him to leave, and sets out the essential facts in relation thereto. He further alleges that he was forced to leave the home of the defendant for fear of bodily harm. These allegations are essential to the plaintiff's cause of action for the purpose of disclosing the alleged reason why the plaintiff has not complied, on his part, with the alleged agreement. Having alleged an agreement to serve defendant during his lifetime and having admitted in his complaint his non-compliance, it is essential to his alleged cause of action that he set forth the wrongful conduct of defendant which caused the breach through no fault of the plaintiff.

NOTE

The Case of the School Board's Lesson. The New York City Board of Education let a contract for work on a school building, containing a condition that the agreement should be binding only if "the comptroller shall indorse hereon his certificate" that appropriated and unexpended funds were on hand to meet the estimated expense. After the contractor had done some preliminary work, the Board "rescinded" the contract. Although it did not question that the required funds were available, it justified its action by the comptroller's failure to certify the contract. He had withheld certification at the Board's request. The contractor sued the Board. From a judgment for the defendant, the plaintiff appealed. *Held*: Reversed. The Board's action could not be justified by the comptroller's failure to certify the contract. "The general rule is, as it has been frequently stated, that a party to a contract cannot rely on the failure of another to perform a condition precedent where he has frustrated or prevented the occurrence of the condition." Kooleraire Serv. & Inst. Corp. v. Board of Ed., 28 N.Y.2d 101, 268 N.E.2d 782 (1971).

Is there any difference, in legal effect, between wrongful prevention of the fulfillment of a constructive condition and similar action with respect to an express condition?

PREVENTION AS BREACH

The success of the claimant in Barron v. Cain, and in the note case, can be ascribed to the doctrine of "prevention." In each case the defendant's conduct was such as to enable the claimant to assert a breach, although a condition qualifying the claimant's right had not been fulfilled. (In Barron v. Cain, the condition was a *constructive* one: that he care for Cain for the rest of his life.)

Sometimes the doctrine of prevention is regarded as a roundabout way of expressing an implied undertaking by the defendant. "It is a general rule of contract law that each party impliedly covenants not to hinder, prevent or make more burdensome the other party's performance. . . . A breach of this covenant may . . . be construed as an actual breach of the contract. . . ." State of California v. United States, 151 F.Supp. 570, 573 (N.D.Cal.1957).[a] On this view, in the Case of the School Board's Lesson, the plaintiff might have charged the board with breach, not for "rescinding" the contract, but for directing the comptroller not to certify it.

Does it matter, in substance, whether the act of prevention is regarded as being itself a breach, or as maturing a further duty of the defendant? In a somewhat comparable case, Justice Holmes said: "The sole difference would be in the form of the declaration." St. Louis Dressed Beef & Prov. Co. v. Maryland Cas. Co., 201 U.S. 173 (1906). After the defendant's first breach in that case, he said, "we think that the plaintiff was entitled to treat the contract as on foot, notwithstanding the defendant's act, and go on with it *cy-près*." But that was a singular case in some ways; it is sometimes risky for the victim of a breach of contract to disregard it, and "go on" with the contract. In the Case of the School Board's Lesson, would the plaintiff have been well advised to proceed with the work, notwithstanding the comptroller's failure to certify the contract? What risks would it run?

NOTE

Early Cases. "The older common law did not uniformly require the promisor to refrain from actively preventing the promisee from performing the condition of the promise. In one early case the defendant had given his penal bond to pay the plaintiff eighty pounds unless the defendant should procure a marriage to take place between the plaintiff and one Bridget Palmer, before a certain day. The defendant pleaded that before that day the plaintiff addressed Bridget in such vile and insulting language that the defendant could not bring about the marriage. The plea was adjudged bad, on the ground that the defendant should show that he used due diligence to bring about the marriage. [Blandford v. Andrews, Cro.Eliz. 694, 78

---

a. And may also, "in some cases, be construed as a failure of a condition precedent, thereby relieving the other party from the duty of counterper-

formance under the terms of the contract, and providing him with a defense to an action on the contract . . . ."

Eng.Rep. 930 (K.B.1599)] . . . These decisions show that the implication of a condition of non-prevention was by no means inevitable." Patterson, Constructive Conditions in Contracts, 42 Colum.L.Rev. 903, 931–2 (1942).

IRON TRADE PRODUCTS CO. v. WILKOFF CO.

Supreme Court of Pennsylvania, 1922.
272 Pa. 172, 116 A. 150.

WALLING, J. In July, 1919, plaintiff entered into a written contract with defendant for the purchase of 2,600 tons of section relaying rails, to be delivered in New York harbor at times therein specified for $41 a ton. Defendant failed to deliver any of the rails, and plaintiff brought this suit, averring by reason of such default, it had been compelled to purchase the rails elsewhere (2,000 tons thereof at $49.20 per ton and 600 tons at $49 per ton), also that the market or current price of the rails at the time and place of delivery was approximately $50 per ton, and claiming as damages the difference between what it had been compelled to pay and the contract price. Defendant filed an affidavit of defense and a supplement thereto, both of which the court below held insufficient and entered judgment for plaintiff, from which defendant brought this appeal.

In effect, the affidavit of defense avers the supply of such rails was very limited, there being only two places in the United States (one in Georgia and one in West Virginia) where they could be obtained in quantities to fill the contract, and that pending the time for delivery defendant was negotiating for the required rails when plaintiff announced to the trade its urgent desire to purchase a similar quantity of like rails, and in fact bought 887 tons and agreed to purchase a much larger quantity from the parties with whom defendant had been negotiating, further averring this conduct on behalf of plaintiff reduced the available supply of relaying rails and enhanced the price to an exorbitant sum, rendering performance by defendant impossible. The affidavit, however, fails to aver knowledge on part of plaintiff that the supply of rails was limited or any intent on its part to prevent, interfere with, or embarrass defendant in the performance of the contract; and there is no suggestion of any understanding, express or implied, that defendant was to secure the rails from any particular source, or that plaintiff was to refrain from purchasing other rails; hence it was not required to do so. The true rule is stated in Williston on Contracts, p. 1308, as quoted by the trial court, viz.:

"If a party seeking to secure all the merchandise of a certain character which he could entered into a contract for a quantity of the required goods, and subsequently made performance of the contract by the seller more difficult by making other purchases which increased the scarcity of the available supply, his conduct would furnish no excuse for refusal to perform the prior contract."

Mere difficulty of performance will not excuse a breach of contract. Corona C. & C. Co. v. Dickinson, 261 Pa. 589, 104 A. 741; Janes v. Scott, 59 Pa. 178, 98 Am.Dec. 328; 35 Cyc. 245. Defendant relies upon the rule stated in United States v. Peck, 102 U.S. 64, 26 L.Ed. 46, that—

"The conduct of one party to a contract which prevents the other from performing his part is an excuse for nonperformance."

The cases are not parallel. Here plaintiff's conduct did not prevent performance by defendant, although it may have added to the difficulty and expense thereof. There is no averment that plaintiff's purchases exhausted the supply of rails, and the advance in price caused thereby is no excuse. The Peck Case stands on different ground. There Peck contracted to sell the government a certain quantity of hay for the Tongue River station, and the trial court found it was mutually understood the hay was to be cut on government lands called "the Big Meadows," in the Yellowstone valley, which was the only available source of supply, also that thereafter the government caused all of that hay to be cut for it by other parties, in view of which Peck was relieved from his contract.

The affidavit "denies that there was any market or market price or current price for such relaying rails" at any time from the date of the contract to the beginning of this suit, but other statements therein amount to an admission of a market price. For example, it speaks of "the trade in Pittsburgh, New York, and other centers of such trade"; also of "the very small quantity of such rails in the market." The affidavit further states that—

"After making the said contract with the plaintiff the defendant began negotiations with the persons from whom the said rails in Georgia and West Virginia might be purchased; and in each of the two cases referred to such negotiations had proceeded so far that defendant could have purchased 2,600 tons of such rails either in Georgia or West Virginia at some such price as that contracted to the plaintiff, or less, or not greatly in excess thereof.

"In fact, the plaintiff bought a quantity of such rails, to wit, 887 tons, and at one time had contracted for the purchase of a much larger quantity thereof, from the same persons with whom the defendant had been negotiating for the same, and at higher prices than had been offered to the defendant by the same persons within the terms of the said contract.

"And affiant, while denying, as aforesaid, that the plaintiff was compelled to purchase the said rails or any of them, avers that, if the plaintiff was so compelled, it was only as the result of plaintiff's own interference with the defendant's performance of the said contract, and avers that but for the said interference the defendant would have made full performance of its said contract."

The above and the admitted facts that plaintiff actually bought the 2,600 tons and had previously resold the same indicate a market value, and the specific averment thereof, in the statement of claim is not sufficiently denied in the affidavit. An affidavit of defense must be considered as a whole, and therein a general denial is of no avail against an admission of the same fact. An affidavit that is contradictory or equivocal is insufficient. See Noll v. Royal Exchange Assurance Corp., 76 Pa.Super.Ct. 510.

The supplemental affidavit avers that when the contract in suit was made plaintiff, to the knowledge of defendant, had resold the 2,600 tons of rails at $42.25 per ton, and, furthermore, that the purchaser at such resale released plaintiff from all claim for damages under the contract. . . . The fact that a vendee has resold the goods contracted for is of no moment unless made a part of the contract; for, if not, he is entitled to the benefit of his bargain, regardless of the disposition he may intend to make of the property involved. To hold otherwise would inject collateral issues in trials for breaches of such contracts.

The assignments of error are overruled, and the judgment is affirmed.

NOTES

(1) *The Rationale.* Could the decision in United States v. Peck be justified without assuming that the Government acted with intent to prevent, interfere with, or embarrass Peck in the performance of his contract? A possible explanation of the case is that the Government's action relieved Peck by reason of a constructive condition. Does the principal case establish the proposition that no condition respecting prevention was attached to the rail purchase contract?

(2) *The Case of the Overbidding Buyer.* Some houses in Brooklyn were about to be offered for sale in a foreclosure proceeding. Patterson was in a favorable position to buy them at the public sale, and Mrs. Meyerhofer was interested in owning them. Therefore they entered into an ordinary sale contract whereby Mrs. Meyerhofer agreed to pay Patterson $23,000 for the property. No mention was made of the fact that he did not own it. When Patterson attended the foreclosure sale Mrs. Meyerhofer was also there, and whenever he made a bid she bid higher. The four houses in question were struck down to her for $22,380. Patterson sued for damages, and it was said that on these facts he was entitled to $620. "In the case of every contract there is an implied undertaking on the part of each party that he will not intentionally and purposely do anything to prevent the other party from carrying out the agreement on his part." Patterson v. Meyerhofer, 204 N.Y. 96, 97 N.E. 472 (1912).

(3) *Alice's Action.* John Alice was invited by the General Services Administration to bid for a contract to supply uniforms to the Government. He telephoned a clothing manufacturer, the Robett Company, to obtain its prices, and Robett at once wrote to Alice as follows: "we are pleased to offer the 3500 shirts at $4 each and the trousers at $3 each

. . . " In fact, an agreement on these terms was reached in the telephone conversation. Alice told Robett that its price would be the basis of his bid to GSA. About ten days later, Robett made its own bid for the contract, offering to produce the uniforms for $7.78 each. The Government accepted this bid. Alice sued Robett for breach of contract. *Held*: Summary judgment granted for the defendant. Robett's letter did not satisfy the statute of frauds (UCC 2–201), for it was only an offer. "Neither does it appear that an offer from a manufacturer, to a supplier who is bidding for resale over to a third party contains an implied term prohibiting the manufacturer from submitting its own bid directly to the third party, in competition with the supplier." Alice v. Robett Mfg. Co., 328 F.Supp. 1377, (N.D.Ga.1970), aff'd mem. 445 F.2d 316 (5th Cir. 1971). (The plaintiff's acceptance of the offer was not found as a fact, but was assumed for purposes of the motion for summary judgment.) Would the decision have been the same if the defendant's letter had been a "firm offer" under UCC 2–205?

KEHM CORP. v. UNITED STATES

United States Court of Claims, 1950.
93 F.Supp. 620.

The Kehm Corporation sued the United States for damages sustained as the result of delays caused by defendant, in performance of plaintiff's contract to manufacture practice bombs for the Navy. On a hearing under a court rule to determine whether defendant is liable for any part of the money sought to be recovered. . . .

Judgment determining plaintiff's right to recover damages in an amount to be determined in future proceedings.

HOWELL, JUDGE. On October 8, 1943, the plaintiff contracted with the United States to manufacture for the Navy 2,800 concrete practice bombs, 2,500 to be 100-pound bombs and 300 to be 1,000-pound bombs. Plaintiff had two plants, one at Miami, Florida, where the 1,000-pound bombs were manufactured, and one at nearby Fort Lauderdale, where the 100-pound bombs were manufactured. The completed bombs were to include tail assemblies which were to be furnished by the defendant. Delivery of the bombs, complete with tail assemblies, was to be made within 45 days, that is, by November 22, 1943. As it turned out, the last shipment was not made until April 12, 1944. Plaintiff has been paid the contract price, and now sues here for an additional $21,737.94 as compensation for losses and damages allegedly sustained as a result of delays caused by the Government which retarded completion of the contract. The period for which damages are sought ended April 7, 1944, and plaintiff's claim was first filed with the contracting officer on April 8, 1944. The case at this stage is limited under our Rule 39(b), 28 U.S.C.A., to a determination of whether the United States is liable for any part of the money sought to be recovered.

The contract did not specify what type of tail assemblies was to be supplied by the Government, nor when. There were two types, service and practice. The methods of manufacturing the bombs differed depending on the type of tail to be used. Practice tails must be cast integrally with the concrete, which means that the bomb cannot be cast until the tail is actually on hand. Service tails are attached after the concrete casting has been completed, and it is feasible therefore to cast the bomb before receipt of the tail. In the initial stage of the negotiations leading up to the contract, it was contemplated that practice tails would be used. Prior to the signing of the contract, however, plaintiff was informed that service tails were desired and would be supplied. The Navy did not have sufficient tail assemblies and had to procure them by special orders. At the time the contract was signed, the Navy had not ordered any service tails for 100-pound bombs, although it had ordered 500 practice tails on September 10. Plaintiff, however, had been led to expect service tails.

On October 16, the Government delivered the 500 practice tails to plaintiff at Fort Lauderdale. Plaintiff had already commenced making molds for bombs to which service tails could be attached. A week was lost while plaintiff attempted to determine whether the delivery of practice tails was a mistake or whether it indicated a change in the last expressed intention of the Navy, which was that service tails would be supplied. Plaintiff was again assured that service tails were wanted and would be furnished for the major part of the bombs. Plaintiff was instructed, however, to proceed with the manufacture of the bombs with the tails at hand, that is, with the practice tails. Plaintiff had previously cast some test sample bombs with practice tails and had about a dozen or two of these molds on hand. Other molds for practice tail bombs were made, and plaintiff had 500 100-pound bombs, equipped with practice tails, ready for delivery by November 22, 1943, the date by which the contract was supposed to have been completed.

Three days earlier, on November 19, two more shipments of tails were received. One shipment, to Fort Lauderdale, was of 500 more practice tails for 100-pound bombs; the other, to Miami, consisted of 500 service tails for 1,000-pound bombs. This was the first shipment of tails for 1,000-pound bombs and was of the expected type. Plaintiff proceeded with the manufacture of 1,000-pound bombs, and the 300 called for in the contract were ready for delivery by the end of December.

No more tails were received by plaintiff until February 23, 1944, when 2,050 service tails for 100-pound bombs were received. These tails had not even been ordered by the Government until November 12, 1943, and an additional shipping order for them had to be issued on January 25, 1944. After receipt of this shipment, manufacture of 100-pound bombs was resumed and all casting was completed at Fort Lauderdale by March 10, 1944. Plaintiff then closed its Fort Lauderdale plant and moved the undelivered 100-pound bombs to Miami. Some of the tails for this last group of bombs were not attached until after the bombs had reached the Miami plant.

Plaintiff was unable to complete manufacture of the bombs by November 22, 1943, because of defendant's delay in furnishing the tails. [Further details of the Navy's delays are here omitted.]

Plaintiff was further delayed by the defendant's failure to accept the bombs as they were completed. [Details are here omitted.]

Behind the defendant's delays in accepting the bombs was the fact that the Navy had lost interest in the concrete bomb program. It was having difficulty in finding storage space for these now unwanted items. Because of the uncertainty created by defendant's confusing deliveries of practice rather than service tails and because of defendant's delays in supplying any tails and in accepting the completed bombs, plaintiff's performance of its contract was delayed until April 12, 1944. For purposes of measuring damages in this case, however, the period of delay will have to be considered as ending on April 7.

Plaintiff has been paid the contract price. Its claim for additional expenses was filed on April 8, 1944. On July 10, 1944, the contracting officer made findings of fact sustaining plaintiff's contentions. His findings were forwarded to the Navy Department, which referred the matter to the Comptroller General, who disallowed the claim on January 26, 1945, on the ground that it was for unliquidated damages and therefore a matter for determination by the courts. The disallowance was reaffirmed on September 7, 1945. We have now to determine not the extent of recoverable damages, if any sustained by plaintiff but whether any recoverable damages were sustained, that is, whether defendant's delays amounted to a breach of contract.

Logic would seem to require that a contract binding one party to fabricate goods for another by a certain time out of material to be furnished by the other must perforce be held also to bind the other party to supply the material sufficiently early for the work to be done as promised and not to be dilatory in accepting the completed goods. The law considers a promise such as plaintiff's to be subject to a "constructive condition of cooperation." Patterson, Constructive Conditions in Contracts, 42 Col.L.Rev. 903. The promisor's undertaking normally gives rise to an implied complementary obligation on the part of the promisee: he must not only not hinder his promisor's performance, he must do whatever is necessary to enable him to perform. United States v. Speed, 8 Wall. 77, 75 U.S. 77, 19 L.Ed. 449.
. . . 5 Williston on Contracts (1937) Sections 1293 A and 1318. The implied obligation is as binding as if it were spelled out. Wood v. Lucy, Lady Duff-Gordon, 222 N.Y. 88, 118 N.E. 214 [p. 234 supra].

[The court here distinguishes the case of United States v. Howard P. Foley Co., Inc., 329 U.S. 64, 67 S.Ct. 154.]

The Government's right under the contract to make changes cannot justify its waiting until February to supply material it was obligated to supply in October or November. [Citations omitted.]

We hold only that defendant's delays breached the contract, prevented timely performance by plaintiff, and resulted in some damage. Plaintiff is entitled to recover the loss it actually sustained as a result of the delay. United States v. Wyckoff Pipe & Creosoting Co., 271 U.S. 263, 46 S.Ct. 503, 70 L.Ed. 938. What these damages were we do not now determine. .   .   .

NOTES

(1) *Influences in Cooperation Cases.* The Patterson article, cited by the court, gives an historical and critical survey of the requirement of cooperation at pp. 928–42. "While not every act or omission by the obligor which may expedite performance by the obligee (of his promise or of a condition) is required, the acts or omissions which are clearly within the obligor's control and which are the normal or obvious means of the obligee's performance, are presumably required of the obligor, or he assumes the risk of their non-occurrence. The justifiable reliance by the obligee, the usages of the trade or activity, the mores of the community, are obviously influential in determining what co-operation is required in a particular transaction. Judicial opinions reveal these influences. The moral notions of carelessness or diligence, malice or inadvertence, have sporadic influence. The avoidance of unjust enrichment seems also influential." Id., pp. 937–8. How many of these "influences" would be relevant in applying Restatement, § 295? Is the phrase "terms of the contract" unduly restrictive, as Patterson suggests?

(2) *Problem.* Why was there not a constructive condition of cooperation in Dickey v. Philadelphia Minit-Man Corp., p. 615 supra, requiring Minit-Man to continue its car-washing business? Compare Levicoff v. Rubin & Co., 413 Pa. 134, 196 A.2d 359 (1964).

(3) *Express Requirements.* Sometimes an express provision is made in a contract for one party to cooperate with the other in bringing about a common objective. When a man engaged an artist to paint portraits of himself and the members of his family he agreed to make himself and them available for sittings.[a] Another example is found in standard liability insurance contracts. It is assumed that the common desire of the parties is to exonerate the insured from claims of liability to third persons. The insurer undertakes to defend suits against him, and, if unsuccessful, promises also to pay the resulting judgments, within policy limits. The following express condition is inserted for the insurer's protection: "The insured shall cooperate with the company and, upon the company's request, shall attend hearings and trials and shall assist in effecting settlements, securing and giving evidence, obtaining the attendance of witnesses and in the con-

---

a. Brockhurst v. Ryan, 2 Misc.2d 747, 146 N.Y.S.2d 386 (Sup.Ct.1955).

duct of suits." If the insured does not comply with this provision the insurer is likely to be relieved of further liability under the policy.

For the view that an insured would be required to cooperate with his insurer in this regard even if the policy had no provision on the subject, see Keeton, Ancillary Rights of the Insured, 13 Vand.L.Rev. 837, 847 (1960).

CORN PRODUCTS REFINING CO. v. FASOLA

New Jersey Court of Errors and Appeals, 1920.
94 N.J.L. 181, 109 A. 505.

BERGEN, J. September 10th, 1918, the plaintiff and defendant entered into a written contract by the terms of which the plaintiff agreed to sell to the defendant "Five hundred cases No. 5 Mazola," to be delivered within sixty days after delivery order. The terms of payment were thirty days net, or two per cent. discount for cash if payment was received by the seller within ten days from date of invoice, subject, however, to the following stipulation: "If at any time before shipment the financial responsibility of the buyer becomes impaired, or unsatisfactory to the seller, cash payment or satisfactory security may be required by the seller before shipment."

Under this agreement the plaintiff shipped to the defendant two hundred of the cases contracted for, and dated the invoice November 12th, 1918, so that payment therefore did not mature, under the contract, until December 12th, 1918. The shipments were made in two lots of one hundred cases each, but the invoices were both dated November, 1918. The defendant, on the 26th day of November, 1918, requested the delivery of the balance of the cases contracted for which the plaintiff refused to honor, and the defendant, claiming a breach of contract, refused to pay for the cases delivered, whereupon the plaintiff brought suit and recovered a judgment for the delivered goods at the contract rate, the court directing the jury to return a verdict for the plaintiff, which is one of the errors alleged in support of this appeal. The facts on this branch of the case are not in dispute and they are: that the plaintiff had been doing business for some time with the defendant, limiting the credit to $3,000; that to comply with the order would extend the credit to about $9,000; that it had been the practice of the defendant to generally discount her bills within ten days to the extent at least of seventy-five per cent. of her purchases, and that this had not been done in the present case when the request was made that plaintiff ship the residue of the cases contracted for.[a] The trial court held that under this contract the seller

---

a. According to the record in the case the trial court said, speaking of earlier dealings between the parties, that Fasola "took advantage of the first provision of the terms of payment in the contract and they discounted it. Now, that is what any good business man would do. Fasola did the right thing because he sweetened the mind of the seller by discounting his bill. There is nothing in the credit world that has a greater effect upon the

had a right to require cash payment or security before further shipment if the financial responsibility of the buyer had become unsatisfactory to the seller, and that the undisputed facts showed a sufficient basis to sustain a want of satisfaction with the financial responsibility of the buyer, and to justify the seller in exercising the option reserved in the contract. The willingness of a seller to extend credit upon being satisfied with the financial responsibility of the buyer must, to a large extent, be committed to the judgment of the seller, and when parties contract that if the responsibility of the buyer becomes unsatisfactory to the seller the latter may require cash payment or satisfactory security before delivery of the goods contracted for, the vendor is entitled to the benefit of his contract and, if for any reason, not pretended or unreal, he becomes dissatisfied with the financial responsibility of his debtor, he may invoke his contract and refuse to ship until secured according to the terms of the agreement. In Gwynne v. Hitchner & Yerkes, 66 N.J.L. 97, it was held that under a contract by a workman to perform his work in a manner satisfactory to his employers the latter had a right to judge for themselves whether his work was satisfactory, and that it was error to leave to the jury the question whether they ought to have been satisfied. The opinion was written for the Supreme Court by Mr. Justice Van Syckel, citing a large number of cases. This case was referred to with approval by Judge Adams in his opinion for this court in Gwynne v. Hitchner & Yerkes, 67 Id. 654, in which case it was held that it must appear, in defence of an action by a discharged employe for want of satisfactory work, that the employer was in fact dissatisfied, and that that was the basis for the discharge. In the instant case the testimony is undisputed that the refusal by the plaintiff to make further shipment was because they had become dissatisfied with the financial responsibility of the buyer, and not for any other reason. It appears in the case that they were perfectly willing to ship the goods upon payment or security, so there was no jury question open on that subject. That the sellers had become dissatisfied with the financial responsibility of their buyer clearly appears, and if they were required to give any reason, those they gave were not unreal or pretended, but sufficient to answer the terms of the contract.

Where a vendor contracts to deliver goods and allows the buyer credit for a term agreed upon, and by the same writing reserves the right to withdraw the credit and demand cash payment or security before the shipment of the goods if the financial responsibility of the buyer becomes unsatisfactory to the seller, the question of the satis-

mind of the seller than to have the purchaser discount his bills for cash. It shows a readiness for payment and a good, sound financial condition apparently. And what occurred after that? Bill after bill came along, discounted, three quarters of them, up to some time in August. And then what happened? Then the discounts were no longer indulged in, or at least to no great extent."

faction of the seller with the buyer's financial responsibility is to be settled by the seller before he parts with his goods, but there must be a real want of satisfaction with the buyer's financial responsibility, and the refusal to ship without payment or security must be based on that reason alone.

If the evidence shows a disputed question whether the seller was in fact dissatisfied or not a jury question is presented. Not whether the seller ought to be satisfied, but whether he was dissatisfied, and acted as he did for that reason. Gwynne v. Hitchner & Yerkes, supra. This result makes it unnecessary to consider defendant's counter-claim. The judgment will be affirmed, with costs.

NOTE

Further Facts in Fasola. According to the record on appeal in this case, Corn Products was the New York based producer of Mazola, which was used as a substitute for olive oil. Mrs. Anna Fasola and her husband did business as a "jobber" in New Jersey, under the name A. B. Fasola Company. Its course of dealing with Corn Products began in February, 1918. As late as November 26th, three months after Fasola stopped discounting its bills (i. e., taking advantage of the discount by quick payment), Corn Products was ready to deliver under the contract of September 10th. On December 3d, Fasola heard from a field salesman for Corn Products that there was "some trouble in the credit department." Fasola telephoned Corn Products at once, and then wrote: "Now today you come along and talk about credit, etc. . . . and refuse to deliver. We give you herewith notice that until said delivery is made to us as agreed upon . . . we will refuse to pay on the 12th of December the two bills which are not yet due . . . [W]e bought from you at 10 days 2 per cent. or 30 days netto, and it is our option and not yours to pay in one of the two ways . . . [I]f you do not mail us delivery order . . . we will refuse payment and will refer all the matter to a jury before our N.J. courts."

On December 9th, Corn Products wrote: "We are willing to give you on our usual open account terms a line of credit of $3,000 or $791.46 more than the two bills you now owe. This new delivery requested comes to $6,456.26 more than this amount and bearer will deliver to you delivery order for quantity of Mazola above mentioned upon your giving him cash or certified check to our order for $6,327.13."

Mr. Fasola testified that the seller's salesman "told me only that the credit department had to cut me down to $3,000 and that is one of the many mysteries of the credit department in the Corn Products Refining Company, they are doing it all over." He said also that the price of Mazola advanced as the Christmas season approached, and that it was in short supply. Should this have been treated as evidence of an unreal or pretended dissatisfaction with Fasola's credit, requiring that the case be submitted to the jury? Fasola's attorney put this question to the salesman:

Q. Wasn't the real refusal to deliver these goods due to the fact that the price had advanced?

A. Oh, no, no. We do not do that, no, sir. No . . . ..

UCC 2–609

The provision in this section for a written demand, and the requirement of a response within thirty days, is a mechanism for securing an expectation of performance that did not exist in pre-Code law. However, the principle on which it rests, as stated in the first sentence, is also expressed in various doctrines much older than the Code, and it is the organizing principle of this section.

To judge by the reported cases, the Code mechanism is not very often deliberately used. What might account for this fact? In spite of it, the section may prove to have an important effect on resolving disputes arising under contracts for the sale of goods. When a party senses a threat to his expectation of the other's performance, and does not react to it, it is possible that a court may later draw a conclusion unfavorable to his interest from his quiescence. Such a conclusion might be expressed in terms of waiver (see p. 770 infra). Do you see how the existence of UCC 2–609 may reinforce such a conclusion?

Is it possible to make a demand for assurance under the section inadvertently, without knowing, that is, of the statutory authorization? The question arises when a party threatened with disappointment responds instinctively with a request for assurance, or by serving an ultimatum on the other party, or by doing something in between. In some circumstances it might be well for him to contend that he cannot have overstepped the section because it applies only when consciously invoked. Probably the section is not so limited, however, for its standards have been referred to in cases where the parties were apparently unaware of it. On that view, does it seem hazardous for a party faced with disappointment to make complaints and threats expressing his insecurity without the advice of counsel? Can contracting parties be expected not to act in this manner often without obtaining legal advice?

Suppose that the Code had been in force at the time of Corn Products Refining Company v. Fasola, supra. Would Fasola's letter of December 3d ("We give you herewith notice . . .") have been regarded as a demand for adequate assurance of due performance by Corn Products? Would Corn Products' letter of December 9th ("will deliver" for cash) have been regarded as such a demand? How might these letters be characterized if they were not authorized by UCC 2–609?

Comment 4 to the section cites the Fasola case and gives the following additional "facts": "at the same time that [the buyer] failed to make his customary 10 days payment, the seller heard rumors, in fact false, that the buyer's financial condition was shaky. Thereupon, the seller demanded cash before shipment or security satisfactory to him. The buyer sent a good credit report from his banker, expressed willingness to make payments when due on the 30 day terms and insisted on further deliveries under the contract." These facts are said to illustrate reasonable grounds for insecurity. Also: "In the absence of the buyer's failure to take the 2% discount as was his custom, the banker's report given in that case would have been 'adequate' assurance under this Act, regardless of the language of the 'satisfaction' clause." (The comment is set out in full in the Supplement.)

The record in the Fasola case shows that in truth there were no rumors, and there was no banker's report.[b] Would the decision in Fasola be warranted under the Code? Would the same result be warranted if the contract had contained no "satisfaction" clause?

NOTES

(1) *Problem.* A buyer of iron rails to be delivered in installments complained that the first two shipments were short, and expressed the wish to be absolved from the contract. The seller answered by letter asking "to know definitely what is your intention." The buyer answered: "You ask us to determine whether we will or will not object to receive further shipments because of past defaults. We tell you we will if we are entitled to do so, and will not if we are not entitled to do so. We do not think you have the right to compel us to decide a disputed question of law to relieve you from the risk of deciding it yourself. You know quite as well as we do what is the rule and its uncertainty of application." On receiving this letter, how should the seller act? See Norrington v. Wright, 115 U.S. 188 (1885). Would he be justified in demanding assurance of due performance under UCC 2–609?

(2) *Demanding Assurance.* Suppose, changing the facts of the foregoing problem, that the buyer had initially written to the seller as follows: "We demand that within ten days you supply us with an inspection report by a surveyor qualified in the trade, showing that you have on hand, or in manufacture, the rails to make up for past short shipments and to meet future deliveries in full." Is it possible that this would justify the seller in cancelling the contract? See UCC 2–610(b). According to Comment 2 after that section, a demand "for more than the contract calls for in the way of counter-performance is not itself a repudiation. . . . However, when under a fair reading it amounts to a statement of intention not to perform except on conditions which go beyond the contract, it becomes a repudiation." Would the buyer be guilty of repudiation if he announced that he would not pay for any more rails unless all those still to

---

b. The Code misstatement of the case appears to have arisen as follows. Article 2 of the Code was preceded by American Law Institute proposals for a "Uniform Revised Sales Act," including a section (99) parallel to UCC 2–609. The reporters (Professors Llewellyn and Mentschikoff) prepared draft comments on selected sections. One on § 99 depicts the facts of an edible oil sale, including rumors and a banker's report, and it refers to the Fasola case, but does not make it clear whether the facts were drawn from the case or were (as they must have been) hypothetical ones devised by the reporters for purposes of illustration. A.L.I., Comments on Council Draft No. 1, Sales Sections (Sales Act) 110–11 (1944). Presumably the redactor who prepared the comments to UCC 2–609 mistook the earlier comment as a report of the Fasola case.

come were shipped at once? Suppose that the first two shipments had not in fact been short, but the buyer thought they were. Would it be a repudiation for the buyer to demand assurance of due performance in that case?

If there is a risk that a demand under UCC 2–609 may amount to a repudiation, how may it be avoided? Would you advise sending the following message?—"We demand whatever assurance of your performance we are entitled to under the Uniform Commercial Code."

Repudiation is considered below in more detail.

DEVELOPMENT OF CONSTRUCTIVE CONDITIONS IN ENGLISH LAW

In a wheat-sale case decided in 1797, the plaintiff buyer alleged that the seller failed to deliver the wheat at the place and time agreed upon, although he, the buyer, was ready and willing to receive it. The defendant objected that the plaintiff should have said something about being ready to pay for the wheat. The court's discussion of the point centered on whether the covenants of the parties—of the seller to deliver and of the buyer to pay—"be or be not independent of each other." As the court ruled that they were dependent covenants, the defendant prevailed. Morton v. Lamb, 7 T.R. 125, 101 Eng.Rep. 890 (K.B.).

In the modern diction of contract law, it might be said that the plaintiff's readiness to pay for the wheat was a condition of the defendant's duty to deliver it. The condition was not one expressed in the agreement, and it might therefore be called an implied condition. But that expression gives an undue emphasis to the unspoken intent of the parties. The existence of the condition may represent that, of course, but it may depend as much or more on an official judgment about "competing legislative grounds . . . some opinion as to policy"—to use Holmesian phrases. Therefore the term *constructive condition,* as suggested by Professor Corbin, has come into use as an explanation for cases like Morton v. Lamb.

To say that a promise sued on is "independent" of the plaintiff's undertaking is still an intelligible way of saying that it is not subject to a constructive condition.

In an earlier period the English courts would have treated the covenants in the wheat-sale case as independent. The element of exchange was less prominent, and the form of words in which a promise was expressed was regarded as more decisive. In 1500, for instance, the Chief Justice of the King's Bench said: "If one covenant with me to serve me for a year, and I covenant with him to give him 20 £., if I do not say 'for the same cause,' he shall have an action for the 20 £. although he never serves me; otherwise, if I say he shall have 20£. 'for the same cause.' " [a]   Doubtless the extension of assumpsit to cases of mutual promises not under seal, in the latter half of the 16th century, had something to do with the abandonment of such views.   The change occurred in stages.   As late as 1669, in Pordage v. Cole,[b] it was held that an action of debt on an agreement to pay for land "was well brought without an averment of the conveyance"—and evidently without an allegation that a deed was tendered.

Lord Mansfield laid the foundation for modern reasoning about constructive conditions of exchange in the opinion reported next. His view (echoed in the wheat-sale case) was that "the dependence or independence of covenants was to be collected from the evident sense and meaning of the parties," and that the sequence of the expected performance was important.   In the wheat-sale case, the delivery of the wheat and payment for it were expected to occur at the same time, and Mansfield referred to that situation as one of "mutual conditions."   In the case before him, the situation was different.

The defendant was in business as a silk mercer, and the plaintiff had entered his business as a "covenant servant," or apprentice.   The articles of indenture provided that after a year and a quarter the defendant would retire from the business.   Thereafter it was to be carried on by the plaintiff and a partner—either a nephew of the defendant or someone else nominated by the defendant.   The plaintiff was to pay for his share of the business in monthly installments of 250 £. (The payments were to represent the value of the inventory, or stock in trade, which was to be fixed at a fair valuation.)   For assuring these payments, the plaintiff agreed to give the defendant "good and sufficient security," approved of by him, "at and before the sealing and delivery of the deeds" conveying the business.

All this was alleged by the plaintiff, and further that he had performed and been ready to perform his covenants, but that the defendant had refused to surrender the business at the appointed time.   The defendant pleaded that the plaintiff did not give sufficient security for the payments.   To this the plaintiff demurred, and arguments ensued as reported below.

KINGSTON v. PRESTON

King's Bench, 1773.
Lofft 194, 2 Doug. 689, 99 Eng.Rep. 437.

On the part of the plaintiff, the case was argued by Mr. Buller, who contended that the covenants were mutual and independent, and therefore a plea of the breach of one of the covenants to be performed by the plaintiff was no bar to an action for a breach by the defendant of one which he had bound himself to perform, but that the

a. Anon., Y.B. 15 Hen. VII. f. 10b, pl.   b. 1 Wms. Saunders 319 (K.B.).
    17.

defendant might have his remedy for the breach by the plaintiff in a separate action.   On the other side, Mr. Gross insisted that the covenants were dependent in their nature, and therefore performance must be alleged: the security to be given for the money was manifestly the chief object of the transaction, and it would be highly unreasonable to construe the agreement so as to oblige the defendant to give up a beneficial business, and valuable stock-in-trade, and trust to the plaintiff's personal security (who might, and, indeed was admitted to be worth nothing), for the performance of his part.

In delivering the judgment of the Court, Lord Mansfield expressed himself to the following effect: There are three kinds of covenants: 1.   Such as are called mutual and independent, where either party may recover damages from the other for the injury he may have received by a breach of the covenants in his favor, and where it is no excuse for the defendant to allege a breach of the covenants on the part of the plaintiff.   2.   There are covenants which are conditions and dependent, in which the performance of one depends on the prior performance of another, and, therefore, till this prior condition is performed, the other party is not liable to an action on his covenant. 3.   There is also a third sort of covenants, which are mutual conditions to be performed at the same time; and in these, if one party was ready and offered to perform his part, and the other neglected or refused to perform his, he who was ready and offered has fulfilled his engagement, and may maintain an action for the default of the other; though it is not certain that either is obliged to do the first act.   His Lordship then proceeded to say, that the dependence or independence of covenants was to be collected from the evident sense and meaning of the parties, and that, however transposed they might be in the deed, their precedency must depend on the order of time in which the intent of the transaction requires their performance.   That, in the case before the Court, it would be the greatest injustice if the plaintiff should prevail: the essence of the agreement was, that the defendant should not trust to the personal security of the plaintiff, but, before he delivered up his stock and business, should have good security for the payment of the money.   The giving such security, therefore, must necessarily be a condition precedent.   Judgment was accordingly given for the defendant, because the part to be performed by the plaintiff was clearly a condition precedent.

NOTE

Serjeant Williams' Rules.   In 1798 Serjeant John Williams sought to rationalize the law of dependency of covenants by stating five rules on the subject, which maintained a certain influence into the present century. According to one rule, if a payment is to be made *after* the day appointed for the thing to be done as consideration for it, the duty to pay is conditional, or "dependent".   By another rule, the duty to pay is dependent if the *same day* is appointed for the two performances.   Not all of the rules are consistent with present understanding, however.

Of these rules Professor Corbin says: "They tended to crystallize the law, when perhaps it should have been flexible. At the same time, they have themselves suffered at the hands of later courts and writers. They show that a Restatement works; but also that even an influential Restatement will require Restating. An attempt to crystallize fails; and the law remains flexible." § 662. See also Williston, §§ 819–23.

TENDER

"A formal tender is seldom made in business transactions," it is said, "except to lay the foundation for subsequent assertion in a court of justice of rights which spring from refusal of the tender." [a] Courts are not often called on to say what is or is not a formal tender of performance under a contract. Partly for that reason, perhaps, as the word "tender" is commonly used it suggests a degree of punctilio in conduct that is seldom achieved. Paradoxically, the strict sense of the word is supported by a set of rules dispensing with the necessity of tender in ordinary contract litigation.

The Code states the requisites, under contracts for the sale of goods, for a seller's tender of delivery (UCC 2–507) and for a buyer's tender of payment (UCC 2–511). A comment after the former section identifies two senses of the word "tender." In the stricter sense, it "contemplates an offer coupled with a present ability to fulfill all the conditions resting on the tendering party and must be followed by actual performance if the other party shows himself ready to proceed." But the comment indicates that something less than this will suffice to put the other party in default, "if he fails to proceed in some manner."

If a buyer has not made an arrangement with the seller for credit, must he proffer payment in money—i. e., "legal tender"? The Code recognizes that it is commercially normal to accept a check from a "seemingly solvent party," and states a rule designed to avoid "commercial surprise." Tendering a check is commonly sufficient under this rule, "unless the seller demands payment in legal tender and gives any extension of time reasonably necessary to procure it." UCC 2–511(2); and see Comments 2–4.

In Lawrence v. Miller, 86 N.Y. 131 (1881), a contract for the sale of land had fallen through, and the buyer sought to recover an initial payment of $2,000. The buyer contended that the seller could retain the money only if he had put the buyer in default by making tender of a deed, and that he had not done so. The court said: "it may be taken that by the term tender is generally meant the actual physical production of the deed, and the reaching it out, with words of offer of it, to the vendee." But the court ruled that the buyer had been put in

---

a. Lehman, J., dissenting, in Petterson v. Pattberg, 248 N.Y. 86, 161 N.E. 428 (1928). For a longer excerpt see Note 4, p. 127 supra.

default without such a ceremony; "the requirement of the law is not cast in a rigid mould. . . ." It appeared that the parties had met twice "with a view to perform." Each time the seller had laid the deed on the table, and the buyer had asked for more time. On the second occasion the seller refused to allow another day. The court's opinion can be understood as saying either that the seller's conduct was a sufficient tender, or that a perfect tender was excused by the buyer's conduct. An exact definition of the word, if it could be achieved, would not be decisive in many cases.

NOTE

The Case of the Party Goers. O'Toole had an option to buy some land from Boelkins which he could exercise by paying $6,000 in cash in 30 days. On the last afternoon they met at a social gathering and O'Toole said he wished to close the transaction. Boelkins promised to be at his home at 7 o'clock for that purpose. When O'Toole went there he had $1,500 in cash and a bank certificate, equivalent to a certified check, for the remainder. Boelkins was not at home. O'Toole waited for more than two hours and left. Later he brought an action for damages because of Boelkins' failure to perform the option. The trial court gave judgment for the defendant because the plaintiff's certificate of deposit was not legal tender. *Held:* Reversed. "Courts should not and have not looked with favor upon the claims of those who seek to evade their obligations in the form of such options by avoiding the optionees until the time of performance has expired. . . . 'A certificate of deposit or certified check is a sufficient tender, if no objection be made on the ground that it is not lawful money.'" O'Toole & Nedeau Co. v. Boelkins, 254 Mich. 44, 235 N.W. 820 (1931).

WALKER & CO. v. HARRISON

Supreme Court of Michigan, 1957.
347 Mich. 630, 81 N.W.2d 352.

SMITH, JUSTICE. This is a suit on a written contract. The defendants are in the dry-cleaning business. Walker & Company, plaintiff, sells, rents, and services advertising signs and billboards. These parties entered into an agreement pertaining to a sign. The agreement is in writing and is termed a "rental agreement." It specifies in part that:

"The lessor agrees to construct and install, at its own cost, one 18' 9" high x 8' 8" wide pylon type d. f. neon sign with electric clock and flashing lamps . . .. The lessor agrees to and does hereby lease or rent unto the said lessee the said SIGN for the term, use and rental and under the conditions, hereinafter set out, and the lessee agrees to pay said rental . . ..

"(a) The term of this lease shall be 36 months . . ..

"(b) The rental to be paid by lessee shall be $148.50 per month for each and every calendar month during the term of this lease; . . . . .

"(d) Maintenance. Lessor at its expense agrees to maintain and service the sign together with such equipment as supplied and installed by the lessor to operate in conjunction with said sign under the terms of this lease; this service is to include cleaning and repainting of sign in original color scheme as often as deemed necessary by lessor to keep sign in first class advertising condition and make all necessary repairs to sign and equipment installed by lessor. . . . ."

At the "expiration of this agreement," it was also provided, "title to this sign reverts to lessee." This clause is in addition to the printed form of agreement and was apparently added as a result of defendants' concern over title, they having expressed a desire "to buy for cash" and the salesman, at one time, having "quoted a cash price."

The sign was completed and installed in the latter part of July, 1953. The first billing of the monthly payment of $148.50 was made August 1, 1953, with payment thereof by defendants on September 3, 1953. This first payment was also the last. Shortly after the sign was installed, someone hit it with a tomato. Rust, also, was visible on the chrome, complained defendants, and in its corners were "little spider cobwebs." In addition, there were "some children's sayings written down in here." Defendant Herbert Harrison called Walker for the maintenance he believed himself entitled to under subparagraph (d) above. It was not forthcoming. He called again and again. "I was getting, you might say, sorer and sorer. . . . Occasionally, when I started calling up, I would walk around where the tomato was and get mad again. Then I would call up on the phone again." Finally, on October 8, 1953, plaintiff not having responded to his repeated calls, he telegraphed Walker that:

"You Have Continually Voided Our Rental Contract By Not Maintaining Signs As Agreed As We No Longer Have A Contract With You Do Not Expect Any Further Remuneration."

[Walker answered by letter, pointing out that the telegram did not "make any specific allegations as to what the failure of maintenance comprises," and concluding:]

"We would like to call your attention to paragraph G in our rental contract, which covers procedures in the event of a Breach of Agreement. In the event that you carry out your threat to make no future monthly payments in accordance with the agreement, it is our intention to enforce the conditions outlined under paragraph G [1] . . .

---

1. (g) Breach of Agreement. Lessee shall be deemed to have breached this agreement by default in payment of any installment of the rental herein provided for; abandonment of the sign or vacating premises where the sign is located; termination or transfer of lessee's interest in the premises by insolvency, appointment of a receiver for lessee's business; filing of a voluntary or involuntary petition in bankruptcy with respect to lessee or the violation of any of the other terms or conditions hereof. In the event of such default, the lessor may, upon notice to the lessee, which notice shall conclusively be deemed sufficient if mailed or delivered to the premises where the sign was or is located, take possession of the sign and declare the balance of the

Unless we receive both the September and October payments by October 25th, this entire matter will be placed in the hands of our attorney for collection in accordance with paragraph G which stipulates that the entire amount is forthwith due and payable."

No additional payments were made and Walker sued in assumpsit for the entire balance due under the contract, $5,197.50, invoking paragraph (g) of the agreement. Defendants filed answer and claim of recoupment, asserting that plaintiff's failure to perform certain maintenance services constituted a prior material breach of the agreement, thus justifying their repudiation of the contract and grounding their claim for damages. The case was tried to the court without a jury and resulted in a judgment for the plaintiff. The case is before us on a general appeal.

Defendants urge upon us again and again, in various forms, the proposition that Walker's failure to service the sign, in response to repeated requests, constituted a material breach of the contract and justified repudiation by them. The legal proposition is undoubtedly correct. Repudiation is one of the weapons available to an injured party in event the other contractor has committed a material breach. But the injured party's determination that there has been a material breach, justifying his own repudiation, is fraught with peril, for should such determination, as viewed by a later court in the calm of its contemplation, be unwarranted, the repudiator himself will have been guilty of material breach and himself have become the aggressor, not an innocent victim.

What is our criterion for determining whether or not a breach of contract is so fatal to the undertaking of the parties that it is to be classed as "material"? There is no single touchstone. Many factors are involved. They are well stated in section 275 of Restatement of the Law of Contracts in the following terms: [quotation omitted.]

We will not set forth in detail the testimony offered concerning the need for servicing. Granting that Walker's delay (about a week

rental herein provided for to be forthwith due and payable, and lessee hereby agrees to pay such balance upon any such contingencies. Lessor may terminate this lease and without notice, remove and repossess said sign and recover from the lessee such amounts as may be unpaid for the remaining unexpired term of this agreement. Time is of the essence of this lease with respect to the payment of rentals herein provided for. Should lessee after lessor has declared the balance of rentals due and payable, pay the full amount of rental herein provided, he shall then be entitled to the use of the sign, under all the terms and provisions hereof, for the balance of the term of this lease. No waiver by either party hereto of the nonperformance of any term, condition or obligation hereof shall be a waiver of any subsequent breach of, or failure to perform the same, or any other term, condition or obligation hereof. It is understood and agreed that the sign is especially constructed for the lessee and for use at the premises now occupied by the lessee for the term herein provided; that it is of no value unless so used and that it is a material consideration to the lessor in entering into this agreement that the lessee shall continue to use the sign for the period of time provided herein and for the payment of the full rental for such term."

after defendant Herbert Harrison sent his telegram of repudiation Walker sent out a crew and took care of things) in rendering the service requested was irritating, we are constrained to agree with the trial court that it was not of such materiality as to justify repudiation of the contract, and we are particularly mindful of the lack of preponderant evidence contrary to his determination. Jones v. Eastern Michigan Motorbuses, 287 Mich. 619, 283 N.W. 710. The trial court, on this phase of the case, held as follows:

"Now Mr. Harrison phoned in, so he testified, a number of times. He isn't sure of the dates but he sets the first call at about the 7th of August and he complained then of the tomato and of some rust and some cobwebs. The tomato, according to the testimony, was up on the clock; that would be outside of his reach, without a stepladder or something. The cobwebs are within easy reach of Mr. Harrison and so would the rust be. I think that Mr. Bueche's argument that these were not materially a breach would clearly be true as to the cobwebs and I really can't believe in the face of all the testimony that there was a great deal of rust seven days after the installation of this sign. And that really brings it down to the tomato. And, of course, when a tomato has been splashed all other (sic) your clock, you don't like it. But he says he kept calling their attention to it, although the rain probably washed some of the tomato off. But the stain remained, and they didn't come. I really can't find that that was such a material breach of the contract as to justify rescission. I really don't think so."

Nor, we conclude, do we. There was no valid ground for defendants' repudiation and their failure thereafter to comply with the terms of the contract was itself a material breach, entitling Walker, upon this record, to judgment.

The question of damages remains. [The court's discussion of this question is omitted.] Judgment was, therefore, rendered for the cash price of the sign, for such services and maintenance as were extended and accepted, and interest upon the amount in default. There was no error.

Affirmed. Costs to appellee.

NOTES

(1) *Drafting Problem.* What might the telegram have said in order to put pressure on Walker without risking liability for the price of the sign?

(2) *Condition v. Promise.* Maintenance of the sign by the plaintiff with some diligence, and in some degree of respectability, was of course a constructive condition of the defendant's duty to keep up the rental payments. The plaintiff's duty of maintenance, as stated in paragraph (d), would not be met by anything less than punctilious performance. But the condition resting on the plaintiff need not be so stringent. Obviously there is some softening effect, or "play", in the process of deriving a condition - from a promise. (See also the cases on substantial performance, in Section

3 infra.) Compare the effect the paragraph might have had if it had been written in terms of an express condition. At the extreme, it might have been written so as to excuse the lessee from all further duties upon any shortcoming in the maintenance services.

Does this difference between express and constructive conditions suggest a preference in interpreting agreements? According to the Restatement, § 261, "Where it is doubtful whether words create a promise or an express condition, they are interpreted as creating a promise . . .." Is there a notion of fairness behind this rule?

Refer again to the drafting problem in the preceding chapter, at p. 649, especially the direction to draft a clause making "sailing with the next wind" the subject of a duty alone. Do you now see a difficulty in doing this, not mentioned in that chapter?

(3) *Question of Law or Fact?* Does the court make its own judgment whether or not Walker's conduct amounted to a material breach? Or does it accept the trial judge's determination as a permissible finding on the evidence? Should the issue of materiality of a breach ever be submitted to a jury? And if so, should they be directed to balance the factors mentioned in Restatement, § 275, or in some similar list? What merit or demerit do you find in treating the issue as a "question of law"? Reconsider your answers after reading the following note.

(4) *The Case of the Carpenter's Payroll.* Knapp-Stiles, Inc. was the general contractor on a housing project, and subcontracted the carpentry work to Baith & Hensley. The contract price was $136,170, plus $4.70 an hour for extras. Owing to a delay in qualifying Baith & Hensley as a subcontractor, the carpentry work went forward for four months under an oral agreement that its workmen would be carried on the general contractor's payroll. After Baith & Hensley was qualified, in mid-August, 1960, it paid its own employees out of a separate account funded by the general contractor. Before that, it had received monthly payments in addition to labor costs, as called for in the contract. At that time these payments were suspended, by agreement, because Baith & Hensley had been overpaid, according to the work completion schedule. Inadvertently, however, Knapp-Stiles made a further non-payroll disbursement to the subcontractor, of some $1,800. In October this was discovered, and Knapp-Stiles reduced its payroll disbursement by this amount. Thereupon Baith & Hensley was unable to pay its employees. Knapp-Stiles refused to let the subcontractor proceed on the job.

Baith & Hensley sued for what it would have earned if it had been permitted to continue. The trial court found that thousands of dollars were due to the plaintiff for extra work and labor, from which Knapp-Stiles could have recouped its overpayment, and gave judgment for the plaintiff.

Two appellate courts (12 judges) examined this judgment in succession. The Michigan Court of Appeals reversed, saying that the plaintiff's failure to meet its payroll on October 14 was a substantial breach, in view of Restatement, § 275. It relied on the following rule: "He who commits the first substantial breach of a contract cannot maintain an action against the other contracting party for failure to perform." Ehlinger v. Bodi Lake Lumber Co., 324 Mich. 77, 36 N.W.2d 311 (1949). The Michigan

Supreme Court reinstated the trial court's judgment. It applied the rule that in law cases, tried without a jury, the judge's findings must be accepted on appeal unless they are against the clear preponderance of the evidence. Three justices dissented. They considered that "when the trial court held that 'said dismissal [of the subcontractor] was not justified under the circumstances' he left the realm of fact finding," and made a conclusion of law.

Although the majority of the Supreme Court referred repeatedly to the trial judge's findings, they appear also to have made a conclusion of their own, as follows: "The instant case does not involve a breach of the original contract, but at most a breach of an oral agreement in regard to accounting. . . . The breach of the oral agreement in regard to accounting does not affect an element so essential as to amount to a breach contemplated by the rule as 'substantial.'" Baith v. Knapp-Stiles, Inc., 380 Mich. 119, 156 N.W.2d 575 (1968). [The Court of Appeals opinion is id. at 2 Mich.App. 305, 139 N.W.2d 781 (1966).] [a]

GILL v. JOHNSTOWN LUMBER CO.

Supreme Court of Pennsylvania, 1892.
151 Pa. 534, 25 A. 120.

[Assumpsit for driving logs under a written contract, the terms of which are set forth in the opinion. Plaintiff agreed to drive some four million feet of logs, and to begin driving at once, "if sufficient natural water, or by the use of splash dams." The trial court directed a verdict for defendant on the ground that the contract was "entire" and that plaintiff had defaulted in that a flood had carried a considerable proportion of the logs past defendant's boom. Plaintiff appeals.]

Opinion by MR. JUSTICE HEYDRICK, October 31, 1892. The single question in this case is whether the contract upon which the plaintiff sued is entire or severable. If it is entire it is conceded that the learned court below properly directed a verdict for the defendant; if severable, it is not denied that the cause ought to have been submitted to the jury. The criterion by which it is to be determined to which class any particular contract shall be assigned is thus stated in 1 Parsons on Contracts, 29–31: "If the part to be performed by one party consists of several and distinct items, and the price to be paid by the other is (1) apportioned to each item to be performed, or (2) is left to be implied by law, such a contract will generally be held to be severable. . . . But if the consideration to be paid is single and entire the contract must be held to be entire, although the subject of the contract may consist of several distinct and wholly independent

---

a. For a case in which a jury's opinion was taken on the issue of materiality of breach by a pro football player, who had flirted with a club in competition with the one entitled to his services, see McLean v. Buffalo Bills Football Club, Inc., 32 A.D.2d 881, 301 N.Y.S.2d 872 (4th Dept.1969).

items." The rule thus laid down was quoted with approval and applied in Lucesco Oil Company v. Brewer, 66 Pa. 351, and followed in Rugg & Bryan v. Moore, 110 Pa. 236, 1 A. 320. It was also applied in Ritchie v. Atkinson, 10 East, 295, a case not unlike the present. There the master and freighter of a vessel of four hundred tons mutually agreed that the ship should proceed to St. Petersburg, and there load from the freighter's factors a complete cargo of hemp and iron and deliver the same to the freighter at London on being paid freight for hemp £5 per ton, for iron 5s. per ton, and certain other charges, one half to be paid on delivery and the other at three months. The vessel proceeded to St. Petersburg, and when about half loaded was compelled by the imminence of a Russian embargo upon British vessels to leave, and returning to London deliver to the freighter so much of the stipulated cargo as had been taken on board. The freighter, conceiving that the contract was entire and the delivery of a complete cargo a condition precedent to a recovery of any compensation, refused to pay at the stipulated rate for so much as was delivered. Lord Ellenborough said: "The delivery of the cargo is in its nature, divisible, and therefore I think it is not a condition precedent; but the plaintiff is entitled to recover freight in proportion to the extent of such delivery; leaving the defendant to his remedy in damages for the short delivery."

Applying the test of an apportionable or apportioned consideration to the contract in question, it will be seen at once that it is severable. The work undertaken to be done by the plaintiff consisted of several items, viz., driving logs, first, of oak, and second of various other kinds of timber, from points upon Stony creek and its tributaries above Johnstown to the defendant's boom at Johnstown, and also driving cross-ties from some undesignated point or points, presumably understood by the parties, to Bethel in Somerset county, and to some other point or points below Bethel. For this work the consideration to be paid was not an entire sum, but was apportioned among the several items at the rate of one dollar per thousand feet for the oak logs; seventy-five cents per thousand feet for all other logs; three cents each for cross-ties driven to Bethel, and five cents each for cross-ties driven to points below Bethel. But while the contract is severable, and the plaintiff entitled to compensation at the stipulated rate for all logs and ties delivered at the specified points, there is neither reason nor authority for the claim for compensation in respect to logs that were swept by the flood to and through the defendant's boom, whether they had been driven part of the way by the plaintiff or remained untouched by him at the coming of the flood. In respect to each particular log the contract in this case is like a contract of common carriage, which is dependent upon the delivery of the goods at the designated place, and if by casus the delivery is prevented the carrier cannot recover pro tanto for freight for part of the route over which the goods were taken: Wharton, Law of Contracts, sec. 714. Indeed this is but an application of the rule already stated. The consideration to be paid for driving each log is an entire sum per thousand feet for the whole distance and is not apportioned or apportionable to parts of the drive.

The judgment is reversed and a venire facias de novo is awarded.

NOTES

(1) *Question.* Into how many parts was the contract divisible? Two parts: one for logs and one for cross-ties? Four parts? One part for each log and cross-tie properly delivered? If some of the oak logs had been driven half way, might the plaintiff have recovered at the rate of 50¢ per thousand feet for them? Why was the contract not divisible by distances?

(2) *The Lowy Case.* A contractor bids for work in developing a tract of land, to consist chiefly of cleaning, grading and compaction, and laying down streets. For the street work (paving, curbs, and gutters) he bids unit prices; e. g., $4 a foot. For the remainder he bids a lump-sum price. The street work cannot be done until the other work is completed. Is there any way to write the contract such that it will not be found "divisible" into two parts?

In Lowy v. United Pacific Insurance Company, 67 Cal.2d 87, 429 P.2d 577 (1967), a contract of this character stated the price for grading, etc., as $73,500 in "Exhibit A." It stated unit prices for paving, etc., in Exhibit B." The court said: "since the consideration was apportioned, the contract was a severable or divisible one. . . . Under the circumstances, the fact that [the contractor] did not perform the second phase of the contract does not prevent his recovering for work done under the first phase."

Suppose the contract had provided that a material default by the contractor in phase two would bar his recovery for work in phase one. Would you expect the courts to implement this provision? Can you improve on it, as a sanction against default by the contractor?

The agreement for street work in the Lowy case was probably not divisible into a paving part, a gutter part, and a curb part, even though a separate price was named for each. A contract for several performances may be "entire," even though the consideration is apportioned among them. The holding in Lowy is not to the contrary, for there were other indications of divisibility not mentioned here. Indeed, the apportionment test does not support the Lowy result very well, inasmuch as the lump price of $73,500 included the *"labor and material* necessary for street improvements" (emphasis supplied).

(3) *Problem.* Paul agreed to erect and maintain six signs for Pete. Four of them were to read "4 miles to Pete's Place," "3 miles to Pete's Place," and so on. One large one was to read, "You are at Pete's Place," and the sixth, "Turn around for Pete's Place." Pete agreed to pay $35 a month for the large sign, and $10 a month for each of the others. Is the contract divisible into six parts? Or divisible at all? How would you write the agreement so as to make it clearly so? How write it to make

it clearly entire? See John v. United Advertising, Inc., 165 Colo. 193, 439 P.2d 53 (1968).

(4) *Employment Contracts.* Work done under a contract of employment for a term may go uncompensated if the employee abandons the job, or is justifiably discharged, before the end of the term. (Quasi-contractual recovery is permitted in some jurisdictions. See Section 2 infra. It would presumably be available anywhere, other circumstances being favorable, if the contract is terminated by death of one of the parties. See Chapter 8 infra. For wrongful discharge, of course, the employee has a contract action.) The loss of wages which occurs when an employer becomes insolvent during the term may also be severe. The doctrine of divisibility, liberally applied, would tend to alleviate all such losses, by permitting the employee to enforce partial payments for units of his work, so much per week for instance, prior to the end of the term. But the doctrine was not, at least in the older cases, liberally applied. Many courts would not be persuaded that wages were to be paid weekly simply by the fact that the contract states the compensation as so much per week. Thus the Ohio court was not persuaded that wages for a farm laborer were to be paid monthly, simply because the agreement required him to work "for six months at eleven dollars per month." Larkin v. Buck, 11 Ohio St. 561 (1860). The employee abandoned work at the end of the first month and brought an action for a month's pay. Recovery was denied. But cf. White v. Atkins, 8 Cush. 367, 62 Mass. 367 (1851) ("$150 per year, payable monthly, if he wishes"), and Oliver v. McArthur, 158 App.Div. 241, 143 N.Y.S. 126 (1913) ("A farm hand is not a capitalist . . .").

Recent cases of this nature are not common, for several reasons: (1) "the great volume of modern employment does not involve contracts for long periods of time, but rather from day to day or week to week"; (2) long-term employees are perhaps more alert to the risk; and (3) "probably the most important practical solution of the problem, has been the passage in many jurisdictions of wage statutes which inexorably clamp divisibility down upon large classes of employment contracts, and thereby take the task of construction from the courts." McGowan, The Divisibility of Employment Contracts, 21 Iowa L.Rev. 50, 67 (1935). As to the statutes, see Note, 43 Harv.L.Rev. 647 (1930); American Mut. Liability Ins. Co. v. Commissioner, 340 Mass. 144, 163 N.E.2d 19 (1959).

PENNSYLVANIA EXCHANGE BANK v. UNITED STATES, 170 F.Supp. 629 (1959). [The United States Army Signal Corps contracted to pay certain sums to Joseph Lerner & Son, Inc., under an "Industrial Preparedness Contract." Lerner's obligation was to equip itself for the production, in volume, of an item called a microwave magic tee. The work was to be done in four steps. Steps I and II entailed acquiring information about and making plans for production, subject to approval, making a pilot run, and going through "all production processes short of procuring tooling and materials and short of actual volume manufacture." Step III required Lerner to acquire certain equipment for which it spent about $38,000.

These steps were substantially completed by October 1, 1953, and the Government had paid Lerner about $128,000. Step IV, which was to be taken only in case of a national emergency, and after receipt of an order from the Government, required "volume production in accordance with previously planned schedules." Lerner was obligated to maintain a status of readiness for this over a six-year period in anticipation of a national emergency. On October 1 Lerner transferred all its assets to assignees for the benefit of creditors, as an alternative to bankruptcy. The assignees sued the Government for about $45,000, the sum owed for completing steps I–III, and the Government counterclaimed for damages.]

WHITAKER, JUDGE. [The court considered the purpose of the contract, as stated in a Signal Corps procurement specification, and said that Steps I, II, and III were] merely incidental to Step IV, which was the ultimate objective. . . . The duty to stand by and be ready to perform Step IV was the essential element of the bargain. The contract was not divisible. . . .

The assignment for the benefit of creditors operates as a present and total breach of the contract, for it is an implied condition in every contract that the promisor will not permit itself, through insolvency or acts of bankruptcy, to be disabled from making performance. Central Trust Co. of Illinois v. Chicago Auditorium Ass'n, 240 U.S. 581, 591, 36 S.Ct. 412, 60 L.Ed. 811; Roehm v. Horst, 178 U.S. 1, 20 S.Ct. 780, 44 L.Ed. 953; Pennsylvania Steel Co. v. New York City R. Co., 2 Cir., 198 F. 721, 743.

[The Government's motion for summary judgment was granted.]

NOTES

(1) *Insolvency.* A person or firm subjected to bankruptcy, or other insolvency proceeding, does not thereby lose the benefit of all his contracts, for his undertaking may yet be performed. See Restatement, § 324: "Insolvency of a promisor is not an anticipatory breach, and his bankruptcy does not have all the effect of such a breach. . . ." It may be profitable for the trustee in bankruptcy, or other official administering his assets, to apply them to performance, in order to earn the counter-performance of the other party. Section 70b of the Bankruptcy Act (11 U.S.C. § 110b) allows the trustee time to consider whether to adopt or to reject executory contracts of the bankrupt. If he rejects one, of course, the other party will commonly be entitled to file a claim in the bankruptcy proceeding.

As the preceding case shows, however, a party may be justified in withholding performance, when the other party, becoming insolvent, has yet to perform all or part of the agreed exchange, unless the insolvent party's performance is "rendered, tendered, or made reasonably certain by security." Restatement, § 287(1). Comment (a) after the section describes the solvent party's protection in terms of a condition: "he is absolved from the duty of giving credit, and may require precedent or concurrent performance or security as a constructive condition."

A liquidation proceeding, such as an ordinary bankruptcy, or an assignment for the benefit of creditors, does not contemplate continued operation of a business for an indefinite period. Therefore the assignees for Joseph Lerner & Son could not well have undertaken complete performance of its "industrial preparedness contract."

(2) *Problem.* A seller of goods, having agreed to give the buyer credit for three months after delivery, hears rumors shortly before the time for shipment of the goods that the buyer has been slow in paying other suppliers. How should he act? One possibility is to ship the goods under a bill of lading, with a "sight draft" attached; by this means the seller can compel the buyer to pay at once if he wishes to take delivery. Would you recommend this procedure? See United States for Use and Benefit of Industrial Instrument Corp. v. Paul Hardeman, Inc., 202 F.Supp. 124 (N.D.Tex.1962), aff'd, 320 F.2d 115 (5th Cir. 1963). If not, what course would you recommend to the seller? See Leopold v. Rock-ola Mfg. Corporation, 109 F.2d 611 (5th Cir. 1940); Koppelon v. W. M. Ritter Flooring Corp., 97 N.J.L. 200, 116 A. 491 (1922).

(3) *Question.* Compare the credit term employed by the seller in Corn Products Refining Co. v. Fasola, p. 686 supra: ". . . cash payment or satisfactory security may be required by the seller before shipment." Does your answer to the foregoing problem indicate that such a term in the contract affords a substantial advantage to the seller?

K & G CONSTRUCTION CO. v. HARRIS

Court of Appeals of Maryland, 1960.
223 Md. 305, 164 A.2d 451.

[A case was stated for appeal in an action by a Contractor against a Subcontractor, and the following facts were given. K & G Construction Company was the owner and general contractor for a housing subdivision project. Harris and Brooks contracted with it to do excavating and earth-moving work on the project. Certain provisions of the agreement were as follows:

"Section 4. (b) Progress payments will be made each month during the performance of the work. Subcontractor will submit to Contractor, by the 25th of each month, a requisition for work performed during the preceding month. Contractor will pay these requisitions, less a retainer equal to ten per cent (10%), by the 10th of the months in which such requisitions are received.[1]

"(c) No payments will be made under this contract until the insurance requirements of Sec. 9 hereof have been complied with.

. . .

"Section 8. . . . All work shall be performed in a workmanlike manner, and in accordance with the best practices.

---

1. This section is not a model for clarity.

"Section 9. Subcontractor agrees to carry, during the progress of the work, . . . liability insurance against . . . property damage, in such amounts and with such companies as may be satisfactory to Contractor and shall provide Contractor with certificates showing the same to be in force."

While in the course of his employment by the Subcontractor on the project, a bulldozer operator drove his machine too close to Contractor's house while grading the yard, causing the immediate collapse of a wall and other damage to the house. Contractor was generally satisfied with Subcontractor's work and progress as required by the contract until September 12, 1958, with the exception of the bulldozer accident which occurred on August 9. The Subcontractor and its insurance carrier refused to repair damage or compensate Contractor for damage to the house, claiming that there was no liability on the part of the Subcontractor.

For work done prior to July 25, the Subcontractor submitted a requisition payable under the terms of the contract on or before August 10. Contractor refused to pay it because the bulldozer damage had not been repaired or paid for. Subcontractor continued to work on the project until September 12, when it discontinued work because of Contractor's refusal to pay the said requisition, but notified Contractor by registered letter of its willingness to return to the job upon payment. Contractor later requested it to return and complete work, which Subcontractor refused to do because of nonpayment of work requisitions of July 25 and thereafter. Contractor had another excavating concern complete the work, for which it paid $450 above the contract price.

Contractor's suit against Subcontractor contained two counts: (1) for the bulldozer damage, alleging negligence, and (2) for $450 as damages for breach of contract. Subcontractor filed a counterclaim for work done and not paid for and for profit it lost by not being permitted to finish the job, totalling $2,824.50. The bulldozer damage claim was submitted to a jury, who found in favor of Contractor in the amount of $3,400, and that judgment has been paid. The other claims were submitted to the trial judge, who allowed the Subcontractor's claim in full. Contractor appealed from this determination.]

PRESCOTT, JUDGE. . . . The vital question, more tersely stated, remains: Did the contractor have a right, under the circumstances, to refuse to make the progress payment due on August 10, 1958?

The answer involves interesting and important principles of contract law. Promises and counter-promises made by the respective parties to a contract have certain relations to one another, which determine many of the rights and liabilities of the parties. Broadly speaking, they are (1) independent of each other, or (2) mutually dependent, one upon the other. They are independent of each other if the parties intend that *performance* by each of them is in no way conditioned upon *performance* by the other. 5 Page, The Law of Contracts, ¶ 2971. In other words, the parties exchange promises for promises, not the *performance* of promises for the *performance* of promises. 3 Williston, Contracts (Rev.Ed.), ¶ 813, n. 6. A failure to perform an independent promise does not excuse non-performance on the part of the adversary party, but each is required to perform his promise, and, if one does not perform, he is liable to the adversary party for such non-performance. (Of course, if litigation ensues questions of set-off or recoupment frequently arise.) Promises are mutually dependent if the parties intend *performance* by one to be conditioned upon *performance* by the other, and, if they be mutually dependent, they may be (a) precedent, i. e., a promise that is to be performed before a corresponding promise on the part of the adversary party is to be performed, (b) subsequent, i. e., a corresponding promise that is not to be performed until the other party to the contract has performed a precedent covenant, or (c) concurrent, i. e., promises that are to be performed at the same time by each of the parties, who are respectively bound to perform each. Page, op. cit., ¶¶ 2941, 2951, 2961.   .   .   .

In the early days, it was settled law that covenants and mutual promises in a contract were *prima facie* independent, and that they were to be so construed in the absence of language in the contract clearly showing that they were intended to be dependent. Williston, op. cit., ¶ 816; Page op. cit., ¶¶ 2944, 2945. In the case of Kingston v. Preston, 2 Doug. 689, decided in 1774, Lord Mansfield, contrary to three centuries of opposing precedents, changed the rule, and decided that performance of one covenant might be dependent on prior performance of another, although the contract contained no express condition to that effect. Page, op. cit., ¶ 2946; Williston, op. cit., ¶ 817. The modern rule, which seems to be of almost universal application, is that there is a presumption that mutual promises in a contract are dependent and are to be so regarded, whenever possible. Page, op. cit., ¶ 2946; Restatement, Contracts, ¶ 266. Cf. Williston, op. cit., ¶ 812.   .   .   .

.   .   . It would, indeed present an unusual situation if we were to hold that a building contractor, who has obtained someone to do work for him and has agreed to pay each month for the work performed in the previous month, has to continue the monthly payments, irrespective of the degree of skill and care displayed in the performance of work, and his only recourse is by way of suit for ill-performance. If this were the law, it is conceivable, in fact, probable, that many contractors would become insolvent before they were able to complete their contracts. As was stated by the Court in Measures Brothers Ltd. v. Measures, 2 Ch. 248: "Covenants are to be construed as dependent or independent according to the intention of the parties and the good sense of the case."

We hold that when the subcontractor's employee negligently damaged the contractor's wall, this constituted a breach of the subcontractor's promise to perform his work in a "workmanlike manner, and in accordance with the best practices." Gaybis v. Palm, 201 Md. 78, 85, 93 A.2d 269; Johnson v. Metcalfe, 209 Md. 537, 544, 121 A.2d 825; 17 C.J.S. Contracts § 515; Weiss v. Sheet Metal Fabricators, 206 Md. 195, 203, 110 A.2d 671. And there can be little doubt that the breach was material: the damage to the wall amounted to more than double the payment due on August 10. Speed v. Bailey, 153 Md. 655, 661, 662, 139 A. 534. 3A Corbin, Contracts, § 708, says: "The failure of a contractor's [in our case, the subcontractor's] performance to constitute 'substantial' performance may justify the owner [in our case, the contractor] in refusing to make a progress payment . . . If the refusal to pay an installment is justified on the owner's [contractor's] part, the contractor [subcontractor] is not justified in abandoning work by reason of that refusal. His abandonment of the work will itself be a wrongful repudiation that goes to the essence, even if the defects in performance did not." See also Restatement, Contracts, § 274; . . . and compare Williston, op. cit., §§ 805, 841 and 842. Professor Corbin, in § 954, states further: "The unexcused failure of a contractor to render a promised performance when it is due is always a breach of contract . . . . Such failure may be of such great importance as to constitute what has been called herein a 'total' breach. . . . . For a failure of performance constituting such a 'total' breach, an action for remedies that are appropriate thereto is at once maintainable. Yet the injured party is not required to bring such action. He has the option of treating the nonperformance as a 'partial' breach only . . . ." In permitting the subcontractor to proceed with work on the project after August 9, the contractor, obviously, treated the breach by the subcontractor as a partial one. As the promises were mutually dependent and the subcontractor had made a material breach in his performance, this justified the contractor in refusing to make the August 10 payment; hence, as the contractor was not in default, the subcontractor again breached the contract when he, on September 12, discontinued work on the project, which rendered him liable (by the express terms of the contract) to the contractor for his increased cost in having the excavating done—a stipulated amount of $450. Cf. Keystone Engineering Corp. v. Sutter, 196 Md. 620, 628, 78 A.2d 191. . . .

[Defendant also contended] that the contractor had no right to refuse the August 10 payment, because the subcontractor had furnished the insurance against property damage, as called for in the contract. There is little, or no, merit in this suggestion. The subcontractor and his insurance company denied liability. The furnishing of the insurance by him did not constitute a license to perform his work in a careless, negligent, or unworkmanlike manner; and its acceptance by the contractor did not preclude his assertion of a claim for unworkmanlike performance directly against the subcontractor.

Judgment against the appellant reversed; and judgment entered in favor of the appellant against the appellees for $450, the appellees to pay the costs.

NOTES

(1) *Questions.* Did the contractor withhold the payment due on August 10 because the subcontractor "did his work in a careless, negligent or unworkmanlike manner"? Or because the insurer denied liability? (It is a customary condition in liability insurance policies that the insured shall not assume any obligation in connection with an accident, except at his own cost.) If the subcontractor and his insurer had conceded liability at once, reserving only the question how much damage was done, would the contractor have been justified in withholding the August payment? Or if the subcontractor had promised at once to repair the damage?

Did the court overlook a clear implication in the contract (§§ 4c and 9) that the contractor's duty to pay was *independent* of isolated acts of carelessness by the subcontractor?[a] What may the subcontractor include in his next contract that would alter the foregoing result?

Would the court's reasoning have been simpler if it had said that the contractor was entitled to set off the bulldozer damage against the requisition payable August 10th? Sound?

(2) *Wrongful Refusal to Make Progress Payments.* If the jury had found that the bulldozer damage was not due to the subcontractor's fault, would the trial court's judgment have been affirmed? The subcontractor discontinued work on September 12, and the last payment he had received was presumably made on July 10. It is not uncommon for disputes to arise about the amount due as a progress payment, leading to a wrongful withholding of all or part of it. If the builder discontinues work, what are his rights?

In one such case where he brought an action against the other party for damages, the defendant requested an instruction that "The delay of defendant to make payments on estimates, in the absence of a positive refusal to pay anything, was not ground for a rescission or termination of the contract by plaintiff," and that plaintiff's remedy was to recover interest on the deferred payments. Instead, the court instructed the jury that if defendant failed to make payments on account as called for by the contract—"a substantial failure, amounting substantially to the withholding of the whole payment, not necessarily the whole payment, but the

---

a. Compare United States v. F. D. Rich Co., Inc., 439 F.2d 895 (8th Cir. 1971), in which a subcontractor was held to be entitled to job earnings, although there were claims against him by laborers and materialmen that exceeded the amount owing, and the contract seemed to make it clear that he was entitled to no recovery in the circumstances. The court "interpreted" the contract in the subcontractor's favor, relying on the contract provision for a payment bond, which had been supplied. The court of appeals suggested to the trial court that it enter judgment in a form assuring the defendant contractor protection against double liability.

bulk of the payment"—such failure constituted a breach on the part of defendant justifying plaintiff in stopping work and entitling him to recover damages (including lost profits) from defendant. A judgment for the builder was affirmed by the Supreme Court, saying: "As is usually the case with building contracts, it evidently was in the contemplation of the parties that the contractor could not be expected to finance the operation to completion without receiving the stipulated payments on account as the work progressed. In such cases a substantial compliance as to advance payments is a condition precedent to the contractor's obligation to proceed." Guerini Stone Co. v. P. J. Carlin Const. Co., 248 U.S. 334 (1919).

For a somewhat divergent view, see Palmer v. Watson Const. Co., 265 Minn. 195, 121 N.W.2d 62 (1963): "We are committed . . . . to the rule that non-payment of installment obligations is not in and of itself such prevention of performance as will make possible suit for loss of profits even though the party entitled to payment may lack working capital." Cf. Integrated, Inc. v. Alec Fergusson Electrical Contractors, 250 Cal.App.2d 287, 58 Cal.Rptr. 503 (Cal.App.1967). On progress payments in general, see Sweet, Legal Aspects of Architecture, Engineering and the Construction Process, § 24.03 (1970).

(3) *Independent Covenants.* Recent cases in which a promise on one side of a bilateral contract has been held to be "independent" are exceptional. For an independent covenant in a trading-stamp contract, see Gold Bond Stamp Co. v. Gilt-Edge Stamps, Inc., 437 F.2d 27 (5th Cir. 1971). As to covenants in leases, see Note 2, p. 806 infra.

(4) *Problem.* The defendants, who were practicing physicians and operated a hospital in X County, sold the hospital to the plaintiffs with a promise that defendants would not compete by operating any hospital in X County for 10 years, in return for which plaintiffs gave, besides the purchase price, their promise to let one of defendants practice medicine in the hospital and bring his patients to it. In a suit by plaintiffs to enjoin defendants from breaking their promise, can the latter defend on the ground that plaintiffs broke theirs? See Johnson v. Stumbo, 277 Ky. 301, 311, 126 S.W.2d 165, 176 (1939) (hospital built 300 yards outside county). See also General Billposting Co. v. Atkinson, [1909] A.C. 118 (House of Lords) (discussing Serjeant Williams' rules).

ANTICIPATORY BREACH OF CONTRACT

In Phillpotts v. Evans, 5 M. & W. 475, 151 Eng.Rep. 200 (1839), a seller sued on a contract for the sale of wheat. The buyer had refused to take delivery. Some time before the seller was required to make delivery, the buyer had given him notice that it would not be accepted. The market price had dropped between then and the last day when the seller could have made a proper tender. The question was whether the damages should be calculated with reference to the market price at the time of the buyer's repudiation, or to the price at the later time. Naturally, the buyer preferred the earlier date. The same issue was presented in Roehm v. Horst, 178 U.S. 1 (1900), which is perhaps the leading American case on anticipatory breach of contract.

In the Restatement, the term "anticipatory breach" is treated as a misnomer: "The full expression would be breach by anticipatory repudiation." Section 318, Comment d. But this diction is not entirely trustworthy; for a repudiation is not always regarded as simply one variety of breach of contract, as will be seen. To make matters worse, the word "repudiation" is sometimes used in the sense of "cancellation." An example is the opinion in Walker & Co. v. Harrison, p. 695 supra, where the court said: "Repudiation is one of the weapons available to an injured party in event the other contractor has committed a material breach." Compare UCC 2–106(4).

By the better usage, an anticipatory repudiation occurs when a promisor *wrongfully* signifies, in advance of the time for his performance, that it will not be forthcoming. The notice given by the buyer in Phillpotts v. Evans was a repudiation in this sense. Under the Code, such a repudiation occurs when a party fails to respond adequately to a justified demand by the other party for an assurance of due performance. UCC 2–609(4).

What are the effects of an anticipatory repudiation? This is the question to be considered next. Sometimes it is assumed that if an anticipatory repudiation has one effect similar to that of a breach it must have other consequences as well. The leading case on the subject, Hochster v. De la Tour, has been criticized for reasoning in that way. After reading the opinion, which follows, consider whether or not the criticism is a fair one.

In any event, the problem of calculating damages that was raised in Phillpotts v. Evans is separable from other issues relating to anticipatory repudiation. More recent materials addressing that problem are presented in a later section of this chapter.

HOCHSTER v. DE LA TOUR

Queen's Bench, 1853. 2 E. & B. 678, 118 Eng.Rep. 922.

[Action of assumpsit.] Declaration: "for that, heretofore, to wit, on 12th April 1852, in consideration that plaintiff, at the request of defendant would agree with the defendant to enter into the service and employ of the defendant in capacity of a courier, on a certain day then to come, to wit, the 1st day of June, 1852, and to serve the defendant in that capacity, and travel with him on the continent of Europe as a courier for three months certain from the day and year last aforesaid, and to be ready to start with the defendant on such travels on the day and year last aforesaid, at and for certain wages or salary, to wit," £10 per month of such service, "the defendant then agreed with the plaintiff, and then promised him, that he, the defendant, would engage and employ the plaintiff in the capacity of a courier on and from the said 1st day of June, 1852, for three months" on these terms; "and to start on such travels with the plaintiff on the day and year last aforesaid, and to pay the plaintiff" on these terms. Averment that plaintiff, confiding in the said agreement and promise of the defendant "agreed with the defendant" to fulfill these terms on his part, "and to be ready to start with the defendant on such travels on the day and year last aforesaid, at and for the wages and salary aforesaid." That, "from the time of the making of said agreement of the said promise of the defendant until the time when the defendant wrongfully refused to perform and broke his said promise, and absolved, exonerated, and discharged the plaintiff from the performance of his agreement as hereinafter mentioned, he, the plaintiff, was always ready and willing to enter the service and employ of the defendant, in the capacity aforesaid, on the said 1st day of June, 1852, and to serve the defendant in that capacity, and to travel with him on the continent of Europe as a courier for three months certain from the day and year last aforesaid, and to start with the defendant on such travels on the day and year last aforesaid, at and for the wages and salary aforesaid; and the plaintiff, but for the breach by the defendant of his said promise as hereinafter mentioned, would, on the said 1st day of June, 1852, have entered into the said service and employ of the defendant in the capacity and upon the terms and for the time aforesaid; of all which several premises the defendant always had notice and knowledge; yet the defendant, not regarding the said agreement, nor his said promise, afterwards and before the said 1st June, 1852, wrongfully wholly refused and declined to engage or employ the defendant in the capacity and for the purpose aforesaid, on or from the said 1st June, 1852, for three months, or on, from, or for, any other time, or to start on such travels with the plaintiff on the day and year last aforesaid, or in any manner whatsoever to perform or fulfill his said promise, and then wrongfully wholly absolved, exonerated, and discharged the plaintiff from his said agreement, and from the performance of the same agreement on his the plaintiff's part, and from being ready and willing to perform the same on the plaintiff's part; and the defendant then wrongfully wholly broke, put an end to, and determined his said promise and engagement," to the damage of the plaintiff. The writ was dated on the 22d of May, 1852.

Pleas: 1. That defendant did not agree or promise in manner, and form, &c.: conclusion to the country. Issue thereon.

2. That plaintiff not not agree with defendant in manner and form, &c.: conclusion to the country. Issue thereon.

3. That plaintiff was not ready and willing, nor did defendant absolve, exonerate, or discharge plaintiff from being ready and willing, in manner and form, &c.: conclusion to the country. Issue thereon.

4.   That defendant did not refuse or decline, nor wrongfully absolve, exonerate, or discharge, nor wrongfully break, put an end to, or determine, in manner and form, &c.: conclusion to the country.   Issue thereon.

On the trial before Erle, J., at the London sittings in last Easter term, it appeared that plaintiff was a courier, who in April, 1852, was engaged by defendant to accompany him on a tour, to commence on 1st June, 1852 on the terms mentioned in the declaration.   On the 11th May, 1852, defendant wrote to plaintiff that he had changed his mind, and declined his services.   He refused to make him any compensation.   The action was commenced on 22d May.   The plaintiff, between the commencement of the action and the 1st of June, obtained an engagement with Lord Ashburton, on equally good terms, but not commencing till 4th July.   The defendant's counsel objected that there could be no breach of the contract before the 1st of June.   The learned judge was of contrary opinion, but reserved leave to enter a nonsuit on this objection.   The other questions were left to the jury, who found for plaintiff.

LORD CAMPBELL, C. J.,[a] now delivered the judgment of the court:

On this motion in arrest of judgment, the question arises whether if there be an engagement between A. and B. whereby B. engages to employ A. on and from a future day for a given period of time, to travel with him into a foreign country as a courier, and to start with him in that capacity on that day, A. being to receive a monthly salary during the continuance of such service, B. may, before the day, refuse to perform the agreement and break and renounce it, so as to entitle A. before the day to commence an action against B. to recover damages for breach of the agreement, A. having been ready and willing to perform it, till it was broken and renounced by B.   The defendant's counsel very powerfully contended that, if the plaintiff was not contented to dissolve the contract, and to abandon all remedy upon it, he was bound to remain ready and willing to perform it till the day when the actual employment as courier in the service of the defendant was to begin; and that there could be no breach of the agreement, before that day, to give a right of action.   But it cannot be laid down as a universal rule that, where by agreement an act is to be done on a fu-

---

a.   John Campbell (1779–1861), a Scotsman of ancient lineage, matriculated at St. Andrews University at the age of eleven.   Upon entering the English bar he predicted that he would become Lord Chancellor.   His name is associated with a number of law reform statutes which he pressed as a member of Parliament, as Attorney General, and in the House of Lords. As a reward for his services to the government, he was made the first Baron Campbell.   He won literary fame with his "Lives of the Lord Chancellors," followed by the "Lives of the Chief Justices."   These works are full of good stories, inaccuracies, and harsh judgments; it was said that they had added a new sting to death.   He held judicial office briefly as Lord Chancellor of Ireland, where he was not popular, and as Chief Justice of England from 1850 to 1859. Then he became Lord Chancellor of England, at the age of eighty.

ture day, no action can be brought for a breach of the agreement till the day for doing the act has arrived. If a man promises to marry a woman on a future day, and before that day marries another woman, he is instantly liable to an action for breach of promise of marriage. Short v. Stone, 8 Q.B. 358. If a man contracts to execute a lease on and from a future day for a certain term, and, before that day, executes a lease to another for the same term, he may be immediately sued for breaking the contract. Ford v. Tiley, 6 B. & C. 325. So if a man contracts to sell and deliver specific goods on a future day, and before the day he sells and delivers them to another he is immediately liable to an action at the suit of the person with whom he first contracted to sell and deliver them. Bowdell v. Parsons, 10 East, 359. One reason alleged in support of such an action is, that the defendant has, before the day, rendered it impossible for him to perform the contract at the day; but this does not necessarily follow; for, prior to the day fixed for doing the act, the first wife may have died, a surrender of the lease executed might be obtained, and the defendant might have repurchased the goods so as to be in a situation to sell and deliver them to the plaintiff. Another reason may be that, where there is a contract to do an act on a future day, there is a relation constituted between the parties in the meantime by the contract, and that they impliedly promise that in the meantime neither will do anything to the prejudice of the other inconsistent with that relation. As an example, a man and woman engaged to marry are affianced to one another during the period between the time of the engagement and the celebration of the marriage. In this very case of traveller and courier, from the day of the hiring till the day when the employment was to begin, they were engaged to each other; and it seems to be a breach of an implied contract if either of them renounced the engagement. This reasoning seems in accordance with the unanimous decisions of the Exchequer Chamber in Elderton v. Emmens, 6 C.B. 160, which we have followed in subsequent cases in this court. The declaration in the present case, in alleging a breach, states a great deal more than a passing intention on the part of the defendant which he may repent of, and could only be proved by evidence that he had utterly renounced the contract, or done some act which rendered it impossible for him to perform it. If the plaintiff has no remedy for breach of the contract unless he treats the contract as in force, and acts upon it down to the 1st June, 1852, it follows that, till then, he must enter into no employment which will interfere with his promise "to start with the defendant on such travels on the day and year," and that he must then be properly equipped in all respects as a courier for a three months' tour on the continent of Europe. But it is surely much more rational, and more for the benefit of both parties, that, after the renunciation of the agreement by the defendant, the plaintiff should be at liberty to consider himself absolved from any future performance of it, retaining his right to sue for any damage he has suffered from the breach of it. Thus, instead of remaining idle and laying out money in preparations which must be useless, he is at liberty to seek service under another employer, which would go in mitigation of the damages to which he would otherwise be entitled for a breach of the contract. It seems strange that the defendant, after renouncing the contract, and absolutely declaring that he will never act under it, should be permitted to object that faith is given to his assertion, and that an opportunity is not left to him of changing his mind. If the plaintiff is barred of any remedy by entering into an engagement inconsistent with starting as a courier with the defendant on the 1st June, he is prejudiced by putting faith in the defendant's assertion; and it would be more consistent with principle if the defendant were precluded from saying that he had not broken the contract when he declared that he entirely renounced it. Suppose that the defendant, at the time of his renunciation, had embarked on a voyage for Australia, so as to render it physically impossible for him to employ the plaintiff as a courier on the continent of Europe in the months of June, July and August, 1852; according to decided cases, the action might have been brought before the 1st June; but the renunciation may have been founded on other facts, to be given in evidence, which would equally have rendered the defendant's performance of the contract impossible. The man who wrongfully renounces a contract into which he has deliberately entered cannot justly complain if he is immediately sued for a compensation in damages by the man whom he has injured; and it seems reasonable to allow an option to the injured party, either to sue immediately, or to wait till the time when the act was to be done, still holding it as prospectively binding for the exercise of this option, which may be advantageous to the innocent party, and cannot be prejudicial to the wrongdoer. An argument against the action before the 1st of June is urged from the difficulty of calculating the damages; but this argument is equally strong against an action before the 1st of September, when the three months would expire. In either case, the jury in assessing the damages would be justified in looking to all that happened, or was likely to happen, to increase or mitigate the loss of the plaintiff down to the day of trial. We do not find any decision contrary to the view we are taking of this case. Leigh v. Paterson, 8 Taunt, 540, only shows that upon a sale of goods to be delivered at a certain time, if the vendor before the time gives information to the vendee that he cannot deliver them, having sold them, the vendee may calculate the damages according to the state of the market when they ought to have been delivered. . . .

If it should be held that, upon a contract to do an act on a future day, a renunciation of the contract by one party dispenses with a condition to be performed in the meantime by the other, there seems no reason for requiring that other to wait till the day arrives before seeking his remedy by action; and the only ground on which the condition can be dispensed with seems to be, that the renunciation may be treated as a breach of contract.

Upon the whole, we think that the declaration in this case is sufficient. It gives us great satisfaction to reflect that, the question being on the record, our opinion may be reviewed in a Court of Error. In the meantime, we must give judgment for the plaintiff.

Judgment for plaintiff.

NOTES

(1) *The Victim's Option.* The implication of the opinion seems to be that the victim of a repudiation may treat it as a breach, or not, as he likes: "the renunciation may be treated as a breach." The element of choice appears in many anticipatory breach cases. Sometimes it is said that the injured party has an election, sometimes that the repudiation amounts to an "offer" of breach to him.

If the injured party disregards the repudiation altogether, will his rights later be determined as if it had never occurred? An English decision of 1872 contains reasoning that is well-known in this country, and indicates that they will. However, that reasoning has also been rejected, at least where it would permit the injured party to pile up damages by proceeding with performance. See Rockingham County v. Luten Bridge Co., p. 503 supra, where the English case (Frost v. Knight) is criticized.

Nevertheless, it is a persistent idea that the injured party has a choice, upon receiving a repudiation, and that he may "keep the contract alive," to use Lord Cockburn's expression, for the benefit of both parties. As an example, see Dunn v. Reliance Life & Accident Ins. Co., 405 S.W.2d 389 (Tex.Civ.App.1966), where the court observed that the injured party did not *accept* the repudiation. The question was whether the statute of limitations began to run on the date the performance was promised, or earlier at repudiation. See also Brewer v. Simpson, 53 Cal.2d 567, 349 P.2d 289 (1960). Could this question be answered without regard to the decision in the Luten Bridge case?

(2) *Disability.* Suppose it appeared, in the trial of Hochster v. De la Tour, that between May 22, when the action was commenced, and June 1, when the employment was to begin, the plaintiff had suffered a crippling injury that would have prevented his serving the defendant for any part of the summer. If damages were denied the plaintiff on those facts, would it be consistent with the court's ruling that "the renunciation may be treated as a breach"? Would it be consistent with the view that a party receiving a repudiation has an election, or option? Would it be unjust to award damages? For indications of the result, see Model Vending, Inc. v. Stanisci, 74 N.J.Super. 12, 180 A.2d 393 (1962); Hodes v. Hoffman International Corporation, 280 F.Supp. 252 (S.D.N.Y.1968).

BERNSTEIN v. MEECH, 130 N.Y. 354, 29 N.E. 255 (1891). [The Jarbeau Comedy Company was engaged to appear in the Academy of Music, a Buffalo opera house, on three days late in December, 1887. The gross receipts were to be divided equally between the plaintiff (representing Jarbeau) and the defendants (representing the Academy). On August 12 the plaintiff sent to the defendants another contract for signature by which the plaintiff would receive 60% of the receipts, and he wrote that he could not think of playing for less. The defendants returned the contract unsigned "for the reason that we have a contract signed by you and do not need any other for the appearance of Vernona Jarbeau and company at our Academy of Music."

In November the defendants received advertising material from the plaintiff, who wrote: "Please keep Miss Jarbeau before the public as much as possible. I want to see her turn them away in your town. . . ." This letter was sent on the 17th but not received at once because of a defendant's absence from Buffalo. He answered it on the 28th, saying that Miss Jarbeau could not play the Academy and expressing surprise that she intended to. This letter did not reach the plaintiff's agent, who was travelling, until after the middle of December. Before the Jarbeau Company arrived, the defendants had booked other performers, and the plaintiff's company was not permitted to appear.

A judgment in favor of the plaintiff, entered on a verdict, was affirmed. The Court of Appeals decided that it was for the jury to determine whether or not the plaintiff's letter of August 12 was a renunciation of the contract.]

BRADLEY, J. . . . But whatever view may have been taken of the right of the defendants to treat the contract for the purposes of its performance as at an end and to act upon that assumption when they received the plaintiff's letter, they disposed of that question by their letter to him. By this it appeared that the defendants elected to keep the contract in force for the purposes for which it was made. This operated alike upon the rights of both parties, and the plaintiff was justified in so understanding it. In that view the contract was kept alive until the time arrived for performance, and the obligations of the defendants no less than those of the plaintiff for that purpose remained effectual. (Johnstone v. Milling, L.R. (16 Q.B.D.) 460; Frost v. Knight, L.R. (7 Exch.) 111; Zuck v. McClure, 98 Pa.St. 541.)

There was no error in the refusal of the court to direct a verdict for the defendants. . . .

[In the remaining portions of the opinion, the court held that plaintiff could recover the amount of his "expenses legitimately and essentially incurred for the purpose" of performing the contract.]

Judgment affirmed.

NOTE

Retraction. An offer to contract and an anticipatory repudiation have virtually nothing in common, except this: each may be withdrawn. In the case of an offer, the appropriate word is "revoke"; in the case of a repudiation the appropriate word is "retract". See UCC 2–611. Inasmuch as a present breach of contract cannot be undone, the view has been expressed that the conception of breach by anticipatory repudiation is anomalous, and cannot be accounted for on "normal contract analysis." G. E. J. Corporation v. Uranium Aire, Inc., 311 F.2d 749, 754 n. 3 (9th Cir. 1963). In the case of an ordinary breach of contract, nothing the defaulting party may do can deprive the injured party of a right of action—although the breach may be so slight that only nominal damages would be granted.

The matter of retraction will be further considered below.

————

PHELPS v. HERRO, 215 Md. 223, 137 A.2d 159 (1957). [In 1955 Herro contracted to sell certain interests, in realty and corporate stock, to Phelps for a price of $37,500. Phelps agreed to pay $5,000 by January 1, 1956, and to give a promissory note for the remainder. This note was to be payable in $5,000 installments, with interest, on the first of each succeeding year until paid in full. The first $5,000 was paid, and in September of 1956 Herro made the transfers called for in the contract. Later he was notified that the rest of the price would not be paid. He had never received the note. On December 7, 1956, he sued for $32,500. A judgment in his favor is the subject of this appeal. *Held:* For Phelps.

The court acknowledged that Herro might have sued Phelps for failure to give the note within a reasonable time, and recovered at least nominal damages, but it held that he was not entitled to installments due after December 7. (Not even the one due on January 1, 1957, apparently, although it was overdue at the time of judgment.)]

Prescott, Judge. . . . We think the proper rule is that the doctrine of anticipatory breach of a contract has no application to money contracts, pure and simple, where one party has fully performed his undertaking, and all that remains for the opposite party to do is to pay a certain sum of money at a certain time or times, and, under the circumstances of this case, this is as far as we need to rule, although some of the cases cited hold that the doctrine of anticipatory breach has no application whatsoever in unilateral contracts, or bilateral contracts that have become unilateral by full performance on one side.

[The court said that a different rule would apply if the contract had required the giving of a note *with security*.]

The appellees argued further that a promise to give a negotiable note stands on the same footing as a promise to furnish security. We find it unnecessary to decide this question; because we think the promise to give a note in this case contemplated a non-negotiable one. . . .

Hammond, Judge (dissenting). . . . I could not bring myself . . . to saddle Maryland needlessly with what I consider to be illogical and unsound law—a doctrine that is more apparent than real, and one that has been repudiated by the ablest judges and scholars. [Judge Hammond conceded that Williston favored an exception to the doctrine of anticipatory breach—"perhaps because of his dislike of the doctrine." However, he quoted from Corbin and others to sustain his view.]

NOTES

(1) *The Rose Bowl Affair.* The Southern California football team played in the Rose Bowl on January 1, 1969. Tickets sold for $20 on the "black market." Before the season began, Roger Diamond had bought an "economy season ticket" from the University, on the promise that he could have a Rose Bowl ticket if the team played there. When it was selected to do so, however, the Tournament of Roses Association allotted to the University fewer tickets than it needed to meet its commitments to season ticket holders, by about 3,500. Early in December, 1968, the University notified Diamond that he and other first-time holders of economy season tickets could not be accommodated. The notice thanked him for his support of Trojan football.

On December 9 Diamond, a lawyer, brought a class action against the University on behalf of himself and others similarly situated, holders of 3,000 tickets. About a week later the University altered its stance and began distributing applications for Rose Bowl tickets to members of the plaintiff's class. In January, the trial court gave summary judgment for the defendant. The plaintiff appealed, for the purpose of establishing his right to an attorney's fee. *Held:* Affirmed. Diamond v. University of Southern California, 11 Cal.App.3d 49, 89 Cal.Rptr. 302 (1970).[a]

The court found several unanswered questions about class actions in the appeal, but passed them by and pinned its result on the rule that "the doctrine of anticipatory repudiation does not apply to contracts which are unilateral in their inception or have become so by complete performance by one party. . . . Plaintiff and the members of his class had done all that they had ever been obligated to do, that is pay the price of a season ticket. Nothing was left but for defendant to furnish the applications for the Rose Bowl tickets. The action was, therefore, premature. . . . We have, admittedly, taken the easy way out and decided to affirm on the basis of a simple principle of contract law. The day may come when that principle, which already is not universally admired . . . will be successfully questioned in another class action, similar in structure, but which presents major considerations of public policy which outweigh the social utility of a technical exception to the doctrine of anticipatory breach. When that day comes, the court concerned with the case can easily confine this decision to its own peculiar facts by noting that easy cases make bad law."

(2) *The Code.* It has been suggested that the Code "demands discontinuance of the artificial distinction between contracts which have been fully performed by one party and those which are completely executory." Taylor, The Impact of Article 2 of the U.C.C. on the Doctrine of Anticipatory

---

a. The trial court made a finding that the University's "sudden affluence in the matter of tickets" was not caused by the plaintiff's suit. Does this affect your judgment about the case? It did not seem to affect the court's.

Repudiation, 9 Bost.Coll.Ind. & Comm.L.Rev. 917, 926–27 (1968). What Code sections are incompatible with the distinction? 2–609 or 2–610? Do any Code sections support it? 2–709?

INSTALLMENT PAYMENT CONTRACTS

In several important classes of contracts there is a commitment to pay money in installments over an extended period of time. Long-term leases are examples. In the event of repudiation by the tenant, what may the landlord recover on account of future payments? A possible answer is nothing, according to the "usual rule that contracts to pay money in installments are breached one installment at a time." Quick v. American Steel and Pump Corporation, 397 F.2d 561 (2d Cir. 1968). There are other answers, which cannot be examined here, except to note that anticipatory breach law has not worked in favor of lessors so well as it has worked for others. The lessor's performance is regarded as complete at the time of the lease; for by the niceties of ancient property law it is a conveyance. If the rent is therefore an independent obligation, the lessor is handicapped in claiming damages. "There must be some dependency of performance in order to make anticipatory breach possible." Sagamore Corp. v. Willcutt, 120 Conn. 315, 180 A. 464 (1935). Yet this rule may not, in practice, handicap lessors so much as it seems to do, as is shown by the case cited.

Like leases, annuity contracts call for long-term installment payments. In a suit for such payments, it is generally accepted that a judgment for the payee should be limited to money owing when the action is brought,[a] or when it reaches trial,[b] or when the judgment is entered, at the latest. The consequence may be that the payee has to assert his rights in successive actions. Dissatisfaction with this state of affairs has suggested at least two remedial measures. One is to apply the doctrine of anticipatory breach, with the effect that the payee has judgment for the immediate recovery of the present value of all future installments. Another is that the court enter an order calling for future payments to be made as they fall due. This procedure amounts to specific performance, and for effectiveness it might require that the court retain the case until completion of the payments.

The former suggestion is plagued by doubt that the calculations would be accurate. Consider, for example, an agreement by which Henry Pollack was to pay $5,000 a year to his brother Charles (in monthly installments) for the life of Charles, except that if Henry died first his estate was to pay Charles $100,000. What is the present value of Charles' rights when Henry repudiates? Does it matter that

---

a. As in Phelps v. Herro, supra.

b. Brix v. People's Mutual Life Ins. Co., 2 Cal.2d 446, 41 P.2d 537 (1935).

Henry is a bit older? In Pollack v. Pollack, 39 S.W.2d 853 (Tex. Com.App.1931), the court directed a calculation on the assumption that Henry would die in 12 years, and Charles three years later.[c]

A more common sort of contract containing health contingencies is illustrated in New York Life Ins. Co. v. Viglas, infra. Still another is an ordinary life insurance contract. If the insurer repudiates while premiums are still to be paid, there is an element of dependency, and the policyholder is commonly entitled to the present value of the death benefit. That value will be relatively large if it is assumed that death is imminent. A policyholder having a serious ailment, Patterson suggested, may play on the court's sympathies to enlarge his recovery. Essentials of Insurance Law § 48 (2d ed. 1957).

After reading the Viglas case, consider whether there is reason for concern about sympathetic distortion of a verdict in that situation.

NOTE

Specific Performance. For the annuitant of a life insurance company, once the company repudiates, what is the advantage of specific performance? If the installment payments are resumed, and stopped again, presumably the payee must apply again to the court for relief. This may seem a remote prospect because of the insurer's need to maintain a reputation.[d] Or because it would fear regulatory sanctions. But if that is so, the objective is gained, is it not, by awarding only accrued installments to the payee? See Fanning v. Guardian Life Ins. Co., 59 Wash.2d 101, 366 P.2d 207 (1961). This case is one of many which limit recovery to accrued installments by following the rule stated in Phelps v. Herro, supra. And this was done although the company denied the existence of the contract; compare the text of Viglas as to "complete repudiation."

"A contract for the payment of money in installments is not ordinarily specifically enforceable, the common law remedies being regarded as adequate." 5 Corbin, 663. But in a few courts an order may be granted for periodic future payments.[e] Corbin argues for more flexibility in this regard, especially in favor of an insured person claiming by right of disability.

---

c. The court said it was "impossible to actually tell, with certainty, which of these parties will die first, but such fact does not prevent the court from ascertaining such fact."

d. Cobb v. Pacific Mutual Ins. Co., 4 Cal.2d 565, 51 P.2d 84 (1935).

e. See Equitable Life Assur. Soc. v. Branham, 250 Ky. 472, 63 S.W.2d 498 (1933); John Hancock Mutual Life Ins. Co. v. Cohen, 254 F.2d 417 (9th Cir. Okla.1958); cf. Wild v. Wild, 360 Mich. 270, 103 N.W.2d 607 (1960).

NEW YORK LIFE INS. CO. v. VIGLAS

Supreme Court of the United States, 1936.
297 U.S. 672, 56 S.Ct. 615, 80 L.Ed. 971.

On Writ of Certiorari to the United States Circuit Court of Appeals for the First Circuit.

Action by Demetrios P. Viglas against the New York Life Insurance Company. To review a judgment of the Circuit Court of Appeals [78 F.2d 829] reversing a judgment of the District Court for defendant, the defendant brings certiorari.

Judgment of the Circuit Court of Appeals reversed, and judgment of the District Court affirmed.

MR. JUSTICE CARDOZO delivered the opinion of the Court.

The case, which is here upon demurrer to a declaration, depends for its solution upon the nature of the breach of contract imputed to the defendant, the petitioner in this court, and upon the measure of the damages recoverable therefor.

From the declaration we learn the following: Respondent received from petitioner on February 7, 1927, a policy of insurance for $2,000 payable at his death. The consideration was a semiannual premium of $38 payable during his life, but for not more than twenty years. If, however, the insured became totally and permanently disabled before the age of sixty, the company, petitioner, was to pay him a monthly income at an agreed rate and was to waive the payment of any premium that would otherwise be due. Disability was to be considered total when the insured was so affected by bodily injury or disease as to be wholly prevented from performing any work, from following any occupation, or from engaging in any business for remuneration or profit. In particular, "the total and irrecoverable loss of the sight of both eyes or of the use of both hands or of both feet or of one hand and one foot" was to constitute "total disability for life." Before making any income payment or waiving any premium, the company might demand due proof of the continuance of total disability, not oftener, however, than once a year after such disability had continued for two full years. Upon failure to furnish such proof, or if the insured performed any work, or followed any occupation, or engaged in any business for remuneration or profit, "no further income payments" were to be made, "nor premiums waived." If, at the time of a default in the payment of a premium, the insured was disabled within the definition of the policy, the insurance was to be reinstated, provided, however, that within six months after the default proofs of such disability were received by the insurer. In any event, reinstatement would be permitted at any time within five years upon evidence of insurability satisfactory to the insurer and upon payment of overdue premiums with interest at 5 per cent. Finally, the insured, though in default, was to have the benefit of surrender values in the form either of cash or of temporary insurance or of participating paid-up insurance according to his choice.

On September 11, 1931, the insured, according to the declaration, lost "the total and irrecoverable use" of one hand and one foot, and became totally and permanently disabled. Upon proof of his condition the company paid him the monthly benefits called for by the policy from October 11, 1931, to July 11, 1933, and during the same period waived the payment of semiannual premiums. It refused to make a monthly payment in August, 1933, and refused the same month to waive a semiannual premium, "asserting to the plaintiff as its ground for such refusal that since it appeared to the defendant that for some time past the plaintiff had not been continuously totally disabled within the meaning of the disability benefit provision of the policy, the defendant would make no further monthly disability payments, and that the premiums due on and after August 7, 1933, would be payable in conformity with the terms of the contract." Later, upon the expiration of a term of grace, "the defendant, on or about September 19, 1933, declared the policy as lapsed upon its records." Plaintiff has elected to treat the defendant's acts "as a repudiation and denunciation of the entire contract," relieving him on his part from any further obligation.

There are two counts to his declaration. In the first, after stating the foregoing facts, he claims the cash surrender value that the policy will have in February, 1969, if he lives until that time, the date being chosen with reference to his expectancy of life under the American Table of Mortality. This value, $1,408, is less than the amount necessary to give jurisdiction in accordance with the Judicial Code. Judicial Code, sec. 24, 28 U.S.C. sec. 41, 28 U.S.C.A. sec. 41. In the second count, after stating the same facts, he claims for damages the total benefits that will be payable to him during the same period of expectancy, if he lives that long and his disability continues. The damages so computed are $15,900. No deduction is made on account of future premiums, for by hypothesis the disability will continue during life. The defendant demurred to both counts, stating in the demurrer that the declaration sets forth a cause of action for the benefits and premiums accruing prior to the date of the writ, and for nothing in excess thereof. In that view the recovery will be only $98, which is less than the jurisdictional amount. The District Court sustained the demurrer, and gave judgment for the defendant. The Circuit Court of Appeals for the First Circuit reversed. 78 F.2d 829. A writ of certiorari issued to resolve a claim of conflict with a decision of this court. 296 U.S. 571, 56 S.Ct. 370, 80 L.Ed. 403.

Upon the showing made in the complaint there was neither a repudiation of the policy nor such a breach of its provisions as to make conditional and future benefits the measure of recovery.

Repudiation there was none as the term is known to the law. Petitioner did not disclaim the intention or the duty to shape its conduct in accordance with the provisions of the contract. Far from repudiating those provisions, it appealed to their authority and endeavored to apply them. If the insured was still disabled, monthly benefits were payable, and there should have been a waiver of the premium. If he had recovered the use of hand or foot and was not otherwise disabled, his right to benefits had ceased, and the payment of the premium was again a contractual condition. There is nothing to show that the insurer was not acting in good faith in giving notice of its contention that the disability was over. Mobley v. New York Life Insurance Co., 295 U.S. 632, 638, 55 S.Ct. 876, 79 L.Ed. 1621, 99 A.L.R. 1166. If it made a mistake, there was a breach of a provision of the policy with liability for any damages appropriate thereto. We do not pause at the moment to fix the proper measure. Enough in this connection that at that stage of the transaction there had been no renunciation or abandonment of the contract as a whole. Mobley v. New York Life Insurance Co., supra; Dingley v. Oler, 117 U.S. 490, 503, 6 S.Ct. 850, 29 L.Ed. 984; Roehm v. Horst, 178 U.S. 1, 14, 15, 20 S.Ct. 780, 44 L. Ed. 953; Pierce v. Tennessee Coal, Iron & R. Co., 173 U.S. 1, 3, 11, 19 S.Ct. 335, 43 L.Ed. 591.

Renunciation or abandonment, if not effected at that stage, became consummate in the plaintiff's view at the end of the period of grace when the company declared the policy "lapsed upon its records." Throughout the plaintiff's argument the declaration of a lapse is treated as equivalent to a declaration that the contract is a nullity. But the two are widely different under such a policy as this.[1] The policy survived for many purposes as an enforceable obligation, though default in the payment of premiums had brought about a change of rights and liabilities. The insurer was still subject to a duty to give the insured the benefit of the stipulated surrender privileges, cash or new insurance. It was still subject to a duty upon proof within six months that the disability continued to reinstate the policy as if no default had occurred. None of these duties was renounced. None of them was questioned. Indeed, there is lacking an allegation that notice of the entry on the records was given to the plaintiff, or that what was recorded amounted to more than a private memorandum. In that respect the case is weaker for the plaintiff than Mobley v. New York Life Insurance Co., supra, decided at the last term. . . .

What the damages would be if there had been complete repudiation we do not now decide. Cf. Kelly v. Security Mutual Life Insurance Co., 186 N.Y. 16, 78 N.E. 584, 9 Ann.Cas. 661; O'Neill v. Supreme Council, A.L. of H., 70 N.J.Law, 410, 415, 57 A. 463, 1 Ann. Cas. 422. For breach short of repudiation or an intentional abandonment equivalent thereto, the damages under such a policy as this

---

1. See the cases collected in Vance on Insurance, 2d Ed., pp. 283, 301, 302.

do not exceed the benefits in default at the commencement of the suit. Full justice will thus be done alike to insured and to insurer. The insured, if he proves that the benefits are due, will have a judgment effective to reinstate his policy. The insurer will be saved from a heavy, perhaps a crushing, liability as the consequence of a claim of right not charged to have been made as a disingenuous pretense. Cf. Armstrong v. Ross, 61 W.Va. 38, 48, 55 S.E. 895. So the courts have held with an impressive concord of opinion.[2] Federal Life Insurance Co. v. Rascoe (C.C.A.) 12 F.2d 693, one of the few decisions to the contrary, was disapproved in Mobley's Case, 295 U.S. 632, at page 639, 55 S.Ct. 876, 878, 79 L.Ed. 1621, 99 A.L.R. 1166, and is now disapproved again.

We have no thought to suggest an invariable rule whereby the full value of a bargain may never be recovered for any breach of contract falling short of repudiation or intentional abandonment. All depends upon the circumstances. Helgar Corporation v. Warner's Features, Inc., 222 N.Y. 449, 452, 453, 454, 119 N.E. 113.[3] There may be times when justice requires that, irrespective of repudiation or abandonment, the sufferer from the breach shall be relieved of a duty to treat the contract as subsisting or to hold himself in readiness to perform it in the future. Roehm v. Horst, supra, 178 U.S. 1, at pages 17, 18, 20 S.Ct. 780, 44 L.Ed. 953; Nichols v. Scranton Steel Co., 137 N.Y. 471, 487, 33 N.E. 561. Generally this is so where the contract is a bilateral one with continuing obligations, as where a manufacturer has undertaken to deliver merchandise in instalments. Norrington v. Wright, 115 U. S. 188, 6 S.Ct. 12, 29 L.Ed. 366; Wolfert v. Caledonia Springs Ice Co., 195 N.Y. 118, 88 N.E. 24, 21 L.R.A.,N.S., 864. Even then, the rights that are his may depend upon the grounds of the rejection or the nature of the default, whether unintentional or wilful. Helgar Corporation v. Warner's Features, Inc., supra. On the other hand, a party to a contract who has no longer any obligation of performance on his side, but is in the position of an annuitant or a creditor exacting payment from a debtor, may be compelled to wait for the instalments as they severally mature, just as a landlord may not accelerate the rent for the residue of the term because the rent is in default for a month or for a year. McCready v. Lindenborn, 172 N.Y. 400, 408, 65 N.E. 208; cf. National Machine & Tool Co. v. Standard Shoe Machinery Co., 181 Mass. 275, 279, 63 N.E. 900; Wharton & Co. v. Winch, 140 N.Y. 287, 35 N.E. 589. With the aid of this analysis, one discovers the rationale of the cases which have stated at times, though with needless generality, that by reason of the subject-matter of the undertaking the rule applicable to contracts for the payment of money is not the same as that applicable for the performance of services

2. [Twenty two cases cited.]

3. For a collection of the cases, see Williston, Contracts, vol. 2, secs. 864,

866, 867, 870, vol. 3, sec. 1290, and cf. Restatement, Law of Contracts, vol. 1, sec. 275.

or the delivery of merchandise.[a] Cf. Roehm v. Horst, supra, 178 U.S.
1, at page 17, 20 S.Ct. 780, 44 L.Ed. 953; Moore v. Security Trust &
Life Insurance Co. (C.C.A.) 168 F. 496, 503; Howard v. Benefit Association of Railway Employees, 239 Ky. 465, 470, 39 S.W.2d 657, 81
A.L.R. 375; Washington County v. Williams (C.C.A.) 111 F. 801,
810; Restatement, Law of Contracts, section 316. The root of any valid distinction is not in the difference between money and merchandise
or between money and services. What counts decisively is the relation
between the maintenance of the contract and the frustration of the
end it was expected to subserve. The ascertainment of this relation
calls for something more than the mechanical application of a uniform formula. To determine whether a breach avoids the contract as
a whole one must consider what is necessary to work out reparation in
varying conditions.

If that test be applied, the declaration will not stand. The plaintiff does not need redress in respect of unmatured instalments in order to put himself in a position to shape his conduct for the future.[b]
If he is already in default for the nonpayment of a premium, he will
not be in any worse predicament by multiplying the defaults thereafter. On the other hand, if his default is unreal because the premiums
had been waived, the insurer will be estopped from insisting upon later premiums until the declaration of a lapse has been canceled or
withdrawn. Besides, if the disability is permanent, there will be nothing more to pay. The law will be able to offer appropriate relief
"where compensation is willfully and contumaciously withheld." Cobb
v. Pacific Mutual Life Insurance Co., 4 Cal.2d 565, 51 P.2d 84, 88.

We have refrained in what has been written from developing the
distinction between an anticipatory breach and others. The line of division between the two has not always been preserved with consistency
or clearness. To blur it is prejudicial to accuracy of thought as well
as precision of terminology. Strictly an anticipatory breach is one
committed before the time has come when there is at present duty of
performance. Roehm v. Horst, supra; Pollock on Contracts, 9th Ed.,
p. 293; Williston, Contracts, vol. 3, sec. 1296, et seq., collecting the decisions. It is the outcome of words or acts evincing an intention to
refuse performance in the future. On the other hand, there are
times, as we have seen, when the breach of a present duty, though only
partial in its extention, may confer upon the injured party the privilege at his election to deal with the contract as if broken altogether.
A loose practice has been growing up whereby the breach on such occasions is spoken of as anticipatory, whereas in truth it is strictly
present, though with consequences effective upon performance in the

a. In a later case, Cardozo said that
the doctrine of anticipatory breach is
not applicable to unilateral contracts,
especially those for the payment of
money. Smyth v. U. S., 302 U.S. 329,
356 (1937).

b. Does this statement sufficiently take
account of the requirement that the
insured submit himself to a periodical
examination?

future.   The declaration in the case at hand makes a showing of a present breach.   It does not make a showing of a breach so wilful and material as to make acceleration of future benefits essential to the attainment of present reparation.   Helgar Corporation v. Warner's Features, Inc., supra.

The judgment of the Court of Appeals should be reversed and that of the District Court affirmed.

It is so ordered.

NOTES

(1) *Insurance Obligations and Anticipatory Breach.*   In many cases where there was a showing of present breach as there was in Viglas, the extent of an insurer's liability has been said to turn on the scope of the doctrine of anticipatory breach.   See Mabery v. Western Casualty & Surety Co., 173 Kan. 586, 250 P.2d 824 (1952) (monthly payments promised in settlement of tort claim).   In that case the court expressed concern, as others have done, about the difficulty of valuing plaintiff's right to future payments.   "Damages are not to be based upon mere conjecture or speculation, and we think plaintiff cannot be heard to claim serious physical permanent disability on the one hand, which condition existed at the time the alleged agreement was made, and at the same time to claim damages based on a normal life expectancy.   Suppose he were to die a year or two from now."

In Greguhn v. Mutual of Omaha Ins. Co., 23 Utah 2d 214, 461 P.2d 285 (1969), the Viglas case was followed, by a divided court, but as to the future it said:

"The verdict and the decision of the trial court amounts to a determination that the plaintiff is entitled to the monthly payments as specified in the insurance policies so long as he is totally and permanently disabled.   Defendants are not relieved of the obligation of making the payments unless the plaintiff should recover or die.   Should the defendants fail in the future to make payment in accordance with the terms of the policies without just cause or excuse and the plaintiff is compelled to file another action for delinquent installments, the court at that time should be able to fashion such relief as will compel performance."

(2) *Problem.*   Oil companies commonly make "dry hole contributions" to the drillers of test, or wildcat, wells.   Having minerals in the neighborhood, the company will be enriched if oil is found.   But so will the wildcatter, who has his own minerals;   and no payment is called for in that event. If no oil is found, he is a loser, but the company will reimburse part of his costs.   For a few thousand dollars, it may thereby save itself the expense of drilling its own well to prove (or disprove) its holdings.

Placid Oil Company made a dry hole contribution contract with a driller, by which it agreed to pay him $25,000 if he put a test well down to 10,000 feet and it proved to be a dry hole.   The driller was required to prove compliance with Texas law in plugging the hole;   this would have cost $2,000.   He spent more than $100,000 and drilled to 10,025 feet without finding more than a trace of oil.   He then asked Placid what to do.   Placid answered with the following telegram: "You are obligated to test all horizons which appear promising. To do so you must set pipe and conduct tests by perforating and sandfacing the following zones [naming eight zones]. The failure of which will be a material breach of agreement and a forfeiture of all your rights." Compliance with this demand would have cost $75,000, and was not required by the contract. Instead the driller went on down a short distance (indicated by the dissenting judge to be three feet) and struck oil. (Fortune smiled on him, said the court, "albeit wanly.") Then he brought an action against Placid for $25,000.

Consider the following issues: (a) Did Placid repudiate the contract? (b) At the time of the telegram, was there an "element of dependency" in the contract? (c) What is the effect on the driller's claim of his failure to plug the well? See Placid Oil Co. v. Humphrey, 244 F.2d 184 (5th Cir. 1957).

SECTION 2. RESTITUTION FOR A DEFAULTING PLAINTIFF

INTRODUCTION

Restitutionary relief, such as recovery in quasi contract, is sometimes available as between persons who have not dealt with one another (see Chapter 1), and sometimes between the parties to negotiations that fall short of a contract (see Chapter 2). As between the parties to an agreement, restitutionary relief is sometimes granted when it appears that the agreement is not enforceable for one reason or another: it is an illegal contract (see Chapter 3, Section 5); it is unenforceable because of the statute of frauds (see Chapter 4, Section 3); or it has become so by impossibility of performance or frustration (see Chapter 8). When there is an enforceable agreement between the parties, and a breach of it, the aggrieved party may prefer restitution to other forms of relief, and it is commonly available to him (see Chapter 5, Section 2).

But what of restitution for a party in breach of an enforceable agreement? If he has performed in part, and is unable to enforce the contract because he has failed to complete his performance, may he resort to an action in quasi contract? Such claims have met serious resistance, especially when the plaintiff's breach may be characterized as "willful." The following remarks represent a traditional response of the courts:

It would be an alarming doctrine, to hold, that the plaintiffs might violate the contract, and because they chose to do so, make their own infraction of the agreement the basis of an action for money had and received. (Ketchum & Sweet v.

Evertson, 13 Johns. (N.Y.) 358 (1816).)   To allow a recovery of this money would be to sustain an action by a party on his own breach of his own contract, which the law does not allow.   .   .   .   That would be ill doctrine.   (Lawrence v. Miller, 86 N.Y. 131 (1881).)

Some other responses are shown in this section.   The following case is a watershed.

BRITTON v. TURNER

Supreme Court of Judicature of New Hampshire, 1834.
6 N.H. 481.

Assumpsit, for work and labor, performed by the plaintiff, in the service of the defendant, from March 9, 1831, to December 27, 1831.

The declaration contained the common counts, and among them a count in quantum meruit, for the labor, averring it to be worth $100.

At the trial in the C. C. Pleas, the plaintiff proved the performance of the labor as set forth in the declaration.

The defense was that it was performed under a special contract; that the plaintiff agreed to work one year, from some time in March, 1831, to March, 1832, and that the defendant was to pay him for said year's labor the sum of $120; and the defendant offered evidence tending to show that such was the contract under which the work was done. Evidence was also offered to show that the plaintiff left the defendant's service without his consent, and it was contended by the defendant that the plaintiff had no good cause for not continuing in his employment.   There was no evidence offered of any damage arising from the plaintiff's departure, farther than was to be inferred from his non-fulfillment of the entire contract.

The court instructed the jury that, if they were satisfied from the evidence that the labor was performed under a contract to labor a year, for the sum of $120, and if they were satisfied that the plaintiff labored only the time specified in the declaration, and then left the defendant's service, against his consent, and without any good cause, yet the plaintiff was entitled to recover, under his quantum meruit count, as much as the labor he performed was reasonably worth, and under this direction the jury gave a verdict for the plaintiff for the sum of $95.

The defendant excepted to the instructions thus given to the jury.

PARKER, J., delivered the opinion of the court.

It may be assumed that the labor performed by the plaintiff, and for which he seeks to recover a compensation in this action, was commenced under a special contract to labor for the defendant the term of one year, for the sum of $120, and that the plaintiff has labored but a portion of that time, and has voluntarily failed to complete the entire contract.

It is clear, then, that he is not entitled to recover upon the contract itself, because the service, which was to entitle him to the sum agreed upon, has never been performed.

But the question arises: Can the plaintiff, under these circumstances, recover a reasonable sum for the service he has actually performed, under the count in quantum meruit? Upon this, and questions of a similar nature, the decisions to be found in the books are not easily reconciled.

It has been held, upon contracts of this kind for labor to be performed at a specified price, that the party who voluntarily fails to fulfill the contract by performing the whole labor contracted for, is not entitled to recover anything for the labor actually performed, however much he may have done towards the performance, and this has been considered the settled rule of law upon this subject. [Citations of Massachusetts, New York and English cases omitted.]

That such rule in its operation may be very unequal, not to say unjust, is apparent. A party who contracts to perform certain specified labor, and who breaks his contract in the first instance, without any attempt to perform it, can only be made liable to pay the damages which the other party has sustained by reason of such non-performance, which in many instances may be trifling; whereas a party who in good faith has entered upon the performance of his contract, and nearly completed it, and then abandoned the further performance, although the other party has had the full benefit of all that has been done, and has perhaps sustained no actual damage, is in fact subjected to a loss of all which has been performed, in the nature of damages for the non-fulfillment of the remainder, upon the technical rule, that the contract must be fully performed in order to [sustain] a recovery of any part of the compensation.

By the operation of this rule, then, the party who attempts performance may be placed in a much worse situation than he who wholly disregards his contract, and the other party may receive much more, by the breach of the contract, than the injury which he has sustained by such breach, and more than he could be entitled to were he seeking to recover damages by an action.

The case before us presents an illustration. Had the plaintiff in this case never entered upon the performance of his contract, the damage could not probably have been greater than some small expense and trouble incurred in procuring another to do the labor which he had contracted to perform. But having entered upon the performance, and labored nine and a half months, the value of which labor to the defendant as found by the jury is $95, if the defendant can succeed in this defense, he in fact receives nearly five-sixths of the value of a whole year's labor, by reason of the breach of contract by the plaintiff, a sum not only utterly disproportionate to any probable, not to say possible damage which could have resulted from the neglect of the plaintiff to continue the remaining two and a half months, but altogether beyond any damage which could have been recovered by the defendant, had the plaintiff done nothing towards the fulfillment of his contract.

Another illustration is furnished in Lantry v. Parks, 8 Cow., N. Y., 63. There the defendant hired the plaintiff for a year, at ten dollars per month. The plaintiff worked ten and a half months, and then left saying he would work no more for him. This was on Saturday—on Monday the plaintiff returned, and offered to resume his work, but the defendant said he would employ him no longer. The court held that the refusal of the defendant on Saturday was a violation of his contract, and that he could recover nothing for the labor performed.

There are other cases, however, in which principles have been adopted leading to a different result.

It is said, that where a party contracts to perform certain work, and to furnish materials, as, for instance, to build a house, and the work is done, but with some variations from the mode prescribed by the contract, yet if the other party has the benefit of the labor and materials he should be bound to pay so much as they are reasonably worth. 2 Stark.Ev. 97, 98; Hayward v. Leonard, 7 Pick., Mass., 181.

. . .

A different doctrine seems to have been holden in Ellis v. Hamlen, 3 Taunt. 52, and it is apparent, in such cases, that if the house has not been built in the manner specified in the contract, the work has not been done. The party has no more performed what he contracted to perform, than he who has contracted to labor for a certain period, and failed to complete the time.

It is in truth virtually conceded in such cases that the work has not been done, for, if it had been, the party performing it would be entitled to recover upon the contract itself, which it is held he cannot do.

Those cases are not to be distinguished, in principle, from the present, unless it be in the circumstance, that where the party has contracted to furnish materials, and do certain labor, as to build a house in a specified manner, if it is not done according to the contract, the party for whom it is built may refuse to receive it—elect to take no benefit from what has been performed—and therefore, if he does receive, he shall be bound to pay the value; whereas in a contract for labor, merely, from day to day, the party is continually receiving the benefit of the contract under an expectation that it will be fulfilled, and cannot, upon the breach of it, have an election to refuse to receive what has been done, and thus discharge himself from payment.

But we think this difference in the nature of the contracts does not justify the application of a different rule in relation to them. The party who contracts for labor merely, for a certain period, does so with full knowledge that he must, from the nature of the case, be accepting part performance from day to day, if the other party commences the performance, and with knowledge also that the other may eventually fail of completing the entire term. If under such circumstances he actually receives a benefit from the labor performed, over and above the damage occasioned by the failure to complete, there is as much reason why he should pay the reasonable worth of what has thus been done for his benefit, as there is when he enters and occupies the house which has been built for him, but not according to the stipulations of the contract, and which he perhaps enters, not because he is satisfied with what has been done, but because circumstances compel him to accept it such as it is, that he should pay for the value of the house.

Where goods are sold upon a special contract as to their nature, quality, and price, and have been used before their inferiority has been discovered, or other circumstances have concurred which have rendered it impracticable or inconvenient for the vendee to rescind the contract in toto, it seems to have been the practice formerly to allow the vendor to recover the stipulated price, and the vendee recovered by a cross-action damages for the breach of the contract. "But according to the later and more convenient practice, the vendee in such case is allowed, in an action for the price, to give evidence of the inferiority of the goods in reduction of damages, and the plaintiff who has broken his contract is not entitled to recover more than the value of the benefits which the defendant has actually derived from the goods; and where the latter has derived no benefit, the plaintiff cannot recover at all." 2 Stark.Ev. 640, 642; Okell v. Smith, 1 Starkie's Rep. 107. . . .

There is a close analogy between all these classes of cases, in which such diverse decisions have been made.

If the party who has contracted to receive merchandise takes a part and uses it, in expectation that the whole will be delivered, which is never done, there seems to be no greater reason that he should pay for what he has received than there is that the party who has received labor in part, under similar circumstances, should pay the value of what has been done for his benefit.

It is said that in those cases where the plaintiff has been permitted to recover there was an acceptance of what had been done. The answer is that where the contract is to labor from day to day, for a certain period, the party for whom the labor is done in truth stipulates to receive it from day to day, as it is performed, and although the other may not eventually do all he has contracted to do, there has been, necessarily, an acceptance of what has been done in pursuance of the contract, and the party must have understood when he made the contract that there was to be such acceptance.

If, then, the party stipulates in the outset to receive part performance from time to time, with a knowledge that the whole may not be completed, we see no reason why he should not equally be holden to pay for the amount of value received, as where he afterwards takes the benefit of what has been done, with a knowledge that the whole which was contracted for has not been performed. In neither case has the contract been performed. In neither can an action be sustained on the original contract. In both the party has assented to receive what is done. The only difference is that in the one case the assent is prior, with a knowledge that all may not be performed; in the other it is subsequent, with a knowledge that the whole has not been accomplished.

We have no hesitation in holding that the same rule should be applied to both classes of cases, especially as the operation of the rule will be to make the party who has failed to fulfill his contract liable to such amount of damages as the other party has sustained, instead of subjecting him to an entire loss for a partial failure, and thus making the amount received in many cases wholly disproportionate to the injury. 1 Saund. 320, c; 2 Stark.Ev. 643. It is as "hard upon the plaintiff to preclude him from recovering at all, because he has failed as to part of his entire undertaking," where his contract is to labor for a certain period, as it can be in any other description of contract, provided the defendant has received a benefit and value from the labor actually performed.

We hold, then, that where a party undertakes to pay upon a special contract for the performance of labor, or the furnishing of materials, he is not to be charged upon such special agreement until the money is earned according to the terms of it, and where the parties have made an express contract the law will not imply and raise a contract different from that which the parties have entered into, except upon some farther transaction between the parties.

In case of a failure to perform such special contract, by the default of the party contracting to do the service, if the money is not due by the terms of the special agreement he is not entitled to recover for his labor, or for the materials furnished, unless the other party receives what has been done, or furnished, and upon the whole case derives a benefit from it. Taft v. Montague, 14 Mass. 282; 2 Stark.Ev. 644.

But if, where a contract is made of such a character, a party actually receives labor, or materials, and thereby derives a benefit and advantage, over and above the damage which has resulted from the breach of the contract by the other party, the labor actually done, and the value received, furnish a new consideration, and the law thereupon raises a promise to pay to the extent of the reasonable worth of such excess.[a] This may be considered as making a new case, one not within the original agreement, and the party is entitled to "recover on his new case, for the work done, not as agreed, but yet accepted by the defendant." 1 Dane's Abr. 224.

If on such failure to perform the whole, the nature of the contract be such that the employer can reject what has been done, and refuse to receive any benefit from the part performance, he is entitled so to do, and in such case is not liable to be charged, unless he has before assented to and accepted of what has been done, however much the other party may have done towards the performance. He has in such case received nothing, and having contracted to receive nothing but the entire matter contracted for, he is not bound to pay, because his express promise was only to pay on receiving the whole, and having actually received nothing the law cannot and ought not to raise an implied promise to pay. But where the party receives value —takes and uses the materials, or has advantage from the labor, he is liable to pay the reasonable worth of what he has received. Farnsworth v. Garrard, 1 Camp. 38. And the rule is the same whether it was received and accepted by the assent of the party prior to the breach, under a contract by which, from its nature, he was to receive labor, from time to time until the completion of the whole contract, or whether it was received and accepted by an assent subsequent to the performance of all which was in fact done. If he received it under such circumstances as precluded him from rejecting it afterwards, that does not alter the case—it has still been received by his assent.

In fact, we think the technical reasoning—that the performance of the whole labor is a condition precedent, and the right to recover anything dependent upon it; that, the contract being entire, there can be no apportionment; and that, there being an express contract, no other can be implied, even upon the subsequent performance of service—is not properly applicable to this species of contract, where a beneficial service has been actually performed; for we have abundant reason to believe, that the general understanding of the community is that the hired laborer shall be entitled to compensation for the service actually performed, though he do not continue the entire term contracted for, and such contracts must be presumed to be made with reference to that understanding, unless an express stipulation shows the contrary. .   .   .

It is easy, if parties so choose, to provide by an express agreement that nothing shall be earned, if the laborer leaves his employer without having performed the whole service contemplated, and then there can be no pretense for a recovery if he voluntarily deserts the service before the expiration of the time.

a. This passage exemplifies the earlier attempts to squeeze a quasi-contractual duty into the Procrustean bed of contract.

The amount, however, for which the employer ought to be charged, where the laborer abandons his contract, is only the reasonable worth, or the amount of advantage he receives upon the whole transaction (Wadleigh v. Sutton, 6 N.H. 15), and, in estimating the value of the labor, the contract price for the service cannot be exceeded. . . .

If a person makes a contract fairly, he is entitled to have it fully performed; and, if this is not done, he is entitled to damages. He may maintain a suit to recover the amount of damage sustained by the non-performance. The benefit and advantage which the party takes by the labor, therefore, is the amount of value which he receives, if any, after deducting the amount of damage; and if he elects to put this in defense he is entitled so to do, and the implied promise which the law will raise, in such case, is to pay such amount of the stipulated price for the whole labor, as remains after deducting what it would cost to procure a completion of the residue of the service and also any damage which has been sustained by reason of the nonfulfillment of the contract. If in such case it be found that the damages are equal to or greater than the amount of the labor performed, so that the employer, having a right to the full performance of the contract, has not upon the whole case received a beneficial service, the plaintiff cannot recover. . . .

Applying the principles thus laid down, to this case, the plaintiff is entitled to judgment on the verdict. The defendant sets up a mere breach of the contract in defense of the action, but this cannot avail him. He does not appear to have offered evidence to show that he was damnified by such breach, or to have asked that a deduction should be made upon that account. The direction to the jury was therefore correct, that the plaintiff was entitled to recover as much as the labor performed was reasonably worth, and the jury appear to have allowed a pro rata compensation, for the time which the plaintiff labored in the defendant's service.

As the defendant has not claimed or had any adjustment of damages, for the breach of the contract, in this action, if he has actually sustained damage he is still entitled to a suit to recover the amount. . . .

Judgment on the verdict.

NOTES

(1) *The Case of the Client Who Quit.* Begovich was charged with murder. He retained Murphy to defend him and paid $2,500. Later Murphy was paid another $4,000 as an advance for legal services to be rendered for Begovich. He consulted with his client, and made two appearances in his behalf, these services not being worth more than $2,500. At that point Begovich committed suicide. The administrator of the estate sued Murphy for $4,000, and Murphy demurred. The court purported to apply Restate-

ment, § 357. What decision? See Begovich v. Murphy, 359 Mich. 156, 101 N.W.2d 278 (1960).

(2) *References.* For an interesting and difficult question of compensation for a lawyer who quit (i. e., refused to conduct litigation for his client to a conclusion as he had agreed), see Moore v. Fellner, 50 Cal.2d 330, 325 P.2d 857 (1958). Part of an intermediate court's opinion in this case was as follows: "The question is whether an attorney who undertakes to render an entire service may quit when an important part of the work remains undone and deserve to be paid for partial performance. As well might a surgeon claim compensation when he had quit in the middle of an operation, or a barber when he had shaved half of a customer's face." The judgment of this court was reversed.

The conflicting but rather faded precedents on the problem of Britton v. Turner are reviewed in Birmingham, Breach of Contract, Damage Measures, and Economic Efficiency, 24 Rutgers L.Rev. 273, 286–289 (1970). The author approves the ruling, with qualifications, as conducive to "proper functioning of the market mechanism." For a general review of the problems of this section, see Lee, The Plaintiff in Default, 19 Vand.L.Rev. 1023 (1966).

KIRKLAND v. ARCHBOLD

Court of Appeals of Ohio, Cuyahoga County, 1953.
113 N.E.2d 496.

[The plaintiff contracted to make alterations and repairs on a dwelling house owned by the defendant. Paragraph 20 of the contract provided: "The Owner agrees to pay the Contractor, as follows: $1,000 when satisfactory work has been done for ten days; an additional $1,000 when twenty days work has been completed; an additional $1,000 when thirty days work has been completed, and $1,000 on completion of the contract. $2,000 shall be paid within thirty days after the completion of the contract." After the plaintiff had worked for two months on the job he was prevented from proceeding further. He claims that he and his sub-contractors had reasonably expended $2,985 at that point; he has been paid only $800; and he sues for damages in the amount of the difference.

[The trial court found that the plaintiff was in default in attempting to plaster the house over wood lath instead of rock lath, and without the use of rock wool. Paragraph 4 of the contract provided: "All outside walls are to be lined with rock wool and rock lathe, superimposed thereon." Thus the defendant was within her rights in preventing the plaintiff from proceeding. However, the court held that her payment of $800 was an admission that the first installment of the price was earned, and gave the plaintiff judgment for $200. The plaintiff appealed.]

SKEEL, PRESIDING JUDGE. . . . The court committed error prejudicial to the rights of plaintiff in holding that the provisions of the contract were severable. The plaintiff agreed to make certain re-pairs and improvements on the defendant's property for which he was to be paid $6,000. The total consideration was to be paid for the total work specified in the contract. The fact that a schedule of payments was set up based on the progress of the work does not change the character of the agreement. Newman Lumber Co. v. Purdum, 41 Ohio St. 373.

The court found that the plaintiff and not the defendant breached the agreement, leaving the job without just cause, when the work agreed upon was far from completed. In fact, the plaintiff by his pleadings and evidence does not attempt to claim substantial per-formance on his part. The question is, therefore, clearly presented on the facts as the court found them to be, as to whether or not the plaintiff being found in default can maintain a cause of action for only part performance of his contract.

The earlier case law of Ohio has refused to permit a plaintiff to found an action on the provisions of a contract where he himself is in default. The only exception to the rule recognized is where the plain-tiff has substantially performed his part of the agreement. . . .

The result of decisions which deny a defaulting contractor all right of recovery even though his work has enriched the estate of the other party to the contract is to penalize the defaulting contractor to the extent of the value of all benefit conferred by his work and mate-rials upon the property of the other party. This result comes from unduly emphasizing the technical unity and entirety of contracts. Some decisions permit such result only when the defaulting contrac-tor's conduct was wilful or malicious.

An ever-increasing number of decisions of courts of last resort now modify the severity of this rule and permit defaulting contrac-tors, where their work has contributed substantial value to the other contracting party's property, to recover the value of the work and ma-terials expended on a quantum meruit basis, the recovery being di-minished, however, to the extent of such damage as the contractor's breach causes the other party. These decisions are based on the theo-ry of unjust enrichment. The action is not founded on the broken contract but on a quasi-contract to pay for the benefits received, which cannot be returned, diminished by the damages sustained because of the contractor's breach of his contract.

The leading case supporting this theory of the law is Britton v. Turner, 6 N.H. 481, 26 Am.Dec. 713. . . .

Williston on Contracts, Vol. 5, p. 4123, par. 1475, says:

"The element of forfeiture in wholly denying recovery to a plain-tiff who is materially in default is most strikingly exemplified in building contracts. It has already been seen how, under the name of substantial performance,[a] many courts have gone beyond the usual principles governing contracts in allowing relief in an action on the contract. But many cases of hardship cannot be brought within the doctrine of substantial performance, even if it is liberally interpreted; and the weight of authority strongly supports the statement that a builder, whose breach of contract is merely negligent, can recover the value of his work less the damages caused by his default; but that one who has wilfully abandoned or broken his contract cannot recover. The classical English doctrine, it is true, has denied recovery altogether where there has been a material breach even though it was due to negligence rather than wilfulness; and a few decisions in the United States follow this rule, where the builder has not substantially performed. But the English court has itself abandoned it and now holds that where a builder has supplied work and labor for the erection or repair of a house under a lump sum contract, but has departed from the terms of the contract, he is entitled to recover for his services and materials, unless (1) the work that he has done has been of no benefit to the owner; (2) the work he has done is entirely different from the work which he has contracted to do; or (3) he has abandoned the work and left it unfinished. The courts often do not discuss the question whether one who has intentionally abandoned the contract did so merely to get out of a bad bargain or whether he acted in a mistaken belief that a just cause existed for the abandonment. Where the latter situation exists, however, it would seem that the defaulter might properly be given recovery for his part performance. It seems probable that the tendency of decisions will favor a builder who has not been guilty of conscious moral fault in abandoning the contract or in its performance."

The drastic rule of forfeiture against a defaulting contractor who has by his labor and materials materially enriched the estate of the other party should in natural justice, be afforded relief to the reasonable value of the work done, less whatever damage the other party has suffered. Such a rule has been clearly recognized in the law of bailment where a defaulting bailee has enhanced the property of the bailor (Dobie on Bailments, Page 139 (1914)) and also by statute a defaulting vendee in a conditional sales contract, where the vendor retakes the property, is entitled to a return of a just proportion of the money paid. G.C. Sec. 8570.

We conclude, therefore, that the judgment is contrary to law as to the method by which the right to judgment was determined.   .   .   .

For the foregoing reasons the judgment is reversed and the cause is remanded for further proceedings.

-----

a. The following section of the case-book presents this doctrine.

NOTES

(1) *Severability.* Would the trial court's treatment of the contract in Kirkland as severable, or divisible, have been justified if the *defendant* had broken the contract rather than the plaintiff? See Fuller v. United Electric Co., 70 Nev. 448, 273 P.2d 136 (1954). The Electric Company sued Fuller for 80% of the contract price of doing the wiring in his new home, which became payable "on the completion of rough-in and inspection thereof." Fuller unjustifiably replaced the Electric Company with another contractor at that point, and apparently the cost of completing the work was well above 20% of the contract price. *Held:* The damages must be ascertained upon the entire contract. "The breach was a total breach and was so treated by plaintiff. The contract was thereby terminated."

(2) *The Case of the Driller's Bond.* J. L. McBride contracted to drill seven well holes at a test site in Nevada for the Atomic Energy Commission. He subcontracted part of the drilling work to the B & B Drilling Company at a stated price per linear foot. The subcontract required B & B to furnish a performance and payment bond. It called for payments on the 15th of each month for progress made to the end of the preceding month. B & B began drilling on May 24 with McBride's approval, although no bond had been posted. About two months later B & B learned that it could not secure a bond, because surety companies will not issue one on a job that is under way. McBride was so informed. B & B continued to drill until August 10, and stopped because no progress payments had been made. McBride refused a demand for payment on August 15, and ordered B & B off the site.

In a suit by B & B against McBride, the trial court gave judgment for some $16,000, based upon the prices and rates of payment stated in the contract. On an appeal by McBride, *held*: Affirmed. Passing the question whether the plaintiff's breach was material and substantial, the court relied on Restatement, § 357. The proper measure of recovery was the "price fixed by the contract for [the] part performance" because the defendant assented to it with knowledge of the plaintiff's inability to procure the bond. American Surety Company v. United States, 368 F.2d 475 (9th Cir. 1966). What other measure of recovery might have been adopted?

THE CODE

When a buyer of goods defaults under a contract of sale, after he has paid all or part of the purchase price, may the seller retain the prepayment? Prior to the enactment of the Code, the law was in some disarray on the point. In Amtorg Trading Corp. v. Miehle Printing Press & Mfg. Co., 206 F.2d 103 (2d Cir. 1953), the court examined the common law of New York, and found no convincing precedent for restitution in favor of the buyer; however, it noted "several trends away from this harsh rule in situations deemed exceptional. . . . " In 1952 the New York legislature provided a generalized right of restitution. This statute was influential in the formulation of UCC 2–718, which replaced it.

In the case cited above, Amtorg contracted to buy 20 printing presses, and made an advance payment of nearly $60,000, or 25% of the total price. It wrongfully refused to take delivery, owing to a change in federal export laws which prevented export of the presses to Russia. Miehle, the seller, then disposed of them to the Bureau of Engraving and Printing for more than Amtorg had contracted to pay. Amtorg sued Miehle for the amount of the down payment, and for the resale profit. If the case had been governed by UCC 2–718, what would Amtorg have recovered, if anything? [a]

NOTES

(1) *Seller's Default.* If a seller delivers part of the goods contracted for, and defaults as to the rest, and has received no payment, is he entitled to the price fixed by the contract for the goods delivered, or to the amount by which the buyer is enriched? See Restatement, § 357; UCC 2–607(1).

(2) *A Mutual Breaching.* In Admiral Plastics Corp. v. Trueblood, Inc., 436 F.2d 1335 (6th Cir. 1971), a contract had been made for the manufacture of some specialized machines to be designed. The design was never completed and very little progress was made on construction. The buyer sued the seller for breach, and the trial court awarded recovery of the amount of its down payment. Both parties appealed, each charging the other with want of good faith and failure of cooperation. *Held:* Affirmed. Both were sufficiently at fault to justify a finding of "mutual breaching of the contract. . . . We construe the parties' actions in this case, illustrated by their failure to cooperate and failure to perform tasks called for by the contract within a reasonable time, as evidence of a mutual rescission."

The down payment was almost $30,000. Can it be said that the judgment was a fair one without knowing what the development costs were for each party to this aborted project?

(3) *Land Sales.* Very few courts, it appears, espouse a firm rule against forfeiture of a land buyer's payments under an installment purchase contract. Yet it is said that cases of "outright forfeiture" are comparatively rare, for one reason or another. Lee, Defaulting Purchaser's Right to Restitution Under the Installment Land Contract, 20 U.Miami L. Rev. 1 (1965). The California development is reflected in Holiday Inns v. Knight, p. 660, supra. [b]

"A contract for the sale of land differs in several material respects from other contracts. It is almost invariably held to be specifically enforceable at the suit of either the vendor or the vendee. Even before any deed of conveyance, the vendee is regarded as having some property interest in the land by virtue of the contract alone . . . All this being true, it can

---

a. The court found a basis for recovery in federal law, and directed "refund of the prepayment, subject to deduction of any expenses proven by defendant if and only so far as they may exceed its profit of $18,765."

b. In one state, by statute, the buyer is given a right to a conveyance not later than when he has paid 40% of the original cash price, on condition that he execute a mortgage for the balance to the seller, on prescribed terms. The statute applies only to land installment contracts, as defined, where the price does not exceed $25,-000. Md.Code Ann., art. 21, §§ 110–116 (1964).

be seen that there are special reasons for refusing to allow the vendee to repudiate the contract of purchase and to recover judgment for restitution of advance instalments paid. Neither by a repudiation nor by mere failure to pay other instalments, when due, can the vendee terminate the vendor's right to payment of the full price—his right to specific performance, his right as holder of a lien for the purchase price. As long as the vendor continues to assert these rights and to remain ready and willing to make conveyance as agreed, the defaulting vendee has no right of restitution; he cannot recover back money that he has paid if it is money that the vendor could still compel him to pay if as yet unpaid. Some of the cases denying restitution to the vendee can be justified on this reasoning, even though the court may not have used it and may not have been conscious of its application." Corbin, The Right of a Defaulting Vendee to the Restitution of Instalments Paid, 40 Yale L.J. 1013, 1016–18 (1931).

Are there circumstances in which the claim of a buyer of goods for restitution under UCC 2–718(2) might be denied on comparable reasoning? See UCC 2–709.

SECTION 3.   CONSTRUCTION CONTRACTS

UNITED STATES v. SPEARIN

Supreme Court of the United States, 1918.
248 U.S. 132, 39 S.Ct. 59, 63 L.Ed. 166.

The case is stated in the opinion.

MR. JUSTICE BRANDEIS [a] delivered the opinion of the court.

Spearin brought this suit in the Court of Claims, demanding a balance alleged to be due for work done under a contract to construct a dry-dock and also damages for its annulment. Judgment was entered for him in the sum of $141,180.86; (51 Ct.Cl. 155) and both parties appealed to this court. The Government contends that Spearin is entitled to recover only $7,907.98. Spearin claims the additional sum of $63,658.70.

a. Louis Dembitz Brandeis (1856–1941) developed a lucrative Boston practice in corporate matters, and at the same time took a reformer's interest in public affairs. The cause of trade unionism was among those he espoused. His nomination to the Supreme Court in 1916 engendered a lengthy controversy; seven former presidents of the American Bar Association declared that he was "not a fit person to be a member" of the Court. On the Court he was frequently associated with Holmes in dissent, although his efforts to educate his older friend in economic and social conditions met with a "fastidious disrelish." The so-called "Brandeis brief" is one that seeks to inform the court of such conditions as bearing on the issue before it. He resigned in 1939. The ideal of personal moral responsibility was central to his thought, and led him to oppose insurance in certain forms, such as bank deposit insurance.

First. The decision to be made on the Government's appeal depends upon whether or not it was entitled to annul the contract. The facts essential to a determination of the question are these:

Spearin contracted to build for $757,800 a dry-dock at the Brooklyn Navy Yard in accordance with plans and specifications which had been prepared by the Government. The site selected by it was intersected by a 6-foot brick sewer; and it was necessary to divert and relocate a section thereof before the work of constructing the dry-dock could begin. The plans and specifications provided that the contractor should do the work and prescribed the dimensions, material, and location of the section to be substituted. All the prescribed requirements were fully complied with by Spearin; and the substituted section was accepted by the Government as satisfactory. It was located about 37 to 50 feet from the proposed excavation for the dry-dock; but a large part of the new section was within the area set aside as space within which the contractor's operations were to be carried on. Both before and after the diversion of the 6-foot sewer, it connected, within the Navy Yard but outside the space reserved for work on the dry-dock, with a 7-foot sewer which emptied into Wallabout Basin.

About a year after this relocation of the 6-foot sewer there occurred a sudden and heavy downpour of rain coincident with a high tide. This forced the water up the sewer for a considerable distance to a depth of 2 feet or more. Internal pressure broke the 6-foot sewer as so relocated, at several places; and the excavation of the dry-dock was flooded. Upon investigation, it was discovered that there was a dam from 5 to 5½ feet high in the 7-foot sewer; and that dam, by diverting to the 6-foot sewer the greater part of the water, had caused the internal pressure which broke it. Both sewers were a part of the city sewerage system; but the dam was not shown either on the city's plan, nor on the Government's plans and blue-prints, which were submitted to Spearin. On them the 7-foot sewer appeared as unobstructed. The Government officials concerned with the letting of the contract and construction of the dry-dock did not know of the existence of the dam. The site selected for the dry-dock was low ground; and during some years prior to making the contract sued on, the sewers had, from time to time, overflowed to the knowledge of these Government officials and others. But the fact had not been communicated to Spearin by anyone. He had, before entering into the contract, made a superficial examination of the premises and sought from the civil engineer's office at the Navy Yard information concerning the conditions and probable cost of the work; but he had made no special examination of the sewers nor special enquiry into the possibility of the work being flooded thereby; and had no information on the subject.

Promptly after the breaking of the sewer Spearin notified the Government that he considered the sewers under existing plans a menace to the work and that he would not resume operations unless the Government either made good or assumed responsibility for the damage that had already occurred and either made such changes in the sewer system as would remove the danger or assumed responsibility for the damage which might thereafter be occasioned by the insufficient capacity and the location and design of the existing sewers. The estimated cost of restoring the sewer was $3,875. But it was unsafe to both Spearin and the Government's property to proceed with the work with the 6-foot sewer in its then condition. The Government insisted that the responsibility for remedying existing conditions rested with the contractor. After fifteen months spent in investigations and fruitless correspondence, the Secretary of the Navy annulled the contract and took possession of the plant and materials on the site. Later the dry-dock, under radically changed and enlarged plans, was completed by other contractors, the Government having first discontinued the use of the 6-foot intersecting sewer and then reconstructed it by modifying size, shape and material so as to remove all danger of its breaking from internal pressure. Up to that time $210,939.18 had been expended by Spearin on the work; and he had received from the Government on account thereof $129,758.32. The court found that if he had been allowed to complete the contract he would have earned a profit of $60,000, and its judgment included that sum.

The general rules of law applicable to these facts are well settled. Where one agrees to do, for a fixed sum, a thing possible to be performed, he will not be excused or become entitled to additional compensation, because unforeseen difficulties are encountered. Day v. United States, 245 U.S. 159, 38 S.Ct. 57; Phoenix Bridge Co. v. United States, 211 U.S. 188, 29 S.Ct. 81. Thus one who undertakes to erect a structure upon a particular site assumes ordinarily the risk of subsidence of the soil. Simpson v. United States, 172 U.S. 372, 19 S. Ct. 222; Dermott v. Jones, 2 Wall., U.S., 1. But if the contractor is bound to build according to plans and specifications prepared by the owner the contractor will not be responsible for the consequences of defects in the plans and specifications. MacKnight Flintic Stone Co. v. The Mayor, 160 N.Y. 72, 54 N.E. 61; Filbert v. Philadelphia, 181 Pa.St. 530, 37 A. 545; Bentley v. State, 73 Wis. 416, 41 N.W. 338. See Sundstrom v. New York, 213 N.Y. 68, 106 N.E. 924. This responsibility of the owner is not overcome by the usual clauses requiring builders to visit the site, to check the plans, and to inform themselves of the requirements of the work, as is shown by Christie v. United States, 237 U.S. 234, 35 S.Ct. 565; Hollerbach v. United States, 233 U.S. 165, 34 S.Ct. 553, and United States v. Utah &c. Stage Co., 199 U.S. 414, 424, 26 S.Ct. 69, where it was held that the contractor should be relieved, if he was misled by erroneous statements in the specifications.

In the case at bar, the sewer, as well as the other structures, was to be built in accordance with the plans and specifications furnished by the Government. The construction of the sewer constituted as much an integral part of the contract as did the construction of any part of the dry-dock proper. It was as necessary as any other work in the preparation for the foundation. It involved no separate contract and no separate consideration. The contention of the Government that the present case is to be distinguished from the Bentley case, supra, and other similar cases, on the ground that the contract with reference to the sewer is purely collateral, is clearly without merit. The risk of the existing system proving adequate might have rested upon Spearin, if the contract for the dry-dock had not contained the provision for relocation of the 6-foot sewer. But the insertion of the articles prescribing the character, dimensions and location of the sewer imported a warranty that, if the specifications were complied with, the sewer would be adequate. This implied warranty is not overcome by the general clauses requiring the contractor to examine the site, to check up the plans, and to assume responsibility for the work until completion and acceptance. The obligation to examine the site did not impose upon him the duty of making a diligent enquiry into the history of the locality with a view to determining, at his peril, whether the sewer specifically prescribed by the Government would prove adequate. The duty to check plans did not impose the obligation to pass upon their adequacy to accomplish the purpose in view. And the provision concerning contractor's responsibility cannot be construed as abridging rights arising under specific provisions of the contract.

Neither sec. 3744 of the Revised Statutes, which provides that contracts of the Navy Department shall be reduced to writing, nor the parol evidence rule, precludes reliance upon a warranty implied by law. See Kellogg Bridge Co. v. Hamilton, 110 U.S. 108, 3 S.Ct. 537. The breach of warranty, followed by the Government's repudiation of all responsibility for the past and for making working conditions safe in the future, justified Spearin in refusing to resume the work. He was not obliged to restore the sewer and to proceed, at his peril, with the construction of the dry-dock. When the Government refused to assume the responsibility, he might have terminated the contract himself, Anvil Mining Co. v. Humble, 153 U.S. 540, 551–552, 14 S.Ct. 876; but he did not. When the Government annulled the contract without justification, it became liable for all damages resulting from its breach.

Second. Both the main and the cross-appeal raise questions as to the amount recoverable. [The Court ruled that Spearin should be, and had been, allowed recovery of all his losses resulting from the breach, including his proper expenditures, less receipts, and his lost profit.]

The judgment of the Court of Claims is, therefore,

Affirmed.[b]

b. For a collection of authorities related to this case, see Anno., 6 A.L.R. 3d 1394 (1966). As to an agency's effort to disclaim accountability for

NOTES

(1) *Problem.* A plumber contracted to install plumbing in a new building, connecting its sewer system to the city system at the curb. The plumber found a pipe at the curb where city records indicated it was, and made the connection there. This was an abandoned pipe, however, the "live" one being a foot deeper and to one side. When the owner discovered his problem, the plumber offered to correct it at cost, but the owner paid another plumber some $650 for the work. When the owner sued the first plumber for that amount, the jury was asked whether the defendant had exercised the degree of skill and care ordinarily exercised by plumbers in the community, and it found that he had. Should judgment be entered for the defendant? See Hennington v. Valuch, 27 Wis.2d 130, 133 N.W.2d 824 (1965).

(2) *The Two-Contractor Situation.* Paccon, Inc. contracted to build 51 houses for the government, at a site on Okinawa, which was to be prepared by the Shimato Construction Company. Lateness and disorganization in Shimato's work caused delay and extra cost to Paccon. In an action against the United States, Paccon claimed more than $150,000 in additional cost. Each contract required the contractor to cooperate with others, and to fit his own work to theirs, "as may be directed by the Contracting Officer." Before Paccon's contract was executed, the government's representatives promised it to impose a schedule of priorities of work on Shimato, coordinated with Paccon's work.

The Armed Services Board of Contract Appeals found that that was the extent of the government's obligation, and that it had lived up to the promise. It ascribed Paccon's loss to its having taken the risk that "Shimato would be a satisfactory contractor and that the Government's plans for coordinating the work and preventing delays and interference would be effective."

On review, this ruling was held erroneous. The Court of Claims said: "we think it clear that the Government did have the obligation to do what it reasonably could to see that Shimato complied with the schedule of priorities." There was a "latent obligation, implicit in the written contract, of the Government to take reasonable steps to coordinate the work." And conversations before the contract was made spelled out a duty on the government to "use reasonable efforts, under its powers of control, to make Shimato comply with a proper priority schedule." Paccon, Inc. v. United States, 399 F.2d 162 (Ct.Cl.1968). Was the court's reliance on pre-contract conversations consistent with the parol evidence rule? Was it essential to the decision?

GOVERNMENT CONTRACT DISPUTES

Disputes arising under government contracts in the normal course of events may not be presented to a court in the first instance. Unless a dispute is settled by the contracting officer or his staff, he is charged with making a written decision, which is conclusive unless

specifications, see Grossbaum, Procedural Fairness in Public Contracts: The Procurement Regulations, 57 Va. L.Rev. 171, 211–12, 224 (1971).

the contractor takes an administrative appeal. Various boards of contract appeals are constituted to conduct hearings, make records, and render decisions, acting as delegates of the departmental heads. (The Armed Services Board, acting for the Secretary of Defense, naturally occupies a strategic position.) Upon a board decision, the parties are then free to institute suit, but the administrative decision is again "final and conclusive" over a broad range of issues.

The procedure just described is specified in standard disputes clauses of government contracts. One sentence common to these clauses is: "The decision of the Secretary or his duly authorized representative for the determination of such appeals shall be final and conclusive unless determined by a court of competent jurisdiction to have been fraudulent, or capricious, or arbitrary, or so grossly erroneous as necessarily to imply bad faith, or not supported by substantial evidence." This language was worked out by Congress as a standard for judicial review, when government contractors protested that the Supreme Court had attached too much finality to administrative determinations in disputes cases. (A case that aroused protest was United States v. Wunderlich, 342 U.S. 98 (1951), and the act that altered the Court's ruling is known as the "Wunderlich Act."[a])

The disputes clauses may not foreclose judicial inquiry into questions of "law". Hence, in the preceding note case, the Court of Claims was free to correct the ASBCA's error about the government's "latent obligation" to coordinate the work of the two contractors. However, the finality of administrative decisions is more imposing than the law-fact distinction might suggest. For one thing, problems of interpreting contract documents are sometimes regarded as being questions of fact, within the meaning of the disputes clause.[b] For another, government contracts usually contain clauses relating to modifications and terminations which envisage a continuous and cooperative relation between contractors and contracting officers, and which commit highly discretionary functions to the latter. A confrontation entailing administrative review is therefore relatively infrequent, and when it occurs it may not be framed in terms of which party is supported by the contract requirements. Instead, it may be framed in terms of whether or not the contracting officer has made an "equitable adjustment" in light of changed conditions, as the contract directs him to do. Naturally, the courts do not find it easy to ascribe capriciousness, bad faith, or the like, to decisions on such an issue. On the other hand, the Court of Claims has maintained a certain level of sur-

a. 41 U.S.C.A. §§ 321, 322. The act was also a response to United States v. Moorman, 338 U.S. 457 (1950).

b. Compare Salem Products Corp. v. United States, 298 F.2d 808 (2d Cir. 1962), with Kayfield Construction Corp. v. United States, 278 F.2d 217 (2d Cir. 1960).

veillance by making innovative decisions on contractors' rights, particularly in the face of unforeseen difficulties they encounter.[c]

The procedure sketched above is fairly productive of snarls, invites unwarranted charges of fraud and the like, and is not a sure safeguard against bureaucratic blunders and worse. In recent years, however, alterations have occurred chiefly at the level of contract drafting, and to make structural improvements in the procedure is a legal challenge of a high order.

Are the procedures for resolving disputes specified in private contracts generally better?

NOTE

"Changed Conditions." Government construction contracts now generally contain a "changed conditions" clause, more or less standard in terms, which would probably require an "equitable adjustment" of the price in circumstances such as those appearing in United States v. Spearin. As to subsoil conditions, in particular, bidders receive data on test borings by the government, and if it proves to be inaccurate an adjustment is called for. The contractor's right to rely on such information cannot be impaired by the government's disclaimer, it is said, in a broadly worded standard term, though the language is unmistakable. Foster Const. C. A. & Williams Bros. Co. v. United States, 435 F.2d 873 (Ct.Cl.1970; commissioner's opinion). The court said there that the government takes the risk of inaccuracy by long-established procurement policy. "The purpose of the changed conditions clause is thus to take at least some of the gamble on subsurface conditions out of bidding." What calculation of benefits might have led the government to adopt such a policy?

As to the important and intricate effect of the changed conditions clause on the doctrine of the Spearin case, see also Jefferson Construction Company v. United States, 392 F.2d 1006 (Ct.Cl.1968), cert. denied, 393 U.S. 842 (1968). Contrast the risk as to subsoil conditions placed on a contractor in private work, in P & Z Pacific, Inc. v. Panorama Apartments, Inc., 372 F.2d 759 (9th Cir. 1967).

STEES v. LEONARD

Supreme Court of Minnesota, 1874.
20 Minn. 494, 20 Gil. 448.[a]

Appeal by defendants from an order of the district court, Ramsey county, denying a new trial.

The action was brought to recover damages for a failure of defendants to erect and complete a building on a lot of plaintiffs, on Minnesota street, between Third and Fourth streets, in the city of St.

----

c. E. g., National Presto Industries, Inc. v. United States, 338 F.2d 99 (Ct.Cl. 1964), cert. denied, 380 U.S. 962 (1965). Compare Natus Corp. v. United States, 178 Ct.Cl. 1, 371 F.2d 450 (1967).

a. The statement of facts is taken in part from the 1882 edition by Gilfillan of 20 Minnesota Reports.

Paul, which, by an agreement under seal between them and plaintiffs, the defendants had agreed to build, erect, and complete, according to plans and specifications annexed to and made part of the agreement. The defendants commenced the construction of the building, and had carried it to the height of three stories when it fell to the ground. The next year, 1869, they began again and carried it to the height as before, when it again fell to the ground, whereupon defendants refused to perform the contract. They claimed that in their attempts to erect the building they did the work in all respects according to the plans and specifications and that the failure to complete the building and its fall on the two occasions was due to the fact that the soil upon which it was to be constructed was composed of quicksand, and when water flowed into it, was incapable of sustaining the building. . . . The specifications annexed to the contract are very full, and provide, (among other things,) that "All the walls shall be of the following thickness: foundation walls, two feet thick, and shall have footings six inches thick, which shall run clear across walls and project six inches on each side of wall above it." The specifications contain no other provisions relating to the character of the foundation for the building. [The plaintiffs alleged that the specifications, signed by both parties to the contract, had been prepared by a firm of architects named Sheire & Bro. Two persons named Sheire were named as defendants along with Leonard.]

The plaintiffs allege . . . that the fall of the building was owing to the negligence and unskilful work of the defendants, and the poor quality of the material furnished by them. Judgment is demanded for the sum of $5,214.80, with interest, as the damages sustained by the plaintiffs; being $3,745.80 paid, pursuant to the contract, during the progress of the work, $1,000 as damages for loss of the use of the lot on which the building was to be erected, and $469, as damages, occasioned by the fall of the building, to an adjacent house of plaintiffs, and property stored therein. . . .

The jury found for the plaintiffs. The defendants moved, upon a bill of exceptions, for a new trial, and appeal from the order denying their motion.

YOUNG, J. The general principle of law which underlies this case is well established. If a man bind himself, by a positive, express contract, to do an act in itself possible, he must perform his engagement, unless prevented by the act of God, the law, or the other party to the contract. No hardship, no unforeseen hindrance, no difficulty short of absolute impossibility, will excuse him from doing what he has expressly agreed to do. This doctrine may sometimes seem to bear heavily upon contractors; but, in such cases, the hardship is attributable, not to the law, but to the contractor himself, who has improvidently assumed an absolute, when he might have undertaken only a qualified, liability. The law does no more than enforce the contract as the parties themselves have made it. Many cases illustrating the application of the doctrine to every variety of contract are collected in the note to Cutter v. Powell, 2 Smith, Lead.Cas. 1 [p. 855 infra].

. . .

School Trustees v. Bennett, 3 Dutcher, N.J., 513, is almost identical, in its material facts, with the present case. The contractors agreed to build and complete a schoolhouse, and find all materials therefor, according to specifications annexed to the contract; the building to be located on a lot owned by plaintiff, and designated in the contract. When the building was nearly completed it was blown down by a sudden and violent gale of wind. The contractors again began to erect the building, when it fell, solely on account of the soil on which it stood having become soft and miry, and unable to sustain the weight of the building; although, when the foundations were laid, the soil was so hard as to be penetrated with difficulty by a pickax, and its defects were latent. The plaintiff had a verdict for the amount of the installments paid under the contract as the work progressed. The verdict was sustained by the supreme court, which held that the loss, although arising solely from a latent defect in the soil, and not from a faulty construction of the building, must fall on the contractor.

. . .

In Dermott v. Jones, 2 Wall., U.S., 1, the foundation of the building sank, owing to a latent defect in the soil, and the owner was compelled to take down and rebuild a portion of the work. The contractor having sued for his pay, it was held that the owner might recoup the damages sustained by his deviation from the contract. The court refer with approval to the cases cited, and say: "The principle which controlled them rests upon a solid foundation of reason and justice. It regards the sanctity of contracts. It requires a party to do what he has agreed to do. If unexpected impediments lie in the way, and a loss ensue, it leaves the loss where the contract places it. If the parties have made no provision for a dispensation, the rule of law gives none. It does not allow a contract fairly made to be annulled, and it does not permit to be interpolated what the parties themselves have not stipulated."

Nothing can be added to the clear and cogent arguments we have quoted in vindication of the wisdom and justice of the rule which must govern this case, unless it is in some way distinguishable from the cases cited.

It is argued that the spot on which the building is to be erected is not designated with precision in the contract, but is left to be selected by the owner; that, under the contract, the right to designate the particular spot being reserved to plaintiffs they must select one that will sustain the building described in the specifications, and if the spot they select is not, in its natural state, suitable, they must make it so; that in this respect the present case differs from School Trustees v. Bennett.

The contract does not, perhaps, designate the site of the proposed building with absolute certainty; but in this particular it is aided by the pleadings. The complaint states that defendants contracted to erect the proposed building on "*a certain piece* of land, of which the plaintiffs then were, and now are, the owners in fee, fronting on Minnesota street, between Third and Fourth streets, in the city of St. Paul." The answer expressly admits that the defendants entered into a contract to erect the building, according to the plans, etc., "on that certain piece of land in said complaint described," and that they "entered upon the performance of said contract and proceeded with the erection of said building," etc. This is an express admission that the contract was made with reference to the identical piece of land on which the defendants afterwards attempted to perform it, and leaves no foundation in fact for the defendants' argument.

It is no defense to the action that the specifications directed that "footings" should be used as the foundation of the building, and that the defendants, in the construction of those footings, as well as in all other particulars, conformed to the specifications. The defendants contracted to "erect and complete the building." Whatever was necessary to be done in order to complete the building, they were bound by the contract to do. If the building could not be completed without other or stronger foundations than the footings specified, they were bound to furnish such other foundations. If the building could not be erected without draining the land, then they must drain the land, "because they have agreed to do everything necessary to erect and complete the building." (3 Dutcher, N.J., 520; and see Dermott v. Jones, supra, where the same point was made by the contractor, but ruled against him by the court.)

As the draining of the land was, in fact, necessary to the erection and completion of the building, it was a thing to be done, under the contract, by the defendants. The prior parol agreement that plaintiffs should drain the land, related therefore, to a matter embraced within the terms of the written contract, and was not, as claimed by defendants' counsel, collateral thereto. It was, accordingly under the familiar rule, inadmissible in evidence to vary the terms of the written contract, and was properly excluded.

[In the remainder of the opinion the court considered evidence offered by the defendants that *after* the work was begun the plaintiffs made promises to drain the site of the building, and that the failure to do so caused the collapse. The court held that the evidence was properly excluded because the defendants had failed to allege consideration for the promises, or justifiable reliance upon them.]

There was, therefore, no error in the exclusion of the evidence offered, and the order appealed from is affirmed.

NOTES

(1) *Loss Questions*. The opinion in Stees seems to proceed on the assumption that a loss traceable to a latent soil condition must fall on either the owner or the builder. If the builder discovers the difficulty when he begins work, and refuses to proceed, what kinds of loss have to be considered? One may be the additional price the owner must pay to have the work done as projected. Evidently the plaintiffs did not claim this type of loss in Stees v. Leonard. Would it have been granted, if such an amount had been proved and claimed?

(2) *Mistake*. There is authority for avoiding a construction contract that the parties made without sufficient information about soil conditions, on the ground of mutual mistake. See Restatement, Restitution, § 9; but see Watkins & Son v. Carrig, p. 271 supra. If a builder has made test borings at the site before contracting, is he in a good position to plead mistake? Should he be allowed to make this defense if the agreement requires him to test the soil, and he has not done so? Compare the reference, in United States v. Spearin, to the "usual clauses requiring builders to visit the site," and so on.

If the contract in Stees v. Leonard had been held voidable for mutual mistake, how many elements in the plaintiff's recovery could have been granted, if any?

(3) *Case Comparisons*. Were the specifications in Stees v. Leonard adequate for the construction of the building on the site specified? Can the decision be distinguished from that in United States v. Spearin? Compare Ridley Investment Co. v. Croll, 192 A.2d 925, 6 A.L.R.3d 1389 (Del.1963), a "soft soil" case in which the contractor prevailed. The court observed that "plans and specifications do not exist in a vacuum; they are made for a particular building at a particular place. The defect in the plans and specifications for the building in question was the failure to make provision for adequate pilings and other support for the floor; the fact that these plans and specifications might provide for an adequate building in some other place does not render the plans and specifications less defective for the location in question."

See also Patterson, Constructive Conditions in Contracts, 42 Colum.L. Rev. 903, 938–39 (1942), where it is said: "The owner ordinarily employs an architect or engineer to prepare the plans and specifications, and thus has control of their adequacy; moreover, the builder's promise requires him to adhere to the plans furnished by the owner. The rub comes when the defective performance is due to a combination of sub-soil obstacles *and* the inadequacy of the owner's plans and specifications in relation to those obstacles. The marked tendency in recent years is to throw the loss on the owner, especially where the owner is the government." [a]

The usual way of distinguishing cases like Stees v. Leonard is to say that "in most, if not all of these, there was a positive and unequivocal undertaking by the contractor to furnish a completed building. Such is not the

a. See also Sweet, Legal Aspects of Architecture, Engineering and the Construction Process, ch. 22 (1970).

In Ridley Investment Co. v. Croll, supra, the court rejected an attempted distinction between public works and private construction projects.

case here." Blue Bell, Inc. v. Cassidy, 200 F.Supp. 443 (N.D.Miss.1961). In Friederick v. Redwood County, 153 Minn. 450, 190 N.W. 801 (1922), the Minnesota court used precisely this formula without bothering to cite its prior decision in Stees v. Leonard.

JACOB & YOUNGS v. KENT

[For the report of this case see p. 477 supra.]

NOTES

(1) *Question.* Would it have been possible for the parties, using a tightly-drawn provision in the contract, to preclude a recovery by the contractor such as this? Consider the provisions that the contract contained, set out in footnote a, p. 478 supra. How could they have been improved upon, as a means of protecting the defendant?

(2) *Conclusive Third-Party Approval.* It has been held that a contractor is exempted from liability for misperformance by a contract provision for the approval of his work by an architect or engineer, when such approval has been certified. If the approval is stated as a condition of payment to the contractor, his failure to obtain it is not necessarily fatal to his claim for payment, as we have seen in the preceding chapter. Given identical terms in the contract about approval, are these rulings consistent? Might the difference be explained in terms of an architect's disposition to side with the owner? See Arc Electrical Construction Co. v. George A. Fuller Company, 24 N.Y.2d 99, 247 N.E.2d 111 (1969).

For one reason or another, it seems that an architect's final certificate is not often helpful to the contractor defensively.[a] The rule of exemption was applied, however, in City of Granville v. Kovash, Incorporated, 118 N.W.2d 354 (N.D.1962). There the city sued the contractor who had laid some water mains for it, after they froze, for failure to place them at the depth required by the contract. It provided for supervision and control of the work by a project engineer, and that after an inspection by him final payment would be made upon his certificate that the work had been "completed in a satisfactory manner and in accordance with the terms of the contract." The engineer had issued such a certificate, and it was held to bar the city's claim.

(3) *Substantial Performance and Quasi Contract.* The function of the rule of substantial performance, as Cardozo explains it, is to "mitigate the rigor of implied conditions." That is also the function of quasi contract, as applied in cases like Kirkland v. Archbold, p. 736 supra. What is the difference in effect between applying the one remedy or the other?

---

a. It is normally binding on the owner only to the extent of establishing the "actual final completion" of the work. Board of Education v. A. Barbaresi & Son, Inc., 25 A.D.2d 855, 269 N.Y.S.2d 823 (2d Dept.1966). So understood, it may serve to foreclose a claim upon a performance bond, yet leave the contractor open to a claim for latent defects. See City of Midland v. Waller, 430 S.W.2d 473 (Tex.1968) (note the A.I.A. standard form provision construed in that sense). Furthermore, a certificate is open to challenge on the ground that its issuance was the result of "fraud", loosely understood, or gross mistake. James I. Barnes Const. Co. v. Washington Township, 184 N.E.2d 763 (Ind.App.1962).

If Cardozo had accepted the principle of Kirkland, could he have said that the "willful transgressor must accept the penalty of his transgression?" In Massachusetts, the rule of substantial performance is thought not to prevail; yet the court there permits a quantum meruit recovery modelled closely on the principle of Jacob & Youngs v. Kent.[b] In some cases it is difficult to tell whether the court is proceeding on the basis of substantial performance or of quasi contract, in giving relief to a defaulting plaintiff. Should the problems in all cases of deviating builders be allowed to "blend into one problem with but one answer?" See Nordstrom & Woodland, Recovery by Building Contractor in Default, 20 Ohio St.L.J. 193, 217 (1959). In some cases the builder's measure of recovery seems to be more generous if he has failed of substantial performance than if he has achieved it.[c] Does that make any sense?

SUBSTANTIAL PERFORMANCE IN CONTEXT

The rule of substantial performance is uniquely associated with building and improvement contracts. It is applied sporadically, however, in litigation over other types of contracts. Indeed, the origin of the rule has been traced to a decision by Mansfield about the sale of a plantation in the West Indies, including land and slaves. Boone v. Eyre, 1 H.Bl. 273, 126 Eng.Rep. 160, Note (K.B. 1777). A leading English case on the subject concerned an indenture of apprenticeship. Ellen v. Topp, 9 Exch. 424, 155 Eng.Rep. 609 (1851). Nevertheless, the rule has found its chief proving ground in suits on construction contracts.[d]

Why should this be so? Several considerations suggest the answer. As for employment contracts, it is usual for an employer to pay wages at short intervals, and to reserve the power of termination at will.[e] Leases of real property have traditionally been regarded as exempt from the usual contract rules of constructive conditions. As for contracts for the sale of goods, the party who is denied a remedy does not suffer an investment loss, ordinarily, in the same degree as a builder whose earnings prove uncollectible. As for land sale contracts, enforcement is regularly sought in a court of equity, in which there are specialized rules serving some of the same objects as the doctrine of substantial performance.

Ordinarily neither party to a construction contract has access to specific performance as a remedy. On the one side, there is an un-

b. Dodge v. Kimball, 203 Mass. 364, 89 N.E. 542 (1909).

c. See Fuller v. Rosinski, 79 Wash.2d 719, 488 P.2d 1061 (1971); Forrester v. Craddock, 51 Wash.2d 315, 317 P. 2d 1077 (1957); cf. White v. Mitchell, 123 Wash. 630, 213 P. 10 (1923); Nordin Construction Co. v. City of Nome, — Alaska —, 489 P.2d 455 (1971).

d. Its relation to contracts for the sale of goods is considered in Section 4, infra.

e. For an application of the material breach rule to an employment contract see Restatement, § 275, Illustration 5.

dertaking to pay money, which may be adequately enforced at law. On the other, there is an undertaking to make improvements. As a rule, a court will not undertake the supervision of such work. For this reason, largely, they will not make a decree requiring performance by a builder—or a painter, repairman, excavator, or the like—any more than they will order performance by an actor or singer. (Exceptions are made, but only in exceptional circumstances, such as the presence of an overriding public interest.) The result is that controversies over imperfect performance by a builder are usually transmuted into money claims, when presented in court.

"Through the doctrine of substantial performance," it is said, "the judges installed themselves as administrators of the execution and discharge of contracts. They freed themselves from rigid rules and adopted a broad standard under which they could apply a policy of making contract effective." [f] This must not be understood to mean that the courts will directly administer the performance of a contract; it means that practical judgments about performance figure in their decisions about money claims. Should the courts undertake a more active role as to construction contracts? Having become "administrators of execution" indirectly, would they find it a short and easy step beyond to order the correction of defective work?

NOTES

(1) *Judicial Barn Building.* An Idaho case illustrates the courts' reluctance to supervise builders' work. It concerned a contract to put up a barn for a dairyman. Not being paid in full, the builder sued the dairyman. The trial court ordered "that the plaintiff shall make the following changes, alterations and repairs in the barn and milk house . . . within thirty days from the date of this Order: —," and specified 14 items for attention. When the work was properly done, the court ruled, "the plaintiff will then be deemed to have substantially complied with the terms of the building contracts between the parties. . . ." Thirty days later the parties were still in contention, and the court appointed a referee to make an inspection and report. He found "minor items that still need some attention," but gave his opinion that the court's order had been substantially complied with. Further controversy ensued, and an appeal. The Idaho Supreme Court manifested extreme displeasure with the trial court's management of the suit. Mackey v. Eva, 80 Idaho 260, 328 P.2d 66 (1958); see also Eldred v. C. L. Folkman Company, 93 Idaho 131, 456 P.2d 775 (1969).

(2) *Willful Breach.* What are the cases of a builder's deviation from the plans agreed upon that should be regarded as intentional or willful misconduct? The use of inferior materials for the purpose of filching a profit?

Professor Corbin has objected to the use of the word *willful* on the ground that it "indicates a childlike faith in the existence of a plain and obvious line between the good and the bad, between unfortunate virtue and

f. Corry, Law and Policy, 41–43 (1959).

unforgivable sin. . . . [T]he enrichment of even an injured man may become unjust." [g] What word is better than "willful" to describe conduct of a builder that will bar him from claiming on the theory of substantial performance?

What if the builder departs from the plans for the purpose of enhancing the value of the structure? To meet unforeseen construction problems? [h] What if it is *impossible* to follow the plans literally? Compare a builder who cannot pay all his laborers and materialmen, as the contract requires him to do, because he lacks funds. [i]

It has been generally held—or at least said—that a "willful" or "intentional" deviation from the terms of the contract will always preclude a finding of substantial performance. [j] This is often said when the facts seem to show a deviation that would be material in any case.

(3) *Problem.* Contractor installs a heating system in a building, and does such poor work that he is accountable to Owner for his loss of $25,-000, calculated on the "diminished value" rule. The misperformance was willful. Owner has withheld $15,000 of the contract price, and Contractor believes he should be held liable only for the difference, $10,000. Should the unpaid price be allowed as a credit upon his liability? See Kirk Reid Company v. Fine, 205 Va. 778, 139 S.E.2d 829 (1965). Compare Di Mare v. Capaldi, 336 Mass. 497, 146 N.E.2d 517 (1957). Willfulness aside, if the cost of correcting the work is greater than $25,000, Jacob & Youngs v. Kent is not an authority for limiting the contractor's liability to that amount, is it? See Bellizzi v. Huntley Estates, 3 N.Y.2d 112, 143 N.E.2d 802 (1957).

(4) *Problem.* A subcontractor for grading and excavating on a building site completes all his work except for hand-raking the site. He refuses to do that work because he believes the contractor is unjustified in withholding part of his earnings. This belief is in error. The contractor does the hand-raking at a cost of $3800. The total contract price is about ten times that amount, and the sub has been paid only $20,000. What are his rights? Has the sub committed a willful breach? See United States ex rel. Johnson v. Morley Const. Co., 98 F.2d 781 (2d Cir. 1938), cert. denied, Maryland Casualty Co. v. U. S., 305 U.S. 651 (1938) (L. Hand). But cf. Malott & Peterson Grundy, Inc. v. Reynolds Const. Co., 472 P.2d 701 (Colo.App. 1970).

---

g. Section 1123; cf. § 1254. And see Shapiro, Inc. v. Bimblich, 101 A.2d 890 (D.C.Mun.App.1954) (petty vengeance).

h. See Shell v. Schmidt, 164 Cal.App. 2d 350, 330 P.2d 817 (1958), cert. denied, 359 U.S. 959 (1959).

i. Cf. Witherell v. Lasky, 286 App.Div. 533, 145 N.Y.S.2d 624 (1955).

j. In Samuel J. Creswell I. Wks. v. Housing Auth. of Camden, 449 F.2d 557 (3d Cir. 1971), a vice-president of the plaintiff contractor testified that it did not intend to comply with the specifications of the contract when bidding for it; the plaintiff was held to be "estopped" from asserting substantial performance.

PLANTE v. JACOBS

Supreme Court of Wisconsin, 1960.
10 Wis.2d 567, 103 N.W.2d 296.

[Eugene Plante contracted with Frank and Carol Jacobs to furnish the materials and construct a house upon their lot in Brookfield, in accordance with plans and specifications, for the sum of $26,765. During the course of construction Plante was paid $20,000. Disputes arose between the parties, the Jacobs refused to continue payment, and Plante did not complete the house. He sued to establish a lien on the property as a way of recovering the unpaid balance of the contract price, plus extras. The owners—who are the appellants—answered with allegations of faulty workmanship and incomplete construction.]

HALLOWS, JUSTICE. The defendants argue the plaintiff cannot recover any amount because he has failed to substantially perform the contract. The plaintiff conceded he failed to furnish the kitchen cabinets, gutters and downspouts, sidewalk, closet clothes poles, and entrance seat amounting to $1,601.95. This amount was allowed to the defendants. The defendants claim some 20 other items of incomplete or faulty performance by the plaintiff and no substantial performance because the cost of completing the house in strict compliance with the plans and specifications would amount to 25 or 30 per cent of the contract price. The defendants especially stress the misplacing of the wall between the living room and the kitchen, which narrowed the living room in excess of one foot. The cost of tearing down this wall and rebuilding it would be approximately $4,000. The record is not clear why and when this wall was misplaced, but the wall is completely built and the house decorated and the defendants are living therein. Real estate experts testified that the smaller width of the living room would not affect the market price of the house.

The defendants rely on Manitowoc Steam Boiler Works v. Manitowoc Glue Co., 1903, 120 Wis. 1, 97 N.W. 515, for the proposition there can be no recovery on the contract as distinguished from *quantum meruit* unless there is substantial performance. This is undoubtedly the correct rule at common law. For recovery on *quantum meruit*, see Valentine v. Patrick Warren Construction Co., 1953, 263 Wis. 143, 56 N.W.2d 860. The question here is whether there has been substantial performance. The test of what amounts to substantial performance seems to be whether the performance meets the essential purpose of the contract. In the Manitowoc case the contract called for a boiler having a capacity of 150 per cent of the existing boiler. The court held there was no substantial performance because the boiler furnished had a capacity of only 82 per cent of the old boiler and only approximately one-half of the boiler capacity contemplated by the contract. In Houlahan v. Clark, 1901, 110 Wis. 43, 85 N.W. 676, the contract provided the plaintiff was to drive pilings in the lake and place a boat house thereon parallel and in line with a neighbor's dock. This was not done and the contractor so positioned the boat house that it was practically useless to the owner. Manthey v. Stock, 1907, 133 Wis. 107, 113 N.W. 443, involved a contract to paint a house and to do a good job, including the removal of the old paint where necessary. The plaintiff did not remove the old paint, and blistering and roughness of the new paint resulted. The court held that the plaintiff failed to show substantial performance. The defendants also cite Manning v. School District No. 6, 1905, 124 Wis. 84, 102 N.W. 356. However, this case involved a contract to install a heating and ventilating plant in the school building which would meet certain tests which the heating apparatus failed to do. The heating plant was practically a total failure to accomplish the purposes of the contract. See also Nees v. Weaver, 1936, 222 Wis. 492, 269 N.W. 266, 107 A.L.R. 1405 (roof on a garage).

Substantial performance as applied to construction of a house does not mean that every detail must be in strict compliance with the specifications and the plans. Something less than perfection is the test of specific performance unless all details are made the essence of the contract. This was not done here. There may be situations in which features or details of construction of special or of great personal importance, if not performed, would prevent a finding of substantial performance of the contract. In this case the plan was a stock floor plan. No detailed construction of the house was shown on the plan. There were no blueprints. The specifications were standard printed forms with some modifications and additions written in by the parties. Many of the problems that arose during the construction had to be solved on the basis of practical experience. No mathematical rule relating to the percentage of the price, of cost of completion, or of completeness can be laid down to determine substantial performance of a building contract. Although the defendants received a house with which they are dissatisfied in many respects, the trial court was not in error in finding the contract was substantially performed.

The next question is what is the amount of recovery when the plaintiff has substantially, but incompletely, performed. For substantial performance the plaintiff should recover the contract price less the damages caused the defendant by the incomplete performance. Both parties agree. Venzke v. Magdanz, 1943, 243 Wis. 155, 9 N.W.2d 604, states the correct rule for damages due to faulty construction amounting to such incomplete performance, which is the difference between the value of the house as it stands with faulty and incomplete construction and the value of the house if it had been constructed in strict accordance with the plans and specifications. This is the diminished-value rule. The cost of replacement or repair is not the measure of such damage, but is an element to take into consideration in arriving at value under some circumstances. The cost of replacement or the cost to make whole the omissions may equal or be less than the difference in value in some cases and, likewise, the cost to rectify a defect may greatly exceed the added value to the structure as corrected. The defendants argue that under the Venzke rule their damages are $10,000. The plaintiff on review argues the defendants' damages are only $650. Both parties agree the trial court applied the wrong rule to the facts.

The trial court applied the cost-of-repair or replacement rule as to several items, relying on Stern v. Schlafer, 1943, 244 Wis. 183, 11 N.W.2d 640, 12 N.W.2d 678, wherein it was stated that when there are a number of small items of defect or omission which can be remedied without the reconstruction of a substantial part of the building or a great sacrifice of work or material already wrought in the building, the reasonable cost of correcting the defect should be allowed. However, in Mohs v. Quarton, 1950, 257 Wis. 544, 44 N.W.2d 580, the court held when the separation of defects would lead to confusion, the rule of diminished value could apply to all defects.

In this case no such confusion arises in separating the defects. The trial court disallowed certain claimed defects because they were not proven. This finding was not against the great weight and clear preponderance of the evidence and will not be disturbed on appeal. Of the remaining defects claimed by the defendants, the court allowed the cost of replacement or repair except as to the misplacement of the living-room wall. Whether a defect should fall under the cost-of-replacement rule or be considered under the diminished-value rule depends upon the nature and magnitude of the defect. This court has not allowed items of such magnitude under the cost-of-repair rule as the trial court did. Viewing the construction of the house as a whole and its cost we cannot say, however, that the trial court was in error in allowing the cost of repairing the plaster cracks in the ceilings, the cost of mud jacking and repairing the patio floor, and the cost of reconstructing the non-weight-bearing and nonstructural patio wall. Such reconstruction did not involve an unreasonable economic waste.

The item of misplacing the living-room wall under the facts of this case was clearly under the diminished-value rule. There is no evidence that defendants requested or demanded the replacement of the wall in the place called for by the specifications during the course of construction. To tear down the wall now and rebuild it in its proper place would involve a substantial destruction of the work, if not all of it, which was put into the wall and would cause additional damage to other parts of the house and require replastering and redecorating the walls and ceilings of at least two rooms. Such economic waste is unreasonable and unjustified. The rule of diminished value contemplates the wall is not going to be moved. Expert witnesses for both parties, testifying as to the value of the house, agreed that the misplacement of the wall had no effect on the market price. The trial court properly found that the defendants suffered no legal damage, although the defendants' particular desire for specified room size was not satisfied. For a discussion of these rules of damages for defective or unfinished construction and their application see Restatement, 1 Contracts, pp. 572–573, sec. 346(1) (a) and illustrations. . . .

Judgment affirmed.

NOTES

(1) *Question.* In what ways does the New York version of the substantial performance rule appear to differ from the Wisconsin court's approach in Plante v. Jacobs?

(2) *Subsequent Wisconsin Cases.* In Reith v. Wynhoff, 28 Wis.2d 336, 137 N.W.2d 33 (1965), a controversy arose between the builder of an apartment house and its owner over supposed defects. In litigation between them, they stipulated for the appointment of two experts by the court: a building contractor to state the cost of correcting matters that could be set right at reasonable expense and without economic waste, and a real estate appraiser to apply the diminished-value rule to other items. The experts agreed on the proper classification of the items for attention, and then *each* of them assessed the builder with the cost of corrections plus amounts they characterized as an "inconvenience factor." The supreme court decided that the builder's recovery should be limited as the experts advised, except that no inconvenience factor should have been applied by the contractor. Was this consistent with the principles of Plante v. Jacobs?

In Kreyer v. Driscoll, 39 Wis.2d 540, 159 N.W.2d 680 (1968), a contractor had agreed to build a home for a family for about $47,000. Controversies arose, apparently over progress payments, and the parties "reached an impasse." Stopping work, the contractor sued the owners. He had done only half the work on each of the following items: plumbing, electrical work, heating, and tile work. He had placed none of the linoleum, and had done only about a quarter of the decorating. The cost of completing these items was $4,650. The trial court gave judgment for the plaintiff for nearly $11,000. It allowed credits to the owners of $740 for imperfect workmanship, and $1,233 for delay in completion. The theory of the recovery was that the plaintiff had substantially performed. The owners appealed. *Held:* Affirmed. "[T]he amount of the judgment found by the lower court was not justified on the theory of substantial performance but is justified on the theory of *quantum meruit* or restitution." Was this consistent with the principles of Plante v. Jacobs? When a builder pulls off the job in Wisconsin, does it make any difference to his rights whether or not he is justified by the conduct of the owner? The court did not discuss the issue of justification in the Kreyer case.

Would the Wisconsin court reach the same result as the New York court did on the facts of Nolan v. Whitney, p. 646 supra? On the same theory?

(3) *Limitations on the Rule.* Real or apparent exceptions to the rule of substantial performance are abundant. In builders' cases, however, none of them seems to command general assent. A short list is as follows:

(a) "The doctrine is essentially a rule of damages . . . [I]ts purpose is not to compel the unwilling acceptance of tendered work that fails to meet contract specifications." Ballou v. Basis Construction Company, 407 F.2d 1137, 1140 (4th Cir. 1969).

(b) "[S]ubstantial performance relates to the degree of completion rather than the date of completion." Todd Shipyards Corporation v. Jasper Electric Service Co., 414 F.2d 8 (5th Cir. 1969).

(c) The rule does not temporize with "structural defects." See Spence v. Ham, 163 N.Y. 220, 57 N.E. 412 (1900), in which the size and placement of girders was faulty, affecting the solidity of the building: these were "deviations from the general plan of so essential a character that they cannot be remedied without partially reconstructing the building, and hence do not come within the rule of substantial performance . . .." Compare Kizziar v. Dollar, 268 F.2d 914 (10th Cir. 1959) ("standard and adequate" foundation for the building, though not equal to that specified).

(d) "Under ordinary circumstances . . . a failure to perform 10 percent of the contract price will not admit of the claim of substantial performance." Rochkind v. Jacobson, 126 App.Div. 347, 110 N.Y.S. 583 (1908). But see Jardine Estates v. Donna Brook Corp., 42 N.J.Super. 332, 126 A.2d 372 (1956) ("The matter is not to be determined on a percentage basis, for the cost of remedying defects may sometimes even exceed the outlay for original construction.").

(4) *The Brick Veneer Problem.* A homeowner, Roper, agreed to pay $535.25 to Armstead for installing brick veneer at Roper's home. Armstead agreed to use new brick matching as closely as possible the color and appearance of Roper's existing brickwork. When the work was done, Roper refused to pay. In an action by Armstead, the trial court found that his work was functionally acceptable, but not esthetically so. On hearing testimony about Roper's "damages," the court assessed them at 50% of the contract price, and gave judgment for Armstead for $267.62. On an appeal by Roper, what decision? See Reynolds v. Armstead, 166 Colo. 372, 443 P. 2d 990 (1968).

STEWART v. NEWBURY

Court of Appeals of New York, 1917.
220 N.Y. 379, 115 N.E. 984, 2 A.L.R. 519.

[Plaintiff, a builder, offered to do the excavation work for defendant's new foundry building at 65 cents per cubic yard; to furnish labor and forms for the concrete work at $2.05 per cubic yard, and to furnish labor to put in re-enforcing (of the concrete) at $4.00 per ton. The defendant accepted this offer. Other necessary facts are stated in the opinion. In the trial court judgment was entered upon a verdict for the plaintiff; this judgment was affirmed in the Appellate Division, and the defendant appealed by permission.]

CRANE, J. Nothing was said in writing about the time or manner of payment. The plaintiff, however, claims that after sending his letter and before receiving that of the defendant he had a telephone communication with Mr. Newbury and said: "I will expect my payments in the usual manner," and Newbury said, "All right, we have got the money to pay for the building." This conversation over the telephone was denied by the defendants.

The custom, the plaintiff testified, was to pay 85 per cent every thirty days or at the end of each month, 15 per cent being retained till the work was completed.

In July the plaintiff commenced work and continued until September 29th, at which time he had progressed with the construction as far as the first floor. He then sent a bill for the work done up to that date for $896.35. The defendants refused to pay the bill and work was discontinued.

The plaintiff claims that the defendants refused to permit him to perform the rest of his contract, they insisting that the work already done was not in accordance with the specifications. The defendants claimed upon the trial that the plaintiff voluntarily abandoned the work after their refusal to pay his bill.

On October 5, 1911, the defendants wrote the plaintiff a letter containing the following: "Notwithstanding you promised to let us know on Monday whether you would complete the job or throw up the contract, you have not up to this time advised us of your intention.
. . . Under the circumstances we are compelled to accept your action as being an abandonment of your contract and of every effort upon your part to complete your work on our building. As you know, the bill which you sent us and which we declined to pay is not correct, either in items or amount, nor is there anything due you under our contract as we understand it until you have completed your work on our building."

To this letter the plaintiff replied the following day. In it he makes no reference to the telephone communication agreeing, as he testified, to make "the usual payments," but does say this: "There is nothing in our agreement which says that I shall wait until the job is completed before any payment is due, nor can this be reasonably implied. . . . As to having given you positive date as to when I should let you know what I proposed doing, I did not do so; on the contrary I told you that I would not tell you positively what I would do until I had visited the job, and I promised that I would do this at my earliest convenience. . . ."

The defendant Herbert Newbury testified that the plaintiff "ran away and left the whole thing." And the defendant F. E. Newbury testified that he was told by Mr. Stewart's man that Stewart was going to abandon the job; that he thereupon telephoned Mr. Stewart, who replied that he would let him know about it the next day, but did not.

In this action, which is brought to recover the amount of the bill presented as the agreed price and $95.68 damages for breach of contract, the plaintiff had a verdict for the amount stated in the bill, but not for the other damages claimed, and the judgment entered thereon has been affirmed by the Appellate Division.

The appeal to us is upon exceptions to the judge's charge. The court charged the jury as follows: "Plaintiff says that he was excused from completely performing the contract by the defendant's unreasonable failure to pay him for the work he had done during the months of August and September. . . . Was it understood that the payments were to be made monthly? If it was not so understood the defendant's only obligation was to make payments at reasonable periods, in view of the character of the work, the amount of work being done and the value of it. In other words, if there was no agreement between the parties respecting the payments, the defendants' obligation was to make payments at reasonable times. . . . But whether there was such an agreement or not, you may consider whether it was reasonable or unreasonable for him to exact payment at that time and in that amount."

The court further said, in reply to a request to charge:

"I will say in that connection, if there was no agreement respecting the time of payment, and if there was no custom that was understood by both parties, and with respect to which they made the contract, then the plaintiff was entitled to payments at reasonable times."

The defendants' counsel thereupon made the following request, which was refused: "I ask your Honor to instruct the jury that if the circumstances existed as your Honor stated in your last instruction, then the plaintiff was not entitled to any payment until the contract was completed."

The jury was plainly told that if there were no agreement as to payments, yet the plaintiff would be entitled to part payment at reasonable times as the work progressed, and if such payments were refused he could abandon the work and recover the amount due for the work performed.

This is not the law. Counsel for the plaintiff omits to call our attention to any authority sustaining such a proposition and our search reveals none. In fact the law is very well settled to the contrary. This was an entire contract. (Ming v. Corbin, 142 N.Y. 334, 340, 341, 37 N.E. 105.) Where a contract is made to perform work and no agreement is made as to payment, the work must be substantially performed before payment can be demanded. [Citations omitted.]

This case was also submitted to the jury upon the ground that there may have been a breach of contract by the defendants in their refusal to permit the plaintiff to continue with his work, claiming that he had departed from the specifications, and there was some evidence justifying this view of the case, but it is impossible to say upon which of these two theories the jury arrived at its conclusion. The above errors, therefore, cannot be considered as harmless and immaterial. [Citations omitted.] As the verdict was for the amount of the bill presented and did not include the damages for a breach of contract, which would be the loss of profits, it may well be presumed that the jury adopted the first ground of recovery charged by the court as above quoted and decided that the plaintiff was justified in abandoning work for nonpayment of the installment.

The judgment should be reversed, and a new trial ordered, costs to abide the event.

NOTES

(1) *Questions.* If the jury believed the plaintiff's evidence about the telephone conversation with Mr. Newbury, does it follow that he was justified in abandoning the work? Would it matter whether this conversation occurred before or after the contract was concluded? If it occurred afterward, what was the consideration for Newbury's promise to pay "in the usual manner"?

(2) *Work Before Pay.* "When the performance of a contract consists in doing (faciendo) on one side, and in giving (dando) on the other side, the doing must take place before the giving. (Langdell's Summary of Law of Contracts, sec. 125.)" Kellogg, J., in Coletti v. Knox Hat Co., Inc., 252 N.Y. 468, 472, 169 N.E. 648, 649–650 (1930). This is said to be based on the "practice of centuries." Restatement, § 270, Comment a; see also §§ 266(3), 268, 272.

———

ALLOCATING CREDIT RISKS

In a schematic analysis of contract policy by Professor Macaulay, he offers support for the rule that "in the typical employment contract the employee must work before the employer must pay for the service—the employer's duty to pay is constructively conditional on the employee's performance." One justification for the rule that he gives is that employers are, as a class, "probably better credit risks than employees paid in advance." Macaulay, Justice Traynor and the Law of Contracts, 13 Stan.L.Rev. 812, 815–16 (1961).

In a sale of goods for cash there is no credit risk in the standard sense. However, Professor Leff has described the buyer's risk that the goods will prove to be defective as being in the nature of a credit risk.[a] The rule placing this risk on the buyer "unless otherwise agreed" is reflected in UCC 2–310(a). Can this rule be justified on the ground that, as a class, sellers are probably better credit risks than buyers who obtain goods on credit?

Does the same consideration tend to justify the rule in Stewart v. Newbury? For repair work on buildings and chattels, and similar modest jobs, payment is commonly withheld until completion. But for sizable construction work it is well-nigh universal practice to agree upon periodic progress payments, or "draws," in favor of the contractor. As security for completion, the owner retains a fraction (usual 10–20%) of the amount earned each month by the contractor, and the

---

a. Leff, Injury, Ignorance and Spite—
The Dynamics of Coercive Collection,
80 Yale L.J. 1, 20–22 (1970).

sums withheld (sometimes called the "retent") are payable only upon completion. Does this practice indicate that contractors are dissatisfied with the rule in Stewart v. Newbury? Is it a reason for discarding the rule?

NOTE

Security Against Credit Risks. Buyers of land and goods who contract to pay in installments, after possession is transferred, are to some extent secured, as Professor Leff noted, against the "credit risk" that the property will prove to be defective. In Chapter 10, Section 3, it will be seen that credit sellers and financing institutions have attempted to deprive buyers of the privilege of stopping payment when they are disappointed. In part, the law has frustrated these attempts, showing its concern to minimize the buyer's risk. Securing payment for contractors (and laborers and materialmen) is a function of mechanics' lien laws (see Note 2, p. 35 supra) and of payment bonds that are commonly required by statute on public projects.

Obviously the doctrine of constructive conditions has not succeeded alone in making a satisfactory allocation of credit risks; but perhaps it has played a useful part in doing so, as Professor Macaulay suggests. Reconsider Kingston v. Preston, p. 692 supra. Does it appear that Lord Mansfield was cognizant of the utility of implied conditions for allocating credit risks?

———

NEW ENGLAND STRUCTURES, INC. v. LORANGER

Supreme Judicial Court of Massachusetts, 1968.
354 Mass. 62, 234 N.E.2d 888.

CUTTER, JUSTICE. In one case the plaintiffs, doing business as Theodore Loranger & Sons (Loranger), the general contactor on a school project, seeks to recover from New England Structures, Inc., a subcontractor (New England), damages caused by an alleged breach of the subcontract. Loranger avers that the breach made it necessary for Loranger at greater expense to engage another subcontractor to complete work on a roof deck. In a cross action, New England seeks to recover for breach of the subcontract by Loranger alleged to have taken place when Loranger terminated New England's right to proceed. The actions were consolidated for trial. A jury returned a verdict for New England in the action brought by Loranger, and a verdict for New England in the sum of $16,860.25 in the action brought by New England against Loranger. The cases are before us on Loranger's exceptions to the judge's charge.

Loranger, under date of July 11, 1961, entered into a subcontract with New England by which New England undertook to install a gypsum roof deck in a school, then being built by Loranger. New England began work on November 24, 1961. On December 18, 1961, New England received a telegram from Loranger which read, "Because of your . . . repeated refusal . . . or inability to provide enough properly skilled workmen to maintain satisfactory progress, we . . . terminate your right to proceed with work at the . . . school as of December 26, 1961, in accordance with Article . . . 5 of our contract. We intend to complete the work . . . with other forces and charge its costs and any additional damages resulting from your repeated delays to your account." New England replied, "Failure on your [Loranger's] part to provide . . . approved drawings is the cause of the delay." The telegram also referred to various allegedly inappropriate changes in instructions.

The pertinent portions of art. 5 of the subcontract are set out in the margin.[1] Article 5 stated grounds on which Loranger might terminate New England's right to proceed with the subcontract.

There was conflicting evidence concerning (a) how New England had done certain work; (b) whether certain metal cross pieces (called bulb tees) had been properly "staggered" and whether joints had been welded on both sides by certified welders, as called for by the specifications; (c) whether New England had supplied an adequate number of certified welders on certain days; (d) whether and to what extent Loranger had waived certain specifications; and (e) whether New England had complied with good trade practices. The architect testified that on December 14, 1961, he had made certain complaints to New England's president. The work was completed by another company at a cost in excess of New England's bid. There was also testimony (1) that Loranger's job foreman told one of New England's welders "to do no work at the job site during the five day period following the date of Loranger's termination telegram," and (2) that, "if New England had been permitted to continue its work, it could have completed the entire subcontract . . . within five days following the date of the termination telegram."

The trial judge ruled, as matter of law, that Loranger, by its termination telegram confined the justification for its notice of termination to New England's "repeated refusal . . . or inability to provide enough properly skilled workmen to maintain satisfactory

---

1. "The Subcontractor agrees to furnish sufficient labor, materials, tools and equipment to maintain its work in accordance with the progress of the general construction work by the General Contractor. Should the Subcontractor fail to keep up with . . . [such] progress . . . then he shall work overtime with no additional compensation, if directed to do so by the General Contractor. If the Subcontractor should be adjudged a bankrupt . . . or *if he should persistently . . . fail to supply enough properly skilled workmen* . . . or . . . disregard instructions of the General Con-

tractor or fail to observe or perform the provisions of the Contract, then the General Contractor may, by *at least five . . . days prior written notice to the Subcontractor* without prejudice to any other rights or remedies, *terminate the Subcontractor's right to proceed with the work.* In such event, the General Contractor may . . . prosecute the work to completion . . . and the Subcontractor shall be liable to the General Contractor for any excess cost occasioned . . . thereby . . ." (emphasis supplied).

progress." He then gave the following instructions: "If you should find that New England . . . did not furnish a sufficient number of men to perform the required work under the contract within a reasonable time . . . then you would be warranted in finding that Loranger was justified in terminating its contract; and it may recover in its suit against New England . . . . [T]he termination . . . cannot, as . . . matter of law, be justified for any . . . reason not stated in the telegram of December 18 . . . including failure to stagger the joints of the bulb tees or failure to weld properly . . . or any other reason, unless you find that inherent in the reasons stated in the telegram, namely, failure to provide enough skilled workmen to maintain satisfactory progress, are these aspects. Nevertheless, these allegations by Loranger of deficiency of work on the part of New England Structures may be considered by you, if you find that Loranger was justified in terminating the contract for the reason enumerated in the telegram. You may consider it or them as an element of damages sustained by Loranger . . . ."[2] Counsel for Loranger claimed exceptions to the portion of the judge's charge quoted above in the body of this opinion.[3]

1. Some authority supports the judge's ruling, in effect, that Loranger, having specified in its telegram one ground for termination of the subcontract, cannot rely in litigation upon other grounds, except to the extent that the other grounds may directly affect the first ground asserted. See Railway Co. v. McCarthy, 96 U.S. 258, 267–268, 24 L.Ed. 693 ("Where a party gives a reason for his conduct and decision touching . . . a controversy, he cannot, after litigation has begun, change his ground, and put his conduct upon . . . a different consideration. He is not permitted thus to mend his hold. He is *estopped* from doing it by a settled principle of law" [emphasis supplied]); Luckenbach S.S. Co. Inc. v. W. R. Grace & Co. Inc., 267 F. 676, 679 (4th Cir.); Chevrolet Motor Co. v. Gladding, 42 F.2d 440 (4th Cir.), cert. den. 282 U.S. 872, 51 S.Ct. 78, 75 L.Ed. 770. See also Rode & Brand v. Kamm Games, Inc., 181 F.2d 584, 587 (2d Cir.); Cummings v. Connecticut Gen. Life Ins. Co., 102 Vt. 351, 359–362, 148 A. 484. In each of these cases, there is reference to estoppel or "waiver" as the legal ground behind the principle.

2. The judge also instructed, "[I]f you find that on the day following the sending of this telegram . . . employees of New England . . . were refused permission to continue that work, then you may consider that as a breach of the contract by Loranger, for Loranger's telegram terminated the contract . . . as of December 26th, [by] the giving of five days notice . . . . . [I]f you find that [employees of] New England . . . reported for work and were only informed that they were to call their office and were not prevented from working then . . . you would be warranted in finding that this was not a refusal on the part of Loranger to permit them to work for the period between the receipt of the telegram and the date of the termination, December 26th."

3. No exception appears to have been claimed to the portion of the charge (see fn. 2) relating to whether Loranger prevented New England from performing work on the subcontract during the period from December 19 to December 26.

Our cases somewhat more definitely require reliance or change of position based upon the assertion of the particular reason or defence before treating a person, giving one reason for his action, as estopped later to give a different reason. See Bates v. Cashman, 230 Mass. 167, 168–169, 119 N.E. 663, 664. There it was said, "The defendant is not prevented from setting up this defense. Although he wrote respecting other reasons for declining to perform the contract, he expressly reserved different grounds for his refusal.[4] While of course one cannot fail in good faith in presenting his reasons as to his conduct touching a controversy he is not prevented from relying upon one good defense among others urged simply because he has not always put it forward, when it does not appear that he has acted dishonestly or that the other party has been misled to his harm, or that he is estopped on any other ground." See Brown v. Henry, 172 Mass. 559, 567, 52 N.E. 1073; St. John Bros. Co. v. Falkson, 237 Mass. 399, 402–403, 130 N.E. 51; Moss v. Old Colony Trust Co., 246 Mass. 139, 150, 140 N.E. 803; Sheehan v. Commercial Travelers Mut. Acc. Assn. of America, 283 Mass. 543, 551–553, 186 N.E. 627, 88 A.L.R. 975; Restatement: Contracts, § 304; Williston, Contracts (3d ed.) § 742 (and also §§ 678, 679, 691); Corbin, Contracts, §§ 762, 1218, 1266 (and also §§ 265, 721, 727, 744, 756). See also Randall v. Peerless Motor Car Co., 212 Mass. 352, 376, 99 N.E. 221.

We think Loranger is not barred from asserting grounds not mentioned in its telegram unless New England establishes that, in some manner, it relied to its detriment upon the circumstance that only one ground was so asserted. Even if some evidence tended to show such reliance, the jury did not have to believe this evidence. They should have received instructions that they might consider grounds for termination of the subcontract and defences to New England's claim (that Loranger by the telegram had committed a breach of the subcontract), other than the ground raised in the telegram, unless they found as a fact that New England had relied to its detriment upon the fact that only one particular ground for termination was mentioned in the telegram.

2. As there must be a new trial, we consider whether art. 5 of the subcontract (fn. 1) afforded New England any right during the five-day notice period to attempt to cure its default, and, in doing so, to rely on the particular ground stated in the telegram. Some evidence summarized above may suggest that such an attempt was made. Article 5 required Loranger to give "at least five . . . days prior written notice to the Subcontractor" of termination.

---

4. The original papers show (record, p. 22) that the reservation was, "The statement of the foregoing [reason] is not to be taken as waiving any other reason for . . . Cashman's refusal to proceed further with the agreement." This distinction from the present case, in our opinion, does not affect the principle that any estoppel to assert a different reason must rest on actual reliance.

If a longer notice period had been specified, one might perhaps infer that the notice period was designed to give New England an opportunity to cure its defaults. An English text writer (Hudson's, Building and Engineering Contracts, 9th ed. p. 530) says, "Where a previous warning notice of specified duration is expressly required by the contract before . . . termination [in case of dissatisfaction], the notice should be explicit as to the grounds of dissatisfaction, so that during the time mentioned in the notice the builder may have the opportunity of removing the cause of objection. . . ." This view was taken of a three-day notice provision in Valentine v. Patrick Warren Constr. Co., 263 Wis. 143, 164, 56 N.W.2d 860, without, however, very full consideration of the provision's purpose. In Corbin, Contracts, § 1266, p. 66, it is said of a reserved power to terminate a contract, "If a period of notice is required, the contract remains in force and must continue to be performed according to its terms during the specified period after receipt of the notice of termination." See Simons v. American Dry Ginger Ale Co. Inc., 335 Mass. 521, 524–525, 140 N.E.2d 649.

Whether the short five-day notice period was intended to give New England an opportunity to cure any specified breach requires interpretation (see Valentine v. Patrick Warren Constr. Co., 263 Wis. 143, 155, 56 N.W.2d 860) of art. 5,[5] a matter of law for the court. See Charles L. Hazelton & Son, Inc. v. Teel, 349 Mass. 617, 621, 211 N.E. 2d 352. It would have been natural for the parties to have provided expressly that a default might be cured within the five-day period if that had been the purpose. See e. g. Mad River Lumber Sales, Inc. v. Willburn, 205 Cal.App.2d 321, 322, 325, 22 Cal.Rptr. 918 (contract specifically gave period in which to cure default).[6]

Strong practical considerations support the view that as short a notice period as five days in connection with terminating a substantial building contract cannot be intended to afford opportunity to cure defaults major enough (even under art. 5) to justify termination of a contract. Such a short period suggests that its purpose is at most to give the defaulting party time to lay off employees, remove equipment from the premises, cancel orders, and for similar matters.

Although the intention of the notice provision of art. 5 is obscure, we interpret it as giving New England no period in which to cure continuing defaults, but merely as directing that New England

5. Article 5 of this subcontract (which is part of a printed form of contract) appears to be based to some extent upon the American Institute of Architects, standard contract, Form A1, art. 22. See Parker and Adams, The A.I.A. Standard Contract Forms and the Law. The purpose of the notice period under this A.I.A. form is not clarified by any commentary.

[See also Supplement, Standard Construction Agreement, Article 25.—eds.]

6. Somewhat analogous provisions sometimes appear in real estate purchase agreements, expressly giving a vendor an extension of time for performance in order to cure title defects. See Swaim, Crocker's Notes on Common Forms (7th ed.) § 814, p. 435, § 852.

be told when it must quit the premises and as giving it an opportunity to take steps during the five-day period to protect itself from injury. Nothing in art. 5 suggests that a termination pursuant to its provisions was not to be effective in any event at the conclusion of the five-day period, even if New England should change its conduct.

If Loranger in fact was not justified by New England's conduct in giving the termination notice, it may have subjected itself to liability for breach of the subcontract. The reason stated in the notice, however, for giving the notice cannot be advanced as the basis of any reliance by New England in action taken by it to cure defaults. After the receipt of the notice, as we interpret art. 5, New England had no further opportunity to cure defaults.

Exceptions sustained.

NOTES

(1) *The Notice Term.* As the court interpreted the five-day notice provision of article 5 (footnote 1), did it have any effect on New England's claim against Loranger? Notice that Loranger's telegram of December 18 stated: "we terminate your right to proceed . . . as of December 26." Was the provision intended to limit what New England might recover, if the termination was wrongful, to damages that such advance notice would not have permitted it to prevent? Was it intended to prevent or limit Loranger's recovery, if its termination was rightful but was not given upon sufficient notice? What other effect might it have? On the purposes of such a provision, see Sweet, Legal Aspects of Architecture, Engineering and the Construction Process, § 26.07 (1970).

(2) *Unconscionability.* Consider this provision in a subcontract, operative upon default by the sub: "the General Contractor shall be at liberty to take possession, for the purpose of completing the work included in this contract, of all materials, tools, scaffolding and appliances thereon." Should it be held unenforceable as unconscionable? See RAO Electrical Equipment Co. v. Macdonald Eng. Co., 124 Ill.App.2d 158, 260 N.E.2d 294 (1970).

(3) *Seriatim Objections.* A builder has put up a dwelling, under contract with the owner of the lot, and considers that he has complied with all the specifications, leaving no defects. If, however, the owner disagrees, the builder hopes to satisfy him with corrective work. The builder wishes to do all such work at one time, before moving his crew and equipment away. How can he elicit a definitive list of the owner's objections? (Compare Sears, Roebuck and Co. v. Jardel Co., p. 311 supra.)

In Cawley v. Weiner, 236 N.Y. 357, 140 N.E. 724 (1923), the owners of a new bungalow moved in before the builder had stopped work, and handed him a list of 17 items that they considered necessary by way of change in or addition to the structure. For about a week after that, apparently, the builder continued work. Not being paid in full, he brought suit against the owners for the price. At the trial, they offered to prove three particulars, not specified in the earlier list, in which the plaintiff had failed of performance. The trial court excluded the evidence on grounds of waiver and estoppel, and gave the plaintiff judgment for virtually the whole amount he claimed. On appeal by the owners, *held:* Reversed. "Unless the plaintiff were in some way harmed by the action of these defendants in furnishing him with a list of the defects, how are they estopped from showing the departures from the plans and specifications?"

In preparing a construction contract, what provision might be made to prevent the owner from raising new objections seriatim? Is this the answer?—"Owner agrees not to move into the house until Contractor receives final payment." See Creith Lumber v. Cummins, 163 Ohio St. 264, 126 N.E.2d 323 (1955).

(4) *Problem.* In Michel v. Efferson, 223 La. 136, 65 So.2d 115 (1953), the owner prepared a list of defects for the builder which he seems to have made some effort to correct. He then told the owner, who needed a place to live, that she could not have the keys unless she accepted the house in its then condition. Finally she accepted the house "as is," saying she guessed she would have to "swallow the plaster." At the time she did not know the extent of the defects in the plaster (as she now says), not having gone upstairs in the house on account of illness. She subsequently brought an action against the builder on account of defective construction. What result?

WAIVER, ESTOPPEL, AND ELECTION

A waiver or estoppel foreclosing a ground for recovery (e. g., Loranger v. New England) is not at all uncommon, but the more usual case is a waiver or estoppel foreclosing a line of defense (e. g., New England v. Loranger). In stating the principles of waiver and estoppel there are unusual difficulties because they are applied with more stringency to some factual patterns than to others. They apply over the whole range of contract relations, and in other contexts as well. Probably their most frequent applications are in aid of suits on insurance policies, by excusing the failure of a policyholder or other claimant to comply with some condition of the contract.[a]

A third principle, election, provides comparable aid. "Election is simply what its name imports; a choice, shown by an overt act, between two inconsistent rights, either of which may be asserted at the will of the chooser alone." Holmes, J., in Wm. W. Bierce, Ltd. v. Hutchins, 205 U.S. 340, 346 (1907). An important instance of election arises under liability insurance policies, in some states, when the insured person is charged with negligence in causing harm, and the insurance company believes that in fact he inflicted the harm intentionally. If he was only negligent, the company must provide a defense for him, and pay any resulting judgment against him, according to a prevalent view. But if the company is right, it need not do either, according to most courts. The rule of election is that if the company provides a defense, and loses, it must pay whatever judgment runs against the policyholder (within the amount of the policy).

a. See Keeton, Insurance Law (Basic Text) 343–45, 423–27 (1971); Morris, Waiver and Estoppel in Insurance Policy Litigation, 105 U.Pa.L.Rev. 925 (1957); Patterson, Essentials of Insurance Law, Ch. 11 (2d ed. 1957).

This rule obtains in New Jersey, where the only way the company can reserve its "no coverage" position against the policyholder, while defending him, is with his express consent. Burd v. Sussex Mutual Ins. Co., 56 N.J. 383, 267 A.2d 7 (1970).[b] Some other courts do not apply the election rule to this situation. See, for instance, Ferguson v. Birmingham Fire Ins. Co., 254 Ore. 496, 460 P.2d 342 (1969). In that case the company offered to defend a suit against its policyholder under a reservation of its right to disclaim coverage if it lost. The policyholder demanded: "We will expect you to defend under the terms of the policy with no reservations." In New Jersey, that would be a proper demand; but the Oregon court regards it as an unwarranted attempt to put the insurer to an election. Other authorities on each side of this issue are collected in texts on insurance law.

Elections are not always called by that name. Quite often, when a contracting party has made a necessary choice between opposing courses of action or legal positions that were open to him, a court will say that he has "waived" one of them. It has been argued that a different kind of waiver occurs when a party submits himself voluntarily to a legal burden in the absence of pressure to do so. That kind of waiver is suggested by the definition, "waiver is an intentional relinquishment of a known right."[c] As an example, a life insurance company might waive its right to an autopsy, where the contract and the circumstances authorize it to make that a condition of payment, simply by saying to the beneficiary of the policy, "we will not require an autopsy." Yet the difference between an ordinary, "intentional" waiver and an election-waiver is a subtle one, at best. As concerns an autopsy, if the insurer does not demand one soon after it learns of the policyholder's death, it may be held to have *elected* not to stand on the condition.

In one respect, an intentional waiver seems to be different from both election and estoppel: there are times when it may be withdrawn. A landlord might say, for example, that he waived prompt payment of the rent, without committing himself indefinitely. If the succeeding installments of rent were not paid on time, the landlord would hardly be permitted to take immediate eviction proceedings. (Is that because he has waived prompt payment? Or because he is estopped to act on the delay?) Yet he would probably be permitted, after some experience of aggravated delays, to reinstate the requirement of prompt payment by saying, in good time, that future installments must be timely. The waiver would be withdrawn.[d] (On closer analysis,

b. See also Three Sons, Inc. v. Phoenix Ins. Co., 357 Mass. 271, 257 N.E.2d 774 (1970).

c. Lee v. Casualty Insurance Co., 90 Conn. 202, 96 A. 952 (1916).

d. Compare Charles Rickards, Ltd. v. Oppenheim, [1950] 1 K.B. 616, [1950] 1

All. E.R. 420. But cf. Lee v. Casualty Insurance Co., footnote c supra, saying that "rights once waived cannot be regained by revoking the waiver." See also Restatement, §§ 88(2), 297, and 311.

it might appear that what is withdrawn is not a waiver, which occurs month by month, but a notice of *intent* to waive. But close analysis of the word "waiver" is not usual in the cases.)

An estoppel, like an election, may sometimes be discerned in a case where the opinion speaks only of waiver. As the Loranger case indicates, an estoppel is thought to arise only when there has been reliance—a change of position, or at least detrimental inaction—in response to conduct or expressions of the party said to be estopped. The reliance must be manifest in some form: it is not enough that the party asserting estoppel has had his expectations aroused, or that "some secret operation of his own mind" was set in motion. Wood v. State, 12 N.Y.2d 25, 186 N.E.2d 406 (1962). An estoppel may be illustrated by these facts: a buyer contracts for goods "to be shipped in wooden crates." Thereafter, he writes the seller: "you may ship in cardboard cartons, instead." After the goods are packed in cardboard, the buyer may not insist on repacking in crates.

Sometimes it is difficult to distinguish an estoppel from a modification of the contract. If the buyer in the foregoing example had *requested* the seller to pack the goods in cardboard, and the seller had begun to do so, it might be inferred that the parties had formed a new contract for a different performance. The distinction is especially difficult to maintain for contracts within Article 2 of the Code because it provides that "An agreement modifying a contract within this Article needs no consideration to be binding." UCC 2–209(1).[e] Under this rule, the buyer supposed above might be bound by an agreement to pay for the goods packed in either way the seller chooses, and be bound whether or not the seller has begun to pack them. The same section of the Code also recognizes the principle of estoppel, however, in subsection (5), by limiting the power to retract a waiver, "in view of a material change of position. . . . " What does the word "waiver" mean in this context?

The efficacy of waivers, estoppels, and elections is limited, in a way not easy to summarize, by a perception that they ought not to be allowed to displace the necessity of a bargain altogether. As an extreme example, a buyer of goods would not be held bound by waiver if he said to the seller, "I will pay for the goods promised whether they are delivered or not." The point is discussed in Corbin, § 752, and in Rennie & Laughlin, Inc. v. Chrysler Corp., 242 F.2d 208 (9th Cir. 1957): "Where substantial rights are involved, it is frequently said that waiver must be supported by either an agreed consideration or by acts amounting to estoppel." Substantial rights are clearly not involved in a life insurer's waiver of an autopsy; but if it could succeed in waiving the payment of premiums on a policy, both the basis of the bargain and some imposing public interests would be seriously im-

e.   See also UCC 2–208.

paired. In other instances, of course, it is not always evident whether or not substantial rights are involved.[f]

Even the principle of estoppel may be impotent to achieve some of the results that are regularly accomplished by bargaining. Cf. Restatement Second, § 90, suggesting a limitation on the remedy in a case of *promissory* estoppel. An important example is the rule often stated that "estoppel cannot be used to enlarge the coverage of an insurance policy." Madgett v. Monroe County Mutual Tornado Ins. Co., 46 Wis.2d 708, 176 N.W.2d 314 (1970) ("Estoppel can block, but it cannot create. It is a barricade. . . . not a bulldozer.") The rule is open to serious challenge,[g] but it indicates that estoppel, like waiver, is still only an ancillary source of contract rights.

NOTES

(1) *The Case of the Rancher's Misjudgment.* Charles Lohmann had an option contract to buy a large ranch that he had occupied under a lease for several years. The lease and option were to expire at the end of August, 1968. The price stated for the purchase was "a price that the Lessor would be willing to accept from another party." As the lease term wore on, the owners named successively lower prices to Lohmann, all of which he rejected as being too high. Being determined to sell, the owners consulted George Hall, a real-estate broker, who told them he thought he could sell the property for $20 an acre. The owners made an offer to Lohmann at that price. He told them to "go ahead and list it; he didn't think it would sell." Early in June, 1968, the owners listed the property with Hall for sale, and Lohmann expressed his willingness to have it shown to prospective purchasers. On June 28, the owners sold the ranch to Hall himself. Lohmann brought an action against them for specific performance of his option contract. His complaint alleged his willingness to pay $19 an acre. (That would be the amount net to the defendants on their sale to Hall, since he was to have a 5% broker's commission.) The trial court dismissed the action after hearing Lohmann's evidence, on two grounds: (a) estoppel of the plaintiff to assert any right under the option contract, and (b) inadequacy of his tender as a specific-performance basis. On Lohmann's appeal, *held*: Affirmed. Lohmann v. Bellah, 441 F.2d 458 (10th Cir. 1971). See also Evelyn v. Raven Realty, Inc., 215 Md. 467, 138 A.2d 898 (1958), a land sale case, where the court undertook to clarify confusion attending the terms "waiver" and "estoppel".

(2) *Waiver Distributed.* It has not been possible to regard waiver as a single-valued concept since a Canadian lawyer, Ewart, published a volume called "Waiver Distributed Among the Departments Election, Estoppel, Contract, Release" in 1917.[h] "The explanation of the somewhat curious

---

f. See National Utility Service v. Whirlpool Corp., 325 F.2d 779 (2d Cir. 1963); United States v. Chichester, 312 F.2d 275 (9th Cir. 1963); Restatement, §§ 88, 297.

g. See Keeton, Insurance Law (Basic Text), § 6.6(b) (1971).

h. He was thinking of changing the title as early as 1905; see Waiver in Insurance Law, 18 Harv.L.Rev. 365, 378. See also Election in Insurance Law, 12 Colum.L.Rev. 619 (1912).

title of the present volume is that although the author commenced to write a book about 'waiver,' he very soon ascertained that there was not enough 'waiver' to write a book about." Id. at p. 3. "For the simple statement that, upon breach of a policy-condition, the insurance company may elect whether to continue or discontinue its liability, substitute that the company has a right to 'waive the forfeiture,' and you have made clear reasoning impossible. . . . The case is purely one of election." Id. at p. 25. Ewart found that waiver was also a common alias for estoppel: "The doctrine of waiver, as asserted against insurance companies to avoid the strict enforcement of conditions contained in their policies, is only another name for the doctrine of estoppel." Insurance Co. v. Wolff, 95 U.S. 326 (1877). However, he granted that waiver is sometimes a serviceable word, even if some other will usually serve the purpose better, and he approved the following proposition: "While one party has time and opportunity to comply with a condition precedent, if the other party does or says anything to put him off his guard, and to induce him to believe that the condition is waived, or that a strict compliance with it will not be insisted on, he is afterward estopped from claiming non-performance of the condition." Underwood v. Farmers' Joint Stock Ins. Co., 57 N.Y. 500, 505 (1874).[i]

(3) *Rights Upon Breach.* The discharge of a "claim or right arising out of an alleged breach" cannot be effected by a simple waiver, although the Code provides a mechanism for discharge that does not require a consideration. UCC 1–107.

PHOENIX INS. CO. v. ROSS JEWELERS, INC., 362 F.2d 985 (5th Cir. 1966). [Burglars cut their way into a retail store operated by Ross Jewelers, Inc., and made away with merchandise worth more than $60,000. All but about $10,000-worth was taken from a vault in the store. The vault had a protective alarm system, as required by insurance on the goods, but the manager's habit was to leave the key in the lock. The policy also required the insured to maintain a "detailed and itemized inventory" of its property. A report was given to the insurer's home office by the General Adjustment Bureau showing that "a detailed and itemized inventory was not kept," "the internal control over the stock was inadequate," and "the detail stock records were not up to date." A week later the supervisor of the insurer's Inland Marine Claim Department wrote to the Bureau, saying that nothing would be paid for contents of the vault, but authorizing a settlement offer for the remainder of the loss. The offer was declined. In a suit brought by Ross Jewelers on the policy, the insurer disclaimed liability altogether, relying on the inventory provision. The trial court gave judgment for the plaintiff for the merchandise lost both from the vault and elsewhere. The insurer appealed.]

---

i. The author of this opinion also said: "The doctrine of estoppel lays at the foundation of the law, as to waiver. . . . I think there can be no waiver of a condition precedent, except there be in the case an element of estoppel. . . . But my brethren are unwilling to express an opinion upon the doctrine of waiver as I have stated it." Id., pp. 505–7.

JONES, CIRCUIT JUDGE: . . . We are in agreement with the district court's holding that the denial of liability by Phoenix upon the sole ground that Ross Jewelers had breached the condition that it would maintain the protective devices . . . operated as a waiver of the defense of the failure of Ross Jewelers to maintain an inventory. . . . The writer of the Phoenix letter stated in an affidavit that he did not, at the time the letter was written, intend to waive the inventory defense. [He testified that he had prepared the letter in haste, without thought of the inventory question.] While it may be said that waiver depends upon intention, the intention may be inferred from acts and conduct. Such inference is fully warranted under the facts here established. [Judgment reversed, however, for redetermination of the amount, so as to eliminate the contents of the vault.] [a]

NOTES

(1) *Waiver-Estoppel.* "Ordinarily, when an insurer, with knowledge of all pertinent facts, denies liability upon a specific ground, all other grounds are deemed to be waived. This waiver is conditioned, however, upon a showing of detriment or prejudice. . . . We find nothing in this case to indicate that the insured acted upon the announced ground or incurred any expense, loss or detriment in reliance upon it." Larson v. Occidental Fire & Cas. Co., 79 N.M. 562, 446 P.2d 210 (1968). Is it possible to reconcile this passage with the foregoing decision? If not, which do you prefer?

(2) *Unfair Advantage?* Waiver and like doctrines produce results at variance with the terms of standardized contracts, determined by particular variations in patterns of facts. Does this consideration reinforce the need for caution in applying theories of waiver and estoppel? In relation to insurance contracts, Professor Keeton observes that they "may produce exceptionally favored treatment for limited numbers of policyholders, giving some a far better bargain than others with the same class of coverage. Moreover, this inequity is not mitigated by broader considerations of fairness, as when a knowledgeable policyholder benefits by an objectively reasonable construction of an onerous provision." Keeton, Insurance Law (Basic Text) 415 (1971).

McKENNA v. VERNON, 258 Pa. 18, 101 A. 919 (1917). [The plaintiff undertook to build a moving picture theatre in Philadelphia for the defendant. The contract price, $8,750, was to be paid in installments of 80% of the work set in place, and the final installment within 30 days after completion of the work. The work was to be done under the direction of an architect, whose certificate of work done was to be the condition of each payment by the defendant. The plaintiff

a. For an extreme application of the doctrine of this case, see Delmar Bank v. Fidelity & Deposit Co., 428 F.2d 32 (8th Cir. 1970). Contrast American Ins. Co. v. Nationwide Mutual Ins. Co., 110 N.H. 192, 270 A.2d 907 (1970).

received several payments, amounting in all to $6,000, and brought this action for the remainder of the contract price. The defendant asserted that the work was defective; but the architect testified that there were no unauthorized departures from the specifications, and the plaintiff received a judgment for $2,500. The defendant appealed on the theory that no right of action existed in the absence of a certificate from the architect of final completion of the building. *Held*: Affirmed.]

STEWART, JUSTICE. . . . All payments were to be made only on certificate of the architect, and yet with a single exception each of the seven payments made as the work progressed was made without a certificate being asked for. With such constant and repeated disregard on the part of the owner to exact compliance with this provision in the contract, it is too late now for him to insist that failure on the part of the plaintiff to secure such certificate before suit defeats his right of action. . . . If he waived it repeatedly, as he did here, during the progress of the work, he cannot complain if he be held to have waived it when he seeks to defend against a final payment for work shown to have been honestly and substantially performed, especially when almost daily he has had the work under his own observation, without remonstrance or complaint at any time with respect to either the work done or materials employed.

NOTES

(1) *The Rationale.* How many payments might the defendant have made before losing, as to the future, the right to insist that the architect's certificates be given? Is it clear that the decision was not based on facts creating an estoppel? See Restatement, § 300. If the plaintiff had asked for and received, early in the course of performance, the defendant's promise that he would not insist on compliance with the condition, enforcement of the promise would present an obvious problem of consideration. Was there any problem of consideration on the facts of McKenna v. Vernon?

(2) *Problem.* How helpful to the defendant-owner's case would it have been if he had had the foresight to insert the following provision in the contract?—"Failure of the owner to insist on full, absolute and complete compliance with any provisions of the contract, in any one or more instances, shall not be deemed as a waiver of owner's right at any and all times thereafter to such compliance." See Few v. Automobile Financing, Inc., 101 Ga.App. 783, 115 S.E.2d 196 (1960) (note the statute). Cf. Dempsey v. Stauffer, 312 F.2d 360 (3d Cir. 1962).

(3) *Good Faith.* Do the instances of waiver given above support the general proposition that "Every contract imposes upon each party a duty of good faith and fair dealing in its performance and its enforcement"? Restatement Second, § 231. Two illustrations given for the section (8 and 10) are situations in which the courts would normally reason in terms of waiver and the like. Do the instances of recovery for substantial performance given above support the proposition? One of the illustrations (6) would normally be reasoned in terms of substantial performance.

Is it possible that the doctrines mentioned would have been unnecessary if there had been an early and generous recognition of the duty of good faith in the performance of contracts? See Childres, Conditions in the Law of Contracts, 45 N.Y.U.L.Rev. 33, 35–36 (1970).

McCLOSKEY & CO. v. MINWELD STEEL CO.

United States Court of Appeals, Third Circuit, 1955.
220 F.2d 101.

Suit by contractor against subcontractor alleging anticipatory breach of three contracts entered into by parties. The United States District Court for the Western District of Pennsylvania, Joseph P. Willson, J., granted defendant's motion for judgment on ground that plaintiff had not made out prima facie case, and entered order denying plaintiff's motion for findings of fact, to vacate judgments and for new trial, and plaintiff appealed. . . .

Order affirmed.

McLaughlin, Circuit Judge. Plaintiff-appellant, a general contractor, sued on three contracts alleging an anticipatory breach as to each. At the close of the plaintiff's case the district judge granted the defense motions for judgment on the ground that plaintiff had not made out a cause of action.

By the contracts involved the principal defendant,[1] a fabricator and erector of steel, agreed to furnish and erect all of the structural steel required on two buildings to be built on the grounds of the Hollidaysburg State Hospital, Hollidaysburg, Pa. and to furnish all of the long span steel joists required in the construction of one of the two buildings. Two of the contracts were dated May 1, 1950 and the third May 26, 1950. By Article V of each of the contracts "Should the Sub-Contractor [the defendant herein] . . . at any time refuse or neglect to supply a sufficiency . . . of materials of the proper quality, . . . in and about the performance of the work required to be done pursuant to the provisions of this agreement . . ., or fail, in the performance of any of the agreements herein contained, the Contractor shall be at liberty, without prejudice, to any other right or remedy, on two days' written notice to the Sub-Contractor, either to provide any such . . . materials and to deduct the cost thereof from any payments then or thereafter due the Sub-Contractor, or to terminate the employment of the Sub-Contractor for the said work and to enter upon the premises . . . .."

There was no stated date in the contracts for performance by the defendant subcontractor. Article VI provided for completion by the subcontractor of its contract work "by and at the time or times hereafter stated to-wit:

---

[1]. The Travelers Indemnity Company, which posted performance bonds on two of the contracts, is a co-defendant in No. 11,422.

"Samples, Shop Drawings and Schedules are to be submitted in the quantities and manner required by the Specifications, for the approval of the Architects, immediately upon receipt by the Sub-Contractor of the contract drawings, or as may be directed by the Contractor. All expense involved in the submission and approval of these Samples, Shop Drawings and Schedules shall be borne by the Sub-Contractor.

"All labor, materials and equipment required under this contract are to be furnished at such times as may be directed by the Contractor, and in such a manner so as to at no time delay the final completion of the building.

"It being mutually understood and agreed that prompt delivery and installation of all materials required to be furnished under this contract is to be the essence of this Agreement."

Appellee Minweld Steel Co., Inc., the subcontractor, received contract drawings and specifications for both buildings in May, 1950. On June 8, 1950, plaintiff McCloskey & Co. wrote appellee asking when it might "expect delivery of the structural steel" for the buildings and "also the time estimated to complete erection." Minweld replied on June 13, 1950, submitting a schedule estimate of expecting to begin delivery of the steel by September 1, and to complete erection approximately November 15. On July 20, 1950 plaintiff wrote Minweld threatening to terminate the contracts unless the latter gave unqualified assurances that it had effected definite arrangements for the procurement, fabrication and delivery within thirty days of the required materials. On July 24, 1950 Minweld wrote McCloskey & Co. explaining its difficulty in obtaining the necessary steel. It asked McCloskey's assistance in procuring it and stated that "We are as anxious as you are that there be no delay in the final completion of the buildings or in the performance of our contract, ..." [2]

2. This letter in full is as follows:

Minweld Steel Company
Incorporated
Shaler and Wabash Streets
Pittsburgh 20, Pa.

July 24, 1950.

McClosky & Company
1620 Thompson Street
Philadelphia 21, Penna.

In re: New Hospital Buildings
Hollidaysburg State Hospital
Hollidaysburg, Pennsylvania

Attention of J. C. McCloskey,
Vice President

Dear Sir:

This will acknowledge receipt of your letter of July 20th, 1950, which was received by us today.

Upon receipt of the architect's specifications, we completed the engineering and erection plans on the said specifications. Immediately after those details were available, we attempted to place orders for the steel with the Bethlehem Steel Company. Our order was held in the offices of the Bethlehem Steel Company for two weeks before we were notified that it could not be supplied. Since that time, we have tried the U. S. Steel Corporation and Carnegie-Illinois, both companies informing us that they were under contract for approximately one year and could not fulfill the order.

The recent directive by the President of the United States, with which we assume you are familiar, has fur-

Plaintiff-appellant claims that by this last letter, read against the relevant facts, defendant gave notice of its positive intention not to perform its contracts and thereby violated same.[3] Some reference has already been made to the background of the July 24th letter. It concerned Minweld's trouble in securing the steel essential for performance of its contract. Minweld had tried unsuccessfully to purchase this from Bethlehem Steel, U. S. Steel and Carnegie-Illinois. It is true as appellant urges that Minweld knew and was concerned about the tightening up of the steel market.[4] And as is evident from the letter it, being a fabricator and not a producer, realized that without the help of the general contractor on this hospital project particularly by it enlisting the assistance of the General State Authority,[5] Minweld was in a bad way for the needed steel. However, the letter conveys no idea of contract repudiation by Minweld. That company admittedly was in a desperate situation. Perhaps if it had moved earlier to seek the steel its effort might have been successful. But that is mere speculation for there is no showing that the mentioned producers had they been solicited sooner would have been willing to provide the material.

Minweld from its written statement did, we think, realistically face the problem confronting it. As a result it asked its general contractor for the aid which the latter, by the nature of the construction, should have been willing to give. Despite the circumstances there is no indication in the letter that Minweld had definitely abandoned all hope of otherwise receiving the steel and so finishing its undertaking.

ther tightened up the steel market so that at the present writing we cannot give you any positive promise as to our ability to obtain the steel or delivery dates.

In view of the directive from Washington and the tightening up of the entire steel industry, we solicit your help and that of the General State Authority in aiding us to obtain the steel for these contracts.

We are as anxious as you are that there be no delay in the final completion of the buildings or in the performance of our contract, but we have nowhere else to turn at the present time for the supply of steel necessary under said contracts, unless through your aid and assistance, and that of the General State Authority, a supplier can be induced to give us the materials needed.

The U. S. Steel Corporation informs us that you have discussed this matter with them and are presently aware of our present difficulties.

If steel is to be supplied to these hospital buildings by governmental directive, we feel that the steel should be supplied to us for completion under our contract.

Very truly yours,

Minweld Steel Company, Inc.
J. A. Roberts
Sales Manager

JAR/fs

c/c Travelers Indemnity Co.,
Hartford, Conn.
General State Authority,
Harrisburg, Penna.

3. Plaintiff cancelled the contracts on July 26, 1950 on the ground that the July 24th letter constituted an admission of defendant's inability to perform the required work.

4. The Korean War broke out on June 24, 1950.

5. The Pennsylvania state agency which represented and owned the Hollidaysburg State Hospital.

One of the mentioned producers might have relented. Some other supplier might have turned up. It was McCloskey & Co. who eliminated whatever chance there was. That concern instead of aiding Minweld by urging its plea for the hospital construction materials to the State Authority which represented the Commonwealth of Pennsylvania took the position that the subcontractor had repudiated its agreement and then moved quickly to have the work completed. Shortly thereafter, and without the slightest trouble as far as appears, McCloskey & Co. procured the steel from Bethlehem [6] and brought in new subcontractors to do the work contemplated by the agreement with Minweld.

Under the applicable law Minweld's letter was not a breach of the agreement. The suit is in the federal court by reason of diversity of citizenship of the parties. Though there is no express statement to that effect the contracts between the parties would seem to have been executed in Pennsylvania with the law of that state applicable. In McClelland v. New Amsterdam Casualty Co., 1936, 322 Pa. 429, 433, 185 A. 198, 200, the Pennsylvania Supreme Court held in a case where the subcontractor had asked for assistance in obtaining credit, "In order to give rise to a renunciation amounting to a breach of contract, there must be an absolute and unequivocal refusal to perform or a distinct and positive statement of an inability to do so." Minweld's conduct is plainly not that of a contract breaker under that test. See also Dingley v. Oler, 1886, 117 U.S. 490, 6 S.Ct. 850, 29 L.Ed. 984. Restatement of Contracts, Comment (i) to Sec. 318 (1932) speaks clearly on the point saying:

"Though where affirmative action is promised mere failure to act, at the time when action has been promised, is a breach, failure to take preparatory action before the time when any performance is promised is not an anticipatory breach, even though such failure makes it impossible that performance shall take place, and though the promisor at the time of the failure intends not to perform his promise." See Williston on Contracts, Vol. 5, Sec. 1324 (1937), Corbin on Contracts, Vol. 4, Sec. 973 (1951).

Appellant contends that its letter of July 20, requiring assurances of arrangements which would enable appellee to complete delivery in thirty days, constituted a fixing of a date under Article VI of the contracts. The short answer to this is that the thirty day date, if fixed, was never repudiated. Appellee merely stated that it was unable to give assurances as to the preparatory arrangements. There is nothing in the contracts which authorized appellant to demand or receive such assurances.

---

6. Bethlehem had originally submitted a bid in competition with Minweld. Its new proposals were dated July 28, 950 and were finally accepted by McCloskey & Co. on August 7, 1950. The long span steel joists required by the third contract were procured from the Frederick Grundy Iron Works.

The district court acted properly in dismissing the actions as a matter of law on the ground that plaintiff had not made out a prima facie case.

The order of the district court of July 14, 1954 denying the plaintiff's motions for findings of facts, to vacate the judgments and for new trials will be affirmed.

NOTES

(1) *The Code.* The possibility cannot be ruled out that if this case were to recur it would be governed by Article 2 of the Code.[a] If it were, would McCloskey's letters of June 8 and July 20 be regarded as demands for assurance of due performance? (See p. 689 supra.) And would the responses be regarded as adequate?

(2) *Forcing the Issue.* A party who is delinquent in performance, or threatened with inability, can surely plead with the other for leniency without being guilty of a repudiation. If pressed, he may hope to skirt a repudiation with cautiously written letters, perhaps drafted with the aid of counsel. How may the other party force the issue? Would it be easier to do so in a face-to-face encounter than by correspondence? Which party is likely to call for a conference? See Plunkett v. Comstock, Cheney Co., 211 App.Div. 737, 208 N.Y.S. 93 (1st Dept. 1925).

(3) *Problem.* Refer to the facts in Stewart v. Newbury, p. 760 supra. Assuming that the plaintiff did not abandon the job, did he repudiate the contract at any time? By sending the bill on September 29? By writing the letter of October 5? Compare Menako v. Kassien, 265 Wis. 269, 61 N.W.2d 332 (1953).

(4) *What Language Constitutes a Repudiation?* There is a suggestion in the Viglas case, p. 720 supra, that a good faith disclaimer of a duty is not a repudiation. Is it satisfactory to require the party receiving a disclaimer to judge whether or not it was made in good faith? The prevailing opinion is that the test is an objective one. The passage referred to in Viglas has been questioned by Williston (§ 1325) and disapproved by Corbin (§ 973) on this ground. On looking at the case again, does it seem that the court would have decided it in the same way if the insurer had acted on some honest but wholly indefensible ground?

By an objective standard it is no better to say "I cannot perform the contract" than to say "I will not perform it." Is it any better to say, "I will try to perform, though I see no prospect of succeeding?"[b] How does that differ from what Minweld wrote to McCloskey, in the main case?

In J. K. Welding Co. v. W. J. Halloren Steel Erection Co., 178 F.Supp. 584 (D.R.I.1959), the court said that "the better rule gives the right of rescission to a party to a contract if the other party thereto manifests doubt as to his willingness or ability to perform his obligations substantially in accordance with the terms of such contract." (Massachusetts law) This proposition is evidently consistent with the main case, because the re-

---

a. See Entron, Inc. v. General Cablevision of Palatka, 435 F.2d 995 (5th Cir. 1970).

b. Compare Avery v. Bowden, 5 El. & Bl. 714, 119 Eng.Rep. 647 (Q.B.1855), aff'd, 6 El. & Bl. 953, 119 Eng.Rep. 1119 (Ex.Ch.)

lief claimed by McCloskey was *damages*, not rescission.[c] What would be an appropriate name for an expression that warrants rescission, but not a damage claim? Do you see any objection to recognizing such an intermediate category of expressions? Do you find evidence of such a category in the Code?

(5) *Election.* If the recipient of a letter of repudiation disregards it for a time, should he be regarded as making an election to proceed with the contract? See Note, 37 Colum.L.Rev. 610 (1937). The argument for election is most persuasive in the case of an inadvertent repudiation by a party who is content with his bargain and willing to perform it. Can you imagine such a repudiation? See Philadelphia Eagles, Inc. v. Armstrong, [1952] 1 D.L.R. 332 (Manitoba). Compare Campos v. Olson, 241 F.2d 661 (9th Cir. 1957), another sporting case.

SECTION 4. SALE OF GOODS

INTERNATIO–ROTTERDAM, INC. v. RIVER BRAND RICE MILLS, INC.

United States Court of Appeals, Second Circuit, 1958.
259 F.2d 137.
Certiorari denied 358 U.S. 946 (1959).

HINCKS, CIRCUIT JUDGE. Appeal from the United States District Court, Southern District of New York, Walsh, Judge, upon the dismissal of the complaint after plaintiff's case was in.

The defendant-appellee, a processor of rice, in July 1952 entered into an agreement with the plaintiff-appellant, an exporter, for the sale of 95,600 pockets of rice. The terms of the agreement, evidenced by a purchase memorandum, indicated that the price per pocket was to be "$8.25 F.A.S. Lake Charles and/or Houston, Texas"; that shipment was to be "December, 1952, with two weeks call from buyer"; and that payment was to be by "irrevocable letter of credit to be opened immediately payable against" dock receipts and other specified documents.[a] In the fall, the appellant, which had already com-

---

c. For an unusual attempt to "manufacture" a sizeable claim for damages by seizing on a supposed anticipatory repudiation, see Bowes v. Saks & Company, 397 F.2d 113 (7th Cir. 1968).

a. A letter of credit is a binding undertaking by a bank that is used in the following manner. Seller in Neartown and Buyer in Farville agree upon the sale of goods, but Seller is reluctant to rely upon the promise of a distant merchant. If Buyer should fail to pay after the shipment had reached Farville, Seller might sustain a substantial loss, even though he might still have the right to the goods. This would be particularly true if they were not readily resaleable or if the market price should drop so that their resale would bring little. Furthermore, suit against a buyer on his home ground is not an attractive possibility for a seller. These difficulties for a seller are of course committed itself to supplying this rice to a Japanese buyer, was unexpectedly confronted with United States export restrictions upon its December shipments and was attempting to get an export license from the government. December is a peak month in the rice and cotton seasons in Louisiana and Texas, and the appellee became concerned about shipping instructions under the contract, since congested conditions prevailed at both the mills and the docks. The appellee seasonably elected to deliver 50,000 pockets at Lake Charles and on December 10 it received from the appellant instructions for the Lake Charles shipments. Thereupon it promptly began shipments to Lake Charles which continued until December 23, the last car at Lake Charles being unloaded on December 31. December 17 was the last date in December which would allow appellee the two week period provided in the contract for delivery of the rice to the ports and ships designated. Prior thereto, the appellant had been having difficulty obtaining either a ship or a dock in this busy season in Houston. On December 17, the appellee had still received no shipping instructions for the 45,600 pockets destined for Houston. On the morning of the 18th, the appellee rescinded the contract for the Houston shipments, although continuing to make the Lake Charles deliveries. It is clear that one of the reasons for the prompt cancellation of the contract was the rise in market price of rice from $8.25 per pocket, the contract price, to $9.75. The appellant brought this suit for refusal to deliver the Houston quota.

The trial court, in a reasoned but unreported opinion which dealt with all phases of the case, held that New York would apply Texas law. Auten v. Auten, 308 N.Y. 155, 124 N.E.2d 99, 50 A.L.R.2d 246. We think this ruling right, but will not discuss the point because it is conceded that no different result would follow from the choice of Louisiana law.

The area of contest is also considerably reduced by the appellant's candid concession that the appellee's duty to ship, by virtue of the two-week notice provision, did not arise until two weeks after complete shipping instructions had been given by the appellant. Thus on

pounded in international trade, to which letters of credit are an indispensable adjunct.

Seller may, therefore, require Buyer to obtain a letter of credit from a Farville bank. The bank, by issuing its letter of credit at Buyer's request, undertakes with Seller that it will pay against Seller's orders in an amount equal to the purchase price, on condition that the orders, known as "drafts" or "bills of exchange," are accompanied by documents affording control over the goods. The documents specified are commonly bills of lading, issued by a carrier. Less commonly they may be documents of other sorts, such as the dock receipts in the present case, that also carry with them power over the goods. When Seller ships the goods, it forwards to the Farville bank its draft together with the specified document covering the goods. The bank then pays the draft and takes up the document. As soon as Buyer reimburses the bank, he may have the document and use it to obtain the goods from the carrier.

brief the appellant says: "[w]e concede (as we have done from the beginning) that on a fair interpretation of the contract appellant had a duty to instruct appellee by December 17, 1952 as to the place to which it desired appellee to ship—at both ports, and that, being late with its instructions in this respect, appellant could not have demanded delivery (at either port) until sometime after December 31, 1952." This position was taken, of course, with a view to the contract provision for shipment "December, 1952": a two-week period ending December 31 would begin to run on December 17. But although appellant concedes that the two weeks' notice to which appellee was entitled could not be shortened by the failure to give shipping instructions on or before December 17, it stoutly insists that upon receipt of shipping instructions subsequent to December 17 the appellee thereupon became obligated to deliver within two weeks thereafter. We do not agree.

It is plain that a giving of the notice by the appellant was a condition precedent to the appellee's duty to ship. Corbin on Contracts, Vol. 3, § 640. Id. § 724. Obviously, the appellee could not deliver free alongside ship, as the contract required, until the appellant identified its ship and its location. Jacksboro Stone Co. v. Fairbanks Co., 48 Tex.Civ.App. 639, 107 S.W. 567; Fortson Grocery Co. v. Pritchard Rice Milling Co., Tex.Civ.App., 220 S.W. 1116. Thus the giving of shipping instructions was what Professor Corbin would classify as a "promissory condition": the appellant promised to give the notice and the appellee's duty to ship was conditioned on the receipt of the notice. Op. cit. § 633, p. 523, § 634, footnote 38. The crucial question is whether that condition was performed. And that depends on whether the appellee's duty of shipment was conditioned on notice *on or before December 17*, so that the appellee would have two weeks wholly within December within which to perform, or whether, as we understand the appellant to contend, the appellant could perform the condition by giving the notice later in December, in which case the appellee would be under a duty to ship within two weeks thereafter. The answer depends upon the proper interpretation of the contract: if the contract properly interpreted made shipment *in December* of the essence then the failure to give the notice on or before December 17 was nonperformance by the appellant of a condition upon which the appellee's duty to ship in December depended.

In the setting of this case, we hold that the provision for December delivery went to the essence of the contract. In support of the plainly stated provision of the contract there was evidence that the appellee's mills and the facilities appurtenant thereto were working at full capacity in December when the rice market was at peak activity and that appellee had numerous other contracts in January as well as in December to fill. It is reasonable to infer that in July, when the contract was made, each party wanted the protection of the specified delivery period; the appellee so that it could schedule its production without undue congestion of its storage facilities and the appellant so that it could surely meet commitments which it in turn should make to its customers. There was also evidence that prices on the rice market were fluctuating. In view of this factor it is not reasonable to infer that when the contract was made in July for December delivery, the parties intended that the appellant should have an option exercisable subsequent to December 17 to postpone delivery until January. United Irr. Co. v. Carson Petroleum Co., Tex.Civ.App., 283 S.W. 692; Steiner v. United States, D.C., 36 F.Supp. 496. That in effect would have given the appellant an option to postpone its breach of the contract, if one should then be in prospect, to a time when, so far as could have been foreseen when the contract was made, the price of rice might be falling. A postponement in such circumstances would inure to the disadvantage of the appellee who was given no reciprocal option. Further indication that December delivery was of the essence is found in the letter of credit which was provided for in the contract and established by the appellant. Under this letter, the bank was authorized to pay appellee only for deliveries "during December, 1952." It thus appears that the appellant's interpretation of the contract, under which the appellee would be obligated, upon receipt of shipping instructions subsequent to December 17, to deliver in January, would deprive the appellee of the security for payment of the purchase price for which it had contracted.[b]

Since, as we hold, December delivery was of the essence, notice of shipping instructions *on or before December 17* was not merely a "duty" of the appellant—as it concedes: it was a condition precedent to the performance which might be required of the appellee. The nonoccurrence of that condition entitled the appellee to rescind or to treat its contractual obligations as discharged. Corbin on Contracts, §§ 640, 724 and 1252; Williston on Sales, §§ 452, 457; Restatement, Contracts, § 262; . . . On December 18th the appellant unequivocally exercised its right to rescind. Having done so, its obligations as to the Houston deliveries under the contract were at an end. And of course its obligations would not revive thereafter when the appellant finally succeeded in obtaining an export permit, a ship and a dock and then gave shipping instructions; when it expressed willingness to accept deliveries in January; or when it accomplished a "liberalization" of the outstanding letter of credit whereby payments might be made against simple forwarder's receipts instead of dock receipts.[1]

The appellant urges that by reason of substantial part performance on its part prior to December 17th, it may not be held to have

---

b. For critical comment on this passage, see Childres, Conditions in the Law of Contracts, 45 N.Y.U.L.Rev. 33, 56–57 (1970).

1. The appellee was not informed that the letter of credit had "liberalized" until after it had rescinded. Moreover, even the liberalized letter did not call for payment of deliveries not made until January.

been in default for its failure sooner to give shipping instructions. The contention has no basis on the facts. As to the Houston shipments the appellant's activities prior to December 17th were not in performance of its contract: they were merely preparatory to its expectation to perform at a later time. The mere establishment of the letter of credit was not an act of performance: it was merely an arrangement made by the appellant for future performance which as to the Houston deliveries because of appellant's failure to give shipping instructions were never made. From these preparatory activities the appellee had no benefit whatever.

The appellant also maintains that the contract was single and "indivisible" and that consequently appellee's continuing shipments to Lake Charles after December 17 constituted an election to reaffirm its total obligation under the contract. This position also, we hold untenable. Under the contract, the appellee concededly had an option to split the deliveries betwixt Lake Charles and Houston. The price had been fixed on a per pocket basis, and payment, under the letter of credit, was to be made upon the presentation of dock receipts which normally would be issued both at Lake Charles or Houston at different times. The fact that there was a world market for rice and that in December the market price substantially exceeded the contract price suggests that it would be more to the appellant's advantage to obtain the Lake Charles delivery than to obtain no delivery at all. The same considerations suggest that by continuing with the Lake Charles delivery the appellee did not deliberately intend to waive its right to cancel the Houston deliveries. Conclusions to the contrary would be so greatly against self-interest as to be completely unrealistic. The only reasonable inference from the totality of the facts is that the duties of the parties as to the Lake Charles shipment were not at all dependent on the Houston shipments. We conclude their duties as to shipments at each port were paired and reciprocal and that performance by the parties as to Lake Charles did not preclude the appellee's right of cancellation as to Houston. Cf. Corbin on Contracts §§ 688, 695; Simms-Wylie Co. v. City of Ranger, Tex.Civ.App., 224 S.W.2d 265.

Finally, we hold that the appellant's claims of estoppel and waiver have no basis in fact or in law.

Affirmed.

NOTE

The Uses of Divisibility. What was the significance in this decision of the finding of divisibility? Would the rice seller have been *justified* in withholding further shipments to Lake Charles after December 17th? If the seller had done so, how would you compare the merits of the buyer's claim with that presented in Gill v. Johnstown Lumber Company, p. 700 supra?

As the Gill case shows, the notion of divisibility of contract sometimes serves to mitigate the rigorous effects that might otherwise follow from the doctrine of constructive conditions. See also Rudman v. Cowles Communications, 30 N.Y.2d 1, 280 N.E.2d 867 (1972). Refer again to Shapiro Engineering Corporation v. Francis O. Day Co., Note 3, p. 502 supra. In that case the question was whether or not damages for a breach of contract must be calculated with reference to the whole performance called for. Corbin lists fourteen questions which have been answered by reference to the distinction between entirety and divisibility, concluding that they cannot be answered by "the application of some simple and uniform test." Section 695. See also Karpinski v. Ingrasci, p. 394 supra; United States v. Clementon Sewerage Authority, 365 F.2d 609 (3d Cir. 1966). As to a right to arbitration reinforced by divisibility, see Prima Paint Corp. v. Flood & Conklin Mfg. Co., 388 U.S. 395 (1967).

CONTINENTAL GRAIN CO. v. SIMPSON FEED CO., INC.

United States District Court, E. D. Arkansas, 1951.
102 F.Supp. 354.
Affirmed 199 F.2d 284 (8th Cir. 1952).

Action by the Continental Grain Company against the Simpson Feed Company, Inc., for breach of a contract for the sale of soybeans wherein defendant filed a cross complaint. On motion of plaintiff for a judgment in accordance with its motion for a directed verdict.

. . .

Judgment for plaintiff in accordance with the opinion.

LEMLEY, DISTRICT JUDGE. [The price of soybeans rose steadily from September 14, 1950, to November 30. On September 14 Continental contracted to buy 10,000 bushels (about 5 carloads) of soybeans from Simpson. Delivery was to be made at any time Simpson named during October or November. As the beans were loaded, Continental was to furnish shipping instructions.

One car was shipped on October 30. Another car was loaded the following day, and Simpson called for shipping instructions. Continental did not give them until November 2, about 48 hours later. (Its testimony indicates trouble getting "clearance" from New Orleans, where it intended to send the beans for export.) Meanwhile, Simpson was under pressure from the railroad to move the car or unload it, and had billed the car to another customer. When the instructions were received, Simpson informed Continental that no more beans would be shipped under the contract.

On December 1, Continental bought four carloads of beans from another supplier, and later brought an action for the difference between the contract price and what it paid. The case was tried to a jury, which was unable to agree on a verdict. Continental moved for a judgment in its favor. The court assumed that the delay in furnishing shipping instructions was a breach of contract, and proceeded to discuss the question of materiality.]

The question of the materiality of a breach of the contract under the sections of the Uniform Sales Act just cited [45(2) and 65] is ordinarily one of fact for the jury, but where the facts are undisputed with respect to the breach, the question becomes one of law for the Court. 46 Am.Jur., "Sales", Section 270; 3 Williston on Contracts, Section 866; Helgar Corporation v. Warner Features, Inc. [222 N.Y. 449, 119 N.E. 113] .   .   .

In determining whether or not a breach on the part of a buyer, with respect to one installment of a contract for the sale of goods to be delivered and paid for in installments, is so material as to justify the seller in refusing to perform further, numerous factors are to be considered. In the Helgar case, supra, the Court was concerned with whether or not a failure on the part of the buyer to pay for certain installments within the time fixed by the contract for such payments justified the seller in refusing to make further deliveries; and the Court said: "The vendor who fails to receive payment of an installment the very day that it is due may sue at once for the price. But it does not follow that he may be equally precipitate in his election to declare the contract at an end. (Citing cases.) That depends upon the question whether the default is so substantial and important as in truth and in fairness to defeat the essential purpose of the parties. Whatever the rule may once have been, this is the test that is now prescribed by statute. The failure to make punctual payment may be material or trivial according to the circumstances. We must know the cause of the default, the length of the delay, the needs of the vendor, and the expectations of the vendee. If the default is the result of accident or misfortune, if there is a reasonable assurance that it will be promptly repaired, and if immediate payment is not necessary to enable the vendor to proceed with performance, there may be one conclusion. If the breach is willful, if there is no just ground to look for prompt reparation, if the delay has been substantial, or if the needs of the vendor are urgent so that timely performance is imperiled, in these and in other circumstances, there may be another conclusion. Sometimes the conclusion will follow from all the circumstances as an inference of law to be drawn by the judge; sometimes, as an inference of fact to be drawn by the jury."

[The court referred to Restatement, § 275, and then concluded "as a matter of law" that the breach was insubstantial; that "neither party was in a particular hurry;" and that Simpson "simply seized upon what was at most an inconsequential breach" as an excuse for release from a disadvantageous contract.]

NOTES

(1) *Question.* What decision in each of the two foregoing cases under the Code? The following sections might be relevant, among others: UCC 2–311(3) (b), 2–319(2), (3), 2–612(3), 2–703(f).

(2) *How to Assert Rights Upon Breach by the Other Party.* There is some hazard for a party complaining of a breach in saying that he elects to rescind the contract. Do you see what it is? See Plunkett v. Comstock, Cheney Co., 211 App.Div. 737, 208 N.Y.S. 93 (1st Dept. 1925). Compare such an announcement with what was said by the injured sellers in the rice case and the bean case. For obvious reasons it is better to announce a *default* than to announce a *rescission.* But see UCC 2–720. The meaning of rescission is discussed in Corbin, §§ 1236–1237.

(3) *When Time is of the Essence.* Whether or not a delay of performance on one side will excuse performance on the other depends largely on the nature of the contract, and on the seriousness of the consequences of the delay. See Restatement, § 276. The matter is treated in Corbin, §§ 713–23; Williston, §§ 845–55; and see Stoljar, Untimely Performance in the Law of Contract, 71 Law Q.Rev. 527 (1955). "Courts of equity have treated stipulations as to time as subsidiary and of comparatively little importance, unless either the language of the parties or the nature of the case imperatively indicated that the date of performance was vital. In courts of common law, however, and especially in mercantile contracts, it is held that time is of the essence of the contract." Williston, § 845. The reference to equity has special application to land sale contracts, specific performance of which may be granted, to prevent injustice, in spite of "considerable delay" on the part of the plaintiff, either vendor or vendee, in tendering his own performance. Restatement, § 276(e). General statements that "time is of the essence," even in reference to mercantile contracts, and even when so provided in the agreement, need not be taken at face value. See Fairchild Stratos Corp. v. Lear Siegler, Inc., 337 F.2d 785 (4th Cir. 1964). "By the blind eye of the common law, it would seem, 'time' is read as a master word in the contract jungle, absolute and uncompromising in its significance and power. It can be asserted with confidence that never were the common law judges so blind as this. . . . [T]here is no absolute and universal rule." Corbin, § 713. There are statutes in some states providing that time is not of the essence unless the contract expressly makes it so. They have been denied application to option contracts. Williston, § 855.

HAYS MERCHANDISE, INC. v. DEWEY

Supreme Court of Washington, 1970.
78 Wash.2d 343, 474 P.2d 270.

FINLEY, ASSOCIATE JUSTICE. This is an appeal from a judgment for the sale price of a number of toys delivered by the Hays Merchandise, Inc., to the appellants Dewey.

Mr. Dewey operated Dewey's Fuller Paint Store in Bremerton, Washington. In the autumn of 1967, he decided to establish and stock a "Toyland" in his store for Christmas trade. Pursuant to this plan, he and his wife and children visited Hays Merchandise, a wholesale toy company, in Seattle. Mr. Woodring, an employee of Hays, met Mr. Dewey and his family at the company's display rooms, where they together selected toys. Almost all of the toys selected at that time were stuffed animals; Mr. Dewey was apparently particularly interested in having a good stock of stuffed or "plush" animals. Mr. Dewey and Mr. Woodring then discussed the purchase of other toy items which Mr. Woodring was to select. It was agreed that the estimated cost for all of the toys, including the stuffed animals, would be approximately $2,500.00 to $3,500.00.

Several shipments of toys were sent to Dewey's Fuller Paint Store during October and November. The number of stuffed animals included in these shipments fell well below the expectations of the Deweys. Indeed, although the question was disputed at trial, the trial court found that less than half of the stuffed animals anticipated by the Deweys were in fact delivered. The purchase price of the animals ordered was found to be a sum not exceeding $500.00. There is substantial evidence in the record to support this finding and it will not be disturbed on appeal.

Mr. Dewey repeatedly called Hays Merchandise, complaining that they were not receiving all of the stuffed animals ordered. He also complained personally to Mr. Woodring on the two occasions that autumn and winter when Mr. Woodring made periodic sales visits to the store. Mr. Dewey was assured each time that the items in question had been "back ordered," and would be forthcoming. Finally, shortly before December 1, Mr. Dewey called Mr. Woodring about the stuffed-animal order. Mr. Woodring gave approximately the same reply, at which point an exasperated Mr. Dewey said that they wanted no more toys.

Apparently this call was too late to stop another shipment of toys which arrived several days thereafter. Mr. Dewey was advised by Mr. Woodring that there would be no problem with this one late unopened shipment which should be sent back. Mr. Dewey kept this shipment, along with a number of other unopened and unmarked boxes of toys. Other toys were priced and put on display for sale.

Several months later, another Hays salesman, Mr. Osterholt, visited the Dewey's store. (Mr. Woodring had been away from work for some time because of illness.) According to the unchallenged finding of fact of the trial court, Mr. Dewey advised Mr. Osterholt that they had authority from Hays Merchandise to return a considerable quantity of unmarked toys, amounting to a value of almost $2,000.00. Mr. Dewey then shipped these toys to Seattle, whereupon Hays Merchandise refused the shipment, and it was returned to Mr. Dewey.

Hays had earlier billed Dewey for $3,598.11, the amount outstanding on the account. When no payment was forthcoming this action was commenced. After trial, judgment was rendered for $3,436.36. The difference in the two sums reflects a minor accounting error by Hays and the freight charges for the shipment of the toys back to Seattle and thence back again to Bremerton. In addition, the judgment provides for an additional $299.98 credit upon the return of the one shipment received after the cancellation. The Deweys appeal from that judgment.

All of the transactions involved took place after the effective date of the Uniform Commercial Code in Washington and, hence, are governed by the provisions of RCW 62A. The trial court held that the delivery of less than one half of the stuffed animals was not a "material breach" of the sales contract. Appellant Dewey contends that this finding is in error. His contention is based largely upon RCW 62A.2–608, which provides as follows:

> *Revocation of acceptance in whole or in part.* (1) The buyer may revoke his acceptance of a lot or commercial unit whose non-conformity substantially impairs its value to him if he has accepted it
>
> (a) on the reasonable assumption that its non-conformity would be cured and it has not been seasonably cured; or
>
> (b) without discovery of such non-conformity if his acceptance was reasonably induced either by the difficulty of discovery before acceptance or by the seller's assurances.
>
> (2) Revocation of acceptance must occur within a reasonable time after the buyer discovers or should have discovered the ground for it and before any substantial change in condition of the goods which is not caused by their own defects. It is not effective until the buyer notifies the seller of it.
>
> (3) A buyer who so revokes has the same rights and duties with regard to the goods involved as if he had rejected them.

There is no question but that Dewey accepted the toys in question. The issue before this court is whether there was an effective revocation of acceptance. This, in turn, is dependent upon (1) whether the nonconformity substantially impaired the value of the total order to Dewey, and (2) whether notice of the revocation took place within a reasonable time.

Appellant presents an ingenious argument on the first of the above questions. He argues that he would have been entitled to initially reject the toys if they failed "in any respect to conform to the contract . . . ." RCW 62A.2–601. He chose not to reject the toys, but rather reasonably assumed "that its non-conformity would be cured . . . ." RCW 62A.2–608. Since the nonconformity was not seasonably cured, he argues that he should be entitled to revoke acceptance on, generally, the same basis for which he could have rejected the toys. Consequently, he contends that the emphasis in RCW 62A.2–608 is properly upon "impairs its value *to him*" rather than upon "*substantially* impairs." In short, appellant would have this court adopt a largely subjective test; *i. e.*, Did the buyer *believe* that the value was substantially impaired?

The question is one of first impression in this court. Indeed, few, if any, appellate courts have considered this precise issue under UCC § 2–608.

Appellant's argument, based upon the need for a logical consistency between RCW 62A.2–608 and RCW 62A.2–601, is not persuasive. We are convicted [sic] that the emphasis is properly upon "substantially impairs . . . value" rather than upon ". . . impairs its value to him." This does not mean that "substantial impairment" is to be determined without reference to the objective needs and expectations of the buyer. *See* RCWA 62A.2–608, Official Comment 2. But it is an objective factual determination of the buyer's particular circumstances rather than some unarticulated desires.

The question of whether or not there is such a substantial impairment is a factual determination to be made by the trial court. This is in accord with the result of most of the few cases which have considered the interpretation of UCC § 2–608. *See, e. g.*, Campbell v. Pollack, 101 R.I. 223, 221 A.2d 615 (1966) (evidence warranted trial court finding that omission of key equipment in sale of car-wash was substantial impairment); Rozmus v. Thompson's Lincoln-Mercury Co., 209 Pa.Super. 120, 224 A.2d 782 (1966) (remanded for factual finding by trial court as to whether defect in car was substantial impairment); L. & N. Sales Co. v. Stuski, 188 Pa.Super. 117, 146 A.2d 154 (1958) (case remanded to allow jury determination of factual question of whether defect in beverage dispensers was substantial impairment). *But see* Lanners v. Whitney, 247 Or. 223, 428 P.2d 398 (1967) (Supreme Court made factual finding of substantial impairment after required de novo review of record in suit in equity).

There are some similarities between the contract in the instant case and a contract which could be clearly described as an installment contract. For example, the trial court found that multiple lot deliveries were contemplated by the parties; and, delivery was in fact made in multiple installments. It is of some passing interest in this connection, by analogy, that RCW 62A.2–612, governing procedures applicable in the event of breach of an installment contract, uses similar language. Under that section, when delivery in separate lots is authorized, to be separately accepted, a nonconforming lot may be rejected only "if the non-conformity *substantially impairs the value* of that installment . . . .." As noted by Wash.L.Rev., The Uniform Commercial Code in Washington 156 (1967), "This differs from the approach taken in non-installment contracts wherein the buyer may

reject 'for any reason.' " The phrase, "substantially impairs
. . . value," is also used in RCW 62A.2–616; it obviously is a
term chosen with care.

We are convinced that the question of "substantial impairment of
value to [the buyer]" is best determined as a factual question by the
trial court based upon all objective evidence properly before that
court. In the instant case, the trial court's finding that there was no
"material breach," while perhaps inartfully phrased, is in essence a
finding that there was no substantial impairment. Our general rule
is that findings of fact must be accepted as verities unless there is no
substantial evidence in the record to support them. Friedlander v.
Friedlander, 58 Wash.2d 288, 362 P.2d 352 (1961). Appellant has
not presented any considerations in the instant case which would lead
this court to depart from that rule.

There remains the question of whether the notice of revocation
was given within a reasonable time. Under the code, there is a distinction between notice of breach (RCW 62A.2–607(3)) and notice of
revocation of acceptance (RCW 62A.2–608(2)). There is no question
but that there was adequate and timely notice of breach. That, however, it is not the question before this court. The notice of revocation
of acceptance need not be in any particular form, but it must at least
inform the seller that the buyer does not want the goods and does not
desire to retain them. With the exception of the last small lot, there
is no indication that the Deweys gave this notice prior to mid-Febru-
ary, when they attempted to return the unmarked and unsold toys.
Indeed, the Deweys advertised the "Toyland" and attempted to sell
the toys during December. It was not until a considerable time after
Christmas that they attempted to return the toys. In view of the sea-
sonal nature of the toy business and the somewhat faddish demand
for certain toys, this delay in giving notice was unreasonable.

Even if the notice of revocation had been given in early December and if this were considered timely, the buyer's subsequent acts of
dominion over the goods are inconsistent with such claimed revocation. The buyer's acts of pricing, displaying, advertising and selling
were for his own account and were not in keeping with his duty to use
reasonable care in holding the goods at the seller's disposition for a
reasonable time. *See* RCW 62A.2–606(1)(c); Holland Furnace Co.
v. Korth, 43 Wash.2d 618, 262 P.2d 772, 41 A.L.R.2d 1166 (1953).

The judgment of the trial court is affirmed.

NOTES

(1) *Waiver?* Would Dewey have been permitted to show, in the defense of this action, or as a ground for damages, that the toys were not of
contract quality, not having mentioned that point before?

If a buyer *rejects* goods he will be well advised to use caution in stating the reason for doing so. If he states that the goods are not of mer-

chantable quality, for example, it may not be open to him to take the position in litigation that they were not properly packaged. In a famous and controversial case it was said: "The principle is plain, and needs no argument in support of it, that if a particular objection is taken to the performance and the party is silent as to all others, they are deemed to be waived." Littlejohn v. Shaw, 159 N.Y. 188, 53 N.E. 810 (1899); see Eno, Price Movement and Unstated Objections, 44 Yale L.J. 782 (1935).

Consult Restatement, § 304 and UCC 2–605; cf. UCC 2–508. What is an example of a case that would be decided one way under these rules and another under the "plain principle" of Littlejohn v. Shaw?

(2) *Timely Notice.* What, if anything, was to prevent Dewey from making a counterclaim for damages arising from Hays' failure to supply as many stuffed animals as the contract called for? See UCC 2–714. Dewey gave timely notice of breach, the court says.

Notice the drastic consequence of a failure to give such notice: UCC 2–607(3)(a). By contrast, in the event of a serious default by a *buyer*, there is little incentive under the Code for the seller to give any notice of his intentions. (See UCC 2–703, 2–706(3); cf. 2–609.) How might this difference be explained? Consider the position of a Seattle seller with respect to toys in Bremerton (or farther away) when a controversy arises shortly before Christmas.

(3) *Installment Contracts.* The court's reference to UCC 2–612 for an analogy may raise more questions than it answers. Why was not the toy sale contract an "installment contract" in the strict sense of that section? And what does it say about Dewey's right to reject? Do you agree with the following comment on the section?—"[It is] a law professor's delight . . . [It] guarantees at least two class hours of wandering through a maze of inconsistent statutory standards and elliptical cross references." Peters, Remedies for Breach of Contracts Relating to the Sale of Goods Under the UCC: A Roadmap for Article 2, 73 Yale L.J. 199, 227 (1963).

Professor Peters comments on the absence of "to him" in UCC 2–612, and she seems to hope that it will be read in. "It is to be hoped that the discrepancy in language between 2–612 and 2–608 is not intended to invoke for the installment contract that mythical character, the good faith objective observer, as the reference for injury, and, hence, the right to abandon." Id. at 225. As you understand the main case, does it read the words "to him" *out* of 2–608?

Regarding the toy sale contract as an "installment contract," does it seem that the deficiency of stuffed animals did not substantially impair the value of the whole contract, but would have permitted Dewey to demand an assurance of "cure" under UCC 2–612(2)? (See UCC 2–508.) On that situation Professor Peters makes these remarks: "But if 'assurances of cure' do not mature into a realization of cure, what then? After the expiration of a reasonable—or unreasonable—period of time, the buyer should be entitled to a belated revocation of his acceptance, as 2–608(1) indicates, which would eventually put him into the same position as to remedies as if he had initially been permitted to reject. In the interim, pending the actual tender of cure, the buyer may invoke the powers given him under 2–609 to suspend his own performance." Id. at 226–27. How can this be squared with UCC 2–608(2): "Revocation of acceptance must occur within a reasonable time after the buyer discovers . . . the ground for it . . . ."?

(4) *Problem.* Seller contracts to supply a quantity of stuffed animals for Buyer's Christmas trade, for $5,000. Ten days before Christmas Seller telephones Buyer to apologize for not shipping the goods earlier, and he adds, "I can ship them today if you still want them." Buyer answers: "Your delay has cost me $2,000. I am going to pay you $3,000 for the goods, and you had better ship them at once." If the buyer is right about his damages, must the seller comply with his demand? See UCC 2–717. If the Code supports the demand, does it open up the possibility of overreaching by buyers?

RELIANCE COOPERAGE CORP. v. TREAT

United States Court of Appeals, Eighth Circuit, 1952.
195 F.2d 977.

Action by Reliance Cooperage Corp. against A. R. Treat for damages for breach of executory contract for sale of goods. The United States District Court for the Western District of Arkansas, John E. Miller, J., entered judgment on verdict of $500 for plaintiff, and plaintiff appealed. . . .

Reversed, and case remanded with directions to grant new trial limited to issue of amount of damages.

SANBORN, CIRCUIT JUDGE. The question for decision is whether the measure of the general damages recoverable by a purchaser for the nonperformance by a seller of an executory contract for the sale of goods is changed or affected by an unaccepted anticipatory repudiation of the contract by the seller.

[Plaintiff, Reliance, on July 12, 1950, entered into a written contract with Treat, whereby Reliance agreed to buy and Treat to sell a quantity of staves "sufficient to aggregate 300,000 white oak bourbon staves of four and one-half average width, to be produced or purchased by seller in Arkansas, Missouri or Oklahoma; 90% of staves when shipped to be 'of bourbon grade' ". "Production shall commence as soon as possible and shall be completed not later than December 31, 1950." The price was $450 per thousand for bourbon grade staves of 4½ in. average width, and $40 per thousand for oil grade staves, same width; all to be delivered f. o. b. freight cars where produced. On August 12, 1950, Treat wrote Reliance a letter in which he stated in substance that he would be unable to produce and deliver staves at the contract price since the market price had risen to $475 or $500 per thousand (for the bourbon grade). (At the trial, however, Treat stated that the fair market value of bourbon staves was, during August, 1950, $400 to $450 per thousand.) At the end of August (or September, as Reliance's witness testified) Treat by telephone informed Reliance that no staves would be delivered at the contract price. On October 6, 1950, Reliance formally notified Treat that "we

[Reliance] are looking forward to your strict compliance with all of the obligations which you have undertaken in your agreement with us", and requested a reply from Treat. No reply was shown. The evidence as to the market price of (bourbon) staves on December 31, 1950, would have sustained a finding of not more than $750 per thousand. No staves were ever delivered by Treat. Reliance brought this action against Treat to recover damages.

At the trial the court refused plaintiff's request to instruct the jury that the plaintiff was entitled to recover the difference between the contract price and the market price on December 31, 1950. Instead the Court charged that if defendant proved that he repudiated the contract prior to December 31, 1950, and that plaintiff by a reasonable effort could have mitigated its damages by the purchase of staves on the open market, without undue risk and expense, at a price in excess of the contract price, then it was plaintiff's duty to do so and mitigate its damages so far as possible, and plaintiff would then be entitled to recover only the difference between the market price at that time and the contract price. The jury returned a verdict for plaintiff for $500. Plaintiff appealed. The Court here summarizes the trial court's instruction and states that the applicable law is that of Missouri. After discussing Missouri cases the Court continues:]

There is no doubt that a party to an executory contract such as that in suit may refuse to accede to an anticipatory repudiation of it and insist upon performance, and, if he does so, the contract remains in existence and is binding on both parties, and no actionable claim for damages arises until the time for performance expires. [Citations omitted.]

It is our opinion that, under the undisputed facts in this case, the unaccepted anticipatory renunciation by the defendant of his obligation to produce and deliver staves under the contract did not impair that obligation or affect his liability for damages for the nonperformance of the contract, and that the measure of those damages was no different than it would have been had no notice of renunciation been given by the defendant to the plaintiff. If there had been no anticipatory repudiation of the contract, the measure of damages for nonperformance by the seller would have been the difference between the contract price and the market price of the staves on the date when delivery was due, and that is the measure which should have been applied in assessing damages in this case.

Moreover, the measure of damages would have been the same had the plaintiff accepted the anticipatory repudiation as an actionable breach of the contract. The plaintiff would still have been entitled to recover what it had lost by reason of the defendant's failure to produce and deliver by December 31, 1950, the staves contracted for, namely, the difference between the market price and the contract price of the staves on that date. The Comment in Restatement of the Law of Contracts, § 338, Measure of Damages for Anticipatory

Breach, contains the following statement (page 549) : "The fact that an anticipatory repudiation is a breach of contract (see § 318) does not cause the repudiated promise to be treated as if it were a promise to render performance at the date of the repudiation. Repudiation does not accelerate the time fixed for performance; nor does it change the damages to be awarded as the equivalent of the promised performance." See, also, Williston on Contracts, Rev.Ed. Vol. 5, § 1397; 46 Am.Jur., Sales, § 688.

It seems safe to say that ordinarily no obligation to mitigate damages arises until there are damages to mitigate. No damages for the nonperformance of the contract in suit accrued before December 31, 1950. Until that time the defendant, notwithstanding his anticipatory repudiation of the contract, was obligated and was at liberty to produce and deliver the staves, and had he done so the plaintiff would have been required to take and to pay for them. There is no justification for ruling that, after the plaintiff was advised that the defendant did not intend to perform, it must hold itself in readiness to accept performance from him and at the same time, at its own risk and expense, buy the staves contracted for upon the open market in the hope of reducing the defendant's liability for damages in case he persisted in his refusal to fulfill his obligations. The plaintiff did nothing to enhance its damages and seeks no special damages.

This same question as to mitigation of damages by a purchaser who insisted upon performance of a contract after a seller's anticipatory repudiation, arose in Continental Grain Co. v. Simpson Feed Co., D.C.E.D.Ark., 102 F.Supp. 354 [reprinted in part, p. 830 infra.] In that case Judge Lemley, we think, correctly decided that the purchaser was not required to attempt to mitigate his damages by buying the commodity contracted for upon the open market. Judge Lemley said [after enunciating the rule just stated by the present court], page 363 of 102 F.Supp.:

"There are two reasons for this rule. First, to require the innocent party to make an immediate purchase or sale upon receipt of notice of the other's repudiation would encourage such repudiation on the part of the seller or of the buyer as the market rose or fell. See Fahey v. Updike Elevator Co., [102 Neb. 249, 166 N.W. 622]. Second, the immediate action of the innocent party might not have the effect of mitigating his damages, but might, on the other hand, enhance them. Williston On Contracts, Section 1397, Callan v. Andrews [48 F.2d 118, 120], and Missouri Furnace Co. v. Cochran, [8 F. 463] both supra."

The doctrine of anticipatory breach by repudiation is intended to aid a party injured as a result of the other party's refusal to perform his contractual obligations, by giving to the injured party an election to accept or to reject the refusal of performance without impairing his rights or increasing his burdens. Any effort to convert the doctrine into one for the benefit of the party who, without legal excuse, has renounced his agreement should be resisted.

The plaintiff is entitled to recover as damages the amount by which on December 31, 1950, the market price of the staves contracted for exceeded their contract price. What the market price of such staves was on that date is a question of fact which has not as yet been determined.

The judgment is reversed and the case is remanded with directions to grant a new trial limited to the issue of the amount of damages.

NOTES

(1) *Damages on Anticipatory Repudiation.* The rule stated by the court in the Reliance Cooperage case seems to have been generally accepted, partly on the argument that the repudiatee should not be called upon to take the risk of price fluctuations in order to save the repudiator money. See Restatement, § 338. But where the commodity involved is one for which there is an established market on which contract rights for future delivery are bought and sold, it has been held that the value of such rights at the time of repudiation is evidence upon which a jury may find the prospective difference between contract price and market price at the time fixed for delivery by the terms of the contract litigated. See Renner Co. v. McNeff Bros., 102 F.2d 664 (6th Cir. 1939), involving a contract for the sale and delivery of hops one, two and three years ahead.

(2) *The Code.* Section 2–713(1) alters the rule of this case—but how? For a discussion of how to determine "the time when the buyer learned of the breach," see Taylor, The Impact of Article 2 of the UCC on the Doctrine of Anticipatory Repudiation, 9 Bost.Coll.Ind. & Comm.L.Rev. 917, 928 ff. (1968). "If the buyer decides to wait a 'commercially reasonable time,' as section 2–610 allows him to, before determining that the seller has really breached, one wonders whether he learns of the breach when the seller repudiates or when he, the buyer, determines that the repudiation is a breach." Is there an implication in the latter section that repudiation is not a "breach," in the Code lexicon? If repudiation is regarded as a species of breach, what is the point of the rule stated in UCC 2–723(1)? For an attempt to reconcile these sections, see Note, 64 Yale L.J. 85, 103 (1954).

Would Reliance have been protected against a subsequent market drop if it had covered by contracting for replacement staves shortly after receiving Treat's letter of August 12? If Reliance covered by contracting with X for the delivery of staves on December 31 *at the market price then prevailing*, would that be consistent with the Code scheme? See UCC 2–712. What would you advise a buyer in the position of Reliance to do under the Code? See generally, Peters, Remedies For Breach of Contracts Relating to the Sale of Goods Under the UCC, 73 Yale L.J. 199, 263 (1963).

If Reliance, the buyer, rather than Treat, had been the one repudiating the contract (the market price of staves having fallen), would the December price of staves have controlled the measure of recovery? The Code seems to say that it would—at least in the usual case of an action coming to trial after the time for performance: section 2–708(1). What alternatives to a damage claim does a seller have? If he has goods in process of manufacture, would he be well advised to complete the process, in the face of a falling market? See UCC 2–704. Comment 2 after that section states: "The burden is on the buyer to show the commercially unreasonable nature of the seller's action in completing manufacture."

UNITED STATES v. SEACOAST GAS CO.

United States Court of Appeals, Fifth Circuit, 1953.
204 F.2d 709.
Certiorari denied 346 U.S. 866 (1953).

Suit against gas company and its surety on gas company's performance bond, for damages alleged to have resulted from an anticipatory breach of contract in nature of notice of intent to cancel contract as of November 15, 1947. The United States District Court for the Southern District of Georgia entered judgment in favor of gas company and surety, and plaintiff appealed. . . .

Judgment reversed, caused remanded with directions.

HUTCHESON, CHIEF JUDGE. Brought against Seacoast Gas Company and the surety on its performance bond, the suit was for damages alleged to have resulted from the anticipatory breach by the Gas Company of its contract with plaintiff to supply gas to a federal housing project during the period from April 15, 1947, to June 15, 1948. The claim was: that on October 7, 1947, while performance of the contract was in progress, Seacoast anticipatorily breached the contract by writing plaintiff unequivocally that, because of plaintiff's breach of the contract, Seacost intended to cancel same as of November 15, 1947; that the plaintiff immediately notified Seacoast that it did not recognize any right in it to cease performance and that it proposed to advertise for bids to insure a continued supply of gas if Seacoast's breach persisted; that, thereafter, having advertised for bids and on November 6th, having received the low bid from Trion Company, it on that date notified Seacoast by letter that unless it retracted its repudiation of the contract within three days from the letter date, Trion's bid would be accepted and Seacost and its surety would be held liable for breach of contract; and that thereafter Seacoast not having retracted within the time fixed, plaintiff on November 10, accepted Trion's bid and, pursuant thereto, began its preparations to execute with Trion a contract for a price in excess of that provided in the Seacost contract, and Seacoast is liable to plaintiff for this excess.

Defendant Seacoast, admitting in its pleading and its testimony that the facts were substantially as claimed by plaintiff, defended on the ground: that it had retracted its notice of repudiation and given assurance of its intention to continue to perform before the plaintiff had actually signed the new contract; and that, since, as it claimed, plaintiff had not then substantially changed its position or suffered any damages as a result of Seacoast's notice to terminate the contract and cease performance under it, the retraction was timely and healed the breach.

Upon the issue thus joined, the cause was tried to the court without a jury, and the court stating the question for decision thus, "The question in this case is as to whether Seacoast Gas Company, Inc. withdrew its notice of cancellation of its contract prior to the rendering of the contract to the Trion Gas Company," found that it had done so. On the basis of this finding and a further finding that on November 13, two days before the termination date which Seacoast had fixed in its notice, Zell, who was president both of Seacoast and of Trion Company, to whom the new contract was awarded, notified the regional counsel for the Public Housing Authority that Seacoast admitted it had no right to cancel the contract and was rescinding its notice, the court held that the anticipatory breach had been healed and plaintiff could not recover.

Appealing from this judgment, plaintiff is here insisting that under the settled law governing anticipatory breaches not only as it is laid down in Georgia but generally, Seacost's retraction came too late to heal the breach, and the judgment must be reversed.

Appellees, on their part, insist that the judgment appealed from was soundly based in law and in fact and must be affirmed.

We do not think so. The undisputed facts establish: that Zell, president of both companies, was present at the opening of the new bids on November 6, 1947, and upon being asked to withdraw Seacoast's notice that it would cease performing the contract, refused to do so; that on that date the Public Housing Administration regional counsel wrote Seacoast by registered mail, addressed "Attention Zell", advising of the steps the government had taken and stating that unless Seacost retracted its repudiation within three days from the date of the letter, Trion's bid would be accepted and Seacoast and its sureties would be held liable for breach of contract; and that having received no response from Seacoast within the three days specified, and Zell again asked on November 10th, to retract the notice of repudiation having refused to do so, the government accepted Trion's bid and proceeded with the execution of the contract. The record standing thus, under settled law [1] not only of Georgia but generally elsewhere,

---

1. Baker v. Corbin, 148 Ga. 267, 96 S. E. 428; Bu-Vi-Bar Petroleum Corp. v. Krow, 10 Cir., 40 F.2d 488, 69 A.L.R. 1295; Finch v. Sprague, 117 Wash. 650, 202 P. 257; Parker v. King, 68 Ga.App. 672, 23 S.E.2d 575; Roehm v. Horst, 178 U.S. 1, 20 S.Ct. 780, 44 L. Ed. 953; United Press Ass'n v. National Newspaper Ass'n, 10 Cir., 237 F. 547; 12 Am.Jur., "Contracts" Sec. 392; Ballantine, Anticipatory Breach and the Enforcement of Contractual Duties, 22 Mich.L.Rev. 329; 17 C.J.S., Contracts, § 472, p. 973; Vold, Withdrawal of Repudiation after Anticipatory Breach of Contract, 5 Tex.L.Rev. 9, 10; Williston on Contracts (Rev. Ed.1936) Sec. 1323, Vol. 5, pp. 3710–3711.

the breach was not healed, the judgment was wrong, and it must be reversed.

A comparison of the briefs and arguments of appellant and appellees will show that the case is in quite small compass. Both agree that Seacoast's letter of October 24th [sic] operated as an anticipatory breach and that unless effectively withdrawn during the *locus poenitentiae* it operated to put Seacoast in default and to render it liable for the loss to the government of the difference in price between the old and the new contract.

Appellees, after quoting from Anson on Contracts, 6th Ed., Sec. 385, p. 444:

"The repudiator has the power of retraction prior to any change of position by the other party, but not afterwards."

go on to say:

"So we see that the authorities seem to be unanimous that a person who gives notice of his intention not to perform a contract may withdraw such notice and offer to perform prior to the time the other party acted or relied thereon."

Based upon these premises, they insist that "the undisputed evidence is that appellant did not 'accept the bid of Trion Gas' until November 17th, which was after the notice of cancellation had been withdrawn in writing."

We think: that this statement is erroneous; that it represents the crucial difference between the parties; and that the error of the statement lies in the fact that it confuses the acceptance of the bid with the signing of the contract.

It is true that the contract was not signed until the 17th, after Seacoast had retracted its notice and if appellees were correct in its position that the date of the signing of the new contract was determinative of this case, they would be correct in their conclusion that the judgment should be affirmed.

But that position is not correct. In fact and in law, when the government took bids and notified Seacoast that unless it retracted within three days it would proceed to accept the Trion bid and award the contract to it, the *locus poenitentiae* ended with these three days. The fact that Seacoast claims that it did not receive the notice is completely immaterial both because it was not necessary for the government to give any notice or fix any time and because Zell, on November 10th, repeated to the Regional Counsel his refusal to retract.

All that is required to close the door to repentance is definite action indicating that the anticipatory breach has been accepted as final, and this requisite can be supplied either by the filing of a suit or a firm declaration, as here, that unless within a fixed time the breach is repudiated, it will be accepted.

Here, in addition to this firm declaration, the record shows the taking of bids and the awarding of the contract to the lowest bidder. The error of the district judge lies, we think, in holding that the *locus poenitentiae* was extended until the 17th, when the contract was signed, and that Seacost having repented before the signing of the contract, had healed the breach and restored the contract to its original vitality.

Whatever of doubt there may be, and we have none with respect to this view, as a matter of strict law, there can be none with respect to the justice or equity of this determination when it is considered; that Zell, the president and practically sole owner of Seacoast, was the organizer, the president and practically sole owner of Trion; that he organized Trion for the sole purpose of the bidding; and that on the date the bids were opened and later on the date the contract was awarded, he, though requested to do so, refused to withdraw Seacoast's repudiation and continued in that refusal until a day or two before the contract was signed.

The evidence showing, as it does, without contradiction, that the signing of the contract was not delayed because of a purpose on the part of the government to extend the time for Seacoast's repentance, but because until that date Trion had not furnished his bond, we think it clear that, in entering judgment for the defendants, the court erred. The judgment is, therefore, reversed and the cause is remanded with directions to enter judgment for plaintiff for the loss Seacoast's breach of contract has caused it.

NOTES

(1) *The Door to Repentance.* There was a substantial change of position by the Government, was there not, on November 10 when it accepted Trion's bid? The filing of a suit against Seacoast would have been such a change of position. The question remaining, then, is whether *without any such step* the Government's firm declaration "accepting" the repudiation would "close the door to repentance." Why should it? See Restatement, § 319.

Cases which assimilate a repudiation to an offer, in that each may be made irrevocable by acceptance, are not uncommon in this country. The other side of the coin is that a repudiation can be ignored by the innocent party: "I have never been able to understand what effect the repudiation of one party has unless the other party accepts the repudiation." (Lord Scrutton) "An unaccepted repudiation is a thing writ in water and of no value to anybody: it confers no legal rights of any sort or kind." (Lord Asquith)[a] Such expressions are not consistent with American law, however. See Note 1, p. 716 supra. They overstate the difference between an "actual breach" and a breach by anticipation. For various differences between an anticipatory repudiation and an offer to rescind, see Corbin, §§ 980–81.

---

a. These observations were quoted and commented on in White and Carter (Councils) Ltd. v. McGregor, [1962] A. C. 413 (H.L.), at 438 and 444.

American cases are somewhat more compatible with the view that a repudiation puts the injured party to an election of cancelling the contract or of keeping it alive, as Lord Cockburn indicated (see the Note referred to). However, the better view is that the injured party may urge that the repudiation be withdrawn—that repentance be made—without committing himself to further performance if it is not. (Note the October notice by plaintiff in Reliance Cooperage Corp. v. Treat, supra.) See Restatement, § 320. Is this consistent with the election imposed on a promisee by § 298? If a seller of goods repudiates his obligation, as in the Reliance Cooperage case, and then seeks to retract after a rise in market prices, should the buyer be privileged to disregard the retraction? Is the retraction some evidence that market price equals contract price? See Gold-Farb v. Campe Coop., 99 Misc. 475, 164 N.Y.S. 583 (City Ct. 1917).

What position does the Code take on these problems? See UCC 2–610(b), 2–611.

(2) *Problem.* An importer of Mexican shrimp was fearful that his supplier would not fulfill their long-term contract. The supplier, a Mexican firm, had repudiated its obligations, but retracted the repudiation on advice of counsel. The importer withheld accrued payments from the supplier as a safeguard against its further default, and sought to justify doing so by suggesting that its rights would not be honored in a Mexican court. The supplier terminated the contract and obtained a judgment for the payments withheld. Refrigeradora Del Noroeste, S. A. v. Appelbaum, 248 F.2d 858 (7th Cir. 1957), cert. denied, 356 U.S. 901 (1958). How might the importer have acted to assure himself of a supply of shrimp?

(3) *Summary.* "Repudiation and its effects [from Restatement Second, § 161, Comment a]. In some cases a repudiation by one party to a contract discharges the duty of the other party (see § 280); in some cases it requires the other to treat as total a breach which might otherwise be partial (see § 317), or it may itself be a total breach (see § 318). See Uniform Commercial Code § 2–610. For these purposes repudiation includes a positive statement by [a promisor] that he will not or cannot substantially perform his duties, or any voluntary affirmative action which renders substantial performance apparently impossible. In some circumstances a statement that he doubts whether he will substantially perform, or that he takes no responsibility for performance, or even a failure to give adequate assurance of performance may have a similar effect."

Reconsider the cases in this chapter with a view to finding support for each of these propositions. Where do you find indications that this pattern is not consistently followed?

SECTION 5.   SALE OF LAND

In actions for specific performance, and especially those based on land sale contracts, constructive conditions of exchange sometimes do not operate with the same effect as in ordinary damage actions. Furthermore, courts of equity have devised some distinctive methods of securing contract expectations in specific performance cases.   This is not to say that the conceptions of performance and breach are radically different in equity and at law, for it is a long-established principle that in determining whether or not a right to performance exists, "equity follows the law."

An example of the equitable standard for tender as a condition is found in McMillan v. Smith, 363 S.W.2d 437 (Tex.1962).   The plaintiffs had contracted to buy a ranch, and tendered what they regarded as the correct price, on a per-acre basis, to the defendants.   The defendants refused to convey, and the plaintiffs sought specific performance.   They deposited in court the amount they believed to be due, and declared that they were ready and able to pay "such further sum as the Court may order."   Ultimately it was decided that the sellers were entitled, upon giving a deed, to a large additional amount— some $28,000.   The court directed that the buyers be given 30 days to deposit the full price, upon which the sellers were to make a conveyance.   Failing full payment, judgment was to be entered for the sellers.   The court said: "Historically, in a suit for specific performance, the question as to the necessity for a tender of performance by a purchaser has been determined according to equitable rules rather than to those applicable to an action at law.   The latter requires the purchaser, as a condition precedent, to tender performance.   Courts of equity, on the other hand, have not been bound by strict and inflexible rules."

Another doctrine peculiar to equity is known as the requirement of "mutuality of remedy."   According to this doctrine, broadly stated, a plaintiff is not entitled to specific performance of his contract unless his own undertaking was such that, if the parties had been reversed, he could have been compelled to render specific performance. The requirement may be regarded as a means of securing the expectation of performance that the contract conferred on the defendant. However, it has often been observed that the requirement is unnecessary for that purpose in many instances, and the doctrine has been largely discredited, at least in the broad form stated above.[a]   Nevertheless, if a plaintiff seeking specific performance has not completed his own performance, the court may hesitate to compel performance

a.   Gould v. Stelter, 14 Ill.2d 376, 152 N.E.2d 869 (1958); but see Rego v. Decker, Alaska, 482 P.2d 834 (1971).

by the defendant and expose him to the risk of a later default by the plaintiff. According to the Restatement, § 373, the court may properly deny the remedy if the plaintiff's performance "is not well secured to the satisfaction of the court." In the comments to this and the following section various forms of decrees are suggested as means of reducing the defendant's risk, including specific performance decrees conditioned on the plaintiff's giving a mortgage or other collateral. "In every case the court will mold its decree in the exercise of sound judicial discretion."

Partly because specific performance is a flexible remedy, and partly because of its history, then, in an action for specific performance the court is not required to follow the analysis of the promises as dependent or not that a court of law might make. This observation is pertinent especially to land sale contracts because equity courts have made a specialty of enforcing them.[b] Nevertheless, as the following cases will show, such contracts are also governed, in part, by general conceptions of performance and breach, including that of constructive conditions.

NOTES

(1) *Buyer's Anticipatory Breach.* Buyer received a preliminary title report on a tract of land he had contracted for, and notified Seller that it was not satisfactory. Seller sought to cure the defects in his title, and called on Buyer with a deed. Buyer declared that he was not then interested in a deed or title: "All I want is an extension." Seller offered Buyer an extension of time to pay, for a price, and gave him time to think it over. Two days later Buyer made a further inquiry about the title. Having no response for two months, Buyer demanded that Seller repay $10,000 that he had deposited when the contract was executed. Seller refused the demand, and Buyer sued for repayment. From a judgment for Seller, Buyer appealed. *Held*: Reversed. Seller's argument centered on the effect of Buyer's statement, "All I want is an extension." The court concluded that if this was an anticipatory repudiation of the contract the buyer had withdrawn it.

The issue was complicated by a provision of the contract for forfeiture of the deposit if the buyer failed to comply with the requirements of the contract. The court said that Buyer would have been "estopped" to withdraw a repudiation if Seller had (a) changed position in reliance on it, or (b) instituted suit asserting a breach, prior to the withdrawal. Seller contended that such a suit was not required, inasmuch as its damages were stipulated to be the amount of the deposit. The court rejected this argument, saying: "It is, we think, the status created from a justiciable assertion being made of the right to claim anticipatory breach and immediate damages, and not the matter alone of resolving the amount of those dam-

---

b. Indeed, the making of such a contract is regarded in equity as a transfer of the beneficial ownership of the property, by a principle known as "equitable conversion." See Note 3, p. 740 supra. The significance of the principle cannot be appreciated fully apart from the context of a course on equity or on real estate transactions.

ages, on which the existence of the estoppel by law against an anticipatory repudiation being retracted depends." Quivirian Development Company v. Poteet, 268 F.2d 433 (8th Cir. 1959).

(2) *Covenants in Leases.* In a lease of real property the lessee usually enjoys the benefit of various covenants (promises) by the lessor, apart from the right of possession. For a material breach of such a covenant, one might expect, the lessee would be privileged to suspend the payment of rent. At least, that is what one would expect on approaching leases from the precinct of contract law. For several reasons, however, the doctrine of dependency of covenants has only qualified application to leases. One reason is the ancient conception of a lease as a grant of a property interest, rather than an exchange of undertakings. (Land sale contracts have a comparable aspect.)

By standard lease law, a tenant may not make needed repairs on the premises and offset the cost against the rent. However, some courts have recently modified this rule. It was held not to apply, for instance, in Garcia v. Freeland Realty, Inc., 63 Misc.2d 937, 314 N.Y.S.2d 215 (Civ.Ct. 1970), in which the tenant repaired flaking walls in a Harlem tenement. The court took judicial notice that the health of his young children was endangered by their eating paint and plaster flakes from the walls. It spoke of modifying landlord-tenant law, "established in the course of a rural society . . . so that it can deal adequately with the realities of modern urban living. Central to this approach is the application of guidelines drawn from the law of contracts to the rigid concept of a lease as strictly a conveyance of an interest in real estate." See also Javins v. First National Realty Corporation, 428 F.2d 1071 (D.C.Cir. 1970). As to the persistence of conveyance theory, however, see Rock County Savings & Trust Co. v. Yost's, Inc., 36 Wis.2d 360, 153 N.W.2d 594 (1967) (business premises).

The Supreme Court has had occasion to say that the states are constitutionally free to treat the undertakings of a tenant and of a landlord as independent rather than dependent covenants; the Constitution "has not federalized the substantive law of landlord-tenant relations." Lindsey v. Normet, 405 U.S. 56, 92 S.Ct. 862, 31 L.Ed.2d 36 (1972).

SITLINGTON v. FULTON

United States Court of Appeals, Tenth Circuit, 1960.
281 F.2d 552.

SAVAGE, DISTRICT JUDGE. . . . Sarah Sitlington and her husband, Thomas O. Sitlington, of Baxter, Kansas, were the joint owners of a farm situated in Grady County, Oklahoma. For some time prior to January, 1956, Jack Ledbetter had been in possession of this farm as a tenant operating a dairy business in partnership with Sarah Sitlington. On or about January 8, 1956, Mr. and Mrs. Sitlington entered into a written contract of sale of the farm to Robert and Ruby

May Fulton, husband and wife.[1] The agreed consideration was $81,000. The sum of $3,000 as earnest money was to be placed in escrow with the contract of sale and the deed.[a] An additional $17,000 was to be paid when the sale was closed, and the balance of the purchase price was to be financed by a note secured by a mortgage. The contract also provided:

"It is further agreed between the parties hereto that as soon as the title has been approved by the second party as acceptable this transaction shall be closed and the second parties shall be entitled to full and complete possession. . . ."

The title was approved on January 17, 1956. The purchaser went into partial possession of the farm on January 10, but the tenant retained possession of the improvements. The seller was unable to deliver complete possession because of the tenant's refusal to vacate the premises and the sale for that reason could not be promptly closed.

Despite the sellers' inability to close the sale, the purchaser continued in partial possession. He purchased 53 steers and placed them on the farm and 30 dairy cows which, because he did not have access to the barns, were put on leased land; he planted 33 acres of barley and arranged for the Soil Conservation Service to fill a canyon, build a pond and fell trees on the farm.

An escrow arrangement provided for in the contract was concluded on February 6, 1956. The sellers delivered to Owen Vaughn, attorney for purchaser, the contract of sale and a warranty deed properly executed. The purchasers delivered to Vaughn a check for $3,000 and a note for $61,000 with a mortgage covering the farm as security therefor. The dates on the note and mortgage were left blank with the understanding that the date of closing would be inserted. The escrow agent upon the closing of the transaction was to deliver the deed to the purchasers, the check, note and mortgage to sellers, and at the same time, purchasers were to make the additional down payment of $17,000.

The seller endeavored in good faith to perform the contract. Unable to settle her difficulties with the tenant, she brought appropriate legal proceedings to oust him. The purchaser was aware of the effort being made by the seller to remove the tenant in order that the sale could be consummated and told her, "to get Ledbetter out just as quickly as you can and I will go ahead and take over."

---

1. Sarah Sitlington will be referred to as the Seller; Sarah and Thomas O. Sitlington will be referred to either as Appellants or Sellers; Robert Fulton will be referred to as Purchaser and Robert and Ruby May Fulton will be referred to as Appellees or Purchasers.

a. "Escrow" has been defined as "the deposit of any written instrument, evidence of title, or thing of value in the hands of a third person, with an instruction to deliver it on the performance of stated conditions in the effectuation of a sale, transfer, leasing, or encumbering of property. In simple terms it may be defined as a title closing mechanism." Aran, Chapter 14 in "California Real Estate Sales Transactions" 506 (1967).

Finally on May 22, the tenant under compulsion of a court order vacated the premises. Promptly thereafter seller tendered full performance of the contract but purchaser insisted as a condition of closing the sale that he be paid $2,400 in damages occasioned by the delay. Upon sellers' refusal to accede to this demand, purchaser repudiated the contract. Sellers thereupon elected to treat the renunciation of the contract as a breach and in due course were restored to possession of the farm.

Some eight months thereafter and on February 25, 1957, the purchasers brought this action seeking specific performance and recovery of damages for breach of the contract. The sellers by counterclaim alleged that the contract had been breached by the purchasers and sought a judgment for damages resulting from such breach. The trial court denied specific performance of the contract but entered judgment for damages against the sellers for "failure to give up possession when agreed" in the sum of $7,675, itemized as follows: $2,500 for loss on steers, $3,750 for loss on dairy cattle, $1,300 soil conservation expense, and $125 barley planting expense.

The appellants complain of the judgment for damages and the denial of relief to them on their counterclaim. The appellees at the hearing on the motions for new trial abandoned their claim for specific performance.

The obligation of the sellers to close the sale and put the purchasers in full and complete possession of the property as soon as the title had been approved is clearly stated in the contract. It is undisputed that the title was approved on January 17, 1956. The sellers' inability to perform the contract by giving complete possession precluded the closing of the sale and constituted a breach of the contract. The purchasers thereupon had a choice of rights or remedies. They could either rescind the contract and bring an action to recover damages for its breach or they could require performance and retain a cause of action for damages suffered by the delay in performance.[2] The rights are inconsistent and the choice of one amounts to an election to surrender the other.[3]

In Oklahoma it is a statutory requirement that, if an injured party elects to rescind, he must do so promptly upon discovering facts which entitle him to do so, and he must restore to the other party everything of value which he received under the contract.[4] Any act by

2. 12 Am.Jur. § 390 at p. 968; Bu-Vi-Bar Petroleum Corporation v. Krow, 10 Cir., 40 F.2d 488, 69 A.L.R. 1295; Kentucky Natural Gas Corporation v. Indiana Gas & Chemical Corporation, 7 Cir., 129 F.2d 17, 143 A.L.R. 484, certiorari denied 317 U.S. 678, 63 S.Ct. 161, 87 L.Ed. 544.

3. Williston on Contracts, Vol. 3, § 683, at p. 1969; Bierce v. Hutchins, 205 U.S. 340, 346, 27 S.Ct. 524, 51 L.Ed. 828.

4. 15 O.S.A. § 235; Commercial Finance Company v. Patterson, 182 Okl. 411, 77 P.2d 133; Smith v. Reinauer, 178 Okl. 4, 61 P.2d 1039; Appliance Distributors v. Mercury Electric Corporation, 10 Cir., 202 F.2d 651.

the injured party indicating an intent to continue performance is deemed a conclusive election.[5] But by the election to continue performance he does not forego his right of action to recover damages caused by the breach.[6]

The purchasers did not promptly rescind the contract. They remained in partial possession of the farm and thus failed to restore something of value which they had received under the contract. The escrow arrangement stipulated for in the contract was completed after the breach and on February 6, 1956. The purchaser encouraged the seller to resort to legal proceedings for eviction of the tenant in order that the contract could be performed. These acts are all indicia of an election upon the part of the purchaser to continue performance of the contract.

The trial court was apparently of the view that the purchasers had the right to rescind the contract in May because of the breach of the contract by the sellers in January. But the purchasers were bound by their election to continue performance and thereby lost their right to stop performance. Conceding a meritorious claim for damages, the purchaser did not have a right to compel payment of any specified amount as a condition of closing the sale. The refusal to close the sale until the unwarranted condition imposed should be satisfied was a breach of the contract by the purchasers.[7]

Thus, it is our conclusion that the purchasers had a right of action for damages for the delay in performance of the contract by sellers, and the sellers had a cause of action for damages for breach of the contract by the purchasers.

We agree with appellants, however, that the trial court did not apply the proper measure of damages. The established measure of damages in Oklahoma for delay in delivering possession of real estate is the value of the use of the land during the time that possession was wrongfully withheld. Special damages could not be recovered unless in contemplation of the parties at the time the contract was executed. The sellers could not have foreseen that the purchaser would buy cattle or incur expenses in planting crops and making improvements on the farm before obtaining complete possession. Moreover the items of damage found by the trial court to have been sustained by the purchaser obviously resulted from his repudiation of the contract when the late performance was tendered by the sellers.

---

5. Kentucky Natural Gas Corporation v. Indiana Gas & Chemical Corporation, supra; 12 Am.Jur. § 390 at p. 968.

6. Williston on Contracts, Vol. 5, § 1334 at p. 3749; 12 Am.Jur. § 390 at p. 968.

7. Page on Contracts, Vol. 5, § 2904; Rest.Contracts, §§ 309, 310; Also see 12 Am.Jur. § 387 at p. 963 where it is said: "Accordingly, the refusal of one party to perform an executory contract unless the other party consents to a modification amounts to a total breach of the agreement. Similarly, refusal to accept title tendered in accordance with the terms of sale constitutes a breach by the purchaser of land of his contract to purchase. . . ."

At a new trial the damages suffered by the appellees should be ascertained in conformity with the views herein stated and damages should be awarded to the appellants on their counterclaim for breach of the contract by the appellees.

Reversed and remanded.[b]

NOTES

(1) *Remedies.* If Sitlington had chosen to demand specific performance, would it have been granted? Would she have been entitled to damages as well? Damages may be awarded in connection with a decree of specific performance, in an appropriate case. However, "the injured party should not be allowed to enforce and receive specific performance and at the same time get judgment for damages for a total breach. Specific performance actually rendered, even though under the compulsion of court decree, prevents the breach from being total." 5 Corbin, 913–14. See Karpinski v. Ingrasci, p. 394 supra.

If specific performance were granted on the facts of the main case, would it be consistent to award damages in addition to *Fulton*?

Was Fulton entitled to specific performance, if he had pressed his claim for that remedy? He was awarded damages, be it noted, although he had wrongfully refused a tender of full performance by the seller.

(2) *Question.* Note the court's view that Fulton "did not have the right to compel payment of any specified amount as a condition of closing the sale." Compare the problem in Note 4, p. 795 supra. Is there a liberty for buyers of goods, in this respect, that land purchasers do not have?

(3) *Election.* The election made by Fulton was a choice between two remedies for the seller's breach. Another kind of election is sometimes required between inconsistent *judicial* remedies, to be made when litigation is begun, or as it proceeds. Are there different reasons for these different sorts of election? If Fulton wished to call off the purchase unless it could be completed in the early spring, could he safely have urged the seller to start eviction proceedings against the tenant? What might he have said, if anything, to avoid making a conclusive election to continue performance?

For some various meanings of election see Restatement, §§ 309, 310; Corbin, §§ 755, 766, 1214.

---

b. On retrial the trial court found that the Fultons had suffered damages in the sum of $1500, the value of the use of the land during the time that they were wrongfully deprived of its possession. It found that the Sitlingtons had suffered damages in the sum of $2504, the amount they expended in removing Ledbetter and providing complete possession for the Fultons. It gave judgment against the Fultons for $1004. On a second appeal by the Sitlingtons the judgment was affirmed. Sitlington v. Fulton, 297 F.2d 458 (10th Cir. 1961).

MITCHELL v. EVANS

Supreme Court of Colorado, 1962.
150 Colo. 568, 375 P.2d 101.

DAY, CHIEF JUSTICE. Plaintiffs in error were sellers in a contract involving real estate. The defendant in error is the executrix of the estate of Evans who in his lifetime offered to purchase the property and who instituted the action to recover the down payment made by him.

We will refer to the parties as sellers and Evans.

Trial was to the court, resulting in a judgment in favor of Evans.

The case was submitted on stipulations. The facts as settled by the parties are that on June 5, 1959, sellers and Evans entered into a purchase contract concerning real property in Larimer County, Colorado. The total consideration to be paid was $23,000.00, payable $500.00 at the time of signing of the contract and $4,500.00 in cash on closing, the sellers to take back a mortgage for the balance. Possession was to be given on closing date, August 1, 1959.

The sellers agreed to convey by a warranty deed free and clear of all liens and encumbrances except 1959 taxes payable in 1960. They were to deliver an abstract of title showing the title to be clear as agreed, but the contract was silent as to procedures to be followed in the event title was found to be unmerchantable.

The contract provided for liquidated damages by way of forfeiture of payments, on ten days' notice, if Evans failed to perform his agreements.

Evans, on June 17, 1959, had made a $500.00 payment bringing the amount then paid to $1,000.00. On August 1, 1959, the closing was not consummated, and the stipulation does not give any reason therefor. On September 1, 1959, Evans made an additional $1,000.00 payment and later in September (the exact date not specified) the parties met in conference with their lawyers, at which time the sellers were told that upon examination of the title Evans' lawyer had rendered an opinion that the title was not merchantable. At least one defect, referred to by the parties as the "Krickbaum defect", was called to the sellers' attention. However, Evans was still interested in the property and wanted further time to raise additional funds. An agreement was reached to close the transaction on September 25, 1959.

A meeting was held on that date at which the "Krickbaum defect" was again discussed. No further payments were made and the closing was not consummated. There was *discussion* not formalized nor made part of the contract, relative to acceptance by Evans of an arrangement under which a portion of the purchase price would be withheld in order to insure quieting of the title by sellers.

Evans did not tender further payment so on October 7, 1959, the sellers served a notice on him which recited, inter alia:

> "Whereas, you have failed to make the payments provided for in said contract, you are hereby notified that unless your obligations under said contract are performed within ten (10) days from the date of service of this notice, the said contract shall be terminated, as provided therein, and all payments heretofore made under said contract will be retained by the sellers as liquidated damages."

In reply to the notice of termination, Evans, by letter dated October 12, 1959, made demand for return of the $2,000.00 which had been paid, and stated no further payments would be made because of unmarketable title, specifying the "Krickbaum defect" as ground for rescission.

The judgment complained of was entered in favor of Evans and held that the sellers were not in a position to declare a forfeiture and retain the money paid as liquidated damages because of the title defect. We hold it to be correct.

The sellers do not deny that title to the property is defective and no steps were taken to correct the defect before declaring forfeiture. Since sellers could not perform, there was no duty on Evans to complete a bad bargain.

On behalf of the sellers it is contended: (1) The sellers have a reasonable time to correct any alleged deficiencies in title; (2) Since Evans was in default in failing to make his payments he could not rescind; and (3) Evans waived the right to rescind by indicating his continued interest in the property in spite of the title defect.

As a general proposition, when a contract contemplates examination of the title and report to the vendor of defects therein, where no fixed time is specified for the remedying of such defects, the vendor has a reasonable time to remove such defects. However, he may be estopped from asserting this right, where his conduct amounts to an election to stand upon the title as tendered. Fruhling v. Ellis, 143 Colo. 162, 352 P.2d 656. In this case the sellers by giving notice of forfeiture and termination to the vendee, elected to stand on the title as tendered.

At the time of the rescission Evans was not in default because no performance was required by him until the deal was closed, and this could not take place until merchantable title was tendered by the sellers. White v. Evans, 120 Colo. 200, 208 P.2d 922. It was not necessary for Evans to tender the balance of the payment before declaring rescission. Heaton v. Nelson, 69 Colo. 320, 194 P. 614.

Evans did not waive his right of rescission. Having discovered the existence of the "Krickbaum defect" he had a right to insist upon its removal from the title or to accept the title conditioned upon its later removal. But he had no chance to make such election. The sellers having served notice of forfeiture and termination, effectively prevented Evans from exercising his election and forced the rescission.

The judgment is affirmed.

NOTES

(1) *Questions.* What would the result have been if the court had ruled that Evans had a choice of rights when he discovered the Krickbaum defect —either to rescind the contract or to require performance and claim damages—and that he could rescind only by doing so promptly? (That view appears in Sitlington v. Fulton, supra, and many other cases.) On that view, was it not too late to rescind on October 7? If it was, the sellers' letter of that date may be regarded as a lucky chance for Evans, giving him another opportunity to rescind. Was there any way, other than rescission, for Evans to recapture his $2,000? Was there any way for him to put the sellers in default without tendering another $3,000? Does it appear that Evans had ready access to such a sum? Would it have paid the sellers to lay out any substantial amount to cure the title defect before giving Evans a ten-day deadline? Could either of the parties have made good use of a right to demand assurance of due performance from the other? If that device is wanted in a land-sale transaction, apparently it must be built into the contract.[a] How would you draft a provision for that purpose?

(2) *The Case of A and B.* Andrews contracted to sell a farm to Blinzler, to be paid for in annual installments. About four years afterward Andrews gave notice of default to Blinzler. The contract provided that on 60 days' notice after default Andrews could resume possession and retain all moneys previously paid by Blinzler, as rent and liquidated damages. Blinzler declared his intent to rescind some 2½ months after receiving the notice. He then sued for rescission. He had failed to pay an installment of the purchase price about a month before the notice of intent to cancel was given, but Andrews had failed to furnish title insurance as he had agreed to do, within a reasonable time after contracting.[b] The title policy was supplied before Blinzler sued. The trial court decreed rescission, concluding that Andrews was guilty of a material breach, and Andrews appealed. *Held:* Reversed (3–2). The court observed that Blinzler had had possession of the farm, tilling it, for four years, and had not requested the title insurance after the initial two years, and that Andrews had taken some steps to clear the title during the life of the contract. "Where a party treats a contract as valid after facts appear which would establish the right to rescind and misleads the other party, the right to rescission is waived. This principle is more clearly established where the party retains dominion over the subject matter of the contract and accepts

a. But see Restatement, § 284.

b. A "title policy" is a contract of insurance, usually paid for by the buyer, insuring him against certain claims of right that may be asserted against

the property, including mortgages, easements, and the like. Outstanding interests that the insurer's search of the record discloses are stated as exceptions or "conditions" in the policy, unless the seller clears them up.

benefits therefrom." Blinzler v. Andrews, 94 Idaho 215, 485 P.2d 957 (1971).

How is this case to be distinguished from Mitchell v. Evans?

(3) *Status Quo Ante.* In the foregoing note case the court said: "One other point ought to be mentioned here, although the issue has been rendered moot by this decision. Rescission exists as an alternate remedy to damages for breach of contract. Williston, Contracts, Rev.Ed., Vol. 5, § 1455. Since these are alternative remedies, both cannot be granted for the same breach. In this case, the district judge granted rescission to the Blinzlers and contract price minus market value as of April, 1964 or benefit of the bargain as a set-off to the Andrews. Since this was a rescission case where the objective is to treat the contract as never having existed and to return the parties to the status quo before the contract was formed, it is improper to grant a measure of damages to any of the parties based on breach of the contract." Is this dictum consistent with Sitlington v. Fulton?

MOUNTAIN VIEW CORP. v. HORNE

New Mexico Supreme Court, 1964.
74 N.M. 541, 395 P.2d 676.

NOBLE, JUSTICE. Defendants have appealed from a judgment requiring specific performance of a real estate contract.

Seller (plaintiff) represented itself to be the fee simple owner of the land, free of defects, liens and encumbrances. It agreed to convey when a specified portion of the purchase price had been paid. At the time of execution of the written contract of sale and purchase, the property was subject to a mortgage and to certain restrictions and easements. The first title policy furnished the escrow agent was subject to those conditions. Purchasers (defendants) defaulted in payment of the first installment required by the contract, and seller brought action for specific performance and was awarded judgment for two installments then due with a provision in the decree for further application to the court if they were not paid within thirty days. The title defects were cleared after commencement of the action, but before judgment, and a title policy free of exceptions was filed with the escrow agent.

We find no merit to defendants' argument that seller's failure to have a clear title at the time of execution of the contract entitled defendants to rescission, nor do we agree that the statement of clear title in the contract amounted to fraud or misrepresentation.

We are clear that the contract in this instance was an executory one for conveyance of the real estate. Seller's assertion therein of ownership free of defects is not necessarily a misrepresentation even though there were defects at the time. The general rule, and the established law in New Mexico, is that failure of a vendor to have the clear title he agrees to convey does not justify rescission or repudiation by a vendee if vendor can perform by delivery of the agreed title at the time required by the contract for such performance. Montgomery v. First Mortgage Co., 38 N.M. 148, 29 P.2d 331; Clark v. Ingle, 58 N.M. 136, 266 P.2d 672. Accordingly, if the seller is able to deliver the title agreed upon when the contract requires conveyance, he may ordinarily compel specific performance by the purchaser. See 22 A.L.R.2d 508, 560.

This contract requires the seller to convey when a certain amount of the purchase price has been paid. No showing has been made either of such payment or of a tender thereof, and seller corrected the defects and was able to convey the title agreed upon before the time required by the contract for vendor's performance. Purchasers have failed to show themselves in a position to rescind or repudiate the contract.

Error claimed as a result of the court's denial of a jury trial is likewise without merit. The action here is clearly one in equity for specific performance, and the parties were not entitled to a jury for the trial thereof. The issue of indebtedness was not one cognizable only in a court of law, but was an issue in the equitable action under equity practice. . . .

It follows that the judgment appealed from should be affirmed.

It is so ordered.

NOTES

(1) *Title Defects.* Is it the rule that a contract for the sale of land does not impose on the seller an obligation that the buyer's expectation of receiving due performance will not be impaired? Or is it enough to meet the buyer's fair expectation that the seller clear his title by the time set for a conveyance? Before that time, a buyer might naturally sense a risk in making payments on the purchase price. How might the contract be drawn so as to require that title be perfected earlier? If a lawyer or title company performs an examination of the seller's title at the inception of the contract, will it have to be done over again at the time of closing? The mechanics of a title search, and the buyer's right to make a record of his contract, must be examined in a course on real estate transactions; but it may be noted here that a title search entails substantial expense.

What function was served by the seller's representation, at the time he contracted, that he then had an unencumbered title to the land? Does it appear that the purchasers failed to pay because of the defects in the seller's title? That they knew or had reason to know of the defects when they contracted? For the possible importance of these questions, see Restatement, § 283.

(2) *Buyer's Remedies.* If the contract required the seller to convey at the time the buyer made the third installment payment, but he had been unable to show a merchantable title at that time, what would the buyer's remedies be? A possibility recognized in many equity cases is specific performance, with an abatement of the purchase price. If the buyer prefers instead to withdraw from the agreement, how should he proceed? In Cohen

v. Kranz, 12 N.Y.2d 242, 189 N.E.2d 473 (1963), the court said: "While a vendee can recover his money paid on the contract from a vendor who defaults on law day without a showing of tender or even of willingness and ability to perform where the vendor's title is incurably defective, a tender and demand are required to put the vendor in default where his title could be cleared without difficulty in a reasonable time. Further, the vendor in such a case is entitled to a reasonable time beyond law day to make his title good."

If a timely conveyance is important to the buyer, and he learns in advance of imperfections in the seller's title, how would you advise him to act?

(3) *Dependency in Installment Sale Contracts.* In Kane v. Hood, 13 Pick. (30 Mass.) 281 (1832), the question was said to be "whether, in a contract between parties relative to the same subject matter, some stipulations may be mutual and independent, and others dependent and mutually conditional." And it was held that they may. The contract was one for the sale of land, to be paid for in three installments, "the deed to be executed at the completing of the last payment." The buyer paid the first two installments. The court said, in dictum, that if he had not the seller might have recovered them without tender of performance or averment of readiness. But the suit was for the third installment. The seller alleged that he had always been ready to convey the land, and offered in court to do so upon payment. Yet he was nonsuited, for failure to allege or prove any tender of the deed. The promise of the final installment was dependent on the seller's promise to convey.

If no payment had been made, and the seller waited to sue until all were due, would the court's dictum still hold good? Or would a tender have been required for *any* recovery? This problem has aroused differences of opinion. See Beecher v. Conradt, 13 N.Y. 108 (1855); Restatement, § 273.

(4) *Problem.* Developer lays out housing lots and a grid of streets on a tract of suburban land he owns, and grades the streets. He contracts to sell a lot to Buyer for $1,000, to be paid in monthly installments over five years. The contract requires Developer to "cinderize" the street in front of the lot, and to give Buyer a deed when his payments are complete. At the end of five years nothing has been done to the streets in the subdivision, and Buyer has paid only half the price. Developer sues Buyer for the balance, tendering a deed, and shows that the stretch of street in front of the lot could be cinderized for less than $50. What result? See Palmer v. Fox, 274 Mich. 252, 264 N.W. 361, 104 A.L.R. 1057 (1936).

Chapter 8

IMPOSSIBILITY OF PERFORMANCE AND FRUSTRATION OF PURPOSE

In a case presented earlier, it was said that hardship, hindrance, and difficulty do not excuse a man from doing what he has agreed to do by a "positive, express contract." That case is Stees v. Leonard, p. 747 supra, in which damages were assessed against a builder for failure to put up a structure on what appeared to be quicksand. Of course there are many contractual undertakings that are not absolute in this sense. A lawyer's duty to his client, for example, is to use a measure of skill, prudence, and diligence in the affair entrusted to him; see Lucas v. Hamm, p. 908 infra. Even in Stees v. Leonard the court acknowledged that eventualities beyond the control of the parties will sometimes excuse the performance of a positive contract. We are now to explore the limits of "absolute" undertakings.

In this chapter, great historical events make their appearance. There is war in the Middle East, leading to closing of the Suez. There is the illness of a king. There is the imposition of wartime rationing. And we begin with Prince Rupert's invasion of England, in the reign of Charles I. But there is also local and private distress: the death of a seaman, the burning of a theater, a crop failure. The aspect of these events that concerns us here is that each of them caused a dislocation of some agreement, and so occasioned a request for relief from an obligation that would otherwise be enforced. Hardship arising from an unexpected event, or at least a plea of hardship, is a common element in the cases that follow. They have some similarities to cases in Chapter 3, Policing the Bargain. Yet the emphasis in that chapter is on harsh and unsavory effects of contracts that are *intended*, by one of the parties at least; whereas in this one the emphasis is on unexpected effects. Of course there are several reasons for refusing to enforce an agreement as it was expressed when an extraneous event has upset a fundamental assumption on which it rested. One is simply to relieve a party from a loss that seems unjust. Another is to prevent an unmerited gain for the other party. More broadly, the object may be to mitigate the disruptive effects of an abrupt change of conditions, when, from the standpoint of the contracting parties, the change is relatively uncontrollable.

The other side of the coin is that agreements must be enforced —*pacta sunt servanda*. For this principle, also, several reasons may be given. Two of them appear in a well-known judgment of the Kings Bench, in 1647: Paradine v. Jane.[a] The plaintiff sued on a lease, for three years' back rent on a place of business. The defendant's plea was that he had been dispossessed by a hostile army under Rupert— "a German prince, an alien born, enemy to the King and kingdom"— and that during his ouster he could not take income from the premises. The court's conclusion was that he ought to pay his rent; the plea was bad. For one reason, the court said that, though the defendant was unable to prevent his eviction, "he might have provided against it in his contract." For another reason, the court added that "as the lessee is to have the advantage of casual profits, so he must run the hazard of casual losses." Evidently the court contemplated that some fortuitous event ("casualty") might have occurred during the term of the lease that would have increased markedly the value of the premises to the defendant. Nothing of that sort would have permitted the lessor to relet the premises, or to charge a higher rent. Hence—to draw out the court's reasoning—the contract imposed matching burdens on the parties. Both of these reasons are echoed in later cases and continue to be effective as argument, on occasion.

Paradine v. Jane has regularly been taken to mean that contract duties are "absolute," in the sense that no excuse based on change of conditions will be recognized.[b] If that was ever the rule, it has long been subject to some important qualifications. The scope and grounds of those qualifications are the subject of this chapter.

TAYLOR v. CALDWELL

King's Bench, 1863.
3 B. & S. 826, 122 Eng.Rep. 309.

[Action for breach of a written agreement by which defendants contracted to "let" the Surrey Gardens and Music Hall, at Newington, Surrey, to plaintiffs, for four days, for the purpose of giving four "grand concerts" and "day and night fetes" in the hall; plaintiffs agreeing to pay £100 at the close of each day. The defendants agreed to furnish a band and certain other amusements in connection with plaintiffs' entertainments, but the plaintiffs were to have all moneys paid for entrance to the music hall and gardens. The plaintiffs alleged the defendants' breach, "Whereby the plaintiffs lost divers moneys paid by them for printing advertisements of and in advertising the concerts, and also lost divers sums expended and expenses incurred by them in preparing for the concerts and otherwise in relation thereto, and on the faith of the performance by the defendants

---

a. Aleyn 26, 82 Eng.Rep. 897 (K.B. 1647).

b. Whether the case could have been understood that way when it was decided, or ever, is questionable; but as with many an early text its importance resides chiefly in its interpretations.

of the agreement on their part". The defendants pleaded that the Gardens and Music Hall were accidentally destroyed by fire on June 11, 1861, without the default of the defendants or either of them. A verdict was returned for the plaintiffs, with leave reserved to enter a verdict for defendants. Further facts are stated in the opinion.]

The judgment of the Court was now delivered by

BLACKBURN, J. In this case the plaintiffs and defendants had, on the 27th May, 1861, entered into a contract by which the defendants agreed to let the plaintiffs have the use of The Surrey Gardens and Music Hall on four days then to come, viz., the 17th June, 15th July, 5th August and 19th August, for the purpose of giving a series of four grand concerts, and day and night fetes at the Gardens and Hall on those days respectively; and the plaintiffs agreed to take the Gardens and Hall on those days, and pay £100 for each day.

[The court interprets the agreement not to be a lease, and concludes that the entertainments provided for in the agreement could not be given without the existence of the Music Hall.]

After the making of the agreement, and before the first day on which a concert was to be given, the Hall was destroyed by fire. This destruction, we must take it on the evidence, was without the fault of either party, and was so complete that in consequence the concerts could not be given as intended. And the question we have to decide is whether, under these circumstances, the loss which the plaintiffs have sustained is to fall upon the defendants. The parties when framing their agreement evidently had not present to their minds the possibility of such a disaster, and have made no express stipulation with reference to it, so that the answer to the question must depend upon the general rules of law applicable to such a contract.

There seems no doubt that where there is a positive contract to do a thing, not in itself unlawful, the contractor must perform it or pay damages for not doing it, although in consequence of unforeseen accidents, the performance of his contract has become unexpectedly burthensome or even impossible. The law is so laid down in 1 Roll. Abr. 450, Condition (G), and in the note (2) to Walton v. Waterhouse, 2 Wms.Saund. 421a. 6th Ed., and is recognised as the general rule by all the Judges in the much discussed case of Hall v. Wright (E. B. & E. 746). But this rule is only applicable when the contract is positive and absolute, and not subject to any condition either express or implied: and there are authorities which, as we think, establish the principle that where, from the nature of the contract, it appears that the parties must from the beginning have known that it could not be fulfilled unless when the time for the fulfillment of the contract arrived some particular specified thing continued to exist, so that, when entering into the contract, they must have contemplated such continuing existence as the foundation of what was to be done; there, in the absence of any express or implied warranty that the thing shall exist, the contract is not to be construed as a positive contract, but as subject to an implied condition that the parties shall be excused in case, before breach, performance becomes impossible from the perishing of the thing without default of the contractor.

There seems little doubt that this implication tends to further the great object of making the legal construction such as to fulfil the intention of those who entered into the contract. For in the course of affairs men in making such contracts in general would if it were brought to their minds, say that there should be such a condition.

Accordingly, in the Civil law, such an exception is implied in every obligation of the class which they call obligatio de certo corpore. The rule is laid down in the Digest, lib. XLV, tit. 1, de verborum obligationibus, 1.33. "Si Stichus certo die dari promissus, ante diem moriatur: non tenetur promissor." The principle is more fully developed in 1.23. "Si ex legati causa, aut ex stipulatu hominem certum mihi debeas: non aliter post mortem ejus tenearis mihi, quam si per te steterit, quominus vivo eo eum mihi dares: quod ita fit, si aut interpellatus non dedisti, aut occidisti eum." The examples are of contracts respecting a slave, which was the common illustration of a certain subject used by the Roman lawyers, just as we are apt to take a horse; and no doubt the propriety, one might almost say necessity, of the implied condition is more obvious when the contract relates to a living animal, whether man or brute, than when it relates to some inanimate thing (such as in the present case a theatre) the existence of which is not so obviously precarious as that of the live animal, but the principle is adopted in the Civil law as applicable to every obligation of which the subject is a certain thing. The general subject is treated of by Pothier, who in his Traite des Obligations, partie 3, chap. 6, art. 3, sec. 668, states the result to be that the debtor corporis certi is freed from his obligation when the thing has perished, neither by his act, nor his neglect, and before he is in default, unless by some stipulation he has taken on himself the risk of the particular misfortune which has occurred.[a]

Although the Civil law is not of itself authority in an English Court, it affords great assistance in investigating the principles on which the law is grounded. And it seems to us that the common law authorities establish that in such a contract the same condition of the continued existence of the thing is implied by English law.

There is a class of contracts in which a person binds himself to do something which requires to be performed by him in person; and such promises, e. g. promises to marry, or promises to serve for a certain time, are never in practice qualified by an express exception of the death of the party; and therefore in such cases the contract is in

a. For a criticism of the Roman law authorities relied upon by Blackburn, J., see Buckland, *Casus* and Frustration in Roman and Common Law, 46 Harv.L.Rev. 1281, 1287–89 (1933).

terms broken if the promisor dies before fulfilment. Yet it was very early determined that, if the performance is personal, the executors are not liable; Hyde v. The Dean of Windsor (Cro.Eliz. 552, 553). See 2 Wms.Exors. 1560, 5th Ed., where a very apt illustration is given. "Thus," says the learned author, "if an author undertakes to compose a work, and dies before completing it, his executors are discharged from this contract: for the undertaking is merely personal in its nature, and, by the intervention of the contractor's death, has become impossible to be performed." . . .

These are instances where the implied condition is of the life of a human being, but there are others in which the same implication is made as to the continued existence of a thing. For example, where a contract of sale is made amounting to a bargain and sale, transferring presently the property in specific chattels, which are to be delivered by the vendor at a future day; there, if the chattels, without the fault of the vendor, perish in the interval, the purchaser must pay the price and the vendor is excused from performing his contract to deliver, which has thus become impossible.

[In Williams v. Lloyd, W. Jones, 179] the count, which was in assumpsit, alleged that the plaintiff had delivered a horse to the defendant, who promised to redeliver it on request. Breach, that though requested to redeliver the horse he refused. Plea, that the horse was sick and died, and the plaintiff made the request after its death; and on demurrer it was held a good plea, as the bailee was discharged from his promise by the death of the horse without default or negligence on the part of the defendant. "Let it be admitted," say the Court "that he promised to deliver it on request, if the horse die before, that is become impossible by the act of God, so the party shall be discharged as much as if an obligation were made conditioned to deliver the horse on request, and he died before it." [b]

It may, we think, be safely asserted to be now English law, that in all contracts of loan of chattels or bailments if the performance of the promise of the borrower or bailee to return the things lent or bailed, becomes impossible because it [sic] has perished, this impossibility (if not arising from the fault of the borrower or bailee from some risk which he has taken upon himself) excuses the borrower or bailee from the performance of his promise to redeliver the chattel.

The great case of Coggs v. Bernard (1 Smith's L.C. 171, 5th ed.; 2 L.Raym. 909) is now the leading case on the law of bailments, and Lord Holt, in that case, referred so much to the Civil law that it might perhaps be thought that this principle was there derived direct from the civilians, and was not generally applicable in English law except in the case of bailments; but the case of Williams v. Lloyd (W.

---

b. But at an earlier period the bailee was not excused. Holmes, The Common Law (1881), 176 et seq.

Jones, 179), above cited, shows that the same law had been already adopted by the English law as early as The Book of Assizes. The principle seems to us to be that, in contracts in which the performance depends on the continued existence of a given person or thing, a condition is implied that the impossibility of performance arising from the perishing of the person or thing shall excuse the performance.

In none of these cases is the promise in words other than positive, nor is there any express stipulation that the destruction of the person or thing shall excuse the performance; but that excuse is by law implied, because from the nature of the contract it is apparent that the parties contracted on the basis of the continued existence of the particular person or chattel. In the present case, looking at the whole contract, we find that the parties contracted on the basis of the continued existence of the Music Hall at the time when the concerts were to be given; that being essential to their performance.

We think, therefore, that the Music Hall having ceased to exist, without fault of either party, both parties are excused, the plaintiffs from taking the gardens and paying the money, the defendants from performing their promise to give the use of the Hall and Gardens and other things. Consequently the rule must be absolute to enter the verdict for the defendants.

Rule absolute.

NOTE

The Doctrine of Implied Conditions. A seller of jute contended that his contracts had become impossible of performance because of a wartime order prohibiting the shipments he had promised. One clause in the contracts was: "Any dispute that may arise under this contract to be settled by arbitration in Dundee." Arbiters were appointed and the question of impossibility was taken up before them. The seller brought an action for a "declarator" that this issue was not within the jurisdiction of the arbiters. Lord Sands [Lord Ordinary of the Court of Sessions] wrote an opinion in which he observed that the House of Lords had steadily expounded the law of impossibility by reference to an express or implied condition in the contract itself. He continued as follows: "Mr. Chree [counsel for the pursuers, or plaintiff] argued that this is a pious fiction—a fiction because it does not correspond with anything that was in the minds of parties at the time; pious because it seeks to do homage to a very sacred legal principle, the sanctity of contract. I confess I have some sympathy with Mr. Chree. It does seem to me somewhat far-fetched to hold that the non-occurrence of some event, which was not within the contemplation or even the imagination of the parties, was an implied term of the contract.[c]

c. Cf. L. Hand: "As courts become increasingly sure of themselves, interpretation more and more involves an imaginative projection of the expressed purpose upon situations arising later, for which the parties did not provide and which they did not have in mind." L. N. Jackson & Co. v. Royal Norwegian Government, 177 F. 2d 694, 702 (2d Cir. 1949), cert. denied, 339 U.S. 914 (1950) (dissent).

. . . No doubt this theory has been developed to square with the rule of the English common law in regard to supervening impossibility. A tiger has escaped from a travelling menagerie. The milkgirl fails to deliver the milk. Possibly the milkman may be exonerated from any breach of contract; but, even so, it would seem hardly reasonable to base that exoneration on the ground that 'tiger days excepted' must be held as if written into the milk contract. But though I sympathise with Mr. Chree's difficulty I am unable to adopt his reasoning." Lord Sands concluded that a question about an implied term was one which "arose under" the contracts, so that the arbiters had jurisdiction. Scott & Sons v. Del Sel, 1922 S.C. [Session Cases] 592, 596–97, aff'd, 1923 S.C. (H.L.) 37.

TRANSATLANTIC FINANCING CORPORATION v. UNITED STATES

United States Court of Appeals, D. C. Circuit, 1966.
363 F.2d 312.

J. SKELLY WRIGHT, CIRCUIT JUDGE. This appeal involves a voyage charter between Transatlantic Financing Corporation, operator of the SS CHRISTOS, and the United States covering carriage of a full cargo of wheat from a United States Gulf port to a safe port in Iran. The District Court dismissed a libel filed by Transatlantic against the United States for costs attributable to the ship's diversion from the normal sea route caused by the closing of the Suez Canal. We affirm.

On July 26, 1956, the Government of Egypt nationalized the Suez Canal Company and took over operation of the Canal. On October 2, 1956, during the international crisis which resulted from the seizure, the voyage charter in suit was executed between representatives of Transatlantic and the United States. The charter indicated the termini of the voyage but not the route. On October 27, 1956, the SS CHRISTOS sailed from Galveston for Bandar Shapur, Iran, on a course which would have taken her through Gibraltar and the Suez Canal. On October 29, 1956, Israel invaded Egypt. On October 31, 1956, Great Britain and France invaded the Suez Canal Zone. On November 2, 1956, the Egyptian Government obstructed the Suez Canal with sunken vessels and closed it to traffic.

On or about November 7, 1956, Beckmann, representing Transatlantic, contacted Potosky, an employee of the United States Department of Agriculture, who appellant concedes was unauthorized to bind the Government, requesting instructions concerning disposition of the cargo and seeking an agreement for payment of additional compensation for a voyage around the Cape of Good Hope. Potosky advised Beckmann that Transatlantic was expected to perform the charter according to its terms, that he did not believe Transatlantic was entitled to additional compensation for a voyage around the Cape, but that Transatlantic was free to file such a claim. Following this discussion, the CHRISTOS changed course for the Cape of Good Hope and eventually arrived in Bandar Shapur on December 30, 1956.

Transatlantic's claim is based on the following train of argument. The charter was a contract for a voyage from a Gulf port to Iran. Admiralty principles and practices, especially stemming from the doctrine of deviation, require us to imply into the contract the term that the voyage was to be performed by the "usual and customary" route. The usual and customary route from Texas to Iran was, at the time of contract, via Suez, so the contract was for a voyage from Texas to Iran via Suez. When Suez was closed this contract became impossible to perform. Consequently, appellant's argument continues, when Transatlantic delivered the cargo by going around the Cape of Good Hope, in compliance with the Government's demand under claim of right, it conferred a benefit upon the United States for which it should be paid in *quantum meruit*.

The doctrine of impossibility of performance has gradually been freed from the earlier fictional and unrealistic strictures of such tests as the "implied term" and the parties' "contemplation." Page, The Development of the Doctrine of Impossibility of Performance, 18 Mich.L.Rev. 589, 596 (1920). See generally 6 Corbin, Contracts §§ 1320–1372 (rev. ed. 1962); 6 Williston, Contracts §§ 1931–1979 (rev. ed. 1938). It is now recognized that " 'A thing is impossible in legal contemplation when it is not practicable; and a thing is impracticable when it can only be done at an excessive and unreasonable cost.' " Mineral Park Land Co. v. Howard, 172 Cal. 289, 293, 156 P. 458, 460, L.R.A.1916F, 1 (1916). *Accord*, Whelan v. Griffith Consumers Company, D.C.Mun.App., 170 A.2d 229 (1961); Restatement, Contracts § 454 (1932); Uniform Commercial Code (U.L.A.) § 2–615, comment 3. The doctrine ultimately represents the ever-shifting line, drawn by courts hopefully responsive to commercial practices and mores, at which the community's interest in having contracts enforced according to their terms is outweighed by the commercial senselessness of requiring performance.[1] When the issue is raised, the court is asked to construct a condition of performance [2] based on the changed circumstances, a process which involves at least three reasonably definable steps. First, a contingency—something unexpected—must have occurred. Second, the risk of the unexpected occurrence must not have been allocated either by agreement or by custom. Finally, oc-

---

1. While the impossibility issue rarely arises, as it has here, in a suit to recover the cost of an alternative method of performance, compare Annot., 84 A.L.R.2d 12, 19 (1962), there is nothing necessarily inconsistent in claiming commercial impracticability for the method of performance actually adopted; the concept of impracticability assumes performance was physically possible. Moreover, a rule making nonperformance a condition precedent to recovery would unjustifiably encourage disappointment of expectations.

2. Patterson, Constructive Conditions in Contracts, 42 Colum.L.Rev. 903, 943–954 (1942).

currence of the contingency must have rendered performance commercially impracticable.[3] Unless the court finds these three requirements satisfied, the plea of impossibility must fail.

The first requirement was met here. It seems reasonable, where no route is mentioned in a contract, to assume the parties expected performance by the usual and customary route at the time of contract.[4] Since the usual and customary route from Texas to Iran at the time of contract [5] was through Suez, closure of the Canal made

---

3. Compare Uniform Commercial Code § 2–615(a), which provides that, in the absence of an assumption of greater liability, delay or non-delivery by a seller is not a breach if performance as agreed is made "impracticable" by the occurrence of a "contingency" the non-occurrence of which was a "basic assumption on which the contract was made." To the extent this limits relief to "unforeseen" circumstances, comment 1, see the discussion below, and compare Uniform Commercial Code § 2–614(1). There may be a point beyond which agreement cannot go, Uniform Commercial Code § 2–615, comment 8, presumably the point at which the obligation would be "manifestly unreasonable," § 1–102(3), in bad faith, § 1–203, or unconscionable, § 2–302. For an application of these provisions see Judge Friendly's opinion in United States v. Wegematic Corporation, 2 Cir., 360 F.2d 674 (1966) [p. 841 infra].

4. Uniform Commercial Code § 2–614, comment 1, states: "Under this Article, in the absence of specific agreement, the normal or usual facilities enter into the agreement either through the circumstances, usage of trade or prior course of dealing." So long as this sort of assumption does not necessarily result in construction of a condition of performance, it is idle to argue over whether the usual and customary route is an "implied term." The issue of impracticability must eventually be met. One court refused to imply the Suez route as a contract term, but went on to rule the contract had been "frustrated." Carapanayoti & Co. Ltd. v. E. T. Green Ltd., [1959] 1 Q.B. 131. The holding was later rejected by the House of Lords. Tsakiroglou & Co. Ltd. v. Noblee Thorl G.m.b.H., [1960] 2 Q.B. 348.

5. The parties have spent considerable energy in disputing whether the "usual and customary" route by which performance was anticipated is defined as of the time of contract or of performance. If we were automatically to treat the expected route as a condition of performance, this matter would be crucial, and we would be compelled to choose between unacceptable alternatives. If we assume as a constructive condition the usual and customary course always to mean the one in use at the time of contract, any substantial diversion (we assume the diversion would have to be substantial) would nullify the contract even though its effect upon the rights and obligations of the parties is insignificant. Nor would it be desirable, on the other hand, to assume performance is conditioned on the availability of *any* usual and customary route at the time of performance. It may be that very often the availability of a customary route at the time of performance other than the route expected to be used at the time of contract should result in denial of relief under the impossibility theory; certainly if *no* customary route is available at the time of performance the contract is rendered impossible. But the same customarily used alternative route may be practicable in one set of circumstances and impracticable in another, as where the goods are unable to survive the extra journey. Moreover, the "time of performance" is no special point in time; it is every moment in a performance. Thus the alternative route, in our case around the Cape, may be practicable at some time during performance, for example while the vessel is still in the Atlantic Ocean, and impracticable at another time during performance, for example after the vessel has traversed most of the Mediterranean Sea. Both alternatives, therefore, have their short-

impossible the expected method of performance. But this unexpected development raises rather than resolves the impossibility issue, which turns additionally on whether the risk of the contingency's occurrence had been allocated and, if not, whether performance by alternative routes was rendered impracticable.[6]

Proof that the risk of a contingency's occurrence has been allocated may be expressed in or implied from the agreement. Such proof may also be found in the surrounding circumstances, including custom and usages of the trade. See 6 Corbin, supra, § 1339, at 394–397; 6 Williston, supra, § 1948, at 5457–5458. The contract in this case does not expressly condition performance upon availability of the Suez route. Nor does it specify "via Suez" or, on the other hand, "via Suez or Cape of Good Hope." [7] Nor are there provisions in the contract from which we may properly imply that the continued availability of Suez was a condition of performance.[8] Nor is there

comings, and we avoid choosing between them by refusing automatically to treat the usual and customary route as of any time as a condition of performance.

6. In criticizing the "contemplation" test for impossibility Professor Patterson pointed out:

" 'Contemplation' is appropriate to describe the mental state of philosophers but is scarcely descriptive of the mental state of business men making a bargain. It seems preferable to say that the promisee *expects* performance by [the] means . . . the promisor expects to (or which on the facts known to the promisee it is probable that he will) use. It does not follow as an inference of fact that the promisee expects performance by *only* that means . . . ." Patterson, supra Note 2, at 947.

7. In Glidden Company v. Hellenic Lines, Limited, 2 Cir., 275 F.2d 253 (1960), the charter was for transportation of materials from India to America "via Suez Canal or Cape of Good Hope, or Panama Canal," and the court held performance was not "frustrated." In his discussion of this case, Professor Corbin states: "Except for the provision for an alternative route, the defendant would have been discharged, for the reason that the parties contemplated an open Suez Canal as a specific condition or means of performance." 6 Corbin, supra, § 1339, at 399 n. 57. Appellant claims this supports its argument, since the Suez route was contemplated as usual and

customary. But there is obviously a difference, in deciding whether a contract allocates the risk of a contingency's occurrence, between a contract specifying no route and a contract specifying Suez. We think that when Professor Corbin said, "Except for the provision for an alternative route," he was referring, not to the entire *provision*—"via Suez Canal or Cape of Good Hope" etc.—but to the fact that *an alternative route* had been provided for. Moreover, in determining what Corbin meant when he said "the parties contemplated an open Suez Canal as a specific condition or means of performance," consideration must be given to the fact, recited by Corbin, that in *Glidden* the parties were specifically aware when the contract was made the Canal might be closed, and the promisee had refused to include a clause excusing performance in the event of closure. Corbin's statement, therefore, is most accurately read as referring to cases in which a route is specified after negotiations reflecting the parties' awareness that the usual and customary route might become unavailable. Compare Held v. Goldsmith, 153 La. 598, 96 So. 272 (1919).

8. The charter provides that the vessel is "in every way fitted for *the voyage*" (emphasis added), and the "P. & I. Bunker Deviation Clause" refers to "the contract voyage" and the "direct and/or customary route." Appellant argues that these provisions require implication of a voyage by the direct and customary route. Actually they

anything in custom or trade usage, or in the surrounding circumstances generally, which would support our constructing a condition of performance. The numerous cases requiring performance around the Cape when Suez was closed, see e. g., Ocean Tramp Tankers Corp. v. V/O Sovfracht (The Eugenia), [1964] 2 Q.B. 226, and cases cited therein, indicate that the Cape route is generally regarded as an alternative means of performance. So the implied expectation that the route would be via Suez is hardly adequate proof of an allocation to the promisee of the risk of closure. In some cases, even an express expectation may not amount to a condition of performance.[9] The doctrine of deviation supports our assumption that parties normally expect performance by the usual and customary route, but it adds nothing beyond this that is probative of an allocation of the risk.[10]

prove only what we are willing to accept—that the parties expected the usual and customary route would be used. The provisions in no way condition performance upon nonoccurrence of this contingency.

There are two clauses which allegedly demonstrate that time is of importance in this contract. One clause computes the remuneration "in steaming time" for diversions to other countries ordered by the charterer in emergencies. This proves only that the United States wished to reserve power to send the goods to another country. It does not imply in any way that there was a rush about the matter. The other clause concerns demurrage and despatch. The charterer agreed to pay Transatlantic demurrage of $1,200 per day for all time in excess of the period agreed upon for loading and unloading, and Transatlantic was to pay despatch of $600 per day for any saving in time. Of course this provision shows the parties were concerned about time, see Gilmore & Black, The Law of Admiralty § 4–8 (1957), but the fact that they arranged so minutely the consequences of any delay or speedup of loading and unloading operates against the argument that they were similarly allocating the risk of delay or speed-up of the voyage.

9. Uniform Commercial Code § 2–614(1) provides: "Where without fault of either party . . . the *agreed* manner of delivery . . . becomes commercially impracticable but a commercially reasonable substitute is available, such substitute performance must be tendered and accepted." (Emphasis added.) Compare Mr. Justice

Holmes' observation: "You can give any conclusion a logical form. You always can imply a condition in a contract. But why do you imply it? It is because of some belief as to the practice of the community or of a class, or because of some opinion as to policy . . . ." Holmes, The Path of the Law, 10 Harv.L.Rev. 457, 466 (1897).

10. The deviation doctrine, drawn principally from admiralty insurance practice, implies into all relevant commercial instruments naming the termini of voyages the usual and customary route between those points. 1 Arnould, Marine Insurance and Average § 376, at 522 (10th ed. 1921). Insurance is cancelled when a ship unreasonably "deviates" from this course, for example by extending a voyage or by putting in at an irregular port, and the shipowner forfeits the protection of clauses of exception which might otherwise have protected him from his common law insurer's liability to cargo. See Gilmore & Black, supra Note 8, § 2–6, at 59–60. This practice, properly qualified, see id. § 3–41, makes good sense, since insurance rates are computed on the basis of the implied course, and deviations in the course increasing the anticipated risk make the insurer's calculations meaningless. Arnould, supra, § 14, at 26. Thus the route, so far as insurance contracts are concerned, is crucial, whether express or implied. But even here, the implied term is not inflexible. Reasonable deviations do not result in loss of insurance, at least so long as established practice is followed. See Carriage of Goods by Sea Act § 4(4), 49 Stat. 1210, 46 U.S.C. § 1304(4); and

If anything, the circumstances surrounding this contract indicate that the risk of the Canal's closure may be deemed to have been allocated to Transatlantic. We know or may safely assume that the parties were aware, as were most commercial men with interests affected by the Suez situation, see The Eugenia, supra, that the Canal might become a dangerous area. No doubt the tension affected freight rates, and it is arguable that the risk of closure became part of the dickered terms. Uniform Commercial Code § 2–615, comment 8. We do not deem the risk of closure so allocated, however. Foreseeability or even recognition of a risk does not necessarily prove its allocation.[11] Compare Uniform Commercial Code § 2–615, Comment 1; Restatement, Contracts § 457 (1932). Parties to a contract are not always able to provide for all the possibilities of which they are aware, sometimes because they cannot agree, often simply because they are too busy. Moreover, that some abnormal risk was contemplated is probative but does not necessarily establish an allocation of the risk of the contingency which actually occurs. In this case, for example, nationalization by Egypt of the Canal Corporation and formation of the Suez Users Group did not necessarily indicate that the Canal would be blocked even if a confrontation resulted.[12] The surrounding circumstances do indicate, however, a willingness by Transatlantic to assume abnormal risks, and this fact should legitimately cause us to judge the impracticability of performance by an alternative route in stricter terms than we would were the contingency unforeseen.

We turn then to the question whether occurrence of the contingency rendered performance commercially impracticable under the circumstances of this case. The goods shipped were not subject to harm from the longer, less temperate Southern route. The vessel and crew were fit to proceed around the Cape.[13] Transatlantic was no less

discussion of "held covered" clauses in Gilmore & Black, supra, § 3–41, at 161. Some "deviations" are required. E. g., Hirsch Lumber Co. v. Weyerhaeuser Steamship Co., 2 Cir., 233 F.2d 791, cert. denied, 352 U.S. 880, 77 S.Ct. 102, 1 L.Ed.2d 80 (1956). The doctrine's only relevance, therefore, is that it provides additional support for the assumption we willingly make that merchants agreeing to a voyage between two points expect that the usual and customary route between those points will be used. The doctrine provides no evidence of an allocation of the risk of the route's unavailability.

11. See Note, The Fetish of Impossibility in the Law of Contracts, 53 Colum. L.Rev. 94, 98 n. 23 (1953), suggesting that foreseeability is properly used "as a *factor* probative of assumption of

the risk of impossibility." (Emphasis added.)

12. Sources cited in the briefs indicate formation of the Suez Canal Users Association on October 1, 1956, was viewed in some quarters as an implied threat of force. See N.Y. Times, Oct. 2, 1956, p. 1, col. 1, noting, on the day the charter in this case was executed, that "Britain has declared her freedom to use force as a last resort if peaceful methods fail to achieve a satisfactory settlement." Secretary of State Dulles was able, however, to view the statement as evidence of the canal users' "dedication to a just and peaceful solution." The Suez Problem 369–370 (Department of State Pub. 1956).

13. The issue of impracticability should no doubt be "an objective determina-

able than the United States to purchase insurance to cover the contingency's occurrence. If anything, it is more reasonable to expect owner-operators of vessels to insure against the hazards of war. They are in the best position to calculate the cost of performance by alternative routes (and therefore to estimate the amount of insurance required), and are undoubtedly sensitive to international troubles which uniquely affect the demand for and cost of their services. The only factor operating here in appellant's favor is the added expense, allegedly $43,972.00 above and beyond the contract price of $305,842.92, of extending a 10,000 mile voyage by approximately 3,000 miles. While it may be an overstatement to say that increased cost and difficulty of performance never constitute impracticability, to justify relief there must be more of a variation between expected cost and the cost of performing by an available alternative than is present in this case,[14] where the promisor can legitimately be presumed to have accepted some degree of abnormal risk, and where impracticability is urged on the basis of added expense alone.[15]

We conclude, therefore, as have most other courts considering related issues arising out of the Suez closure,[16] that performance of this

tion of whether the promise can reasonably be performed rather than a subjective inquiry into the promisor's capability of performing as agreed." Symposium, The Uniform Commercial Code and Contract Law: Some Selected Problems, 105 U.Pa.L.Rev. 836, 880, 887 (1957). Dealers should not be excused because of less than normal capabilities. But if both parties are aware of a dealer's limited capabilities, no objective determination would be complete without taking into account this fact.

14. Two leading English cases support this conclusion. The Eugenia, supra, involved a time charter for a trip from Genoa to India via the Black Sea. The charterers were held in breach of the charter's war clause by entering the Suez Canal after the outbreak of hostilities, but sought to avoid paying for the time the vessel was trapped in the Canal by arguing that, even if they had not entered the Canal, it would have been blocked and the vessel would have had to go around the Cape to India, a trip which "frustrated" the contract because it constituted an entirely different venture from the one originally contemplated. The lower court agreed, but the House of Lords (see Lord Denning's admirable treatment, [1964] 2 Q.B. at 233), "swallowing" the difficulty of applying the

frustration doctrine to hypothetical facts, reversed, holding that the contract had to be performed. Especially relevant is the fact that the case expressly overruled Societe Franco Tunisienne D'Armement v. Sidermar S.P.A. (The Massalia), [1961] 2 Q.B. 278, where a voyage charter was deemed frustrated because the Cape route was "highly circuitous" and cost 195s. per long ton to ship iron ore, rather than 134s. via Suez, a difference well in excess of the difference in this case.

In Tsakiroglou & Co. Ltd. v. Noblee Thorl G.m.b.H., supra Note 4, the difference to the seller under a C.I.F. contract in freight costs caused by the Canal's closure was £15 per ton instead of £7.10s. per ton—precisely twice the cost. The House of Lords found no frustration.

15. See Uniform Commercial Code § 2–615, comment 4: "Increased cost alone does not excuse performance unless the rise in cost is due to some unforeseen contingency which alters the essential nature of the performance." See also 6 Corbin, supra, § 1333; 6 Williston, supra, § 1952, at 5468.

16. Appellant seeks to distinguish the English cases supporting our view. The Eugenia, supra, appellant argues, in-

contract was not rendered legally impossible. Even if we agreed with appellant, its theory of relief seems untenable. When performance of a contract is deemed impossible it is a nullity. In the case of a charter party involving carriage of goods, the carrier may return to an appropriate port and unload its cargo, The Malcolm Baxter, Jr., 277 U.S. 323, 48 S.Ct. 516, 72 L.Ed. 901 (1928), subject of course to required steps to minimize damages. If the performance rendered has value, recovery in *quantum meruit* for the entire performance is proper. But here Transatlantic has collected its contract price, and now seeks *quantum meruit* relief for the additional expense of the trip around the Cape. If the contract is a nullity, Transatlantic's theory of relief should have been *quantum meruit* for the entire trip, rather than only for the extra expense. Transatlantic attempts to take its profit on the contract, and then force the Government to absorb the cost of the additional voyage.[17] When impracticability without fault occurs, the law seeks an equitable solution, see 6 Corbin, supra, § 1321, and *quantum meruit* is one of its potent devices to achieve this end. There is no interest in casting the entire burden of commercial disaster on one party in order to preserve the other's profit. Apparently the contract price in this case was advantageous enough to deter appellant from taking a stance on damages consistent with its theory of liability. In any event, there is no basis for relief.

Affirmed.

volved a time charter. True, but it overruled The Massalia, supra Note 14, which involved a voyage charter. Indeed, when the time charter is for a voyage the difference is only verbal. See Carver, Carriage of Goods by Sea 256–257 (10th ed. 1957). More convincing is the argument that Tsakiroglou & Co. Ltd., supra Note 4, involved a contract for the sale of goods, where the seller agreed to a C.I.F. clause requiring him to ship the goods to the buyer. There is a significant difference between a C.I.F. contract and voyage or time charters. The effect of delay in the former due to longer sea voyages is minimized, since the seller can raise money on the goods he has shipped almost at once, and the buyer, once he takes up the documents, can deal with the goods by transferring the documents before the goods arrive. See Tsakiroglou & Co. Ltd., supra Note 4, [1960] 2 Q.B. at 361. But this difference is not so material that impossibility in C.I.F. contracts is unrelated to impossibility in charter parties. It would raise serious questions for a court to require sellers under C.I.F. contracts to perform in circumstances under which the sellers could be refused performance by carriers with whom they have entered into charter parties for affreightment. See The Eugenia, supra, [1964] 2 Q.B. at 241. Where the time of the voyage is unimportant, a charter party should be treated the same as a C.I.F. contract in determining impossibility of performance.

These cases certainly are not distinguishable, as appellant suggests, on the ground that they refer to "frustration" rather than to "impossibility." The English regard "frustration" as substantially identical with "impossibility." 6 Corbin, supra, § 1322, at 327 n. 9.

17. The argument that the Uniform Commercial Code requires the buyer to pay the additional cost of performance by a commercially reasonable substitute was advanced and rejected in Symposium, supra Note 13, 105 U.Pa.L.Rev. at 884 n. 205. In Dillon v. United States, 156 F.Supp. 719, 140 Ct.Cl. 508 (1957), relief was afforded for some of the cost of delivering hay from a commercially unreasonable distance, but the suit was one in which the plaintiff had suffered losses far in excess of the relief given.

NOTES

(1) *Shipment via Suez.* Suppose the charter had given the Government a right to notice of the progress of the vessel by requiring the master to send it a telegram "on passing Suez." Such a provision appeared in "The Massalia," one of the more controversial of the Suez cases. The charter was for a voyage from India to Genoa. Note the court's reference to the case (and to its overruling) in footnote 14.

In footnote 7 the court uses the Glidden case, in the Second Circuit, for support. The charter there gave the shipper power to designate a destination (on the Atlantic seaboard) "not later than on Vessel's passing Gibraltar." But a more interesting feature of this case was that the ship-owner had asked for a clause excusing it in the event the Canal was closed, and that the shipper had rejected any such term. These facts, taken together, make the case a near-perfect example of the type described in the last sentence of footnote 7, do they not? Do you agree with the court that the doctrine of impossibility is better applicable in that situation than in the case before it?

As the court notes, all of these cases were rather different from the problem in Tsakiroglou, mentioned in footnotes 4, 16 and 17, where the contract was one of *sale.* The seller had agreed to ship groundnuts from the Sudan to Hamburg, paying the cost, insurance and freight (c.i.f.). The contract was entered into on October 4, and called for shipment in November or December. The House of Lords sustained an award of damages for his failure to perform. As regards the custom of shipment via Suez, Lord Radcliffe said: "A man may habitually leave his house by the front door to keep his appointments; but, if the front door is stuck, he would hardly be excused for not leaving by the back."

Professor Harold Berman has argued that the doctrines of impossibility and frustration are out of place in relation to international trade transactions. Examining the standard terms they employ, he infers that the parties rely not on the peculiar doctrines which might excuse performance in this or that country, but on the sanctity of contract, "their surest defense," plus their own precautionary drafting of special clauses. A charter party, for instance, is not a "hit-or-miss effort to foresee the future," but a "serious attempt to exhaust the possible allocations of risks." [a] Berman, Excuse for Nonperformance in the Light of Contract Practices in International Trade, 63 Colum.L.Rev. 1413 (1963).[b] Does the court reject that view in the main case?

(2) *Reprise.* The Canal was closed again on June 5, 1967. At that time the tanker Washington Trader was about 84 miles from Port Said, on a voyage from Beaumont to Bombay. As in the main case, the claimant (owner

---

a. Compare Lord Sumner's opinion in Larrinaga & Co. v. Société Franco-Americaine des Phosphates de Medulla, [1923] 92 L.J.K.B. 455, 464; 39 T.L.R. 316: "In effect most forward contracts can be regarded as a form of commercial insurance, in which every event is intended to be at the risk of one party or another."

b. For less stringent views, see Birmingham, A Second Look at the Suez Canal Cases, 20 Hast.L.J. 1393 (1969) (providing an economic analysis), and Schlegel, Of Nuts, and Ships, and Sealing Wax, Suez, and Frustrating Things, 23 Rutgers L.Rev. 419 (1969), both suggesting a graduated response to differing equities.

of the vessel) sought to charge the charterer with the additional cost of the voyage around the Cape: about $132,000. This sum was almost a third of the freight paid at the agreed rate, as compared with the 14% overrun in Transatlantic. The closing took the Washington Trader more than 8,000 miles out of her way. (Note the example used in footnote 5 of the main case, of a vessel that has "traversed most of the Mediterranean Sea.") These figures did not persuade the court that the charterer should pay more than it had contracted for.

The owner sought to distinguish Transatlantic on the ground that a flat rate was contracted for there, whereas in the present case the freight was calculated on the basis of a prevailing rate (per ton) applicable to transport through the Canal. Again the court was unpersuaded. Trading & Pro. Corp. v. Shell Internat'l Marine Ltd., 453 F.2d 939 (2d Cir. 1972).

INTERNATIONAL PAPER CO. v. ROCKEFELLER, 161 App. Div. 180, 146 N.Y.S. 371 (3d Dept., 1914). [Action for breach of contract to deliver pulpwood to plaintiff. Defense, that the pulpwood was to be cut from green spruce wood growing on a particular tract of land, and that the uncut spruce wood on this land was in 1903 destroyed by fire, except about 550 cords upon the top of a high mountain, which could be cut and delivered only at an expense of $20 per cord, as compared with the contract price of $5.50 per cord. The evidence to support defendant's contention that the parties "contemplated" delivery from this land was: The written contract, the one sued upon, referred to this tract of land and recited that the buyer "is desirous of purchasing wood now on said lands from [the seller] which the latter is willing to sell if he acquires the title to said lands under" a certain contract with the Kingsley Lumber Company; the contract sued upon was made as a result of the negotiations of one Hibbard for the purchase of these lands from the Kingsley company; and although the contract called for delivery of 6000 cords the first year and 10,000 cords in each of the next five years (ending in 1905), the plaintiff wrote defendant protesting against the cutting of spruce on this tract for any other purposes. The trial court held the defendant was bound unconditionally to deliver the entire quantity of pulpwood, and plaintiff recovered judgment for the difference between the contract price and the market price of the quantity not delivered, amounting to $48,000. Defendant appealed.]

KELLOGG, J. (after stating the facts): While not free from doubt, it seems to me that it was contemplated that the wood to be furnished was to be cut on the Kingsley lands. The statement that the plaintiff was desirous of purchasing the wood now on the lands and that the defendant was willing to sell it if he acquired the lands; the fact that the contract was conditional upon the purchase and that the first deliveries in 1899 were dependent upon the connection with the Chateaugay road which came within a very short distance but would not immediately serve any other woodlands, and the fact that

Hibbard was the moving spirit in the matter, was understood to be the party getting out the wood and apparently had no other relations with the defendant than in lumbering this tract, indicate that the parties had in mind, in making the contract, the lumbering of this tract. We need not say that the defendant could not have furnished like wood of equal quality from other lands, but the contract, read in connection with the known facts, shows the source from which the parties contemplated the wood should be furnished, and when the source is destroyed the defendant is excused from further performance. The defendant did not contract to deliver the wood unless he acquired the Kingsley lands. If all the wood upon the Kingsley lands had been destroyed by fire immediately after the contract was executed, the parties would have been in substantially the same position they would have occupied if the defendant had not acquired the lands. The real reason which induced the contract and upon which it depended would have failed.

. . . The defendant is not excused from delivering the live spruce suitable for pulpwood which survived the fire by the mere fact that its location upon the tract is such that it would be very expensive for him to deliver it.

The judgment and orders are reversed on law and facts and a new trial granted, with costs to the appellant to abide the event.

NOTES

(1) *Parol Evidence.* If the seller had offered to prove an oral agreement, at the time the written one was executed, that all of the pulpwood was to come from the Kingsley lands, would the evidence have been admissible? See Colonial Operating Corp. v. Hannan Sales & Service, 265 App. Div. 411, 39 N.Y.S.2d 217 (1943). What if the seller had offered evidence that the buyer had agreed not to hold him bound in the event of a fire consuming the timber in question? The admission of such evidence was held not to be prejudicial error in Ontario Deciduous Fruit Growers' Association v. Cutting Fruit-Packing Company, 134 Cal. 21, 66 P. 28 (1901).

In the case as it stands, notice the sources, in and out of the written contract, from which the court drew the conclusion that "the parties had in mind, in making the contract, the lumbering of this tract." If the writing had made no reference to the Kingsley lands, should the court have reached a different result?

(2) *The Reverse Claim.* Suppose that the market price of pulpwood had declined, that the seller had tendered pulpwood from another tract, and that the buyer had declined to take it. Would that have been a breach by the buyer? See Patterson, The Restatement of the Law of Contracts, 33 Colum.L.Rev. 397, 423 (1933). On this and foregoing questions, see also Note 1, p. 839 infra.

CANADIAN INDUSTRIAL ALCOHOL CO. v. DUNBAR MO-LASSES CO., 258 N.Y. 194, 179 N.E. 383, 80 A.L.R. 1173 (1932). [At the end of 1927 the plaintiff Alcohol Company contracted with

Dunbar to purchase a quantity of molasses, shipments to begin after the following April 1, and to be spread out during the warm weather. The goods were described as "approximately 1,500,000 wine gallons Refined Blackstrap (Molasses) of the usual run from the National Sugar Refinery, Yonkers, N.Y., to test around 60 per cent sugars." While the contract was in force that refinery produced much less molasses than its capacity—less than half a million gallons. Dunbar shipped to the Alcohol Company its entire allotment of the refinery's output (344,083 gallons), but failed to deliver any more molasses. Upon being sued for damages, Dunbar contended that its duty was conditioned, by an implied term, on the refinery's producing enough molasses to fill the plaintiff's order. From a judgment for the buyer, Dunbar appealed.]

CARDOZO, CH. J. . . . The contract, read in the light of the circumstances existing at its making, or more accurately in the light of any such circumstances apparent from this record, does not keep the defendant's duty within boundaries so narrow. . . . The defendant does not even show that it tried to get a contract from the refinery during the months that intervened between the acceptance of the plaintiff's order and the time when shipments were begun. It has wholly failed to relieve itself of the imputation of contributory fault (3 Williston on Contracts, sec. 1959). So far as the record shows, it put its faith in the mere chance that the output of the refinery would be the same from year to year, and finding its faith vain, it tells us that its customer must have expected to take a chance as great. We see no reason for importing into the bargain this aleatory element. The defendant is in no better position than a factor who undertakes in his own name to sell for future delivery a special grade of merchandise to be manufactured by a special mill. The duty will be discharged if the mill is destroyed before delivery is due. The duty will subsist if the output is reduced because times turn out to be hard and labor charges high. . . . [Affirmed.]

ALLOWING FOR CONTINGENCIES BY CONTRACT

In earlier chapters some mechanisms have been suggested by which contractual commitments may be adjusted to allow for the impact of changing circumstances. One illustration was the term inserted by the United States in the set of contracts it made for the purchase of trap rock in Sylvan Crest Sand & Gravel Co. v. United States, p. 242, supra: "Cancellation by the Procurement Division may be effected at any time." The government's objective was to improve an airport; and if further planning for the project showed it to be unduly expensive, that would seem to be a suitable occasion for invoking the power to cancel. In the absence of the provision, it would hardly be thought that a cost projection would justify the government in crying off its bargain for trap rock.

In that case the court ruled that the Government might be accountable to the seller for failing either to request delivery of the rock or to give a seasonable notice of cancellation. Even this risk can be dispelled by using the classic mechanism of an option contract to purchase (or sell, as the case may be). If a dealer in trap rock, for example, has an option contract to sell a given quantity, he is in a peculiarly favorable position, for he cannot suffer by a run-up in the prices he pays, or by an unexpected blockage in his source of supply.

Since an ordinary offer does not subject the offeree to any duties, he is also immune—in a sense—to the burdens of changing circumstances. The owner of a business interested in selling it sometimes promises a fee to a broker for finding a purchaser and arranging the sale. If the promise is stated as an offer to be accepted only by complete performance, the theory of unilateral offers is that no duty attaches to the broker. If the buyer he finds is disabled, for any reason, the broker will not be compensated for his efforts, but at least he need not fear liability to the promisor.

More precise planning for changing circumstances is reflected in a variety of pricing provisions. A building contractor unwilling to assume the risk that he must excavate more rock than is anticipated may insist on a unit price (per cubic yard, say) for that component of the work. See Depot Construction Corp. v. State, 19 N.Y.2d 109, 224 N.E.2d 866 (1967). If he is unwilling to assume the risk even of changing labor and material costs, he may insist on a cost-plus contract. Similarly, buyers and sellers of goods may use "flexible pricing" terms in lieu of discounting all the risks of price movement in the market. As for anticipating events that may affect the quantity of goods to be sold, see the materials at pp. 238 and 606 supra on requirements and output contracts.

Still another way to contract out of burdens cast by unforeseeable events is to address the problem frontally, with a *force majeure* clause. The following example comes from a three-year contract for a supply of natural gas by a producer to a distributor: Nondelivery by the seller was to be excused—

> if the same shall arise from any cause or causes beyond Seller's control, including but not restricted to: acts of God, war, accident . . ., or exhaustion, reduction or unavailability of liquified petroleum gas at the source of supply from which deliveries are normally made hereunder.

Although the techniques mentioned here may all serve to allow for unknown contingencies, they do so in various ways, and at varying costs. They are by no means interchangeable. A three-year supply contract with a liberal *force majeure* clause is feasible; but a three-year offer is unheard of (see UCC 2–205). A liquidated damages clause in a modest amount might serve the purposes of a party about as well as a *force majeure* clause, but the latter may be far preferable in light of the legal risks associated with underliquidated damages. See Better Food Markets v. American District Tel. Co., p. 368 supra.

In general, there are distinctive legal problems associated with each of the techniques mentioned. In the example of a "unilateral offer" to a broker, given above, the offeree runs the risk of revocation before his performance is complete. Requirements contracts, flexible-pricing terms, and cost-plus contracts are bedevilled by problems of drafting, and of measuring recovery. An unrestricted power of cancellation, as in the trap-rock case, invites an argument that the contract is illusory. And, finally, it is easy to raise a suspicion of overreaching in connection with an exchange that appears to be one-sided. (As for a charge of duress in procuring a cost-plus contract, see United States v. Bethlehem Steel Corporation, 315 U.S. 289 (1942).)

It must also be understood that an astute bargainer will rarely insist on the most risk-free position that the law would allow. For instance, a dealer undertaking to supply goods may be able to reserve a certain power of cancellation, but meet stiff sales resistance if he stipulates broadly against "force majeure." In Canadian Alcohol Co. v. Molasses Co., p. 833 supra, Cardozo remarked that if the buyer had been told that its right to delivery was contingent on the seller's ability to obtain the goods from the refinery, the buyer "would very likely have preferred to deal with the refinery directly, instead of dealing with a middleman."

NOTES

(1) *The Case of the Five Mill Formula.* A producer of plywood appointed a sales company as distributor of the product, and contracted to honor the company's orders at "market price." For determining that price the parties agreed on a so-called five-mill pricing formula: "the published market price listed to jobbers by the following plants [listing five] shall be for the purposes of this agreement the 'market price'." (Apparently the listed prices were to be averaged.) The formula soon became unworkable: some of the mills listed went out of business, and others failed to publish prices. After a time the producer refused to honor further orders. In an action brought by the sales company, the trial court determined that the failure of the formula caused the contract to be unenforceable, and gave judgment for the defendant. The sales company appealed, contending that prices could be determined by the general market. *Held*: Affirmed. "When the five-mill formula, intended here as the only binding method of fixing price, became indeterminable, the contract became unenforceable." Interstate Plywood Sales Co. v. Interstate Container Corp., 331 F.2d 449 (9th Cir. 1964). What provision in the agreement would have preserved the seller's commitment, despite the failure of the pricing formula?

(2) *Modifying Agreements.* In Chapter 3 some examples were given of modifying an agreement to allow for a contingency not foreseen when it was made. The occasion for such a modification may be a strike of a

contractor's employees,[a] the discovery of rock in ground to be excavated,[b] a general collapse of prices,[c] or the offer to an employee of higher pay in another job.[d] Some of these events would, in an appropriate case, justify a court in excusing performance by the burdened party, on principles of impossibility and frustration. Nevertheless, as has been seen, the law does not take an altogether benign attitude to modifications giving relief to such a party; they may run afoul of the pre-existing duty rule. On the other hand, in a number of cases where that rule was pushed aside it is evident that the court was actuated by a sense that a supervening event or discovery impaired the fairness of the original bargain. See Blakeslee v. Board of Water Commissioners, 106 Conn. 642, 139 A. 106 (1927) ; Watkins & Son v. Carrig, p. 271 supra.

CASUALTY LOSS IN RELATION TO SALES

One of the parties to a contract of sale must usually absorb a loss, on account of physical injury to the subject of the sale, if it is injured (or destroyed) by casualty before the contract is consummated. (For this note it will be assumed that the loss is not traceable to the fault of someone who can be held accountable.) It is common to insure against the risk of such loss.

The seller of improved land may have his fire insurance policy endorsed with the name of the purchaser, usually without charge, so that the purchaser's interest is also insured until he arranges his own insurance. In the event of loss in the interim, the proceeds will be allocated between the parties "as their interests may appear." Similarly, a dealer in personal property sometimes insures not only his unsold inventory, but also goods "sold but not removed." So written, the policy amounts to a contract for the benefit of unnamed third parties, his customers, to the extent that they bear the risk of damage to the goods. In the absence of some policy provision of this character, it is the general rule that insurance held by one of the contracting parties is not available to the other. Insurance on property is "personal" to the named insured. Therefore a buyer may find that he must pay the agreed price for goods or improvements he has contracted for, even if they are no longer in existence and the seller has been compensated for their loss through his insurance. In that event, part or all of the payment goes to reimburse the insurer, through "subrogation" to the seller's claim. A certain number of buyers are unaware of the threat of loss that these rules impose on them, and are grievously surprised when it eventuates.

Insurance aside, how does the law allocate a casualty loss occurring while a sale of the property is exectuory? For real property, an an-

a. As in Arzani v. People, p. 266 supra.

b. As in Watkins & Son v. Carrig, p. 271 supra.

c. See note, Leases and Economic Adversity, p. 269 supra.

d. As in Schwartzreich v. Bauman-Basch, Inc., p. 263 supra.

swer was developed under the aegis of equity courts, which conceived of the purchaser as "owner" of the property from the time of contracting. As such, he is required to pay the purchase price without abatement for the casualty. In a number of jurisdictions, however, the classical rule no longer holds, whether by judicial [a] or legislative [b] reform.

For sales of goods, the answers are codified in the Uniform Commercial Code, §§ 2–509, 2–510, and 2–613, with possible supplementation from §§ 2–615 and 2–616. Pre-Code law asserted that a buyer was accountable for the price of damaged goods if, and only if, title in them had passed to him prior to the casualty; and the Uniform Sales Act contained elaborate rules and presumptions for locating title. In dissociating risk of loss and "title," the Code worked a major change.

Two aspects of UCC 2–613 may be noted here. First, since it assumes that the risk of loss is on the seller, the relief it affords is for his benefit, in the main. Second, it cannot apply to the usual contract for a sale of goods to be produced or procured by the seller, or even of goods to be selected from his stock of merchandise: e. g., a contract to sell a carload of alfalfa seed. Until a carload is "identified" to the contract, that is, the destruction by flood of all the seed in the vicinity would leave the seller obligated to make delivery. This proposition has its soft spots, as will be seen, and the Code states a qualification in § 2–615. But none of the other Code sections purports to relieve such a seller. (For rules about when "identification" of goods occurs, see UCC 2–501(1)—noting the provision about crops.)

In UCC 2–510 there is a Code innovation designed to spread the advantages of insurance, in special circumstances, where it is held by the "wrong" party to the sale. The treatment of insurance here has been criticized thoughtfully in McCoid, Allocation of Loss and Property Insurance, 39 Ind.L.J. 647 (1964). However, there is a strong and supportive doctrine of equity, having somewhat the same effect in relation to real property sales. If a building subject to a sale contract burns before the deed is given, and the seller is provided with fire insurance, many courts will abate the purchase price to the extent of the insurance proceeds.[c] The seller's insurance claim is said to be held in constructive trust for the purchaser. The doctrine is discordant with the personal character of fire insurance generally, and has been ascribed to "layman's ideas of equity." [d]

a. See Anderson v. Yaworski, 120 Conn. 390, 181 A. 205, 101 A.L.R. 1232 (1935); Potwin v. Tucker, 128 Vt. 142, 259 A.2d 781 (1969).

b. See 9C Uniform Laws Annotated 313 et seq. (1957).

c. Or impose a constructive trust on the seller's insurance proceeds for the buyer's benefit. See Vogel v. Northern Assur. Co., 219 F.2d 409 (3d Cir. 1955).

d. Brownell v. Board of Education, 239 N.Y. 369, 146 N.E. 630, 37 A.L.R. 1319 (1925).

A fuller treatment of these topics must be deferred to other courses. But at least one section of the Code (2–615) should be examined closely as a modern formulation of the case-law principle of "commercial impracticability."

NOTES

(1) *A Visit to the Farm.* Crop failures have prompted a series of cases in which an impossibility of delivering specified farm products was asserted. Comment 9 after UCC 2–615 is as follows: "The case of a farmer who has contracted to sell crops to be grown on designated land may be regarded as falling either within the section on casualty to identified goods or this section, and he may be excused, when there is a failure of the specific crop, either on the basis of the destruction of identified goods or because of the failure of a basic assumption of the contract." A more acute issue is presented by an agreement for the sale of farm products (e. g., 5,000 bushels of corn, to grade 3Y) which does *not* designate the land from which it is to come. See Unke v. Thorpe, 75 S.D. 65, 59 N.W. 2d 419 (1953) (600 to 800 bushels of seed). If the seller is a farmer, being sued for non-delivery, should he be permitted to testify that the agreement was executed at his farm, after the buyer had inspected his growing crop? Should the buyer be permitted to testify that he insisted on the quantity term, and explained to the seller that he intended to resell against the contract? Both pieces of evidence might shed light on the "basic assumptions" of the contract, might they not?

Nevertheless, in the case cited above, evidence of a conversation was said to be inadmissible, in the face of the written agreement. An interesting case for comparison is Snipes Mountain Co. v. Benz Brothers & Co., 162 Wash. 334, 298 P. 714, 74 A.L.R. 1287 (1931), which involved the sale of a hundred tons of potatoes. The court effected a reformation of the writing, in order to deny the buyer's claim. After the word "potatoes," it wrote in the words "grown during the year 1929 on the following described premises: [here describing the seller's crop land]." Some courts would regard equitable relief as unnecessary. Barkemeyer Grain & Seed Co. v. Hannant, 66 Mont. 120, 213 P. 208 (1923); and see Note 4, p. 587 supra. On a stricter view, crop shortage is no excuse to a producer if he might have supplied the goods from another source; e. g., Eskew v. California Fruit Exchange, 203 Cal. 257, 263 P. 804 (1928).

If the seller is a dealer in the product being sold, a crop failure is somewhat less likely to afford him an excuse for non-delivery. As an explanation it has been said that a dealer is "in a position to spread the risk of a single crop failure among his customers." Note, 53 Colum.L.Rev. 94, 102 (1953). Presumably a farmer is less able to adjust his prices to allow for a liability he might suffer, when his crop fails. On this reasoning, does if follow that a farmer who has insured his crop against the destruction it suffered should be liable for non-delivery, whereas his uninsured neighbor, contracting on the same terms, should not?

As for excusing a dealer in case of crop failure, see Pearce-Young-Angel Co. v. Charles R. Allen, Inc., 213 S.C. 578, 50 S.E.2d 698 (1948), and UCC 2–615, Comment 4.

(2) *Unassumable Risk?* If the possibility of a widespread crop failure arises in negotiations for the sale of a carload of corn, may the parties

agree that any such risk lies with the seller? The first phrase of UCC 2–615 seems to give a categorical answer; but the comments after the section suggest reservations. They speak of "adjustments" required by other sections and by equitable principles when the flat decision, "no excuse" (or "excuse"), is opposed by sense and justice (Comment 6). They also indicate that 2–615 is not meant as an "exhaustive expression" of the underlying principle (Comment 2). See also footnote 3 in Transatlantic Financing Corporation v. United States, p. 823 supra.

If a grower of corn, in disposing of his expected harvest, guarantees its quantity and quality, is the contract subject to avoidance under UCC 2–613, by reason of casualty? See §§ 1–102(3), (4), and 2–509(4). What evidence would be helpful in determining whether or not the guarantee is unconscionable (UCC 2–302)?

---

407 EAST 61ST GARAGE, INC. v. SAVOY FIFTH AVE. CORP.

Court of Appeals of New York, 1968.
23 N.Y.2d 275, 244 N.E.2d 37.

[For the report of this case, see p. 619 supra.]

NOTES

(1) *Specific Performance.* It seems clear from the opinion in this case that the plaintiff could not have required Savoy to keep the hotel open, by bringing an action for specific performance. Financial disability might have prevented the enforcement of such a decree. However, that is not of itself a sufficient reason for denying specific relief, according to Christy v. Pilkinton, 224 Ark. 407, 273 S.W.2d 533 (1954). In that case a buyer of real property was ordered to pay the unpaid part of the purchase price, although his evidence showed that he had no means to pay or to borrow that amount.[a]

(2) *Subjective Impossibility.* The Restatement defines "subjective impossibility" as impossibility "not due to the nature of the performance, but wholly to the inability of the individual promisor." Section 455. A characteristic example is the case of a promisor disabled by financial reverses. But if his financial difficulties are traceable to an "objective" event, not envisaged at the time of contracting, the promisor has a more plausible ground for excuse. Even so, performance has often been required, on the general view that a promise should be honored, as the court says above, regardless of financial hardship. See Twin Harbors Lumber Co. v. Carrico, 92 Idaho 343, 442 P.2d 753 (1968).

a. But see Valley Associates Corp. v. Rogers, 4 Misc.2d 382, 158 N.Y.S.2d 231 (1956). The buyer there sought an order that the seller convey property as he had contracted to do. He had only a half interest. His sister had the other, she had refused to go along with the contract, and she was not a party to the action. The court said it was "not in a position" to direct the seller to convey the entire title: "The court will not attempt to decree the impossible." The serious issue in the case was whether or not the buyer could obtain a *half* interest upon paying *part* of the price. The subject of "specific performance with abatement" is not apposite to a basic contracts course.

For a criticism of the distinction between subjective and objective impossibility, see Patterson, The Apportionment of Business Risks through Legal Devices, 24 Colum.L.Rev. 335, 349 (1924).

(3) *Problem.* The Chrysler Motor Company discontinued the manufacture of its DeSoto cars in 1960, owing to public disfavor. Dealers holding Chrysler franchises for the distribution of DeSotos bring damage claims against it for failing to maintain a supply. The defense is "impossibility" of performance. What result? See Buono Sales, Inc. v. Chrysler Motors Corp., 363 F.2d 43 (3d Cir. 1966), cert. denied, 385 U.S. 971 (1966); id., 449 F.2d 715 (3d Cir. 1971).

UNITED STATES v. WEGEMATIC CORP.

United States Court of Appeals, Second Circuit, 1966.
360 F.2d 674.

FRIENDLY, CIRCUIT JUDGE. The facts developed at trial in the District Court for the Southern District of New York, fully set forth in a memorandum by Judge Graven, can be briefly summarized: In June 1956 the Federal Reserve Board invited five electronics manufacturers to submit proposals for an intermediate-type, general-purpose electronic digital computing system or systems; the invitation stressed the importance of early delivery as a consideration in determining the Board's choice. Defendant, a relative newcomer in the field, which had enjoyed considerable success with a smaller computer known as the ALWAC III–E, submitted a detailed proposal for the sale or lease of a new computer designated as the ALWAC 800. It characterized the machine as "a truly revolutionary system utilizing all of the latest technical advances," and featured that "maintenance problems are minimized by the use of highly reliable magnetic cores for not only the high speed memory but also logical elements and registers." Delivery was offered nine months from the date the contract or purchase order was received. In September the Board acted favorably on the defendant's proposal, ordering components of the ALWAC 800 with an aggregate cost of $231,800. Delivery was to be made on June 30, 1957, with liquidated damages of $100 per day for delay. The order also provided that in the event the defendant failed to comply "with any provision" of the agreement, "the Board may procure the services described in the contract from other sources and hold the Contractor responsible for any excess cost occasioned thereby." Defendant accepted the order with enthusiasm.

The first storm warning was a suggestion by the defendant in March 1957 that the delivery date be postponed. In April it informed the Board by letter that delivery would be made on or before October 30 rather than as agreed, the delay being due to the necessity of "a redesign which we feel has greatly improved this equipment"; waiver of the stipulated damages for delay was requested. The Board took the request under advisement. On August 30 defendant wrote that delivery would be delayed "possibly into 1959"; it suggested use of ALWAC III–E equipment in the interim and waiver of the $100 per day "penalty." The Board also took this request under advisement but made clear it was waiving no rights. In mid-October defendant announced that "due to engineering difficulties it has become impracticable to deliver the ALWAC 800 Computing System at this time"; it requested cancellation of the contract without damages. The Board set about procuring comparable equipment from another manufacturer; on October 6, 1958, International Business Machines Corporation delivered an IBM 650 computer, serving substantially the same purpose as the ALWAC 800, at a rental of $102,000 a year with an option to purchase for $410,450.

In July 1958 the Board advised defendant of its intention to press its claim for damages; this suit followed. The court awarded the United States $46,300 for delay under the liquidated damages clause, $179,450 for the excess cost of the IBM equipment, and $10,056 for preparatory expenses useless in operating the IBM system—a total of $235,806, with 6% interest from October 6, 1958.

The principal point of the defense, which is the sole ground of this appeal, is that delivery was made impossible by "basic engineering difficulties" whose correction would have taken between one and two years and would have cost a million to a million and a half dollars, with success likely but not certain. Although the record does not give an entirely clear notion what the difficulties were, two experts suggested that they may have stemmed from the magnetic cores, used instead of transistors to achieve a solid state machine, which did not have sufficient uniformity at this stage of their development. Defendant contends that under federal law, which both parties concede to govern, see Cargill, Inc. v. Commodity Credit Corp., 275 F.2d 745, 751–753 (2 Cir. 1960), the "practical impossibility" of completing the contract excused its defaults in performance.

We agree with the defendant that the decisions most strongly relied on by the Government are not controlling; much of the seeming confusion in this field of law stems from failure to make necessary distinctions as to who is suing whom for what. Thus Day v. United States, 245 U.S. 159, 38 S.Ct. 57, 62 L.Ed. 219 (1917), and Fritz-Rumer-Cooke Co. v. United States, 279 F.2d 200, 6 Cir. (1960), involved no question of nonperformance but an attempt by a contractor who had fully performed to secure added compensation for surmounting unexpected difficulties. While Austin Co. v. United States, 314 F.2d 518, 161 Ct.Cl. 76, cert. denied, 375 U.S. 830, 84 S.Ct. 75, 11 L.Ed.2d 62 (1963), did involve failure by a manufacturer to perform because of engineering problems, it was not an effort to resist damages, which the Government did not seek; the contractor was attempting to recover costs incurred prior to termination under a special clause in the contract without which, as Professor Corbin has noted, it "would not have had the shadow of a claim." 6 Corbin, Contracts § 1328 n. 40 (1964 Pocket Part). Consolidated Airborne Systems, Inc. v. United States, 348 F.2d 941 (Ct.Cl.1965), was a case of financial inability peculiar to the contractor and is distinguishable under the doctrine of "subjective impossibility," that a promisor's duty is never discharged "by the mere fact that supervening events deprive him of the ability to perform, if they are not such as to deprive other persons, likewise, of ability to render such a performance." 6 Corbin, Contracts § 1332, at 361 (1962). And in Carnegie Steel Co. v. United States, 240 U.S. 156, 36 S.Ct. 342, 60 L.Ed. 576 (1916), which is most nearly apposite in that it concerned a claim by the promisee for delay occasioned by an unanticipated technological problem encountered by the promisor, the precise issue was whether the difficulty came within a clause excusing delays resulting from "unavoidable causes, such as fires, storms, labor strikes, action of the United States, etc." 240 U. S. at 163, 36 S.Ct. at 344. On the other hand, the mere fact that the Government's cases do not dictate decision in its favor does not mean that defendant wins; it means only that we must seek guidance elsewhere.

We find persuasive the defendant's suggestion of looking to the Uniform Commercial Code as a source for the "federal" law of sales. The Code has been adopted by Congress for the District of Columbia, 77 Stat. 630 (1963), has been enacted in over forty states, and is thus well on its way to becoming a truly national law of commerce, which, as Judge L. Hand said of the Negotiable Instruments Law, is "more complete and more certain, than any other which can conceivably be drawn from those sources of 'general law' to which we were accustomed to resort in the days of Swift v. Tyson." New York, N. H. &. H. R. Co. v. Reconstruction Finance Corp., 180 F.2d 241, 244 (2 Cir. 1950). When the states have gone so far in achieving the desirable goal of a uniform law governing commercial transactions, it would be a distinct disservice to insist on a different one for the segment of commerce, important but still small in relation to the total, consisting of transactions with the United States.

Section 2–615 of the UCC, entitled "Excuse by failure of presupposed conditions," provides that:

"Except so far as a seller may have assumed a greater obligation . . . delay in delivery or non-delivery . . . is not a breach of his duty under a contract for sale if performance as agreed has been made impracticable by the occurrence of a contingency the nonoccurrence of which was a basic assumption on which the contract was made . . ."

The latter part of the test seems a somewhat complicated way of putting Professor Corbin's question of how much risk the promisor assumed. Recent Developments in the Law of Contracts, 50 Harv.L.

Rev. 449, 465–66 (1937) ; 2 Corbin, Contracts § 1333, at 371. We see no basis for thinking that when an electronics system is promoted by its manufacturer as a revolutionary breakthrough, the risk of the revolution's occurrence falls on the purchaser; the reasonable supposition is that it has already occurred or, at least, that the manufacturer is assuring the purchaser that it will be found to have when the machine is assembled. As Judge Graven said : "The Board in its invitation for bids did not request invitations to conduct a development program for it. The Board requested invitations from manufacturers for the furnishing of a computer machine." Acceptance of defendant's argument would mean that though a purchaser makes his choice because of the attractiveness of a manufacturer's representation and will be bound by it, the manufacturer is free to express what are only aspirations and gamble on mere probabilities of fulfillment without any risk of liability. In fields of developing technology, the manufacturer would thus enjoy a wide degree of latitude with respect to performance while holding an option to compel the buyer to pay if the gamble should pan out. See Austin Co. v. United States, 314 F.2d 518, 521, 161 Ct.Cl. 76, cert. denied, 375 U.S. 830, 84 S.Ct. 75, 11 L. Ed.2d 62 (1963). We do not think this the common understanding— above all as to a contract where the manufacturer expressly agreed to liquidated damages for delay and authorized the purchaser to resort to other sources in the event of non-delivery. Contrast National Presto Industries, Inc. v. United States, 338 F.2d 99, 106–112, 167 Ct.Cl. 749 (1964), cert. denied, 380 U.S. 962 (1965). If a manufacturer wishes to be relieved of the risk that what looks good on paper may not prove so good in hardware, the appropriate exculpatory language is well known and often used.

Beyond this the evidence of true impracticability was far from compelling. The large sums predicted by defendant's witnesses must be appraised in relation not to the single computer ordered by the Federal Reserve Board, evidently for a bargain price, but to the entire ALWAC 800 program as originally contemplated. Although the record gives no idea what this was, even twenty-five machines would gross $10,000,000 if priced at the level of the comparable IBM equipment. While the unanticipated need for expending $1,000,000 or $1,500,000 on redesign might have made such a venture unattractive, as defendant's management evidently decided, the sums are thus not so clearly prohibitive as it would have them appear. What seemingly did become impossible was on-time performance; the issue whether if defendant had offered prompt rectification of the design, the Government could have refused to give it a chance and still recover not merely damages for delay but also the higher cost of replacement equipment, is not before us.

Affirmed.

NOTE

The Government and Development Costs. The Court of Claims occupies a strategic position in determining the effect of mishaps under production contracts that require novel technology in performance. Government procurement programs readily give rise to claims by suppliers for additional compensation for such performance, and the views of that court are usually authoritative. The following four grounds are recognized bases for recovery: (a) when the Government authors the specifications, it warrants that if they are complied with satisfactory performance will result, and the warranty includes a right to rely on the indicated method of manufacture; (b) when the Government possesses vital information indispensable to satisfactory performance, and the supplier should not be expected to perceive it, the Government has a duty of disclosure; (c) commercial impracticability justifies a reallocation of costs; and (d) mutual mistake as to a material fact, the risk of which was not assumed, justifies a reallocation if it appears that the Government would have assented to it at the outset if it had known the truth.

A striking decision embodying the latter principle is National Presto Industries, Inc. v. United States, 338 F.2d 99 (Ct.Cl.1964), cert. denied, 380 U.S. 962 (1965). A particular departure of the case is that the court ordered a determination of the unexpected costs attributable to the mistake, and directed that the supplier recover half of them, so that it would bear the loss equally with the Government. Is proration an equally appropriate solution under the other three principles mentioned above? Is it *more* appropriate in a case of commercial impracticability? Refer again to the Suez-closing case, p. 823 supra: would the claimant there have made a more appealing case if it had limited its claim to *half* the additional expense of the long haul 'round the Cape? (See footnote 17 in that case.)

Some branches of the Government are commonly willing to pay costs of experimentation with new processes that may prove, as they know, to be unusable. In the case last cited, the Army's Ordnance Department evinced such a willingness. Presumably the Federal Reserve Board is rarely willing to bear development costs for its equipment. In the Wegematic case, the court accepted the Board's suggestion that a federal rule for the case be derived from the Code. Considering UCC 2–615, does it seem equally adaptable for use in relation to ordnance development contracts?

Even in a research and development contract, it seems, the supplier may commit himself to make a "breakthrough" in the state of the art, such that he is in default if the Government's specifications prove impossible to meet. See Aerosonic Instrument Corp., 1959–1 Board of Contract Appeals ¶ 2115 (contract to produce a lightweight tachometer for the Air Force). But see Smith Engineering Co. v. Rice, 102 F.2d 492 (9th Cir. 1938), cert. denied, 307 U.S. 637 (1939) (private contract; note the statute).

––––––––

MINERAL PARK LAND CO. v. HOWARD, 172 Cal. 289, 156 P. 458 (1916). [Action for breach of contract. Defendants agreed to take from plaintiff's land all the gravel and earth necessary in the construction of a bridge, and to pay for it at a stated rate. Defendants actually used 101,000 cubic yards of earth and gravel, only 50,131 of which they took from plaintiff's land, having procured the rest elsewhere. The court found this was all the material on plaintiff's land which was above water level; that defendants removed "all that could have been taken advantageously to defendants, or all that was practical to take and remove from a financial standpoint"; and ruled that this fact did not excuse defendant's failure. Defendants appealed.]

SLOSS, J. . . . The parties were contracting for the right to take earth and gravel to be used in the construction of the bridge. When they stipulated that all of the earth and gravel needed for this purpose should be taken from plaintiff's land they contemplated and assumed that the land contained the requisite quantity, available for use. . . . And, in determining whether the earth and gravel were "available," we must view the conditions in a practical and reasonable way. Although there was gravel on the land, it was so situated that the defendants could not take it by ordinary means, nor except at prohibitive cost. To all fair intents then, it was impossible for defendants to take. . . . We do not mean to intimate that the defendants could excuse themselves by showing the existence of conditions which would make the performance of their obligation more expensive than they had anticipated, or which would entail a loss upon them. But where the difference in cost is so great as here, and has the effect, as found, of making performance impracticable, the situation is not different from that of a total absence of earth and gravel.

Judgment reversed.

NOTE

The Case of the Rock Trap. The State of New York contracted to pay $6 million for the construction of a hospital building, including rock excavation. The contract price was to be adjusted, however, in the event that more than specified yardages of rock was required to be excavated: the additional amount was to be either 10 or 22 dollars a cubic yard of excess, depending on the location. The builder was required to excavate as much as 1,100 yards without additional compensation. Test borings at the site by the State were relied on for estimates, but the State carefully disclaimed any representation about the amount of rock there. As it turned out the rock excavation required amounted to 2,982 yards. The builder made a claim for this work in an amount based on its reasonable value, which was found to be greater than the unit prices would yield. Accepting this basis, the Court of Claims awarded almost $88,000 for additional rock excavation. On an appeal by the State, the Appellate Division found a "mere quantitative change" and reduced this element of the award to $9,017. The builder then appealed. *Held:* Affirmed. Depot Construction

Corp. v. State, 19 N.Y.2d 109, 224 N.E.2d 866 (1967).[a] Does it seem that the builder might have been well advised to omit the unit-price feature from its bid on the job? Did the builder's claim violate the principle stated in the final paragraph of the opinion in Transatlantic Financing Corporation v. United States, p. 823 supra?

KRELL v. HENRY

Court of Appeal, [1903] 2 K.B. 740.

[By a contract in writing of June 20, 1902, the defendant agreed to hire from the plaintiff a flat in Pall Mall, London, for June 26 and 27, on which days it had been officially announced that the coronation processions (i. e., to be held in connection with the coronation of Edward VII) would take place and pass along Pall Mall. The contract contained no express reference to the coronation processions, or to any other purpose for which the flat was taken. A deposit was paid when the contract was entered into. As, owing to the serious illness of the King, the processions did not take place on the days originally fixed, the defendant declined to pay the balance of the rent.]

VAUGHN WILLIAMS, L. J. The real question in this case is the extent of the application in English law of the principle of the Roman law which has been adopted and acted on in many English decisions, and notably in the case of Taylor v. Caldwell, (3 B. & S. 826). . . .

I do not think that the principle of the civil law as introduced into the English law is limited to cases in which the event causing the impossibility of performance is the destruction or non-existence of some thing which is the subject matter of the contract or of some condition or state of things expressly specified as a condition of it. I think that you first have to ascertain, not necessarily from the term of the contract, but, if required, from necessary inferences, drawn from surrounding circumstances recognized by both contracting parties, what is the substance of the contract, and then to ask the question whether that substantial contract needs for its foundation the assumption of the existence of a particular state of things. If it does,

---

a. The Court of Claims had found that the borings were taken haphazardly. The contract referred to them as follows:

"Test holes have been drilled on the site, at locations shown on the Plot Plan drawing. The test hole data shown on the plans are not guaranteed by the State in any respect, nor represented by it as being worthy of reliance. They are made available to the Bidders, who shall make their own in-dependent determination as to what value to assign to them. The State makes them available as information in its possession without intent or attempt to induce the Bidders to rely thereon."

For the court's animadversions on this paragraph, see Depot Construction Corp. v. State, 41 Misc.2d 764, 246 N.Y.S.2d 527 (1964).

this will limit the operation of the general words, and in such case, if the contract becomes impossible of performance by reason of the non-existence of the state of things assumed by both contracting parties as the foundation of the contract, there will be no breach of the contract thus limited.   Now what are the facts of the present case? The contract is contained in two letters of June 20 which passed between the defendant and the plaintiff's agent, Mr. Cecil Bisgood. These letters do not mention the coronation, but speak merely of the taking of Mr. Krell's chambers, or, rather, of the use of them, in the daytime of June 26 and 27, for the sum of 75*l*., 25*l*. then paid, balance 50*l*. to be paid on the 24th.   But the affidavits, which by agreement between the parties are to be taken as stating the facts of the case, show that the plaintiff exhibited on his premises, third floor, 56A, Pall Mall, an announcement to the effect that windows to view the Royal coronation procession were to be let, and that the defendant was induced by that announcement to apply to the housekeeper on the premises, who said that the owner was willing to let the suite of rooms for the purpose of seeing the Royal procession for both days, but not nights, of June 26 and 27.   In my judgment the use of the rooms was let and taken for the purpose of seeing the Royal procession.   It was not a demise of the rooms, or even an agreement to let and take the rooms.   It is a license to use rooms for a particular purpose and none other.   And in my judgment the taking place of those processions on the days proclaimed along the proclaimed route, which passed 56A, Pall Mall, was regarded by both contracting parties as the foundation of the contract; and I think that it cannot reasonably be supposed to have been in the contemplation of the contracting parties, when the contract was made, that the coronation would not be held on the proclaimed days, or the processions not take place on those days along the proclaimed route; and I think that the words imposing on the defendant the obligation to accept and pay for the use of the rooms for the named days, although general and unconditional, were not used with reference to the possibility of the particular contingency which afterwards occurred.   It was suggested in the course of the argument that if the occurrence, on the proclaimed days, of the coronation and the procession in this case were the foundation of the contract, and if the general words are thereby limited or qualified, so that in the event of the non-occurrence of the coronation and procession along the proclaimed route they would discharge both parties from further performance of the contract, it would follow that if a cabman was engaged to take someone to Epsom on Derby Day at a suitable enhanced price for such a journey, say 10*l*., both parties to the contract would be discharged in the contingency of the race at Epsom for some reason becoming impossible; but I do not think this follows, for I do not think that in the cab case the happening of the race would be the foundation of the contract.   No doubt the purpose of the engager would be to go to see the Derby, and the price would be proportionately high; but the cab had no special qualification for this particular occasion. Any other cab would have done as well.

Appeal dismissed.

NOTES

(1) *The Doctrine.* The foregoing decision is the best-known example of a doctrine known as "frustration of purpose," or commercial frustration. As opposed to impossibility, the label *frustration* signifies that nothing has happened to impede performance of the defendant's undertaking. After the King's illness, as before, it was perfectly possible for the defendant to pay the agreed price—and indeed for him to occupy the rooms. Other instances of frustration claims are given below. Was the issue raised in Paradine v. Jane (p. 818 supra) one of impossibility or of frustration?

"Whether the basis for commercial frustration rests on failure of consideration as suggested by 6 Williston, Contracts (Rev. ed.) § 1954, p. 5480, note 14, or on equitable principles of allocation of risks as suggested by Corbin is not made entirely clear by the decided cases. Thus in 6 Corbin, Contracts, § 1322, p. 256 (1951) it is said that the 'problem is that of allocating, in the most generally satisfactory way, the risks of harm and disappointment that result from supervening events.' " Perry v. Champlain Oil Co., 101 N.H. 97, 134 A.2d 65 (1957). Compare Patterson, The Apportionment of Business Risks, 24 Colum.L.Rev. 335, 345 (1924). Does the choice of one basis or the other suggest any difference in the scope of the doctrine?

(2) *Problems.* D promised to pay $400 in return for a wedding dress to be made by P. D and X were to be married on June 15, and P promised to have the dress ready a week before. X was accidentally killed after the dress was ready but before it could be delivered. Is D's duty to take and pay for the dress discharged? Assuming the gown can be sold to someone else at a greatly reduced price, who should bear the loss? Compare the situation with that of the cab engaged for Derby Day. Is either of these cases within section 288 of the Restatement?

SWIFT CANADIAN CO. v. BANET

United States Court of Appeals, Third Circuit, 1955.
224 F.2d 36.

Action to recover from buyer of goods, for breach of contract. In the United States District Court for the Eastern District of Pennsylvania, George A. Welsh, District Judge, each party moved for summary judgment upon stipulated facts, and the buyer's motion was granted. The seller appealed to the Court of Appeals. . . .

Judgment reversed with instructions to enter judgment for plaintiff.

GOODRICH, CIRCUIT JUDGE. This is an action on the part of a seller of goods to recover against the buyer for breach of contract. In the trial court each party, following the filing of a stipulation of facts, moved for summary judgment. The court granted the motion of the defendant. Plaintiff here says that it should have had the summary judgment or, at the worst, that the case should be remanded for trial on the facts.

The one point presented is both interesting and elusive. The seller is a Canadian corporation. It entered into an agreement with defendant buyers who do business as Keystone Wool Pullers in Philadelphia. By this contract Keystone agreed to purchase a quantity of lamb pelts at a stipulated price. Part of the quantity was delivered on board railroad cars at Toronto and shipped to Keystone in Philadelphia. On or about March 12, 1952, Swift advised Keystone of its readiness to deliver the remaining pelts to the buyer on board railroad cars in Toronto for shipment to Philadelphia. The parties have stipulated that on or about that day the government of the United States by its agency, the Bureau of Animal Industry, had issued stricter regulations for the importation of lamb pelts into the United States. The parties have stipulated that "pursuant to these regulations, the importation into the United States of these lamb pelts by Keystone was prevented." They have also stipulated that for the reasons just stated Keystone then and thereafter refused to accept delivery of the pelts and the loading and shipment of the car did not occur.

From an inspection of the contract made between the parties it appears that the seller agreed to sell the pelts:
"all at $3.80 each U. S. Funds
F. O. B. Toronto."
Below this an approximate time was stipulated for shipment and then there were shipping directions in the following form:

"Note _____ Frankford

Via: Buffalo-Penna. R. R. to

~~Broad & Washington Ave.~~

Freight Sta. Penna. R. R. Delivery."

Following this appears the terms and method of payment.

Two additional conditions of sale should be stated. There was a provision that neither party is to be liable for "orders or acts of any government or governmental agency . . ." And there was a provision that "when pelts are sold F.O.B. seller's plant title and risk of loss shall pass to buyer when product is loaded on cars at seller's plant."

The one question in this case is the legal effect of this agreement between the parties. If the seller's obligation was performed when it delivered, or offered to deliver, the pelts to the railroad company in Toronto, we think it is entitled to recovery. If the seller did fulfill its obligation, when it did so deliver, of course it is clear that when it failed to load the pelts because the buyer had signified his refusal to accept them, the seller may assert the same rights as though he had loaded them. A party is not obligated to do the vain thing of performing, assuming that he is ready to perform, when the other party has given notice of refusal to accept performance. 3 Williston on Sales, § 586 (Rev. ed., 1948); Restatement, Contracts, §§ 280, 306; Leonard Seed Co. v. Lustig Burgerhoff Co., 1923, 81 Pa.Super. 499. See also Uniform Commercial Code, § 2–610(c); Pa.Stat.Ann. tit. 12A, § 2–610(c) (1954).

The argument for the buyer must rest on the fact that the shipping directions in the contract showed that what the parties had in mind was such kind of performance by the seller as would start the goods to the buyer in Philadelphia. This coupled with the stipulation that, in consequence of the stiffening of federal regulations, "the importation into the United States of these lamb pelts by Keystone was prevented," forms the basis for the argument that the carrying out of the agreement was prevented by governmental agency and the buyer is therefore excused.

The validity of this argument depends upon what effect we give to a provision for shipment of the goods to the buyer via Pennsylvania R. R., destination Philadelphia. We do not think that this is any more than a shipping direction which the buyer could have changed to any other destination in the world had it so desired. Suppose the buyer had found that it wanted the goods in New York, could it not have directed such a change in destination without any violation of the contract? Could the seller have insisted that it would ship to Philadelphia and nowhere else? We think that authority in general regards these shipping directions as simply inserted for the convenience of the buyer and subject to change by him. Dwight v. Eckert, 1888, 117 Pa. 490, 12 A. 32; Hocking v. Hamilton, 1893, 158 Pa. 107, 27 A. 836; Richter v. Zoccoli, 1930, 150 A. 1, 8 N.J.Misc. 289; 1 & 2 Williston on Sales, §§ 190, 457 (Rev. ed., 1948). See also Uniform Commercial Code, § 2–319(3); Pa.Stat.Ann. tit. 12A, § 2–319(3) (1954).

If the contract in this case had called for performance "F.O.B. seller's plant" a provision of the contract itself would clearly have indicated when the seller's responsibility was finished and the buyer's had begun.[1] Here the provision in the earlier part of the contract was simply "F.O.B. Toronto" and it was not specifically provided that the sale was delivery at the seller's plant. We think the provision shows what the parties meant by "F.O.B." and can see no difference,

---

1. See the second additional condition of sale quoted in the text above.

so far as this expressed meaning goes, between F.O.B. at seller's plant and F.O.B. Toronto.

The general rule on this subject is pretty clear. Williston points out that when goods are delivered "free on board" pursuant to contract the presumption is that the property passes thereupon. Williston on Sales, § 280(b) (Rev. ed., 1948). It is agreed that this is a presumption and that the phrase F.O.B. is not one of iron-clad meaning. Seabrook Farms Co. v. Commodity Credit Corp., 206 F.2d 93 (C.A.3, 1953). There is nothing in this case, however, to counteract the effect of such a presumption. When the shipper had made his delivery he was to send bill of lading and draft through a Philadelphia bank. His part of the agreement would have been fully performed when the goods were delivered F.O.B. at Toronto. We think both the risk of loss and the possibility of profit if the market advanced, were in the buyer from then on. Even if the goods could not be imported into the United States under the then existing regulations, the rest of the world was free to the buyer, so far as we know, as destination for the shipment. If he did not care to accept them under the circumstances and his expectation of a profitable transaction was disappointed, nevertheless, the seller having performed or being ready, able and willing to perform, was entitled to the value of his bargain.

[The court finds that the law of Pennsylvania and that of Ontario were identical on the issue involved here, and that the seller's damages were sufficiently proved.]

The judgment of the district court will be reversed with instructions to enter judgment for the plaintiff for the difference between the contract price and the price at which the goods were sold.

NOTES

(1) *The Code.* Can the Uniform Commercial Code be faulted because it contains no rule excusing a buyer of goods in the event of commercial impracticability? Cf. UCC 2–615; and see Gilmore, 2 Security Interests in Personal Property, § 41.7 (1965).

(2) *"F.O.B. Philadelphia."* Would the decision have been different if the sale contract had provided for delivery f. o. b. Philadelphia rather than Toronto? As to the seller's obligation in that case see UCC 2–319(1) (b). If the seller failed to deliver in accordance with such a contract because of United States import regulations, would that necessarily be a breach of his duty?

(3) *Export Licenses.* If Canada had regulated the *export* of lamb pelts, so as to require a license, would the Canadian seller have borne the risk that one could not be obtained? See Amtorg Trading Corp. v. Miehle Printing Press & Mfg. Co., 206 F.2d 103 (2d Cir. 1953).

LAW OR FACT?

When an issue of impossibility or frustration is presented, should it be decided as an ordinary question of fact? If not, what role can findings of fact (jury verdicts in particular) play in the disposition of such issues?

In Mitchell v. Ceazan Tires, Ltd., 25 Cal.2d 45, 153 P.2d 53 (1944), it was held that a war rationing system for tires and tubes did not discharge a lease of premises for the conduct of an automobile tire business "and other related businesses such as automobile supplies." The tenant contended that the question of frustration was one of fact, which had been resolved in his favor by the trial court. The Supreme Court said: "The excuse of frustration, however, like that of impossibility, is a conclusion of law drawn by the court from the facts of a given case, and although the trial court found both as a finding of fact and as a conclusion of law that the defendant's business was 'frustrated' and 'unlawful' and 'impossible,' the evidence does not establish that the sale of new tires was made illegal or impossible, or that the purpose of the lease was frustrated." See also Poussard v. Spiers and Pond, 1 Q.B.D. 410 (1876): the jury "must have made a mistake in law as to what was a sufficient failure of consideration to set the defendants at liberty, which was not a question for them." But see Oosten v. Hay Haulers Dairy Employees, etc. Union, 45 Cal.2d 784, 291 P.2d 17 (1955), cert. denied, 351 U.S. 937 (1956).

In the Mitchell case, if the trial court had made more concrete findings of fact, might its judgment have been affirmed by the Supreme Court? Suppose it had found that an abnormal change of circumstances occurred, that the parties contracted with reference to normal business conditions, and that the tenant did not assume the risk of the change by failing to provide against it in the contract. In Housing Authority, etc. v. East Tennessee L. & P. Co., 183 Va. 64, 31 S.E.2d 273 (1944), a jury made findings somewhat like these. (The contract was for supplying natural gas for heating; the change in circumstances was the depletion of the seller's gas reserves.) The appellant Housing Authority complained about the charge to the jury, but apparently did not make the point that juries are incompetent to grapple with the sort of issue submitted. Are they?

NOTES

(1) *Problem.* A one-year lease of a farm to a rice grower provided for a rental of 20% of the gross crop proceeds, or in any event a minimum of $2,500. The grower planted no rice on the rented tract that year, but put in a crop on a tract he owned, of the same size. He did not plant both tracts because, after the lease was entered into, by order of the Department of Agriculture he was prohibited from planting more than 50% of the acreage he had expected to cultivate. He now contends that the order discharged his duties under the lease. What may the lessor recover

as rent, if anything? See County of Yuba v. Mattoon, 160 Cal.App.2d 456, 325 P.2d 162 (1958). What weight would attach to a jury verdict in favor of the lessee?

(2) *Problem.* Given the same lease, assume that the grower has no other acreage. He is prohibited from planting rice on half of the leased tract. If he wishes to cultivate the remainder, may the *lessor* declare the contract terminated by frustration of purpose? See. Perry v. Champlain Oil Co., 99 N.H. 451, 114 A.2d 885 (1955); 101 N.H. 97, 134 A.2d 65 (1957).

ENFORCEMENT *CY PRES* AFTER IMPOSSIBILITY OR FRUSTRATION

When it appears that a promisor's undertaking will no longer be enforced in full measure, owing to a change of circumstances, what alternatives are there to excusing further performance by the promisor altogether? May the promisee salvage something of his bargain by offering a suitable concession to the promisor? Or would that be to infringe the principle that one contracting party may not impose new terms on the other without his consent?

The question is closely connected with the matter of contract revision by the courts. In some instances, when an agreement has been disrupted by events, the court has directed that the parties fulfill its general objects on terms that the court dictates. That is not the customary judicial practice, certainly; but the doctrine of *cy pres* has a certain place in contract law. An instance is Miller v. Campello Cooperative Bank, 344 Mass. 76, 181 N.E.2d 345 (1962). There the court considered an installment contract for the purchase of a house. The buyer had occupied it for a quarter of a century, making regular payments. Taxes and other charges against the payments had increased to the point where it appeared that the unpaid balance of the price would never be satisfied out of the buyer's payments. The court summarily turned the sale agreement into a 30-day option contract.

Other instances may be classified as cases of "partial" and "temporary" impossibility. See Restatement, §§ 462–464; UCC 2–615(b); Patterson, Temporary Impossibility of Performance of Contract, 47 Va.L.Rev. 798 (1961). In a case of the latter type, the decision may be to extend the time allowed for full performance, or to postpone the scheduled dates for performance. There are good reasons, however, for courts to be cautious in choosing to enforce part of an agreement and not others, or to give other partial relief. When a builder meets with unanticipated difficulty, performing under a fixed-price contract, would circumstances ever justify a court in directing him to continue work, and the owner to receive it, on a cost-plus basis?

Returning to the original question, it seems there is even more reason for caution in permitting a promisee to determine what parts of his agreement remain effective in a case of temporary or partial impossibility. That is the tendency, however, of the reasoning in some cases. See, for example, Lloyd v. Murphy, 25 Cal.2d 48, 153 P. 2d 47 (1944). In that case a dealer in new cars suffered from wartime restrictions, and ultimately vacated his Wilshire Boulevard location. Before that, however, the landlords had offered to reduce the rent and to waive prohibitions in the lease against uses they had not consented to, and against subletting. In ruling that the lease was not "frustrated," Justice Traynor emphasized the value of the landlords' concession.[a] The inference might be that the defendant (promisor) was bound to his lease or not, as the promisee might choose to refashion its terms or not. See also UCC 2–613(b) for a rule of "buyer's option."

NOTE

Problem. A, an inventor, licensed B, a manufacturer, to produce and sell his patented washing machine, on paying a royalty of 20¢ each. A agreed not to license any other producer of the machine, and B agreed to pay a royalty of at least $5,000 a year, after the first three years. Five years into the term of the contract, the Government prohibited further manufacture of washing machines for an indefinite term, as part of a program of total mobilization for war. (Nine years thereafter, when A's patent will expire, his permission will no longer be required for exploiting his invention.) Does the Government's order terminate the license contract, or does it only suspend B's duty to pay the minimum royalty? Or should the war-caused loss be divided between A and B in some more imaginative way? See Patch v. Solar Corp., 149 F.2d 558 (7th Cir. 1945), cert. denied, 326 U.S. 741 (1945).

CUTTER v. POWELL

Court of King's Bench, 1795.
6 T.R. 320, 101 Eng. Reprint 573.

[Assumpsit for work and labour performed by plaintiff's intestate. Defendant had given the following note: "Ten days after the ship 'Governor Parry,' myself master, arrives at Liverpool, I promise to pay Mr. T. Cutter the sum of thirty guineas, provided he proceeds, continues and does his duty as second mate in the said ship from hence to the port of Liverpool. . . ." The ship sailed from Kingston on August 2, with T. Cutter on board, and arrived at Liverpool on October 9. Before this, on September 20, Cutter had died. The usual wage for a second mate on such a voyage was £4 per month.]

a. This opinion is a major statement in the law of commercial frustration. As to Justice Traynor's supposed conservatism on that subject, see Macau-

lay, Justice Traynor and the Law of Contract, 13 Stan.L.Rev. 812, 833–38 (1961).

LORD KENYON, CH. J. . . . But it seems to me at present that the decision of this case may proceed on the particular words of this contract, and the precise facts here stated, without touching marine contracts in general. That where the parties have come to an express contract none can be implied has prevailed so long as to be reduced to an axiom in the law. Here the defendant expressly promised to pay the intestate thirty guineas, provided he proceeded, continued and did his duty as second mate in the ship from Jamaica to Liverpool; and the accompanying circumstances disclosed in the case are that the common rate of wages is four pounds per month, when the party is paid in proportion to the time he serves; and that this voyage is generally performed in two months. Therefore if there had been no contract between these parties, all that the intestate could have recovered on a quantum meruit for the voyage would have been eight pounds; whereas here the defendant contracted to pay thirty guineas provided the mate continued to do his duty as mate during the whole voyage, in which case the latter would have received nearly four times as much as if he were paid for the number of months he served. He stipulated to receive the larger sum if the whole duty were performed, and nothing unless the whole of that duty were performed; it was a kind of insurance.

Judgment for defendant.

NOTES

(1) *Death and Illness.* A duty to perform services that are "personal" —i. e., non-delegable—is excused when the promisor suffers death or disabling illness. Also, the death of an employer will terminate a contract the performance of which depends on his conduct. For a doubtful case where the death of a racehorse owner terminated the rights of a jockey he had employed, see Graves v. Cohen, 46 T.L.R. 121 (1929). A clearer example resulted from the death of Nat King Cole, who had employed the claimant for a year as a "musical director in connection with my personal appearances." In ruling that the claimant's salary is terminated by the death, it may be confusing to say that the defense is "impossibility", for money payments can readily be continued. The defense may be characterized as "failure or (sic) consideration" or, more precisely, as "frustration of purpose."

If a performer's agent arranges a personal appearance for him, and dies before it occurs, the agent's representatives may well be entitled to a commission for his services, as agreed. See Peaseley v. Virginia Iron, Coal and Coke Co., 5 N.C.App. 713, 169 S.E.2d 243 (1969) (salesman on commission). And for a real estate broker it may even be that his executor can earn commissions by finding a buyer under an agreement that the owner made with the broker. See Phoenix Title and Trust Co. v. Grimes, 101 Ariz. 182, 416 P.2d 979 (1966).

Not only illness, but the "apprehension" of illness, may excuse a performer from making an appearance. See Wasserman Theatrical Enterprise, Inc. v. Harris, 137 Conn. 371, 77 A.2d 329 (1950) (Walter Huston, the actor, suffered a minor throat ailment.) But of course under a contract for the services of a famous performer, his illness does not excuse either party if suitable provision is made for an understudy. See Terry v. Variety Theatres Company, 44 T.L.R. 451 (1928).

(2) *Self-Induced Impossibility.* A party who willfully disables himself from performing an undertaking is in no position to assert impossibility as a defense. To some extent, not fully examined, his carelessness in permitting a disabling event to occur may have a similar effect. "Some day it may have to be finally determined whether a prima donna is excused by complete loss of voice from an executory contract to sing if it is proved that her condition was caused by her carelessness in not changing her wet clothes after being out in the rain." Viscount Simon, in Joseph Constantine S. S. Line v. Imperial Smelting Corp., [1942] A.C. 154, [1941] 2 All Eng. 165.

If a disabling event has been proved, must the promisor go further, to make good his defense, and establish that it was no fault of his? Or is it then for the promisee to come forward with evidence on the fault issue? Who has the burden of persuasion? On the latter point, see Blount-Midyette & Co. v. Aeroglide Corporation, 254 N.C. 484, 119 S.E.2d 225 (1961), disagreeing with the rule of the English case cited above. See also Arnold v. Ray Charles Enterprises, Inc., 264 N.C. 92, 141 S.E.2d 14 (1965); 6 Corbin, § 1329.

GOLD v. SALEM LUTHERAN HOME ASS'N, 53 Cal.2d 289, 347 P.2d 687 (1959). [The defendant Association maintained a home for the aged, for whom it would agree to provide lifetime care. On August 1, 1956, it admitted Nicholas Chouvaldjy for a trial period of two months. Toward the end of September, he and the Association executed a life care contract dated October 1, for which he paid $8,500. He died on September 28. His executors brought an action against the Association to recover the sum paid.]

McComb, Justice. . . .

Question: *Since performance of the contract was not to commence until October 1, 1956, and Mr. Chouvaldjy died before performance was to commence, (a) was there a failure of consideration for the contract, or (b) was the doctrine of frustration applicable?*

No. (a) . . . Defendant's promise to furnish food, lodging, and care to decedent "for the remainder of his life" constituted consideration for the agreement, and the fact that decedent died before performance of the contract was to commence did not give his estate the right to recover the amount paid under the agreement on the ground that there was a failure of consideration. . . .

(b) The doctrine of frustration is not applicable to the facts in the present case . . . ..

That death may at any unexpected time overcome a man of decedent's age, 84 years, is by common observation readily classified as "reasonably foreseeable." In the present case each party to the contract had clearly assumed the risk of variation of the life span from that predicted by the mortality tables. Therefore, the doctrine of frustration is not applicable here. (Cf. Coyne v. Pacific Mut. Ins. Co., supra, 8 Cal.App.2d at page 109, 47 P.2d at page 1081.)

[A judgment for the Association was affirmed. PETERS, J., dissented on the ground that no "annuity relationship" was to exist until October 1. The contract was "subject to an implied condition that decedent be able to become a life member" on that date.]

NOTES

(1) *Mistake.* If Chouvaldjy's life had been threatened by a fatal illness, unknown to him, when he contracted with the Association, his executors would presumably have based their claim on an additional ground: mistake. (In fact he suffered a stroke the day before his death.) Would the claim have been materially stronger if based on that fact? See Woodworth v. Prudential Ins. Co., 258 App.Div. 103, 15 N.Y.S.2d 541 (1939), aff'd, 282 N.Y. 704, 26 N.E.2d 820 (1940), and comment on that case in Palmer, Mistake and Unjust Enrichment 53–57 (1962).

(2) *Restitution.* In Cutter v. Powell, Lord Kenyon said that the employment contract was "a kind of insurance." An annuity contract and a lifetime care contract are also comparable to insurance contracts. "An ordinary annuity contract provides for the payment of a fixed-dollar annual benefit commencing at a specified date and continuing as long as the annuitant lives. Such a contract is in many contexts treated as a form of insurance." Keeton, Insurance Law (Basic Text) 18 (1971).

Seaman Cutter's contract was arguably different, in that his death cut short performance of a *duty* on his part. Ordinarily a recipient of personal services must pay their value, even though he does not receive the full performance he was promised by reason of "impossibility" such as the death or illness of the promisor. A recovery for the promisor (or his estate) is an instance of a general rule of restitution: see Restatement, § 468. Of course, the decision in Cutter v. Powell must be an exception to that rule, if it is sound. Do the words of the contract there show that the rule was not meant to apply? For criticism of the case see Stoljar, The Great Case of Cutter v. Powell, 34 Can.Bar.Rev. 288, 298–9 (1956).

(3) *Problem.* A lawyer agrees to defend a client's title to Blackacre for $25,000 if successful, and for $5,000 if not. At a trial, the client's title is vindicated, through the lawyer's efforts. The adverse claimant takes an appeal, and the lawyer dies before the appeal is heard. In an action by the lawyer's estate against the client, how should the recovery be measured? Should the amount depend on how the appellate decision goes? See Morton v. Forsee, 249 Mo. 409, 155 S.W. 765 (1913) (4–3 decision). How should the recovery be measured if the controversy is compromised without a decision on appeal?

See also Clark v. Gilbert, 26 N.Y. 279 (1863) ("The recovery in such a case cannot exceed the contract price, or the rate of it for the part of the service performed"), and Matter of Buccini v. Paterno Construction Co., 253 N.Y. 256, 170 N.E. 910 (1930) ("The question to be determined is the benefit to the owner in advancement of the ends to be promoted by the contract").

WEST LOS ANGELES INST. FOR CANCER RESEARCH v. MAYER, 366 F.2d 220 (9th Cir. 1966), cert. denied, 385 U.S. 1010 (1967). [The facts and holding in this case are indicated in Note 2 at p. 417 supra. The additional fact may be noted that the agreement permitted the Mayers to recapture the business upon a "default" by the Institute, as defined. Also, the trial court found that "Ward Mayer did not accept the default provisions as adequate protection against an adverse tax ruling but requested assurances that the property would be returned if the tax assumptions underlying the transaction were challenged, and that he was given such assurances by representatives of the Institute."]

BROWNING, CIR. J. . . . The ultimate question in every case is "whether or not proper interpretation of the contract shows that the risk of the subsequent events, whether or not foreseen, was assumed by the promisor. If it appears from the nature of the contract as well as from the surrounding circumstances that, although they were reasonably foreseeable, the promisor did not assume the risk of the subsequent events, the contract shows a gap subject to supplementation in accordance with rules of objective law." Smit, Frustration of Contract: A Comparative Attempt at Consolidation, 58 Colum.L.Rev. 287 (1958) . . . . [I]t would be untenable to conclude that the parties intended that the Mayers should assume the risk of an adverse tax ruling simply because such a ruling was, in a sense, "foreseeable" . . .

[Affirmed.]

NOTES

(1) *Gap-Filling.* Where Professor Smit's article reads, "the contract shows a gap subject to supplementation," would it not be simpler to say, "the contract *is* subject to supplementation?" He answers, in part, as follows: "Broad terms do not cover unforeseen contingencies. . . . What would seem the inestimable advantage of the gap filling doctrine is that it effectively and permanently eliminates the erroneous assumption that recognition of the legal relevance of frustration requires deviation from the express contractual terms." Op. cit. supra at pp. 313, 315.

(2) *Case Comparisons.* In Mayer's case the court seemed to accept a California decision as authoritative on the issue of frustration, but it did not mention Gold v. Salem Lutheran Home Ass'n. The court said flatly there: "Frustration is no defense if it was reasonably foreseeable." Compare the tax ruling with the "first step" toward a defense of impossibility, as stated in Transatlantic Financing Corporation v. United States, p. 823 supra: "a contingency—something unexpected—must have occurred." Should that be an element of "frustration" also? And if so was it present in Mayer's case? For the view that the element of foreseeability is "not very important," see Aubrey, Frustration Reconsidered, 12 Int. & Comp. L.Q. 1165 (1963). There it is observed: "Many people foresaw the Suez crisis, for example."

In Miller v. Bank, a case cited in the Note on Enforcement *Cy-pres*, p. 854 supra, an increase of real-property taxes on a house was one circumstance leading to revision of a sale contract. That was a case of a rather evident "gap" in the agreement of the parties. What inconvenience would you foresee if every change in a tax law were held to vary the commitments under every executory contract affected by the change? In truth, of course, changes of law and other acts of government that increase the burdens of a contracting party commonly do not excuse his performance. See Lloyd v. Murphy, 25 Cal.2d 48, 153 P.2d 47 (1944) (rationing of automobiles); M. A. Felman Co. v. WJOL, Inc., 104 Ill.App.2d 66, 243 N.E.2d 33 (1968) (FCC regulation); Hungarian People's Republic v. Cecil Associates, 127 F.Supp. 361 (S.D.N.Y.1955) (closure of consulate).

Reconsider your answer to the problem at p. 855 supra. What is distinctive about the facts of the problem?

YOUNG v. CITY OF CHICOPEE

Supreme Judicial Court of Massachusetts, 1904.
186 Mass. 518, 72 N.E. 63.

HAMMOND, J. This is an action to recover for work and materials furnished under a written contract providing for the repair of a wooden bridge forming a part of the highway across the Connecticut river. While the work was in progress the bridge was totally destroyed by fire without the fault of either party, so that the contract could not be performed. The specifications required that the timber and other woodwork of the carriageway, wherever decayed, should be replaced by sound material, securely fastened, so that the way should be in "a complete and substantial condition." As full compensation both for work and materials, the plaintiff was to receive a certain sum per thousand feet for the lumber used "on measurements made after laying and certified by the engineers"; or, in other words, the amount of the plaintiff's compensation was measured by the number of feet of new material wrought into the bridge. That the public travel might not be interfered with more than was reasonably necessary, the contract provided that no work should be begun until material for at least one-half of the repairs contemplated should be "upon the job." With this condition the plaintiff complied, the lumber, which, at the time of the fire had not been used, being distributed "all along the bridge" and upon the river banks. Some of this lumber was destroyed by the fire. At the trial the defendant did not dispute its liability to pay for the work done upon and materials wrought into the structure at the time of the fire (Angus v. Scully, 176 Mass. 357, 57 N.E. 674, 49 L.R.A. 562, 79 Am.St.Rep. 318, and cases there cited), and the only question before us is whether it was liable for the damage to the lumber which was distributed as above stated and had not been used. It is to be noted that there had been no delivery of this lumber to the defendant. It was brought "upon the job," and kept there as the lumber of the plaintiff. The title to it was in him, and not in the defendant. Nor did the defendant have any care or control over it. No part of it belonged to the defendant until wrought into the bridge. The plaintiff could have exchanged it for other lumber. If at any time during the progress of the work before the fire the plaintiff had refused to proceed, the defendant, against his consent, could not lawfully have used it. Indeed, had it not been destroyed, it would have remained the property of the plaintiff after the fire. Nor is the situation changed, so far as respects the question before us, by the fact that the lumber was brought there in compliance with the condition relating to the commencement of the work. This condition manifestly was inserted to insure the rapid progress of the work, and it has no material bearing upon the rights of the parties in relation to the lumber. It is also to be borne in mind in this connection that the compensation for the whole job was to be determined by the amount of lumber wrought into the bridge. The contract was entire. By the destruction of the bridge each party was excused from further performance, and the plaintiff could recover for partial performance. The principle upon which the plaintiff can do this is sometimes said to rest upon the doctrine that there is an implied contract upon the owner of the structure upon which the work is to be done that it shall continue to exist, and therefore, if it is destroyed, even without his fault, still he must be regarded as in default, and so liable to pay for what has been done. Niblo v. Binsse, *40 N.Y. 476; Whelen v. Ansonia Clock Co., 97 N.Y. 293. In Butterfield v. Byron, 153 Mass. 523, 27 N.E. 669, 12 L.R.A. 571, 25 Am.St.Rep. 654, it was said by Knowlton, J., that there was "an implied assumpsit for what has properly been done by either [of the parties], the law dealing with it as done at the request of the other, and creating a liability to pay for it its value." In whatever way the principle may be stated, it would seem that the liability of the owner in a case like this should be measured by the amount of the contract work done which at the time of the destruction of the structure had become so far identified with it as that, but for the destruction, it would have inured to him as contemplated by the contract. In the present case the defendant, in accordance with this doctrine, should be held liable for the labor and materials actually wrought into the bridge. To that extent it insured the plaintiff. But it did not insure the plaintiff against the loss of lumber owned by him at the time of the fire, which had not then come into such relations with the bridge as, but for the fire, to inure to the benefit of the defendant, as contemplated by the contract. The cases of Haynes v. Second Baptist Church, 88 Mo. 285, 57 Am.Rep. 413, and Rawson v. Clark, 70 Ill. 656, cited by the plaintiff, seem to us to be distinguishable from this case.

The exceptions therefore must be sustained, and the verdict set aside. In accordance with the terms of the statement contained in the bill of exceptions, judgment should be entered for the plaintiff in the sum of $584 damages, and it is so ordered.

NOTES

(1) *Repair v. Building.* If Young had contracted to erect a bridge from scratch, rather than to repair one, the risk of its destruction by casualty, before completion, would have rested entirely on him, in the absence of an agreement to the contrary.[a] So far from recovering for a part performance, he would have been accountable for breach if he did not begin again. "It is well established law, that, where one contracts to furnish labor and materials, and construct a chattel or build a house on land of another, he will not ordinarily be excused from performance of his contract by the destruction of the chattel or building, without his fault, before the time fixed for the delivery of it." Butterfield v. Byron, 153 Mass. 517, 27 N.E. 667 (1891). According to Corbin: "This is the rule that is applied to contracts for the erection of buildings and bridges, the driving of tunnels, the building of dams, the manufacture of goods." 6 Corbin, § 1338. What might account for the difference, in this respect, between construction contracts and repair contracts?

(2) *The Case of the House Halfway.* Owner contracted with Mover to have his building on Third Street relocated on First Street, at a fixed price. When Mover had gotten it about halfway, and quit work for the night, it was consumed by fire, through no fault of his. Owner disclaimed any liability, and Mover sued for the fair value of his services rendered in the work down to the time of the fire. Mover obtained a judgment on a jury verdict (amount unspecified), and Owner appealed. *Held:* Affirmed. Angus v. Scully, 176 Mass. 357, 57 N.E. 674 (1900).

(3) *Pre-Existing Duty.* A fire at a building site destroyed materials and equipment that had been placed there by an electrical subcontractor. The sub replaced the materials and completed his work, after being assured by the general contractor that he would be reimbursed for the fire loss. The fire was not caused by either party, and the subcontract did not specify who should bear such a loss. Not being reimbursed, the sub sued the general contractor. *Held:* For the defendant. The assurance, or promise, was given without consideration, for the plaintiff's undertaking to do the work imposed on him the risk of damage to the materials. Mainland v. Alfred Brown Company, 85 Nev. 654, 461 P.2d 862 (1969).

(4) *Insurance and Supplies.* Buildings under construction are commonly insured in "builder's risk" policies. The policies insure not only the structure itself, but also (for example)

> materials, equipment and supplies of all kinds incident to the construction of said building or structure and, when not otherwise covered by insurance, builders' machinery, tools and equipment owned by the Insured or similar property of others for which the Insured is legally liable [while on the premises].

The policy may be written so as to name both the builder and the owner as "the insured," reducing the incidence of problems like that in the main case.

---

a. For a collection of cases, indicating a minor strain of dissent, see Anno., 28 A.L.R.3d 788 (1969).

That was the situation in Transamerica Ins. Co. v. Gage Plumbing and Heating Co., 433 F.2d 1051 (10th Cir. 1970). The insurer refused to pay, however, for a fire loss to supplies at the job site that belonged to Gage, a subcontractor. Gage was not named as an insured in the policy: it claimed to be an unnamed insured by reason of the clause set out above. Keeping in mind the general rule that insurance policies are construed against the interest of the insurer, in case of doubt, do you see a way of sustaining Gage's claim?

RESTITUTION IN ENGLISH LAW

In English law an accrued obligation—that is, a duty of performance owing at the time of the event discharging the contract—has always been treated as absolute to the same extent as a prior payment would be regarded as final. Chandler v. Webster, [1904] 1 K.B. 493 (one of the so-called "coronation cases," to be compared with Krell v. Henry, p. 847 supra). However, sums are recoverable from a party who has received payment under the contract, or has obtained a valuable benefit by reason of another party's performance, before the time of the discharge by impossibility or frustration. This doctrine dates from 1943, when the House of Lords permitted a Polish company to recover £1,000 which it had paid to an English maker of textile machinery, in the summer of 1939. When Poland was invaded it became impossible for the seller to make delivery of the machines as required by the contract. Fibrosa Spolka Akcyjna v. Fairbairn Lawson Combe Barbour, Ltd., [1943] A.C. 32, 144 A.L.R. 1298. If the seller had done any fruitless work on the machines, it was said that no offset could be allowed for that.

The case suggested to Parliament that a more equitable solution might be achieved, and the response was the Law Reform (Frustrated Contracts) Act, 1943. One of its chief effects was to alter the position of one who has received an advance payment, but has also incurred expenses going toward his own performance: "the court may, if it considers it just to do so having regard to all the circumstances of the case, allow him to retain [part of the prepayment], not being an amount in excess of the expenses so incurred." Section 1(2).

NOTES

(1) *Equal Division?* In the Fibrosa case, how much of the prepayment could the seller justly retain, if it had expended £800 in manufacturing the machines (now unsalable) before the contract was discharged? The proponents of the Act thought he should have to repay £200. The Lord Chancellor (Simon) said, "I think that will commend itself to everybody as good sense," in giving such an example. But Professor Glanville Williams has argued that he should have to return £600, shouldering half of the unavoidable loss. "Either natural justice, on my understanding of it, is altogether silent on a case of this sort, or it decrees that the distribution of loss shall be equal. Equal division of loss is also economically

sounder than the placing of loss on one party only, for each of the two parties may be able to bear half the loss without serious consequences when the whole loss might come close to ruining him." See Williams, Law Reform (Frustrated Contracts) Act, 35–6 (1944).

This argument assumes that the seller did not contract for the early payment of £1,000 in order to protect himself against discharge of the contract by the law of impossibility, but rather against the risk of insolvency: "It is not often that parties contemplate that performance of their contract will become impossible. If they do contemplate the latter event, their usual reaction is to take out a policy of insurance, not to provide for payment in advance." Id., 36.

(2) *Problem.* A contracted to build showcases and other fixtures for B's projected store in a new shopping center, and was paid $1,000 in advance. He has done work reasonably worth $2,000, when B informs him that the sponsors of the shopping center will not let B have space there. B refuses to make further payment for the fixtures. What prospect do you see in a claim by A?

In English law, unless A can enforce the contract, he has no claim, presumably. (But he might well retain the $1,000.) Are his prospects better in American law? Compare the case with Young v. City of Chicopee, and with the case in Note 2 thereafter: Angus v. Scully. See Wallace Studios, Inc. v. Brochstein's, Inc., 297 S.W.2d 218 (Tex.Civ.App.1956), error refused n. r. e.

If A has no claim, is it possible that he must repay the $1,000 to B? See Restatement, § 468.

(3) *Loss Apportionment.* Statutes apportioning the consideration "according to the benefit" appear in some states, e. g., Cal.Civ.Code, § 1514. In a Note at 69 Yale L.J. 1054 (1960), a statute is proposed which broadly defines the "apportionable loss" and, with certain limitations, permits the court to apportion it among the parties equally, or "in any manner it deems just". Losses compensated by insurance would not be apportionable. Is it clear that the common law cannot adapt to the demands of justice in these situations? For an ingenious loss-apportionment without benefit of statute, see Kinzer Const. Co. v. State, 125 N.Y.S. 46 (Ct.Cl.1910), aff'd, 145 App. Div. 41, 129 N.Y.S. 567 (1911), aff'd, 204 N.Y. 381, 97 N.E. 871 (1912).

M. AHERN CO. v. JOHN BOWEN CO.

Supreme Judicial Court of Massachusetts, 1956.
334 Mass. 36, 133 N.E.2d 484.

WHITTEMORE, JUSTICE. This is an action of contract to recover for labor and materials furnished by the plaintiff as a subcontractor, to the defendant as general contractor, in connection with the construction in Boston, by the Commonwealth, of the Chronic Disease Hospital and Nurses' Home. The case was tried in the Superior Court without a jury and the judge found for the plaintiff. The defendant excepted (1) to the refusal of the trial judge to rule that upon all the evidence the defendant was entitled to judgment, (2) to the finding for the plaintiff, and (3) to the exclusion of certain evidence. There was no error.

The essential facts are not in dispute. The labor and materials had been furnished under a partially performed contract, the further performance of which had become impossible because of the decision of this court in Gifford v. Commissioner of Public Health, 328 Mass. 608, 105 N.E.2d 476, declaring void the underlying general contract between the defendant and the Commonwealth. The amount claimed due, apart from interest, was the difference between the value of the materials and labor furnished and the sums paid by the defendant to the plaintiff under the terms of the contract prior to the Gifford decision.

The subject contract provided in part for the plaintiff's "furnishing all labor, material, equipment, insurance, etc., to do all plumbing as called for in . . . [stated parts of the general contract and contract documents] all in accordance with the plans and specifications . . . and perform all work to the satisfaction of the governing authorities and John Bowen Co., Inc. [the defendant]"; also that "You as subcontractor, further agree to be bound to us, the general contractor, by the terms of the special form of construction contract for projects under jurisdiction of Mass. Public Building Commission, the general conditions, drawings and specifications, and to assume toward us all the obligations and responsibilities that we, by those documents, assume toward the owner. . . . Terms of payment are to be the same as our terms of payment with the owner, all as outlined under . . . [the relevant part of the construction contract]. It is understood . . . that we [the defendant] accept no clause, reservation, or agreement other than those herein mentioned."

Prior to learning that it had no contract under which it could continue work, the defendant had been paid by the Commonwealth the amounts called for in three requisitions, less ten per cent as provided in the contract, and the defendant had paid the plaintiff the amount allowed in these requisitions for plumbing work less ten per cent. The amount found due represents, as to principal, the retained ten per cent plus additional work done and materials furnished, not covered in the honored requisitions.

The evidence to the exclusion of which the defendant excepted consisted of certain papers in two cross actions between the defendant here and the Commonwealth. The defendant offered to show that these cross actions had been tried together, and that the judge had ruled that neither party could recover from the other, that is, the defendant could not recover from the Commonwealth for the fair value of materials and labor furnished up to the time work ceased, including materials and labor furnished by the plaintiff here, and the Commonwealth could not recover the amounts paid to the defendant on the honored requisitions; also that following the findings by the judge there was "in each case . . . an agreement . . . of the parties to accept his decision" evidenced by the filing of the agreements for judgment.

It is plain that the defendant does not owe the plaintiff any sum under the contract and that the plaintiff after the Gifford decision could have done nothing to mature an obligation of the defendant under its terms. But the absence of an express provision in the contract to cover the unexpected contingency has not deterred this court or other American courts from giving recovery in cases of excusable impossibility for such performance as has been received. Butterfield v. Byron, 153 Mass. 517, 521, 522, 27 N.E. 667, 12 L.R.A. 571; Angus v. Scully, 176 Mass. 357, 358, 57 N.E. 674, 49 L.R.A. 562; Young v. Chicopee, 186 Mass. 518, 72 N.E. 63; Herbert v. Dewey, 191 Mass. 403, 411, 77 N.E. 822; Eastern Expanded Metal Co. v. Webb Granite & Construction Co., 195 Mass. 356, 362–363, 81 N.E. 251; Vickery v. Ritchie, 202 Mass. 247, 250–251, 88 N.E. 835, 26 L.R.A.,N.S., 810; Williston, Contracts (Rev.Ed.) §§ 1975–1977. Restatement: Contracts, § 468.

These decisions are not, as the defendant argues, based in the ultimate analysis on the principle of unjust enrichment which underlies restitution cases wherein recovery is limited to benefits received. Restatement: Contracts, § 348; Restatement: Restitution, § 155. Our decisions have spoken of "an implication that what was furnished was to be paid for", Vickery v. Ritchie [supra], or have indulged the fiction of an implied contract that the subject matter will continue to exist so that even though the defendant is without fault in fact he is to be regarded as in default and hence liable to pay. Young v. Chicopee [supra]. In commenting upon the "benefit" theory Williston (Contracts [Rev.Ed.] § 1977, pages 5553–5554) says, "It is sometimes said that the defendant is liable for the benefit which he has received, but unless the word 'benefit' is given a meaning wider than is natural, the statement is inadequate. In the first place, the word 'benefit' suggests that the matter is to be examined as it exists after the impossibility has supervened; but . . . the American law seems clear that where the defendant has received part performance regarded as valuable under the contract between the parties, the fact that this value has been destroyed by the very circumstances which make full performance of the contract impossible will not preclude recovery. A second reason for discarding the use of the word 'benefit,' in this connection, is because it suggests that what has been received by the defendant must be of pecuniary advantage to him. This seems unnecessary. . . . Accordingly, it is well settled that a recovery on a quantum meruit or quantum valebat should prima facie be such a proportion of the price as the work which the plaintiff has done bears to the full amount of the work for which the contract provided." And see idem, § 1972A, page 5541. Restatement: Contracts, § 468(3), gives "benefit" an appropriately limited meaning in saying, "The value of performance within the meaning of Subsections (1, 2) is the benefit derived from the performance in advancing the object of the contract, not exceeding, however, a ratable portion of the contract price." . . .

In Gillis v. Cobe, 177 Mass. 584, 59 N.E. 455, on which the defendant relies, the plaintiff did not show himself free of fault in respect to his nonperformance of the contract, 177 Mass. at page 597, 59 N.E. at page 459. The distinction between that case and the line with which this case stands was noted by the court in that opinion, 177 Mass. at page 592, 59 N.E. at page 457 and reaffirmed in Vickery v. Ritchie [supra].

It is no longer necessary to find implications of a contract to support recovery. The implications are undoubtedly found in each case in accordance with what the court holds to be fair and just in the unanticipated circumstances and it is in order to proceed at once to that issue.

This is not a case where the defendant stands fully apart, as the plaintiff does, from the circumstances which caused the unexpected destruction of the subject matter of the contract. The defendant did those things with respect to the subbids discussed in Gifford v. Commissioner of Public Health [supra], which caused its bid to appear the lowest, although in fact it was not. The Gifford decision has held that what the defendant did was not properly done. Even though we assume, as the defendant urges here, that it acted in good faith, and in respects as to which the prescribed course was not clear, the fact is that its actions, in a field where it had a choice, had a significant part in bringing about the subsequent critical events—the awarding to it of an apparent contract which turned out to be void and the ensuing decision of this court. In the circumstances it is plain that this is not a case of fully excusable impossibility. The defendant's part in the train of events is amply sufficient to offset the consideration that it has suffered uncompensable loss. Whatever might be said against the application of our established rule (and we do not intend any suggestion) to a case where the contract subject matter is destroyed by an event completely unconnected with either party and where both parties were equally interested in making the contract for mutual profit, and neither, by insurance or otherwise, could have provided against the risk of the unexpected loss and there is no final benefit, it is clearly fair and just to say in the instant case that "It is enough that the defendant has actually received in part performance of the contract something for which when completed he had agreed to pay a price." Williston, Contracts (Rev. ed.) § 1976, page 5551.

The plaintiff's contract was with the defendant, not with the Commonwealth. East Side Construction Co., Inc., v. Town of Adams, 329 Mass. 347, 353, 108 N.E.2d 659. There are in it necessarily, important references to the underlying contract. And it is clear that, while the contract continued, the plaintiff would become entitled to payment only as the defendant was paid by the Commonwealth under the general contract. But there is no express provision that the plaintiff is to be paid only if the defendant is paid, regardless of what happens to the general contract. There is no basis for saying what the parties would have done if they had thought of the matter. But the implication of the circumstances (that is, fairness in the circumstances) is against such a construction.

What has been said disposes of the exception to the exclusion of evidence. The liability of the defendant did not depend upon whether the defendant had or would receive payment from the Commonwealth for the labor and materials for which the plaintiff here makes claim.

Exceptions overruled.

NOTES

(1) *Subsequent Litigation.* The Boston Plate & Window Glass Company contracted to do the glass and glazing work on the same hospital. Before the work was actually begun, it was advised by the John Bowen Company not to proceed, for the reason given in the main case. The Glass Company had incurred some expenses in preparing to do the work, and it brought an action against Bowen on the contract. The trial court concluded that it should recover the "cost of estimates, drawings, labor and all other expenses inclusive of allocable overhead charges relative to plaintiff's contract with the defendant, but exclusive of any profit."

On appeal, the court rendered judgment for Bowen, holding that it was not liable for breach of the contract. It said: "We need not consider—and intend no intimation—whether and to what extent, under appropriate pleadings, in an extension of the principle established in M. Ahern Co. v. John Bowen Co. . . ., recovery may be had for payments made or obligations reasonably incurred in preparation for performance of a contract after it has been executed and delivered and is reasonably understood to be in effect. See Williston on Contracts (Rev. ed.) § 1976. . . . [T]he damages awarded included items outside such categories." Boston Plate & Window Glass Co. v. John Bowen Co., 335 Mass. 697, 141 N.E.2d 715 (1957).

The Albre Marble and Tile Company was in a position much like that of the Glass Company. It brought an action against Bowen for the value of work and labor furnished at Bowen's request. Their contract provided that Albre would "furnish and submit all necessary or required samples, shop drawings, tests, affidavits, etc., for approval, all as ordered or specified. . . ." The court decided that Albre should recover the "fair value of those acts done in conformity with the specific request of the defendant as contained in the contract", and justified the decision by reference to a "combination of circumstances peculiar to this case". Two excerpts from its decision follow:

"Although the matter of denial of reliance expenditures in impossibility situations seems to have been discussed but little in judicial opinions, it has, however, been the subject of critical comment by scholars.

See Fuller and Perdue, The Reliance Interest in Contract Damages, 46 Yale L.J. 52, 373, 379–383. Note, 46 Mich.L.Rev. 401. In England the recent frustrated contracts legislation provides that the court may grant recovery for expenditures in reliance on the contract or in preparation to perform it where it appears *'just to do so having regard to all the circumstances of the case'* (emphasis supplied). 6 & 7 George VI, c. 40." [a]

". . . We are mindful that in Young v. Chicopee [p. 860 supra], recovery of the value of materials brought to the construction site at the specific request of the defendant therein was denied. But in that case the supervening act rendering further performance impossible was a fire not shown to have been caused by the fault of either party. We are not disposed to extend that holding to a situation in which the defendant's fault is greater than the plaintiff's.

"Moreover, the acts requested here by their very nature could not be 'wrought into' the structure. In Angus v. Scully [Note 2, p. 862 supra], recovery for the value of services rendered by house movers was allowed although the house was destroyed midway in the moving. The present case comes nearer to the rationale of the Angus case than to that of the Young case." Albre Marble and Tile Co. v. John Bowen Co., 338 Mass. 394, 155 N.E.2d 437 (1959); 343 Mass. 777, 179 N.E.2d 321 (1962) (second appeal).

(2) *Reliance Expenditures.* It is interesting to speculate that courts sometimes give rein to their sympathies rather than apply rules which would saddle a party with unforeseen losses in the form of work and expense in preparation for his performance under a contract. Do the cases show a "covert influence of the desire to reimburse detrimental reliance"? Certain cases in which a promised performance was not excused by unforeseen circumstances may be explained this way. Raner v. Goldberg, 244 N.Y. 438, 155 N.E. 733 (1927). Compare Tube-Art Display v. Berg, 37 Wash.2d 1, 221 P.2d 510 (1950), with Claude Neon Federal Co. v. Meyer Bros., 150 So. 410 (La.App.1933). Other cases are collected by Fuller and Perdue at 46 Yale L.J. 373, pp. 379–82. However, they could find no case in a common-law jurisdiction where a fair sharing of the loss was expressly said to require recovery of the plaintiff's reliance interest. The decision in Albre Marble and Tile Co. v. John Bowen Co., Note 1 supra, has met that description, and confirmed their analysis.

(3) *Problem.* James Moore was indicted for passing counterfeit money. Robinson, a lawyer, contracted with Thomas, James' brother, to defend him for $1,000, of which $600 was paid. Thomas gave a note to Robinson for the remainder of his fee, not to be enforced if he did not win an acquittal in 1875. James was never tried, apparently having "skipped bail," but not until Robinson had spent some time on the case. What is the legal position of the contracting parties? See Moore v. Robinson, 92 Ill. 491 (1879).

a. This is not accurate, is it?

Chapter 9

THIRD PARTY BENEFICIARIES

The modern development of third party beneficiary law, at least in this country, is usually dated from Lawrence v. Fox, decided in 1859 (see p. 873 infra). Long before then, however, claims on contracts had been made by persons who were not parties to them. The results were mixed. In 17th century England it was successfully argued that a promise to pay a woman £1,000 was enforceable by her, although it was made to her father, and although she gave nothing in exchange for the promise. Later this case was disapproved. According to a 19th century English judge, "It would be a monstrous proposition to say that a person was a party to the contract for the purpose of suing upon it for his own advantage, and not for the purpose of being sued." [a]

As the case law has developed in this country, it is generally accepted that an action may be maintained on a contract, in an appropriate case, by one who had no part in creating it. The contract in such a case is said to be a "third party beneficiary contract." Probably the class of these contracts most familiar to the public at large is contracts of life insurance. It is perfectly well understood that the beneficiary of a life insurance policy may enforce his right to the death benefits even though he did not apply for it, pay for it, or have any other connection with it.

Of course, many contracts are not in this category, and often a claimant's attempt to seize an advantage under a contract between other parties meets with failure. The Restatement of Contracts has popularized the term "incidental beneficiary" for a third party who, though he may enjoy an advantage through the performance of a contract, has no enforceable interest in its performance. A clear—though admittedly bizarre—example may be helpful. Blake and Sullivan were colleagues in an attempt at armed robbery, and were apprehended. Blake pleaded guilty to a charge of assault, by agreement with the district attorney. Part of the agreement (it was said) was that the D.A. would not call Blake to testify against Sullivan. In the prosecution against Sullivan it was held that he could not claim the benefit of this agreement. If it was a contract at all, Sullivan was only an incidental beneficiary of it. [b]

a. Crompton, J., in Tweddle v. Atkinson, 1 B. & S. 393, 121 Eng.Rep. 762 (Q.B.1861).

b. People v. Sullivan, 271 Cal.App.2d 531, 77 Cal.Rptr. 25 (1969), cert. denied, 396 U.S. 973 (1969). Blake was called to the stand, but refused to say who his companion was. Sullivan was of course convicted.

A beneficiary who has an enforceable interest in performance of the contract may be variously known as a "donee beneficiary," a "creditor beneficiary," or simply as an "intended beneficiary."

Several bodies of law exist, apart from third party beneficiary law, by which a contract may create such an interest in a party who is not named or addressed in it. By the law of agency, for example, an undisclosed principal of one of the named parties may enforce a contract made on his behalf. In some situations various doctrinal ideas work in tandem to the same end. The following example is given in the Restatement Second: "the rights of employees under a collective bargaining agreement are sometimes treated as rights of contract beneficiaries, sometimes as rights based on agency principles, sometimes as rights analogous to the rights of trust beneficiaries. Or the collective bargaining agreement may be treated as establishing a usage incorporated in individual employment contracts, or as analogous to legislation."

The Restatement Second also refers to certain "overriding social policies" that may determine the stake of third parties in an agreement. Such policies are beyond the scope of the Restatement and of this book. For instance, the range of warranties accompanying sales of goods is not explored here. The business of this chapter is to identify third party interests in performance, as determined by the general law of agreements, and to indicate some qualities of those interests.

Through the power of contracting parties to create rights in others many needs have been met, some commercial in nature, others not; and there are "procedural" conveniences as well in recognizing third party claims in contracts. Nevertheless, there are complications and inconveniences in the law of third party beneficiaries. It will be well, in going through the chapter, to consider both aspects of the subject. When disadvantages are encountered in granting a third-party claim, it may be possible to think of an alternate arrangement that would serve the purpose better. And in many of the cases there is a challenge to skill in drafting, so as to remove doubts and to promote the objects of the agreement.

NOTES

(1) *The Unborn Beneficiary.* In 1956 a federal antitrust prosecution of the IBM Corporation resulted in an important consent decree, whereby IBM was obliged to alter some of its business practices: e. g., to permit its customers to buy as well as rent its machines ("hardware"). One theory of the decree was that computer users would then be free to acquire ancillary products and services ("software") from other suppliers. It appears that the decree gave rise to an entirely new industry, including a firm called Data Processing. Many years later, this firm brought an action against IBM alleging its violation of the decree, in particular that it had failed to offer its hardware for sale "upon terms and conditions which shall not be substantially more advantageous to IBM than the lease charges,

terms and conditions for such machines." The amount of the claim was 315.5 million dollars. Data Processing represented itself as a third party beneficiary of the settlement between IBM and the United States. The trial court ruled against the claimant on this theory, striking the references to the decree in the complaint. It described the claimant as an "unborn" beneficiary, referring to the fact that it did not exist at the time of the IBM decree. Data Processing appealed. *Held:* Affirmed, per curiam. Data Proc. Fin. & Gen. Corp. v. Int. Bus. Mach. Corp., 430 F.2d 1277 (8th Cir. 1970).

(2) *A Mix-up.* In a case involving sensitive issues of public policy, or one for which there is sparse precedent, third party beneficiary theory may sometimes be of service to a resourceful counsel, or to a court, in arriving at a satisfactory result. An example is Bossier Parish School Board v. Lemon, 370 F.2d 847 (5th Cir. 1967), cert. denied, 388 U.S. 911 (1967). A holding there was that Negro airmen stationed in Louisiana could assert their children's rights to desegregated public education as third party beneficiaries of "contractual assurances" given by the local school board to the United States, in return for heavy grants of financial aid.

The result may be a mix-up in the law, of course. This case has been carelessly cited in a purely commercial context, even though the court did not rely primarily on third party beneficiary theory, and added: "Contract rights are not involved in this case." See also Todd v. Joint Apprenticeship Com. of Steel Wkrs., 223 F.Supp. 12 (N.D.Ill.1963), vacated for mootness, 332 F.2d 243 (7th Cir. 1964), cert. denied, 380 U.S. 914 (1965) (victims of racial discrimination claiming under fair-employment contracts).

(3) *Express Trust.* An express trust is defined as "a fiduciary relationship with respect to property, subjecting the person by whom the property is held to equitable duties to deal with the property for the benefit of another person, which arises as a result of a manifestation of an intention to create it." The requisite to be noticed here is that there be some property—a *res*—as the subject matter of the trust. An instance that is given in the next main case is a quantity of lead: X has promised a pig of lead to A, and he entrusts lead to B who undertakes to make it into a pig and deliver it to A. In such a case A has a property interest in the lead which will be recognized and vindicated by special procedures in equity, chancery courts being the historic guardians of trusts, The property may be a bag of money as well as a pig of lead; or it may be an intangible such as a contract right. But in any event, in the case of a trust "there is always some property which is the subject matter of the trust, and which is held by the trustee for the benefit of the cestui que trust." 1 Scott on Trusts, § 2.6 (3d ed. 1967).

(4) *The Promisee as "Agent."* Courts reluctant to subscribe wholeheartedly to the third party beneficiary doctrine frequently support a factually appealing suit by the third party on the theory—or fiction—that the promisee was acting as agent for the third party in making the contract. Two interesting Massachusetts illustrations of this are Gardner v. Denison, 217 Mass. 492, 105 N.E. 359 (1914), and Green v. Green, 298 Mass. 19, 9 N.E.2d 413 (1937). For a comparison of agency and trust relationships with those growing out of third party beneficiary contracts, see Restatement Second, § 133, Comment f.

LAWRENCE v. FOX

Court of Appeals of New York, 1859.
20 N.Y. 268.

Appeal from the Superior Court of the City of Buffalo. On the trial before Mr. Justice Masten, it appeared by the evidence of a by-stander that one Holly, in November, 1857, at the request of the defendant, loaned and advanced to him $300, stating at the time that he owed that sum to the plaintiff for money borrowed of him, and had agreed to pay it to him the then next day; that the defendant, in consideration thereof, at the time of receiving the money, promised to pay it to the plaintiff the then next day. Upon this state of facts the defendant moved for a nonsuit, upon three several grounds, viz.: That there was no proof tending to show that Holly was indebted to the plaintiff, that the agreement by the defendant with Holly to pay the plaintiff was void for want of consideration, and that there was no privity between the plaintiff and defendant. The court overruled the motion, and the counsel for the defendant excepted. The cause was then submitted to the jury, and they found a verdict for the plaintiff for the amount of the loan and interest, $344.66, upon which judgment was entered, from which the defendant appealed to the Superior Court, at General Term, where the judgment was affirmed, and the defendant appealed to this court. The cause was submitted on printed argument.

H. GRAY, J. The first objection raised on the trial amounts to this: That the evidence of the person present, who heard the declarations of Holly giving directions as to the payment of the money he was then advancing to the defendant, was mere hearsay and, therefore, not competent. Had the plaintiff sued Holly for this sum of money no objection to the competency of this evidence would have been thought of; and if the defendant had performed his promise by paying the sum loaned to him to the plaintiff, and Holly had afterwards sued him for its recovery, and the evidence had been offered by the defendant, it would doubtless have been received without an objection from any source. All the defendant had the right to demand in this case was evidence which, as between Holly and the plaintiff, was competent to establish the relation between them of debtor and creditor. For that purpose the evidence was clearly competent; it covered the whole ground and warranted the verdict of the jury.

But it is claimed that notwithstanding this promise was established by competent evidence, it was void for the want of consideration. It is now more than a quarter of a century since it was settled by the supreme court of this state—in an able and painstaking opinion by the late Chief Justice Savage, in which the authorities were fully examined and carefully analyzed—that a promise in all material respects like the one under consideration was valid; and the judgment of that court was unanimously affirmed by the court for the correction of errors. Farley v. Cleveland, 4 Cow. 432, 15 Am.Dec. 387; s. c. in error, 9 Cow. 639. In that case one Moon owed Farley and sold to Cleveland a quantity of hay, in consideration of which Cleveland promised to pay Moon's debt to Farley; and the decision in favor of Farley's right to recover was placed upon the ground that the hay received by Cleveland from Moon was a valid consideration for Cleveland's promise to pay Farley, and that the subsisting liability of Moon to pay Farley was no objection to the recovery. The fact that the money advanced by Holly to the defendant was a loan to him for a day, and that it thereby became the property of the defendant, seemed to impress the defendant's counsel with the idea that because the defendant's promise was not a trust fund placed by the plaintiff in the defendant's hands, out of which he was to realize money as from the sale of a chattel or the collection of a debt, the promise although made for the benefit of the plaintiff could not inure to his benefit. The hay which Cleveland bought of Moon was not to be paid to Farley, but the debt incurred by Cleveland for the purchase of the hay, like the debt incurred by the defendant for money borrowed, was what was to be paid.

That case has been often referred to by the courts of this state, and has never been doubted as sound authority for the principle upheld by it. Barker v. Bucklin, 2 Denio 45, 43 Am.Dec. 726; Canal Co. v. Westchester County Bank, 4 Denio 97. It puts to rest the objection that the defendant's promise was void for want of consideration. The report of that case shows that the promise was not only made to Moon but to the plaintiff Farley. In this case the promise was made to Holly and not expressly to the plaintiff; and this difference between the two cases presents the question, raised by the defendant's objection, as to the want of privity between the plaintiff and defendant. . . .

But it is urged that because the defendant was not in any sense a trustee of the property of Holly for the benefit of the plaintiff, the law will not imply a promise. I agree that many of the cases where a promise was implied were cases of trusts, created for the benefit of the promisor. The case of Felton v. Dickinson, 10 Mass. 287, and others that might be cited are of that class; but concede them all to have been cases of trusts, and it proves nothing against the application of the rule to this case. The duty of the trustee to pay the cestui que trust, according to the terms of the trust, implies his promise to the latter to do so. In this case the defendant, upon ample consideration received from Holly, promised Holly to pay his debt to the plaintiff; the consideration received and the promise to Holly made it as plainly his duty to pay the plaintiff as if the money had been remitted to him for that purpose, and as well implied a promise to do so as if he had been made a trustee of property to be converted into cash with which to pay. The fact that a breach of the duty imposed in the one case may be visited, and justly, with more serious consequences than in the other, by no means disproves the payment to be a duty in both.   The principle illustrated by the example so frequently quoted (which concisely states the case in hand) "that a promise made to one for the benefit of another, he for whose benefit it is made may bring an action for its breach," has been applied to trust cases, not because it was exclusively applicable to those cases, but because it was a principle of law, and as such applicable to those cases.

It was also insisted that Holly could have discharged the defendant from his promise, though it was intended by both parties for the benefit of the plaintiff, and, therefore, the plaintiff was not entitled to maintain this suit for the recovery of a demand over which he had no control.   It is enough that the plaintiff did not release the defendant from his promise, and whether he could or not is a question not now necessarily involved; but if it was, I think it would be found difficult to maintain the right of Holly to discharge a judgment recovered by the plaintiff upon confession or otherwise, for the breach of the defendant's promise; and if he could not, how could he discharge the suit before judgment, or the promise before suit, made as it was for the plaintiff's benefit and in accordance with legal presumption accepted by him (Berly v. Taylor, 5 Hill, 577–584 et seq.), until his dissent was shown?

The cases cited and especially that of Farley v. Cleveland, established the validity of a parol promise; it stands then upon the footing of a written one.   Suppose the defendant had given his note in which for value received of Holly, he had promised to pay the plaintiff and the plaintiff had accepted the promise, retaining Holly's liability. Very clearly Holly could not have discharged that promise, be the right to release the defendant as it may.   No one can doubt that he owes the sum of money demanded of him or that in accordance with his promise it was his duty to have paid it to the plaintiff; nor can it be doubted that whatever may be the diversity of opinion elsewhere, the adjudications in this state, from a very early period, approved by experience, have established the defendant's liability; if, therefore, it could be shown that a more strict and technically accurate application of the rules applied, would lead to a different result (which I by no means concede), the effort should not be made in the face of manifest justice.

The judgment should be affirmed.

JOHNSON, CH. J., DENIO, SELDEN, ALLEN and STRONG, JJ., concurred.   JOHNSON, CH. J., and DENIO, J., were of opinion that the promise was to be regarded as made to the plaintiff through the medium of his agent, whose action he could ratify when it came to his knowledge, though taken without his being privy thereto.

COMSTOCK, J. (dissenting).   The plaintiff had nothing to do with the promise on which he brought this action.   It was not made to him, nor did the consideration proceed from him. If he can maintain the suit, it is because an anomaly has found its way into the law on this subject. In general, there must be privity of contract. The party who sues upon a promise must be the promisee, or he must have some legal interest in the undertaking. In this case, it is plain that Holly, who loaned the money to the defendant, and to whom the promise in question was made, could at any time have claimed that it should be performed to himself personally. He had lent the money to the defendant, and at the same time directed the latter to pay the sum to the plaintiff. This direction he could countermand, and if he had done so, manifestly the defendant's promise to pay according to the direction would have ceased to exist. The plaintiff would receive a benefit by a complete execution of the arrangement, but the arrangement itself was between other parties, and was under their exclusive control. If the defendant had paid the money to Holly, his debt would have been discharged thereby. So Holly might have released the demand or assigned it to another person, or the parties might have annulled the promise now in question, and designated some other creditor of Holly as the party to whom the money should be paid. It has never been claimed that in a case thus situated the right of a third person to sue upon the promise rested on any sound principle of law. We are to inquire whether the rule has been so established by positive authority. .   .   .

If A. delivers money or property to B., which the latter accepts upon a trust for the benefit of C., the latter can enforce the trust by an appropriate action for that purpose. Berly v. Taylor, 5 Hill, 577. If the trust be of money, I think the beneficiary may assent to it and bring the action for money had and received to his use. If it be of something else than money, the trustee must account for it according to the terms of the trust, and upon principles of equity. There is some authority even for saying that an express promise founded on the possession of a trust fund may be enforced by an action at law in the name of the beneficiary, although it was made to the creator of the trust. Thus, in Comyn, Dig. "Action on the Case upon Assumpsit," B. 15, it is laid down that if a man promise a pig of lead to A., and his executor give lead to make a pig to B., who assumes to deliver it to A., an assumpsit lies by A. against him. The case of Delaware & H. Canal Co. v. Westchester County Bank, 4 Denio 97, involved a trust because the defendants had received from a third party a bill of exchange under an agreement that they would endeavor to collect it, and would pay over the proceeds when collected to the plaintiffs. A fund received under such an agreement does not belong to the person who receives it. He must account for it specifically; and perhaps there is no gross violation of principle in permitting the equitable owner of it to sue upon an express promise to pay it over. Having a specific interest in the thing, the undertaking to account for it may be regarded as in some sense made with him through the author of the trust. But further than this we cannot go without violating plain rules of law. In the case before us there was nothing in the nature of a trust or agency. The defendant borrowed the money of Holly and received it as his own. The plaintiff had no right in the fund, legal or equitable. The promise to repay the money created an obligation in favor of the lender to whom it was made and not in favor of any one else. . . .

The judgment of the court below should, therefore, be reversed, and a new trial granted.

GROVER, J., also dissented.

Judgment affirmed.

NOTES

(1) *An Indemnity Agreement.* Phillips & Associates was an unincorporated business association having six members. Needing funds, the firm obtained a loan from Charles Jett, and gave him a promissory note for $16,000. Three members of the association signed the note as makers, so as to be individually accountable to Jett. The other three members later executed an agreement in favor of the association, agreeing "that they will jointly and severally guarantee payment of the said promissory note to Charles C. Jett. . . ." This agreement recited that its three signers "will benefit from said loan," and that the three who had signed the note "would not have guaranteed" it but for the expected adherence of all members of the association.

The note was not paid when due, and Jett brought an action against all members of the association.[a] As against those who signed the note, he was entitled to judgment, the court ruled.[b] But the other members were held not to be liable to Jett. Their "intent and purpose," it was found, was to share with the makers of the note their liability on it, "and with no intent to benefit the holder of the note," Jett. He was only an incidental beneficiary of their undertaking. Jett v. Phillips & Associates, 439 F.2d 987 (10th Cir. 1971).

A technical name for the members who did not sign the note is "indemnitors." They agreed to *indemnify* the signers against a portion of their liability on the note. A contract of indemnity is often contrasted with a third party beneficiary contract. A "third party indemnity clause," such as that in Pacific Gas & Elec. Co. v. G. W. Thomas Drayage & R. Co., p. 582 supra, does not necessarily confer rights on third parties.

What purpose was served by limiting Jett's recovery to the members who signed the note? Upon paying the judgment, the signers will presumably be entitled to a pro rata contribution from those who made the indemnity agreement.

If the indemnity agreement is enforced, does it require a special exception to the usual requirement of consideration?

a. Actually, Jett himself had been admitted to membership in connection with the loan, but that circumstance is unimportant for present purposes.

b. One of these, Phillips, had died, and no judgment ran against him.

(2) *Problem.* Vendor contracts to sell a parcel of land for $100,000. The contract recites that Vendor has retained the services of Broker in arranging the sale, and continues: "Vendor covenants that he will pay Broker any fee or commission to which he may be entitled by reason of this sale, and further covenants to hold Purchaser harmless from any liability to said Broker for such fee or commission." Broker sues Vendor for a commission of $5,000, alleging that to be a reasonable and customary compensation for his services. He has no writing signed by Vendor, other than the sale contract, to support his claim, and a statute makes a promise of a commission to a real estate broker unenforceable unless it is expressed in such a writing. What result? See Robertson v. Hansen, 89 Idaho 107, 403 P.2d 585 (1965).

SEAVER v. RANSOM

Court of Appeals of New York, 1918.
224 N.Y. 233, 120 N.E. 639, 2 A.L.R. 1187.

Action by Marion E. Seaver against Matt. C. Ransom and another, as executors, etc., of Samuel A. Beman, deceased. From a judgment of the Appellate Division (180 App.Div. 734, 168 N.Y.S. 454), affirming judgment for plaintiff, defendants appeal. Affirmed.

POUND, J. Judge Beman and his wife were advanced in years. Mrs. Beman was about to die. She had a small estate consisting of a house and lot in Malone and little else. Judge Beman drew his wife's will according to her instruction. It gave $1,000 to plaintiff, $500 to one sister, plaintiff's mother, and $100 each to another sister and her son, the use of the house to her husband for life, and remainder to the American Society for the Prevention of Cruelty to Animals. She named her husband as residuary legatee and executor. Plaintiff was her niece, 34 years old, in ill health, sometimes a member of the Beman household. When the will was read to Mrs. Beman, she said that it was not as she wanted it. She wanted to leave the house to the plaintiff. She had no other objection to the will, but her strength was waning, and, although the judge offered to write another will for her, she said she was afraid she would not hold out long enough to enable her to sign it. So the judge said, if she would sign the will, he would leave plaintiff enough in his will to make up the difference. He avouched the promise by his uplifted hand with all solemnity and his wife then executed the will. When he came to die, it was found that his will made no provision for the plaintiff.

This action was brought, and plaintiff recovered judgment in the trial court, on the theory that Beman had obtained property from his wife and induced her to execute the will in the form prepared by him by his promise to give plaintiff $6,000, the value of the house, and that thereby equity impressed his property with a trust in favor of the plaintiff. Where a legatee promises the testator that he will use property given him by the will for a particular purpose, a trust arises. O'Hara v. Dudley, 95 N.Y. 403, 47 Am.Rep. 53; Trustees of Amherst College v. Ritch, 151 N.Y. 282, 45 N.E. 876, 37 L.R.A. 305; Aherns v. Jones, 169 N.Y. 555, 62 N.E. 666, 88 Am.St.Rep. 620. Beman received nothing under his wife's will but the use of the house in Malone for life. Equity compels the application of property thus obtained to the purpose of the testator, but equity cannot so impress a trust, except on property obtained by the promise. Beman was bound by his promise, but no property was bound by it; no trust in plaintiff's favor can be spelled out.

An action on the contract for damages, or to make the executors trustees for performance, stands on different ground. Farmers' Loan & Trust Co. v. Mortimer, 219 N.Y. 290, 294, 295, 114 N.E. 389. The Appellate Division properly passed to the consideration of the question whether the judgment could stand upon the promise made to the wife, upon a valid consideration, for the sole benefit of plaintiff. The judgment of the trial court was affirmed by a return to the general doctrine laid down in the great case of Lawrence v. Fox, 20 N.Y. 268, which has since been limited as herein indicated.

Contracts for the benefit of third persons have been the prolific source of judicial and academic discussion. Williston, Contracts for the Benefit of a Third Person, 15 Harvard Law Review, 767; Corbin, Contracts for the Benefit of Third Persons, 27 Yale Law Review, 1008. The general rule, both in law and equity (Phalen v. United States Trust Co., 186 N.Y. 178, 186, 78 N.E. 943, 7 L.R.A.,N.S., 734, 9 Ann.Cas. 595), was that privity between a plaintiff and a defendant is necessary to the maintenance of an action on the contract. The consideration must be furnished by the party to whom the promise was made. The contract cannot be enforced against the third party, and therefore it cannot be enforced by him. On the other hand, the right of the beneficiary to sue on a contract made expressly for his benefit has been fully recognized in many American jurisdictions, either by judicial decision or by legislation, and is said to be "the prevailing rule in this country." Hendrick v. Lindsay, 93 U.S. 143, 23 L.Ed. 855; Lehow v. Simonton, 3 Colo. 346. It has been said that "the establishment of this doctrine has been gradual, and is a victory of practical utility over theory, of equity over technical subtlety." Brantly on Contracts, 2d Ed., p. 253. The reasons for this view are that it is just and practical to permit the person for whose benefit the contract is made to enforce it against one whose duty it is to pay. Other jurisdictions still adhere to the present English Rule (7 Halsbury's Laws of England, 342, 343; Jenks' Digest of English Civil Law, sec. 229) that a contract cannot be enforced by or against a person who is not a party. Exchange Bank v. Rice, 107 Mass. 37, 9 Am.Rep. 1. But see, also, Forbes v. Thorpe, 209 Mass. 570, 95 N.E. 955; Gardner v. Denison, 217 Mass. 492, 105 N.E. 359, 51 L.R.A.,N.S., 1108.

In New York the right of the beneficiary to sue on contracts made for his benefit is not clearly or simply defined. It is at present confined: First. To cases where there is a pecuniary obligation running from the promisee to the beneficiary, "a legal right founded upon some obligation of the promisee in the third party to adopt and claim the promise as made for his benefit." [Cases cited.] Secondly. To cases where the contract is made for the benefit of the wife (Buchanan v. Tilden,[a] 158 N.Y. 109, 52 N.E. 724, 44 L.R.A. 170, 70 Am.St.Rep. 454; Benton v. Welch, 170 N.Y. 554, 63 N.E. 539), affianced wife (De Cicco v. Schweizer, 221 N.Y. 431, 117 N.E. 807, Ann. Cas.1918C, 816), or child (Todd v. Weber, 95 N.Y. 181, 193, 47 Am. Rep. 20; Matter of Kidd, 188 N.Y. 274, 80 N.E. 924) of a party to the contract. The close relationship cases go back to the early King's Bench case (1677), long since repudiated in England, of Dutton v. Poole, 2 Lev. 211 (s.c., 1 Ventris, 318, 332). See Schemerhorn v. Vanderheyden, 1 Johns, 139, 3 Am.Dec. 304. The natural and moral duty of the husband or parent to provide for the future of wife or child sustains the action on the contract made for their benefit. "This is the furthest the cases in this state have gone," says Cullen, J., in the marriage settlement case of Borland v. Welch, 162 N.Y. 104, 110, 56 N.E. 556.

The right of the third party is also upheld in, thirdly, the public contract cases [cases cited] where the municipality seeks to protect its inhabitants by covenants for their benefit; and, fourthly, the cases where, at the request of a party to the contract, the promise runs directly to the beneficiary although he does not furnish the consideration [cases cited]. It may be safely said that a general rule sustaining recovery at the suit of the third party would include but few classes of cases not included in these groups, either categorically or in principle.

The desire of the childless aunt to make provisions for a beloved and favorite niece differs imperceptibly in law or in equity from the moral duty of the parent to make testamentary provision for a child. The contract was made for the plaintiff's benefit. She alone is substantially damaged by its breach. The representatives of the wife's estate have no interest in enforcing it specifically. It is said in Buchanan v. Tilden that the common law imposes moral and legal obligations upon the husband and the parent not measured by the necessaries of life. It was, however, the love and affection or the moral sense of the husband and the parent that imposed such obligations in the cases cited, rather than any common-law duty of husband and parent to wife and child. If plaintiff had been a child of Mrs. Beman,

---

a. The defendant in this case was the nephew of Samuel J. Tilden, who succeeded in "breaking" a portion of his uncle's will. He had promised to share the recovery with the plaintiff, who was, by adoption, a niece of Governor Tilden. The promise was made to her husband in return for arranging advances for use in prosecuting the will contest.

legal obligation would have required no testamentary provision for her, yet the child could have enforced a covenant in her favor identical with the covenant of Judge Beman in this case. De Cicco v. Schweizer, supra. The constraining power of conscience is not regulated by the degree of relationship alone. The dependent or faithful niece may have a stronger claim than the affluent or unworthy son. No sensible theory of moral obligation denies arbitrarily to the former what would be conceded to the latter. We might consistently either refuse or allow the claim of both, but I cannot reconcile a decision in favor of the wife in Buchanan v. Tilden, based on the moral obligations arising out of near relationship, with a decision against the niece here on the ground that the relationship is too remote for equity's ken. No controlling authority depends upon so absolute a rule. In Sullivan v. Sullivan, 161 N.Y. 554, 56 N.E. 116, the grandniece lost in a litigation with the aunt's estate, founded on a certificate of deposit payable to the aunt "or in case of her death to her niece;" but what was said in that case of the relations of plaintiff's intestate and defendant does not control here, any more than what was said in Durnherr v. Rau [135 N.Y. 219, 32 N.E. 49], on the relation of husband and wife, and the inadequacy of mere moral duty, as distinguished from legal or equitable obligation, controlled the decision in Buchanan v. Tilden. Borland v. Welch, supra, deals only with the rights of volunteers under a marriage settlement not made for the benefit of collaterals. Kellogg, P. J., writing for the court below, well said:

"The doctrine of Lawrence v. Fox is progressive, not retrograde. The course of the late decisions is to enlarge, not limit, the effect of that case."

The court in that leading case attempted to adopt the general doctrine that any third person, for whose direct benefit a contract was intended, could sue on it. [Next the court referred to a number of later New York precedents, some stating the doctrine in general terms, and others narrowing its application.]

But, on principle, a sound conclusion may be reached. If Mrs. Beman had left her husband the house on condition that he pay the plaintiff $6,000, and he had accepted the devise, he would have become personally liable to pay the legacy, and plaintiff could have recovered in an action at law against him, whatever the value of the house. . . . That would be because the testatrix had in substance bequeathed the promise to plaintiff, and not because close relationship or moral obligation sustained the contract. The distinction between an implied promise to a testator for the benefit of a third party to pay a legacy and an unqualified promise on a valuable consideration to make provision for the third party by will is discernible, but not obvious. The tendency of American authority is to sustain the gift in all such cases and to permit the donee beneficiary to recover on the contract. Matter of Edmundson's Estate (1918) 259 Pa. 429,

103 A. 277. The equities are with the plaintiff, and they may be enforced in this action, whether it be regarded as an action for damages or an action for specific performance to convert the defendants into trustees for plaintiff's benefit under the agreement.

The judgment should be affirmed, with costs.

Judgment affirmed.[b]

NOTES

(1) *Restatement Revision.* The Restatement Second introduces the term "intended" beneficiary to designate claimants who (like the plaintiff in Lawrence v. Fox) are permitted to enforce contracts to which they are not party. Section 135. Other beneficiaries of a contract are "incidental"; and such a beneficiary "acquires by virtue of the promise no right against the promisor or the promisee." Section 147. Lawrence would have been called a *creditor* beneficiary under § 133 of the original Restatement; but the terms "creditor" and "donee" are discarded in this connection by Restatement Second. It is not altogether clear what is gained by the new diction. The new text begins: "(1) Unless otherwise agreed between promisor and promisee, a beneficiary of a promise is an intended beneficiary if recognition of a right to performance in the beneficiary is appropriate to effectuate the intention of the parties and . . . (a) the performance of the promise will satisfy a duty of the promisee to the beneficiary. . . ." It seems that Lawrence may now be called a "subsection (1)(a) intended beneficiary."

As to the former donee beneficiary consult § 133(1) (b). In applying the rule stated here is it a material issue whether or not the claimant enjoyed the love and affection of the promisee? Whether or not the claimant was closely related to the promisee? Should these issues be material?

For a criticism of intention as the criterion of actionability by a third party, see Note, 54 Va.L.Rev. 1166 (1968).

(2) *English Law.* Though there were early precedents to the contrary,[c] it seems to have become settled in the common law of England that contracts may not confer enforceable rights on third parties as such.[d] For discussion of the rule, see Beswick v. Beswick, [1967] 3 W.L.R. 932, [1967] 2 All E.R. 1197, in which a widow sued on a promise of payments to her that the defendant had made to her husband. The House of Lords ruled that she was entitled to specific performance, in her capacity as administratrix of her husband's estate, but it was conceded that she had no claim as an individual.[e] Lord Reid hinted that he would be prepared to

---

b. The case might not now be decided as it was, apparently, owing to a New York statute requiring that a contract to bequeath property or make a testamentary provision of any kind "be represented by a writing." Gen.Obl. L., § 5–701(7). Do you regard this statute as an improvement in the law? See Redke v. Silvertrust, 6 Cal.3d 94, 490 P.2d 805 (1971).

c. See the note introducing this chapter.

d. Statutory exceptions have been made in relation to certain insurance contracts.

e. Much of the law lords' discussion was directed to a "consolidation act" of 1925, and they concluded that it did not make a sweeping alteration in the rights of third parties.

For discussion prompted by the case, see Baker, Note, 83 Law Q.Rev. 465 (1967); Comment, Third Party Beneficiary Contracts in England, 35 U. Chi.L.Rev. 544 (1968).

reconsider the common-law rule, except that Parliamentary reform may be anticipated.

An American scholar has said that the English courts are "very ready to torture a contract into a trust" because they feel the injustice of denying a remedy to the beneficiary of a contract. Scott on Trusts, Vol. 1, § 14.4 (3d ed. 1967).

(3) *Intention and Motivation.* The intention requisite to create rights in a third party is sometimes said to be apparent on "the face of the contract." E. g., Shillman v. Hobstetter, 249 Md. 678, 241 A.2d 570 (1968). And the requisite intention is sometimes contrasted with the *motivation* of the promisee. E. g., James Stewart & Co. v. Law, 149 Tex. 392, 233 S.W. 2d 558, 22 A.L.R.2d 639 (1950); Socony-Vacuum Oil Co. v. Continental Cas. Co., 219 F.2d 645 (2d Cir. 1955). On such reasoning, third party beneficiary claims are recognized when it is perfectly apparent that the promisee was moved by nothing but self-interest in bargaining as he did. As Corbin repeatedly insisted, it is not necessary for the claimant to demonstrate that the promisee had an altruistic or philanthropic purpose in obtaining the promise sued upon. Nevertheless, the category "incidental beneficiary" is sometimes enlarged through a process of reasoning by exclusion: if performance of the promise will satisfy no duty of the promisee, and if no benevolent purpose on his part is apparent, then the claimant must be an incidental beneficiary. See, for example, Olney v. Hutt, 251 Iowa 1379, 105 N.W.2d 515 (1960): "If they were third party beneficiaries at all, they were only incidental beneficiaries and not entitled to recover."

Naturally, a promise enforceable by a third party beneficiary may also be enforced, normally, in an action by the promisee. The damages flowing from a breach may not be the same for the promisee as for the third party, however. In a case like Seaver v. Ransom, for instance, the promisee has no economic interest in the performance. Hence it is said that the damage remedy is inadequate, and that specific performance may be an appropriate remedy for the promisee (or his representative). See Drewen v. Bank of Manhattan, 31 N.J. 110, 155 A.2d 529, 76 A.L.R.2d 221 (1959), and Beswick v. Beswick, cited in the preceding note. As to the appropriate person to enforce a separation agreement made for the benefit of the children, see Forman v. Forman, 17 N.Y.2d 274, 217 N.E.2d 645 (1966).

H. R. MOCH CO., INC. v. RENSSELAER WATER CO.

Court of Appeals of New York, 1928.
247 N.Y. 160, 159 N.E. 896, 62 A.L.R. 1199.

Appeal from Supreme Court, Appellate Division, Third Department.

Action by the H. R. Moch Company, Inc., against the Rensselaer Water Company. From a judgment of the Appellate Division (219 App.Div. 673, 220 N.Y.S. 557), reversing an order of the Special Term, and granting defendant's motion for judgment dismissing the complaint for failure to state facts sufficient to constitute a cause of action, plaintiff appeals. Affirmed.

See, also, 127 Misc. 545, 217 N.Y.S. 426.

CARDOZO, C. J. The defendant, a waterworks company under the laws of this state, made a contract with the city of Rensselaer for the supply of water during a term of years. Water was to be furnished to the city for sewer flushing and street sprinkling; for service to schools and public buildings; and for service at fire hydrants, the latter service at the rate of $42.50 a year for each hydrant. Water was to be furnished to private takers within the city at their homes and factories and other industries at reasonable rates, not exceeding a stated schedule. While this contract was in force, a building caught fire. The flames, spreading to the plaintiff's warehouse near by, destroyed it and its contents. The defendant, according to the complaint, was promptly notified of the fire, "but omitted and neglected after such notice, to supply or furnish sufficient or adequate quantity of water, with adequate pressure to stay, suppress, or extinguish the fire before it reached the warehouse of the plaintiff, although the pressure and supply which the defendant was equipped to supply and furnish, and had agreed by said contract to supply and furnish, was adequate and sufficient to prevent the spread of the fire to and the destruction of the plaintiff's warehouse and its contents." By reason of the failure of the defendant to "fulfill the provisions of the contract between it and the city of Rensselaer," the plaintiff is said to have suffered damage, for which judgment is demanded. A motion, in the nature of a demurrer, to dismiss the complaint, was denied at Special Term. The Appellate Division reversed by a divided court.

Liability in the plaintiff's argument is placed on one or other of three grounds. The complaint, we are told, is to be viewed as stating: (1) A cause of action for breach of contract within Lawrence v. Fox, 20 N.Y. 268; (2) a cause of action for a common-law tort, within MacPherson v. Buick Motor Co., 217 N.Y. 382, 111 N.E. 1050, L.R.A. 1916F, 696, Ann.Cas.1916C, 440; or (3) a cause of action for the breach of a statutory duty. These several grounds of liability will be considered in succession.

(1) We think the action is not maintainable as one for breach of contract.

No legal duty rests upon a city to supply its inhabitants with protection against fire. Springfield Fire & Marine Ins. Co. v. Village of Keeseville, 148 N.Y. 46, 42 N.E. 405, 30 L.R.A. 660, 51 Am.St.Rep. 667. That being so, a member of the public may not maintain an action under Lawrence v. Fox against one contracting with the city to furnish water at the hydrants, unless an intention appears that the promisor is to be answerable to individual members of the public as well as to the city for any loss ensuing from the failure to fulfill the promise. No such intention is discernible here. On the contrary, the contract is significantly divided into two branches: One a promise to the city for the benefit of the city in its corporate capacity, in which branch is included the service at the hydrants; and the other a promise to the city for the benefit of private takers, in which branch is included the service at their homes and factories. In a broad sense it is true that every city contract, not improvident or wasteful, is for the benefit of the public. More than this, however, must be shown to give a right of action to a member of the public not formally a party. The benefit, as it is sometimes said, must be one that is not merely incidental and secondary. Cf. Fosmire v. National Surety Co., 229 N.Y. 44, 127 N.E. 472. It must be primary and immediate in such a sense and to such a degree as to bespeak the assumption of a duty to make reparation directly to the individual members of the public if the benefit is lost. The field of obligation would be expanded beyond reasonable limits if less than this were to be demanded as a condition of liability. A promisor undertakes to supply fuel for heating a public building. He is not liable for breach of contract to a visitor who finds the building without fuel, and thus contracts a cold. The list of illustrations can be indefinitely extended. The carrier of the mails under contract with the government is not answerable to the merchant who has lost the benefit of a bargain through negligent delay. The householder is without a remedy against manufacturers of hose and engines though prompt performance of their contracts would have stayed the ravages of fire. "The law does not spread its protection so far." Robins Dry Dock & Repair Co. v. Flint, 275 U.S. 303, 48 S.Ct. 134.

So with the case at hand. By the vast preponderance of authority, a contract between a city and a water company to furnish water at the city hydrants has in view a benefit to the public that is incidental rather than immediate, an assumption of duty to the city and not to its inhabitants. Such is the ruling of the Supreme Court of the United States. German Alliance Ins. Co. v. Homewater Supply Co., 226 U.S. 220, 33 S.Ct. 32, 57 L.Ed. 195, 42 L.R.A.,N.S., 1000. Such has been the ruling in this state   .   .   .   though the question is still open in this court. Such with few exceptions has been the ruling in other jurisdictions. Williston, Contracts, sec. 373, and cases there cited; Dillon, Municipal Corporations (5th Ed.) sec. 1340. The diligence of counsel has brought together decisions to that effect from 26 states. [Cases cited.] Only a few states have held otherwise. Page, Contracts, sec. 2401. An intention to assume an obligation of indefinite extension to every member of the public is seen to be the more improbable when we recall the crushing burden that the obligation would impose. Cf. Hone v. Presque Isle Water Co., 104 Me. 217, at p. 232, 71 A. 769, 21 L.R.A.,N.S., 1021. The consequences invited would bear no reasonable proportion to those attached by law to defaults not greatly different. A wrongdoer who by negligence sets fire to a building is liable in damages to the owner where the fire has its origin, but not to other owners who are injured when it spreads. The rule in our state is settled to that effect, whether wisely or unwisely.   .   .   .   If the plaintiff is to prevail, one who negligently omits to supply sufficient pressure to extinguish a fire started by another assumes an obligation to pay the ensuing damage, though the whole city is laid low. A promisor will not be deemed to have had in mind the assumption of a risk so overwhelming for any trivial reward.

The cases that have applied the rule of Lawrence v. Fox to contracts made by a city for the benefit of the public are not at war with this conclusion. Through them all there runs as a unifying principle the presence of an intention to compensate the individual members of the public in the event of a default. For example, in Pond v. New Rochelle Water Co., 183 N.Y. 330, 76 N.E. 211, 1 L.R.A.,N.S., 958, 5 Ann.Cas. 504, the contract with the city fixed a schedule of rates to be supplied, not to public buildings, but to private takers at their homes. In Matter of International R. Co. v. Rann, 224 N.Y. 83, 85, 120 N.E. 153, the contract was by street railroads to carry passengers for a stated fare. In Smyth v. City of New York, 203 N.Y. 106, 96 N.E. 409, and Rigney v. New York Cent. & H. R. R. Co., 217 N.Y. 31, 111 N.E. 226, covenants were made by contractors upon public works, not merely to indemnify the city, but to assume its liabilities. These and like cases come within the third group stated in the comprehensive opinion in Seaver v. Ransom, 224 N.Y. 233, 238, 120 N.E. 639, 2 L.R.A. 1187. The municipality was contracting in behalf of its inhabitants by covenants intended to be enforced by any of them severally as occasion should arise.

(2) We think the action is not maintainable as one for a common-law tort. . . .

(3) We think the action is not maintainable as one for the breach of a statutory duty. . . .

The judgment should be affirmed with costs.

NOTES

(1) *Scope of Duty.* With the rules limiting the rights of third parties in a contract, compare those limiting the types of damages that may be claimed by a party to a contract (e. g., Hadley v. Baxendale, p. 524 supra). What similarity of function do you see?

(2) *Authorities.* For a more recent decision in the same vein as Moch, see Clark v. Meigs Equipment Co., 10 Ohio App.2d 157, 226 N.E.2d 791 (1967).

Water companies have usually been shielded from tort claims as well as contract claims, in actions to recover private fire losses. However, in Doyle v. South Pittsburgh Water Co., 414 Pa. 199, 199 A.2d 875 (1964), a complaint alleging negligence by failing to maintain service at fire hydrants was sustained. The opinion relied on the opinion by Cardozo in MacPherson v. Buick Motor Co., 217 N.Y. 382, 111 N.E. 1050 (1916), and said of his opinion in the Moch case that "at this point Homer nodded." (Two of the seven judges concurred in the result and two dissented.) See Note, 65 Colum.L.Rev. 169 (1965).

There are decisions contrary to the Moch case, notably in Kentucky and North Carolina, but it represents the prevailing view. In Kansas there is dictum that a similar decision "is no longer to be regarded as sound and should be disapproved." Anderson v. Rexroad, 157 Kan. 676, 266 P.2d 320 (1954). But see Earl E. Roher Co. v. Water Co., 182 Kan. 546, 322 P.2d 810 (1958). The loss in the Anderson case was a fire loss, but the defendant was a contractor, making improvements for a city. He had agreed to be liable "for all damages to buildings . . . or other property. . . . The contractor, at his expense, shall repair, replace or reconstruct such property or otherwise make amicable settlement for such damage claims within thirty days after the claim is filed." [a] The court said that the waterworks cases were distinguishable, and in a class by themselves. In what ways might they be distinguished?

(3) *Strikes.* Through interrupting service by an employer, a strike may cause widespread economic loss among his customers, and beyond, for which he is not accountable. If the strike violates a collective bargaining agreement, does it follow that the victim has a claim against the union? This question was seriously discussed in Isbrandtsen Co. v. Local 1291, etc., 204 F.2d 495 (3d Cir. 1953), where the claimant was a shipowner, whose ship was tied up by a longshoremen's strike. The strike was against a stevedore employed by a charterer of the vessel. In Jamur Productions Corporation v. Quill, 51 Misc.2d 501, 273 N.Y.S.2d 348 (1966), a strike that paralyzed New York City's public transport gave rise to a comparable claim against the Transport Workers Union for business losses. The claim was brushed aside. (A claim based on the Universal Declaration of Human Rights was also rejected.)[b]

INSURANCE

According to the Restatement Second, one of the factors that may make a third-party claim inappropriate is "the availability of alternatives such as insurance." This remark has interesting implications. If all the property owners of a city (and tenants and so on) were in fact fully insured against fire losses, very little could be said for enforcing a claim such as that of the Moch Company. In Burford v. Glasgow Water Co., 223 Ky. 54, 2 S.W.2d 1027, 62 A.L.R. 1195 (1928), decided one month before the Moch case, the Water Company was held not liable on similar facts because the action was brought on behalf of Burford's insurers. The court said that if it allowed recovery, "property owners will not only pay for fire protection premiums sufficient to cover the risk assumed, but will also pay higher water rates for the purpose of relieving the insurance companies of the liability

---

a. Compare the contract provisions concerning damage in the contract here with those in Lundt v. Parsons Construction Company, 181 Neb. 609, 150 N.W.2d 108 (1967).

b. Other examples of ingenious, but unsuccessful, third party beneficiary claims are as follows: Finch v. Rhode Island Grocers Ass'n, 93 R.I. 323, 175 A.2d 177 (1961); Shubitz v. Consolidated Edison Co., 59 Misc.2d 732, 301 N.Y.S.2d 926 (1969) (tenant injured in hallway during electrical blackout); and Creedon v. Voting Machine Corp., cited in the next main case.

which they have been paid to assume." This observation is questionable, however, for fire insurance premium rates would presumably be adjusted downward to reflect any "relief" from liability that insurers enjoy.

Insurers commonly stipulate that in the event of payment of an insured lost they are subrogated to claims, based on the loss, that the insured person may have against others. (And the right of subrogation may exist apart from a policy provision.) The courts have exhibited a good deal of hostility to insurers' subrogation claims. A notable example is Anderson v. Rexroad, 180 Kan. 505, 306 P.2d 137 (1957) (a later phase of the case cited in Note 2). The court had already given recognition to a claim by a homeowner for loss against a firm engaged in making street improvements, much like the claim in the main case. But when it appeared that the house was partially insured against the loss, the court limited the recovery to the amount of the loss exceeding the amount of insurance. Hence there was no possibility that the insurer could recoup its payment to the insured owner from the construction firm. On the other hand, an uninsured neighbor whose house was similarly damaged would presumably have full recovery from the firm under its contract with the city. Do you see objections to this state of affairs? See McCoid, Allocation of Loss and Property Insurance, 39 Ind.L.J. 647 (1964).

PROBLEMS

(a) An operator for a telephone company neglected to report a fire to a fire department, in violation of an agreement the company had made with its customers, when one of them called "central." In consequence, a neighbor's house burned. Does the neighbor have a contract claim against the company? See Christenson & Arndt, Inc. v. Wisconsin Tel. Co., 264 Wis. 238, 58 N.W.2d 682 (1953).

(b) The owner of a commercial building arranged to lease it to a newspaper publisher, upon building an addition to it. A builder contracted with the owner to construct the addition in less than 80 days, knowing that the tenant expected occupancy after that. The addition was not completed until some eight months after the contract. The builder was held liable to the owner for the reasonable rental value of the structure for the period of the delay. The publisher also made a claim against the builder, as a third party beneficiary, for its loss of anticipated profits. What result? See McDonal Construction Co. v. Murray, 5 Wash.App. 68, 485 P.2d 626 (1971).

(c) The Exercycle Corporation contracts with a dealer in Michigan, giving him the exclusive right to sell its product there. Similarly, it contracts with a dealer in Illinois. Each of the dealers undertakes "not to sell Exercycles in any territory other than that assigned to him by the Company." The Illinois dealer violates this promise by making sales in Michigan. Does the Michigan dealer have a remedy under the Illinois dealer's contract? If the Illinois dealer had been appointed first, would that make a difference? See Exercycle of Michigan, Inc. v. Wayson, 341 F.2d 335 (7th Cir. 1965).

LA MOUREA v. RHUDE

Supreme Court of Minnesota, 1940.
209 Minn. 53, 295 N.W. 304.

Action on a contract by Henry E. La Mourea against Jens O. Rhude and others, copartners doing business as Rhude, Fryberger and MacDonell. From an order overruling a demurrer to the complaint, defendants appeal.

STONE, JUSTICE. The one question is whether plaintiff may recover on a contract, to which he was not a party, between the city of Duluth and defendants whereby the latter obligated themselves to do certain work of sewer construction. Plaintiff seeks recovery for consequential damage to his nearby real estate caused by the blasting operations of defendants.

The contract contemplated excavation in solid rock, and that the work could be done only "by the use of heavy charges of explosives . . . the use and effect of which might, and very probably would be felt and cause damage . . . in the immediate vicinity." In consequence it made defendants "liable for any damages done to the work or other structure or public or private property and injuries sustained by persons" in the operations.

The claim for defendant is that this promise was one to indemnify the city and nothing more. So, the conclusion is, plaintiff has no cause of action against defendants. That argument we consider unsound.

The question of when and under what circumstances the beneficiary of a contract, not himself a party thereto, may recover thereon has been the subject of much and conflicting decision law. For long it was held that a stranger to a contract between others, in which one of the parties promises to do something for the benefit of such stranger, there being nothing but the promise, no consideration from such stranger, and no duty or obligation to him on the part of the promisee, cannot recover upon it. Jefferson v. Asch, 53 Minn. 446, 55 N.W. 604, 25 L.R.A. 257, 39 Am.St.Rep. 618.

That rule recognized that the "stranger" could recover if the promisee owed him a duty against which he, the promisee, undertook to protect himself by the contract. In such case, the beneficiary could recover even though not a party to the contract. Even with the qualifications stated, the doctrine of Jefferson v. Asch has been subject to so much attrition in succeeding cases that, in the interest of accuracy, it is in need of restatement.

1. That restatement is found in Restatement of the Law of Contracts, secs. 133–147. The rule is there declared that donee and creditor beneficiaries may recover, but an incidental beneficiary cannot.

The incidental beneficiary is illustrated by a contract such as that where "B contracts with A to buy A a new Gordon automobile." The Gordon Company is an incidental beneficiary without right of recovery.

2. It is no bar to recovery by the beneficiary, if he be donee or creditor of the promisee, that the promise in his favor is conditioned, as here, upon a future event, such as damage to his property. Id. sec. 134.

3. Neither is it essential to the right of donee or creditor beneficiary that he be identified when the contract containing the promise is made. Id. sec. 139.

4. All that fits this case. The city exacted from the defendants a promise that they should be "liable for any damages done to . . . private property" in connection with the work. It is immaterial that the obligation was also in effect one to indemnify the city against claims for such damage.

Such promises, made to a municipality for the benefit of its citizens, are put in a special category by the Restatement, sec. 145. Provisions of that section would allow recovery in the instant case. The comment states the obvious conclusion that it is but a special application of the principles of sec. 133 concerning the rights of donee and creditor beneficiaries. The courts of Michigan and Arizona have expressly adopted the rule of sec. 145. Bator v. Ford Motor Co., 269 Mich. 648, 257 N.W. 906; Cole v. Arizona Edison Co., Inc., 53 Ariz. 141, 86 P.2d 946. And two lower New York courts have indicated approval, Wilson v. Oliver Costich Co., Inc., 231 App.Div. 346, 247 N.Y. S. 131; Creedon v. Automatic Voting Machine Corp., 243 App.Div. 339, 276 N.Y.S. 609, following a line of earlier cases in that state which allowed recovery in situations covered by that section and analogous to the instant case. . . .

We affirm plaintiff's right to sue as a beneficiary of the contract. An opposite holding would defeat obligation where obligation is not only intended but also expressed and paid for. Implicit in such holding would be the indefensible hypothesis that, although a party to a contract may stipulate for such benefits to himself as he wants and the other party will allow, yet the two of them by the same process and for the same consideration cannot secure similar benefit to a stranger. In the contractual promise for the benefit of one not a party, there is nothing illegal or contrary to public policy. The promise is within the right of one party to exact and the other to make. No reasonable ground can be suggested for its not being enforceable according to its expressed intent.

The contrary doctrine, now altogether if not quite outmoded, was put in the main upon factors of consideration and privity. . . . Consideration for a promise is demanded by the law solely as a test of actionability. It is determinative of the presence of enforceable obligation but ordinarily not of its quantity or the identity of obligee. For the latter two, we usually look not to source of consideration but exclusively to the terms of the contract. It is common to find enforceable obligation in favor of a contracting party who has furnished no consideration. So it is no objection to an action on the contract by a donee or creditor beneficiary that he did not furnish any of the consideration.

5. Many cases dealing with recovery by a third party beneficiary have also required and discussed the element of privity as prerequisite to recovery. Those dealing with promises to a public corporation for the benefit of its citizens have found that factor in the "obligation to protect its inhabitants" resting on a governmental unit in making public contracts. . . . Under the rule as we view it, such obligation is immaterial. Privity, in the law of contracts, is merely the name for a legal relation arising from right and obligation. For example, A, by contract, secures a promise from B. A may transfer his right of enforcement to C. C thereby succeeds to A's right of action, and, in consequence, comes into the relationship with A and B which we call privity of contract. Instead of waiting to do it by assignment, A may, at the outset, exact from B the same promise in favor of C. It is enforceable by C, who thereby has come directly into legal relationship with B. That illustrates the normal course of things resulting in privity of contract, which is but a descriptive term, designating effect rather than cause. In short, privity of contract is legal relationship to the contract or its parties. To affirm one's right under a contract is therefore to affirm his privity with the party liable to him.

That simple truth removes the difficulty arising from the complicated notions expressed by judges and text writers concerning privity of contract. The term has been much mis-used. In consequence, we have the process referred to by Chief Judge Cardozo in Ultramares Corp. v. Touche, 255 N.Y. 170, 174 N.E. 441, 445, 74 A.L.R. 1139, when he said: "The assault upon the citadel of privity is proceeding in these days apace. How far the inroads shall extend is now a favorite subject of juridical discussion." [b] Mr. Page, in respect to the right of a beneficiary of a contract, asserts that the true explanation is that no privity is necessary between beneficiary and promisor. 4 Page, Law of Contracts, 2d Ed. 1920, p. 4211, sec. 2388. It is said, concerning the right of a beneficiary to recover: "The very essence

[b]. This well-known passage continues: "In the field of the law of contract there has been a gradual widening of the doctrine of Lawrence v. Fox, 20 N.Y. 268, until today the beneficiary of a promise, clearly designated as such, is seldom left without a remedy. Seaver v. Ransom . . . Even in that field, however, the remedy is narrower where the beneficiaries of the promise are indeterminate or general. Something more must then appear than an intention that the promise shall redound to the benefit of the public or to that of a class of indefinite extension. . . . Moch Co. v. Rensselaer Water Co. . . . . "

of the American rule is that such privity is not necessary." Annotation, 81 A.L.R. 1289. The truth is, says Mr. Williston, "that through this travail [of the conflicting notions of judges and text writers] the common law has given birth to a distinct, new principle of law which takes its own place in the family of legal principles, and gives not only to a donee beneficiary, but also to a creditor beneficiary, the right to enforce directly the promise from which he derives his interest." 2 Williston, Contracts, Rev.Ed., sec. 357, p. 1049.

Our submission is that all such discussion (including this) has no more than academic value because, the beneficiary's right to recover established, with the resulting obligation of the promisor in his favor, there arises the relation we call privity. Anyway, privity or no privity, the overwhelming weight of authority and the entire weight of all inherent factors of the problem speak for recovery by this beneficiary.

Affirmed.

NOTES

(1) *Insurance.* Would this case have been decided differently if it had appeared that the plaintiff (La Mourea) was fully insured against the damage he complains of? If it had appeared further that he had been compensated in full by the insurer? (A claim to which an insurer is subrogated is frequently prosecuted by the insurer in the name of the insured person, as ostensible plaintiff—though the practice is regarded in some courts as contrary to a "real party in interest" rule. Why would an insurer prefer not to appear as the claimant?)

(2) *Drafting.* If you had advised the city in preparing the contract, and its desire was to facilitate claims such as La Mourea brought, could you have improved on the language that the court quotes? How? See Lundt v. Parsons Construction Company, 181 Neb. 609, 150 N.W.2d 108 (1967); Pacific Northwest Bell Telephone Co. v. DeLong Corp., 246 Ore. 369, 425 P.2d 498 (1967).

(3) *Problem.* An oil prospector buys the mineral interest in a farm, together with the right to drill on it. The drilling operation ruins a crop belonging to a sharecropper on the farm. The prospector's contract with the owner provides that he "shall be responsible for all damages caused by drilling operations." Does the sharecropper (tenant) have a contract claim against the prospector? See Andrepont v. Acadia Drilling Co., 255 La. 347, 231 So.2d 347 (1969).

(4) *Problem.* The owner of a valuable coin collection deposited it in a coin-operated locker at a municipal airport. Before his return the locker was rifled, and the collection stolen. The lockers were serviced by a company under contract with the city that operated the airport, and it contained this term: "The Locker Company agrees to indemnify the City against all liabilities of whatever kind or character for which either party may be legally liable, resulting from or in any way connected with the lawful use of lockers, and also against all claims for loss of or damage to articles checked in lockers." If the victim of the theft cannot recoup his loss from

the city, and cannot establish any negligence on the part of the locker company, is the company liable to him as a third party beneficiary of the contract? See Silton v. Kansas City, 446 S.W.2d 129 (Mo.1969). If the contract also required the company to provide locking mechanisms such as to "assure adequate security against forcible entry," does that term establish the company's liability? Ibid.

VISINTINE & CO. v. NEW YORK, CHICAGO & ST. LOUIS R. CO.

Supreme Court of Ohio, 1959.
169 Ohio St. 505, 160 N.E.2d 311.

The amended petition of the plaintiff, Visintine & Company, to which a demurrer was filed by each of the defendants, alleges two causes of action, one for breach of contract and one for negligence. The demurrers were sustained by the Court of Common Pleas.

The Court of Appeals reversed the judgment of sustention as to the contract cause and affirmed such judgment as to the tort cause.

Plaintiff's amended petition, containing as it does extended quotations from the contracts involved, is too long to set out in full here. The allegations of the petition are very fairly and succinctly summarized in the opinion of the Court of Appeals, as follows [155 N.E.2d 683]:

"Prior to 1950 railroad tracks of each of the defendant companies, The New York, Chicago & St. Louis Railroad Company and The Baltimore & Ohio Railroad Company, crossed United States Route 23 at grade on Wood Street in the City of Fostoria, Ohio. In August, 1949, the City of Fostoria passed an ordinance giving its consent to the grade crossing elimination and agreed to bear certain costs of the improvement. In May of 1950 the Director of Highways for the State of Ohio, by official entry, declared that the separation of grades was reasonably necessary and expedient. Following this, on the 17th day of July, 1950, the Director of Highways entered into a contract with the City of Fostoria and the defendant railroad companies, which contract set up the proportion of costs of the grade crossing elimination to be borne by each of the parties thereto, and also provided for certain work to be performed by the defendant companies. These contracts with the City of Fostoria and the railroads did not cover all the necessary work to be done on the project, the balance of which was to be performed under a separate contract and which was accordingly entered into at a later date, between the plaintiff-appellant Visintine Company, and the State of Ohio. Each of the separate contracts provided that the work should be performed in accordance with the plans and specifications submitted for the project and in the sequence designated. The nature of the work was such that none of the parties could perform its part in a single operation, but numerous ones were required and the time when each was to be performed was specified and spelled out in the plans and specifications agreed upon. These contracts were subsequently carried out and the project completed. Plaintiff now claims damages against the railroad companies as the result of said project and claims in the amended petition that the defendant railroad companies failed to perform their work as required by their contract with the State of Ohio."

The cause is before this court upon the allowance of motions to certify the record filed on behalf of both defendants and plaintiff.

PER CURIAM. It is conceded that there was no actual contract between the plaintiff and either of the defendants. The theory of plaintiff upon which it seeks to recover is that it was a third party beneficiary to the contracts of July 17, 1950, between the state of Ohio and each of the defendants.

In Restatement of the Law of Contracts, Section 133, a third party beneficiary is said to be either (a) a creditor beneficiary (b) a donee beneficiary or (c) an incidental beneficiary. An incidental beneficiary under a contract to which he is not a party may not recover from the promisor. . . .

According to . . . Section 133, a person is a creditor beneficiary if the performance of the promise will satisfy an actual, supposed or asserted duty of the promisee to the beneficiary and is not intended as a gift.

Although this Restatement definition distinguishes between a creditor beneficiary and a donee beneficiary, such distinction has little materiality so far as liability to the beneficiary is concerned because it is generally held that either type of beneficiary may recover. 11 Ohio Jurisprudence (2d), 429, 431. Familiar examples of recovery by third party beneficiaries, without any attempt to distinguish between creditor or donee, are by the beneficiary of a life insurance policy, by a person injured by the holder of a liability insurance policy, and by a materialman from a surety indemnifying an owner of a construction project against the defaults of a contractor.

The most frequent examples of the creditor-beneficiary situation outlined in the texts are those where one person contracts to pay the debts of another. But such need not always be the case. It is pointed out, as follows, in 4 Corbin on Contracts, 97, Section 787:

"The promises on which a creditor beneficiary has been given judgment are nearly all cases where the consideration was executed and the promisor is a money debtor. The term 'creditor,' however, may properly be used broadly to include any obligee to whom the promisee owes a duty. There seems to be no good reason for restricting the rule to cases where the third party is a creditor in the narrow sense of one to whom the promisee owes a liquidated debt. Thus, if the promise is to perform labor or deliver goods instead of to pay money, or is to pay claims for unliquidated damages, the obligee should be able to maintain suit against a promisor who has assumed the duty."

The state of Ohio owed certain duties to plaintiff under the contract entered into between them. Among those duties was that of providing plaintiff with a site on which it could perform its work without hindrance or delay and of doing those things which it promised to do at such time and in such manner as would not hinder or delay the plaintiff. Even though the state, because of governmental immunity, can not be sued for its failure to perform those duties, the duties nevertheless existed. The performance of those duties was undertaken by the defendants under their contracts with the state of Ohio. Since the contracts between defendants and the state, in addition to the performance of certain obligations assumed by the defendants for the benefit of the state, provided, also, for the performance of certain obligations owed by the state to the plaintiff, it would seem that plaintiff falls squarely within the definition of "creditor beneficiary."

Plaintiff's petition alleges that the contracts between defendants and the state of Ohio set out the standard specifications of the state of Ohio which specifically stated that those contracts and that between the state and plaintiff were entered into pursuant to the accomplishment of a single project, and that it was the duty of all contractors to co-operate and to co-ordinate their work. The petition alleges also and sets out in detail a schedule of construction contained in all contracts, whereby mutual and reciprocal obligations were placed on the defendants and plaintiff to perform their respective portions of the work on time and in sequence.

It is urged by the defendants that the contracts between them and the state of Ohio do not clearly show an intent to benefit the plaintiff, and that such an intent cannot be implied. And several cases from outside Ohio to that effect are cited to us by the defendants. However, there appears to be no unanimity of opinion on this subject. In 4 Corbin on Contracts, 20, Section 776, the following is said about the intention to benefit the third party:

"It is clear that if the 'primary' and 'paramount' purpose seems to be to benefit the third person, as in the case of all sole and donee beneficiaries, he should have an enforceable right as the court says. But rights have not been limited so narrowly as this. In the case of most creditor beneficiaries, it is the purpose and intent of the promisee to procure the discharge of his obligation. The attainment of this end involves benefit both to himself and to his creditor. This 'benefit' he intends to bring about as an entirety, having no idea in his own mind as to its division between the persons receiving it or as to 'primary' or 'paramount' purpose. Neither should the court make such a division. It should content itself with bringing about the entire result that the promised performance would attain. That result was the 'paramount' object of desire and that result was the 'primarily' intended result, including not only the ultimate end in view but also the means used to bring it about. The great majority of the courts attain this desired result in full by giving a remedy to the creditor against the promisor. The question is not 'whose interest and benefit are primarily subserved,' but what was the performance contracted for and what is the best way to bring it about."

In the light of that statement, we concur in the analysis by the Court of Appeals, where, in the opinion by Judge Miller, it is said:

". . . We are of the opinion that in considering the railroad contracts and the plans and specifications and sequence of work specifications it is apparent that it was intended to benefit the contractor, as they all provided for cooperation in order that the job might be completed as scheduled. . . . Throughout all contracts it was made plain that the work of Visintine was dependent upon the performance by the railroads of their contractual obligations and vice versa. By each performing their obligations in the proper sequence a benefit was incurred upon the other by permitting them to complete their work in accordance with the terms of their various contracts."

Taken altogether, we believe the allegations of the petition are sufficient, as against demurrer, to qualify plaintiff as a beneficiary under the contracts between the defendants and the state of Ohio, particularly in view of the fact that the state is immune from suit for any alleged violations of the duties it assumed under its contract with plaintiff.

We agree with the Court of Appeals in its affirmance of the sustaining of the demurrer to the tort cause of action. Tort is based on a duty owed by one party to another. The duty owed here by the defendants was to the state of Ohio, not to the plaintiff. The duty arising out of contract upon which plaintiff may rely in its first cause of action was that owed to it by the state. If defendants are liable to plaintiff it is due to a breach of the contracts they made with the state of Ohio and not to the violation of any duty owed directly to the plaintiff upon which a tort action may be based. Wymer-Harris Construction Co. v. Glass, 122 Ohio St. 398, 171 N.E. 857, 69 A.L.R. 517.

Judgment affirmed.

TAFT, JUSTICE (dissenting). See Brotherton v. Merritt-Chapman & Scott Corp., 2 Cir., 1954, 213 F.2d 477; . . . Restatement of the Law of Contracts illustration under Section 147,[a] 12 American Jurisprudence, 834, Section 281.

---

a. This illustration is as follows: "A, an owner of land enters into a contract with B, a contractor, by which B contracts to erect a building containing certain vats. C contracts with B to build the vats according to the specifications in the contract. The vats are installed in the building, but, owing to defective construction, leak and cause harm to A. C is under no

NOTES

(1) *Cautionary Considerations.* At what point would it be too late for the state, city, and railroads to modify their contract, so as to reduce the obligations of the railroads to the Visintine Company? Such a modification would occur, for example, if the state undertook to do some of the work previously assigned to the railroads, and the costs were reapportioned accordingly. Another kind of "modification" would occur if disputes arose between the state and the railroads in the course of performance, and they agreed to a settlement on which the work might go forward in the spirit of letting bygones be bygones. If the rights of the Visintine Company were held to be unaffected by subsequent agreements such as these, the state and city might well find themselves locked into unsatisfactory contracts with the railroads—contracts that would be variable to fit changing circumstances except for the necessity of Visintine's consent. The termination of a beneficiary's right by agreement between the parties who created it in the first place is not always permitted; see Restatement, § 143, and Restatement Second, § 142. (This topic is developed below.)

One of the reasons given for caution in recognizing third party beneficiary claims on government contracts on behalf of members of the public is that it may upset "arrangements for governmental control over the litigation and settlement of claims." Restatement Second, § 145, Comment a. To some extent the same consideration makes it doubtful that Visintine should be recognized as a third party beneficiary. The decision does not have impressive support in many other courts, and has been distinguished on comparable facts. See C. H. Leavell & Co. v. Glantz Contracting Corp., 322 F.Supp. 779 (E.D.La.1971).

(2) *Problem.* A subcontract for electrical installations in a building under construction requires the subcontractor (S) to fulfill the specifications about wiring found in the contract between the prime contractor (P) and the building owner (O). S installs defective wiring; in consequence the building burns; and O makes claim for his loss against S, as third party beneficiary of the P–S contract. (P is insolvent.) What result? See Vogel v. Reed Supply Company, 277 N.C. 119, 177 S.E.2d 273 (1970); but see Cox v. Fremont County Public Building Authority, 415 F.2d 882 (10th Cir. 1969).

(3) *Question.* In what circumstances would a subcontractor be a third party beneficiary of the prime contract? Compare Thomas G. Snavely Co. v. Brown Construction Co., 16 Ohio Misc. 50, 239 N.E.2d 759 (1968), with International Erectors, Inc. v. Wilhoit Steel Erectors & R. Serv., 400 F.2d 465 (5th Cir. 1968) (claim by sub-sub-sub against subcontractor, on defendant's contracts both up and down).

(4) *Promoting a Common Cause.* One of the undoubted merits of third party beneficiary theory is that it permits a group of persons to give legal backing to a common interest that they have. As an illustration

duty to A who is only an incidental beneficiary of the contract between B and C, since C's performance is not given or received in discharge of B's duty to A."

Is there a substantial difference between this example and the situation in the main case? See also 4 Corbin, pp. 102–105.

there is the case of a group of merchants, all tenants in a shopping center, who, together with the landlord, were interested in promoting the center and fostering ethical business practices. To advance such ends they formed a tenants' association, run on democratic principles. A provision in each lease required the tenant to be a dues-paying member. It was held that the association was a third party beneficiary of the leases, entitled to specific performance of this term against some tenants who were outvoted. Moorestown Management, Inc. v. Moorestown Bookshop, Inc., 104 N.J.Super. 250, 249 A.2d 623 (1969).

A more usual illustration is a composition among creditors. Frequently the creditors of a debtor who is unable to pay his debts as they mature are willing to scale down their claims, or extend the time for paying them, or both. A voluntary agreement among them to such an effect is called a "composition." It is enforceable by the debtor (absent any vitiating circumstance such as fraud or nonperformance on his part), and an explanation often given is that he is a third party beneficiary of the mutual promises of his creditors. On this theory, he need not have joined in the agreement. (If he is a party to the agreement, what consideration does he give for the creditors' promises of forbearance? See Massey v. Del-Valley Corp., 46 N.J.Super. 400, 134 A.2d 802 (1957).)

(5) *Immunities as Benefits.* The benefit conferred on a debtor by a composition among his creditors is in the form of a release (or postponement) of liability. That is, he obtains an immunity to suits, in whole or in part. Contracts conferring this sort of benefit on a third party are more widespread than is usually appreciated. For one example, consider this term in the contracts between a dealer in manufactured products and his customers: "Warranties by manufacturers are limited to repair and replacement." In K & C, Inc. v. Westinghouse Electric Corporation, 437 Pa. 303, 263 A.2d 390 (1970), the court held that such a term barred an action by a buyer against a manufacturer for special or consequential damages resulting from a defect in the goods. The court said: "A clearer case of a contract made for the benefit of another would be hard to imagine . . . ." See also Ison v. Daniel Crisp Corp., 146 W.Va. 786, 122 S.E.2d 553 (1961).

MASSENGALE v. TRANSITRON ELECTRONIC CORPORATION

United States Court of Appeals, First Circuit, 1967.
385 F.2d 83.

[Prior to 1962, McClellan and Burck, Inc. was a New York corporation engaged in the business of planning and effecting mergers of business corporations. One of its clients was a Minnesota firm, Thermo King Corporation. Ultimately, in August, 1961, many efforts it had made on behalf of Thermo King resulted in its acquisition by the Westinghouse Electric Corporation. At that time, Thermo King paid McClellan and Burck $325,000 for its services.

The present action is one against Transitron Electronic Corporation, which had been interested in acquiring Thermo King in 1960. It was brought by McClellan and Burck, and continued by Massengale, as trustee for the stockholders of the firm after its dissolution. That firm is referred to hereafter as "Burck". (The court's opinion also refers to the plaintiff as "Burck".)

In July, 1960, both Westinghouse and Transitron had become interested, through Burck's efforts, in acquiring Thermo King. Burck and Thermo King entered into a letter agreement about Burck's compensation, which was fixed as a percentage of the sale price, not to exceed $325,000. The fee was expected to be paid by the acquiring company, and its amount was to be approved (at Thermo King's insistence) by the acquiring company. The compensation was agreed upon, in Burck's words, "in the event a transaction is consummated with any company where our firm has originated the transaction." A month later, negotiations had focussed on Transitron. Burck wrote to Thermo King stating its willingness to accept a reduced fee of $300,000— only in connection with the Transitron purchase—"to be due and payable when and if the proposed transaction with Transitron is consummated."

In October Transitron and Thermo King entered into an agreement for the sale of Thermo King's assets. The price was to be paid in Transitron stock, Thermo King was to be dissolved, and the stock distributed to its shareholders. The execution of the sale was subjected to various conditions, including the taking of certain corporate actions such as a favorable vote by the seller's stockholders. The agreement recited Thermo King's agreement to pay Burck's fee "in the event that the said transactions are consummated, but not otherwise. Such fee shall be paid by Transitron if and when such transactions are effected."

In December Transitron sent Thermo King a notice terminating the agreement on the grounds of a material adverse change in Thermo King's business, and the failure of Thermo King to call a stockholders' meeting.

Several years later, the present action was brought to recover the $300,000 fee from Transitron. The plaintiff alleged that the termination was without justification, and was a willful breach of the agreement, and was a violation of Transitron's obligation to Burck; also that Transitron "wrongfully prevented the effecting and consummation of the transaction." [a]

The trial court, though sitting in Massachusetts, gave effect to a provision in the Transitron agreement that it should be "governed by Minnesota law." In the present appeal, this ruling was approved. The court said that to apply Minnesota law, including its recognition

a. Immediately after the termination, Burck wrote to Westinghouse, seeking to revive its interest in Thermo King. This letter stated that the Transitron sale was aborted by a precipitous drop in the market value of Transitron stock, which eroded the price by almost 40%.

of third party beneficiary claims, did not offend substantial Massachusetts public policy.[b]

The trial court nevertheless granted a motion by Transitron for summary judgment, on two grounds. One was that Burck's receipt of $325,000 on account of the Westinghouse transaction discharged any claim it may have had against Transitron. (In this connection the court attempted to distinguish Olds v. Mapes-Reeve Construction Co., herein at p. 519 supra.) The other ground was that none of the agreements contemplated payment of a fee to Burck, in relation to the Transitron sale, if it was not consummated. In this connection the court refused to accept an implication drawn from two Minnesota cases: Huntley v. Smith and Flower v. Davidson. According to the appellate court, these cases "allowed recovery to a broker of a fee contingent on consummation when his seller-principal arbitrarily refused to consummate a transaction." The trial court refused to extend the principle of these cases to the present one, finding no Minnesota case that had applied it in favor of a third party beneficiary. The plaintiff appealed.]

COFFIN, CIRCUIT JUDGE.

. . . [W]e cannot say that Burck has advanced no cause of action. Appellee acknowledges that Minnesota law confers upon a third party beneficiary the right to assert such claims against a promisor as he has against a promisee. The district court recognized this when it declared that Transitron's obligation to Burck was co-extensive with Thermo King's. Appellee implicitly and the court explicitly accepted the principle of La Mourea v. Rhude [p. 889 supra]. But both failed to pursue the implications of this landmark case.

The court read *La Mourea* as merely giving Burck the right to maintain an action, without shedding light on the nature of its rights. It therefore, as we have noted, refused to apply Huntley v. Smith, supra, and Flower v. Davidson, supra, because ". . . in this case [Burck] and [Transitron] had no relationship apart from the Transitron-Thermo King agreement." In similar vein appellee relied heavily on Kramer v. Gardner, 104 Minn. 370, 116 N.W. 925, 22 L.R.A.,N. S., 492 (1908), which held that a promise by the purchaser of a business to a second mortgagee to pay off the first mortgage gave no rights to the first mortgagee, there being no privity between the two mortgagees, no obligation on the part of the second mortgagee to the first mortgagee, nor any consideration moving from the beneficiary (first mortgagee) to the promisor.

Leaving aside the factual differences between *Kramer* and the case at bar, *La Mourea* specifically overruled the "outmoded" doc-

---

b. Citing Restatement Second, of Conflict of Laws, §§ 332(2), 332a (and comment g), and 346 (and comment c).

trine of Kramer v. Gardner and in so doing, dealt fatal blows to the traditional concepts of both consideration and privity.   .   .   .

La Mourea was not an accident.   It was foreshadowed by the concurring opinion of Justice Royal Stone in Peterson v. Parviainen, 174 Minn. 297, 219 N.W. 180 (1928), who, twelve years later, wrote the opinion in *La Mourea* for a unanimous court.   See de Werff, Third Party Beneficiary Contracts in Minnesota, 29 Minn.L.Rev. 436, 441–45 (1945).[1]   See also 25 Minn.L.Rev. 523 (1941) ; Mitchell v. Rende, 225 Minn. 145, 147, 30 N.W.2d 27, 29 (1947).

To use the language of *La Mourea*, Burck in the case before us "has come directly into legal relationship with" Transitron.   This is no surprise to anyone, for Burck drafted its fee agreement letter knowing it would be shown to the acquiring company; Thermo King accepted the fee agreement only on condition that Transitron approve; in fact subsequent discussions between Thermo King and Transitron resulted in a reduction in fee for that transaction; and Transitron in its contract with Thermo King assumed the obligation to pay Burck's commission.   But, apart from the express characterization of the direct relationship just quoted, the entire import of *La Mourea* is that, regardless of such labels as "consideration" and "privity", Transitron stands in the same position toward Burck as does Thermo King.   The district court, while formally accepting this concept in referring to Transitron's obligation as "co-extensive" with Thermo King's, for all practical purposes diminished it by applying traditional concepts of consideration and privity when it refused to extend to Transitron the principle that arbitrary refusal to consummate a transaction could mature its obligation as fully as could consummation.

This principle is to be distinguished from the undertaking by Thermo King and Transitron in their contract to use "best efforts" to bring about the transaction.   We do not reach the issue whether, as the district court said, this obligation was reciprocal only, for there is a large difference between the positive duty to use best efforts and the negative duty to refrain from termination for unjustifiable cause.

On what basis of reason should there be a difference between the liability of a seller and a buyer, each of whom had undertaken to pay a brokerage fee in the event of consummation and each of whom wrongfully refuses to consummate a transaction?   Or, to put it more concretely, why should Thermo King be obliged to pay Burck if it cap-

1.   We are told that in the valedictory of Justice Stone, his last opinion—a dissent—he wrote of the third party beneficiary contract doctrine: "It illustrates the fact that the common law is not a matured, rigid, and inert mass.   It is rather a live and growing organism, self-adapting to new problems and new truths.   While avowing respect for precedent, it owes no allegiance either to ancient error or any concept invalidated by progress." Farmers State Bank v. Burns, 212 Minn. 455, 472, 5 N.W.2d 589, 591 (1942), quoted in 29 Minn.L.Rev., supra at 436, n. 3.

tiously aborted the transaction while Transitron would be under no such obligation for the same conduct leading to the same result? We cannot see any basis—other than "privity"—for making a distinction.[2] Nor can we see the distinction drawn by the district court between a fee agreement contingent on "consummation" and one contingent on specified preconditions to consummation ,as well as final consummation itself. . . .

We recognize that the Minnesota courts, so far as we are aware, have not had occasion to rule on the obligation of an arbitrarily defaulting promisor to a third party beneficiary in such a case as that at bar. But we feel that they would today be constrained to recognize a cause of action.[3] The most pertinent case that has been cited to us is Chipley v. Morrell, 228 N.C. 240, 45 S.E.2d 129 (1947), where, on demurrer, a broker hired by a seller, was held entitled to sue an arbitrarily reneging buyer despite the absence of any undertaking to pay the fee on the part of the buyer. This case is, a fortiori, persuasive authority for that at bar since we have here an explicit undertaking by the buyer to pay the fee. . . .

The second ground of the district court's decision—that Thermo-King's payment for the Westinghouse transaction satisfied any liability of Transitron—is based on the concept that all that was bargained for was one fee for one transaction. In a sense this is true. Prospectively, Burck and Thermo King contemplated only one completed transaction. There obviously could be only one completed merger. But what is alleged by the complaint to have happened is something beyond the contemplation of the parties, i. e., the unjustifiable refusal by Transitron to consummate the first transaction. This, as we have concluded, gives rise to an obligation. The broker has in such case earned a commission just as if the merger had been completed. When its subsequent services, which it was under no compulsion to render, resulted in a completed transaction, a second commission was earned. This is not, as appellant properly notes, an action against an employer for damages caused by wrongful discharge, in which damages would be mitigated by plaintiff's subsequent earnings.

---

2. That a broker's right to his commission should not turn on whether the sale falls through because of the default of the seller or buyer seems clear from Blanken v. Bechtel Properties, Inc., 194 F.Supp. 638 (D.D.C.1961) in which Judge Holtzoff thoughtfully reviews a wide range of authorities, citing, among others, Restatement (Second) of Agency § 445, comment d, ill. 1, and 4 Williston, Contracts § 1030A (1936).

3. We are conscious of the fact that both Huntley v. Smith, supra, and

Flower v. Davidson, supra, contain dicta that a broker is not entitled to a commission if the failure to complete the sale rested on the purchaser's refusal to carry out the contract of sale. While no underlying reason was given in either case, the concepts of privity and consideration, so unequivocally laid low by La Mourea, supra, must have made the proposition appear too obvious to warrant discussion. We cannot believe that these dicta would today be accepted as law in Minnesota.

In sum, while only one transaction was originally contemplated, the allegedly wrongful withdrawal of Transitron matured one commission-producing occurrence and the completion of the Westinghouse transaction matured another. Appellant therefore does not seek double compensation for a single debt but one payment for each of two separate debts.

Judgment will be entered reversing the judgment of the District Court and remanding the action for further proceedings not inconsistent herewith.

NOTES

(1) *Release and Modification.* Suppose that Transitron had not declared a termination of its agreement with Thermo King, but had obtained Thermo King's consent to a rescission, on the eve of consummating the agreement. Would Burck have had a claim against either of them for its fee? If they had agreed to reduce the purchase price by a substantial amount, would that have affected Burck's right to the fee? On this controversial point, a comment in the Restatement Second has this to say: "Even though there is no novation and no change of position by the beneficiary, the power of promisor and promisee to vary the promisor's duty to an intended beneficiary is terminated when the beneficiary manifests assent to the promise in a manner invited by the promisor or promisee." (Comment h to § 142) This proposition marks a retreat from the original Restatement position taken in § 142; but it strengthens the hand of a *creditor* beneficiary as stated in the first Restatement, § 143. On both points, see McCulloch v. Canadian Pacific Railway Co., 53 F.Supp. 534 (D.Minn.1943).

The proposition does not quite answer the questions posed above, however. Was it Thermo King's duty to Burck not to release Transitron from its undertaking to pay the fee? Nothing in the main case indicates that a release would not be effective, except that both parties contracted to use their "best efforts" to bring about the transaction. Possibly this provision created a duty to Burck that could not be altered without its consent. According to the Restatement Second a duty to an intended beneficiary is *irrevocable* if it is created by a promise prohibiting its discharge or modification through subsequent agreement of the parties. See § 142, Comment a.[c]

(2) *Mortgagee as Third Party Beneficiary.* Note the facts in Kramer v. Gardner, as stated in the main case. (And note that the doctrine of the case was rejected.) That case is one variant of a problem which has been a proving-ground for the law of third party beneficiaries. The more usual instance concerns a purchase of mortgaged property, in which the buyer undertakes to maintain the scheduled mortgage payments. Whether or not he does so, he stands to lose the property in case of default. (The case of a sale in which the seller's mortgage is retired is excluded from this discussion.) The mortgagee is entitled to a "deficiency judgment" if, upon foreclosure, the proceeds of the property do not satisfy his claim. If the buyer does not assume the mortgage, but takes the property only "subject

c. But another comment (§ 140, Comment c) hints that the promisor's duty may not be so irrefragible as this one indicates. Compare § 170(2).

to" it, the deficiency judgment may run against the seller, but cannot run against the buyer. Mortgage assumption agreements are regularly implemented, and a usual ground has been that the mortgagee is a third party creditor beneficiary.

There may indeed be a "chain" of assumptions: A buys the property (assuming the mortgage), and B buys from him (assuming the mortgage). The A–B contract is enforceable by the mortgagee: A is the promisee, just as the original mortgagor was the recipient of A's promise. But suppose there is a break in the chain: A did *not* assume the mortgage, but required B to do so. Is B personally subject to the mortgagee's claim? The Restatement has always taken a position generally favorable to the mortgagee.[d] But in some states there are crystallized rules that may be exempt from general argumentation about third party rights. The topic is not further noticed here, partly because it is threshed over in casebooks on real estate transactions.[e]

———

IRREVOCABLE BENEFICIARY DESIGNATIONS

An irrevocable duty is thought to be created by an ordinary life insurance policy, payable to someone other than the estate of the policyholder, unless it contains a term permitting him to change the beneficiary. But an irrevocable beneficiary designation is rarely encountered in current policies: When a policyholder wishes to divest himself of incidents of ownership, for tax reasons, the usual mode of doing so is through an assignment of the policy, or an "ownership" designation. See McGill, Legal Aspects of Life Insurance 131–36 (1959). The rights of minors under contracts for their benefit are also held, sometimes, to be immune from variation by agreement of the parties. Plunkett v. Atkins, 371 P.2d 727 (Okla.1962). But see Lehman v. Stout, 261 Minn. 384, 112 N.W.2d 640 (1961).

Apart from "family" arrangements, is there any purpose to be served by irrevocable beneficiary designations, that cannot be served just as well by a simpler legal device? If Transitron had been willing to undertake an irrevocable duty toward Burck, the simpler method would have been a promise running directly to Burck. (Supplying consideration for such a promise would not have been a difficulty, would it?)

Reconsider Note 1 after the Visintine case, at p. 893 supra. Do the facts of that case suggest that the railroads had irrevocable duties toward the plaintiff, Visintine?

NOTE

Problem. Mr. X's employer agreed, upon a sufficient consideration, to secure a policy of insurance on X's life payable to Mrs. X. Later the agree-

---

d. See § 144, Illustration 2 of the original; Illustration 3 of the Second.

e. E. g., Axelrod, Berger, & Johnstone, Land Transfer and Finance 161–74 (1971).

ment was changed so that X got a raise in salary instead. When X dies uninsured, does Mrs. X have a claim against the employer? Compare Weiner v. Physicians News Service, 13 A.D.2d 737, 214 N.Y.S.2d 474 (1961), with Cory v. Troth, 170 Kan. 50, 223 P.2d 1008 (1950).

SURETYSHIP BONDS FOR CONTRACTORS

Sizeable construction projects are frequently undertaken by contractors whose financial resources are thin. It is an ordinary precaution for the owner to require the backing of a bonding company as a condition to letting the contract, and similarly a contractor will commonly require his subcontractors to furnish bonds. The practice is indeed so prevalent that contractors of unquestioned financial integrity apply for bonds as a matter of course, and naturally charge the premiums to the owner as part of their costs.[a] In undertaking public works they must furnish bonds which satisfy the statutes and ordinances found at all levels of government. The expression "Miller Act bond" is shorthand for the contract of suretyship required for most federal projects.

The Miller Act (40 U.S.C.A. §§ 270a–e) requires that the contractor furnish two bonds: a performance bond and a payment bond. Each of them is a tripartite contract, the parties being the *principal* (i. e., the principal obligor), or contractor, the *surety*, and the *obligee*, who is the United States or its agency. A performance bond gives assurance that the work undertaken by a contractor will be completed. A payment bond gives assurance that he will discharge obligations related to the work, notably that debts he incurs for labor and materials will be paid. Sometimes these commitments are combined in a single bond.

A question that naturally arises when a payment bond is required by an owner or contractor is: What was his object? The obligee is not personally responsible for the payment of labor and material claims incurred by the principal—at least not by any contractual arrangement between them. There are, however, at least three explanations for the existence of the bond that may be explored: (1) The obligee may be a contractor who has undertaken by agreement with the owner that the subcontractor will satisfy his laborers and materialmen. [If this is so, the question is only pushed back one step: Why should the owner require that?] (2) The obligee may be accountable by statute for the payment of such claims. A characteristic mechanics' lien statute permits laborers and materialmen to file notices of their

a. In Electro-Kold Sales Corp. v. General Cas. Co., 174 Wash. 555, 25 P.2d 572 (1933), a contractor's bond is quoted as follows: "Note: The attention of Owners and Architects is called to the provisions [which give] direct right of suit against the Surety to all subcontractors and materialmen having direct contracts with the Contractor, and will generally involve the Owner in an added premium."

claims with the effect of fixing liens on the improved property. If the owner does not satisfy such a lien it will be foreclosed after the fashion of a mortgage. [Variations from state to state make it unsafe to generalize far.] (3) Failing other explanations, the obligee may have required a payment bond as an act of benevolence toward laborers and materialmen, who are characteristically not well placed to shoulder the risk of the contractor's insolvency. [For the relation of bonds to social policy see 4 Corbin, pp. 177–8.]

In the case of a payment bond in favor of the United States—and the same may be said of public authorities generally—the first two explanations do not apply. As the Supreme Court has said, "nothing is more clear than that laborers and materialmen do not have enforceable rights against the United States for their compensation. . . . They cannot acquire a lien on public buildings . . . and as a substitute for that more customary protection, the various statutes were passed which require that a surety guarantee their payment." [b] The Miller Act provides explicitly that persons furnishing labor and materials *shall have the right to sue* on the payment bond.[c]

With respect to state and local projects, and private ones, the rights of subcontractors, laborers and materialmen against bonding companies which have issued bonds to contractors largely depend on the common law of contracts, as applied to the bond language. Even under payment bonds, some courts have denied the status of third party beneficiary to such parties. There has been a tendency to differentiate private bonds from those issued to public authorities. An intent to benefit the unpaid claimant is more readily inferred from the latter; as the public authority lacks the self-interest of protecting itself against mechanics' liens (see Note 2, p. 35 supra), it may be said that "the bond could have no other meaning" than to confer benefits on third parties.[d] This distinction, however, is not generally maintained, and by the prevailing view laborers and materialmen may sue upon both public and private payments bonds written in common form.

b. United States v. Munsey Trust Co., 332 U.S. 234, 241 (1947). But cf. Pearlman v. Reliance Ins. Co., 371 U.S. 132, 141 (1962): "We therefore hold . . . that the Government had a right to use the retained fund to pay laborers and materialmen; that the contractor, had he completed his job and paid his laborers and materialmen, would have become entitled to the fund; and that the surety, having paid the laborers and materialmen, is entitled to the benefit of all these rights to the extent necessary to reimburse it."

c. 40 U.S.C.A. § 270b(a) (emphasis supplied). This right of action is not limited to persons who have furnished labor and materials to the principal on the bond; hence one who has dealt with a subcontractor may by giving a prescribed notice to the contractor qualify for a right of action upon *his* bond. See Wallick and Stafford, The Miller Act, 29 Law & Contemp.Prob. 514 (1964).

d. See the Rainer case, cited below.

An excerpt from a bond for both performance and payment is as follows (referring to the contractor as *principal*) :

> Now therefore the condition of this obligation is such that (1) if the principal shall faithfully perform the contract on his part, and (2) satisfy all claims and demands incurred for the same, and (3) shall fully indemnify and save harmless the owner from all cost and damage which he may suffer by reason of failure so to do, and (4) shall fully reimburse and repay the owner all outlay and expense which the owner may incur in making good such default, and (5) shall pay all persons who have contracts directly with the principal for labor and material, then this obligation shall be null and void; otherwise it shall remain in full force and effect.

As to the archaic form of such bonds, see p. 535 supra.

What arguments would you make that this language expresses an undertaking by the obligor, bonding company, to see that payment is made to laborers and materialmen, which they may enforce as third party beneficiaries? What arguments would you make to the contrary? See Fidelity & Deposit Co. v. Rainer, 220 Ala. 262, 125 So. 55, 77 A.L.R. 13 (1929).

NOTES

(1) *Intent to Benefit?* The issue just described is commonly decided without the aid of extrinsic evidence about the purpose or intent of the payee in exacting the bond. Indeed, the terms of his contract with the principal obligor (contractor) seem to be a subsidiary consideration in some cases. See Jacobs v. Northeastern Corporation, 416 Pa. 417, 206 A.2d 49 (1965); LaSalle Iron Works, Inc. v. Largen, 410 S.W.2d 87 (Mo.1966). In the latter case the court found an intent to benefit the claimants in the wording of the bond itself—"insofar as an intent of the parties may be necessary." In ascertaining their intent, should the amount of the premium paid by the contractor be taken as an indicator? [e] Would you expect premiums to be affected markedly by the applicable law of third party beneficiaries?

A chapter of the Restatement of Security is devoted to the rights of those furnishing labor or materials against a contractor's surety. There it is said that the applicable rules "have been established to such an extent that they can no longer be considered merely rules of interpretation." (Introductory Note to Ch. 7.) The Supreme Court of Oregon, which follows the minority rule that materialmen are not third party beneficiaries of a payment bond, has acknowledged criticism of the rule. But it adheres to it because of the "untold numbers of surety contracts" entered into in reliance on previous decisions, and the "repercussions that could occur within the

---

e. As to using the amount of insurance premiums as an aid in interpreting policies, see Douglas Equipment Company v. Hartford Accident & Indem. Co., 435 F.2d 1024 (7th Cir. 1970); B. Schwartz & Company v. Hepburn, 302 F.2d 576 (7th Cir. 1962); Keeton, Insurance Law (Basic Text), § 6.3(b) (1971).

construction industry by an abrupt reversal of the rule." James A. C. Tait & Co. v. D. Diamond Corp., 228 Ore. 602, 365 P.2d 883 (1961). What repercussions can you conceive of?

The Massachusetts legislature has come to the aid of suppliers of labor and material, by providing them with rights of action on certain private payment bonds.[f] Before that, the Massachusetts court had evolved a unique doctrine for them to stand on,[g] although it has been reluctant to subscribe to third party beneficiary doctrine in general.[h] (In Massengale v. Transitron Electronic Corporation, p. 898 supra, note the importance to the plaintiff of making reference to Minnesota law.)

(2) *Problem.* In Sanders v. American Casualty Company, 269 Cal. App.2d 306, 74 Cal.Rptr. 634 (1969), a supplier of materials to a contractor did not learn that a payment bond had been executed for his benefit until it was too late for him to sue on it: the bond prescribed a limitation of one year from the time the contractor ceased work. The materialman sued on the bond despite the condition, and argued that it was unfair for him to be bound by it "where he was unaware of the existence of the contract itself." What result?[i]

(3) *Bid Bonds.* A builder has performed a contract except that he has failed to pay his suppliers, as the contract requires him to do. Before contracting, he supplied the owner with a bid bond, assuring the owner that he would execute the contract, and also a payment bond, if his bid was accepted. But the owner did not insist on the payment bond. Is the surety company that wrote the *bid* bond accountable to the suppliers, as third party beneficiaries, on the reasoning that their claims could have been satisfied from the payment bond if one had been provided? See Wisner, Recent Developments in The Law of Bid Bonds, 1971 Ins.Couns.J. 565.

LUCAS v. HAMM, 56 Cal.2d 583, 364 P.2d 685 (1961). [In a complaint against a lawyer, L. S. Hamm, some plaintiffs made the following allegations: They were designated as beneficiaries in a will prepared by the defendant for Eugene Emmick, deceased. The will had placed certain assets in trust, and specified that the plaintiffs were to have a 15% interest in it. After the will was probated, the

---

f. Mass.Gen.L., ch. 149, § 29A (1965).

g. See Johnson-Foster Co. v. D'Amore Const. Co., 314 Mass. 416, 50 N.E.2d 89, 148 A.L.R. 353 (1943), permitting enforcement of a payment bond on behalf of subcontractors, materialmen, and the like, on the theory that it was a "standing offer of security to all who, in reliance upon it, should accept the offer by bringing themselves within its terms," through furnishing services or materials. In what case would the "standing offer" theory fail to produce the same result as recognizing the rights of claimants as third party beneficiaries?

An echo of the reliance notion may be found in Restatement Second, § 133, Comment d.

h. See Estate of Porter v. C. I. R., 442 F.2d 915 (1st Cir. 1971). But see Canter v. Schlager, — Mass. —, 267 N.E.2d 492 (1971).

i. Cf. General Insurance Co. of Am. v. State Highway Commission, 147 Mont. 450, 414 P.2d 526 (1966); Coleman Capital Corp. v. Travelers Indemnity Company, 443 F.2d 47 (2d Cir. 1971).

lawyer had advised the plaintiffs that the trust provision was invalid under the California Civil Code. The plaintiffs were compelled to enter into a settlement with Emmick's blood relatives, by which they received a share of his estate that was $75,000 less than what they would have received if the will had been properly prepared. They sought recovery from the lawyer in that amount, basing the claim on his negligence, and on breach of his contract with Emmick. The action was dismissed, and the plaintiffs appealed.]

GIBSON, CHIEF JUSTICE. . . . It was held in Buckley v. Gray, 110 Cal. 339, 42 P. 900, 31 L.R.A. 862, that an attorney who made a mistake in drafting a will was not liable for negligence or breach of contract to a person named in the will who was deprived of benefits as a result of the error. . . . For the reasons hereinafter stated the case is overruled. [The court's discussion of the tort claim is omitted.]

Neither do we agree with the holding in Buckley that beneficiaries damaged by an error in the drafting of a will cannot recover from the draftsman on the theory that they are third-party beneficiaries of the contract between him and the testator.[1] Obviously the main purpose of a contract for the drafting of a will is to accomplish the future transfer of the estate of the testator to the beneficiaries named in the will, and therefore it seems improper to hold, as was done in Buckley, that the testator intended only "remotely" to benefit those persons. It is true that under a contract for the benefit of a third person performance is usually to be rendered directly to the beneficiary, but this is not necessarily the case. (See Rest., Contracts, § 133, com. d; 2 Williston on Contracts (3rd ed. 1959) 829.) For example, where a life insurance policy lapsed because a bank failed to perform its agreement to pay the premiums out of the insured's bank account, it was held that after the insured's death the beneficiaries could recover against the bank as third-party beneficiaries. Walker Bank & Trust Co. v. First Security Corp., 9 Utah 2d 215, 341 P.2d 944, 945 et seq. Persons who had agreed to procure liability insurance for the protection of the promisees but did not do so were also held liable to injured persons who would have been covered by the insurance, the courts stating that all persons who might be in-

---

1. It has been recognized in other jurisdictions that the *client* may recover in a contract action for failure of the attorney to carry out his agreement. (See 5 Am.Jur. 331; 49 A.L.R. 2d 1216, 1219–1221; Prosser, Selected Topics on the Law of Torts (1954) pp. 438, 442.) This is in accord with the general rule stated in Comunale v. Traders & General Ins. Co., 50 Cal.2d 654, 663, 328 P.2d 198, 68 A.L.R.2d 883, that where a case sounds in both tort and contract, the plaintiff will ordinarily have freedom of election between the two actions.

[In Schirmer v. Nethercutt, 157 Wash. 172, 288 P. 265 (1930), S was a student of law in N's office. He employed N to draw up a will for his grandmother, for which S paid. The grandmother instructed N to provide a substantial legacy for S. N prepared the will and had it witnessed by S—thereby costing him the legacy. S recovered his loss from N.—Eds.]

jured were third-party beneficiaries of the contracts to procure insurance.   Johnson v. Holmes Tuttle Lincoln-Merc., Inc., 160 Cal.App.2d 290, 296 et seq., 325 P.2d 193; James Stewart & Co. v. Law, 149 Tex. 392, 233 S.W.2d 558, 561–562, 22 A.L.R.2d 639.   Since, in a situation like those presented here and in the Buckley case, the main purpose of the testator in making his agreement with the attorney is to benefit the persons named in his will and this intent can be effectuated, in the event of a breach by the attorney, only by giving the beneficiaries a right of action, we should recognize, as a matter of policy, that they are entitled to recover as third-party beneficiaries.   See 2 Williston on Contracts (3rd ed. 1959) pp. 843–844; 4 Corbin on Contracts (1951) pp. 8, 20.

Section 1559 of the Civil Code, which provides for enforcement by a third person of a contract made "expressly" for his benefit, does not preclude this result.   The effect of the section is to exclude enforcement by persons who are only incidentally or remotely benefited. See Hartman Ranch Co. v. Associated Oil Co., 10 Cal.2d 232, 244, 73 P.2d 1163; cf. 4 Corbin on Contracts (1951) pp. 23–24.[a]   As we have seen, a contract for the drafting of a will unmistakably shows the intent of the testator to benefit the persons to be named in the will, and the attorney must necessarily understand this.

Defendant relies on language in Smith v. Anglo-California Trust Co., 205 Cal. 496, 502, 271 P. 898, and Fruitvale Canning Co. v. Cotton, 115 Cal.App.2d 622, 625, 252 P.2d 953, that to permit a third person to bring an action on a contract there must be "an intent clearly manifested by the promisor" to secure some benefit to the

---

a.   The impact of statutes on third party beneficiary law is summarized in the following extract from a Note, The Third Party Beneficiary Concept, 57 Colum.L.Rev. 406, 414–15 (1957).

"Legislation has had only a limited effect on the enforcement of contracts for the benefit of third persons.   California, Idaho, Montana, North Dakota, Oklahoma, and South Dakota have the code provision that 'a contract made expressly for the benefit of a third person may be enforced by him at any time before the parties thereto rescind it,' but it has been liberally construed. Although the language of their statutes differ *inter sese*, Georgia, Louisiana, New Jersey, and Virginia have given legislative recognition in liberal terms to the prevailing theory that a person for whose benefit a contract is made may sue thereon.   [A Michigan statute, rephrased in 1962, provides: "A promise shall be construed to have been made for the benefit of a person whenever the promisor has undertaken to give or to do or to refrain from do-

ing something directly to or for said person."]   The standard used to determine when the promisor has so undertaken has been called an objective one, determined from the form and meaning of the contract itself.   However, the key word 'directly' is left undefined, and Michigan courts could, by reasoning from the form and meaning of the agreement, unwarrantedly broaden the future application of the rule.   In contrast, West Virginia has tightly restricted recovery to actions on a '. . . promise . . . made for the sole benefit of a person with whom it is not made. . . .'   In addition to these general provisions, statutes of limited substantive coverage frequently give rights of action to beneficiaries of three general types: beneficiaries of life insurance policies, laborers and materialmen on statutory bonds posted by public contractors, and persons injured by the negligence of a bonded public official." (Footnotes to this passage are omitted.)

third person. This language, which was not necessary to the decision in either of the cases, is unfortunate. Insofar as intent to benefit a third person is important in determining his right to bring an action under a contract, it is sufficient that the promisor must have understood that the promisee had such intent. (Cf. Rest., Contracts, § 133, subds. 1(a) and 1(b); 4 Corbin on Contracts (1951) pp. 16–18; 2 Williston on Contracts (3rd ed. 1959) pp. 836–839.) No specific manifestation by the promisor of an intent to benefit the third person is required. The language relied on by defendant is disapproved to the extent that it is inconsistent with these views.

We conclude that intended beneficiaries of a will who lose their testamentary rights because of failure of the attorney who drew the will to properly fulfill his obligations under his contract with the testator may recover as third-party beneficiaries.

[The court went on to rule, however, that the complaint did not allege any error by Hamm that was not excusable in a well-informed lawyer. The supposed invalidity of the trust depended on rules about perpetuities and restraints on alienation—subjects which "have long perplexed the courts and the bar." In view of the state of the law, and the nature of the supposed error, "it would not be proper to hold that defendant failed to use such skill, prudence, and diligence as lawyers of ordinary skill and capacity commonly exercise." Judgment affirmed.]

NOTES

(1) *Lucas v. Hamm Revisited.* In Heyer v. Flaig, 70 Cal.2d 223, 449 P.2d 161 (1969), the court had to decide when the statute of limitations began to run on a claim such as that in the foregoing case: when the will was prepared, or when the testator died. In choosing the latter date, the court said that, under Lucas, the third party can recover on a tort theory. Of the third party beneficiary theory, it said: "This latter theory of recovery, however, is conceptually superfluous since the crux of the action must lie in tort in any case; there can be no recovery without negligence." [b] Does this mean that a lawyer cannot contract with his client to achieve a given result, even though a careful effort might fail?

(2) *The Case of the Charity Chilled.* William Overlock sued the Central Vermont Public Service Corporation, making the following allegations. While working as a lineman for the corporation he had fallen from a tree, suffering a permanent disability. "Certain persons interested in the welfare of the Plaintiff decided to take up a collection" among his neighbors for his benefit. But the defendant, "in order to induce these persons not to take up the collection, promised them that there was no need to take up the collection because the Defendant would take care of the Plaintiff for the rest of the Plaintiff's life." The suit was based on the corporation's failure to perform this promise. As the defendant should have expected, "in justifiable reliance on that promise these persons ceased all efforts to take

---

b. See also Knepper, Some Observations, etc., 38 Ins.Couns.J. 39, 43 (1971).

up the collection," with the result that the plaintiff lost the expected proceeds. The defendant refused to perform its promise.

The trial court certified the question to the supreme court whether or not these allegations stated a cause of action. *Held:* They did not. The court said that the asserted forbearance in reliance on the promise was "illusory". It quoted from Boyer, Promissory Estoppel: Requirements and Limitations of the Doctrine, 98 U.Pa.L.Rev. 459, 465 (1950): "It asks too much of a promisor to require that he consider whether or not his promise will induce action by a *third party.*" [c]

Do you agree? Boyer continues: "Yet some courts have seen fit to enforce gratuitous promises because they were considered to have induced the making of similar promises by other subscribers to a charity . . . ." Was Overlock's case different in any important way from the situation mentioned by Boyer? See Note, 30 U.Pitt.L.Rev. 174 (1968). If so, do you consider it stronger or weaker?

THIRD PARTY CLAIMS AGAINST LENDERS

Financial institutions are a favorite target of third party beneficiary claims. In a period such as the recent past, when the building industry has suffered heavily from the unavailability of construction financing, many participants in a job, or prospective ones, may have their expectations aroused by a bank's making a loan commitment. When such expectations are dashed, it is natural for them to make claims based on the commitment, although in terms it runs to another party. A series of recent cases, all involving savings and loan associations, exemplify a protective measure that they have taken; their loan contracts contain the following provision: "This agreement is made for the sole protection of the Borrower and the Lender (Association), and no other person or persons shall have any right of action hereon." [a]

Although the provision seems to have been useful, it is hard to tell whether or not it is ever decisive, for loan commitments are rarely held to be third party beneficiary contracts in the absence of such a reservation. A usual case is one in which the financer withholds the promised loan proceeds because of some real or supposed default on the part of its customer. The customer is commonly a developer or contractor, and is in financial straits. The claimant may be a person (contractor or sub-contractor) who is dependent on the loan proceeds for payment. There are cases, of course, in which the financer's con-

---

c. But see Restatement Second, § 90, Comment d.

a. For the provision, in slightly varying terms, see Pioneer Plumbing Sup. Co. v. Southwest Sav. & L. Ass'n, 102 Ariz. 258, 428 P.2d 115 (1967); Gordon Building Corp. v. Gibraltar Savings & Loan Ass'n, 247 Cal.App.2d 1, 55 Cal.Rptr. 884 (1966); and Seaboard Const. Co. v. Continental Mortgage Investors, 298 F.Supp. 579 (S.D. Ga.1969).

duct was justified on the terms of the contract.[b]   In such a case the court can avoid making a determination whether or not there are any third party beneficiaries.   Doubtless most lenders would prefer a broader ruling, such as that in Mortgage Associates, Inc. v. Monona Shores, Inc., 47 Wis.2d 171, 177 N.W.2d 340 (1970) : "The loaning of money to finance the construction of a building and thus pay contractors is not a third-party-beneficiary contract." [c]

But in the following note case a lender was on each side of the fence.

NOTES

(1) *Bank v. Bankers Life.*   There is a division of function among financial institutions lending on real property: long-term ("permanent") financing is commonly arranged with savings and loan associations and life insurance companies, among others; and short-term financing through commercial banks, chiefly.   The latter is used for a construction loan, when improvements are to be made.   Such a loan commonly has an "interim" character, in that it may not be drawn down until an arrangement for permanent financing is made.

The Republic National Bank of Dallas made a construction loan on the strength of a loan commitment that the borrower had obtained from a life insurance company.   The bank was not repaid, and it attributed its loss to the insurer's failure to make advances under the commitment.   In an action against the insurer, the bank was faced with the difficulty that the commitment was directed only to the prospective borrower, a developer; and the bank was forced to resort to third party beneficiary theory. The bank was defeated.

Would the bank have succeeded if it had shown that the insurer knew, in making its commitment, that the bank would rely upon it as it did?   In the trial, a bank vice-president gave testimony describing "the practice of Republic and banks generally by which applicants for interim loans are required to furnish 'take out commitments' from responsible lenders thus assuring a source of repayment of the interim loans."   And the court said: "As to the matter of custom and usage we may assume   .   .   .   it is a common occurrence for insurance companies and savings and loan associations to give their commitments that such companies will fund a permanent loan." The court based its ruling, however, on the text of the commitment.   (Apparently it would have ruled out parol evidence of the insurer's intent.) Does this case establish that a "custom" or "usage" cannot be the source

b. E. g., L. B. Herbst Corporation v. Northern Illinois Corporation, 99 Ill. App.2d 101, 241 N.E.2d 125 (1968) (conditions); Ted Spangenberg Co. v. Peoples Nat. Gas, 439 F.2d 1260 (8th Cir. 1971) (conditions—and modification?).

(Mo.App.1967).   The latter case relied both on a default by the prospective borrower, a developer, and on the broader ground that the claimant, a paving contractor, was only an incidental beneficiary.

c. See also Burns v. Washington Savings, 251 Miss. 789, 171 So.2d 322 (1965); Stephens v. Great Southern Savings & Loan Ass'n, 421 S.W.2d 332

Cf. McConnico v. Marrs, 320 F.2d 22 (10th Cir. 1963); Robert Wise Plumbing & H., Inc. v. Alpine Develop. Co., 72 Wash.2d 172, 432 P.2d 547 (1967).

of a third-party claim? See Republic Nat. Bank v. National Bankers Life Ins. Co., 427 S.W.2d 76 (Tex.Civ.App.1968).

(2) *Parol Evidence.* Professor Corbin, no friend to the parol evidence rule, thought it should permit an extrinsic showing that a written contract was intended for the benefit of a third party. But his view has been characterized as more "liberal" in that respect than that of the New York courts. Hylte Bruks Aktiebolag v. Babcock & Wilcox Co., 399 F.2d 289 (2d Cir. 1968) (footnote 6).

In Ridder v. Blethen, 24 Wash.2d 552, 166 P.2d 834 (1946), the curious question was whether or not parol evidence was admissible to establish that one of the plaintiffs was *not* a third party beneficiary of a contract his father had made, by the express terms of which he appeared to be a donee beneficiary. The court indicated that such evidence is commonly required to show whether or not the parties had a donative purpose. It referred to the Restatement, § 133(1)(a). That section speaks of the promisee's purpose, as it appears "from the terms of the promise in view of the accompanying circumstances." Would it be proper, under this test, to take testimony from the promisee about his purpose? Compare Restatement Second, § 133. What forms of parol evidence are admissible under that rule?

INSURANCE STATUTES PROVIDING THIRD PARTY CLAIMS

Except in a few states, it has traditionally been a choice for each motorist whether or not to insure himself against liability for road injuries. If he chooses to insure, however, he must usually insure not only against his own liabilities, but also against those of "permittees" —drivers to whom he entrusts his car. This requirement results partly from statutes, and partly from the manner in which insurers choose to designate the persons insured in their standard contracts. The so-called *omnibus clause* has been the chief instrument for extending protection to permittees. The clause was initially developed to serve the self-interest of the premium payer, and his altruistic interest in friends and relations. But the object of legislation on the subject is doubtless to increase the prospect that *victims* of road injuries—not permittees—will have access to insurance benefits.[a] The object of such a statute, it has been said, is to protect "that ever changing and tragically large group of persons who while lawfully using the highways themselves suffer grave injury through the negligent use of the highways by others." Atlantic National Ins. Co. v. Armstrong, 65 Cal.2d 100, 416 P.2d 801 (1966). Even in the absence of such a statute it has been argued that an insurer should not offer automobile insurance lacking an omnibus clause; but see the case at Note 3, p. 349 supra.

Other forms of legislation designed for the same broad purpose are directed to situations in which a liability insurer is entitled to re-

[a]. See Keeton, Insurance Law (Basic Text) § 4.7(a) (1971).

scind the contract, or otherwise resist a claim within its coverage, because of some act or neglect of the insured person. The insurer may find that it is nevertheless obliged to respond to a victim's claim against the insured. See Allstate Ins. Co. v. Dorr, 411 F.2d 198 (9th Cir. 1969), where a constitutional objection to such a statute was overcome. Automobile policies recite, in a "compliance" paragraph, that they are to be applied in accordance with such a law. And they further provide: "The insured agrees to reimburse the insurer for any payment it is required to make by such law, if it would not have had to pay except for the agreement in this paragraph." The net effect is that compensation for the third party, having been provided by the "promisor" company, may be recouped from the "promisee" insured.[b]

It is a developing statutory trend, as this is written, that motorists must insure themselves, and various groups such as their passengers, against certain losses caused by motoring generally, including those caused by the torts of other motorists. The shift is from a system of compensation based on fault to a "nonfault" system—although there are many forms of compromise. One of the precursors of this development was an insuring agreement (still prevalent) called Uninsured Motorist Coverage. It goes some distance toward indemnifying a driver who buys it against losses caused by the fault of another driver, who is uninsured, and may be penniless. This coverage is also widely supported by statutes. See Note, p. 348 supra.

Incontestability. Life insurance contracts are another class of contracts in which third party benefits are commonly mandated by statute. When the policy has been in force for a certain period, usually two years, it is no longer open to the insurer to contend that it is unenforceable by reason of fraud in procuring it or the like. Furthermore, the insurer may lose the advantage of certain qualifications on its promise that may have been written into the policy. All ordinary life policies express this intention in the form of an "incontestability clause;" but the policy claimant may assert a right broader than the one stated if it is supported by an applicable statute. The policy claimant is usually a third party beneficiary, of course, but is sometimes the person who procured the policy. For debatable decisions on this topic, see Simpson v. Phoenix Mut. Life Ins. Co., 24 N.Y.2d 262, 247 N.E.2d 655 (1969), and First Pennsylvania Bank & Trust Co. v. United States Life Ins. Co., 421 F.2d 959 (3d Cir. 1969).

The Barrera Case. In California, an analogue to the incontestability clause has been announced by the supreme court for application against automobile liability insurers. They have a duty to investigate the insured person's insurability with reasonable promptness aft-

---

b. As to the effectiveness of such a provision, however, see the California case quoted above.

er the issuance of the policy, not waiting until the occasion of an accident. Under this doctrine, the policy may be enforced even though the insured deceitfully misrepresented his driving record in applying for insurance. The insurer's duty of investigation inures, of course, "directly to the benefit of third persons injured by the insured." And the court hinted that the insured might be held ultimately accountable for the claim. Barrera v. State Farm Mutual Automobile Ins. Co., 71 Cal.2d 659, 456 P.2d 674 (1969).

NOTE

Problems. Victims of road injuries have sought compensation through an interesting variety of contracts other than insurance policies. What merit do you see in the following *contract* claims?—(a) Against an insurance broker, who had agreed to effect liability insurance for a customer; the customer negligently injured the claimant, and proved to be uninsured. See Gothberg v. Nemerovski, 58 Ill.App.2d 372, 208 N.E.2d 12 (1965).[c] (b) Against a road repair firm, which had undertaken in its contract with the state to place appropriate warning signs at the site; the claimant was injured when he failed to notice an unmarked detour. See Davis v. Nelson-Deppe, Inc., 91 Idaho 463, 424 P.2d 733 (1967).[d] (c) Against a driver for injury he caused to the claimant when he violated a traffic law; the supposed contract arose at an interview he had with a state official about possible withdrawal of his license to drive; in the course of it he agreed to abide by the traffic laws. See Hayrynen v. White Pine Copper Company, 9 Mich.App. 452, 157 N.W.2d 502 (1968).

Note that the latter two situations suggest an alternate claim for negligence. What reasons for pressing a contract claim can you envisage?

ROUSE v. UNITED STATES

United States Court of Appeals for the District of Columbia, 1954.
94 U.S.App.D.C. 386, 215 F.2d 872.

Action by United States, which had taken assignment of F. H. A. note which was in default, to recover from purchaser who had bought house from maker of note. The United States District Court for the District of Columbia, Burnita Shelton Matthews, J., struck purchaser's defenses and granted summary judgment for plaintiff and purchaser appealed.

EDGERTON, CIRCUIT JUDGE. Bessie Winston gave Associated Contractors, Inc., her promissory note for $1,008.37, payable in monthly

---

c. Compare American Credit Co. v. Stuyvesant Insurance Co., 7 N.C.App. 663, 173 S.E.2d 523 (1970).

d. According to this case, highway construction and repair contracts are generally not considered to be for the benefit of third persons, "absent a manifested intent to the contrary;" proof of negligence was required. See also Stewart v. Arrington Construction Company, 92 Idaho 526, 446 P.2d 895 (1968); Fannin v. Cubric, 21 Ohio App.2d 99, 255 N.E.2d 270 (1970), and cases cited.

installments of $28.01, for a heating plant in her house. The Federal Housing Administration guaranteed the note and the payee endorsed it for value to the lending bank, the Union Trust Company.

Winston sold the house to Rouse. In the contract of sale Rouse agreed to assume debts secured by deeds of trust and also "to assume payment of $850 for heating plant payable $28 per Mo." Nothing was said about the note.

Winston defaulted on her note. The United States paid the bank, took an assignment of the note, demanded payment from Rouse, and sued him for $850 and interest.

Rouse alleged as defenses (1) that Winston fraudulently misrepresented the condition of the heating plant and (2) that Associated Contractors did not install it satisfactorily. The District Court struck these defenses and granted summary judgment for the plaintiff. The defendant Rouse appeals.

Since Rouse did not sign the note he is not liable on it. D.C.Code 1951, § 28–119; N.I.L. Sec. 18.[a] He is not liable to the United States at all unless his contract with Winston makes him so. The contract says the parties to it are not "bound by any terms, conditions, statements, warranties or representations, oral or written" not contained in it. But this means only that the written contract contains the entire agreement. It does not mean that fraud cannot be set up as a defense to a suit on the contract. [3 Williston, Contracts § 811A (Rev. Ed.1936).] Rouse's promise to "assume payment of $850 for heating plant" made him liable to Associated Contractors, Inc., only if and so far as it made him liable to Winston; one who promises to make a payment to the promisee's creditor can assert against the creditor any defense that the promisor could assert against the promisee. [2 Williston, § 394.] Accordingly Rouse, if he had been sued by the corporation, would have been entitled to show fraud on the part of Winston. He is equally entitled to do so in this suit by an assignee of the corporation's claim. It follows that the court erred in striking the first defense. We do not consider whether Winston's alleged fraud, if shown, would be a complete or only a partial defense to this suit, since that question has not arisen and may not arise.

We think the court was right in striking the second defense. "If the promisor's agreement is to be interpreted as a promise to discharge whatever liability the promisee is under, the promisor must certainly be allowed to show that the promisee was under no enforceable liability. . . . On the other hand, if the promise means that the promisor agrees to pay a sum of money to A, to whom the promisee says he is indebted, it is immaterial whether the promisee is actually indebted to that amount or at all. . . . Where the promise

---

a. "No person is liable on the instrument whose signature does not appear thereon, except. . . ." UCC 3–401

(1): "No person is liable on an instrument unless his signature appears thereon."

is to pay a specific debt . . . this interpretation will generally be the true one." [2 Williston, § 399.]

The judgment is reversed and the cause remanded with instructions to reinstate the first defense.

Reversed and remanded.

NOTES

(1) *Rouse: The Second Defense.* If it is found, on remand, that the heating plant was installed so poorly as to be worthless, but that Bessie Winston made no misrepresentation about it, should Rouse be made to pay? The inference might be that when the house was sold both Winston and Rouse acted on the mistaken premise that Winston had no defense to a claim on the note by Associated Contractors. For such a case the Restatement authorizes the promisor to invoke the rules making contracts voidable for mistake: § 144. The corresponding section of Restatement Second is to the same effect. But Comment b to that section states that nonexistence of the supposed duty does not necessarily establish a "mistake". In other words, the promisor's undertaking may be one to perform a duty that might be asserted against the promisee, whether or not it would prove to be enforceable against him. Contrast an undertaking to perform whatever duty may be binding on the promisee. (Which of these undertakings is more like an indemnity contract?)

Sometimes the facts underlying a third party beneficiary claim permit the promisor to set up a series of defenses, with good effect: his promise was to pay only what the promisee owed; or (if it was more extensive) the undertaking is voidable for a mistake shared by him and the promisee; or (if there was no mutual mistake) the promisee was guilty of fraud in exacting the promise. See, for example, the facts in Lindler v. McClure, 292 S.W. 2d 381 (Tex.Civ.App.1956).

(2) *Standard Mortgagee Clause.* A provision generally found in policies of insurance on buildings is entitled "standard mortgagee clause," and in part it reads as follows: "If a mortgagee is named in the Declarations, . . . this insurance, as to the interest of the mortgagee only therein, shall not be invalidated by any act or neglect of the mortgagor or owner of the within described property . . . ; provided, that in case the mortgagor or owner shall neglect to pay any premium due under this policy, the mortgagee shall, on demand, pay the same." See General Credit Corp. v. Imperial Cas. Co., p. 650, supra.

When this clause applies, the mortgagee can properly be regarded as a third party beneficiary of the insurer's undertaking, which usually runs to the owner-mortgagor as the "named insured." If the owner destroys his own property by design, he does not have a claim on the policy, but the mortgagee does. If the owner knowingly converts the property to a more hazardous use, the insurance is commonly suspended as to him, but not as to the mortgagee. If the owner procured the policy by fraud upon the insurer, it is voidable as to him, but not as to the mortgagee.

All of these effects are somewhat exceptional, in a general view of third party beneficiary law. As a rule, the beneficiary's right, "like that of an assignee, is subject to limitations inherent in the contract, and to supervening defenses arising by virtue of its terms." Restatement Second § 140, Comment c. The effects stated above for the standard mortgagee clause are clearly intended by this section, for another comment (b) states: "The agreement may effectively provide that the right of the beneficiary is not to be affected by the act or neglect of the promisee." (Oddly, however, the text of the section seems to state precisely the opposite rule, just as § 140 of the original Restatement does.)

If an imposter applies for an insurance policy, pretending to be the person who owns the property, it might be supposed that the contract is a nullity. And that no claim could be based on such a document, even under the standard mortgagee clause. The right of a third party beneficiary is "created by contract, and in the absence of contract there is no such right." Restatement Second, § 140, Comment a. But this supposition is not necessarily safe, for the courts sometimes refer to the clause as creating an "independent contract" between the insurer and the mortgagee. And see Great American Ins. Co. v. Southwestern Finance Co., 297 P.2d 403 (Okl.1956), as to the imposter case.

(3) *Rouse: The First Defense.* In the Rouse case the court said: "one who promises to make a payment to the promisee's creditor can assert against the creditor any defense that the promisor could assert against the promisee." What qualification should be placed on that proposition, to account for the effects of a standard mortgagee clause? Cf. Aetna Ins. Co. v. Eisenberg, 188 F.Supp. 415 (E.D.Ark.1960), aff'd, 294 F.2d 301 (8th Cir. 1961); noted, 13 Stan.L.Rev. 926 (1961).

(4) *Problem.* Allan, an apple grower, was indebted to Paul. He contracted to deliver a load of apples to Dan, in exchange for Dan's promise to pay the debt to Paul. When Dan received the apples, he found them to be wormy, but kept them anyway. Can he escape paying the debt in full, if Paul sues him, by showing that the apples were worth only half what they should have been, if sound? If he had rejected the apples, for what amount would he have been liable to pay Paul? See Alexander H. Revell & Co. v. C. H. Morgan Grocery Co., 214 Ill.App. 526 (1919); First Carolinas Land Bank v. Page, 206 N.C. 18, 173 S.E. 312 (1934).

THE COAL STRIKE CASE

In the early 50's, the United Mine Workers struck the nation's coal operators, including the Benedict Coal Company. Considering that the union had violated a collective bargaining agreement, Benedict claimed damages. It also withheld certain royalties that the agreement would have required it to make, if performed, to the UMW Welfare and Retirement Fund. Although the Fund was created by the collective bargaining agreement, it was administered by its own trustees. They sued Benedict for the sums withheld. In defense, Benedict contended that the duty to pay royalties to the trustees was conditioned on performance by the union of its promises, or at least that the amount of the company's damage claim against the union should be set off against the trustees' recovery. In Lewis v. Benedict Coal Corp., 361 U.S. 459 (1960), the Supreme Court rejected both of these contentions. Its reasoning emphasized the peculiar character of an industry-wide collective bargaining agreement. Under a more "typical" third party beneficiary contract, it indicated, when the promisor has a damage claim against the promisee it may be fair to assume that the beneficiary's claim should be correspondingly reduced. But such a design, the Court ruled, must have been expressed in "unequivocal words" before it could be applied to the agreement in question. For one of its grounds, the Court found an expression of "national labor policy" in the Taft-Hartley Act, indicating that a union, like a corporation, should be the "sole source of recovery for injury inflicted by it."

In one interesting passage the Court remarked: "Using terms like 'counterclaim' or 'setoff' in a third-party beneficiary context may be confusing." What is confusing about it? The Restatement Second describes a setoff situation (§ 140, Illustration 9), and it says: "Partial defenses by way of recoupment for breach by the promisee may be asserted against the beneficiary, unless precluded by the terms of the agreement or considerations of fairness or public policy." (Comment c)

NOTE

Collective Agreements as Contracts. Students of labor law have often commented on the interplay, or lack of it, between the law of collective bargaining agreements and the law of contracts as represented in the treatises and the Restatements. One such comment advances these conclusions, among others: "contract rules which attempt to define with some specificity or detail rights and duties of parties are largely useless and often misleading when applied to collective agreements.[a] . . . [W]hile we may gain little insight into collective agreements by looking upon them as contracts, we can achieve significant insights into the nature of the law of contracts by viewing it from the perspective of collective agreements."[b] Compare the emphasis in Cox, The Legal Nature of Collective Bargaining Agreements, 57 Mich.L.Rev. 1 (1958), quoted in the Note at p. 625 supra. The passage set out in footnote a there was quoted by Justice Frankfurter in his dissent in the coal strike case.

SEARS, ROEBUCK AND CO. v. JARDEL CO.

United States Court of Appeals, Third Circuit, 1970.
421 F.2d 1048.

[For a partial report, including the facts, of this case, see p. 311 supra. The opinion (by VAN DUSEN, CIRCUIT JUDGE) continues as follows.]

Having correctly found the release to cover the claim involved here as to Robbins, Inc., the District Court held the release binding

---

a. Summers, Collective Bargaining and the Law of Contracts, 78 Yale L.J. 525, 538 (1969). On the third-party aspect of collective agreements, see pp. 538–41.

b. Id., 527.

upon Jardel by disregarding the separate entities of the two corporations. . . .

Courts of Pennsylvania and Delaware do not easily pierce the corporate veil. [But the court avoided a decision on the District Court ruling, and found another reason for affirmance.]

Even if the corporate veil of Jardel were not disregarded, it cannot entirely separate itself, for the purpose of this suit, from the activities of Robbins, Inc. Jardel's claim against Hirsch is based upon Hirsch's duties arising out of Robbins, Inc.'s subcontract with it. In its third-party complaint, Jardel alleged the contract as the basis for its suit: "Defendant is informed and believes and thereon alleges that Hirsch breached its agreement with the contractor [Robbins, Inc.] . . .." But just as Jardel did not sign the release, so too it was not a signatory to the underlying Robbins, Inc.-Hirsch contract.

Because the contract explicitly contemplated the provision of services by Hirsch to Jardel,[1] Jardel has rights under the contract as a third-party creditor beneficiary. See, e. g., Van Cor, Inc. v. American Cas. Co., 417 Pa. 408, 413, 208 A.2d 267, 269 (1965). Professor Williston defines a third-party creditor beneficiary contract as one in which:

> " 'no purpose to make a gift appears from the terms of the promise in view of the accompanying circumstances and performance of the promise will satisfy an actual or supposed or asserted duty of the promisee to the beneficiary . . ..'
>
> "The promisee's object in the contract to discharge his debt must always be primarily, and generally solely, to secure his own advantage. He wishes to be relieved from liability, and he exacts a promise to pay the third person only because that is a way of relieving himself."

2 S. Williston, Law of Contracts, § 361, at 863 (3rd Ed., 1959) [quoting Restatement of Contracts § 131(1)(b) (1932)] (footnotes omitted).[2] As general contractor, Robbins, Inc. had a duty to provide Jardel with certain specified services; it chose to fulfill part of that duty by subcontracting with Hirsch, Hirsch thereby promising to complete the plumbing, heating and air-conditioning work. Because courts have "instinctively recogniz[ed] the creditor's [Jardel's] interest in such a promise," Williston, supra, § 361, at 864–65, the third-

---

1. Article I of the Robbins, Inc.-Hirsch contract provided:
"The word 'Owner' shall mean JARDEL CO., INC., the Owner of the building [or buildings, Art. XXIV] of which the Sub-Contractor's [Hirsch's] work forms a part."

2. Also see 4 A. Corbin, Contracts § 787, at 95 (1951):
"If the promisee in a contract contemplates the present or future existence of a duty or liability to a third party and enters into the contract with the expressed intent that the performance contracted for is to satisfy and discharge that duty or liability, the third party is a creditor beneficiary."

party creditor beneficiary can sue the promisor (in this case, Hirsch) directly.[3]

Once a third-party beneficiary contract has been made however, the beneficiary's rights are not unlimited.[4] In this case, the terms of § 143 of the Restatement of Contracts require the conclusion that the release satisfied the promisor's obligation to the creditor beneficiary (Jardel) as well as to the promisee (Robbins, Inc.) :

> "A discharge of the promisor by the promisee in a contract or a variation thereof by them is effective against a creditor beneficiary if,

> (a) the creditor beneficiary does not bring suit upon the promise or otherwise materially change his position in reliance thereon before he knows of the discharge or variation, and

> (b) the promisee's action is not a fraud on creditors."[5]

Professor Williston has adopted the Restatement rule, distinguishing the creditor beneficiary situation from that of the donee beneficiary,[6]

3. Article XIV of the Robbins, Inc.-Hirsch contract provided that Hirsch "shall indemnify and save harmless the Owner . . . against all claims of damage to persons or property growing out of the execution of [Hirsch's] work." Hirsch also agreed to "indemnify and save harmless" Jardel from any damage arising out of Hirsch's work that could be asserted against the general contractor, Robbins, Inc. The parties' intention that Hirsch's performance was to carry out the obligations of Robbins, Inc. to Jardel also appears in Articles I, II, XVI, XVIII, and XXIV. These provisions make clear that " 'both parties to the contract . . . [intended that Jardel be a beneficiary] . . and [indicated] that intention in the contract . . . .' " See Van Cor, Inc. v. American Cas. Co., supra, at 413, 208 A.2d at 269.

4. For example, since the beneficiary's rights depend on the contract, if for some reason the contract is invalid, "no rights can arise in favor of anyone." Id. § 364A, at 873; accord, Restatement of Contracts § 140 (1932). See, also, Williston, supra, § 395, at 1066. Thus, in Williams v. Paxson Coal Co., 346 Pa. 468, 31 A.2d 69 (1943), a promisor agreed to look only to the dividends of three named shareholders for enforcement of a demand note given him in exchange for the transfer of property to the corporation. After the named shareholders sold their entire interest in the corporation, the promisor sued the corporation to enforce the note. The corporation argued that it was obligated to satisfy the note only if it should declare dividends to the original shareholders. Treating the corporation under its new owners as a donee beneficiary and the original shareholders as promisees to the agreement, the court held that because the promisees had made enforcement of the agreement impossible by removing their names from the shareholder list, there was a failure of consideration by the promisees, and thus the corporation, as third-party beneficiary, could not enforce the agreement.

5. Illustration 1, accompanying § 143, provides:
"B contracts with A to pay C $200 which A owes C. C learns of this contract and expresses satisfaction but does not make a novation with B, or begin an action to enforce a right against B, or change his position in reliance on the contract. Later, in consideration of a horse worth $200 given him by B, A releases B from his contract. C, after learning of the release, cannot enforce a right against B. . . ."

6. The distinction between a creditor and donee beneficiary, restricting the right of the promisor in the donee situation to be released, is based on reasoning that the creditor beneficiary's right "is purely derivative." Williston, supra, § 397, at 1074.[7]

This is the rule that Pennsylvania would adopt. Not only do Pennsylvania courts rely upon the Restatement and Professor Williston in establishing the law of third-party beneficiary contracts, e. g., Williams v. Paxson Coal Co., 346 Pa. 468, 470, 471, 472, 31 A.2d 69, 70, 71 (1943),[8] but they apparently have adopted § 143. In Clardy v. Barco Construction Co., 205 Pa.Super. 218, 224–225, 208 A.2d 793, 796 (1965), the court found that a release did not bar the third-party creditor beneficiary's claim by reason of § 143, because the creditor had relied on the contract in completing his duties. In Miller v. Travelers Insurance Co., 143 Pa.Super. 270, 17 A.2d 907 (1941), the court adopted the rule of § 143, although it actually cited § 140[9] as authority. Plaintiff's husband contracted with his employer to have deductions taken from his wages to support a group life insurance policy that the employer took out with the defendant insurance company. After giving notice to the employees, the employer cancelled the policy. Upon her husband's death, the plaintiff sued the insurance company as a third-party beneficiary, arguing that the contract be-

---

the theory that only the donee beneficiary (and not the promisee) has so substantial an interest in the contract that he can enforce it. See, e. g., Tasin v. Bastress, 284 Pa. 47, 57, 130 A. 417, 421 (1925). Professor Corbin, however, argues that the creditor beneficiary's rights are similar to those of the donee beneficiary, since the creditor beneficiary is "given" the right to look not only to the promisee for enforcement of his contract, for which he had originally bargained, but also to the promisor. "It seems best, therefore, that the discharge by the promisee should be operative as against the beneficiary only in case he learns of the discharge before he has assented to the contract or has acted in reliance upon it." Corbin, supra, note 19, § 815, at 260; see e. g., Hughes v. Gibbs, 55 Wash.2d 791, 350 P.2d 475 (1960).

The proposed Second Restatement of Contracts, to which Professor Corbin served as Consultant, adopts his view that the promisee and promisor have no power to modify or release the promisor's duties to the beneficiary after the beneficiary has assented to their contract. Restatement (Second) of Contracts § 142 (Tent. Draft No. 3, 1967). However, this tentative draft has been adopted by neither the American Law Institute nor the courts of Pennsylvania.

7.   Also see R. J. Cardinal Co. v. Ritchie, 218 Cal.App.2d 124, 32 Cal.Rptr. 545, 552–553, 561 (1963); Davis v. Nelson-Deppe, Inc., 91 Idaho 463, 424 P.2d 733, 737 (1967); Britton v. Groom, 373 P.2d 1012, 1015–1016 (Okl.1962); Morstain v. Kircher, 190 Minn. 78, 250 N.W. 727 (1933). In commenting on Morstain, one student authority relied on § 143: "Since the [creditor beneficiary's] right seems only derivative, . . . it appears better to permit a release if the creditor has not materially changed his position in reliance on the [promisor's] agreement." 47 Harv. L.Rev. 1065, 1066 (1934).

8.   Also see note [4], supra.

9.   Restatement of Contracts § 140 provides:
"There can be no donee beneficiary or creditor beneficiary unless a contract has been formed between a promisor and promisee; and if a contract is conditional, voidable, or unenforceable at the time of its formation, or subsequently ceases to be binding in whole or in part because of impossibility, illegality or the present or prospective failure of the promisee to perform a return promise which was the consideration for the promisor's promise, the right of a donee beneficiary or creditor beneficiary under the contract is subject to the same limitation."

tween the employer and the insurance company could not have been cancelled without her husband's consent. The court held:

> "The insured employee or his beneficiary have no greater rights than are provided in the policy, certainly no vested right which would prevent cancellation by mutual agreement between the insurer and the employer, especially where reasonable notice of cancellation is given to the employee. A third party beneficiary in an ordinary contract is subject to the limitation of its terms as he has no greater rights under it than are provided in the contract itself: Restatement of the Law, Contracts, § 140 . . .."

Id. at 273, 17 A.2d at 908.[10]

Application of § 143 to this case bars not only the recovery by Jardel under a contractual theory, but its suit in negligence as well. Under § 143 the release was also a "variation," expressly precluding "all, and all manner of, actions and causes of action" arising from the contract between Robbins and Hirsch. Pennsylvania courts have uniformly honored such contractual provisions where they are entered into by "free bargaining agents," [citations omitted].

Applying the above-stated rule to Jardel would not work an "injustice," as Jardel has argued.[11] Should Jardel not have an actionable claim against Hirsch, it can still sue the general contractor, Robbins, Inc., whose obligation to Jardel remained unchanged by the subcontract or the release. See, e. g., National Fire Ins. Co. of Hartford v. Westgate Constr. Co., 227 F.Supp. 835 (D.Del.1964). Indeed, Jardel's separate existence was justified in part by the necessity of keeping its assets apart from those of its parent, and thus suit against its parent would be more than a futile gesture in this instance.[12]

Accordingly, we hold that Jardel is bound by the release, since the record does not show any material change of position by it in reliance on the promise prior to the variation of the contract by the

---

10. Another bar to the recovery of the creditor beneficiary occurs in the situation where the promisee recovers a judgment under the contract against the promisor:

"Whatever the hardship upon the promisor may be in being liable to two persons when he promised but one, most courts have found it the simpler alternative, a recovery by either party being a bar to an action by the other."

Williston, supra, § 392, at 1057 (footnotes omitted); cf. Parker v. London Guar. & Accident Co., 30 F.2d 464 (E.D.Pa.1927) (federal common law). We need not reach the question whether the rule would be accepted by Pennsylvania or whether it applies to the facts of this case.

11. Of course, the parties can contract that a release given the promisor shall not be binding on the creditor beneficiary. See Beaver Falls B. & L. Ass'n v. Allemania Fire Ins. Co., 305 Pa. 290, 157 A. 616 (1931).

12. It is irrelevant that Jardel's action against Robbins, Inc. may now be barred by the applicable statute of limitations. It seems reasonable to surmise that Jardel would not have let the statute of limitations run had not Robbins, Inc. been its sole stockholder.

release.[13] See Morstain v. Kircher, 190 Minn. 78, 250 N.W. 727, 728 (1933),[14] where the court said:

" . . . [The plaintiff] paid no consideration for defendant's agreement to pay the mortgage debt, nor had she in reliance on the assumption contract placed herself in a position from which she could not retreat without loss. [citing § 143] . . ."

For the foregoing reasons, the District Court order of December 9, 1968, will be affirmed.

NOTES

(1) *Questions.* Does the court's footnote 6 indicate that the result would be different under Restatement Second, § 142? See Note 1, p. 903 supra. If so, which rule seems preferable?

(2) *Problem.* John Sunday and his wife contracted to sell a house for $37,500, to be paid by George Rheims. The contract document named Mrs. Annette Oman as purchaser, however, rather than Rheims, for he intended to give the house to her. All the parties mentioned signed the document. Rheims gave a check for earnest money (10% of the contract price) to a lawyer acting for the other parties. The check was presented for payment, but was returned marked "NSF" (not sufficient funds). About a month after the agreement was made, Rheims died. The Sundays refused to convey to Mrs. Oman, and made a settlement with the Rheims estate, whereby the executor allowed their claim for $3,750 as liquidated damages. Does Mrs. Oman have a claim against either Rheims' estate or the Sundays? See Oman v. Yates, 70 Wash.2d 181, 422 P.2d 489 (1967).

13. In a supplemental brief to this court, Jardel claims that it paid Robbins, Inc. in reliance on the Robbins, Inc.-Hirsch contract, so that Robbins, Inc. could pay Hirsch. Such an allegation, if proved, might well be a defense to a claim by Hirsch against Jardel for payments owed to Hirsch by Robbins, Inc. Cf. Clardy v. Barco Constr. Co., supra. We do not believe, however, that in the posture of this case such a payment represents a material change of position, as contemplated by § 143.

Since Robbins was the president of Jardel when he signed the release on behalf of Robbins, Inc., Jardel simultaneously had knowledge. Jardel did not bring suit on the contract before the release was signed, nor can we find any evidence that Robbins, Inc.'s action in executing the release was a fraud upon its creditors.

14. See, also, Britton v. Groom, supra, note [7], 373 P.2d at 1016.

Chapter 10

ASSIGNMENT AND DELEGATION

Today most contract rights having commercial value are transferable. The proposition is, indeed, something of a truism, for commercial worth is attributable to a right largely *because* of its transferability. Broad recognition of the principle is commonly found in statutes, as for instance in § 13–101 of the New York General Obligations Law which begins, "Any claim or demand can be transferred, except in one of the following cases. . . ." [a]

Section 1 of this chapter presents some fundamental propositions about assignments of contract rights, including the necessity of taking certain simple steps in order to effect the transfer of such a right. The topic of non-commercial (i. e., gift) assignments is featured here. The section demonstrates the primary function of an assignment: by this means a creditor may institute a duty running directly from his debtor to a third party, the assignee.

Section 2 focusses on sales of businesses, although lessons learned from other types of transaction are brought to bear on this one. When a business is sold, the buyer commonly acquires not only its tangible properties, such as plant and equipment, but also its intangibles, including accounts receivable. In addition, the buyer commonly undertakes to perform the duties of the seller under contracts that the seller has made, but not yet performed. From the seller's point of view, this transaction amounts to a delegation of his duties, which may be to render service to his customers, or to supply goods to them, or to render some other variety of performance. Of course, the right to be paid for such a performance is also transferred to the buyer— assigned to him. With respect to an executory contract, then, a seller of a business typically makes both an assignment of the contract rights and a delegation of its duties. The section considers the limits of assignability and delegability in this context.

Section 3 concentrates on a problem loosely described as the "holder in due course" problem. May a credit sale transaction be so arranged that, upon an assignment by the seller of the right to be paid, the assignee can override defenses of the buyer that would have

---

a. "1. Where it is to recover damages for a personal injury;

"2. Where it is founded upon a grant, which is made void by a statute of the state; or upon a claim to or interest in real property, a grant of which, by the transferrer, would be void by such a statute;

"3. Where a transfer thereof is expressly forbidden by a statute of the state, or of the United States, or would contravene public policy."

West's Ann.Cal.Civ.Code, § 1458: "A right arising out of an obligation is the property of the person to whom it is due, and may be transferred as such."

defeated or limited a claim against him by the seller? (Not only contracts for the sale of goods, but services contracts and others present the problem.) The issue has been highly controversial, especially in relation to "consumer" transactions. Banks and finance companies provide financing for consumer credit, backed by assignments purporting to give them a specialized legal advantage. Successes and failures in this attempt are examined here.

Section 4 turns to the role of financing institutions in relation to commercial credit. Manufacturers and merchants obtain financing on the strength of assigning their accounts receivable. Contractors obtain financing through assigning their anticipated job earnings. Farmers assign anticipated crop earnings. A large and complex body of law bears on the value of these assignments. In part it is case law; in part it is the Code and other state legislation; in part it is federal law, particularly the Bankruptcy Act. The financer (and its counsel) have to think of multiple risks, in addition to the prospect that the person expected to pay may be financially unable to do so. For one thing, he and the assignor may indulge in dealings without regard to the financer's interest, and prejudicial to it. For another, the payment may be intercepted by other creditors of the assignor, or his bankruptcy trustee, or someone else claiming under him. These risks, and the measures available to limit them, are examined in this section.

NOTE

Evolution of Assignments. Contract rights of many kinds, known as "choses in action," were not transferable in an early stage of English law. Legal historians have delighted in tracing the process by which this rule was overthrown. As usually recounted, it employed the device called a "power of attorney." That device is still in use to enable lawyers and collection agencies to proceed against debtors on claims turned over to them by their creditor-clients, for collection only. Characteristically the agent suing on the claim does so in the name of the client, his principal. So used, the device does not involve an assignment of a claim. There was a time, however, when the device was employed to implement assignments indirectly, apparently to circumvent the rule that a chose in action is not transferable. The critical point in this evolution was passed when the creditor, having given a power of attorney for that purpose, could no longer prevent his "agent" from using his name in the agent's suit.

"Although a person to whom a contract right was owed could not transfer it to one to whom the obligor was not bound in privity, he could appoint an agent or attorney to collect in his place or stead. In time the fictitious agency became irrevocable and the nominal owner, after notice of the assignment to the obligor, lost any power to interfere with the assignee's rights. Thus by the typically muddle-headed process of thinking known as the genius of the common law, assignments of intangibles were made effective in fact while basic theory still proclaimed them to be legal impossibilities." Gilmore, 1 Security Interests in Personal Property 202 (1965). Sections 7.3 and 7.4 of this work provide references to the historical studies, and an entertaining account of their differences.

SECTION 1. GENERAL PRINCIPLES

What is the effect of an assignment? Consider the following example:

> A has a right to $100 against B. A assigns his right to C. A's right is thereby extinguished, and C acquires a right against B to receive $100. (Restatement Second, § 149, Illustration 1)

On these facts alone, the Restatement goes on to say, C's right does not amount to much, except the power to enforce the claim without the cooperation of A.[a] (Real-party-in-interest statutes are germane here.) For C's right is subject to extinction by any of the following events: revocation of the assignment by A; death of A; re-assignment by A of the same right to D. Revocability is characteristic of many assignments. (Until revocation, however, C may disable A from giving an effective discharge to B, by notifying B of the assignment.)

Assignments that are not "gratuitous" are not revocable, as a rule. And only some gift assignments are revocable. In Restatement terms, the issue in the following case was whether or not a gratuitous assignment was made irrevocable.

ADAMS v. MERCED STONE CO.

Supreme Court of California, 1917.
176 Cal. 415, 178 P. 498, 3 A.L.R. 928.

Suit by Edson F. Adams, as executor of the estate of Thomas Prather, deceased, against the Merced Stone Company. From a judgment for defendant and order denying new trial plaintiff appeals. Reversed.

SHAW, J. . . . The court found that during the last sickness of Thomas Prather, to wit, on April 17, 1913, said Thomas Prather made a gift to his brother Samuel D. Prather, of all of the indebtedness due from the defendant to said Thomas, being the indebtedness sued for by the plaintiff herein. That at that time Samuel was the president, the general manager, and a member of the board of directors of the defendant, said defendant being a corporation, and Thomas Prather knew that Samuel held said offices and by reason thereof had full and exclusive charge and control of defendant's books of account, including power to make or direct the making of entries and transfers in said books, and knew that by reason thereof Samuel D.

---

a. On the historical antecedents of this proposition, see Restatement Second, § 164, Comment a.

Prather had the means of obtaining possession and control of the said indebtedness so given to him. . . . It is admitted that the asserted gift was made during the last sickness of Thomas Prather, two days before his death, which event occurred on April 19, 1913, and was therefore a gift in view of death. It is also admitted that no change was made upon the books of the defendant regarding said indebtedness, up to the time of the trial of this action, and that when the action was begun the account books of the defendant showed it to be indebted to the said Thomas Prather in the sum claimed in the complaint.

The only evidence of the gift asserted in the answer is found in the testimony of Samuel D. Prather, and is as follows: "In talking business matters my brother said to me, 'Now, in reference to the account of Thomas Prather in the Merced Stone Company, I want to give you that account, all that is due me from that account. I don't know just how to do this, but I give it to you.' . . . A little further in the conversation my brother said to me, 'I give you the keys to my office, the combination of my safe and keys to my desk, and with these I give you all accounts, books, papers, letters, documents, furnishings, pictures, everything that belongs to me in that office. It is yours.' "

[The court quoted California Civil Code, § 1147: "A verbal gift is not valid, unless the means of obtaining possession and control of the thing are given, nor, if it is capable of delivery, unless there is an actual or symbolical delivery of the thing to the donee." The court rejected defendant's construction of the section.] It contemplates that the donor shall do something at the time of making the gift which has the effect of placing in the hands of the donee the means of obtaining the control and possession of the thing given. That the fact that the thing was already in possession of the donee at the time of declaring the gift is not enough, is well settled by the authorities. . . .

In order to comply with the section the "means" must be "given." In the connection in which these words occur the effect is that such means must be given by the donor to the donee. This giving of the means is authorized, where the thing given is not capable of delivery, as a substitute for the actual or symbolical delivery of the thing by the donor to the donee required in cases where such thing is capable of delivery. No good reason can be given for supposing that a transmission or delivery by the donor to the donee of the means was not intended to be as essential in the case of intangible property, as the delivery, actual or symbolical of the thing itself, where it is tangible.

In the case of a chose in action not evidenced by a written instrument, the only means of obtaining control that is recognized by the authorities is an assignment in writing, or some equivalent thereof. . . .

In the present case it is true that Samuel D. Prather was possessed of the physical power and of the official authority, by reason of his relation to the defendant, to make the necessary changes on its books to show that the indebtedness was due to him and not to the decedent. But this power did not emanate from the decedent. Samuel possessed it before the asserted gift as well as after. The decedent did not even authorize him to make such changes, nor suggest that the gift might be effected in that way. It was not shown that such method was in the mind of the donor. The fact that it was a book account, or that a change might be made in the name of the debtor, was not even mentioned in the conversation. The law intends something more than a mere power to make physical entries in the books of the debtor in such a case. The authority to make the change, or cause it to be made, must be vested in the debtor by reason of some act or direction of the creditor. If verbal gifts could be made in such loose manner as this it would open the door to innumerable frauds and perjuries. . . . For this reason the authorities hold that something more than mere physical power is necessary; something more than the previous possession of the property or of the means of obtaining it; something emanating from the donor which operates to give to the donee the means of obtaining such possession and control. . . .

The conclusion of the court below upon the facts found was not in accordance with the law, and its finding of the ultimate fact that Thomas Prather transferred the debt to Samuel D. Prather by way of a verbal gift is not supported by the evidence. Consequently the judgment and order cannot be upheld.

The judgment and order are reversed and the cause is remanded, with directions to the court below to enter judgment upon the findings in favor of the plaintiff for the amount prayed for.

NOTES

(1) *Death-Bed Gifts.* If there had been other witnesses to the conversation between Thomas and Samuel, does it seem that the result would have been different? Would the court have been satisfied with anything less than a writing, containing the decedent's signature? "Speaking for myself," said a lord chancellor of England, "I do not look with any particular favor on these death-bed gifts." [a] The Restatement agrees with the ruling in the main case; see § 158.

Suppose that Thomas Prather wishes to make the gift to his other brother, Paul. Instead of speaking to Paul about it, Thomas says to Samuel: "I want you, as president of the Merced Stone Company, to agree that after my death the Company will pay to Paul all that it owes me. In exchange for your promise, I will release the company from its indebtedness to me." Samuel agrees, acting as the company's authorized agent. After Thomas' death, may his executor (Adams) make a successful

---

a. Ashbourne, quoted in Williston,
Gifts of Rights, 40 Yale L.J. 1 (1930).

claim for the amount owing? What arguments would you make in favor of Paul? Is there anything about the transaction that tends to remove the suspicion commonly surrounding an oral death-bed gift?

(2) *Symbolic Documents.* Probably the most common way of making an irrevocable gift assignment is by compliance with Restatement, § 158 (1)(b): delivery of a "tangible token or writing" of the kind specified there. Examples of documents that can be delivered with such effect are promissory notes and life insurance policies; Williston spoke of documents that are "ordinarily kept in a safe deposit box." The Restatement Second indicates that a pass book representing a checking account is not so significant: see § 164, Illustration 7.

That section refers to writings "of a type customarily accepted as a symbol or as evidence of the right assigned." The delivery or possession of such a writing has consequences not only for a donee but for assignees generally, under §§ 170(4) and 174.[b]

(3) *Writing and Revocability.* The Uniform Commercial Code provides that certain assignments are not enforceable against the assignor or third parties unless he has signed a "security agreement." Section 9–203 (1)(b). This section does not speak of assignments in terms, but it clearly applies to all transactions that are "financing" assignments, in a broad sense. For certain "sale" assignments, other than those effected by security agreements, the Code requires a signed writing in Section 1–206. Nothing in the Code applies to a gift assignment. By statute in New York, the absence of consideration does not entail the conclusion that an assignment is revocable, if it is in writing and signed by the assignor.[c] For the Restatement rules on revocability of gift assignments see § 158 of the first Restatement, and § 164 of the Second.

(4) *A Case of Two Wives.* After his second marriage, John Cassiday brought home from the office a folder containing two certificates of insurance on his life, and placed it in a dresser drawer. His former wife, Margaret, was named as beneficiary on these certificates, and that designation was never changed. Yet when he brought them home John said to his wife, Edytha: "the beneficiaries are changed . . . and he also said he didn't want that woman [Margaret] to have any more of his money." After John died, a contest arose between the two women over the proceeds, and the insurer brought an interpleader action. From a judgment for Margaret, Edytha appealed. *Held:* Affirmed. It was found that John had made no parol assignment or gift of the two policies in question to Edytha. "He did not say: 'Edytha, I give you these policies.' He did not say: 'Edytha, these policies are yours.' . . . [H]e exhibited no intention either to give or assign the policies to Edytha." Cassiday v. Cassiday, 256 Md. 5, 259 A.2d 299 (1969).

Even if John had said what the court suggested, Edytha's claim would probably have failed in some courts, for want of delivery of the certificates to her. On the other hand, a symbolic or a "constructive" delivery some-

---

b. Cf. Grant v. Colonial Bank and Trust Co., 356 Mass. 392, 252 N.E.2d 339 (1969). Here the court said that a savings bank book "falls short of being a negotiable instrument." And see Restatement Second, § 174, Comment f.

c. N.Y.Gen.Obl.L. § 5–1107. Compare § 5–701(9).

times meets the requirement. In the attempt to apply these conceptions, especially to intangible assets, the courts have made some refined distinctions. See Brooks v. Mitchell, 163 Md. 1, 161 A. 261, 84 A.L.R. 547 (1932); Rohan, Delivery in the Law of Gifts, 38 Ind.L.J. 1 (1962), 470 (1963). If John had handed the insurance certificates to Edytha for her to place in the dresser drawer, should that be regarded as a sufficient delivery?

FORM OF ASSIGNMENT

For making an assignment, it is agreed, no particular expression or form of words is required. However, it may be helpful to consider an excerpt from a form of assignment prepared by the American Bankers Association. The form is designed for use by a bank in taking an assignment of a life insurance policy from a borrower, as security for a loan:

> For Value Received the undersigned hereby assign, transfer and set over to ————, its successors and assigns, (herein called the "Assignee") Policy No. ———— issued by ————
> (herein called the "Insurer") . . . and any supplementary contracts issued in connection therewith . . ., upon the life of ———— . . . and all claims, options, privileges, rights, title and interest therein and thereunder
> . . . .

According to Restatement Second, § 156, "It is essential to an assignment of a right that the obligee manifest an intention to transfer the right to another person without further action or manifestation of intention." The manifestation is usually made to the "other person," but it may also be made to a third person on his behalf; e. g., a borrower might make an assignment of an insurance claim to a bank by a suitable indication to the insurer. However, in such a case, special problems arise in characterizing the terms used. If obligee (A) says to obligor (B), "I direct you to pay what you owe me to C," is that an assignment? If he says, "I authorize you to discharge your debt to me by paying C," is that an assignment? The Restatement Second states that an order to pay may be an assignment, but only in special circumstances. See section 157. The following illustration is given:

> A writes to B, "Please pay to C the balance due me." This is insufficient to establish an assignment . . . But the letter would be an effective assignment if delivered to C to pay or secure a debt owed by A to C.

Assignments have often been contrasted with promises to make payments. See Christmas v. Russell's Executors, 81 U.S. 69, 84 (1871): "An agreement to pay out of a particular fund, however clear in its terms, is not an equitable assignment . . . ."

NOTES

(1) *Problem.* Which of the following documents, if any, constitutes an assignment?

(a) The owner of a store suffers a large loss when a Navy jet crashes into it. As a result he has a claim against his insurance company and also a tort claim against the United States. The insurer makes a loan to him for immediate repairs, in the amount of $100,000, and he gives it a document in this form: "In consideration of the loan, I will pay you all sums paid to me by the United States on account of my loss up to the amount of $100,-000." See Arkwright Mutual Ins. Co. v. Bargain City, U. S. A., Inc., 251 F. Supp. 221 (E.D.Pa.1966).

(b) A real estate broker (A) earns a commission, with the help of another (C), and before it is paid gives him this signed document: "In consideration of $1 I hereby agree with C that he is entitled to one-half of the commission earned from the sale of Blackacre." See Donovan v. Middlebrook, 95 App.Div. 365, 88 N.Y.S. 607 (Sup.Ct. 1904).

(c) A sends a signed document to his tailor (C) reading: "First Bank. Pay to the order of C $100 (One Hundred) Dollars." A has a large checking account in First Bank. See UCC 3–409(1): "A check or other draft does not of itself operate as an assignment . . . ."

How would you redraft each of the foregoing documents so as to make it clear that an assignment has been given?

(2) *Legal Effect Without Assignment.* If none of the documents set out in the preceding note is an assignment, it does not follow that they are all legally insignificant. It is clear, for instance, that a bank may charge the checking account of a customer upon payment of a check properly drawn by him, issued, and indorsed and presented by the payee. Do you find the elements of a contract in any of the transactions described above? There is even a possibility that a right to payment may become subject to a security interest, of sorts, by an agreement between its owner and a creditor of his, though it does not embody an assignment. At best, such an interest, known as an equitable lien, is of limited value to the creditor, and the precedents supporting it are unstable. For an elaborate essay on the doctrine, see Warren Tool Co. v. Stephenson, 11 Mich.App. 274, 161 N.W.2d 133 (1968).

FUTURITY

An aspect of many contract claims that has been a recurrent blight on the expectation of assignees may be called "futurity." According to the Restatement, a right expected to arise in the future can be effectively assigned, but the rule is qualified in important ways. See section 154.[a]

a. The rule stated here is slightly liberalized in the corresponding section of the Restatement Second: section 153. See especially Illustration 5.

The problem may be illustrated by the facts in Shiro v. Drew, 174 F.Supp. 495 (D.Me.1959), which grew out of the financial difficulties of the American Fiberlast Company. Fiberlast borrowed some $2,000 from Drew on or about November 1, 1956, and gave him the following letter: "To Gordon L. Drew: Whereas the American Fiberlast Co. has received a contract for a 21' Radome from Hazeltine Electronics Corp. totaling $4900 but is unable to finance the purchase of the necessary materials and labor to construct the dome—the American Fiberlast Co. agrees that any money advanced by Mr. Drew for the specific expense of manufacturing the Radome will be paid immediately to Mr. Drew upon receipt of Hazeltine's remittance irrespective of any other demands from other creditors."

This letter was not needed to establish Drew's right to repayment of the loan. Its object was, rather, to provide him with a right of repayment out of the proceeds of the Radome contract, to the exclusion of other creditors of Fiberlast. In other words, it was designed to give Drew a security interest. The enactment of the Uniform Commercial Code has removed any doubt that a lender can achieve that object by complying with Article 9, on Secured Transactions. As late as 1942, however, a New York lender very nearly came to grief in relying on the security of the borrower's executory contracts.[b] In that case the court first ruled that the security agreement was ineffectual. The lender's petition for rehearing was supported by several New York banks, as amici curiae. According to Corbin, the banks "showed the court that in the period of one week the banks had lent to wartime contractors the amount of $600 million on no other security than an assignment of the contractors' rights to future payments by the Government, all of the rights so assigned being conditional on performances still to be rendered by the assignors. . . . The shock produced by this showing caused the two majority judges (men of the very highest honor and ability) to reverse their decision." Corbin, § 903, Supp.

A creditor may seize his debtor's right to a contract payment through the process of garnishment or (as it is known in some states) attachment, creating a lien on it for the satisfaction of his claim. Unless an assignment of the right is effectual in foreclosing garnishment of it, it fails of its essential purpose. Before the Code was widely enacted, an enormous volume of financing was subject to a certain risk owing to the doubts that courts entertained about assignments of "future" rights. When Fiberlast borrowed from Drew, of course, it had already contracted with Hazeltine, and had an existing "contract right." This term is defined in the Code as a right to payment not yet earned by performance.[c] Subsequently, Fiberlast completed con-

b. Rockmore v. Lehman, 128 F.2d 564 (2d Cir. 1942), reversed on rehearing, 129 F.2d 892 (1942), cert. denied, 317 U.S. 700 (1943).

c. UCC 9–106.

struction of the Radome, thereby acquiring an earned right to payment. Such a right is called an "account" in the Code,[d] and the power to assign it has long been established. Obviously Fiberlast could not wait until it had an account to make an assignment, for it needed loan money to turn its contract right into an account.

A more acute problem of "futurity" is presented when funds are obtained on the strength of contracts not in existence, but which the borrower expects to make later. There is a deep-seated conceptual difficulty about recognizing a present transfer of a non-existent right. However, there is a commercial need for obtaining funds in reliance on anticipated contracts. Many merchants who extend short-term credit to their customers have accounts receivable on their books at all times, which may be large and fairly constant in amount. From month to month, however, the specific accounts outstanding are different. Many merchants, both dealers and manufacturers, obtain liquid capital from financial institutions which rely, for security, on assignments of such accounts. If an assignment had no prospective effect, the security would rapidly be depleted by payments of the accounts outstanding at the time of the assignment. Rather than taking a new assignment each month, or oftener, the lender will wish to be secured by new accounts as they arise, so that the security is continually replenished. The following form of "assignment" is suggested in the Restatement Second: Merchant assigns as security "all the book debts due and owing or which may during the continuance of this security become due and owing" to the merchant.[e] The Restatement uses quotation marks on the word "assignment" to indicate that the lender is not truly an assignee at the time of the agreement, as to accounts yet to arise. "Strictly there cannot be an effective assignment of a right not yet in existence."[f]

If that were the whole story, the lender could not be effectively protected against creditors of the merchant who might levy writs of garnishment on the "future" accounts. However, means have been found to make the assignment effectual, under both judicial and legislative auspices. The judicial approach is to treat the "assignment" as a contract to make an assignment of each account as it arises, and to implement the contract as if it had been performed. According to Restatement Second, § 162, the effect of a contract to make an assignment is "determined by the rules relating to specific performance . . . ." If the promisee is entitled to specific performance, his right "resembles that of an assignee, and it is sometimes referred to as an 'equitable assignment' or 'equitable lien.' "[g]

The Uniform Commercial Code appears to renounce this approach, although there is controversy about the extent to which equi-

---

d.   Ibid.

e.   Section 162, Illustration 7.

f.   Restatement Second, § 163, Comment b.

g.   Id., § 162, Comment c.

table liens are compatible with the Code.[h] In any event, it provides a mechanism by which an agreement for a security interest in an account or contract right not yet in existence may preempt the claims of creditors of the assignor. Some features of this mechanism are described in the Note, Assignments, Bankruptcy, and Creditors, p. 1017 infra. The result is that, for transactions within the Code, it is both unnecessary and undesirable to rely on the equity doctrine referred to above. Proposals were made in 1971 to amend Article 9 of the Code so as to achieve an even greater assimilation of prospective rights to existing ones, with the following comment: "This Article rejects any lingering common law notion that only rights already earned can be assigned."[i]

The unstable effects of an "assignment" of rights not yet in existence are partly traceable to historical factors and to conceptual difficulties. But a more suitable ground for giving it a limited effect may sometimes be found in a "public policy which seeks to protect the assignor and third parties against transfers which may be improvident or fraudulent." Restatement Second, § 153, Comment b. Such a policy is especially prominent in relation to an employee's assignment of earnings that are not matured claims.[j]

NOTES

(1) *Assigning Proceeds.* Refer again to the terms of Fiberlast's letter to Drew: it agreed that "any money advanced by Mr. Drew . . . will be paid immediately to Mr. Drew upon receipt of Hazeltine's remittance . . . ." Could better language have been chosen to express an assignment of the contract right? Consider the following rule: "the assignment of after-acquired proceeds of a claim is generally considered an assignment only of a future right and, therefore, the assignment does not give the assignee priority over lienors who have attached before the proceeds have come into existence." Harold Moorstein & Co. v. Excelsior Ins. Co., 25 N.Y.2d 651, 254 N.E.2d 766 (1969).

The court that stated the foregoing rule also adheres to the view that an effective transfer of a "present" claim is possible, although it has not yet matured, or is disputed, or is dependent upon future conditions.[k] Do you see a way of reconciling these views?[l] Outside the range of the Code,

h. See Warren Tool Co. v. Stephenson, 11 Mich.App. 274, 161 N.W.2d 133 (1968).

i. Final Report, Review Committee for Article 9, Permanent Editorial Board for the UCC, 46 (1971). See, generally, Gilmore, 1 Security Interests in Personal Property, §§ 7.10–.12 (1965).

j. See Commodore v. Armour & Co., 201 Kan. 412, 441 P.2d 815 (1968); New England Merchants Nat. Bank v. Herron, 243 A.2d 722 (Me.1968).

Assignments of future wages are generally prohibited in some states, and are regulated in one way or another in almost all others, especially as they may be used as security for small loans. A compilation of statutes appears in Restatement Second, Tentative Draft No. 3, at 150 (1967).

k. Note the court's reliance, in the case last cited, on Stathos v. Murphy, cited below.

l. See State Farm Mut. Auto. Ins. Co. v. Pohl, 255 Or. 46, 464 P.2d 321

the subject continues to defy understanding. For an impressive essay on the subject, see the opinion of Justice Breitel, in Stathos v. Murphy, 26 A.D.2d 500, 276 N.Y.S.2d 727 (1st Dept.1966), aff'd, 19 N.Y.2d 883, 227 N.E.2d 880 (1967).

Even for transactions within the Code, specialists in the law of creditors' rights detect continuing problems of futurity, connected with the federal Bankruptcy Act. See p. 1020 infra.

(2) *Problem.* After Fiberlast has completed construction of the Radome, and before Hazeltine has paid it the price, a bank sues Fiberlast on an overdue loan and serves a writ of garnishment on Hazeltine. Drew intervenes, asserting a superior interest in the proceeds of the contract. Should the court direct Hazeltine to pay Drew or the bank?

SPEELMAN v. PASCAL

Court of Appeals of New York, 1961.
10 N.Y.2d 313, 178 N.E.2d 723.

DESMOND, CHIEF JUDGE. Gabriel Pascal, defendant's intestate who died in 1954, had been for many years a theatrical producer. In 1952 an English corporation named Gabriel Pascal Enterprises, Ltd., of whose 100 shares Gabriel Pascal owned 98, made an agreement with the English Public Trustee who represented the estate of George Bernard Shaw. This agreement granted to Gabriel Pascal Enterprises, Ltd., the exclusive world rights to prepare and produce a musical play to be based on Shaw's play "Pygmalion" and a motion picture version of the musical play. The agreement recited, as was the fact, that the licensee owned a film scenario written by Pascal and based on "Pygmalion". In fact Pascal had, some time previously, produced a nonmusical movie version of "Pygmalion" under rights obtained by Pascal from George Bernard Shaw during the latter's lifetime. The 1952 agreement required the licensee corporation to pay the Shaw estate an initial advance and thereafter to pay the Shaw estate 3% of the gross receipts of the musical play and musical movie with a provision that the license was to terminate if within certain fixed periods the licensee did not arrange with Lerner and Loewe or other similarly well-known composers to write the musical play and arrange to produce it. Before Pascal's death in July, 1954, he had made a number of unsuccessful efforts to get the musical written and produced and it was not until after his death that arrangements were made, through a New York bank as temporary administrator of his estate, for the writing and production of the highly successful "My Fair Lady". Meanwhile, on February 22, 1954, at a time when the license from the Shaw estate

(1970). As to assigning the proceeds of a projected auction sale, see Rural Gas, Inc. v. Shepek, 205 Kan. 397, 469 P.2d 341 (1970); Wilkie v. Becker, 268 Minn. 262, 128 N.W.2d 704 (1964).

still had two years to run, Gabriel Pascal, who died four and a half months later, wrote, signed and delivered to plaintiff a document as follows:

"Dear Miss Kingman [a]

"This is to confirm to you our understanding that I give you from my shares of profits of the Pygmalion Musical stage version

a. In earlier litigation it had been decided to admit the following instrument, in Pascal's handwriting, to probate as a will:

"To Zaya Kingman-Speelman
        470 Park Avenue, N. Y.
This is my will if I
should die on this
my trip to India
You are my sol heiress.
                Signed the 22 february 1954
Witnesses
[signatures]   [signature] Gabriel Pascal
Daisy Haang
Y. T. Kan
[oriental calligraphy]"

However, it was construed as ineffectual to dispose of any part of Pascal's property. His projected trip to India was not made, and he died in a New York hospital. He had been separated from his wife, Valerie, since about the time he met the plaintiff, Speelman, in March, 1953. Valerie sued him for divorce in California in February, 1954. A property settlement was reached in March, and an interlocutory decree granted on June 15. The divorce was not final at the time of Pascal's death. Valerie was appointed administratrix of his estate, and is the present defendant. See In re Pascal, 309 N.Y. 108, 127 N.E.2d 835, 52 A.L.R. 2d 1202 (1955); 2 Misc.2d 337, 152 N.Y.S.2d 185 (Surr.Ct., N.Y.County 1956), aff'd, 4 A.D.2d 941, 167 N.Y.S. 2d 1002 (1st Dept. 1957), leave to appeal denied, 4 A.D.2d 1021, 169 N.Y. S.2d 419 (1957), 4 N.Y.2d 674, 171 N.Y.S.2d 1027 (1958); 15 Misc.2d 767, 182 N.Y.S.2d 927 (Sup.Ct. N.Y.County 1959), aff'd, 10 A.D.2d 619, 197 N.Y.S. 2d 424 (1st Dept. 1960), affirmed in the opinion reproduced here.

In 1970 Valerie Pascal published a book about her life with Pascal, of whom Shaw wrote, "The man is a genius: that is all I have to say about him." The book, called *The Disciple and His Devil*, does not mention Zaya Kingman-Speelman by name; she is referred to as the Woman of Shanghai, and the Woman of Park Avenue. She is represented as a dealer in the occult, the Irish-Chinese widow of a Dutch banker. Pascal emerged (he said) from the Transylvanian peasantry to become the producer-director of *Pygmalion* and other films. He was a devotee of an Indian holy man who obeyed a vow of silence, and he planned a visit to this avatar before his final illness. Mrs. Pascal (now Mrs. George Delacorte), had a career in Hungarian films before the first of her three marriages. Her second marriage, to Pascal, occurred in 1947. She resembled Bergman, one of the many celebrated friends of the Pascals.

Pascal's will, in favor of Zaya, was held to be inoperative a month after the opening of *My Fair Lady*. Although he had died penniless, his estate increased to "well over the mark of $2 million," according to Mrs. Pascal. It was divided between her and Pascal's brother.

The transactions in question in the main case are described in her book at pp. 297–98. The Woman of Shanghai had made loans to Pascal, and pawned jewelry to enable him to keep alive his *Pygmalion* musical rights. The assignment (Mrs. Pascal wrote) "presented a gift . . . designed to calm her worry over the loans." The will and the document litigated in the main case were written on the same day, about a year after Pascal became acquainted with the plaintiff. His deathbed, in a New York hospital, was surrounded by the impenetrable intrigue of three women. Evidently, he was a man of great personal magnetism.

Shaw envisaged Valerie as playing in one of his films, and suggested a coach in English diction. He prized Pascal for his faithfulness to the Shavian texts.

five per cent (5%) in England, and two per cent (2%) of my shares of profits in the United States.　From the film version, five per cent (5%) from my profit shares all over the world.

　　"As soon as the contracts are signed, I will send a copy of this letter to my lawyer, Edwin Davies, in London, and he will confirm to you this arrangement in a legal form.

　　"This participation in my shares of profits is a present to you, in recognition for your loyal work for me as my Executive Secretary.

"Very sincerely yours,

"Gabriel Pascal."

The question in this lawsuit is: Did the delivery of this paper constitute a valid, complete, present gift to plaintiff by way of assignment of a share in future royalties when and if collected from the exhibition of the musical stage version and film version of "Pygmalion"? A consideration was, of course, unnecessary (Personal Property Law, Consol.Laws, c. 41, § 33, subd. 4).[b]

　　In pertinent parts the judgment appealed from declares that plaintiff is entitled to receive the percentages set out in the 1954 agreement, requires defendant to render plaintiff accountings from time to time of all moneys received from the musical play and the film version, and orders defendant to make the payments required by the agreement.　[Certain submissions for the defendant were rejected by the court, including one based on the difference between Pascal Enterprises and Gabriel Pascal individually.]

　　The only real question is as to whether the 1954 letter above quoted operated to transfer to plaintiff an enforcible right to the described percentages of the royalties to accrue to Pascal on the production of a stage or film version of a musical play based on "Pygmalion".　We see no reason why this letter does not have that effect.　It is true that at the time of the delivery of the letter there was no musical stage or film play in existence but Pascal, who owned and was conducting negotiations to realize on the stage and film rights, could grant to another a share of the moneys to accrue from the use of those rights by others.　There are many instances of courts enforcing assignments of rights to sums which were expected thereafter to become due to the assignor.　A typical case is Field v. Mayor of City of New York, 6 N.Y. 179.　One Bell, who had done much printing and similar work

---

b.　Carried forward as General Obligations Law, § 5–1107: "An assignment shall not be denied the effect of irrevocably transferring the assignor's rights because of the absence of consideration, if such assignment is in writing and signed by the assignor, or by his agent."　Cf. Restatement, § 158 (1) (a).
"The kind of writing which is necessary in order to transfer a chattel without delivery may differ in the various states.　At common law presumably a sealed instrument was necessary, but doubtless, at least in states where seals have been abolished, and very likely in many other states, a formal unsealed writing, or perhaps even an informal writing, would be sufficient." Williston, Gifts of Rights, 40 Yale L.J. 1, 2 (1930).

for the City of New York but had no present contract to do any more such work, gave an assignment in the amount of $1,500 of any moneys that might thereafter become due to Bell for such work. Bell did obtain such contracts or orders from the city and money became due to him therefor. This court held that while there was not at the time of the assignment any presently enforcible or even existing chose in action but merely a possibility that there would be such a chose in action, nevertheless there was a possibility of such which the parties expected to ripen into reality and which did afterwards ripen into reality and that, therefore, the assignment created an equitable title which the courts would enforce. . . . The cases cited by appellant (Young v. Young, 80 N.Y. 422; Vincent v. Rix, 248 N.Y. 76, 161 N.E. 425; Farmers' Loan & Trust Co. v. Winthrop, 207 App.Div. 356, 202 N.Y.S. 456, mod. 238 N.Y. 477, 144 N.E. 686) are not to the contrary. In each of those instances the attempted gifts failed because there had not been such a completed and irrevocable delivery of the subject matter of the gift as to put the gift beyond cancellation by the donor. In every such case the question must be as to whether there was a completed delivery of a kind appropriate to the subject property. Ordinarily, if the property consists of existing stock certificates or corporate bonds, as in the Young and Vincent cases (supra), there must be a completed physical transfer of the stock certificates or bonds. . . . In our present case there was nothing left for Pascal to do in order to make an irrevocable transfer to plaintiff of part of Pascal's right to receive royalties from the productions. . . .

The judgment should be affirmed, with costs.

NOTES

(1) *A Distinction.* Compare the contest in this case, between the assignee (Speelman) and the widow (Pascal), with a contest between an assignee and a creditor of the assignor. Contests of the latter type are illustrated in the problem immediately preceding the case. Do you see why the main case might not be a powerful precedent against a *creditor?* The case was not even cited by Justice Breitel in Stathos v. Murphy, Note 1, p. 937 supra.

(2) *Question.* Reconsider the problem in Note 2, p. 925 supra. How plausible would it be for Mrs. Oman to pitch her claim against the Sundays on an assignment to her of Rheim's interest in the contract? (In the case cited there, Speelman v. Pascal is distinguished.)

COOPER v. HOLDER, 21 Utah 2d 40, 440 P.2d 15 (1968). [Davis Holder obtained a contract with the city of Moab, Utah, for engineering services. Then he borrowed $10,000 from Joe Cooper, and assigned his rights to payment under the contract to Cooper, as security for the loan. Cooper served a notice of assignment on the mayor of Moab, who signed an acknowledgment that payment would be made in accordance with the assignment. But it was not: "For some reason" the city paid Holder instead. Cooper sued the city for $5,000, the unpaid balance of the loan. The city's defense was based on state statutes about the duties and powers of its officials. One provision was that "all propositions to create any liability against the City" must be voted on and approved by the city council. The trial court gave judgment against the city, and it appealed.]

CROCKETT, CHIEF JUSTICE: . . . The obligation of a debtor to honor an assignment of a right to receive money payable is plainly something quite different in nature from the negotiation for and the entering into a contract for goods, property, or services in the first instance. In this case the problems involved in whether the City should enter into the contract for water and sewer improvements had been resolved when the original contract was entered into with Holder. Our concern is only with the payment by the City of money it owed for his services. Once he had acquired the right to receive the money, it was his prerogative to assign it to whomsoever he chose. When this has been done it is not essential that the debtor agree to that arrangement.[1] Except under unusual circumstances, where the assignment relates to personal services, or something of a unique character where a party would be put to a distinct disadvantage, when the obligor receives proper notice of the assignment, he must honor it. It has been specifically so adjudged where the debtor is a municipal corporation and money due under a contract is assigned.[2]

The question then becomes whether notice to the mayor should be deemed proper notice to the City. A study of the authorities dealing with this question indicates that the requirement of proper notice is satisfied by serving it upon an official whose duty it would be to either act upon it himself or to communicate it to others who had such duty. . . . There should be no question but that this doctrine would apply to the mayor of Moab. He is the chief executive officer of the City, Sec. 10–6–23, U.C.A.1953; is affirmatively charged with the duty of giving the council information concerning the business of the City, Sec. 10–6–24, U.C.A.1953.

Judgment affirmed. Costs to plaintiff (respondent).

NOTES

(1) *Question.* As a result of this decision, Holder has been paid in full for his services, his debt has been paid with $5,000 of the city's money, and it is out of pocket in that amount. What basis might there be for a claim by the city against Holder? See Newark Ins. Co. v. United States, 181 F.Supp. 246 (Ct.Cl.1960).

1. 6 C.J.S. Assignments § 75, p. 1127.

2. See People's Bank of Weir v. Attala County, 156 Miss. 560, 126 So. 192

(1930); Hartford Accident & Indemnity Co. v. Village of Milan, 176 F. Supp. 84, District Court of Illinois, 1959.

(2) *Problem.* Cooper writes to the mayor of Moab, as follows: "I am about to lend $10,000 to Davis Holder, and I intend to take an assignment of his rights under the contract he has with the city as security for the loan. Please acknowledge." When the mayor does so, Cooper makes the loan, takes the assignment, and deems himself secure. In fact, he is courting disaster. What would you advise him to do? See UCC 9–318(3), p. 1008 infra; C. I. T. Corporation v. Glennan, 137 Cal.App. 636, 31 P.2d 430 (1934); Time Finance Corporation v. Johnson Trucking Company, 23 Utah 2d 115, 458 P.2d 873 (1969).

(3) *Acceptance.* The Arrow Construction Company, general contractors for a building, subcontracted the glass work to the Border Glass Company. Border assigned its expected earnings on the job to the Bank of Yuma as security for loans. The bank presented the assignment to Arrow, which signed an "acceptance" in these words: "the undersigned agrees to pay all moneys due under said [glass] contract, to the Bank of Yuma . . . with the understanding that acceptance of this assignment places no greater burden upon the undersigned than if this assignment had not been accepted . . ." Arrow received checks for the glass work from time to time, which it endorsed in such a way that Border could use them to pay the firm supplying it with glass. As a result, the bank's loans were not repaid, and it sued Arrow. From judgment for the defendant, the plaintiff appealed. *Held:* Reversed. Arrow argued that the terms of its acceptance relieved it of the necessity of indorsing the checks specially, so that they could not be cashed without the bank's signature. The court said: "This argument is fallacious. When notice of an assignment is given to and received by the debtor, he becomes liable to pay the assignee, whether he accepts the assignment or not." Arrow was held liable to pay the bank the amount of its unpaid loans. Bank of Yuma v. Arrow Construction Co., 106 Ariz. 582, 480 P.2d 338 (1971).

(4) *Discharge After Assignment.* "Except as stated in this Section, notwithstanding an assignment, the assignor retains his power to discharge or modify the duty of the obligor to the extent that the obligor performs or otherwise gives value until but not after the obligor receives notification that the right has been assigned and that performance is to be rendered to the assignee." Restatement Second, § 170(1).[a] Ensuing subsections state some qualifications, one of which has to do with possession of "symbolic documents."[b]

---

a. On what constitutes receipt of notification, see Comment e. Notification cannot be given for this purpose by a filing in a public office; see Illustration 4.

b. If a claim is represented by a symbolic document, it is not safe for the obligor to render performance to the original obligee without requiring him to produce it: "Non-production has the same effect as receipt of notifica-

tion of assignment . . . . In addition, the obligor who performs without surrender or cancellation of or appropriate notation on the writing takes the risk of further obligation to an assignee who takes possession of the writing as a bona fide purchaser. The latter rule may be regarded as an application of a broader doctrine of estoppel." Restatement Second, § 170, Comment h. See also § 174, Comment f.

SECTION 2.   ASSIGNMENT AND DELEGATION IN CONNECTION WITH THE SALE OF A BUSINESS

CRANE ICE CREAM CO. v. TERMINAL FREEZING & HEATING CO.

Court of Appeals of Maryland, 1925.
147 Md. 588, 128 A. 280, 39 A.L.R. 1184.

Action by the Crane Ice Cream Company against the Terminal Freezing & Heating Company.   Demurrer to the declaration was sustained, and from the judgment entered thereon against plaintiff, it appeals.   Judgment affirmed.

PARKE, J.   The appellee and one W. C. Frederick entered into a contract for the delivery of ice by the appellee to Frederick, and, before the expiration of the contract, Frederick executed an assignment of the contract to the appellant; and on the refusal of the appellee to deliver ice to the assignee it brought an action on the contract against the appellee to recover damages for the alleged breach.   .   .   .

The contract imposed upon the appellee the liability to sell and deliver to Frederick such quantities of ice as he might use in his business as an ice cream manufacturer to the extent of 250 tons per week, at and for the price of $3.25 a ton of 2,000 pounds on the loading platform of Frederick.   The contractual rights of the appellee were (a) to be paid on every Tuesday during the continuation of the contract, for all ice purchased by Frederick during the week ending at midnight upon the next preceding Saturday; (b) to require Frederick not to buy or accept any ice from any other source than the appellee, except in excess of the weekly maximum of 250 tons.   .   .   .

Before the first year of the second term of the contract had expired Frederick, without the consent or knowledge of the appellee, executed and delivered to the appellant, for a valuable consideration, a written assignment dated February 15, 1921, of the modified agreement between him and the appellee.   The attempted transfer of the contract was a part of the transaction between Frederick and the appellant whereby the appellant acquired by purchase the plant, equipment, rights, and credits, choses in action, "good will, trade, custom, patronage, rights, contracts," and other assets of Frederick's ice cream business which had been established and conducted by him in Baltimore.   The purchaser took full possession and continued the former business carried on by Frederick.   It was then and is now a corporation "engaged in the ice cream business upon a large and extensive scale in the city of Philadelphia, as well as in the city of Baltimore, and state of Maryland," and had a large capitalization, ample resources, and credit to meet any of its obligations "and all and singular the terms and provisions" of the contract; and it was prepared to pay cash for all ice deliverable under the contract.

As soon as the appellee learned of this purported assignment and the absorption of the business of Frederick by the appellant, it notified Frederick that the contract was at an end, and declined to deliver any ice to the appellant. Until the day of the assignment the obligations of both original parties had been fully performed and discharged. . . .

The basic facts upon which the question for solution depends must be sought in the effect of the attempted assignment of this executory bilateral contract on both the rights and the liabilities of the contracting parties, as every bilateral contract includes both rights and duties on each side while both sides remain executory. Williston on Contracts, sec. 407. If the assignment of rights and the assignment of duties by Frederick are separated, they fall into these two divisions: (1) The rights of the assignor were (a) to take no ice, if the assignor used none in his business, but if he did (b) to require the appellee to deliver, on the loading platform of the assignor, all the ice he might need in his business to the extent of 250 tons a week, and (c) to buy any ice he might need in excess of the weekly 250 tons from any other person; and (2) the liabilities of the assignor were (a) to pay to the appellee on every Tuesday during the continuance of the contract the stipulated price for all ice purchased and weighed by the assignor during the week ending at midnight upon the next preceding Saturday, and (b) not directly or indirectly, during the existence of this agreement, to buy or accept any ice from any other person, firm, or corporation than the said Terminal Freezing & Heating Company, except such amounts as might be in excess of the weekly limit of 250 tons.

Whether the attempted assignment of these rights, or the attempted delegation of these duties must fail because the rights or duties are of too personal a character, is a question of construction to be resolved from the nature of the contract and the express or presumed intention of the parties. Williston on Contracts, sec. 431.

The contract was made by a corporation with an individual, William C. Frederick, an ice cream manufacturer, with whom the corporation had dealt for 3 years, before it executed a renewal contract for a second like period. The character, credit, and resources of Frederick had been tried and tested by the appellee before it renewed the contract. Not only had his ability to pay as agreed been established, but his fidelity to his obligation not to buy or accept any ice from any other source up to 250 tons a week had been ascertained. In addition, the appellee had not asked in the beginning, nor on entering into the second period of the contract, for Frederick to undertake to buy a specific quantity of ice or even to take any. Frederick simply engaged himself during a definite term to accept and pay for such quantities of ice as he might use in his business to the extent of 250 tons a week. If he used no ice in his business, he was under no obligation to pay for a pound. In any week, the quantity could vary from zero to 250 tons, and its weekly fluctuation, throughout the life of the contract, could irregularly range between these limits. The weekly payment might be nothing or as much as $812.50; and for every week a credit was extended to the eighth day from the beginning of every week's delivery. From the time of the beginning of every weekly delivery of the ice to the date of the payment therefor the title to the ice was in the purchaser, and the seller had no security for its payment except in the integrity and solvency of Frederick. The performances, therefore, were not concurrent, but the performance of the nonassigning party to the contract was to precede the payments by the assignor.

When it is also considered that the ice was to be supplied and paid for, according to its weight on the loading platform of Frederick, at an unvarying price without any reference either to the quantity used, or to the fluctuations in the cost of production or to market changes in the selling price, throughout 3 years, the conclusion is inevitable that the inducement for the appellee to enter into the original contract and into the renewal lay outside the bare terms of the contract, but was implicit in them, and was the appellee's reliance upon its knowledge of an average quantity of ice consumed, and probably to be needed, in the usual course of Frederick's business, at all times throughout the year, and its confidence in the stability of his enterprise, in his competency in commercial affairs, in his probity, personal judgment, and in his continuing financial responsibility. The contract itself emphasized the personal equation by specifying that the ice was to be bought for "use in his business as an ice cream manufacturer," and was to be paid for according to its weight "on the loading platform of the said W. C. Frederick."

When Frederick went out of business as an ice cream manufacturer, and turned over his plant and everything constituting his business to the appellant, it was no longer his business, or his loading platform, or subject to his care, control, or maintenance, but it was the business of a stranger, whose skill, competency, and requirements of ice were altogether different from those of Frederick. The assignor had his simple plant in Baltimore. The assignee, in its purchase, simply added another unit to its ice cream business which it had been, and is now, carrying on "upon a large and extensive scale in the city of Philadelphia and state of Pennsylvania, as well as in the city of Baltimore and state of Maryland." The appellee knew that Frederick could not carry on his business without ice wherewith to manufacture ice cream at his plant for his trade. It also was familiar with the quantities of ice he would require, from time to time, in his business at his plant in Baltimore, and it consequently could make its other commitments for ice with this knowledge as a basis.

The appellant, on the other hand, might wholly supply its increased trade acquired in the purchase of Frederick's business with its ice cream produced upon a large and extensive scale by its manufactory in Philadelphia, which would result in no ice being bought by the assignee of the appellee, and so the appellee would be deprived of the benefit of its contract by the introduction of a different personal relation or element which was never contemplated by the original contracting parties. Again, should the price of ice be relatively high in Philadelphia in comparison with the stipulated price, the assignee could run its business in Baltimore and furnish its patrons, or a portion of them, in Philadelphia with its product from the weekly maximum consumption of 250 tons of ice throughout the year. There can be no denial that the uniform delivery of the maximum quantity of 250 tons a week would be a consequence not within the normal scope of the contract, and would impose a greater liability on the appellee than was anticipated. 7 Halsbury's Laws of England, sec. 1015, p. 501.
. . .

While a party to a contract may as a general rule assign all his beneficial rights, except where a personal relation is involved, his liability under the contract is not assignable inter vivos, because any one who is bound to any performance whatever or who owes money cannot by any act of his own, or by any act in agreement with any other person than his creditor or the one to whom his performance is due, cast off his own liability and substitute another's liability. If this were not true, obligors could free themselves of their obligations by the simple expedient of assigning them. A further ground for the rule is that, not only is a party entitled to know to whom he must look for the satisfaction of his rights under the contract, but in the familiar words of Lord Denman in Humble v. Hunter, 12 Q.B. 317, "you have a right to the benefit you contemplate from the character, credit, and substance of the person with whom you contract." For these reasons it has been uniformly held that a man cannot assign his liabilities under a contract, but one who is bound so as to bear an unescapable liability may delegate the performance of his obligation to another, if the liability be of such a nature that its performance by another will be substantially the same thing as performance by the promisor himself. In such circumstances the performance of the third party is the act of the promisor, who remains liable under the contract and answerable in damages if the performance be not in strict fulfillment of the contract. . . .

However, the analysis of the facts on this appeal leaves no room for doubt that the case at bar falls into the category of those assignments where an attempt is made both to transfer the rights and to delegate the duties of the assignor under an executory bilateral contract whose terms and the circumstances make plain that the personal qualification and action of the assignor, with respect to both his benefits and burdens under the contract, were essential inducements in the formation of the contract, and further, that the assignment was a repudiation of any future liability of the assignor. The attempted assignment before us altered the conditions and obligations of the undertaking. The appellee would here be obliged not only to perform the subsequent stipulations of the contract for the benefit of a stranger and in conformity with his will, but also to accept the performance of the stranger in place of that of the assignor with whom it contracted, and upon whose personal integrity, capacity, and management in the course of a particular business he must be assumed to have relied by reason of the very nature of the provisions of the contract and of the circumstances of the contracting parties. . . .

Judgment affirmed.

NOTES

(1) *Question*. Suppose that Terminal's contract with Frederick had provided that, upon demand by Terminal Freezing, he would pay cash for any ice he ordered, not later than its delivery at his loading platform. And suppose it provided that Terminal might terminate the contract immediately, upon discovering that Frederick had bought ice from another source (without having taken 250 tons from Terminal that week).[a] Given these provisions, would the decision have been different?

(2) *The Code*. Would the reasoning or the result of the case be any different now that Maryland has adopted the Code? See UCC 2–210. According to Comment 4, "This Article and this section are intended to clarify [the problem of assignability of rights], particularly in cases dealing with output, requirement and exclusive dealing contracts. In the first place the section on requirements and exclusive dealing removes from the construction of the original contract most of the 'personal discretion' element by substituting the reasonably objective standard of good faith operation of the plant or business to be supplied. Secondly, the section on insecurity and assurances . . . frees the other party from the doubts and uncertainty which may afflict him under an assignment of the character in question by permitting him to demand adequate assurance of due performance without which he may suspend his own performance. [In subsection 5] the word 'performance' includes the giving of orders under a requirements contract. Of course, in any case where a material personal discretion is sought to be transferred, effective assignment is barred by subsection (2)." Cf. Robbins v. Hunts Food & Industries, Inc., 64 Wash.2d 304, 391 P.2d 713 (1964).

With slight alterations, the phrasing of subsection (2) has been copied into Restatement Second, § 149(2)(a). See also § 166, and especially Illustrations 3 and 6 thereafter.

(3) *The Reverse Action*. Does the court hold, in the main case, that Frederick committed a breach of his contract with Terminal Freezing?

_____

a. Would this provision be enforceable as written? See UCC 1–208.

Suppose, for example, that after the sale of his business Terminal could find no buyer for its ice for more than $3 a ton, and that (for some reason) it preferred not to sell to Crane. Aside from any "duty" to mitigate damages by dealing with Crane, would Terminal be permitted to hold Frederick accountable for its damages?

Whatever the case implies about this problem, the Code rather clearly indicates a way for Terminal to establish a damage claim against Frederick. See UCC 2–210(5) and the final clause of 2–609: ". . . is a repudiation of the contract." The following case (arising prior to the Code) is exceptional in that the assignor did not wait for a demand for assurances; it was in haste to repudiate.

The Code sections cited above permit the non-assigning party to demand assurances from *both* the assignee and the assignor in a proper case, do they not? If only one of them responds, but he is unquestionably willing and able to perform, should that count as an "adequate assurance" on behalf of both?

(4) *Incorporation.* Suppose that Frederick had transferred his business—plant, contract and all—to a corporation he formed, of which he is the principal officer, and the sole stockholders are himself and his wife. Would the court have said, in that case, that the assignment was a "repudiation of any future liability" by Frederick? Or would it have permitted the corporation to enforce the contract? See Milton L. Ehrlich, Inc. v. Unit Frame & Floor Corp., 5 N.Y.2d 275, 157 N.E.2d 495 (1959); Restatement Second, § 150, Illustration 8 (dissolution of close corporation).

These questions suggest that an assignment may be effective or not, depending upon the personality of the assignee. Is that proposition compatible with the rules of the Restatement? See sections 151(a) and 160(3). A measure of support for the proposition may be found in Meyer v. Washington Times Co., 64 App.D.C. 218, 76 F.2d 988 (1935), cert. denied, 295 U.S. 734 (1935), involving a contract for the supply of newspaper features such as "Dick Tracy."

WESTERN OIL SALES CORP. v. BLISS & WETHERBEE, 299 S.W. 637 (Tex.Com.App.1927). [A contract was executed by a partnership of oil well owners (McCamey, Sheerin and Dumas) and the Western Corporation. Western undertook to connect certain wells with tanks by laying gathering lines. All the oil produced from the wells for six months after they were connected up was to be sold to Western, which agreed to pay a "posted" price for crude oil, plus 25 cents per barrel premium. "This agreement shall extend to and be binding on the parties hereto, their heirs, executors, administrators, successors, and assigns." After about three months Western assigned the contract to the American Oil Company, American acquiring all rights and assuming all obligations of Western under the contract. Western notified the partnership of the assignment, declaring that American would be responsible to pay for future deliveries of oil and that Western would not. American made demand for deliveries (it was then solvent), but the sellers refused to deliver except on condition that Western should recognize its liability under the contract. When Western refused to do so, the sellers treated the contract as terminated. They assigned all claims growing out of the contract to Bliss & Wetherbee, who brought suit against Western for damages. Damages of $4,420.25 were awarded, and Western brought error.]

HARVEY, P. J. . . . The mere fact that a contract is invested, by consent of the parties or otherwise, with the quality of assignability, does not signify that either party may, by assigning the contract, release himself from liability under it. When a contract is assignable, a party may assign the benefits of his contract to another, and delegate to his assignee the performance of his obligations under the contract; but he remains liable for the proper performance of those obligations, unless the other party to the contract consents for the assignment to have the effect of releasing him. 5 C.J. § 45, p. 878, and authorities there cited.

The Western Corporation was not released from its contract by the assignment to the American Oil Company. The unexecuted portion of the contract remained constituted, as it was in the beginning, of the mutual promises of the contracting parties. When, therefore, the corporation repudiated all liability for future deliveries of oil, it committed an anticipatory breach, and the sellers thereupon became entitled to terminate the contract. . . .

The contract having been thus terminated, the sellers' obligation to make future deliveries of oil under it was released; and the sellers were under no obligation which required them to substitute the promise of the American Oil Company for that of the Western Corporation which had been repudiated. Nor was it the duty of the sellers, in order to minimize their damage, to waive the breach and continue to deliver oil to the oil company under the contract. Nor is the evidence such as to establish, as a matter of law, that the sellers, or the plaintiffs, failed to exercise ordinary prudence and diligence to mitigate the damage flowing from said breach.

We recommend that the judgment of the Court of Civil Appeals affirming the judgment of the trial court be affirmed.

CURETON, C. J. Judgments of the district court and Court of Civil Appeals both affirmed, as recommended by the Commission of Appeals.

NOTES

(1) *Novation?* If the partnership had made deliveries to American as demanded, after notice of the assignment, what would the legal position of the parties have been? See Dowling v. Parker, 221 Ala. 63, 127 So. 813 (1930), and Restatement Second, § 161(2).

(2) *An Accidental Assignment.* J. R. Miller contracted to do tile flooring in a new school building. Before performing, he incorporated his business as "Miller Floor Co., Inc." The corporation carried out the job.

Miller's contract with the builder provided: "The Subcontractor shall not assign or transfer this contract or any part thereof or any interest therein, without the written consent of the Contractor." The builder gave no consent, written or oral. In an action that did not involve either Miller or his company, the court ruled that the events constituted an effective equitable assignment of the subcontract to the corporation—"even though Miller testified that he made no *formal* assignment." Ruberoid Co. v. Glassman Construction Co., 248 Md. 97, 234 A.2d 875 (1967).

When an agreement is made for the substitution of one obligor for another, such that the obligee is entitled to the same performance, but the original obligor is released, the agreement is one of a class called "novations." See Restatement, § 428. The assent of the obligee is indispensable. It may be inferred from his conduct, of course. But when an obligor delegates performance of his duty, and the obligee does no more than indicate that he will "go along" with it, as a rule he is not understood as agreeing to release of the original obligor. See Bank of Fairbanks v. Kaye, 227 F.2d 566 (1955).

(3) *The Pizza Shop Case.* The court that decided the Crane Ice Cream case later returned to the problem in a case where the defendants operated a chain of pizza shops: Macke Company v. Pizza of Gaithersburg, Inc., 259 Md. 479, 270 A.2d 645 (1970). The plaintiff, Macke, bought the assets of a company that had contracted to install and service cold-drink vending machines in the pizza shops. The defendants contended that the sale had deprived them of the "personalized" service of the former owner. Further particulars of this case are given below: Note 3, p. 961. In part, the court relied on the following excerpt from a California case:

"All painters do not paint portraits like Sir Joshua Reynolds, nor landscapes like Claude Lorraine, nor do all writers write dramas like Shakespeare or fiction like Dickens. Rare genius and extraordinary skill are not transferable, and contracts for their employment are therefore personal, and cannot be assigned. But rare genius and extraordinary skill are not indispensable to the workmanlike digging down of a sand hill or the filling up of a depression to a given level, or the construction of brick sewers with manholes and covers, and contracts for such work are not personal, and may be assigned." Taylor v. Palmer, 31 Cal. 240, at 247–248 (1866).

DELEGATION DISPUTED

The making of an assignment "in general terms" may invite an unnecessary dispute. An illustration suggested in the Restatement Second concerns a contract for the sale of oil by the Ace Oil Company to Buyer. Before delivery is made, Ace sells its refinery to the Deuce Company. Referring to Buyer's contract, this sale agreement provides that "Ace assigns all its right, title and interest in said contract to Deuce." Buyer does not receive the oil he has contracted for, and sues Deuce for nondelivery.[a] Is it a sufficient defense for Deuce that it made no promise to deliver the oil?

---

a. The illustration referred to is Restatement Second, § 160, Illustation 1. The facts given here are a free adaptation.

For this simple problem an answer may be found in UCC 2–210(4). According to Comment 5, this subsection "lays down a general rule of construction . . . ." A comparable rule, expressed as one of interpretation, is stated in Restatement, § 164. However, even before the Restatement was promulgated it became evident that some courts might not accede to it. In Langel v. Betz, 250 N.Y. 159, 164 N.E. 890 (1928), the court quoted from the rule (in draft), giving it emphasis as follows: "Acceptance by the assignee of such an assignment is interpreted . . . as a promise *to the assignor to assume the performance of the assignor's duties.*" The court said: "This promise to the assignor would then be available to the other party to the contract. Lawrence v. Fox [p. 873 supra]." It also cited Seaver v. Ransom, p. 878 supra, and seemed sympathetic to the draftsmen's purpose. Perhaps, it said, the proposed rule is "more in harmony with modern ideas of contractual relations than is 'the archaic view of a contract as creating a strictly personal obligation between the creditor and debtor.' (Pollock on Contracts, 9th Ed., 232), which prohibited the assignee from suing at law in his own name and which denied a remedy to third party beneficiaries." Nevertheless, the court said, "The proposed change is a complete reversal of our present rule of interpretation as to the probable intention of both parties. . . . [T]he law remains that no promise of the assignee to assume the assignor's duties is to be inferred from the acceptance of an assignment of a bilateral contract, in the absence of circumstances surrounding the assignment itself which indicate a contrary intention."

The facts in Langel v. Betz were notably different from the illustration of a refinery sale, given above, and it would be possible for any court to make an intelligible distinction between the two situations. Langel, the plaintiff, had contracted to sell certain real property to two individuals. They assigned the contract to Benedict, who in turn assigned it to Betz, the defendant. In form, these were assignments of the assignors' "right, title and interest in and to the said contract." Betz refused to perform on the date set for closing, and Langel brought an action against him for specific performance. From a judgment for the plaintiff, defendant appealed. *Held*: Reversed. "The mere assignment of a bilateral executory contract may not be interpreted as a promise by the assignee to the assignor to assume the performance of the assignor's duties, so as to have the effect of creating a new liability on the part of the assignee to the other party to the contract assigned." Langel v. Betz, supra.[b] In the

---

b. Additional facts in the case were these: "The date for performance of the contract was originally set for October 2d, 1925. This was extended to October 15th, 1925, at the request of the defendant, the last assignee of the vendees. The ground upon which the adjournment was asked for by defendant was that the title company had not completed its search and report on the title to the property." The plaintiff based an argument on this request, which the court also rejected.

case of the oil-sale contract, how would you argue for Buyer, distinguishing Langel v. Betz?

The rule of the case has had continuing recognition in New York and elsewhere, and is not always confined to land-sale cases. However, the revisers of the Restatement considered that contracts for the sale of land may be regarded as distinctive for this purpose. (For possible justification, see Chapter 3, Section 2, and Chapter 7, Section 5, supra.) In preparing the Restatement Second, they were agreed that the original Restatement rule should be carried forward, as rephrased to parallel the language of UCC 2–210(4), except in relation to such contracts. As limited to land-sale contracts, the rule of Langel v. Betz presented the revisers with a dilemma. They found much authority to support it, and none directly contrary. A draft subsection (in new § 160) was therefore prepared to reflect the case-law rule. On the other hand, they were not in sympathy with it, and would have preferred to state a single rule embracing all types of contracts. Further consideration led to the drafting of a "caveat." [c] In using this technique, the Restatement simply avoids pronouncement on a debatable point. In 1967 the American Law Institute voted on the choice between the caveat and the draft embodying the (land sale) rule of Langel v. Betz. The caveat won, 47–44. It reads: "The Institute expresses no opinion as to whether the rule stated in Subsection (2) applies to an assignment by a purchaser of his rights under a contract for the sale of land."

In both UCC 2–210(4) and Restatement Second, § 160(2), the undertaking imputed to assignees is qualified by this phrase: "unless the language or the circumstances indicate the contrary." By this language it is possible to explain why, when a contractor obtains funds from a bank for a house-building job, and assigns it "the contract," the owner may not hold the bank accountable to put up the house. It explains also why, when a merchant assigns his sale contracts as security for a loan, his customers may not hold the lender accountable for nondelivery of the goods. Something more than a "financing assignment" in general terms would be required to charge a financial institution with such a duty.

Naturally, cases arise in which the indications of a financing assignment are ambiguous. An example is Chatham Pharmaceuticals, Inc. v. Angier Chemical Co., 347 Mass. 208, 196 N.E.2d 852 (1964). Angier (the company) had given an exclusive license to Chatham for the making of a product patented by the company. The contract permitted Chatham to give up the license and resell to the company, at an agreed price, all the product it had on hand. The company owed large sums to some of its stockholders, and it gave them an assignment of "all of its right, title and interest" in the Chatham contract. Evidently this entitled the assignees to royalties under the Chatham

---

c.   See Reporter's Notes to § 160.

contract. When Chatham gave up the license and called for performance under its sale option, the company refused to perform. In an action against the company and its assignees, Chatham obtained a favorable decree, and the assignees appealed. (What does this suggest about the solvency of the company?) *Held*: Decree modified by dismissing the bill against the assignees. What circumstances, if any, indicated that the assignees were not to pay for the left-over inventory? If the company were shown to have been insolvent at the time of the assignment, would that fact tend to reinforce the court's conclusion? If the assignees had paid the company a substantial sum for the assignment, what inference might be drawn from that fact?

NOTES

(1) *Problems.* Prepare a form of assignment making it clear that the assignees of the Chatham contract are not obliged to pay for the inventory. Prepare one making it clear that they *are*. If the contract to be assigned is one governed by UCC 2–210, and the assignee means to undertake the assignor's duties of performance, what practical value is there in including a statement to that effect in the assignment?

(2) *The Eau d'Or Case.* The owner of a mare named Eau d'Or leased her for breeding purposes and agreed to refund the breeder's payment if she failed to produce a foal in a certain time. The owner encountered financial difficulties and sought to mollify one of his creditors by transferring to the creditor his interest in the mare and the lease contract. When the mare failed to foal, the breeder sued the creditor for the amount of his payments. The trial court gave judgment against the defendant, saying, "If there was an assignment made you not only assume the benefits but you also assumed any obligations and you cannot have one without the other." On appeal by the creditor, *held:* Reversed and remanded for the resolution of a question of interpretation—"ordinarily more a question of fact than of law." Keyes v. Scharer, 14 Mich.App. 68, 165 N.W.2d 498 (1968). Does the court's remark about "question of fact" mean that the creditor should be allowed to testify about his intention in taking the assignment? If he is held not liable, does it follow that he may reclaim the mare, paying nothing to the breeder?

(3) *The Code.* Consult UCC 2–210(4) in relation to the following case: "A sells and delivers an automobile to B, the price to be paid in installments, and assigns to C for value 'all A's rights under the contract.' After B has made all the payments, the automobile is discovered to have been stolen and is retaken by the owner. C is not liable to B for breach of warranty of title; A is." Restatement Second, § 160, Illustration 3. How can it be explained, under the Code, that C is not liable to B? Note the parenthesis in the Code section. The Restatement comment, to which the illustration is appended, directs attention (via other sections) to UCC 1–201 (37), the third sentence.

ARNOLD PRODUCTIONS, INC. v. FAVORITE FILMS CORP.

United States Court of Appeals, Second Circuit, 1962.
298 F.2d 540.

LUMBARD, CHIEF JUDGE. Arnold Productions, Inc., the owner of two motion pictures, "Hangmen Also Die" and "It Happened Tomorrow," on May 27, 1947 entered into a distribution agreement with Favorite Films Corp., which granted Favorite "the sole and exclusive right to reproduce, lease, license, sub-license, exhibit, rent, distribute and exploit [the films] . . . for reissue purposes, for a period of seven (7) years," and similar rights for the same period "to lease, license, sub-license, rent, distribute and exploit [the films] . . . through and by television." In return Favorite agreed "to use its best efforts diligently and in good faith to exploit the said photoplays and to obtain as wide a distribution thereof and as many exhibitions and bookings thereof as possible." It was further provided that "This agreement is personal and cannot be assigned by the Licensee voluntarily, by operation of law or otherwise, without the consent in writing of the Licensor first obtained." Favorite was to retain 62½ percent of the receipts from the exploitation of the films, and Arnold was to receive the remainder.

On March 14, 1949, Favorite entered into an agreement with Nationwide Television Corp., co-defendant in this action, constituting Nationwide its "sole and exclusive agent for the television distribution of the films" on terms substantially the same as those of the Arnold-Favorite contract. Nationwide, in turn, orally subleased the television distribution rights to its wholly-owned subsidiary, Film Equities Corp., which was subsequently succeeded by another subsidiary of Nationwide called Unity, Inc. These subsidiaries handled the actual distribution of the films and accounted directly to Favorite, retaining 25 percent of all proceeds.[1]

This is a diversity action brought by Arnold, a Delaware corporation, against Favorite and Nationwide, both New York corporations; New York law applies. Arnold claims that Nationwide was guilty of fraud against it, and that Favorite broke the contract in failing to use its "best efforts" in television distribution and in delegating the television distribution to Nationwide; it also seeks an accounting from Favorite. No question is raised of Favorite's performance of that part of the contract covering the reissue of the films for theatre showings. Judge Murphy, in his opinion reported at 176 F. Supp. 862, granted judgment for Nationwide and for Favorite, except to the extent of requiring Favorite to account for its receipts from the licensing of the two films since the date of the last financial report to Arnold in 1955. We affirm the judgment.

---

1. Since Nationwide, Film Equities and Unity all had common ownership and common personnel, we shall treat them as one entity, as did the court below.

[The court said there was no evidence to suggest fraud on the part of Nationwide. As to its claims against Favorite, Arnold presented three arguments. The court rejected the first two of them.]

Arnold's third assignment of error, and that with which we are here primarily concerned, is that Favorite violated the contract by delegating its performance to Nationwide rather than handling the distribution itself as agreed. We find no error in Judge Murphy's holding that Favorite did not assign the contract to Nationwide or abandon its duties under it, and thus committed no breach.

It is clear that Favorite did not technically "assign" its contract in its entirety, but merely delegated a part (the extent of which we shall presently discuss) of its duties. Favorite did not purport to divest itself of its ultimate responsibility to Arnold. Although it made Nationwide its "sole and exclusive agent," it maintained certain supervisory powers over it. It reserved "the right to designate . . . a Representative, to whom you agree to submit for approval or rejection, each and all of your proposed license or sub-license agreements with respect to the Photoplays," and it appointed its president as such representative. Thus there was no breach of the specific covenant against assignment. Rather the question is whether the delegation of performance deprived Arnold of any right to Favorite's own services which it may have acquired explicitly from the provision that "this agreement is personal" or implicitly from the "best efforts" clause and the inherent nature of the contract.[2]

We do not find it necessary to consider whether New York would impose the same implied duty of personal service upon a contracting corporation as it would on an individual under the same circumstances, or whether this contract by its explicit terms gave Arnold the right to demand Favorite's own services.[3] Even if we assume that only Favorite was to give the performance called for by the contract, which was the "exploitation" of the films and the "obtaining" of bookings, we do not believe that this performance excluded such use of Nationwide's services as Favorite made. The contract must be interpreted in light of what the record reveals about the practices of

2. "In a contract for a sales agency, the personal performance of the agent is practically always a condition precedent to the duty of the principal and employer," and the agent cannot discharge his obligation by furnishing a substitute. 4 Corbin, Contracts 444–45 (1951); see, Paige v. Faure, 229 N.Y. 114, 127 N.E. 898, 10 A.L.R. 649 (1920); cf. Nassau Hotel Co. v. Barnett & Barse Corp., 162 App.Div. 381, 147 N.Y.S. 283 (1st Dept. 1914), aff'd mem., 212 N.Y. 568, 106 N.E. 1036 (1914). Plaintiff has made no claim that Favorite's duty should be determined by principles of actual agency, and we see no reason to treat the duty as more than contractual.

3. There is some reason to believe that the New York courts would not permit such an implication in the case of a corporation. Wetherell Bros. v. United States Steel Co., 200 F.2d 761 (1 Cir. 1953); New York Bank Note Co. v. Hamilton Bank Note Engraving & Printing Co., 180 N.Y. 280, 293, 73 N.E. 48, 52 (1905); New England Iron Co. v. Gilbert Elevated Ry. Co., 91 N.Y. 153, 166–167 (1883).

the business in which the parties were engaged, and especially what it reveals about the general understanding and course of dealings between them.

It is significant that under this contract Favorite's duties with respect to reissue of the two films to theatres were exactly the same as the television distribution duties here in question. There is no dispute that it was understood that little if any of the actual theatre distribution (possibly that in New York City, at the most) was to be done by Favorite itself; most was to be delegated to various "franchise holders" in various parts of the country, who were to do the actual work of selling films to local exhibitors. There is no indication that Favorite's supervision over these franchise holders was any greater than its supervision over Nationwide's television distribution. Favorite maintained the right to reject any agreements suggested by Nationwide, and there was sufficient evidence that on occasion its president actually did so with respect to television distribution, to justify Judge Murphy's finding that there was no abdication of responsibility. There is no suggestion that Arnold was endangered by lack of financial responsibility on Nationwide's part, or in any other way not having to do with the quality of the performance it received. In any event, the concession that under the same contract distribution through franchise holders was contemplated is sufficient to foreclose any inference that Favorite's employees were expected to do all television distribution personally. There is, indeed, testimony which would support a finding that throughout most of the term of the contract Arnold acquiesced in Favorite's delegation of sales duties.

Affirmed.

NOTES

(1) *Demand for Assurances?* Was there, in this case, any "assignment which delegates performance," as that expression is used in UCC 2–210? The exact issue could not arise in relation to a film-distribution agreement, presumably, unless it were characterized as a transaction in goods under Article 2 of the Code. But if the provision *were* applicable, the question would be whether or not it entitled Arnold to demand assurances from Nationwide (or from Favorite) under section 2–609, because of the arrangement between Favorite and Nationwide. It is risky to make a demand for assurances, of course, unless the Code clearly authorizes it; for an unwarranted demand may itself constitute a repudiation. The Code expression, "assignment which delegates performance," might be read narrowly, justifying a demand only when the contract has been assigned in its entirety—and the court says Favorite did not do that. Would you support a broader reading? How broad?

For discussion of this and other questions arising out of the Code treatment of assignments, see Note, 105 U.Pa.L.Rev. 836, 906–20 (1957). (In some respects the Code text has been altered since this study.)

(2) *Corporate Successors.* In the Bank Note case, cited by the court in footnote 3, it was said: "It is true that in dealing with corporations a

party cannot rely on what may be termed the human equation in the company. The personnel of the stockholders and officers of the company may entirely change. [But] a substitute for personal character is the charter rights of the corporation, the limits placed on its power, especially to incur debt, the statutory liability of its officers and stockholders. These are matters of great importance when, as at present, many states and territories seem to have entered into the keenest competition in granting charters; each seeking to outbid the other by offering to directors and stockholders the greatest immunity from liability at the lowest cash price."

In the Wetherell case, also cited, a Massachusetts corporation holding a sales agency contract was dissolved, and its three stockholders transferred the assets to the plaintiff, a Pennsylvania corporation of the same name. The other party to the contract, a steel producer, did not learn of the assignment until after it had received certain orders for steel procured by the plaintiff. It refused to fill these orders, but later made its own sales to the same customers. In an action against the steel producer, it was held to be justified in treating the contract as terminated by the liquidation of the Massachusetts corporation. Also, it was held not liable on a theory of quasi contract, for two reasons. "First, because no benefit was conferred on defendant under the prevalent conditions of a seller's market. Second, because the [plaintiff] acted officiously or as a volunteer, in forwarding the steel orders without disclosing its true identity or the fact of the purported assignment. Restatement, Restitution (1937) § 2."

THE BRITISH WAGGON CO. AND THE PARKGATE WAGGON CO. v. LEA & CO.

Queen's Bench Division, 1880.
5 Q.B.D. 149.

COCKBURN, C. J. This was an action brought by the plaintiffs to recover rent for the hire of certain railway waggons, alleged to be payable by the defendants to the plaintiffs, or one of them, under the following circumstances:

By an agreement in writing of February 10th, 1874, the Parkgate Waggon Company let to the defendants, who are coal merchants, fifty railway waggons for a term of seven years, at a yearly rent of £600 a year, payable by equal quarterly payments. By a second agreement of June 13th, 1874, the company in like manner let to the defendants fifty other waggons, at a yearly rent of £625, payable quarterly like the former.

Each of these agreements contained the following clause: "The owners, their executors, or administrators, will at all times during the said term, except as herein provided, keep the said waggons in good and substantial repair and working order, and, on receiving notice from the tenant of any want of repairs, and the number or numbers of the waggons requiring to be repaired, and the place or places where it or they then is or are, will, with all reasonable despatch, cause the same to be repaired and put into good working order."

On October 24th, 1874, the Parkgate Company passed a resolution, under the 129th section of the Companies Act, 1862, for the voluntary winding up of the company. Liquidators were appointed, and by an order of the Chancery Division of the High Court of Justice, it was ordered that the winding up of the company should be continued under the supervision of the Court.

By an indenture of April 1st, 1878, the Parkgate Company assigned and transferred, and the liquidators confirmed to the British Company and their assigns, among other things, all sums of money, whether payable by way of rent, hire, interest, penalty, or damage, then due, or thereafter to become due, to the Parkgate Company, by virtue of the two contracts, and all the interest of the Parkgate Company and the said liquidators therein; the British Company, on the other hand covenanting with the Parkgate Company "to observe and perform such of the stipulations, conditions, provisions, and agreements contained in the said contracts as, according to the terms thereof were stipulated to be observed and performed by the Parkgate Company." On the execution of this assignment the British Company took over from the Parkgate Company the repairing stations, which had previously been used by the Parkgate Company for the repair of the waggons let to the defendants, and also the staff of workmen employed by the latter company in executing such repairs. It was expressly found that the British Company have ever since been ready and willing to execute, and have, with all due diligence, executed all necessary repairs to the said waggons. . . .

The main contention on the part of the defendants, however, was that, as the Parkgate Company had, by assigning the contracts, and by making over their repairing stations to the British Company, incapacitated themselves to fulfill their obligation to keep the waggons in repair, that company had no right, as between themselves and the defendants, to substitute a third party to do the work they had engaged to perform, nor were the defendants bound to accept the party so substituted as the one to whom they were to look for performance of the contract; the contract was therefore at an end.

The authority principally relied on in support of this contention was the case of Robson v. Drummond, 2 B. & Ad. 303, approved of by this court in Humble v. Hunter, 12 Q.B. 310. In Robson v. Drummond a carriage having been hired by the defendant of one Sharp, a coachmaker, for five years, at a yearly rent, payable in advance each year, the carriage to be kept in repair and painted once a year by the maker—Robson being then a partner in the business, but unknown to the defendant—on Sharp retiring from the business after three years had expired, and making over all interest in the business and property in the goods to Robson, it was held, that the defendant could not be sued on the contract—by Lord Tenterden on the ground that "the defendant might have been induced to enter into the contract by reason of the personal confidence which he reposed in Sharp, and therefore have agreed to pay money in advance, for which reason the defendant had a right to object to its being performed by any other person"; and by Littledale and Parke, JJ., on the additional ground that the defendant had a right to the personal services of Sharp, and to the benefit of his judgment and taste, to the end of the contract.

In like manner, where goods are ordered of a particular manufacturer, another, who has succeeded to his business, cannot execute the order, so as to bind the customer, who has not been made aware of the transfer of the business, to accept the goods. The latter is entitled to refuse to deal with any other than the manufacturer whose goods he intended to buy. For this Boulton v. Jones, 2 H. & N. 564, is a sufficient authority. The case of Robson v. Drummond comes nearer to the present case, but is, we think, distinguishable from it. We entirely concur in the principle on which the decision in Robson v. Drummond rests, namely, that where a person contracts with another to do work or perform service, and it can be inferred that the person employed has been selected with reference to his individual skill, competency, or other personal qualification, the inability or unwillingness of the party so employed to execute the work or perform the service is a sufficient answer to any demand by a stranger to the original contract of the performance of it by the other party, and entitles the latter to treat the contract as at an end, notwithstanding that the person tendered to take the place of the contracting party may be equally well qualified to do the service. Personal performance is in such a case of the essence of the contract, which, consequently, cannot in its absence be enforced against an unwilling party. But this principle appears to us inapplicable in the present instance, inasmuch as we cannot suppose that in stipulating for the repair of these waggons by the company—a rough description of work which ordinary workmen conversant with the business would be perfectly able to execute—the defendants attached any importance to whether the repairs were done by the company, or by any one with whom the company might enter into a subsidiary contract to do the work. All that the hirers, the defendants, cared for in this stipulation was that the waggons should be kept in repair; it was indifferent to them by whom the repairs should be done. Thus if, without going into liquidation, or assigning these contracts, the company had entered into a contract with any competent party to do the repairs, and so had procured them to be done, we cannot think that this would have been a departure from the terms of the contract to keep the waggons in repair. While fully acquiescing in the general principle just referred to, we must take care not to push it beyond reasonable limits. And we cannot but think that, in applying the principle, the Court of Queen's Bench in Robson v. Drummond went to the utmost length to which it can be carried, as it is difficult to see how in repairing a carriage when necessary, or painting it once a year, preference would be given to one coachmaker over another.

Much work is contracted for, which it is known can only be executed by means of subcontracts; much is contracted for as to which it is indifferent to the party for whom it is to be done, whether it is done by the immediate party to the contract, or by some one on his behalf. In all these cases the maxim Qui facit per alium facit per se applies.

In the view we take of the case, therefore, the repair of the waggons, undertaken and done by the British Company under their contract with the Parkgate Company, is a sufficient performance by the latter of their engagement to repair under their contract with the defendants. Consequently, so long as the Parkgate Company continues to exist, and, through the British Company, continues to fulfill its obligation to keep the waggons in repair, the defendants cannot, in our opinion, be heard to say that the former company is not entitled to the performance of the contract by them, on the ground that the company have incapacitated themselves from performing their obligations under it, or that, by transferring the performance thereof to others, they have absolved the defendants from further performance on their part.

That a debt accruing due under a contract can, since the passing of the Judicature Acts, be assigned at law as well as equity, cannot since the decision in Brice v. Bannister, 3 Q.B.D. 569, be disputed.

We are therefore of opinion that our judgment must be for the plaintiffs for the amount claimed.

NOTES

(1) *Offer to the Wrong Person.* The court distinguishes Boulton v. Jones, the case of the leather pipe hose stated in Note 3, p. 32 supra, and Robson v. Drummond, the case of the carriage, admitting that the latter "comes nearer to the present case." It should be noticed that the two cases cited are analytically quite different. In the former the court held that there was no contract. In the latter there was an unquestioned contract between the coachmaker and his customer. Might the outcome in Boulton v. Jones have been different if Jones' order for hose had been handled differently?

Suppose that A, wishing to buy a used truck that he has seen, writes an offer to B, whose name is painted on it. The truck belongs in fact to "B Corporation," a company wholly owned by B. B likes the offer, and does not want to give A a chance to change his mind. Advise B. Would there be any advantage in having A readdress his offer to the company, if he will do it?

In connection with the analytical difference between the cases referred to, compare what was said in United States v. Braunstein, Note 2, p. 572 supra: "It is true that there is much room for interpretation once the parties are inside the framework of a contract, but it seems that there is less in the field of offer and acceptance."

(2) *The Boston Ice Case.* An old and well-known case about a buyer of ice for home use has recently been restated as follows: "Potter, who had dealt with the Boston Ice Company, and found its service unsatis-

factory, transferred his business to Citizens' Ice Company. Later, Citizens' sold out to Boston, unbeknown to Potter, and Potter was served by Boston for a full year. When Boston attempted to collect its ice bill, the Massachusetts court sustained Potter's demurrer on the ground that there was no privity of contract, since Potter had a right to choose with whom he would deal and could not have another supplier thrust upon him." The case is Boston Ice Co. v. Potter, 123 Mass. 28 (1877).

The case has been "roundly criticized" by Corbin, and it is said that modern authorities do not support the result. Macke Co. v. Pizza of Gaithersburg, Inc., 259 Md. 479, 270 A.2d 645 (1970) (source of the quotation above). Would you support a quasi-contract claim against Potter? A contract claim? On the facts, which of the following cases does this one resemble most?—the British Waggon case, Boulton v. Jones, or Robson v. Drummond?

(3) *The Pizza Shop Case (Continued).* This case is cited in the preceding note, and partially briefed in Note 3, p. 950 supra. Vending machines had been installed in the pizza shops by the Virginia Coffee Service, Inc., under one-year agreements requiring Virginia to "maintain the equipment in good operating order and stocked with merchandise." The Pizza Shops attempted to terminate the contracts after Virginia assigned them to the Macke Company, saying they preferred the way Virginia conducted its business: that "the president of Virginia kept the machines in working order, that commissions were paid in cash, and that Virginia permitted them to keep keys to the machines so that minor adjustments could be made when needed." The trial court denied recovery for Macke, in a suit against the Pizza Shops; but the judgment was reversed on appeal. The court relied on the British Waggon case. Also, it seemed to disapprove the Boston Ice case. Should the court have distinguished the latter case? Would you have advised the Pizza Shops, given their strong preference for Virginia, not to repudiate the contracts abruptly, but to wait and see what quality of service Macke would provide?

(4) *Code Influence.* The British Waggon case is the basis for an illustration after Restatement Second, § 152. The original Restatement standard of a permissible delegation—§ 160(3)(a)—has been made more congruent with the Code standard in the Second Restatement: see UCC 2–210(1) and § 150 of the latter. Which of the foregoing cases would be affected by the Code provision?

(5) *The Case of the Dancer's Faux Pas.* Mr. and Mrs. Philip Seale signed up with the Dale Dance Studio, a corporation, for a series of lessons, paying some $200. They became dissatisfied, and Dale arranged for them to complete the lessons at the Bates Dance Studio, also a corporation. At the end of this series they contracted with Bates for another series of 600 lessons. These lessons were interrupted by illness, and when the Seales returned they found that Bates has assigned the contract to the Dale Studio which undertook to complete performance for Bates. They were told that the entire Bates organization was transferred to Dale, and that they would have the same instructors and instruction as before. However, the Seales found the lessons unsatisfactory and made unsuccessful complaints: the rooms were small, crowded and noisy, and the couple had to share an instructor, a Mr. Ritchie. After some 30 sessions at the Dale Studio they

stopped attending, and subsequently sued Bates and Dale to recover the cost of the lessons. *Held:* For the defendants.

"The argument of plaintiffs that this was a personal service contract and therefore non-assignable without their consent is valid. . . . Had they refused to receive instruction from Dale and had they taken the position that their contract was with Bates and no other, there would be substance to their present contention that this violation justified the rescission. [But they accepted the assignment.] While we sympathize with Mr. Seale's preference for Miss Valie over Mr. Ritchie, we do not consider this a breach of a promise implicit in the contract. . . . It is probable that Mrs. Seale preferred to be taught by Mr. Ritchie. It thus appears to us that the proper remedy for this problem is an express stipulation in the contract requiring a partner of the opposite sex." Seale v. Bates, 145 Colo. 430, 359 P.2d 356 (1961). See also Purnell v. Atkinson, 451 S.W.2d 734 (Ark.1970).

STANDARD CHAUTAUQUA SYSTEM v. GIFT, 120 Kan. 101, 242 P. 145 (1926). [Anna Gift and others formed a committee to arrange a Chautauqua assembly at Mankato, Kansas, in 1924. A talent bureau, Midland Chautauqua, contracted to supply performers, a tent, advertising matter and the like. The committee agreed to furnish grounds and pay enumerated local expenses. They were to give the bureau hearty support and cooperation, and to pay it $750 on the opening day. Proceeds of the assembly were to be divided between the parties according to a prescribed formula. The bureau undertook to provide Midland quality lecturers, entertainers and musicians. "This agreement includes no oral promises, and it cannot be changed, modified, or canceled except by written mutual consent, and, when signed by fifteen persons, and accepted and signed by (bureau), is valid, and shall bind and benefit the parties thereto, their successors and assigns."

[About a month before the projected Chautauqua, Midland assigned the contract to the plaintiff, Standard Chautauqua System, and the committee was notified that Standard assumed responsibility for the bureau's performance. The plaintiff alleged the foregoing facts, and others recited in the opinion.]

JOHNSTON, C. J. . . .

The plaintiff also suggested to defendants that it would present two plays, "Friendly Enemies," and "The Gorilla," the Loveless Concert Company, St. Cecilia Singing Orchestra, and a novelty trio, and three splendid lecturers that were named. The plaintiff alleged that the proposed program was of the same or better quality than that of the Midland Chautauqua, and the talent to be furnished was high class in every respect. It was further alleged that the plaintiff came on and furnished everything that was required by the contract on August 21, 1924, but that the defendants and each of them refused and neglected to assist in any way whatever, and neglected to carry out their part of the agreement in any particular. They therefore asked for damages in the sum of $950.

A demurrer to the petition was sustained by the trial court on the ground that a cause of action had not been stated. The principal contention of the defendants is that the contract was so personal in character that it was nonassignable, and that, under the provisions contained in the contract, a change or modification of it could not be made without the written consent of the defendant.

There was no error in the ruling.   .   .   . Relying on the skill, discretion, and integrity of the managers of the bureau, defendants were willing to allow it to choose the talent, believing that they could do so and conduct an educational, entertaining, and successful assembly. The contract therefor involved personal and confidential relations to which liabilities were attached. While rights under ordinary contracts are assignable, there are well-recognized exceptions, and it is generally held that rights arising out of contracts involving a relationship of personal credit and confidence are not assignable by one party unless the other consents to the transfer.

[The court also rejected the plaintiff's contention that the word "assigns" as used in the contract signified that the duties and responsibilities of either party might be transferred without the consent of the other.]

NOTES

(1) *Personal Services Contracts.* It is frequently said that contracts for personal services are not assignable. The following questions may suggest some limitations on that proposition: (a) Would the Chautauqua decision necessarily have been the same if the Midland bureau had delegated only *part* of its duties to Standard? (b) If Midland had transferred only its rights to payment under the contract, and had tendered its own performance, would the assignee's claim be objectionable? (c) Is it clear that the defendants—members of the committee—could not delegate their duties without the consent of the bureau?

(2) *Two Senses of "Assignability."* In a much-cited case, a right to the delivery of lead ore was held nonassignable where it appeared that the seller and buyer were to cooperate in the assaying of the ore, the price to be ascertained after the assaying. During the assaying, the only security the seller had was the buyer's solvency. Clearly, the seller might not be willing to rely on the assignee's assaying or to trust the assignee with title and possession of the ore before payment. Arkansas Valley Smelting Co. v. Belden Mining Co., 127 U.S. 379 (1888). Is the issue in bilateral contract cases like this one essentially a question of assignability of the assignor's *rights* under the contract (i. e. to receive the ore) or a question of the delegability of the assignor's *duties* (i. e. to cooperate in assaying and furnish personal security)? Many, perhaps most, judicial references to "nonassignable contracts" concern not the nature of the rights being transferred but the nature of the duties which the transferor wishes to delegate to another.

(3) *Drafting.* When referring to John Doe in drafting a contract, would you expect to convey much meaning by adding, "and his assigns"? "Contracts often refer to the 'assigns' of one or both parties. A purported promise by a promisor 'and his assigns' does not mean that the promisor can terminate his duty by making an assignment, nor does it of itself show an assumption of duties by any assignee. It tends to indicate that the promised performance is not personal, just as a promise to a promisee 'and his assigns' tends to indicate that the promisor is willing to render performance to an assignee. Whether there is a manifestation of assent to assignment or delegation, however, depends on the interpretation of the contract as a whole." Restatement Second, § 155, Comment b.

CITY OF NORTH KANSAS CITY v. SHARP, 414 F.2d 359 (8th Cir. 1969). [The City of North Kansas City, Missouri, contracted for professional engineering services in connection with a proposed sewer project. The other party was a partnership of two consulting engineers, Riddle and Sharp. They were to make surveys and perform other preliminary services, and then, if a bond issue passed, were to prepare a design and contract documents, to supervise the work, and give the city general assistance. The first stage of the work was satisfactorily performed. Before the second stage was entered, a new partner was admitted to the firm, and Riddle withdrew. Sharp and the new partner advised the city that they had acquired his interest in the "former firm." They also wrote to the mayor that "there has been no dissolution of the partnership." The city attorney responded: "The City has been advised by their legal counselors that the dissolution of the partnership works a termination of any previous agreement or understanding." The city solicited new bids for completion of the engineering work from various firms, including Sharp and his partner, and Riddle. Still another firm got the job, and the Sharp firm brought an action for breach of its contract. From judgment for the plaintiff, the city appealed.]

BLACKMUN, CIRCUIT JUDGE. . . . *The assignability of the contract.* The City's argument is that the [original] partnership was one of professional people; That upon the assignment of a partner's interest in a contract with a client, the client has the option to abrogate the contract; that professional service is a very personal matter; that civil engineers are to be classified, in this respect, with attorneys. . . .

Despite the trial court's concern with the paucity of precedent, we have no difficulty in agreeing with its conclusion on this issue. We may, of course, generally accept the City's statement as to the law with respect to professional service contracts and, without deciding, we may assume for present purposes that professional engineers, in contracting for sanitary sewer work, come within that classification. But this acceptance and this assumption do not provide or compel an answer favorable to the City.

[The court mentioned an aggregation of eight items in support of the decision below. Two of them were as follows.] Although the City claims it was not so advised, there is evidence in the record that Riddle agreed to hold himself available to complete contracts outstanding between clients and the firm and that, if asked to do so, he would have worked with [his former partners] on the city contract. . . . The essence of the professional service cases is that the critical partner, for one reason or another, is no longer available to render those services. Here the critical partners were available and the record indicates . . . that they were able to, and did function collectively.

[The court was also influenced by indications that some city officials were disposed to place the contract with a firm that Riddle expected to join. The trial court had found that the mayor and Riddle were "evidently friendly," and that the other firm, "on its promise to take in Mr. Riddle, was recommended by the Mayor for employment at a substantially higher fee than that provided in the original contract." The court of appeals remarked that these findings "tell a sorry story." Affirmed.]

NOTES

(1) *Questions.* How may this case be reconciled with Standard Chautauqua System v. Gift? Does the present case suggest a way in which Standard Chautauqua might have obtained an effective assignment of the Midland contract?

(2) *Clean Hands.* In August, 1969, the owners of the Oakland "Oaks" basketball club contracted to sell all its assets to the Washington Capitols Basketball Club, Inc. One of its assets, valued at three-quarters of a million dollars, was a contract for the services of their star player Richard "Rick" Barry. He had signed with the Oaks for a three-year term in 1967. The day after the sale, Barry contracted to play for the San Francisco "Warriors." The Washington club brought an action against him in equity, seeking an injunction against his playing for the Warriors.

One of the defenses was based on the curious events of 1967, leading up to Barry's contract with the Oaks. It appears that he had previously had a contract with the Warriors club, and that the owners of the Oaks had induced him to play for them in violation of that contract. An objection to the injunction, then, was based on the maxim: "He who comes into equity must come with clean hands." (See Note 2, p. 417 supra.) The court granted a preliminary injunction, ruling that the suitor, Washington, should not be barred by the offense of its assignor, the Oakland Club. The relation between an assignee and his assignor is relatively remote, the court said, for purposes of the maxim. Washington Capitols Basketball Club, Inc. v. Barry, 304 F.Supp. 1193 (N.D.Cal.1969). (The court observed that the Warriors club had had Barry enjoined from playing with the Oaks in 1967–68.)

How can it be supposed that a contract so "personal" as this one was assignable at all? The opinion discusses the point.

SECTION 3.   FINANCING CONSUMER CREDIT

Mr. John Q. Public buys a new Thunderwagen car from the Potluck Motor Company. The purchase is on "time," because John does not have cash enough to pay the full price at once. He signs a promissory note in favor of the Motor Company for the price of the car, interest, and certain other charges, less the down payment. It calls for equal monthly payments over the course of two years. At the same time both the Motor Company (as Seller) and John (as Customer) sign a "Conditional Sale Contract." The critical feature of the contract is this sentence: "Title to the car is retained by Seller until said time balance is fully paid in money to the holder hereof (meaning Seller or its assignee if this contract is assigned) when title shall pass to Customer." The contract is lengthy, and contains many clauses in rather fine print. Permission for the Seller to seize the car in the event of John's default is expressly reserved.

The Motor Company wishes to maintain a full inventory of cars. Since it has to pay cash to the manufacturer before delivery, it does not have the additional funds necessary to finance its customers. For this purpose it has a long-standing arrangement with a finance company, the Thunderwagen Acceptance Corporation (TACO). In accordance with this agreement, TACO credits the Motor Company with all of the time balance owing under the conditional sale contract, less a "discount." In return, the Motor Company executes a "Dealer's Assignment" form appearing on the back of the contract, indorses John's note, and delivers both instruments to TACO. The first sentence of the assignment form is as follows: "We hereby sell and assign the contract on the reverse side and all interest in the car . . . to you . . . with full power to you in your or our name to collect and discharge the same and to take all such legal or other proceedings as we might take, save for this assignment." TACO sends notice to John that he should make the monthly payments directly to it. It encloses a handy coupon book for keeping the account straight. Steps may be taken, depending on local law, to file notice in a public office, or to make a notation on John's certificate of title, reflecting the fact that the car is subject to an encumbrance, or security interest. When John completes his payments, he then has the car free of TACO's security interest and can obtain a suitable record of his unencumbered title.

A transaction more or less like the one described occurs in connection with most consumer purchases of cars in this country, and the volume of credit generated is enormous. Sometimes the security agreement taken by the dealer and assigned to the finance company takes the form of a chattel mortgage rather than a conditional sale contract. Not only automobile purchases, but also purchases of many kinds of durable consumer goods (furniture, appliances, etc.) are similarly financed. And so it is with the purchase of items of business equipment ranging from barber chairs to drilling rigs. Some finance companies specialize in particular lines of business—the name TACO suggests an affiliation with the manufacturer of Thunderwagen cars. Others are not specialized, and commercial banks generally engage in financing on the same basis.

NOTES

(1) *Dealer's Finance Agreement.* By the agreement between the Motor Company and TACO, the assignment of John's contract might be made "without recourse," so that the Motor Company would be under no liability to TACO in the event of the customer's default in making payments. However, certainly with respect to a new-car sale, it would more probably be agreed that the Motor Company would repurchase the car from TACO if it be repossessed as a result of the customer's default. The amount credited to the Motor Company in connection with the assignment of John's contract would depend on that and a number of other factors. "In automobile financing under a repurchase arrangement, the financing agency ordinarily pays into a reserve account a portion of the finance charge on paper purchased from a particular dealer. Such payments continue until the account reaches either a minimum dollar amount or, more commonly, a percentage of the dealer's outstanding paper (usually three percent). Upon default by a buyer and repossession by the financer, the dealer is obligated to repurchase the vehicle, and the unpaid balance of the note is charged to the reserve account. . . . Once the stipulated reserve account balance is attained, subsequent sums payable under the dealer-participation agreement are periodically distributed to the dealer. Since the dealer's share of the finance charges typically ranges from one-fifth to one-third, dealer participation constitutes a major element of his income." Warren, Regulation of Finance Charges, 68 Yale L.J. 839, 859 (1959).

(2) *Assignee's Rights.* The principal problem of this section may be stated as follows: after the assignment, is the contract, in the hands of TACO, subject to the defenses that John might have made against the dealer? On the facts so far given, the answer is certainly "yes." When sued by the assignee, the buyer's defense is most often based on breach of warranty by the seller, or other non-performance, or on a misrepresentation inducing the buyer to contract. All these and many other defenses are available to the buyer to the same extent they would be if the dealer itself were suing for the purchase price.

If an assignee bank or finance company finds that the contract is unenforceable by reason of the seller's conduct it will invariably have a claim against him. The claim may be based on an implied warranty of the assignor; see Restatement Second, § 165. Or it may be based on express warranties accompanying the assignment. For examples of such warranties see Warner v. Seaboard Finance Company, 75 Nev. 470, 345 P.2d 759 (1959), concerning the assignment of an installment contract for storm windows and awnings. Among other things, the dealer warranted to the finance company that the contracts he assigned would be valid and enforceable obligations of the customer, signed by him, and that "ethical and proper selling practice will be followed."

The assignee must consider the possibility, however, that the dealer will be unable to respond to such a claim, by reason of insolvency, when the time comes to enforce it. For this reason, chiefly, financing institutions have not been content to take assignments of contracts "subject to defenses" that the customer, or obligor, may have against the assignor. The law has traditionally provided means for them to "take free" of such defenses, and the efficacy of these means is to be considered in this section. In most of the cases presenting the issue there is a loss attributable to substandard performance by a dealer in goods or services, and it must be allocated either to the customer or to the financing assignee. If the dealer is available for suit, and able to pay a judgment, the problem is not an acute one. In considering the materials to follow, you should assume that that is not the case.

WAIVING DEFENSES AND HOLDING IN DUE COURSE

Two principal arrangements are available for permitting an assignee to take free of an obligor's defenses against the assignor. Each requires a specialized form of expression for the obligor's undertaking. One relies upon the law of negotiable instruments, and the object is to give the assignee status as a "holder in due course." This arrangement is illustrated in Mutual Finance Co. v. Martin, p. 970 infra, and the basic rules of negotiability are important to an understanding of that case. The other arrangement relies on a term in the assigned contract known as a "waiver of defense" clause. For consumer transactions, such clauses are now more commonly used than negotiable instruments. However, the issues they raise are similar to those associated with negotiability. By a quirk of language, the phrase "holder in due course" has come to be applied to both the arrangements described here. Even careful students of the law are sometimes heard to say that a holder-in-due-course problem exists in a case where a waiver clause is in question. Accurately speaking, of course, there can be no such problem unless something that might pass for a negotiable instrument has been executed.

The following example of a waiver of defense clause is taken from Unico v. Owen, 50 N.J. 101, 232 A.2d 405 (1967), which concerned a contract signed by a New Jersey couple for 140 record albums, to be delivered and paid for in installments (with a "free" record player thrown in):

> Buyer hereby acknowledges notice that the contract may be assigned and that assignees will rely upon the agreements contained in this paragraph, and agrees that the liability of the Buyer to any assignee shall be immediate and absolute and not affected by any default whatsoever of the Seller signing this contract; and in order to induce assignees to

purchase this contract, the Buyer further agrees not to set up any claim against such Seller as a defense, counterclaim or offset to any action by an assignee for the unpaid balance of the purchase price or for possession of the property.

The buyers received the record player, and 12 albums; but the remainder were never received because the seller became insolvent. The buyers stopped their monthly payments after a year, and were then sued by a finance company as assignee of their contract.

The same buyers had also signed a promissory note, negotiable in form, for the entire purchase price of the albums, payable in installments. The note had also been transferred to the finance company, and it sought to recover on the note as a holder in due course, in the technical sense. The case is unusual in that the documents were designed to give the finance company the advantages both of a waiver clause and of negotiability; but the object was the same: to deprive the buyers of defenses such as failure of consideration.

The definition and effects of negotiable instruments are now stated in Article 3 of the Uniform Commercial Code. For about half a century before the Code was drafted, the subject was governed by the Negotiable Instruments Law (NIL), the first of the "uniform laws." And for perhaps two centuries before that the essential characteristics of negotiable instruments were established in the common law.

When the obligation on the instrument takes the form of a promise, the instrument is known as a *promissory note* or simply a *note*. UCC 3–104(2)(d). In order to be *negotiable*, however, the note must meet a number of other requirements: it must be signed by the maker, it must contain an unconditional promise to pay a sum certain in money, it must be payable on demand or at a definite time, and it must be payable to order or to bearer. UCC 3–104(1). Only if it meets these requirements is the note invested with the special characteristics of a negotiable instrument.

Chief among these characteristics is the protection of a good faith purchaser against defenses. When a negotiable instrument payable to bearer is transferred by delivery or when a negotiable instrument payable to order is transferred by a valid indorsement followed by delivery, the transfer is known as *negotiation* and the transferee is known as a *holder* of the instrument. UCC 3–202. The holder will qualify as a *holder in due course* if, in addition, he takes the instrument for value, in good faith, and without notice that it is overdue or has been dishonored or of any defense against or claim to it. UCC 3–302(1). Thus in order to be a holder in due course, he must show: first, that the instrument is negotiable; second, that he took by negotiation, as a holder; and third, that he took in due course. If he can do all this, then he "takes the instrument free from   .   .   . all defenses of any party to the instrument with whom the holder has not dealt," with the exception of certain rare defenses known as *real* defenses, such as incapacity, duress, and some types of fraud. UCC 3–305. He takes free of all other defenses, known as *personal* defenses, including such common matters as want of consideration, failure of condition, breach of warranty in the sale of goods, and most cases of fraud. See UCC 3–306.

NOTE

New Phase. The case that follows, Mutual Finance Co. v. Martin, was decided under the NIL. The Code does not depart from the rules of this law in any respect material here. The decision proved to be a seminal one; together with the Arkansas and California cases that the court cited, it opened a new chapter in the law on the "holder in due course" problem.

MUTUAL FINANCE CO. v. MARTIN

Supreme Court of Florida, Division B., 1953.
63 So.2d 649, 44 A.L.R.2d 1.

Action by finance company on note. The Circuit Court for Hillsborough County, I. C. Spoto, J., entered judgment for maker, and company appealed.

Judgment affirmed.

DREW, JUSTICE. On July 5, 1949, at Homeland, Florida, one W. A. Highsmith, an appliance dealer from Tampa, Florida, sold a Tyler Deep Freezer and a meat saw to F. J. Martin, doing business at Homeland, Florida, as Martin's Grocery (appellee here, defendant below, and to whom we shall hereafter refer as Martin). On the same day the parties entered into a conditional sale agreement and Martin executed a promissory note attached to said conditional sale agreement by perforations, said note being in the principal sum of $1,405.68, payable monthly. The note was for the balance due on the equipment. On the following day the conditional sale agreement and promissory note were assigned and endorsed, respectively, by Highsmith to Mutual Finance Company (appellant here, plaintiff below and hereafter called the finance company) for the sum of $1,255.

On February 10, 1950, no part of the promissory note above referred to having been paid, the finance company filed its complaint in the lower court seeking a judgment against Martin for the amount thereof, interest, attorneys' fees and costs. Martin answered alleging, among other things, that the finance company was not the holder in due course of the note and that because the deep freezer was not as represented and was wholly valueless for the purposes it was sold to Martin, there was a failure of consideration in the original transaction, which resulted in the execution of the note.

As a result of two pre-trial conferences and the highly commendable efforts and co-operation of the attorneys representing the respective parties in simplifying the issues, the following facts were agreed to and are incorporated in the record:

1.   That the note sued on is a negotiable instrument under the laws of Florida.

2.   (a) That the promissory note was executed to secure the balance due on the freezer and saw.

(b) That the price of the freezer was $1,495, the saw $390, carrying charges $150.68 and that Martin paid $625 in cash at time of closing, leaving a balance due of $1,405.68.

(c) That the note and conditional sale agreement were executed concurrently and as a part of the same transaction.

3.   The finance company admits that it prepared and furnished to W. A. Highsmith the printed forms for the conditional sale agreement and promissory note described in the pleadings herein; that said printed forms designate the finance company as the specific assignee of said conditional sale contract and note, and shows its name in bold type at the top and throughout the body of said contract and note; that the finance company's office is designated as a place of payment of said contract and note; that on the day before said transaction took place, the finance company investigated Martin's credit standing, approved the terms of, and agreed to purchase the contract and note involved herein in the event the transaction between Martin and W. A. Highsmith was consummated; that by said printed assignments the finance company took said contract and note contemporaneously by purchasing the same from W. A. Highsmith the day following the execution thereof.

4.   That the finance company paid Highsmith $1,255 for the note and conditional sale agreement by delivery to him $1,129.50 cash and crediting his (Highsmith's) reserve account with the finance company the balance of $125.50, said sum to be paid Highsmith upon the completion of the payments by Martin.

5.   That the finance company, to the extent set forth herein, provided financing for the said W. A. Highsmith in his operation as a dealer on a "Floor Plan" basis for a period commencing June 14, 1946 and terminating January 24, 1950.   The finance company received from the said W. A. Highsmith a total of 18 "Floor Plan" notes secured by mortgages on the various articles held for resale by the said W. A. Highsmith, 8 of which loans were made in 1946, 4 of which were made in 1947, 4 of which were made in 1948, one of which was made in 1949 and the last of which was made January 24, 1950.

6.   Subject to the specific understanding that it is not intimated or suggested that the finance company had any actual knowledge or information concerning any fraudulent representations or failure of consideration, the finance company admitted that prior to the pur-

chase of said personalty and on or about July 1, 1949, Martin was approached by one Luther Keen, who represented himself to be the lawful agent of said Highsmith; that said Luther Keen then and there represented to Martin that said Highsmith desired to sell to Martin a new model Tyler Deep Freezer, and that said Highsmith owned stock in the finance company, which said company would finance said sale.

That thereafter on or about July 4, 1949, and before the purchase of said personalty, said Highsmith personally approached Martin and represented to him that he was an authorized Tyler Deep Freezer dealer, that said Tyler Deep Freezer so offered by him for sale to Martin was the very latest and best model, that it was suitable for the keeping of ice cream on display in its upper exposed portion, and that it was efficient for its intended purpose of keeping all frozen foods and selling them on display.

That all of said representations so made to Martin by said Luther Keen and said Highsmith were false, were known by them to be false, were acted upon and relied upon by Martin in and about the purchase of said personalty, to his detriment, and that Martin would not have purchased said personalty but for said false representations.

That said Tyler Deep Freezer was and is wholly unfit for the purpose for which it was intended and represented, that said Freezer was and is in truth and in fact an old, inefficient, completely outmoded model; that it has never maintained the necessary temperature required by its own specifications for its proper and efficient use; that Martin suffered losses of large quantities of ice cream and other foods; and by reason whereof Martin suffered a total failure of consideration for his purchase of said Freezer.

That thereafter by reason of said fraud and of said failure of consideration, and after many unsuccessful attempts by said Highsmith to make said Freezer work, and after the finance company undertook to make said Freezer work, and failed in performing said undertaking that Martin on or about January 15, 1950, gave final notice of his rescission of said conditional sale agreement, and ceased trying to use said Freezer; and that Martin therefore owes no money to the finance company.

7.   That in December of 1949 the finance company, in order to prevent rescission of said conditional sale agreement, undertook to remedy the defects of said deep freezer and Martin agreed, in consideration thereof, to pay the amount of two installments each month until the payments became current; that the finance company failed to remedy said defects and because thereof Martin ceased using said deep freezer, rescinded said conditional sale agreement but the finance company refused to take said freezer back.

8.   That the deep freezer was of no value to Martin.

9.   That the finance company relies upon its contention that it is a bona fide holder of the note, in due course, in that said note is not subject to the defense of fraud and failure of consideration.

After the above facts had been agreed to by the parties, the lower court entered its order finding that no genuine issue of any material fact remained in the case and entered a summary final judgment finding that, and we quote verbatim, "under the admitted facts and the law the plaintiff Mutual Finance Company, a corporation, is not a holder of the note in due course, and is therefore subject to the defense of fraud and failure of consideration and allowing credit for the purchase price of the Tyler Deep Freezer, that there is no balance due on the note." It is from this final judgment that this appeal is prosecuted.

The Uniform Negotiable Instruments Act was the result of many years of work on the part of business men, banks, bar associations, jurists, and the citizens in general. The object sought was to produce uniformity in the Country, so far as possible, in the law relating to the subject. The Act, as finally agreed upon, was finished in 1896 and, only a few months later, in the Spring of 1897, it became part of the Statute Law of Florida. It is now in force in all of the States and Territories of the United States and the District of Columbia. See 7 Am.Jur. 801. There have been few changes in the Act since its adoption more than fifty years ago. It is interesting to note that the Sections of the Act primarily involved here are viz.:

Section 674.59, F.S.A., which reads:

"A holder in due course holds the instrument free from any defect of title of prior parties, and free from defenses available to prior parties among themselves, and may enforce payment of the instrument for the full amount thereof against all parties liable thereon."

Section 674.54, F.S.A., which reads:

"A holder in due course is a holder who has taken the instrument under the following conditions:

"(1) That it is complete and regular upon its face;

"(2) That he became the holder of it before it was overdue, and without notice that it had been previously dishonored, if such was the fact;

"(3) That he took it in good faith and for value;

"(4) That at the time it was negotiated to him he had no notice of any infirmity in the instrument or defect in the title of the person negotiating it."

Section 674.58, F.S.A., which reads:

"To constitute notice of an infirmity in the instrument or defect in the title of the person negotiating the same, the person to whom it is negotiated must have had actual knowledge of the infirmity or defect, or knowledge of such facts that his action in taking the instrument amounted to bad faith."

have never been amended in any respect since the original Act, Chapter 4524, Acts of 1897, was adopted.[a]

The question presented on this appeal is whether, under the admitted facts as stated above, the finance company was a bona fide holder in due course of Martin's note under the provisions of the Negotiable Instruments Law above quoted, and, therefore, not subject to personal defenses interposed by Martin.

This proposition has not heretofore been answered by this Court. An examination of the authorities reveals a sharp conflict in the decisions. In some States the rule is that in a suit on a note executed concurrently with and as a part of the conditional sale agreement, retain title contract or similar instrument, personal defenses, such as fraud or failure of consideration may be interposed. . . .

On the other hand, many respectable authorities take an entirely different viewpoint. They hold that under such circumstances personal defenses are not available to the maker of the note. . . .

So far as negotiability is concerned, we see no reason why the concurrent execution of a retain title contract, conditional sale agreement, or similar instrument, along with a promissory note for the balance of the purchase price of personal property, should enter into the picture, or in any way affect any of the characteristics of the note which give it commercial value. We have so held in Voges v. Ward, 98 Fla. 304, 123 So. 785; Fowler v. Industrial Acceptance Corp., 101 Fla. 259, 134 So. 60; Robertson v. Northern Motor Securities Co., 105 Fla. 644, 142 So. 226. Nor do we see that it makes any difference whether the note is executed simultaneously on a separate piece of paper or is attached to the conditional sale agreement or retain title contract by perforations.

We have carefully examined the many cases dealing with this matter in the light of modern conditions and we are not in accord with either of the rules which we have previously mentioned. We think, *so far as the admitted facts in this case are concerned,* that the better rule is that approved in Commercial Credit Co. v. Childs, 199 Ark. 1073, 137 S.W.2d 260–261, 128 A.L.R. 726, wherein the Arkansas Court said:

" . . . The note and contract are attached and constitute one instrument covering an agreement of the sale and purchase of the automobile in question. . . . The note, contract and assignment were all executed and signed the same day. The instrument was pre-

---

a. The three sections quoted are sections 57, 52, and 56, respectively, of the Negotiable Instruments Law. Corresponding provisions of the Code are found at UCC 3–305, 3–302, and 3–304; cf. UCC 1–201(25).

pared and delivered to the Arkansas Motors, Inc., by appellant to be used by it in the sale and purchase of cars. Appellant financed the deal.

"We think appellant was so closely connected with the entire transaction or with the deal that it can not be heard to say that it, *in good faith,* was an innocent purchaser of the instrument for value before maturity. . . . Rather than being a purchaser of the instrument after its execution it was to all intents and purposes a party to the agreement and instrument from the beginning. . . ." (Emphasis supplied.)

For an interesting analysis and discussion of the above decision see 53 Harvard Law Review, 1200. See also Commercial Credit Corp. v. Orange County Machine Works, 34 Cal.2d 766, 214 P.2d 819, 822, where the Supreme Court of California said:

"When a finance company actively participates in a transaction of this type from its inception, counseling and aiding the future vendor-payee, it cannot be regarded as a holder in due course of the note given in the transaction and the defense of failure of consideration may properly be maintained. Machine Works never obtained the press for which it bargained and, as against Commercial, there is no more obligation upon it to pay the note than there is to pay the installments specified in the contract."

To paraphrase the last sentence of the above quotation to fit the instant case, "Martin never obtained the deep freezer he bargained for, and, as against the finance company there is no more obligation upon him to pay the note than there is to pay the installments specified in the conditional bill of sale."

We therefore hold that *under the facts shown in this record* the finance company had such notice of the note's infirmity as is contemplated under Section 674.54(4), F.S.A., and that the defenses interposed by Martin were proper and lawful defenses to the action.

The argument has been advanced by appellant that this cause should be reversed and that this Court should hold the finance company to be a holder in due course of the note and that personal defenses are unavailable against it. Appellant says that unless this is done it "will destroy the long established precedent of the State of Florida and thereby seriously affect 'a certain mode of transacting business adopted throughout the State in reliance thereon.' " It may be that our holding here will require some changes in business methods and will impose a greater burden on the finance companies. We think the buyer—Mr. & Mrs. General Public—should have some protection somewhere along the line. We believe the finance company is better able to bear the risk of the dealer's insolvency than the buyer and in a far better position to protect his interests against unscrupulous and insolvent dealers. Even in this case the record shows that the finance company retained from the purchase price of the note and conditional sale agreement the sum of $125 "to be paid to Highsmith upon the completion of the payments by Martin." Obviously it was retained to protect the finance company against loss on the note.

If this opinion imposes great burdens on finance companies it is a potent argument in favor of a rule which will afford protection to the general buying public against unscrupulous dealers in personal property. See Buffalo Industrial Bank v. DeMarzio, 162 Misc. 742, 296 N.Y.S. 783; Industrial Loan & Trust Co. v. Bell, 300 Ill.App. 502, 21 N.E.2d 638; Taylor v. Atlas Security Co., 213 Mo.App. 282, 249 S.W. 746; United States v. Hansett, D.C., 30 F.Supp. 455.

For the reasons herein stated the judgment of the lower court is Affirmed.

NOTES

(1) *Question.* What possible interest might Highsmith have had in the resolution of this controversy?

(2) *A Disclosure Order.* The Federal Trade Commission took proceedings against a firm selling and installing aluminum siding, and found it guilty of unfair and deceptive practices, including "bait and switch" advertising. The Commission ordered the firm to cease and desist from various practices, including this:

> Failing to disclose orally prior to the time of sale, and in writing on any conditional sale contract, promissory note or other instrument of indebtedness executed by a purchaser, and with such conspicuousness and clarity as is likely to be read and observed by such purchaser, that:

> Any such instrument, at the firm's option and without notice to the purchaser, may be discounted, negotiated or assigned to a finance company or other third party to whom the purchaser will thereafter be indebted and against whom the purchaser's claims or defenses may not be available.

On a petition for review by the firm, the court approved the order, saying that it was "peculiarly justifiable here because of the nature and prevalence of All-State's deceptions." All-State Industries of North Carolina, Inc. v. F.T.C., 423 F.2d 423 (4th Cir. 1970), cert. denied, 400 U.S. 828 (1970).

Compare the sanction imposed on All-State with that imposed (indirectly) on Highsmith, in Mutual Finance Co. v. Martin. Was it a less severe sanction for a more serious delinquency?

(3) *A Proposed Statute.* One of the provisions of the National Consumer Act (p. 357 supra) is billed as destroying "once and for all the doctrine of 'holder in due course.' " [a] Part of the provision is as follows: "No merchant shall take or otherwise arrange for the consumer to sign an

---

a. Section 2.405, Comment 2. Of course the provision does not accomplish this, for (among other things) the Act excludes transactions in which the amount financed exceeds $25,000. Section 1.202(4).

References to the Act in this note are to the "First Final Draft," of 1970.

instrument payable 'to order' or 'to bearer' as evidence of the credit obligation of the consumer in a consumer credit transaction." [b]

As applied to the main case, it would have been violated by Highsmith, entailing a penal liability to Martin of at least $300, and other consequences. The definition of "consumer" in the Act would embrace Martin. The definition of "merchant" embraces lenders as well as sellers. Hence the provision would also have been violated by Martin's bank, if it had made a loan to him for the purchase of the equipment, and had taken his promissory note, in negotiable form, for the indebtedness. The provision might also be violated in an ordinary sale by a retailer, on an installment payment plan, if he takes a check in part payment. Might these effects help to explain why the Act has nowhere been adopted?

(4) *Variant Local Rules.* In a number of states there is now a rule supporting a buyer of consumer goods (and perhaps a buyer of services as well) when he seeks to make good a defense, against a financing institution relying on a waiver clause or negotiable note. Some such rules are statutory, often embodied in legislation called "retail installment sales acts." [c] An example of a more particularized statute is set out at p. 985 infra. The rules vary in scope, and in a single jurisdiction there may be a variety of rules applicable to different sorts of transaction. Some are elaborated in considerable detail; others are fairly indistinct. The enactment of the Code did not displace statutes regulating retail installment sales. A special note in Article 9 (following UCC 9–102) declares that "it does not prescribe regulations and controls which may be necessary to curb abuses arising . . . in the financing of consumer purchases on credit. Accordingly there is no intention to repeal existing regulatory acts [in that field]. See Section 9–203(2) and the Note thereto."

For the rule applicable to a particular transaction, therefore, it is often necessary to make a careful examination of local statutes and cases.

(5) *Fact Estoppels.* "Retail installment sales acts sometimes protect innocent assignees against particular hazards. In many States, for example, the buyer's written acknowledgement of delivery of a completed copy of the contract is conclusive or presumptive evidence in an action by or against an assignee that a requirement of such delivery has been met." Statutory Note, Restatement Second, Chapter 7.

Apart from statutory requirements, a buyer's defense may rest on an assertion that something did not occur; the buyer of a car, for instance, may resist a suit for the price on the ground that it was not delivered to him. If the contract contains a recital, over his signature, that the car was delivered, is he estopped to deny delivery, in a suit by a good faith assignee of the contract for value? Even if the applicable law would override a waiver of defenses by the buyer, it might conceivably enforce an estoppel against him. However, claims based on this ground have not been well received. See Parker v. Funk, 185 Cal. 347, 197 P. 83 (1921).

---

b. Section 2.405(1).

c. For a compilation of retail installment sales acts, see Statutory Note in

Restatement Second, Tentative Draft No. 3, at 155 (1967).

POLICY CONSIDERATIONS

Are there distinctive considerations of policy that underlie the rule in Mutual Finance Co. v. Martin, and the cognate rules mentioned above? To some extent these rules reflect only concern about the more general problems of adhesion contracts: an absence of choice, an absence of intelligent assent, and inequality of bargaining power. However, there have been attempts to show that the "holder in due course problem" is a singular one, deserving of specialized rules. The following considerations figure in the argument.

(1) Financing institutions are in a superior position, by comparison with ordinary consumers, to evaluate a merchant's responsibility. The prospect of disappointment in dealing with a merchant is partly a function of his usual business practices, his reputation for fair dealing, and the risk of his becoming insolvent. On all these matters a bank or finance company supplying him with funds is equipped to make judgments more accurately than his ordinary customers.

(2) A merchant's customers are poorly situated to exercise discipline against him for substandard business practices, whereas corrective measures may readily be forced on him by a financer if his retail operations give rise to an undue number of complaints. Hence a rule imposing on financers the risk of customer disappointment will effectively engage them in the function of "policing" against irresponsible merchandising.

(3) Pooling of information is an effective means of reducing substandard performance by merchants. Financing institutions are capable of organizing exchanges of information, such that a merchant who proves unworthy of trust will be promptly foreclosed from the credit market. By contrast, information exchanges among consumers are feebly organized, so that a merchant may maintain a certain reputation with the public even though many of his customers suffer from his delinquencies. Not only so, but he may also be able to escape their wrath by a change of business name, or of location. Financing institutions can more easily penetrate disguises. Furthermore, when such an institution undertakes collections for a merchant, the wrath of a disappointed customer is likely to be deflected from the merchant to his assignee.[a] Hence, the argument runs, it is appropriate to align the assignee with the customer as a party aggrieved by the merchant's delinquency. That is the effect when the assignee is deprived of holder-in-due-course status, and deprived of the benefit of a waiver of defense clause.

None of these arguments need be taken at face value, of course. What countervailing considerations are there? It has been forcefully

a. See Leff, Injury, Ignorance and Spite—The Dynamics of Coercive Collection, 80 Yale L.J. 1, 35 (1970).

argued that, if merchants cannot give the assurances to financing institutions described as holder-in-due-course status, they will find
credit more expensive, or inaccessible, and that the cost to merchants
must be reflected in retail prices.   How do you appraise this argument?   If a rule against cutting off defenses has any such consequence, would you expect it to affect only credit prices, or cash prices
as well?   Suppose that the sale in Mutual Finance Company v. Martin had been for cash.   If the goods were worthless, and Martin had
paid Highsmith in full, what would his remedy have been?   Presumably any remedy you suggest would have been available to Martin on
the facts as they were.   Do you conclude that a disappointed cash
buyer never has a better prospect of relief than one who pays by a
negotiable note, and often has a worse one?   Does this state of affairs make any sense?   You should reconsider these questions after
reading further in this section.

If there is to be a rule against cutting off defenses, to what
transactions should it apply?   To a doctor's purchase of a car for
professional use?   To the purchase of a yacht for $50,000, with 10%
down?   The Commissioners on Uniform State Laws would implement
a waiver clause in each of these contracts.   (For the doctor's case,
the rule is stated in UCC 9–206(1).   For the yachtsman's case, the
rule is stated in UCCC 2.403, 2.404.[b])   Are the considerations the
same in these two cases?   How do they compare with the contract in
Mutual Finance Company v. Martin?

NOTES

(1) *Gaps in the Fictional Fence.*   The following excerpt is from Unico
v. Owen, 50 N.J. 101, 232 A.2d 405 (1967).   The contract sued on in this
case was for a sale of record albums, as described in the Note, Waiving
Defenses p. 968 supra, and contained the waiver clause quoted there.   Unico,
the assignee of the contract, sued Owen, the buyer, and lost in the trial
court.   On successive appeals, the judgment was twice affirmed.   The
Supreme Court of New Jersey wrote an elaborate opinion, referring to
Henningsen v. Bloomfield Motors (p. 335 supra) and Williams v. Walker-
Thomas Furniture Co. (p. 373 supra), among other cases.   It summarized
some of them as follows:

"The courts have recognized that the basic problem in consumer goods
sales and financing is that of balancing the interest of the commercial community in unrestricted negotiability of commercial paper against the interest of installment buyers of such goods in the preservation of their
normal remedy of withholding payment when, as in this case, the seller
fails to deliver as agreed, and thus the consideration for his obligation
fails.   Many courts have solved the problem by denying to the holder of

---

b. More accurately, the UCC states the
rule for the yachtsman's case.   The
Uniform Consumer Credit Code establishes a different rule for buyers of
consumer goods in the sections cited;
but its provisions do not apply to a

transaction in which a credit of more
than $25,000 is extended.

UCCC 2.404, it should be noted, offers a
choice to the several legislatures about
the terms of the "different rule."

the paper the status of holder in due course where the financer maintains a close relationship with the dealer whose paper he buys; where the financer is closely connected with the dealer's business operations or with the particular credit transaction; or where the financer furnishes the form of sale contract and note for use by the dealer, the buyer signs the contract and note concurrently, and the dealer endorses the note and assigns the contract immediately thereafter or within the period prescribed by the financer. [Citations omitted.]   Other courts have said that when the financer supplies or prescribes or approves the form of sales contract, or conditional sale agreement, or chattel mortgage as well as the installment payment note (particularly if it has the financer's name printed on the face or in the endorsement), and all the documents are executed by the buyer at one time and the contract assigned and note endorsed to the financer and delivered to the financer together (whether or not attached or part of a single instrument), the holder takes subject to the rights and obligations of the seller.   The transaction is looked upon as a species of tripartite proceeding, and the tenor of the cases is that the financer should not be permitted 'to isolate itself behind the fictional fence' of the Negotiable Instruments Law, and thereby achieve an unfair advantage over the buyer.   [Citations omitted.]"

In this case the New Jersey court also considered the effect of a negotiable note given by Mr. Owen, on which Unico asserted rights as a holder in due course.[c] In General Investment Corp. v. Angelini, 58 N.J. 396, 278 A.2d 193 (1971), the court returned to the question of negotiability, this time in relation to a home improvement contract. It gave effect to failure of consideration as a defense, and rejected the finance company's contention that it had taken the note without notice of the defense, and in good faith. The court spoke of "unique policy considerations attendant upon consumer home repair transactions."

After first making provision against negotiability in home-repair contracts, the New Jersey legislature acted to negate holder-in-due-course status in a broad range of installment sale contracts, and to permit recoveries by injured buyers from assignees of such contracts of payments made on the contracts—excepting from the latter provision, however, down payments on new car purchases. N.J. Laws 1971, Ch. 399.

(2) *Administrative Action.* In the absence of legislative action, are the problems discussed in the foregoing materials more amenable to solution by an administrative agency than by a court? Given the magnitude of

---

c. On this point see also Jones v. Approved Bancredit Corp., 256 A.2d 739 (Del.1969), a case said to be "especially analogous" to Unico v. Owen, and Rosenthal, Negotiability—Who Needs It?, 71 Colum.L.Rev. 375, 378–80 (1971). The Unico case was successfully defended for the Owens by private counsel, who accepted a "small fee" for representing them in the trial court.   Unico appealed to an intermediate court, and then to the state supreme court. (What would justify this expense to a finance company? Was it worth it?)   The Owens could not pay for appellate representation, but their lawyers espoused their cause through both appeals, plus supplementary briefing and argument requested by the supreme court. "We, of course, did not realize what we were getting into; however, once we were involved we had no choice but to proceed to the ultimate conclusion." During the proceedings Mr. Owen died, leaving his family without means, and they moved back to their former home in another state. The foregoing incidents are as reported in a letter to the editors from counsel for the Owens.

the interests involved, is it likely that an administrative solution will be durable? If such an agency is charged with controlling deceptive practices by merchants, is its mandate broad enough to deal adequately with waiver of defense clauses? The Federal Trade Commission has held hearings on a proposed rule about buyers' defenses in consumer installment sales.

THE CODE

In Section 9–206, part of which is set out below, the Code contains a three-part rule relating to the problems in the foregoing cases. First, the section broadly validates waiver of defense clauses, in favor of certain assignees. Second, the section places a transferee of a negotiable instrument on at least as strong a footing as an assignee relying on a waiver of defense clause. (Note that the section does not require that the transferee be a holder, taking the instrument by negotiation.[d]) Third, the section begins with a curious qualification referring to non-Code law. This phrase is explained in Comment 2 as follows: "This Article takes no position on the controversial question whether a buyer of consumer goods may effectively waive defenses by contractual clause or by execution of a negotiable note." Early drafts of the Code show that this formula was achieved only after intense debate.

UCC 9–206. *Agreement Not to Assert Defenses Against Assignee; . . .*

(1) Subject to any statute or decision which establishes a different rule for buyers or lessees of consumer goods, an agreement by a buyer or lessee that he will not assert against an assignee any claim or defense which he may have against the seller or lessor is enforceable by an assignee who takes his assignment for value, in good faith and without notice of a claim or defense, except as to defenses of a type which may be asserted against a holder in due course of a negotiable instrument under the Article on Commercial Paper (Article 3).[e] A buyer who as part of one transaction signs both a negotiable instrument and a security agreement makes such an agreement.

NOTES

(1) *Question.* In Mutual Finance Co. v. Martin, was the defendant a buyer of "consumer goods"? Does the decision there "establish a rule for buyers of consumer goods" that is different from the rule for buyers of commercial goods, as laid down in the Code? What does the court signify by its reference to "Mr. & Mrs. General Public"?

(2) *Unconscionability.* A contract for the sale of commercial equipment provides that if the seller assigns his right to payment the buyer will assert no defense against the assignee that he might otherwise make against

---

d. But see Cheshire Commercial Corp. v. Messier, 6 Conn.Cir. 542, 278 A.2d 413 (1971).

e. As to the exceptional "real" defenses, see the Note on Waiving Defenses and Holding in Due Course, p. 968 supra.

the seller. The buyer fails to pay the price and the seller sues, not having made an assignment. The buyer's defense is that the waiver of defense clause is unconscionable, under UCC 2–302, so that the court should deny enforcement of the contract. Is this defense plausible? If the seller had made an assignment, would it be a plausible defense against the assignee? Would it be more so if the buyer were to assert also that the equipment was worthless, and that he had a defense based on breach of warranty?

Answers favorable to the buyer are suggested in United States Leasing Corp. v. Franklin Plaza Apartments, Inc., 8 UCC Rep. 1026 (N.Y.Civ.Ct. 1971).[f] The court said: "the agreement is unconscionable if the user must pay for something he can't use without the right to assert a meritorious defense or set-off." The case concerned a lease of equipment, rather than a sale. Although UCC 2–302 does not purport to apply to genuine leases, the court found support for its ruling there. Would the court have been better advised *not* to refer to the Code? Does UCC 9–206 have any bearing on these questions? As to the Code's neutrality on consumer credit issues, see Skilton and Helstad, Protection of the Installment Buyer of Goods under the UCC, 65 Mich.L.Rev. 1465 (1967).

WAIVER OF DEFENSE CLAUSES

Working with pre-Code materials, several courts have reached the position that a waiver of defense clause is ineffective, at least in a conditional sale contract. A threefold argument along these lines appears in a number of cases: (1) a statute or local policy is found to intend protection for buyers, on conditional sale, against installment sellers; (2) reference is made to the usual statute or rule relating to defenses against an assignee; and (3) the NIL is cited, with the assertion that it provides the only means for imparting negotiability to an instrument, and the suggestion that trying to give a contract this quality by a waiver clause is illicit.[g]

In cases using this triad of reasons, evidently no great confidence is put in any of them. In truth, all of the statutes implicated in these arguments are rather old ones, and do not speak directly to the problem. The policy of the NIL, if accurately stated here, has of course been altered by UCC 9–206(1).

When a buyer has been induced to make a purchase by fraud, and an assignee relies on a waiver of defense clause to overcome that defense, the buyer should contend that the fraud vitiates the entire contract, *including* the waiver clause. In other words, such clauses are most dependable in relation to defenses, such as breach of warranty, that require the defendant to affirm the existence of the contract. See Note, 42 Tex.L.Rev. 1072 (1964).

---

f. Cf. Unico v. Owen, 50 N.J. 101, 232 A.2d 405 (1967).

g. Representative cases are Quality Finance Co. v. Hurley, 337 Mass. 150, 148 N.E.2d 385 (1958); Unico v. Owen, supra. See also Fairfield Credit Corporation v. Donnelly, 158 Conn. 543, 264 A.2d 547 (1969), referring to the Code and to a mass of consumer-protection legislation.

NOTES

(1) *Good Faith and Notice.* There is general consensus that an assignee does not take free of defenses unless he takes his assignment for value, in good faith, and without notice of a claim or defense by the obligor. For assignees of commercial contracts, at least, the elements of "good faith" and "notice" are critical. Consult the definitions in UCC 1–201(19) and (27). Are they generally helpful to assignees? Are they consistent with the references to good faith and notice in Mutual Finance Co. v. Martin? Many cases appear to impute notice, or want of good faith, to a finance company because of a pattern of involvement between it and its assignor, without proof relating to the individual transaction in question. What commercial values are sacrificed by such decisions? The Connecticut Home Solicitation Sales Act, set out below, makes the elements of good faith and lack of notice inconsequential in transactions that it governs. Is the technique of the statute preferable to that of the courts as described above? On what ground?

(2) *The Case of the High-Pressure Seller.* Mr. and Mrs. Ingel contracted for the installation of aluminum siding on their home by Allied Aluminum Associates, Inc., and signed a negotiable note for the price. Allied negotiated the note to the Universal C.I.T. Corporation, and upon default by the Ingels C.I.T. sued them on the note. As evidence that the plaintiff was not a holder in due course, the defendants offered a credit report that C.I.T. had received on Allied some three months before the note was negotiated. Portions of the report were as follows: "The subject firm is engaged in the sale of storm windows [and other products]. They are reported to employ high pressure sales methods for the most part . . . . They have been criticized for their advertising methods, and have been accused of using bait advertising, and using false and misleading statements. The Boston Better Business Bureau has had numerous complaints regarding their advertising methods, and have reported same to the Attorney General. FHA . . . have warned the firm to stop their practice." The trial court gave judgment for the plaintiff, refusing to receive the credit report in evidence, and the Ingels appealed. *Held:* Affirmed. Nothing in the report would give C.I.T. "reason to know" of any fraud in the Ingels contract, the court ruled, citing UCC 1–201(25) and 3–302(1). Universal C.I.T. Corp. v. Ingel, 347 Mass. 119, 196 N.E.2d 847 (1964). [By a subsequent enactment in Massachusetts, the taking of a negotiable note in such a transaction has been prohibited.]

(3) *Financing Home Improvements.* "Home improvement dealers operate in one or more of the following ways: the dealer solicits door-to-door and completes the entire transaction in the buyer's home; the dealer calls or receives calls from potential customers and then visits the home where the contract is signed; the dealer visits the home prior to the buyer's agreement to the contract, but the contract is completed at the seller's office; the entire transaction is completed at the seller's place of business. The first method and probably the second are within the definition of home solicitation in the Connecticut Act.

"After the contract is signed the seller often goes to a distributor and purchases the goods or materials he needs to complete the contract.

The dealer may either pay the distributor on a job-by-job basis or arrange for a line of credit. If the dealer needs workmen, he may be able to hire some at the distributor's office; otherwise he completes the work himself or with his own workmen.

"Interlacing the process of solicitation, sale, obtaining materials, and doing the work is the question of financing. In most situations the buyer is either unwilling or unable to pay cash and some form of credit must be arranged. The seller, however, may need cash immediately for personal reasons or in order to get the materials; or he may be reluctant to carry the administrative burdens of long-term installment contracts. Furthermore, dealers of any size may make a greater profit from immediate reinvestment of proceeds in their business than they do from interest on outstanding debt. Since both parties desire to make a contract, the financing difficulties are worked out by resorting to a third party for assistance, and financial institutions play this role.

"The need for financial assistance has resulted in several different financing arrangements involving the financer, the dealer, and the buyer. The major distinction is between "indirect" and "direct" loans. A direct loan involves only the financial institution and the buyer; the buyer goes to the financing agency and takes out a loan in his own name. An indirect loan, on the other hand, involves in the first instance only the buyer and the seller. The buyer signs a note along with the sales contract promising to pay the price in installments. The seller then sells the note to the financing agency, which collects the installments from the buyer as they fall due. The financer has effectively made a loan to the buyer, paying the proceeds directly to the seller; the loan is then repaid in installments.

"In making indirect loans, banks often do business only with a certain list of dealers, and they supply these dealers with a package of forms—blank note forms, completion certificates, and traditional credit applications—to be used in each credit sale. When the contract is signed, the buyer normally signs a note providing for installment payments and completes a credit application. The dealer forwards the credit application to the bank, which then decides whether to grant its approval to the indirect loan. Usually approval is granted as a matter of course to dealers who work regularly with the bank. When the work is completed, the buyer executes a completion certificate. The dealer then presents the completion certificate to the bank and negotiates the note. Often the entire transaction is completed with one trip to the bank, as the credit application, note, and completion certificate may all be signed by the buyer at the same time." Note, A Case Study of the Impact of Consumer Legislation: The Elimination of Negotiability and the Cooling-Off Period, 78 Yale L.J. 618, 624–28 (1969).[h]

h. Footnotes omitted. Reprinted by permission of The Yale Law Journal Company and Fred B. Rothman & Company from The Yale Law Journal, Vol. 78, pp. 624–628.

HOME SOLICITATION SALES ACT

Conn.Gen.Stats. §§ 42–135 et seq. (1968 Supp.)
[excerpt]

[The Act defines "home solicitation sale" so as to include a sale of goods or services solicited and arranged at the buyer's home, in which any part of the purchase price is payable in installments.]

§ 42–136.　Note or evidence of indebtedness given by buyer

(a) Any note or other evidence of indebtedness given by a buyer in respect of a home solicitation sale shall be dated not earlier than the date of the agreement or offer to purchase. Any transfer of a note or other evidence of indebtedness bearing the statement required by subsection (b) of this section shall be deemed an assignment only and any right, title or interest which the transferee may acquire thereby shall be subject to all claims and defenses of the buyer against the seller arising under the provisions of this chapter.

(b) Each note or other evidence of indebtedness given by a buyer in respect of a home solicitation sale shall bear on its face a conspicuous statement as follows: THIS INSTRUMENT IS BASED UPON A HOME SOLICITATION SALE, WHICH SALE IS SUBJECT TO THE PROVISIONS OF THE HOME SOLICITATION SALES ACT. THIS INSTRUMENT IS NOT NEGOTIABLE.

(c) Compliance with the requirements of this section shall be a condition precedent to any right of action by the seller or any transferee of an instrument bearing the statement required under subsection (b) of this section against the buyer upon such instrument and shall be pleaded and proved by any person who may institute action or suit against a buyer in respect thereof.

(d) A promissory note payable to order or bearer and otherwise negotiable in form issued in violation of this section may be enforced as a negotiable instrument by a holder in due course according to its terms.

NOTES

(1) *Negotiability Preserved.* The last clause of this section has an ominous sound for consumers; but there is less in it than meets the eye, probably. Any financing institution having regular commercial relations with a firm engaged in home solicitation selling could hardly fail to be aware of that fact, and would almost certainly be charged with notice that its customers' notes *should* bear the legend, "This instrument is not negotiable," whether they do or not. It is therefore probable that the last clause has its principal application in situations where a financer of first instance, such as a country bank, re-discounts its paper by negotiating notes in bulk to a major city bank. In that situation it is possible that the second transferee may enforce the note against its maker; but in practice the prospect seems a remote one. Contrast the National Consumer Act, § 2.405 (2).

(2) *Effects of the Statute.* The editors of the Yale Law Journal made a "case study" of the impact of this legislation, over the first year of its operation, on the home improvement business. (For an excerpt see Note 3, p. 983 supra.) Many of their findings had to be expressed tentatively because they depended largely on unverified responses of persons associated with the business. Interviews with dealers produced estimates that as many as 50 or 60 "found it virtually impossible since the Act to obtain any financing at all and have been forced out of business." Very few dealers reported that they had "shifted sales away from the home in any way." The predominant mode of accommodation to the Act by dealers was apparently to reduce the percentage of credit sales. Finance institutions supplying funds to dealers exerted a marked "squeeze," terminating many dealer relationships, and stiffening the terms of credit for others. Yet it appeared, for reasons not wholly clear, that sales volume had not been adversely affected. In part, the explanation offered was that dealers intensified their efforts to find customers who could afford to pay cash. One bank reported success with a program of increased advertising of its cash loans to homeowners. A resulting advantage was, that "since the elimination of negotiability does not change the bank's legal position on direct loans, the borrower's obligation to repay on a direct loan is not conditioned on adequate performance by the dealer."

The Connecticut act quoted above also provided for a "cooling off" period. (As to the character of such a provision, see p. 390 supra.) As first enacted, it permitted the cancellation of a home solicitation sale only up to midnight of the first business day after signing. Very little use of the cancellation right was reported. But the study concluded that the shift from indirect to direct loans, so far as it was detected, "appears to work against sharp dealing and fraud. . . . The buyer is not likely to sign a cash contract until he has gone to a financial institution and secured a loan. This gives the buyer an automatic 'cooling-off' period after the sales pitch, and it may induce him to consider alternative purchases. . . .

"The shift to direct loans, however, may have an adverse effect on low-income consumers. Such persons are frequently hesitant to enter into dealings with bankers. Also, before the Act, as part of a larger on-going business arrangement with dealers, financers were willing to purchase the notes of customers to whom individually they would either charge very high rates or refuse credit altogether. Since low-income buyers are dependent on credit merchandising to secure their small share of consumer goods, such buyers might be seriously hurt by the general switch to direct loans." Note, A Case Study of the Impact of Consumer Legislation: The Elimination of Negotiability and the Cooling-Off Period, 78 Yale L.J. 618, 654–55 (1969).

(3) *Methodology.* Some limitations on the study just described were as follows: "(1) the names of dealers solicited had to be taken from only five sources; (2) completed questionnaires were returned by less than one-third of the dealers and sales finance companies contacted. . . ." For an assessment of research of this character, see Shuchman, Empirical Studies in Commercial Law, 23 J.Leg.Ed. 181 (1970). The inquiry is characterized here as asking the wolves what has been the effect of the new anti-wolf device. Credit is given the sponsors, however, for their explicit warnings about deficiencies in the study.

SPECIOUS CASH SALES

Buyer bought a television set from Seller, paying $500, a sum which he borrowed for that purpose from First Bank on an installment loan. Now, some four months after the purchase, he has repaid $100 to the bank. The set has ceased to function, owing to a defect in its manufacture. Seller has become insolvent and gone out of business. Is Buyer liable to the bank for the $400 balance? May he recover from the bank the $100 that he has paid?

A 1971 enactment in New York (and comparable statutes in a few other states) may support Buyer on the first point. The central provision of the New York statute is as follows:

> *Consumer defenses.* A creditor, who made a consumer loan the proceeds of which were primarily used in a consumer sale, shall be subject to all of the defenses of a consumer arising from such consumer sale, provided that the creditor knowingly participated in or was directly connected with such consumer sale. The creditor's liability under this article shall not exceed the amount owing to the creditor at the time the defenses of the consumer are asserted against the creditor. Rights of the consumer under this article can only be asserted as a matter of defense to or set-off against a claim by the creditor. The creditor shall be subrogated to the rights of the consumer arising from the consumer sale and shall have recourse against the seller to the extent of any liability incurred by the creditor pursuant to this article.—N.Y.Gen.Bus.L. § 253.

Notice that the second and third sentences of this provision present obstacles to the buyer's claim against the bank. However, decision should be reserved on their meaning until the following case is read.

The New York act contains definitions of several terms used in the section quoted above. In particular, "consumer sales" is defined so as to embrace contracts to furnish certain services. It also contains elaborate provisions for determining whether or not a creditor has "knowingly participated in or [been] directly connected with" the sale. For example, if the seller is a business firm, and the creditor is under common control with it, or if either controls the other ("directly or indirectly"), the act establishes a rebuttable presumption that the necessary participation or connection existed. So also if forms used to evidence the loan were prepared by the seller, or supplied to it by the creditor.

If there is no presumption favoring the buyer, what sort of facts might he seek out to connect the lender with his purchase? One possibility is to show that he informed the lender, at the time of the loan, of his intended use of the loan proceeds. Another is to show that the merchant he dealt with is, or has been, a regular user of commercial credit supplied by the lender. Should either or both of these facts be taken to support a finding that the creditor "knowingly participated in or was directly connected with" the sale? If not, would it help to show also that the creditor was aware of numerous consumer complaints arising from the merchant's business? [a]

NOTE

Effects of the Statute. If the bank, in the problem given above, is subject to the buyer's defenses arising from the sale, does it follow that the entire unpaid balance of the loan is uncollectible? If the set can be repaired for $50, and the sale contract effectively limited the buyer's remedy to the cost of repair (see UCC 2–719), would the bank be permitted to enforce its claim in a reduced amount?

Usually, however, the buyer can refuse to pay for the set if he is willing to give it up. If the set was misrepresented to the buyer, he may rescind the contract, and in some circumstances he may revoke his acceptance of the set. If he wishes to do this, at whose disposition should he hold the set? At the seller's? Or at the bank's? See UCC 2–602, 2–608, 2–721. Might the buyer's position be damaged by tendering the set to the seller? Note the subrogation provision of the statute quoted above.

VASQUEZ v. SUPERIOR COURT OF SAN JOAQUIN COUNTY

Supreme Court of California, 1971.
4 Cal.3d 800, 484 P.2d 964.

MOSK, JUSTICE. We consider whether a group of consumers who have bought merchandise under installment contracts may maintain a class action seeking rescission of the contracts for fraudulent misrepresentation on behalf of themselves and others similarly situated, against both the seller of a product and the finance company to which the installment contracts were assigned. We conclude that such an action will lie against the seller under the principles set forth in Daar v. Yellow Cab Co. (1967) 67 Cal.2d 695, 63 Cal.Rptr. 724, 433 P.2d 732, and that the assignee of the contract is a proper party to such an action under the circumstances presented here.

The action was brought by 37 named plaintiffs on behalf of themselves as well as others who are residents of San Joaquin and

---

a. A Massachusetts statute, along the same lines, is more stringent. If the proceeds of as many as two loans made by the creditor in any calendar year have been used in transactions with the same seller, and if the creditor was "specifically recommended" by the seller to the aggrieved borrower (and in other circumstances as well), the creditor is "deemed to have participated" in the sale. Mass.Gen.L., Ch. 255, § 12F. (Supp.1970).

This statute explicitly affords defenses to a user of a credit card, arising out of the sale transaction, against the issuer of the card, in certain circumstances; whereas the New York statute does not apply to credit card transactions. Who will bear the costs imposed by the Massachusetts law on credit card issuers?

Stanislaus Counties and who purchased frozen food and freezers from Bay Area Meat Company. They each executed two retail installment sales contracts to finance the purchases, one in payment of the food, and the other for the freezer, and a binder contract. These contracts were assigned by Bay Area to three finance companies, Avco Thrift, Sterling Finance Corporation, and Beneficial Finance Company of Turlock, which were also named as defendants.[1] Defendants demurred to the complaint on the ground that it did not state a cause of action, and the demurrers were sustained without leave to amend insofar as the complaint alleged a class action for fraud but were overruled on the fraud count as to the named plaintiffs. A second cause of action, also alleged as a class action, charged violation of the Unruh Act (Civ.Code, § 1801 et seq.) in that the installment contracts failed to meet the requirements of that act. The demurrers of all defendants were overruled as to the second cause of action.

In upholding the demurrers to the class action aspect of the fraud count, the trial court made it clear that it was not concerned with the sufficiency of the particular allegations to assert a class action but, rather, that in its view a class action for fraud may not be maintained by consumers.[2]

Plaintiffs seek a writ of mandate to compel the trial court to vacate its order sustaining the demurrers to the first cause of action as a class action and to order the court to allow them to proceed to try the cause of action for fraud as a class action.

.   .   .   .

Protection of unwary consumers from being duped by unscrupulous sellers is an exigency of the utmost priority in contemporary society. According to the report of the Kerner Commission, many persons who reside in low income neighborhoods experience grievous exploitation by vendors using such devices as high pressure salesmanship, bait advertising, misrepresentation of prices, exorbitant prices and credit charges, and sale of shoddy merchandise. State laws governing relations between consumers and merchants are generally utilized only by informed, sophisticated parties, affording little practical protection to low income families. (Report of National Advisory Commission on Civil Disorders (Bantam ed. 1968) pp. 275–276; Hester, Deceptive Sales Practices and Form Contracts—Does the Con-

1. For literary convenience, defendants in the trial court who are real parties in interest will be referred to hereinafter either as defendants or as Bay Area, Avco, Sterling, or Beneficial. The reference to "plaintiffs," who are petitioners in this proceeding, will, unless otherwise stated, refer collectively to both the named plaintiffs and the unnamed class members.

2. After analyzing some California cases on the subject of class actions, the court stated in its ruling that many state decisions appear to have been unsympathetic to consumer class actions, that these cases may be outmoded and class actions may be permitted, but that appellate courts are better suited to decide this question than a trial court.

sumer Have a Private Remedy? 1968 Duke L.J. 831.) The alternatives of multiple litigation (joinder, intervention, consolidation, the test case) do not sufficiently protect the consumer's rights because these devices "presuppose 'a group of economically powerful parties who are obviously able and willing to take care of their own interests individually through individual suits or individual decisions about joinder or intervention.' " (Dolgow v. Anderson (E.D.N.Y.1968) 43 F.R.D. 472, 484.)

Frequently numerous consumers are exposed to the same dubious practice by the same seller so that proof of the prevalence of the practice as to one consumer would provide proof for all. Individual actions by each of the defrauded consumers is often impracticable because the amount of individual recovery would be insufficient to justify bringing a separate action; thus an unscrupulous seller retains the benefits of its wrongful conduct. A class action by consumers produces several salutary by-products, including a therapeutic effect upon those sellers who indulge in fraudulent practices, aid to legitimate business enterprises by curtailing illegitimate competition, and avoidance to the judicial process of the burden of multiple litigation involving identical claims. The benefit to the parties and the courts would, in many circumstances, be substantial.

. . . . .

VI

Liability of Finance Company Defendants

The final question is whether the finance company defendants to which the sales contracts were assigned are proper parties defendant in the action.[3] In the instant case, as in many situations in which consumers have been defrauded by a seller, a judgment against the seller alone would represent a Pyrrhic victory because the defrauding seller is insolvent and the victorious consumers remain liable to the finance companies, which as the assignees of the installment contracts claim that they are entitled to payment even if the seller acted fraudulently. Bay Area merely filed a demurrer and answer in the trial court and has indicated no inclination to oppose the action further. Obviously, if plaintiffs are to be made whole for the wrongs allegedly done to them, the finance company defendants must be held liable as assignees if Bay Area is culpable.

The lenders contend, however, that even if plaintiffs prove that Bay Area was guilty of fraud they are nevertheless entitled as as-

---

3. Strictly speaking, it is not necessary to decide the question at this time. The trial court has concluded, at least for the purpose of ruling on the demurrers, that the finance companies are proper parties defendant since it overruled their demurrers to the fraud cause of action insofar as the individual plaintiffs are concerned. However, the issue has been briefed extensively, the question of the finance company defendants' liability will undoubtedly arise at the trial, and we discuss the matter here in order to guide the trial court in its conduct of the action.

signees to payment under the contracts because they enjoy the privileges of a holder in due course and take free of plaintiffs' defenses against Bay Area. Although it is not entirely clear from the record, this claim apparently rests on a clause in the contracts signed by plaintiffs waiving all defenses against assignees.[4]

It seems clear under both statute and established legal principles that the finance company defendants would not be deemed holders in due course under the allegations of the complaint, even if they were holding an ordinary promissory note. The complaint alleges that Avco, Sterling and Beneficial had actual or constructive knowledge of Bay Area's fraudulent practices. Under section 3302, subdivision (1)(c), of the Commercial Code, one who takes with notice of a defense against an instrument is not a holder in due course. (See Norman v. World Wide Distributors, Inc. (1963) 202 Pa.Super. 53, 195 A.2d 115, 118.)

Moreover, it has long been settled in California that a financial institution may be denied the status of a holder in due course because of its close connection with the seller. (Commercial Credit Corp. v. Orange Co. Mach. Works (1950) 34 Cal.2d 766, 214 P.2d 819; see Morgan v. Reasor Corp. (1968) 69 Cal.2d 881, 895, 73 Cal.Rptr. 398, 447 P.2d 638.)[5] In *Commercial Credit* we held that since the assignee of a contract and note advanced money to the seller with the understanding that these instruments would be assigned to it, supplied the contract forms to the seller, and actively participated in the transaction from its inception, it could not claim holder-in-due-course status. The complaint in the present case contains allegations aimed at bringing the finance companies within these principles.[6]

Under section 9206 of the Commercial Code, a clause in a contract waiving defenses against an assignee is only effective when the assignee takes in good faith and without notice of defenses and not even then as to such defenses as may be raised against a holder in due course. The section provides, however, that it is subject to any statute which establishes a "different rule" for buyers of consumer goods.

4. The Unruh Act prohibits the execution of a note by a buyer which will when separately negotiated cut off as to third parties any right of action or defense which the buyer may have against the seller. (Civ.Code, § 1810.9.)

5. Avco claims that *Morgan* was overruled by the enactment of section 1801.4 of the Civil Code in 1969. (Stats. 1969, ch. 554, § 1.) Section 1801.4, a provision of the Unruh Act, merely states that the act does not apply to any contract for the construction and/or sale of a residence or commercial building or for the sale of real property.

6. It is alleged that Bay Area followed a regular business practice of assigning to Avco substantially all of its contracts in San Joaquin and Stanislaus Counties, of assigning all poor credit risks to Sterling, and a "substantial number" of contracts to Beneficial. Moreover, it is alleged, Bay Area was the agent of these lenders and used contract forms supplied by Avco.

We must next inquire whether a "different rule" is set forth in section 1804.2 of the Civil Code, which is a provision of the Unruh Act. The section provides, "Except as provided in Section 1812.7,[7] an assignee of the seller's rights is subject to all claims and defenses of the buyer against the seller arising out of the sale notwithstanding an agreement to the contrary, but the assignee's liability may not exceed the amount of the debt owing to the assignee at the time that the defense is asserted against the assignee. The rights of the buyer under this section can only be asserted as a matter of defense to a claim by the assignee."

The finance companies contend that under this section plaintiffs may not bring an affirmative action against them for rescission but may only assert their defense of fraud in an action by the finance companies to collect on the contracts and then only to the extent of the amount still owing. Upon analysis, however, a number of considerations militate against such a restrictive interpretation of the section as to assignees who take with notice of defenses against an instrument or who bring themselves within the rationale of *Commercial Credit*.

The purpose of the Unruh Act is to protect consumers, and it should be liberally construed to that end. (Morgan v. Reasor, supra, 69 Cal.2d 881, 889, 73 Cal.Rptr. 398, 447 P.2d 638.) If we were to adopt the concept of the finance companies it would, by virtue of section 1804.2, bestow upon them immunities and privileges against consumers unavailable to them in the ordinary commercial transaction. (Cf. Unico v. Owen (1967) 50 N.J. 101, 232 A.2d 405, 417–418.)

It is suggested by amicus curiae that section 1804.2 was intended to eliminate the possibility that by depriving assignees of any right to take free of the buyer's defenses against the seller despite an agreement to the contrary, the section might subject assignees to products liability suits which might involve personal injuries and large damage claims.[8]

---

7. Section 1812.7 of the Civil Code provides: "In case of failure by any person to comply with the provisions of this chapter, such person or any person who acquires a contract or installment account with knowledge of such noncompliance is barred from recovery of any finance charge or of any delinquency, collection, extension, deferral or refinance charge imposed in connection with such contract or installment account and the buyer shall have the right to recover from such person an amount equal to any of such charges paid by the buyer."

8. The section is taken from the Uniform Consumer Credit Code (§ 2.404, Alternative A), which model legislation has not been adopted in this state. The co-reporter-draftsman of this code, who assisted in the preparation of an amicus curiae brief, asserts that he actively participated in the discussions of the commissioners in the drafting of the section, that their concern was to avoid product liability claims against assignees, and that there was no discussion of the possibility that the provision could deprive a buyer of his right to bring an action to rescind a contract fraudulently induced.

It would be ironic indeed if a provision in an act intended to benefit consumers could be invoked to their detriment to such an extent that they would stand in a less advantageous position than others in the commercial arena. (See Consumer Viewpoints: Critique of the Uniform Consumer Credit Code, vols. 1, 2, p. 445.) We are constrained to conclude that the limitations on a buyer's rights set forth in section 1804.2 are not applicable if an assignee has taken the contract with notice of defenses of the buyer against the assignor or if the assignee's relationship with the assignor comes within the rule set forth in *Commercial Credit*.

The finance companies advance numerous policy arguments in support of their claim that they should not be held liable for Bay Area's alleged fraud. It is asserted that a finance company is in no position to police the seller's activities, cannot know whether the goods which are the subject of the contract are reasonably priced, and should not be required to make such a determination. Moreover, if the finance company takes too active a part in the seller's business he becomes subject to liability under the *Commercial Credit* doctrine. Financial institutions are also victimized by fraudulent sellers and they have strong incentive to refrain from tacitly participating in a seller's fraud.

It must be emphasized that the complaint alleges the finance company defendants were aware of Bay Area's fraud and under the law one who accepts an instrument with notice of a defense against it is not a holder in due course. If, despite the allegations of the complaint—admittedly true on demurrer—we were to adopt the views of the finance companies, we would be according to financial institutions greater commercial advantage against consumers than they enjoy with reference to all others.[9] Such a result cannot be justified.[10]

As far back as 1953, the Florida Supreme Court warned that the burden on finance companies may "require some changes in business

---

9. The Attorney General as amicus curiae urges that consumer installment contracts should not, for reasons of public policy, be viewed as negotiable instruments. The question whether lenders purchasing installment contracts should be deemed holders in due course has been vigorously debated in the law reviews. (See, e. g., Jordan and Warren, Uniform Consumer Credit Code (1968) 68 Colum.L.Rev. 387, 436; Murphy, U3C and Negotiability (1968) 29 Ohio St.L.J. 667; Note (1970) 55 Cornell L.Q. 611.) We need not discuss this problem in view of our conclusion that the finance company defendants may not in any event be deemed holders in due course under the allegations of the complaint.

10. Defendants also contend that serious unfavorable consequences for consumers would ensue if lenders are held liable for the seller's fraud. It is claimed that lenders would be required to insure themselves against the risk of being deprived of holder-in-due-course status and would do so by accepting contracts from only the most select sellers, thus depriving the buyer of a competitive market, that sellers would receive less money for the contracts assigned to lenders, and the lower return would be reflected in higher price to consumers. These arguments were rejected in *Morgan* with regard to a somewhat analogous matter. (Morgan v. Reasor, supra, 69 Cal. 881 at p. 890, 73 Cal.Rptr. 398, 447 P.2d 638.)

methods." But, said the court, "the finance company is better able to bear the risk of the dealer's insolvency than the buyer and in a far better position to protect his interests against unscrupulous and insolvent dealers." (Mutual Finance Co. v. Martin (Fla.1953) 63 So.2d 649, 653.) Zeal is originally employed by the seller in investigating the credit of the buyer; only a modicum of additional zeal by the lender should be necessary to investigate the good faith of the seller. If any hardship results from the rule we adopt, it is only that hardship inherent in the insistence of the law that honesty and enterprise must remain compatible.

The writ is granted, and the trial court is directed to vacate its judgment dismissing the first cause of action as a class action, to vacate its order sustaining the demurrers without leave to amend, to overrule the demurrers, and to proceed in a manner consistent with the views expressed herein.

NOTES

(1) *Questions.* In Mutual Finance Co. v. Martin, p. 970 supra, the defendant had made a down-payment of $625 at the time of his purchase. It does not appear that he sought to recover that amount from the plaintiff finance company. Does the rule of the foregoing case mean that he could have done so if he had established fraud on the part of the seller, W. A. Highsmith? Or does it mean that he could have done so only by establishing fraud on the part of the *finance company*?

On the latter interpretation, the Vasquez rule hardly seems a surprising one. But if it creates a vicarious liability of a finance company for misdeeds of its merchant-customer, it is a novel development in the law. Consider the case of a merchant doing business in corporate form, and holding all of the shares in the corporation. It is the received tradition that he is not accountable, as an individual, for fraud, breach of warranty, or other liabilities of the corporation.[a] Would it make sense to adhere to this rule, but to impose the corporate liabilities on a finance company to which the firm had assigned its contracts? If the finance company is accountable for the seller's misdeeds, should they also be chargeable to a bank that supplies general credit to the seller?

How many of the problems in this section might be dealt with effectively by the licensing and regulation of finance companies? See Warren, Regulation of Finance Charges, 68 Yale L.J. 829 (1959).

(2) *The Case of the Flimsy Franchise.* In 1967 the plaintiff, Marion Weil, paid more than $7,000 for dance lessons, pursuant to three contracts with "New York Dance, Inc.," a dance studio holding a franchise from Arthur Murray, Inc. Marion had previously taken dancing instruction, over some six years, offered by the Arthur Murray Dance Studio in the same quarters, from the same instructors. She claimed reimbursement of the sums paid under the three contracts, asserting that these contracts violated statutory prohibitions, and that the payments were for "unused"

a. See O'Neal, Close Corporations, §§ 1.09, 109a (1971).

lessons.   (It appeared that when asked to sign a new contract Marion always had an entitlement to unused instruction under a previous one.)

The whole series of contracts was in identical form, but in the three in question the name "Arthur Murray, Inc." had been stamped out, and "New York Dance Studio, Inc." stamped over it before Marion signed them. Arthur Murray contended that to hold it liable for a franchisee's dereliction "would make a continuation of a franchising system impossible." *Held:* Arthur Murray was accountable for Marion's payments.   The court said: "the control maintained by this defendant over its franchisees, and their transferability from one location to another, so transcends the ordinary and normal franchisor-franchisee relationship that, in effect, the franchisees became the alter egos of this defendant in the conduct and operation of its studios."   Weil v. Arthur Murray, Inc., 324 N.Y.S.2d 381 (City Court, 1971).

SECTION 4.   FINANCING COMMERCIAL CREDIT

NOBLETT v. GENERAL ELECTRIC CREDIT CORPORATION

United States Court of Appeals, Tenth Circuit, 1968.
400 F.2d 442, cert. denied, 393 U.S. 935 (1968).

CHRISTENSEN, DISTRICT JUDGE.   In this diversity action General Electric Credit Corporation obtained summary judgment against Ernest V. Noblett for rentals under a bowling equipment "Rental Lease", which had been assigned to the corporation by the lessor, Bowl-Mor Company.

Whether the case was factually ripe for summary judgment and whether Noblett in the rental agreement validly waived defenses as against the assignee as a matter of law, are the problems presented by this appeal.

Noblett's answer as amended had raised among other defenses that of failure of consideration by reason of alleged breaches of an express warranty against defects, an implied warranty of fitness and the obligations of the lessor to furnish advertising and training assistance.

The rental agreement included the following provision:

> "The lessor may assign all its right, title and interest under this lease, including the payments due hereunder, but the assignee shall not be held responsible for any of the lessor's obligations.   The obligations of the Lessee shall, however, continue in full force and effect."

Applying Massachusetts law in accordance with the terms of the rental agreement, and being of the view that Noblett thereby had waived the pleaded defenses, General Electric Credit Corp. v. Noblett,

268 F.Supp. 984 (W.D.Okl.1967), the trial court granted summary judgment for the balance of the rentals in the sum of $64,389.91, together with interest of $3,541.45, $11,814 attorney's fees and costs of the action.

Section 9–206, Chapter 106, of the General Laws of Massachusetts, based upon the Uniform Commercial Code, provides:

[See p. 981 supra for the text as set out here.]

The equipment did not constitute "consumer goods" within the meaning of the Act.

The appellant Noblett contends that under any view of the Massachusetts law this case was not ripe for summary judgment since there was an issue of fact whether the assignee credit corporation took the assignment "for value, in good faith, and without notice of a claim or defense"; if not, under the terms of the Code no waiver agreement would be recognized.

In support of its motion for summary judgment the credit corporation filed below an affidavit from one R. N. Lamy, who stated that he was a Credit Specialist for General Electric Credit Corporation; that on the 24th day of May, 1965, General Electric Credit Corporation took an assignment from Bowl-Mor Company, Inc., for "good and valuable consideration" of the lease in question and "that said assignment was taken by General Electric Credit Corporation in good faith and without notice of any claim or defenses which Ernest V. Noblett might have against Bowl-Mor Company, Inc.".

We are not unmindful of the practical difficulties of establishing by affidavit in strict compliance with Rule 56(e), F.R.Civ.P., a lack of notice on the part of a corporation having numerous officers, managing agents and employees. A reasonable application is all that is required. It is apparent that in any view this affidavit did not conform with the requirements that such an affidavit be made on personal knowledge, state facts which would be admissible in evidence and show affirmatively that affiant was competent to testify to the matters therein stated. [But the court ruled that the trial judge was justified in giving credit to the affidavit, as the defendant had not challenged its assertions before it was entered. The court said: "there is a more dispositive reason why the summary judgment cannot stand."]

The trial court determined that in agreeing that "the Assignee shall not be held responsible for any of the Lessor's obligations", and that "the obligations of the Lessee shall, however, continue in full force and effect", Noblett effectually indicated "that he will not assert against an assignee any claim or defense which he might have against the . . . Lessor" within the contemplation of § 9–

206(1), and, hence, that he was barred from asserting against the appellee his defense of failure of consideration and related defenses.[1]

Our attention has been directed to two unpublished decisions of courts in other states holding that the precise language used in the form of the lease in question is valid and binding under Massachusetts law for the purpose.[2] And we are mindful that in Straight v. James Talcott, Inc., 329 F.2d 1 (10th Cir. 1964), this court held that an agreement of a buyer that he would settle all claims against the seller directly with him and would not set up any such claim against his assignee, operated to waive defenses in a suit brought by the assignee.

No Massachusetts decision has been called to our attention, nor can we find any, defining how far from the precise language of the authorizing statute an agreement might depart and still be effective as a waiver. Neither the decision of the trial court nor any of the cases cited come to grips expressly with the most persuasive phase of appellant's argument—that the intent manifested by the quoted provision of the lease agreement was not to waive defenses as allowed by § 9–206(1) of the Uniform Commercial Code but to relieve the assignee of the duty of affirmative performance of the lessor's obligations under the lease with reference to an entirely different section of the Code. It is provided in § 2–210:

> "(4) An assignment of 'the contract' or of 'all my rights under the contract' or an assignment in similar general terms is an assignment of rights and unless the language or the circumstances (as in an assignment for security) indicate the contrary, it is a delegation of performance of the duties of the assignor and its acceptance by the assignee constitutes a promise by him to perform those duties. This promise is enforceable by either the assignor or the other party to the original contract."

The provisions of the lease agreement which speaks in terms of obligations is peculiarly suited to an indication for the purposes of § 2–210(4) that there was no "delegation of the performance of the du-

---

1. "Whether the allegations in the answer and amendment thereto, to-wit: breach of warranty of fitness of the machines; disregard of the agreement to provide 'on the job training'; and failure to make allowance for advertising and signs, be technically designated as 'defenses', 'counterclaim' or 'set-off' and regardless of whether defendant seeks rescission of the contract or affirmance with damages to him because of the alleged breach, it is clear that all of the omissions complained of by him were obligations of Bowl-Mor, not plaintiff. It seems further to be clear from the contract that plaintiff is exonerated from responsibility for all of these complaints unless the contract provision allowing same be invalid".

2. General Electric Credit Corporation v. Brick Plaza Lanes, Inc., et al, Superior Court of New Jersey Law Division, Ocean County, Docket Number L25891-64, A-13908 (1966), and Baldino v. ABC Appliance Service, 83 Pa. Dist. & Co., 305 (Philadelphia County, 1952).

ties of the assignor" or a "promise by him to perform those duties." Indeed, more apt language for this purpose could hardly be devised than was used in the lease agreement. But with respect to waiver of defenses, the language at best is indirect and unclear and at its worst misleading or entrapping. The question of the appropriateness of language, however, is not the worst of the problem, which goes deeper into the very substance of the legal concepts involved.

An assignment in general terms under the Uniform Commercial Code, and, hence, under the present Massachusetts law, is an assignment of rights, and unless the language or the circumstances indicate the contrary, it is also a delegation of performance of the duties of the assignor and its acceptance by the assignee, constituting a promise by him to perform those duties. The promise is enforceable by either the assignor or the other party to the original contract. In general, whether there is a delegation of duties as well as rights in and of itself does not affect defenses available to the other original contracting party. If there is a delegation of obligations, failure of consideration remains a defense, and the same is true even though there is no delegation of obligation to the assignee in the absence of waiver; the assignee stands in the shoes of the assignor as far as the right to recover is concerned in either event. Moreover, if there is a delegation of obligation to the assignee, this in and of itself does not relieve the assignor from the obligation of performance. If the assignor is required to respond to the other contracting party after duties have been delegated by the assignor, the assignee may be rendered liable to the assignor, which is a reason why a nondelegation agreement may be important to the assignee in the absence of a waiver of defenses.[3]

The point of these general principles is that defenses are available against the assignee in the absence of waiver, not because of the delegation or non-delegation of duties but because the assignee in either event must claim under the original contract and is subject to the defenses allowed thereby. The fact that the lease recited that the lessee should continue to be bound to his contracted obligations despite any assignment does not suggest in context that he agreed to waive defenses any more than the agreement that responsibilities of the assignor were not to be deemed delegated had anything to do with the waiver of defenses. The intent and meaning of the lease in this respect is made all the more clear by Bowl-Mor's assignment to the credit corporation which simply provides on the point that "Assignee shall have no obligations of lessor under said lease."

3. See generally William D. Hawkland, A Transactional Guide to the U.C.C. (A.L.I.) (1964), § 1.25 p. 150 et seq.; 6 Am.Jur.2d Assignments, § 102, p. 282; 3 Williston on Contracts (Third Ed.-Jaeger), Sec. 432, pp. 177, et seq. Cf. Nickell v. United States, etc., 355 F.2d 73 (10th Cir. 1966); Denver United States Nat. Bank v. Asbell Bros. Constr., 294 F.2d 289 (10th Cir. 1961); Imperial Refining Co. v. Kanotex Refining Co., 29 F.2d 193 (8th Cir. 1928).

Whether responsibilities of the assignor were or were not delegated pursuant to § 2–210(4), or as a matter of general law, the rule continued operative that failure of consideration could be raised as a defense either against the assignee or the assignor in the absence of a waiver as authorized by the other provision of the Code. There was no such waiver. To enlarge the agreement concerning the non-delegation of obligation into such a waiver would be not only unwarranted but unfair. When appellant consented to the non-delegation to the assignee of obligations of the assignor under the lease, whether viewed from the standpoint of one learned in the law and capable of appreciating these distinctions, or as one only generally aware of the meaning of language, he reasonably could have assumed that the purpose was what it purported to be and was not to preclude his defenses should he not receive the consideration for which he bargained. We are of the opinion that as a matter of law there was no waiver of defenses.[4]

We see nothing in Straight v. James Talcott, Inc., 329 F.2d 1 (10th Cir. 1964), supra, that warrants a contrary conclusion. There Oklahoma law was involved; the language which was employed more specifically sustained the conclusion reached and was not apparently designed for another purpose; it was not expressly questioned that the provision was intended to waive defenses, and the primary issue was whether such an agreed waiver would be valid under Oklahoma law. Massachusetts law governs the result here. In view of considerations discussed above and the general policy expressed in Quality Finance Company v. Hurley, 337 Mass. 150, 148 N.E.2d 385 (1957) it is fairly to be predicted that in the interpretation of the subsequently adopted Uniform Commercial Code an agreement that an assignment would not constitute a delegation of duties would not be so broadly construed as to be accepted in that state as a waiver of defenses under § 9–206(1).

Reversed and remanded for further proceedings not inconsistent with this opinion.

On Petition for Rehearing

PER CURIAM. Appellee has filed a petition for rehearing, its only contention justifying further notice being that the court has held in effect that the "Sales" provisions of the Uniform Commercial Code govern "Secured Transactions". In other words, it is argued that "the application of Section 2–210(4) was erroneous" and would open

---

4. Even if the contract had been ambiguous on this point, summary judgment would have been inappropriate, since the appellant would have had the right to be heard on the question of intent as a matter of fact, and to resort to intrinsic aids to establish that intent at the trial. The lease agreement bears the letterhead of the lessor and appears to be on its printed form, and the rule of interpretation that in such event ambiguities are to be resolved against the drafter could well apply.

all secured transactions to question by indicating that in the absence of specific negation the obligation of performance would be placed upon the security holder as a matter of course. It should have been enough to preclude such misunderstanding to quote, as we did, Section 2–210(4) which states among other things that there is a delegation of performance "unless the language or the circumstances (*as in an assignment for security*) indicate the contrary" (emphasis added). We did not refer to Section 2–210(4) to indicate that the "Sales55 provisions of the Code necessarily governed Secured Transactions in the absence of language so providing but rather to demonstrate that waiver of affirmative performance is not the same as waiver of defenses for non-performance by a party to the original contract.

Far from justifying the appellee's claim that we misconceived the relationship of the Sales provisions to the Secured Transactions provisions of the Code, we simply pointed up in our opinion the basic misconception implicit in appellee's argument that language in the rental agreement which would have been appropriate for purposes of Section 2–210(4) relating to Sales could serve the entirely different purpose of satisfying the waiver of defense requirements established in Section 9–206(1) concerning Secured Transactions.

Finally, appellee sees in the language of the rental agreement that "the assignee shall not be responsible for any of lessor's obligations", an enigma if it is not held to constitute a waiver of defenses by the lessee since in a secured transaction an assignment does not delegate performance in any event. Perhaps appellee is in the best position to explain this supposed enigma; in the assignment by which it took the security it was again stipulated that "assignee shall have no obligation of lessor under the lease". The same question applies —why, if there would be no such obligation anyway, was this specifically provided there? No matter the reason, such language does not operate as a waiver of defenses under Section 9–206(1) and this is the determinative point.

The petitions for rehearing and for rehearing en banc are denied.

NOTES

(1) *Problem.* Prepare a term for inclusion in a rental lease that would be operative as a "waiver of defenses" by the lessee. If your provision is used, in leases of business equipment, can the assignee (finance company) count on obtaining summary judgment in other cases like the main one?

(2) *Assignees as Third Party Beneficiaries.* When an assignee succeeds in making claim against the obligor on the strength of a waiver of defense clause, and would not have succeeded otherwise, what is the theory of the recovery? The Restatement sections on assignments skirt the issues raised by such clauses. However, in Comments f and g to § 168 of the Restatement Second, three theories are offered for their efficacy, including estoppel. Strangely, it is not suggested that the assignee may enforce the

clause as a third party beneficiary. Would that construction be a sound basis for his claim, in an appropriate case?

To characterize an assignee as (also) a third party beneficiary would not be a novelty; but in the absence of a waiver of defense clause it would not contribute much to his standing. In Restatement Second § 140, Comment c, a comparison is made between a beneficiary's position and that of an assignee after notice to the obligor of the assignment. As to the effect of a waiver clause, the comparison seems incomplete. In the chapter on assignments, a comment says that "if the agreement not to assert defenses or claims is itself voidable or unenforceable, the assignee takes subject to the defect."[a] Can this be reconciled with the provisions about a beneficiary?[b] See Note 2, p. 918 supra, on the standard mortgagee clause.

When UCC 9–206 applies so as to override a "claim or defense" by a buyer (or lessee), the assignee need not appeal to third party beneficiary law, of course: he has *statutory* support for his claim. On that basis, however, he can succeed only if he took his assignment "for value," etc. Suppose that an assignee cannot meet the requisites of that section for enforcing a waiver of defense clause: Is it possible that he may nevertheless enforce it under the general principles of third party beneficiary law? Note that the Code is "supplemented" by the general principles of law and equity (§ 1–103)—*unless* they are "displaced by the particular provisions of this Act." The question, then, becomes how far the law of third party beneficiaries is displaced by UCC 9–206. And the answer is clear: it is so far displaced that an assignee who does not meet the requisites of that section may not enforce such a clause.

GENERAL ELECTRIC CREDIT CORP. v. SECURITY BANK, 244 A.2d 920 (D.C.Ct.App.1968). [A builder of shell homes, Le-Wood, Inc., contracted to build a home for Peyton Bailey. Needing construction funds, Le-Wood sought an interim loan from the Security Bank. Upon completing the home, Le-Wood expected to receive Bailey's installment note for the price, and to sell it to the General Electric Credit Corporation. By a standing agreement between them, G.E. Credit would pay Le-Wood for its customers' notes, and it was bound to pay $8,200 for the Bailey contract, upon completion of the work. Le-Wood offered the bank security for the loan it sought, in the form of an assignment of its right to this sum. (Similar contracts with other customers were also involved.)

The bank made an inquiry of G.E. Credit, to be described below, and subsequently granted the loan. It was never repaid. Le-Wood went out of business. G.E. Credit obtained possession of Bailey's note but it refused to pay the purchase price to the bank. It relied on the terms of its agreement with Le-Wood by which it was entitled to withhold disbursements to secure Le-Wood's obligations to G.E.

---

a. Section 168, Comment f.   b. Compare especially Illustration 10
                                               after § 168 with Illustration 7 after
                                               § 140.

Credit.   These obligations arose from home-sale contracts on which Le-Wood's customers defaulted: on demand by G.E. Credit, Le-Wood was bound to repurchase any customer's note on which two install-ments were overdue.   When the bank demanded payment for the Bailey contract, Le-Wood had been presented with "repurchase re-quests" by G.E. Credit amounting to $60,000.   Suing G.E. Credit, the bank obtained a directed verdict, and the defendant appealed.

Two issues were discussed: (1) whether or not G.E. Credit had a right of set-off against Le-Wood at the time of the assignment, and (2) if so, whether or not G.E. Credit was estopped to assert it against the bank.   The supposed estoppel rested largely on events just be-fore the loan.   At that time a bank vice-president telephoned G.E. Credit "to find out that everything was all right," and was told (as he testified) "it was okay."   The bank also wrote to G.E. Credit, referring to its purchase agreement and listing certain accounts, including that of Bailey in the sum of $8,200.   The letter requested that G.E. Credit "signify your acceptance of the assignment by sign-ing and returning the enclosed copy."   The copy was returned, en-dorsed as "Received and accepted . . .."   The loan and assign-ment ensued.

On the issue of set-off the court cited Restatement, § 167(1): "We are cognizant of the general rule that an assignee of a chose in action takes it subject to all defenses, including any valid set-off based on facts existing at the time of the assignment . . .   but not to set-offs acquired after notice thereof to the obligor."   The decision was rested on another ground, however.]

KELLY, ASSOCIATE JUDGE . . . .   [I]n our view Credit Cor-poration was estopped to claim a set-off against the bank by its own unqualifed commitment to pay the assigned debt.   We there-fore attach little significance to the disputed telephone conversa-tion. . . .

All of the evidence in this case points up the fact that in making the loan to Le-Wood the bank placed sole reliance on Credit Corpora-tion's assurances that the loan would be repaid.   It was for this reason that . . .   the bank placed a telephone call to Credit Cor-poration to see that everything was all right. . . .   Whether or not Credit Corporation had a duty to inform the bank of the underly-ing agreement it had with Le-Wood or, at the very least, of the out-standing repurchase requests, which we think it clearly had, the fact is that the accepted assignment represented that the Peyton Bailey account correctly set forth an *undisputed* account, and that upon completion Le-Wood *was entitled to receive the full amount* of the designated account from Credit Corporation.   It is true that the as-signment contains no specific waiver of defenses, yet in the face of the unequivocal representations made it can hardly be said that Credit Corporation's agreement to "disburse any and all funds due" Le-Wood was a qualification upon the promise to pay which allows it a set-off against the bank's claim. . . .

Affirmed.

NOTES

(1) *Case Comparisons.* Comparing its experiences with Noblett, in the preceding case, and with the bank, in this one, G. E. Credit might conclude that the gods are vindictive. As obligor, it loses defenses without making a "specific" waiver; but as assignee it cannot override an obligor's defenses without exacting a waiver in the most explicit terms. However, defenses without exacting a waiver in the most explicit terms. What alternative explanations do the two cases suggest?

(2) *The Security Bank Transaction.* The repurchase agreement that Le-Wood made with G. E. Credit was a form of "recourse" against him. Recourse financing is so prevalent that a bank official must be very ill-informed if he is not aware of its general characteristics. It is therefore a questionable aspect of the Security Bank's claim that the inquiries it put to the Credit Corporation were as vague as they were: "Is everything all right?" A more pointed question would be: "What agreement do you have with Le-Wood about recourse in the event of a default on a note?" The answer to this question would either have warned the bank away from the transaction, or have created a firmer basis for estoppel, it would seem. Do you think that the court reads too much into the defendant's notation on the bank's letter: "Received and accepted . . . "? That the defendant had a duty of disclosure about the repurchase agreement?

SET–OFF OF UNMATURED CLAIMS

At the time an obligor learns of an assignment, a claim that he has against the assignor, giving rise to a potential set-off, may be in any one of several stages of maturing. At best, his claim may be matured, in the sense that he has a right to immediate performance by the assignor. Short of that, his claim may be a right to performance at a future date, or a right to performance conditioned on an event that may occur in the future.

For an assignee, the distinction between matured and unmatured claims may be critical. "Set-off against an assignee has sometimes been limited to cases where both offsetting claims were fully matured at the time of assignment." [a]

Note, however, that the Security Bank case states a rule more burdensome to the assignee: he is subject to "any valid set-off based on facts existing at the time of the assignment." Consider a note current at the time of the assignment, but dishonored after Le-Wood went out of business. Under this rule, it is arguable that (apart

---

a. Restatement Second, § 168, Comment
c.

from any estoppel) the Credit Corporation could set off its investment in such a note against the bank. After all, the repurchase
agreement, on which its set-off claim is based, existed at the time of
the assignment. This rule is derived from the original Restatement:
see § 167(1). It has substantial support in case law.[b]

Yet the Restatement Second adopts a different formulation:
"The right of an assignee is subject to any defense or claim of the obligor which *accrues* before the obligor receives notification of the assignment . . ." (§ 168(2); emphasis supplied) The source of
this expression is obviously UCC 9–318 (reproduced below, at p. 1008).

When a contract for the sale of goods calls for payment 30 days
after delivery, is the seller's claim for the price accrued when the
contract is made? Upon delivery? Thirty days thereafter? When a
note is payable on demand, is the payee's claim on it accrued before
demand? One of the architects of the Code, Professor Gilmore, pro-
fesses not to understand the Code expression any better than he un-
derstands the first Restatement rule.[c] The comments in Restatement
Second are somewhat equivocal. Under the usual statute or rule of
court, it is said, the obligor "cannot . . . set off an unrelated
claim which matures after notification is received." Section 168,
Comment d.

Local and somewhat differing statutes, much older than the Uniform Commercial Code, may govern a particular controversy about
set-off, or another defense. A valuable compilation of such statutes
appears as a prefatory note to Chapter 7 of the Restatement Second.
It is said that there are 40 states in which such a statute provides
that an assignment is without prejudice to any set-off or defense existing before notice of the assignment. But some of these statutes
apply only to limited types of claim.

NOTES

(1) *G. E. Credit v. Bank: Accrual.* It may be a reasonable guess that
G. E. Credit had an accrued claim against Le-Wood, when it was notified of
the assignment, as to any note it held on which two installment payments
(by the maker, i. e., homeowner) were then overdue. Perhaps it is significant, in this connection, that the Credit Corporation's duty of disclosure
to the bank (as declared by the court) extended, "at the very least," to the
outstanding repurchase requests.

(2) *Question.* Did the Credit Corporation receive "notification of the
assignment" at the time of the telephone conversation with the bank, or
when it received the bank's letter enclosing copies of the assignments?

b. See Maryland Cooperative Milk Producers v. Bell, 206 Md. 168, 110 A.2d
661 (1955).

c. Gilmore, 2 Security Interests in Personal Property 1091 (1965).

For a troublesome set-off problem arising out of a series of construction contracts, see Algernon Blair, Inc. v. National Surety Corporation, 222 Ga.
672, 151 S.E.2d 724 (1966).

(3) *Drafting.* Upon receiving notice of an assignment, the obligor may be well advised to send a carefully expressed acknowledgement to the assignee. Some firms having experience with assignments attempt to forestall assertions of estoppel against them in this way. What language would you suggest for the obligor's protection? See Federal Nat. Bank & Trust Co. v. Owen, 389 F.2d 457 (10th Cir. 1968); Worthen Bank & Trust Co. v. Franklin Life Ins. Co., 370 F.2d 97 (8th Cir. 1966). Better yet, as in the latter case, the obligor may succeed in having the assignment made on a form that he prepares. How many risks can the obligor throw off on the assignee by proper design of the documents?

NECESSARY ADVANCES

As a rule, an assignee's rights against the obligor are not impaired by the fact that the obligor, having notice of the assignment, makes a payment in disregard of the assignment. If the obligor is so unwise as to deal with the assignor after notice, the assignee may commonly require him to make a second payment of the assigned claim. See Cooper v. Holder, p. 940 supra.

An important qualification on this rule is suggested by a handful of cases that may be described as involving "necessary advances." Two of them are outlined in this note: Argonaut Insurance Co. v. United States, 193 Ct.Cl. 483, 434 F.2d 1362 (1970), and Fricker v. Uddo & Taormina Co., 48 Cal.2d 696, 312 P.2d 1085 (1957).

The Argonaut Insurance case concerned a contract for surfacing part of an Alaskan highway. For this work the United States contracted to pay some $478,000 to the Watkins Company. Argonaut issued performance and payment bonds on behalf of Watkins. It had an interest in Watkins' job earnings, which would be available to reimburse it for any outlay that Argonaut might have to make under the bonds. (Probably it held an assignment from Watkins for security, and in any event it would be subrogated to Watkins' rights upon performing its duties.)

In the second summer of the work, the United States made a progress payment amounting to nearly $90,000, over Argonaut's objection. Watkins had encountered financial difficulty and Argonaut had met some of its payrolls. It had also assigned its earnings to a bank for a loan. Upon learning this, Argonaut urged the Government to declare Watkins in default and terminate the contract. Instead, it allowed the work to be completed, and made the payment in question to the bank. Upon completion, there was an unpaid balance owing by the Government of about $150,000. Argonaut claimed that amount, and more, having met large claims under its payment bond. The bank made a conflicting claim, but the balance was awarded to Argonaut by virtue of subrogation—sometimes called an "equitable assignment."

Argonaut also sought to charge the Government for the amount of the progress payment. The court's ruling suggests, by inference, that an obligor may properly safeguard his own interests, in some circumstances, by making a payment in disregard of an assignment. It ruled for the Government, saying:

> During performance, the Government's role is substantially different from that of a mere stakeholder of a final contract payment. [It] has an important interest in the timely and efficient completion of the contract work. In furtherance of this interest, the Government contracts for a broad range of rights which are designed to promote continuation of the contract work. These provisions give the Government considerable discretion and flexibility in administering the contract. Public policy supports this flexibility in light of the various unforeseen circumstances which may hinder performance. . . . It is not necessary to define the limits of the Government's discretion in this case, because the plaintiff has failed to show an abuse of that discretion. On the contrary, the facts are sufficient to show that the Government's refusal to terminate the contract and its determination that the payment of Progress Payment No. 3 to Wells Fargo Bank was essential to the continued performances and timely completion of the contract, were well within the range of discretion conferred on the contracting agency by the terms of the contract and the applicable regulations.

In Fricker v. Uddo & Taormina Company, supra, the assignee was more fortunate than Argonaut. The parties were a canning company (defendant), a farmer (George Kikuchi), and a creditor of his (plaintiff). Kikuchi contracted to sell his 1952 tomato crop to the defendant company, and his harvest produced earnings for him of about $77,000. Unhappily the venture was unprofitable for him, inasmuch as he incurred obligations during the season of more than $84,000. Most of this was advanced to him by the canning company, as a charge against his "crop account." By early spring it had already advanced Kikuchi $27,000. Then he sought to buy soil fumigant from Fricker, on credit. The canning company was informed, and wrote to Fricker: "This will confirm that we have accepted a crop order instructing us to pay to you $4,074.91 from the return due George Kikuchi from tomatoes delivered by him to us during the 1952 season." The crop order was treated, in the subsequent litigation, as a partial assignment of Kikuchi's right to payment for the tomatoes.

Thereafter the canning company made other large advances to Kikuchi, so that the total was more than he earned by supplying tomatoes. Not being paid, Fricker sued the company. His complaint was that the latter advances were made in disregard of the assignment.

The company argued that its advances were necessary to enable Kikuchi to perform his contract; and the court accepted the view that payments by an obligor of this character, in disregard of an assignment, are justified. Such a rule, it said, is "obviously an exception to the general rule relating to assignments." But the canning company, it said, was required to make a showing of necessity. To a considerable extent, it did so. After accepting the crop order, it had advanced Kikuchi some $42,000 which was actually used for producing the crop. (Installment payments on his farm machinery were thought to be among the allowable costs.) However, advances beyond this sum were held to violate Fricker's rights as assignee. Some of the advances were used by Kikuchi for living expenses of his family. The court ruled that such sums could not be treated as having been used for the purpose of tomato production. Advances by the company prior to the crop order, plus "necessary" ones thereafter, amounted to less than $70,000. Since the gross return from the crop exceeded this amount by more than the plaintiff's fumigant bill, a judgment for the plaintiff was affirmed.

NOTES

(1) *Authorities.* The doctrine of "necessary advances" has been developed in the following California cases: St. Paul Fire & Marine Ins. Co. v. James I. Barnes Const. Co., 59 Cal.2d 691, 381 P.2d 932 (1963); ibid., 267 Cal.App.2d 931, 73 Cal.Rptr. 618 (1968); and Walker v. Nitzberg, 13 Cal. App.3d 359, 91 Cal.Rptr. 526 (1970).[a] These two cases concern construction work, and are not easy to reconcile.

(2) *The Case of Bannister's Boat.* A shipowner, Bannister, contracted to pay £1375 to John Gough, in installments, for the building of a vessel. On October 27, 1876, two installments of £250 each had been earned, but Bannister had already advanced sums that were necessary for Gough to pay his workmen and the cost of materials employed on the job, amounting to £1015. On that date Gough assigned to William Brice, a solicitor, £100 out of money due or to become due under the contract, and notice of the assignment was given to Bannister. Subsequently Bannister made payments to Gough of more than £100, and refused to pay anything to Brice. Gough would not have been able to complete the vessel without these payments. Brice brought an action against Bannister upon the assignment. *Held*: For Brice. One of the judges expressed doubt that the decision would have been the same if Bannister had made the subsequent payments in response to a threat by Gough not to finish the vessel. Brett, L. J., dissented, saying this of the transaction between Gough and the defendant: "if what they do is done bonâ fide and in the ordinary course of business, I cannot think

a. See also Hoover v. Agriform Chemical Company, 268 Cal.App.2d 818, 74 Cal.Rptr. 325 (1969) (not a construction case); Honolulu Roofing Company v. Felix, 49 Haw. 578, 426 P.2d 298 (1967). The complexities of these cases cannot be represented here.

their dealings ought to be impeded or imperilled . . . , and it seems to me the purchaser of a ship and the builder might have cancelled the contract even after this assignment. Why may they not modify it? If they cannot modify it, it seems to me to denote a state of slavery in business that ought not to be suffered . . . " Brice v. Bannister, L.R. 3 Q.B.D. 569 (1878). How may this case be distinguished from the one in the preceding note?

UCC 9–318

Defenses Against Assignee; Modification of Contract After Notification of Assignment; Term Prohibiting Assignment Ineffective; Identification and Proof of Assignment.

(1) Unless an account debtor has made an enforceable agreement not to assert defenses or claims arising out of a sale as provided in Section 9–206 the rights of an assignee are subject to

> (a) all the terms of the contract between the account debtor and assignor and any defense or claim arising therefrom; and
>
> (b) any other defense or claim of the account debtor against the assignor which accrues before the account debtor receives notification of the assignment.

(2) So far as the right to payment under an assigned contract right has not already become an account, and notwithstanding notification of the assignment, any modification of or substitution for the contract made in good faith and in accordance with reasonable commercial standards is effective against an assignee unless the account debtor has otherwise agreed but the assignee acquires corresponding rights under the modified or substituted contract. The assignment may provide that such modification or substitution is a breach by the assignor.

(3) The account debtor is authorized to pay the assignor until the account debtor receives notification that the account has been assigned and that payment is to be made to the assignee. A notification which does not reasonably identify the rights assigned is ineffective. If requested by the account debtor, the assignee must seasonably furnish reasonable proof that the assignment has been made and unless he does so the account debtor may pay the assignor.

(4) A term in any contract between an account debtor and an assignor which prohibits assignment of an account or contract right to which they are parties is ineffective.

NOTES

(1) *Questions.* How does the rule of subsection (2) compare with the doctrine of necessary advances, as stated in the Fricker case?

As you understand the second sentence of the subsection, does it authorize an agreement that binds an obligor not to assent to any modification whatever? If not, does the section make such an agreement impossible, in situations to which it applies?

(2) *Restatements.* The original Restatement contains no provision comparable to the Code subsection; but Restatement Second states a closely parallel rule, in § 170(2). Comment f after the section states: "Contrary agreement between obligor and assignee is effective." The inference is clear that a "contrary agreement" between obligor and assignor is *ineffective.* But Comment a after § 142 states: "The parties to a contract . . . can by agreement create a duty to a beneficiary which cannot be varied without the beneficiary's consent." How is it possible to reconcile these rules?

(3) *An Illustration.* "A Company contracts to supply electricity to B for twenty years. Later A assigns to C for value certain fixed monthly payments to be made by B under the contract. After ten years B ceases to require electricity and A and B agree in good faith to terminate all performance under the contract. B is not liable to C for payments which would have accrued thereafter." Illustration 6 to Restatement Second, § 170.

(4) *A Stand-Pat Position.* In UCC 9–318(2), the standards for a modification or substitution, effective against a notifying assignee, are that it be "made in good faith and in accordance with reasonable commercial standards." At this point there is a variance in the New York version of the Code, which adds: "and without material adverse effect upon the assignee's rights under or the assignor's ability to perform the contract."

Does this addition make a worthwhile limitation on the power of the contracting parties to alter their relations? The Permanent Editorial Board for the Code thinks not.[a]

———

SCOPE PROVISIONS FOR UCC ARTICLE 9

For many reasons it may often be important to determine whether or not a given assignment is one to which the rules of Article 9 apply. Some of the scope provisions are as follows:

Section 9–104. Among the transactions excluded from Article 9 by this section are assignments "as part of a sale of the business out of which they arose," and the assignment of an unearned payment "to an assignee who is also to do the performance under the contract."

Section 9–102(1). With certain stated exceptions, "this Article applies . . . to any sale of accounts, contract rights or chattel paper." (The principal limitations on this sweeping statement are those found in section 9–104.)

Section 1–201(37), defining "security interest." As defined, the term "includes any interest of a buyer of accounts, chattel paper, or contract rights which is subject to Article 9." Therefore, where the

a. Final Report, Permanent Editorial
Board for the UCC, Review Committee
for Article 9, 215 (1971).

article provides (with exceptions) that "A financing statement must be filed to perfect all security interests"—UCC 9–302(1)—it signifies that a *buyer* of accounts or contract rights must often make a public filing in order to perfect his interest.

NOTES

(1) *Filing.* Consider again the "illustration" assignment, in Note 3, p. 1009 supra. We are not told whether C acquired the rights of A to secure an obligation, or acquired them to satisfy an obligation, or simply "bought" them. In the two latter cases, the assignment would be a sale; but in any event it would be subject to Article 9.

Despite this conclusion, C may have a perfected interest in the assigned rights without filing a financing statement, according to the following rule: "A financing statement must be filed to perfect all security interests except the following: . . . an assignment of accounts or contract rights which does not alone or in conjunction with other assignments to the same assignee transfer a significant part of the outstanding accounts or contract rights of the assignor." UCC 9–302(1)(e). Owing to the fact that filing is an easy and inexpensive procedure, C would probably not be well advised to rely on the rule quoted; there is a serious risk of error in assuming that C's assignment covers an insignificant part of A's rights.

(2) *Statute of Frauds.* An assignment within the scope of Article 9 is not enforceable against the assignor or anyone else unless the assignor has signed a writing containing a "description of the collateral." UCC 9–203 (1). But see Spurlin v. Sloan, 368 S.W.2d 314 (Ky.1963).[b]

ALLHUSEN v. CARISTO CONSTRUCTION CORP.

Court of Appeals of New York, 1952.
303 N.Y. 446, 103 N.E.2d 891, 37 A.L.R.2d 1245.

Herman Allhusen, as assignee, sued the Caristo Construction Corp. for money due plaintiff's assignor under a contract with defendant. The Special Term, New York County, Botein, J., entered an order granting defendant's motion for summary judgment dismissing the complaint, and plaintiff appealed. The Appellate Division, 278 App.Div. 817, 104 N.Y.S.2d 565, by a divided court, affirmed the judgment, and plaintiff appealed. . . .

FROESSEL, JUDGE. Defendant, a general contractor, subcontracted with the Kroo Painting Company (hereinafter called Kroo) for the performance by the latter of certain painting work in New York City public schools. Their contracts contained the following prohibitory provision: "The assignment by the second party [Kroo] of this contract or any interest therein, or of any money due or to become due by reason of the terms hereof without the written consent of the first party [defendant] shall be void." Kroo subsequently assigned cer-

---

b. An expansion of the exclusion stated in UCC 9–104(f), so as to embrace cases like this one, is proposed. Op. cit. footnote a, supra.

tain rights under the contracts to Marine Midland Trust Company of New York, which in turn assigned said rights to plaintiff. These rights included the "moneys due and to become due" to Kroo. The *contracts* were not assigned, and no question of improper delegation of contractual duties is involved. No written consent to the assignments was procured from defendant.

Plaintiff as assignee seeks to recover, in six causes of action, $11,650 allegedly due and owing for work done by Kroo. Defendant answered with denials, and by way of defense set up the aforementioned prohibitory clause, in addition to certain setoffs and counterclaims, alleged to have existed at the time of the assignments. It thereupon moved for summary judgment under rule 113 of the Rules of Civil Practice, and demanded dismissal of plaintiff's several causes of action on the sole ground that the prohibitory clause constituted a defense sufficient as a matter of law to defeat each cause of action. Special Term dismissed the complaint, holding that the prohibition against assignments "must be given effect." The Appellate Division affirmed, one Justice dissenting on the ground that the "account receivable was assignable by nature, and could not be rendered otherwise without imposing an unlawful restraint upon the power of alienation of property." 278 App.Div. 817, 104 N.Y.S.2d 565, 566.

Whether an anti-assignment clause is effective is a question that has troubled the courts not only of this State but in other jurisdictions as well, Burck v. Taylor, 152 U.S. 634, 14 S.Ct. 696, 38 L.Ed. 578; State St. Furniture Co. v. Armour & Co., 345 Ill. 160, 177 N.E. 702, 76 A.L.R. 1298 [other citations omitted].

Our courts have not construed a contractual provision against assignments framed in the language of the clause now before us. Such kindred clauses as have been subject to interpretation usually have been held to be either (1) personal covenants limiting the covenantee to a claim for damages in the event of a breach as e. g., Manchester v. Kendall, 19 Jones & Sp. 460, affirmed 103 N.Y. 638; Sacks v. Neptune Meter Co., 144 Misc. 70, 258 N.Y.S. 254, affirmed 238 App.Div. 82, 263 N.Y.S. 462, or (2) ineffectual because of the use of uncertain language, State Bank v. Central Mercantile Bank, 248 N.Y. 428, 162 N.E. 475, 59 A.L.R. 1473. But these decisions are not to be read as meaning that there can be no enforcible prohibition against the assignment of a claim; indeed, they are authority only for the proposition that, in the absence of language clearly indicating that a contractual right thereunder shall be nonassignable, a prohibitory clause will be interpreted as a personal covenant not to assign.

In the Manchester case, supra, it was held, 103 N.Y. at page 463, that the words, " 'This contract not to be assigned, or any part thereof, or any installments to grow due under the same' ", must be construed as an agreement not to assign, the breach of which would give rise to a claim for damages by the covenantee. The court stated, 103

N.Y. at page 463, that the quoted words "would not make the assignment void." In the clause now before us, however, it is expressly provided that the "assignment . . . shall be void." In the State Bank case, supra, 248 N.Y. at page 431, 162 N.E. at page 476, 59 A. L.R. 1473, which involved the assignment of certificates of deposit which were "not subject to check" and were "payable only to himself [depositor] . . . on return of this Certificate properly endorsed", we held that such language did not make the certificates nonassignable, and that nonnegotiable certificates of deposit are assignable *in the absence of an agreement to the contrary.* Judge Pound, writing for a unanimous court, added, however, 248 N.Y. at page 435, 162 N.E. at page 477: "Clear language should therefore be required to lead to the conclusion that the certificates are not assignable. 1 Williston on Contracts, § 422. We cannot deduce such consequences from uncertain language. Scheffer v. Erie County Sav. Bank, 229 N.Y. 50, 127 N.E. 474. The plainest words should have been chosen so that he who runs could read, in order to limit the freedom of alienation of rights and prohibit the assignment. It might have been stipulated on the face of the certificates that they should be 'nontransferable' or 'nonassignable.' "

In Devlin v. Mayor of City of N. Y., 63 N.Y. 8 at pages 17, 20, we said: "Parties may, in terms, prohibit the assignment of any contract ["and the interest of the contractor under it"] and declare that neither personal representatives nor assignees shall succeed to any rights in virtue of it, or be bound by its obligations." In Fortunato v. Patten, 147 N.Y. 277, 41 N.E. 572, where the contract with the city provided in substance that the contractor shall not assign the contract, or any moneys payable thereunder, without the consent of the city, we noted, 147 N.Y. at page 281, 41 N.E. at page 573: "it was inserted in the contract solely for the benefit of the city, and prevents any claim being asserted against it in the absence of consent."

In the lower courts, Sacks v. Neptune Meter Co., supra, expresses the view, and Morkel v. Metropolitan Life Ins. Co., App.Term, 1st Dept., 163 Misc. 366, 297 N.Y.S. 962, and Reisler v. Cohen, 67 Misc. 67, 121 N.Y.S. 603, hold that, where the agreement provides that the claim is nonassignable, the assignee may not recover. This is in harmony with Restatement of the Law of Contracts (§ 151): "A right may be the subject of effective assignment unless . . . (c) the assignment is prohibited by the contract creating the right." See, also, 2 Williston on Contracts, § 422, pp. 1217–1218.

In the light of the foregoing, we think it is reasonably clear that, while the courts have striven to uphold freedom of assignability, they have not failed to recognize the concept of freedom to contract. In large measure they agree that, where appropriate language is used, assignments of money due under contracts may be prohibited. When "clear language" is used, and the "plainest words . . . have been chosen", parties may "limit the freedom of alienation of rights and prohibit the assignment." State Bank v. Central Mercantile Bank, supra, 248 N.Y. at page 435, 162 N.E. at page 477, 59 A.L.R. 1473. We have now before us a clause embodying clear, definite and appropriate language, which may be construed in no other way but that any attempted assignment of either the contract or any rights created thereunder shall be "void" as against the obligor. One would have to do violence to the language here employed to hold that it is merely an agreement by the subcontractor not to assign. The objectivity of the language precludes such a construction. We are therefore compelled to conclude that this prohibitory clause is a valid and effective restriction of the right to assign.

Such a holding is not violative of public policy. Professor Williston, in his treatise on Contracts, states (Vol. 2, § 422, p. 1214): "The question of the free alienation of property does not seem to be involved." The New York cases do not hold otherwise, State Bank v. Central Mercantile Bank, supra, 248 N.Y. at page 435, 162 N.E. at page 477, 59 A.L.R. 1473. Plaintiff's claimed rights arise out of the very contract embodying the provision now sought to be invalidated. The right to moneys under the contracts is but a companion to other jural relations forming an aggregation of actual and potential interrelated rights and obligations. No sound reason appears why an assignee should remain unaffected by a provision in the very contract which gave life to the claim he asserts.

Nor is there any merit in plaintiff's contention that section 41 of the Personal Property Law, Consol.Laws, c. 41,[a] requires that the prohibitory clause be denied effect. Because the statute provides that a person may transfer a claim, it does not follow that he may not contract otherwise. Countless rights granted by statutes are voluntarily surrendered in the everyday affairs of individuals. In Rosenthal Paper Co. v. National Folding Box & Paper Co., 226 N.Y. 313, 325–326, 123 N.E. 766, 770, we noted: "The general rule now prevailing . . . that any property right, not necessarily personal, is assignable, *is overcome only by agreement of the contracting parties* or a principle of law or public policy. [Citing cases.] In this jurisdiction the statute, in effect, so provides [referring to the predecessor of section 41 of the Personal Property Law]." (Emphasis supplied.)

The judgment should be affirmed, with costs.

NOTES

(1) *Status of the Rule.* The Restatement acknowledges that an assignment may be proscribed, as in the foregoing case, but only in a rather grudging way: § 176. See also Restatement Second, § 154.

a. The statute referred to has been carried forward as General Obligations Law, § 13–101. See p. 926 supra.

Holmes observed that it is one thing to permit a contracting party to confine his obligation to narrow limits, but quite another to permit him to make the other party's right (such as it is) inalienable. The buyer of a horse may not contract in such a way that he may not later transfer the horse; the parties to the sale may not deprive him of the *power* of resale. According to Holmes, "it is not illogical to apply the same rule to a debt that would be applied to a horse"—and he applied it. He observed that sometimes assignability is "sustained on the ground that the provision against assignment is inserted only for the benefit of the [obligor]. Whether that form of expression is accurate or merely is an indirect recognition of the principle that we have stated, hardly is material here." Portuguese-American Bank of San Francisco v. Welles, 242 U.S. 7 (1916).

In sympathy with Holmes's view, the Code invalidates anti-assignment clauses within its purview: see section 9–318(4), p. 1008 supra. It reverses the rule of the main case.[b]

"The no assignment right is one of those peculiar legal rules which are honored almost exclusively in the breach." Gilmore, Good Faith Purchase, 63 Yale L.J. 1057, 1118 (1954). Both here and in drafting UCC comments Professor Gilmore criticized Allhusen as a monument to conceptualism and a throwback to ancient law. "The cases are legion in which courts have construed the heart out of prohibitory or restrictive terms and held the assignment good. . . . This gradual and largely unacknowledged shift in legal doctrine has taken place in response to economic need: as accounts and contract rights have become the collateral which secures an ever-increasing number of financing transactions, it has been necessary to reshape the law so that these intangibles, like negotiable instruments and negotiable documents of title can be freely assigned." Comment to UCC 9–318(4).

Should commercial accounts receivable be accorded the quality of negotiability as a matter of law? See Gilmore, op. cit. supra, 1120.

(2) *Protection for the Obliger.* Consider some of the reasons a contracting party might have for insisting upon a term prohibiting an assignment of rights by the other party: (a) He anticipates equivocal action by the other party—a questionable notice or the like—which leaves doubt about the person to whom his own performance is due. (b) He is concerned about the other party's financial needs and the risk involved in meeting those needs—after notice of an assignment—with prepayments and advances. (c) He foresees circumstances that might make it desirable to modify the contract in a way affecting the interest of the assignee adversely—a hazardous course to take without the assignee's assent. Are there other possible reasons for prohibiting an assignment?

How much does the Code do to satisfy these objectives of the obligor? Is it enough to offset the rule that a prohibition on assignment is ineffective?

(3) *Problem.* Kroo Painting Company makes an assignment of its job earnings to First Bank, without Caristo's consent. Then it makes another assignment of the same earnings—fraudulently—to Second Bank, this time

---

b. But in the drafting of Article 2 the rule of Article 9 seems to have been overlooked. Note the first three words of section 2–210(2): what can they possibly mean?

obtaining written consent from Caristo. When both banks claim the proceeds, Caristo interpleads them and deposits the fund into the court. Does it follow from the main case that Second Bank will prevail, because the first assignment was "void"? See Fox-Greenwald Sheet Metal Co. v. Markowitz Bros., Inc., 452 F.2d 1346 (D.C.Cir. 1971). What is the difference between Restatement, § 176 and Restatement Second, § 154(d), in relation to this problem?

ASSIGNMENTS IN RELATION TO CONSTRUCTION CONTRACTS

Assignments are a customary and prominent by-product of contracts for construction, improvement, and repair work. The role of banks and other institutions financing such work is largely dependent on the effectiveness of assignments for security purposes. In general, the problems connected with such assignments arise out of the insolvency of an assigning contractor or subcontractor.

Two main types of controversy must be distinguished. One source of resistance to the financer (assignee) is the owner or contractor from whom the assigned payments are expected. (Such a person will be called an "employer" in this note, without any intention to suggest that he is empowered to direct performance of the work as a true employer is.) The other source of controversy is a set of persons who have claims derived from the contractor (assignor). This group includes a person taking a competing assignment, a surety company that has written a bond for his performance of the work, and a representative of his creditors—usually his trustee in bankruptcy.

Controversies of the first type are illustrated by Monroe Banking & Trust Company v. Allen, 286 F.Supp. 201 (N.D.Miss.1968). In that case the defendant was a builder who had subcontracted a painting job. The painter had obtained financing from a bank, assigning for security his right to payment. After notice of the assignment, the builder sold materials to the painter on credit. When the bank sought to enforce the assigned claim, the builder asserted the right to set off the unpaid price of the materials. The bank was not informed of the credit sales until it appeared that the painter could not repay the bank's advances.

Controversies of the second type are illustrated by interpleader cases, in which an employer seeks direction about how to allocate payment for a contractor's work, as between competing claimants. If the contractor is a bankrupt, one of the claimants is likely to be the trustee, who is vested with the bankrupt contractor's "title" by Section 70a of the Bankruptcy Act. Another may be a bonding company which has had to pay claims of laborers and materialmen for their contribution to the work. Banks and others who finance contractors on the strength of assignments must regularly anticipate competing claims from these quarters.

As against a bankruptcy trustee, the key to victory for an assignee lies chiefly in his compliance with the filing requirements of the Uniform Commercial Code, Article 9. The statute provides for filing in one or more public offices of a document called a "financing statement." In relation to assignments, the statement amounts in essence to a notice that an assignment has been made, or is contemplated, between the lender and the borrower. Their names, signatures, and addresses must appear on it, but virtually no additional particulars are required. (Further description of the Code impact on assignments is given below. The filing system embraces far more than assignments connected with construction contracts.[a])

In contests with bonding companies, financing banks have suffered a series of recent reverses. They have sought to exploit the fact that bonding companies commonly do not make filings under the Code so as to perfect assignments of job earnings.[b] However, in their capacity as sureties for contractors, bonding companies have usually preempted bank assignments of those earnings by relying on the principle of subrogation. See In re J. V. Gleason Co., 452 F.2d 1219 (8th Cir. 1971).

Bankruptcy trustees are also subjugated to bonding companies, through subrogation, in situations to which the Code is not applicable. The leading case is Pearlman v. Reliance Insurance Company, 371 U.S. 132 (1962), involving earnings under a Government contract.[c]

Like bonding companies, banks have not been content to rely altogether on their status as assignees. A technique sometimes used to advantage is to procure an "acceptance" of the assignment by the contractor's employer. The acceptance may have no import except to signify prompt notification of the assignment to the obligor. But it may include terms open to a more helpful construction. For example, the employer sometimes undertakes to make progress payments by check payable jointly to the contractor and to the financer. If he fails to do so, and in consequence funds are improperly diverted by the contractor, the financer is in a position to claim indemnity from the employer. Of course, it is well for a financer to lay a careful predicate, in advance, for such a claim. Several cases concern "acceptances" addressed solely to the contractor (assignor): the employ-

---

a. With respect to certain international accounts receivable, a security interest "may only be perfected by notification to the account debtor." UCC 9–103(5).

b. For an explanation, see Hoffman, Jacobs—Sureties' Panacea or Narcosis?, 1967 Ins.Couns.J. 387, 391–92.

c. See also Canter v. Schlager, —— Mass. ——, 267 N.E.2d 492 (1971); Travelers Indemnity Co. v. Clark, 254 So.2d 741 (Miss.1971) (receiver). Each case concerns the filing problem. The former gives references to controversies between banks and sureties.

er, for example, promises *him* to issue checks payable to his bank. In such a case it is necessary for the bank to develop a theory to overcome the lack of privity. Can you suggest such a theory? [d]

NOTES

(1) *Problem.* In Monroe Banking Co. v. Allen, briefed above, the bank's claim was held not to be subject to the contractor's set-off. Before advancing funds to the painter, the bank had obtained an acceptance of the assignment from the contractor. Was that fact essential to the result? Do you consider that additional facts might have dictated a different result? If so, what facts?

(2) *The Case of the Intrepid Bank.* A bank made an arrangement with a subcontractor whereby it would make direct payments to his suppliers, for building materials that he needed. The subcontractor executed an assignment of his earnings on the contract to the bank, on the understanding that the main contractor would be asked to "accept" it. The subcontract provided: "This contract shall not be assigned by the Subcontractor, nor shall he assign any moneys due or to become due to him hereunder, without the previous written consent of the Contractor." [e] The bank asked the main contractor to accept the assignment, but was met with a refusal. Nevertheless, the bank paid for the building materials. Not being reimbursed, the bank brought an action against the contractor for the sub's earnings. *Held:* For the defendant. Merchants & Farmers Bank v. McClendon, 220 So.2d 815 (Miss.1969). The court indicated that an assignment to the bank as security for a loan might have been effective, but characterized the bank's assignment as a "general" one. How would the case have been decided in New York, to judge by the Allhusen case, p. 1010 supra? Was the decision compatible with UCC 9–318(4)? (The opinion did not mention the Code.)

ASSIGNMENTS, BANKRUPTCY, AND CREDITORS

A firm wishing to use its account receivables to obtain funds from a financing institution, either by selling them or borrowing against them, will be required to sign a "financing statement." This is a document intended for filing in a public office, from which inquirers can learn that the firm has assigned its accounts, or at least that it contemplates doing so. The simple requisites of the document are stated in UCC 9–402: it must contain the names, addresses, and signatures of the assignor and the assignee, and an indication of the type of asset ("collateral") to be transferred. The same form is used

d. If so, you may wish to consider whether or not your theory offers a way for financing banks to avoid the necessity of filing financing statements under Article 9. For materials on this rather arcane subject, see Gilmore, 2 Security Interests in Personal Property, § 41.3 (1965). See also

Wolters Village Manage. Co. v. Merchants & P. Nat. Bank, 223 F.2d 793 (5th Cir. 1955). Cf. Citizens National Bank of Orlando v. Vitt, 367 F.2d 541 (5th Cir. 1966).

e. As construed by the court.

to make a record of security interests in equipment and inventory, suitably varying the description of the collateral.[f]

Failure to file an appropriate financing statement has two principal consequences for the assignee: (1) his interest in the accounts is "subordinate to the rights of . . . a person who becomes a lien creditor without knowledge of the [assignment] and before [filing] ;[g] and (2) another person holding an assignment of the same accounts, whenever made, has priority of right if he makes an earlier filing.[h] The more important stimulus to prompt filing is the first point. The situation of conflicting assignments of the same right most often arises from bad-faith conduct on the part of the assignor, and a financer would not usually depend on a public filing to protect him against that risk. He will hardly advance funds until he is satisfied of the assignor's good character. The problem of ranking is examined further in Note 2, p. 1023 infra.

A "general" creditor, as such, may not complain that his debtor has made assignments of which he had no notice. He becomes a "lien creditor," entitled to the protection of the Code, by taking proceedings on his claim such as directing a writ of garnishment to an "account debtor"—one who is indebted on an assigned account.[i] Even the threat of subjection to an individual creditor's rights, through garnishment or levy, is not the principal concern of a financing assignee, except as it expresses itself in the law of bankruptcy. Bankruptcy is the preeminent type of an insolvency proceeding, in which the assets of a business are parcelled out among its creditors. Few creditors, except those who have effective liens and security interests, can expect to share substantially in the distribution. For an assignee of accounts, or other secured party, the ultimate test of his position is whether or not he can retain his collateral against a trustee in bankruptcy of the debtor's estate.

f. Further information has to be elicited by inquiry. See UCC 9–208. With certain exceptions (see especially UCC 9–104f), a sale of accounts gives rise to a "security interest" for the purpose of the Code. UCC 1–201(37), 9–102(1)(b). So also does a sale of contract rights. "Account" and "contract right" are defined in UCC 9–106. "[I]n most situations the same rules apply to both accounts and contract rights." Comment to UCC 9–106. This note focusses on accounts receivable. Financing institutions purchasing such accounts have been known as "factors." However, their services amount to financing, functionally speaking, and for many purposes there is not a sharp distinction between lending on the security of accounts and purchasing them.

g. UCC 9–301(1)(b). This section, like many others cited in this note, is not confined to accounts receivable, but applies to security interests in other types of collateral as well.

h. UCC 9–312(5)(a).

i. "Account debtor" is defined in UCC 9–105(1)(a). The term includes a person obligated on a contract right.

"A 'lien creditor' means a creditor who has acquired a lien on the property involved by attachment, levy or the like and includes an assignee for benefit of creditors from the time of assignment, and a trustee in bankruptcy from the date of the filing of the petition or a receiver in equity from the time of appointment. . . ." UCC 9–301(3).

The Bankruptcy Act, a federal statute, sets high standards for testing the validity of transfers, including assignments, that the debtor may have made. If the transferee has neglected to file a financing statement, as required by the Code, the trustee may avoid the transfer.[j] A financing assignee will, in that event, rank only as a general, unsecured creditor. By the terms of the Act, the assignor's trustee is made a sort of apotheosis of all the challenges that his individual creditors might make to an assignment. Not only so, but the trustee has bankruptcy power to avoid certain assignments (and other transfers) that are not vulnerable to individual creditors.

Since before World War II there has been continuing skirmishing between financing assignees and unsecured-creditor interests, focussing principally on the Bankruptcy Act.[k] For creditors, represented by the trustee, Section 60 of the Act is the most potent weapon; it provides for avoiding many transfers that are not "perfected," in a special bankruptcy sense, within four months before the proceedings are begun. For assignees of accounts receivable this provision is especially embarrassing because, on any given date, commonly, many of the accounts in hand will not have been in existence for as long as four months. If this fact signifies that, as to them, the transfer has not been "perfected" for so long, it may not survive the trustee's avoiding power under Section 60.

A word about the central function of Section 60 will be in order. As creditors who are not adequately secured, or not secured at all, become aware that the debtor is slipping toward financial ruin, they will naturally seek to save themselves by obtaining speedy payment, or by obtaining security for their claims. (Taking either payment or a security interest from a debtor amounts to a "transfer" as defined in the Bankruptcy Act, and a preference, as defined in Section 60, is a species of transfer.) In the circumstances described it will have the effect it is meant to have unless it is set aside in an insolvency proceeding: it gives the creditor a greater percentage of his claim than other creditors, less alert, will receive. This is an instance of "grab law," by which the race is to the swift. The main object of Section 60 is to reverse that effect, within limits, by avoiding certain preferences. One characteristic of a preferential transfer is that it be for antecedent debt; a transfer for adequate current value does not deplete the debtor's assets. However, as noted above, giving cur-

---

j. This effect follows from Section 70e of the Bankruptcy Act, together with UCC 9–301(1)(b). See also Sections 60 and 70c of the Act. (These section numbers are the ones commonly used; they refer to the Chandler Act of 1938. The United States Code references are 11 U.S.C. §§ 96, 110.)

See also the definition of lien creditor, supra.

k. For notable episodes, see Corn Exchange National Bank & Trust Co. v. Klauder, 318 U.S. 434 (1943), and Miami National Bank v. Knudsen, 300 F.2d 289 (5th Cir. 1962). The statutory context of each of these cases has been altered, however.

rent value for a transfer will not save it if the transferee has neglected a required step to "perfect" it, as by filing a financing statement. Section 60 provides that a transfer is deemed made on the date of its perfection. In this way it permits the trustee to avoid even a long-standing transfer if it is not perfected until shortly before bankruptcy, when the transferee has cause to believe the debtor is insolvent. If it were not so, a secured creditor might maintain secrecy about his interest until bankruptcy was imminent, and then make a last-minute filing.

The possibility was mentioned above that some of the assigned accounts may have come into existence shortly before the bankruptcy. In itself, this fact does not suggest anything so obviously offensive as obtaining a brink-of-bankruptcy assignment for antecedent debt, or as keeping an old assignment secret. Yet it is possible to discern transfers (for antecedent debt) in the ongoing effect that an assignment agreement usually has on the debtor's accounts as they arise from day to day. A threat is thereby posed by Section 60 to a customary business practice, openly conducted. Two features of the Code tend to protect financing institutions from this threat. One is the privilege it gives to file a financing statement in advance of the time of taking an assignment, or other security interest.[1] Some courts seem to regard such a filing as accomplishing perfection of the interest, contrary to the diction of both the Bankruptcy Act and the Code.[m] More to the point, the Code contains a controversial section (UCC 9–108[n]) designed specifically to preserve security interests against the threat of Section 60 in the situation described above. Arguably, that section is inconsistent with the Bankruptcy Act, and so invalid, in part, under the supremacy clause of the Constitution.[o] However, by the end of the 60's, case law seemed to have established that, on one ground or another, the purpose of UCC 9–108 could be reconciled with the Act.

NOTES

(1) *Caveat.* The preceding note depicts an elaborate statutory pattern in a cursory and incomplete way. But the moral for assignees is a simple

l. UCC 9–402(1).

m. See In re King-Porter Company, 446 F.2d 722 (5th Cir. 1971), reviewing cases.

n. "Where a secured party makes an advance, incurs an obligation, releases a perfected security interest, or otherwise gives new value which is to be secured in whole or in part by after-acquired property his security interest in the after-acquired collateral shall be deemed to be taken for new value and not as security for an antecedent debt if the debtor acquires his rights in such collateral either in the ordinary course of his business or under a contract of purchase made pursuant to the security agreement within a reasonable time after new value is given."

o. This view is espoused in Countryman, Code Security Interests in Bankruptcy, 75 Comm.L.J. 269 (1970), 4 UCC L.J. 35 (1971), referring to an extensive literature on the issue.

one: take care, in good time, to comply with the Code prescriptions for filing a financing statement, found in sections 9–401 et seq.

Some alterations in the pattern are in prospect, but its main outlines are not likely to be affected. Section 60 may in time be amended to comport with UCC 9–108. Also, the Permanent Editorial Board for the Code recommends an amendment to UCC 9–301, further delimiting the class of lien creditors whose claims outrank that of a secured party. In each case, it will be noted, the interests of financing assignees would be advanced.

(2) *Payment to Assignee.* Beyond this point the legal issues must be left for study in a course on creditors' rights or secured transactions, except for a word about payment to an assignee. It is sound bankruptcy principle that an effectively and fully secured creditor cannot be unduly favored over general creditors by receiving payment of his claim. This proposition constitutes one of the chief values of having an assignment, or other security interest. Without it, the monthly payments that debtors commonly make to their secured creditors would very often be voidable for a four-month period. The point was involved in Shiro v. Drew, 174 F.Supp. 495 (D.Me.1959). For the background of this case, see the note on Futurity, p. 934 supra. Additional facts were these: Drew's loan was repaid by Fiberlast on February 11, 1957. At this time it was insolvent, and Drew had reasonable cause to believe it. Before the month was out, Fiberlast was in bankruptcy. Its trustee, Shiro, brought an action against Drew to recover the payment as a voidable preference. Owing to the proposition stated above, the result should depend on Drew's status as assignee prior to the date of payment. May Shiro recover? Does the answer depend on whether or not Drew made an appropriate filing of a financing statement?

(3) *Problem.* Suppose these facts: Drew made the Fiberlast loan on an agreement, written and signed, that when the Radome money was earned he would be secured by Fiberlast's right to payment. He promptly filed a financing statement appropriate for the perfection of such an interest. At the juncture when the money was earned, Fiberlast was insolvent and Drew knew it, and its bankruptcy ensued within four months. Who is entitled to the earnings, the bankruptcy trustee or Drew?

McDOWELL, PYLE & CO. v. HOPFIELD, 148 Md. 84, 128 A. 742, 52 A.L.R. 105 (1925). [The Commercial Credit Company was in the business of purchasing accounts receivable on the "non-notification basis." In July, 1923, it purchased some accounts from the Wirth Concord Ade Company, of Rhode Island. They represented sales made to a customer in Baltimore, McDowell, Pyle & Company. On August 13, Carl Hopfield, a salesman for Wirth, brought an action against it in Maryland, claiming that his services had not been paid for. Jurisdiction was based on the "presence" of Wirth's claim in Maryland, and a writ of attachment which Hopfield served on its debtor, McDowell. The next day, McDowell answered, admitting its indebtedness. On September 20 a default judgment was entered, Wirth not appearing, to be enforced against its claim. (By Maryland practice, the judgment was entitled a "condemnation".) Not receiving payment of the accounts as it expected, Commercial Credit notified McDowell of its assignments on October 8. Ten days later it learned from McDowell of the attachment and judgment. On October 20 both Commercial Credit and McDowell filed petitions asking that the judgment be stricken. The petitions were denied, and they appealed.

[The court first examined the character of a garnishor's judgment in Maryland, and concluded that equitable considerations might require it to be reconsidered, in the court's discretion, upon an application made before the close of the term.]

WALSH, J. . . . In the present case the equities of the situation are clearly with the assignee. It purchased the accounts for a valuable consideration, and in deference to the assignor, which was to collect and forward the money, it did not notify the original debtor of the assignment until after the accounts had all matured. When payment was not received through the assignor in the usual course of business the assignee within two weeks of the final maturity notified the debtor, and now both the assignee and debtor (the garnishee) are asking that the judgment in favor of the attaching creditor be stricken out. This creditor dealt with the assignor on the basis of the latter's general credit, and not with any special reference to these accounts, while the assignee advanced money on these specific accounts, and it is the almost universal rule that under such conditions the assignee has the better claim, unless the judgment of condemnation alters the rule. . . . The judgment in this case has not been paid, nor has any execution been issued on it, and the garnishee against whom it was entered applied within the term to have it stricken out. Considering all the circumstances of the case, and the legal principles which we deem properly applicable thereto, we think that the judgment should have been stricken out and the assignee allowed to intervene as claimant.[a]

NOTES

(1) *Levy and the Like.* The Uniform Commercial Code, which would now govern this case, does not specify the procedure requisite for acquiring a "lien" on a debtor's property, further than to say "by attachment, levy or the like." § 9–301(3). To serve a writ of garnishment (called attachment or trustee process in some states), as Hopfield did, is commonly regarded as a lien-creating step. However, a close examination of creditors' remedies may be required for a confident opinion about the law of a particular jurisdiction. Certainly a lien is established by an appropriate service of a writ of execution, following judgment.

Whatever the requisites may be, the essential rule of the preceding case is unquestioned: a creditor of the assignor who has taken no such step is in

a. The original Restatement rule on an attaching creditor's position vis-a-vis the assignee has been revised to follow the rule of this case. See Restatement Second, § 173(2), and the Reporter's Note.

no position to challenge the interest of an assignee. Like other transfers, an assignment may be a fraud upon creditors of the transferor, and voidable by them. A gratuitous assignment, in particular, is open to challenge by the assignor's creditors. See Restatement, § 172. But a judicial process, either a levy or something comparable, is an essential step in the challenge. The "something comparable" may be filing a bankruptcy petition: that is said to amount to a general levy on the debtor's assets.

(2) *Successive Assignees from the Same Assignor.* The Restatement states a complex rule for the problem of ranking conflicting assignments, in § 173. It is carried forward in Restatement Second, § 174, without change of substance. (The quotations that follow are from comments to that section.) The problem was much reduced in importance by the enactment of the Code and legislation that preceded it. "The subject is now largely governed by the Uniform Commercial Code, except in cases of wage claims, rights under insurance policies, bank accounts, and certain other excluded types of transactions. See § 9–104." As has been noted, the sequence of filing is the chief factor in ranking "conflicting security interests" under the Code.[b] In this connection, it is well to observe that parties who contemplate entering into an assignment in the future (or other Code security agreement in many forms) may effect a filing before the transaction is executed. There is no name for the status that such a filing confers on the prospective assignee; it certainly gives him no present interest in anything. Yet it is an important step in practice, for it will surely warn off any wary financer who might otherwise be inclined to give value for an interest within the description of the financing statement.

The Restatement rule is known as the "four horsemen" rule. If both A and B have bought a claim from a double-dealing assignor, in that order, and B collects it, the rule permits B to retain the proceeds against A,[c] and in any one of three other circumstances it permits B to recover and retain the proceeds.

"In England and in a number of states, aside from statute, a different rule has been followed, giving priority to the assignee who first gives notice to the obligor, regardless of the order in which the assignments were made. That rule stems from the leading case of Dearle v. Hall, 3 Russ. 1, 48 (1828), involving successive assignments of the interest of a beneficiary of a trust. The English rule has consequences similar to that of a system of public filing, except that the obligor acts as the filing office; it is somewhat more convenient where a single obligor is involved such as a trustee or the owner or prime contractor on a construction project than in cases of multiple obligors, as where a business concern assigns its accounts receivable."[d]

---

b. "An unperfected security interest is subordinate to the rights of a person who is not a secured party to the extent that he gives value for accounts, contract rights or general intangibles without knowledge of the security interest and before it is perfected. § 9–301." But the usual contest between two assignees of the same claim is one between two *secured parties*, if it is governed by the Code at all.

c. B must have given value, in good faith.

d. Restatement Second, § 174, Comment b.

INDEX

References are to Pages
